Short Story
Criticism

Guide to Gale Literary Criticism Series

For criticism on	Consult these Gale series
Authors now living or who died after December 31, 1999	*CONTEMPORARY LITERARY CRITICISM (CLC)*
Authors who died between 1900 and 1999	*TWENTIETH-CENTURY LITERARY CRITICISM (TCLC)*
Authors who died between 1800 and 1899	*NINETEENTH-CENTURY LITERATURE CRITICISM (NCLC)*
Authors who died between 1400 and 1799	*LITERATURE CRITICISM FROM 1400 TO 1800 (LC)* *SHAKESPEAREAN CRITICISM (SC)*
Authors who died before 1400	*CLASSICAL AND MEDIEVAL LITERATURE CRITICISM (CMLC)*
Authors of books for children and young adults	*CHILDREN'S LITERATURE REVIEW (CLR)*
Dramatists	*DRAMA CRITICISM (DC)*
Poets	*POETRY CRITICISM (PC)*
Short story writers	*SHORT STORY CRITICISM (SSC)*
Black writers of the past two hundred years	*BLACK LITERATURE CRITICISM (BLC)* *BLACK LITERATURE CRITICISM SUPPLEMENT (BLCS)*
Hispanic writers of the late nineteenth and twentieth centuries	*HISPANIC LITERATURE CRITICISM (HLC)* *HISPANIC LITERATURE CRITICISM SUPPLEMENT (HLCS)*
Native North American writers and orators of the eighteenth, nineteenth, and twentieth centuries	*NATIVE NORTH AMERICAN LITERATURE (NNAL)*
Major authors from the Renaissance to the present	*WORLD LITERATURE CRITICISM, 1500 TO THE PRESENT (WLC)* *WORLD LITERATURE CRITICISM SUPPLEMENT (WLCS)*

ISSN 0895-9439

Volume 44

Short Story Criticism

Criticism of the
Works of Short Fiction Writers

Justin Karr
Editor

GALE GROUP
TM
THOMSON LEARNING

Detroit • New York • San Diego • San Francisco
Boston • New Haven, Conn. • Waterville, Maine
London • Munich

STAFF

Lynn M. Spampinato, Janet Witalec, *Managing Editors, Literature Product*
Kathy D. Darrow, Ellen McGeagh, *Product Liaisons*
Justin Karr, *Editor*
Mark W. Scott, *Publisher, Literature Product*

Anja Barnard, *Editor*
Madeline S. Harris, *Assistant Editor*
Jenny Cromie, Mary Ruby, *Technical Training Specialists*
Deborah J. Morad, Joyce Nakamura, Kathleen Lopez Nolan, *Managing Editors*
Susan M. Trosky, *Director, Literature Content*

Maria L. Franklin, *Permissions Manager*
Margaret Chamberlain, *Permissions Specialist*

Victoria B. Cariappa, *Research Manager*
Sarah Genik, *Project Coordinator*
Ron Morelli, Tamara C. Nott, Tracie A. Richardson, *Research Associates*
Nicodemus Ford, *Research Assistant*

Dorothy Maki, *Manufacturing Manager*
Stacy L. Melson, *Buyer*

Mary Beth Trimper, *Manager, Composition and Electronic Prepress*
Carolyn Roney, *Composition Specialist*

Michael Logusz, *Graphic Artist*
Randy Bassett, *Imaging Supervisor*
Robert Duncan, Dan Newell, Luke Rademacher, *Imaging Specialists*
Pamela A. Reed, *Imaging Coordinator*
Kelly A. Quin, *Editor, Image and Multimedia Content*

Library of Congress Catalog Card Number 88-641014
ISBN 0-7876-4704-7
ISSN 0895-9439
Printed in the United States of America

10 9 8 7 6 5 4 3 2 1

Contents

Preface vii

Acknowledgments ix

Walter Abish 1931- 1
Austrian-born American short story writer, novelist, and poet

Akutagawa Ryunosuke 1892-1927 40
Japanese short story writer, novelist, poet, translator, and critic

Feodor Dostoevsky 1821-1881 92
*Russian novelist, short story writer, and essayist; single-work entry on
the novella* Dvoynik (The Double)

Sarah Orne Jewett 1849-1909 178
*American short story writer, novelist, and poet; single-work entry on
the short story "A White Heron"*

James Joyce 1882-1941 234
*Irish short story writer, novelist, playwright, poet, memoirist, and critic;
single-work entry on the short story "Araby"*

Dylan Thomas 1914-1953 320
Welsh poet, dramatist, short story writer, and essayist

Israel Zangwill 1864-1926 363
*English novelist, short story writer, dramatist, essayist, critic, translator,
lecturer, and poet*

Literary Criticism Series Cumulative Author Index 395

SSC Cumulative Nationality Index 471

SSC-44 Title Index 473

Preface

*S*hort Story Criticism (*SSC*) presents significant criticism of the world's greatest short story writers and provides supplementary biographical and bibliographical materials to guide the interested reader to a greater understanding of the authors of short fiction. This series was developed in response to suggestions from librarians serving high school, college, and public library patrons, who had noted a considerable number of requests for critical material on short story writers. Although major short story writers are covered in such Gale series as *Contemporary Literary Criticism* (*CLC*), *Twentieth-Century Literary Criticism* (*TCLC*), *Nineteenth-Century Literature Criticism* (*NCLC*), and *Literature Criticism from 1400 to 1800* (*LC*), librarians perceived the need for a series devoted solely to writers of the short story genre.

Scope of the Series

SSC is designed to serve as an introduction to major short story writers of all eras and nationalities. Since these authors have inspired a great deal of relevant critical material, *SSC* is necessarily selective, and the editors have chosen the most important published criticism to aid readers and students in their research.

Approximately eight to ten authors are included in each volume, and each entry presents a historical survey of the critical response to that author's work. The length of an entry is intended to reflect the amount of critical attention the author has received from critics writing in English and from foreign critics in translation. Every attempt has been made to identify and include the most significant essays on each author's work. In order to provide these important critical pieces, the editors sometimes reprint essays that have appeared elsewhere in Gale's Literary Criticism Series. Such duplication, however, never exceeds twenty percent of an *SSC* volume.

Organization of the Book

An *SSC* entry consists of the following elements:

- The **Author Heading** cites the name under which the author most commonly wrote, followed by birth and death dates. Also located here are any name variations under which an author wrote, including transliterated forms for authors whose native languages use nonroman alphabets. If the author wrote consistently under a pseudonym, the pseudonym will be listed in the author heading and the author's actual name given in parentheses on the first line of the biographical and critical introduction. Uncertain birth or death dates are indicated by question marks. Single-work entries are preceded by the title of the work and its date of publication.

- The **Introduction** contains background information that introduces the reader to the author and the critical debates surrounding his or her work.

- A **Portrait of the Author** is included when available.

- The list of **Principal Works** is ordered chronologically by date of first publication and lists the most important works by the author. The first section comprises short story collections, novellas, and novella collections. The second section gives information on other major works by the author. For foreign authors, the editors have provided original foreign-language publication information and have selected what are considered the best and most complete English-language editions of their works.

- Reprinted **Criticism** is arranged chronologically in each entry to provide a useful perspective on changes in critical evaluation over time. All short story, novella, and collection titles by the author featured in the entry are printed in boldface type. The critic's name and the date of composition or publication of the critical work are given at the beginning of each piece of criticism. Unsigned criticism is preceded by the title of the source in which it appeared. Footnotes are reprinted at the end of each essay or excerpt. In the case of excerpted criticism, only those footnotes that pertain to the excerpted texts are included.

- Critical essays are prefaced by brief **Annotations** explicating each piece.

- A complete **Bibliographical Citation** of the original essay or book precedes each piece of criticism.

- An annotated bibliography of **Further Reading** appears at the end of each entry and suggests resources for additional study. In some cases, significant essays for which the editors could not obtain reprint rights are included here. Boxed material following the further reading list provides references to other biographical and critical sources on the author in series published by Gale.

Cumulative Indexes

A **Cumulative Author Index** lists all of the authors that appear in a wide variety of reference sources published by the Gale Group, including *SSC*. A complete list of these sources is found facing the first page of the Author Index. The index also includes birth and death dates and cross references between pseudonyms and actual names.

A **Cumulative Nationality Index** lists all authors featured in *SSC* by nationality, followed by the number of the *SSC* volume in which their entry appears.

A **Cumulative Title Index** lists in alphabetical order all short story, novella, and collection titles contained in the *SSC* series. Titles of short story collections, separately published novellas, and novella collections are printed in italics, while titles of individual short stories are printed in roman type with quotation marks. Each title is followed by the author's last name and corresponding volume and page numbers where commentary on the work is located. English-language translations of original foreign-language titles are cross-referenced to the foreign titles so that all references to discussion of a work are combined in one listing.

Citing *Short Story Criticism*

When writing papers, students who quote directly from any volume in the Literature Criticism Series may use the following general format to footnote reprinted criticism. The first example pertains to material drawn from periodicals, the second to material reprinted from books.

Henry James, Jr., "Honoré de Balzac," *The Galaxy* 20 (December 1875), 814-36; reprinted in *Short Story Criticism,* vol. 5, ed. Thomas Votteler (Detroit: The Gale Group), 8-11.

Linda W. Wagner, "The Years of the Locust," *Ellen Glasgow: Beyond Convention* (University of Texas Press, 1982), 50-70; reprinted and excerpted in *Short Story Criticism,* vol. 34, ed. Anna Nesbitt Sheets (Farmington Hills, Mich.: The Gale Group), 80-82.

Suggestions are Welcome

Readers who wish to suggest new features, topics, or authors to appear in future volumes, or who have other suggestions or comments are cordially invited to call, write, or fax the Managing Editor:

Managing Editor, Literary Criticism Series
The Gale Group
27500 Drake Road
Farmington Hills, MI 48331-3535
1-800-347-4253 (GALE)
Fax: 248-699-8054

Acknowledgments

The editors wish to thank the copyright holders of the excerpted criticism included in this volume and the permissions managers of many book and magazine publishing companies for assisting us in securing reproduction rights. We are also grateful to the staffs of the Detroit Public Library, the Library of Congress, the University of Detroit Mercy Library, Wayne State University Purdy/Kresge Library Complex, and the University of Michigan Libraries for making their resources available to us. Following is a list of the copyright holders who have granted us permission to reproduce material in this volume of *SSC*. Every effort has been made to trace copyright, but if omissions have been made, please let us know.

Walter Abish
1931–

Austrian-born American short story writer, novelist, and poet.

INTRODUCTION

Abish is known as an inventive experimentalist intent on examining the role of language in the construction of reality. He brings to his fiction the techniques of games, puzzles, cinema, pop art, and deconstructive textual subversion, as well as skepticism about the capacity of language to convey truth. These techniques create works that, as they present themselves as conceptual, self-referential, and abstract, also anatomize, satirize, and criticize contemporary social institutions and attitudes.

BIOGRAPHICAL INFORMATION

Abish was born in Vienna, Austria, in 1931 to middle-class Jewish parents. The family fled Vienna for Nice, France, in 1938 and sailed to Shanghai, China, in 1940, just ten days before Germany invaded France. There they lived in a European quarter of the city, and Abish attended a European school. In 1949 the family emigrated to Israel. Despite the surrounding danger, turmoil, and dislocation, Abish reports he led a routine and rather monotonous, even stifled, existence in his youth, which he suggests is partly responsible for his rebelliousness as a writer. His mother, he reports, was "efficiently cool and remote," while his father was an "energetic" businessman. In Israel Abish began writing poetry in English, and, after completing the compulsory military service, studied architecture and worked designing small communities. In Israel, too, he met an American city planner, Cecile Rubin, who was to become an important sculptor and photographer. They were married and moved to England and then to the United States, where Abish worked as a city planner and began writing fiction. After the publication in 1974 and 1975 of *Alphabetical Africa* and *Minds Meet*, he taught or was a writer-in-residence at a number of American universities, including Columbia, Brown, Yale, and Cooper Union. He has also been the recipient of many honors and grants, among them awards from the New Jersey State Council on the Arts, the National Endowment for the Arts, the Guggenheim Foundation, the MacArthur Foundation, the American Academy and Institute of Arts and Letters, and the Lila Wallace-Reader's Digest Foundation.

MAJOR WORKS OF SHORT FICTION

Abish's short stories probe the relationship between language, reference, and representation, and explore the role

of fiction in the construction of reality. They also sometimes serve as preliminary versions of his novels. Abish wrote *Alphabetical Africa*, for example, after *Minds Meet*, imposing the same discipline upon its composition. *How German Is It* (1980), considered by many to be his best work, while free of stringent rules of composition, uses the Holocaust as a centering device for perception, experience, and interpretation, as does his short story "The English Garden," of which it is an expansion. Both works consider problems of memory, treachery, terrorism, and authenticity. The novel *Eclipse Fever* also owes much to the short form, presenting numerous juxtaposed sections that are unified by montage rather than by a sweeping narrative arc. In addition to being representations of "how we live now," Abish's short stories also represent formal experimentation, as in *99: The New Meaning*, (1990) where text is created from recycling and recombining previous texts from other writers. His short story "This is not a film, this is a precise act of disbelief" is a critical and ironic homage to the French new wave filmmaker Jean Luc Godard.

1

CRITICAL RECEPTION

Abish's early works like *Minds Meet* and *Alphabetical Africa* earned him a reputation as an important experimental writer, playful and trenchant. He was awarded the PEN/Faulkner prize for his second novel, *How German Is It,* and the equally prestigious MacArthur "genius" grant. His third novel *Eclipse Fever* appeared in 1993 to a mixed reception. The daily reviewers found it unsatisfactory, seeing it as a more or less traditional novel with avant-garde quirks, but without the bite they had come to expect from Abish. But critic Harold Bloom called it an essential work of the 1990s, seeing in it important extensions of Marcel Proust and Franz Kafka. Critics have also noted Abish's apparent move away from experimentalism in *Eclipse Fever* as opposed to, for instance, *99: The New Meaning,* the collection of stories that appeared shortly before it.

PRINCIPAL WORKS

Short Fiction

Minds Meet 1975
In the Future Perfect 1977
99: The New Meaning 1990

Other Major Works

Duel Site (poetry) 1970
Alphabetical Africa (novel) 1974
How German Is It (novel) 1980
Eclipse Fever (novel) 1993

CRITICISM

Jerome Klinkowitz (essay date 1977)

SOURCE: "Walter Abish," in *The Life of Fiction,* University of Illinois Press, 1977, pp. 62–70.

[*In the following survey of Abish's fiction, Klinkowitz argues that Abish uses postmodern and absurdist techniques and draws attention to them in order to undermine the uses of language that constrict rather than reveal meaning.*]

Despite his foreign background and experiences, Walter Abish is nonetheless thoroughly Americanized. Like Donald Barthelme, he plays with substitutions and inversions in the modern American landscape, taking our ha-

bitual mores and exposing the silliness they mask. Knowing he's from Vienna makes it all the more fun. In his story **"More by George"** from the *New Directions #27* (1973) anthology, a couple together with hitchhiker and camper travel from Vienna, Maryland, to Vienna, Georgia (pop. 3,718). There the people are about to celebrate "the anniversary marking the defeat of the Turks, as well as, one hundred fifty years later, the publication of a slim volume of poetry entitled *Rambles of a Viennese Poet,* a book that was promptly outlawed when it first appeared in print." For the occasion a replica of the Stefan's Turm has been erected. "It was only one fifth the size of the original, but three times as large as the one in Vienna, Maryland, which had a population of 420."

Abish is also concerned with language. Often it is the subject of the story itself, as in **"Minds Meet."** Other times his characters treat the topic, as in **"Crossing Friends,"** published for the first time in *Minds Meet*: "He presses his knife against Doug's throat because he found it difficult to rely solely upon language. Language contains all kinds of secret impediments. Language constricts."

The characters in Abish's stories who are concerned with or confused about language are usually confused in their personal lives as well. The stories center on this confusion. "All those courses in psychology have not prepared me for a locked door," the narrator of **"The Second Leg"** (*Paris Review #55,* Fall 1972, collected in *Minds Meet*) confesses. "Logic 1. and 2. has not helped me achieve a measure of tranquility." Characters such as this narrator are constantly self-reflective, measuring every move they make; since their actions and (more often) musings constitute the core of the story, Abish's fiction itself becomes self-reflective. But never with the ponderous seriousness of Beckett. For some reason when American fictionists use this technique the result is more exuberantly funny. It never happens with the confessional poetry of Lowell, Plath, or Berryman; but put it in prose and the result is literary hysteria. "So far she has not made one single reference to sex. It must be my imagination . . . my restless, troubled mind that is plaguing me. . . . It must be my imagination . . . all the same I can hear her quite distinctly enunciate the ejaculatory words: fuck, balls, cunt. . . ."

Barthelme puts his characters through similar rigors; like Abish, he is drawn to the paranoiacally self-conscious narrator who undermines the seriousness of what he has to say by the way he goes about saying it. The art, of course, is in the way it is said; that much is held in common with Beckett and the French New Novelists. But as Barthelme has written of them in *Location* (Summer 1964), "The French new novelists, Butor, Sarraute, Robbe-Grillet, Claude Simon, Philippe Sollers, have . . . succeeded in making objects of their books without reaping any of the strategic benefits of the maneuver—a triumph of misplaced intelligence. Their work seems leaden, self-conscious in the wrong way." There is humor, even of an American variety, in Beckett—Buster Keaton, perhaps, especially as

Michael Stephens uses him for *Still Life*. The appropriate model for Walter Abish's characters, however, would be the comedian Woody Allen, because as the story develops, a self-reflexive narrative figure has been created whose own self-doubting attributes are the story's point.

Abish's protagonists are forever being excluded from the party. It's usually a matter of sex, as in **"The Second Leg."** In **"The Istanbul Papers"** (*New Directions #23*, 1971, collected in *Minds Meet*), Abish tells of a minor diplomatic functionary who attended Harvard with John Kennedy and Norman Mailer—and who is forever excluded from that company. "Don't you want to show them up," a colleague taunts, "and stride shoulder to shoulder with Norman and Jack down the corridors of power?" His ticket of admission is unlikely: an affair with Hitler's daughter. "Hitler Jugend be damned. If Jack can profess to be a Berliner, I don't see why I can't be the lover of Hitler's daughter." Again, the narrator becomes the excluded party, as the real issue becomes the interests of his colleague and the stamping of the girl's passport. "I often think of those hectic days, standing shoulder to shoulder with Norman and Jack in the quadrangle," he concludes. "Only their dreams have come true."

There is a possible reason why the self-reflexive character in fiction so often plays the buffoon. Among Communists the confessional strain is provided for by the structure of self-criticism, an adaptable tool for any political writing; Catholics (accounting for most of the confessional poets) have examination of conscience, and Confession itself. But without such a structure, the result is pure solipsism, drifting every so often into rampant paranoia. When it is either substanceless or hopelessly naive, it's funny. As are most of Walter Abish's stories.

The best of Abish's fiction offers a loony mix of the aesthetic with the ethic. His diplomat from **"The Istanbul Papers"** reflects, "Unfortunately, the Embassy library leaves a lot to be desired. But there are so many other rewards. I am carried away by the slow emollient pace of the city . . . by the magnificent mosques with their sunbasked courtyards . . . by the serene flow of the river, and by the shiny eager faces of the young boys who beg for a livelihood. Seldom has anything so succeeded in inspiring me. Tomorrow I'm to meet Hitler's daughter." Often disconcerting things will be converted to an aesthetic, not as a form of escape, but to make them manageable; then we as readers can come back to life (as we inevitably will) with a better appreciation. It's a question of long-term versus short-term gains. It is instructive to note the silliness of people who make something over nothing—confusing the ethical with the aesthetic. The converse is the silliness of making nothing over something.

Walter Abish's first novel, *Alphabetical Africa*, includes his customary interest in the inability of people to communicate. An example from Chapter E shows both technique and theme at work:

> Demure damsel eagerly clutches at Emperor's defenses, but Emperor, deeply embarrassed, draws back, coughing, a bit calculatedly, cough, cough, but by coughing

Emperor accidently creates a complex code designed by bombing consultant. As Emperor considers balling Edna again, airplane erroneously bombs beleagured Ethiopian capital, eliminating everything below. Capital becomes antiquity dated A.D.

Abish's skepticism of understanding, which he feels is so often lacking in human communication, becomes in *Alphabetical Africa* "a determining factor upon which the flow of the narrative was largely predicated." His subject matter—Western uncertainty personified—is the white man's view of Africa.

Abish has pushed both language and idea farther than one thought they could go. His Africa, colonized and exploited by two centuries of Europeans and Americans, is described as actually shrinking. The map itself changes colors, as one country after another wins its independence; hence when one new nation makes war against another, the prime weapons are paint and brushes, used to transform the landscape to the aggressor's hue.

Abish's novel is "about" Africa only in the sense that certain notions about that continent provide a field in which Abish can generate the energy of his fiction. Ronald Sukenick has asked that fiction be appreciated in terms of its principles and elements of composition—like a painting, or like a piece of music. One can appreciate abstract art, or virtually any music, without recourse to the old debilitating question always asked of fiction: what is it about? Or, what does it mean? Only film is so monotonously subjected to the same question. Abish's special use of language—within the topographically familiar surfaces of the world we share—works to discredit the question. His stories reflect the methods of filmmaker Peter Kubelka, a fellow Viennese. Kubelka's films are based on the idea that their substance is not a panoramic view of the world thrown upon the screen, but the phenomenon of light passing through a celluloid stencil twenty-four times per second. Sequentially moving celluloid frames may very easily accommodate a realistic narrative, just as may the sequential arrangements of words upon a page. But that's just one of many things film and fiction may do; to restrict them to that sole function is to ignore the very makings of their art.

Therefore both Kubelka and Abish draw attention to their form of composition. A film catalogue description states that "Kubelka formulates the rhythm of his cuts, and counterpointing of imagery and soundtrack, the repetition and subtle variation of his imagery, playing a very similar role to the main theme or melody within a fugue." Kubelka gives us what has been called a "vertical montage" of sound against image. In a similar manner, Abish focuses his art on the words and phrases of our language. His sentences are often composed of radically different words and thoughts which collide at the caesura. By these collisions, the story moves forward: its subject is nothing other than itself. The subject of Kubelka's major work is also itself: it is titled *Our Trip to Africa*.

"This is not a film, this is a precise act of disbelief" is Abish's novella, first published in *Seems* (#5, 1975) and subsequently collected in the volume *Minds Meet.* Its field of action is a small American town, run by a small-town oligarchy—mayor, businessman, architect, developer—who control the surfaces which reflect their needs. Within these needs are the absolute truths of their lives; but the surfaces are only introductions, familiar at first but slightly unstable, until the skeletons in the closets rattle too loudly.

In story after story Abish uses a few key elements: the familiar surfaces, the lurking needs, and ultimately the sexual provocation which shows the vertical montage when one is counterpointed with the other. Abish disrupts the smooth system of language, so that superficial conventions are revealed as just that. As Sukenick says, good art deconditions us from our accepted view of reality. When we live only on the surface, we find our needs too easily satisfied by the perfect home, the perfect job, the perfect place for a new table, chair, or plant. In **"The English Garden"** (*Fiction International* #4/5, 1975) Abish takes his epigraph from John Ashbery's *Three Poems*: "Remnants of the old atrocity subsist, but they are converted into ingenious shifts in scenery, a sort of 'English Garden' effect, to give the air of naturalness, pathos and hope." Abish's own story is about a modern German town, with bright new buildings full of neatly planned apartments in turn filled with nicely arranged furniture—all built on the site of a former concentration camp, the topography of which has been effaced by a newer surface. The narrator compares it to the stenciled coloring book he buys as a souvenir; all is jolly and smiling, all is facade, and nothing is intrinsic "until it receives its color." In **"This is not a film . . ."** Bontemps shoots his films in color so that people will remember his images; the opposite are the unpenetrating citizens who simply polish the surfaces of their lives, understanding little beyond the brand names and commercial lifestyles around them, and hence not communicating at all. "Rudolf Arnheim speaks of order as anything the human mind is to understand," Abish has said; "I think by undermining order, as we in our culture understand it, writers bring about a new understanding."

Humanism in a literary context is a surface phenomenon, then, when it imposes itself as the necessary grand subject matter for fiction. No matter how worthy its aims, it is only one more system; and systems, as Sukenick and Abish and Stephens have told us, make it impossible for us to communicate the needs which lie beyond them. As Sukenick has said in his *Digressions,* language is a self-contained system, "But the art of fiction and poetry lies precisely in opening that system up to experience beyond language" as it has become systematized. "The obligation of fiction," one must recall, "is to rescue experience [for Abish, read "our needs"] from history, from politics, from commerce, from theory, even from language itself—from any system, in fact, that threatens to distort, devitalize, or manipulate experience. The health of language depends on its contact with experience, which it both embodies and helps to create."

Alain Arias-Misson (essay date 1980)

SOURCE: "The Puzzle of Walter Abish: *In The Future Perfect*," in *Sub-Stance,* Vol. IX, No. 2, 1980, pp. 115–24.

[*In the following essay, Arias-Misson argues that Abish deconstructs language by using devices like listing and counting the words used in his texts in order to show "the fictitious nature of our truths."*]

Combinations, copulations, permutations, deletions, transferences, transgressions, substitutions, cross-references, doublings: Walter Abish fabricates puzzles—puzzles of sex, puzzles of minds, puzzles of death—and words and images, letters and numbers are the matter of a puzzle. In his first novel, astonishingly amusing *Alphabetical Africa,* section A is assembled only with words beginning with a, section B only with a's and b's, C only with a's, b's, and c's and so on to Z, then into reverse, deleting first all z words, then z's and y's until in the last section, A, only a's are left again. A fabulous letter-land thus expands and shrinks, even describing a shrinking Africa progressively colored orange in the second part, in a linguistic slapstick where meaning jumps from word to event and character and back again to words and trapdoors fly open in the text with real persons falling through, all with the verse and speed of a Marx Brothers ad-lib. Under the extraordinary constraints exercised on the language, WA displays a virtuoso mastery of articulation; under the pressures of *alphabet* (the dual, structuring principle of language: phonetics/writing), his fictions constantly collapse into syntax and semantics and are as constantly resuscitated.

In the Future Perfect, WA's third work of fiction, a collection of stories, enriches the alphabetical instrumentarium with numbering-cogs and wheels and tightens the humour to a razor-cutting edge. The "puzzles of life" are brought to disquieting incandescence. If the labyrinth is the matrix symbol of a Borges, WA has put the *puzzle* at the obscure heart of his own fiction. The peculiar interest of an examination of his work is the ultra-violet light it sheds on the problems of contemporary fiction.

In the Future Perfect is not written in the future perfect. In the gap between the tense of the title and the tense of the book lies a puzzle. More exactly, the future perfect *is* the tense of the puzzle—the tense of the ready-made possible. Kierkegaard said, "Poetry commands the possible"; WA puts the stress on *commands*. The future perfect is determinative. In one of the stories WA writes, "The immediate future, the immediate, immaculate future lies mapped out in the brain cells." Persons and events lock into place like pieces in a puzzle. Essential to the puzzle is that its artificial itineraries, slots, sums provide predetermined solutions. In his *Self-Portrait*[1] WA writes, "I read over and over again a story by Borges, called *Death and the Compass* which bears a resemblance to a mathematical equation $a \div b \div c = x$. On first reading the story one is unprepared, accepting at face value the contrivance that entices the detective in the story to move from a to b then to c, finally as surprised as the reader to die at x." The arbitrariness of WA's constructions, their superdetermination, corresponds to the intrinsic indeterminacy or randomness of character and action.

In the Future Perfect is a book of ultra-chic furniture—gleaming surfaces, luxurious implements, push-button controls: a super-developed, American dream-world—a muffled nightmare. This perfection shines forth from the photos of thick, glossy fashion and interior decorating magazines, in the Fifth and Madison and Lexington Avenue plate-glass shop windows, inside the color television sets strewn throughout WA's fiction. Flatness and surface are the constant properties of his fictive world. The American perfection lies in the future, the "immediate" future: the images of opulence (things, sex, lives) which beckon just beyond the audience's reality-screen. Little wonder that the Muriels and Maudes and Janes (almost all the dominant characters are women—sexual images of the images of desire) and Hildas, who pick their way precisely, knowingly through this cosmetic rubble, have so keen a sense of smell of unreality. "Imprinted on her brain were a succession of faces, interiors and the sound of voices. All she had to do was switch channels." The "heroine" from **"In so many words"** is not named, this story being the only such case in a fiction where proper names constitute the one barrier between their characters and the pervasive flatness. **"In so many words"** is *about* perfection, and "she" is absorbed quickly, remorselessly into the succession of images. Her apartment, her days, her sex-life are brightly, coldly outlined; bold flat coloring included. The story begins with her "standing at one of the elongated windows, munching a Sara Lee croissant (quite delicious), she is taking in the American perfection, the American splendour—absolutely no irony is intended. It is true. From a certain height and perspective, the eighth floor of her building, America is convulsed with perfection." It ends with her taking her pleasure with three black-leather jacketed small-town thugs, sitting in a row on her brand new leather couch, "not oblivious of the perfection of her furniture, her lighting fixtures, the paintings on the walls, the view of the horsemen in the park below." At one point in the story she is disturbed by Whitehead's admonition, "Even perfection will not bear the tedium of indefinite repetition." The fastidiously accumulated, sheer weight of this perfection delivers a nearly imperceptible but most murderous, ideological razor-stroke across the baby-smooth skin of America.

But the *Future Perfect* is a *tense,* a category of language, of grammar, before being a ratio of reality. The flawless furniture of the American mind is interiorized, is the interior decoration in WA's precise, minimal line of diction. None of that *messiness* of speech which is an esthetic category of a characteristic American literature, consecrated in a Henry Miller and enshrined in innumerable material-hungry literary reviews, an esthetic seeking salvation in the brute massiveness and numbers of its own prolixity, a looseness and "richness" which once seemed to reproduce the chaos and energy of American life but today only capitulates to journalistic myth and publicity-image. *Prolixity* of language in the best contemporary users does draw attention to itself as prolixity of *language*; but an internal contradiction debilitates the correlation between a superabundant language and the superfluities of American life, since the *life of the fiction* can only be left over as the *residue* of such a correlation—and how can this residue be communicated in a welter of language? (That the life or energy of fiction be communicated as a *direct* product, as "superlife," of such a language is only conceivable in a Whitman, at the latest in the pre-war naïveté of a Miller, in the superalienation[2] of the 1960s and 1970s not at all). To find WA's roots one would have to go back, behind the self-conscious American literature (which sought as much its "literariness" as its "americanness") to the paradoxically unself-conscious writing of a James. The marginal life allowed in WA's stories, the fictive energy which feeds, animates his characters, their landscapes, the events, is a precise function of the sparse economy of his phrasing. The muffled universe described above finds its muffled echo in sheer and toneless constructions of his grammar. A pathological sameness of tone carries from descriptive passages to the direct speech of characters—which is never enclosed in quotation marks—and these characters, their conversations, their acts, the polished interiors and exteriors, and the *ex cathedra* annotations of the narrator blend into the same textual tissue. Questions and exclamations usually end with a period; even when characters cry out or groan, the text does not rise above a measured, polite, conversational tone: "Oh, no, cried Gregory. Not again. It's going to be one of those long drawn-out melodramas. I can't take it. I simply can't take it. Not at four in the morning." It is like watching television with the sound turned off. This soundless speech has a name: it is *writing.* Writing is language slowed to almost-zero, a near-immobility of language, *frozen language.* Derrida has taken an extreme, nihilistic position on this "second nature" of language as the full autonomy of text. consequently "logocentrism," the basis of classic, western ontology, is split and collapses. That is, *logos* can no longer represent Being in its transparency. A doubling, a destructive ambiguity stretches down into the roots of the Beginning; language exhibits in its phonetic spacings the articulations of writing. This is the *reflection,* the *double* of language that WA calls attention to constantly. The minute, precision-work of WA's elegant phrasing is a shield against its terror—terror of the abyss beneath the words, of an ontological caving-in. The reflexivity of his writing tunnels into and undermines the molar figures on the surface. Subversion of the "fictive truths" of his own fiction is already achieved in the molecular stresses of grammar and diction.

"The English Garden," the first story of this collection, perhaps exhibits the double and its terror with the starkest simplicity. **"The English Garden"** is quoted from Ashbery's *Three Poems*: "Remnants of the old atrocity subsist, but they are converted into ingenious shifts in scenery, a sort of 'English Garden' effect, to give the required air of naturalness, pathos and hope." I have requoted WA's quote of Ashbery because there is no literal "English Garden" in his story, only this literary one "lifted" from another text—the typical gap between language and referent, like a decalcomania, leaves a translucid tracing in the ensuing story where its content should have been. The story is the narrator's visit to a German city, Brumholdstein, ostensibly to interview the experimental writer, Wilhelm Aus. There is a puzzle under the surface however, as *this* WA plays an insignificant role in the story, much more attention being given to the local librarian, Ingeborg Platt, with whom the narrator has an affair, and to the city itself. The "ingenious shifts in scenery" become evident as we learn that the new, model German city was built on the site of a former concentration camp, Durst, demolished because "it would not attract a sufficient number of tourists to warrant the extensive repairs." The vanished camp imperceptibly pervades the busy, pleasant garden-city. One thinks of Walter Benjamin's characterization of Baudelaire: "The construction of his verse is the map of a big city, in which one can move about discreetly, covered by blocks of buildings, gates and squares. On this map are words, like conspirators at the outbreak of a revolt, their positions exactly indicated. Baudelaire conspires with language itself. . . ." Benjamin's intuition has come full circle in the new fiction; here the city, Brumholdstein, *is* a text, a sinister double of the "real" city; instead of conspirators the former inmates and torturers hover in the background like shadows of the present, model citizens, the "cheerful faces, massive faces . . . faces colored various shades of satisfied red." WA, the *narrator*, picks his way through the "German Garden"-city and the characters that people it with a lethal accuracy of tone, every word calculated and positioned precisely as if the Garden were a mine-field, barely hinting, by a shadow in the voice, at the horror and menace beneath. Like clues planted in a detective story, one by one pieces of the puzzle fall into place, although the "mystery" is never really elucidated, never "given" as in the detective story, its configuration only suggested. "Why did he refuse to take off his shirt? Because he is hiding something. What could he be hiding under his shirt," we are told after his affair with Ingeborg Platt in pedantic, puzzle-book type questions-and-answers, with a switch from the narrator's first person account to the third person, abruptly dropping the drama to a text level. Shortly afterwards Ingeborg disappears, and we learn that she had revealed to the narrator that her father had been commander of the Durst concentration camp. In the next to last paragraph, a photograph is found in her apartment of a "group of skeleton-like men standing in a row, posing for a photograph" in front of a building of the former camp. "Under a magnifying glass I could clearly make out the numbers tatooed on their forearms." What might be called the macro-puzzle emerges tenebrously, as *we* are obliged to fit the pieces together in a complicity with the narrator. So far, the obliqueness, the savagery beneath the delicate phrasing, mark what might be a typical if notable example of contemporary fiction. At the heart of this story however lurks a quintessential Abishian invention which separates his work out as a unique undertaking: a *language-machine*.

There is a language-machine in every one of WA's stories. Much has been made of WA as one of the foremost *experimental* writers today, a title which he disavows with some embarrassment—"I'm not really concerned with language. As a writer I'm principally concerned with meaning," he declares, with some duplicity as well, in one of his stories. But to these language-machines the label "experimentation" must be affixed, because they are imposed from "outside" upon his subjects, his material, his data, like some device, an input-output model, a black box. In this story the black box is a child's coloring book—an innocuous-looking device to apply to this "literary" visit to a German town built on the ruins of a concentration camp. The coloring book is acquired by the narrator upon arriving at the German airport. It depicts a jolly, gemütlich Germany, "almost everything that could be said to exist in the mind of a child." It is a machine because it generates language, or better a certain *activity in the text*. It might be more accurate to say that it *degenerates* the text. The presence of the coloring book is most obvious at the beginning of the story, the arrival in Germany; it serves as a sort of guide to Germany. "The question one keeps asking oneself is: How German is it? And, is this the true color of Germany?" Bright, chatty comparisons are made between coloring book and Germany until it is no longer clear when the narrator is speaking of the one or the other: those model Germans—"Many of the cars contain families on their way home from a Sunday outing . . . faces colored various shades of satisfied red. Cheerful faces, massive faces, glum faces." Coloring book and "real" Germany are, again, a *doublet*. It is in the pages of the coloring book that we first meet Brumhold, the hopelessly profound philosopher-Professor after whom the city is named, a Wittgensteinian or is it Heideggerian archetype who ponderously, asininely echoes WA's own preoccupations with words and "Things" in pseudo-conceptual counterpoint to the "colors" of the story. Gradually explicit reference to the coloring book is phased out of the story, but it has been so solidly lodged at the reality-base of the story that its energy eats away subliminally at the macro-puzzle. Embedded in the phrase-work of the story, it is a micro- or subpuzzle which disintegrates the macro-figures emerging from the story-frame and reduces them to bits and pieces of a puzzle, merely, or here to a coloring book. Any reference to color in the story-fiction is charged with this energy and immediately deconstructs the molar figures in its proximity. After the affair with Ingeborg Platt, for example, the narrator finds her "bright-colored silk scarf made in India. It has been left behind to remind me of an event that had taken place in this third-floor apartment." The neutral, "colorless" language of the "event" is *colored* only by the scarf; later when the narrator visits WA the avant-garde writer, "There are white tiles on the floor of their apartment. The metal railing on the staircase is black. The stairs like the exterior of the building are also made of red brick." As WA's apartment is colored in, it collapses onto the page of the coloring book. When Ingeborg disappears at the end of the story, all that marks the disappearance is "an ivory-colored dress with gold buttons" she wore on her evening at a restaurant with the narrator, the night before. "The coloring book," points out the narrator, "simply activates the desire of most people to color something that is devoid of color." The language-machine (or micro-puzzle, or double) re-converts the figures and events of a staged, fake Germany to language. With the narrator's straight-faced evocations of Professor Brumhold's impenetrable inanities in the background, "He started his philosophical inquiry by simply asking: *What is a thing,*" one might think of another famous, and mad, professor—Nietzsche, who, considering the "cogito ergo sum," found that the only certainty was that "I speak." And Clavel,[3] questioning this grammatical faith, suggests "why say 'I' speak, why not 'it' speaks in what I call 'me'. . . ."

SEXUAL EQUATION

We have approached the dark heart of WA's puzzles; before descending more deeply into this tissue of words, the spongy labyrinth of language, surely *sex* in should provide some relief, an antidote to words? In his *Self-Portrait,* WA speaks of "allowing the I to resuscitate itself by immersing its I in the attractiveness of a story-line or a screen or a page . . . there is also always sex. . . . As it fucks the I is temporarily expunged, only to reassert itself afterwards, a bit feebly it is true, as it addresses the other, saying: I love you." There appears to be an equation here. WA's fiction has been said to be erotically obsessive; it would be truer to speak of the absence of sex—or of its presence in the eye.

> Ingeborg is attempting to give me pleasure. She is doing it in a completely selfless and unselfconscious manner. It is, admittedly, not an entirely new experience, but the familiarity of the experience is colored by the unfamiliar world around me, a world housing unfamiliar things, that the remoteness, the polite distance between Ingeborg and myself serves only to intensify, although what I interpret as distance may merely be due to the way we *express* or fail to *express* ourselves in both English and German.

> (my italics)

Sex in WA's fiction is voyeuristic, divested of any sensual imagery, cold if mildly interested or amused, cerebral—it is a *combinatoire*. Composed of the observer and the object(s) (never subjects) observed, it interposes a membrane between them as impenetrable and transparent as writing between reader and event. The reflexiveness of the narrator—or whoever the observer may be—strips the communication of experience—except the experience of alienation of desire—precisely communicated because nothing of sexual experience is communicated. The experience of sex is diaphanously substituted for by *language-about* sex. "Knees are for supporting the body in a crouching position," a female character reflects in the middle of "the act" in another story; the mechanics are observed in a language reminiscent of a manual or instructions-for-assembling. Sex is a machine similar to the language-machine: it deconstructs people, separating them into parts. "Alva and his loved one entangled in a familiar routine of love, combining heads and legs, but all a bit mechanical, a bit staged, a bit fake. . . ." An articulation of writing?

WA never touches, penetrates the phenomenal level in his stories, but slips, glides over a film. The normal *seeing* of the reader—unself-conscious, absorbed, merged with the eyes of the characters, immersed in the seen—is converted by WA into the detached if fascinated *looking* of the voyeur, a literary voyeurism which stands outside the fiction looking in, which invests the world with eroticism, horror, eccentricity. "Thanks to language, thanks to maps, thanks to a few signs on the road, the brain can digest the surface of the areas that lie just beyond the familiar. In that way the familiar is expanded. . . ." This *de*-familiarization occurs when language is no longer purely transparent, or rather when self-aware, self-reflexive, it becomes quasi-visible as *writing*. It mirrors its own grammar, its own semantic projections in the trembling double of its writing. If WA's sex is *textual,* his text is no less *sexual*: just as the neutrality, the disassociation, the depersonalization of voyeuristic sex produce a febrile excitement, so the meticulous mechanics and static grammar of WA's "observed" prose create an inexplicable tension. The eye transgresses an erotic barrier in sex analogous to *writing* in language. "Barriers appear in my writings more frequently than they deserve," writes WA in a story. "Language is not a barrier," he says in the same paragraph, tongue-in-cheek. Writing, as *fictive act,* is the radical transgression of the new novel.

There is an absolute barrier to language: the image. I do not mean the "literary" image which is a fulfillment of language. For just that reason much contemporary fiction, including WA, strips its language of imagery. Some new novelists and "visual" poets use "real" (reproduced) images, blocking out or paralyzing the imagination of language. Language is murdered by the image, displaced and made superfluous by the mechanical abstraction and mimicry of "life." This image may be interiorized in fiction: as language-about photos, film, television. A subtle *blur* is produced in the fiction as a result. Fictive persons, events, landscapes are unchanged between the space of fictive language and an *other,* frozen and flat space: "At what stage does the Southern Californian convert the world around him into the flatness that resembles a movie screen." WA makes the conversion constantly in his fiction by means of these *machines of artifice*: "Has she become a part of Maxwell's scenario for the afternoon," a character asks. In this story, **"Ardor/Awe/Atrocity,"** a television series, *Mannix* (man X?), saturates the physical and "human" environment of the "real" characters. The images of visual media—flattened, hard, exact—become the language of WA's entire fiction. WA compares his writing to Rosenquist: "The realism of being screwed by three men in leather jackets. The overlapping was not disharmonious. If anything it resembled a painting by Rosenquist." While recognizing the discontinuities which WA might share with Rosenquist, I prefer to compare the hyper- or photorealists—the pellucid quality, sheen, esthetic functionality of phrase line coincide with photorealism in the reproducing of "reproduction." Precise detail and hard surface did not bring visual art back to the figure of course, but doubly removed it. Photorealism produced a picture of reproducibility—just as WA produces language-about language. Susan Sontag has said that the photographic image is language. More precisely, it is a *writing*. In WA's fiction, these "images" are an image of writing.

CROSS-WORD PUZZLE

The artifices of WA's language have become sufficiently apparent; these are doubled to a power X^2 by his *languages of artifice*. The paradox of his fiction is disclosed here. The model of the puzzle has been shown to articulate his entire fiction. The combining of characters and event sequences and identities throughout his stories, the mini-plots of sex, the micro-structural unravelings of image, find their analog in the effort to identify and unscramble letter and number games. There are two kinds of writing in WA's fiction: a warm and a cold current. **"The English Garden"** is an example of the former: the puzzle, the structuring-destructuring device, however pervasive, is married or blended more smoothly with the "fiction," is more implicit and "literary" (in the nature of an extended image). In the cold current, the puzzle hardens, becomes entirely visible, *visual,* and clearly imposed upon the fiction from the "outside." The mysterious heart of the puzzle is revealed in such stories: this most trivial of intellectual diversions, this distraction from the serious, meaningful concerns of life becomes a metaphysics of nihilism.

"In so many words," the contents of which I outlined in the first part of this essay, has such a puzzle applied onto it. The text is divided into pairs of paragraphs: the first in italics consists of a list of words in alphabetical order; the second in ordinary print is the regular, on-going text of the story. Each paragraph is also headed by a number. One notes first that the words in the alphabetical series are all found in the regular paragraphs; next that the alphabetical paragraphs are always shorter than the regular paragraphs; finally that the numbers heading the paragraphs correspond to the number of words each respectively contains, and that these naturally differ since certain words given only once in the alphabetical series, particularly prepositions, articles and pronouns, are repeated in the other paragraph.

Even if we wish at first to skip over the disturbing, italicized paragraphs to find out *what is happening* in the story, our eye is tripped and slowed down by the opaque blocks of (meaningless) alphabetical paragraphs and foreign bodies of the numbers. Events, people, scenes and their words are inexorably split apart, subjects and acts are broken down. However even in the next-to-zero velocity of one- and two-word concrete poems, a flicker of life is preserved; like gravestones with their pithiest of biographies, name, date of birth and death, the shadow of a man is fleetingly recalled—especially when one reviews these fossilized stones serially, the cemetery comes faintly, remotely alive with the murmur of their momentarily concrete presences. It is provocative in this regard to reiterate the importance WA places on names (particularly of the women): the female automats that people his pages are de-fined sexually and as personalities solely (almost) by the phonetic symbols that compose their names: the peculiar resonances of *Irma, Maude, Muriel*. In any case, since word and meaning cannot be fully amputated, we never read WA's prose like the succession of words and letters he keeps impressing (by means of print) upon us, but the presence of disintegration is always there, and his characters and landscapes threaten at every instant to crumble into the flatness and bloodlessness of their lettered likenesses—and they *know* it.

On the face of it, this alphabetical and numbering clockwork appears to be purely mechanical and external. On closer examination the puzzle is seen to participate in the persons, their acts and love-making, in a cold and horrifying, pseudo-intrinsic way: the number at the top of the ordinary paragraphs in its ratio with the number of the alphabet series stands for the *number* of the words which brought them—persons, events, etc.—*into being*. The *number* thus contains them like their cipher. The alphabetical order of the words which represent these beings serializes them arbitrarily but in a coherent, other universe. The senselessness of their "own" world is purely mirrored in this arbitrary order. The rigidity of the alphabet reflects the determinism of their lives. The perfections of America so dazzlingly projected in this story are translated, encapsulated in the arithmetical series. The pure structure of alphabet and number reproduce, in their insidious relationship to character and event and landscape, the elegance of a perfect, meaningless world.

In another "cold" story, **"Ardor/Awe/Atrocity,"** the trip of "Jane" through Southern California and her adventures, mostly sexual, finally murderous, are described in the first half; in the second half, "Bob Down's" arrival in Southern California and elusive pursuit of "Jane." The subject of the story is as much the psychic landscape of CA, intimately pervaded, colored by the detective series, *Mannix*. The story is divided into 26 paragraphs, each headed by three numbered words: the first is Ardor[1] Awe[2] Atrocity[3], the second Byouan[4] Bob[5] Body[6], the third California[7] Color[8] Cut[9] and so on down the alphabet to Zoo[76] Zodiac[77] Zero[78] at the end. In the body of each paragraph several words are numbered, and the words and numbers which at first appear quite random are found to coincide with a corresponding word/number couple in one of the paragraph headings. The triplicate titles, at first seemingly arbitrary, are felt to cast a sheen, an aura which sets the atmosphere of the story.

The highly contrived and artificial *look* of the puzzle immediately makes its point, as a language of artifice. The letters and numbers scattered through the various paragraphs are like coordinates, ordering events, parts of events, particles of persons *somewhere else*. In our effort to solve and combine the puzzle, we become accomplices of WA in fixing or framing (the criminal connotation) characters in a situation they are *ignorant* of; we move above them. The author's—and our—self-exclusion in the coldness of the medium, is over-compensated for by this hovering, shadowy presence through the grid of alphabet and number.

So far we have looked at the negativity of the (written) word and the ruinous effects of the puzzle. Having penetrated into these interstices of language, an unexpected inversion takes place. By reducing "things" to words, to symbols, WA has gained power over them; by sacrificing the expressive, i.e., *magic* property of words, WA gains a *magic,* incantatory power over the intractable world. Deconstructing the continuum of language to an inebriate excess by lettering and numbering, WA produces an alchemistry of the anguishing "everyday" world; breaking it down into its molecules, it may now be chemically recombined— the new compounds hinted at by letter/number couples. Having recognized the non-translatability of "reality" into language, WA performs instead a magical or Kabbalistic letter-meditation on his fiction; a sort of *Holhmath hatseruf* or "science of the combination of letters" such as the Sephardic Abulafia elaborated in the 13th century. In his search for a method of meditation which would enable the soul to shut out and see beyond the sensible forms of this world, Abulafia found the mystical contemplation of the letters of the Hebrew alphabet. Among the conceptions he studied was *gematria,* the numerical value of words (surely a future perfect fiction of WA will number the letters of words!), and the extraordinary *dillug,* a jumping from one conception to another, a species of discontinuity thoroughly familiar to WA! Now of course the whole aim of this "mystical logic" for Abulafia was the movement to God in ecstasy. In WA however, the use of our degraded alphabet, and the schizophrenic condition (doubling) of our superalienation which his fiction so mordantly represents, point in the opposite direction. It is well known, in fact the popular misconception, that Kabbalism tended to slide from a translucent meditation into magic. Are WA's puzzles a magical rite, by means of which he exorcizes the mindless horrors of our future perfect world and substitutes an alternative reality: mysterious, poetic, opaque to the one described? A magical manipulation and domination of the everyday world?

SOLUTION

This essay has been an attempt to solve the puzzle. The letters of the words of events and personalities have been inserted into their numbered slots, and seen to lock together. The puzzle may have been solved but it has not been resolved.

What "real life" is left in **"In the Future Perfect"**? Well, there is WA himself, the narrator/author present throughout his fictions. I have labeled him with his initials, feeling authorized by WA himself in his *Self-Portrait*: "Kafka . . . took refuge behind one of the letters of our alphabet. It so happened that the letter he picked was the initial of his family name . . . a formal link to the exteriority of his self"—a link similar to the pseudo-intrinsic relationship of letters and numbers to the words of his world. In the un-

raveling of the puzzle we thus see WA play amidst the letters he assembled. WA is both actor in and author of the fiction. In **"The English Garden"** he colors in the picture book which generates the story. He appears at the end of **"Awe/Ardor/Atrocity"** as a "Mannix nut" and author of a book set in Southern California, in which this story takes place. In **"In so many words,"** one of his real-life books, *Alphabetical Africa,* inexplicably finds its way into the heroine's perfectly furnished apartment. And throughout, *ex cathedra,* WA lets us know about compositional problems and itineraries in the movement of the fiction. His entrances "on stage" are discreet, like a Hitchcock's. He is an innocent onlooker in a voyeuristic prose, mildly sympathetic to the ravenous and soulless characters peopling his pages. WA is a real person as we know from his extraordinary *Self-Portrait*: born in Vienna, raised in China where he lived through World War II, then eight years in Israel, where he served in the army, and where he also had a chance to become well acquainted with the Negev Desert. Incidents, friends' and acquaintances' names, objects shift back and forth between biography and fiction. A friend of WA's disappeared exactly like Ingeborg Platt in **"The English Garden."** The photograph "of Irma on a west side pier" which generated the story, **"Parting Shot,"** is to be seen on the second shelf of WA's bookcase, as described at the end of the story, "sitting on the second shelf is a photograph I took. . . ." On the other hand, his apartment is far from the perfect, antiseptic interiors of his characters; I am glad to say it is quite messy and comfortable and gemütlich.

I am not sure whether WA's presence tends to soften or "gentle" this hard and glassy world, or to ensure simply that every exit is securely locked. In effect there is no way *out* of his world of surfaces, a world with no inside to start with and an outside which is nowhere. Sex itself has been experienced as impenetrable: seamless, perfectly jointed, it allows no crack, no surface rupture, no way to penetrate to the other. His characters do rarely, briefly, recognize imperfection: ". . . in bed something else besides perfection was wanted, needed, desired," but that need is quickly overcome in the headlong rush into the future perfect. In only one story is there something like an opening, a rent in an otherwise seamless fabric: at the end of **"The English Garden,"** WA "tossed the coloring book and the crayons into a garbage can. The man who stamped my passport said: Come back soon. *Auf Wiedersehen.*" The gesture negates, contemptuously, the very stuff of this fictitious culture: the German farewell, ironic self-contradiction, betrays the passion WA has kept just below the surface of this particular story, and which does not surface elsewhere. But the rent allows no light to pierce through, and opens out onto nothing.

RESOLUTION?

What is missing in WA's fiction is any moment of ecstasis, a standing-out from the world. And this exactly defines its closure, its perfect circularity. The analysis of this essay is constructed on the concentric circles of WA's grand puzzle. The master-puzzler manufactures the fictive truths (identity, act, origin) and this verbal act constitutes the truth of his mastery. There is a metaphysics implicit in WA's fiction; it is the metaphysics of an active nihilism. Through the subtle relations, hierarchies, figures of his lettered and numbered geometry of the mind, WA deconstructs ordinary language and builds, projects a mathematical, artificial language in its place, one which exactly spells out the fictitious nature of our truths, dispels these truths, and numbering, recollects them in the mesh of its finely webbed construction. The mastery of the whole vibrates in a polarity with the will to master. A. Glucksmann has shown how this Nietzschean circle of domination is rooted in traditional western metaphysics[4]: "the double question: what is being? is formulated on the one hand: what is (in general) being? and on the other hand it is formulated: what (which) is (absolutely) being?" (Heidegger). Shades of Prof. Brumhold! WA, the Grand Puzzler, holds his puzzlebook up like a decoding grid to the light of everyday, an alphabet and an arithmetic to decipher the world—and *encodes* the world as a puzzle. To take the last image of the last story in *In the Future Perfect,* to cast a last—light?—on this puzzle: at the end of **"Crossing the great void,"** Zachary, the hero, "is bound for the center of the desert," a place (topos) which has had mythic (?) importance in WA's "real" life, "and every step he has taken is bringing him closer to the center, and every step he has taken in the past has led to his being here. Even before he was aware of the center's existence, he was traveling towards it." Two lines further, he declares that "the emptiness which he expects to encounter at the center will be no different from the emptiness he might experience in the interior of his room after it had been denuded of all his possessions, stripped of all the things he had clung to with such persistence, such tenacity, such great effort, as if all his entire life depended on it." The eerie beauty of this final image points to some content of the puzzle, to something like a resolution. Or is the image voided by the "emptiness"? Or isn't "emptiness" an image of the voided imagery? In the bible, the desert is seen as the place of spirits, not of the Spirit. The desert lies beyond language, a white page. It has been seen how WA's writing oscillates with the tensions of an absent sexuality, or the sexuality of absence. This absence, that emptiness, has a name: cruel, half-hidden at the sharp corner of the last letter of the last phrase, the jocular grin of Death.

Notes

1. "Self-Portrait," W. Abish, published in *Individuals: Post-Movement Art in America* (New York: Dutton, 1977).

2. *Superalienation* is a concept I developed in a recent essay, "The Ideology of Fiction," as the ideological framework of the new fiction, in particular "superfiction." Based on M. Clavel's thinking, and Foucault and Derrida, I described the "text" of our culture, which—having become autonomous and universal, the voided metaphysical assumptions about man embedded in the forms of culture, co-extensive with

language itself—can no longer be "read" by man today; he can no longer recognize himself in this "text."

3. Maurice Clavel, seminal thinker and first of the "nouveaux philosophes," in *Ce que je crois* (Paris: Grasset, 1975), and *Dieu est Dieu nom de Dieu* (Paris: Grasset, 1976).

4. André Glucksmann, *Les Maîtres Penseurs* (Paris: Grasset, 1977).

Gabriel Josipovici (review date 1984)

SOURCE: "Another Old Atrocity," in *Times Literary Supplement,* No. 4234, March 25, 1984.

[*In the following review, Josipovici dismisses Abish's stories as banal and vulgar exercises in "American pseudo-experimentalism."*]

"Remnants of the old atrocity subsist, but they are converted into ingenious shifts in scenery, a sort of 'English Garden' effect, to give the required air of naturalness, pathos and hope." These words of John Ashbery's form the epigraph to the first story in Walter Abish's collection [*In the Future Perfect*]. They are menacing and haunting precisely because they are so simple, so clear. What old atrocity? we wonder, and who converts and who requires? The passage is troubling precisely because we all seem to be implicated, because it suggests that all patterning, no matter how innocent, is a way of concealing; but, by the same token, that all patterning, however innocent, carries the tell-tale signs of its origins.

Unfortunately this is by far the best thing in the book. Abish follows it, for example, with a story of awful banality, about a writer—not so different, we guess, from Abish himself—who comes to a clean new German town to interview a local author. Of course it turns out that the town is built on the site of an old concentration camp; of course the visitor's ex-wife turns out to have been in this very camp (it is even suggested, with plonking obviousness, that the visitor himself, since he does not take off his shirt when he makes love to the immediately willing daughter of—of course—the ex-camp commandant, has something on his arm he wishes to hide); of course the Germans he meets don't want to remember; of course the ex-commandant's daughter is suddenly struck with guilt or remorse and vanishes; of course her friends silently blame the visitor for disturbing their settled way of life.

The story is nothing but a string of clichés. We are never made to ponder motive or asked to grapple with the complexity of the issues involved. Malcolm Bradbury, in his enthusiastic introduction, compares Abish to Peter Handke, but to my ear they are worlds apart. Handke's neutral prose is, like Kleist's, resonant with suppressed emotion, and his books convey a sense of deep understanding and compassion, as well as a fierce delight in the one weapon left him in a terrifying world: writing itself.

Abish, by contrast, seems to want to present us with the neutrality of adult cartoons, combined with the New American Pseudo-Experimentalism. This means that he writes in short paragraphs, which often have little relation to each other; that he eschews all punctuation except the full stop; that he is fond of numbering words in order to draw our attention to their recurrence at different points in the piece, or running through the alphabet with the initial letters of the words of a paragraph. But the style never seems to be dictated, as it is in Handke or, say, Georges Perec, by the exigencies of the theme, while the formal constraints are too slack to be interesting. If, for example, in using the alphabet as generator, you leave yourself free to repeat letters as often as necessary, and even to leave some out, it is like writing a sonnet sequence with poems of anything from twelve to sixteen lines, and in any rhyme scheme, or none; one wonders why the writer has bothered with the form in the first place.

Part of the answer is that Abish is clearly uneasy with the given forms of narrative but doesn't quite know what to do about it. The result is a continuous attempt at "alienation effect", plus an excruciating whimsy, as in the opening to the fourth story: "In the cradle of civilization men and women habitually sat face-to-face. They sat on stone benches or on the ground. The art of costume design was already well-advanced, although, I might add, these events preceded the invention of the door-knob and the window-pane."

Yet such writing, like that of Coover or Barthelme, is highly regarded in America, where clearly both style and content find echoes in many hearts. Fiction which deals, though, only with people whose principal interests are sex, being unpleasant to their spouses or blowing people up, even if this is an authentic image of present-day America, makes for tedious reading. The attempt to inject pathos by the use of resonant epigraphs and concentration camps turns the tedious into the unpleasantly vulgar.

Jerome Klinkowitz (essay date 1984)

SOURCE: "The Self-Apparent Word," in *The Self-Apparent Word: Fiction as Language/Language as Fiction,* Southern Illinois University Press, 1984, pp. 86–95.

[*In the following excerpt, Klinkowitz examines the techniques Abish has employed to create an "awareness of the author's role in the composition" of his fictions.*]

The novella **"This Is Not a Film. This Is a Precise Act of Disbelief"** forms the centerpiece to the author's first collection, **Minds Meet.**[1] How we live, what our needs may be, and the form our hopes will take are all determined by the available surface of things surrounding us, this piece of fiction argues. Strongly narrative in form, it

uses the methods of city planning (the trade which brought Abish to America after living in Austria, China, Israel, and England) to show how the structures available to us actually create, rather than serve, our needs. The occasion is the planning of a new shopping mall, which a French film director very much like Jean-Luc Godard[2] has come to study as an example of decadent American capitalism. The mall developer is part of a group which runs the town; within its population can be found a network of relationships, financial and sexual, which determine how things will happen. "This is a familiar world," the novella begins, announcing a strategy parallel to Abish's theory in **"On Aspects of the Familiar World as Perceived in Everyday Life and Literature"** and just as systematic as the alphabet in *Alphabetical Africa.* "It is a world crowded with familiar faces and events. Thanks to language the brain can digest, piece by piece, what has occurred and what may yet occur" (p. 31). The developers plan malls, and the builders construct them according to plan—a comfortable arrangement of surfaces. The lowest worker in the story takes delight in forklifting cases of soda pop from shelves in the warehouse to pallets in the parking lot. (He also enjoys table tennis, just as his bosses enjoy bouncing their designs along the town's surface.) Disruptions of routine are moved aside, whether it be a retarded child shunted off to an institution or a corpse hidden behind locked doors. Whatever might be hidden beneath this clean and shiny surface is as important to Abish's work as to Poe's, and is a recurrent device to suggest how the systems which regulate our surface lives screen the less workable complications within the depths.

Much of **Minds Meet,** however, is playfully comic, toying with the inadequacies of a bumbling narrator. In **"The Istanbul Papers"** he is an embassy official seduced into giving Hitler's daughter a visa to the United States. **"The Second Leg"** finds this same type of figure as the odd-man-out at his girlfriend's apartment, where he plots out the doings in syntactic fashion.

> All evening I master forebearance. I decline to inquire into their true relationship. Why should it matter to me, a kind of stretched-out week-end guest, what she and Victor do in the bathroom. It is so simple to jump to an erroneous conclusion. First Victor excuses himself, and leaves the table. Then she goes to the kitchen to fetch the dessert and coffee. Don't run off and desert me, I say jokingly. The next thing I hear is their boisterous shouts, their unabashed shrill laughter. They do nothing to restrain their mirth . . . or the sound of running water. It is seeping through from under the bathroom door when I get up to investigate. I keep myself in check and do not bring it to their attention. All things considered . . . not to overlook the soaked bedroom slippers, as well as the inexplicable presence of the two damp pillows on the toilet seat. I am at an utter loss for an explanation. Is this all being done for my exclusive benefit? I am resolved not to take too dark a view of all this horseplay.

> (P. 111)

Still other stories verge on abstraction, as in **"With Bill in the Desert"** and **"Non-Site."** In the former piece a desert trek seems to be taking place in a small room lit by an un-shaded bulb, Abish's fictive reaction to a work of conceptual art by Terry Fox where "the light formed a topography of the interior that was, at once, a familiar romantic configuration in which the tent became the emotive key to a kind of disturbance of things past, and another in which one's physical presence, one's emotions, were measured (and partly activated) by one's proximity to that light" (p. 103). It is in such conceptual artwork that Abish finds the true connection between surface and depth and indicates the direction his own work pursues.

In the Future Perfect,[3] Abish's second collection, shows the wide range of the author's methods, from the sign-fixated topology of **"The English Garden"** (which anticipates *How German Is It*) to a series of shorter pieces which experiment with structural forms even more complexly determining than that of *Alphabetical Africa*. In **"Ardor/ Awe/Atrocity,"** for example, block paragraphs are titled by a trinity of alphabetically ordered words, seventy-eight in all, which are in turn identified by superscript numbers (of their ordinal ranking according to the alphabet). The subtitles introduce us to the words before their narrative sense, and their superscription when they do appear reminds us that they are first of all lexical devices and only secondly signifiers of an other reality. The story line itself discusses the surface of the "perpetual present" along which Californians propel themselves, acquiring styles from hit TV shows and acting them out along the boulevards, freeways, and beaches of their streamlined land. Without such shows as guidance, the story insists, the land and its people would be bereft of distinction. Citing the private detective hero, Abish notes that "keeping an eye on Mannix is one way of watching the smoothly functioning process of a culture prepared for any eventuality" (p. 49), as if the entire world has been converted to a movie screen. Breaking down this technique even further in the story **"In So Many Words,"** Abish titles his paragraphs by the number of words they contain, and then mixes the contents up before repeating them in proper order. Hence the reader again encounters the words apart from any combinatory meaning; and even when the meaning emerges on the second reading through, there will still be a sense of each word's individuality remaining from the first self-apparent encounter. In similar manner the emerging story features a young woman around whom meaning slowly takes shape as the sense of her syntax forms itself: "They know nothing about her except what is on view. What is on view is splendidly displayed. It is, furthermore, on view in order to be appreciated" (p. 94), and that act of appreciation must be constructed according to rules of visual grammar, just as Abish unscrambles each paragraph's words to make sense.

Three of Abish's more recent stories are even more radical in their methods of self-apparency. Prefacing the first, Abish explains his intent.

> In constructing **"Inside Out"** I pretended that all books published in English represented a vast dictionary that made sentences (instead of just words) available to a

writer. More or less at random I selected one sentence, and sometimes part of a sentence, from eighty authors. The numbers on the page indicate the number of words taken (and I cannot think of a more appropriate word) from each writer. The selection of the sentence, the sequence I followed and the idea to undertake this exercise are mine, but the story . . . ?[4]

The piece which follows does have a sense of progression to it, as a narrator describes his position, activities, and re-actions—all of which is amazing because we have been told first off that the author has not composed these sentences but chosen them at random. This method is less shocking when we are reminded that there are such things as dictionaries of symbols which writers may use to create stories and which critics may in turn refer to for interpretation. But Abish's achievement is considerable when we note that words lose their self-apparency (and had in fact in his earlier experiments) just at the point of their combination into sentences. In **"Inside Out"** and the author's other variations in this mode the sense of opaqueness is expanded to include the sentence and then the paragraph, all the while maintaining a humanly interesting story.

"Ninety-Nine: The New Meaning"[5] and **"What Else"**[6] show Abish perfecting his theory and also moving toward longer selections, so that a fully new meaning for each sentence may be assumed from its new context. The first consists of ninety-nine selections each from page ninety-nine of books available in Abish's library, including two of his own. **"What Else"** allows the freedom of scanning fifty other books for passages that seem to be of use, although the story does not assume final form until all the selections are placed in Abish's "order." Such a technique—using others' sentences rather than his own—would seem to be the extreme of abstraction in composition. But Abish's device in fact produces the opposite effect, for so rich are words and their associations that even plucked so randomly they still allow the author to compose with great human significance. "What tense would you choose to live in?" this latter story concludes, and answers: "I want to live in the imperative of the future passive participle—in the 'what ought to be.' I like to breathe that way. That's what I like. It suggests a kind of mounted, bandit-like equestrian honor" (p. 119), much like the sense of vitality Abish's work entails.

Notes

1. Walter Abish, *Minds Meet* (New York: New Directions: 1975.

2. In the original manuscript later changed for publication by *Seems* magazine, Abish named his character Jean-Luc Godard.

3. Walter Abish, *In the Future Perfect* (New York: New Directions, 1977).

4. Walter Abish, "Inside Out," *Personal Injury,* No. 4 (1977), pp. 57–68.

5. Walter Abish, "Ninety-Nine: The New Meaning," *Renegade,* No. 1 (1979), pp. 2–15.

6. Walter Abish, "What Else," *Conjunctions,* No. 1 (Winter 1981–82), pp. 105–19.

Robert Siegle (excerpt date 1987)

SOURCE: "On the Subject of Walter Abish and Kathy Acker," in *Literature and Psychology,* Vol. XXXIII, Nos. 3 & 4, 1987, pp. 38–57.

[*In the following excerpt, Siegle examines how Abish uses language to undermine subjectivity, which, Abish argues, encourages the projection of presumed meaning onto ready surfaces, and prevents the discovery of the actuality of things in themselves.*]

Part of the attraction of Walter Abish's work is the extent to which it carries forward the rethinking of subjectivity, rescuing many immediate experiences we know to be part of the contemporary subjective reality instead of dispersing them along with the theory of selfhood that had supported their fictional manifestations. He tells Jerome Klinkowitz in an interview that "I avoid the intentional and sometimes unintentional hierarchy of values that seems to creep in whenever lifelike incidents are depicted," and goes on to explain that

> language ceases to be a "tool" that facilitates the realization of a lifelike atmosphere, and concomitant creation of "real" people . . . it also ceases to intensify the immediacy of action, thereby diminishing the somewhat misleading proximity between words and what they signify.
>
> (Klinkowitz, *Life of Fiction,* 65)

But of course "realistic" places, situations, encounters, "people" are throughout a collection like *In the Future Perfect,* but partly, perhaps, because his foregrounding of various cultural languages reoccasions the vitality of those situations without their distance from language and belief systems diminishing.

In terms of subjectivity, then, Abish does indeed dispense with the illusion of the Self as a regal authority with power, and thus responsibility, to determine its thoughts, actions, the assumptions underlying them, and the means by which they are exercised. Behavior is a complex interaction of systems and structures which exist in no simple internal/external or cause/effect relation with the "subject," but perhaps in one of mutual *supplement.* Fiction seems to have become an ideal site in which Abish arranges encounters between history, systems, and subjectivity. Always in those encounters the latter fails to function in ways predictable by its classic formulation. Relationships, for example, are mediated by systems of which consciousness (language) and history (state policy) are woven. "Self-awareness" is contingent upon the ability of given elements to resonate within accessible frame(s) of reference.

Subjectivity is dwarfed by larger structures like History, the State, popular culture, private and collective myths, all evolving from the cultural process—and all of which, of course, are not to be conceived, as they often have been, within the metaphysics of the Subject (intention, identity, etc.), but as themselves undercoded, asymmetrical, and self-differing codes-in-formation which are latent within the overdetermined and hence infinitely complex events of experience.[1] **"In the Future Perfect"** is an ideal title for Abish because it underscores the extent to which futures are perfected, completed, by the systems and structures by which they are determined. The danger of oversimplifying a cultural model is present, of course, and Abish works against that not with the "humanism" of traditional realism with its illusion of infinite depth, but rather with the facets and glints of surfaces, their emphasis being upon the two-dimensional semiotic planes of billboards, silver screen, *House Beautiful,* and television.

The result is a significant interplay of immediate elements and mediating cultural forms, of individual and collective scales of reference. In **"The English Garden,"** perhaps the most often mentioned of the stories, one of many interesting incarnations of that interplay is to be seen. In effect, the story is about the stakes, often ideological, in the naturalized relation between sign and referent. In that most accessible and ideological dimension, the story undoes the attempt to repress a concentration camp by building a model city upon it. The "English Garden" metaphor is at first glance inappropriate, since anything but a natural paradise is erected: what we really find is a prefab city, gleaming, urban, perfect. But since an English garden, on second thought, is also anything but natural, is in fact a Central Park built stone by shrub or a Yorkshire sculpted by a landscape designer, the metaphor points towards prefabricated and mechanized "perfection" as what a semiotically hyperactive culture takes as its Nature.

What happens, of course, is that the concentration camp stalks the collective memory, a constant source of anxiety to its politicians, writers, and survivors (from both sides of the line). The Mayor snubs the narrator, the Writer tears up an old photo of camp inmates in front of him and works instead in avant-garde surfaces and the predictable and half-domesticated mildly left politics of the intelligentsia, and the commandant's daughter becomes "desperate" (her word) in her effort to maintain the contemporary facade and drops out of sight. In the public world History, in the private world Memory, each work against the ideological closure which the preplanned city is designed to impose upon the fertile ground of the old camp's site. The new system overcoded onto the old system preserves, perhaps, too much of the latter's reduction of people to objects, its management of dissonance with the final solution of exterminating traces of any perceived threat to its hegemony. That is to say, the history of systems is sedimented into their current morphologies despite our best efforts.

But that buried past is not the only lever used to dislocate the perhaps hegemonic sway of the reigning codings. Abish makes much of the after-thought of naming the new town after a philosopher, Brumhold, an unmistakably Heideggerian philosopher in his queries about "the *thing*" and its "metaphysical" or "intrinsic" meanings. These two labels, of course, resist a reigning assignment of significance by opposing to it a Real or True meaning in the classic idealist tradition, a tradition whose traces in Heidegger's metaphysical nostalgia are equally unmistakable:

> In the great tradition of Greek and German philosophy Brumhold has questioned the meaning, the intrinsic meaning of a *thing* as it manifests itself in the context of metaphysics. There is, moreover, if one stretches the mind a little bit, a certain correlation between a *thing* as we know and understand it to be so and 2,500 apartment units, not to mention the additional services, the fire department, post office, library, school . . .
>
> (8)

The context of metaphysics is different from that of city planning, just as the thing-in-itself (the apartments, or the camp for that matter) is different from the thing "as we know and understand it to be so"—i.e., as it functions within a given semiotic coding or, if you prefer, discursive regime. Brumhold raises similar questions as a WWII draftee:

> If we assume that this is merely a *thing,* he said pointing at his rifle, and this is a *thing,* pointing at his uniform, and each and all of us are doing our *thing,* then our actions, whatever they might be, and whatever they might be called if we were to use the prevailing military terminology, are formulated by our grasp of the *things* around us.
>
> (8–9)

Abish has great fun, of course, with his narrator's parody of Brumhold (particularly when the incongruity surfaces between such speculation and the surrounding destruction), so that the apolitical quietism of idealist speculation is made unmistakable. But equally important is the revolutionary potential Brumhold's Idealist—that is, ahistorical and anti-ideological (itself, of course, an ideology) loosening of reigning codings from their naturalized authority. As "our grasp" changes, so change our actions and our understanding of everything around us. Brumhold's belief in "the profound need and urge to *think*" is a license to recode the present in terms of a metaphysical, "meditative," idealist, ontological, or other order alternative to the dominant.

The effect of the parody of Brumholdian style, the juxtaposition of his questions with the historical reality of WWII death and destruction, and the inevitably already completed passage of the *thing* into a grasp or a thing "as we understand it," is to see his thought not as the freeing of things from codings, but simply as another coding. The master metaphor of such coding is that of the coloring book the narrator buys, a metaphor no commentator on the story misses (see, for example, Klinkowitz 69, Arias—Misson 118). As he considers the stylized shapes and the implications of coloring them German, the narrator indexes in the course of the story a number of functions the book serves.

To begin with it is, of course, an instrument by which children are socialized with certain values and assumptions: "the coloring book accurately depicts almost everything that could be said to exist in the mind of a child" (1). Moreover, "nothing that is depicted in the coloring book will force them to think in either" the calculative or meditative modes, but instead everything simply asks to be colored as "details whose sum is perfection," a nice image of the totalization of both these cognitive alternatives beyond which the story strives to push. And since its contents include only things "that will never arouse anyone's disapproval," it "simply activates the desire of most people to color something that is devoid of color. In this particular instant it is the normal everyday activity of people in the process of going about their tasks" (5), an apt reference to the coding of Heidegger's Everydayness. Since "dislike has been permanently effaced from the world of this coloring book" (17), it serves the current social goals of homogenization and pacification, just as the 1940 coloring books, we're told, emphasized tanks and "strange salutes." History has shifted from *lebensraum* to *altäglichkeit,* but the culture's means of filling the minds of its (childlike?) citizenry remain the codings in popular media.

That media operates by two crucial dimensions of meaning in its semiotic media. The first we might call, following Eco, the segmentation of the content continuum (Eco 50–58). Coloring books, as those of us with no artistic talent experienced early on, are often one of the earlier experiences of the Law, of boundary, of arbitrarily recognized or constituted entities naturalized by the force of cultural institutions. One has to take as authoritative its pictures of the world, and one has to confine one's play within the boundaries it authorizes. Until one becomes a Brumholdian philosopher or an avant-garde artist, the possibility does not occur to one to rethink those circumscriptions of the actual, to alter its selection, its decisions about margins and categories, its accentings of the stress in garments or experiences.

The faces and scenes, we're told, are "by no means . . . characteristically German faces. Nothing is intrinsically German, I suppose, until it receives its color" (1); it corresponds to western culture's general segmentation of reality, but not yet to the specific networks of historical coding we call characteristically "German." Just as significant, then, are the emotional tonalities that govern their combination, their vitality, their emergence as a vibrant and living (realistic?) whole. The narrator decides of the pages that

> all they need is a bit of color to come to life and embrace each other, and then, in the best of humor, stroll over to a nearby cafe and have a *Bratwurst* or some other kind of *Wurst,* and then, to top it off, see a good film, a satisfying film shot in bright color, the bright color of Germany around them, the color that still remains to be added to these pages, the color that in the film isolates details, the details whose sum is perfection . . .
>
> (4–5)

The passage equates the colors by which the book is colored "German," of the colorful life of "ethnic" German pastimes, of popular film (the adult world's coloring book?), and of the world outside as perceived. It also suggests that "color" represents the network of connotation by which film, art, landscape, and other cultural forms weave meanings by connecting their various meaning-clusters, their semiotic strands, their systems—the mechanics, in other words, of coding their values, hierarchies, and assumptions about what is "natural" in the "Germany around them."

But this story is only one of those by which Abish draws a box around all the activities of a story's participants and includes them within the systematic quality of contemporary semiotic mores. In the New Germany of the collection's opening story, the product of such activity is a disquieting world in which repressed contradictions lead to constricted relations, whether social, artistic, or sexual. The narrator keeps his shirt on when making love to the commandant's daughter, Ingeborg Platt the librarian, no doubt "hiding" the metaphorical stenciled numbers he wears as an inmate of a global camp of ideological control that is the alarming counterpart to those literal numbers worn by the wraiths in the old photo. The rest of the stories open a fascinating range of perspectives upon this global "city planning" of the collective consciousness.

In **"Ardor/Awe/Atrocity,"** for example, Abish is up to tricks reminiscent of *Alphabetical Africa* with a story of twenty-six sections, alphabetically arranged, each of whose three keywords are superscripted. The story then superscripts each word when it appears, perhaps to signify, by means of the absent footnotes to which we expect superscripts to refer, the often unacknowledged diacritical nature of its meaning. The tactic thus denaturalizes the medium and prevents our minds from disappearing into plot. That is important, of course, if we are not to repeat the fate of the principal characters who disappear into the plots of popularized pathways. Jane, that is, goes to L.A. over the misgivings of her parents, makes it (literally) in pornographic movies, and dies (also literally) to her old acquaintances, murdered by her success. Aside from a commentary on the fundamentally voyeuristic appeal of popular film and its (ab)use of its starlets and upon the reduction of women to male sex objects—a theme pervasive in the volume—Jane's fate is also a reading of the surprise characters experience when they try to follow too literally the prescriptions of popular stereotypes.

Everyone in the story, for example, looks to Mannix (manics?) as "one way of watching the smoothly functioning process of a culture prepared for any eventuality, any disaster" (49). Such a culture is, of course, engaging in the basic project of semiosis, perceiving experience as signifying elements within a coherent system, though at the frenetic pace imaged in the story by the freeway network with its menace of death at high speed for those, like Jane, who fail to navigate by its signs with sufficiently well-trained apparently "spontaneous" responses. Hence Bob

Down's parents, trying to understand another East Coast emigrant, "realize that they needed someone like Mannix to get to the heart of the problem, to determine what was the matter with their son"—they too watch Mannix for guidance. Indeed, just as Jane is reduced to the object of the voyeuristic lens, so is she reduced in the second half of the story to no more than the contents of a suitcase by which Bob Downs converts his outsider status, thanks to its $14K, to marriage with someone he met at the "house of two dear and close friends of his" he met that weekend—a not inconsequential conjunction of capital and the commodified Image as subject. Indeed, every (metaphorical) Californian is similarly reduced:

> At what stage does the Southern Californian convert the world around him into the flatness that resembles a movie screen. Everything the mind focuses on may be something it might have, on a prior occasion, spotted on a screen. In time, the Southern Californian will no longer ask, can I also do it? Instead he or she will want to know where, at what movie house, can it be seen?
>
> (50)

In the place of the depth of the intending subject we have the two-dimensionality of the self as public screen figment, its inner and outer actions both within the sphere of commodified simulations. It is a short distance indeed from the coloring book of **"English Garden."**

In **"Read Only Memory,"** we encounter a series of characters—from the President's wife reading French novels in translation, to a stable boy dreaming of the last cavalry charge, to Harry who seeks the maid who fits the shoe he finds in the bowery—for whom internalized fantasy incapacitates any ability to relate directly to experience or even to share parts of so fragile an internal mythology. No doubt such fantasies compensate for what personal experience lacks—in private license for a public figure, in heroism for a laborer, in a Romance role for the wide bottomed protagonist—and thus function in ways similar to the repression of historical contradictions masked by the conception of Brumholdstein. But they also stress the concomitant function of popularized forms in programming the desires of the culture's subjects. It's not for nothing that the President's wife names her dog Madame Bovary.

"Access" shifts the emphasis slightly to the logic of conventional coding. Its title stands in a significant contrast to its subtitles (all of which include the word "Barrier") that undoes the logic of oppositions, that emphasizes the extent, that is, to which binary oppositions are in fact redundancies. Something of a shorthand, perhaps, for certain deconstructive themes, **"Access"** presupposes barriers which surround it and to which it is a perhaps temporary exception, just as "barrier" denotes a temporarily barred access. More generally, then, language, or any of the "larger" semiotic systems to which the stories in the collection allude, is an access that is simultaneously a barrier or, perhaps more profoundly, (and in keeping with the collection's repeated reference to language as the medium of "dread"), a barrier that marks a (desired) access blocked by the ellipses or aporia—it's difficult always to tell which—in the culture and the signifying systems through which it is manifested.

Each of the "barriers" denominated by the story's subtitles grows out of a transgression of a social law—the "emotional" violation of the (working class) garbageman who attends the (upper middle class) party, a clash of Class and Party mores; the "absolute" barrier of a husband who arrives home a day earlier than announced to find his wife absent and, as it turns out, swinging; the "physical" barrier of $50 that Hilda (the wife) interposes between her available body and two briefcase-carrying businessmen who had expected freer access; the "acquisition" barrier Hilda has faced in trying to cultivate a boutique owner (Marthe) with whom one kind of relationship (as customer) defers another (as lover); the "language" barrier that Mark, the husband Hilda leaves, encounters when she moves in with "Marthe" now called "Paul"; and the barrier of cataloging or categorizing *we* face by the ease with which virtually any of these labels could be applied to any of the cases summarized in the story.

Language, it seems, and the social codings which share their structure with it, permit a certain kind of access as long as rules are agreed upon and scrupulously observed. But experience, reading, writing, thinking, interpretation, history, all seem at times to surprise the barriers necessarily imposed in its structuring of the content continuum, with the result that the access those barriers may be intended to channel is blocked by the gap between Reality and Signifying System, and that cultural "inside" to which one is granted access turns out to lack what the entrant seeks. Perhaps nowhere is this radically semiotic understanding of our collective experience so memorably portrayed as in **"Crossing the Great Void."** Zachary has always been told by his Mafiosi uncle and beautiful mother that his father was lost in the WWII desert as a Captain on a heroic secret mission. Dependent upon a hearing aid, Zachary still does not hear well—particularly the undercurrents. The picture he is shown (and treasures) is of a hotel doorman in Rome, and he is unwittingly in the position of Hamlet, his mother his uncle's lover, his own position usurped, his father displaced. Forced to work in a garage, he bombs his uncle's car and heads for the desert oasis in which his father has, reportedly, been seen, though not before he has a not entirely satisfactory sexual relationship with a beautiful girl on whose back is tatooed a map of the desert with Blitlu, the oasis in question (and an anagram for bullit?), at its center.

The story, then, is not difficult to "interpret." By the time he reaches the town nearest Blitlu, his hearing aid battery is dead, the only available batteries said to be at Blitlu. The hotel doorman, suspiciously like an older version of the photograph he has of his father, hails the cab in which he rides off toward Blitlu:

> Now he is bound for the center of the desert, and every step he is taking is bringing him closer to the center, and every step he has taken in the past has led to his

being here. Even before he was aware of the center's existence, he was traveling towards it. . . . After all, the emptiness he expects to encounter at the center will be no different from the emptiness he might experience in the interior of his room after it had been denuded of all his possessions, stripped of all the things he had clung to with such persistence, such tenacity, such great effort, as if his entire life depended on it.

(113)

He has taken as his reality a myth, a reordering of facts fabricated by his uncle in order to obtain the object of his desire with the least disturbance. His room, its maps and photos a shrine to the absent Father, is like the desert, an experience of absence, but the informing myth on which his life depends. His whole upbringing is like that of any citizen of the culture—a steady training in the expectation of a certain mythic center from which the Father beckons (compare Alice Jardine's use of the story as her allegorical emblem in *Gynesis*).

But it is a center in the void, and it is a center which is a semiotic black hole sucking into itself the psychic power of every experience to which he is exposed: the mind-liberating drugs he hears are sold there, the Father who is said to be there, the past the stories of which are the means by which, whispering to him in the night, his mother soothes him into sleep, the erotic totem of the girl on whose back is the map and whose directions he follows to the Center. All are subsumed in the paradigmatically logo-centric myth of a center that the story marks as both regressive and delusional. Perhaps one might well conclude that every Abish story is about the desire for such a Center and the discovery of a metaphysical or intrinsic Void at the heart of every semiotic linkage, a marker of the ideological interests of the sign-wielders and managers of discursive regimes, a pointer to the absence of the *thing* the Greek and German traditions have taught us to expect of language. Each story is a variation upon a tracing of the semiotic strands of which the stuff of subjects is woven and the tragic rending of those strands by those who take them literally enough to act fully upon them, rather than cataloging peacefully in the library, governing politely like the Mayor of Brumholdstein, operating along the spokes of the semiotic webbing like the Mayor's brother-in-law, WA the writer, or the photographer-narrator of **"A Parting Shot"** whose stylized photograph of a bathing beauty facilitates both the disappearance of a husband in whom it awakens unfilled desires and his own taking of that husband's place with a woman who, apparently, fills his.

Note

1. Such a statement illustrates my debts to theorists like Foucault, Eco, Jameson, and Althusser, debts whose theoretical implications are acknowledged at great length in *The Politics of Reflexivity*.

Works Cited

Abish, Walter. *In the Future Perfect*. New York: New Directions, 1977.

Arias-Misson, Alain. "The Puzzle of Walter Abish: *In the Future Perfect.*" *SubStance* 27 (1980), 115–124.

Eco, Umberto. *A Theory of Semiotics.* Bloomington: Indiana University Press, 1976.

Klinkowitz, Jerome. *The Life of Fiction.* Urbana: University of Illinois Press, 1977.

Christopher Butler (essay date 1988)

SOURCE: "Walter Abish and the Questioning of the Reader," in *Facing Texts: Encounters between Contemporary Writers and Critics,* edited by Heide Ziegler, Duke University Press, 1988, pp. 168–85.

[*In the following essay, Butler argues that although Abish's fiction challenges the idea that there can be an authoritative, self-centered narrative, it does not surrender a quest for meaning or for representing a reality beyond the text itself.*]

The title *How German Is It* calls attention to a preoccupation, in this case Germany. It's a highly charged issue. Most of us have responses to Germany as we do to so much else. In general, readers compliantly accept what they are offered. Their chief concern is, "how readable is the text". For the most part, novels about Germany, or those simply located in Germany, without having to raise the question of, 'How German is it?' resolve the unspoken question by explaining Germany. In one way or another, they explain Germany away and thereby provide satisfaction. I have avoided an explanation. I have introduced German signs to create and to authenticate a "German" novel.[1]

One might imagine a collective of writers of innovative fiction getting together in their own Geneva and coming out with a communiqué that says:

> At some stage the readers (too few) of our sort of fiction have got to shape up to the world; and we really mean to the world, and not just to those marvelous theoretical implications of our own techniques of writing, which are so flattering to the critic. They thus have a great deal more work to do than they thought: of course they can't treat writers like us as authorities who will tell them what to think. To that extent Barthes is right to say that "a text is not a line of words releasing a single 'theological' meaning (the 'message' of the Author-God) but a multidimensional space,"[2] but his further argument that we are all mere unoriginal citers of past texts cannot be sustained. If it were we would stop writing. Even when the author attempts a disappearance into intertextuality, the arranger's hand remains as much his own as did that of Joyce.

> Nor can readers go looking in our work for soluble modernist puzzles, in which the kindly writer has tried to provide a solution for as many of the interpretative problems that he at least could foresee. The critic for us can't be a Budgen or a Gilbert. Our world doesn't

make sense in that kind of way, and nor do our texts. It is not presented like Joyce's Dublin, Musil's Vienna, or even Kafka's Prague: it is a collage, and often enough an absurdist or alienating one.

One might translate some of this imagined declaration into "academic" terms by arguing that postmodern innovative writers often present evidence that is fragmented or skewed by its play within the web of independent semiotic systems, and the reader has to work matters out from there. What their texts demand, in the first instance, is not so much criticism or interpretation as cooperation in putting them together. Whether the reader is able to share such a cooperative reading with anyone else is not a primary concern. Experimentalists like Abish are not, after all, academics who have to keep that kind of talk going. If his texts do not easily create any consensus as to their interpretative meaning, then they may well be accurate symptoms of a subjectivity, a relativism, and even a confusion in the "postmodern" zeitgeist, to which more attention still needs to be paid.

However, I wish to argue that books like ***Minds Meet*** and *How German Is It* show us how this disruptive relationship of the text to our assumed knowledge of the world can still have a moral effect over which we might be able to agree. For central to Abish's writing is, I think, the way in which he can convict us of harboring prejudices, which he seems positively to encourage us to hold. This is a dangerously Swiftean use of experimental technique, and it has very few parallels. Since Abish achieves his effects essentially through irony and humor, we may find a way into the problems his work raises by considering the joke. If we laugh at a joke about Poles, or Jews, or WASPS changing a lightbulb, in the very act of "getting the point" we momentarily share the (often aggressive) prejudice that powers it:

> How many WASPS does it take to change a light bulb?

> Two. One to mix the martinis while the other calls the repairman.

And the same goes for the metajoke, which can only work, like Abish's metafictions, once a genre is established:

> How many feminists does it take to change a light bulb?

> That's not funny.[3]

Walter Abish's attacks on what he calls the "familiar" world work in very much this way. As we enter the contemporary German world of his novel with Ulrich Hargenau, we are slyly asked what a (French) visitor would notice.

> Undoubtedly the cleanliness. The painstaking cleanliness. As well as the all-pervasive sense of order. A reassuring dependability. A punctuality. An almost obsessive punctuality. Then of course there is the new, striking architecture. Innovative? Hardly. Imaginative? Not really. But free of that former somber and authori-

tative massivity. A return to the experimentation of the Bauhaus? Regrettably no. Still, something must be said in favour of the wide expanse of glass on the buildings, the fifteen-, twenty-story buildings, the glass reflecting not only the sky but also acting as a mirror for the older historical sites, those clusters of carefully reconstructed buildings that are an attempt to replicate entire neighbourhoods obliterated in the last war.[4]

This use of discomforting detail to build up the world of the book, which itself, we notice, incorporates some artfully chosen mirrors of past history, is a central feature of the book. So too are the narrator's many questions; for example: "But why this curious predilection for black leather?" (*HGI,* p. 3), which is the twelfth such question in the first three pages. However much we may like to think we can resist Abish's obliging anatomy of cultural stereotypes, in the very act of recognizing them we are made their accomplices.

Abish is thus an insidiously didactic and even moralizing writer, and this sense of engagement underlies much of his experimental technique in writing. Despite the modish emphasis of some of his interpreters upon his subject's being language, I feel that his texts are about something, even if this "something" is made strange or unfamiliar in narratives that often center on the important themes of cultural relativity, of skepticism, and of our proneness to be comically misled by the language that reader and writer both have to use.

Abish thus occupies that middle position described by Alan Wilde (who sees many surfictionists, by contrast, as uninvolved in the world and lost in a self-reflexivity and play which have given up the effort to engage the world through language). For Wilde discerns in postmodernism a mode of "midfiction" that still seeks, even if indirectly and ironically, to be referential:

> Midfiction describes a narrative form that negotiates the oppositional extremes of realism and reflexivity (both their presuppositions and their technical procedures). Further, it seeks to reveal the extraordinariness of the ordinary, frequently and paradoxically by trafficking in limit situations—thereby subjecting to interrogation the very foundations of the writer's (and the reader's) beliefs. And finally, it invites us not *through* but *in* the relationships and actions of its characters—and by way of some strategic *écart* or swerve in its fabric—to perceive, obliquely and ironically, the moral perplexities of inhabiting a world that is itself, as "text," ontologically ironic, contingent, and problematic.[5]

I believe that Abish belongs in this central postmodernist tradition. His main concerns seem to me to be three: (1) an attack on the notion of the self wishing to order the world in its own interests, (2) the defamiliarization of the world that results once the incorporating self is dethroned, and (3) the uncertainties thus produced, in his characters and in the reader, by the sense of relativism and conflict of cultures that results from this new relation.

Abish sees the self as perpetually attempting to make the world familiar, comfortable, and conformable to its organizing desires. Thus in traditional fiction, "We read a text and world falls into place. Both Proust and Henry James provide psychologically valid explanations that enable the reader to maneuver in their world and grasp the emotional content of what is at stake."[6] We feel, and feel secure, through a narrator whose consciousness and growing control of his material allows the reader to stand in for him. Thus Marcel conquers the "otherness" of the Guermantes way, or Lambert Strether finally decodes others' deceptions and finds out what they mean for him. Indeed, such a narrator attempts to possess his world in quite a straightforward linguistic sense, for "All that is required to depict the 'familiar' is that the possessive pronoun, singular or personal, be introduced in a sentence or attached to a word: Our doorway, our neighbourhood, my grandeur, his view."[7]

Abish often uses the metaphor of the house and its furniture for this sense of "possession," which he then disrupts. Thus his aptly titled **"This is not a film, this is a precise act of disbelief"** begins: "This is a familiar world. It is a world crowded with familiar faces and events. Thanks to language the brain can digest, piece by piece, what has occurred and may yet occur. It is never at a loss for the word that signifies what is happening this instant. In Mrs Ite's brain the interior of the large house with a view of the garden and the lake are surfaces of the familiar."[8] And Michael Bontemps, who replicates landscapes in his films and has come to America "to make a film exploring American needs," and indeed to concentrate on the shopping mall as the "museum of need," also chooses "to arrange the furniture and thereby create a topography for his daily needs" as do two other characters: Frank Ol and Mrs Ite. But this topography is not allowed to last in the story.[9]

Abish clearly feels that trust in the language we use, as the one that "truly" articulates the world, is often misplaced. Indeed, it may lead to a moral failing, for "the 'self' persists in regarding the world as an extension of its very being and its vocabulary."[10] The result of this is that many of Abish's protagonists fail to meet the post-Kantian moral demand that they achieve insight into another's point of view (a demand that is essential to the liberal tradition of the novel). Much of his writing indeed consists in the comic demonstration of the fact that too much reliance on our own way of engaging in linguistic transactions with others may prove, in a world governed by the contingent and the absurd, to be deeply unreliable.

This is a theme of all his work, but it is perhaps most directly shown in his ironically entitled story **"Minds Meet,"** which is full (among much else) of messages going wrong (astray, misinterpreted) and coming into contradiction. As modes of ordering reality they somehow comically and significantly fail to be agreed between sender and receiver. "Not infrequently the writer of notes will feel impelled to address a larger audience. He may, on his way home, stop at one of the public conveniences in the subway and write in capital letters above the urinal: Does the past leave any room for the future? The writer will have the satisfaction of knowing that many men will ponder this question as they stand with legs apart on the brink of an incertitude that nothing will relieve."[11] These failed messages disconcert Abish's characters, and the reader, because they are in ironic contrast to the apparent clarity and certainty displayed by the helpfully explanatory narrator, who goes on to anatomize, in the following sections of his story, being "taken aback" by the message, being "abased" by the message, being "abashed" while receiving it, and so on in alphabetical order. For paradoxically enough, the narrator of the text seems to look at the world in wide-eyed innocence, and yet also to be the master of reported anecdote. Thus, for example,

> Harry discovers Gwen in bed with Tobias and is taken aback. He says to himself, I am taken aback. His face more or less confirms this. Dubiously he inspects his face in the bathroom mirror. He is filled with a profound melancholy as well as distrust. How confusing, he thinks, Do I mistrust my melancholy, or am I melancholy because I am riddled with mistrust?
>
> Most men feel frustrated by the time they reach thirty because there are only so many ways of making love. While the lower part of the body is actively engaged during this act of passion the face questions the veracity of its own existence. In its distress it beams all kinds of signals to the other face. These signals are by no means reliable. One might say that the faces are immersed in the self.
>
> (*MM*, pp. 6f.)

Here the self, as the supposedly certain, single origin of the "message," or of introspection, or of its "own" lovemaking, experiences itself as divided. It is a decentered self like that proposed by much contemporary theory, subject to contradictory beliefs derived from habitual behavior and ideology. This pathetic division in consciousness is comically paralleled here, in a rather Beckettian manner, by that between the mind and body in making love. For the self may be stricken by doubt at the most embarrassing moments. Thus Harry is "abashed" while receiving his message, which is a surprisingly equivocal reply to the kind of order that is supposed to be pretty clear:

> Harry steps into a bank in Queens and points a pistol at the bank teller. Let's have all your dough, he says. Dough, mocks the teller. What do you think this is, a bakery. Next thing you'll be asking for bread. Harry blushes furiously. He is being mocked. He feels abashed. It is a familiar quandary, so he shoots the bank teller, and then hops on the first passing bus outside the bank. Killing is a stabilising factor in this society. But in no time Harry is again filled with a familiar panic, he doesn't know in which direction the bus is headed.
>
> (*MM*, p. 10)

What Abish does is to translate our distrust of language and our mishaps in trying to make it work for us into a fictional model of human relationships. Harry's bus is as ambivalent for him as the "dough" he fails to acquire. Frames of reference and language games get across one another and mixed up. Abish thus uses his writing to contest the "perception of the everyday predicated on an unquestioning affirmation of the function and role of the 'self' in society, as rigidly governed by the 'reality principle' and as subsumed by the logic of everyday existence as we are. What the innovative novel must disavow is a self centered world in which the 'self' continues to reign supreme."[12] By a highly inventive and sustained poetic fiction of anecdotes he shows us what the world would be like if. . . . For the characters in many of his stories variously and comically misunderstand messages and significant expressions, and even doubt their own introspective judgments. They are led into contradiction and absurdity by the differing interpretations that can be put on them. They adopt incompatible strategies of comprehension and so deconstruct their own intentions and situations. They also enact the reader's own uncertainty, as he or she attempts to interpret signs within the story, looking within the narrative for a consistency and coherence that simply is not there, because all the old reliable methods of realist narrative are (partially) allowed to break down, along with their communicative codes.

These themes remain central to Abish's work subsequent to **"Messages,"** such as **"Ardor/Awe/Atrocity," "How the comb gives a meaning to the hair,"** and **"Crossing the Great Void,"** which develop them in a more complex and indirect manner. These texts are perhaps most significant for what they conceal, of situations and motivation. They are, Abish tells me, "energized by sexuality," which is a key to the "subversive" meanings that lie just below the surface. These teasingly repel and invite those neo-Freudian explanations preferred by so many critics. They are almost, but not quite, case studies—as Marcel Proust in **"How the Comb . . ."** goes rat hunting in the Hotel Marigny in Albuquerque, and "starved for Albertine" plans to have her "trampled to death by a horse in the fifth volume of the English edition" of his novel (*MM*, p. 150). But Albertine hotly contests her fate and dies when her single-engined plane explodes over the desert. A similar fate awaits the detested uncle of Zachary, the hero of **"Crossing the Great Void"** (in the collection *In the Future Perfect*). His car is blown up by his nephew, with him in it, on the Cross Bronx, perhaps because he is Zachary's mother's lover. This story, which is a family romance of sorts, also concerns Zachary's search for his Italian Fascist father, who disappeared behind enemy lines in the North African desert in 1941. Perhaps deliberately cut off from others by deafness, he has been obsessed since his school days by deserts: of which the "authoritative study" is *Crossing the Great Void* by one Major Klip D. Jars.

He is aided in his quest by his lover, Track, who has a map of the oasis Blitlu, in which his father disappeared, tattooed on her back.

> Your back?
>
> She had taken him by complete surprise. He was dumbfounded. He was also unprepared for what was to follow that evening at her place. He had no prior experi-

ence, no knowledge upon which he could base an appropriate response when hours later, at her house, she unbuttoned her blouse and began to take it off. With the lights off, it was too dark in her bedroom to see the map of Blitlu. In addition to your hearing aid you seem to need glasses, she said matter-of-factly. He was convinced that her remark was devoid of malice. It was not an accusation, but merely a statement of fact.

(*IFP*, p. 105)

Once in North Africa, he passes a hotel doorman who curiously resembles an old photograph of his father; he then sets off for Blitlu where, he thinks, he may be able to find the batteries he needs for his hearing aid. The story concludes with a stripping away of the furniture of the familiar world:

Now he is bound for the center of the desert, and every step he is taking is bringing him closer to the center, and every step he has taken in the past has led to him being there. Even before he was aware of the center's existence, he was traveling towards it. Everything he has encountered so far appears familiar, as if at some time in the past his mother must have described it to him as she spoke of his father in the Italian Expeditionary Forces crisscrossing the desert. Consequently he feels convinced that what lies ahead will also prove to be familiar. After all, the emptiness he expects to encounter at the center will be no different from the emptiness he might experience in the interior of his room after it had been denuded of all his possessions, stripped of all the things he had clung to with such persistence, such tenacity, such great effort, as if his life depended on it.

(*IFP*, p. 113)

Such Kafkaesque allegorical quests are of course open to all sorts of interpretations, but to none that are certain, for the characters of stories like **"Minds Meet," "Parting Shot," "Access,"** or **"Crossing the Great Void"** are comic rather as they are in Beckett or Pinter. We can see that what they think and do has absurd consequences and so are tempted to feel superior to them. But insofar as they cumulatively reveal to us the instability of all communication (in a way that my quotations only feebly exemplify), we do not manage to feel so superior. Within the illogical world presented by the text we cannot solve their problems for them, any more than we can those of Estragon and Vladimir. This impotence and anxiety is part of our sense of the metaphysically absurd, as originally conceived by writers like Kafka, Sartre, and Camus. But in a post-theological age in which all philosophies, including the existentialist, are suspect, this sense of alienation has become centered on the linguistically absurd. Where metaphysical props are taken away, only language, which as Wittgenstein so brilliantly demonstrated can bewitch our intelligence, remains. This is painfully funny, since it abandons traditional comedy, where the audience can usually grasp a rational solution to the cross-purposes of the plot and so feel superior to the dramatis personae. In a world like that presented by Abish there are no such solutions. (These considerations would apply equally well, I think, to much of the work of Apple, Barthelme, and Coover.)

The insecurities to which Abish subjects his characters are passed on to the reader by the defamiliarization of the world he presents. This is brought about not only by the estranging effects wrought by his perpetual asking of questions and his authorial commentary, but by his very mode of description. This can be deliberately simplified. A children's copybook style is presented, sometimes quite explicitly (as in the coloring book introduced in *How German Is It*, pp. 176ff.). We are invited to see it as unreliable or naive, and above all, as politically unaware or innocent.

The air in such passages is one of patient explanation, or of what Abish often calls in his subheadings "An Introduction" to the extraordinary:

The number of cars on the F train is considered adequate. During the early morning rush hour at least eight people are crushed each day. This number is considered tolerable. The following day the next of kin can pick up the morning paper and on the front page compare the accomplishments of their loved one to the accomplishments of the other victims. It has become common practice for the newspapers to embellish these accomplishments. For a slight remuneration the victim can receive a one-day posthumous honorary membership in the Yale or Princeton eating clubs. . . . The people who disagree that the number of F cars on the train are adequate have been forced to go underground. They are said to exist as a movement.[13]

This example is chosen pretty well at random and may seem, in isolation, merely anecdotal, whereas it is Abish's skill at working observations like this into complex narratives that makes him such a distinguished writer. In this example and in many others that might be cited, such extraordinarily detached descriptions of bizarre situations are part of fictional worlds that are, to say the least, at a peculiar angle to our own, as for example in the story **"Life Uniforms,"** where buildings collapse each day, and an electric company records this, noting their loss of electricity-consuming customers (*MM*, pp. 21ff.).

There is thus a defamiliarizing withdrawal and detachment in Abish's presentation, even when he deals with situations that would naturally prompt us to consider their real-life analogues, and that the reader might expect to be emotionally involving. In this he follows one of his most important predecessors, for as he points out: "Disfamiliarisation was Kafka's intuitive response to any situation that demanded his emotional attention."[14] His central characters are deprived of "depth," as in so much postmodern experimental writing. But unlike Handke, and like Barthelme, Abish combines this withdrawal with a sense of humor. This implies a peculiarly behavioristic description in his writing, a pretense that the bizarre behavior of others is beyond psychological or moral explanation, or simply doesn't need it. What is more, his characters' reflections on their predicaments often have a relevance to them that is, to say the least, oblique.

These considerations apply most strikingly to his descriptions of sex, as for example in his short story **"Parting**

Shot," which depends on one of Abish's many triangular or quadrangular relationships. Here Gregory, a literary critic who is an expert on Maupassant, falls in love with a photograph of Irma and leaves his wife Maude. In section 14 of the story

> Without the slightest trepidation Maude enters the room in which two men are sitting on the couch with Irma. No one prevents her from walking to the window and looking at the West Side Drive, as she pretends not to notice that the two are quite openly caressing Irma's small white breasts, breasts that resemble her own breasts. In order not to see the men and Irma, she is compelled to partly close her eyes, or focus them elsewhere, on the wallpaper for instance. It is a pity about the wallpaper. The wallpaper destroys the room. It makes the room smaller and less attractive. Obviously Irma had little sense for colour or design. Maude would have suggested a bolder pattern. But Irma had an incredible body. Most men noticed her body. Irma, at their first encounter, had quite casually mentioned that her legs were her best feature. What an amazing thing to say, Maude had thought at the time. For some reason the two men were not touching Irma's legs. Perhaps, it occurred to Maude, they were saving Irma's legs for some other time. Perhaps they were satisfied to look at the legs while concentrating on other parts of Irma's anatomy. Who can say? Who can tell what is on the mind of a man who is caressing a woman.
>
> *(IFP,* pp. 38f.)

We are back in the world of **"Minds Meet"**: these men have purposes that Maude cannot know, and Abish won't tell us. They are, after all, "sunk in the self," and their division of attention neatly parallels and subverts that which Abish exploited in the earlier story. But it is only the willingness of the author to include the irrelevant along with the "moving," to observe the scene in a nonvoyeuristic but not anaesthetized manner (for Maude has good reasons, as can be seen from other parts of the story, for noticing the details, and in particular the legs that she does), that can leave the matter wholly up for the judgment, rather than the participation, of the reader.

The unemotional manner of Irma's description is ipso facto defamiliarizing, even as it picks out familiar detail, and it is deeply expressive of Maude's alienation. It is "inappropriate" for Maude to be thinking about wallpaper, and a more conventional writer would leave the matter as a simple gesture of self-protection, the noticing of something irrelevant because one cannot "face the situation." Abish does allow for this, of course, as an essentially compassionate writer, but he does more. Since Maude is not developed in the narrative as a conventional character (this is virtually all we see of her), she seems to us to be divided or decentered in some more profound way. She observes sexual acts, with us, but she has to conclude that she simply doesn't know "what is on the mind of a man who is caressing a woman." We grasp and sympathize with this disassociation and division within her, because these men, as described by Abish, don't seem to have any emotional involvement either. Even within the most intimate of contexts, cross-purposes still abound.

Like Brecht, Abish thus denies us "the culinary theatre of the emotions" and refuses that kindly liberalizing commentary that would allow us to impose "our" values on the text, to hierarchize his descriptions with them and so make "familiar" moral judgments on a world arranged, as his is not, to obey our wishes.

Thus, as Jerome Klinkowitz remarks, with reference to *How German Is It*: "All hierarchical values are removed from Abish's perceptions, not so that we see the thing in itself (a *nouveau roman* attitude he satirizes through the philosopher Brumhold) but rather to emphasize the opaque nature of the sign. Once we humanize, Abish implies, we become subject to the same flawed rules of communication from which his characters suffer."[15]

This unreliability of the sign is exploited by Abish in many virtuosic ways, as we have already partly seen, but I wish to pursue here one of its most important effects, that of making us aware of the trickiness and indeed playfulness of our perception of signs as they function between different cultures, with reference to *How German Is It* and to his present work in progress, *House on Fire*. Abish warns us that in reading texts like these, the reader is invited to consider their mode of narration, rather than to make facile judgments on contemporary political history. For he doesn't simply rely on his own or the reader's cleverness in matching *histoire* and history, but on his or her awareness of a much more slippery common bond, that of language:

> Essentially, I am questioning how we see and write about something. Levi Strauss, wherever he went in Brazil, embodied Western culture. How could he avoid that? He reduced everything to *signs* in order to comprehend it. At the same time his own cultural as well as personal history may distort the signs he uses by attaching a particular Western significance to them. Perhaps that is why I feel that the text I write lies between me and the experience.[16]

The underlying chain of events is thus meant to be much less important than the dislocated manner of their narration. And yet the accessibility of the book does partly depend on its running very close to a conventional narrative, concerning Ulrich Hargenau, who is the son of a soldier implicated in the plot against Hitler of 1944, and his brother Helmuth, a successful architect, in and of the "new Germany." Ulrich has helped to convict by his court testimony the Einzieh left-wing terrorist group, in which his wife Paula, now living in Geneva, was implicated. The activities of this group threaten the buildings Helmuth designs. A post office is blown up. When Ulrich returns to visit him in Brumholdstein, he meets Franz, a former servant of the Hargenaus now working as a waiter, who is also designing a building, this one a matchstick model of the Durst concentration camp, which was in fact on the site of the present Brumholdstein. This begins to open up another of Abish's themes, which is indeed the relationship of the new Germany to its past. Later in the novel one of its few dramatic events of obvious symbolic significance takes place: a street caves in, and a mass grave is discovered beneath the town.

Ulrich also becomes involved in a number of those interlocking sexual relationships we find in Abish's other stories: Egon, who lives in a house designed by Helmuth, is unfaithful to his wife Gisela and takes up with Rita Tropf-Umwert, a photographer. But Helmuth also seduces Rita.

In the final part of the novel we are by the sea with Ulrich, Egon, and Gisela, at Ganzlich near the East Frisian islands. While they are all there, Gottfried, the keeper of a bridge between the islands and the shore, and who has possibly been recruited by Paula's Einzieh group, shoots two policemen. His bridge is blown up. In the last scene of the book Ulrich visits a doctor for hypnotherapy, recounts his childhood, admits that he is a bastard and not a Hargenau, and under hypnosis begins to raise his hand in what may well be a Nazi salute. The novel ends with a final question: "Is it possible for anyone in Germany, nowadays, to raise his right hand, for whatever the cause, and not be flooded by the memory of a dream to end all dreams?" (*HGI*, p. 252).

It is the sections inset into this narrative, whose effect is primarily metafictional, that reinforce Abish's theme of the sign, and of the dreams, or hidden purposes, or suppressed past history, that might underlie it. These metafictional episodes include the memorial meeting for the recently dead philosopher Brumhold (very like Heidegger indeed), and Helmuth's speech on him (*HGI*, pp. 164ff., 169f.); the section on the coloring book *Das Neue Deutschland*, which is sent to Ulrich by Daphne (*HGI*, pp. 176ff.); and the section on the purposes of an antiterrorist film (*HGI*, pp. 243ff.).

All of these place the main line of the narrative in a very problematic light indeed. The novel slyly invites the cooperation of the reader, who lives after all in his own "familiar" ordered world, to assess an imagined German society, which only *seems* to be subject to an "all pervasive sense of order" (*HGI*, p. 2). This "order" is a characteristic that runs directly contrary to a narrative mode that thrives on the doubtful perspectives of internal mirroring and ironic self-qualification, and so threatens to lead us into self-deconstruction and contradiction. For example, Ulrich Hargenau himself slyly resembles his author: he proves to be writing a book called *The Idea of Switzerland*: "where only a few years ago Nabokov lived, as much a prisoner of the past as I am a prisoner of the present" (*HGI*, p. 54), and this is indeed the title of this part of *How German Is It*. Ulrich's book is as concerned as Abish's own, it seems, to diagnose a culture through its products, and to contrast the idealized, stereotypical, and treacherous "idea" with the reality of the exemplar: "it's based on something I read about Paganini. Apparently Berlioz loved the idea of Paganini but was revolted by his music" (*HGI*, p. 52). This contrast of "idea" and "revulsion" may well lie at the heart of Abish's novel.

The lesson given by Ulrich's lover Anna Heller to her young pupils on the "familiar" (*HGI*, pp. 119ff.) also stands at an interesting remove from the main narrative and helps to expose its method: for the familiar here relates to the comfortable matching of cultural stereotype to external reality but also makes, we might think, a barrier: "We want to visit museums and monuments and ruins that we only know from reproductions in books. Having seen the photographs of what we have come to visit, we naturally know what to expect. So the ruins, the works of art, the foreign cities are not entirely unfamiliar" (*HGI*, p. 120). Nor indeed are the scenes Abish describes. And yet he almost literally digs below this level of response, in revealing the camp Durst hidden below the new German town of Brumholdstein; and so there is no little irony when Anna also explains that something her pupils often see, like the railway station of Durst, behind which lies the history of the camp it once supplied with prisoners, may become so terribly familiar that "we stop seeing it" (*HGI*, p. 120).

Abish's method in *How German Is It* is I think most clearly exposed in his chapter on Egon and Gisela, who are indeed "representatives" of his imagined new society of the postwar years. Their picture and the article on them in the magazine *Treue* depends on all sorts of illusions. Their stereotypical description (*HGI*, pp. 123ff.) conforms so well to an image of what the new Germany "must" be like that even as they project a way of life for the admiration of the readers of a magazine, they at the same time inspire distrust in the readers of Abish's novel, particularly if those readers are aware of the type of analysis to which Barthes has subjected this kind of material. This is because Egon and Gisela as described here are too perfect, too close to what "everyone" believes (informed as they so often are by nothing better than just such journalism, with its glamorized notions of the quotidian). Our image of Gisela and Egon thus derives from that "manuel scolaire" of *idées reçues* that Barthes ridicules.

It is most important to realize that such a mode of narration does not simply play with theory and make the narcissistic demand that we theorize in interpreting it. Instead, it exploits the relationship between stereotype and prejudice to disturb the reader. It goes beyond Barthes, because his theory is really a very comfortable one from the critic's point of view, insofar as it allows those who accept it to feel that they are somehow superior to the delusions encoded by "bourgeois" realistic texts, the popular media, and so on. Abish destroys any such complacency in the reader by ensnaring us in prejudice and stereotype from the start. After all, we know what "black leather," and "cleanliness," and "the innate German upper-middle class instinct to combine 'perfection' with the 'menacing'" (*HGI*, p. 127) really "mean" . . . or do we? Even if the text is parodic here, it entraps us as surely as the joke does.

These themes are beautifully orchestrated in our extract from Abish's latest novel, which begins once more with a question: "Is this really you?" The reader is put on the defensive in confronting a reborn and reconstructed "German" world, where trees die from industrial poisoning, under conditions ironically described as "normal." This serene country-side is the setting for "passionate love" and also "Ah stability!" It is a land populated by the *Wirtschaftswunder,* the true pioneers of this present peace." We are once more in an imagined country, more "precise in detail" than Austria or Italy, where the trains run on time. For the reader of Abish's earlier work, this is indeed a "familiar world," but as treacherous to the reader's presuppositions as ever.

Abish likes societies where things seem to work but which have an underlying unease, and he likes the source of that unease to be a past history, and bygone ideologies that haunt the present (for the philosopher Brumhold soon makes a reappearance here). "But to what end? What purpose is served by endlessly unearthing the signs of an earlier disaster: in trying to read the labored handscratched markings that constitute a primitive calendar (but what year?) on some moist stone wall that happily, once again, serves a more peaceful purpose: the storage of Rhein wines." It is our answer to this question that will, presumably, justify the whole novel.

Abish's problem here is to find new topics for this type of political and yet playful analysis, for that is what it is in essence. His writing here has all the signs (a treacherous word, interpreted in poststructuralist manner) of aiming at a greater depth of suggestion as to what might underlie it. This chapter sets the scene for an investigation, in which: "Signs fall into place. *Hubschrauberlandeplatz,* Heliport, *Mittelstreckenrakete,* medium range missile, *Höhepunkt,* pinnacle. And words fall into place. *Grundverfassung,* basic state. *Alltäglichkeit,* everyday life, *Nichtmehrdasein,* no-longer-being-there, *zweideutig,* ambiguous."

These military features, which we might just fail to find on a map, and the all-embracing network of words, might be expected to come together at some point, but they are here subjected to that skepticism concerning their marriage that is a central theme of postmodernism. A common language, whether it be the English of this text or that of contemporary Germany, is inherently treacherous, even when, as we are told, it is shared by tram conductors and third-year students of philology. The latter may indeed be studying the present hospitality of German to "guest words" of American origin. But such divisions within language are echoed by and encode the social divisions of the past and of the present. Every door and paving stone may carry the "trace" (another theoretically loaded word) of "that at one time violently enforced 'solution.'" This sort of comment runs the risk for Abish of being too overt, but it is indeed the risk of this type of writing that it should willy-nilly become politically engaged.

So here we are in the town of Selten, which is pored over by elderly female tourists, observed by the far-from-touristic eye of Abish. They pass Altneu, the site of Brumhold's log cabin home, from which "in 1944 he scrupulously avoided reading a moral disintegration into the stream of refugees and . . . concentration camp inmates" who were passing by him. There is a further problem here,

which arises not just from the painful potential of engagement with this part of history. Abish's writing scrupulously and ironically exploits a metalanguage, with its references to "signs," "traces," "reading," and so on. We are aware that this metalanguage is indeed at a remove from historical reality. Brumhold shouldn't have been doing nothing more than "reading" the events that were immediately present to him, even if he was a mere philosopher. But the text almost conspires with him, to keep the events of history at a distance from the author's story. It is once more the reader who is expected to outdo Brumhold and to "see through" this ironically distanced and metafictional language, to history, to make the critically much-disputed transition from language to reference.

This preliminary tour d'horizon can no more claim a disengagement from the presentation of the scene of politics than can Conrad's at the opening of *Nostromo.* At this point, of course, like the most naive reader of a realist text, we await the stirrings of plot. About this little can be said. Much is already in place: but as yet no Ulrich-like antihero. There is indeed the society of a revived Germany, with its business and its architecture of past and present, including the Stahl-Eins building and the Baroque Residenz of Selten, restored after a thorough Allied bombing aimed "to reduce accident as a factor in survival." But it is presented through Abish's metaphors, which after all may attempt to match universes of discourse to one another and find interesting ways of failing to do so. Thus he describes the Allied invasion after the war as a conflict or competition between languages: "In the main it was the Russian, the English, and the American—if indeed the American can be distinguished from the English—the three language groups that were penetrating the German linguistically dominated space, that were intruding into the German awareness, presenting, if only subliminally, a kind of choice." But the nature of this choice, as it might await a character in a novel, or us as readers, will have to await the publication of the full text. This will no doubt develop very significantly the problematic, based on cultural relativism and linguistic unreliability, of Abish's earlier work, and this is in itself sufficient promise.

This problematic seems to me to be of considerable importance, because experimental fictions like this are competing with others for mental space, and they are inherently more liberating than many others, because they leave us so many choices. They leave the finding of the truth up to us, having set the questions correctly, and thus confront the terrible simplifications of moral, sexual, and political doctrine, which are so powerfully transmitted by politicians and the media they control. We need, I think, to take Abish's fictions very seriously, given this type of contrast. It is one to which he himself points, with typical good humor and depth of ironic perception:

> SL: In a sense the production of the "Holocaust" is the right answer to the German problem.
>
> WA: It's the popular answer. The Walt Disney answer. It's the only answer possible. Walt Disney is our truth.

SL: History returns not as a comedy or tragedy: a cartoon.

WA: The Germans had Wagner to designate their space in the world. We have Walt Disney. Where is the grave of all this. In Hollywood?[17]

This "grave in Hollywood" may prove to be as sinister in its way as the one Abish led us to discover in Brumholdstein. His writing is an eloquent protest against its existence.

Notes

1. Walter Abish, interview with Sylvere Lotringer, *Semiotext(e)* 4, no. 2 (1982): 160f.

2. Roland Barthes, "The Death of the Author" in *Image Music Text,* ed. Stephen Heath (London, 1977), p. 146.

3. Ted Cohen, "Jokes" in Eva Shaper, ed., *Pleasure, Preference and Value* (Cambridge, 1983), pp. 120–37. The examples are cited from pp. 127f.

4. Walter Abish, *How German Is It* (New York, 1980), pp. 2f. Cited from here on as *HGI,* with references in the text.

5. Alan Wilde, "Strange Displacement of the Ordinary: Apple, Elkin, Barthelme, and the Problem of the Excluded Middle," in *Boundary* 2, no. 10, p. 192.

6. Walter Abish, "On Aspects of the Familiar World as Perceived in Everyday Life and Literature," a paper delivered at a conference on Innovation and Renovation, University of Wisconsin, Milwaukee, in 1981.

7. Ibid.

8. Walter Abish, *Minds Meet* (New York, 1975), p. 31.

9. Ibid. Cf. pp. 32, 33, 36, 41, and 66.

10. Abish, "On Aspects."

11. Abish, *Minds Meet,* p. 5. Subsequently cited in the text as *MM.*

12. Abish, "On Aspects."

13. Walter Abish, "Read Only Memory," *In the Future Perfect* (New York, 1977), p. 59f. Subsequently cited in the text as *IFP.*

14. Abish, "On Aspects."

15. Jerome Klinkowitz, *The Self Apparent Word* (Carbondale and Edwardsville, Ill., 1984), p. 131. Compare the description of Ulrich and Anna making love in *HGI,* ch. 29, pp. 172ff.

16. Abish, interview in *Semiotext(e),* p. 162. I have written at greater length about these aspects of *HGI* in my "Scepticism and Experimental Fiction," *Essays in Criticism* 36, no. 1 (January 1986): 47–67.

17. Abish, interview in *Semiotext(e),* pp. 174f.

Jerry A. Varsava (essay date 1990)

SOURCE: "Walter Abish and the Topographies of Desire," in *Contingent Meanings: Postmodern Fiction, Mimesis, and the Reader,* Florida State University Press, 1990, pp. 82–108.

[*In the following essay, Varsava argues that a major theme in Abish's fiction is the tension between a superficial perfection and a profound moral and emotional void.*]

Viennese Jews, Walter Abish and his family fled Hitler's Austria for China. Unbeknown to him, there lurked below Vienna's surface decorum, concealed by the refinement and prosperity of a former imperial center, a most virulent ethno-racial hate. And how did such a world appear to a boy of seven or eight? Life, Abish tells us, was very much an affair of surfaces for him, a mistaking of the *apparent* for the *real.* Reassured by the props of his childhood— favorite toys, a comfortable home, a supportive family— Abish viewed life as a harmonious arrangement of people and objects. Writing recently in a lengthy essay on his Viennese roots, Abish, referring to himself in the third person, retrospects:

> . . . from the very beginning he sensed a smoothly functioning world in which his needs were taken care of with a scrupulous attention to detail, a world in which pleasure had to be negotiated, in which the gramophone, the radio, the telephone as much as the tiny bell on the underside of the dining table, the bell with which his mother summoned the maid, highlighted the perfection of a designed world. Everything was always planned, all contingencies *appeared* to be covered. Nothing was left to accident . . .

("The Fall of Summer," 121–22)

In its various allusions to perfection, familiarity, orderly surfaces, and naive confidence, this brief passage highlights key thematic interests of Abish's innovative short stories, collected in ***Minds Meet*** (1975) and ***In The Future Perfect*** (1977), and his novels, *Alphabetical Africa* (1974) and, most notably, *How German Is It,* winner of the Faulkner/Pen award for the best fictional work of 1980.[1]

PLEASING SURFACES

Abish's fiction depicts the surfaces of things, of people, of events, compelling the reader to ponder the moral and psychological interests that shape life's visible contours and condition our response to them. He attributes his reluctance to intrude with "clarifying" narratorial commentary to his own perception of the world, while growing up, as "bewildering in its profusion of stylized drama . . . a drama that remained forever highly elusive" (Klinkowitz, "Walter Abish," 97). In Abish's view, we, in the twentieth century, present images of order and perfection to ourselves in order to assuage the demands of psyche and conscience for emotional and moral solvency. The world of Abish's fiction is preeminently urban, a not surprising preoccupation given Abish's professional training as an urban planner. The characters that populate this world strive for urbanity, a presentation of self suggesting confident mastery of the codes of bourgeois taste and personal comportment. "Taste," in this narrow context, involves the recuperation of familiar standards of social grace, the repetition of an unreflective "perfection."

Abish's characters strive to achieve "familiarity" and "perfection." They dexterously arrange objects in space, from domestic bric-a-brac and furniture to major institutional architecture, in an effort to present iconically the values and achievements most revered in the late twentieth century: self-confidence, material success, taste, stability, and power. Whether involving the markers of bourgeois affluence—designer clothes, a "good education" for our children, fashionable holidays—or the signs of sociopolitical prowess—sleek technologies, polished executive performances, well-publicized philanthropies—we live in an image-conscious era in which style, artfully and strategically, subverts substance, in which the ephemeral often supplants the ethically responsible. Whether considering our collective preoccupation with appearances in the context of personal crises, as he does in many of the short stories, or in light of a major historical issue such as contemporary attitudes toward the Nazi pogroms, as in *How German Is It,* Abish, a subtle social critic, always returns to a single question: "Is there any other way to live?" (Klinkowitz, "Walter Abish," 96).

Abish's work, like the fictions of Pynchon, Handke, Vonnegut, and many Latin American writers, effectively rebuts the argument that contemporary, innovative writers neglect history in their preoccupation with formalistic vanguardism and (what Jameson cites as) postmodern stylization of "past-ness" ("Postmodernism," 66–71). As in the best postmodern fiction, technique and content are interactive in Abish's work. The discernment of the "familiar" is a central imperative in Abish's fiction, for it is only through discernment that the "familiar" can be displaced by something more morally profound, more profoundly insightful. Abish would risk unintended, unfortunate self-parody were he to discuss the "familiar" in familiar literary-generic terms. The "familiar" can only be effectively depicted through a representational mode that denudes it of its familiarity, making of it something foreign, something unsettling, something perhaps even hateful to the reader.

Abish's most succinct statements on his narrative aesthetic come in interviews, one in 1974, the other in the early 1980s, each appearing after the publication of a novel. In the earlier interview, he analyzes the uninflected description that figures so prominently in *Alphabetical Africa* and *Minds Meet* (and that we also see in later work):

> In my writing I try to strip language of its power to create verisimilitude that in turns shields the reader from the printed words on the page that are employed as markers. Writing as close as possible to a neutral content, everything, the terrain, the interiors, the furniture, the motions of the characters are aspects of a topography that defines the limits of the situation being explored.

(Klinkowitz, "Walter Abish," 96)

Though indicating a concern for the empirical, this statement quite obviously defines no standard mimetic realism, nor indeed a neonaturalism. Abish's realism, really an "experimental realism" as Jerome Klinkowitz has observed, presents a highly nuanced vision of a world only superficially stable (*The Self-Apparent Word,* 128–31). Unlike conventional realists who supplement description with much straightforward narratorial analysis and commentary, Abish manipulates language and images in a more self-conscious, subtle manner in order to show the capacity of communicational codes to constrict thought and to preempt moral introspection.[2]

Structurally, both in the stories and the novels, we find an emphasis on spatiality. Not a great deal happens in Abish's fiction, typically. He juxtaposes a series of short, narrowly enframed scenes involving, for example, a character considering the contents of a shop window, or a sparse narratorial description of an interior, or a bland conversational exchange. His realism offers no expansive, slice-of-life tableaux. His is the art of the photographer, not the mural painter (and we find frequent references to photographs and photographers in his fictions). Abish's verbal vignettes flaunt the surfaces of life. Abish is not after a deep, hidden truth. For him, "everything is on the surface" (Lotringer, 165). Characters are presented to the reader very much as people present themselves to us in our daily interactions with them, replete with apparent goodwill and not always scrutable motivations and desires. Yet, though he offers neither conventional psychological analysis nor exemplary characters, Abish, in a resolutely Bakhtinian spirit, consistently manipulates an understated irony to deride the superficiality of our age. Unlike Robbe-Grillet, for example, Abish pursues "neutral content" in order to achieve a value-charged end. His fictions relate the epistemological to the moral.

As has been suggested above, in order to isolate phenomena, and therein render them less "familiar," Abish uses a kind of scenic enframement in his fictions roughly analogous to the spatial limits placed upon a photographic image by the aperture of a camera lens. Abish, like many twentieth-century writers and philosophers, is acutely aware of another "enframing" device—language. As we find with other modern, native-born Austrian writers like Musil, Thomas Bernhard, and Handke (all of whom are mentioned by Abish from time to time), Abish interrogates the constrictive function of language. Through the isolation and repetition of clichés—the verbal bedrock of human interaction—Abish considers language's seductive capacity to domesticate objects and events in the world by reducing them to the rhetorically familiar. Abish's characters take refuge in language, allowing the reassuring rhythms of trite conversation to lull them into intellectual and moral apathy.[3] In *How German Is It,* for example, the weather inspires an often repeated exchange that, incidentally, has embedded within it a reference to the war the characters are attempting to forget.

A glorious German summer.

Oh, absolutely.

A scent of flowers in the air.

Isn't it marvelous.

Easily the most glorious summer of the past thirty-four years [since 1944].

And how relaxing.

(54)

The unreflective use of language represents, of course, an affirmation of the status quo and this affirmation has obvious and profound moral implications. At the conclusion of **"Access,"** the narrator remarks both on the malaise of stereotyped speech patterns and the writer's capacity to effect partial remedy:

> I'm not really concerned with language. As a writer I'm principally concerned with meaning. What, for instance, does being a writer mean in the context of this society . . . writers perform a vital task, they resuscitate words that are about to be obliterated by a kind of willful negligence and general boredom. Writers frequently are able to inject a fresh meaning into a word and thereby revitalize the brain cells of the reader by feeding the brain information it does not really require.
>
> (*Future Perfect,* 72–73)

And, by helping overcome the intellectual entropy begot of formulaic language, the writer may also have a moral impact.

Though, as Wolfgang Holdheim has pointed out, "The boundary between ethical blindness and intellectual obtuseness has never been precisely defined," we may nonetheless consider Abish's fictions as preliminary cartographic efforts to draw this line of demarcation (147).[4] Before considering the novel *How German Is It,* his longest and most successful work, let us turn first to the short fiction and Abish's portrayal therein of contemporary urban society.

THE SHORT FICTION

A materialistic society is controlled by the manipulation of, and its own absorption in, the apparent. It practices a crude, impatient phenomenology that "understands" through reduction and typification. A priori notions of perfection render invisible the nuances of the moment. **"This Is Not a Film This Is a Precise Act of Disbelief,"** the lengthiest of Abish's collected stories, starts off with some *apparently* reassuring observations:

> This is a familiar world. It is a world crowded with familiar faces and events. Thanks to language the brain can digest, piece by piece, what has occurred and what may yet occur. It is never at a loss for the word that signifies what is happening this instant. In Mrs. Ite's brain the interior of her large house with a view of the garden and the lake are surfaces of the familiar. . . . To some degree the objects in the familiar interior of her house channel the needs.
>
> (*Minds Meet,* 31)

The passage suggests, as Abish says of it, "the dubiousness of the familiar" (Klinkowitz, "Walter Abish," 96). Its naively confident tone excites in the reader the suspicion that all is not as it appears to be, that the verbal surface of the story must be attended to closely. As the story illustrates, Mrs. Ite's "understanding" of the world around her is based on myopia. She understands very little about the circumstances in which her life is enmeshed. This opening section concludes with Mrs. Ite remarking to her son Bud that something is missing, something normally present "among the familiar setting of her furniture" (*Minds Meet,* 31). Her son responds wanly that it couldn't be anything "terribly familiar," investing the scene with comic absurdity for, in fact, it is her husband who has disappeared.

Three years after his father's disappearance, son Bud discovers the keys to Mr. Ite's locked study. Upon casual investigation he and Mrs. Ite discover Mr. Ite's body, the seeming victim of foul play (though the cause of his fate is never identified). Mr. Ite, an architect by profession, was professionally engaged in the creation of new surfaces. At the time of his death he was involved in the design of the local mall, a fixture in the landscape of contemporary America. A mall, of course, bears testimony to our capacity (and desire) both to neutralize nature and to implant our own stylized vision on the world. (And, lest we doubt the compelling nature of this vision, there were, in 1985, more enclosed malls in the United States than cities, four-year colleges, or television stations, and almost as many as county courthouses [Kowinski, 20].)

In the story, a French Marxist film director who has come to "use" the mall as a set for a movie—actually to blow it up as a gesture of proletarian self-righteousness—refers to the new mall as a "Museum of Need," noting generally the "surfaceness of all American things" (*Minds Meet,* 34). Abish's story shows us that the mall must be read as a sociological marker. Apparently a "museum" that bequeaths to its clientele usable cultural artifacts, it represents, at the same time, equally apparently (if we defamiliarize "mall-ness" for a moment, as Abish does), the most recent stage in the commercialization of modern life. The architects of such structures are also, in concert with developers, retailers, etc., the would-be architects of our desires. Barthes, in the essay on the Eiffel Tower—another architectural paean to "progress"—notes that architecture has always been "dream and function, expression of a utopia and instrument of a convenience" (239). It remains of crucial importance that we consider self-consciously the dream, the utopia, the mall's authors are, quite literally, selling and that, if we accept this dream, we do so volitionally.[5]

Like many postmodern writers, Abish rarely puts forward exemplary ethical postures in his fiction. As noted earlier, his characters exhibit bad faith and bad moral judgment, typically. In **"This Is Not a Film"** the various characters represent different classes, varying intellectual interests, and conflicting political positions; therein, they serve as foils for one another. Yet, in the end, the cast behaves in a frighteningly undifferentiated way. The working class—represented by Hank notably—and the controlling bourgeoisie have essentially the same values, a situation that denies the Marxist claim—at once romantic and hopeful—that the workers are closer to historical truth than any other class. Hank, a worker in a local bottle plant, accepts unquestioningly both his wife's lavish wardrobe and the ease with which he himself receives well-remunerated employment. Hank, like his bourgeois masters, affirms a statement made by Cas Ite shortly before his death: "We're all trapped by our needs" (60). Hank's needs, emotional ones that are serviced by material well-being, compel him to overlook the source of his prosperity—his wife's efforts to copulate her way up the social ladder, a circumstance happily exploited (and paid for) by the town's oligarchy of professionals and businessmen.

In addition to class difference, there are two other noteworthy oppositions in the story though neither admits significant moral differentiation. Merce Ite, the brother of architect Cas, appears to be markedly dissimilar to his brother and the latter's cronies. A man of culture, a cosmopolitan, Merce seems admirable in his sensitivity to books and theater and his general aloofness from the maneuverings of the provincial business world. However, these aesthetic interests—call them "needs"—merely indulge a hedonism indistinguishable from those of his peers, a hedonism that is underwritten in part by brother Cas, who provides Merce funds for fine suits and trysts in Boston with male prostitutes. Finally, the seemingly disparate priorities of culture and corporation are subsumed by a common foundational priority—the satisfying of personal need. After seeing his sister-in-law and his brother's business associate Frank Ol together in a Boston hotel, Merce opts for the preservation of surface harmonies and does not inform his brother of the infidelity. Cas's death, though never definitely explained—was it murder or was it suicide?—seems most likely attributable to the treachery of Ol and Mrs. Ite, a treachery inadvertently abetted by Merce's moral passivity.

Completing this pattern of immorality in **"This Is Not a Film"** is the character Michel Bontemps, a leftist filmmaker after the fashion of Godard, who serves as a foil to businessman Frank Ol and his associates. As with the oppositions discussed above, Abish plays with stereotypes in this juxtaposition of the "Marxist revolutionary" and the captains of commerce. Written in the early seventies, **"This Is Not a Film"** rejects the fatuous assumption (more current then perhaps than in the opportunistic eighties) that antiestablishment rhetoric serves as the only necessary surety for ethico-political idealism. Though purportedly intent on producing an agitprop film depicting the general corruptness of American values—values that are embodied by Ol and Cas Ite—Bontemps' cinematic project is more an act of self-promotion than of social critique. The narrator makes clear in introducing Bontemps that the latter has developed a personality cult around himself by carefully fashioning a public image. Dark sunglasses, a myriad of affairs, temper tantrums, fifteen "innovative films," and the

interior of his apartments are the markers that define "Michel Bontemps" (32). As his surname suggests, Bontemps is after a "good time"; he is a hedonistic media star, not a Marxist ideologue.

Bontemps and his aides—the unnamed narrator and his fiancée—have installed themselves in a local hotel:

> The hotel room is our center, our HQ . . . our books, our papers, our black-and-white photographs of Che and Mao have diminished the bleak uniformity of the surfaces in our room. We have, for the duration of our presence, imposed on the neutral hotel surface the dynamics of our ideas and intentions.
>
> (37)

The narrator suggests that their alteration of the hotel's surface establishes a moral difference between themselves and small town America. Their actual behavior, however, contradicts this implicit claim. In his development of a glamorous public persona, Bontemps does not indulge in the revolutionary's characteristic self-denial. Significantly, when Bontemps unexpectedly leaves the town, he takes along the narrator's Gillette razor, thirty-five of his Seconals, and the narrator's fiancée, Jill. In a farewell note, Bontemps admits having bedded Jill, while denying that she holds any physical appeal for him. The note's recurrent use of the pronoun "I" unambiguously denotes Bontemps' central concern in life. The narrator remains in America to work out filming details. Feeling that the film may improve mall business, Frank Ol agrees to certain "eccentricities"—to allow Bontemps to blow up a few houses, to burn a pile of consumer goods, and even to destroy a portion of the mall. Paradoxically, the film, which intends to destroy corporate America, may well accomplish the opposite end of financially buttressing it (a situation, incidentally, that often occurs when "antiestablishment" books, recordings, and films are successfully marketed through mainstream corporate entities).

Bontemps is a poseur, a conventional bourgeois artist for whom self expression and personal accomplishment are primary goals. In his films the aesthetic overwhelms the ethical.[6] The narrator points out this contradiction. Bontemps, he tells Frank Ol, "subverts the destruction of his enemies by his aesthetic concerns. In other words, the placement, the color, the objects, the motions, the juxtaposition of faces all combine to diminish the revolutionary content" (58). In Bontemps' films, aesthetic novelty produces a strong visceral reaction, produces an aesthetic frisson, and undermines his ostensible theme(s). This is a danger that every innovative artist courts. Unusual formal designs can dominate semiosis rather than aid it, can produce a formalistic reception. And we can legitimately ask how an innovative story such as **"This Is Not a Film"** succeeds notwithstanding the risks inherent in experimentation.

First of all, the "experimental realism" of the story obviously builds on the elements of conventional realism, the latter a mimetic form readily accessible to readers. Clearly defined characters occupy a clearly defined time and place. Charactral introspections are totally neglected. Settings such as domestic interiors and the mall serve as obvious symbols of a human desire for order at whatever moral price. The plot is progressive with few violations of natural chronology. Yet, notwithstanding these features, the fluidity of the conventional realist fiction is not apparent here. A number of elements block narrative flow and compel an active engagement on the part of the reader. **"This Is Not a Film"** has a complexity of plot unusual for a story or even a novella. There are a number of subplots that require contextualization within the main story. Relationships between people, for example, are only hinted at, requiring the reader to scrutinize the "surface" of the narrative carefully for clues indicating, variously, a love interest, corporate machinations, or a betrayal of trust. The three parts of the story are broken up into a total of thirty-one sections, a structure that further fragments the narrative, with the reader forced to relate each part and each section to the others, forced to fill in what Wolfgang Iser calls "blanks," those points in a story where focus shifts—sometimes subtly, sometimes radically (166–70; 190–203). In the absence of guiding narratorial commentary, the preoccupation with surface description results in an allusivity one associates more with the mystery tale than with a realist milieu study. And of course, as noted already, there is no moral center in the story, no exemplary character, no foil to define virtuous conduct. In **"This Is Not a Film,"** as in other of his works, Abish skillfully marries fragmentation and allusivity to such conventions of realism as natural plot chronology, symbolism, and surface description. This marriage of the disparate yields a *relatively* original narrative that valorizes neither form nor content and thus avoids both aestheticism and an aesthetically barren tendentiousness. The story defamiliarizes both the reassuring surfaces of conventional realist fiction and the reassuring surfaces of the quotidian.

In **"This Is Not a Film This Is a Precise Act of Disbelief,"** characters take considerable emotional and moral solace in the aura of order that emanates from the surfaces of their surroundings and the surfaces of their lives. They remain scarcely aware of the sexual predation, the avarice, the manipulation, the general misanthropy that motivate their behavior. The mall, Bontemps' films, and Hank's apartment all serve as calming, familiar surfaces to be recognized; they conspire to perpetuate moral and epistemological obtuseness. Similarly, in other stories, Abish uses such highly structured phenomena as contrastive symbols to highlight a desire, often distinctly neurotic, on the part of his characters to protect themselves from the contingencies of their existence. These contrastive symbols—photographic portraits, maps, mosques, formal gardens, and chic living quarters are notable—all present to the viewer a superficially ordered world. They offer a world enframed, one reduced to essence. Each symbol in its own way lies and conceals: the portrait, for example, seeking in a single glance to characterize; the map offering its custodian an illusory sense of mastery over space, its two-dimensionality emphasizing surface; the mosque and the formal garden

objectifying metaphysics; the chic apartment exhibiting a tenuous self-assurance. These symbols bear closer scrutiny.

For the narrator-protagonist of **"The Second Leg,"** mosques, actually photographs of them, provide endless fascination. Though he has never visited a Muslim country, mosques are part of his "turf" (*Minds Meet,* 105). On the other hand, the turf of Ludmilla, a former lover with whom he is staying while visiting New York, is "insidious sex." As the story unfolds, the protagonist and Ludmilla act out a sadomasochistic melodrama in which mosques, his images of completeness, and Ludmilla's misshapen leg, a living allusion to imperfection and death, provide symbolic polarity. Having failed in marriage and having been spurned by Ludmilla, the protagonist turns to his mosques. "Love," he observes, "does not have the resolute perfection of the courtyard of the Great Mosque of Kairouan" (117). The illustrations give him order, however vicarious and fragile. At the same time, they present a past that is neutral and hence not psychologically oppressive for him. He passes an ingenuous confidence: "Unlike most passionate involvements with the past, illustrations, it seems to me, are not necessarily regressive. I find this reassuring. I have no wish to be imprisoned in a Parthenon of rosy memories" (118). In fact, the protagonist's own past has enshrined in his mind oppressive memories of marital failure, of sexual confusion, of an enigmatic relationship with his mother.

The orderly volumes of the mosque, its pillars, its many naves, the striking chromatic contrast between the mosque's whiteness and the perfect blue of the Mediterranean sky, all these write a topography of his desires, a need for clear delineation and confident restraint and physical prowess:

> I now can clearly see the egg-white ribbed dome, the cobalt blue frames of the crosshatched windows and the gleaming white walls. . . . The eye is so tremendously selective. The exterior of the mosque is covered with many layers of whitewash, and when viewed below, the walls stand out in sharp contrast to the Mediterranean sky above.
>
> (118)

The protagonist's eye is indeed "selective," his mosque "fantastic" (118). He takes in surface detail without considering the mosque as a time-conditioned artifact. Just as his own dispiriting circumstances are forgotten in his contemplation of the mosque, so too is the mosque's cultural specificity overlooked when it is translated into a mere *objet d'art* existing beyond the contingent within the covers of the coffee-table book. In **"The Second Leg,"** "culture," as it does in much of Abish's work, becomes a refuge for the emotionally (and morally) weak. In serving up time-honored analogues of perfection, that is, predefined "masterworks" stripped of cultural context, culture risks becoming an opiate that dulls the sensibilities. **"The Second Leg"** concludes, uncharacteristically enough for Abish's fiction, with the protagonist achieving some degree of self-understanding. The protagonist and Ludmilla sit contemplating her legs, first the healthy one, then the misshapen one. "Poor Ludmilla, no amount of loving will replace your deformed leg," he confides to himself, acknowledging, symbolically, the imperfections of his own life (124). The story ends with the protagonist and Ludmilla in emotional union, the former having accepted "the second leg," an emblem of the contingency and death that his mosques had striven to negate.

A numbing concern for perfection also surfaces in stories of the second collection, *In the Future Perfect.* The same quote from Whitehead occurs in two of them, **"Parting Shot"** (25) and **"In So Many Words"** (79, 87): "Even perfection will not bear the tedium of infinite repetition."[7] Both stories are set in chic Manhattan. The characters in both have not come to terms with Whitehead's remark. In each instance they use money to achieve "perfection" repetitively, unconsciously calling into question of course, at the same time, the very notion of perfection. Television, shop displays, glossy magazines, the small private galleries, all these mold notions of value, identity, and world:

> Did Whitehead know that wealth enables people to acquire the perfect apartment, the perfect country house, the perfect haircut, the perfect English suits, the perfect leather and chrome armchair, the perfect shower curtain, the perfect tiles for the kitchen floor, and a perfect quiche available only from a small French bakery near Madison Avenue, and the perfect Italian boots that look like English boots but are more elegant, and the perfect mate, and the perfect stereo, and the perfect books that have received or undoubtedly are just about to receive a glowing review in the *Saturday Review.* Wealth makes it easier to have the perfect encounter with a stranger, enjoy the perfect afternoon, make perfect love, a sexual encounter that is enhanced by the objects that are in the room, objects that may at one time have attracted a good deal of attention while on display in a Madison Avenue shopwindow.
>
> *(Future Perfect,* 25)

The narrator's mock rebuttal of Whitehead's statement illustrates well Abish's technique of defamiliarization, in this case of a crassly materialistic view of perfection. In response to Whitehead's succinct, seemingly credible assertion, the narrator offers a droning anatomy of "perfection" as construed by an upper-middle-class urban milieu. The appending of "perfect" to a great number of mundane objects ultimately derides the values that define "perfection" in this context. The litany of "perfect" objects is interlarded with references to human relationships, indicating of course that some equate the two or, more accurately, emotional satisfaction is, for some, a mere derivative of bourgeois faddishness. Objects combine in their settings to serve as a panoply to protect their proprietors from the vagaries of open, forthright relationships. Perfection is accomplished only through reification of self and others. People wear brand names, rather than clothes. People become "generic," mere mannequins posturing within "sets" appropriated from shop windows and department store displays.

In the tastefully appointed prison houses of the urban chic, stylish perfection is an end in itself. In **"Parting Shot,"** Maud acknowledges, from her midtown Manhattan apartment, that she and her husband have become "two collectors of the perfect experience, assessing the degree to which we have arrived at the state of perfection" (26). Maud herself is an object on display. At her parties she serves as another prop within the fashionable ensemble of her apartment. Certainly, the "perfection" of her surroundings in no way protects her from sexual frustration and a general sense of displacement any more than it does the heroine of **"In So Many Words."** She too seeks, and fails to find, ecstasy in the perfection of surfaces:

> Standing at one of the elongated windows, munching a Sara Lee croissant (quite delicious) she is taking in the American perfection, the American splendor—absolutely no irony intended. It is true. From a certain height and perspective, the eighth floor of her building, America is convulsed with perfection.
>
> *(Future Perfect,* 75)

Again, name brand consumer goods are the primary patrons of this perfection, e.g., Abercrombie and Fitch binoculars, Gillette and Schick razors, Sara Lee pastries, and Draino. Yet, these fail to neutralize the existential malaise that envelops her. (Or do they enhance it?) At story's end, in a desperate attempt to escape the "familiar perfection" of her social set, she invites three leather-jacketed men from small town Arizona into her bed for "in bed something else besides perfection was wanted, needed, desired" (97). Finally, the familiar, perfected topography of her milieu yields to long repressed desire.

HOW GERMAN IS IT: PERFECTING NOTIONS OF GERMAN-NESS

The Nazi reign of terror remains, decades after its defeat, an enduring nightmare. It crops up regularly as a primary theme in various artistic media as well as in contemporary current events.[8] There is, as Elie Wiesel tells us, a double moral imperative to remember—to honor the innocent victim (living and dead), and to ensure that history never again takes such a vile turn. And indeed, in the face of a fundamental human inclination to gloss over the savage, there can never be too many reminders. *How German Is It* is Walter Abish's reminder. Abish first considers the Holocaust in **"The English Garden,"** a story which provides the setting and general tone of the novel. The "garden" of the story's title has a symbolic rather than ontic presence in the story, appearing as it does only in an epigraph that Abish takes from John Ashbery's *Three Poems:*

> Remnants of the old atrocity subsist, but they are converted into ingenious shifts in scenery, a sort of "English Garden" effect, to give the required air of naturalness, pathos and hope.
>
> *(Future Perfect,* 1)

Both the short story and *How German Is It* explore how the "English Garden effect" strives today in contemporary

West Germany to subdue an unseemly past.[9] Since the novel's techniques and themes subsume, for the most part, those of the story, I will focus on it.[10]

"The presentation of the 'familiar world' is not," notes Abish, "an innocent one."

> To me, the familiar details are also *signs* of a familiar world. In projecting these *signs* I am aware of my own preoccupation with the "familiar" and the presentation of it. Essentially, I am questioning how we see and write about something. . . . I feel that the text I write lies between me and the experience.
>
> (Lotringer, 162)

How German Is It studies how the familiar signs of the world—linguistic, kinetic, iconic, etc.—are perceived and processed. For Abish's characters, just as for Abish himself and the reader, the variegated "textual" signs that the world offers us help configure our general attitudes. The world looms as a dynamic semiotic field, one that is open to manipulation, one that demands of us an interpretive gesture. Both the manipulation of the semiotic field and the interpretation of it have obvious ethical ramifications. *How German Is It* considers the production, maintenance, and reception of the field of signs in the context of a small West German town in the seventies, paying particular mind to the ideological bias that responses to signs betray.

Abish uses a number of techniques to defamiliarize the milieu of the novel: the detailed listing of "typical" features; unaccentuated references to the past and the past in the present; the posing of blunt, leading questions; and the double entendre. In part 1 of the novel, entitled "The edge of forgetfulness," the protagonist, Ulrich Hargenau, Jr., a writer, returns home to Würtenburg after an extended French sojourn. "The edge of forgetfulness" offers a subtly ironic catalogue of what, for the native German or the returning expatriate or the tourist, constitutes "German-ness." Like a tour book or a Chamber of Commerce pamphlet, the images presented strive earnestly for typicality. Great emphasis is placed on the visible splendors of Germany's past but, as the narrator observes in **"This Is Not a Film This Is a Precise Act of Disbelief,"** the brain is "highly selective" (*Minds Meet,* 36). The typical portrait of German typicality is indeed laudatory. Germany *is* culture: Gothic and Baroque architecture; Wagner and Beethoven festivals; Dürer and Cranach and Holbein and Grünewald; and Goethe, *natürlich.* Germany *is* punctiliousness: clean streets, obedient trains, civic order, well-stocked shops, and precision-engineered automobiles coursing along precision-engineered *Autobahnen.* Germany *is* economic progress (if not "economic miracle"): industrial plants, well-designed dams and bridges, modern farms, and new urban centers. These are the familiar signs of German typicality that greet one pondering "this smooth and agreeable surface" (3). These are the familiar signs that present German history as an unbroken series of achievements and civilized national gestures.

Yet, punctuating this familiar, univocal semiotic system, we find brief, hushed allusions to the "atypical," to past events and current attitudes that lie beyond the conventionally familiar. In these passages, Abish strictly controls the flow of information, presenting only a superficial description and, consequently, leaving the reader to his or her own resources. Ulrich von Hargenau, Sr., Ulrich's *apparent* father, a Nazi officer executed in 1944 for treason—he is not "familiar," remaining for many ever a traitor to national ambitions. Passing mention is made of a local Jewish furrier who converted to Catholicism earlier in the century (6). Why? Perhaps to escape the wrath of anti-Semitism, and perhaps not. Abish compels the reader to consider the bare facts of the anecdote, i.e., its "surface," and to postulate their implications. The narrator does not guide the reader through commentary. Pointing out the many "tall blond men and women" wearing leather coats and jackets, the narrator asks, "But why this curious predilection for leather?" (3). The linking of fabled Aryan racial traits to leather overwear stirs images of Hitler Youth donning martial leather. Or does it? Again, Abish neither confirms nor denies such readerly associations. It is only through a slow accretion of such allusive references and images that the reader becomes suspicious that traditional notions of German typicality are compromised by a strategic blindness to certain "obvious"—at least in Abish's defamiliarized context—moral failings. Indeed, these unsettling references to an immoral recent history, and its residual influence, are largely beyond the ken of the protagonist who, until the novel's conclusion, disregards visible suggestions of a dark past—collective or private—preferring to write self-indulgent autobiographical novels about male-female relationships.

At the end of part 1, Ulrich plays the *boulevardier,* drinking beer, observing others, and taking in the sights. But Abish allows the reader no such anesthetized point of view. He heightens the reader's sensitivity to his thematic concerns through questions and the double entendre. The narrator probes: "The question remains, do the Germans still expect to be asked embarrassing questions about their past and about their present and what, if any, ideas they may have about their future?" (7). And, as Ulrich considers the reconstructed version of a bridge destroyed in the war, the narrator ironically acknowledges that "replicas of this kind testify to a German reverence for the past and for the truth, a reverence for the forms and structures upon which so many of their ideals have been emblazoned" (7). We will later learn that this interest in replicas is "highly selective" and that it does not extend to replicas of Durst, the local Nazi death camp that now lies in ruins (7). At the conclusion of "The edge of forgetfulness," a series of questions focuses unequivocally on the novel's key interests. The last two questions are central: "What is seen? And what is said" (9). Most of the novel focuses on the major disjunction between, precisely, what the eye recognizes, and what the mouth reports.

In parts 2 ("The idea of Switzerland") and 3 ("Sweet truth"), the setting shifts from the "Old World" splendor of Würtenburg to a new town, Brumholdstein, with Ulrich spending a brief interlude in Geneva. Brumholdstein is a civic embodiment of Ashbery's "English Garden" effect in very many ways. Constructed as it is on the site of Durst, it literally covers the "surface" of an unsavory remnant of Germany's Nazi past. Brumholdstein offers a clean, new topography. The town emblematizes the "New Germany," presenting a revision of "typical" qualities, ones apparently at odds with those honored in the thirties and forties. The novel of course will demonstrate that now, as in the period of the most heinous persecution of innocent people, there exists a conspiracy of silence that, effectively, puts the best face on the past and the present. In the only concentrated description of Brumholdstein (77–82), the narrator shifts registers continually, modulating with these shifts the degree of irony within the respective sections. These registers range from a bald promotional tone to objective description to a subtle criticism of the townspeople's "forgetfulness." The town has become a modest center of culture offering concerts and operas, international films, and lectures on such compelling topics as excavations in Outer Mongolia (79). Brumholdstein also happens to be home to author Bernard Feig, whose novels Burghermeister Kahnsitz-Lese praises for not being "immersed in the past," and for offering characters "happily free of that all too familiar obsession with the 1940–45 period of our life" (82). Feig is, as his name indicates, "cowardly" and "fainthearted" in his forgetfulness of history. Ulrich's views on authorship suggest his own aversion to plumbing the unhappy depths of his nation's past. In comments given in an interview in Geneva, Ulrich denies for his own novels any political import, or at least any politically revisionist function. The novel is not, Ulrich tells us, "a process of rebellion," but rather "it validates and makes acceptable forms of human conduct, it also validates and makes acceptable societal institutions" (53). In viewing writing as an apology for the status quo, Ulrich's views are obviously at odds with Abish's.[11] Like Feig and the good citizens of Brumholdstein, Ulrich neglects the archeological study both of local historical "treasures" and of the soul, preferring to concentrate on the surface of a temporally disembodied present.

Brumholdstein is named after "Germany's greatest contemporary thinker," a world-renowned philosopher who happens to be a native of its environs (80). Over his long career, Brumhold has concentrated mostly on ontology except during the thirties when social ethics and political philosophy attracted his attention. Notwithstanding the tribute paid him by his fellow citizens, this august figure, now in venerable old age, refuses to mix with the good burghers of Brumholdstein, eschewing the highways and byways of urban society in order to pursue his contemplative life amid the fields and forest paths (*Holzwege*) of a rural setting, in order to advance his study of *Dasein* and "thinking." "The forest continues to beckons us," writes Brumhold.

> For in the forest are located our innermost dreams and desires. In order to reestablish our roots and our purpose and return to a simplicity of life that can no longer be found in the German community, we turn to the forest. We wander off by ourselves, packs on our backs

> . . . confident that in what we are doing, we are coming closer to our past, to our history, to our German spirit.

> (167)

And, like Martin Heidegger whose words these echo, and on whom the character Brumhold is based, the latter returns to university teaching after an enforced absence, "the result of too many reckless speeches in the '30s and '40s, speeches that dealt with the citizen's responsibility to the New Order" (19).[12]

Abish harbors ambivalent feelings toward Heidegger.[13] Though admitting the astuteness of Heidegger's observations on the linguisticality of being—"Language is the house of Being. In its home man dwells" ("Letter on Humanism," 193)—Abish is openly scornful of Heidegger's philosophy of history:

> His [Heidegger's] history, as I see it, was always a universal history that he somehow managed to locate in his own beloved forest. But was his history not shaped by specific historical events? When Heidegger, a most remarkable thinker, touches on German history he verges on the banal. That is perplexing.

> (Lotringer, 169)

Though *How German Is It* offers no rigorous critique of Heidegger's rapprochement/cooperation with Nazism—Heidegger's famous 1933 rectorial address calls Hitler the "greatness and glory of this new [national] dawn"—it makes a number of suggestive observations through its characterization of Brumhold (quoted in "Only A God Can Save Us," 269).[14]

Heidegger and Brumhold both appeal to German "rootedness," what in his *Discourse on Thinking* Heidegger calls *Bodenständigkeit*, to support their views of German history and national destiny (48–49). Brumhold's withdrawal from society emulates Heidegger's; both retire to the *Schwarzwald* to seek philosophical clarity in its foggy reaches.[15] Isolation in the German countryside allows each to recuperate that special relationship between spirituality and the land that makes Germans special. Of the German spirit Heidegger writes:

> For "spirit" is neither empty cleverness, nor the noncommittal play of wit, nor the endless drift of rational distinctions, and especially not world reason; spirit is primordially attuned, knowing resoluteness toward the essence of Being. And the *spiritual world* of a people is not the superstructure of a culture . . . it is the power that most deeply preserves the people's strengths, which are tied to earth and blood, and as such it is the power that most deeply moves and most profoundly shakes its being (*Dasein*).

> ("Self-Assertion," 474–75)

Like much of the *Rektoratsrede,* this passage represents a strange amalgam. Here, to the philosopher's sincere affirmation of the importance of truth, Heidegger weds an appeal to an obscure romantic nationalism, one that is not much elevated above the tabloid editor's, the soapbox sage's, or indeed the populist politician's. National-racial pride is not far removed here, if it is at all, from a banal chauvinism.

In his characteristically deflated way, Abish satirizes the preoccupation with "rootedness" and what is for Brumhold an overweening concern for the etymological purity of the German language, the latter issue also important to Heidegger as both his Germanophilia and his often ingenious, often interminable "word studies" would seemingly suggest.[16] Indeed, for Brumhold, the special relationship between "earth and blood," between land and race, is enhanced by the unique character of the German language itself.

> Their language, *die deutsche Sprache,* as once before is again absorbing words from other languages. Still, notwithstanding the doubtful foreign elements in the language today, the German language remains the means and the key to Brumhold's metaphysical quest; it is a language that has enabled him, the foremost German philosopher, to formulate the questions that have continued to elude the French- and English-speaking metaphysicians. How German is it? Brumhold might well ask of his metaphysical quest, which is rooted in the rich dark soil of *der Schwarzwald,* rooted in the somber, deliberately solitary existence that derives its passion, its energy, its striving for exactitude from the undulating hills, the pine forests, and the erect motionless figure of the gamekeeper in the green uniform. For that matter, Brumhold might well ask of the language, How German is it still? Has it not once again, by brushing against so many foreign substances, so many foreign languages and experiences, acquired foreign impurities, such as *okay* and *jetlag* and *topless* and *supermarket* and *weekend* and *sexshop,* and consequently absorbed the signifiers of an overwhelmingly decadent concern with materialism?
>
> (5)[17]

In this seemingly neutral, innocent engagement with key ideas of Brumhold the narrator identifies a number of questionable elements in his world view: his intellectual chauvinism, his obscure religious attachment to German topography, his linguistic xenophobia, and an undergirding nostalgia for a simpler, premodern time. Interestingly, we find guarding over Brumhold's Baden idyll the gamekeeper, whose uniform is a subtle reminder of the Germanic need for order, and often order at any price, as history documents.[18]

The reception of Brumhold by his fellow Germans is marked by strategic oversight and self-congratulation. Brumhold's writings are read by few and understood by fewer yet. His major public political addresses, unable to take refuge in abstraction and terminology, are "platitudinous": "We have completely broken with a landless and powerless thinking" (19).[19] Yet, upon death, he becomes another national treasure. Helmuth Hargenau, Ulrich Jr.'s brother, a celebrated architect, delivers a memorial address at a service for Brumhold, who dies midway through the novel. His speech can be read on two levels—as a straightforward eulogy or as a clear instance of "indirect authorial word," to borrow from Bakhtin. Viewed from the latter perspective, Brumhold's views exemplify neither virtue nor insight, particularly, but rather ethnic arrogance, irrationalism, and romantic obfuscation.

Helmuth links Brumhold's "metaphysical quest for *Dasein*" to a concern for "universal history" (170–71), tying Brumhold to a metaphysical-idealistic tradition that phenomenology, Heidegger's certainly, seeks to undermine, though not always with success as Adorno points out in *The Jargon of Authenticity.* Helmuth's speech contributes to Brumhold's canonization as an important cultural artifact, comparable to other German cultural "goods" such as Bach, Grünewald, and Hölderlin. For Helmuth, as for his auditors, Brumhold becomes another signifier within the semiotic field of "German-ness." Adorno offers some trenchant comments on this sort of commodification of one's national cultural legacy (and obviously it is not an exclusively German tendency, by any means):

> Those who most loudly proclaim Kant, Goethe or Beethoven as German property as a rule have the least concern for the content of these authors' works. They register them as possessions despite the fact that what these writers taught and produced precludes transformation into something that can be possessed. The German tradition is violated by those who neutralize it into a cultural property which is both venerated and yet has no consequence. Meanwhile those who know nothing about the implications of these ideas are quickly seized with indignation when even the slightest critical word is dropped about a famous name which they want to confiscate and exploit as a brandname product "made in Germany."
>
> ("On the Question," 122)

"Brumhold," rendered less than human at this point by idealization, contributes to the *familiar* and favorable stereotype of the intelligent, civilized Teuton and in so doing serves as yet another instrument of official culture. Yet, as Abish maintains throughout *How German Is It,* official culture is forgetful or, as Heidegger would have it, "lethetic." Neglecting many of the colors of the historiographer's palette, Helmuth—an exponent of universal history—presents a portrait of Germany that is too reliant on pastels, that neglects the delicate chiaroscuro that best captures the variegated story of any nation.

In his address, Helmuth actually identifies, inadvertently, a typical German "dualism," as Thomas Mann calls it—the coexistence, historically, of the "boldest [philosophical] speculation" and "political immaturity" (188–89). While the magnificence of German achievements in the arts and letters is undeniable, the German record in social and governmental reform is far from exemplary. Even the briefest survey documents the regressive, reactionary tenor of German political history, a tradition that long resisted substantive democratic reforms and general social reorganization.

Certainly, the leader cult is not an isolated post-Versailles phenomenon that culminates in the Hitlerian *Führerkultus,* a point Heinrich Mann makes in his sardonic novel *Der Untertan,* which ridicules the Kaiser cult and therein the average German's blind commitment to "order and duty" (*Ordnung und Pflicht*). Helmuth's historiography fails to write these chapters in German history, ones that would compromise the superficial harmonies of his own definition of German-ness. Certainly, such a revisionist project would have to contend with four hundred years of political autocracy, a trend already highlighted, as Thomas Mann notes, by Martin Luther's betrayal of the peasants (186–89). Such a project would acknowledge the slow development of what Mann calls "social maturity":

> The Germans are always too late. They are late, like music which is always the last of the arts to express a world condition—when that world tradition is already in its final stages. They are abstract and mystical, too, like this, their dearest art—both to the point of criminality.
>
> (193)

Though Helmuth does not acknowledge it, Brumhold's immersion in philosophy after his political phase in the thirties and forties is an escape from social responsibility and a flight to the security of the "ivory tower." Brumhold effects a kind of Faustian pact wherein he acquires philosophical knowledge but fails to exercise the moral and social leadership one might expect of a great mind, the kind of leadership exercised, for example, by Sartre. Helmuth concludes his speech by praising Brumhold for enabling Germans to see themselves as they really are, indicating that the philosopher's meditations are both exemplary and illuminating (171). Yet, in the context of *How German Is It,* this is at best ambivalent praise. Read as double entendre, Helmuth's claim becomes an indictment of the German nation.

As noted, we can transvalue many of Brumhold's seemingly positive attributes, seeing his writings, and life-style generally, as reprochable—his spiritual unworldliness can be viewed as a flight from social problems, his preoccupation with German culture as simple chauvinism, his ontological meditations in the Black Forest as dreamy, self-indulgent romanticism. Similarly, though most of the key figures in the novel are cultivated, intelligent, and professionally accomplished, they remain nonetheless morally myopic, both in their relations with others and in their neglect of their national past. Quite simply, they separate intellection and ethics. The examples are many. Ironically, Anna Heller, a schoolteacher, attempts to sensitize her students to the world around them through a phenomenological study—she does an ontology of chalk—yet she opts to marry Jonke, bookstore owner and collector of Nazi memorabilia, not out of love but because she does not wish to become an old maid.

Intelligence and cultivation are alienated from moral vision in the cases of Egon and Gisela as well. Egon, a book

publisher and therein a patron of the arts, is a paradigm of the "New Germany," a prosperous, civilized democracy that has apparently conquered its past. Indeed, a popular magazine—suggestively entitled *Treue,* which can mean either "honesty" or "loyalty"—runs a photographic essay on Egon and Gisela that extends to its subscribers an "invitation . . . to reinterpret Germany":

> A new Germany. Certainly not the Germany that was once firmly ensconced (the saddle, after all, is an appropriate metaphor) in the Prussian tradition of honor and obedience, old money and authority, the saber, the crumbling castle overlooking the Rhine.
>
> (129)

However, concealed beneath the topography of civility that the photos write lies an unmistakable recidivism. In comments given to a photo-journalist from the magazine, Egon, seemingly an exponent of a politically reformed Germany, offers a crypto-fascist political philosophy. For him, democracy has become depleted of "its meaning, its energy, its power" (131). "If anything can be said to represent the new Germany," he explains, "it is the wish, the desire, no, the craving to attain a *total harmony*" (131; my emphasis). (And the very term "New Germany" carries with it an unfortunate but, in the context of the novel, symptomatic echo of another slogan, Hitler's "New Order.") Curiously, neither phenomenologist Anna nor Egon nor their peers reach beyond the surface of the familiar to grapple with difficult moral issues; they use the artifacts of culture and material prosperity to fashion for themselves a "New Germany," a topography that leaves them reassured and unthreatened.[20]

Though offering an unflattering view of right-wing politics, *How German Is It* does not see in leftist extremism a tenable alternative. Throughout the novel, the Einzieh group, a leftist terrorist cell, conducts various violent acts, many of which involve, or appear to involve, Ulrich's former wife, Paula. Yet, the blowing up of public property has no clearly delineated purpose other than to disrupt public life. The Einzieh group issues no manifesto and seems to find its incendiarism an end in itself. Events at the end of the novel suggest that the group has little genuine sympathy for the working class, the constituency whose causes it apparently wishes to champion. With the aid of the very ambiguous Daphne (who is in turn Ulrich's lover and apparently Paula's, who may be a terrorist or a counterterrorist agent or even a double agent), Paula recruits a simple drawbridge attendant, Gottfried Mühler, to blow up the bridge where he works.

> When Daphne and Paula visited his [Mühler's] control room on the tower, it was Paula who asked him: Is this what you will be doing for the rest of your life? Raising the bridge for yachts, the pleasure boats, and nothing to show for it except a small pension at the end of thirty-five years? He pointed out that most of the boats during the off season were fishing trawlers, not yachts.
>
> (222–23)

Clearly, the destruction of the bridge will cause more harm to working men and women than to vacationers and the monied leisure class. Though it is by no means obvious exactly how, Paula is able to trigger some latent rage in Mühler. She is able to "draw him in," to "recruit" him, to "draft" him—all meanings of the German verb "einziehen," from which of course the Einzieh group takes its name. Ultimately, in what seems more Gidean-Camusian *acte gratuit* than political statement, Mühler does indeed destroy the bridge and gun down two policemen. And, as he and Paula laughingly acknowledge earlier while discussing the destruction of the bridge, the result of his act is simply public inconvenience (and needless carnage), and not the overthrow of the government (217).

Ulrich, along with the reader, considers the politico-moral alternatives outlined in the action of the novel. On one side, we have leftists who seek to overthrow the status quo while failing to offer a compelling vision of social progress; on the other, we find right-wing traditionalists who blindly ape the (in)glories of the past. The implication in the novel, certainly in its conclusion, is that the individual must carefully attend to the issues of the day and not be swept along by either a corrupt tradition or by corrupt visions of progress and futurity. There is obviously an existentialist overtone here and, we might say, Ulrich's tribulations throughout the novel clear the way for what is depicted at the end of the novel as an inchoate process of moral self-determination.

Protagonist Ulrich, not coincidentally a former student of Brumhold, is, until the end of the book, a study in bad faith/inauthenticity, one study among many in *How German Is It.* A writer, ideally one gifted in seeing and describing what others cannot, Ulrich consistently defines his world in terms of culture, fleeing the contingency of the moment for the assurance of the aesthetically pure. The primary preoccupation of his writing as well as his life is private relationships. Yet, paradoxically, he avoids a crucial personal issue until the penultimate chapter of the book. Having long suspected that the man from whom he takes his name was not his actual biological father, having long suppressed his curiosity about the matter, Ulrich finally contends with his doubts by consulting a psychoanalyst. He admits that he has been afraid to learn who his father was and what role he played in the war. To seek out his father's identity would have violated "convention" and "good taste," and Ulrich, like his fellow citizens, has obsequiously guarded the harmonious topography of the "New Germany" through his reticence (250). The book concludes with his analyst using hypnosis to unearth Ulrich's suppressed past. Ulrich's right hand slowly rises and he nods as it does so, the entire scene marking an incipient process of historical recollection, the recollection of Hitler's "dream to end all dreams" (252).

"LIVING IN THE MATERIAL WORLD"

Though devoid of Madonna's panache and hysteria, Walter Abish's fictions too explore what it means to live in the "material world." Abish investigates how our desire for an untroubled self-consistency and social harmony manifests itself in the perceptible surfaces of our lives. In documenting the visible markers of our conformity—as apparent in our speech patterns, for example, the shape we give our physical environment, and the use we make of cultural goods—he divests these familiar surfaces of their familiarity and therein encourages us to interrogate our own values. In *For a Critique of the Political Economy of the Sign,* Baudrillard identifies consumption as a universal value of contemporary Western society and illustrates its operation as a morality and instrument of power. Though Abish does not share Baudrillard's sympathy for leftist politics, he does consider, like the latter, our material world and the ethical implications of consumption.[21] In his essay, "Self-Portrait," Abish addresses the issue of moral reformation in a typically postmodern way: "If we were to receive a message from outer space that read: Is there any other way to live? Our reply might be: No, there is not, but we try" (13). The pessimism revealed here is obviously qualified, and is not sustained in the bulk of his fiction, which has a clear moral tendency without being merely tendentious. Though Abish depicts humankind as the product of many powerful determinisms—objects, language, history, instinct—his fiction does not depict these determinisms as incorrigible or purely self-perpetuating. They are open to revision, to the influence of human agency. His fictions are not simply exercises in formalistic legerdemain.

In the 1982 interview, Lotringer characterizes *How German Is It* as a "machine made of broken pieces of mirror that flash elements of meaning to attract the birds" (177). Abish's response indicates his clear disagreement with this characterization (which seems to imply the absence of a clear moral center to the novel): "I wouldn't write in order to trap or fool the reader. To elicit a false response deliberately or intentionally mislead would be to reduce the meaning this book has for me as a literary accomplishment" (177). In this remark Abish effectively ties the aesthetic to the moral and implies that a "good" novel always does so.[22] Though Abish rejects traditional humanism because he feels, as does Heidegger of course, that it imposes a scheme of arbitrary, absolute values upon the historically conditioned circumstances of life, he does not advance the skepticism that is much in fashion in contemporary criticism and contemporary philosophy.[23](Clearly, as Butler points out, the subject matter of *How German Is It* does not permit playful distortions of historical fact [64–65].) Abish realizes that life is full of moral quandaries, of inexplicable situations, yet, at the same time, he acknowledges that these aporias elicit from us interpretive responses. Abish's fictions are his response to these aporias. Though his works offer the reader few positive moral paradigms, they do suggest various moral courses that we should eschew.

Notes

1. For brief analyses of *Alphabetical Africa,* a work I will not discuss here, see Martin (230–33) and my review essay "Walter Abish."

2. Though brief, Messerli's discussion of Abish's seemingly objective point of view in *How German Is It* is helpful (298–300).

3. On this same subject of language's capacity to shape personal ethics Adorno writes: "Fascism was not simply a conspiracy—although it was that—but it was something that came to life in the course of a powerful social development. Language provides it with a refuge. Within this refuge a smoldering evil expresses itself as though it were salvation" (*The Jargon of Authenticity*, 5).

4. I mostly agree with Holdheim, though one might regard Melville's "Benito Cereno," for example, contrary to Holdheim's view, as a case in which, arguably, an author has delineated with some acuity the relationship between morality and plain stupidity. I am thinking particularly, of course, of Captain Delano.

5. Incidentally, William Kowinski cheerfully speculates that the amalgamation of malls and condominiums, i.e., "the Mallcondo Continuum," may well be the way of the future: "The new challenge is to create the ever-beckoning Eden of the frontier within the internal worlds of the planned town, the megastructure, the dome, the mall. It's enclosing time in the Garden of the West" (388). Many will find this vision of Fortress Suburbia "post-Edenic," even dystopian. Are we approaching the day when an entire life will be lived within an emporium? The thought gives chilling new meaning to the notion of a "captive clientele."

6. In the McCaffery/Gregory interview, Abish cites the influence of Godard's early films on his fiction. Bontemps appears to be modeled on Godard, whose films, Abish notes in the interview, develop an "uneasy relationship between his revolutionary fervor and his aesthetic concern," though the two never quite "merge" (24). Incidentally, like Bontemps' film, Godard's *Vent d'Est* also involves the physical destruction of shopping malls and their patrons. Throughout Abish's fiction we find the same themes that pervade Godard's films: gratuitous violence, materialism, and the exploitation of women. Political extremism also figures prominently in many of Godard's films as it does in "This Is Not a Film" and *How German Is It*.

7. A paraphrase of this same statement appears in *How German Is It*, but, strangely, Whitehead is introduced there as an "American thinker" (15).

8. The many recent films and literary works dealing with this subject are well known. In world affairs, Nazi atrocities continue to be a focal point. One can cite, for example, Wiesel's receipt of the 1986 Nobel Peace Prize as well as the ongoing efforts of various national and international bodies to identify and prosecute Nazi war criminals. In recent years, in unrelated cases, two Canadian anti-Semites, Jim Keegstra and Ernst Zundel, have been prosecuted for violation

of Canadian hate laws (Quinn; Aikenhead). (Both Keegstra and Zundel were initially convicted; an appellate court threw out the former's conviction on a legal technicality while Zundel's conviction was upheld by an Ontario Appeal Court ruling, with both appellate judgments occurring coincidentally in June 1988.) And, of course, there is the 1985 Bitburg incident when Ronald Reagan visited a West German cemetery to honor 1,900 German war dead among whom were 49 soldiers of the infamous Waffen-SS. Reagan rankled many people by suggesting that members of Hitler's armed forces were also victims of a "vicious ideology" (quoted in Rentschler, 88). Rentschler's article provides an excellent analysis both of the Bitburg incident and of current attitudes toward Nazism, particularly as presented by the news media and film.

9. Formal English gardens are mentioned recurrently in the novel, e.g., Munich's Englischer Garten (16), Geneva's Jardin Anglais (47), and the Englischer Garten of Egon's city (127).

10. The principal formal differences between the story and the novel are, first, that the former has a first person narrator and the latter a third person, and, second, consistent with the necessary economy of the form, the action of the short story is brisker and more concentrated. The suppression of historical truth is, of course, the primary theme of both. Brumhold, Durst, and the Holocaust's victimized Jewry are emphasized more in "The English Garden" than in the novel. See Arias-Misson for a discussion of "The English Garden" (117–18).

11. In "On Aspects of the Familiar World as Perceived in Everyday Life and Literature," an unpublished conference paper from 1981, Abish emphasizes the disruptive purposes of experimental fiction: "The innovative novel is, in essence, a novel of disfamiliarization, a novel that has ceased to concern itself with the mapping of the 'familiar' world" (quoted in Martin, 238).

12. In fairness to Heidegger, it should be noted that, in contrast to those of the fictitious Brumhold, his "reckless speeches" are confined to a brief ten-month period. His 1933 Rector's address at Freiburg, "The Self-Assertion of the German University," is of course the most famous and noteworthy exemplar in this particular genre. Heidegger offers a spirited defense of himself in the 1966 *Spiegel* interview, published posthumously in 1976, in which, while acknowledging a brief infatuation with Nazism, he depicts himself as the victim of "slander," misinformation, malice, and misquotation. As Heidegger admits in the interview, it was his view in 1933 that, given the "general confusion of opinions and of the political trends of twenty-two parties," Hitler would bring national political cohesion (270). Published first in 1933, the *Rektoratsrede* was not republished until 1983 at which time it was accompanied by a foreword by Heidegger's son Hermann. The first (and

only, so far as I know) English translation of the address is Karsten Harries's in 1985. In addition to his remarks in the *Spiegel* interview, Heidegger's "The Rectorate 1933/34: Facts and Thoughts," written in 1945 after the collapse of the Third Reich, also serves as self-apology. (The latter was first published in the early eighties; Harries's translation of it accompanies the translation of the *Rektoratsrede*.)

Predictably, Heidegger's involvement with the Nazis has inspired much commentary. See Gillespie for an overview of the various positions up until the early eighties (198–99 n. 38). We are entering a new period of investigation with the recent appearance of Victor Farias's highly critical study, *Heidegger et le Nazisme* (1987). See Wolin for an analysis of the Farias book and reactions to it. *New German Critique* has recently published translations of other public political statements Heidegger made in 1933 and 1934; the same issue provides translations of two essays by Heidegger's former student, Karl Löwith. Neither Harries nor Löwith accepts Heidegger's claims, and those of later apologists, that his embracing of Nazism was a temporary, politically expedient move. Harries's "Heidegger as a Political Thinker" argues convincingly that, far from being a philosophical aberration, Heidegger's political views in the thirties build on notions developed in *Being and Time*: "Once we recognize that authenticity demands the subordination of the individual to a common destiny, it becomes impossible to see the *Rektoratsrede* as diametrically opposed to *Being and Time*" (651). Löwith also sees an organic link between Heidegger's ontology and politics: "The possibility of a Heideggerian political philosophy was not born as a result of a regrettable 'miscue,' but from the very conception of existence that simultaneously combats and absorbs the 'spirit of the age'" ("Political Implications," 132). Indicative of renewed interest in Heidegger's political views, *Critical Inquiry* devoted much of its Winter 1989 issue to the subject of "Heidegger and Nazism."

13. Heidegger has not been flatteringly characterized in imaginative literature. In Borges's "Guayaquil" (1970) and Grass's *Dog Years* (*Hundejahre* [1963]), Heidegger is depicted as a Nazi apologist and irrational idealist, respectively. In his lengthy essay *The Jargon of Authenticity* Adorno emphasizes both these points. In Bellow's *Herzog* (1964), the protagonist includes Heidegger in his gallery of intellectual foes. Rebuking the philosopher for his denigration of the "quotidian," Herzog claims that every person's moral worth is centered in quotidian behavior and quotidian values, not in learned abstraction: "Dear Doktor Professor Heidegger, I should like to know what you mean by the expression 'the fall into the quotidian.' When did this fall occur? Where were we standing?" (49; 106). Heidegger discusses the falling of *Dasein* and its causes—"idle talk," "curiosity," and "ambiguity"—in *Being and Time* (210–24).

14. Heidegger's most explicit statement regarding the promise and historical destiny of the Nazis occurs at the very end of the rectorial address. The conclusion of the speech is unmistakably supportive of the Nazis though in it Heidegger makes his familiar claims about the imminent collapse of Western culture and the exemplarity of the classical Greek tradition: "But no one will even ask whether we do or do not will [the centrality of the German university in German society], when the spiritual strength of the West fails and the joints of the world no longer hold, when this moribund semblance of a culture caves in and drags all that remains strong into confusion and lets it suffocate in madness. Whether this will happen or not depends alone on whether or not we, as a historical-spiritual people, still and once again will ourselves. Every individual *participates* in this decision, even he, and indeed especially he, who evades it. But we do will that our people fulfill its historical mission. We do will ourselves. For the young and the youngest strength of the people, which already reaches beyond us, *has* by now *decided* the matter. But we fully understand the splendor and the greatness of this setting out only when we carry within ourselves that profound and far-reaching thoughtfulness that gave ancient Greek wisdom the word: 'All that is great stands in the storm' (Plato, *Republic*, 497 d, 9)" (479–80).

15. And, we should note, the very name "Brumhold," drawing as it seems to from *brume,* a French term for heavy fog, is in itself an authorial judgment on Brumhold's views, which are arguably "fogbound."

16. Obviously, the German belief that language shapes national consciousness and, consequently, national values predates the twentieth century. Herder, Fichte, and Humboldt, among others, make the same claim much earlier. See Stambrook for a discussion of the language issue in the context of German nationalism in the nineteenth century (16–28).

17. Curiously, Adorno, not unlike Brumhold, maintains that German is uniquely suited to philosophical meditations, that "there is a specific, objective quality of the German language" ("On the Question: 'What is German?'" 130). I am ill-equipped to say if this is simple chauvinism or an exile's nostalgia for the *Vaterland* or the truth of the matter.

18. In Abish's story, "I Am the Dust Under Your Feet," Rainer, a gamekeeper, is a reassuring presence: "Even his twill knee-length trousers, his leather vest, his broad leather belt, his worn bone-handle hunting knife, his heavy socks, scuffed resoled boots, were a means of mapping the topography" (8).

19. In Karl Löwith's view, Heidegger, for his part, mastered the art of rhetorical equivocation well in his political addresses, which, Löwith observes, left his auditors unsure whether they should take up the study of the pre-Socratics or enlist in the Storm Troopers (quoted in Megill, 130). Megill provides a succinct

overview of Heidegger's political texts from the thirties (128–36).

20. "Just When We Believe That Everything Has Changed" and "I Am the Dust Under Your Feet," two excerpts from Abish's next novel, continue his discussion of the "New Germany."

21. Though its emphasis is entirely different, Toni Morrison's *The Bluest Eye* also investigates the signifying practices of the material world. In that novel, black children learn racial self-loathing through the models of perfection offered by a dominant white culture. A number of images promote their self-loathing: the domestic harmony of a white household as represented in the "Dick and Jane" reading primers; the sheer "cuteness" of child film star Shirley Temple whose visage decorates a cup; blue-eyed Caucasian dolls; and even the picture of a pretty little white girl on a candy wrapper.

22. Here, it seems to me, Abish's position is very similar to Sartre's when the latter says that there is no such thing as a *good* anti-Semitic novel or a *good* novel that oppresses workers or blacks or colonial peoples (*What Is Literature?* 58).

23. The relationship between skepticism and the "forgetting" of history is a topic of some concern today in critical circles given the recent (1987) de Man disclosures ("Yale Scholar's Articles"). For early contributions to the de Man debate, see articles by David Hirsch, Wiener, Hartman, and Barbara Johnson. See also the various essays in *Critical Inquiry* 15.4 (Summer 1989).

William Doreski (essay date 1991)

SOURCE: A review of *99: The New Meaning*, in *The Literary Review*, Vol. 35, No. 1, Fall, 1991, pp. 163–64.

[*In the following review, Doreski praises Abish's experimental artifice in constructing narratives from previously used sentences in* 99: The New Meaning.]

Walter Abish's new book [*99: The New Meaning*] invokes the convention of the *pensée*, the isolated, reified "thought," to underscore the tendency of all fine or literary writing to privilege the sentence or paragraph and thus undermine the author's intention of rendering cohesive larger entities—short stories or novels. His procedure is to select and arrange fragments of narrative from various authors—ninety-nine of them in the title piece, fifty in **"What Else,"** and so on—and by juxtaposing these fragments create oddly shifting dramas of emotional introspection. The results suggest novels like *Nausea* composed of fictional diary or journal entries in which rhetorical discontinuity embodies strain or anxiety.

Abish, somewhat disingenuously, claims an emotional rather than an aesthetic or critical purpose: "In using se-

lected segments of published texts authored by others as the exclusive 'ready made' material for these five 'explorations' I wanted to probe certain familiar emotional configurations afresh, and arrive at an emotional content that is not mine by design." Yet the strategies of design, the empowerment of context over content, dominates the book. Abish, after all, has not written (in the ordinary sense) the content: he has merely appropriated it. But in juxtaposing one passage to another, utterly foreign one, he externally redetermines the emotional and aesthetic significance of that content. He shows us that fiction is dependent not only on the content of sentences and paragraphs but on their relationship to each other, or to whatever context we find them in. This both rebukes the critical establishment, with its tendency to isolate passages for examination, thus depriving them of context, and affirms some of its recent insights into the complexity of structure and texture.

In **"What Else"** most of the excerpts are paragraph-length, while in **"Inside Out"** most are sentence-length. The other three pieces mix excerpts of varied length, some as brief as four words, some containing more than a hundred words. The longest excerpts stand almost as complete essays, rather than as little stories or parables, while the short ones most resemble the *pensée*, the convention that gives the book its air of critical meditation. Many of them, long and short, comment on writing itself, or the situation of the writer, such as this one from **"What Else"**:

88

Here is a whole nervous breakdown in miniature. We came on Tuesday. Sank into a chair, could scarcely rise; every thing insipid; tasteless, colorless. Enormous desire for rest. Wednesday—only wish to be alone in the open air. Air delicious—avoided speech; could not be read. Thought of my own power of writing with veneration, as of something incredible, belonging to someone else never again to be annoyed by one. Mind a blank. Slept in my chair. Thursday. No pleasure in life whatsoever; but felt perhaps more attuned to existence.

This passage (I don't know from which author's work it derives) exemplifies certain qualities that attract Abish in his compilation: the diary motif, the air of discontinuity, the speaker's uncertainty and lack of purpose, and the fragmentary style. From a thematic view, the entire series of "found" *pensées* suggests a "whole nervous breakdown in miniature." The real challenge, however, is not thematic but structural. Abish requires the reader to suspend the conventional idea of fiction as continuous narrative, to suspend as well the ordinary notions of creativity, and to confront the challenge of the text as endlessly manipulable object rather than inviolable whole. Other authors, from Joyce through Beckett to our own time, have asked something of the sort, but Abish, with a panache already familiar to admirers of his earlier work (especially the brilliant *How German Is It*), pushes the boundaries of fiction still further, challenging settled notions of language and structure and redefining the generic possibilities of his art.

Paul Metcalf (essay date 1991)

SOURCE: "Among the Casualties," in *American Book Review,* Vol. 12, No. 6, 1991, pp. 16, 19.

[*In the following review of* 99: The New Meaning, *Metcalf discusses the importance of displacement and detachment in Abish's work.*]

No man can quite emancipate himself from his age and country, or produce a model in which the education, the religion, the politics, usages and arts of his time shall have no share. Though he were never so original, never so willful and fantastic, he cannot wipe out of his work every trace of the thoughts amidst which it grew. . . . Above his will and out of his sight he is necessitated by the air he breathes and the idea on which he and his contemporaries live and toil, to share the manner of his times.

—Ralph Waldo Emerson

On May 31, 1970, an earthquake and avalanche struck Peru, devastating a 125-mile-long valley between two Andean ranges, the Cordillera Negra and the Cordillera Blanca. With an estimated 75,000 casualties, it was the worst disaster in recorded New World history. Emotional and spiritual responses, among the survivors, were manifold, from the suicidal to the euphoric; but one particular reaction came to be known as *desprendimiento de las cosas,* detachment from things, and this had its counterpart in a kind of "social nakedness," an experience of anonymity, loss of identity. (These notes are taken from *No Bells To Toll,* by Barbara Bode [Scribners, 1989]).

Walter Abish, author of *99: The New Meaning,* was born in Vienna in 1931. He says, in an interview, "I spent my childhood in China, seeing an incredibly corrupt society slowly disintegrate. It was as if all the life processes were accentuated and crowded into the period of time I lived in Shanghai." He now lives in New York City.

For Walter Abish, born in dying Vienna, making a childhood escape from Hitler, and growing up in decadent Shanghai, the twentieth century must have seemed like one endless earthquake-avalanche, inducing an inescapable *desprendimiento.*

Abish again: "I have always thought that all the life networks that enable us to proceed wherever we are going, or prevent us from doing so, are predicated on a system we called language."

Again: "I try to strip language of its power to create verisimilitude that in turn shields the reader from the printed words on the page that are deployed as signifiers." This is crucial, not only to Abish, but to other contemporary prose writers and poets. To undo the traditional work of language. And the *idea* of this process becomes obsessive to the author.

One section of *99: The New Meaning* is called "Skin Deep," and Abish refers to this as a "literary infringe-ment." A feeding back on his own European heritage. Paul Bowles once wrote a story ("Here to Learn") about a Moroccan girl, born into ignorance and poverty, who is rescued by an American, flown to Europe and eventually to Los Angeles. Crossing the Atlantic, in the middle of the night, she becomes convinced that the plane is not moving. "We're standing still. The plane is stuck." And Claude Levi-Strauss tells of having, in flying from Europe to *any* point in the Western Hemisphere—New York, the Brazilian jungle—a kind of mental adjustment, a click in his brain, as the plane touches down. A new dimension. *Desprendimiento . . .* and reconnection.

In an earlier volume, ***In the Future Perfect,*** a collection of short stories, Abish writes a more conventional prose. But already the process of dismantling is apparent. In story after story, the only sure connection between characters is through sex—what Quentin Crisp calls "the epidermal felicity of two featherless bipeds in desperate congress." All other connections, all other ways in which human beings interact, are suspect.

Desprendimiento. Anonymity. Following are quotations from *99: The New Meaning*:

"I'm aware that a good many perfectly intelligent people can't stand parenthetical comments while a story's purportedly being told."

"The more a story is told in a proper well-spoken straightforward way, in an even tone, the easier it is to reverse it, to blacken it, to read it inside out."

"(I am breaking the process into its components for the sake of analysis.)"

"Suppose I wanted to replace all the words of my language at once by other ones; how could I tell the place where one of the new words belong? Is it images that keep the places of the word?"

"Neither is there any end: you never leave a woman, a friend, a city in one go. And then everything looks alike: Shanghai, Moscow, Algiers, everything is the same after two weeks."

"The self is not only hateful: there is no place between *us* and *nothing.*"

"And how much fine joy, how much graciousness ever do we owe precisely to our contempt!"

"I loathe unexpectedly catching sight of myself in a mirror. . . ."

"What is thought, but disease of action."

In his preface, Abish speaks admiringly of Kafka, in *The Castle* naming his protagonist, simply, "K.," thereby voiding "any necessity to provide or explain the character's antecedents. Kafka's marked disinclination to furnish K.'s credentials—K. has no identifiable or censoriously traceable past—greatly contributed to the heightened immediacy of *The Castle.*"

And elsewhere he speaks of the hotel guest who had no memory: each time he entered the lobby the desk clerk had to tell him his name, and which room he occupied.

After the Peruvian earthquake, each survivor, almost without exception—his city a *tabula rasa*—wanted to rebuild on the exact site of his original home. These instincts—the sense of history, the sense of place—run deep in human experience. In the work of Walter Abish—making Literature rather than Life the subject of the work—they are among the casualties.

FURTHER READING

Criticism

Karl, Frederick R. *American Fictions: 1940–1980*. New York: Harper and Row, 1983, pp. 551–55.

Discusses *How German Is It* in a survey of modern experimental fiction.

Messerli, Douglas. "The Role of Voice in Nonmodernist Fiction." *Contemporary Literature* 25, No. 3, 1984.

Considers Abish's narrative techniques in a discussion of contemporary narrative voices.

Semrau, Janusz. "Magritte, Godard, and Walter Abish's Architectonic Fiction." *Studia Anglia Posnaniensia: An International Review of English Studies* 22, 1989, pp. 141–52.

Considers Abish's method of constructing narratives in the context of self-referential visual and cinematographic art.

Additional coverage of Abish's life and career is contained in the following sources published by the Gale Group: *Contemporary Authors*, Vol. 101; *Contemporary Authors New Revision Series*, Vol. 37; *Contemporary Literary Criticism*, Vol. 22; *Dictionary of Literary Biography*, Vol. 130.

Akutagawa Ryunosuke
1892–1927

(Born Niihara Ryunosuke) Japanese short story writer, novelist, poet, translator, and critic.

INTRODUCTION

Akutagawa is considered one of the foremost writers of Japan's modern era, a period that began in 1868 under the rule of the Emperor Meiji. His works, particularly his short stories, contributed greatly to his generation's thoughtful consideration of such issues as the function and merits of different literary genres and the artist's role in contemporary Japanese society. They also proved instrumental in extricating Japanese literature from what critics consider the morass of gossip and tedious didacticism into which it had fallen before the Meiji Restoration.

BIOGRAPHICAL INFORMATION

Akutagawa was born in Irifunecho, a district within Tokyo. His father was the enterprising owner of five dairies by the time Akutagawa was born. Shortly after Akutagawa's birth, his mother, who suffered from mental illness, lapsed into a schizophrenic state from which she never recovered. Memories of his mother's insanity and the resulting fear that he may have inherited her mental condition preyed upon Akutagawa his entire life; these factors also strongly influenced his writing, often serving as themes in his fiction. After his mother's death, his mother's elder brother and his wife, who gave the boy their family name, Akutagawa, adopted him. His adoptive parents had remained largely untouched by Western culture, and they instilled in him a reverence for Japanese traditions, particularly in literature. Akutagawa developed a fondness for ancient legends and tales of the grotesque, both of which later figured significantly in his work. However, he was a voracious reader, and by the time he reached middle school he was reading the works of Henrik Ibsen, Rudyard Kipling, and Anatole France, among others. Akutagawa attended Tokyo Imperial University, where he excelled in his studies of English literature, translated many Western works, and became active in publishing a student-produced literary periodical, as well as regularly participating in a discussion group conducted by the renowned novelist Natsume Sōseki. Akutagawa had begun publishing short stories in periodicals by the time he graduated in 1916, and he was widely acclaimed as one of the brightest newcomers on the literary scene. He accepted a part-time teaching position at the Naval Academy at Yokosuka, meanwhile strengthening his reputation during 1917 by publishing his stories in various magazines and in two collections. In 1918 Akutagawa married the niece of a friend he had known since childhood; in the same year he also entered into a contract with a Japanese newspaper to publish his fiction. This enabled him to resign his post at the Naval Academy and devote himself entirely to his writing. In 1921 Akutagawa was sent to China by his newspaper as an "overseas observer," an assignment that proved to be a turning point in his life. Never having enjoyed sound health, he suffered during his travels from a number of debilitating illnesses that left him weakened, depressed, and helpless to combat a developing mental illness brought on by fears of a deterioration similar to his mother's. His writing, which up to this point was firmly rooted in history and legend, grew introspective and autobiographical. Akutagawa's fear of madness became obsessive, and he sought temporary respite from both psychological and physical troubles through the use of drugs. Following the mental breakdown of a close friend, Akutagawa committed suicide in 1927.

MAJOR WORKS OF SHORT FICTION

While Akutagawa did not confine himself to any particular genre during his career, his greatest work was done in the short story form. He consistently attempted to examine predictable and universal patterns of human behavior, and to depict those natural aspirations and illusions that transcend barriers of space and time. Conflicts between the natural inclinations of human beings and the demands imposed by ordered societies, as well as humanity's struggle with baser propensities, echo throughout Akutagawa's works. For example, "Rashomon," which has come to be synonymous with its author's name in part because of the 1950 film version by director Kurosawa Akira, depicts the moral collapse of a man driven to assault and thievery by the horror he witnesses in a society that has itself collapsed and lives by the savage morality of expediency. In this story Akutagawa portrayed the psychological drama of humanity caught in the confrontation between circumstantial chaos and structured morality, an approach unceasingly fascinating to him, in one of the ancient settings he had always found so effective as dramatic background. His second volume of short stories, *Tobako tu akuma* (1917; *Tobacco and the Devil*), featured stories set in medieval Japan and drew heavily on Asian legends in form and theme. "Kumo no Ito" ("The Spider's Thread") deals allegorically with one man's pervasive egoism, a flaw that proves fatal both to himself and to others. While Akutagawa's subjects constitute faithful representations of both the grim and the foolish aspects of human behavior, they are not always devoid of humor. "Hana" ("The Nose"), one of Akutagawa's best-known stories, addresses egoism by relating the predicament of a Buddhist monk who has succeeded in shortening his enormous nose, the bane of his existence and, as he sees it, the impediment to his social acceptance, but his vanity is penalized by disfigurement of his face and coldness from his peers.

CRITICAL RECEPTION

After his death Akutagawa was largely neglected in Japan by critics who considered his style affected and his poetic approach to fiction overly refined—as evidenced, for example, in his subtle characterization. If not for the lively interest of a Western audience, which was removed from Japanese literary debate and which found in his work a fresh Eastern perspective on dilemmas long familiar in Western literature, Akutagawa might have been completely forgotten. The history of Akutagawa's critical reception is far more complex; due to neglect by Western readers of the later stories, and a tendency in Japan to rate the author's efforts purely in terms of personal preference, more comprehensive critical estimations of Akutagawa's career were largely nonexistent for a time. However, more recent commentators have found that Akutagawa's stories are skillfully written and demonstrate scope unrestricted to his own time and culture, and for that reason widened the dimensions of their genre and helped make short stories a more important part of Japanese literature. Through his early work as a translator and his later concern with important critical issues, he helped introduce and foster the tradition of the European novel in his own country, where, according to some critics, the novel form might otherwise have degenerated. Far from being dismayed by the differences between East and West, Akutagawa used them as sources for both the content and spirit of his work; the result was a significant achievement in the development of modern Japanese literature.

PRINCIPAL WORKS

Short Fiction

Rashomon [*Rashomon, and Other Stories*] 1916
Tobaku tu akuma [*Tobacco and the Devil*] 1917
The Puppeteer 1919
Tales Grotesque and Curious 1930
Jigoku Hen [*Hell Screen and Other Stories*] 1948
Japanese Short Stories 1961
Exotic Japanese Stories: The Beautiful and the Grotesque 1964

Other Major Works

Kappa (novel) 1947

CRITICISM

Glenn W. Shaw (essay date 1930)

SOURCE: Introduction to *Tales Grotesque and Curious* by Akutagawa Ryunosuke, translated by Glenn W. Shaw, The Hokuseido Press, 1930, pp. i-vii.

[*In the following essay, Shaw gives an account of Akutagawa's influences and development as a short story writer.*]

[Akutagawa's] graduation thesis was entitled, *Wiriamu Morisu Kenkyū (A Study of William Morris)*.

He was like Morris in his surrender to the fascination of the Middle Ages, but he had none of the practical reforming tendencies of that artist socialist. He has been more aptly compared to Flaubert for the seriousness with which he took his art and the preciousness of his style. And the post-bellum point of view has been expressed by a Japanese social worker who, at his death, compared him, as a man with a keen sense of humor and knowledge of human nature and "an arbiter of elegance in the vicious society in which he lived," to Petronius.

He says of himself while at the University that he did not attend classes very well and was an idle student, but we may take this for the expression of a sincere wish to be more like some of his hardier classmates, for Kikuchi Kan, one of them and today the literary Crœsus of Japan, says that Akutagawa went to his classes faithfully and had the confidence of his professors.

Kikuchi first came to admire Akutagawa when, with a few others at the University, they began in 1914 the publication of the third series of the magazine *Shinshichō*. His maiden effort appeared in the first issue, attracting no particular attention. But in the following year he published in the magazine *Teikoku Bungaku* two stories, the second of which, **"Rashōmon,"** became the title story of his first volume . . . and is now always associated with his name. It is a gruesome thing concerning the old two-storied south gate of Kyōto in the days when that landmark was falling into decay with the rest of the ancient capital toward the end of the twelfth century. By way of lame extenuation, this much, at least, may be said for the story (which is the fourth in this volume), that in other tales, Akutagawa has written with even more disgusting realism of this truly distressing period.

In December, 1915, while still at the University, Akutagawa became a disciple of the preeminent writer of the day, Natsume Soseki, who probably had a greater influence than any other man on his literary life. Mori Ogai, the versatile army surgeon, who tried his hand at so many things in the literary field during the periods of Meiji and Taishō, has been credited with having had the next greatest influence on him.

In 1916, in a fourth revival of the magazine *Shinshichō*, Akutagawa published **"Hana"** (**"The Nose"**), the second story in this book, which drew from Natsume the highest praise. He told his young disciple that if he would write twenty or thirty more stories like it, he would find himself occupying a unique position among the writers of his country, a prophecy which came true. Out of old material, with the greatest attention to detail and to the atmosphere of the period of which he wrote, Akutagawa had produced a grotesquely amusing thing, writing into it some modern psychology and the little lesson that ideals are precious only so long as they remain ideals. This new way of treating historical material in Japan attracted the attention of his countrymen and became characteristic of much of Akutagawa's work. Of this sort of tale, **"Lice"** and the Chinese story, **"The Wine Worm,"** go one step further in grotesquery, while **"The Pipe"** turns to lighter and more wholesome humor.

In 1917, when Akutagawa published his second volume of short stories, *Tobako to Akuma* (*The Devil and Tobacco*), he had already established himself as one of the foremost writers of the day. The title story of the volume is the opening story in this book. In it we see an Oriental saturated with western literature playing with an old theme in a highly amusing and clever way. (Incidentally Akutagawa was himself an inveterate cigarette smoker.) It is one of the many stories he wrote about the early Catholic missionaries of the sixteenth century, one of them so cleverly that it fooled Japanese students of the period into believing that it was a translation from an old Latin text, nonexistent, but called by Akutagawa *Legenda Aurea.*

[There] can be no doubt that he had more individuality than any other writer of his time and has left in Japanese literature a mass of artistic work, often grotesque and curious, that, while it undoubtedly angers the proletarian experimenters who now hold the stage and fight with lusty pens and a highly developed class consciousness against all that he stood for, will continue to live as long as men go on treasuring the fancies their fellows from time to time set down with care on paper.

Robert Halsband (essay date 1953)

SOURCE: "Fresh Tales from Japan," in *The Saturday Review,* Vol. XXXVI, No. 10, March 7, 1953, pp. 59–60.

[*In the following review, Halsband offers high praise for the English translation of* Rashomon.]

The recent success in this country of the Japanese film *Roshomon* probably explains why there has now been published ***Roshomon and Other Stories,*** by Ryuonsuke Akutagawa. The six stories which it contains need no recommendation except their own merits—which are fresh and striking. Their themes are varied: a pair of stories deal with murder and with seduction and rape; a pair are comic, about a glutton cured by gorging, and a mischievous priest deceived by his own deception; the remaining two relate the robbing of a thief, and the martyrdom of a saintly boygirl. All are brief and incisive, yet with a wealth of overtone which enlarges their meanings beyond specific people and places. The sensibility with which they are presented by Akutagawa—who died a suicide in 1927—is cynical and subtle.

Here, obviously, is no pretty-pretty playing with Japanese garden life, but a relentless stripping of character and motive. The rationalization of a ghoulish thief is as bitterly sensitive as the thoughts of an unfaithful wife who prepares to substitute herself for her husband to be killed by her lover. The translation by Takashi Kajima, except for a few clumsy phrases, is clean and lucid; and the volume itself is tastefully printed, illustrated, and priced. The unusual excellence of the stories suggests that more of contemporary Japanese literature deserves publication in English.

Patricia M. Lewis (essay date 1971)

SOURCE: "Akutagawa's Rashomon: The Development of the Theme Through Setting and Symbolism," in *Literature East and West,* Vol. 15, No. 4, December, 1971, pp. 867–71.

[*In the following essay, Lewis examines the meaning of the story "Rashomon" through its setting and symbolism.*]

In **"Rashomon,"** a short story by Ryunosuke Akutagawa, the central theme—the destruction of conventional morality—is skillfully conveyed primarily through patterns of imagery and the setting. Through a combination of casual events and psychological justifications, the protagonist shatters the facade of noble principles that would eventually result in his death by his realization that his resurgent doubts about the immorality of stealing in order to live are merely symptomatic of a harsher reality—that principles are only fabrications of social convenience with little validity when measured against survival itself.

The author constructs and embellishes this theme by establishing the setting in conventional symbols and images: it is a cold, rainy evening, and the servant has taken refuge from the weather (and his plight) in the Rashomon, the deserted gate in Kyoto's outer wall, itself symbolic of the decline of ancient values. The physical features of the setting are vehicles, both on a literal, casual plane and also on the symbolic level, of the destruction of the servant's traditional views of honor and morality. This tradition is emphasized by the fact that the protagonist has been released from his function as the servant of a samurai, the literal and symbolic figure of traditional Japanese life and custom. The old order has been disrupted: the servant has been discharged, and the time-honored code of morality has been displaced. On a larger scale, the decaying Rashomon is representative of the declining prosperity of Kyoto, and it is this decline that has resulted in the servant's dismissal. Thus, it is subtly significant that he should take refuge in an edifice that is suffering, as he is, from the effects of economic pressures. These pressures precipitate his confrontation with his own moral precepts just as they precipitate the desecration of the Buddhist images which are sold as firewood. The setting at the gate is also important because it is on the perimeter of the city and opens out to the unknown, the significance of which will be discussed later in this paper.

But the decaying state of the Rashomon is not the only symbolic indication of future realizations. The deathly ominous red sky "in the afterlight of the departed sun," the depressing effect of the rain, the "howling wind in the evening dusk," and the presence of the "white droppings of crows"[1] dotting the crumbling stones, all contribute to the realistic setting of the story, but also operate on a symbolic level to portend the transformation of the servant into an absurd here devoid of metaphysical anchorage. The symbolic death of metaphysics is intensified by the ghostly aura created by the presence of the unwanted corpses as well as by the image of "a fat black cloud impaling itself on the tips of the tiles jutting out from the roof on the gate."

It is the presence of the bodies in the surreal flickering light which magnifies his receptivity to the nightmarish confusion of reality with appearance: "He caught sight of a ghoulish form bent over a corpse." This confusion is paralleled by his vacillation between the alternative of death and good or the alternative of life and evil, but the confusion is subliminally negated by the red, festering pimple which, like his final commitment to evil, is resolutely emerging. But the conventional view of evil as the absence of good is torturously inverted. For the servant, good becomes the absence of evil, or at best, a superfluous construct of appearances superimposed on a reality that makes no distinctions. It is therefore his commitment to reality instead of appearance that supplants his original conflict. And it is his realization of this distinction expressed in the "certain courage [which] was born in his heart," that designates his emergence as an absurd figure.

His emergence is also conveyed by the author on an imagistic level. When the servant first sees the light in the tower, he is described as "huddling, cat-like . . ." When creeping to the tower to investigate the light, he is compared to a lizard. But after his acceptance of the absurd and his resultant detachment from conventional codes, he is ironically elevated to the level of mythological powers by the image of thundering footsteps pounding in the hollow tower.

Animal imagery is also employed in describing the old woman: she is compared to a monkey killing the lice of her young; her arms have "no more flesh on them than on the shanks of a chicken"; she gazes at the servant with the "sharp red eyes of a bird of prey"; and, a "sound like the cawing of a crow came from her throat." It is significant that these images are drawn during the servant's moments

of confusion between appearance and reality, until he is aware that she is "A ghoul no longer; only a hag. . . ." It is during these moments of confusion that the significance of the sword becomes evident.

The servant's sword, reminiscent of traditional bonds and samurai ritual, is a conventional symbol of violence, but violence tempered by a code of honor. Because the servant never considers selling the sword in order to buy food, the importance of the sword and its tradition is indirectly emphasized. It is ironic that the sword subdues the woman and thereby frees the servant from the illusion that he battles a ghoul. When the servant sheathes his sword and raises his hand to touch the pimple on his cheek, his metamorphosis from honor to the absurd is nearly complete.

The motif of appearance and reality is further exemplified by the old woman stealing from the corpses hair that will be made into wigs. Not only does the initially apparent desecration of the bodies serve to horrify the servant and thus act as catalyst to his epiphany, but the idea of wig-wearing also carries with it overtones of artificiality, subterfuge, a deliberate attempt to mask reality with an artifact of appearance. And it is ironic that the old woman's words, ". . . I pull out the hair . . . to make a wig . . . ," banish the unknown—the realm of appearance.

This same motif is apparent in the depiction of the bodies: "Some of them were women, and all were lolling on the floor with their mouths open or their arms outstretched showing no more signs of life than so many clay dolls. One would doubt that they had ever been alive, so eternally silent they were. Their shoulders, breasts, and torsos stood out in the dim light; other parts vanished in shadow." The fusion of clay dolls with shadow again juxtaposes appearances and reality, inducing them to merge in the bizarre, surrealistic, limbo-like setting. It is in limbo that life and death are no longer dichotomous.

Perhaps the most complex image and symbol pattern lies in the recurrence of "the unknown." The first instance where this occurs is when the servant is climbing the board lacquered stairs leading to the tower over the gate. He is halfway up the stairs when he sees a flickering light in the tower. "What sort of person would be making a light in the Rashomon . . . and in a storm? The unknown, the evil terrified him." The second instance occurs after the servant has stolen the old hag's clothes and disappeared into the night: "Shortly after that the hag raised her body from the corpses. Grumbling and groaning, she crawled to the top stair by the still flickering torchlight, and through the gray hair which hung over her face, she peered down to the last stair in the torch light. Beyond this was only darkness . . . unknowing and unknown."

The images are inverted: the servant, in a state of moral conflict, sees the light in the tower as he climbs the stairs and fears an unknown that awaits him; the hag, who has resolved, or perhaps denied moral conflict, looks down the stairs into the darkness. And there lies the unknown for her. Because the images are inverted, their symbolism must likewise be inverted. As the servant transcends the unknown by his metamorphosis to the absurd and his implied commitment to life (conveyed by the light imagery, ghostly though it may be), the old hag, now faced with the consequences of her amoral "non-code" turned back upon her, must undergo a reversal of the servant's metamorphosis from conventional morality to valueless existence. She is no longer detached from a code of values because her encounter with the servant has altered her perception of reality. For her, the darkness beyond the stairs is death. And therein lies the despair of this story.

Although a congruity of theme, action, character and imagery exists within the story proper, the entire incident is beyond the confines of rational or normal experience. But the bizarre seems less so when placed in a nebulously remote time.[2] Like the servant's pimple, the author has established a festering poetic truth that is not contingent on a believable, or rather, mundane setting.

Notes

1. Parenthetically, it should be noted that the crows, conventional symbols of death, are not present in the Rashomon while the servant is there. Death will not be his choice.

2. The setting in antiquity is established first by the fact that it is in the Rashomon itself, and second by the intrusion of the author in the references to "Old chronicles say . . . ," and "As rumor has said. . . ."

Makoto Ueda (essay date 1976)

SOURCE: "Akutagawa Ryunosuke," in *Modern Japanese Writers and the Nature of Literature,* Stanford University Press, 1976, pp. 111–44.

[*In the following essay, Ueda discusses Akutagawa's interest in literary criticism and the representation of the artist's life in his short stories.*]

Akutagawa Ryūnosuke (1892–1927) was a writer who could easily have become a scholar or literary critic. An extremely self-conscious man, he never failed to criticize the artist within himself, usually with unforgiving scrutiny. Naturally the basic problems of art and artist are abundantly reflected in his works. **"The Hell Screen,"** a masterpiece of his early period, centers on a painter caught between the conflicting demands of life and art. *Kappa,* a major work of his later years, has a poet, an aphorist, and two composers among its main characters. A sizable number of his other major pieces, such as **"Absorbed in Letters," "Withered Fields," "Genkaku Sanbō," "Cogwheel,"** and **"A Fool's Life,"** also have artists for their principal characters and deal with problems relating to art. As an essayist, too, Akutagawa wrote a good deal about literature, from the casual and polemic "Literary, Too Literary" to the more theoretical "Ten Rules for Writing a Novel," "Literature: an Introduction," and "On the Appreciation of Literature." There can be no doubt that, like his mentor Sōseki before him, he devoted many hours to pondering the nature of literature.

TAMING A MONSTER

One of Akutagawa's clearest definitions of literature appears in his essay "Literature: an Introduction," where he calls literature "an art that uses words or letters for its medium." He continues: "To elaborate, it is an art that transmits life by means of three elements: (1) the meaning of words; (2) the sound of words; (3) the shape of ideograms." This definition reveals two factors that are basic to Akutagawa's concept of literature. The first is his emphasis on the medium of literature, namely, language. The second is his assumption that literature aims to "transmit life."

Of course, literature does use language for its medium. But Akutagawa seems a bit overemphatic on that point. In a definition of literature as brief as this, one would usually forgo mention of sound and meaning; certainly, one would not want to refer to the visual effect of ideograms. To Akutagawa, however, those formal elements of language were so important that he could not help bringing them in. This fact is substantiated in the essay itself: two of its three sections are devoted to words, letters, sounds, ideograms, structures, etc. Although the shape of ideograms was hardly a universal issue, Akutagawa could not bear to leave it out. For him, literature was above all an art of words.

The reason for his emphasis on words is explained in the same essay. It is that words, when arranged in an orderly fashion, create form, without which contents cannot exist. "Contents that lack a form are like a desk or chair without its form," he wrote. A work of literature could exist only when it took on a form, just as a desk was a desk by virtue of its form. Life, before it had been given form by the artist, was nothing but crude material, just as a desk was coarse lumber without the carpenter. Words were the very means by which wild nature was molded into form and given a place in human life.

As might be expected, Akutagawa favored unambiguous words and lucid syntax. Explaining his principles of composition, he once said:

> More than anything else, I want to write clearly. I want to express in precise terms what lies in my mind. I try to do just that. And yet, when I take up my pen, I can seldom write as smoothly as I want to. I always end up writing cluttered sentences. All my effort (if I can call it that) goes into clarification. The quality I seek in other men's writings is the same as the one I seek in my own. I cannot admire a piece of composition lacking in clarity. I am sure I could never bring myself to like it. In matters of composition, I am an Apollonian.

What aspects of life should the literary artist try to clarify with the words that are his shaping tools? Akutagawa's answer is implied in the word he used for "life" in the definition of literature already quoted. The Japanese word is *seimei,* usually translated as "life" but primarily referring to "the source of life." Akutagawa chose this word in preference over *seikatsu,* which can also be translated as "life," but which more precisely means "activities in life." Seimei is energy, vitality, the inner biological force that keeps a living thing alive and vigorous. Seikatsu is the outer manifestation of seimei—eating, drinking, talking, walking, running, fighting, and every other kind of human behavior. Literature, Akutagawa seems to be saying, should transmit the source of life; it should not aim merely to copy outward manifestations of that source.

As can be imagined, Akutagawa was against those who insisted that a novel should copy the tangible realities of life as they are. In one of the first critical essays he published, he attacked a school of tanka, quite influential at the time, that was known as the Seikatsu School. "I know I am being rude in saying this," he wrote, "but I cannot understand what makes those distinguished poets write exclusively in the style of that school. If they wish to express nothing more than those plain—if the word is offensive, I would be willing to say 'realistic' or 'plebeian'—those plain feelings, they need not go to all the trouble of confining themselves to the 31-syllable form. Instead, they might as well choose such forms as free verse or the novel, which are more conducive to narration." Akutagawa was saying, in effect, that the Seikatsu School poets presented seikatsu but not seimei. He made the same point about fiction, a literary form that by his own admission was more conducive to description of everyday life. A target of his attack was Flaubert, then one of the reigning deities among Japanese novelists. After citing Flaubert's words that an artist should be like God, manifesting Himself in all His creations but remaining invisible to man, Akutagawa caustically remarked: "For that very reason his *Madame Bovary* lacks emotional appeal, even though it creates a microcosm." The author of *Madame Bovary,* he thought, might well have succeeded in his creative task, but why had he concealed himself so thoroughly, as if he wanted nothing to do with his readers? There was such a thing as being too godlike. As a commentary on Flaubert, this is hardly just. But Akutagawa was aiming his barbs at the Japanese naturalists of his day, who had made Flaubert an idol, and here he was much nearer the mark. The Japanese naturalists, as he correctly pointed out, wrote boring novels because, with all their attention to surface facts, they had neglected the one essential ingredient: the source of life itself.

But where was this all-important "source of life" to be found? Akutagawa's answer is best expressed in his works of fiction. However, there are answers of a sort to be found throughout his other writings. Among them is the following, which appears in a letter he wrote to a friend when he was still an undergraduate student:

> These twain, sprung from the same homeland, are named Good and Evil. They were given these names by folk who knew nothing of their homeland. Let us

now rename them, to mark their common origin. Shall their name be Logos? A high-sounding name, you say. But Logos pervades the universe. Logos is in all men. The Greater Logos moves the constellations; the Lesser Logos moves the human heart. Those who reck not of Logos shall surely perish! Such behavior, for want of a better name, we call evil. Logos is neither emotion nor intellect nor will. If we have to define it, we might say it is Supreme Intellect. Good and Evil are only utilitarian concepts that vaguely define men's conduct in terms of their relation to Logos. Sometimes I feel as if the stars are mixed in my blood and circulating in my veins. The founders of astrology must have felt as I do, only more strongly. Unless we know the Logos, there is no health in us. Whatever we write must partake of its influence, else it will be worthless. It is only by and through the Logos that a work of art becomes meaningful.

Clearly, whatever Akutagawa meant by "Logos," it was neither good nor evil; rather, it was the prototype of them both. It was not an external power like fate; rather, it was part of one's very existence, as familiar—and as close—as one's own heartbeat. From this point of view, his "Supreme Intellect" was a misnomer.

Akutagawa stressed that art must partake of this Logos, this power that lies deep in the existence of man. Most of his major stories can be interpreted as attempts in this direction. **"Rashōmon"** is a study of how man's survival instinct supersedes moral values. **"In a Grove"** takes the reader into a subterranean world of sex and death where the so-called facts and truths of the daylight world disappear in the murk. The priest's monstrous nose in **"The Nose"** is symbolic of an incurable deformity in human nature—a deformity with which every man has to live. The hero of **"The Hell Screen"** has a more tragic fate: *his* deformity is the artist's irresistible passion to copy the dark hell that is human life. Akutagawa's Logos finds even more direct expression in **"Doubts,"** the story of a man who kills his wife when he is unable to release her from under a fallen beam in their burning house. He chooses to beat her to death with a few swift and savage blows rather than leave her to meet a slower, more painful end in the fire. After the incident, however, doubts begin to fill his mind that, somewhere deep within him, he had always wanted to kill her, because she had not been a sexually ideal wife for him. His doubts grow more serious and more importunate with time, until he has a nervous breakdown. "I may be a lunatic," he finally reflects, "but, then, wasn't my lunacy caused by a monster that lurks at the bottom of every human mind? Those who call me a madman and spurn me today may become lunatics like me tomorrow. They harbor the same monster."

The young Akutagawa, after dutifully pursuing his Logos, found such a monster waiting for him in the end. Seimei, the "source of life" that made men want to go on living, turned out to be a monstrous force capable of driving a man to bludgeon his wife to death. An ordinary person does not do such things simply because he has never been faced with an extreme situation. This dreadful wisdom casts an even darker shadow on Akutagawa's stories as time goes by. The heroine of **"A Clod of Earth,"** known to her entire village as a model of diligence, is a merciless, egotistical monster at home; her industry and her egotism spring from the same internal source. **"Genkaku Sanbō"** is a story filled with monsters: the old painter who often wishes for his concubine's death; his invalid wife who is silently jealous not only of the concubine but of her own daughter; his grandson who in his childish innocence hurts everyone who gets close enough to him; and his sickroom nurse who takes a sadistic pleasure in watching others suffer. *Kappa* is not a social satire, as has often been claimed; it is the story of a man who has become awakened to the monstrous "source of life" (symbolized by kappas),[1] and who eventually goes insane as a result. Doubts, anxiety, and fear about the weird forces that underlie human existence make up the atmosphere of **"Cogwheel."** "It is unspeakably painful to live with these feelings," says the hero at the end of the story. "Isn't there anyone who would kindly strangle me to death while I am asleep?"

Akutagawa's last thoughts about "the source of life" are unmistakably expressed in his famous suicide note entitled **"Note to an Old Friend."** "What is known as the source of life is in reality nothing more than animal energy," he wrote near its end. "I, too, am one of the human animals." Finally, he confesses that when he was young he wanted to think of himself as God, but that at last he realized he was wrong. No doubt he was recalling his student days—the days when he believed in the Supreme Intellect as the source of human life. Now he found that what he had taken to be divinity was no more than animality.

For Akutagawa, then, to depict nature was to depict the monstrous animality that was the source of human life. The agreeable part of nature—the part that was pleasing to the eye and mind—was all on the surface, even though it might be all that an ordinary person saw in his daily life. Akutagawa would have no part of such superficiality. He wanted extreme circumstances under which man would be forced to face his own monstrous nature. His tales are full of such circumstances for that very reason. He himself wrote in explanation:

> . . . suppose I have a theme and would like to make it into a novel. In order to give it an artistically powerful expression, I need some extraordinary incident. But the more extraordinary I imagine it to be, the less plausible today's Japan becomes as a setting for it. If I give it a contemporary setting, I will most likely strain my readers' credulity. This will probably ruin my chances of getting the theme across. I already suggested one solution to this problem when I said it was difficult to place an extraordinary incident in a contemporary setting. The solution is nothing other than this: to make the incident happen in some remote past (the use of the future for this purpose would be possible but rare), or in a country other than Japan, or both.

The microcosm created by Akutagawa in his fiction was simply a means to an end, namely, illustration of his theme;

it was not an end in itself. Here he differed from Tanizaki, with whom he otherwise had much in common. Tanizaki created a world of fantasy according to the dictates of his imagination; Akutagawa first conceived his theme, then made up a fantasy world to suit the theme.

The reason why Akutagawa took this attitude is clear enough: he had a stronger faith in the power of words as such. A novelist, he thought, could penetrate to and express the source of life through his mastery of words. Unfortunately for Akutagawa, mastery of words proved no substitute for mastery of life. His definition of literature thus fell prey to conflicting principles. Literature, he said, was an art that used words to transmit life. But what if life should resist transmission by words? Language is Apollonian, life Dionysian. Akutagawa wanted art not merely to imitate nature, but to conquer it. He wanted too much.

The Novelist Must Be a Poet

It follows from Akutagawa's concept of literature that a novelist needs two qualifications above all else: command of words, and deep feeling. He is a verbal artist, but he is also sensitive enough to penetrate the surface of life and reach the source of human vitality beneath.

That a novelist must be a competent prose writer is a truism. Probably for that reason, Akutagawa did not stress this point in his essays. In "Ten Rules for Writing a Novel," he put style in seventh place. Nevertheless, he held up an ideal of literary craftsmanship.

> Literature is an art that depends on language for its expression. It goes without saying, then, that a novelist must work hard to improve his writing. If he finds himself indifferent to the beauty of language, he must realize he lacks one of a novelist's chief qualifications. Saikaku gained the nickname "Saikaku the Dutchman" not because he broke the contemporary rules of fiction, but because he had learned the beauty of words by writing *haikai.*[2]

The passage is noteworthy for its rather peculiar reference to Saikaku. This seventeenth-century novelist has often been praised for his sturdy prose style (Shiga, as we have seen, admired him in this respect), but rarely for his quaint vocabulary. Akutagawa here seems to be advocating a highly individual style, including an unusual vocabulary, together with a certain disregard of ruling literary conventions.

Akutagawa's high regard for individuality in writing probably accounts for some unique advice of his: "High school students wanting to become writers should waste as little time as possible on such subjects as Japanese literature or Japanese composition." He did not want aspiring novelists to produce model schoolroom compositions or imitate the styles of famous writers. Instead, he recommended that they concentrate on two subjects usually loathed by young would-be writers in Japan: mathematics and physical education. The choice is interesting because it seems to reflect

Akutagawa's concern with language as an organizer of chaos rather than as a means of communication. Just as mathematics creates an arbitrary universe completely controllable by discursive reason, so physical education provides the means of controlling physical circumstance. In both cases, the theme of control is paramount. In Akutagawa's view, a novelist works on human experience in the same manner as a mathematician works on his universe of mathematical concepts or an athlete on his physical constitution. In short, he saw the creative process as strenuous and deliberate.

> The artist's creative activities are conscious, however much of a genius he may be. Take, for instance, the case of Ni Yün-lin, who drew a pine tree with all its branches outstretched in one direction.[3] I do not know if he knew why the stretching of the branches produced a certain effect in the painting. But I am certain he was fully aware that the extended branches would produce that effect when he drew them. If he had done it without knowing what the result would be, he would have been no more than a robot. So-called unconscious creative activities remind me of the imaginary seashell vainly sought by the nobleman in the old story.[4] Rodin despised *l'inspiration* for that reason.

According to Akutagawa, the creative process was to represent the human life-force, in the sense discussed. The second of the artist's two chief qualifications was that he has plenty of that force in himself; otherwise he would never be able to grasp it, far less give expression to it. Akutagawa once wrote that someone who composed a work of literature must be a barbarian deep down, no matter how cultivated he might be on the surface. By "barbarian" he meant a man with superabundant animal vitality. He used an English word, "brutality," to describe the dominant quality of the medieval Japanese tales collected in *Ages Ago*.[5] Akutagawa gave that quality to Yoshihide, the painter-hero of "**The Hell Screen**," who originally appeared in *Ages Ago*. The painter is described by Akutagawa as creating a "weird, truly bestial impression" with his ugly appearance, particularly his bright red lips. This appearance has earned him the nickname of Yoshihide the Monkey. A pet monkey that appears in the same story is also named Yoshihide, and the close relationship between the painter and the animal is unmistakable. The same sort of animality is seen in Bakin, the novelist-hero of "**Absorbed in Letters**," another major Akutagawa story about an artist. Bakin is sixty years of age in the story, yet he is described as showing "an awesome flash of vigorous animal force" on his cheeks and around his mouth. It should be noted, however, that Akutagawa gives noticeably more animal vitality to Yoshihide the painter than to Bakin the novelist. Yoshihide has headstrong energy and barbarous pride that make him sneer at the tyrannical ruler of the country. Bakin, on the other hand, is put out when a frivolous gossiper in a public bathhouse adversely criticizes his work. The difference can be attributed to several factors, not the least important of which is that one is a painter and the other a novelist. A painter, Akutagawa believed, could express himself more freely than a novelist. Indeed,

Bakin is described as being envious of a painter because the latter did not have to worry about government censorship.

There is evidence that painting, to Akutagawa, was a better medium than prose for embodying the human life-force. The novel, he thought, was a rather impure art form. The very first item in his "Ten Rules for Writing a Novel" is an affirmation to that effect: "One should realize that the novel is the least artistic of all literary genres. The only one that deserves the name of art is poetry. The novel is included in literature only for the sake of the poetry in it. In other respects, the novel differs not at all from history or biography." Of course the question here is what Akutagawa meant by "poetry." This is made somewhat clearer in the second of the rules: "The novelist is a historian or biographer, in addition to being a poet. Hence he is compelled to relate himself to the human life (of a given age and of a given country). This fact is proved by the works of Japanese novelists, from Lady Murasaki to Ihara Saikaku." Akutagawa seems to be implying that a poet is the only kind of literary artist who does not depend on contemporary society for his subject matter. A novelist can and should be a poet, but he is also obligated to be a historian or biographer, and that makes him an impure poet. In this respect, a painter has more artistic freedom than a novelist, because he can be more subjective, and therefore more faithful to the source of vitality within him.

Akutagawa's term "poetic spirit," which became a subject of controversy in his famous quarrel with Tanizaki, can be interpreted in the same light. Akutagawa did not explain the term clearly—not to Tanizaki's satisfaction, anyway—but he must have meant the poetic residue of the novel, after the elements of history and biography had as it were evaporated from it. The poetry corresponded to his conception of what life ultimately was, as opposed to what it had been on such and such an occasion. The theme of human bestiality is present here, but perhaps not fully realized. At any rate, this is what is suggested by Akutagawa's remark to Tanizaki that "by poetic spirit I mean lyricism in its broadest sense." Elsewhere he suggested that the most lyrical examples of Japanese poetry were to be found in the tanka of *The Collection of Ten Thousand Leaves*, primitive poems of the eighth century and earlier that expressed "simple feelings in a moving way." In another essay he recalled how touched he was one day when he heard a deer's cry in the mountains. "It seemed to me," he continued, "that all lyric poetry must have had its origin in such a cry—the cry of a male deer calling for his mate." Akutagawa's unconscious syllogism is here complete: the poetic spirit, in its purest form, is contained in lyrics; lyrics originate in a male animal calling for a female; therefore, poetic spirit has its source in animal instinct. "Poetic spirit" ultimately goes back to animal instinct.

If this interpretation is accepted, it follows that a novelist should nurture the beast in him, for it is the very source of his artistic creation. He should try to improve his physical condition by exercising, as Akutagawa advised high school students who aspired to become writers. The weaker the artist's health, the weaker his creative urge. The artist with failing health would inevitably meet a tragic end, like Tok, the poet in *Kappa* who kills himself while longing to reach the Valley of Life where clear water flows and medicinal herbs flower. Akutagawa himself committed suicide when he felt he had lost the "animal force" in himself. "I, too, am one of the human animals," he wrote in his suicide note. "But I seem to be losing the animal force. Witness the fact that I have lost my appetite for food and for women."

Loss of animal force is a characteristic ailment of modern man, surrounded as he is by the products of human intellect. A novelist, Akutagawa thought, should resist these pressures and never lose sight of human bestiality. The ninth of Akutagawa's ten rules for writing a novel touches on this point:

> A person aspiring to be a novelist should always be cautious not to respond to philosophical, scientific, or economic theories. No ideology or theory is capable of controlling man's entire life, as long as he remains a beast in human form. A person who responds (knowingly, at least) to such theories will meet needless inconveniences in following his life's course—the animal life.

This is a sad verdict on the role of ideas. But Akutagawa in later life seems to have reached a point at which he was forced to acknowledge the powerlessness of modern learning in the face of man's biological nature. In *Kappa,* for instance, Mag the stoic philosopher cannot quite overcome his sexual drives; Gael the millionaire businessman is at the mercy of his wife; the doctors in kappaland have not found an effective way of controlling undesirable hereditary traits. In short, the products of human intellect are no match for basic human animality, and a wise artist should put no trust in them.

It is ironic that Akutagawa, who stressed the intellectual power of language and the artist's command over it, eventually had to face up to the powerlessness of intellect. Akutagawa began by regarding the novelist as a specialist in language on the one hand and a seeker after experience on the other. As it turned out, the two functions were incompatible. After all, to the extent that the novelist was still a historian or biographer—which he could not help being part of the time—he continued to depend on the generalizing power of intellect. This was the heart of his dilemma. If he became too much of a historian or a biographer, the poet within him would be overwhelmed and his work would lose its "poetic spirit." On the other hand, if the poet within him grew too powerful, he would not be able to relate to the outside world; he would end up as a social misfit, a misanthrope, or a madman. According to Akutagawa, then, there could not be a happy novelist.

Akutagawa offered three solutions to this dilemma, none of which was very attractive. One was not to become a novelist, or at least to stop being one. "If a person wants to live a relatively happy life," he said, "the best course he can take is not to become a novelist." The second was suicide, the course taken by Yoshihide the painter, Tok the poet, and, finally, Akutagawa himself. The third was prolonged perseverance. Bakin, the other notable artist-hero in Akutagawa's fiction, is an example of this: he keeps repeating to himself: "Learn! Don't get upset! And endure harder!" Each of these solutions is so drastic that it is clear Akutagawa regarded the novelist's situation as desperate. This tragic view may well be a reaction to his earlier optimism (if not arrogance), when he thought the chaos of human reality could be given order by means of language, a human invention. He thought a novelist could overcome the world with mere words. The world proved to be too powerful, and Akutagawa was too perceptive not to realize when he was beaten. He could not console himself with belief in the redemptive power of ethics, religion, or Marxism; he had too clear a view of human bestiality. On the other hand, he was also too proud, or too afraid, to embrace the powers of chaos. He was too much of an intellectual to accept the prospect of insanity, of being a burden to others simply in order to stay alive. His ideal of the novelist, then, had to be a tragic one—as tragic as his own life.

GAUGUIN VERSUS RENOIR

Akutagawa's dualistic concept of art is also reflected in his ideal of beauty. On the one hand, he was very much attracted to the primitive, dynamic type of beauty that is created by an artist with more natural vitality than formal training. On the other hand, he could not help feeling an affinity with the elegant, urbane type of beauty produced by the professional artist who is completely at home in modern society. This, then, was yet another of his dilemmas.

Akutagawa made his views on art abundantly clear in two successive sections of his long essay "Literary, Too Literary." These two sections are entitled "The Call of the Wild" and "The Call of the West." In the first, he recalls how repelled he was when he first saw Gauguin's painting of a Tahitian woman who was, as he felt, "visually emitting the smell of a barbarian's skin." He then goes on to say that, despite his initial reaction, he gradually became fascinated with this orange-colored woman. "Indeed," he wrote, "the power of the image was such that I felt almost possessed by the Tahitian woman." Why he was so enchanted by her is clear enough. He saw in her a "source of life," the vigorous life of primitive people. "Gauguin—at least as I see him—meant to show us a human beast in that orange-colored woman," he reflected. "Furthermore, he showed it to us with more power than the painters of realistic schools." Naturally he recognized the same type of beauty in the works of other Postimpressionist painters. He saw it, for instance, in Van Gogh's paintings of the Arles period. He especially adored Matisse, of whom he said: "What I am seeking is his type of art, the kind of art that is brimming with vitality, like grass in the sunshine vigorously growing toward the sky."

Akutagawa also recognized a "Tahiti School" in literature. His subtitle, "The Call of the Wild," is obviously a reference to Jack London's novel, though there is no clear evidence to show how much he liked it. The strongest expressions of his enthusiasm in this regard are directed at *Ages Ago*, Bashō, and Shiga Naoya.

Akutagawa has generally been considered the "discoverer" of *Ages Ago* for modern Japanese readers. That massive collection of old tales had attracted little attention through the centuries, until Akutagawa published an essay called "On *Ages Ago*," praising it in the highest terms. The chief value he found in *Ages Ago* was what he termed "the call of the wild," which he explained as follows. "I finally discovered the sterling worth of *Ages Ago*. The artistic value of *Ages Ago* lies not only in its vigor. It lies in its beauty— the beauty of *brutality*, if I may borrow a word from the English. It is the type of beauty farthest removed from anything elegant or delicate." He then cited a tale from *Ages Ago* that he thought exuded this brutal beauty. The tale was about a man who was suddenly gripped by sexual passion while traveling alone in the countryside. Unable to calm it in any way, he at last pulled out a large turnip from a field by the road and satisfied himself with it. Some time later the turnip was picked up and eaten by a young maiden who had no knowledge of how it had been used by the traveler. In due time she became pregnant and gave birth to a baby boy. The story makes clear what Akutagawa meant by "brutal beauty": it was an artless, low-brow, crude type of beauty, tempered by bawdy humor. Certainly, as Akutagawa noted, it was far removed from elegant or exquisite beauty. Also noteworthy was the way in which the story revolved around the traveler's virility: primitive vigor—the vigor of the life-force—is an essential ingredient in "brutal beauty."

Akutagawa has also been credited with throwing new light on Bashō. Before he published "Miscellaneous Notes on Bashō," the seventeenth-century haiku poet had been visualized as a lean, travel-worn sage who had no interest in mundane affairs. Akutagawa presented a new image of Bashō by describing him as a sturdy, energetic man with a great many fleshly interests, including heterosexual and even homosexual ones. Here, for instance, is his condensed version of Bashō's biography: "He committed adultery and thereupon eloped from his native province Iga; arrived at Edo, where he frequented brothels and other such places there; and gradually evolved into one of the age's great poets." As an example of Bashō's superabundant energy, Akutagawa quoted a haiku of his:

> In the summer woods
> I kneel before the divine footwear:
> my journey's start.[6]

Akutagawa did not spell this out, but it is obvious that the poem, with its images of summer trees, giant footwear, and a traveler just setting out, gave him an impression of vigorous life far removed from exquisite, graceful, or delicate beauty.

The same type of beauty can be found in the works of Shiga Naoya, who, as we saw in the last chapter, tried to capture the beauty of a healthy animal vigorously pursuing its natural way of life. Largely for that reason, Akutagawa admired Shiga's works more than those of any other contemporary Japanese writer. "Mr. Shiga's works," he once wrote, "show they are by a writer who, above all, is living a wholesome life in this world." He went on to point out that they show "poetic spirit" and that Shiga was a poet as well as a novelist. Referring to a scene of *Voyage Through the Dark Night* where the hero enjoys a night with a prostitute, Akutagawa commented: "Only a poet could have sung 'It's a rich year! It's a rich year!' at the sight of a woman's voluptuous breasts. I feel a little sorry for my contemporaries, who have given relatively little attention to the sort of 'beauty' that Mr. Shiga has created." Again the beauty Akutagawa spoke of is not elegant or urbane. Though not as "brutal" as that of *Ages Ago*, it has the natural appeal of animal good health and vitality—the call of the wild.

Yet, with all his admiration for a dynamic, masculine beauty, Akutagawa did not produce a literary oeuvre in which that quality predominates. He did write stories about primitive, violent men—**"The Robbers,"** for example, and **"Lord Susanoo"**—but they are not among his more successful efforts. He also wrote a number of tales based on *Ages Ago*, **"Rashōmon"** and **"The Nose"** among them, but they are noticeably lacking in the beauty of "brutality." As has been pointed out, his friend Tanizaki noticed this fact and told him that he could not write stories like Shiga's because he lacked the physical strength. Akutagawa himself admitted that none of the contemporary imitators of Shiga, including himself, had succeeded in emulating Shiga's "poetic spirit." The hero of **"Cogwheel,"** who is obviously Akutagawa himself, confesses that *Voyage Through the Dark Night* has turned out to be a frightening book for him. Akutagawa listened to the call of the wild, but his own work does not have it.

Why was this so? Tanizaki's explanation is surely inadequate. Akutagawa may have been fascinated with the call of the wild, but he was also drawn to an opposing force, a force that he termed "the call of the West." It is this latter force that seems to predominate in his works of fiction, though he says less about it in his essays. The reason may well be that Akutagawa himself was somewhat at a loss to explain this other "call" in analytical terms. In fact, he called it "mysterious."

> Underlying the West, as we call it, is ever-mysterious Greece. As an old saying goes, one cannot know the temperature of water until one drinks it. The same applies to Greece. If someone were to ask me for a concise explanation of Greece, I would advise him to look at the few examples of Greek pottery on display in Japan. Or I might recommend that he study photographs of Greek sculpture. The beauty of those works is the beauty of Greek gods.

"The call of the West," then, seems to be the call of ancient Greek civilization, of the Hellenism that lies at the roots of Western culture. If that is the case, Akutagawa's attraction to the West is quite consistent with his admiration for Supreme Intellect, the force that conquers chaos. As we have seen, he called himself an Apollonian. The Western style of beauty is, above all, the beauty of intellect organizing chaos into order. Applied to a literary work, it is the beauty of a tale with a logically ordered structure that gives form to the chaos of raw life and the human psyche.

Akutagawa's stories, especially his early ones, show this type of beauty. **"Rashōmon," "The Nose,"** and **"Yam Gruel"** all have a well-ordered structure patterned on the hero's thinking. They have a beginning, a middle, and an end. Progression from beginning to end is attained through analysis of the hero's psychology; the general effect is of light thrown on the dark corners of the mind until everything is revealed. The weird, uncanny part of the human mind is brought under control; fear of the dark is dispelled. The servant in **"Rashōmon,"** who is at a loss when the story begins, clearly knows what to do at its close. At the same time, the reader learns how to behave in a chaotic, war-ridden society. The priest in **"The Nose,"** unable at first to tolerate his grotesque nose, finally makes peace with himself as he comes to know his mind better. The petty official in **"Yam Gruel,"** who makes himself ridiculous by his fondness for yam gruel at the tale's beginning, succeeds in overcoming his weakness, whereupon the tale ends. The reader of these stories is left with the feeling that life, chaotic and uncontrollable though it may seem, can be brought under control by intelligence and self-knowledge.

Intellect, in reordering the conventionally ordered world, sometimes begets humor and irony. In some of his tales, Akutagawa laughs at people who are important only because they are wedded to the existing social order. In **"The Handkerchief,"** he gives a highly satirical picture of what really goes on in the mind of an internationally known philosopher and moralist. In **"The General,"** he shows a greatly respected general to be petty, inconsiderate, and vainglorious. In **"Lice,"** he has fun with the spectacle of some ostensibly courageous samurai being completely stripped of their dignity when attacked by lice. Akutagawa once remarked: "According to Pascal, man is a thinking reed. Does a reed think? I really can't say. But I do know that a reed, unlike a man, does not laugh. I cannot imagine a man being serious—or, indeed, having any humanity—unless I can also imagine him laughing." By "humanity" he must mean intellect; only a creature with intellect can laugh. Akutagawa's stories, especially his early ones, are often humorous because of their intellectuality.

Human intellect, while begetting humor and irony on the one hand, evolves elegance and delicacy on the other when it functions as an aesthetic principle. A man-made world is self-insulated; having no room for such "animal" activities as procreation, it tends to cut itself off from the roots of life. Art in such a world is, above all, artificial. It therefore

has no greater goal than its own refinement. The artist, however confident of his dexterity, has to make his work meticulously artificial in order to prove it. Such elegant beauty is a mark of civilization in the sense that it shows a distance from barbarism. Akutagawa liked elegant, sophisticated beauty; he had to, as long as he approved the progress of civilization. While attracted to Gauguin and Van Gogh, he confessed he was also fascinated by the works of Renoir and Redon. "Like all art lovers of my generation," he recollected, "I was first an admirer of those moving, powerful works of Van Gogh. But slowly I began to develop a taste for Renoir's works, the ultimate in elegant beauty." He drew a similar parallel between Gauguin and Redon. "I feel the call of the wild in Gauguin's orange-colored woman," he wrote. "But I also feel 'the call of the West' in Redon's 'Young Buddha.'" He attributed his fondness for an elegant, sophisticated style of beauty to the fact that he was a city dweller. His claim that a civilized person like himself could never really understand Gauguin or Van Gogh seems at times to proceed from a genuine inferiority complex. At other times, however, he seems to have been overcome by a sense of superiority before such "barbarous" works.

Of all Akutagawa's works, the one that shows elegant, urbane beauty in its most touching form is **"The Lady Roku-no-miya."** This court lady, precisely because of her courtly refinement and elegance, is lacking in the will to live and eventually has to meet a passive death. An elegant, courtly atmosphere also prevails in **"Heichū, the Amorous Genius,"** and its hero, who is a courtly, sophisticated Don Juan, meets a similar fate. Indeed, the Akutagawan protagonists who are urban dwellers with delicate sensitivities and impaired vitality outnumber the more primitive and vital ones. The stories in which the latter appear do not always produce a graceful effect, but none creates a crude or vulgar impression, either. If one is to make a comparison, they are closer to Renoir than to Van Gogh.

If elegance and sophistication are marks of advanced culture, so are pluralism and complexity. The more intellectual a person is, the more skeptical he tends to become. Akutagawa liked to create deliberate ambiguity in his stories, because he did not believe in simple truths. In an aphorism entitled **"Interpretation,"** he wrote:

> Any interpretation of a work of art presupposes a degree of cooperation between artist and interpreter. In a sense, the interpreter is an artist who, using another artist's work for his theme, creates his own work of art. Hence, every famous work of art that has withstood the test of time is characterized by its capacity to induce a multiplicity of interpretations. But, as Anatole France has pointed out, the fact that a literary work has the capacity to induce multiple interpretations does not make it ambiguous in the sense that the reader can easily give it any interpretation he likes. Rather, it means that a good work is like Mount Lu; it is many-sided, and therefore encourages viewing from many angles.[7]

A work of art, Akutagawa is saying, is the better for being many-sided and multilayered, because life is many-sided and multilayered. A simple-hearted rustic may see all human life in black-and-white terms, but a modern intellectual would not and should not do so. Truth in human life is always complex, always elusive. A good work of literature recognizes that fact and creates a complex effect.

The multilayeredness of Akutagawa's stories is well known. The most famous is **"In a Grove,"** in which the same event is narrated in such widely different ways by its three participants that the reader is left wondering what really happened. The reader knows exactly what is going to happen in **"Kesa and Moritō,"** but he also knows that Kesa (or her ghost), Moritō, Wataru, and others will have widely differing interpretations of it when it happens. In **"Doubts,"** the hero is unable to decide on his true motive for killing his wife and finally goes insane. The hero of **"Cogwheel"** cannot look reality in the face because phantasmal cogwheels in his eyes obstruct his sight; as a result, he has difficulty distinguishing between what he sees and what he imagines. The painter in **"Dreams,"** likewise, cannot discern reality from dreams, and the reader also does not know what really happened to the model who just disappeared. *Kappa,* a story narrated by a mental patient, has inspired a good many controversies about its meaning. In **"The Painting of an Autumn Mountain,"** multiplicity of interpretation is itself the main theme: the famed Chinese painting of the title gives such different impressions at different times that the on-lookers are not sure if they have seen the same painting.

It can be said that this skeptical disposition of Akutagawa, while it gave his fiction complexity of meaning, prevented him from pursuing "the call of the wild" with wholehearted devotion. He was torn between "the call of the wild" and "the call of the West," as he himself conceded. The tales he wrote show, as a result, neither the vigorous strength of the former nor the graceful beauty of the latter—or, at least, not as much as he would have liked them to show. Many of them are both logical in conception and orderly in construction. Nevertheless, something raw and weird remains lurking beneath the surface. Other tales of his try to present human animality in its primitive form, and yet they lack a strong lyrical appeal because the theme has been intellectualized. It was Akutagawa's unhappy fate as an artist to pursue two conflicting sets of aesthetic ideals without being able to reconcile them. In the final analysis, however, the best of his works—**"The Hell Screen," "In a Grove,"** *Kappa,* **"Cogwheel"**—derive their basic appeal from that conflict. These stories move the reader by showing a penetrating intellect desperately trying to cope with the murky, chaotic realities of the human subconscious and ending in failure. Despite their author's nostalgic longing for ancient Greek civilization, their beauty is not that of classicism. Rather, it leans toward the grotesque.

FORM FOR A VERSATILE WRITER

Akutagawa revealed his ideas on the structure of the novel in the course of his famous controversy with Tanizaki, even though he did it in a somewhat haphazard way and invited misunderstandings as a result. As against Tanizaki, who argued that a novel would be better for having an ingenious, well-constructed plot, Akutagawa maintained that plot itself has no artistic value, and that a novel without a complicated plot can be a fine work of art if it has plenty of "poetic spirit." As the controversy became famous, he came to be considered the champion of the "plotless" novel, in spite of his repeated insistence that he did not necessarily regard it as the best form of fiction.

Akutagawa's use of the term "plot" was also widely misunderstood. Certainly he did not mean a novel without structure. "I am not insisting that every writer should write a novel lacking a plotlike plot," he stressed. "In fact, most of my own works have a plot. Without *dessin,* there cannot be a work of painting. It is through plot that every work of fiction comes into being." Here Akutagawa was using the word "plot" to mean "structure," and he approved of plot in this sense without reservation. When he talked about the "plotless" novel, he had a different type of plot in mind: it was a more "plotlike" plot, a plot with a sequence of events the reader would find interesting (Akutagawa once used the term "shocking" in this context and was consequently misunderstood still further). Roughly, it meant a story in the popular sense. In advocating a "plotless" novel, Akutagawa was advocating a novel without a "good story."

What he meant by the plotless novel becomes clearer when one reads his argument in favor of the plotless play: "Now I am sick and tired of watching a playlike play—that is to say, a play with plenty of dramatic interest. I want to see a play as free as air, a play that hardly has a plot." This is an unusually forthright statement for a diffident man like Akutagawa; perhaps he found it easier to make because he was talking about a genre to which he was an outsider. What he was objecting to was the "well-made," Ibsenesque plot, with its series of clashes between protagonist and antagonist. He liked a more lyrical plot—a plot with "poetic spirit," as he would have said. He expressed his sympathetic approval of a certain Japanese producer whose favorite Western playwright had changed from Ibsen to Maeterlinck to Andreev.

The form of prose fiction Akutagawa advocated, then, was a poetic, and not dramatic, novel. It might or might not have a protagonist. In all likelihood, it would not have an antagonist. It might or might not present a series of events; when it did, the events would not be sensational ones, and they would be arranged loosely rather than with tight dramatic logic. There would be no single story line that would hold the different parts of the novel together. In general, it would create the impression that the novelist wrote it in a casual mood, digressing whenever he felt like it. Ostensibly, the structure was so loose that a careless reader might think the novel had not ended when it actually had.

Have there been such works of fiction? Akutagawa cited Jules Renard's "Ways of the Philippes" and Shiga Naoya's "The Fires" as leading examples. "Ways of the Philippes," included in *The Winegrower in His Vineyard,* is a short story made up of some dozen brief episodes with a rustic vinedresser's family for their common characters. The episodes are varied in their time, setting, and subject matter. The first is a casual conversation exchanged between Philippe and his wife concerning their centuries-old house, with the narrator cutting in from time to time. The second episode takes place a few months later: it describes the Philippes waiting in vain for their soldier son to come home for the New Year. In the third episode, the Philippes are seen butchering a pig. In the fourth they have just been married. The bridegroom eats fourteen plates of food at the wedding dinner, while the bride sits there silently with no appetite at all. Other episodes are of similar nature, all dealing with the daily events of life normally following their course in a peaceful French village. The same uneventfulness is also seen in Shiga's "The Fires," though it ranges over a much shorter span of time and space. The story describes the happenings of just one day in the life of a man building a cottage with his wife and friends near a lake in the woods. They play cards in the morning since it is rainy, but they begin working on the cottage when the sky clears in the afternoon. After supper they go boating on the lake. When it gets dark they make a bonfire on the shore; as they sit around the fire one of them tells a strange experience he had the previous year. That is all.

"Ways of the Philippes" and "The Fires" seem to fit well with Akutagawa's idea of a plotless novel. Certainly, the reader would not read them for their story's sake. In both instances, the plot is loose or nonexistent; various episodes from the life of an ordinary Frenchman or a Japanese are just put together, seemingly at random. Pervading the episodes are the personalities of the dramatis personae, who are all simple, honest, sincere people (in the case of Philippe, this simplicity of character is developed to the point of naiveté). Together they create a warm, congenial atmosphere in a rustic setting. The reader visualizes good-natured, simple-hearted people leading wholesome lives entirely removed from the strains and stresses of "keeping up with the times." The sincerity of their basic attitude creates a lyrical mood. That mood, and not a well-developed story line, is the unifying principle in these works.

Akutagawa did make a few efforts to write in the vein of Renard and Shiga, notably in a series of short autobiographical pieces that have Yasukichi, a teacher of English at a naval academy, for their common hero. The results are largely unsuccessful because the characters are far from attractive, and the narrator's observations are too unimaginative to animate the trite events he describes. Markedly more successful in this genre are several works of his last years, notably **"On the Seashore"** and **"The Mirage,"** both of which describe the leisurely life of a recent college graduate who is vacationing at a beach resort for a few days. Most of the scenes in these two stories show the young man walking and talking on the sandy shore with friends from his college days; that is all. Yet the stories impress because the few incidents they depict, while trivial

in themselves, are presented through the eyes of a hypersensitive young man, a young man abnormally sensitive to decay, death, ghosts, and the dark side of life in general. The young man is totally different in personality from Philippe or the narrator in "The Fires," yet he grips the reader's attention by his uncanny capacity to sense weird things hidden from the ordinary eye. His presence creates an eerie mood that holds the different episodes together. Admittedly, **"On the Seashore"** and **"The Mirage"** have somewhat more structure than "Ways of the Philippes" or "The Fires." But of all Akutagawa's works they are the ones that best embody his idea of the plotless novel.

Nevertheless, the fact remains that those pieces constitute only a small proportion of Akutagawa's canon. He himself admitted that most of his works had a story to tell. Even when arguing most vehemently in favor of the plotless novel, he still declared that he had no intention of confining himself to writing essaylike stories. It would be misleading, then, to conclude that Akutagawa's concept of plot centered on the plotless novel. If he seemed to have become its champion at the time of the famous controversy, it was partly because Tanizaki drove him into that position, and partly because he associated the idea of an intriguing plot with the "popular" novel, which he detested. His stand in favor of the plotless novel was never so strong that he had to label other kinds as inferior. He championed the essaylike novel mainly because Tanizaki appeared to overpraise the novel that had an interesting story to tell.

In the final analysis, what Akutagawa really wanted to say in his controversy with Tanizaki seems to be that novels can have different types of structure, and that it is wrong to say one type is better than another. As a novelist, he did not like to be restricted in form; he wanted to be completely free to use any kind of structure he saw fit. Life, he thought, had many layers of meaning. Since literary works should present many types of life, it followed that novels should have many types of form and structure.

Akutagawa did write stories in a wide variety of forms. To mention only the principal types, he wrote essaylike stories like **"On the Seashore"** and **"The Mirage"**; dramatic pieces like **"In a Grove"** and **"Kesa and Moritō"**; märchen like **"The Spider's Thread"** and **"Tu Tzu-ch'un"**; traditional tales like **"The Robbers"** and **"The Hell Screen"**; lyrical stories like **"The Mandarin Oranges"** and **"Flatcar"**; fantasies like **"Strange Island"** and *Kappa*. Akutagawa also tried his hand at many literary forms besides prose fiction. He was one of the period's major haiku poets. He also wrote poems in the tanka form, and revived an obsolete verse-form called *sedōka* that had a 5–7–7–5–7–7 syllable pattern. He had some free verse to his credit, too. In the area of nonfiction, he made lasting contributions with his aphorisms and journals. His aphorisms, serialized in a magazine under the title *Maxims of a Midget,* attracted a great deal of attention at the time. His journals were also quite popular; some readers who do not like his fiction consider his *Records of a Journey to China* to be his finest work.

It can even be said that one of the main charms of Akutagawa's writings lies in the great variety of literary forms that he employed. He was a versatile writer, and he enjoyed displaying his versatility. In fact, he once said he had become a novelist because it gave him the opportunity to do so. "I write prose fiction," he explained, "because it is more all-embracing than any other form of literature, allowing me to toss in anything and everything." Accordingly, his idea of plot had to be a comprehensive one.

The same applies to his idea of prose style. He did not say it specifically, but it is obvious that he wanted to see a great variety of styles in prose fiction. His own works are, indeed, sufficiently varied in this respect. **"Ogata Ryōsai's Affidavit"** and **"The Old Murder"** are written in a certain style that used to be employed in the official language of the past. **"The Martyr"** and **"St. Christopher's Life"** have a very peculiar style, apparently modeled after the language of sixteenth-century Japanese Christians. In **"The Hell Screen"** and *Heresy,* though they are written in modern Japanese, he tried to convey the flavor of the language spoken by an ancient Japanese courtier. **"A Clod of Earth"** and **"Genkaku Sanbō"** are written in a simple, matter-of-fact style, stripped of all the decorative elements usually associated with literary language. **"The Dog Shiro"** and **"The Three Treasures"** show stylistic features reminiscent of a tale for children. **"On the Seashore"** and **"The Mirage"** are, as can be imagined, written in a lucid, precise style that approaches Shiga's.

Akutagawa never attempted to classify Japanese prose styles in a methodical manner, but he did set up two examples at opposite stylistic poles: Shiga and Sōseki. He thought that Shiga and his followers "wrote in the manner of speaking," while Sōseki was a writer who "spoke in the manner of writing." By the former he meant simply a colloquial style, that is, a style that reproduces the vocabulary and rhythm of daily speech. But the meaning of the phrase "spoke in the manner of writing" is more ambiguous. He did not mean a bookish style, for that would have been to "write in the manner of writing." A short essay of his entitled "Composition That Makes One Visualize" throws light on this point:

> I like the kind of composition that makes the reader visualize the scene. I detest the kind that does not do so. In my view, there is a fundamental difference in sensibility between a person who writes "The sky is blue," and one who writes "The sky is blue like steel." While the former feels the color as merely "blue," the latter feels it as "blue like steel." He added the phrase "like steel" not because he was a better technician in composition; he did so because he had a more accurate grasp of what he saw. Sōseki had such a grasp and, as can be seen from his writings, it was of a highly individual and yet superb kind. Here is the opening sentence of "Snake," from his *Spring Miscellanies:* "As I opened the wooden door and stepped outside, I saw a horse's tracks, large and brimming with rainwater." With just one sentence, the impression of a country road full of rain puddles is vividly created. I like this type of writing.

In an ordinary conversation one does not say "The sky is blue like steel," or "As I opened the wooden door and stepped outside, I saw a horse's tracks, large and brimming with rainwater." These sentences are too calculated in their effect to be spoken extemporaneously, at least by an ordinary person. Yet what they lose in spontaneity, they gain in accuracy and individuality. Since they make more use of similes, metaphors, and symbols, they also gain in vividness. Their meaning is at once more complex and more accurate, as any figurative language is. In short, the style that "speaks in the manner of writing" is the style of poetry (one recalls that Sōseki was himself a writer of haiku).

It goes without saying that Akutagawa, who stressed the importance of "poetic spirit" in the novel, favored the style that "speaks in the manner of writing." Indeed, his typical style is the polar opposite of the style that "writes in the manner of speaking." It is anything but spontaneous; indeed, Akutagawa was a perfectionist. He once reflected:

> I know I overtax my nerves unnecessarily in composing a piece. I cannot help it. There are certain words that I simply cannot bring myself to use on certain occasions. The tone of certain phrases disturbs me too much. For instance, I find it difficult to use a place name like Yanagihara ("willow-field")[8] because, to my mind, it makes the entire passage green; I cannot use the word unless the passage includes a word of another color to tone down that green.

Akutagawa was here talking about the writing of prose fiction, but what he said can be applied, with equal aptness, to the writing of haiku. Haiku poets take great care to create a harmony of colors, sounds, tactile sensations, etc., and they often go about doing so in a very self-conscious manner. Akutagawa's style is deliberate in the same way as the language of haiku is deliberate.

Akutagawa was often criticized for his artificiality by contemporary critics, many of whom were admirers of Shiga's more natural style. Always sensitive to criticism, the young Akutagawa tried hard to write more spontaneously, but without satisfactory results. One day he brought this problem to the attention of his mentor, Sōseki, and asked how he could possibly learn to write like Shiga. Sōseki answered: "He [Shiga] can write in the way he does because he writes spontaneously, without trying to create a piece of prose," and added that he, too, could not write like Shiga. Later on, however, Akutagawa seems to have been more confident of his own style. He remarked, for example, "My friends tell me: 'Your writings are too deliberate. Don't be so deliberate.' But I don't recall ever having been more deliberate than necessary. More than anything else, I want to write clearly." He went on: "No matter what other people may say, I shall go on trying to produce composition as clear-cut as calcite, one that permits the minimum amount of vagueness." Consciously or unconsciously, he did what he said. Even when he wrote such Shiga-like pieces as **"On the Seashore"** and **"The**

Mirage," his style remained somewhat less spontaneous than Shiga's. Given his view of language, this was probably inevitable. He considered words—and the arrangement of words known as style—as so many tools with which to organize the chaos of life. As long as he held such an Apollonian view of literature, he had to be an Apollonian in matters of style, too.

NEGATION OF A NEGATIVE SPIRIT

Akutagawa was adamant in repudiating the idea that literature was merely play or entertainment. For him, a literary work written to amuse the reader was "popular" literature, a product of commercialism that had nothing to do with "genuine" novelists. He wrote:

> Today I stopped by the roadside to watch a fight between a rickshaw man and a motorist. I found myself watching it with a certain interest, and wondered what kind of interest it was. No matter how hard I tried to convince myself otherwise, I could not but feel that it was the same sort of interest I would have in watching a fight on the kabuki stage. . . . I have no intention of denying the value of literary works that produce this sort of interest. But I believe there can be interest of a kind higher than this.

The main question is what Akutagawa meant by a "higher" kind of interest. Instead of explaining, he simply observed that the first few pages of **"Kylin,"** an early Tanizaki tale, produced that kind of interest. **"Kylin"** is the story of how Confucius, in his old age, toured China to propagate his teachings. Its first few pages describe his encounter with a venerable Taoist sage and then his travel to the state of Wei. There are no fights, nor any other kind of sensational incident. All that happens is a brief discussion on human happiness between Confucius, a disciple of his, and the Taoist sage. This is followed by a description of life in the state of Wei, where people are starving while the ruler and his beautiful wife indulge in luxury. The interest generated by these few pages is philosophical and moral to the highest degree, leaving no doubt about Akutagawa's meaning.

Indeed, Akutagawa repeatedly emphasized the didactic use of literature. "In a way, all novels are textbooks in the art of living," he once said. "Therefore, they can be said to be educational, in a very broad sense of the word." On another occasion, he called the poet "a microphone created by God." His reason was that "in this world of men no one proclaims the truth. It is the poet who amplifies people's whispers in an instant." Akutagawa was most persuasive on this point in his autobiographical story entitled **"The Youth of Daidōji Shinsuke"**:

> Shinsuke learned everything through books. At least, he could not think of anything he did not owe to books in some degree. As a matter of fact, he never tried to improve his knowledge of life by watching people in the street. Rather, he tried to read about men's lives in order to watch people in the street. A roundabout way to learn about life, you may say. But for him real-life people were merely passersby. In order to know them—to know their loves, hatreds, and vanities—he had no means other than to read books.

Shinsuke may have had a rather more withdrawn personality than the average person. A more extroverted person may learn more directly from actual life. Yet Shinsuke was also a man with a greater thirst for knowledge than the average person. He was not satisfied with a superficial knowledge of men; he had to know love, hatred, vanity, and all the other emotions hidden in their hearts. Good books present the facts of life at a level deeper than everyday events. A person like Shinsuke, who seeks hidden truths about men, goes to books rather than to actual life.

Literature, however, is far more than a mere supplier of knowledge. The point is made unobtrusively by Akutagawa a little later in the same story. Here, beauty rather than truth is the issue:

> "From books to reality" was an unchanging truth for Shinsuke. In his past life, he had not been without some women he found himself in love with. Yet none of them showed him what feminine beauty was. At least, none showed him anything more than what he had read about feminine beauty. Thanks to Gautier and Balzac and Tolstoy, he noticed the beauty of a woman's ear glowing translucent in the sunlight, or of her eyelash casting a shadow on her cheek. He could still remember her beauty because of that. If he had not read these books, he might have seen nothing in a woman but a female animal.

In this instance, books taught Shinsuke how to look at life. Life might be ugly, but it could be beautiful if looked at in a certain way. The woman might not be beautiful, but her partner could see in her an image of his favorite heroine in Gautier, Balzac, or Tolstoy. Literature might reveal hidden truths that were better left hidden. But it might also reveal beauty such as an ordinary person would never see in his lifetime. A literary work could depict people as more beautiful or noble than the reader had ever thought they were. In this way, it could give him support and encouragement in fighting the battle of life itself.

From his earliest youth, Akutagawa seems to have considered art a guiding light. As a young man of twenty-four who had not yet established himself as a writer, he wrote to a friend of his: "At some moments I find myself in the presence of a current that flows through life and art. The next moment, I lose sight of it again. And the instant I lose sight of it, I am overcome by the immense darkness and solitude that loom around me." This is the same current that Bakin, the novelist-hero of **"Absorbed in Letters,"** eventually discovers "flowing like the Milky Way in the sky"—a sight that drives away all the unhappy thoughts from his troubled mind. Yoshihide, the artist-hero of **"The Hell Screen,"** is so swept up by that current he forgets that the model being burnt to death before his eyes is his beloved daughter. The Akutagawa-like narrator of **"Cogwheel,"** depressed, nervous, and on the brink of insanity, reads *Voyage Through the Dark Night* and gains peace of mind for a while.

Another revealing testimonial to the power of art is given by Akutagawa in an essay that records his experiences in the ruins of Tokyo immediately after the great earthquake of 1923. He was walking among the debris of fire-ravaged buildings with a heavy heart, when suddenly he heard the voice of a youngster in a nearby moat. He was singing "My Old Kentucky Home." "I felt strangely moved," Akutagawa later recalled. "I felt something within me that wanted to join in with the youngster. No doubt he was simply enjoying himself singing a song. Yet the song, in a trice, overcame the spirit of negation that had gripped my mind for some time." Akutagawa went on to reflect on the uses of art. He concluded: "What I saw was something that even the flaming fire could not destroy." That "something" was the power of art, a strange power that could overcome the darkest of negative spirits. Even a simple song by Stephen Foster could do that; great masterpieces of literature should be able to do the same or more.

At this point art approaches close to religion—that is, if the purpose of religion is to overcome the spirit of negation. Akutagawa—at least the young Akutagawa—thought so. For instance, he wrote in a letter to a friend in 1914: "There is no need to force oneself to seek faith in God. One is compelled to debate whether or not there is a God because one thinks of faith only in terms of faith in God. I have my faith—a faith in art. I cannot believe that the exaltation I gain through this faith of mine is inferior to the exaltation gained through other faiths."

Could art really be a religion, in the sense Akutagawa thought it could? The available precedents were not very hopeful. There was the case of Bashō, who tried to unite art and religion, but failed because religion required him to be passive before the Supreme Being while art wanted him to be an active creator. Akutagawa, who was the first to point out that dichotomy in Bashō, came down firmly on the side of art. "Goethe once said he was possessed by a daemon while he was writing poetry," he wrote. "Wasn't Bashō too much under the influence of a poetic daemon to become a religious recluse? Wasn't the poet within Bashō more powerful than the religious recluse within him?" Akutagawa's answer was, of course, in the affirmative. For him, Bashō exemplified the sad fate of a poet who wrote poetry in the belief that it brought him closer to religion, but who finally came to the realization that he was wrong. How, then, did Akutagawa try to resolve a dilemma that had defeated Bashō?

Akutagawa's proposed solution was the opposite of Bashō's. While Bashō tried to bring poetry close to religion by writing a passive kind of poetry, Akutagawa attempted to humanize religion and thereby bring it closer to art. Increasingly interested in Christianity in his later years, he wrote essays describing the Holy Scriptures as literature. Jesus, he thought, was more human than divine. "Christianity," he once wrote, "is a poetic religion rich in ironies, a religion that Jesus himself could not practice. He laughingly threw away his life, even, for the sake of his genius. No wonder Wilde discovered in him the first of the romantics." "Christ became an early-day journalist," he wrote in another instance. "He also became an early-day

Bohemian. His genius marched on in leaps and bounds, overriding the social codes of his time. On occasions, he grew hysterical with disciples who did not understand him." He added:

> Jesus would ask his disciples, "What am I?" It is not difficult to answer that question. He was both a journalist and a subject for journalism; or, to put it another way, he was the author of short stories called "The Parables" as well as the hero of fictional biographies called the *New Testament*. A number of other Christs, it appears, had similar characteristics.

By "other Christs" Akutagawa meant Goethe, Tolstoy, Ibsen, and all other "journalists" who were possessed by a "daemon," and who kept on writing about themselves as they searched for something nobler than human bestiality. For Akutagawa, the Holy Ghost that fathered Jesus was merely another name for that "daemon," which also moved Jesus to teach, preach, and be crucified. In that sense, Jesus was a writer like the others. "In the final analysis, Christianity is a work of art, a didactic literature created by Jesus," Akutagawa concluded. "The works of Tolstoy's last years come closest to this ancient work of didactic literature [the Bible], though they lack the romantic color he (Jesus) added." Here, Akutagawa was implying not only that the Bible is literature if Tolstoy's *Resurrection* is literature, but also that *Resurrection* is a religious classic if the Bible is a religious classic.

Thus Akutagawa attained a unification of literature and religion by making the former include the latter. Religion, in his way of thinking, was a type of literature, a romantic type. This was, of course, far more than a literary judgment, and should not be judged on literary grounds. The only question one can legitimately ask in a biographical context is whether Akutagawa did actually derive from literature the religious consolation he apparently demanded from it.

Ostensibly, the answer must be in the negative. Admittedly, the young Akutagawa seems to have found in art the kind of exaltation that a religion might give. Thus the writer Bakin attains "mysterious joy" and "ecstatic, moving exaltation" by means of art, and the painter Yoshihide shows the "splendor of ecstatic joy" on his face as he works at creating a masterpiece. Yoshihide eventually commits suicide, but this is depicted as a triumph because he leaves behind him a masterpiece that is immortal. And yet, Akutagawa seems to grow less and less confident in the saving power of art as he grew older. The suicide of Tok the poet is described in *Kappa* as being far less glorious than Yoshihide's: there are obvious indications that poetry failed to function as a redeemer for Tok. The neurotic narrator of **"Cogwheel"** does get solace from reading *Voyage Through the Dark Night,* but it is a temporary solace. And, of course, Akutagawa himself committed suicide. Does this not indicate that his religion of art had failed him? Could he not have lived on if he had become a Christian, for example?

From Akutagawa's point of view, his suicide indicates neither that art had failed him nor that religion could have saved him. To him, it appeared that even Jesus had died a suicidal death. And as Jesus had died because he would not compromise his ideals, so did Akutagawa. He had a lofty ideal of man in his youth, and he kept on refusing to abandon it, even when he grew older and came to discover bestiality at the source of human life. He chose to keep believing that man was considerably nobler than a beast. Unfortunately, his health rapidly deteriorated in his later years, threatening to reduce or even incapacitate his intellectual power. He could have lived on, had he been ready to accept a less intellectual life for himself. He could have stopped being a writer, if he found himself unable to write. He could have lived on in retirement, as a good-for-nothing, or even as a mental patient. But he was too proud; he could not and would not compromise his idea of human nobility. Likewise, he could have lived on as a Christian. But, in his view, becoming a Christian would have meant surrendering his humanity to God; it would have meant recognizing an existence higher than man. His religion, which was art, dictated that man be his own master in death as in life. His suicide, in this context, was therefore a vindication of art; it was comparable to the suicide of Yoshihide in **"The Hell Screen."** Yoshihide the man died, but his hell screen, a proof that man is not a mere beast, remained. And so it is with Akutagawa: he killed himself, but his works remain as the record of his struggles to prove human nobility.

Notes

1. Kappa is an aquatic monster that appears in Japanese folklore. It looks like a large frog, with a saucerlike receptacle growing on its head. "Weird" is the adjective Akutagawa uses most often to describe this creature in *Kappa*.

2. Saikaku was a writer of *haikai*, a popular form of linked verse, before he began writing prose fiction. As a haikai writer he shocked his contemporaries by the use of quaint, unconventional words, so much so that he was nicknamed "Dutchman." His use of unconventional words in his fiction was just as striking.

3. Ni Yün-lin (1301–74), also known as Ni Tsan, was a leading painter in the late Yüan period and was especially skilled in landscape painting. He also wrote many volumes of poetry.

4. In a ninth-century Japanese tale called *A Tale of a Bamboo-Cutter*, the beautiful heroine gives a test to each of her wooers. She asks one suitor to bring her a seashell that does not exist in reality.

5. *Ages Ago* is a collection of more than 1,200 tales compiled in the early twelfth century. Unlike most of the literary works that preceded it, the collection was intended to appeal to a large segment of the contemporary Japanese populace. Accordingly, it did not shy away from presenting vulgar or even bawdy aspects of life in a direct, unsophisticated manner.

6. The haiku was written by Bashō in the summer of 1689, when he visited a rural temple at the beginning of his long journey to the far north. Enshrined in the temple was a mountain priest noted as a tireless traveler through the wilderness. Unlike other holy statues, that of the priest normally wore wooden shoes.

7. In *The Garden of Epicurus* Anatole France remarked that words in a book were magic fingers that played on the harp strings of the reader's brain, and that the sounds thus evoked depended on the quality of the strings within each individual reader. Mount Lu is a famous mountain located near the Yangtze River. Because of its scenic beauty and its close associations with Buddhism, it provided fitting material for poetry and the arts through the centuries.

8. Yanagihara is the name of a district in Tokyo. It is written with two characters meaning "willow" and "field," respectively.

Beongcheon Yu (essay date 1976)

SOURCE: "The Flight to Parnassus," in *Akutagawa: An Introduction*, Wayne State University Press, 1972, pp. 15–42.

[*In the following essay, Yu examines major themes in Akutagawa's short stories, focusing on "The Nose" as the starting point of his fiction career.*]

1

Of Akutagawa's early writings, only a handful—translations of France and Yeats,[1] and pieces like **"The Old Man"** (written in 1914) and **"Youths and Death"** (1914)—appeared in the third *New Thought*. None of these writings attracted critical attention; nor did his more ambitious **"Rashomon"** (1915), which he managed to place in another little magazine. Even **"The Nose"** might have suffered the same fate but for Soseki's personal blessings. Upon reading this story in the first issue of the fourth *New Thought*, Soseki at once wrote a congratulatory letter to the young author: "I found your piece very interesting. Sober and serious without trying to be funny, it exudes humor, a sure sign of refined taste. Furthermore, the material is fresh and eye-catching. Your style is well-polished, admirably fitting." The elder novelist did not forget to add a word of advice: "Go on and produce twenty or thirty stories like this one. You will soon be incomparable in literary circles. **'The Nose'** alone may not attract many readers. Even if it does, they may let it pass quietly. But without worrying about it, you must go on. Ignore the crowd—the best way of keeping your integrity." Through the arrangement of one of Soseki's disciples, the story was reprinted in the May issue of the influential *New Fiction*, making Akutagawa's first success all the more secure.

Set in ancient Japan, the story portrays a Buddhist priest of great renown and piety who suffers, not knowing what to do with his six-inch long nose. Although outwardly indifferent, he is much mortified, feeling that his concern about such a mundane matter does not become his priestly dignity. (He can never be a Cyrano de Bergerac who knows how to capitalize on his grotesque nose.) While searching for precedents in scripture, he subjects himself to all sorts of cures, such as boiling and stamping, and finally succeeds in shrinking his nose, but his success merely redoubles his embarrassment and shame as he now attracts even more attention. Then, much to his relief, sheer chance restores it to its original size. "Now, no one will laugh at me any more," he mutters to himself as he enjoys the breeze of an early autumn morning.

"The Nose" is based mainly on an episode about the famous long-nosed priest, found in the *Konjaku* and *Ujishui*,[2] two ancient collections of stories and tales; in psychological treatment it was inspired by Gogol's story of the same title. Yet Akutagawa's story retains nothing of the crudely simple narration and earthy humor of the original anecdote; nor does it echo the bizarre twist and sardonic laughter of the Russian writer. Sober and serious, as Soseki said, the tone is ironic, and this sense of irony derives from the author's angle of vision, the uncertainty of being human in a fickle world. The story revolves around the very attitude of the author who neither condemns nor condones. Using the human nose as a focal point Akutagawa pits his protagonist against the world and shows that neither side wins or loses completely. While his clear-eyed intelligence does not miss the slightest shade of psychological tension, his subtle comic sense contemplates human frailty with serene pity.

Already apparent in "The Nose" are three motifs: the manipulation of the absurd; the uncertainty of being human; and the morbidity of obsession. Each of these motifs is carried further in Akutagawa's later stories. The first motif is evident in "Lice" (1916), which concerns solemn-faced samurai warring over lice, and "The Dragon" (1919), in which the credulous masses gather to witness the ascent of a dragon. The second motif appears in "The Wine Worm" (1916) and "The Dream of Lusheng" (1917), both of which suggest the futility of attempting to change what one is born with, and the third in "Yam Gruel" (1916), which exposes the extremity of a human obsession fearful of its own realization.

Uniquely Akutagawa, "The Nose" refuses classification with any of the three literary schools that dominated the contemporary literary scene: naturalism, aestheticism, and idealism. Like "Rashomon," it was written in an effort to get over a recent disappointment in love, and Akutagawa meant to be pleasant and remote from reality. Fresh in conception, dexterous in execution, and cumulative in effect, the story both puzzled and delighted the reading public.

2

Although "The Nose" made Akutagawa famous virtually overnight, he was too ambitious an artist to merely indulge in his first success. His literary activities during the next few years fully indicate his ability to turn his sudden fame

into something more solid and permanent. The period 1916–1919 marked in many ways perhaps the happiest years of his life, resulting in three collections of short stories, *Rashomon, Tobacco and the Devil,* and *The Puppeteer.*

The thirty-odd stories collected in these volumes are typical of Akutagawa, rich in variety and impressive in scope. In addition to conventional short stories, there are dramas, satires, fairy-tales, prose poems, and sketches—set in Japan, China, India, and imaginary lands. The Japanese stories, for instance, range from remote antiquity to the contemporary world, from the early Japanese Christian to the Edo period. Depending on his subject matter his narrative form is varied—dramatic, epistolary, allegorical, and objective—as is his style—pseudo-classical, early Christian, Chinese, and modern. Fantastic in imagery, tender in sentiment, biting in ridicule, and startling in direction, these pieces are all experimental, demonstrating the author's determination to explore and exploit different genres. Some are perhaps precious but none amateurish. Whether precocious or mature, they all attest to a high degree of literary intelligence at work.

Contemporary critics, sympathetic or hostile, quickly noted Akutagawa's intelligence and craftsmanship. One critic, designating the essence of Akutagawa's art as a combination of intelligence and humor, stressed his pose as a detached outsider observing the kaleidoscope of life. While regretting that Akutagawa's analytical power sometimes failed to go beyond common sense, the critic nonetheless lavished praise on the author's artistic integrity and his unerring sense of language. All in all, Akutagawa seemed to him to be the kind of writer who would proceed from emphasis on form to concern with content. Another critic found one of Akutagawa's central themes to be the sense of fear that inevitably follows our fulfilled expectations; he pointed out the author's capacity for perfect form, contemplation, and aesthetic distance, all of which combined to make his art unique in contemporary literature. A third critic suggested that Akutagawa's primary virtue was the purity of his aesthetic contemplation, apparent in the best of his stories, and that these stories were often almost too pure to excite the general reader long spoiled by impure works—works immature in aesthetic contemplation. Probably for this very reason his works appeared to lack in raw strength, what the critic called the throbbings of life. Despite their varied observations the critics concurred on one point: perfect form compensates for insufficient content.[3] Whatever the validity of such a verdict, it was the view generally shared by Akutagawa's contemporaries since they were prompt to label him a neo-intellectualist, neo-classicist, neo-mannerist, and the like.

Akutagawa rejected such labels designed only for the convenience of reviewers and critics because they were all too neat and simple to characterize what he was trying to do. He took every opportunity to clarify his intent: to go his own way as best he could—the only sure way of growing. In reply to the question, "Why do you write?" he said he wrote neither for money nor for the public but because something vague and chaotic within himself demanded a certain form which was at once clear and precise. Declaring that art is, first of all, expression, he challenged the general critical assumption that a writer starts with content and then frames it in some sort of form, as though there were two separate and separable processes. The common critical clichés, "stylistic obsession," "too deft" or "too dexterous," were meaningless to Akutagawa. Form, he said in effect, does not wrap content in a neat package; form lies in content, and *vice versa*. To one who cannot understand this basic truth, art will forever remain another world. Art begins and ends in deliberate expression. Write with your soul or with your life—all these gilded sermons had better be addressed to high school students. All creative activities, even those of a genius, are conscious; he is perfectly aware of what effect his single touch, his single stroke will create; if not, then he is no better than an automaton.

In Akutagawa's view, then, it would be a mistake to assume the primacy of either form or content. In the same reflections on art he in fact warned that stressing form would be equally harmful, and that in practice it might be even more harmful than stressing content, a warning apparently against a typical Japanese tendency toward the decorative or a refined preciousness. The point here is Akutagawa's passion for perfection, the quality which struck the three critics referred to above. The artist, in Akutagawa's view, must strive to perfect his work; otherwise his devotion to art amounts to nothing. For moral exaltation the reader might as well turn to sermons, but for aesthetic pleasure he must go to a work of art. And to secure this pleasure the artist must pursue his dream of perfection. It was in this vein that Akutagawa also wrote: "There is in the kingdom of art no room for the unperfected"; "A work of art, when perfected, becomes timeless"; and "In the religion of art self-reliance is the only key to salvation."

"One who has a correct view of art does not necessarily create a better work. Such a reflection makes me sad. Am I the only one in this? I pray this is not the case"—so Akutagawa wrote in "Art, etc." The truth is that Akutagawa not only had a "correct" view of art but also wrote "better" works because of it. In reference to Poe's "Philosophy of Composition" he observed that the American poet wrote his poems and stories just as a brick layer would go about his job.[4] Then turning to his own manner of writing. Akutagawa said in the preface to *Tobacco and the Devil*:

> To speak of my feelings while I am at work, it seems like growing rather than making something. Every phenomenon, human and otherwise, follows its own unique course of development in that it happens in the way it must. So as I write I proceed from point to point, from moment to moment. If I miss one step, then I am stuck. I can not go even one step further. If I force myself, something is bound to go wrong. I must always be alert. No matter how alert, it often happens that I miss it. That is my trouble.

This, according to Akutagawa, explains why a work of art in progress sometimes refuses to follow the artist's own plan, however well calculated, "just as the world may have gone out of God's hands, much as he tried to adhere to his original plans of creation." Thus, despite his insistence on conscious intelligence, Akutagawa recognized that the artist was fallible, but this human frailty was no excuse for not striving for perfection.

3

Although it is obvious that in theory and practice Akutagawa put a high premium on literary intelligence, the matter apparently was not so obvious to many of his contemporary critics who, taking the term intelligence differently, charged that with Akutagawa intelligence often degenerated into book learning and antiquarianism. The implication of their charge was that his art is all imitation, devoid of a sense of life. For example, the narrative substance of **"The Nose"** derived entirely from either the *Konjaku* or *Ujishui*, and for psychological analysis it followed Gogol's piece of the same title. The same is true of other stories like **"Rashomon,"** which again relied heavily on the *Konjaku*, and **"The Dragon,"** which in turn was based on the *Ujishui*. Likewise, both **"The Wine Worm"** and **"The Dream of Lusheng"** drew from well-known Chinese materials, and **"Lice"** admittedly had an oral source. Clearly, it was assumed, Akutagawa's art was bookish, and his originality, if any, was only in form, not in content. To these critics who took the terms originality and imitation in a narrow sense, Akutagawa's presumed lack of originality indicated the fatal paucity of his inner life which his art was used to camouflage.

According to Yoshida Seiichi's investigations,[5] at least sixty-two of Akutagawa's stories reveal a varying degree of indebtedness to known literary sources, Japanese, Chinese, Indian, and Western. His Western sources in particular show a wide range—the Bible, Caxton, Swift, Defoe, Goethe, Poe, Bierce, Browning, Butler, Gogol, and Dostoevsky, as well as Flaubert, Régnier, Mérimée, Loti, Strindberg, France, Synge, and others. Although Akutagawa's habit of borrowing—from mere inspiration to outright plagiarism—becomes less conspicuous as he proceeds, the proportion of borrowings to his total output of some 150 stories is very high indeed, even if one grants that such borrowing is not uncommon among writers and that reading, as a form of experience, is a very important part of any writer's life. If the practice reflected Akutagawa's omnivorous reading, it was also what made his admirer Hori Tatsuo say of him: "He finally ended without any original masterpiece. In all of his masterpieces, in every single one of them, linger the shadows of previous centuries."[6]

The question of imitation and originality could hardly have disturbed earlier Eastern and Western critics who usually showed an enviable degree of permissiveness toward such practices, over-stressing neither originality as a cardinal virtue nor imitation as a deadly sin. Even in the present century, at least in the West, we have since Joyce and Eliot, learned to accept imitation as a common phenomenon. Yet, to the modern Japanese the question still has a special significance because of their oft-alleged racial propensity to imitation, and also because of the peculiar influence of naturalists and humanists who insisted on the primacy of life over art, an attitude central to the *shishosetsu* tradition.

Akutagawa sharply disagreed with his critics on the question and affirmed the validity of literary imitation. "I am not at all ashamed to imitate the geniuses of all ages and to appropriate their crafty methods and devices." The preface to *Tobacco and the Devil* also indicates that he was fully aware of the implications of his critics' charge. It is true, writes Akutagawa, that he frequently draws from old materials with which his early education familiarized him. But it is not true that he read them with an eye to extracting possible materials for his stories. Although he does not consider such a manner of reading a serious vice, the fact is that while reading he often comes upon some interesting materials he can use later. Discovery of such materials does not insure stories since materials are just materials. As Akutagawa points out, he cannot write unless he becomes one with his material as his mind penetrates into it. And when such a union will occur, he himself cannot predict. But when it happens he knows it because his vision suddenly clears up.

From this it is apparent that Akutagawa takes reading as a major source of his literary inspirations. Especially revealing is what he has to say about the creative process, the process from reading to creation, when he describes how a story grows out of his union with a given source. **"Spiderthread"** (1918) may serve as an example of his personal method. The story is brief enough to be quoted in full:

I

One day in Paradise, Buddha was alone strolling around the Lotus Pond. The flowers were now in their pearly white bloom with an exquisite fragrance radiating from their golden crowns. It was morning in Paradise.

Soon Buddha paused by the edge of the pond and peered down through the lotus leaves overgrowing the water. Deep beneath the Lotus Pond lay the pit of Hell, and through the crystal-clear water the River Styx and the Mountain of Needles appeared vividly.

There at the bottom of Hell he noticed a man named Kantada writhing among his fellow sinners. Although he was a notorious robber who had committed arsons, murders, and other sins, he had done one good deed in his lifetime. Once while passing through a dense forest he came upon a tiny spider crawling along the path. Raising his foot, he was about to crush it, when he checked himself: "No, it isn't right. Tiny as it is, it must also have its life. It would be cruel of me to kill it for no good reason." So he let the creature go unharmed.

While observing Hell beneath, Buddha recalled Kantada's charitable deed to the spider and decided to rescue him out of Hell as a reward. It so happened that Buddha noticed a spider of Paradise weaving its beautiful silvery web over the sapphire-colored lotus leaves nearby. Taking this spiderthread gently, he lowered it through an opening amid the pearl-white lotus flowers all the way down to the shadowy bottom of Hell.

2

In the Lake of Blood at the pit of Hell, Kantada was bobbing up and down with the other sinners. Whichever way he looked, all was dark—except for the occasional glimmer of sharp steel from the Mountain of Needles—a scene which was ghastly beyond description. Moreover, all was as still as the grave but for the faint sighs and groans rising every now and then from those wretched sinners, utterly exhausted with every known kind of infernal torture, indeed too exhausted even to cry out. The notorious robber Kantada was no exception. Choked with blood in this Lake of Blood, he was struggling in desperation like a dying frog.

Then, he happened to glance up at the sky above the Lake of Blood, and he saw the silvery spiderthread coming down from the far, faraway sky, glimmering as stealthily as if it feared the watchful eyes of the sinners. At the sight of this thread Kantada clapped his hands for joy. If he could only cling to it and climb up as far as he could, it seemed that he would surely get out of Hell. And if things were to go well, he might be able to get into Paradise. Then, he wouldn't have to be hauled up the Mountain of Needles or be cast down into the Lake of Blood.

Trembling with hope, Kantada at once grasped the thread in both hands and began to pull himself up with all his strength. Having been a great robber, he was thoroughly at home in this sort of thing.

However, Paradise rises tens of thousands of miles above Hell, too long a way for him to make it for all his eagerness. Having climbed up for a while, Kantada became so weary that he couldn't pull himself an inch further. With nothing else to do now, he took his breath, hanging onto the thread and peering below.

His strenuous climb had been rewarded. The Lake of Blood, which he had left behind a while ago, was no longer visible in the darkness. The dreadful Mountain of Needles was only faintly glimmering way below. At this rate of ascent he might easily escape from Hell. Lacing both hands around the thread, Kantada exclaimed: "I've done it!" and laughed aloud for the first time in many years. Then suddenly he noticed right below him a myriad number of sinners climbing up and up the same thread close on his heels, diligently like a procession of ants. Kantada was stunned, his mouth agape and his eyes rolling like a dumbfounded idiot. How could this slender thread, already strained to the breaking point under his own weight, possibly sustain the crushing weight of so many? And what if the thread snaps off now? Then, he himself, after all his strenuous ascent, would be hurled back headlong into his former gloom in Hell. That would be even more frightening. While he was thus paralyzed with this prospect, hundreds and thousands of sinners kept climbing up, in a single file, along the silvery thread—after swarming out of the dismal Lake of Blood. Something had to be done at once. Otherwise, it would snap off halfway, hurling him back down to the pit of Hell.

"You damn'd sinners," Kantada shouted aloud. "This thread is mine, mine alone. Who said you could climb up? Get down, all of you get down."

At that very moment the thread snapped. All was over with Kantada. Down he plunged, whirling like a top, deep into the gloomy pit of Hell.

All that was left behind now was the faint gleam of the spiderthread hanging midair in the moonless and starless space.

3

Having seen all this through to the point at which Kantada sank to the bottom of the Lake of Blood, Buddha turned away from the edge of the Lotus Pond, and with a saddened look resumed his stroll. He must have pitied the shameless Kantada who, for his very lack of charity, was cast down to his former abode in Hell.

But those lotus flowers in Paradise seemed not at all affected by what had just happened in the world below. The pearly white flowers keep waving their calyxes around the feet of Buddha, still with their golden crowns radiating an exquisite fragrance. In Paradise it is now nearly midday.

Although even a sinner, through a small deed of charity in the past, deserves a chance to be saved, it is selfishness again that ruins him as well as others. In thesis and spirit the story is a Buddhist parable; in language and tone it is a fairy tale. As Akutagawa admitted, it required the greater care because of its brevity. Even though his lucid, elegant style suffers in translation, Akutagawa's essentially cinematic method is apparent. Masamune Hakucho missed the point when, comparing the story with *Gulliver's Travels,* he said: "Never venturing beyond common sense, it merely accepts the well-defined world of order. Granted it is meant to be a fairy tale, the author's mind too seems to indulge in the world of fairy tale."[7] Whatever this well-defined world of order, our real concern is with the source Akutagawa used for this story. For this nine out of ten readers would turn to some Buddhist source; and all ten would be surprised that it was adapted from a simple episodic parable—a thoroughly Christian one at that—in Dostoevsky's *The Brothers Karamazov,* which Akutagawa had recently read. The episode appears in "An Onion," the third chapter of Book VII, where Grushenka engages in conversation with Alyosha. The story, which Grushenka learned from her cook when she was a child, is as follows:

Once upon a time there was a peasant woman, and a very wicked woman she was. And she died and did not leave a single good deed behind. The devils caught her and plunged her into the lake of fire. So her guardian angel stood and wondered what good deed of hers he could remember to tell to God; "she once pulled up an onion in her garden," he said, "and gave it to a beggar woman." And God answered: "You take that onion then, hold it out to her in the lake, and let her take hold and be pulled out. And if you can pull her out of the lake, let her come to Paradise, but if the onion breaks, then the woman must stay where she is." The angel ran to the woman and held out the onion to her. "Come,"

said he, "catch hold and I'll pull you out." And he began cautiously pulling her out. He had just pulled her right out when the other sinners in the lake, seeing how she was being drawn out, began catching hold of her so as to be pulled out with her. But she was a very wicked woman and she began kicking them. "I'm to be pulled out, not you. It's my onion, not yours." As soon as she said that, the onion broke. And the woman fell into the lake and she is burning there to this day. So the angel wept and went away.

[Constance Garnett's translation]

So completely recast, **"Spiderthread"** as it stands leaves almost no trace of the original. By juxtaposing both versions we may sufficiently understand what Akutagawa meant by his union with the materials. Of course, he is not always so successful as in this instance. But with such a felicitous adaptation few would raise the question of imitation and originality.

4

Related closely to the question of imitation is Akutagawa's dependence on history, an early interest of his. It is his use of history as a fictional frame that led his critics to confound his intelligence with his learning and antiquarianism, and dub him a writer of historical fiction. Some forty stories, over a quarter of his total output, and all of his best pieces in the first half of his writing career fall under the category of what may loosely be called historical fiction. Akutagawa himself, in reference to **"The Nose,"** warned against such simplistic labeling, and he was right. Today we would certainly hesitate to regard this and other stories in the same vein as historical tales.

"Rashomon" (1915), one of his earliest attempts in this genre, may help to clarify the matter. (Incidentally, the film version is actually a combination of this piece and **"In a Grove"** [1921].) Akutagawa's source for **"Rashomon"** is found again in the *Konjaku* collection. The original is a brief, simple and straightforward episode:[8] A certain rustic, having arrived in the capital to begin a career of robbery, makes his way to the great gate of Rashomon to spend the night. In this shelter he chances upon an old shrivelled woman prowling among unclaimed corpses, plucking hair for the wig market. He strips the hag and her victim and runs off. The point of the episode is the sense of fright and horror both the man and the old woman experience in their brief encounter.

Akutagawa, following his source, sets his story in the Heian period, and his narrative method here, as in **"Spiderthread,"** is cinematic. The deserted gate of Rashomon looms in an evening storm, a symbol of the capital long deteriorating under a series of natural calamities. A man appears, a former servant who has recently been dismissed. Although armed, he is undecided whether to choose robbery or starvation. Among the scattered corpses beneath the gate he comes upon an old ape-like woman busily plucking a dead woman's hair.[9] Curious and frightened at first, he becomes indignant and demands an explanation.

She tells him that she gathers hair in order to survive, and that her victim, a rapacious vendor, deserves no better treatment. As indignation gives way to desperate courage, he snatches her clothes, and leaving the old woman naked among the corpses, disappears into the darkness.

Correcting the general view that egoism is the story's central theme, one critic said: "It neither affirms nor asserts egoism. Rather in order to negate it, the author, in extreme terms, scorns and satirizes its hideousness."[10] Another critic, in the light of what he called the logic of starvation, suggested that the story expressed the anarchist position that became prevalent soon after 1910.[11] Neither critic seems really convincing, however, because both mistake the part for the whole. More likely Akutagawa tried to strike at something deeper and more basic than human egoism or the logic of starvation. And this "something" is the self that harbors those irresistible impulses of life, ultimately transcending the notions of good and evil. The theme of the story, then, is the uncertainty of the human ego which often finds itself at the mercy of those impulses whenever life asserts its primacy. The nameless characters are no better than those corpses—all completely overshadowed by the towering gate. The real protagonist is the great gate itself, which stands for the human soul impregnated with uncertain and unpredictable elements, and the atmosphere hovering over its massive structure makes **"Rashomon"** a powerful piece of writing. (Akutagawa felt so confident as to use it as the title story of his first collection.) More fittingly than **"The Nose," "Rashomon"** marks the start of his career over which it cast its long, dark shadow.

Literary historians generally agree that Mori Ogai is the founder of historical fiction in modern Japanese literature (meaning he was the first to modernize the genre), and that his legacy was further developed by Kikuchi Kan and Akutagawa. In scope, however, Akutagawa goes far beyond Kikuchi and Ogai. While the majority of Ogai's historical novels are set in Japan, in the Tokugawa period (1600–1868), Akutagawa's tales exhibit a wider range from antiquity to the modern era, and are set in Japan, Korea, China, India and 19th century Russia. His Japanese stories in particular cover virtually all the major periods, from the mythological, Heian, early Christian, and Tokugawa down to the enlightened Meiji. At one time or another Akutagawa, if we take the narrator of his autobiographical story **"Cogwheels"** literally, even conceived of something like an epic novel consisting of some thirty pieces arranged chronologically, from the Nara down to the Meiji period, with the people of each period as its own characteristic protagonist.

The historical novel, such as would serve to express an author's paradoxical view of life, was peculiar to the period following 1910, and the use of history for creative purposes was common to the tradition of Ogai, Kikuchi, and Akutagawa. Although Ogai's historical novels successfully created an ideal image of the feudal world of samurai, he strove to portray the past faithfully—as faithfully as contemporary realists would claim to describe their own period. To this end Ogai approached historical materials with scientific accuracy and objectivity, so that the "nature" inherent in them might unfold itself, and this refusal to alter the "nature" in history, philosophical in intention though it was, often resulted in mere documentation. By concentrating on moments of crucial significance he pursued history for its own sake, not as a backdrop for his fiction. It is this emphasis on the "nature" in history that separated Ogai from his successors in the field.

Both Kikuchi and Akutagawa were alike in turning to history as a fictional frame. Defining his kind of historical fiction Kikuchi remarked:

> In historical records there is many an incident—described in a matter-of-fact manner—which, once projected into our own subjective mind, would gain a sudden illumination as an episode of human life. In other words, if, aided by our refined modern sensibility, we retrace the past our forebears lived with little awareness, we often come across those gems of life which they let pass without notice.[12]

And what Kikuchi aimed to provide in his historical novels was a fresh interpretation of the past in the light of modern sensibility. To a large extent this seems to apply to Akutagawa too. Many of his historical tales are short, and present historical figures in new perspective often at the expense of historical convention and accuracy.

While agreeing in the main with Kikuchi's definition, Akutagawa took the term historical fiction less broadly. Although he accepted as a rule that there is no historical novel without some measure of fidelity to the general mores of a particular era, he also suggested the possibility of the kind of novel which would thematically focus on only certain unique aspects of it, say, its moral aspect. For example the Heian concept of sexual relationship differs considerably from the modern. According to Akutagawa, a writer should present this older concept in a detached manner as if he were a contemporary eyewitness and let the story produce its effect through the resulting contrast. To this category belong some of the historical novels of Mérimée and France. In Akutagawa's view there were yet no Japanese works comparable to them. Instead, there were only those that presented a glimpse of humanity common both to the ancient and to the modern. He hoped to see some young talent explore something different.

As for his own practice, Akutagawa explained the role of "a by-gone era" in his stories as a sort of fictional frame—as an equivalent of "once upon a time" or "long, long ago" of the fairy tale, and what he had to say about the matter is important to an understanding of his art.

> Let us suppose that I, seizing on a certain theme, set out to write a story. In order to give the theme great artistic power I must have an uncommon incident. Considering the uncommonness of such an incident I cannot possibly set it in modern Japan. If I do, it may only appear unnatural to the reader, and thus destroy my

theme. The best way to avoid such a waste, then, would be . . . to set it in the past (rarely in the future) or somewhere outside Japan—even ancient Japan. In most of my stories I was driven by the need to avoid unnaturalness. Consequently I looked for settings in by-gone eras because, unlike the fairy tale, novelistic conventions prohibit the use of 'once upon a time' or 'long, long ago.' Once this choice of a suitable period is made, I take the next step, that is, I introduce various contemporary social conditions to make my setting appear natural. This point, that in no sense do I aim at an exact and detailed recreation of a bygone era, I think, separates mine from the so-called historical novel.

His turning to by-gone eras, added Akutagawa, does not mean that he cherishes nostalgic longings for them. He is perfectly happy to have been born in modern Japan. True, our universal interest in things exotic may have to do with his selection of uncommon incidents, and likewise the very beauty of a by-gone era may conceivably affect his selection. While these exotic and aesthetic factors may find their way into the picture, Akutagawa emphasized that it is still the role of "long, long ago" that the past plays in his stories.

There is a group of stories executed more or less in the spirit of epic or legend, such as **"The Robbers"** (1917), **"Heresy"** (1918), **"St. Christopher"** (1919), **"Susano-ono-mikoto"** and **"The Aged Susano-ono-mikoto"** (both 1920). Set in the Heian, the late Heian, the early Christian, and the mythological eras respectively, these stories each conjure up those by-gone days with their peculiar atmospheres of savage flight and splendor, primitive faith and valor. The first, inspired by both the *Konjaku* and Mérimée's *Carmen,* the third, based on the Caxton version, and the last two, fashioned after the *Kojiki,* the earliest Japanese chronicle,—all have specific thematic concerns. The second story, for instance, depicts the confrontation between the native way of life and the Christian God. In the group as a whole, however, Akutagawa's thematic interest is somehow overshadowed by his exotic and aesthetic interest in the periods in which the stories are set.

There is another group of historical stories dealing with early Japanese Christians, some fifteen in all, written at various times throughout Akutagawa's career. In these Japanese Christian stories, as they might be called, theme and frame are hardly distinguishable. The subject itself was new, being one of the discoveries of the Taisho period to which contemporary scholars and artists turned with increasing fascination. Akutagawa was no exception, and he returned frequently to the newly-found materials. He was irresistibly drawn to them, no doubt, for what he called exotic and aesthetic reasons, but we cannot dismiss these Japanese Christian stories merely as the product of his alleged dilettantism. Pieces like **"Tobacco and the Devil"** (1916), **"The Wandering Jew"** (1917), and **"Lucifer"** (1918) couldn't possibly have been written without his antiquarian learning. Yet these and other pieces, such as **"Ogata Ryosai's Memorandum"** (1916), **"The Martyr"**

(1918), and **"Juliano Kichisuke"** (1919), reveal something deeper and more personal than mere exoticism and aestheticism.[13]

"Ogata Ryosai's Memorandum" treats in a form of official report a village doctor's awe at the miraculous revival of a dead peasant girl by a Jesuit missionary. **"Juliano Kichisuke"** relates the life of a servant—the "holy idiot" whom Akutagawa loved best of all Japanese Christian martyrs—whose love for his mistress assumes the quality of religious devotion. And **"The Martyr"** traces the strange career of a girl who passes as a boy and is accused of fathering a child until her true identity is revealed in an attempt to rescue the child from a burning house.[14] Although few of these attain the level of his best stories, they are nevertheless significant for their themes, a variety of religious passion. Originated in the period that marked the first Japanese contact with Christianity, these materials may have served Akutagawa as he tried to reach out towards the West. Perhaps more than that, these early Japanese Christians, to him, embodied the will to transcend their frail human selves and conquer death. Their age, the 16th and 17th centuries, reminded him of the Middle Ages in Europe, a period of religious faith, miracle, and martyrdom. Akutagawa turned to this period not so much for a fictional frame as for its pervasive spiritual intensity. Or rather that was what he found in the early Japanese Christian materials.

Akutagawa's own account, quoted earlier, that he first seizes on a theme and then seeks a suitable setting for it, suggests two valuable points: the extent to which intelligence is allowed to play in his creative process, and the manner in which a theme gains clarity and intensity through its proper setting. From his declared procedure of coming upon potential materials, rather than seeking them out in old books, and since almost all of his historical stories draw from written sources, it would seem that his theme, far from being abstract, is already embedded in a germinal story or episode, and as he further develops the germinal piece the theme emerges in sharper focus.

There is still another group of stories portraying historical personages, in some of which the author's theme tends to override his other considerations. In **"Saigo Takamori"** (1917), for instance, he is particularly concerned to detach this recent national militaristic hero from the historical context. An elderly skeptic confounds a young historian with his thesis that Saigo, contrary to history, did not fall in the last battle of the Seinan Rebellion. The old man's sophistry in juggling actuality and probability is so persuasive that the young scholar becomes almost convinced of Saigo's survival. But the *tour de force* of the story reveals itself in the sophist's final statement:

> "I am quite satisfied to be a disciple of Pyrrho. We can never be sure about anything, even about ourselves—much less about Saigo Takamori's survival or death. Therefore, when I write a history I don't pretend to write a history free of lies. I would be perfectly content to write a history which would seem only probable and

beautiful. As a young man I thought of becoming a novelist. Had I become one, I would have been writing such stories. That might have suited me better than being a historian. At any rate, I am quite satisfied to be a sceptic."

The sophist was perhaps not meant to express the author's view of history as such; even so, it suggests something of his attitude. History is regarded not simply as what happened but more broadly as what might have happened. It is certainly the artist's view of history in that it is still fluid rather than established. In this Akutagawa stands a world apart from Ogai.

What has been said amounts to this: Akutagawa uses history only as a fictional frame and is thus more concerned with its utility than its actuality. Because he uses history only to serve his artistic purposes, those who criticize his tales on the basis of historical distortion or inaccuracy go wrong. For example in his portrait of Oishiuchi Kuranosuke, the leader of the celebrated forty-seven samurai (1917),[15] Akutagawa shows no interest whatever in tracing the hero's career from the time he and his men begin plotting up to their final act of vendetta. Rather he concentrates on Oishiuchi in the aftermath of the event—at the moment he is basking in serene satisfaction while waiting for the order of harakiri that is sure to come. But his serenity is suddenly upset as he learns that his group set an unsavory pattern for vendetta-mongers, whereas others are branded as cowards or renegades for their failure to do the same. With the deeds of his group being praised for the wrong reasons, he begins to suspect that not all of his motives were pure and honorable; he even questions whether or not his feigned debaucheries resulted from selfish motives on his part. The story gives only a partial portrait of Oishiuchi, to be sure; hence the title **"One Day of Oishiuchi Kuranosuke."** What emerges from the series of dramatized reflections is not a shining exemplar of feudal loyalty, but an honest man with common frailties capable of self-doubt, a man of flesh and blood made all the more appealing to the modern reader. By disregarding much of the historical detail and developing the psychological conflict, Akutagawa rescues his protagonist from the myth which has long apotheosized his heroic vendetta.

In **"Kesa and Morito"** (1918) Akutagawa is even less concerned with actual history. Here through two dramatic monologues, we get a glimpse of the interior of the ancient lovers' minds. Awaiting the appointed time to kill Kesa's husband, Morito reflects: "I despise her. I fear her. I hate her. And yet—and yet, all this may be because I love her." On the other hand, Kesa, deciding to die in her husband's place, confesses: "I am going to die, but not for my husband. I am going to die for my own sake—yes, for having my pride hurt and my body defiled. Oh, my life has been unworthy, and so, too, will be my death." Although, according to Akutagawa, the original episode in *The Rise and Fall of the Minamoto and Taira Clans* indicates that the lovers' relationship was a sordid sexual affair, tradition has turned Kesa into a heroine who chose death for the sake of her honor.[16] When a reader protested

his iconoclastic rendering, Akutagawa, referring specifically to the original version, replied that it is a sheer bourgeois myth to idolize this wretched, fallen woman as if she were some sort of superhuman paragon of chastity. In stories like these Akutagawa attempted to liberate man from all-powerful myth, and he often ran counter to tradition. When he penetrates the complex interior of humanity, history simply provides the initial frame, thus making the label "historical fiction" meaningless.

This is especially true with **"In a Grove"** (1921). Here again Akutagawa turns to the *Konjaku* for a usable episode but to Browning's *The Ring and the Book* for a suitable narrative mode, and he exploits his imagination to the fullest extent. (It has also been suggested that the central situation of a ravished wife came from his talk with a fellow writer.)

The story opens rather matter-of-factly with official testimonies by four witnesses: a woodcutter who chanced upon the dead body of a young samurai on a wooded hillside; a traveling priest who saw him on the road with his wife accompanying him on horseback; a constable who apprehended the murder suspect, a notorious robber; and an old woman who, identifying the slain samurai as her daughter's husband, added that the young couple was bound for their home in the country.

After these factual testimonies, the story turns sharply to another series of three mutually conflicting accounts of what really happened in the grove. As the robber defiantly admits, he did indeed slay the samurai in a duel which the ravished wife demanded with the winner to take her as his own. This version is at once contradicted by the woman's tearful confession at a temple, that she killed her husband for having witnessed her shame and then tried in vain to kill herself. But even this version turns out to be totally unreliable when the murdered husband, through a medium, reveals that his wife urged the robber to kill him, and when the robber refused he decided to take his own life.

Proceeding from the four testimonies to the three conflicting accounts of what happened, the story relentlessly develops an emotional vortex: lust, love, hate, suspicion, jealousy, anger, contempt, and resignation. It finally suggests that, as a victim of these elemental passions, man must wander hopelessly in his world of uncertainty, forever blind to the ultimate truth. The innocuous grove becomes a symbol of life itself which is dark with human ambiguities. (It is to Kurosawa's credit that in his film he made full use of certain affinities between this story and **"Rashomon."**[17] The setting is ancient, but the theme is modern, and from their peculiar combination the story draws its savage intensity.

5

There is finally a group of stories portraying famous artists as heroes. If the so-called artist stories together constitute a unique genre in modern literature, they also occupy a special place in Akutagawa's art. Being intensely conscious of his trade, he wrote more than a dozen stories about art and the artist, and most of them understandably in the early years of his career. Besides those unguardedly autobiographical reminiscences of his literary adolescence, such as **"On the Seashore"** (1925) and **"Those Days"** (1918), there are allegories satirizing critics and writers such as **"Mensura Zoili"** (1916) and **"The Strange Island"** (1923); there are also stories about works of art, such as **"Noroma Puppets"** (1916), **"The Marshland"** (1919), and **"An Autumn Mountain"** (1920). Some of the stories such as **"Withered Fields"** (1918), **"The Ball"** (1919), and **"The Solitary Snipe"** (1920), dealing with the death of Basho, the casual appearance of Pierre Loti, and the encounter of Tolstoy and Turgenev, respectively, are simple episodes. Others come to grips directly with artists at their moment of creation and here the author's theme triumphs over his historical frame.

Perhaps most typical of this series is **"Creative Frenzy"** (1917), a portrait of Takizawa Bakin, a great Edo novelist working on his masterpiece, *The Romance of Eight Dogs*. Based on Bakin's own diaries and written somewhat in the manner of **"One Day of Oishiuchi Kuranosuke,"** this story was most popular among Akutagawa's friends and he himself took no little pride in it, saying that he "borrowed Bakin to write what was on his own mind."

Bakin as he appears in the story is over sixty, though with his prominent cheekbones, sturdily-set jaws, and somewhat large mouth, all suggesting his enormous vitality, he seems more like a man in his prime. Akutagawa describes in detail a typical day of Bakin's life at its peak, from his morning visit to the public bath to his lonely midnight work. Out of the massive accumulation of details gradually emerge Akutagawa's manifold themes: the conflict between the artist and his readers who are enthusiastic but remain unappreciative of his intentions; the relationship of the artist and his critics who, accusing him of imitating old masters, always lump his works with those of mediocre writers; the unsatisfactory association of the artist with his greedy, unscrupulous publishers who tempt him to prostitute his artistic integrity; the ironic relation of the artist and young aspirants who, resenting his refusal to read their manuscripts, repay him with insults and slanders; the trouble between the artist and censors who pose as the guardians of public morality and detect nothing but eroticism in his characters; and finally the sympathy between the artist and his colleagues who share his devotion to artistic pursuit.

Such a list of themes might create the impression that Akutagawa's story is merely an artist's manifesto, certainly interesting but a bit too obvious. All of these themes, no doubt, had personal implications for Akutagawa, then fresh from the first round of his literary struggle. Many contemporary readers and critics did in fact take the story as a personal manifesto. But what helps lift the story above documentary status is the author's ability to dramatize his themes with concrete daily events and thereby create a cumulative effect. As we are led into the story we perceive with increasing clarity that it extends over three concentric circles: in the outer stand the general public which remains alien to Bakin; in the middle his family and a few fellow artists who care for him and his ideals; and in the inner, Bakin himself, alone as every artist must be when he faces his work. He is oblivious to everything else, his public, his family, and even the shared pledge with his painter-friend Watanabe Kazan that they will go on fighting unto death. Once in this magic circle he is free of his usual frustrations and doubts. Akutagawa describes it thus:

> When he finally lowered his brush to paper, some faint light was glimmering in his mind. And as he wrote ten, twenty lines, and more, the light grew larger and larger. What this was, Bakin knew from experience and kept at his writing with the greater care. Divine inspiration was in no way different from fire. Once kindled, it may go out quickly unless one knows how to feed it.

> "Don't be impatient! And think deeply—as deeply as you can," Bakin kept whispering to himself, trying to restrain his brush which tended to run ahead in eagerness. What had earlier seemed to be but shattered stars, was now flowing through his mind more swiftly than a river, gaining force every moment urging him forward, whether he liked it or not.

> No longer did he hear the chirping of crickets outside; nor did he have to strain his eyes in the dim light of the round paper lamp. His brush, by its own momentum, began gliding on paper without a pause. He kept on desperately as though in a mortal struggle with some supernatural power.

> The stream within, like the Milky Way across the sky, came flowing from some unknown, inexhaustible source. He feared that his strength could no longer bear its torrential force. Gripping his brush firmly, he said to himself time and again: "Keep on writing to the utmost limits. If what you are writing you do not write now, you may never be able to write again."

> The misty stream of light would not ebb. It swept over him, drowning everything in its dizzy rush until at last he became its helpless captive, oblivious to all, as his brush carried him along the course of the flood.

> At that moment he was a sovereign whose vision transcended thoughts of gain and loss, love and hate, and whose mind remained indifferent to clamors of fame and slander. With all vanished, he was alone, experiencing only a sense of marvelous joy, a sublime ecstasy.

To this Akutagawa adds: "How could anyone alien to this heightened feeling possibly appreciate the inmost ecstasy of creative frenzy or fathom the writer's supreme spirit? In this very moment *life,* cleansed of its dregs, begins to shine before the eyes of the artist, with the brilliance of a new gem." This addition, though perhaps unnecessary, reaffirms Akutagawa's profound conviction that artistic creation is indeed a supreme human act bordering on divine mystery and that this sense of ecstasy is the highest reward any artist can hope to win.

The greatest of all of Akutagawa's artist stories, and in fact the greatest of all of his stories written during his early period is **"The Hell Screen"** (1918). Again drawing from old materials, this time from two different sources— one of a painter rejoicing as his house burns down and the other of a painter working on a screen depicting hell (neither episode runs to more than a dozen lines),[18] this novella portrays a tragic artist who sacrifices everything to complete his masterpiece. Incomparably better than in his Bakin story, Akutagawa here succeeds in creating an ideal artist driven by his daemon and obsessed with his dream of perfection, because here at last Akutagawa found the material that matched his gift, and both author and material achieved a rare union. It is this piece, **"The Hell Screen,"** that elicited Masamune Hakucho's praise: "the very best of Akutagawa's stories" and "a masterpiece which gains special brilliance in post-Meiji Japanese literature."[19]

Yoshihide, or Monkey Yoshihide as he was nicknamed, is eccentric—greedy, indolent, impetuous, shameless, and above all arrogant. Odious as he is, he is a supreme artist, the greatest painter of his time. His other saving personal virtue is his passionate love for his only daughter, who is his exact opposite in every way—sweet, innocent, and obedient. Moreover, she has a quick turn of mind such as is apparent in her saving a mischievous pet monkey called Yoshihide from an impending punishment by her witty reference to the creature's nickname. After this incident the girl and the monkey become fast friends. One day the patron lord commands the artist to paint a scene of Hell on a screen. For several months he locks himself up in his studio, working on the project. As he becomes engrossed with the subject, all sorts of wild, fantastic rumors begin to spread concerning his nightmare-ridden sleep, his binding an apprentice in chains for sketches, and many other bizarre actions. Finally one day Yoshihide presents himself before the lord and reports that the picture has been completed except for the central scene featuring a magnificent carriage falling in midair. As he further explains:

> "In the carriage an exquisite court lady, in the midst of raging flames, writhes in agony, with her black hair flowing loose. Choked with the burning smoke, she turns her face up toward the roof of the carriage, with her brows tightly drawn. Perhaps her hands that grip the ripped-off screen are trying to ward off the rain of flames. And a score of ominous-looking birds flutter around the carriage, clacking their beaks. Ah, such a court lady in a flaming vehicle, I cannot paint."

With this Yoshihide makes the extraordinary request that such a carriage be burned before his very eyes, and if possible—with a young lady in it. In apparent madness that matches Yoshihide's, the lord grants the request. The appointed night arrives and everyone is invited to a deserted palace for the occasion. With the stage thus set, a carriage is drawn into the courtyard, and in it is a young lady bound in chains, exactly as Yoshihide requested. As the carriage is set afire the torches reveal that the lady is Yoshihide's daughter. The artist, horrified by the terror and death agony of his beloved daughter, is dumb-founded and cannot move to save her. Then, as the pet monkey leaps into the flames to join its mistress, an awesome change occurs in Yoshihide.

> In front of the pillar of fire Yoshihide, who was suffering infernal tortures a moment ago, stands rooted. But what a marvelous transformation! His wrinkled face now radiates a kind of blissful ecstasy as he stands, with his arms folded, oblivious to the presence of the Grand Lord. No longer does his vision reflect the image of his daughter's death agony. He seems supremely delighted with the beautiful color of the flames and the form of the woman writhing within.

It is a marked contrast to the lord's own transformation. He is now a completely changed person, pale and livid with foam gathering at his mouth, gripping his robed knees with both hands, panting like a thirsty animal. Not long after, Yoshihide completes the masterpiece which has caused so much sorrow and horror. And on the night following its completion the artist hangs himself.

All this is narrated by an eyewitness of the whole drama. Being a retainer in service of the lord, the narrator is always deferential and obsequious, consciously and unconsciously interpreting everything in favor of his master, as when he tends to gloss over the relationship between the lord and Yoshihide's daughter:

> The most prevalent rumor was that the Lord was motivated by his spurned love. But most probably he meant to punish the perversity of Yoshihide, who was so anxious to paint the Hell Screen even at the sacrifice of a court carriage and a human life. As a matter of fact, this was what I heard from his own lips.

Toward Yoshihide, on the other hand, he is uncharitable and supercilious. Because of his social prejudice and lack of perception, the narrator never understands what he observes, which only intensifies the abysmal gap between the artist and worldly authorities. To this narrative point of view the story owes much of its ambiguity, depth, complexity, and vitality.[20] Consider also the role of the pet monkey: as its nickname suggests, the creature represents Yoshihide the father. Its leap into the flames symbolizes in Yoshihide the separation of father and artist. Yoshihide the artist can now transcend his own personal tragedy, if only momentarily. The separation insures his triumph, whereas the lord suffers a complete defeat. Once within this circle of divine madness the artist, far beyond the boundary of secular power, stands alone on the lofty summit of art where he is immune and invulnerable. As a portrait of his ideal artist **"The Hell Screen"** marks the moment of Akutagawa's artistic triumph.

The singular intensity that pervades the novella derives from the complete identity between the author and his hero-artist. This hero's passion for artistic perfection which becomes sheer madness is also Akutagawa's. The story evokes horror and illustrates what Akutagawa meant by the beauty of savage, naked brutality, the terms with which he attempted to define the artistic essence of the *Konjaku*.[21] It was only natural that he set the story in the same Heian period that produced the *Konjaku*. It was to his credit that in that period he discovered not only the spirit of tenderness and elegance—as many usually do, but at the same time the undercurrent of savage brutality, the quality we seldom associate with the period.

In the context of the story Yoshihide's suicide would seem to be the only logical and satisfactory solution, because it suggests the paradoxical nature of the artist who, driven by his own daemon, must transcend himself. It is this paradox inherent in his creative activities that endows his art with a sense of tragic grandeur. There is, however, something more to Yoshihide's suicide than this; because of Akutagawa's unmistakable identity with his hero, we are tempted, as Akutagawa himself was in his last days, to see Yoshihide's suicide in the light of his own. While, as Miyamoto Kenji pointed out, Akutagawa the artist has his hero experience an artistic triumph, Akutagawa the man cannot leave him forever in that sublime ecstasy; and his own later suicide, like his hero's, is what results inevitably from the very conflict within himself between the artist and the man.[22] In this sense Akutagawa was never an artist for art's sake, a writer content to remain in his enchanted circle.

Notes

1. For his translations of France, Yeats, Gautier, and Voltaire, see *Zenshu*, VIII, pp. 200–70, and for those left unfinished, see *Zenshu*, XV, pp. 134–44.

2. The full titles of these collections are *Konjaku Monogatari* and *Ujishui Monogatari*. The former, compiled in the 11th century, contains over a thousand tales in three sections, Indian, Chinese, and Japanese. The latter, a smaller collection of the Kamakura period, includes slightly less than two hundred tales. For the *Konjaku* and its relationship with the *Ujishui*, see S. W. Jones's introductory essay to *Long Ago: Thirty-Seven Tales from the Konjaku Monogatari Collection* (Cambridge, Mass., 1959), and also D. E. Mills's to *A Collection of Tales from Uji: A Study and Translation of Uji Shūi Monogatari* (Cambridge, 1970).

3. See the essays by Eguchi Kiyoshi, Tanaka Jun, and Ishizaka Yohei, all collected in *Annai*, pp. 55–69.

4. Akutagawa's interest in Poe is borne out by the notes for his two lectures, "Poe as a Short Story Writer" and "One Aspect of Poe" (*Zenshu*, XIX, pp. 82–92), and by some of his stories, such as "The Case of a Modern Murder" (1918). See also Toyoda Minoru, "Akutagawa Ryunosuke and Edgar Allan Poe," *Bungaku Kenkyu* (January 1934).

5. See his appended essay to *Akutagawa Ryunosuke*, pp. 279–86.

6. Quoted in Yoshida, *Akutagawa Ryunosuke*, p. 279.

7. "Akutagawa Ryunosuke," *Annai*, pp. 177–78.

8. This tale and another, Akutagawa's partial source, do not appear in Jones's *Long Ago*. For the original tales used for "Rashomon," "The Nose," and "The Hell Screen," see Yuseido's annotated edition, *Akutagawa Ryunosuke*, ed. Yoshida Seiichi (Tokyo, 1963).

9. For an accurate description of corpses Akutagawa is said to have visited the Medical School (Yoshida, *Akutagawa Ryunosuke*, p. 64), and this visit is mentioned in "Cadavers," the ninth chapter of "The Life of a Fool."

10. Wada Shigejiro, *Akutagawa Ryunosuke* (Osaka, 1956), p. 39.

11. Iwakami Junichi, quoted in Yoshida, *Akutagawa Ryunosuke*, p. 63.

12. Quoted in Yoshida, *Akutagawa Ryunosuke*, p. 291. See also Inakaki Tatsuro, "Akutagawa Ryunosuke as a Historical Novelist," *Kenkyu* (A), pp. 155–71. Ogai's view of history is conveniently found in Chikuma Shobo edition, *Mori Ogai: Collected Stories* (Tokyo, 1953).

13. Cf. Shibukawa Gyo: "His exoticism finally ended in no more than an intellectual curiosity" ("Exoticism and Akutagawa," *Kenkyu* [A], p. 253). For a study of this period of Japanese history, see C. R. Boxer, *The Christian Century in Japan 1549–1650* (Berkeley, 1951).

14. In the postscript to this story Akutagawa cited a fictitious source which caused a great sensation among contemporary historians and collectors. See Yoshida, *Akutagawa Ryunosuke*, pp. 123–26.

15. The dramatic treatment of this celebrated vendetta is discussed in Shioya Sakae, *Chûshingura: An Exposition*, 2nd ed. (Tokyo, 1956).

16. The movie *Gate of Hell* is based on Kikuchi Kan's version. In this connection it is interesting to read Lafcadio Hearn's in *Glimpses of Unfamiliar Japan* (Boston & New York, 1894), II, pp. 577–78.

17. For the filmscript, see Kurosawa Akira and Hashimoto Shinobu, *Rashomon*, Film Book Series (New York, 1969).

18. The original version in the *Ujishui* reads:

Once upon a time there was a man called Ryōshu [Yoshihide], a painter of Buddhist subjects. A fire having broken out next door to his house, he ran out into the highway because the wind was blowing in his way. There was in his house a Buddha which someone had ordered. Also his clothes, his garments, his wife and children, etc. were in the house unthought of. Heedless of that, he made it his business simply to run out; and as he stood on the opposite side and looked the fire had already passed on to his house; and he gazed till the smoke and flames were thick, whereupon people came to condole saying: "What a pity." But he disturbed himself not. Though people wondered at him, he looked at the burning of his house, nodding and sometimes laughing, "Oh, what a gain I have made," he said. "Oh how badly I painted it for years!"

Then those who had come to condole him said: "What is this? What a pity it is that you should thus stand here. Are you possessed?" "Why should I be possessed?" said he scornfully laughing and continuing to stand there. "I had for years painted the Holy Fudō's flames badly. As I now look, I have understood that it is thus that fire burns. Ah, this is indeed a gain. Supposing I live having brought this art to perfection, I can have a hundred houses, if only I paint Buddha well" (Basil Hall Chamberlain's translation, quoted in W. H. H. Norman, *Hell Screen and Other Stories,* Tokyo, 1948, p. 8).

The other episode, from the *Kokin chobunshu,* features another painter called Hirotaka, and only its opening passage is relevant to Akutagawa's story: "Hirotaka, in his screen painting of hell, presented a demon from the tower piercing a man with his halberd; and seeing the scene so vivid and real, he said to himself: 'Perhaps my days are numbered.' Indeed not long after he passed away."

19. "Akutagawa Ryunosuke," *Annai,* p. 180.

20. Ishimitsu Shigeru, however, believes that the presence of this ambiguous narrator actually weakens the total effect of the story. See his study of "The Solitary Hell" and "The Hell Screen," *Kenkyu* (A), p. 270. In response to Kojima Masajiro's similar objection, Akutagawa wrote: "There is, I believe, something to be said for 'the explanatory element in the story.' My narration progresses as two lines of explanation intertwine. While the one takes the positive line to which belong many of your examples, the other proceeds negatively, continuously rejecting (actually affirming) the love relationship between the lord and Yoshihide's daughter. Inasmuch as both lines accentuate each other in building up the narration, neither can be taken out of the story" (Letter of June 18, 1918. *Zenshu,* XVI, pp. 257).

21. In a letter of November 20, 1918 Akutagawa also mentions his increasing fascination with the "civilized brutality" of the Chinese, a quality so abundant in such pornographic works as *Chin P'ien Mei* (*Zenshu,* XVI, pp. 273).

22. "Literature of Defeat," *Kenkyu* (B), pp. 148–49.

Noriko Mizuta Lippit (essay date 1980)

SOURCE: "From Tale to Short Story: Akutagawa's Toshishun and It's Chinese Origins," in *Reality and Fiction in Modern Japanese Literature,* M. E. Sharpe Inc., 1980, pp. 39–54.

[*In the following essay, Lippit argues that Akutagawa's use of traditional existing stories allows him to shift his focus away from the problems of modern storytelling and instead deal more directly with the story elements themselves.*]

Following in the path of Mori Ogai and Natsume Sōseki, writers whom he especially admired, Akutagawa Ryunosuke (1892–1927) started his writing by rejecting the confessional self-revelation and open self-search which characterized Japan's I-novelists, including the naturalistic writers like Katai and the idealistic Shirakaba writers. Akutagawa, who was also strongly influenced by Western fin-de-siècle literature, chose the short story as his form from the start, and studied Poe, Anatole France, de Maupassant, Gautier, and Merimée, among others.

Although the short story has been the dominant form in modern Japanese literature, it was often—particularly in realistic works—meant only to be a short form of the novel. In fact, the Japanese term *shōsetsu* is used to refer to both the novel and the short story. Such writers of the I-novel as Shiga Naoya (who wrote major novels) and Kajii Motojiro (who wrote short fiction exclusively) excelled in using the short-story form to present situations which led to the height of the author's or protagonist's perception and to a moment of profound realization in his daily-life experiences. Precisely for this reason, however, precisely because they used the short-story form to explore openly the self and life, centering on the protagonist-author's self-search and self-expression, the form of their short stories was no different from that of the novel, except in length. For writers pursuing self-growth, the novel is definitely a more suitable form, and even Kajii, who was devoted to the genre of the short story, turned to the novel just before his untimely death.

Akutagawa, on the other hand, approached the short story in a manner completely different from the I-novelists. First of all, the short story for him was a modern form of storytelling and had to center around the story element (the lack of which characterizes the work of the I-novelists). Second, the stories had to present a self-sufficient world of their own. The art of the short-story writer, therefore, had to concentrate on creating in the works a perfectly autonomous "architectural structure," to borrow Tanizaki's phrase (which, ironically, he used in his debate with Akutagawa).

The most characteristic feature of Akutagawa's short stories is the fact that they are based almost exclusively on other stories: classical tales, foreign tales, the works of other writers, and so forth. In other words, Akutagawa's short stories do not usually deal with human reality directly, but with materials which have already been fictionalized in tales or stories. On the rare occasions when he dealt with situations in his own experience, they were almost invariably limited to those in his childhood. He did deal with historical situations, learning much from Mori Ogai, but even there his interest was not in dealing with the actual human experience, but in the use of stories which had already been told in history.

The borrowing of old stories or the use of someone else's stories, immediately and on a superficial level, frees the writer from having to confront the epistemological question of how to know, grasp and present reality, a question which has been vital to modern fiction. The reality in Akutagawa's works is one or two steps removed from the reality of the author and the reader, and the reality in his twice-told tales is replaced by the "story," temporarily solving the problem of the relation between reality and art. Moreover, the story element, which he made central, helps to create the structure of the works and to make them self-contained. Their perfection can be evaluated in terms of the narrative structure, that is, by the art of storytelling and the extent to which the story presents a world complete in itself.

The borrowing of old stories also exempts the author from confronting directly the question of self-expression in his works. He is a storyteller, one whose business is to mediate between the readers and the story. Not only does the story give shape and boundaries to the world of his works, but it also defines the author's identity in relation to his works as a storyteller, both inside and outside the works. Akutagawa was amazingly unconcerned with the question of the relationship between the author and the work. He often appears openly as a narrator in his works (as in **"Rashomon"**), and the author as narrator is surprisingly free from self-consciousness in his intrusion into the world of the story.

Thus, the use of existing stories, particularly old stories, whose credibility the author did not have to defend, enabled Akutagawa to circumvent dealing directly in his works with the two vital problems of modern fiction, reality and self, and to avoid the deadlock which the I-novelists reached in dealing with these problems. In Akutagawa's short stories, the question of reality and fiction and that of their relation to the search for the self in literature are temporarily suspended because of the dominance of the story itself. In that world of story, the questions of reality and the self are converted into technical or aesthetic problems of narration.

This does not mean that Akutagawa lacked concern with the problems of reality and self or that he tried to avoid dealing with them. By borrowing stories and taking the reader away from the immediate reality, Akutagawa sought to present symbolic situations relevant to all human reality. A self-avowed literary cosmopolitan, Akutagawa was confident of the universal validity of his works, confident that his works transcended the particular time and place in which they were set. Most of Akutagawa's works deal with complex psychological situations that exist in human relations, and they often reveal his fundamental skepticism about human life and belief in the relativity of human relations. In other words, Akutagawa's borrowing of the stories was a device for dealing with the modern human situation and psychology. The borrowed story provided the distance of time and space which helped give universality to the situation with which he was dealing. In this sense, the story provided only a convenient framework.

Moreover, Akutagawa's consistent use of old stories, stories twice or thrice told, reveals his belief in or reliance on

archetypal literary themes and patterns of human life. Often in his stories, the narrator evades the responsibility even for being the witness or providing firsthand information on the story. By relying on the archetypal patterns of his stories, Akutagawa was able to expand his imagination to present his own story. In fact, his short stories are characterized by the exceptional integration of storytelling with the presentation of modern psychological reality.

In depending on earlier literary works, Akutagawa was certainly not alone among Japanese authors; such dependence has been one of the major techniques of Japanese (and Chinese) literature. Japanese fiction in particular, including the *monogatari, setsuwa* and short fiction of Saikaku and Ueda Akinari, has relied extensively on the use of earlier works as source materials. In utilizing earlier works, therefore, Akutagawa was only revitalizing a deep-rooted tradition of Japanese fiction, and in doing so, he countered the dominant trend of his time which treated the short story as a form of direct self-search and self-expression or as the presentation of a slice of life, a form without a story. In the Western short story too, the development of the modern genre involved liberal borrowing from earlier stories as, for example, in the case of Edgar Allan Poe, often regarded as the father of the modern short-story genre.

Furthermore, Akutagawa was far from indifferent to the question of self-expression or the author's ego. Indeed, he admired and envied Shiga Naoya and Goethe, both of whom openly exposed their internal lives as the materials for their literature and the subject of their literary pursuit. Considering himself a poet, Akutagawa was strongly inclined toward the pursuit of self-exultation and self-transcendence. His persistent concern with egotism, particularly the egotism of the artist, was reflected in various ways in his works, but most often in the recurring theme of conflict between the decadent pursuit of art and beauty and the humanistic acceptance of the self as part of humanity. **"Jigokuhen"** (**"The Hell Screen,"** 1918) is the most brilliant dramatization of the conflict. By assuming the role of a storyteller, therefore, Akutagawa was only wearing a mask which would hide the author's ego in the archetypal drama contained in the stories. In fact, it can be said that the development of modern fiction is the history of the authors' search for the appropriate masks in which to confess.

Mishima Yukio, who is the proper successor to Akutagawa in this respect, reveals plainly the mechanism of the confession of a mask. Unlike Mishima, however, Akutagawa was never successful in dramatizing the self in different personae; not only was the short-story form decidedly unsuitable for it, but also the narrative structure in which the narrator assumed the role of storyteller imposed inherent limitations on such dramatization.

The plot controversy between Akutagawa and Tanizaki, which took place in the last year of Akutagawa's life, sheds considerable light on these issues. In this dispute,

Akutagawa, almost negating his entire literary achievement, advocated the writing of stories without a story and the expression of the author's "poetic spirit" as the purpose of literary expression rather than the creation of an autonomous world of fiction with architectural beauty. The dispute took place at a point when Akutagawa's confidence as a storyteller was deeply shaken and he had come to doubt whether storytelling was an adequate form to provide the mask for the search for the self and the meaning of life. . . . Although it would be too simple to take his last work, **"Aru ahō no isshō" ("A Fool's Life,"** 1927), as a straight confessional, autobiographical work, the change of his literary stance and form of expression, the open and direct dealing with himself at the time of his mental crisis, only impresses us the more with his earlier effort to hide his vulnerable self under the mask of a story-teller.

Such critics as Saeki Shōichi have pointed out that Akutagawa's failure as a storyteller in his later years was due mainly to his failure to clarify the relation between the narrator and the author himself. Such modern writers as Henry James, Mauriac and Jean-Paul Sartre have long cast doubt on the ontological legitimacy of the author assuming the role of narrator, and in contemporary fiction, the narrator has become nothing but a fictional character. Akutagawa's turning to the story without a story, therefore, was only the result of his doubt about having the author assume the role of narrator and of his recognition of the problems which became acutely felt in the modernist era. Akutagawa was thus anticipating, in his later years, the direction which modern fiction itself would take.

In this sense, Akutagawa's early works present a happy union of storytelling and the presentation of the psychological or inner reality of human beings, a union between the architectural beauty of a self-sufficient, artificial world of art and the human condition. In other words, Akutagawa found in his stories, his twice-told tales which borrowed from earlier works, a means of overcoming the dichotomy between art and life, a dichotomy which was the major literary and aesthetic concern of the fin-de-siècle writers.

Akutagawa was an indefatigable experimenter in his expression and in his effort to develop the poetics of the short story. Each story, therefore, reveals not only his unending search for new materials, but also his awareness of the problems of narration. One of the genres he successfully developed was stories for young adults, the most representative of which is the famous **"Kumonoito" ("The Thread of the Spider's Web,"** 1915). He wrote about eleven such stories, all during the middle period of his writing career (1918–1924), a period in which he was especially concerned with the relations between art and life.

The Taisho period (1912–1926) was a time when stories for children were seriously pursued as a new genre. Such writers as Ogawa Mimei and Suzuki Miekichi turned completely to children's literature and led the movement to raise the genre to the level of art. Other writers, including Uno Koji, Kubota Mantaro and Sato Haruo, were also devoted to the genre. Akutagawa wrote the stories for young adults under the influence of Suzuki Miekichi, who was one of the pupils of Sōseki. Akutagawa's *dowa* (*Tales for Children*), like most of his other works, were based on a wide range of old and legendary stories, including Buddhist, classical Chinese and Japanese tales, and Western fairy tales. Since they were ostensibly written for young adults, however, they enabled Akutagawa to express more openly his own ethical views and attitude toward life, and his lyrical appraisal of innocence and purity.

"Toshishun," which was published in 1920 in *Akai Tori* (*The Red Bird*), a journal of children's literature edited by Suzuki Mickichi, is not only one of the masterpieces of children's literature but also occupies a significant place in Akutagawa's literature. The work is an adaptation of a tale, or *ch'uan-ch'i,* of T'ang China entitled "Tu Tzu-chun," which falls into a major category of supernatural tales in the *ch'uan-ch'i* genre. Although Akutagawa followed the basic plot and story of "Tu Tzu-chun," essentially retelling the story to young adults, by changing several key elements in the story he converted the Chinese tale into a quest-story of his own.

The original Chinese story is about a young man, Tu Tzu-chun, who dissipated his inheritance. A good-for-nothing wastrel who neglected all his duties, he is deserted by his relatives and friends when he loses his money. At this point he meets at the city gate an old man who gives him money to restore his former life of dissipation. When he again wastes his money within a few years, the same old man appears and gives him a still larger amount of money. He intends to do something good with the money, but the minute he receives it he resumes his decadent life. When he receives money for the third time, Tu Tzu-chun is determined to use it to promote public welfare, and after attending to his worldly affairs in this way, to place himself at the old man's disposal. After spending a year helping orphans and widows and contributing to the social good in other ways, he goes on the appointed day to see the old man at the appointed place. The old man takes him to his mansion on a mountain which penetrates deeply into the clouds. In the mansion there is a cauldron for making holy medicine. The old man, returning in his Taoist's clothing, tells Tu Tzu-chun not to utter a single word at the trials he is about to experience, for whatever he experiences will not be real.

Subsequently, Tu Tzu-chun is tortured by soldiers, attacked by ferocious animals, and tortured by monsters and ogres who boil him and cut up his limbs. Through all this, Tu Tzu-chun utters not a single word. Next his wife is brought before him and cut up inch by inch. Tzu-chun survives this too without saying anything. After this, Tzu-chun is killed and sent to hell. Having gone through the torture of hell, he is sent back to this world as a daughter of a family in Sung-chun. She is a mute woman who suffers pain and illness silently. A man marries her, and they have a son. Angered by his wife's remaining silent even when she sees their son, the husband bangs the son's head against a stone, cracking it. When she sees this, she feels love in her heart and utters, "A!" in spite of herself.

Tu Tzu-chun finds himself once more at the cauldron beside the old man. The old man is grieving and tells him that he failed to become immortal. He tells Tzu-chun that he was successful in repressing such human feelings as joy, anger, sorrow, fear and desire, but not love. He then sends Tzu-chun back to the world. Tzu-chun is ashamed of his failure to assist his benefactor and once more tries to seek him out to offer his services, but he can never find him again.

In the original Chinese tale, the life of man, searching vainly for unattainable immortality, is portrayed as absurd. The tale is filled with obvious Taoist ethical teachings. Tu Tzu-chun is not selected by the old man for the test because he is a Taoist interested in becoming an immortal, nor is he selected because he requested it. He goes through the test simply because he is "told" to do so. In the story, he is asked to find the old man deep in the mountains, and when he arrives, he is asked by the old man to sit down and neither to move nor to utter a single word. In other words, when he was put to the test, he knew nothing about the nature of the test and was therefore following the Taoist principle of purposelessness, or the Buddhist principle of mindlessness. The test was a direct experiment on human nature, and only human will, not intention, would help one succeed in it. In addition, Tzu-chun was selected because he had been a spend-thrift, a parallel of the prodigal son whose return was especially blessed because he had sinned.

The nature of the old man's test, therefore, can be understood as an ironic statement on the vulnerability of the human will, which is so closely connected to human relations with others. Success in the test—or rather, the attainment of immortality—lies in the elimination of all the human attachments which detain man so powerfully on the mortal level. The achievement of immortality, therefore, requires the filtration of all human sediments, enabling the protagonist to reach the realm of "non-man" and the ultimate "silence."

Tu Tzu-chun's being mute in the test is a second mask laid over the first, which is created by his conversion into a woman. Being a mother, he experiences the maternal human nature of love for his/her child. Being mute, however, he/she experiences an initial non-attachment to worldly matters. She grows up

> With incomparable beauty, but mute. Her family treated her as a born mute. There were indecent relatives who intimidated her in many ways, but she made no response.

In other words, being mute is a mask which protects her from responding to human experiences. Unfortunately, the mask is ripped asunder at the moment when she sees her child dashed to his death.

Although Akutagawa's **"Toshishun"** appears to follow "Tu Tzu-chun" quite faithfully, it differs from its source story in two fundamental respects. The first difference is in Toshishun's motive for leaving the human world; the second is in the attitude of the *sennin* (old man) toward Toshishun's attempt to become an immortal *sennin* himself.

In the original story, Tu Tzu-chun becomes ashamed of his wasteful life, and when he is made rich for the third time, he spends money for public welfare. Toshishun, to the contrary, never becomes ashamed of his life of luxury; nor does he spend any of the money he receives for the social benefit. Moreover, Akutagawa describes in detail the gorgeousness of Toshishun's life and the decadent beauty in which he indulges himself. This does not exist in the original. When the pensive Toshishun is asked by the old man whether it is the luxurious life itself that he has become tired of, he answers positively no and refuses to live a life of poverty. It is not a distaste for luxury that made him dissatisfied with life, but the fact that he had "given up on man." He then asks the *sennin* to make him his pupil and to train him to be a *sennin* of high virtue, to enable him to transcend human life. Tu Tzu-chun, on the other hand, wishes to place himself at the Taoist's disposal, to assist him in making an elixir, in order to return the favor the Taoist did for him. Moreover, this takes place after Tzu-chun has established himself as a virtuous and respectable social existence, restoring his respect as a human being. Although both Tzu-chun and Toshishun were disillusioned by people who were nice to them when they were rich and deserted them when they were poor, Tzu-chun's return of the favor is fundamentally different from Toshishun's despair over humanity as far as the motive for leaving the human world is concerned.

From the start, Akutagawa's **"Toshishun"** presents the languid, melancholy air of a decadent life, and Toshishun is portrayed as a man who, disillusioned with the pursuit of beauty and luxury, searches for the meaning of life. Akutagawa's opening narration conveys this sense immediately:

> It was a spring day; nightfall was approaching. At the west gate of Lo Yang, the capital of T'ang, a young man was gazing vacantly up at the sky.

Then he describes a busy street of this gorgeous, prosperous city, contrasting it with the lonely, pensive Toshishun who stands leaning against the gate, looking vacantly at the sky. When the old man appears before Toshishun, he asks him what he is thinking. Toshishun just answers him, "Me? I was thinking about what I should do, since I do not even have a place to sleep tonight." In the original, the old man hears Tzu-chun's complaint about his cold-hearted friends and relatives, and offers him money.

Akutagawa's Toshishun is, indeed, a decadent hero, who, turning his back on morality, has stoically pursued a life of beauty and luxury and become disillusioned by his pursuit. He is presented as a quester-hero, who, having seen and been disgusted with everything about men and life, desires to transcend human life, to be above human beings. He is not a naive Tzu-chun who is simply weak at the temptation of luxury and a lazy life and has just learned a lesson about the selfishness of people. Through his experiences, Tzu-chun turns into a morally and socially respectable man, even an honorable man who does not forget to show his gratitude by returning the favor done him. What Toshishun learns is disillusionment with human life.

Akutagawa wrote two other works which contain the story of a man who was made rich instantly by meeting a wizard. The first of these, **"The Sennin"** (1914), also takes place in China. One of his earliest works, it is a story about a street magician who endures poverty and rigorous training for the moment of glory when his skill in his art will reach its height and the audience will throw him money in excitement. At the end of the story, the protagonist, his performance over, is walking on the deserted street, his magic tools on his shoulder, wet in the evening drizzle. He meets an old man to whom he tells his life's sufferings and hardships, and the old man, who is a wizard, makes him rich instantly. In another story of the same title written in 1922, an honest idiot who wishes to become an immortal works without pay for a greedy doctor who promises to make him one at the end of a long period of service. Although the doctor has no power to make him an immortal, the doctor's wife suggests at the end of the promised years of service that he try flying, and the idiot flies away as an immortal. It is evident, therefore, that the theme of **"Toshishun"** was one with which Akutagawa was consistently concerned.

Akutagawa was obsessed with the theme of the "condensed life," a life comprised of moments of intense feeling. His often-quoted saying that life is not worth a line of Baudelaire's poetry indicates not only his ideal of art for art's sake, but also his desire for a short but brilliant life. "Fireworks in a dark sky" was how he envisioned his own life. Indeed, many of Akutagawa's protagonists risk the destruction of their social and moral integrity for the sake of brilliant, intense moments of experience. One of Akutagawa's masterpieces for young adults, **"Torokko"** (**"The Truck,"** 1922), describes a boy who pursued the excitement of coasting downhill in a truck (a coal-car on rails). He offers to help miners push the truck up the hill for the thrill of coming down. After the pursuit of excitement, he finds out that he has come too far away from home to return in the daylight. The story ends with a brilliant description of the boy running back home in fear, barefooted in the twilight, and of his outburst of crying when he finally reaches home.

Akutagawa's Toshishun pursues a life of luxury and beauty at the risk of his social and moral destruction, and his gorgeous, decadent life is not the result of his weakness as in the case of Tu Tzu-chun. He has no intention of living the long and dull life of a morally upright, socially respectable

philanthropist. When he becomes disillusioned with the life he envisioned, he desires to leave human life, to go beyond human experience. His request to the *sennin* to make him a *sennin* too, therefore, is a quest for an above-human existence, not an effort to return the wizard's favor. The ordeal he goes through—the same maintenance of silence in the face of physical and mental agony—is clearly a trial through which a quester-hero must pass to attain his ideal. The tortures which Toshishun has to bear are much more simple than those to which Tu Tzu-chun is subjected. The wife does not appear at all, and he is not reincarnated as a woman. Although both heroes break their oaths because of concern for loved ones, in Toshishun's case it is the torturing of his parents in hell that he finally cannot bear and that causes him to break his silence.

The ending of **"Toshishun"** is also fundamentally different from that of the original. Both stories are about the failure to attain immortality, the transcendence of human life, because of human love. Although both Tzu-chun and Toshishun fail in the face of human love, however, Toshishun's happiness with his failure contrasts sharply with Tzu-chun's shame. Above all, the *sennin* in Akutagawa's **"Toshishun"** tells Toshishun that if he had not said anything when his parents were in agony, he would have killed Toshishun instantly. The Taoist monk in "Tu Tzu-chun," on the other hand, laments over Tzu-chun's failure and sends him back to the world. Tzu-chun tries again to transcend human existence, while Toshishun is reborn as a new human being with a new vision of life. He decides to live truthfully as a human being, and the *sennin* assists him in doing so by giving him a house with a plot of land for farming.

> "If you had remained silent, I was determined to take your life instantly. I imagine you no longer wish to be a *sennin*. You have already become disgusted with the life of a rich man. Then what do you think you would like to be from now on?"
>
> "Whatever I become, I intend to live an honest life, a humane life." In Toshishun's voice there was a tone of cheerfulness which hitherto was absent.
>
> "Do not forget your word. Then I will not see you again from today." Tekkanshi [the *sennin*] began walking away while saying this, but he suddenly stopped and turned to Toshishun, adding cheerfully,
>
> "Oh, fortunately I just remembered that I have a house at the southern foot of Taizan [Taishan]. I will give you the house together with the plot of land next to it for farming. Go and live there. Just now peach flowers must be in bloom all around the house."

Toshishun attains his desire to be human, and his quest for a meaningful life ends with his regaining trust in humanity. Here immortality is the negation of humanity, and Toshishun learns the value of being human through his effort to become immortal. The *sennin*, representing the point of view of the story, maintains that it is not worthwhile to attain immortality by negating humanity.

The dichotomy between immortality and humanity is the central theme of both the Chinese and Japanese stories.

The Taoist monk in "Tu Tzu-chun" tells Tzu-chun that he successfully conquered all human feelings except love. Tzu-chun's failure is that of a common Chinese pursuing immortality. His trial is not a heroic quest because the tale lacks the grandeur to portray him as a hero. Indeed, it emphasizes Tzu-chun's awareness of a sense of shame when he is thrice financed by the old man, but only to add to his personality the element of human dignity, a virtue perhaps, but one of common mortals. His failure shows the existence of an unbridgeable gap between the realm of mortals and the realm of immortals. The harder human beings try to attain the unattached immortal realm, the more they realize their unbreakable ties to their human surroundings. This is why the Taoist monk finally sighs:

> "Alas, how hard it is to find the talent with the potential to become immortal! I can make my medicine once again, but you will have to go back to the human world. I wish you well."

Both the Taoist monk and Tu Tzu-chun consider the pursuit of immortality to be positive, and there is no moral statement in "Tu Tzu-chun" with regard to humanity. But Akutagawa, by contrast, tells us that it is not human to conquer love, and that we should be human.

Akutagawa's **"Toshishun"** thus is a story of a quest for the meaning of life, a quest which leads to humanity itself. Humanity is weighed against immortality and art, or the decadent life which pursues art for art's sake. Toshishun's attempt to attain immortality was doomed from the start, for the *sennin* would not have granted it in any event, even if he had remained silent until the end. Therefore he did not fail the trial, but passed it. His quest was actually for humanity, and his attempt at immortality was a necessary part of his quest.

It is worth noting here that in a Ming version of "Tu Tzu-chun" which appears in *Hsing shih heng yen* (*Lasting Words to Awaken the World*), collected by Feng Meng-lung in 1627, Tzu-chun does finally attain immortality with his wife in the most glamorous manner, even after failing the test. The change may be attributable to the storytelling tradition in which the storyteller always attempts to satisfy his audience, mainly unsophisticated merchants and commoners, with a happy ending. Indeed Tzu-chun's attainment of immortality in the Ming version appears more ludicrous than instructive. The Taoist monk, instead of retaining his identity as a symbol of higher transcendence, becomes Lao Tzu, the Taoist god commonly known to lay followers of the Taoist religion. Consequently, the story is degraded to a mere instance of Taoist didacticism, advising people to give away their belongings to achieve immortality. Compared to the T'ang tale, the Ming version lacks tragic intensity.

In contrast to the original "Tu Tzu-chun," Akutagawa's **"Toshishun"** has a clear message for the reader: To learn the value of being human is the meaning of life; to be human means to be true to one's feelings and to accept the life of emotions. The humble recognition of joy and sorrow, and submission to love as the substance of human life is what saved Toshishun from the life of decadence and inhuman immortality. The *sennin* in the story is a moral teacher. Among art, immortality and life (humanity), humanity receives the highest value. When he wrote **"Toshishun,"** Akutagawa had just finished writing **"The Hell Screen,"** whose central theme is the conflict between art and life. The painter in the story sacrifices love and human life for the sake of art. The work of art which was produced through this negation of humanity, however, stands as a brilliantly true work of art. Akutagawa condemns the artist as a human being, but never dismisses the value of his art, which demands perfection and purity in the sacrifice of human emotion. In **"The Hell Screen,"** therefore, the dichotomy between art and life is left unsolved. In **"Toshishun,"** the conflicts presented are among the selfish pursuit of beauty (art), the transcendence of life (immortality), and humanity (life). Akutagawa clearly states that the aspiration for humanity is more valuable than the other two.

Akutagawa was torn between art and life throughout his life. Unlike Tanizaki, who chose to live in a way that would serve his art, and Shiga Naoya, who used art to attain a higher realization of life, Akutagawa despaired of life in human society from his early years and wished to live the condensed life of a line of poetry, while remaining aware of and torn by the sacrifice of humanity such a life would demand.

In one of his later works, **"Shūzan zu"** (**"The Autumn Mountain,"** 1921), Akutagawa even considers art to be an illusion; a masterpiece of art is certainly the product of man's imagination dreaming of the ideal, perfect beauty, but the actual work may not exist at all. The conflict between art and life presented in the case of **"The Hell Screen"** no longer exists here. Art is meaningful not because of itself but because man aspires for it. The question of realism Akutagawa raised in **"The Hell Screen,"** the question of the artist's need to see reality in order to paint it, is also dismissed here. The significance of art is reduced to the point of denying art, for art without visible work is no longer art. **"Toshishun"** reflects Akutagawa's turning toward life, moving away from his belief in art for art's sake.

The central theme of **"Toshishun"** is indeed a theme in Akutagawa's own life as an artist. In the place of realism and confession, Akutagawa used an old tale to dramatize his own search. He thus converted the classical Chinese tale into a short story which contained his own quest and his own clear message. By confining the work clearly within the framework of the ancient tale and directing it to young adults, Akutagawa was able to avoid being didactic despite the existence of a moral. In **"Toshishun,"** Akutagawa successfully combined brilliant storytelling with the presentation of a symbolic situation in which the quest of modern man can be dramatized. In his search for a method to dramatize his quest for reality and self, Akutagawa revived the tradition of storytelling in fiction, a tradition which had been lost in the era of modern realism and naturalism.

Donald Keene (essay date 1984)

SOURCE: "Akutagawa Ryunosuke," in *Dawn to the West: Japanese Literature of the Modern Era,* Henry Holt and Company, 1984, pp. 556–93.

[*In the following essay, Keene presents an overview of Akutagawa's short stories and his place in modern fiction.*]

The most striking literary figure of the fifteen years of the Taishō era was Akutagawa Ryūnosuke (1892–1927). He established his reputation early in his brief career, and even when his style and manner had greatly changed he retained his hold on the mass of readers. His short stories, especially those of the early period, have acquired the status of classics, and are read in the schools and frequently reprinted. He was also the first modern Japanese writer to attract wide attention abroad, and most of his important works have been translated. His writings, together with those of Natsume Sōseki and Mori Ōgai, "constitute the basic elements in the literary background of modern Japanese."[1]

Akutagawa was born in Tokyo, the son of a dairyman named Niihara Toshizō. Most of his father's customers were foreigners, and that, no doubt, was why the Niiharas were one of only three Japanese families living in the Irifune foreign concession. It has often been suggested that Akutagawa's fascination with the exotic reflected this early background, but considering that he left the foreign concession when still an infant, this seems improbable. About seven months after Akutagawa was born his mother went insane, and she remained in this condition until her death in 1902. In the autobiographical stories written toward the end of his life Akutagawa often referred to his mother. **"Tenkibo"** (**"Death Register,"** 1926), the most revealing account, opens in this fashion:

> My mother was a madwoman. I never once experienced anything resembling maternal affection from her. She would always be sitting by herself in the family house in Shiba, her hair twisted around a comb, puffing away at a long-stemmed pipe. Her face and body were both very small. Her face—I can't explain this—was always an ashen color, with no suggestion of living vitality. . . .
>
> My mother never looked after me in any way. I remember that once when I went upstairs to her room with my foster mother to say a word of greeting, if nothing else, she suddenly hit my head with her pipe. But most of the time my mother was an extremely well-behaved lunatic.[2]

Akutagawa was adopted by his mother's brother after she went insane, and that is why he took her maiden name.

The aunt who became his foster mother and a maiden aunt who lived with her treated the child with affection, and the atmosphere of his adopted home was cultured, quite unlike that of his real father; but Akutagawa's references to his mother in his most personal works reveal how deeply he was affected by his loss, and how constrained he felt whenever he recalled the circumstances of his adoption. The fear of insanity, which at the time was believed to be directly attributable to heredity, constantly haunted him; he alluded to his insane mother in a suicide note.

As a child Akutagawa excelled in his studies and became an avid reader, at first of Japanese and Chinese classics, such as Bakin's *Biographies of Eight Dogs* and *Shui Hu Chuan (Water Margin)* in Bakin's adaptation; later of such middle-Meiji writers as Ozaki Kōyō and Kōda Rohan; and eventually of near contemporaries like Izumi Kyōka, Natsume Sōseki, and Mori Ōgai. His tastes in European literature, formed while in high school, included the works of Maupassant, Anatole France, Strindberg, and Dostoevski. Elements in his stories have been traced to all these readings.

In 1913 Akutagawa entered the English Literature Department at Tokyo Imperial University and soon afterward began to publish in the third series of *Shinshichō (New Thought Tides)*, a university literary magazine, beginning with his translation (from an English version) of France's "Balthasar." He himself later referred slightingly to his still immature style, but it was in fact more distinguished than that employed by most translators at the time. His first original story, **"Rōnen"** (**"Old Age,"** 1914), which also appeared in *Shinshichō*, already suggested the crisp, precise style of his major works.[3]

An unhappy love affair in 1914–1915 led Akutagawa to neglect his university studies in favor of unrelated readings, in the effort to find distraction from his woes. He later described the genesis of his first two successful stories in these terms:

> The stories I wrote at the time, in my study which [with its clutter of books] was like a symbol of my mind, were **"Rashōmon"** and **"The Nose."** As the result of a love affair that had dragged on unhappily for six months, I felt depressed whenever I was alone so, by way of reaction, I wanted to write stories that would be as remote as possible from my circumstances at the time and as cheerful as possible. That is how I happened to write these two stories, borrowing my materials from *Konjaku Monogatari*. I only published one, **"Rashōmon";** the other, **"The Nose,"** I broke off halfway through and did not finish for some time.[4]

If **"Rashōmon"** really seemed like a "cheerful" story to Akutagawa, it is not hard to imagine the depths of his depression! It is noteworthy, in any case, that Akutagawa at this time did not use his writings to express even indirectly his personal circumstances. Unlike the case of many modern Japanese writers, it is possible to discuss these works without reference to Akutagawa's life.

"Rashōmon" appeared in the November 1915 issue of *Teikoku Bungaku (Imperial Literature)*, another Tokyo Imperial University literary magazine. Akutagawa's friends were merciless in their criticism; one even wrote him a letter, urging Akutagawa to give up writing altogether.[5] Such criticism induced him to make various alterations in the manuscript, mainly deletions in the interest of concision,[6] but it is extraordinary that Akutagawa's closest friends should have been so insensitive to what became one of his most popular and admired stories.

The description of the Rashōmon gate in *Konjaku Monogatari,* the twelfth-century collection of tales from which Akutagawa had derived his basic material, is extremely brief, only a dozen or so lines; he augmented it from other sources. The setting of "Rashōmon" is Kyoto in the twelfth century, when the great buildings of the capital were sometimes broken up for firewood, and desperate men turned to banditry or even murder in order to stay alive in a time of disorder and violence. Akutagawa's "Rashōmon" opens as a man (described as an "underling") takes shelter from a rainstorm at the great gate at the southern entrance to the capital. The man has reluctantly reached the conclusion that he may have to become a bandit, but as yet has committed no crime. He climbs to the upper story of the gate and finds there an old woman squatting amid corpses, victims of an epidemic. The old woman is pulling out one by one the hairs from the head of a corpse lying before her. She intends to make a wig she can sell. This horrifying sight destroys the man's last compunctions. He rips the filthy rags the old woman is wearing from her body and rushes off to sell them, a criminal now like the others. The old woman stares as he disappears into the distance.

The story is given its effectiveness by the vividness of Akutagawa's evocation of the age, as much as by the details he found in *Konjaku Monogatari*. He borrowed also from the descriptions in *Hōjōki (An Account of My Hut)* of the famine and other disasters of the time, but it is apparent on examination that his story owed comparatively little to such borrowings; the psychology of the man and the overtones of the story owe more to Akutagawa's readings in European literature.[7] Akutagawa some years later explained why he had set such works as "Rashōmon," which are essentially modern in outlook, in the distant Japanese past:

> Supposing I have thought of some particular theme and decide to write a story about it. In order to express this theme as artistically and strikingly as possible, I must include unusual incidents. The more unusual the incidents, the harder it will be to describe them convincingly as events of present-day Japan. If an author nevertheless insists on making a modern story out of such events, it generally seems unnatural to readers, and the result is that his carefully chosen theme drops by the wayside. A short story, unlike a fairy tale, has certain requirements peculiar to the genre; the author simply cannot write "once upon a time" and let the background go at that. In practice this means that something akin to restrictions of period are established, and it becomes necessary therefore to introduce social conditions of the time, at least to the degree of satisfying the requirement that the story seem natural and plausible. Stories of this kind can be distinguished from "historical novels" in that they in no sense aim at a re-creation of the past. I might mention in this connection that—as the reader will easily guess from the above—I feel no great yearning for the past even when I write about distant times. I am far luckier to have been born in present-day Japan than in the Heian or Edo periods.[8]

Most of Akutagawa's popular stories were set in the past. His favorite historical periods were the twelfth century, when Kyoto was wasted by disasters; the late sixteenth century, when Christian influence was at its height in Nagasaki; and the beginning of the Meiji era, when European culture was uncritically adopted, especially in Tokyo, the new capital. Akutagawa was always at pains to create an impression of verisimilitude by supplying details—often harsh or cruel—drawn directly from accounts in such works as *Konjaku Monogatari*. Sometimes his fondness for unusual effects (suggested by the passage quoted above) induced him to indulge in sensationalism. When this method was successful, as in "Rashōmon" and a dozen other stories, Akutagawa created unforgettable vignettes of the past, as filtered through the mind of a modern Japanese who knew Western literature well. Sometimes he tried too hard. One of his longest stories, "Chūtō" ("The Bandits," 1917), is set in the same period as "Rashōmon," and opens with the description of a sultry summer day in Kyoto:

> The tracks of an ox-cart that had passed by not long before wound off into the distance. A small snake, run over by the cart, for a time had twitched its tail, the flesh of its gaping wound turning green, but now it lay motionless, not a scale stirring, its greasy belly exposed. If there was one spot of moisture visible on this dusty street, under the burning sky, it was the raw-smelling, putrescent liquid oozing from the snake's wound.[9]

The snake, a symbol of the city of Kyoto, mortally wounded and festering, recurs again and again in the story, together with another symbolic figure, a sick woman, apparently a victim of the epidemic, who lies more dead than alive in a wretched hut, her body marked by toothmarks from ravenous hounds. Some children find the snake lying in the dust, and a mischievous little boy slings it into the sick woman's hut. "The greenish, greasy belly slapped against the woman's cheek, and the tail, wet with putrescent liquid, slid over her face."[10]

The reader is sooner or later numbed by the reiteration of such details, and the rest of the story is on the same level. Akutagawa's evaluation of this story was given in a letter written in March 1917:

> "The Bandits" is terrible. It's like a cheap picture book. There's one scene in which somebody tries to force a pregnant woman to swallow an aborticide. People will wonder if I can be serious. And there are lots of other idiotic implausibilities. The characteriza-

tion is utterly inconsistent. When I was sick in bed with a fever the grain of the wood of the ceiling looked like marble, but now it merely looks like wood. That's the difference between before and after writing **"The Bandits."** It's my worst work.[11]

Akutagawa's inability to make something more impressive of his longest story suggests his limitations as a writer, and clearly demonstrates that a mere accumulation of the kind of details that made **"Rashōmon"** memorable was not enough to make a work succeed.

Not all of Akutagawa's early stories are in this ghastly vein. His first popular success, in fact, was scored with **"Hana"** (**"The Nose,"** 1916), an amusing story of a priest whose nose is five or six inches long, and of his efforts to shorten the nose. He eventually finds a painful but effective method, only to discover that people, who previously had sympathized with him for the misfortune of having such an extraordinary nose, were now laughing at him for his vanity. Depressed by this unexpected result, he becomes disagreeable toward all around him, especially the priest who helped shorten the nose. One night he feels a swelling in his nose, and the next morning it is once again its former length. The priest is relieved, sure that nobody will laugh at him now.

"The Nose" was also derived from *Konjaku Monogatari,* and there may have been influence from Gogol's story **"The Nose"** (1835). But the composition as a whole owes much to Akutagawa's ability to combine the grotesque and the humorous without being too obvious. Natsume Sōseki read the work in *Shinshichō* and was so impressed that he wrote Akutagawa a letter expressing his admiration. The story was subsequently reprinted in the major literary review *Shinshōsetsu* (*New Fiction*), marking the beginning of Akutagawa's fame.

Praise from Sōseki was undoubtedly more welcome than from any other source. Sōseki, the commanding figure in the literary world, had gathered around him a circle of disciples, some of whom later became well-known writers and critics. Akutagawa had admired Sōseki ever since he was a middle-school student, and early in December 1915 he and his friend, the novelist Kume Masao (1891–1952), finally mustered the courage to attend one of Sōseki's regular Thursday afternoon sessions with his disciples. From then on Akutagawa went fairly often, though he confessed that he was so hypnotized by Sōseki's presence that he was almost incapable of relaxing and enjoying the experience.[12] Sōseki's letter, written in February 1916, praised the novelty of the materials, the skill of his terse style, and Akutagawa's ability to be humorous without forcing. He urged Akutagawa to write more stories in the same vein, cautioning him that he must not worry even if **"The Nose"** failed at first to attract much attention. Sōseki predicted that if Akutagawa could write twenty or thirty such stories he would establish an absolutely unique reputation. He urged Akutagawa to follow his own path without taking into account the possible reactions of the mass of readers.[13]

Akutagawa was grief-stricken when Sōseki died in December 1916, just a year after Akutagawa's first visit, and in later years he sometimes returned to the study where Sōseki had received him, in order to renew old memories.[14] Critics have claimed to detect resemblances between Sōseki's late works and those stories by Akutagawa that deal with the problem of egoism.[15] In **"Karenoshō"** (**"Withered Fields,"** 1918), for example, Akutagawa described Bashō's disciples gathered around the bedside of their dying master in these terms:

> Even as they were watching over the last moments of their teacher, each was absorbed with thoughts of possible repercussions of the master's death on other schools, the advantages and disadvantages to his own pupils, and similar calculations of self-interest that were not directly related to their master, now in his last moments. . . . The disciples were grieving not for their teacher but for themselves, for having lost their teacher.[16]

Such analyses of self-interest had preoccupied Sōseki, but egoism as a theme need not have been learned from Sōseki: no writer has gone beyond La Rochefoucauld in detecting the base considerations that influence people even when they seem to be acting in the most disinterested or noble manner. Clearly Akutagawa had his own personal interest in the problem of egoism, but it may have been because of Sōseki that he continued to emphasize it as a theme of his writings.

Typical of this interest is one of Akutagawa's most celebrated stories, the brief **"Kumo no Ito"** (**"The Spider's Thread,"** 1918), about the robber Kandata who, after his death, has sunk to the deepest recess of hell for his many crimes. The all-merciful Buddha, hoping to save even such a man, recalls that Kandata once spared the life of a spider that had crossed his path. He causes the spider to spin a single thread that extends far down into hell. Kandata, in the Sea of Blood, notices the thread and starts to climb it; but even as he is making his way up the immense distance separating hell from heaven, he sees that other sinners are behind him, climbing the same thread. Fearful lest the thread break under their weight, Kandata orders the others to let go of his thread. At that moment the thread breaks, plunging all, including Kandata, back into hell. But for his egoism not only he but the others would have been saved.

Akutagawa was more conspicuously influenced by Mori Ōgai. The style of his early works is so indebted to Ōgai's that one critic believed it would be more accurate to speak of imitation, rather than of influence.[17] This critic, the novelist Nakamura Shin'ichirō, went on to state:

> Akutagawa Ryūnosuke's special virtue as a new writer lay, more than in anything else, in his dry, intellectual manner of dealing with his subjects. The strongest influence Mori Ōgai exerted on Akutagawa, in fact, was embedded in the very foundations of Akutagawa's creative formation as an author. It may be detected, for example, in the way he preserved his distance from his subjects. If this analysis is correct, it means that Ōgai

handed over to Akutagawa the key for unlocking the secrets of modern literature, and that *Ōgai created Akutagawa*. In that case, this event brought about an important advance in the stages of the Japanese absorption of Western literature.[18]

Letters from Akutagawa to his friends written as early as 1913 plainly reveal with what special interest he read Ōgai's historical fiction.[19] The attitudes the two men adopted with respect to historical materials were, however, fundamentally quite dissimilar. Ōgai's historical fiction, even at its freest, never ignored historical fact, but Akutagawa used the past mainly as the springboard for elaborations and inventions, and he was attracted to distant times and places because of the possibilities they afforded to treat the unusual, the supernatural, or the miraculous. His art has been compared to that of the waka poets of the past who, borrowing some theme familiar from earlier poetry, imparted to it their distinctive, modern sensibility.[20]

The success of **"The Nose"** encouraged Akutagawa to write other historical works with comic overtones. The most popular was **"Imogayu"** (**"Yam Gruel,"** 1916), the first work he wrote after his graduation from Tokyo Imperial University. Like so many other early stories, **"Yam Gruel"** had its origins in *Konjaku Monogatari* (*Stories of Times Now Long Ago*), but Akutagawa's ironic attitude toward his materials owed little to this source.[21] This is the story of Goi, a scruffy, minor official who normally eats mainly the leavings from the banquets of his superiors. Goi's dream is to eat his fill of yam gruel, a dish that was probably more appetizing than it sounds. Another official, a rough and powerful man, promises to provide Goi with all the yam gruel he can eat. The two men travel a great distance to the other man's estate where, as promised, an immense quantity of yam gruel is prepared for Goi's delectation. But the sight of so much yam gruel quite takes away Goi's appetite; as so often in Akutagawa's stories, the realization of a dream brings not satisfaction but disillusionment.

Akutagawa was obviously not interested in presenting a convincing portrayal of life among the petty officials of the late Heian period. Goi is a not unfamiliar figure in contemporary society, and his disillusion is described in the literary works of every country; no doubt it was this universality that so appealed to Akutagawa in the theme. Sōseki wrote Akutagawa his impressions of **"Yam Gruel"** not long after it appeared. He found the plot "too labored," and the style overingenious. But he praised Akutagawa's techniques, saying they were second to no writer's.[22] Akutagawa's mastery of the short story won him an exceptionally large following for so young a writer, but he was most often admired for his faults: the overingenuity that Sōseki criticized, his seeming inability to resist adding a surprise ending where none was needed.

Another, more crucial weakness was Akutagawa's lack of originality. He was likened, even by admiring critics, to a mosaicist, piecing together fresh masterpieces out of the materials gleaned from many books. Sometimes the list of

"sources" for a single story, as uncovered by diligent scholars, is so extensive that one can only marvel that any author could fuse together so many disparate elements. Even the miniscule **"The Spider's Thread"** was apparently derived from two entirely distinct sources, a section of the Buddhist canon as described in an American work, *The History of the Devil and the Idea of Evil from Earliest Times to the Present Day* by Paul Carus, and an anecdote related in *The Brothers Karamazov*.[23] The longer **"Hōkyōjin no Shi"** (**"Death of a Martyr,"** 1918) apparently was indebted to *Jocelyn* by Lamartine, *Le crime de Sylvestre Bonnard* by Anatole France, *Vengeance* by Henri de Régnier, Mori Ōgai's translation of *Improvisatoren* by Hans Christian Andersen, *Quo Vadis* by Henryk Sienkiewicz, Friederich Hebbel's play *Judith,* and various Japanese works.[24] It may be hard to believe that *all* these influences are present in a story only ten pages long in most editions, but there is no question that Akutagawa relied more on books than on his imagination or his personal experiences when writing the short stories of this period. Later in his career a seeming inability to invent materials forced him to draw on even the most trivial incidents of his life. One critic went so far as to suggest that despair over his lack of imaginative resources may have been an important cause of Akutagawa's suicide.[25]

Too much should not be made, however, of Akutagawa's reliance on foreign sources. Even when a scholar has identified to his own satisfaction the origins of some section of an Akutagawa story, there is generally no question of direct imitation. Shimada Kinji, for example, believed that the climactic scene in Akutagawa's story **"Jigokuhen"** (**"Hell Screen,"** 1918)—the burning alive of a beautiful woman in a court carriage—was inspired by the novel by D. S. Merezhkovski, *The Forerunner, the Romance of Leonardo da Vinci*. Shimada's arguments are persuasive, but even if a Japanese translation of Merezhkovski's novel inspired Akutagawa, his central theme—that the artist must personally experience what he describes, though this may entail the most terrible sacrifices—was surely Akutagawa's conviction anyway. The apparent identification of the author with Yoshihide, the painter in **"Hell Screen,"** gives this story a moving quality absent from most other works of this period, however skillfully constructed or stylistically distinguished.[26]

"Gesaku Zammai" (**"A Life Spent at Frivolous Writing,"** 1917) is also an account of the trials an artist suffers. The aged novelist Bakin is the central figure, and the action takes place in 1831, mainly at a public bath in Edo. Akutagawa derived his information about the personal life of Takizawa Bakin (1767–1848) from the selections from Bakin's diaries published in 1911. He conveyed very well Bakin's feelings after a lifetime devoted to writing gesaku fiction, but he was totally uninterested in suggesting more than the psychological aspects of the material found in the diaries. He even disregarded the startling fact that Bakin so detested going to the public bath that he never went more than five or six times a year.[27] Akutagawa, it will be recalled, read Bakin's works with great admiration as a boy, and that may be why he chose him as a convenient figure to whom he could ascribe his own views on literature and his own attitudes toward his admirers, detractors, and publishers. In a letter written in 1922 Akutagawa wrote,

> I have read your kind words about **"A Life Spent at Frivolous Writing."** I would be glad if you interpreted my Bakin as merely a figure I have borrowed to express my own feelings. . . . I believe that such an experiment is justifiable, but if people think it is wrong to distort historical facts, I think I can defend myself. I might mention also that at present I do not consider the writing of tanka and haiku to be an unworthy occupation for a man.[28]

The last remark refers to a passage in the story where Bakin explains why he does not write poetry.

> He did not suppose he was incapable of composing waka or hokku; he felt quite confident that he was sufficiently informed on matters of poetic technique. However, he had long since felt a kind of contempt for forms of arts that were too short to permit him to pour himself entirely into them. No matter how skillfully a waka or a hokku might be composed, it could not express more than a few lines of one of his novels, whether a disclosure of human emotions or a description of nature. Such art, as far as he was concerned, was second-class.[29]

It might be mentioned in passing that Akutagawa wrote not only waka and hokku but even the archaic *sedōka,* as well as modern poetry. These compositions have been much praised, and Akutagawa was proud of his poetry, but he was essentially a prose writer, and that may be why he attributed such comments to Bakin.

At one point in **"A Life Spent at Frivolous Writing"** Bakin overhears a customer at the bathhouse abuse his writings:

> In the first place, Bakin uses only the tip of his brush, as if he had nothing whatsoever behind it. Even if he has, it's probably nothing more than the kind of pedantry you might expect from a country schoolmaster expounding on the Four Books and the Five Classics. He still hasn't learned a thing about what's going on in the world today. The proof of it is that he's never once written about anything except what happened a long time ago.[30]

This was precisely the kind of criticism to which Akutagawa himself had been exposed, especially from the Naturalists, but like Bakin in the story, he was not easily swayed by such criticism; his distance from his materials in fact gives Akutagawa's early stories their unchanging appeal.

Another of Bakin's tormentors, his publisher, visits Bakin after he has returned home from the bath. The man talks familiarly about the various writers he publishes, comparing Bakin unfavorably to Shunsui, who writes much faster,

or to Tanehiko, whose works have more appeal. Bakin, unable to bear the man's impertinent chatter, retorts, "Shunsui and I are not the same kind of man." He calls the maid and informs her that the publisher is leaving.

A last visitor, a welcome one, is the painter Watanabe Kazan. Bakin expresses his envy of painters because they need not worry about the censors, a source of fear for writers of the day, but he is confident that long after the censors are forgotten his masterpieces will still be read. After Kazan leaves, Bakin turns back to his manuscript, which looks more and more like a disaster, and his little grandson enters the room. A surge of love for the child restores Bakin's courage to face the manuscript again. His brush begins to write almost of its own, and he feels the joy and pride of the artist. If **"Hell Screen"** reveals the agonies the artist must suffer, **"A Life Spent at Frivolous Writing"** suggests the reward of artistic devotion.

Another important group of historical stories is set in Nagasaki during the period of greatest Christian influence, at the end of the sixteenth century. **"Death of a Martyr"** is written in a style closely modeled on that of a version of *The Tale of the Heike* published at that time by the Jesuit Mission Press. Akutagawa attempted to convey with this style the compelling innocence of the legends of the saints. The young Lorenzo, who has mysteriously appeared at the Church of Santa Lucia in Nagasaki, revealing nothing of his past, is accepted as a monk and leads a life of conspicuous sanctity. One day, however, a girl of the town, also a Christian believer, declares that Lorenzo is her lover. He denies this, but when the girl reveals she is pregnant, no one believes his gentle protestations. Lorenzo is ordered to leave the church and takes shelter in a wretched hovel nearby, scorned and detested by all. Some months later a fire breaks out in the house where the unmarried girl and her baby live. In the confusion she forgets the baby. Another priest, a man of unusual strength, braves the flames, intending to rescue the baby, but the blazing heat forces him back. Suddenly Lorenzo appears and, dashing into the flaming house, retrieves the baby. The contrite girl now reveals she has lied—Lorenzo is not the father of her child. But her confession comes too late. Lorenzo is dying, badly burned. As people gather around him, marveling at his fortitude and self-sacrifice, his tattered garment falls apart, revealing a woman's breasts. All cry out in astonishment at this unanswerable proof that Lorenzo was unjustly accused and punished, and they kneel before the dying woman. With a smile on her lips she breathes her last, confident in her salvation.

The reverence with which Akutagawa treated Christian materials contrasts with the cynicism he often displayed toward Japanese heroes and paragons of samurai behavior. He found something especially appealing in beliefs that transcended the realm of ordinary human virtue, about which he had grave doubts, and envied people of the Middle Ages whose religion enabled them to make sense of the seemingly irreconcilable elements in ordinary daily life. Egoism could be transcended through divine grace, but not by a careful observance of any code of etiquette.

In **"Hankechi"** (**"The Handkerchief,"** 1916), a story with a contemporary setting, a woman relates in casual tones and with a smile on her lips the death of her son. The son's old professor, listening to the story, is amazed by her composure. His fan accidentally drops to the floor and, as he retrieves it, he notices that despite her smile the woman has been clenching the handkerchief on her lap, so convulsively that she seems to be weeping with her whole body. The professor, who is convinced that bushidō, "the way of the warrior," is not only the proper spiritual guide for Japan in a day when the old morality had deteriorated but is also closely akin to the spirit of Christianity, is profoundly impressed by this splendid example of samurai fortitude. He looks forward to telling his wife, an American woman who understands and loves Japan, about this example of the bushidō of a Japanese woman. The experience has filled him with happiness and renewed his faith. A few hours later, however, when he returns to the book by Strindberg he was reading when his visitor arrived, his eyes fall on a passage where Strindberg states that an actress who tears her handkerchief even as she is smilingly telling of some personal tragedy is an affected and bad performer. The professor puts down the book, his happiness shattered by this unpleasant denial of the stoical action that had so impressed him.[31] Akutagawa's cynicism was here directed at the high-minded professor whose ideals are so easily challenged. In the story **"Shōgun"** (**"The General,"** 1922) he satirically dealt with the normally sacrosanct person of General Nogi, another incarnation of bushidō. But Akutagawa's treatment of Christianity was respectful, a presage perhaps of his absorption during his last years with the person of Christ.

Akutagawa's third variety of historical fiction treated the Japan of the early Meiji era. These stories are colored by a nostalgia for what seemed to be a remote age, though it was only forty or fifty years before. During the 1870s and 1880s fashionable Japanese ladies and gentlemen built themselves homes modeled on Victorian domestic architecture, dressed in Western-style clothes, chatted knowingly about European fashions, and prided themselves on their associations with titled foreigners. In Akutagawa's day, however, the Japanese lived in Japanese-style homes with perhaps one foreign room, tended to wear kimonos, and had very few social contacts with Europeans. The extreme adulation of the West of the early Meiji era had come to seem picturesque, and Akutagawa described it with almost the same sense of distance as in his accounts of sixteenth-century Nagasaki. **"Kaika no Satsujin"** (**"A Murder During the Age of Enlightenment,"** 1918) was the first of his stories set in this period. It is absurdly overplotted, reminiscent of the early Izumi Kyōka, and cannot be taken seriously as a work of literature.

"Butōkai" (**"The Ball,"** 1919) is more successful. Akiko, who has just turned seventeen this year of 1886, is taken by her father to a ball at the Rokumeikan. She has learned some French, knows ballroom dancing, and wears her elegant Western gown with assurance. A young French naval officer asks permission to dance with her. When she has

tired they sit outside talking. He remarks that the ball at the Rokumeikan is exactly like one in Paris, or anywhere else. As they talk, they see fireworks, a part of the evening's entertainment. The young Frenchman, watching the sky-rockets cascade, compares their brief moment of brilliance to human life itself. In the concluding section of the story a young novelist meets Akiko, now Mrs. H, in the autumn of 1918, and she tells him about that night at the Rokumeikan. He asks if she remembers the name of the French officer. "Indeed I do," she says, "his name was Julien Viaud." "Then, he was Loti, the author of *Madame Chrysanthème*." "No," Mrs. H replies, "his name was not Loti. He was called Julien Viaud."

Akiko is uninterested in the historical fact that Viaud and Loti were the same person. He has lived so long in her memory as Julien Viaud that it is of no significance to her that the Viaud she knew later became the famous novelist Loti. Akutagawa's manner of treating the past was similar; his aim was always poetic truth, rather than historical accuracy. The young French officer's comparison of human life to fireworks also represented one of Akutagawa's convictions. He used the image of fireworks again and again as a simile for human life, especially in his late works, and otherwise expressed his belief that a whole life may be contained in one perfect moment. Elsewhere he stated, "Human life cannot compare with a single line by Baudelaire."[32]

Akutagawa's reputation as a writer continued to grow in the 1920s, even though none of the stories published after **"Hell Screen"** could match its intensity and unmistakable individuality. Editors of magazines fought for the privilege of publishing his stories, especially in the New Year's issue. He worked hard to satisfy their demands, but in March 1921 he took a vacation, traveling to China as a special correspondent of the *Ōsaka Mainichi Shimbun*. His visit was marred by recurring bouts of illness, but on the whole he enjoyed his four months in China, even if they did not noticeably enrich his works. The deterioration in his health was perhaps the most conspicuous result of the journey.[33]

When Akutagawa returned to Japan he wrote an account of his travels, but he devoted himself mainly to efforts to recover his health. Despite some improvement, he continued to be plagued by nervous exhaustion and insomnia. He was able nevertheless to write the stories that appeared simultaneously in the New Year's issues of four magazines in 1922. They included **"Yabu no Naka"** (**"Within a Grove"**), one of his most striking works, the satirical **"The General,"** and two stories that Uno Kōji, Akutagawa's close friend, dismissed as failures.

"Within a Grove" demonstrated that Akutagawa retained his skill at handling historical materials. Once again he turned to the *Konjaku Monogatari* for the basic story, but he gave the materials depth and freshness by arranging them in the form of testimony from various persons concerning an event in which three of them—a samurai, his wife, and a bandit—had directly participated. The accounts differ widely, each person naturally describing his actions in the most favorable manner. It has been suggested that Akutagawa's technique of narrating a single story from several viewpoints was inspired by Robert Browning's *The Ring and the Book*.[34] But even if this work influenced the conception of **"Within a Grove,"** Akutagawa's contribution can hardly be disputed. The most striking of the seven accounts of the crime is given by the dead samurai who, speaking through the mouth of a medium, relates how he was tricked by the bandit, trussed, then forced to watch as the bandit violated his wife. He accuses the wife of having not merely been a willing victim but of having urged the bandit to kill him. He finally describes how the bandit ran off, appalled by the wife's inhumanity, and how he himself committed suicide with the dagger his wife had dropped, unable to endure the humiliation.

"Within a Grove" was made in 1950 into the prize-winning film *Rashōmon*, directed by Kurosawa Akira. The film is artistically superior to the original story, partly because it introduces, as a major narrator, a woodcutter who witnessed from his hiding place the events so differently related by the three participants. It would seem that he must be telling the truth, since he was a mere bystander, but even the woodcutter lies when he is asked what happened to the valuable dagger with which the samurai killed himself. The film, produced in Japan while the war crimes trials were still fresh in people's memories, suggested the difficulty of ever establishing from the testimony of witnesses what really had taken place.[35]

Akutagawa's health continued to deteriorate in 1922. He complained in a letter written to a friend toward the end of the year that he was suffering from nervous exhaustion, stomach cramps, intestinal catarrh, antipyrine poisoning, and heart palpitations. The letter also listed the various ailments from which his wife, two sons, and adopted parents were suffering.[36] He managed nevertheless to continue writing. The stories written at this time are in a distinctly different vein from his earlier fiction. **"Torokko"** (**"The Hand Car"**) is the deceptively simple story of a boy who helps some railway workmen push a hand car. At first he is exhilarated by the ride, especially when the car coasts downhill, but after they have traveled a considerable distance the two men reveal that they are not making a return trip and they leave the boy. Bewildered, he is assailed by such loneliness and fear that he all but bursts into tears as he makes his way home alone in the gathering darkness. **"The Hand Car"** is strikingly like Shiga Naoya's short story "Manazuru" (1920), which tells of two small brothers who have gone to a nearby town to buy presents for themselves and are overtaken by darkness on the way home. Both stories are set on the Izu Peninsula,[37] and surely it was no coincidence that Akutagawa chose a theme so similar to Shiga's.

There can be no question of Akutagawa's profound interest in Shiga's writings; at times he despaired of ever equaling Shiga. He wrote a friend in 1917, "Ever since reading *Reconciliation* I have felt disgusted with writing fiction."[38]

In his journal he mentioned how easy it was to become the willing captive of Shiga's distinctive manner;[39] and in the late work **"Haguruma"** (**"Cogwheels,"** 1927) this is how he described his feelings when reading Shiga's *A Dark Night's Passing*: "The hero's spiritual conflict was heartrending for me at every moment. I felt what an idiot I was, compared to the hero, and before I knew it I was weeping. At the same time, the tears brought some peace."[40]

Akutagawa and Shiga did not know each other well. According to Shiga, they met barely seven times during the seven years of their acquaintance.[41] Shiga noted that Akutagawa was a faithful reader of his works, but confessed that he himself had not read much of Akutagawa's. He objected to certain of Akutagawa's stylistic techniques, such as his withholding from the readers information known to the author, as in **"Death of a Martyr,"** where Akutagawa kept the sex of Lorenzo a secret until the very end.[42] Shiga seems to have been unaffected by his readings in Akutagawa's works, but Akutagawa, even though he despaired of emulating Shiga, learned much.

The stories that immediately followed **"The Hand Car"** included two set in the past, the Heian period and the early Meiji era, but these were Akutagawa's last mining in familiar veins. **"The Hand Car,"** on the other hand, was the forerunner, especially in its quiet, undramatic manner, of a series of autobiographical stories, which were no doubt influenced by Shiga's success with his "I novels." In these stories Akutagawa called himself Yasukichi, and he related mainly his experiences as an English instructor at the Naval Engineering College in Yokosuka from 1916 to 1919. **"Yasukichi no Techō kara"** (**"From Yasukichi's Notebooks,"** 1923) is typical of the series, an almost plotless work that is awkwardly constructed and generally uninteresting. Why, we may wonder, should a master of the short story have produced such a dreary work? Probably his poor health had taken its toll: Akutagawa seems to have been too exhausted to attempt to work with more imaginative materials, and writing about himself may have been the one way out of what was otherwise a hopeless impasse.[43]

Akutagawa was only too aware, however, of his failure to rival Shiga in achieving the maximum with the barest of means. His pages on Shiga in "Bungeiteki na, amari ni Bungeiteki na" ("Literary, Excessively Literary," 1927) expressed his profound admiration, especially for the fineness of touch in Shiga's realism; in this respect, Akutagawa stated, Shiga was superior even to Tolstoy. "Moreover," he continued, "he has infused this realism with a poetic spirit that is derived from oriental tradition. Surely there can be no disputing that it is in this respect that his *epigonen* most conspicuously fail to attain his heights. His is a special quality which we—at any rate, I—find it most difficult to match."[44] Akutagawa seems in this passage to be identifying himself as an "epigone" of Shiga; but he recognized that Shiga's Confucian, aristocratic self-awareness was quite unlike the individualism that he himself had imbibed from Western authors. Unlike

Shiga, moreover, Akutagawa had no sense of an incorruptible integrity that he felt obliged to preserve and assert; he lacked any such confidence in himself or his writings.[45]

Akutagawa nevertheless found himself being drawn closer to the kind of stories for which Shiga was celebrated, the evocations of seemingly inconsequential personal experiences, related in such a manner as to leave a lasting, poignant impression. The brief **"Mikan"** (**"Tangerines,"** 1919) describes an incident aboard a train. A girl of twelve or thirteen enters the compartment where the narrator is seated, just as the train is about to pull out. She irritates him by her unattractive, countrified features, her stupidity in not realizing that she cannot ride in a second-class compartment with a third-class ticket, and especially by her insistence on opening the train window, even though black smoke from the engine fills the compartment when the train enters a tunnel. The girl seems the incarnation of the trivial, vulgar matters he has been reading about in the newspaper he carries. Suddenly the train emerges from the tunnel. At a level crossing three little boys, dressed in shabby clothes that seem a part of the gloomy atmosphere of the place and the weather, are waiting for the train, and when they see the girl they call to her. Leaning out of the window, she throws them some tangerines, spots of warm color in the dreary landscape. The narrator becomes aware at that instant that the girl is going to the city as a servant, and that she had brought the tangerines with her to express her thanks to her little brothers for seeing her off. The story concludes, "I felt then I could forget for a while my unspeakable fatigue and ennui, and the inexplicable, vulgar, boring nature of life itself."

For years Akutagawa had been urged by critics to discard his literary pretensions and to bare his naked self. His intimate friend Kume Masao had put forth the doctrine that "the true path of the art of prose is the watakushi shōsetsu ['I novel'],"[46] but Akutagawa professed in several essays his disagreement. He did not dispute that an "I novel" could be a masterpiece, but insisted that not all masterpieces of Japanese prose fell into this category. Probably, in any case, Akutagawa did not feel much confidence in his Yasukichi stories. Only in the "I novels" written during the last two years of his life did he achieve real distinction with his autobiographical fiction. Even then he was still reluctant to espouse the "I novel" in the manner of Kume Masao.

Akutagawa's dispute in 1927 with Tanizaki Jun'ichirō, surely one of the least heated and least focused of literary disputes, arose from Akutagawa's stated doubts about the aesthetic value of plot in a work of fiction, and his subsequent attempts to justify stories that lack a clear-cut plot or structure. "Literary, Excessively Literary" opens:

> I do not consider that a work of fiction without a recognizable plot is the finest variety; consequently, I do not urge others to write nothing but plotless stories. I might mention that most of my own stories have plots. A picture cannot be composed without a *dessin*. In precisely the same way, a work of fiction stands or fails on its plot. . . . To put it more exactly, without a plot there can be no work of fiction.[47]

With this concession Akutagawa tried to disarm critics like Tanizaki who believed that a plot was essential to any story; but his emphasis was, rather, on what follows: "There are also works of fiction that are close to poems in prose. . . . I do not consider such works to be the highest form of fiction, but in terms of 'purity,' they are the 'purest' examples of fiction, if only because they lack conventional interest."[48] He cited Shiga Naoya as the outstanding Japanese exponent of this kind of poetic fiction. Clearly he hoped that his own autobiographical works, especially of the last years, would achieve the poetic intensity of Shiga's even though they lacked the thematic interest of his early successes.

The Yasukichi stories are occasionally moving, but they do not possess the unique overtones of Shiga's works. Akutagawa could not follow in Shiga's footsteps, but the neurotic "I novels" of his last period are almost unbearably affecting. Even the brief **"Kyō"** (**"Ill Omens,"** 1926), scarcely a page in length, is unforgettable because of Akutagawa's incredibly evocative descriptions of three apparitions that have filled him with dread.[49]

Shiga was Akutagawa's chief "rival" once Akutagawa had lost the magical touch of his early stories, but he had to take cognizance also of another, quite dissimilar group of "rivals," the writers of proletarian fiction who first emerged into prominence in 1921 with the publication of their magazine *Tane Maku Hito* (*The Sower*). The details of the proletarian literature movement are discussed elsewhere; suffice it to say here that it acquired such authority in a short period of time that Akutagawa felt obliged to respond to its announced principles. In January 1923 he published the essay "Puroretaria Bungei no Kahi" ("Pros and Cons of Proletarian Literature"). The tone, as the opening sentences indicate, was conciliatory: "Literature is not so unrelated to politics as many people suppose. It might more properly be said that the special characteristic of literature is that it can be related even to politics. Proletarian literature, which has finally got underway only recently, has been much too slow in making its appearance."[50]

Akutagawa cited the examples of Victor Hugo and Rai Sanyō as authors who were more likely to be remembered for their political convictions than for their poetic skill. Of course, he continued, advocates of art for art's sake will always look down on literature that is remembered for its political content, and he himself respected such views; nevertheless, he felt it was preferable to share the griefs and joys of the common people, rather than stand aloof and take pride in the filigree perfection of one's style.

Having thus established his willingness to praise proletarian literature, Akutagawa stated his objections:

> The one thing I hope is that spiritual freedom, whether of the proletariat or the bourgeoisie, will not perish. This means that one must see through the egoism not only of one's enemies but of one's friends. . . . If all members of the proletariat were good, and all bour-

geois were evil, this would truly be a simple world. It would certainly be simple, but hasn't the Japanese literary world undergone the baptism of Naturalism?[51]

Akutagawa followed this typical bit of wry commentary with an expression of his doubts as to whether or not humankind is really progressing. He breaks off this train of thought to declare, "I respect freedom of the spirit more than anything else." The essay is ineptly written, shifting from facetious remarks to proclamations of ideals with almost no transition, and ending with the egregiously silly statement that he favors perfectionism of any kind, even if it is a perfectionism of massage techniques. But it is obvious from his general tone that he was not in sympathy with proletarian literature. In his late work *Kappa* (1927) Akutagawa satirized capitalism, established morality, and various other aspects of contemporary society that were also attacked by the proletarian writers. On occasion too he indicated interest in Marxism and contributed manuscripts to left-wing magazines. But he was essentially uninterested in fighting capitalism; he was too aware of his isolation from other writers to join in common action, and too nihilistic to hope for an improvement in people's lots as the result of revolution.[52]

Akutagawa's last two works of fiction, **"Ikkai no Tsuchi"** (**"A Clod of Earth,"** 1923) and **"Genkaku Sambō"** (**"Genkaku's Villa,"** 1927), mark a conspicuous departure from earlier stories.[53] The first is about Otami, a farmer's wife who has been left a widow with a small son. Her mother-in-law, Osumi, expects that Otami will remarry after an appropriate time, but she refuses to consider another husband. Instead, she works like a man in the fields, all but turning herself into a "clod of earth," because she wants her son to inherit the land intact. At first Osumi admires her willingness to perform backbreaking labor, but gradually she realizes that as a result she herself is now responsible for the house and for Otami's son, and that she will therefore never be able to relax and enjoy old age. She becomes hostile toward Otami, and even seeks to turn the boy against his mother, though Otami is praised throughout the village as a model daughter-in-law. In the end, to Osumi's joy, Otami dies of typhoid fever. With Otami's savings augmented by contributions from the admiring neighbors, Osumi should at last be able to enjoy old age, but she now feels ashamed of herself, and whispers to the "new Buddha," "Otami, why did you die?" Apart from the satirical touch at the end and the paradox in most of the story—the model daughter-in-law is detested for precisely the qualities the world admires—little suggests the writer of the historical tales. Akutagawa's sudden interest in the lives of people who work the soil may indicate influence from the proletarian literature movement, though the manner of narration is characteristically his own.

"Genkaku's Villa" is as close as Akutagawa came to writing a Naturalist story. He informed his friend Uno Kōji in 1927 that the material for the story had been provided by the nurse who took care of his brother-in-law in the hospital.[54] Composition of the work was painfully slow. It took Akutagawa over two weeks to write the first section, though it is less than a page in printed text. His slowness was occasioned partly by the terrible complications in his family life after another brother-in-law had committed suicide in the wake of burning his own house in order to collect the insurance money. The brother had thrown himself under a train and Akutagawa, who was close to a nervous collapse even before this event and was acutely suffering from hemorrhoids, had to go to fetch the body. He also was saddled with the responsibility of providing for his sister and her children, who were now destitute. But the slowness of the composition was also the result of his determination to write a work of major importance. He was well aware of the oppressive nature of the story; he wrote Murō Saisei, "I am now writing an extremely gloomy work that is draining all my strength. I don't know if I'll be able to finish it."[55]

"Genkaku's Villa" is indeed a gloomy story; Uno Kōji believed that it evoked hell more powerfully than stories by Akutagawa like **"Hell Screen,"** which have hell for their subject matter.[56] Yet with one exception all the characters are decent and well meaning. The exception is the nurse, Miss Kōno, a cold and malicious woman who surely was an exceedingly warped version of the nurse who told Akutagawa the story! The events surrounding the death of the painter Genkaku are related objectively, and the foibles of each person in the household are subjected to the author's dispassionate scrutiny. The character who emerges most favorably is Genkaku's mistress, Oyoshi, who arrives with the son she has borne Genkaku and stays to look after the dying man. However, the nurse's cold machinations and the natural malice of Genkaku's grandson (who is about the same age as his illegitimate son) make life daily more unendurable for her in the household. At last Genkaku dies, and there is an elaborate funeral. Jūkichi, his son-in-law, rides in the horse-pulled hearse together with a cousin, a university student, who even as the carriage is lurching along is busy reading an English translation of the *Memoirs* of Wilhelm Liebknecht, the German socialist leader. At the end of the story Jūkichi and his wife discuss briefly what is likely to happen to Oyoshi, now that Genkaku is dead. The story concludes:

> His cousin was silent. He was painting in his imagination the picture of a fishing village on the Kazusa coast. And of Oyoshi and her child who would live in that fishing village. . . . His expression suddenly grew severe. In the sunlight, which had broken through the clouds not long before, he once again turned to his copy of Liebknecht.

Akutagawa explained the conclusion of the story in a letter sent to Aono Suekichi (1890–1961), a critic closely associated with the proletarian literature movement. He wrote on March 6, 1927:

> I felt that at the end I wanted to bring the tragedy that had occurred in Genkaku's house into contact with the outside world. (That is why the entire story, with the

exception of the last section, takes place inside the house.) I also thought I would like to hint that the outside world held the promise of a new age. Chekhov, as you know, at the end of *The Cherry Orchard* sketched in a student of the new generation, only to have him fall from his room upstairs. I am unable to bestow the resigned laughter of a Chekhov on the new generation. But, on the other hand, my feelings of sympathy are not intense enough for me to join in a mutual embrace with the new generation. Liebknecht, as you know, in his *Memoirs* sighed at times when he recalled his meetings with Marx and Engels. I wanted to cast Liebknecht's mournful shadow over my student. I fear that this effort may have failed.[57]

Akutagawa's reference to Liebknecht aroused considerable speculation and controversy.[58] His conception of the "new generation" (*shin jidai*) seems vague, and he may have meant nothing more than that he hoped life would be more cheerful for the next generation than it was for the members of Genkaku's unspeakably gloomy household. But his mention of Liebknecht rather than, say, Tolstoy, suggests that he had been affected by the proletarian literature movement. When **"Genkaku's Villa"** was reviewed by a group of nine critics in the March 1927 issue of the literary magazine *Shinchō* (*New Tides*), almost everyone was an advocate of proletarian literature, evidence of the authority that the movement had acquired.[59]

Most of Akutagawa's remaining stories were openly autobiographical. The chief exception is the novella *Kappa*, a satire rather in the vein of Anatole France's *Penguin Island*. The mistakes and hypocrisy of human society are ridiculed by the distorted or exaggerated forms they take in a nonhuman world. The kappa, a kind of water sprite, figures prominently in Japanese folktales. Despite their grotesque appearance—part human, part bird, part reptile—they are sufficiently human to seem plausible when fulfilling the roles of artists, capitalists, students, and so on in Akutagawa's imaginary world. Some passages are amusing, making telling thrusts at current mores, but on the whole *Kappa* is a depressing work, not only because its humor is so joyless, but because it betrays a lack of resourcefulness that would have been unthinkable in the earlier Akutagawa. When *Kappa* appeared it was generally discussed as a work of social criticism, but he described in a letter his irritation with people who had pointed out the inadequacy of his social awareness:

> Of all the criticism that has appeared about *Kappa* your article was the only one to move me. I am especially pleased because it came from someone I have never met. *Kappa* was born out of my *degoût* with respect to everything, especially myself. All the other criticism of *Kappa* has elaborated on the "lighthearted wit" and so on, as if deliberately to make me the more miserable.[60]

Akutagawa followed *Kappa* with two surrealist film scenarios, *Yūwaku* (*Temptation*)[61] and *Asakusa Kōen* (*Asakusa Park*), both bewildering yet fascinating explorations of the fluidity of associations. Neither scenario seems to have been filmed, perhaps because of the astonishing metamorphoses that Akutagawa's texts require.

The sequence of autobiographical works begins with **"Daidōji Shinsuke no Hansei"** (**"The Early Life of Daidōji Shinsuke,"** 1924). The story contains fictitious elements, but was perhaps as close to true autobiography as Akutagawa could come at that time. The sections bear subtitles such as "Cow's Milk," "Poverty," "School," "Books," and "Friends," each one designating a formative element in Shinsuke's character. "Cow's Milk," for example, conveyed his feelings of deprivation:

> Shinsuke never once drank his mother's milk. His mother had always been frail, and even immediately after she gave birth to her only child, she never had a drop of milk for him. The family was moreover much too poor for there to be any question of hiring a wet nurse. That is why Shinsuke drank cow's milk from the time he was born. He could not help resenting this fate. He loathed the bottles of milk delivered every morning to the kitchen, and was envious of friends who, whether they were aware of it or not, had never drunk milk except from their mother's breast.[62]

The section called "Poverty" considerably exaggerates the financial hardships under which Akutagawa grew up, and probably also the resentment he felt for having been forced to endure poverty. He described himself as a product "not of the poverty of the lower classes but of the poverty of the lower middle class, which has to endure hardships for the sake of keeping up appearances."[63]

He describes next his school and the useless information with which he had to fill his head. A tyrannical teacher beat him because he read Kunikida Doppo and Tayama Katai, but he continued to receive good marks despite his rebelliousness. The most affecting part of **"Daidōji Shinsuke"** discusses the books he read. "There was not one single thing which he had not learned from books." He learned from late nineteenth-century European novels and plays but also from Genroku haikai poetry. He confesses, "During the early part of his life he fell in love with any number of women, but none taught him anything about the beauty of women; at any rate, he was taught nothing about feminine beauty that he had not already learned from books."[64]

The last section, on his friends, is mocking. "He always found it rather agreeable to be described as 'an unpleasant guy.'" He was reluctant to have intimate friends, but those he selected were always the brightest in the class, friends who inspired hatred as well as love. **"Daidōji Shinsuke"** breaks off with the promise Akutagawa never fulfilled to extend the manuscript to three or four times its present length. Opinions differ about **"Daidōji Shinsuke"**; no doubt it would seem more impressive if Akutagawa had not written far more powerful works in a confessional vein.

The next autobiographical work, **"Tenkibo"** (**"Death Register,"** 1926), is written in the first person. It opens with the haunting description of his insane mother quoted at the beginning of this chapter. It must have cost Akutagawa a great deal of pain to write this shattering episode. It is followed by the almost sunny description of Ohatsu, the elder sister he never knew, whose name was inscribed in the family "death register" before he was born. Akutagawa recalls the touching little anecdotes told about Ohatsu, all she left behind in the world, and he writes with a tenderness rare in his works.

He turns next to his father, the third name in the "death register." He describes how he was given in adoption to his mother's family, how his father unsuccessfully tried to take back his son, how the boy was reared by his maiden aunt, a woman he loved and hated. This account leads to a description of the death of his father, when Akutagawa felt an intimacy with him for the first time, even though his father's mind was wandering at the very end. His last words were to order Akutagawa to salute a warship with flying pennants, which he saw steaming toward them.[65]

"**Death Register**" concludes with the short account of Akutagawa's visit to the family grave. As he stares at the monument under which the remains of his mother, father, and sister lie, he wonders who of the three was the happiest, and recalls a haiku by Bashō's disciple Naitō Jōsō, composed when he visited his master's grave:

> *kagerō ya*
> *tsuka yori hoka ni*
> *sumu bakari*
> Shimmering haze—
> All I do is go on living
> Outside the grave.

Akutagawa, like Jōsō, felt he was merely biding his time until he joined the others in the grave and in the death register.

The remaining autobiographical works were published post-humously after Akutagawa killed himself on July 27, 1927, by taking a lethal dose of sleeping medicine. His suicide came as a profound shock but not as a surprise to his family and friends. He had spoken of suicide often, and he seemed to be at the end of his strength. A photograph taken in June 1927, his last, shows a gaunt face, hollow eyes, a wrinkled forehead, and an expression of despair accentuated by the mouth twisted around a cigarette. In March he published "**Shinkirō**" ("**The Mirage**"), the account of an almost pointless experience that is given an unforgettable intensity by the eerie apprehension of death; and in June he published "**Mittsu no Mado**" ("**Three Windows**"), in which he described, under the strange allegory of two battleships being repaired at the Yokosuka Dock Yard, how deeply the nervous breakdown of Uno Kōji had upset him, apparently precipitating the decision to commit suicide. This was the last story published during his lifetime.

Among the unpublished materials Akutagawa left behind was the autobiographical "**Cogwheels**," perhaps his masterpiece. He portrays himself in a state of acute mental tension, seemingly schizophrenic, finding peculiar significance in certain colors, or in people casually glimpsed in the street. Such experiences induce the hallucination of semitransparent cogwheels that increase in numbers until they all but blot out his vision. Every now and then the outside world impinges on his fantasies. He learns by telephone that his brother-in-law has thrown himself under a train, and must break off the story he has been writing in a hotel room to go and claim the body. Matter-of-fact conversations alternate with terrifying visions, with little attempt made to distinguish between reality and hallucinations. In between bouts of fantasy he reads Shiga Naoya, Strindberg, and Dostoevski. The whole is a nightmare, impossible to summarize, and filled with a terror that mounts until the final cry: "I lack the strength to write any more. Living with such feelings is an indescribable torment. Will no one have the goodness to strangle me in my sleep?" After reading "**Cogwheels**" we can only marvel that Akutagawa did not kill himself sooner. But it is not only its poignant content that makes "**Cogwheels**" so memorable a literary work. The style, the choice of details, the counterpoint of reality and fantasy all contribute to the indelible impression the work leaves in the reader's mind.

"**Aru Ahō no Isshō**" ("**The Life of a Certain Idiot**") was written on June 20, 1927, as we know from the prefatory note addressed to Kume Masao, asking him to decide if the manuscript should be published. He noted, "I have not attempted to defend myself in this manuscript—not intentionally, at any rate." The work is divided into fifty-one short sections. Here is the sixth section, "Sickness."

> The sea wind kept blowing interminably, but he managed nevertheless to open the unabridged English dictionary.
>
> "Talaria. Shoes or sandals that have sprouted wings.
>
> "Tale. A story.
>
> "Talipot. A palm native to the East Indies. The trunk attains a growth of fifty to one hundred feet, and the leaves are used for umbrellas, fans, hats, etc. It blossoms once in seventy years."
>
> In his imagination he could vividly picture the palm flowers. He felt an itching in his throat he had never previously experienced. Before he knew it, he had spat on the dictionary. He spat?—But that was not spit. Remembering how short his own life was, he once again visualized the palm blossoms, palm blossoms on towering trees on the other side of the distant ocean.[66]

Other sections describe corpses, unhappy memories of childhood, ennui, the author's dread of society, death. He recalls books he has read, a woman he once loved, quarrels. The last section is entitled "Defeat":

> His hand holding the pen began to shake. That was not all. He began to drool. His head was never clear except after waking from sleep induced by 0.8 veronal. And even when it was clear, this state never lasted longer than half an hour, or an hour at most. He went on living day to day in semidarkness. Or, one might say, the blade of the slender sword with which he had propped himself had been nicked.[67]

A short collection of cryptic reflections *Jippon no Hari* (*Ten Needles*) came next, and then two essays on Christianity, "Saihō no Hito" ("The Man from the West") and the sequel "Zoku Saihō no Hito." During Akutagawa's last moments, as he drifted into sleep, he read the Bible, and it seems clear from these late works that in his desperation he had turned to Christianity for solace, attempting to understand the contemporary relevance of the person of Christ. He compared, for example, Christ's peregrinations as a child to the child of a naval officer whose station is constantly shifted, wondering if His "Bohemian" nature did not originate in these early experiences. It is not clear, however, if Christianity represented more to Akutagawa than an intriguing possibility of salvation. In **"Cogwheels"** he described an old man he used to visit, a wise man who knew why Akutagawa's mother had gone mad, why his father had repeatedly failed in business, and why he himself was being punished. The old man urged Akutagawa to become a Christian.

> "Can even someone like me become one?"
>
> "There's nothing difficult about it. All you have to possess is faith in God, in Christ His Son, and in the miracles Christ worked. . . ."
>
> "I can believe in the devil. . . ."
>
> "Then, why don't you believe in God? If you believe in shadows, you can't help but believe in light."
>
> "But there must be some darkness even without light."[68]

Akutagawa opened "The Man from the West" with the statement that he loved Christianity for its artistic qualities. He was especially attracted to Catholicism, as might be deduced from his Nagasaki stories. He admitted that his interest in Catholicism had germinated from the seeds of exoticism scattered by the poets Kitahara Hakushū and Kinoshita Mokutarō, who were fascinated by the atmosphere surrounding the days of the Portuguese in Japan. But his interest went deeper than theirs, to the universal qualities of the religion. "The psychology of the martyr had a morbid attraction for me, like the psychology of every other kind of fanatic." He declared that he was totally uninterested in historical or geographical facts relating to Christianity; he was drawn instead to the dramatis personae, and the many short sections making up "The Man from the West" and its sequel consist of epigrammatic characterizations of Christ and those who surrounded Him. One section begins, "Christ, like all Christs, was a Communist in spirit. Christ's words, if read with a Communist's eyes, would probably turn into the *Communist Manifesto*."[69]

It is difficult to evaluate "The Man from the West." It and its sequel reveal not only careful reading in the New Testament but an acquaintance with the Old Testament and evidence of much pondering over what he had read. Ultimately, however, Akutagawa found insufficient comfort in Christianity.

His last composition, "Aru Kyūyū e okuru Shuki" ("Memorandum Sent to an Old Friend"), was his final testament. It was addressed to Kume Masao and described the circumstances leading up to his suicide. One phrase became famous: *bon'yari shita fuan* (a vague uneasiness), the direct cause of his death. Akutagawa related that for the previous two years he had thought of nothing but killing himself. He mentioned that he had already expressed in **"The Life of a Certain Idiot"** almost everything he had to say about himself. "However," he continued, "I deliberately refrained from describing in that work the social conditions—the feudal age—that had cast a shadow over me. If I had to analyze what made me refrain from mentioning them, it was because even today we human beings are to some extent still in the shadow of the feudal age." It is not clear what Akutagawa was referring to specifically. Perhaps it was to his family background. He confessed that, since he was living within the social condition (*shakaiteki jōken*), he could not be sure he understood it perfectly.

The suicide memorandum passed next to the debates he had with himself over the manner and place of suicide, ending with his decision on aesthetic grounds not to hang himself, though he believed it was the least painful way out. He revealed also that a certain woman wished to join him in suicide, but he had decided against this, both out of consideration for his wife and because dying alone would be easier to arrange. After disposing in this manner of the technical aspects of his suicide, he became more discursive:

> We human beings are human beasts, and that is why, in animal fashion, we fear death. What is called *élan vital* is nothing more than another name for brute strength. Like everyone else, I too am a human beast. But, when I note that I have lost all interest in food and sex, I realize that I am gradually losing my animal vitality. I am living in a sick world of nerves that has become as transparent as ice. Last night, when I talked to a certain prostitute about her wages (!), I felt profoundly the pathos of human beings like ourselves who "go on living in the only way they can go on living." I am sure that if I am allowed, of my own free will, to drift into an eternal sleep, it will bring me peace, if not happiness. But it remains a question when I shall be able to muster the courage to kill myself. In the meantime, in my present state, nature looks more beautiful than ever. You will doubtless laugh at the contradiction of loving nature and planning at the same time to kill myself. But the beauty of nature is apparent to me only because it is reflected in my eyes during my last hours. I have seen, loved, and understood more than most men. That thought brings some satisfaction, even amid the agonies I have repeatedly endured. Please do not publish this letter for some years after my death. It is quite possible that my suicide may appear like a death from natural causes.[70]

The letter concludes with a postscript mentioning that he had been reading the life of Empedocles, who wanted to become a god. Akutagawa himself no longer had any such desire, but he remembered how, twenty years before, Kume and he, sitting under a bo tree,[71] had talked about Empedocles. Akutagawa's last words were, "In those days I wanted to make myself into a god."

This was not Akutagawa's only suicide note. In the spring of 1927 he had left one for his friend, the painter Oana Ryūichi, attributing the cause of his unhappiness to the affair he had with a certain married woman when he was twenty-nine. He also expressed regret that he had for so long acted like a filial son toward his adopted parents, who never allowed him to do anything he wanted. Now, he says, he will commit the self-indulgent act of a lifetime by killing himself. The letter concluded, "But I see that I am, after all, the son of a lunatic. At present I feel disgust toward the whole world, myself most of all."[72]

Perhaps remembering this previous farewell message, Akutagawa feared that he might not have the courage to kill himself, even after writing Kume. But he prepared the fatal dose and drank it. When his wife found him the next morning it was too late.

Akutagawa disclaimed any desire to become a god, but he became one anyway. His life was interpreted as the archetypal fate of the artist, and his suicide deeply shocked not only those who were personally acquainted, but even people outside the literary world, who knew him solely by reputation. The suicide of Arishima Takeo in 1923 had also created a sensation, and many people recalled this event after Akutagawa's death, but it was explicable in the conventional terms of a love-suicide, in the manner of Chikamatsu's plays; Akutagawa's death was interpreted instead as a symbolic act, an expression of profound anxiety over the state of the times, or of personal inability to resolve the conflicting attractions of Japanese tradition and the wave of the future, represented by proletarian literature.[73]

Akutagawa's suicide naturally affected writers most powerfully: the sudden shift to the left of Kataoka Teppei has been directly attributed to the suicide, and for Yokomitsu Riichi it was the turning point of his whole life.[74] Even Shiga Naoya, whom Akutagawa revered above all contemporaries, seems to have been stunned into silence for years. And many lesser writers began to doubt the value of literature itself, if a man so favored with talent and fame by the gods, who was close to being a god himself, had spurned literature in favor of death. But Akutagawa's writings continued to find new readers, and he came to be a god in a special sense: the Akutagawa Prize, founded in 1935 to honor his memory by his friend Kikuchi Kan, the editor of the magazine *Bungei Shunjū*, became the most sought-after accolade for every young writer, the recognition of a god.

Akutagawa's stories were translated into European languages even during the long arid period from the early 1920s to the mid-1950s, when hardly any modern Japanese literature was translated, and his name was known abroad. His early stories do not always stand up to repeated readings, but their effectiveness, even in translation, is undeniable. The works of the middle period, as yet little translated, are often hardly more than sketches brought to life by a single haunting touch, an unforgettable observa-

tion, or a devastating association. But it is the autobiographical works of the late years that are probably Akutagawa's most enduring testament, though they lack the brilliance of the earlier works. No one can read them without recognizing in Akutagawa a quality at once peculiarly modern and peculiarly tragic. In his last works he surrendered the skills that were his birthright and gained with his death a lonely immortality.

Notes

1. Ōoka Shōhei, "Kaisetsu," for *Akutagawa Ryūnosuke,* in Nihon no Bungaku series, p. 516.

2. *Akutagawa Ryūnosuke Zenshū* (henceforth abbreviated *ARZ*), III, p. 305.

3. Sekiguchi Yasuyoshi, *Akutagawa Ryūnosuke no Bungaku,* p. 33.

4. *ARZ*, VI, pp. 310–11.

5. *Ibid.,* p. 311.

6. See Sekiguchi, *Akutagawa,* pp. 40–41, for examples of the revisions.

7. Kobori Keiichirō traced the background of "Rashōmon" to a story by the obscure French writer Frédéric Boutet, which appeared in a translation by Mori Ōgai in the October 1913 issue of *Mita Bungaku.* See Kobori, "Akutagawa Ryūnosuke no Shuppatsu," pp 60–65. However, Akutagawa turned to the Japanese classics for details of the period.

8. *Chōkōdō Zakki,* in *ARZ*, IV, p. 149.

9. *ARZ*, I, p. 136.

10. *Ibid.,* I, p. 143.

11. *Ibid.,* VII, p. 131.

12. *Ibid.,* VI, p. 312.

13. Sekiguchi, *Akutagawa,* p. 59.

14. See *ARZ*, IV, pp. 330–31.

15. See Ooka, "Kaisetsu," p. 518, and Sekiguchi, *Akutagawa,* p. 112; but Nakamura Shin'ichirō, in *Akutagawa Ryūnosuke no Sekai,* p. 73, declared, "Akutagawa Ryūnosuke received almost no *literary influence* from Natsume Sōseki."

16. *ARZ*, I, p. 315.

17. Nakamura, *Akutagawa no Sekai,* p. 69.

18. *Ibid.,* p. 71.

19. See *ARZ*, VII, p. 32; also, Naruse Masakatsu, "Akutagawa to Ōgai," p. 48.

20. Kobori, "Akutagawa no Shuppatsu," p. 55.

21. See Uno Kōji, *Akutagawa Ryūnosuke,* p. 79, where he points out resemblances between "Imogayu" and Gogol's *The Overcoat.* Of course, the basic source of "Imogayu" is to be found in *Konjaku Monogatari,* but Akutagawa's story is not merely a modernization of the early story but a new interpretation, enriched

by his readings in Western literature, and fully as-similated into his own personal style. See also pp. 81, 269.

22. Sekiguchi, *Akutagawa*, p. 74.

23. Shimada Kinji, "Akutagawa Ryūnosuke to Roshiya Shōsetsu," pp. 278–79, gives the account of the story.

24. See Miyoshi Yukio, "Hōkyōjin no Shi," p. 208, in Inagaki and Itō, *Hihyō to Kenkyū.*

25. Ōshima Maki, "Akutagawa Ryūnosuke no Sōsaku to Anatōru Furansu," p. 256.

26. Ōoka Shōhei, however, denied the resemblance be-tween Yoshihide and Akutagawa, stating that Akuta-gawa never sacrificed his real life for his art in the manner of Yoshihide. Ōoka, "Kaisetsu," p. 525.

27. Hasegawa Izumi, *Kindai Meisaku Kanshō*, p. 213.

28. *ARZ*, VII, pp. 344–45.

29. *Ibid.*, I, p. 220.

30. *Ibid.*, I, p. 222.

31. Nitobe Inazō (1862–1933), the model for the profes-sor, wrote in English a book called *Bushido, the Soul of Japan.* "Hankechi" has not often been mentioned as one of Akutagawa's best works, but Mishima Yukio stated, without elaborating on his opinion, that it was "the ultimate" in short stories. ("Akutagawa Ryūnosuke ni tsuite," p. 64). Elsewhere (in "'Hankechi,' 'Nankin no Kirisuto' hoka," p. 162), Mishima wrote that it was Akutagawa's most fully realized *conte*. He compared the beauty of Akutaga-wa's *manière* to the brilliance of certain moments in Nō, but regretted the ending, which he thought had been tacked on by Akutagawa in his usual spirit of irreverence toward acts of heroism or noble gestures. The incident related in "Hankechi" was apparently conveyed to Akutagawa by his friend Kume Masao.

32. See Nakamura, *Akutagawa no Sekai*, pp. 16–19.

33. Hasegawa, *Kindai*, p. 227.

34. *Ibid.*, p. 230.

35. See *ibid.*, pp. 236–41, for a comparison between the story and the film. Possible sources are discussed by Asai Kiyoshi in "Yabu no Naka," p. 63. The wood-cutter appears briefly at the opening of the original story and may be the person who draws from the wound the sword the samurai has used to kill him-self.

36. *ARZ*, VII, p. 377. It may have been at this time that Akutagawa began taking veronal, which he used when committing suicide.

37. Akutagawa apparently was given the materials for his story by a writer from Izu. See Miyoshi Yukio, "Sakuhin Kaisetsu," p. 252.

38. *ARZ*, VII, p. 157. *Reconciliation* is *Wakai* in the original.

39. *Ibid.*, IV, p. 137.

40. *Ibid.*, VI, p. 26. *A Dark Night's Passing* is *An'ya Kōro* in the original.

41. *Shiga Naoya*, II, p. 301.

42. *Ibid.*, p. 305.

43. See Tsuge Teruhiko, "Dōjidai e no Sembō," p. 120.

44. *ARZ*, V, p. 135.

45. Tsuge, "Dōjidai," p. 120.

46. See "Watakushi Shōsetsu Shōken," in *ARZ*, V, p. 61.

47. *ARZ*, V, p. 130.

48. *Ibid.*

49. *Ibid.*, IV, p. 384.

50. *Ibid.*, V, p. 23.

51. *Ibid.*

52. Sekiguchi Yasuyoshi, "*Kappa* kara *Saihō no Hito* e," p. 114. Miyamoto Kenji, later secretary of the Japa-nese Communist party, in 1929 published a sympa-thetic appraisal of Akutagawa's writings in the essay "Haiboku no Bungaku" (The Literature of Defeat), though his conclusion was that "We must at all times possess the fierce enthusiasm to criticize thoroughly Akutagawa's writings. Have we not examined the defeatist course of his writings in order to make our-selves the stronger? We must go forward, stepping over the literature of defeat and the soil of class con-sciousness." See *Kindai Bungaku Hyōron Taikei*, VI, p. 243.

53. Uno, *Akutagawa Ryūnosuke*, p. 252, writes that when he first read *Ikkai no Tsuchi* he could not believe it was by Akutagawa.

54. *ARZ*, VIII, p. 84. See also Uno, *Akutagawa Ryūno-suke*, pp. 308–09.

55. *ARZ*, VIII, p. 77.

56. Uno, *Akutagawa Ryūnosuke*, p. 319.

57. *ARZ*, VIII, pp. 88–89.

58. See Ebii Hidetsugu, "Genkaku Sambō," pp. 81–83.

59. See *Akutagawa Ryūnosuke Annai*, pp. 94–97, for se-lections from the discussion.

60. Letter to Yoshida Yasushi in *ARZ*, VIII, p. 90. In other letters Akutagawa compared *Kappa* to *Gulliv-er's Travels* and *Reinecke Fuchs* (*ARZ*, VIII, pp. 84–85), and expressed surprise at the speed with which he had been able to write what for him was an un-usually long manuscript. An especially revealing let-ter, sent on Feb. 27 to the novelist Takii Kōsaku, stated that of the three works he had been writing concurrently, "Genkaku Sambō" had cost him the greatest effort. *Kappa* was the easiest to write and "Shinkirō" was the one in which he felt greatest con-fidence. He repeated the gist of these remarks in a letter sent on March 28 to Saitō Mokichi, which oth-erwise is devoted mainly to complaints about ex-treme exhaustion. (See also pp. 88–89.)

61. Translated by Arthur Waley as *San Sebastian,* and included in his collection *The Real Tripitaka and Other Pieces.*

62. *ARZ,* III, p. 230.

63. *Ibid.,* pp. 233–34.

64. *Ibid.,* p. 237.

65. *Ibid.,* p. 308.

66. *Ibid.,* IV, p. 54.

67. *Ibid.,* p. 66.

68. *Ibid.,* p. 31.

69. *Ibid.,* V, p. 211.

70. *Ibid.,* VIII, p. 116.

71. The tree mentioned, *bodaiju,* is the Japanese name for the bo tree, under which Shakyamuni Buddha gained enlightenment. It is also the name for the linden. Possibly Akutagawa and Kume actually sat under a linden rather than a bo tree, but the latter, suggesting a sudden revelation of the truth, goes better with Akutagawa's story.

72. *ARZ,* VIII, pp. 117–18.

73. See the statements by Hirotsu Kazuo, made in 1929, as quoted in Miyoshi Yukio, *Nihon Bungaku no Kindai to Han-Kindai,* p. 207.

74. *Ibid.,* p. 206. Kataoka and Yokomitsu were both prominent in the New Sensationalist movement, but their paths diverged after this time.

Florence Goyet (essay date 1991)

SOURCE: "Akutagawa and the 'Western' Short Story," in *Revue de Litterature Comparee,* Vol. 65, No. 2, April, 1991, pp. 175–83.

[In the following essay, Goyet contends that Akutagawa's short stories are stylistically and thematically situated in-between the standards of Western and Eastern short fiction.]

The Japanese did not have a special word for "short story" before the last years of the XIXth century. Up to that time, the same word *monogatari* was used indifferently: e.g., for the *Genji monogatari* and its thousands of pages, and for the *Ugetsu monogatari* of Ueda Akinari, tales of a few pages each. Length had never been a criterion for judging a prose work. Even at the end of the XIXth century, when the opening of the country to the Western world brought about new trends in Japanese literature, the emerging modern literature was slow to pay attention to the criterion of length. The word chosen to name the new-born "novel": *shôsetsu,* was made up of the two sino-japanese characters for "short" (*shô*) and "story" or "apologue" (*setsu*), although the works in question, such as the programmatic *Floating cloud, Ukigumo,* of Futabatei Shimei, were often full-length novels. The specific word for "short story",

tanpen shôsetsu, was created later, in response to the multitudinous translations of Western short stories, by adding *tanpen,* "brief", to the word *shôsetsu,* "novel".

By the second quarter of the XXth century, however, the new word, *tanpen shôsetsu,* is widely used, and Akutagawa was recognized, from the beginning of his very successful career, as a master of the short story genre. He still is, as we are reminded by the "Akutagawa prize", that most famous of Japan literary prizes, awarded each year to enable an author to dedicate his full time to the writing of short stories. Does this mean that when Akutagawa writes "short stories", he is creating something very close to the Western stories, and renouncing, in a way, his native tradition? Our very first contact with his texts provides an easy answer: full of Japanese local colour, his stories differ widely from those of Maupassant or any of the European Naturalists. But if we address ourselves, beyond the themes and motives, to the structure of the stories, our answer might be more ambiguous. On the one hand, a very large number of his stories are built, in fact, in the same way as Western Naturalist short stories. On the other hand, a whole series of texts seem to have little in common with the "story" as Europe or America then knew it. Nonnarrative, they do not tell a regular tale with a beginning, a middle and an end, and they renounce the very way short stories in the West are usually made. Rather they relate to the very old and profoundly Japanese genre of the *zuihitsu,* the *following the brush* essay. Such a parallel, however, should not distract us from another connection, this time to the widespread "stream of consciousness". Akutagawa is standing at a crossroads. They could be thought of as the diverging paths of Western and Eastern traditions. But they could as well be conceived as the diverging paths of the genre itself, short stories divided between narrative and non-narrative texts.

1. THE "WESTERN" STRUCTURE

Akutagawa sometimes claimed the influence of Maupassant on his stories. This might seem strange at first sight, many of them being set in ancient Japan or using Japan or China Classical texts. If we address ourselves to the structure of these texts, though, rather than to their themes and settings, many of them are analogous to European Naturalist stories of the end of the XIXth century. Characteristic is the regular appearance of two features: antithetic structure and paroxystic characterization, visible even in stories based on the very Japanese themes taken from the Classical *Konjaku monogatari.*

Let us first take an obviously "Western-like" short story, **"Mikan," ("The Tangerines")**[1]. As one of a relatively smaller series of texts in which Akutagawa sets his stories in modern life, it is closer to the *nouvelles* of Western Naturalists like Maupassant. At the same time it is very typical of Akutagawa's narrative stories. The narrator, getting on a commuter train to return to Tôkyô, is in a mood as gloomy as the light of this snowy winter day. While he is waiting for the train to depart, a young girl suddenly rushes into his car. She has the disgusting appearance of a peasant girl, and he resents her coarse features and clothes. He resents even more her desperately trying to open the window, and doing so precisely when the train enters a tunnel. Coughing, half choked, he is to scold her rudely, when she reaches for some tangerines she had in her blouse and throws them to a few little boys along the track. To the narrator, things become suddenly very obvious: the girl is evidently going to Tôkyô to a "place", the boys are her brothers come to see her off; and suddenly, he feels more warmly disposed toward the monotonous life he is part of: her greeting to the little brothers has enlightened his day.

Behind the Western themes (the train, the suburbs, etc.), what is very clear here is the way Akutagawa structures his narratives. The story is a neat little scene, which deftly takes us through a well-made scenario and leaves us with a feeling of fulfillment. Five pages are enough for us to enter a narrative world, grasp what is at stake, see vividly the terrible boredom and share the irritation of the narrator, and be content with a resolution that leaves nothing unanswered. How Akutagawa was able, as the Naturalist story does, to present such a nicely rounded little narrative, is in fact relatively simple to understand.

The first feature is the antithetic structure of the story. It takes us smoothly from a sharply defined starting point to a resolution that is its exact opposite. Thus it creates a strong antithesis perceptible at once by the reader, who will need nothing more to feel that the tale is perfected. The first words show the narrator buried in the melancholy feeling of the hideous monotony of life, while the last ones explicitly state that, having seen the young girl greet her loyal brothers, he comes to an undefinable feeling of serenity. His mood has changed and a small miracle has taken place:

> Watashi wa kono toki ajimete, iiyô no nai hirô to kentai to o, sôshite mata fukakai na, katô na, taikutsu na jinsei o wazukani wasureru koto ga dekita no de aru.

> For the first time I could forget a little my inducible fatigue and ennui, and also life's absurdity, vulgarity and monotony.

The words used here: *hirô*, "fatigue"; *kentai*, "ennui"; *fukakai na, katô na, taikutsu na jinsei,* "absurdity, vulgarity, monotony of life", are the same used in the beginning of the text to state his prodigious boredom with modern life. Between these, the whole course of the narrative can be comprised and mentally organized by the reader. In this case, the symmetry is deliberately made easy to grasp. The throwing of the tangerines is what the German criticism on the *Novelle* used to call after Tieck the *Wendepunkt,* the turning-point, and which it tried to establish as the main characteristic of the genre. The tension between the filthy darkness and the tangerines is in fact central to the next. The warm hue of the tangerines confronts the darkness of night and of the train's smoke. The tangerines will finally substitute for the missing sun: their colour is that of the sun and they fall on the boys "from heaven", fertilizing the world and eventually the narrator's own mind.

The second remarkable point is the paroxystic treatment of the materials. To put up sharp contrasts and use them in a structure that will give the short story its fulfilling effect, to leave the reader content with the show that has taken place in front of him, and give the text its organical closure, Akutagawa imparts to everyone of the features he uses a tremendous intensity. What we see here is not "any" gloom, or "any" peasant girl. The girl is shown as profoundly, perfectly disgusting; the smoke, the dirt, the melancholy aspect of the place, are such that they could not be worse. The gloom is painstakingly characterized in the beginning of the short story as a sort of metaphysical absence of light. This text, as is often the case in Akutagawa's works, is verging on allegory; it will explicitly state that all the narrator sees is a "symbol" (*shôchô*):

> Kono tonneru no naka no kisha to, kono inakamono no komusume to, sôshite mata kono heibon na kiji ni uzumatte iru yûkan to—kore ga shôchô de nakute nande arô. Fukakai na, katô na, taikutsu na jinsei no shôchô de nakute nan de arô.

> This train in a tunnel, this peasant girl, and then this evening paper full of commonplace events—if these were not symbols, what were they? The symbols of life's absurdity, vulgarity and monotony.

This story verges on allegory without ceasing to be, at the same time, a very successful narration. This, to my feeling, is due to the fact that a narrative story will use paroxystic states anyway: characters defined by very few qualities, but possessing them in the supreme degree.

Such a structure can be seen in short stories by Akutagawa where the subject is drastically different, much more "Japanese". The "historic" tales are composed on the same lines, and rely on the same treatment of narrative material to give that neat, satisfying effect. In **"Hana,"** (**"The Nose,"**) a high rank monk is shown obsessed by the desire to make his nose smaller. The antithesis will confront the never ending efforts he makes to reduce his nose length, and the melancholy effect of his finally succeeding: years of paroxystically described care of his nose reveal their essential vanity; profoundly relieved, he welcomes his five inch nose when it suddenly grows back again. In **"Kareno shô,"** (**"The Withering Moors,"**) the characters are the disciples of Bashô, assisting the haikai master on his deathbed. The Japanese revere them in proportion of the veneration they have for their master. The story will show for each of them, with many details, that his reaction to the death of his master is the exact opposite of what one would expect. It is interesting that the "turning-point" here does not confront the beginning and the end of the story, but takes place within each of the portraits of the disciples, drawing a sharp contrast between the expected attitude and the actual one. Not a feature of the surface level[2], it is nevertheless a powerful organizing principle for the whole of the story. As was the case in **"Mikan,"** as it is in **"Hana,"** and countless other tales, it will allow the reader to feel the text as a small gem of a story, rounded and perfected.

To be used in an antithesis that can leave us content with the perfection of the story, the basic facts of the story are also "larger than life": subject to the paroxystic treatment we saw in **"Mikan."** In **"Hana"** the length of the priest's nose—a good five inches . . .—is the subject of *all* conversations in the Capital . . . His obsession pervades *everyone* of his activities, and his tremendous vanity is emphazised by the contrast with what is expected of a monk. In **"Kareno shô,"** the devotion of Bashô's disciples to their master, as well as their cold-heartedness at his death bed, are shown as much more powerful than the usual bonds and reactions; Bashô is *the* master, and they feel *totally* devoid of the anticipated emotion.

In these short stories, Akutagawa is very near to what could be characterized as the tradition of Western narration. The brief and strongly effective narrative, of which Maupassant, for instance, albeit with very different themes and preoccupations, produced hundreds of examples. They, too, take us deftly from a sharply defined beginning to a resolution, playing in between on sharp contrasts to establish a strong and fulfilling structure. I cannot, of course, demonstrate here that this was true of in the vast majority of short stories at the end of XIXth century,[3] but such a structure is clear enough in, for example, the "Normand" tales or the "tales of employees" by Maupassant.

2. THE "JAPANESE" TRADITION

The main point is that among Akutagawa's texts, some diverge dramatically from this mode of story-telling. Master of the neatly manufactured little gem, of the sharply drawn narrative, Akutagawa is also the writer of a number of stories of "no shape", deprived of a clear beginning, middle and end.

Japanese critics tend to feel that when Akutagawa wrote such texts, he returned to a more indigenous tradition. They even sometimes hint that his choosing to make well rounded short stories, of the kind I myself linked with the Naturalist short story, is in fact a renouncement of the more "Japanese" genre so well illustrated by Shiga Naoya at that time[4]: Akutagawa would have avoided a genre where Shiga Naoya had so excelled that his own writings could look poor. This comment at least underlines the difference between the two series of texts, and hints to the importance, for the "non-narrative" stories, of Japanese traditions.

As a matter of fact, a number of these texts, especially toward the end of Akutagawa's life, remind us of a Japanese genre that gets to the heart of the indigenous tradition: the *zuihitsu,* the *following the brush essay*[5]. Such texts as **"Aru hô no isshô,"** (**"The Life of an Idiot,"**) **"Shuju no kotoba,"** (**"The Words of a Dwarf,"**) or **"Geijutsu sono ta"** (**"Of Art and Other Things,"**) show a mere succession of paragraphs, a series of very short descriptions and comments on any topic whatsoever, generally preceded by a title, and not linked in any logical or thematic way. This calls to mind those most famous texts in Japanese litera-

ture: Sei Shonagon's *Makura no sôshi,* (*Notes of the pillow*), and Urabe Kenko's *Tsurezuregusa,* (*Idle hours*). Here, too, the topics are many, follow one another with that same absence of logical link, and reveal that same occasional triviality. As in the "non-narrative" stories of Akutagawa, the focus changes with every separate fragment, and the result, contrary to the "narrative" story, is that each of these fragments is considered in itself, each calls for the reader's exclusive attention, and in a way prevents him from feeling the whole as a whole. Contrary to the classical narrative of Western tradition, the reader will not follow a plot, however complex it may be, through to a resolution untying the knot set up in the beginning. Rather, he will follow the changing mood which goes from the memory of the mad mother to that of a conversation in a cafe, to that of the feelings at one's child's birth in **"Aru hô no isshô,"** as it went, in Kenko's *Tsurezuregusa,* from opinions about ladies and wine to points of courtly etiquette or comments on the issues of the day. Akutagawa, of course, especially at the end of his life, did nothing so light-hearted, and **"Haguruma,"** (**"Gears,"**) or **"Yasukichi no techô kara,"** (**"Excerpts from the diary of Yasukichi,"**) for example, are texts of a desperate pessimism. But the general principle is the same, there is a typical lack of interest in anything like a logical concatenation between the various elements presented to the reader.

The *zuihitsu* was not forgotten in Akutagawa's time. Midway between a personal diary and a newspaper chronicle, it was still a part of the authors' works: Shimazaki Tôson, for example, at the very end of his life, published daily in a paper his *Six feet for a sick man's couch.* The narrative's capricious ways, and its triviality, are here emphazised by the very subject of an ill man's pains and interests. Nor did the readers consider it an outdated mode of writing; the text had great success. Akutagawa practiced the genre, too[6]. Does this mean that when turning to non-narrative texts, Akutagawa is using indigenous traditions to get out of the frame that Western literature offered him? This could be a viable point. The struggle between the opposing concepts of the Eastern and Western worlds was central to Akutagawa's painful last years, and it has been said that his suicide was partly due to his not being able to reconcile them in himself.

But although it might be important not to forget the presence of such genres in Akutagawa's orientations, they must not be isolated. One of the most important features of these texts can be compared to that of the "stream of consciousness", or related to the modes of the Fantastic tales throughout the world. Closely following the very movement of the man's fantasy, recording his thoughts, his dreads and his sometimes crazy comments, they present themselves as the emanation of an often sick man's brain, obeying no other law than that of its own capricious ways. The one unifying principle in such texts tends to be the very mind it comes from, that of the "dwarf" in **"Shuju no kotoba,"** or that of the young man Akutagawa in the last, autobiographic, **"Aru hô no isshô."** Even when they follow the chronological order of events, as in **"Hagu-ruma,"** (**"The Gears,"**) the outcome is dramatically dif ferent from that of stories like **"Mikan"** or **"Kareno shô."** The reader witnesses the slow degradation of a mind and the emergence of a crazy world, where we could never be sure that a slipper did not disappear all by itself, where ghosts could very naturally sit in front of you at noon, and gears endlessly mill all that gets into the man's eyes. Nothing in those texts will be resolved at the end: in fact no tension will have been created that could lead to a resolution. Narrative is the absent dimension of such narrations. Similarly, a neat structure is the absent dimension of their elaboration. Their stake is different, much nearer to that of the fantastic tales or, again, of the "stream of consciousness": to watch one idiosyncratic and often erratic way of perceiving the outer world.

Another indication of the fact that Akutagawa did not simply revert to indigenous traditional tones is the presence in his work of another type of non-narrative text: the "lyrical" story. Moreover, these stories verging on the prose poem genre go back to a very early point in his career, in fact, to his very first compositions (**"Oogawa no mizu,"** or even the school-time **"Shisô."**) The most beautiful one is possibly **"Bisei no shin,"** (**"The Faith of Wei Cheng"**)[7], in which a man, waiting on a river-bed for a woman who never comes, finally drowns in the rising water. Here again, we see none of the features that characterize the narrative stories. The most striking is that this quite unusual situation (to wait endlessly for a woman in a river-bed without ever trying to escape) is in no way shown as strange or uncommon. Even the waiting is not made to seem extraordinary; the only comments on his impatience are:

yaya machidoi: somewhat impatient

Kewashiku mayu o hisomenagara: sombrely frowning

nan do mo hashi o sora he me o yata: several times he looked at the sky above the bridge

Neither the water nor the landscape is characterized with any particular tension. That is, there is no paroxystic treatment of the elements here. And as a consequence, no antithesis will emerge.

Contrary to the texts that resemble the *zuihitsu,* though, this one has a strong structure; but it is a structure very close to that of the musical "rondo", with a refrain:

Onna wa imada ni konai: But the lady still does not come.

This difference is important, because what we get is, in fact, nearer to the effect of music or of poetry. There is nothing here like the well-rounded little narrative we first saw. But nothing either like the texts of "no-shape" which we could parallel with the *zuihitsu.*

So Akutagawa presents us with two distinct modes of non-narrative tales, a genre which he explored from the very

beginning of his career. From the beginning then, he concurrently creates both nicely rounded stories that follow the Western way of telling tales, and others that choose a totally different approach[8].

What, finally, are we left with? Beneath Japanese costumes, the narrative tales of Akutagawa offer striking resemblances with the Western tradition of the tale-telling. On the other hand, he sets up "stories" that renounce this same mode of telling neat narratives. He thus finds himself very near to a tradition of his own literature, which very early established genres, like the *zuihitsu,* which show a totally different approach to narrative, with no clear structure and no logical concatenation. However, by so doing, Akutagawa is not returning to a very narrow notion of his work hidden from the rest of the world. He is not returning to an indigenous tradition as a withdrawal from the open world. On the contrary, he is concurring in what might be said to be the broadest movement of the XXth century, when the very categories of the mind and the essential orientations of its representations were questioned.

Notes

1. *Akutagawa Ryûnosuke zenshû,* Iwanami shôten, Tôkyô, 1954, v. 3, p. 95–99. Trans. Kojima Takashi, Tuttle Books, 1981, but translations of the excerpts are my own.

2. Which could explain why this theory was subject to so much criticism, in Germany and elsewhere: looking for it on the surface level, critics often did not find that turning-point, or found too many. But its effect is all the more powerful when, not apparent as a "narrative reversal", antithesis is an organizing principle on a deeper level.

3. Which I shall do in my forthcoming book at Presses Universitaires de France. *La Nouvelle,* series "Ecriture", based on a survey of more than a thousand stories in France, Italy, Russia, Japan and America.

4. With very similar themes, *Mikan,* and *The Ashen Moon,* by Shiga Naoya, are a very good example of these diverging ways to conceive the "story".

5. I know of no work by Japanese critics on that possible link between *zuihitsu* and non-narrative stories of Akutagawa. But scholars like Pr Kato Shuichi or Pr Tsuji Kunio were interested in the idea.

6. See *Akutagawa zenshû,* Iwanami shôten, v. 10.

7. *Akutagawa zenshû,* v. 4, p. 44–46.

8. Clare Hanson dedicated a whole book to this difference between narrative and what she calls "plotless" short stories in the Western tradition. My own work led me to somewhat similar conclusions. I would however be more drastic about the very definition of "non-narrative" texts. A story like *The Escape,* by Katherine Mansfield, is not non-narrative in that it

relates the anecdote of a couple's trip. This is not so important when structure alone is concerned. But it can be shown that what is really at stake behind these problems of structure is the very attitude the short story has toward its subject, the stand it takes to judge the show it presents. In narrative stories the reader is invited to share the author's critical distance on his subject. In non-narrative texts, when they are truly so, it can be shown that the distance is abolished and the reader's stand is very close to the one he takes in the lyrical text. In *The Escape* the reader is invited by the entire text, and especially by the way the characters are shown, to distance himself critically from the lady, paroxystically selfish and ridiculous.

FURTHER READING

Criticism

Allen, Louis. "Dark Estrangements." *Times Literary Supplement* (28 April 1989): 466–67.
    Includes translations of Akutagawa's short stories in an overview of modern Japanese fiction.

Lippit, Seiji M. "The Disintegrating Machinery of the Modern: Akutagawa Ryunosuke's Late Writings." *The Journal of Asian Studies* 58, No. 1 (February 1999): 27–50.
    Reevaluates Akutagawa's late fiction, as well as his ideas about modern fiction writing, to interpret his thoughts on purity in fiction.

Additional coverage of Akutagawa's life and career is contained in the following sources published by the Gale Group: *Contemporary Authors,* **Vols. 117, 154;** *Dictionary of Literary Biography,* **Vol. 180; and** *Twentieth-Century Literary Criticism,* **Vol. 16.**

Dvoynik

Feodor Dostoevsky

(Also translated as Fedor, Fyodor; also Dostoyevsky, Dostoievsky, Dostoevskii, Dostoevski, Dostoiewsky, Dostoiefski, Dostoievski, Dostoyevskiiy, Dostoieffski) Russian novelist, short story writer, and essayist. The following entry presents criticism of Dostoevsky's novella *Dvoynik* (1846; *The Double*). For information on Dostoevsky's short stories, see *SSC,* Vols. 2 and 33.

INTRODUCTION

One of Dostoevsky's most controversial works, *Dvoynik* (1846; *The Double*), remains puzzling for both readers and critics, in part because of its author's own ambivalent feelings toward it. As Dostoevsky's second published piece of fiction, *The Double* has variously been considered immature, experimental, and predictive of the greatness of Dostoevsky's later works.

PLOT AND MAJOR CHARACTERS

The Double tells the story of Yakov Petrovitch Golyadkin, also called Golyadkin Senior, and his descent into paranoia and madness as he becomes obsessed with a man who is his exact likeness. A mid-level office worker, Golyadkin loses all sense of self and reality when his double, who shares his name and is referred to as Golyadkin Junior, comes to work at the same office. But Golyadkin Senior is a man of so little consequence or individuality that no one notices the striking resemblance between the two. As his double's actions gradually ruin his reputation and social standing, Golyadkin Senior falls deeper into insanity, eventually becoming convinced that he is surrounded by doubles in a waking nightmare.

MAJOR THEMES

Dostoevsky's purpose in writing *The Double* remains unclear. As the story progresses, the narrative becomes more rambling, dream-like, and repetitive, and themes that had been clearly established are forgotten, reversed, or abandoned altogether. *The Double* begins with themes that were pervasive in nineteenth-century European literature, including those of the Romantic *doppelganger* and the downtrodden Russian office clerk. But as Golyadkin Senior's life spins out of control, the themes become more ambiguous. Notions of selfhood, objective reality, and existential meaning break down as Golyadkin Senior suc-

cumbs to paranoia and psychosis, and the reader becomes increasingly disoriented with the text.

CRITICAL RECEPTION

Early reviews of *The Double* were for the most part negative. Critic Visarion Belinskij complained in an 1846 review that the circularity and repetition of *The Double* "wearies and bores." Subsequent critics were no more forgiving of Dostoevsky's difficult text. It was not until the post-Freudian era of the twentieth century that critics began to recognize the complexity and psychological perception of the novella. Dostoevsky himself never felt satisfied with what he had accomplished in *The Double*. He revised it fifteen years after the first writing, but still he wrote, "I was again convinced that it wasn't successful." Nonetheless, *The Double* continues to be studied both for its own merits and for the insights it provides into Dostoevsky's later works.

PRINCIPAL WORKS

Short Fiction

Bednye lyudi [*Poor Folk*] 1846

Dvoynik [*The Double*] 1846

"Gospodin Prokharchin" ["Mr. Prokharchin"] 1846

"Khozyaika" ["The Landlady"] 1847

"Roman v devyati pis'makh" ["A Novel in Nine Letters"] 1847

"Belya nochi" ["White Nights"] 1848

"Chestnyi vor" ["The Honest Thief"] 1848

"Chuzhaya zhena i muzh pod krovat'yu" ["Another Man's Wife and a Husband under the Bed"; also translated as "The Wife of Another and the Husband under the Bed"] 1848

"Elka i svad'ba" ["A Christmas Tree and a Wedding"; also translated as "A Christmas Party and a Wedding"] 1848

"Polzunkov" 1848

"Slaboe serdtse" ["A Faint Heart"; also translated as "A Weak Heart"] 1848

"Malneki geroi" ["A Little Hero"] 1857

"Dyaduskin son" ["Uncle's Dream"] 1859

"Selo Stepanchikovo i ego obitateli" ["The Village of Stepanchikovo"; also translated as "The Friend of the Family," "The Hamlet of Stepanchikovo," and "The Manor of Stephachikovo"] 1859

Zapiski iz podpolya [*Notes from Underground*] 1864

"Krokodil. Neobyknovennoe sobytie, ili Passazh v passazhe" ["An Unusual Occurrence"] 1865

"Vechny muzh" ["The Eternal Husband"] 1870

"Krotkaya" ["A Gentle Spirit"; also translated as "The Meek One" and "A Gentle Creature"] 1876

"Muzhik Marei" ["The Peasant Marey"] 1876

Podrostok [*A Raw Youth*] 1876

"Son smeshnogo cheloveka" ["The Dream of a Ridiculous Man"; also translated as "The Dream of a Ridiculous Fellow"] 1877

The Short Novels of Dostoevsky 1945

Short Stories of Dostoevsky 1946

Other Major Works

Ynizhenye i oskorblenye [*The Insulted and Injured*] (novel) 1861

Zapiski iz myortvogo domo [*Buried Alive* or *Two Years Life of Penal Servitude in Siberia,* 1861; also translated as *The House of the Dead* or *Prison Life in Siberia*] (novel) 1862

Igrok [*The Gambler*] (novel) 1866

Prestuplenye i nakazanye [*Crime and Punishment*] (novel) 1866

Idiot [*The Idiot*] (novel) 1869

Besy [*The Possessed*; also translated as *The Devils*] (novel) 1872

Brat'ya Karamazovy [*The Brothers Karamazov*] (novel) 1880

CRITICISM

Stanley M. Coleman (essay date 1934)

SOURCE: "The Phantom Double. It's Psychological Significance," in *British Journal of Medical Psychology,* Vol. 14, 1934, pp. 254–73.

[*In the following excerpt, Coleman finds similarities between the treatment of doubles in the works of Dostoevsky and Guy de Maupassant and examines the psychological implications of doubles overall.*]

> Still ist die Nacht, es ruhen die Gassen,
> In diesen Hause wohnte mein Schatz:
> Sie hat schon längst die Stadt verlassen,
> Doch steht noch das Haus auf demselben Platz.
> Da steht auch Mensch und starrt in die Höhe,
> Und ringt die Hände vor Schmerzengewalt;
> Mir graust es, wenn Ich sein Antlitz sehe,
> Der Mond zeigt mir meine eig'ne Gestalt.
> Du Doppelgänger, du bleicher Geselle,
> Was äffst du nach mein Liebesleid,
> Das mich gequält auf dieser Stelle
> So manche Nacht, in alter Zeit?
>
>   —Heine, *Der Doppelgänger.*

Among nineteenth-century writers it would be difficult to discover two novelists more dissimilar than Guy de Maupassant and Fyodor Dostoevsky.

Maupassant, materialist and atheist, was a master of style and clear thinking. He wrote austerely and with complete detachment. In later years, with the inroads of psychosis, sentimentality, self-pity and self-portrayal became increasingly evident. But in his best period he described exactly what he saw, used a minimum of words, added no comments and told nothing about his own thoughts or feelings. He was a realist.

Dostoevsky, on the contrary, was essentially the introspectionist. Neurotic, hypochondriac and epileptic, his mind was a seething mass of incompatibilities and contradictions. Every critic of this author, Gide[1], Carr[2] and Mirsky[3] for instance, has stressed this state of conflict. For Gide the struggle was essentially ethical, one between good and evil. Freud saw in the rich personality of Dostoevsky four distinct facets: "the creative artist, the neurotic, the moralist and the sinner." Dostoevsky's style is verbose and awkward; his novels are usually badly constructed and unwieldy. Sometimes, as in *A Raw Youth* and *The Possessed,* his ideas overflow and totally obscure the original plot.

There is no coherence in Dostoevsky, no trite philosophy of life. In his writings, as in his life, all that is most despicable in human thought and conduct jostles cheek by jowl with the most lofty ideals.

It is not without interest, therefore, that for these two very different men the phenomena of doubles should have had a special significance. In the case of Maupassant it was not an active interest; the experience was forced upon him as an hallucination. Nowhere in his writing is there any direct reference to the experience, though it will be seen later that a whole series of horror tales bear directly on the phenomena. With Dostoevsky it was otherwise: there is neither evidence that he ever had any hallucination nor that his interest in doubles was anything more than a convenient device for giving expression to his subjective experience of intrapsychic conflict. [. . .]

THE DOUBLE OF FYODOR DOSTOEVSKY

This story, written in the pre-Siberian period, is considered by Mirsky, Lavrin[4] and by Dostoevsky himself to be a work of great significance. Carr is more sparing with his praise, pointing out that as a work of art it has the defect of holding an uneasy course somewhere between the macabre and the psychopathological. Narrated in the first person, the 'double' is presented as a tangible objective fact; but it is repeatedly indicated and is finally patent that this 'double' is a pure projection of the narrator's imagination.

Petrovitch Golyadkin is a petty official of insignificant appearance. He is without self-confidence, irresolute and burdened with an overwhelming feeling of inferiority. As first introduced he is rising from his bed one morning in a definitely clouded state. He feels ill and his brain is in the utmost confusion and chaos. It is soon clear that he is on the verge of a mental breakdown. Gradually it is divulged that he believes that people shout at him in the street; that something is being got up against him by his colleagues at the office; that there is a conspiracy afloat and that malignant enemies have sworn to ruin him.

On this morning, instead of proceeding to the office as was his custom, he astonishes his manservant by ordering a cab. After driving about indefinitely for some hours, he suddenly decides to visit his doctor. The latter, who had been frequently pestered by him of late, now regards his behaviour with some uneasiness. Petrovitch, on his side, is none too certain that the doctor is not in the gang and even suspects that the medicine may be poison. On this occasion it is advised that he should lead a less introverted and a-social life. He is recommended to try and get out of himself, see more people, have a little gaiety and so on. This gives Petrovitch an idea.

It appears that his former patron and benefactor is to give a ball this very night in honour of his daughter Klara's birthday. Petrovitch, though uninvited and on account of his recent behaviour under a cloud, drives up to his patron's house. He is refused admission and subjected to insults from the footmen, but finally succeeds in gaining entrance to the house by means of a side door. For several hours he lurks about in dark corridors in the vicinity of the ballroom, not daring to venture farther. There is an acute mental conflict taking place between his normal, timid, self-effacing personality and a new, until now unappreciated, urge to be in the limelight. Suddenly, almost against his will, he finds himself projected into the ballroom, stammering and floundering congratulations and birthday wishes to Klara. The girl, anything but pleased, moves away in the crowd. Repeated attempts by the butler to induce Petrovitch to leave the ballroom quietly are unavailing. Bewildered and confused, he is nevertheless dominated by one idea. At last he again sees Klara at the other end of the hall. Pushing violently through the crowd of dancers, this wild and dishevelled man again confronts her and implores her to dance with him. At this point Petrovitch is ignominiously propelled from the ballroom and then thrown into the street.

In a highly excited and wrought up state he wanders about St Petersburg far into the night. He hardly knows what he is doing nor where he is going. Exhausted at last he leans against the railing beside a canal. He is vaguely uneasy and frightened, he has the presentiment that something terrible is about to happen. Though the streets are deserted, he has a feeling that there is someone quite close to him. Presently he sees a figure hurrying towards him. As the stranger passes Petrovitch is struck by indescribable terror and, turning, he runs after the stranger. Catching him up at the next lamp-post his worst fears are confirmed. This stranger is his double. Fascinated, he is, in spite of himself, impelled to follow; what is his horror when the unknown stops before and finally enters the house in which Petrovitch lodges.

On the following day at the office 'the double' makes his second appearance. He is sitting opposite to Petrovitch at his desk. In the evening he accompanies him home and does not leave him all night. Poor Petrovitch indulges in an alcoholic debauch and on waking next morning is astonished to find his enemy has departed. There is not even a trace of the bed in which he had slept.

During the next few days 'the double' subjects Petrovitch to innumerable humiliations. In a café he behaves in an unseemly way, wolfs eleven pies, leaving the indignant Petrovitch to foot the bill. At the office he snatches his papers from him, presents them to the chief and so obtains all credit. He ingratiates himself with the other officials, delighting to make Petrovitch appear ridiculous before his colleagues. With an unseemly grimace and "quite unexpectedly under the pretence of caressing him, he pinches his chubby cheek with two fingers." The victim stands rigid and besides himself with fury while his enemy is "patting him two or three times on the cheek, tickling him two or three times, playing with him for a few seconds in this way." Finally "with a most revolting shamelessness" he gives the unfortunate man a playful poke in his rather prominent stomach. 'The double' sees fit to misconduct himself with women, the blame, of course, always falling on the unlucky Petrovitch.

Yet, despite the rascally behaviour of 'the double', our hero cannot get rid of a sneaking regard for him; he would like to be his friend, and constantly tries to make up to him, only to receive some fresh humiliation for his pains. At other times Petrovitch gives full vent to his hatred for his double, describing him as a scoundrel, of a horrid playful disposition, a nimble fellow, a toady, a lick spittle and as being impudent and shameless with something Bacchanalian in his mental make-up.

In this state of mind, Petrovitch receives or imagines he receives a letter from Klara; for later when he wishes to justify his subsequent conduct the letter has disappeared. He learns she is to be married against her will and he is implored to save her. She begs him to elope with her, naming the time and place for a meeting.

The last scene of this fantastic story finds Petrovitch at the appointed spot. It is pouring with rain and he awaits his beloved outside her house. Suddenly he is convinced that there are eyes at every window, gazing maliciously at the place where he is concealed. Then the door of Klara's house opens, and the hated double again makes his appearance.

Presumably for a period Petrovitch's conscious volition is submerged and he is totally under the domination of the second personality. For, on regaining consciousness, he is in Klara's house surrounded by a crowd of curious strangers. He is in an acutely confused and hallucinated state; there is ringing in the ears and darkness before the eyes. It seems that "an infinite procession, an unending series of precisely similar Golyadkins were noisily bursting in at every door of the room." Lastly, he sees a terrible person making towards him with a malicious gleam in his eyes; it is his own doctor. In a carriage on the way to the lunatic asylum the double is still present, hanging on to the carriage door and poking his head into the window.

The Double was written in 1848 about three years after Dostoevsky had scored his first success with *Poor Folk* at the age of 24. There can be no doubt that the sudden change in his circumstances, resulting from instantaneous popularity, had turned the young author's head. *The Double* represents in an exaggerated manner his own bitter reflections at the foolish way in which he had behaved at that time.

Occupying a lowly position in a government department, knowing no one and without financial resources, Dostoevsky was suddenly plunged into society, fêted everywhere and introduced to everyone as a second Gogol. The following extract from a letter written to his brother in 1845 gives a clear idea of his state of mind:

"Well, brother, I think my glory will never reach such a climax as now. Everywhere unbounded respect and extreme curiosity about me. . . . Prince Odoevsky begs me to favour him with a visit, and Count S. tears his hair in despair. Panoev told them that a genius had appeared who will trample them all in the dust. . . . Everybody receives me as a prodigy. I cannot open my mouth without its being reported that Dostoevsky has said this or Dostoevsky wants to do that. . . . I am full of ideas, but I cannot tell any of them even to Turgenev, without its being known next day in every corner of Petersburg that Dostoevsky is writing so and so. Well, brother, if I were to recount to you all my successes, I could not find enough paper. . . ."

Shy, sensitive, introverted and inhibited, the immediate result of success had been to bring to the surface just such a nasty, bombastic and unseemly individual as Golyadkin the second. The foolish young man boasted and strutted, ranting about his wild life and giving everyone to believe that he kept mistresses; "Minnas, Klaras and Marianes" who "cost a pile of money." In actual fact there is ample evidence to show that he was extremely awkward and reserved with women in the pre-Siberian days, and had no love affairs, beyond a sentimental attachment for a Madame Panoeva to whom he was too shy ever to declare his passion. Is it too presumptuous to see in this episode the prototype of the Klara-Petrovitch relation?

Dostoevsky never lived down this unfortunate phase of his career. He became known as the "literary pimple," and it is related by Carr that "an anecdote gained currency that he insisted on *Poor Folk* being printed with a special border to distinguish it from the other contents of the Almanack."

Whatever the intrinsic value of *The Double* may be as a work of literary craftsmanship, it has a very special interest in that it is the first of the author's novels to present the idea of the mind in conflict, of dual personality. For Dostoevsky the divided mind is never alternating personality, that is repression with amnesia. Dostoevsky depicted what he himself subjectively experienced, the simultaneous presentation of conflicting feelings and impulses. It is this state of mind that he projected into his most famous characters, Rasholnikov, Dmitri, Myshkin and Versilov. In his last novel, it is true, the process of decomposition is made use of to portray this state of conflict. As Alexander has pointed out, the four brothers Karamazov represent the four pathological attitudes towards parricide, *i.e.* the neurotic character, the hysterical, the psychotic, and the criminal.

Dostoevsky was a man possessed of amazing insight into the workings of his mind, the dissociated state that absorbed him was therefore essentially a schizophrenic rather than a hysterical mechanism. Writing of *The Double* many years later Dostoevsky states that it was "the greatest and most important social type which I was the first to discover and proclaim." Carr writes that in this novel the author "was feebly groping for the first time after a figure which was eventually to become one of his most profound and characteristic creations; the figure of a man crushed by circumstances or driven by his temperament in upon himself; of the introvert who compensates himself for habitual self control by violent sallies of self-assertion."

Freud, in his study of Dostoevsky with special reference to *The Brothers Karamazov,* has attempted to trace the author's epilepsy, neurotic symptoms and gambling mania to an Oedipus conflict and sense of guilt brought into evidence as a result of his father's murder. It is interesting to note that several of Dostoevsky's most important works besides *The Brothers Karamazov,* have some bearing on this traumatic event. *Crime and Punishment* is concerned with the moral justification of murder. *A Raw Youth* depicts a conflict between the son and father for the same women, while in *The Possessed* the argument is lifted on to the political sphere depicting a nihilist plot against the Czar and state. There is a careful analysis of the reactions of the various conspirators, one of the young men voluntarily sacrificing himself by suicide, so absolving the rest from suspicion.

Only once again in **A Raw Youth** does Dostoevsky revert to the conception of a 'double' in order to elucidate the state of mental disharmony. Much of the subject-matter in this novel is autobiographical. In the *Raw Youth* himself there is little difficulty in recognizing the prototype of the author's own profligate and ungrateful stepson, while in Versilov, the man who preached religion and ran after half-fledged girls, the author himself is clearly depicted. Sofia Andreyevsia, the peasant woman, is drawn from his first wife; while the scene of the disputed will, his relations with the general's daughter and with Lidya Ahmakov are all drawn from post-Siberian experiences. The stepson in a final attempt to explain his father's inconsistent and bizarre conduct towards the woman they are both attracted to, brings forward the following concept:

> "Gradually, I have come to a certain explanation: in my opinion, at these moments, on that last day and on the day before, Versilov was simply incapable of having any fixed purpose and even, I think, did not reason at all, but was under the influence of a sort of whirlwind of feelings. Of course, I do not at all admit real insanity, the more so, as he is not now in the least insane. But the 'double' I do admit certainly. What then precisely is the 'double'? The 'double,' at any rate according to a medical work by an expert which I afterwards read for the purpose, is nothing but the first stage in some serious mental derangement which may lead to a pretty bad conclusion. Indeed, Versilov himself, in the scene at Mama's, explained to us with the most extreme frankness the then 'bifurcation' of his feelings and his will."

Just as in the earlier novel, it is an erotic conflict that is responsible for the dissociated state; in this case it is between the moral sense and the sexual impulse, while in the former study it was the sense of inferiority that was responsible for the conflict. In the earlier tale it is the essentially libidinous significance of the 'double' that is of special interest. Petrovitch is a humble and retiring individual, sentimentally in love with Klara, but much too shy to declare his passion. He has been in poor health for some

time, he realizes that something is wrong with his mind and is consulting a medical man. One day, against his own volition, he is forced into the presence of Klara, to find himself making a ridiculous exhibition of himself. It is only after this episode that the 'double' becomes a separate entity. This second personality, primitive, freakish and instinctive, has control of his mind and body; the real Petrovitch is only a passive and unwilling spectator. Finally fantasy takes the upper hand completely. It is imagined that the beloved has made an assignation and it is only when he is once again in the presence of Klara and about to be conducted to the asylum that he regains some degree of control of his conduct.

It will be seen, therefore, that the 'double' as it occurs in the case of Maupassant and Dostoevsky is due to very different processes.

In Maupassant, the extravert, the hallucinated double is a projection mechanism, the result of repression and amnesia concerning a constellation of ideas centred about the feared results of sexual excesses. In the case of the introverted Dostoevsky there is no evidence that a double was ever experienced as an hallucination. The writer recognized within himself the presence of conflicting forces; libidinous impulses out of harmony with his moral and self-regarding sentiments. In his novels he attempted to give expression to this state of disharmony by making use of the concept of doubles. This state of mind is essentially one of partial dissociation and must be regarded as being that of a schizoid personality.

References

1. Gide, André. *Dostoevsky.* Dent.

2. Carr, Edward K. *Dostoevsky.* Geo, Allen and Unwin, Ltd.

3. Mirsky, D. S. *Modern Russian Literature.* Oxford Univ. Press.

4. Lavrin, Janko. *Russian Literature.* Benn, Ltd.

Clarence A. Manning (essay date 1944)

SOURCE: "The Double of Dostoevsky," in *Modern Language Notes,* Vol. 59, No. 5, May, 1944, pp. 317–21.

[In the following essay, Manning provides a brief analysis of The Double.*]*

The Double marks Dostoyevsky's first attempt to delve deeply into the mysteries of human psychology, but, despite the high hopes with which he published the book, it did not prove successful and many years later in the *Journal of a Writer,* November, 1877 (ed. Lazhechnikov, p. 456), he confessed,

> This story positively did not succeed, but the idea was quite brilliant, and I never introduced into literature anything more serious than this idea. But the form of

this story was absolutely not successful. I corrected it afterwards strongly, fifteen years later, for the then "Complete Collection" of my works, but I was then again convinced, that this thing was completely unsuccessful, and if I should now work on this idea and express it again, I would choose a completely different form; but in '46 I had not found this form and was not master of the story.

It is a frank admission of failure, but unfortunately at no time did Dostoyevsky definitely tell us what idea he was endeavoring to set forth and critics have been no more successful in defining it than in coming to an agreement as to the reality of the second Golyadkin. Many have seen the idea as having some sociological or social content, but it may be merely an attempt to picture objectively the mental disintegration of a man by objectifying his thoughts and aspirations and delusions. The story is almost impossible to visualize and the strange way in which the second Golyadkin appears and disappears will confuse the most careful reader.

Let us look first at a few points in it. At the opening we find Ivan Petrovich Golyadkin in a bad way physically and still more psychically. He has even been to consult a physician, Krestyan Ivanovich, who tells him that he must change his manner of living and not be afraid of society. Apparently in an effort to do this, he hires a carriage to attend the party in honor of Klara Olsufyevna, to which he has not been invited and from which he is turned away for some unexplained reason. After his discomfiture, he wanders around the streets and becomes aware of another man who walks home to his own apartment. He is sure that "his nocturnal visitor was no other than himself Mr. Golyadkin himself, a second Mr. Golyadkin but completely as he, himself—in a word, what is called his double in all relations." (Ed. Lazhechnikov, p. 218 f.)

The next morning this second Golyadkin appears in his office, directly facing him. It arouses no interest among the other officials that there should be two men of the same name in the office. Dostoyevsky implies that the second is a new man (cf. p. 225), but the conversation of Golyadkin and Anton Antonovich does not take the form which we should expect, had the second Golyadkin been an apparition or had the older Golyadkin made a mistake as to the identity or name of the new official.

That same evening Golyadkin invites his new friend home and the stranger tells a story which is almost certainly that of Golyadkin himself, of his unjust treatment in the provinces, of his coming to Petersburg and of his first assignment to duty in the capital. Yet we have no reason to believe that the senior Golyadkin is now wearing a borrowed uniform or is unsure of his position except for his peculiar illness, his fear of unnamed enemies, and his unexplained scandalous conduct with Karolina Ivanovna. As so often in his early works, Dostoyevsky avoids a consistent picture of the events preceding the story and plunges into the action without making clear at any time what is the genesis of the present situation. We are asked to accept Golyad-

kin's attitude and to see everything through his eyes, but the author does not explain to us the real situation.

The two Golyadkins spend the night together, but by morning the guest has disappeared without a trace and Petrushka grimly remarks to his master that "the master is not at home" and only later does he grunt out that the other had left an hour and a half before. Later he makes the cryptic remark "Good people live honorably, good people live without falsehood, and are never doubles" (cf. p. 282). The servant may be alluding to the double or to the intrigues into which his master pushes so zealously.

After this night, the role of the second Golyadkin changes. He is no longer the friendly suppliant. He is rather the successful careerist accomplishing without an effort all that the older man could not gain by intrigue and double-dealing and at the same time the cynical revealer of all that lurks in the back of the senior's mind. He knows at each moment how to exasperate and annoy the first Golyadkin and how to compel him to display to his associates all of his bad sides. Yet it is interesting and perhaps a consequence of the official's insanity that he never notices his rival talking with the other men in the office and the second Golyadkin only appears when he can annoy his rival.

This leads the first Golyadkin to the interchange of letters, but these are never delivered and we are left in the dark as to whether they really exist and whether Petrushka is actually sent to deliver them, or tries to do so.

The confusion continues until Golyadkin is retired and again we are not sure whether this retirement is because of insanity or because of the scandal with Karolina Ivanovna. Then comes the fatal letter from Klara with whom Golyadkin imagines himself in love and by whose father he has apparently been greatly helped. Bem considers this like the others imaginary, Osipov (Dvoynik, "Petersburgskaya Poema," in A. L. Bem, O Dostoyevskom, I, 44), believes that it may be a practical joke on the part of some rough practical jokers. This is hardly probable for it would introduce a completely extraneous note into the story.

Golyadkin has already had his dream of achieving success and then being confused by his rival who possesses those qualities that he himself is desirous of acquiring. In a sense Golyadkin feels toward the double as Salieri does to Mozart in the little drama of Pushkin, *Mozart and Salieri*. It is a recognition that his own ideals are better than his reality, an unconscious tribute to those sides of his character which he refuses to recognize.

It precipitates however the final tragedy. Golyadkin visits his Excellency and then through a doorway which he took for a mirror appears the second Golyadkin and dominates him exactly as he had dreamed. From there he dashes to the house of Olsufy Ivanovich, and again finds there Andrey Semenovich and the second Golyadkin, whom for a moment he pardons. But then Krestyan Ivanovich appears and takes him off to the insane asylum, while the face of the double long remains behind him in the carriage, until he drops into forgetfulness.

All this makes the second Golyadkin a strange figure. He is treated as definitely real and yet there is no proof that he has a real existence outside of the ideas of the first Golyadkin. He is and he is not almost at one and the same moment. The two Golyadkins really represent the two sides of the character of the first man, the mean and sordid and intriguing official and the collection of memories of the past and hopes for the future that throng around his unhappy head.

It was a startling device that the young author assayed, but it is no more fantastic, even if less palpable, that the assumption of magic caps which render the wearer invisible as in Pushkin's *Ruslan and Lyudmila.* or of the paraphernalia in any tale of magic and of the supernatural. Yet it cannot be convincing. The human intellect is not prepared to see people separate into two beings and move in the same environment. Dostoyevsky never tried it again. Hereafter to express his doubles, he employed devices as in *A Raw Youth,* where Versilov changes from one side of his nature to the other behind the scenes, or in the *Brothers Karamazov,* where the devil appears to Ivan when he is alone and mocks him by throwing at him his own words. Or, as in the **"Land Lady,"** he presents his hero as in a state of delirium where anything is possible.

The goal of Dostoyevsky in this novel is really intelligible. It is to present in objective form the lucid and illucid reactions of an insane man in his social and business life. It is to express in objective form the actions and the aspirations of a man in conflict with himself. Yet the device chosen is unsuccessful. The human mind cannot visualize this kind of existence. We demand that the second Golyadkin be a real person or an apparition. He is neither and both at the same time. It is idle to discuss whether the letters are real or imaginary. It is idle to discuss whether there are two or one man in the apartment and in the office. We can only read the story and accept the reality as Golyadkin accepted it without asking questions or seeking for definite answers to the question.

We have a real picture of a paranoiac with his delusions and his moments of lucidity. We have one man and two and if we can accept the stories of magic that have existed since the earliest ages of man, we must read this with the same confidence in the integrity and intentions of the author. Our minds refuse to do this. Dostoyevsky himself realized this after the novel was published. He admitted his failure and he went on to find other devices for thus revealing the deepest sides of human psychology, but he did not try again to present them simultaneously to the public in two different but similar bodies. *The Double* is a milestone on the way to his greater works, but it represents a false step which has remained to produce discussion and baffle the reader and the scholar.

Charles E. Passage (essay date 1954)

SOURCE: "The Double," in *Dostoevski the Adapter: A Study in Dostoevski's Use of* The Tales of Hoffmann, University of North Carolina Press, 1954, pp. 14–37.

[*In the following essay, Passage explores possible literary influences on Dostoevsky's* The Double.]

Dostoevski's point of departure in the creation of *The Double* was clearly enough Poprischchin, hero of Gogol's *The Diary of a Madman,* a short story. Upon this fundamental figure, now rechristened Golyadkin (Poordevil), it was his intention to graft the whole lore of "Doppelgängerei" and his own analysis of that lore. The prime difficulty, which he could not resolve, was the disparity of the two things. The lore of "Doppelgängerei" implied whole volumes, not only stories and novels, but even philosophical tracts, for the theme itself, so far as it entered literature, was but an elaborated detail out of the complex of German Romantic thought. Yet he went ahead with the almost impossible task of forcing so much matter into the compass of a short novel, drawing from sources which were, to be sure, related in theme, but widely different in artistic form. The finished work as we have it may be defined as a combination of the basic character and theme from Gogol's *Diary of a Madman,* a brief bit of Gogol's *The Nose,* possibly another brief bit from "Pogorel'ski's" *The Double, or My Evenings in Little Russia,* an episode from Hoffmann's *Kater Murr* (a novel), important features from Hoffmann's *Die Abenteuer der Sylvesternacht* (a short story), and still more important features from Hoffmann's *Die Elixiere des Teufels,* a full-length and complex novel. The wonder is that the result was not a hopeless hodge-podge. It must be admitted that the work is not crystal clear, but it must also be admitted that the twenty-four-year-old author had in mind a conception of sheer genius,—which lay just beyond his technical powers at that stage of his life. In the completed work trivialities are juxtaposed with passages of astonishing force and grandeur, and in the last analysis it is the latter which prevail.

The thirteen chapters of *The Double* occupy a time-span of four days, of which the first and fourth far transcend the second and third in importance. (Compare the structure of *The Idiot.*) Essentially there is only one character, as in the crucial Gogol tales, *The Diary of a Madman* and *The Overcoat,* all other persons being seen only as they appear to the hero. The true scene of action is the hero's mind, the whole tragedy is an inner tragedy. We behold despair in the act of tearing the edifice of Reason down to ruin.

On the morning of the first of the four days Yakov Petrovich Golyadkin, a titular councillor, is discovered in the act of waking. It is striking that on the very first page of this "realistic" narrative such a point should be made of the hero's uncertainty as to whether he is awake or asleep. A state of waking dream was a favorite Romantic and Hoffmannian subject. Golyadkin does awaken, and into a quite habitual world, a real and sorry world of shabby clothes, shabby furniture, and shabby existence. The reader craving realism may at this point feel assured that he is not being misled into some Romantic fantasy.

Yet why do things look at Mr. Golyadkin, rather than he at them?

> The dirty green, smoke-begrimed, dusty walls of his little room with the mahogany chest of drawers and chairs, the table painted red, the sofa covered with American leather . . . , and the clothes taken off over night and flung in a crumpled heap on the sofa, *looked at him familiarly.*

On the following page of the story Mr. Golyadkin examines his bill-fold:

> . . . the roll of green, grey, blue, red, and particolored notes *looked at Golyadkin,* too, with approval.

Things in this room seem to be alive with a life of their own:

> . . . the samovar standing on the floor was beside itself, fuming and raging in solitude, threatening every minute to boil over, hissing and lisping in its mysterious language, to Mr. Golyadkin something like, "Take me, good people, I'm boiling and perfectly ready."

In a truly realistic story things are not "looking" and "talking" like the animated objects that fill the houses of Archivarius Lindhorst or Prosper Alpanus. However, the realism-craving reader of 1846 might take comfort that the room was filled with objects that were perfectly normal, exactly identified and minutely described.

Mr. Golyadkin is attended by a rascally servant named Petrushka, blood brother to the rascal Selifan who attended Chichikov in *Dead Souls* and to the barber in *The Nose,* but even before summoning him Mr. Golyadkin darts out of bed to look into the little round looking-glass that stood on the chest of drawers:

> "What a thing it would be," he exclaims, "if I were not up to the mark today, if something were amiss, if some repulsive pimple had made its appearance. . . ."

The second section of Gogol's *The Nose,* that parody of Hoffmannian "Doppelgängerei," begins:

> Kovalyov the collegiate assessor woke up early . . . stretched and asked for a little looking-glass that was standing on the table. He wanted to look at a pimple which had come out upon his nose the previous evening. . . .

Upon looking into that little mirror Kovalyov was horrified to behold that "there was a completely flat space where his nose should have been." During the remainder of the story he has to contend not only with his marred countenance but with the nose itself which turns up in public dressed in the uniform of a civil councillor to play against him all the nasty tricks of an *antagonistic double.* Happily Mr. Golyadkin finds only reassurance in *his* mirror.

Now *The Nose,* while it reduced "Doppelgängerei" to an absurdity, drew part of its subject matter from Hoffmann's *Die Abenteuer der Sylvesternacht,* particularly from the last section of that tale which dealt with Erasmus Spikher's lost mirror-image, one of the many variants of the "double" theme. Dostoevski's story is related twice over to the *Sylvesternacht,* directly, and through the Gogolian derivative, and it is by no accident that Mr. Golyadkin's first action on this day is to run to look into his mirror. More than once he will encounter mirrors and mirror-like reflections, and with subtle indirection it is implied that his Double, the second Mr. Golyadkin, is his mirror-image.

After the state of waking dream, the objects with life of their own, and the dubiously Romantic motif of the mirror, the story continues in pure Gogolian vein as Mr. Golyadkin inspects the second-hand livery which Petrushka has acquired for this special day. Dressed now in his best clothes, he has the servant drive him into the center of the city. They pass some insolent young puppies of clerks who act much as similar young clerks used to act with Akaki Akakievich. Mr. Golyadkin is outraged at their insolence. His employer also passes, and Mr. Golyadkin is filled with the same anxious servility that used to mark the poor clerk Poprischchin. As the scene becomes more urban we are aware that this is to be, in Gogol's sense, a "Petersburg story." The subtitle, in fact, is "A Petersburg Poem."

The destination, surprisingly enough, of this trip is the office of Krestyan Ivanovich Rutenspitz, Doctor of Medicine and Surgery. "Rutenspitz" (whip-tip) is surely not intended as very friendly humor, and "Krestyan" may well be a bilingual pun: "Christian," a German name, and "krest'yanin," the Russian word for peasant. Quite possibly the doctor represents a fragment of autobiography and sarcasm, recalling a German doctor named Riesenkampf who had been a fellow-roomer with Dostoevski in the dark days just after graduation from the Engineering Academy in 1843.

Chapter II gives an account of Mr. Golyadkin's visit to the doctor. It is a very strange call. Utterly at a loss for words, he cannot for the life of him tell Rutenspitz why he has come. Obviously he is not a stranger to the doctor and the latter clearly considers him a nuisance. The prescription is to be as before: go out with friends, "not to be hostile to the bottle," avoid solitude. To all this Golyadkin keeps insisting that he is "quite all right," "just like other people." Launched into speech now, he talks faster and faster, overwhelming the bewildered doctor with office gossip, tales of enemies that surround him, of the plots they hatch to destroy him, but coming back to the assertion that he is "quite all right," "just like other people." What is more, he is a man of action, he can take care of himself. The doctor is all at sea; after all, Dostoevski implies, he is only a German. Suddenly Golyadkin fixes him with his eye, stares, then bursts into tears and sobs uncontrollably. For an instant reality is present to his conscious mind, he *knows* he is unbalanced, and he weeps for hopelessness and help-lessness. The final speech of Poprishchin in the madhouse is moving, but this passage is ten times more terrifying and more moving. The strange interview ends. As he passes out the door Golyadkin loses his feeling of utter surrender. Arrogantly he says to himself: "That doctor is extremely silly. He may treat his patients all right, but still . . . he's as stupid as a post."—This scene with an actual doctor, even though the doctor does little, shows Dosto-evski's awareness of the medical nature of schizophrenia and removes his hero from all dualism of a merely sym-bolic nature. This man is beset with a real mental illness, not a division of alliances between the Real and the Ideal or between the Good and the Bad. This chapter had no lit-erary source, it was based on direct observation from life.

From the doctor's office Golyadkin goes on a fantastic shopping tour. (Chapter III.) He visits various stores, prices articles, changes money into smaller denominations, or-ders furniture enough to supply six rooms, but winds up his business with the actual purchase of only a pair of gloves and a bottle of perfume. In his dream world he is preparing for marriage with his employer's daughter, Klara Olsufevna, again paralleling Poprishchin's infatuation with *his* employer's daughter. Golyadkin next goes to a restau-rant for lunch and there he examines himself anew in the restaurant mirror.

Now he is ready for the real errand of the day, a call at the home of his employer Olsufi Ivanovich. It is Klara Olsufe-vna's birthday and a party is being given. Mr. Golyadkin has no invitation but he believes it is his right to appear. Petrushka drives him to the door, he enters, and is refused admittance by the servants. In the presence of arriving guests he is told, in fact, that the master has given strict orders *not* to admit him. Precipitately he rushes back to the carriage and orders Petrushka to drive home. In the next moment he reverses the command and they drive back to the house,—a superb symbol for a mental fixa-tion,—but even as they do so, Golyadkin is stricken with terror and once again, without even stopping, the carriage swings out into the street and disappears.

Up to this point the story has presumably presented realis-tic facts and actions. This realism is none the less ambigu-ous. It would be more correct to say that the story has pre-sented the eerie unreal world seen by a man in the shadow of madness. These events are Mr. Golyadkin's fantasy. The fantasy is about to pass into delirium.

Several hours later Klara Olsufevna's birthday party is in full swing. (Chapter IV.) But Mr. Golyadkin is to be found huddled in the darkness and bitter cold—on the back stairs to his employer's apartment! He has been there a long time. And all that time he has been debating how he can slip in and join the party, for he is "all right," he is "quite well," he is "just like everyone else," he belongs here. Fi-nally he summons the courage and darts in, throwing aside his coat as he goes. The whole company is appalled. His

prepared speeches die on his lips, he can say nothing. The women retreat from him, the men sneer, his employer is shocked, Klara hides. All this is seen through Golyadkin's eyes and the kaleideoscope turns of his mind make a bril-liant passage of imaginative writing. The impressions of the room mingle with impressions gained from books he has read. He recalls the French minister Villesle, the Turk-ish minister Martsimiris, the beautiful Margravine Luise, the Jesuits, his own room, Petrushka. He thinks that if the chandelier were suddenly to fall how he would rush to save Klara. The butler approaches. Golyadkin tells him one of the candles is about to fall out of the chandelier. The butler assures him that the candle will not fall and says that someone outside wishes to speak at once with Mr. Golyadkin. They argue. A tear glitters on Golyadkin's eyelash. He will not go. He feels like an "insect," yet he turns and walks straight toward Klara Olsufevna and asks her to dance with him. The young lady shrieks, everyone rushes toward them, Golyadkin is torn away from her and propelled laughing, talking, explaining, apologizing, out into the vestibule. His hat and coat are thrust upon him. Then he feels himself falling, then lying in the outer court-yard, while the orchestra within strikes up a new piece. He stands perplexed, then

> he started off and rushed away headlong, anywhere, into the air, into freedom, wherever chance might take him.

To some degree this scene is an intensified version of Dos-toevski's own feelings about refined soirées and his place in them. On one occasion he had been so mortified by an ill-timed argument with the young and somewhat patroniz-ing Turgenev that he rushed out of the house. When his coat was held for him he was so excited that he could not get his arms into the sleeves. In utter exasperation he seized the coat and ran out into the night in precipitate flight.

But here may be seen an example of how autobiographical experience is blended with literature to the transformation into something quite new.

In more than one story of Hoffmann's the hero turns from an "impossible situation" and flees as fast as his feet will carry him from the scene. In the opening section of *Die Abenteuer der Sylvesternacht* the narrator, identified only as the "travelling enthusiast," attends a New Year's Eve party at the home of the Justizrat. Among the guests is Julie, his former beloved,—she will become Giulietta, the Venetian courtesan of Act II of Offenbach's opera,—who treats him so heartlessly that he becomes desperate. Her repulsive husband, the frivolousness of the dancing and card-playing guests increase his desperation until he sud-denly leaves the party and runs "out—out into the stormy night." The next section, *Die Gesellschaft im Keller,* be-gins:

> To walk up and down Unter den Linden may at other times be pleasant, but not on St. Sylvester's Night (i.e. New Year's Eve) amid a good sound frost and snow-

squalls. Bare-headed and coatless as I was, I finally realized that as icy shivers pierced through my feverish heat. Away I went across the Opera Bridge, past the Palace—I turned a corner, ran across the Schleusenbrücke past the Mint.—I was on Jägerstrasse close by Thiermann's store. . . .

Just so, at the beginning of the new chapter (V), Mr. Golyadkin

> ran out on the Fontanka Quay, close to the Izmailovski Bridge,

and later, after his adventure with the stranger, discovered that he

> had run right across the Fontanka, had crossed the Anichkov Bridge, had passed part of the Nevski Prospekt, and was now standing at the turning into Liteini Street,

whence he goes eventually down Italianski Street to his own house on Shestilavochni Street. Hoffmann was the poet of Berlin and Gogol and the young Dostoevski were the poets of Petersburg. How uncannily all three authors meet again here: the "travelling enthusiast," Akaki Akakievich, and Mr. Golyadkin, all know the streets of the capital on a night of wind and snow and bitter cold, when a fierce emotion drives them to their fates. When Akaki Akakievich stumbled out of the office of the Person of Consequence into the stormy night, he found that

> In an instant it (the storm) had blown a quinsy into his throat, and when he got home he was not able to utter a word;

while Dostoevski describes this flight of Golyadkin's as taking place on

> an awful November night—wet, foggy, rainy, snowy, teeming with colds in the head, fevers, swollen faces, quinsies, inflammations of all kinds and descriptions.

The verbal echo is from Gogol, but the party, the flight, and the destination are paralleled in Hoffmann. The "travelling enthusiast" finally entered a beer-cellar where all the mirrors were draped over with cloth out of deference for the client Erasmus Spikher, who had surrendered his mirror-image to the temptress Giulietta and therefore could not bear to look into mirrors where he could not see himself. With him is Peter Schlemihl, the man who had sold his shadow. (Hoffmann here borrows him wholesale out of Chamisso's famous fairy-tale.[1])

In short, the "travelling enthusiast" encounters two men who have lost their doubles. Mr. Golyadkin is about to lose his, not just his shadow or his mirror-reflection, but the half of his psychologically sundered self.

The plan of the *Sylvesternacht,* which the story has now begun to parallel, is here interrupted but will be resumed later. At this particular juncture Dostoevski's mind may be seen to swerve suddenly to another scene from Hoffmann's

works where the hero does not simply encounter other men with doubles,—and lost doubles at that,—but encounters for the first time his own double. It is the fine passage toward the end of Part I, Section 2 of the novel *Kater Murr,*[2] where Kreisler abruptly flees from a somewhat different kind of "impossible situation" and rushes out into the palace gardens of Sieghartshof. It is late afternoon.

> Kreisler paused in the middle of the bridge which led across a broad arm of the lake to the fisher-hut and looked down into the water, which reflected with magic shimmer the park, with its wonderful groups of trees, and the Geierstein which towered above them and which bore its white-shining ruins upon its brow like a crown. The tame swan that answered to the name of Blanche was paddling about the lake, its lovely neck proudly held aloft, rustling its flashing wings. "Blanche, Blanche," cried Kreisler aloud as he stretched out both his arms, "sing thy loveliest song and do not think that thou wilt then die!" . . .

> Dark clouds were moving up and throwing broad shadows across the mountains, across the forest, like black veils. Muffled thunder was rolling off to the south, louder rushed the night wind, rushed the brooks, and simultaneously individual tones of the weather-harp resounded like organ tones. Startled, the birds of the night arose and swept through the thicket shrieking.

> Kreisler awoke from his dreaming and glimpsed his dark form in the water. It seemed to him as though Ettlinger, the mad painter, were looking up at him from the depths. "Hoho," he shouted down, "hoho, are you there, beloved Double, old comrade?—. . . . If they have sent you down undeservedly to Orcus, I'll pass on all sorts of news to you!—Know, honored madhouse inmate, that the wound which you dealt that poor child, the beautiful Princess Hedwiga, still has not healed. . . . Do not attribute it to me, my good fellow, that she takes me for a ghost, specifically for your ghost.—But when I am at leisure to prove to her that I am no disgusting spook, but the Kapellmeister Kreisler, along comes Prince Ignatius cutting across my path, who is obviously laboring under a 'paranoia,' a 'fatuitas,' 'stoliditas,' which, according to Kluge is a very pleasant kind of actual folly.—Don't ape all my gestures, painter, when I am talking seriously to you!—Again? If I weren't afraid of a head cold, I would jump down to you and beat you properly.—Devil take you, clownish mimic!"

> Kreisler quickly ran away.

The identity of the mad painter Ettlinger is one of the points left by the author for clarification in the third and last part of the novel, but that part was never written. Some scholars have deduced that he was the actual father of Kreisler and hence that his madness foreshadows that of Kreisler, but these are unresolved questions. Kreisler standing on the bridge and looking at his own image in the water below addresses the image as "Double," yet speaks to him as though he were the mad Ettlinger who had attacked and wounded the Princess Hedwiga.

The first drops of a beginning rain drive Kreisler immediately afterward to seek shelter in the fisher-hut where his friend, the wise Meister Abraham, lives. As he approaches the cottage he receives a shock:

> Not far from the door, in the full glow of the light, Kreisler caught sight of his own image, his very self (sein eigenes Ich), walking along beside him. Seized by the profoundest horror, Kreisler plunged into the cottage and sank pale as death into the arm-chair.

To behold one's double signified, according to folk beliefs, one's approaching death. Meister Abraham inquires what has happened to affect his friend so strongly:

> With difficulty Kreisler got possession of himself, then spoke in a hollow voice: "It cannot be otherwise, there are two of us—I mean I and my Double, who leaped out of the lake and pursued me here.—Have mercy, Master, take your dagger and strike the rascal down—he is mad, believe me, and can destroy us both. He conjured up the storm outside.—Spirits are abroad in the air and their chorale rends the human heart!—Master—Master, lure the swan here—it shall sing—my song is frozen, for the Double (der Ich) has laid his white cold hand upon my heart, he will have to take it away if the swan sings—and go down again into the lake."

Meister Abraham laughs and quickly explains away his friend's terrors: the sounds are made by the wind in the weather-harp,—a sort of giant æolian harp made of tuned steel strings and stretched between buildings in the open,—and the vision of the Double walking beside him was an optical illusion created by the lighted lamp and the concave mirror in the entryway. To convince Kreisler, Abraham steps outside and immediately two Abrahams may be seen in the twilight. For the moment, the whole episode seems to be reduced to comic error caused by an optical illusion. What Hoffmann might have made of it in the unwritten part of the novel no one can say, but it is surely meant to be more than a comic error. It symbolizes Kreisler's present fear of madness and his sense of impending catastrophe and undoubtedly prefigured some future situation in reality; in other words, potentiality pressing forward to become fact.

In the case of Mr. Golyadkin, madness and catastrophe are also potentialities pressing forward to become fact, not in the future but at the present moment. His frantic and random flight from Klara Olsufevna's party into the stormy darkness brought him, when "it was striking midnight from all the clock towers in Petersburg," to the Izmailovski Bridge.

> At last Mr. Golyadkin halted in exhaustion, leaned on the railing in the attitude of a man whose nose had suddenly begun to bleed, and began looking intently at the black and troubled waters of the canal. There is no knowing what length of time he spent like this. All that is known is that at that instant Mr. Golyadkin reached such a pitch of despair, was so harassed, so tortured, so exhausted, and so weakened in what feeble faculties were left him that he forgot everything. . . .

Suddenly terror strikes him. "Was it my fancy?" he asks himself. The import of the question is not disclosed to the reader immediately, but presently a stranger passes, at sight of whom Mr. Golyadkin's terror increases. Again the figure approaches, makes no answer to Mr. Golyadkin, and vanishes. Mr. Golyadkin begins to run. The figure appears anew running parallel to him. As they approach Mr. Golyadkin's house it outdistances him, goes up his stairway, through his doorway, is received by Petrushka without question, and when Mr. Golyadkin arrives in his room, there is the figure sitting on his own bed. The figure is identical to himself in every detail. It is his Double. Here the chapter and the first day of the story end, with all clarification postponed,—in good Hoffmannian fashion,—until another time.[3]

The two-fold connecting link between the two stories and with the *Sylvesternacht* was undoubtedly the mirror-image. Kreisler had identified his reflection in the water with the reflection in the concave mirror in Abraham's vestibule and believed that his Double had risen from the lake to follow him. In all likelihood Dostoevski conceived originally of a reflection of Mr. Golyadkin in the waters of the canal but this became impossible when he placed the time at midnight in the midst of storm. Yet it is on a bridge that the second Mr. Golyadkin first appears to him and then, as in Kreisler's case, reemerges later to follow him home.

For Mr. Golyadkin, however, no swan shall sing, that is the Heavenly Grace of music is not vouchsafed to him, nor shall any Meister Abraham comfort him. Dostoevski's hero, in contrast to Hoffmann's, is utterly alone. He differs from his prototype further in that it is understood, despite the *coming* of the Double, that the self has split under the strain of anguish, has broken in two, and that the Double is Mr. Golyadkin's illusion. It is a part of his personality which has escaped the control of his rational mind and now seems to have a separate existence. The author's "clinical" attitude was new in fiction in 1846, yet it is prefigured in several respects in the most elaborate of Hoffmann's "Double" stories, the novel *Die Elixiere des Teufels,* and from that work Dostoevski now proceeded to draw further materials for the amplification of his theme.

The second period of twenty-four hours in our story occupy Chapters VI and VII and are pitched in a much lower key than the preceding section.

When Mr. Golyadkin awakes the morning after his midnight encounter on the Izmailovski Bridge, he recalls the previous events but dismisses them as more intrigues on the part of his enemies at the office. After delaying over several pipes he goes to work as usual. Scarcely is he settled at his desk when a door opens and through it comes his Double, the second Mr. Golyadkin. The latter is a clerk too, and he will work at a desk just *opposite* the real Mr. Golyadkin, that is in the position of a mirror image. (Is the reader intended to imagine that a mirror hangs on the office wall?) Cold sweat stands out on Mr. Golyadkin. When the Double goes briefly into the inner office Mr. Golyadkin takes the opportunity of speaking with the chief clerk, Anton Antonovich. The latter acknowledges the presence of a new office member who bears a striking resemblance to Mr. Golyadkin—(Does Dostoevski mean to say that all clerks look alike as a class?)—and asks him whether they are related. To Mr. Golyadkin it seems preposterous "to talk of a family resemblance when he could see himself as in a looking-glass." The talkative Anton Antonovich rambles on about Doubles and remarks that an aunt on his mother's side saw her Double just before her death. At the end of the office day Mr. Golyadkin makes haste to leave his work, but there in the street inexplicably his Double is to be found walking beside him. Humbly, deferentially, in halting sentences such as the real Mr. Golyadkin would have used, the new clerk requests his friendship, and Mr. Golyadkin, touched by the request, asks him home to supper.

Chapter VII presents the supper scene. It is a comico-pathetic one of a very lonely and friendless man who has had to create a second self to bear him company. At this point the situation strikingly resembles the beginning of "Pogorel'ski's" *The Double or My Evening in Little Russia,* where the author's Double appears for just this reason to the lonely nobleman and bachelor on his remote Ukrainian estate. The "Evenings" are the account of the discussions they had and the stories they told each other.[4] But where these two Antoni's were much concerned with philosophy and literature, the two Golyadkins find much pleasure in chit-chat about the city. Theirs is a cozy feast of small talk. Before long they call each other "Yasha,"[5] make mutual confessions, and even plot a little counter-conspiracy to confound the intriguers at the office. From the concluding paragraphs it is clear that Mr. Golyadkin is drunk and for a moment it looks as though the whole story might prove an alcoholic hallucination. The second day stands as a comic interlude in the whole work.

On the morning of the third day Mr. Golyadkin awakes to find no trace at all of his guest. (Chapter VIII.) When Petrushka brings the tea his manner is so ambiguous and he speaks so strangely about "the other one" that Mr. Golyadkin is alarmed. After the brief *entente cordiale* the dualism is about to enter its antagonistic phase.

Arriving at the office, Mr. Golyadkin finds his worst fears confirmed. His Double, last night so friendly, so confiding, has preceded him and already is busy at the task of destroying his reputation with his superiors. He blithely takes credit for the work which Mr. Golyadkin performs subserviently; he taunts him for his slowness, his shyness, his bald spot, his middle-aged paunch-belly; he makes a fool of him before the other clerks; he exposes all his fears, all his wounded pride, for the whole world to see. In the face of such treatment Mr. Golyadkin meekly bows and even takes a certain satisfaction from his deliberate humility.

It is clear that the new Mr. Golyadkin is the latent aggressive phase of Mr. Golyadkin's character and that this phase is slipping from his control. The Double is clever, he is successful, he is both sly and gay, he is a man of action, in short, a devil of a fellow. He has another trait, which since

Dostoevski's time has come to be thought of as a commonplace in schizophrenics: he is implacably hostile to the milder phase of the split personality. His sole aim is to destroy the antithetical self. A struggle to the death is the only possible course now.

It is in this deadly struggle of the antithetical selves that we find embodied much of the matter of Hoffmann's novel *Die Elixiere des Teufels,* not in the form of story elements now, though some of these will enter presently also, but rather as a distilled essence. *Die Elixiere des Teufels* relates the life of the runaway monk Medardus from the time of his apparent sainthood in his monastery, through his flight into the world and the mad course of passion and crime he pursued there, to his ultimate return to the monastery and his holy death. In this case the Double of Medardus is not a hallucination but an actual person, Count Viktorin, half-brother to the monk. Not only do they look absolutely identical, but there is at times an interpenetration of their personalities and experiences that goes beyond a rational explanation. At each stage of Medardus's strangely guided journey through the world Viktorin appears, and each time the deadly enmity between the two comes close to destroying the sinning, yet never fatally lost Medardus.

When first they meet, Viktorin is discovered sitting on the edge of a mountain cliff overlooking the Devil's Chasm. The monk, seeing him there apparently in a position ready to fall, attempts to save him, but at the touch of his hand Viktorin does fall and Medardus is horrified to think that he has actually caused the young man's death. Presently a groom appears, greets Medardus as his master, and from his talk it becomes plain that Viktorin had been planning to adopt monk's garb, pose as the Confessor of Euphemie, the adulterous wife of a certain Baron von F., and carry on his nefarious love affair under the cloak of religion. Straightway Medardus allows the groom to guide him to the castle of Baron von F. and there lives out Viktorin's evil plans. The result is tragedy thrice compounded and eventually Medardus flees from the house with the guilt of two murders upon him. Just outside the gate, when the pursuit is hot behind him, Medardus once again meets Viktorin's groom whom "chance" has prompted to come to his master with horses, coach, and a complete wardrobe.

On the way to the "mercantile city" the coachman loses his way in the darkness and Medardus is forced to become the guest of a forester. In the forester's house lives a half-mad monk in whose habit is sewn the name-tag: Medardus. His biography as retold by the forester is the story of Medardus's own childhood,—just as the life-story told by the second Mr. Golyadkin to the first in Chapter VII was actually the life story of the real Mr. Golyadkin. When Medardus, now dressed as a nobleman, is shown this fugitive monk, who is, of course, Viktorin, the latter passes into a kind of frenzy of hatred and screams:

> "Come up to the roof-top. There we shall wrestle with each other, and whoever throws the other down shall be king and drink blood!"

The spectacle fills Medardus with horror, and of himself, he says:

> "More than ever divided within myself, I became ambiguous to myself, and an inner horror came over my own being with a destructive power."

The "monk" Viktorin, who of late had been quite calm and lucid, now reverts to a bestially raving madness so that the forester decides he must be sent away lest he harm some member of the family in the forest-house.

Considering himself well rid of this creature "whose appearance reflected his own Self with features distorted and ghastly," Medardus continues his travels, coming eventually to a *Residenzstadt,* where he is presented at court. To the same court comes Aurelie, whom Medardus knew and loved at the home of her father, Baron von F. and whose brother, Hermogen, he had murdered. She denounces him as her brother's murderer, with the result that he is arrested and imprisoned. With lies born of desperation, he steadfastly maintains he is a Polish gentleman on his travels, but he is caught in the web of his own falsehoods until, suddenly, Viktorin is discovered in a madhouse of the same city and the crime is fastened upon him. Medardus is set free. In meditation of the state of affairs, he says:

> ". . . the conviction arose in me that it was not I who had been the ruthless criminal at the castle of Baron von F., who slew Euphemie, Hermogen, but rather that that deranged monk whom I had met at the forest-house had committed the deed. . . ."

Once his "innocence" is established, a wave of good fortune pours over the unrepentant sinner. Aurelie retracts her accusation and now admits that she loves Medardus. Their wedding day is set. It coincides precisely with the day appointed for the execution of Viktorin, and as the ceremonies begin, the hangman's cart passes the palace with the victim. Glimpsing Medardus at the window, the wretched Double cries:

> "Bridegroom, bridegroom! Come . . . come up to the roof . . . to the roof . . . there we shall wrestle with each other and whoever throws the other down shall be king and drink blood!"

The sight and the challenge of his other self sting Medardus into telling the truth. He laughs as he wildly declares his true identity, then turns, stabs Aurelie, leaps out of the window, cuts the prisoner's bonds with the same dagger, and vanishes through the crowd. That night in a dark forest Medardus drops to the ground from exhaustion. As he makes an effort to rise he is seized from behind by Viktorin, still in monk's garb. "You can't run," he laughs, "you can't run, you've got to carry me!" Then begins a fierce struggle which goes on and on in the darkness until consciousness is lost.

Three months later Medardus comes to himself:

> A gentle warmth pervaded my inner being. Then I felt a movement and a prickling in all my veins. This feeling was transformed into thought, but *my Self was di-*

vided hundredfold. Every member had its own movement, its own awareness of life, and the head commanded the members in vain. Like faithless vassals, they refused to assemble under its leadership. Now the thoughts of the separate parts began to circle like gleaming dots faster and faster, until they formed into a fiery circle. This became smaller as the speed increased, until at last it seemed a motionless ball of fire.
> . . .
>
> These are my limbs that are stirring, I am waking up.

He is in a monastery in Italy. He is lying in bed dressed in the habit of a monk. In the habit is sewn the name-tag: Medardus.

A long section of Italian adventures follows, until Medardus finally arrives at the monastery in Germany from which he had originally set out. His arrival is even more dramatic than if he had come simply from his own adventures, for a few days previously a beggar in rags had presented himself at the monastery gate, declaring himself to be Medardus the runaway. He was taken in but the prior doubted the alleged identity. Then illness came upon the man and, with death imminent, he summoned the prior and confessed that he was not Medardus but Count Viktorin. His confession is one of the most striking passages in the novel.

> "It seems to me that I must soon die, but first I must unburden my heart. You have power over me, for however much you try to conceal it, I perceive that you are St. Anthony and that you know best what evils your elixirs cause. I had high plans in mind when I determined to represent myself as a clerical gentleman with a big beard and a brown cowl. *But when I actually looked into myself, the strangest thoughts seemed to arise from within me and embodied themselves in a corporeal form which was horrible and which was my own Self.* This second self had fearful power and hurled me down, as from out of the black stones of the deep chasm the princess, snow-white, rose out of the swirling, foaming waters. The Princess took me up into her arms and washed my wounds, so that presently I felt no pain. I had indeed become a monk, but the Self of my thoughts was stronger and drove me on so that I had to murder the Princess who had rescued me and whom I loved very much, and to murder her brother as well. They threw me into a dungeon, but you yourself know, holy Anthony, in what way you carried me off through the air after I had swilled your accursed drink. The green Forest-King entertained me badly, despite the fact that he recognized my princely rank. *The Self of my thoughts appeared at his home and did all sorts of hateful things to me, and since we had done everything together, wanted to remain in a joint relationship with me.* That was arranged, but soon after, as we were running away from there, because people wanted to *cut off our head,* we separated again. When the foolish Self, however, kept trying always and forever to feed upon my thoughts, I knocked it down, whipped it hard, and took its coat away."[6]

Shortly after this confession Viktorin apparently dies, but his death, like his confession, was illusion. His body, brought to the monastery courtyard preparatory to burial, mysteriously vanishes. He returns for the great solemnities at which Aurelie is to take the veil of a nun. While Medardus undergoes his last and hardest temptation, watching, as a humble monk among fellow-monks, his beloved becoming the bride of Christ, Viktorin suddenly appears in the throng of worshippers, rushes into the sanctuary, and fatally stabs Aurelie, thus fulfilling the act once before attempted by Medardus. As Aurelie, now the nun Rosalia, dies, the murderer vanishes as suddenly as he had appeared. Not long afterwards Medardus dies, a manifest saint.

If the complex and melodramatic events of this novel seem remote from Mr. Golyadkin's situation, it must be remembered that Dostoevski was deliberately transposing this romantic subject matter into what he considered Gogolian comedy and that he was doing this within the confined limits of a short story about an obscure office employee. In Chapter XIII we shall see a more concrete borrowing from Hoffmann's novel, but just now we should keep in mind that the intensity of the Medardus-Viktorin conflict underlies the antagonism of the two Golyadkins. It should be noted further that Dostoevski has not given roughly equivalent will to both phases of the divided personality but that the "real" Mr. Golyadkin meekly suffers while his aggressive Double is wholly active. Typical of this is the conclusion of Chapter VIII where, having emerged together from the office on this difficult day, the insolent Double is seen suddenly departing gaily in a cab while Mr. Golyadkin is left standing forlorn and alone by a lamp post.

With Chapter IX the story reverts to the general outline of *Die Abenteuer der Sylvesternacht.* After the "travelling enthusiast's" unhappy evening at the soirée of the Justizrat and after his wild flight through the streets of Berlin, he arrived coatless and exhausted in a certain beer-cellar where he encountered Peter Schlemihl, the man without a shadow, and Erasmus Spikher, the man without a mirror-image, that is to say, two men whose Doubles were lost. Mr. Golyadkin now goes to a restaurant and there has a new encounter with his Double.

He is very hungry when he arrives. He orders a pie, sits down and eats it. Then he goes to pay the cashier. With astonishment he is told that he has consumed not one but eleven pies. He protests indignantly, but, not wishing to make a scene, he agrees to pay. All of a sudden he becomes aware of the reason for his plight:

> In the doorway of the next room, almost directly behind the waiter and facing Mr. Golyadkin, in the doorway which, till that moment, our hero *had taken for a looking-glass,* a man was standing—not the original Mr. Golyadkin, the hero of our story, but the other Mr. Golyadkin, the new Mr. Golyadkin.

As we would now say, Mr. Golyadkin, with his meek phase predominant, had cautiously eaten according to his poverty, then with a shift of his aggressive phase into predominant position, he had eaten ten more pies, not so much from hunger as from the will to torment and to humiliate his other Self.

The remainder of the chapter departs again from the *Sylvesternacht* pattern to take Mr. Golyadkin home to write a letter of protest about his Double's conduct. Here Dostoevski does not play quite fair with the reader. In each of several details he is evasive when we would most like to know precisely what happens. Petrushka, for example, merely laughs slyly when his master gives him the letter to deliver. While waiting for his return with the answer, Mr. Golyadkin walks to the home of his employer but does not enter. He comes back home and falls asleep. When Petrushka does finally return, the fellow is thoroughly drunk and unable to answer any questions. He declares at one minute that he delivered the letter and in the next minute says there *was* no letter. Golyadkin indignantly dismisses him. Then his eye catches something on the table. It is a letter, the answer to his protest. It tells him that he is a fool. He immediately writes a reply in which he urgently requests an interview in which to explain himself. When he awakes next morning this letter has disappeared. The question rises as to whether there ever were any letters except as Mr. Golyadkin composed them, both originals and replies. Quite possibly he maintained both parts of the correspondence himself. Or, still more probably, there is simply no rational explanation. The episode surely represents Dostoevski's version of that part of *The Diary of a Madman* where Poprishchin acquires the very informative letters written by the two dogs, Madgie and Fido, to each other. At any rate, the episode shows once again that Dostoevski was indeed writing his story with *The Diary of a Madman* for a basis.

In the same way, Chapter X shows that most closely related in his mind to the Gogol basis was Hoffmann's *Sylvesternacht,* for now the strange dreams that beset Mr. Golyadkin as he sleeps from the third far into the fourth and last day of his story are the exact counterpart of Chapter 3 of the Hoffmann tale. After his encounter with Schlemihl and Spikher in the beer-cellar, the "travelling enthusiast" repaired to a room at the "Golden Eagle" for the night. There, as he slept until far into the morning, he was beset with strange dreams.

The dreams take the form of a phantasmagorical recapitulation of the New Year's Eve party at the home of the Justizrat. There, the "travelling enthusiast" reports,

> . . . I was sitting on the ottoman next to Julie. But presently it seemed to me as though the whole company were a funny Christmas display at Fuchs's store, or Weide's, or Schloch's, or some other, and the Justizrat a dainty sugar-plum figure with a note-paper jabot. . . .

The siren Julie again offers him the goblet of steaming punch from which the blue flame rises. Erasmus Spikher in the form of a squirrel leaps upon his shoulder and warns him that Julie is a figure come to life out of the monitory paintings of Breughel, Callot, and Rembrandt. With his squirrel tail he beats the blue flame and cries: "Drink not! Drink not!"

> But now all the sugar-plum figures of the display came alive and moved their hands and feet comically. The sugar-plum Justizrat tripped up to me and in a faint little voice cried: "Why all the fuss, my good fellow, why all the fuss? Stand on your own good feet, for I've been noticing for some time now how you are walking around in the air over the chairs and tables."

Again Julie tempts. This time it is Peter Schlemihl who cries to the "travelling enthusiast": "This is Mina who married Rascal." (Characters out of Chamisso's *Peter Schlemihl*.) In approaching to say this, Schlemihl has stepped on several of the sugar-plum figures, causing them to groan aloud.

> These now multiplied by the hundreds and by the thousands and tripped up around me and up my person in a motley and loathsome throng. They buzzed around me like a swarm of bees.
>
> The sugar-plum Justizrat clambered as far as my collar, which he clutched tighter and tighter. "Accursed Justizrat!" I cried, and started up awake.

It is a bright clear day and already eleven o'clock in the morning.

Mr. Golyadkin's dreams also review the past. He beholds his superior Andrei Filipovich in an attitude of condemnation. He sees himself a distinguished guest in a distinguished gathering, until, just as his success is most brilliant, the other Mr. Golyadkin comes to spoil it. He sees himself rushing out into the street to hail a cab,

> but with every step he took, with every thud of his foot on the granite of the pavement, there leaped up as though out of the earth a Mr. Golyadkin precisely the same, perfectly alike, and of a revolting depravity of heart. And all these precisely similar Golyadkins set to running after one another as soon as they appeared, and stretched in a long chain like a file of geese, hobbling after the real Mr. Golyadkin, so there was nowhere to escape from these duplicates—so that the real Mr. Golyadkin, who was in every way deserving of compassion, was breathless with terror; so that at last a terrible multitude of duplicates had sprung into being; so that the whole town was obstructed at last by duplicate Golyadkins, and the police officer, seeing such a breach of decorum, was obliged to seize all these duplicates by the collar and to put them into the watch-house, which happened to be beside him. . . . Numb and chill with horror, our hero woke up. . . .
>
> It seemed as though it were rather late in the day. It was unusually light in the room. The sunshine filtered through the frozen panes and flooded the room with light. . . .
>
> It actually was one o'clock.

The motif of the multiplying doubles will occur again at the dénouement.[7]

We are now at early afternoon of the fourth and last day. The rest of Chapter X is devoted to another office sequence, unfortunately not very well differentiated from the former one. At the end of the day Mr. Golyadkin invites his Double and rival to a coffee house for a serious consultation. Their colloquy there (Chapter XI) is very interesting from the viewpoint of modern psychology, and it has no connection whatever with Hoffmann. The Double constantly makes off-color remarks about the waitresses and also flirts shamelessly with them, while the real Mr. Golyadkin lowers his eyes and confesses that he is "absolutely pure." The sexual suggestions sink deep into consciousness. The two leave the coffee house, take a cab together and drive to the home of Olsufi Ivanovich. There the Double goes in, while the real Mr. Golyadkin flees away. He goes to a tavern, and while there draws from his pocket a letter which he had no idea existed. How it came into his pocket he cannot imagine. (The motif of the Madgie-Fido letters from *The Diary of a Madman* again.) It is an appeal from Klara Olsufevna to rescue her that night from her tyrannical parents and a hated suitor. Mr. Golyadkin is intensely preoccupied by this letter, so much so that he occasions a scandalous scene in the tavern by attempting to leave without paying his bill. The bill paid, he hurries home to plan the rescue of Klara. At home he finds the official notice of his discharge from his position, and Petrushka is packing his effects preparatory to leaving his service.

Feverishly brooding over his plans for rescuing Klara, Mr. Golyadkin takes a cab (Chapter XII) and tells the driver to take him to the Izmailovski Bridge. No sooner started in that direction than he changes his mind and has the driver take him to the home of "His Excellency," one of his higher superiors. It is now early evening.

His Excellency has guests. But, no matter. Mr. Golyadkin goes right into the midst of the assembled guests. The light is so brilliant that he is dazzled.

> At last our hero could distinguish clearly the star on the black coat of His Excellency, then by degrees advanced to seeing the black coat and at last gained the power of complete vision. . . .

The mirror-reflection of every shiny surface now fascinates him. Readers of Hoffmann's *Sylvesternacht* will recall how Erasmus Spikher shrank from the sight of a highly polished snuff-box because it resembled a mirror. Mr. Golyadkin's gaze is held by the flashing star, then it is caught by the patent leather shoes on His Excellency's feet. His words are, of course, utterly unintelligible to His Excellency. The situation becomes more desperate by the minute, and now, "through a door which our hero had taken for a looking-glass" comes the impertinent Double to delight in his discomfiture. With his eyes on His Excellency's patent leather shoes and his mind pondering the nature of leather, polish, rays of light in artists' studios, Mr. Golyadkin is lost in a morass of gibberish. Suddenly he feels himself seized, propelled toward the door. "Just as it was at Olsufi Ivanovich's," he thinks. And so it is. His coat is tossed into the street after him. Then he finds himself in a cab. To the driver he cries to drive to the Izmailovski Bridge.

It is not clear just what Dostoevski intended by this fixation of Golyadkin's to return to the Izmailovski Bridge. Perhaps the unfortunate hero wished to return to the place where the Double went forth from him, in the hope of inducing the Double to return to him once more.

The foregoing chapter (XII), interesting as it is, is nevertheless regrettable in that it makes for repetition both of Chapter IV and the final Chapter XIII. No doubt Dostoevski wished to convey the impression of reality spinning about Mr. Golyadkin's consciousness in faster and faster tempo. Unfortunately, the reader sometimes feels as though he were spinning too.

The grand climax of *Die Elixiere des Teufels* occurs at the ceremonies where Medardus watches with renunciation while his beloved Aurelie is made a nun. In religion she takes the name Rosalia for the saint whose intercession for Medardus and for his sinning ancestors has been a recurrent theme of the book. The monastery church is full of people for the occasion, music rolls through the incense laden air, masses of flowers adorn the high altar. It is as though all the senses were receiving their consecration. As the bride of Christ, her vow spoken, waits to have her hair shorn, suddenly the wild Viktorin makes his way to her and stabs her to death by the altar. He escapes forever, but manifest miracle attends the death of the beautiful nun, while to Medardus comes the mysterious painter in his customary purple mantle to speak the final words of consolation. The painter is actually the monk's sinful ancestor five generations removed, whose sin is now expiated and whose miraculously prolonged life may now find rest. Heaven and Hell are present at this culminating scene of the novel, which has the form of a saint's legend, for this is the triumphant overthrow of the works of Evil by the Powers of Good.

The final chapter of **The Double** is not *like* this scene, but it is *analogous* to it. This whole finale, at which Mr. Golyadkin appears once again at the home of Olsufi Ivanovich, presents neither a realistic room nor realistic guests. The previous visit in Chapter IV may be called realistic in so far as it correctly portrayed what a half demented man saw, but this time Dostoevski is not merely repeating himself. Mr. Golyadkin here appears before a kind of Last Judgment.

Not only the drawing-room but the entire house is described as being full to overflowing. There are "masses of people, a whole galaxy of ladies." They are there, row on row, like the heavenly hosts. Klara Olsufevna is there, dressed in white, with a white flower in her hair,—like an angel. Olsufi Ivanovich is enthroned in an arm-chair like a heavenly judge. Mr. Golyadkin's office superiors are there and they gather about the judge. A solemn hush falls. The Double stands in the throng at some remove from the soul

awaiting judgment. White, dazzling light pervades the whole place. At a sign from the superiors, the perfidious Double takes Mr. Golyadkin's hand, then bends and kisses him "with his Judas kiss":

> There was a ringing in Mr. Golyadkin's ears, and a darkness before his eyes; it seemed to him that an infinite multitude, an unending series of precisely similar Golyadkins were noisily bursting in at every door of the room.

The door does indeed open and the Double, with vicious delight, identifies the newcomer as "Krestyan Ivanovich Rutenspitz, doctor of medicine and surgery, your old acquaintance." Judgment has been passed, and this stern policeman of heaven will take him away to outer darkness. He is led down the stairs:

> Faint with horror, Mr. Golyadkin looked back. The whole of the brightly lighted staircase was crowded with people; inquisitive eyes were looking at him from all sides; Olsufi Ivanovich was sitting in his easy-chair on the top landing, and watching all that took place with deep interest. . . .

It is the condemned soul's last lingering look backwards toward Paradise.

And now, a final touch from *Die Elixiere des Teufels*. When Medardus, elegantly dressed as a nobleman and travelling about the world, met his Double in monk's garb at the home of the forester, the effect was to send the wretched Viktorin back to his previous state of raving madness, so that the forester felt compelled to send him away for safety's sake. Medardus watched his departure:

> When I came down, a rack-wagon bedded down with straw was standing in front of the door ready to leave. The monk was brought out. With face deathly pale and distorted, he allowed himself to be led along quite patiently. He answered no question, refused to take anything to eat, and scarcely seemed aware of the persons about him. They hoisted him into the wagon and tied him fast with cords, inasmuch as his condition seemed doubtful and they were not at all sure there would not be a sudden outburst of his inwardly repressed fury. As they secured his arms, his face became convulsively distorted and he emitted a low groan. His condition pierced my heart. He had become closely related to me, indeed it was only to his ruin that I owed my salvation. . . . Only as they started to drive away did his glance fall upon me, and he was suddenly seized with profound astonishment. Even when the wagon was disappearing into the distance (we had followed it as far as the wall) his head remained turned and his eyes directed toward me.[8]

So, now, as Mr. Golyadkin is conducted down the shining stairs from the white light to the waiting darkness, "the malignant Mr. Golyadkin junior in three bounds flew down the stairs and opened the carriage door himself," and once the doomed man is seated inside and the vehicle gets under way, several persons, including the Double, run alongside. But "Mr. Golyadkin's unworthy twin kept up longer than anyone," and he follows the carriage for some distance, gesticulating and throwing farewell kisses.

Mr. Golyadkin, half suffocated with fright, finally addresses Rutenspitz:

"I believe . . . I'm all right, Krestyan Ivanovich. . . ."

But a great voice "stern and terrible as a judge's sentence" rings out:

"You get free quarters, wood, with light, and service, the which you deserve not."

Two fiery eyes stare at him from the darkness.

He is on his way to the madhouse, a real madhouse, like the one to which Poprishchin was sent. But he is also in Hell, the outer darkness pierced by two eyes of a watchful demon.

Our hero shrieked and clutched his head in his hands. Alas! For a long while he had been haunted by a presentiment of this.

So ends the remarkable story.[9]

Notes

1. This famous tale of the luckless fellow who sold his shadow to the "man in grey" originally appeared as *Peter Schlemihl's wundersame Geschichte* mitgeteilt von Adelbert von Chamisso und herausgegeben von Friedrich Baron de la Motte Fouqué, 1814. Its fame was almost instantaneous. Hoffmann's *Sylvesternacht*, which introduces Schlemihl into a new setting together with a patently imitated figure who has lost his mirror-image, was composed in the first week in January,—hence directly after New Year's Eve,—in the year 1815. On the night of the 13th Hoffmann gave a reading of the new work to a group of friends, of whom Chamisso was one.

2. *Kater Murr*, Erster Band, zweiter Abschnitt; the 8th "Makulaturblatt."

3. For a notable instance of such procedure, which may not be unrelated to this chapter-close, see *Die Elixiere des Teufels*, end of the Erster Abschnitt des zweiten Teils, where the pair of Doubles wrestle all night in deadly combat in the forest until Medardus loses consciousness. It is never explained how he managed finally to elude his antagonist. The beginning of the following section (Zweiter Teil, Erster Abschnitt—*Die Busse*) describes Medardus coming to consciousness—three months later.

4. See Notes 4 and 7 to the preceding chapter.

5. Yasha is the diminutive of Yakov (James). The hero's full name is Yakov Petrovich Golyadkin.

6. Note the interpenetration of the lives of Medardus and Viktorin. This confession reads like the experiences of *Medardus* seen through the medium of a deranged mind.

7. Medardus, in a passage previously quoted, describes his waking in the Italian monastery by saying ". . . my Self was divided hundred-fold."

In this connection, another Tale of Hoffmann may be mentioned, *Die Brautwahl*, the opening chapters of which deal with the adventures of the hapless Privy Councilor Tusmann in the streets of Berlin on the night of the autumnal equinox. Tusmann has for opponents certain persons who control very potent magic and who have undertaken certain "operations" to forestall his marriage to the heroine, Albertine Vosswinkel, who is thirty years his junior. At one stage of the "operations" he finds himself compelled to waltz up and down the Spandauerstrasse with a broomstick (Chapter 3). Suddenly the place around him "teemed with Privy Councillor Tusmanns," all of them waltzing with broomsticks.—A page or two previously he had tried to enter his own house, but there at the door he met "himself" and "stared wildly at himself with the same large black eyes as are located in his own head."

Tusmann's adventures will be used by Dostoevski as the partial basis for *An Unpleasant Predicament*, a short story of 1862, and it is quite likely that *Die Brautwahl* is to be included in the various Hoffmann works which contributed details to *The Double*. The primary point of connection would be the bizarre nocturnal adventures of the middle-aged hero in the streets of the capital.

8. It should be observed that this passage is paralleled *within* Hoffmann's novel by the scene where the would-be bridegroom Medardus looks down from the palace window to behold his Double being carried in the hangman's cart to execution. Undoubtedly both scenes are to be related to the final pages of Dostoevski's story.

9. Complex as this analysis has been, it has not wholly exhausted the elements that went into Dostoevski's story.

See V. V. Vinogradov: *Evoliutsiya russkago naturalizma*, Leningrad, 1929, a series of six articles; Article 5: *K Morfologii natural'nogo stilya. Opyt lingvisticheskogo analiza Petersburgskoi poemy "Dvoinik,"* pp. 239 ff., fills four pages with linguistic and stylistic parallels between *The Double* and Gogol's *Dead Souls*.

See also S. Rodzevich: *K Istorii russkago romantizma* in *Russki Filologicheski Vestnik*, LXXVII (1917), pp. 194–237. On page 223 Rodzevich mentions that Hoffmann's *Klein Zaches* and *Prinzessin Brambilla* have bearing on *The Double*, but does not elaborate his statement. The case for *Prinzessin Brambilla* is dubious except in so far as it deals with the interlocked worlds of reality and "higher reality," in which respect it would run competition from various other works of Hoffmann. From *Klein Zaches* could very plausibly come the motif of Zaches's fateful fairy-gift of receiving credit for every good thing said or done by anyone in his presence. This would apply to the passages where Mr. Golyadkin Junior gets credit at the office for the work done by the staid Mr. Golyadkin Senior.

Lawrence Kohlberg (essay date 1963)

SOURCE: "Psychological Analysis and Literary Form: A Study of the Doubles in Dostoevsky," in *Daedalus,* Vol. 92, No. 2, Spring, 1993, pp. 345–62.

[*In the following essay, Kohlberg presents a psychoanalytic interpretation of doubles in Dostoevsky's works.*]

> Psychology is a knife that cuts both ways.
>
> —*The Brothers Karamazov*

> Illness, delirium, amnesia, but why were you haunted by just those delusions and not by any others?
>
> —*Crime and Punishment*

To the psychologist looking at contemporary literature, there is a rather paradoxical discrepancy between the impact of psychoanalysis upon creative and upon critical writing. While it is almost impossible to find a serious modern novel or drama which would not be profoundly different without the existence of psychoanalytic concepts, this can hardly be said for modern literary criticism.

A major factor in the impact of psychoanalytic ideas upon creative writing is the ability of psychoanalysis to breathe new life into old myths and literary forms. This invigorating effect springs in large part from the psychoanalytic balance of concern for inward forces and outward action, each revealing something otherwise mysterious about the person. In contrast, the introspectionism of the Jamesian psychological novel leads to an essential meaninglessness of action, while the Hemingway or "new wave" behaviorism is a complete denial of the meaning of the internal.

The revivifying effect of psychoanalysis upon old literary forms is most clearly apparent in tragedy, which the Freudian world-view makes meaningful for a scientifically oriented and morally relativistic culture. Faithful to necessities apparent in its early Athenian form, tragedy requires a crime to be committed which is both willed and unwilled; both free and foreordained, a fated act for which the actor is yet responsible. As tragic crime is foreordained but willed, so tragic punishment is both doom and self-discovery of evil. In Athenian tragedy, the fated aspects of crime and punishment were the result of cruel but moral external forces. In the modern "psychoanalytic" form of tragedy, the fated aspects of crime and punishment are the products of uncontrolled and unconscious internal forces. The crime is the fated result of immutable instinctual impulses; the inevitable doom which follows the crime is the result of unconscious and inescapable needs for punishment. Other "scientific" worldviews, such as the sociological determinism embodied in Dreiser's *American Tragedy,*

provide a sense of the inevitability of crime and punishment. This inevitability, however, is the product of purely external and amoral forces, and cannot be combined with the willed self-discovery and repentance characteristic of classic tragedy.

In contrast with its revolutionary impact upon creative writing, psychoanalysis seems of only minor importance to modern literary criticism. The common awareness of psychological sickness and symbol in a literary work is believed to detract, rather than add to, understanding and appreciation of the work. Critics who feel that this awareness can be used constructively, such as Burke, Guerard, Hyman, Kazin, Trilling, and Wilson use psychoanalysis primarily as myth, as one element or world-view among many which sensitize the reader of a work of art to its meaning. The construction and "proof" of a detailed psychoanalytic interpretation seems out of place in such literary criticism.

Critical articles in the professional psychiatric journals present a striking contrast. In these, the literary meaning of the work of art is not considered as central to the analytic task. In contrast with the critical use of psychoanalysis as sensitizing "myth," the professional psychoanalyst attempts to use psychoanalytic theory to provide a comprehensive and true explanation of why a given writer wrote just what he did. He brings to literature the habits of the clinic which require that a decision or diagnosis be made, and the habits of a scientist which require that a hypothesis be judged, not as inspiring, but as true or false.

Of all writers, none has elicited more of this case-study approach than Dostoevsky, that archetype of the psychopathological genius. Some of these studies, diagnosing Dostoevsky on the basis of biographical data, as if he were a case to be committed to a hospital or a course of therapy, have come to such conclusions as, "Dostoevsky was an epileptic, schizophrene, paranoid type, complicated by hysterical overlay."[1] Other studies focus upon Dostoevsky's unconscious conflicts as projected into his novels. The classic example of this type of study is Freud's essay on Dostoevsky,[2] in which he views Dostoevsky as preoccupied by parricidal impulses and resultant guilt, a conflict projected into Dmitri and Ivan Karamazov. Still other studies focus upon the analysis of a specific character in a novel as if he were a real person, coming to such conclusions as that "Raskolnikov was an autistic personality with traces of the manic depressive"[3] or that "Raskolnikov's murder was a result of efforts to appease unconscious guilt due to an incestuous attachment to his sister."[4]

Both academic psychologist and humanist question this sort of study. In the first place, it is impossible to know whether these interpretations are true. The characters are not real people, the biographical data on the author is inadequate, and a novel is not a psychological projective-test response by an author. Even if the case data were adequate, one could not achieve scientific certainty in the interpretation of a single case. Few would disagree with

Kris[5] that "It would seem as well demonstrated as any conclusion in the social sciences that the struggle against incestuous impulses, dependency, guilt, and aggression has remained a recurrent topic of Western literature from Sophocles to Proust." The ubiquity of certain themes in myth and literature, though undeniable, does not, however, contribute to certainty of interpretation of any individual case.

The second reservation is an even more crucial one. What difference does it make to the intelligent reader's understanding of a novel to know that Dostoevsky had parricidal impulses or was an epileptic schizophrene? Even Freud seems to agree with this caveat, since he begins his essay on Dostoevsky as follows:

> Four facets may be distinguished in the rich personality of Dostoevsky—the creative artist, the neurotic, the moralist and the sinner. How is one to find one's way in this bewildering complexity? The creative artist is least doubtful. *The Brothers Karamazov* is the most magnificent novel ever written. . . . Before the problem of the creative artist, analysis must, alas, lay down its arms.

Freud would feel that his analysis of Dostoevsky helps explain the power of Dostoevsky's novel in that "It can scarcely be owing to chance that three of the masterpieces of all literature *Oedipus Rex, Hamlet,* and *The Brothers Karamazov* should all deal with the same subject, parricide." In Freud's view, "parricide is the principal and primal crime of humanity as well as of the individual, and the main source of the sense of guilt"; and in some sense the power of *The Brothers Karamazov* lies in its confrontation of the reader with his own guilt-laden impulses in a situation in which identification with the hero is at a sufficient distance to allow "catharsis through pity and fear." Even if one granted this interpretation, it hardly explains the difference between murder in Dostoevsky and murder in Mickey Spillane.

The present paper is an effort to show that psychoanalysis need not entirely "lay down its arms" before Dostoevsky, the creative artist; it will use a psychological analysis to clarify two literary problems important in the appreciation and understanding of Dostoevsky's novels: the first, his use of Doubles; the second, his particular and unique moral ideology.

In recent years, literary critics have come to believe that an understanding of Dostoevsky's use of Doubles is the key to an understanding of the structure of his novels, a key which radically revises early critical views of Dostoevsky's novels as "badly constructed and unwieldly." An example of such a recent structural or "technique" interpretation of the Doubles is Beebe's analysis of *Crime and Punishment:*

> If we approach *Crime and Punishment* with a knowledge of Dostoevsky's character and method of writing, we are likely to be surprised at the disciplined skill the structure of the novel reveals. It meets the test of unity in action; all the parts contribute to the whole and the parts may be fully understood only when the whole is known. One of the ways in which Dostoevsky unified his novel is through his technique of "doubles." The dual nature of his heroes is, of course, a commonplace of criticism. Because his protagonists are usually split personalities, the psychological and philosophical drama in a Dostoevsky novel is expressed in terms of a conflict between opposite poles of sensibility and intelligence, self-sacrifice and self-assertion, God-Man and Man-God, or sometimes "good" and "bad." To dramatize this conflict, Dostoevsky often gives his characters several alter-egos or doubles, each projecting one of the extremes of the split personality. Even when the hero is not present in the scene, he may represent the center of interest because the characters present, represent different facets of his personality. According to most interpretations of *Crime and Punishment,* the struggle within Raskolnikov becomes physical external action as he wavers between Svidrigailov, epitome of self-willed evil, and Sonia, epitome of self-sacrifice and spiritual goodness.

> [J. M. Beebe, "The Three Motives of Raskolnikov," in E. Wasiolek (editor), *Crime and Punishment and the Critics* (San Francisco: Wadeworth, 1961).]

Dostoevsky's Doubles, however, are not mere portrayals of ties between stereotyped representatives of good and evil to be found throughout good and bad fiction. They obviously contain much personal symbolic meaning and are intended to have a psychopathological basis. They not only express ideological values and requirements of plot but enact or express murders of kin, rapes of little girls, spider fantasies, mutilation themes, epileptic attacks, suicide, necrophilia and hallucinations, and were viewed by Dostoevsky himself as forms of psychopathology. The *Raw Youth* says: "What then precisely is the 'double'? The 'double,' at any rate according to a medical work by an expert which I read for the purpose is nothing but the first stage in some serious mental derangement which may lead to a bad conclusion, a dualism between feeling and willing."

Not only does Dostoevsky view his Doubles as "psychopathological," but his preoccupation with Doubles precedes the ideological and structural use he was to make of them in his later novels. This preoccupation on a purely psychological level is expressed in Dostoevsky's second novel, written before his Siberian exile and entitled **The Double,** a novel which he said "contained a great deal of myself."

The hero of this novel, Golyadkin, is one of Dostoevsky's typical, socially isolated petty officials desperately striving to maintain some appearance of respectability in spite of poverty, social incompetence, and deep feelings of inferiority. He awakes in a clouded state, on the verge of a breakdown, believing that something is being got up against him by his colleagues at the office, that there is a conspiracy afloat, that his reputation has been blackened and that his enemies are trying to ruin him.

After consulting his doctor he decides to attend a ball that evening given by his former patron ("who has been a father to him") in honor of his daughter. Golyadkin has not been invited and is under a cloud because of some unspecified recent behavior. He is refused admission by the footman, but enters the house surreptitiously and lurks in the corridor. Suddenly in contradiction to his usual self-effacement, some mysterious brazen impulse "projects" him into the ballroom and leads him to insist on dancing with the daughter. He is ignominiously thrown out on the street.

He then wanders about the streets and contemplates suicide by drowning. He has an uncanny feeling that there is someone near, and in terror recognizes the presence of a Double, a figure exactly like himself, who accompanies him home.

The next day, he finds the Double ensconced at a desk at his office, as if he had always worked there, ingratiating himself with his colleagues and superiors, and ridiculing Golyadkin. All of this Golyadkin II's misconduct is blamed on Golyadkin I, while Golyadkin II gets credit for all of Golyadkin I's efforts. Golyadkin views the Double as an indecent, shameless, malevolent toady but nevertheless attempts to be friendly with him and is insulted and humiliated for his pains.

After agonies of humiliation, rage, fear, and suspicion, Golyadkin believes a solution awaits him. He believes he has received a note from the daughter of his patron asking him to elope with her and arranging a rendezvous. He awaits her at the appointed time in hiding outside her house, just as he had in the episode preceding the emergence of the Double. His Double trots out and hustles him into the house where a crowd is gathered, staring at him. He is suddenly surrounded by an "infinite procession of Golyadkins noisily bursting in at every door of the room." He is carried away to the lunatic asylum by his own cruel doctor while the Double hangs on to the carriage door and pokes his head in the window.

In this tale, Dostoevsky's use of the Double theme of Hoffman and Gogol does not achieve any grand artistic purpose, but it does offer a compelling picture of psychopathology. Accordingly, we shall attempt to settle the purely diagnostic questions about the Double phenomena it presents before considering the literary meanings of the Double themes.

The only serious treatment of *The Double* from a psychopathological view is provided in a monograph written in the early twenties by Otto Rank, Freud's "most gifted follower."[6] Rank proclaims the novel to be a classic portrayal of a paranoid state. There are indeed strong resemblances between the phenomena presented in *The Double* and familiar psychiatric phenomena of paranoid states. Paranoid delusions or hallucinations of persecutory figures emerge from feelings of shame and pathologically low self-esteem. These delusions are presumed to be the result of the defence mechanism of "disowning projection." Shameful impulses and tendencies toward self-accusation are denied as belonging to the self and are projected upon external imagined enemies. Obviously Dostoevsky intended Golyadkin II to be a hallucination representing the assertive, shameless impulses which first "propelled" Golyadkin I into his patron's ballroom, since the novel ends with the double propelling him again into the same ballroom. Golyadkin I's sense of low esteem, his feeling that he is being intrigued against, his life in a world in which he makes and receives veiled threats and innuendoes, are indeed striking portrayals of the paranoid attitude.

It also seems likely that *The Double* may have expressed one of Dostoevsky's states at the time of the writing of the novel, a state of feeling humiliated and "persecuted" in connection with the outbreak of previously unsuspected or unacknowledged qualities in his own personality. Just previous to writing *The Double,* the success of *Poor Folk* had completely turned his head and transformed him from a shy, sensitive, aloof romantic to someone capable of writing such statements as the following to his brother:

> Well brother, I believe my fame is just now in its fullest flower. Everybody looks on me as a wonder of the world. If I but open my mouth the air resounds with what Dostoevsky said, what Dostoevsky means to do. . . . Bielinky declares Turgenev has quite lost his heart to me. . . . All the Minnas, Claras, Mariannas, etc., have got amazingly pretty, but cost a lot of money.[7]

The reaction of his acquaintances to this sort of bombast was to nickname Dostoevsky "the literary pimple." Indeed, *The Double* commences with Golyadkin saying: "A fine thing if something untoward had happened today and a strange pimple had come up." Presumably his double was the "literary pimple" which erupted that day from within Golyadkin's personality.

In spite of these considerations, *The Double* is not the portrayal of a genuine psychiatric phenomenon of paranoia, as Dostoevsky himself may have believed. While the feelings of persecution and the disowning of part of the self portrayed in *The Double* have psychiatric parallels in paranoid states, the experience of a hallucinatory duplicate of the self is not explained by, or consistent with, a paranoid psychosis. The typical paranoid concept is one of a spotless self being unjustly blamed and tortured by evil others. In contrast, Dostoevsky's hallucinatory or semi-hallucinatory Doubles persecute their creators by asserting their identity with them, and usually their creators are aware that the Double is their "other self." Stavrogin says of his hallucinations (in the suppressed chapter of *The Possessed*):

> It shows different faces and characters yet it is always the same. I know it is different aspects of myself splitting themselves off yet it wants to be an independent devil so an independent devil it must be.

Such self-awareness is quite alien to the paranoid state. If the paranoid persecutors were to be experienced as duplicates of the self, the defensive function of the hallucinations would break down, since they would no longer protect the self against the awareness that it is the possessor of shameful impulses.

Another "popular-psychiatry" concept often used by literary critics, the "split personality," is equally inadequate as an accurate interpretation of the Double phenomenon. This concept is suggested by Versilov in *The Raw Youth* who says:

> I am really split in two mentally, and I am horribly afraid of it. It is just as though one's *second self* were standing beside one; one is sensible and rational oneself, but the other self is compelled to do something perfectly senseless and sometimes very funny; and suddenly you notice you are longing to do that amusing thing, goodness knows why. I once knew a doctor who suddenly began whistling in church, at his father's funeral.

These divided selves of Dostoevsky do not, however, correspond to psychiatric notions of the "split personality." The most common psychiatric conception of the "split personality" refers to the hysterical phenomenon of multiple personalities, the *Three Faces of Eve;* each living a Jekyll and Hyde existence in independence of one another. Unlike such multiple personalities, the "selves" within any of Dostoevsky's figures are simultaneously aware of one another. These "split selves" have equally little to do with schizophrenia, in the sense in which this has been misleadingly mistranslated as "split personality."

Dostoevsky's consciously "split" characters do present classical symptoms of the obsessive-compulsive character, however. The "split" is not a separation of selves, it is an obsessive balancing or undoing of one idea or force with its opposite. Most characteristically, a sacred idea compulsively arouses a degrading idea; the sacredness of the father's funeral compels the impulse to whistle. The hero of *Notes from Underground* says, "At the very moment when I am most capable of feeling every refinement of all that is good and beautiful it would, as though by design, happen to me not only to feel, but to do, such ugly things."

Not only impulse and counter-impulse, but belief and disbelief are opposed and simultaneously felt in a compulsion neurosis. According to Ivan's devil, "Some can contemplate such depths of belief and disbelief at the same moment that sometimes it really seems as if they are within a hairbreadth of being turned upside down."

Psychoanalysts view these obsessional oppositions as representing conflicts derived from a battle of wills in early childhood, centering around training conflicts. According to Erikson's *Childhood and Society,* this conflict is between autonomy and shame or doubt. Shame, Erikson says, "is an emotion insufficiently studied because in our culture it is so early and easily absorbed by guilt. Shame supposes that one is completely exposed and conscious of being looked at, i.e. self-conscious. It is essentially rage turned against the self."

The "Underground" man tells us:

> With an intense acute pang I was stabbed to the heart by the thought that ten years, twenty years, forty years would pass and even in forty years I would remember with loathing and humiliation those filthiest, most ludicrous, and awful moments of my life. No one could have gone out of his way to degrade himself more shamelessly, and I fully realized it, fully, and yet I went on.

In the self-abasers, feelings of shame are responded to by further self-abasement, since such self-lowering debases and denies the others before whom shame is felt. Fyodor Karamazov says, "I feel when I meet people that I am lower than all and that they all take me for a buffoon, so I say let me play the buffoon for you are, every one of you, lower than I."

The psychoanalytic notion of the obsessional character focused on a conflict between autonomy and shame helps us understand a very puzzling aspect of the literary structure of *Notes from Underground.* The book is composed of two quite different parts: the first an ideological discussion, the second a presentation of some excursions in self-degradation. The ideological portion is an assertion of the need for free will, rational or irrational, against the rational determinism of Western scientific thought. The other half of the work is the expression of the "shame-humiliation syndrome." Some unity in these two parts of the book is provided by the emotional congruity of a personality type in whom the desperate need for freedom from domination or control is linked to the cycle of shame and denial of others.

This analysis of Dostoevsky's "split personalities" as related to obsessional ambivalence and shame does not directly aid us in understanding his Doubles. There is, however, a very direct psychiatric parallel to the kind of hallucination described in *The Double.* This parallel is the "autoscopic syndrome," a syndrome with no relationship to paranoid states. A typical case is that of Mrs. A:

> Mrs. A returned home from her husband's funeral and when she opened the door to her bedroom, she immediately became aware of the presence of somebody else in the room. In the twilight she noticed a lady in front of her. Under the light she noticed that the stranger wore an exact replica of her own coat, hat, and veil. Mrs. A was neither surprised nor afraid and began to undress. The lady in black did exactly the same. Only then looking into the stranger's face, did Mrs. A become aware that it was she herself, as if in a mirror, that it was her 'double,' her 'second self' looking at her. She felt it was more alive and warm than she was herself. Feeling tired and weary, she lay down on her bed. As soon as she closed her eyes, the apparition disappeared. She felt stronger and when she opened her eyes, the apparition was not visible. Since that evening she had been visited almost daily by her 'astral body,' as she called it, mostly at dusk when she was alone. Of the double she says, 'In a detached intellectual way I am fully aware that my double is only a hallucination.

Yet I see it; I hear it; I feel it with my senses. Emotionally I feel it as a living part of myself. It is me split and divided. It is all so confusing.'[8]

Almost everything Mrs. A says is echoed by one or another of Dostoevsky's Double-haunted figures. The physical details of the appearance of Dostoevsky's hallucinatory Double are very close to those described by autoscopic patients. Ivan's satanic Double has frozen in his trip through space, and is underdressed in summer clothes, though it is winter; autoscopic Doubles are typically cold, often described as bringing "a breeze of cold air." As in autoscopic experiences, Dostoevsky's Doubles appear at dusk or night, typically when the subject is alone in his bedroom. Like them, Dostoevsky's Doubles tend to be colorless, to be described in shades of grey.

Surprisingly, the likelihood of Dostoevsky's having experienced the autoscopic syndrome has not been mentioned in the extensive psychological literature on Dostoevsky. Nevertheless, there is good reason to believe that he actually had these experiences. While the autoscopic syndrome is rare, it is often linked with severe epilepsy of the sort known to have affected Dostoevsky. The syndrome is extremely puzzling since it is found associated with a variety of conditions, usually organic (epilepsy, parietal brain damage, and severe migraine) but occasionally purely emotional (schizoid personality, depressions).

There is reason to believe that an unusual number of writers have experienced autoscopic hallucinations. Maupassant definitely had hallucinations of a duplicate self in the middle stages of his syphilitic or paretic psychosis,[9] hallucinations quite faithfully described in *Le Horla*. Some writers without organic pathology definitely experienced the autoscopic syndrome, including Hoffman, de Musset, Richter and probably Poe.[10] The phenomenon represents a projection of the body-image into space, or a loss of bodily coordinates of the body image. The variations in reported emotional reactions to autoscopic hallucinations are striking: sometimes satisfaction, sometimes sadness, sometimes dread, sometimes indifference. There does not seem to be a single emotional meaning or genesis common to all cases of the autoscopic syndrome. While the psychiatric label provides a basis for understanding Dostoevsky's preoccupation with Doubles, it does not seem to specify their meaning to him or to his novels.

To cast further light on this problem, we must consider the variety of Doubles in Dostoevsky's other novels. We may best begin with some findings from a statistical study of Dostoevsky's characters. Our study made use of a method called "Q technique,"[11] designed to bring some objectivity of inference into the analysis of the single case. Both Dostoevsky and his characters were rated on a large number of traits, both psychoanalytic and ideological. The results were factor analyzed to define types of character in relation to Dostoevsky's own personality.

Undoubtedly this effort to control statistically the psychology which "cuts both ways" would cause its subject to repeat in anguish the famous statement in *Notes from Underground* about "life in the Crystal Palace":

> All human actions will then be tabulated according to these laws, mathematically, like tables of logarithms. But man still is man and not the key of a piano and even if it were proved to him by science and mathematics that he were nothing but a piano key, even then he would not become reasonable but would purposely do something perverse simply to gain his point; if necessary, he will contrive destruction and chaos and sufferings and launch a curse upon the world. If you say all this, too, can be calculated and tabulated—chaos, darkness, and curses, so that the mere possibility of calculating it all beforehand would stop it all, and mathematical reason would reassert itself—then man would purposely go mad in order to be rid of reason and gain his point!

The "chaos, darkness, suffering and curses" of Dostoevsky's characters proved quite amenable to tabulation and defined very stable, clearcut types in the factor analysis. These types were the same (*i.e.*, characters were divided into the same groups) whether psychoanalytic or ideological traits were used as the basis for type formation.[12]

The types which resulted are not likely to make the conventional literary critic "defy mathematical reason," since they are not very different from those familiar in the Dostoevsky criticism.

The types [of characters] . . . are useful in sketching out the meaning of Dostoevsky's Doubles. The most unique of Dostoevsky's Doubles are hallucinations (Golyadkin II in *The Double* and the devils in *The Possessed* and *The Brothers Karamazov*). These hallucinations persecute their flesh and blood counterparts by insisting on the fundamental identity of the two. These hallucinatory Doubles are all our Type I "bad Doubles," and they are imagined by our Type V "will murderers." Raters assigned high scores to Type I characters on the traits: "A mysterious and sinister affinity to another character," "Is a Double who is an intellectual inferior, a caricature of his alter-ego," "Is a persecuting Double." Type V characters tended to be rated high on the complementary traits, e.g., "Is persecuted by a Double."

A second type of Double is defined by the figures of Smerdyakov in *The Brothers Karamazov* and Pyotr Verkhovensky in *The Possessed*. These flesh and blood characters were distinct from the hallucinatory Doubles on the psychoanalytic traits but not the ideological. They are "psychopathic" figures who carry out murders wished for by the "paranoids" Ivan and Stavrogin, and are mysterious "half-brothers" to them.

Still a third type of Double is represented by the Christ-figures of our Type II. These Christ-figures, with the exception of Sonia in *Crime and Punishment,* have alter-egos among our Type VI impulsives. These relations, like those last mentioned, are described in a terminology of "brother" and "sister," real or spiritual. Prince Myshkin has a mysterious affinity to Rogozhin and to Nastasya in *The Idiot,* both an attraction and a feeling of a linkage of fate. Alyosha Karamazov is, in a somewhat similar sense, an alter-ego to his brother Dmitri who enacts sexual and aggressive impulses which Alyosha somehow shares. Dmitri tells him:

> I want to tell you now about the insects to whom God gave sensual lust. I am that insect, brother, and all we Karamazovs are such insects, and, angel as you are, that insect lives in you, too, and will stir up a tempest in your blood.

Like Myshkin, Alyosha knows his impulsive Double will attempt murder, dreads it, but is strangely paralyzed or passive about preventing it. In some sense, Type VI, the impulsives, seem to represent or enact the impulses of Type II, the Christ-figures, just as Type I figures enact the impulses of Type V, the "paranoid" will-murderers. The relationship between Types I and V is explicit and consciously intended by Dostoevsky, while the relationship between Type II and VI is much more cloudy and undefined.

Our statistically derived map shows many clear-cut and recurring aspects to Dostoevsky's Doubles. These are not the result of the requirements of structure of a particular book since they are repeated from novel to novel. They are also not explained, however, by mere knowledge that Dostoevsky may have experienced the autoscopic phenomenon. The autoscopic Doubles are assigned a definite evil personality constant from book to book and are in some mysterious way part of a world including good-and-evil, flesh-and-blood alter-egos.

To enrich our notion of the meaning of these facts in relation to the autoscopic syndrome, we may turn to Otto Rank's discussion of "The Double as Immortal Self" in his last book, *Beyond Psychology.* No better example of the fact that "psychology is a knife which cuts both ways" can be provided than Rank's two writings on the Double. His first treatment is an orthodox psychoanalytic interpretation; his second written thirty years later is part of his own effort to form a theory which is "Beyond Psychology," *i.e.,* beyond psychoanalysis.

Rank's last discussion of literary Doubles is based on his postulation of a universal striving for immortality or rebirth in man's noninstinctual but irrational will. This striving is especially strong in the artist type, says Rank in *Art and the Artist,* since the urge to create is essentially the urge to immortalize the self. While the average individual takes himself as given, the artist (and the neurotic who is essentially an artist manqué) cannot. The artist is continually striving to remold his ego in terms of self-created ideals, in order to perpetuate or immortalize himself. This perpetually recreated or reborn self is projected and justified in the art work.

In *Beyond Psychology,* Rank also postulates the immortalizing tendency as underlying social ideologies and forms of social organization, through which the individual attains collective immortality. Rank believes that one point at which the individual, self-immortalizing needs of the artist intersect with collective ideologies is in the literary use of the Double. This literary use parallels genuine folk-beliefs in many primitive cultures, as well as mythological themes. In these primitive cultures there is an equation of the individual's soul when alive, his ghost after death, and his actual shadow. This shadow-soul survives the individual's death, and may sometimes leave the body in sleep, etc. There may, however, be some differences in appearance and character between the actual self and the ghostly Double.

Rank points out that in modern literature, the Double is usually a symbol of a character's past, his evil tendencies and his death rather than of future immortality, as in naive folk-beliefs. A typical example is E. T. A. Hoffman's *Story of the Lost Reflection,* in which the hero sells his mirror reflection (his "immortal soul") to a devil-figure. This reflection takes on a life of its own and persecutes its former owner until the victim attempts to kill it and so kills himself. (Wilde's *Picture of Dorian Grey* presents a similar theme.) Rank explains the modern negative attitude toward the Double as due to modern man's over-rationalistic alienation from life and death and from his own fundamentally irrational will.

Rank sees folk-beliefs and myths of the Double as related to the wide-spread mythology of twins. A common theme of myth is that of twins who have creative powers and who found cities and cultures (e.g., Romulus and Remus). Often in these myths, one twin is killed by the other, or is killed in his place. Rank interprets this as indicating a concept of the twins as Doubles, one of whom becomes immortal and creative through the death of his mortal counterpart. According to Rank, primitive cultures see Doubles and twins as duplicate selves necessary for immortality, just as patriarchal cultures see the son as a duplicate of the father, necessary for immortality.

Rank applies these suggestive ideas to Dostoevsky's Doubles in only a vague, brief and superficial fashion. Their importance, however, is suggested by the clinical literature on the autoscopic syndrome.[13] A number of the cases reported are like those of Mrs. A, cases in which the Double first appears immediately after the death of a significant person. In some sense the Double seems to be a substitute or resurrection of the lost person. In other cases, the Double represents, not a "resurrected self" but the self as dead. De Musset, just after walking through a cemetery, saw a hallucination of "a mysterious stranger which he recognized with terror as *himself,* twenty years older, with features ravaged by debauchery, eyes aghast with fear." A clinical case is reported of a woman in great anxiety, about to enter the hospital for surgical completion of a miscarriage, who was suddenly confronted by a realistic vision of herself lying in a coffin. This was the first appearance of a recurring mirror-like hallucination of a Double.[14]

Our discussion suggests a close connection between Double or autoscopic experiences and epilepsy on the one hand, and concern about death and immortality on the other. Dostoevsky's extreme concern with death and immortality was expressed both in ideological and in symptomatic behavior.

On the ideological level, he wrote: "Without a superior idea, there cannot exist either the individual or the nation. But here on earth we have only one superior idea—the *immortality of the soul* because all other superior ideas have their source in this idea."[15]

On the symptomatic level, his fear of death was associated with his epileptic attacks. An attack was triggered off by passing a chance funeral procession. The association of death and epilepsy led him to fears of being buried alive, of being closed in for eternity. He would leave notes that he should not be buried for five days after an attack. His own Siberian sentence he viewed as a living burial after his near execution: "It is difficult to express how much I have suffered. These four years I look upon as a time of living burial. I was put in a coffin."[16] These feelings suggest that he feared not only death, but his own ghostly immortality in the face of his apparent death to the world.

Dostoevsky told his friends that his epileptic attacks were associated not only with fear of death and ghostly immortality, but with the joyful experiences of eternal life described by his epileptic figures Myshkin and Kirrilov.

The association we would expect between epilepsy, experiences of immortality, and the Double phenomenon is found in the grouping of these traits in Dostoevsky's characters. A number of both the Type II good Doubles (Myshkin, Kirrilov, Alyosha) and the Type I bad Doubles (Smerdyakov) have epileptic or epileptic-like seizures, while none of the other characters are portrayed as epileptic. In the good Doubles epilepsy is connected with a high rating on the trait, "Joyful experience in which eternal life is collapsed into an instant." All the Type II good Doubles are rated high on the trait, "Lives for and believes in positive immortality." Of Alyosha, Dostoevsky says: "As soon as he reflected seriously, he was convinced of the existence of God and immortality and instinctively said to himself: 'I want to live for immortality and I will accept no compromise.'"

If Dostoevsky's Type II good Doubles express his ideas, concerns and experiences of positive immortality, his Type I bad Doubles express his ideas and experience of negative immortality, of living burial. Svidrigailov says: "We always imagine eternity as something beyond our conception, something vast. But why must it be vast? Instead of all that, what if it is one little room, like a bathhouse in the country, black and grimey and spiders in every corner, and that's all eternity is?"

Dostoevsky intended this to be a reflection of his Siberian "living burial" and wrote of *Crime and Punishment*, "My Dead House was really most interesting. And here again shall be a picture of a hell, of the same kind as that 'Turk-

ish Bath in the Prison' (a chapter in the *House of the Dead* on the horrors of a multitude of naked, filthy bodies closely packed together in the prisoners' weekly steambath)."[17]

Svidrigailov in *Crime and Punishment* and Stavrogin in *The Possessed* are flesh and blood characters who are sinister alter-egos to others. Both also experience hallucinations which are directly said to represent the ghosts or resurrections of dead or murdered persons. In the passage on eternity just mentioned, Svidrigailov discussed his hallucinations of his dead wife Marfa (whom he has mistreated and probably murdered) and of a servant whom he drove to suicide. These hallucinations are not only experienced but believed in by Svidrigailov, who says, "I agree that ghosts only appear to the sick, but that only proves they are unable to appear except to the sick, not that they don't exist."

Stavrogin also has two related sets of hallucinations (described in the suppressed chapter of *The Possessed*). One is of the devil, the other is of the twelve-year-old girl whom he seduced and led to suicide.

At first sight, hallucinatory Doubles in the novels would seem to be one thing, and flesh and blood alter-egos another. The line of thinking we have pursued suggests, however, that the "living" bad Doubles may have a meaning similar to that of the "hallucinatory" bad Doubles. As in the case of Mrs. A, the Double is both a resurrection of a dead person and is the self.

Notes

1. P. C. Squires, "Fyodor Dostoevsky, A Psychopathographical Sketch" in *Psychoanalytic Review*, 24 (1937), pp. 365–388.

2. Sigmund Freud, "Dostoevsky and Parricide" in *Collected Papers*, Vol. V (London: Hogarth, 1950).

3. Smith and Isotoff, "Dostoevsky: the Abnormal from Within" in *Psychoanalytic Review*, 22 (1935), pp. 385–403.

4. Edna C. Florance, "The Neurosis of Raskolnikov; A Study in Incest and Murder" in *Archives of Criminal Psychodynamics*, 1 (1955), pp. 344–396.

5. E. Kris, *Psychoanalytic Exploration in Art* (New York: International University Press, 1952), Chapter 1. This chapter provides a good summary of recent psychoanalytic "ego-psychology" approaches to literature.

6. Otto Rank, "Der Doppelgänger" (Vienna: Internationale Psychoanalytische Verlag, 1925). Translated into French as "Don Juan, une étude sur le double" (Paris, 1932).

7. *The Letters of Fyodor Dostoevsky* (New York: Horizon, 1961).

8. N. Lukianowicz, "Autoscopic Phenomena" in *Archives of Neurology and Psychiatry*, 80 (1958), p. 199. This article is perhaps the best summary of clinical data on this phenomena, along with Reference 10.

9. S. Coleman, "The Phantom Double, Its Psychological Significance" in *British Journal of Medical Psychology,* 14 (1934), pp. 254–273.

10. J. Todd and K. Dewhurst, "The Double: Its Psychopathology and Psychophysiology" in *Journal of Nervous and Mental Diseases,* 122 (1955), pp. 47–56.

11. W. Stephenson, *Q Technique: The Study of Behavior* (Chicago: University of Chicago Press, 1953).

12. The detailed methods and results of this study will be reported in a professional psychological journal.

13. Lukianowicz, *op. cit.*

14. Todd and Dewhurst, *op. cit.*

15. *Diary of a Writer* (New York: Braziller, 1954).

16. *The Letters of Fyodor Dostoevsky.*

17. *Loc. cit*

Roger B. Anderson (essay date 1972)

SOURCE: "Dostoevsky's Hero in *The Double*: A Re-Examination of the Divided Self," in *Symposium,* Vol. 26, Summer, 1972, pp. 101–13.

[*In the following essay, Anderson examines Golyadkin's conception of himself as a divided personality.*]

Dvojnik [*The Double*] has always occupied a unique place in Dostoevsky scholarship because of its multiple levels of meaning and its complexity. In one respect it presents an almost clinical profile of the hero's confused mind drifting into paranoia and schizophrenia. It can also be examined in its relation to developing social activism in Russia at the time of its publication in 1846. Literary depictions of innately good but disadvantaged urban poor in Russia were firmly established through the influence of George Sand, Dickens, Balzac, and Hugo. The strong philanthropic current in Dostoevsky's first novelette *Bednye ljudi* [*Poor Folk*] certainly primed critical expectations for a continuation of that tendency in *The Double.* On yet another level the hallucinatory texture of the work, built around the *Doppelgänger* theme, presents a Hoffmann-like dimension to the work.[1] The unexplained, often paradoxical events of the plot unite with the fantastic and eerie descriptions of St. Petersburg to create a strong phantasmagorical effect on the reader. As with much German-inspired romantic prose, dreams and fantasies compete with and eventually displace everyday reality for Dostoevsky's hero.

Seemingly a hybrid, the novel initially disappointed some critics and confused others. Some condemned the work outright as nothing more than crudely disguised plagiarism of various tales by Gogol.[2] Belinsky gave it scant praise because he saw the work as inconsistent and repetitious. For him, the novel lacked esthetic symmetry and failed to distinguish adequately between the hero's clinical madness and the "real" social environment that Belinsky saw fos-

tering his problem.[3] Belinsky's objections are well founded in that Dostoevsky's point of emphasis in drawing his hero, Golyadkin, is basically different from that of the philanthropists. For writers like N. F. Pavlov (e.g., "Demon" [*"The Demon"*], 1839), or Ya. A. Butkov (e.g., *Petersburgskie veršiny* [*Petersburg Attics*], 1845–46) the ill-used hero of one civil service department tended to be interchangeable with any number of other exploited inhabitants of the harsh city. Instead, Dostoevsky creates in Golyadkin a complete and distinct individual whose material and social problems in life uniquely accentuate the deeper personal questions of his very being.

To further the distance between Dostoevsky's hero and most literary victims of organized social injustice one need but glance at Golyadkin to see that he is not poor (he has 700 rubles in cash). Nor does his personality evoke conventional sympathy.[4] He is given to fits of meanness and scheming, and is capable of thoroughly vile behavior toward people who have done him no harm.[5] Try as one may, it is difficult to see Golyadkin as spiritually noble and held back by the unfair distribution of wealth and political power as philanthropists were prone to present their heroes.[6]

Our purpose here is to assess the nature of Golyadkin's contradictory personality and determine a consistent meaning underlying his seemingly chaotic joust with himself. Of central importance to these questions is his creation of two distinct images of himself, one assertive against authority, the other submissive before that same authority. Each image arises from the hero's deep need to find meaning in life beyond his humdrum existence. The confrontation of these images develops simultaneously on two planes, one bureaucratic, one religious. Through an analysis of the two levels of conflict and by pointing out their close relationship, much that traditionally has appeared paradoxical in the work becomes clear.

Only the advantages of time and the reading of Dostoevsky's later novels allow us to appreciate more fully what *The Double* has to offer. In it the young Dostoevsky approaches the basic issue of man's existential compulsion to be free of externally imposed social labels and to thereby identify himself, the "person within the man." As in later works, that internal drive, although dimly understood by the hero, separates him from his fellows and their ordinary social role-playing. He is subject to an increasingly desperate introversion that holds the key to his very life. External living conditions, money, nature, career, relationships with other people, all come to function as the raw material out of which he gradually formulates a purely subjective perception of himself.

The precise causes of Golyadkin's estrangement are hidden from us; his adventures begin *in medias res.* Society has already denied his existence as a person, relegating him to the purely functional status of clerk. As a result, Golyadkin is interesting primarily as his knowledge of that low position unconsciously triggers an elaborate, profoundly human compensation reaction in his psyche. We observe his response to non-being (what Shklovsky calls the "hollow nut" named Golyadkin)[7] as he creates his own *raison d'être*.

Like the hero, we have no access to any experience of external people or events, except as they refer to the subjective compulsions and distortions that dominate Golyadkin. His world is a closed one in which he assumes all possible roles, in which he alone lives. Our impression of entanglement in his painful unconscious is greatly enhanced by Dostoevsky's choice of narrative point of view. Instead of a reliable interpreting author who explains the confusing events for us, we have a limited narrator whose vision seldom transcends that of Golyadkin himself. We, like the hero, are totally absorbed in the interplay of his psychic needs as he seeks to affirm his own existence in a mechanistic society that ignores him.[8] As the narrator says of Golyadkin, he is a rag "no vetoška-to . . . s oduševleniem i čuvstvami i—daleko v grjaznyx skladkax ètoj vetoški skrytymi, no vse-taki s čuvstvami" ["but a rag . . . invested with a soul and feelings—hidden away in the folds of this rag, but with feelings just the same"].[9]

A. L. Bem has charted part of Golyadkin's struggle for self-definition, terming it a rebellion. The suffocating anonymity of the hero's life leads to aggression in the sublimated form of his double. The purpose is to wrench from his milieu a higher status thereby escaping his own insignificance.[10] Bem draws special attention to the deeply serious quality of Golyadkin's rebellion. Purposely parodying Gogol's "Nos" ["The Nose"], claims Bem, Dostoevsky attempts to portray Golyadkin's tragic need to be free of his office's caste system (pp. 149–50). Dmitri Chizhevsky also emphasizes the hero's rebellion as the work's central message. The "real" Golyadkin is inert, says Chizhevsky. His role is to portray the passive victim of social exploitation. His "unreal" double expresses all the hero's sublimated assertiveness. Falling back on Belinsky's philanthropic criterion of the work, Chizhevsky subordinates the question of the double to social commentary: "Golyadkin is, so to say, the passive bearer of the rational principle and its victim. He, like the other clerks depicted by Dostoevsky, is devastated, exploited by the rational principle, embodied in the government of the period of Emperor Nicholas I."[11] Like Bem, Chizhevsky ignores Golyadkin's strenuous attempt to counteract his double's rebellion. As we shall see, Golyadkin, in his meek image, becomes a self-appointed advocate of the very system against which his double rebels.

M. M. Bakhtin's theory of the dialogic structure of Dostoevsky's art is more helpful in explaining the basis of Golyadkin's dualism. Like heroes of later novels, Golyadkin is subject to an irreducible inner dialectic of potentials. These potentials mix with one another and constantly exist in tension with one another throughout the novel.[12] For Bakhtin, each maintains its own integrity or "voice" (p. 337): each requires the resistance of its opposite to achieve expression. "When the dialog ends, everything [for the character] ends" (p. 338). The result of the inner dialectic is

the painful, solipsistic process of self-definition. As Bakhtin remarks, "Two voices are the minimum of life, the minimum of being" (p. 339). Bakhtin's principle of inner dialog, autonomous voices locked in continual confrontation, comes to life in Golyadkin. In response to his double's rebellion, Golyadkin projects another image of himself, an antidote of meekness (referred to as Golyadkin Sr.). That image seeks a humble role before society's authority figures at all costs; he eagerly *chooses* the role of *abulia*. Some of the most typical phrases of Golyadkin Sr. are "I am nothing," "I am by myself," "I am on the side." The "real" Golyadkin is lost to us as readers. All we see is a counterpoint of the two combating images he actively creates of himself, one aggressive toward authority, the other humbly anonymous before it.[13]

Golyadkin's perception of himself as meek is complicated in its relation to his power-grabbing double. Bem correctly links it to the question of guilt, but oversimplifies the issue by attributing that guilt to the sexual question of Golyadkin's shabby use of his land-lady.[14] Otto Rank's theory of will psychology sheds more light on our understanding of the hero's guilt and its necessary link with the question of will. Guilt in the individual, says Rank, is the necessary result of his expression of personal will in society. The will was a positive virtue for man in primitive cultures; it marked the leader, the seer, and drew admiration from others. With a more sophisticated culture, complete with strict social and bureaucratic hierarchies (e.g., St. Petersburg under Nicholas I) the willful individual, especially from a lower class, poses the threat of disruption. The natural remedy, Rank suggests, is for society (through its authority figures) to invoke taboos unconsciously in the individual that check his natural potential for expressing that personal will.[15] Rank considers that Dostoevsky presents the most insightful literary profile of the double theme in Western literature.[16] Within society's institutionalized repression of personal will, the individual experiences a severe *angst* when his will, and its resultant aggression, periodically arise. Speaking directly of Dostoevsky, Rank states: "The most prominent symptom of the forms which the double takes is a powerful consciousness of guilt which forces the hero no longer to accept the responsibility for certain actions of his ego, but to place it upon another ego, a double, who is either personified by the devil himself or [as in other authors] is created by making a diabolical pact."[17]

By simultaneously revolting against authority and effacing himself before its representatives, Golyadkin tampers with the uncharted region of the soul's dialectic that Dostoevsky was to explore so searchingly for the rest of his life. Golyadkin never consciously grasps the dynamics of his competing needs. Unlike the rebel heroes of later novels, Golyadkin cannot face either his assertive compulsion or its concomitant burden of anxiety and guilt. Instead, he builds an elaborate set of symbolic value judgments that clarify for him his aggression and fear. His displaced attempts at giving meaning to his inner dialectic take shape on two analogous levels, one bureaucratic, the other religious. While they are most clearly visible when discussed separately, they tend to intertwine and even occur simultaneously.

On the bureaucratic plane, Golyadkin expresses his aggression in his attempt to seize a higher status than his lowly station can justify. He translates his fear of rebelliousness into zealous loyalty to the wisdom of the authority that has designated him a low subordinate. The bureaucratic expression of Golyadkin's divided self is visible from the opening pages of the story, as he tries to decide how to act toward a superior he meets on the street. There are indications that the incident holds more than usual significance for him, as he stares open-eyed and flushes to the roots of his hair. He is transfixed by the magnetism of his chief's eyes. If he bows he expresses a certain boldness, an acknowledgment not only of his superior's presence, but of his own independent presence as well. By mumbling to himself, "Ja, ničego, . . . ja sovsem ničego, èto vovse ne ja, Andrej Filippovič, èto vovse ne ja, ne ja, da i tol'ko" ["Don't mind me, . . . don't mind me at all; this isn't me, Andrey Filippovich, this isn't me, isn't me, and that's a fact"] (p. 214), he seeks to retreat from any hint of independence into a self-imposed anonymity, ultimately a denial of his own will.

The same dumb show of inner struggle takes place at a ball given by Golyadkin's immediate superior, Olsufy Ivanovich. Having been refused entrance, Golyadkin feels the need to assert his independence before his chief and forcibly enters the party reasoning, "Idti ili net? Nu, idti ili net? Pojdu . . . otčego ž ne pojti? Smelomu doroga vezde!'" ["'Shall I go in or not? Well, shall I go in or not? I'll go . . . why shouldn't I? To the bold the way is always open!'"] (p. 241). Golyadkin regrets his rashness immediately, however, when the ball stops and everyone watches him. His assertiveness turns to self-denial as it had in the coach and he casts "a humble and imploring" look at Andrey Filippovich who is also there. "Mašinal'no osmotrelsja krugom: emu prišlo bylo na mysl' kak-nibud', ètak pod rukoj, bočkom, vtixomolku uliznut' ot grexa, ètak vzjat'—da i stuševat'sja, to est' sdelat' tak, kak budto by on ni v odnom glazu, kak budto by vovse ne v nem bylo i delo" ["He looked around mechanically. The thought came to him all of a sudden to sneak off from the whole thing on the sly, to efface himself, that is to make out as if he had nothing to do with the whole thing"] (pp. 245–46). Golyadkin's adventure ends in disaster as he is bodily thrown out of the house. The trauma is a profound one because neither of his psychic needs has been satisfied. His assertiveness does not lead to a higher status among his superiors; his humility before them buys him nothing but laughter and ridicule.

As Golyadkin flees into the night with his mind all but destroyed, finding no resolution to his oscillating view of himself, he reaches the breaking point. "Gospodin Goljadkin ne tol'ko želal teper' ubežat' ot sebja samogo, no daže sovsem uničtožit'sja, ne byt', v prax obratit'sja" ["Mr. Golyadkin wanted now not only to run away from himself, but to be completely obliterated, to cease to be, to turn into dust"] (p. 250). In a sense, Golyadkin does die. Amidst the apocalyptic description of the snow, the rain, and all the nameless terrors of the city's terrible weather, he splits into two distinct beings, physically the same but diametrically opposite in temperament. With the appearance of the second Golyadkin, the hero experiences a kind of relief from his need to decide between the two roles. Even though the intensity of the choice continues to mount throughout the story, Golyadkin now at least is in a position to distinguish and label his assertive and meek potentials, attributing one to his double, keeping one for himself. Initially he vacillates in his choice of which "Golyadkin" is to fulfill which psychic need. When he first meets his double, ostensibly a new clerk in his department with the same name, Golyadkin Sr. perceives Jr. as the perfect embodiment of benign humility, reserving for himself the assertive role of mentor. The next morning Golyadkin switches roles and begins to ascribe more and more of his repressed assertiveness to his alter ego and reserves the meek role for himself.

When Golyadkin Sr. meets his double at the office a most important confrontation takes place, one which virtually crystallizes his compulsion to affix definitive labels to his own divided tendencies. When they meet, Golyadkin Jr. steals a report from the hero and presents it to the department head, Andrey Filippovich, as his own. He uses the report to great success as a means of currying favor with those above him. Golyadkin Sr., once he realizes Jr.'s intentions, also takes an equally fixed role as one who has ultimate faith in the wisdom of authority. His first reaction is to turn the matter over to his superior for solution. The roles also take on the added clarity of possessing a distinct moral coloration. Sr. interprets his opponent as morally outrageous, a "Grishka Otrepev," an imposter who deserves severe punishment. Feeling protected by his own righteousness, Golyadkin Sr. decides that he will succeed through meekness.

From this point forward, each Golyadkin relates to civil authority in a thoroughly consistent way. Jr. continues to insinuate himself into ever higher places until he finally has the ear of His Excellency himself. He travels on special commissions for that august representative of authority and even attends his parties. Sr. retreats ever more into a tenacious sense of his own loyalty to authority, seeking the solution to his problem of the double by laying it before Andrey Filippovich and His Excellency. He tries desperately in the meantime to dissociate himself from his sense of shame and responsibility for the aggressive behavior of his twin: "Nu, vot on podlec budet, a ja budu čestnyj,—i skažut, čto vot ètot Goljadkin podlec, na nego ne smotrite, i ego s drugim ne mešajte; a ètot vot čestnyj, dobrodetel'nyj, krotkij, nezlobivyj, ves'ma nadežnyj po službe i k povyšeniju činom dostojnyj; vot ono kak!" ["Well, so he'll be a scoundrel, but I'll be honest; and they will say that this Golyadkin is a scoundrel, don't take any notice of him and don't mix him up with the other one; and this one is virtuous, noble, gentle, completely to be relied on in his work and worthy of promotion. That's how it will be!"] (p. 297). He reinforces his desire to be cleansed of his rebellious alter ego by identifying it as a threat to civil authority, saying of Jr.'s assertive rise through the bureaucratic ranks: "takie otnošenija zapreščeny strogo zakonami, čto, po moemu mneniju, soveršenno spravedlivo, ibo vsjakij dolžen byt' dovolen svoim sobstvennym mestom" ["such behavior is strictly forbidden by law, which in my opinion is perfectly just, for everyone ought to be satisfied with his own place"] (p. 313). He completes his pathetic attempt at self-denial by terming passivity before civil authority a moral imperative (p. 313).

By turning directly to civil authority with his garbled protestations of loyalty,[18] Golyadkin seeks an official certificate of acceptance, a powerful support in gaining a semblance of stability in his life. Most important, it would mean a release from his sense of guilt and a way of ridding himself of his rebellious twin. Golyadkin first turns to Andrey Filippovich with his muddled condemnation of "that notorious person" and an equally muddled plea to his superior to acknowledge and accept his loyalty to established civil authority (p. 330). Predictably, the department head understands nothing of the hero's inner struggle and ignores him, leaving him without the benefit of an easy solution to his problem. Golyadkin then bursts in upon that ultimate authority, His Excellency, still incoherently condemning his enemy and professing his own loyalty. Almost blinded by His Excellency's magnificence, Golyadkin makes his final attempt at exorcising his sense of guilt by prostrating himself before the judge he hopes will protect him from it. Again, the belabored hero finds no relief. He is forcibly ejected without achieving a solution. As always, his search for external answers to the question of his inner division fails.

In the final scenes of the novel, Golyadkin, now hopelessly insane, bursts in upon a second party given by a superior. His desperate quest to be recognized as loyal and humble miraculously seems to be achieving success, at least in his deranged mind. All the guests are caught up in tearful good will toward Golyadkin Sr.; he feels that he has finally tamed his aggressive and iconoclast alter ego. At the fateful moment the peaceful scene explodes as Golyadkin Jr. betrays the hero by refusing a reconciliation. Golyadkin is carried out for the last time, still failing to establish his desired image of probity.

There is no help for Dostoevsky's hero. Nor can there be. The harder he tries to break out of society's strictures and become a "somebody" through his double, the more he tries to hide behind his vision of passive humility before authority. The two needs complement one another perfectly in a classic rhythm of masochism. As Jr. he ridicules his other self, sensing the power of self-assertion in the act. A resultant sense of punishment in Sr. helps him achieve an outlet for his guilt, connected with that self-assertion. At the same time, Sr. seeks to avoid guilt by perceiving himself as an upholder of the doctrine of "keep-ing in one's place," and from there he morally condemns his double's assertiveness. Such self-deprecation in the hero in turn stimulates his need for aggression in the form of Jr. Golyadkin is thus locked in a self-sustaining system of masochism that destroys him from within. His numerous references to himself as a suicide are perfectly applicable, for each of his projected personalities seeks to destroy the other. As Rank points out, the problem of the double "is nourished by a powerful fear of death and creates strong tendencies toward self-punishment, which also imply suicide."[19]

Throughout his convoluted relationship with bureaucracy, Golyadkin consistently uses the world of his office as a screen against which he projects the primal urges of aggression and *angst* that shake his soul. The process of using external reality as a convenient vehicle for giving form to the dialog of one's inner being, as Bakhtin points out, is basic to Dostoevsky's general method. Golyadkin, however, repeats the role-assigning process on a religious plane as well. As Golyadkin's compulsion to be free of his willful second self mounts, he phrases his conflict in terms of Christian mythology. The presence of the religious metaphor in the novel is a solemn reminder of the serious implications of that struggle in man's soul.[20] The bureaucratic arena might be taken as social criticism or even as a naturalistic case study of clinical schizophrenia. But, by implying a religious dimension in Golyadkin's destruction, Dostoevsky emphasizes the spiritual tragedy of the soul's contrary needs that link *The Double* to his later, more mature works.

Golyadkin Sr.'s principle of "keeping one's own place" gradually becomes associated with Christ's acceptance of God's authority. Golyadkin Jr., that "willful and godless person," comes to represent Christ's enemy, a mixture of Antichrist and Judas. As unusual as the parallel of religion might seem, several elements of the identification are present. His Excellency has all the distance and austerity of a superior being, in Golyadkin's mind. Sr.'s need to justify his adoration of authority, his identification of himself as its meek servant, become holy principles for him as they were for Christ. Jr. assumes the role of Christ's enemy who seeks to displace and discredit "the meek one." Jr.'s assertiveness gradually takes on the coloration of heresy and blasphemy for Sr.

The first hint that Golyadkin's inner division carries a religious reference occurs early in the work as he visits his physician, Dr. Rutenshpits. After meeting Andrey Filippovich by chance on the street and exhibiting the desire to appear independent before his superior and yet sensing guilt at the thought, Golyadkin feels an urgent need to see the doctor "dlja sobstvennogo že spokojstvija" ["for his own peace of mind"] (p. 215). Rutenshpits is described as "like a confessor" (p. 215) and possesses such remarkable eyes that he has the power to rout disease. It is before Dr. Rutenshpits that Golyadkin first seeks to "confess" his dual potentials. He delivers a speech in which, like Christ, he denounces the ways of the world with its duplicity, social climbing, masks, and egocentrism: "doroga moja otdel'no idet" ["my path lies apart"] (p. 218). He obviously seeks approbation for his self-assigned spiritual excellence as he "obratilsja ves' v zrenie i robko, s dosadnym, tosklivym neterpeniem ožidal otveta Krest'jana Ivanoviča" ["looks intently and meekly, with anxious and agonized impatience, and waits for Krestyan Ivanovich's answer"] (p. 221). When Dr. Rutenshpits fails to give his blessing, Golyadkin releases his hostility by flippantly treading on his earlier spiritual humility. He schemes, slanders, wears masks, and in general appears like the bantering and irreverent society dandy whom he had just denied. Here, in spiritual terms, are the essential factors that characterize Golyadkin's attitude toward civil authority.

After the double's appearance, the Christian roles take on increasing definition. Golyadkin Sr. is described as suffering unjust derision: "uže gonjat v tolčki blagonamerennogo gospodina Goljadkina, i uže sypljut ščelčki v izvestnogo ljuboviju k bližnemu, nastojaščego gospodina Goljadkina!" ["already they poked at the loyal Mr. Golyadkin, and already they rained blows on the one so well known for his love for his neighbor, the real Mr. Golyadkin!"] (p. 316), a play on Christ's precept of brotherly love even at a time of personal persecution. The cynicism Jr. exhibits is heavily emphasized as "ignoble," "treacherous," "vile," "depraved," "willful and godless" throughout the story. He is a "false friend," a Judas. Through each encounter with his double, Sr. maintains the aura of martyrdom; he bears all with meekness: "vot ono kak! protestovat' tam kakimnibud' obrazom tože ne budu, vse s terpeniem i smireniem snesu," ["and so it is! I shall not protest in any way and shall bear it all with patience and humility"] (p. 335). Sr. is constantly ready to forgive his enemy, in the office, tea room, and during the last scene of near-reconciliation. He is drawn to the Christ-like posture of overcoming evil with kindness: "nevinnost' sil'na už svoeju nevinnost'ju" ["innocence is strong by its very innocence"] (p. 313). At one point Golyadkin Sr. is moved by a compassion close to that of the Good Samaritan as he is ready to shelter the "poor, lost, frightened" Golyadkin Jr. (p. 296). Such magnanimity is, for Sr., in keeping with the will of divine Providence (p. 297). Ready-made Biblical images of righteousness triumphing over evil come readily to the narrator as he describes Sr.: "sokrušit' rog gordyni" ["to shatter the horn of arrogance"] (p. 291) is similar to Psalm 75:4 with its reference to the boastful lifting up their horns and being insolent. Sr. feels it his duty "razdavit' zmeju, gryzuščuju prax v prezrenii bessilija" ["to crush the snake which gnaws the dust in contemptible impotence"] (p. 291) in keeping with the Biblical parallel between evil and the serpent. The power of prophesy sounds through the narrator's remark that "rok-to uvlekal" ["fate drew him on"] (p. 244). Sr.'s constant repetition of trusting in "divine Providence," and his association of it with the "fathers" of bureaucratic authority (e.g., p. 333) are suggestive of Christ's own mixing of prophesy, divine law, and the "fatherhood" of God.

There are also striking parallels between Golyadkin Sr. and Christ as each prepares for his final judgment. In his own version of Gethsemane, behind the woodstack in Olsufy Ivanovich's courtyard, Golyadkin's soliloquy is reminiscent of Christ's prayer. A willingness to accept each's ordained destiny sounds clearly in each.[21] Golyadkin's climax of self-perceived persecution comes after his agony of the vigil as it does for Christ. For both, their enemy, Judas, treacherously exposes them to their judges. Golyadkin Jr. leads the hero into the house and, before the watching crowd, gives his Judas kiss and the betrayal is complete. In the suffering of his destruction after the kiss, Golyadkin Sr. marks the moment with the words "ja gotov . . . ja vverjajus' vpolne . . . i vručaju sud'bu moju Krest'janu Ivanoviču . . ." ["I am ready . . . I trust fully . . . and entrust my fate to Krestyan Ivanovich (Rutenshpits)"] (p. 374). Dr. Rutenshpits, we have noted, is associated with superior spiritual power in the hero's mind. The passage's parallel to Christ's words at His crucifixion (i.e., "Father! Into your hands I commit my spirit" [Luke 23:46]) is clear.

Golyadkin Sr.'s final betrayal and "death" scenes are integral to the broader issue of his feelings of guilt. No matter how hard Sr. unconsciously tries to hide behind the purity of the Christ image, the scene repeats his failure to convince higher authority of his meek morality. Golyadkin Sr. is, after all, a part of the dialectic, a necessary counterpoint to the assertive Golyadkin Jr. Sr. cannot successfully disavow his double and totally withdraw behind his projected humility, be it secular or religious. Thus the judgment scene is more than the cruel and unfair destruction of "the meek one." It contains also the element of punishment for the hero's failure to exorcize his own latent rebellion. Just as Sr. was unable to overcome his alter ego before Andrey Filippovich and His Excellency, so he fails to overcome it before his spiritual superior, Dr. Rutenshpits. At the very moment of his double's Judas kiss, the doctor enters the room. Sr.'s first words to him are: "Ja nadejus', čto zdes' net ničego . . . ničego predosuditel'nogo . . . ili moguščego vozbudit' strogost'" ["I hope there is nothing here . . . nothing worthy of blame . . . that can call for severity"] (p. 374). Rutenshpits has God-like stature in Golyadkin's eyes and is the source of his final judgement and condemnation.[22] When we last see the hero, he is being carried off by the doctor into a new and hellish existence: "Napravo i nalevo černelis' lesa; bylo gluxo i pusto. Vdrug on obmer: dva ognennye glaza smotreli na nego v temnote, i zloveščeju, adskoju radostiju blesteli èti dva glaza" ["Dark woods wound to the right and the left of the unknown road; it was desolate and deserted. Suddenly he froze: two fiery eyes were staring at him in the darkness; these two eyes glittered with sinister and hellish glee"] (p. 375). The gaze is the doctor's, and Golyadkin's punishment is near. The anagram in Rutenshpits' name indirectly supports his punishing image (i.e., the reversal of "*Rutenshpits*" is "*shpitsruten*" or a rod for whipping, in Russian). Golyadkin has been consigned to hell and he now sees his doctor as the angel of death, his guide into the pit. The meek role Golyadkin has desperately tried and failed to assume throughout the novel works no better now: "'Krest'jan Ivanovič, ja . . . ja, kažetsja, ničego, Krest'jan

Ivanovič,'—načal bylo robko i trepešča naš geroj, želaja xot' skol'ko-nibud' pokornostiju i smireniem umiloserdit' užasnogo Krest'jana Ivanoviča" ["'Krestyan Ivanovich, I . . . I think . . . I'm all right now Krestyan Ivanovich,' our hero was beginning timidly in a quavering voice, wishing to placate the terrible Krestyan Ivanovich a little by his meekness and submissiveness"] (p. 375). The final words by Rutenshpits are characterized as a stern and terrible condemnation. That final judgment is understood and accepted by Golyadkin; a suppressed sense of guilt at his unrecognized revolt has never left the hero and "Uvy! on èto davno uže predčuvstvoval!" ["Alas, he had felt that this would happen for a long time!"] (p. 375).

Golyadkin's projection of two selves results from his desperate attempt to transcend society's imposed limits. It is a short step from his fumbling efforts to the Underground Man's manifesto of liberation from similar strictures. The crucial ingredient lacking in Golyadkin, which is present in later Dostoevskian heroes, is self-awareness. This hero never perceives the causes of either his aggression or his sense of guilt. His two images, the matter and antimatter of his being, collide on bureaucratic and religious terms, but fail to lead him to any heightened ontological understanding. They simply happen to Golyadkin. It is for later works (e.g. *Crime and Punishment*) to investigate the weighty implications of rebellion and the question of guilt. Despite the relatively crude phrasing of the dialectic in **The Double**—especially when compared with those later works—Dostoevsky was undoubtedly justified in saying years later that its idea was illuminating and that he had never written anything more serious.[20]

Notes

1. See Otto Rank, *The Double: A Psychoanalytic Study*, tr. Harry Tucker (Univ. of North Carolina Press, 1971), pp. 8–34 for a short survey of the double motif in Western literature, and esp. pp. 27–32 for a discussion of Dostoevsky's handling of the theme within the general European tradition. C. E. Passage has a much longer analysis of various Russian practitioners of the double idea, including Dostoevsky, in his book *The Russian Hoffmannists*, (Mouton, 1963), esp. pp. 197–201.

2. See K. S. Aksakov, *Moskovskij literaturnyj i učenyj sbornik na 1847 god* (otd. kritiki), pp. 33–34, as discussed in R. I. Avanesov's article "Dostoevskij v rabote nad Dvojnikom," *Tvorčeskaja istorija* (M., 1927), p. 158.

3. See V. G. Belinskij, *Pol. sobr. soč.*, Vol. IX (Ak. Nauk, 1953–1956), pp. 563–65.

4. See V. Ja. Kirpotin, *Molodoj Dostoevskij* (M., 1947), p. 235 for a discussion of how Golyadkin violates the credentials of the "positive" or "sympathetic" hero of the typical philanthropic tale of the time.

5. There is ample evidence to indicate that he has taken advantage of his honest landlady before the story begins. He apparently promised to marry her, only to desert and slander her in the hope of paying court to a woman of higher social rank, his superior's daughter.

6. For more background about the question of Dostoevsky's rejection of Belinsky's theory of innate nobility in man see V. L. Komarovich's article "Junost' Dostoevskogo," IV (*Brown University Slavic Reprints*, 1966), pp. 73–117.

7. V. B. Šklovskij, *Za i protiv* (M., 1957), p. 61.

8. As Konstantin Mochulsky says in his book *Dostoevsky*, tr. M. A. Minihan (Princeton U. Press, 1967), p. 48, "The schema of human values was replaced by the table of ranks. All civil servants were indistinguishable one from another, and their significance was determined not inwardly by their respective worth, but externally by their position, by their function. Relations between people became purely mechanical, and people themselves were transformed into mere objects."

9. F. M. Dostoevskij, *Pol. sobr. soč.*, eds. L. P. Grossman, *et al.* (M., 1956), 10 VV., V. I, p. 292. For convenience, all further references to this volume will be made in text with appropriate pagination.

10. See A. L. Bem, "'Nos' i *Dvojnik*," *O Dostoevskom*, III (Praga, 1929–1936) 3 VV., pp. 139–63.

11. Dmitri Chizhevsky, "The Theme of the Double in Dostoevsky," *Dostoevsky*, ed. Rene Wellek (Prentice Hall, 1962), p. 124.

12. See M. M. Baxtin, *Problemy poètiki Dostoevskogo*, izd. 2-oe (M., 1963), pp. 11–12, 62–63.

13. See Temira Pachmuss' discussion of Golyadkin's dream logic in her book *F. M. Dostoevsky: Dualism and Synthesis of the Human Soul* (University of Southern Illinois Press, 1967), pp. 24–25, 30.

14. See A. L. Bem, *O Dostoevskom*, III, p. 154.

15. See Otto Rank, *Psychology and the Soul*, tr. W. D. Turner (University of Pennsylvania Press, 1950), pp. 148–60.

16. See Rank, *The Double*, p. 27.

17. *Ibid.*, p. 76.

18. N. S. Trubetskoj, in his article "The Style of *Poor Folk* and *The Double*," *American Slavic and East European Review*, 7, 2, (1948), 150–70. (Page 166) points out Golyadkin's increasing difficulty in coherently verbalizing his thoughts to authority figures like His Excellency. Golyadkin's speech becomes virtually incomprehensible because he is sure that such important people must already know his thoughts without his having to explain them—again an attempt to defer any situational power to his superiors.

19. Rank, *The Double*, p. 77.

20. Compare Golyadkin's words: "'Bože moj! Bože moj! . . . podaj mne tverdost' duxa v neistoščimoj glu-

bine moix bedstvij! Čto propal ja, isčez soveršenno—v ètom už net nikakogo sommenija, i èto vse v porjdadke veščej, ibo i byt' ne možet nikakim drugim obrazom'" ["'My God! My God! . . . give me strength of soul in the immeasurable depths of my sorrow. That I am finished, vanished utterly, there can be no doubt, and this is all in the natural order of things since it cannot be otherwise'"] (p. 362) with Christ's words: "Father, if thou be willing, remove this cup from me: nevertheless not my will, but thine, be done," (Luke 22:42).

21. N. E. Osipov, in his article "Dvojnik. Petersburgskaja poèma F. M. Dostoevskogo," *O Dostoevskom,* I (Praga, 1929), 3 VV, p. 60, makes the enticing remark that "Christ in his essence of man and Judas are doubles." Unfortunately, Osipov leaves the implications of his insight unexplored. Shklovsky, in his *Za i protiv (op. cit.,* p. 76), provides the biographical information of Dostoevsky's search for a religious faith while he was writing *The Double.* Failing to work out a satisfactory belief at the time, says Shklovsky, Dostoevsky contemplated renouncing Christianity.

22. Passage refers to the scene as representing heavenly judgment with Rutenshpits playing the role of the "grim angel." See Passage, *The Russian Hoffmannists,* pp. 200–201.

23. See F. M. Dostoevskij, *Dnevnik pisatelja 1877 god,* Chap. XII, pp. 297–98.

Joseph Frank (essay date 1976)

SOURCE: "The Double," in *Dostoevsky: The Seeds of Revolt, 1821–1849,* Princeton University Press, 1976, pp. 295–312.

[*In the following essay, Frank provides an overview of* The Double, *including its place in Dostoevsky's canon and its relation to his other works.*]

To attain a proper perspective on Dostoevsky's minor fiction in the 1840s after *Poor Folk* is by no means an easy task. It is impossible, of course, to agree with the almost totally negative evaluation of his contemporaries, especially since we can discern, with the benefit of hindsight, so many hints of the later (and much greater) Dostoevsky already visible in these early creations. On the other hand, in rejecting what seems to us the distressing myopia of his own time, we should not fall into an equally flagrant and perhaps less excusable error. We should not blur the line between potentiality and actuality, and read this earlier work as if it *already* contained all the complexity and profundity of the major masterpieces. Some of the more recent criticism, especially outside of Russia, has fallen into this trap; and these slight early works—*The Double* is a good case in point—have sometimes been loaded with a burden of significance they are much too fragile to bear.

It should be stated at once that Dostoevsky's production between 1846 and 1848 can boast of no work that matches *Poor Folk* as a successful and fully rounded creation. Indeed, at the time of his imprisonment he was generally considered a writer who had failed lamentably to live up to his earlier promise. This prevalent opinion was of course unjust and untrue; but it is not as outrageous as it may seem at first sight. Between 1846 and 1848 Turgenev published a good many of the stories included in *A Sportsman's Sketches;* Herzen produced *Who Is To Blame?* and a series of brilliant short stories; Goncharov made his impressive début with *An Ordinary Story,* and followed it with a chapter from his novel in progress, "Oblomov's Dream"—and we have not yet mentioned either Grigorovich's two novels of peasant life, *Anton Goremyka* and *The Village,* or A. V. Druzhinin's *Polinka Sachs,* which raised the banner of female emancipation. Compared to the array of such works, Dostoevsky's publications seemed very small potatoes indeed; and the longer book that he counted on to reestablish his credit with the reading public, *Netotchka Nezvanova,* was never completed because of his arrest.

Part of Dostoevsky's problem was unquestionably his straitened circumstances, which required him to turn out work too quickly. Part was also his artistic restlessness and ambition, which impelled him to abandon the vein of sentimental Naturalism and, after the triumph of *Poor Folk,* to shift disconcertingly to what seemed an unhealthy fascination with mental disorder and to lyrical explorations of the theme of *mechtatelnost.* It is clear to us now that Dostoevsky was experimenting with styles and character-types that he was later to fuse together superbly. But it was difficult at the time not to feel that, compared with the other young writers on the rise, he had simply lost his way.

2

Dostoevsky's next important work, which followed hard on the heels of *Poor Folk,* was *The Double.* In May 1845, while putting the finishing touches to his first novel, he tells Mikhail that he already has "many new ideas"[1] for other works; and the initial conception of *The Double* was probably among them. From other references in letters, we know that he discussed the novel (as he called this long story) during the summer of 1845, and got down to work on it seriously in the fall. In a letter of October 1845, parodying the speech-style of the main character, he informs Mikhail that "*Yakov Petrovich Golyadkin . . .* [is] a rascal, a terrible rascal! He will not agree, under any circumstances, to finish his career before the middle of November. He has just cleared things up with Your Excellency, and, if it comes to that (and why not?), is ready to hand in his resignation."[2] But, as was to become usual with Dostoevsky, work dragged on longer than expected, and he was still revising at the end of January 1846 just a few days before the magazine version was published.

The origins of the novel, both in Dostoevsky's personal life and in literary tradition, are not difficult to discern. It is interesting to note that, in a letter referring to *Netotchka Nezvanova,* he remarks that this projected novel "will also be a confession like *Golyadkin,* but in another tone and style."[3] This observation is made in a context of some personal self-criticism which reminds one of Golyadkin because of Dostoevsky's protest against the view taken of him by others. "I am ridiculous and disgusting, and I always suffer from the unjust conclusions drawn about me."[4] Like his character again, Dostoevsky was subject to "hallucinations" which may very well have included delusions similar to Golyadkin's; and he was shy to a degree bordering on the abnormal. From Belinsky's already-quoted remark to Annenkov that, like Rousseau, Dostoevsky was also "firmly convinced that all of mankind envies and persecutes him," we know that he exhibited more than a trace of Mr. Golyadkin's paranoia.

Such aspects of self-portraiture in *The Double,* however, furnish only one element of its composition; others were provided both by Dostoevsky's own earlier work and by external literary influences. There is, in the first place, an obvious continuity between the character of Devushkin and that of Golyadkin. During one of the crucial moments of *Poor Folk*—at the point where Devushkin, in complete despair, is summoned for his interview with the General—his feelings are described as follows: "My heart began shuddering within me, and I don't know myself why I was so frightened; I only know that I was panic-stricken as I had never been before in all my life. I sat rooted to my chair—as though there was nothing the matter, as though it were not I" (1: 92). Here is exactly the reaction of terror that leads to the splitting of Golyadkin's personality and the appearance of the double: the internal process is simply given dramatic reality.

Poor Folk thus constitutes the most obvious literary source for *The Double*; but there are several others that should be mentioned. Dostoevsky's employment of the device of the *Doppelgänger* links his new novel with E. T. A. Hoffmann; and the possible relations between *The Double* and various Hoffmannian prototypes have been thoroughly investigated.[5] The direct influence of Hoffmann, however, is much less important than his assimilation by the Russian Hoffmannists as it came to Dostoevsky particularly in the writings of Gogol. V. V. Vinogradov has defined the subject of *The Double,* formally speaking, as consisting of "a naturalistic transformation of the Romantic 'doubles' of Russian Hoffmannism,"[6] presumably on the analogy of the naturalistic transformation of the sentimental epistolary novel in *Poor Folk.* But *The Double* is much less original in this respect. Gogol himself—not to mention others—had already begun this process of "naturalistic transformation," and Dostoevsky simply carries it one step further.

Golyadkin's courtship of the appetizing Klara Olsufyevna recalls the similar infatuation of Gogol's Poprischin, in the *Diary of a Madman,* with the daughter of *his* office-chief. The young lady pays no more attention to him than to the furniture in her father's bureau, and the baffled Romeo ends up in a madhouse firmly believing himself to be the King of Spain. In another of Gogol's stories, *The Nose,* this irreplaceable organ becomes detached from its proper location on the face of collegiate assessor Kovalyov (who prefers the military title of major) and darts about town in the uniform of a much more exalted rank under the bewildered eyes of its former possessor. Both stories use the same technique of the fantastic grotesque combined with themes of social ambition that we find in Dostoevsky, who clearly is working in the same tradition.

These two stories, however, are by no means the only Gogolian sources for *The Double.* There is external evidence that Dostoevsky himself (as well as others) thought of his new work primarily in relation to *Dead Souls.* "Golyadkin is ten times better than *Poor Folk,*" he writes Mikhail jubilantly on the day his new work was published. "They [Belinsky and the pléiade] say that after *Dead Souls* nothing like it has been seen in Russia. . . . You will like it even better than *Dead Souls,* that I know."[7] Dostoevsky evokes this linkage quite self-consciously in his original subtitle, *The Adventures of Mr. Golyadkin,* which recalls Gogol's *The Adventures of Chichikov.* Just as Gogol had written a mock-heroic account of Chichikov's "adventures" in trying to rise in the world, so Dostoevsky was doing the same for Mr. Golyadkin. The relation between *The Double* and *Dead Souls* has been more or less neglected because, in revising the story nineteen years later, Dostoevsky eliminated most of the traces pointing from one to the other. But the best way to understand *The Double* is to see it as Dostoevsky's effort to rework *Dead Souls* in his own artistic terms, just as he had already done with *The Overcoat.*

The effect he obtains, nonetheless, is quite different in the two cases, even though both are part of the same artistic endeavor to penetrate into the psychology of Gogol's characters and depict them from within. Golyadkin may be described as a composite of the timidity and pusillanimity of Poprischin imbued with the "ambition" of Chichikov; but the closeness of vision, the descent into his inner life, hardly creates any feeling of sympathy. The mock-heroic tonality taken over from *Dead Souls,* which Gogol used for purposes of broad social satire, is now applied to a world shrunk to the level of slightly off-color vaudeville farce; the picaresque adventure involves the search, not even for a large fortune, but for a slightly higher office post and acceptance into the charmed circle of a corrupt bureaucratic hierarchy. Dostoevsky thus once again takes his departure from a Gogolian model and intensifies its effect; but this time his aim is not to bring out more unequivocally the "humanitarian" component of the original. Rather, it is to reinforce Gogol's acute perception of the grotesque effects on character of moral stagnation and social immobility. The result is a new synthesis of Gogolian elements, transformed and recast not by sentimentalism but by a deepening of Hoffmannian fantasy into a genuine exploration of encroaching madness. In this way, Dostoevsky accentuates the humanly tragic aspect of Gogol's still relatively debonair portrayal of social-psychic frustrations.

3

In *The Double,* we are once more in the same *chinovnik* atmosphere, and confront the same world of the St. Petersburg bureaucracy, as in *The Overcoat* or *Poor Folk.* But Golyadkin is by no means an Akaky Akakievich or a Devushkin, living at the very edge of poverty and destitution. On the contrary, he is not impoverished at all, lives in his own flat with his own servant (rather than in a "corner" somewhere behind a screen), and has piled up a tidy sum in savings which he keeps at hand to gloat over for reassurance. Golyadkin's position in the bureaucratic hierarchy is by no means exalted, but he is nonetheless the assistant to the chief clerk of his office. As the story opens, he has just hired a carriage, outfitted his servant Petrushka with a livery, and is nervously making preparations to crash the birthday party of Klara Olsufyevna to which he has carefully *not* been invited.

In other words, Mr. Golyadkin has climbed high enough on the social ladder, at least in his own estimation, to aspire to climb a bit higher; he is suffering not from grinding poverty but from "ambition." Dostoevsky thus breaks the connection maintained in *Poor Folk* between Devushkin's poverty and his struggle for self-respect, and now emphasizes this latter motif. His focus, becoming internal and psychological, concentrates on the effort of Golyadkin to assert himself; but this inevitably brings him into opposition with the existing rigidities of the social order. And Dostoevsky's theme now becomes the crippling inner effects of this system on the individual—the fact that, to quote his feuilleton, Golyadkin "goes mad out of *ambition,* while at the same time fully despising ambition and even suffering from the fact that he happens to suffer from such nonsense as ambition."

The first several chapters of *The Double* give a brilliant picture of Golyadkin's split personality before it has disintegrated entirely into two independent entities. On the one hand, there is Golyadkin's evident desire to pretend to a higher social station and a more flattering image of himself—hence the carriage, the livery, the simulated shopping spree for elegant furniture as if he were a new bridegroom, even the marvelous detail of changing his banknotes into smaller denominations to have a fatter pocketbook. His pretension to the favors of Klara Olsufyevna is only an expression of this urge for upward mobility and ego-gratification, not its cause. Indeed, the novel originally contained a passage that explicitly motivates Golyadkin as indulging in ego-enhancing daydreams. Mr. Golyadkin, Dostoevsky wrote, "very much loved occasionally to make certain romantic assumptions touching his person; he liked to promote himself now and then into the hero of the most ingenious novel, to imagine himself entangled in various intrigues and difficulties, and, at last, to emerge with honor from all the unpleasantnesses, triumphing over all obstacles, vanquishing difficulties and magnanimously forgiving his enemies" (1: 335). Mr. Golyadkin as first conceived thus had a streak of Don Quixote in him, or, if one prefers, Walter Mitty.

This motivation was part of the original mock-heroic framework of the novel, which was eliminated in the revised version we are familiar with. Each chapter, for example, was introduced by a series of parodistic descriptive sentences outlining, in a format that began with *Don Quixote,* the action to come. "Of the awakening of the titular councilor Golyadkin," we read in the first chapter. "Of how he outfitted himself, and set forth on the path that lay before him. Of how he justified himself in his own eyes, and then correctly concluded that it was best of all to act boldly and openly, though not without nobility. Of where, finally, Mr. Golyadkin arrived to pay a call" (1: 334). This parody of the heroic convention is supplemented, in the unaltered last chapter, by another parody of the romantic intrigue of the sentimental adventure novel, with its eloping lovers escaping the vigilance of recalcitrant parents and Golyadkin cast in the role of reluctant seducer.

With one part of his character, then, Mr. Golyadkin likes to imagine himself as an all-conquering hero; but with another he knows that he is quite incapable of sustaining such a role, and is, in fact, as timid as a mouse. He shrinks from the sight of two young colleagues in the street as he is rolling along impressively in his carriage, and is positively petrified when overtaken by the smart droshky of his office superior, Andrey Filippovich. His reaction to this event releases the psychic mechanism—the same one we have already seen in Devushkin—that will soon lead to the appearance of the double. "'Bow or not? Call back or not? Recognize him or not,' our hero wondered in indescribable anguish. 'Or pretend that I am not myself, but somebody else strikingly like me, and look as though nothing were the matter. Simply not I, not I—and that's all'" (1: 113). Golyadkin is pathetically unable to live up to the part he is trying to play, and can only escape from it by this evasion of responsibility; but the moment Andrey Filippovich disappears, the all-conquering hero comes to the surface again. "Then, suddenly recalling how taken aback he had been, our hero flushed as hot as fire, frowned, and cast a terrible defiant glance at the front corner of the carriage, a glance calculated to reduce all his foes to ashes" (*ibid.*).

It is clear from the very start that Mr. Golyadkin, for all his assumed heroism, is not setting out on the road to adventure with a light heart. And his visit to his German doctor, Krestyan Ivanovich Rutenspitz, reveals some of the reasons for his discomfiture. A young competitor, the nephew of Andrey Filippovich, has received the office promotion to which Mr. Golyadkin aspired, and is now the leading (and far more suitable) aspirant for the hand of the beauteous Klara. Mr. Golyadkin, unable to control his displeasure at these frustrating events, had created a scandal only a day or so before by overtly displaying his hostility to his rival and the latter's powerful uncle. Moreover, Golyadkin is also aware that word has gotten round of some disreputable behavior in his own past involving the German landlady of a lodging house where he had once lived. At the beginning of the novel, he is desperately trying to suppress his awareness of both these disturbing events, and has already transferred them, with paranoiac logic, into the idea that he is being hounded and persecuted, and that only *he* is acting openly, straightforwardly and honestly. The scene with the doctor thus serves to fill in the background of the action, to indicate that Mr. Golyadkin's behavior is distinctly abnormal, and to reveal the pathos of his plight when he suddenly breaks down and starts to weep.

Mr. Golyadkin's crisis is precipitated by his efforts to gain admittance to Klara's birthday party. The wonders of this occasion are described by the narrator in a splendid outburst of Gogolian mockery underlining the ludicrous mediocrity of the sphere to which Mr. Golyadkin aspires. "Oh, if I were a poet! Such as Homer and Pushkin, I mean, of course; with any lesser talent one would not venture—I should certainly have painted all that glorious day for you, O my readers, with a free brush and brilliant colors," etc. (1: 128). This passage is worth dwelling on for a moment because, aside from its interest as an example of Dostoevsky's rhetorical skill, it is also of some thematic importance. For the narrator makes clear, amidst all his flowery, self-negating phrases, that the group being celebrated is really a hotbed of bribetaking and corruption. The worthy Olsufy Ivanovich, Klara's father and Golyadkin's patron, "is a hale old man and a privy councilor, who had lost the use of his legs in his long years of service and been rewarded by destiny for his devotion with investments, a house, some small estates, and a beautiful daughter," etc. (1: 129). Mr. Golyadkin's rival Vladimir Semyonovich, who has been promoted because of nepotism, inspires the remark that "everything in that young man . . . from his blooming cheeks to his assessorial rank, seemed almost to proclaim aloud the lofty pinnacle a man can attain through morality and good principles" (1: 130). Compared to such hardened reprobates, Golyadkin himself is the soul of innocence and virtue.

It is after Mr. Golyadkin has been ignominiously evicted from this worthy gathering that his double finally materializes. The arrival is preceded by another rhetorical set-piece, a parody of the style of the historical novel. "It was striking midnight from all the clock towers in Petersburg when Mr. Golyadkin, beside himself, ran out on the Fontanka Quay," etc. (1: 138). And the double comes on the scene when, as we are told explicitly, "Mr. Golyadkin was killed—killed entirely, in the full sense of the word" (*ibid.*). When he first looms out of the darkness of the stormy night, the double of Mr. Golyadkin unquestionably seems a purely psychic phenomenon. But there are certain scenes (such as those in the office) where the presence of an actually existing double is affirmed by other characters; and Dostoevsky deliberately keeps the reader in a state of uncertainty about how much of what occurs is the result of Golyadkin's hallucinations and growing loss of objective awareness. Whether the double is psychic or material, however, his function is never left in doubt: he is used to confront Mr. Golyadkin with everything the latter cannot endure to contemplate about himself and his own situation. This situation has been caused by his social temerity,

the suspicions about his tawdry peccadillo in the past, and his fear of the consequences of having offended his superiors. Golyadkin's relation with his double mimics one or another of these three facets of his position vis-à-vis himself and his world, and sometimes several of them blended together in a superbly subtle admixture.

4

The first five chapters of *The Double* describe the "adventures" of Mr. Golyadkin trying to assert himself in the real world. The remainder, which begin a new sequence, depict his unsuccessful struggle to keep from being replaced by his double everywhere and finally sinking into madness. At first, the double is deferential, ingratiating, obsequious, and begs Mr. Golyadkin for protection. Such comportment is probably meant to recapitulate the start of Mr. Golyadkin's own career, when he must have behaved in the same fashion; the sad tale told by the double of early poverty and humiliation may be taken as a flashback to Golyadkin's own life. The subordinate status of the double expresses the position of relative self-confidence that Mr. Golyadkin has just managed to attain and which has nourished his "ambition." But then, after the double worms his way into Mr. Golyadkin's confidence and learns all his secrets, the double "betrays" him (as Mr. Golyadkin is "betraying" his superiors by his insubordination) and begins to act out Mr. Golyadkin's mingled hopes and fears.

The double obtains all the success in the office that Mr. Golyadkin would like to have had, constantly humiliates him by allusions to his amorous dalliance with the German landlady ("'he's our Russian Faublas, gentlemen; allow me to introduce the youthful Faublas,' piped Mr. Golyadkin junior, with his characteristic insolence"), is on the best of terms with Klara Olsufyevna, and baffles and frustrates the real Mr. Golyadkin in every possible way (1: 195). Some of the episodes are purely slapstick—such as the consumption of ten pies by the double on the sly, which requires Golyadkin, who has eaten only one, to pay for eleven and to suffer the embarrassment of a reprimand. But, for the most part, the double's behavior both mirrors the suppressed wishes of Mr. Golyadkin's subconscious and objectifies the guilt feelings which accompany them.

During the first part, Mr. Golyadkin's "ambition" dominates his feelings of inferiority and guilt and manages to keep them in check. The movement of the action shows him, however unsuccessfully, still trying to impose himself on the world despite its rebuffs. Once the double appears, however, the process is reversed, and we find Golyadkin striving by every means possible to prove himself a docile and obedient subordinate, who accepts the dictates of the authorities ruling over his life as, literally, the word of God. It is in this latter part of the work that Dostoevsky's social-psychological thrusts become the sharpest. Golyadkin struggles against becoming confused with his double, who behaves in a fashion that the real Golyadkin would dearly like to emulate but which he has been taught to believe is morally inadmissible. The double is of course "a rascal," but the *real* Golyadkin is "honest, virtuous, mild, free from malice, always to be relied on in the service, and worthy of promotion . . . but what if . . . what if they get us mixed up" (1: 172)! The possibility of substitution leads Mr. Golyadkin to accuse his double of being "Grishka Otrepeev"—the famous false pretender to the throne of the true Tsars in the seventeenth century—and introduces the theme of impostorship, so important for Dostoevsky later and (with its evocation of *Boris Godunov*) so incongruous in this context.

The more threatened Mr. Golyadkin feels because of the machinations of his double, the more he is ready to surrender, give way, step aside, throw himself on the mercy of the authorities and look to them for aid and protection. He is ready to admit that he may even truly be "a nasty, filthy rag"—though, to be sure, "a rag possessed of ambition . . . a rag possessed of feelings and sentiments" (1: 168–169). The inchoate phrases that tumble off his tongue are filled with the mottoes of the official morality of unquestioning and absolute obedience encouraged by the paternal autocracy. "'I as much as to say look upon my benevolent superior as a father and blindly trust my fate to him,'" he tells Andrey Filippovich, in his desperate efforts to "unmask the impostor and scoundrel" who is taking his place. "At this point Mr. Golyadkin's voice trembled and two tears ran down his eyelashes" (1: 196). As the double, "with an unseemly little smile," tells Golyadkin in the important dream-sequence of Chapter 10: "What's the use of strength of character! How could you and I, Yakov Petrovich, have strength of character? . . ." (1: 185.)

This depressing process of Mr. Golyadkin's capitulation is lightened somewhat, in the final chapters, by his belief that he has received a letter from his beloved Klara setting a rendezvous for an elopement. Since Poprishchin was able to read the delightfully chatty correspondence of the two dogs Madgie and Fido in the *Diary of a Madman,* there is no need to speculate, as so many commentators have done, about the ontological status of the epistle that represents Mr. Golyadkin's heart's desire. Or does it really? Some of the most genuinely amusing moments in the novel occur as Mr. Golyadkin, taking shelter from the pouring rain under a pile of logs, sits waiting in the courtyard of Klara's house for her to keep their supposed assignation—and, at the same time, inwardly protests against such an unforgivable breach of the proprieties.

"'Good behavior, madame'—these are his ruminations—'means staying at home, honoring your father and not thinking about suitors prematurely. Suitors will come in good time, madame, that's so. . . . But, to begin with, allow me to tell you, as a friend, that things are not done like that, and in the second place I would have given you and your parents, too, a good thrashing for letting you read French books; for French books teach you no good,'" etc. (1: 221). The original version of *The Double* concludes shortly thereafter as Mr. Golyadkin is driven off in a carriage by his doctor, Krestyan Ivanovich, who suddenly becomes a demonic figure and—but we are left hanging in the air! The work is abruptly cut short at this point on a note of Gogolian flippancy and irresolution: "But here, gentlemen, ends the history of the adventures of Mr. Golyadkin" (1: 431).

5

The haunting brilliance of Dostoevsky's portrayal of a consciousness pursued by obsessions of guilt and ultimately foundering in madness has been recognized from the very first moment that *The Double* was published. What occurs in the novella is clear enough in its general outline; but there has been continual controversy over just how to interpret its significance. Does Mr. Golyadkin's double represent, as one Soviet critic has put it, "the meanest and most degrading qualities of [Golyadkin's] soul"?[8] Or does the double, as another has argued, represent only a hallucinatory image of the external social forces that threaten Golyadkin's existence as an individual?[9] It seems to me impossible to choose between such alternatives because, if Golyadkin's existence *is* threatened socially, it is precisely because he has dared to assert himself in a manner that *does* reveal something about his soul (or his subconscious).

Such disagreements arise, however, because it is genuinely difficult to pinpoint Dostoevsky's moral focus in *The Double.* It is, for example, clearly impossible to identify with Golyadkin sympathetically to the same degree as with the kindhearted and self-sacrificing Devushkin. If nothing else, the nature of his "ambition" as revealed through his double is hardly one of which Dostoevsky wishes us to approve unconditionally—as he makes amply clear by the unflagging mockery of his narrative tone. At the same time, the radical critic of the 1860s, N. A. Dobrolyubov, is undoubtedly right in characterizing Golyadkin as one of the early Dostoevsky's "downtrodden people," struggling desperately to assert their dignity and individuality in a social hierarchy that refuses to acknowledge their right to the luxury of such sentiments.[10] But how can we reconcile Dostoevsky's irony with his compassion?

One way of dealing with this problem has already been indicated in passing. For all his taunts at Golyadkin, Dostoevsky is even more sarcastic about the exalted eminences of the bureaucratic realm that glimmer before Golyadkin as his unattainable ideal. *They* are clearly corrupt to the core, and lack even that minimum of moral self-awareness responsible for Golyadkin's plight.[11] Golyadkin at least *believes* in the pious official morality to which everybody else gives lip service; and his struggle with the double is an effort to defend that morality from being betrayed. In fighting off the double, Golyadkin is really fighting off his own impulses to subvert the values presumably shared by his official superiors. This is probably what Valerian Maikov meant when he said that Golyadkin perishes "from the consciousness of the disparity of particular interests in a well-ordered society," i.e., his realization of the impossibility of asserting himself as an individual without violating the morality that has been bred into his bones and which keeps him in submission.

Such an answer, however, is only partially satisfactory, and still leaves in the dark the question of why Dostoevsky should have treated Golyadkin satirically at all. Here, it seems to me, we must have recourse to a document that has been neglected in this connection—Dostoevsky's remarks on "necessary egoism" in his feuilleton. Russian life, he said there, offered no outlet for the ego to assert itself normally, and the Russian character as a result tended not to exhibit a sufficient sense of its own "personal dignity." Such an analysis contains exactly the same mixture of sympathy and critical reserve that he incorporates in *The Double*: there is commiseration for Golyadkin's desire to rise, but also a certain disdain for his inability to sustain the combat and for the paltriness of his aims. Dostoevsky's genuine indignation at the crippling conditions of Russian life, in other words, did not turn him into a moral determinist willing to absolve the victims of all responsibility for their conduct. Indeed, his very portrayal of a figure like Devushkin implied that debasing social conditions were far from being able entirely to shape character. As a result, Dostoevsky's work of this period often contains a puzzling ambiguity of tone because a character is shown *simultaneously* both as socially oppressed and yet as reprehensible and morally unsavory because he has surrendered too abjectly to the pressure of his environment.

The same ambiguity of attitude is also reflected in the narrative technique of the story, which has attracted a good deal of attention in Soviet criticism. Both Bakhtin and Vinogradov have rightly noted that, while the narrator begins as an outside observer, he becomes more and more identified with Golyadkin's consciousness as the story progresses.[12] More recently, it has been stressed with equal justice that this identification is never total: the narrator keeps his distance by parodying Golyadkin, even when he uses the character's own speech-style and seems to limit himself to Golyadkin's horizon.[13] This mixture of identification and raillery creates the peculiar blend of tragicomedy in *The Double* that most readers find so difficult to accept (if we are to judge from the inclination of critics to read the work exclusively in one or the other perspective), and yet which exactly translates Dostoevsky's own point of view.

6

As we know, Dostoevsky's high hopes for the success of *The Double* were quickly dashed. The work met with a withering fire of criticism for two main reasons. One was simply because—to quote the Russian Symbolist Andrey Bely, both a connoisseur of Gogol and an admirer of Dostoevsky—"*The Double* recalls a patchwork quilt stitched together from the subjects, gestures, and verbal procedures of Gogol."[14] In this respect *The Double* suffered from being too imitative; but in another it was too original to be fully appreciated. For the complexities of Dostoevsky's

narrative technique did pose a special problem for the readers of his time.

The Double is narrated by an outside observer who gradually identifies himself with Golyadkin's consciousness and carries on the narrative in the speech-style of the character. Its verbal texture thus contains a large admixture of stock phrases, clichés, mottoes, polite social formulas, and meaningless exclamations, which are obsessively (and excessively) repeated as a means of portraying the agitations and insecurities of Mr. Golyadkin's bewildered psyche. This is a remarkable anticipation, unprecedented in its time, of Joyce's experiments with cliché in the Gerty McDowell chapter of *Ulysses,* and of what Sartre so much admired in John Dos Passos—the portrayal of a consciousness totally saturated with the formulas and slogans of its society. The effect in *The Double,* however, was a tediousness and monotony that Dostoevsky's readers were not yet prepared to put up with either for the sake of social-psychological verisimilitude or artistic experimentation.

And even though Dostoevsky's narrative technique *per se* no longer creates any barrier for the modern reader, the complexity of Dostoevsky's attitude still creates problems of comprehension. In isolating Golyadkin's imbroglio from any overt social pressure, and by treating both Golyadkin *and* the world he lives in with devastating irony, Dostoevsky tends to give the impression that Golyadkin is simply a pathological personality who has only himself to blame for his troubles. Even Belinsky, who might have been expected to grasp the social implications of Golyadkin's psychology as Dostoevsky had explained them in his feuilleton, remarked that his life would not really have been unbearable except "for the unhealthy susceptibility and suspiciousness of his character" which was "the black demon" of his life.[15] In other words, Dostoevsky was simply portraying a case of paranoia and mental breakdown with no larger significance than that of a case history.

This judgment set the pattern for a view of Dostoevsky's early work (and for much of his later work as well) that dominated a good deal of Russian criticism until the end of the nineteenth century. In 1849 P. V. Annenkov, echoing Belinsky, accused Dostoevsky of being the leader of a new literary school (which included his brother Mikhail Dostoevsky and Butkov) specializing in the portrayal of "madness for the sake of madness."[16] Annenkov severely criticized this unhealthy taste (as he saw it) for rather sensational and grotesque tragicomedy, in which he could discern no more serious or elevated artistic aim. Such an accusation was of course unfair to Dostoevsky, whose "abnormal" and "pathological" characters can all be seen, on closer examination, to make a social-cultural point. But Dostoevsky perhaps relied too much on the reader to grasp the ideological implications of his psychology, and to understand that the "abnormalities" of his characters derived from the pressure of the Russian social situation on personality. The result was an artistic lack of balance that led to a good deal of misunderstanding, and has caused unceasing critical disagreement.

7

The overwhelmingly hostile reaction to *The Double* spurred Dostoevsky to think of revising it almost from the moment of its publication. This did not prove possible before his arrest, however, and he could only return to the project in the 1860s. His notebooks contain a series of jottings, not so much for a revision as for an entire recasting of *The Double,* with the same characters and sentimental intrigue but with new ideological motifs deriving from this later period. Golyadkin would become a radical, attend a meeting of the Petrashevsky circle, "dream of being a Napoleon, a Pericles, the leader of the Russian revolt," learn about science and atheism—and his double would denounce the radicals to the authorities.[17] These notes show how the double-technique had begun to expand in Dostoevsky's imagination, and to incorporate the major ideological motifs that would characterize his post-Siberian creations. But he never got around to rewriting *The Double* as he had intended, perhaps because the same artistic impulse was already being channeled into new productions. It was only while finishing *Crime and Punishment* in 1866 that he revised *The Double,* and gave it the form it has retained ever since.

For the most part, Dostoevsky's revisions consist in little more than cutting out many of the verbal repetitions that were the butt of so much criticism.[18] More important, however, is that he also eliminated the entire mock-heroic framework. He struck out all the chapter headings, and for the original subtitle—*The Adventures of Mr. Golyadkin*—substituted *A Petersburg Poem.* This concealed the stylistic relation to *Dead Souls,* and was perhaps meant to dissociate *The Double* from the elements of radical social critique and the memories of Belinsky still connected with Gogol's novel. The new subtitle did not betray the work (Golyadkin *was* a Petersburg type), and was vague and noncommittal enough not to be compromising; it had the further advantage of correctly assigning *The Double* its place in the Russian literary tradition initiated by *The Bronze Horseman.*

In addition, Dostoevsky shortened the work by a full chapter and simplified the intrigue, excising almost entirely the motif of the double as "Grishka Otrepeev" (this was given much more space in the original), and truncating Golyadkin's xenophobic fear of being poisoned in a plot woven by his German ex-landlady in cahoots with the equally German Krestyan Ivanovich. Some passages connected with this poison-motif are much more obscure in the final version. By contrast, the central social-psychological emphasis was strengthened by a change in the ending, which now provides chilling confirmation of Golyadkin's madness and ultimate destination, along with a last thrust of his sense of guilt: "You get free quarters, wood, with light and service, which you deserve not" (1: 229).

Despite his dissatisfaction with *The Double,* Dostoevsky always continued to maintain his belief in its great significance. Writing to Mikhail in 1859 about his plans to im-

prove it, and to publish it with a new preface, he says: "They [his critics] will see at last what *The Double* really is! Why should I abandon a first-rate idea, a really magnificent type in terms of its social importance, which I was the first to discover and of which I was the herald?"[19] Twenty years later, in the *Diary of a Writer,* he confessed that "my story was not successful"; but he continued to claim that "its idea was clear enough, and I have never contributed anything to literature more serious than this idea. But I was completely unsuccessful with the form of the story."[20] Just what Dostoevsky means by "form" here is unclear; but one suspects that he was referring to the "fantastic" aspect of *The Double,* the uncertain oscillation between the psychic and the supernatural. The double as an emanation of Golyadkin's delirium is perfectly explicable; the double as an actually existing mirror-image of Golyadkin, with the identical name, is troubling and mysterious. Dostoevsky never leaves any doubt in the future about this alternative: his doubles will either be clear-cut hallucinations, or they are what may be called "quasi-doubles"—characters who exist in their own right, but reflect some internal aspect of another character in a strengthened form.

It is not difficult to understand, though, why Dostoevsky thought the "idea" embodied in *The Double* to have been of such importance. Golyadkin's double represents the suppressed aspects of his personality that he is unwilling to face; and this internal split between self-image and truth—between what a person wishes to believe about himself, and what he really is—is Dostoevsky's first grasp of a character-type that became his hallmark as a writer. Golyadkin is the ancestor of all of Dostoevsky's great split personalities, who are always confronted with their quasi-doubles or doubles (whether in the form of other "real" characters, or as hallucinations) in the memorable scenes of the great novels. The similarity of personality-structure between Golyadkin and his successors—such as the underground man, Raskolnikov, Stavrogin, and Ivan Karamazov—has led some critics to interpret *The Double* as if all the philosophical and religious themes of the mature Dostoevsky were *already* present in its pages;[21] but this is an untenable anachronism. The Dostoevsky of the 1840s is not that of the 1860s and 1870s, and his frame of reference in *The Double* is still purely social-psychological.

The mature Dostoevsky later felt that the discovery of this "underground" type, whose first version is Golyadkin, constituted his greatest contribution to Russian literature. For such a type represented, in his view, the true state of the Russian cultural psyche of his time, hopelessly split between competing and irreconcilable ideas and values. In this early phase of Dostoevsky's work, Golyadkin's intolerable guilt feelings at his own modest aspirations disclose the stifling and maiming of personality under a despotic tyranny. Later, the same character-type will be employed to exhibit the disintegrating effect of the atheistic radical ideology imported from the West on what Dostoevsky believed to be the innately moral-religious Russian national character, with its instinctive need to believe in Christ and God.

Notes

1. *Pisma,* 1: 78; May 8, 1845.

2. *Ibid.,* 81; October 8, 1845.

3. *Ibid.,* 108; January-February 1847.

4. *Ibid.*

5. The most recent study is Natalie Reber, *Studien zum Motiv des Doppelgängers bei Dostoevskij und E. T. A. Hoffmann* (Geissen, 1964); also Charles Passage, *Dostoevski the Adapter* (Chapel Hill, N.C., 1954). Passage's book is vitiated by the idea indicated in the title—that Dostoevsky did nothing else but "adapt" Hoffmann.

6. Vinogradov, *Evolutsiia,* 214.

7. *Pisma,* 1: 81; February 1, 1846.

8. G. M. Fridlender, *Realizm Dostoevskogo* (Moscow-Leningrad, 1964), 70.

9. F. Evnin, *"Ob Odnoi Istoriko-Literaturnoi Legenda,"* *Russkaya Literatura* 2 (1965), 3–26.

10. See his influential article "Zabitie Liudi" in *DRK,* 58–94.

11. This is a point well brought out in Evnin's article (note 9 above), though he reads the work much too exclusively in the Dobrolyubov tradition for me to accept his view as a whole.

12. Bakhtin, *Problemy Poetiki Dostoevskogo,* 291–292; Vinogradov, 261–267.

13. See Terras, *The Young Dostoevsky,* 206–212; M. F. Lomagin, "K Voprosu o Positsii Avtora v 'Dvoinike' Dostoevskogo," *Filologicheskie Nauki* 14 (1971), 3 13; most recently, Wolf Schmid, *Der Textaufbau in den Erzählungen Dostoevskijs* (Munich, 1973), 85–146.

14. Cited in A. L. Bem, *U Istokov,* 143.

15. V. G. Belinsky, "Petersburgskii Sbornik," in *DRK,* 27.

16. P. V. Annenkov, *Vospominania i Kriticheskie Ocherki,* 3 vols. (St. Petersburg, 1879), 2: 23.

17. These notes are now in 1: 432–435; they have been translated in *The Unpublished Dostoevsky,* ed. Carl R. Proffer (Ann Arbor, Mich., 1973), 1: 15.

18. A detailed study of these revisions can be found in the article by P. I. Avanesov, "Dostoevskii v rabote nad 'Dvoinikom,'" in *Tvorcheskaya Istoria,* ed. N. K. Piksanov (Moscow, 1927), 154–191.

19. *Pisma,* 1: 257; October 1, 1859.

20. *DW* (November 1877), 882–883.

21. This tendency is regrettably manifest in the otherwise classic study of Dimitri Chizhevsky, "The Theme of *The Double* in Dostoevsky," in *Dostoevsky,* ed. René Wellek (Englewood Cliffs, N.J., 1962), 112–129.

Asya Pekurovskaya (essay date 1986)

SOURCE "The Nature of Referentiality in *The Double,*" in *Dostoevski and the Human Condition after a Century,* Alexej Ugrinsky, Frank S. Lambasa, Valija K. Ozolins, eds., Greenwood Press, 1986, pp. 41–51.

[*In the following essay, Pekurovskaya discusses "the nature of referentiality"* in The Double.]

With a notable persistence (more than thirty times)[1] number "two," both cardinal and ordinal, appears in Dostoevski's narrative as the most explicit tool of executing the theme of the double referred to by the title of the novel. If his persistence is not gratuitous, which is a matter of simple certainty, one should be able to speak of some laws, governing the multiple usage and meaning of the word-sign "two." And indeed the list of textual reference just reproduced suggests, not without an accord with the general concept of "two," that all word-signs pertaining to the notion of "two," denote either a simultaneity ("two gentlemen," "two rows," "both chairs," "a twin") or a sequence ("two hours," "two steps," "second floor"). Yet, no general concept of two supports the idea that all these word-signs denote either spatiality or temporality, respectively, the former manifested by a precise figure: mathematical symbol or a collective linguistic word-sign ("a couple," "a twin"), whereas the latter—by a pendulate integer susceptible to a confusion with its closest integers, "one" and "three" ("a thing or two," "two or three officers") as well as with the figure of spatiality.[2]

The lack of a clear-cut distinction between the basic functions of the word-sign "two" was presumably the source of a general belief that the theme of the double was introduced into modern discourse as a borrowing from Romanticism. Yet a close textual reading with a provisional view as to a heterogeneity of the "two"-concept, leads to an observation that to a certain type of discourse, no matter whether it is regarded as romantic or modern by tradition, the theme of the double, understood as a simultaneity concept,[3] will be foreign. Let us call a discourse which dispenses with the notion of simultaneity in favor of sequence a modern text and, hence, let us question its historically determined continuity with the concept of the "Doppelganger." It will appear then that the theme of the double is appropriated by the modern text not as a borrowing from romanticism accountable in descriptive terms, but as an usurpation which can be described in dialectical terms, encroaching upon the romantic notion of referentiality.[4]

It appears thus, that to speak of romantic referentiality in modern terms means already to discard the notion of referent in favor of the notion of non-referent, insofar as the latter notion constitutes the perspective from which modern man invariably commences his reading of literature. Let us observe *The Double* from the perspective of its (non)referentiality.

The narrative strategy can be described by a term of replication which points to the fact that parts of the narrative are to reappear as if in order to make more sense than their counterparts. For example, Golyadkin's monologue, recorded in Chapter 2 as an undecipherable "confession" to Dr. Rutenspitz, reappears as soon as Chapter 4 (numerically congruent with the rule of doubling) in the form of a lucid description of a dinner party. As this replication-strategy realizes only during one's second reading, "Golyadkin's monologue" may be regarded not as a source, but a sequel and, in fact, a condensation of the re-iterated "description." This suggests a certain reversed procedure according to which a recourse to "the description" will precede one's reading of "the monologue."

In the description-part the discourse produces a novel character who is the narrator himself expressing his wish to be a poet "Homer or Pushkin," and confessing his present lack of eloquence, which amounts to his failure to "possess the secret of elevated and forceful style." As the latter hinders the fulfillment of the basic narrative task, to wit, depicting the "beautiful and modifying moments of mortal existence" (p. 53), the narrative code undergoes an essential transformation. The dramatized narration is supplanted by a pictorial code, foreign to the code of narrativization by definition. In this pictorial code, introduced by the formula "I will say nothing but will point out," the picture of "Vladimir Semyonovich, Andrey Filippovich's nephew," functions as a kernel unit, generating a series of other pictures: "the tearful eyes of the parents of the Queen of Festives, the proud eyes of Andrey Filippovich, the modest eyes of the Queen herself, the rapturous eyes of the guests and the decorously envious eyes of certain colleagues of this brilliant man" (p. 54). Presumably, the effect registered within the pictorial narrative ("tears," "pride," "ecstasy," "decorum," and so on) can very well compensate for the effect of the eloquent story-telling, which means that the figure of "Vladimir Semyonovich" can be viewed as one called for to supplant the narrator's figure in its basic task: verbalization. (The fact that "Vladimir Semyonovich" is the one whose function in the picture is to propose a toast, supports this point as well.)

As congruent with the pictorial code, furthermore, the nominal word-signs become ritualized with the effect of their suppressed semantic value: just as the notion of "young man" appears to mean the same as "old man," a relation of synonymy is to be established among such word-signs as "rank," "rosy cheeks," "lofty heights" and "good manners": "I will say nothing although I cannot help observing that everything about this young man—who, let it be said in his favor, is more like an old man than a young one—everything, from his rosy cheeks to the rank of Assessor with which he is invested, speaks at this triumphant moment of the lofty heights to which one may be elevated by good manners!" (p. 54). And with a notable persistence all these "ritualized synonyms" appear to be the ones clarifying the reference to "Vladimir Semyonovich, Andrey Filippovich's nephew," whose central position in "the narrative description" is emphasized, as he is the one to displace the narrator in his basic function. The narrator not only annihilates his own ego, just as his protago-

nist does later on prior to meeting his own double,[5] but also dilapidates his style by a disguised reference to the Gogolian code.

> How can I, the humble chronicler of the adventures of Mr. Golyadkin, which are, however, very curious in their way, depict this singular and seemly medley of beauty, brilliance, decorum, gaiety, amiable sobriety and sober amiability . . . depict all the daughters and wifes, who, I mean this as a compliment, are more like fairies thant ladies, with their pink and lily-white shoulders and faces . . . and—to use a grand word—homoeopathic feet?
>
> (p. 56)

This hidden indication of the Gogolian *skaz*-code concealed behind an authentic object-language of the story, serves not only to a narrator/character confusion, but also to an entanglement between referential and meta-discursive functions of the narrative language, especially in view of the fact (the entree of which has been procured only by the modern reader) that the recognition of the Gogol-code cannot be acknowledged apart from an indication to a Formalist reading of literary text. Indeed, the Dostoevski dialogue with Gogol appears to be concurrent with that of Eikhenbaum who held that Gogol uses the word "hemorrhoidal," just as Dostoevski's narrator uses the word "homeopathic," not as an authentic sign pertaining to its object-language, but as a meta-discursive sign, referring to another sign ("grandiose and fantastic"[6]).

Apart from being a catalyst of narrator's mortification the Gogol-code functions as a strategical nucleus at which "the narrative description" can be regarded as the one superimposed with the "Golyadkin monologue" previously referred to as undecipherable. Spacial limitations that had prevented me from quoting the "narrative description" in full, force me to limit myself to reference to a concluding segment of the "Golyadkin monologue" as follows:

> Yes, a certain intimate acquaintance of mine was congratulating another very intimate acquaintance of mine, who was, moreover a close friend of mine, "a bosom friend" as the saying is, on his promotion to the rank of Assessor. The way he chanced to put it was: "I'm heartily glad of this opportunity of offering you my congratulations, my sincere congratulations, Vladimir Semyonovich, on your promotion—the more so since nowadays, as all the world knows, those who push their favorites[7] are no more." . . . That's what he said, Doctor, and he looked at Andrey Filippovich, the uncle of our dear Vladimir Semyonovich. But what does it matter to me his being made an Assessor? Is this any business of mine? And there he is wanting to get married and his mother's milk still wet on his lips, if you'll pardon the expression
>
> (p. 33).

It would be difficult if not impossible to persuade the reader familiar exclusively with the fragment just quoted that the narrator's reference to "a certain intimate acquaintance of mine" is none other than a self-reference semantically conflicting with its succeeding reference ("another very intimate acquaintance of mine") the latter being in fact a reference to "Vladimir Semyonovich, the nephew of Andrey Filippovich." Yet, an inference as to a confusion between the two referents, the "I" and "Vladimir Semyonovich," is not only a probable, but rather a predictable narrative turn by which the theme of the double is being executed. Indeed the retroactive familiarity with the description-code where the "Vladimir Semyonovich" figure is realized to supersede the narrator, prevents one from confusing identical signifiers and dissociating the distinct ones. It follows that the signifier "he" in "That's what he said, Doctor," and the signifier "me" in "But what does it matter to *me* his being made an Assessor?" would invariably point to a single referent, precisely, the I/he of the narrator signified by the name of "Golyadkin," the narrator and the acting persona of the story.

So far it can be said that my choice to juxtapose the description-code with the monologue-code was justified insofar as both codes deal with the notion of the suppressed ego, be it an "I" of "the humble chronicler of the adventures of Mr. Golyadkin," supplanted by the figure of "Vladimir Semyonovich, Andrey Filippovich's nephew," or a "he" of Golyadkin the character who buries his monological first-person reference under the third-person self-reference. But even though a discovery that the referent behind the "I" of Golyadkin the narrator is the same as that of the "he" of Golyadkin the character is possible only retroactively, and only retroactively is one to explain the subsequent transition for the initial "he" into a generic, i.e., pertaining to the monologue-form, "I," the key to the discursive meaning should be searched by way of a reciprocal movement from description to monologue and from monologue to description.

This rule of reciprocity (a hermeneutical rule indispensible for deciphering the theme of the double in its modern execution) has various manifestations in modern discourse from the slips of the tongue, pertaining to the language of a character to what can be called a discursive figure of anticipation.[8] I shall presently concentrate my attention on the slips of the tongue which occur in the concluding lines of the Golyadkin monologue to Dr. Rutenspitz which I restrained from quoting so far for the reason that the slips of the tongue make it possible not to just witness the non-referential codification in modern discourse, but also to interpret the very meaning of non-referents along with the narrative intention imbedded in it. Let us recall the lines in question: "But to kill two birds[9] with one stone, after I'd given the young man a start with that bit about pushing favorites [fortune-telling grandmothers] I turned to Klara Olsufyevna, who'd just been signing a tender ballad—all this was the day before yesterday, at her father's—and I said: 'Your singing is full of tenderness, but those who listen haven't got pure hearts'" (p. 34).

What I interpret as the slip of the tongue in the first place is the case of misusing the Russian idiom "*ubit' dvukh zaitsev odnim kamnem*" (literally, "to kill two hares with

one stone"), in view of which an engimatic substitution occurs of the word "hare" by the word "sparrow." I am inclined to ascribe to this substitution an important mental process, namely, the narrator's desire to repress his sexual anxiety. It appears that in its proverbial function the word-sign "sparrow" has an overt erotic connotation[10] in the Russian language.

A tendency to neutralize the terminology pertaining to the language of eroticism, futhermore, is not the only interfering tendency capable of bringing itself to expression in a perverted form. The twice reiterated reference to the "fortune-telling grandmothers," interfering with the narrator's direct address to "Vladimir Semyonovich, Andrey Filippovich's nephew," suggests the meddling of the allusion by omission that betrays the complex of the Gogolian minor official, manifested in a formula: "I should like to know why I'm a Titular Councillor? Why especially a Titular Councillor?" Consequently, a distinction in quality, an order or a rank (of Assessor) achieved through (the) patronage (of Andrey Filippovich, the departmental head) constitutes another source of the narrator's anxiety, comparable with the erotic drive and looming behind the foregoing allusion.

From both these sources of anxiety one can reconstruct the interfering tendency which conditions the appearance of the narrator's first double, "Vladimir Semyonovich, Andrey Filippovich's nephew," whose name is especially suitable for the chosen role. Precisely, "Vladimir" signifies one of the two Russian orders established in 1782 for civil services and endowed all its cavaliers, regardless of degree, with the inheritable nobility; "Semyon" is derived from the root common to a number of words, pertaining to the notion of "seed" of "progeny," and, by extention, "sexuality."

Hence, in a search of support for a modern definition of the non-referential reference, two narrative fragments have been selected, one replicated by another, while reproducing it in a condensed and undecipherable form, existing as a substitute for its repressed self.[11]

Roughly speaking, the phenomena just described have already been detected under the name of mental process par excellence by Sigmund Freud[12] in view of which "Golyadkin's monologue" appears to be a repressed wishful impulse which continues to exist in "the narrative description": in the former case as the workings of subconsciousness (a dream, a joke, or a slip of the tongue), and in the latter case—as a conscious "facade behind which/the thinking process/lies concealed."[13] A necessity for such detection can be now declared as an interpretative condition according to which a claim can be made that prior to the appearance of Golyadkin's double incarnate, i.e., Golyadkin junior, and even prior to the appearance of Golyadkin's double by involuntary desire ("Vladimir Semyonovich's" case), doubling becomes a meaning-generating mechanism. And in its executive strategy of self-unfolding the most authentic Golyadkin's double appears to be what Freud could have called a double by "transferrence," to wit, Dr. Rutenspitz[14] who functions as the one to subject the character to a psychoanalytic treatment (one should not forget that Golyadkin's first appearance in Dr. Rutenspitz's office is referred to in the narrative as his second appearance) resulted in what Francesco Orlando calls the "Freudian negation."[15] Golyadkin the patient negates all his repressed instincts and secret wishes ["I have no gift for fine phrases" (p. 25); "I am no great talker" (p. 26); "I don't like odd words here and there, miserable double-dealing I can't stand, slander and gossip I abominate" (p. 28)] that make their way to the surface only unvoluntarily: through his dreams, jokes, or slips of the tongue which in fact are no longer semantically segregated, insofar as they all are manifestations of the working of the unconscious, all constituting the forces seeking liberation from the repression. And even this semantic indifferentiation characteristic of the unconscious goes in accord with the Freudian understanding of the thinking process:

> Similarly, contraries are not kept apart from each other but are treated as though they were identical, so that in the manifest dream any element may also stand for its contrary. Certain philologists have found that the same holds good in the oldest languages, and that contraries such as "strong-weak," "light-dark," "high-deep" were originally expressed by the same roots, until two different modifications of the primitive word distinguished the two meanings. . . .[16]

At this point I wish to conclude that the nature of referentiality in **The Double** is the double itself detectable from the narrative strategy of deceptive replications. Yet, along with this conclusion I am tempted to resume the theme of the double by a recourse to the concept of the "two" viewed as a spacial versus temporal concept. I claim that the modern feature of temporality, in contradistinction to romantic speciality derived from the notion of the "Doppelganger," does not tolerate the polarized view of the world based on the notion of perceptual evidence.[17] And so does modern discourse in general.

As the last resort, I may say that the consequences of not segregating romantic and modern codes would have been only theoretically predictable were it not for the fact that they are quite tangible already. Notably, the two twentieth century interpreters of **The Double,** both belonging to a category of distinguished contributors of the Dostoevski scholarship, speak of the same "narrative effects" in seemingly incompatible terms. Namely, what for the formalist Vinogradov, presumably brought up in the spirit of romanticism, appears to have a comic effect (an effect of "ironic stylization"[18]), for the structuralist Kramarenko, presumably prejudiced against romanticism as a modern man, becomes a manifestation of tragedy. ("Thus, the character's tragedy," he says, "is permanently accompanied by noise, music, and festive guests."[19]) However, a recourse to Freud and after him to Kierkegaard and a number of modern thinkers, will help us to observe that modern mentality does not know any distinction between comedy and trag-

edy, in view of which one of Golyadkin's doubles, his servant Petrushka can be said to be a predecessor of one of Stravinskij's doubles, "Petrushka," the latter carrying comedy and tragedy of our time.

Notes

1. I shall draw a few examples and leave the rest for the reader to discover: "For two minutes or so he lay motionless in bed," (p. 11); "he had encountered two of his colleagues" (p. 17); "I have come to bother you a second time and for a second time I venture to ask your indulgence." (p. 24). Fyodor Dostoevski, *The Double,* trans. George Bird (Bloomington: Indiana University Press, 1966). Page references to this edition are given parenthetically in the text.

2. I call "spatial," as opposed to "temporal," any reference that can be called authentic due to its being verifiable by senses, such as, for example, a reference to "one or two," "a word or two," "two or three people," taken from E. T. A. Hoffman "Automata," in E. F. Bleiler, ed., *The Best Tales of E. T. A. Hoffman,* (New York: Dover Publications, 1967), p. 90: "When he had heard *one or two* of the Turk's answers, he took the exhibitor aside and whispered *a word or two* in his ear. The man turned pale, and shut up his exhibition as soon as the *two or three* people who were in the room had gone away." Here all the nominal word-signs and numbers point to a narrator's attempt to reproduce an exact picture of what has happened. The notion of exactitude is not only not tottered by a reference to imprecise figures, but even reinforced by them, for the narrative truth is assumed to be ascertained via narrator's sincere effort to tell the truth.

   By contrast, the same signifiers can be said to lose their referentiality in modern discursive convention. In an example from Dostoevsky that follows: "He saw *one or two* people as well. Or rather he didn't. He was no longer aware of anybody. Propelled by the same spring that had brought him bounding into a ball to which he had not been invited, he continued to advance steadily." *The Double,* p. 61, the signifier "one or two people" refers to neither "one" or "two," but a great many with whom the "he" of the narrative is destined to communicate in a non-conventional way, so that "one or two" can be identified with no immediate signified, but with a number of syntagmatically conjoined signifiers that turn into synonyms. What makes them synonyms if the nature of discursive predication which cancels their referentiality by abolishing the means of sensual perception: "he saw . . . or rather he didn't . . . noticing none of this or, more accurately, noticing it, but not looking . . ."

3. The meaning of simultaneity and a grammatical bond between the "double" and the "two" is supported by word etymology. *DOPPELGANGER. "Das diesen Wortern zugrunde liegende lat. Adjectiv du-plus 'zwie- faltig" ist gebildet aus duo 'zwei' und dem*

Stamm **pel- 'falten' (wie dt. Zweifel; vgl. ferner duo und* falten: *s.a.Diplom*) . . . *Doppelganger m* (1976 by Jean Paul *'wer sich selbst an einem andern Ort* [gehen] *sieht', heute varallgemeinert zu 'einem andern zum Verwechseln ahnlicher Mensch')." Duden ed' Paul Grebe (Dudenverlag: Bibliographisches Institut, Mannheim), Band 7, p. 115.

4. Todorov's attempt to identify Gogol's *Nose* as a "limited case" of the fantastic genre comprised exclusively of romantic texts has created unsurmountable difficulties. To incorporate a modern discourse into the body of romantic ones, Todorov was bound to loosen up his theoretical assumptions which still did not help him to avoid imprecision and even confusion in his reading of Gogol. Suggesting, as he did, that "the narrative does not observe the first condition of the fantastic, that hesitation between the real and the illusory or imaginary be present, and it is therefore situated from the start within the marvelous," *The Fantastic,* trans. Richard Howard (Ithaca, N.Y.: Cornell University Press, 1970), p. 72, Todorov permits himself to ignore the fact that such "hesitation" is linguistically present in the text yet maintained at the level of characters' perception. To still support his argument in favor of Gogol's place among the fantastic narratives Todorov is found to assume a non-semiological position from which he states that Gogol "describes the life of Saint Petersburg down to its most mundane details" (p. 72). Finally, he welcomes such contradictory notions as "allegorical" and "literal," (the latter being employed in both literal and figurative sense) in order to conclude: "What Gogol asserts is precisely, non-meaning" (p. 73), as if "meaning and non-meaning" were categories clarified by way of asserting or negating them.

5. The appearance of the "double" is gradually prepared by the narrative Golyadkin either decides to conceal his identity as a matter of his strategy of behavior or he assumes a self-effacing philosophy characteristic of his existential doubts: "'Shall I pretend it's not me, but someone extraordinarily like me, and just look as if nothing has happened? It really isn't me, it *isn't* me, and that's all there is to it. . . .'" (p. 19); "'I'm a simple man. There's no outward show about me. On this point, Doctor, I lay down my arms—or to continue the metaphor, I surrender.'" (p. 24); "He had no more life in him. He was finished in the full sense of the word, and if at that moment he was still able to run, it was only by some incredible miracle." (p. 71); Mr. Golyadkin wanted to annihilate himself completely, to return to dust and cease to be" (p. 73).

6. B. M. Eikhenbaum, "How Gogol's 'Overcoat' Is Made," in *Gogol from the Twentieth Century,* ed. by Robert A. Maguire, (Princeton, N.J.: Princeton University Press, 1974), p. 279.

7. For the purposes which will become clear further on I have to clarify the essentially correct translation of

this segment. The original version of it, to wit: "*vyvelis babuski kotorye vorozat,*" (literally: "the fortune-telling grandmothers are no more") constitutes an abbreviation of the idiomatic expression "*khorosho tomu zhit' u kogo babushka vorozhit*" (literally, "with a fortune-telling grandmother one can be doing fine"). The sense of this idiom no longer immediately identified by the modern reader, has been transmitted by the translator as "those who push their favorites."

8. There are two kinds of "anticipation"-figure in Dostoevsky discourse: "anticipation" through a recourse to the familiar: ["Everything looked back at him familiarly" (p. 11); "he turned to look at Dr. R . . . windows. It was as he thought! The doctor was standing at one of them," (p. 37); "But he was now almost sure it was someone he knew. He'd seen him often. He'd seen him somewhere quite recently even." (p. 78); "Mr. Golyadkin, we must add, knew this man perfectly well, knew his name even." (p. 79)], and secondly, anticipation as a form of knowing the future ["He had sensed that if he once stumbled everything would immediately go to the devil. And so it did." (p. 62); "Mr. Golyadkin knew, felt and was quite convinced, that some new evil would befall him on the way, and that some fresh unpleasantness would burst upon him: that there would be, for instance, another meeting with the stranger," (p. 80); "'Still, I anticipated all this,' thought our hero. 'And I've anticipated what it'll say.'" (p. 159); "'This isn't the way to the door,' flashed through his mind, and indeed, it was not." (p. 245)"].

Quite congruent with its major function, the figure of anticipation negates itself by the end of the narrative, just as the narrator and protagonist did in anticipation of their respective doubles, and it does it in a bifurcated fashion as well. This means that it deactivates both its figures, a "recourse to the familiar": ["But what our hero had apparently been fearing, did not happen" (p. 246)] and "knowing the future" one: ["At this point something unexpected occurred. The door flew open with a bang, and on the threshold stood a man whose very appearance made Mr. Golyadkin's blood run cold" (p. 250)].

9. Literally, "two sparrows."

10. Compare such idioms as "*Sam s vorob'ja a serdtse s koshku*" ("Himself as little as a sparrow, his heart as big as a cat"); "*Za obedom solovej, a posle obeda vorobej*" ("At dinner sings like a nightingale, after dinner—like a sparrow"); "*Starogo vorob'ia na mjakine ne obmanesh'*" ("An old sparrow is not caught with chaff") in Vladimir Dal', *Tolkovyj slovar' zivogo velikorusskogo jazyka,* Vol. 1, (Moscow: Akademiia Nank, 1955), p. 242.

11. Replication patterns are hierarchical, as they comprise either a scope of the entire novel viewed as a replica of Golyadkin's dream (pp. 166–171), or a single symbol, say, a phallic symbolism of Golyad-

kin's "confession", i.e., "*umejut podnesti koku s sokom*— translated, unsuccessfully, I believe, as "know how to spring an old surprise" (p. 32)—replicated in narrator's comment on Anton Antonovich's toadyism—"an old man as grey as a badger, crows like a cock and speaks some jolly verses (pp. 54–55)."

12. See *A General Introduction to Psychoanalysis,* trans. Joan Riviere (New York, New York: A Clarion Book, 1963); *An Outline of Psychoanalysis,* trans. James Strachey (New York: The Norton Library, 1963); *Five Lectures on Psycho-Analysis,* trans. James Strachey (New York: Norton Library, 1952); *Jokes and Their Relation to the Unconscious,* trans. James Strachey (New York: The Norton Library, 1960).

13. Freud, *Outline of Psychoanalysis,* p. 47.

14. The narrative choice for a doctor to be German as well as its choice of German names for all real and fantasized aphrodisiac objects of Golyadkin's desire: form a German landlady, Karolin Ivanovna, to a German waitress and German-sounding name for his imaginary fiancee suggests a hidden dialogue with romanticism always associated with Germany and understood as literary cliche to which modern discourse always responds.

15. *Towards a Freudian Theory of Literature With an Analysis of Rasine's Phedre,* Trans. Ch. Lee (Baltimore: Johns Hopkins University Press, 1979), p. 10.

16. Freud, *Outline of Psychoanalysis,* p. 53.

17. Hoffmann's title of *The Doubles* strikes me as hitting the essence of the distinction between romantic and modern discourse by its choice of plurality. Here, two distinctly real people both mistaken one for another are eventually "recognized" for what each of them should actually be. The idea is that from the concept of "mistake" and "recognition" one is to derive a concept of infallable truth supported by a polarized mode of thinking: *good* versus *bad,* "Hohenflug" versus "Sonsitz," "Golden Ram" versus "Silver Lamb" and so on.

18. V. V. Vinogradov, "K morfologii natural'nogo stilja," *Poetika russkoj literatury* (Moscow: Nanka, 1976), p. 129.

19. M. Kramarenko, "Prostranstvo i vremja v povesti F. M. Dostoevskogo '"Dvojnik,'" p. 19.

David Ayers (essay date 1988)

SOURCE: "Two Bald Men: Eliot and Dostoevsky," in *Forum for Modern Language Studies,* Vol. XXIV, No. 4, October, 1988, pp. 287–300.

[*In the following essay, Ayers explores the influence of* The Double *on the works of T. S. Eliot.*]

Students of the influence that one author has had on the work of another have at all times had reason to be careful, not to give too much importance to the superficial resemblance, the odd verbal parallel, while seeking deeper structural affinities—without, that is, making one or two centuries of high-brow literary effort appear to have repeatedly produced the same thing.

In the case of Eliot, possibly the most influence-prone writer of an age, the scholar must be doubly careful. At all points Eliot seems to have anticipated the influence-hunter's search and to have laid false trails—I say "seems" because, once possessed of the notion of Eliot's duplicitousness, it becomes impossible not to take it into consideration at every stage—what started life as a phantom becomes an everyday reality.

The notorious "Notes on the Wasteland"—hard to take seriously, hard to ignore—are perhaps a prime example of this. Many of Eliot's essays, while purporting to be objective criticism seem, under scrutiny, to be oblique meditations about the influence that an author might have had on Eliot's own work. The 1918 Lecture, "From Poe to Valery", finds in the work of Poe "nothing but slipshod writing, puerile thinking unsupported by wide reading or profound scholarship, haphazard experiments in various kinds of writing . . ."[1] Yet Eliot admits that he shall "never be sure" what influence Poe's work has had on him. The essay then proceeds effectively to mitigate the effect of this influence by refracting Poe through Baudelaire, Mallarmé and Valéry—far more elegant peers than the stylistically crude and obsessive Poe.

Examining the influence of Dostoevsky on Eliot might seem a potentially fraught task. The first attempt to do so was an article by John C. Pope, "Prufrock and Raskolnikov," which appeared in *American Literature* in 1945.[2] Pope gives weight to some very slight verbal parallels between Eliot's poem and Garnett's translation of *Crime and Punishment,* and additionally points out parallels of symbolic language—fog, streets, stairs (fairly ubiquitous phenomena, on any account) and references to Hamlet and Lazarus.

While Pope's intuition was undoubtedly correct, he had made one fatal mistake, which Eliot himself pointed out in a personal letter. "The Love Song of J. Alfred Prufrock" had been completed in the summer of 1911, several years before any English translation of *Crime and Punishment* had appeared. This made nonsense of Pope's verbal parallels, as Pope himself acknowledged. However Pope did draw from Eliot the valuable information that he *had* been reading Dostoevsky in French translation, under the influence of his French tutor, Alain Fournier, while writing "Prufrock", although Eliot carefully disperses the question of influence on the poem by pointing out that parts of the poem, including the reference to Hamlet, were written *before* he had encountered Dostoevsky. Further, in addition to *Crime and Punishment,* he claims to have read *The Idiot* and *The Brothers Karamazov.*[3]

A study of the possible influence of Dostoevsky's early novel *The Double* on "Prufrock" and later works of Eliot seems then to have a profound obstacle in its path—Eliot does not admit to having read the book. This at first seems disabling, but in fact it is liberating. It is possible that Eliot was misleading Pope while at the same time seeming to help the influence-hunters—just as the "Notes on the Wasteland" seem to do. The French edition of *The Double,* had already in the Winter of 1910 run to several editions, and would have been easily available to Eliot. Even discounting this possibility, *The Double,* dating from before Dostoevsky's exile, had an acknowledged effect on the work of his later period, and indeed he was working on a revised version of *The Double* some twenty years after its first publication—working at the same time on *Crime and Punishment.* So the question of influence might then be a question of refracted influence. Just as Poe was received by Eliot refracted through the French symbolistes, perhaps he received *The Double* (a tale with Gothic elements possibly drawn from Poe, and immature in style) refracted through Dostoevsky's later and allegedly greater works. Yet there remains the tantalizing possibility, that Eliot's silence about *The Double,* like his distancing himself from Poe, is the product of a guilty affinity.

The hero of *The Double,* Titular Councillor Golyadkin, Yakov Petrovich to his friends, is a balding civil servant who is every bit as belated, indecisive, evasive and impotent as J. Alfred Prufrock himself. The narrative of the tale, which playfully blends the comic and the Gothic, brings Golyadkin into collision with his exact double, who comes to work in his office, impresses himself on his superiors in a way that Golyadkin has never done, and finally drives Golyadkin to madness. The story of Golyadkin finds its ancestry in Gogol's *The Nose,* Pushkin's *The Bronze Horseman,* and Cervantes' *Don Quixote,* but in its narrative method it is profoundly modern, blending the comic monologue of Dickens—a style itself sometimes named as the precursor of the stream-of-consciousness method in English—with a prediction of Jamesian point-of-view narration. The result is that rather than witness the decline of Golyadkin into madness the reader is inextricably involved in that decline. Much of what occurs is presented in Golyadkin's own words. Even when this is not so, the narrative voice increasingly adopts Golyadkin's own phrases and expressions, and as the persecution inflicted on him by his double grows, there is no relief for the reader who would seek to distinguish the projections of Golyadkin's own fevered mind from a sober and objective understanding of events. Indeed, the status of the reader with respect to the reality of the narrative mimics Golyadkin's own relationship to his double—each is shown a reality which, however implausible, becomes the only possible reference point.

The Double opens with Titular Councillor Yakov Petrovich Golyadkin awakening from a long sleep, and finding himself unable to decide "whether what is happening around him is real and actual, or only the continuation of his disordered dreams".[4] This blurring of the distinction between reality and fantasy, subjective and objective, is in its various forms the archetypal romantic legacy for both Dostoevsky and Eliot alike, refracted through Baudelaire, transported to Dostoevsky's Dickensian St Petersburg or Eliot's Dickensian London, and rendered ineluctable. Although Golyadkin quickly shakes himself awake to the grimy reality of St Petersburg, out of the "far-distant realm" of his dream, he will find the confusion recurring in his waking life, as he is forced to pinch himself to test his own wakefulness, considers pinching others also (but dare not), and is cruelly pinched on the nose and cheek by the taunting double.

For the moment, however, Golyadkin's possession of self and reality seems not to be threatened. He begins the morning by taking possession of his own image in the mirror. Considering what is about to happen, it is a greatly ironical moment, and one which enacts in microcosm the troubled heart of the Golyadkinesque dilemma:

> Although the sleepy, short-sighted, rather bald figure reflected in the glass was of such an insignificant character that nobody at all would have found it at the least remarkable at first glance, its owner was evidently quite satisfied with all he saw there. 'It would be a fine thing if something was wrong with me today, if a pimple had suddenly appeared out of the blue, for example, or something else disastrous had happened; however, for the moment, it's all right; for the moment everything is going well.'[5]

In the heart of the metropolis the individual is utterly anonymous, the civil servant like any other good Russian citizen must dedicate his life to the service of his country, and entrust his fate to the authorities as to the father. The self then can only be recognised as an individual in its own eyes, it can only possess itself as an image, a mirror-image perhaps, or an imagined one, but always one mediated by that of which it is an image. The self and the self-image can never coincide, just as the individual in the parental state must go always unacknowledged, and the result is an interminable anxiety which can only increase the more the incomplete and never self-sufficient self tries to cross the gap. This, roughly expressed, seems to be the Dostoevskian formula not only for Golyadkin—whose name is derived from goli − "naked"—but for mass urban man in general. The nakedness of Golyadkin is in his very typicality, a typicality arrived at by stripping urban man to a core of anxiety, stripping his language down to a mixture of state-inspired platitudes and romance-inspired desires. Indeed the self-satisfaction of Golyadkin contemplating himself in the mirror is presented in terms of a platitudinous satisfaction with reality which Golyadkin continually reproduces throughout the novel as his situation deteriorates with increasing speed.

Golyadkin's possession of self and reality alike appear, even at this early stage of the narrative, to be tenuous. On waking, Golyadkin had looked around his room at his furniture and clothes which "all looked familiarly back at him". After looking in the mirror he takes out a bundle of notes in a wallet, which also seems "to look back at Mr Golyadkin in a friendly and approving fashion".[6] This is the pathetic fallacy—the objects in question look approvingly back at Golyadkin only as a projection of his own self-satisfaction. Yet a reality seen in this way can equally become a menace. What if the pact with reality is broken by reality itself, approval for Golyadkin withdrawn, and a pimple erupts or some worse disaster takes place? As if to underline this threat, Golyadkin's samovar is found "raging and hissing fiercely, almost beside itself with anger and threatening to boil over any minute, gabbling away in its strange gibberish, lisping and babbling to Mr Golyadkin." Yet perhaps this too is a projection of Golyadkin—during the course of the narrative he too frequently threatens to boil over with anger, is almost metaphorically beside himself, and is finally literally beside himself. Golyadkin's consciousness attempts equally to contain a potentially explosive reality and a potentially explosive self. When the attempt at containment fails, Golyadkin's grasp on reality and on his self-image depart together, the self-image conspiring with a malevolent reality to expose the thoroughly dispossessed Golyadkin to his own naked anxieties.

These first pages then present a microcosmic view of the whole tale, although it is not at first apparent how out of hand Golyadkin's affairs already are, let alone how far astray they are going to go. Indeed most of the action of the story has taken place already, and the narrative deals only with the final dissolution. The first incongruities emerge when Golyadkin looks for his servant, Petrushka. Golyadkin is only a minor civil servant in a dingy fourth floor apartment, yet his aspirations to social position, arising from his sheer lack of position, lead him to keep a manservant who must sleep behind a partition, and who accords Golyadkin no respect whatsoever, despite frequent admonitions that he should do so. This morning Golyadkin finds Petrushka joking with other servants, he surmises about himself, and dressed in a ridiculously ill-fitting livery for the purpose of a coach-journey which he is to undertake with his master. For someone of Golyadkin's status, a journey with a liveried coachman is inappropriate. One purpose of the journey is a shopping expedition at the fashionable Arcades of the Nevsky Prospect. It is a ghost expedition: Golyadkin orders many items, some destined for a lady, promises a deposit, and leaves without giving his address: in short, an almost maniacal social masquerade born of Golyadkin's deep-seated wish to be someone. Yet at the same time, an incident on the journey from his own home shows exactly the opposite impulse. First, Golyadkin sees two younger colleagues from his own department. They are surprised to see him dressed up and in a carriage, clearly beyond his station, and call out to him. He hides in the corner of the carriage but consoles himself with aggressive thoughts:

> "I know them, they're nothing but schoolboys still in need of flogging . . . I'd have something to say to the lot of them, only . . ."[7]

Golyadkin's self-communion of consolation rests on knowing the others already, feeling able to look down on and contain them in a fantasy of domination, and on the security that he *would* have something to say, even though he hasn't said it, if only . . . his remarks trail off in suspension points.

The suspension of "only . . ." serves to isolate the most common rhetorical device of Golyadkin's almost constant patter of self-justification. It is not suspended because Golyadkin is lost for argument—indeed later passages show that his rhetoric of the conditional provides him with an unlimited fund of argument—but that a second encounter provides a sharp intrusion into his interior monologue. He encounters his immediate superior in the Department, Andrey Phillipovich, in a carriage travelling in the opposite direction. He is in anguish trying to decide whether or not to greet the other, or to take refuge in self-effacement:

> ". . . shall I pretend it's not me but somebody else strikingly like me, and look as if nothing's the matter?" . . . "I . . . it's all right," he whispered, hardly able to speak, "it's quite all right; this is not me at all, Andrey Phillipovich, it's not me at all, not me, and that's all about it."

Once his boss has passed, Golyadkin is consumed by anger at his own pusillanimity, and directs "a terrible challenging stare at the opposite corner of the carriage, a stare calculated to reduce all his enemies to dust".[8]

This is a fascinating incident, and a crucial one. The urge to self-effacement is born ultimately from the guilt of Golyadkin's desires, both for social status and for the respectable lady whom, it later emerges, he would like to marry. Thus the rhetoric of satisfaction and summary finality—"it's all right . . . that's all about it"—is an anxious attempt to contain the anxiety of an incomplete desire, one that is embarrassed by its own incompletion in the face of the seemingly self-sufficient other. Golyadkin's guilty reaction to his own embarrassment—a reaction he repeats several times during the course of the narration, always belatedly—projects enmity on to a reality which is merely uncompliant to his fantasy, and expresses a desire to exterminate that reality and replace it with fantasy. Indeed, Golyadkin's interior monologue throughout the narrative claims a knowledge, and very often a foreknowledge, of events, particularly of the thoughts and words of others, which it does not and cannot possess. In an effort to contain the other, the self attempts to substitute itself for the other—but only belatedly. In the face of an otherness which appears increasingly hostile to the desire of the self, the self steps sideways evasively—"this is not me at all".

Golyadkin is caught in an anxious oscillation between the wish to manifest his individuality—in whatever this may consist—and wish to conceal it—often expressed as the wish to hide in a mousehole, or as assertions about the normality and acceptability of his own actions or situation. This oscillation becomes a general indecisiveness on his part which almost entirely paralyses his will. This begins to become clear during the encounter with Andrey Phillipovich, and assumes its extreme form during Golyadkin's next encounter—with his new Doctor, Christian Ivanovich Rutenspitz. The visit to Rutenspitz is an impromptu one, impulsively decided upon after the encounter with Andrey Phillipovich and seemingly arising from that. On the way there, Golyadkin is tortured by doubts about the correctness and acceptability of his action, in that language of self-questioning which becomes the most persistent index of his character:

> "Will it be all right though? . . . will it be all right? Is it a proper thing to do? Will this be the right time? However, does it really matter?" he continued as he mounted the stairs, breathing hard and trying to control the beating of his heart, which always seemed to beat hard on other people's stairs; "does it matter? I've come about my own business, after all, and there's nothing reprehensible in that . . . it would be stupid to try and keep anything from him. So I'll just make it appear that it's nothing special, I just happened to be driving past . . ."[9]

It will be seen from this extended quotation that Golyadkin's habitual discourse with himself, the precursor of the staircase torment of Raskolnikov, is like a perpetual attempt to judge himself from an alternative viewpoint. He always wonders "what people might think", and substitutes his own voice for the voice of the imagined others. Yet while the later Dostoyevskian hero is troubled by issues that seem much weightier, Golyadkin's doubts are about almost nothing at all. That "almost nothing" is Golyadkin's own lack, that incompletion which is the anxious heart of urban man. This anxiety reproduces itself in an endless rhetoric of doubt. Indeed, it is about his state of anxiety that Golyadkin wishes to see his doctor. But the will to self-revelation is countered by the will to self-obliteration—to be no-one in particular, self-sufficient, seen by others to be merely going about his own business, as Golyadkin construes the self-sufficiency of others. What results is the paralysis of the will by choice, and this is dramatically enacted by Golyadkin at the door of his doctor's house:

> Coming to a halt, our hero hastily tried to give his countenance a suitably detached but not unamiable air, and prepared to give a tug at the bell-pull. Having taken hold of the bell-pull, he hastily decided, just in time, that it might be better to wait until the next day, and that meanwhile there was no great urgency. But suddenly hearing footsteps on the stairs, Mr. Golyadkin immediately changed his mind again and, while still retaining a look of the most unshakeable decision, at once rang Christian Ivanovich's bell.[10]

The self is both subject and object—its own object and the object of the other, menacingly present here in the footsteps of the doctor's footman, ready to answer the door.

It is Golyadkin's constant claim that he is not duplicitous, that he makes himself plain, that he does not beat about the bush, that he does not wear a mask like others and, in short, that his objective image and his subjectivity are entirely coincident. It is a claim which is manifestly un-

true—the incident at the door of Christian Ivanovich portrays a dramatic rupture between the oscillating anxiety of the self and the mask of "unshakeable decision" which Golyadkin presents. More than this, when Golyadkin goes to his superiors to explain himself, first about his designs on Carolina Ivanovich, daughter of the wealthy Olsufi Ivanovich, and later about the outrageous activities of his double, his rhetoric of self-revelation serves to so far defer and delay the actual moment of self-relevation that he is dismissed with impatience before any revelation has been made.

To complete this picture of Golyadkin before the appearance of his double—and it is a picture which accounts for most of his activities after the double appears—it need only be added that Golyadkin's linguistic attempt to contain the other and bend it toward his self-completion and self-sufficiency in the eyes of others is bound to fail, and continued frustration develops into a paranoia which sees enmity everywhere. Indeed, Golyadkin's rhetorics of self-questioning and of self-revelation are accompanied by an equally prolific and self-sustaining rhetoric of enmity. Not satisfied with one enemy, the allegation of enmity slips from one to another, frustrated of a final object, as Golyadkin is frustrated of his final revelation, another endless rhetoric of incompletion.

This is the prelude to the appearance of the double. The final precipitation is an abortive sexual encounter at a ball thrown by Olsufi Ivanovich, whose daughter has been wooed by a younger colleague of Golyadkin's, and in whose person therefore the whole of Golyadkin's anxiety of incompletion is embodied. Golyadkin is definitively not invited to the ball, and after a first abortive attempt at entry he is politely ejected. Instead of going home, he goes around to a rear entrance, and stands for three hours "in the cold among every kind of trash and lumber" assuring himself that his presence there means nothing, he could go in if he wanted to, it is not that he dare not, just that he does not choose to at the moment, and so on. Having finally decided to go in and stepped up to the door, he retreats again into hiding. Having decided that he will go home, not only because he would like a warm cup of tea but also because his prolonged absence might upset his manservant, Golyadkin states summarily "I'll go home, and that's all about it!"[11] and steps straight inside the house. He proceeds to embarrass himself in the eyes of all present, and resorts to that device of self-detachment which enabled him to pretend not to be himself, this time to pretend to be merely a casual onlooker, and not a part of any scandal. Golyadkin's indecision and self-detachment, as well as his self-revelation when he tearfully tries to explain his presence in the sincerest manner, all reach their logical limit and, cast out on the streets of St Petersburg on a stormy night, Golyadkin first encounters his double, and follows him back to his own flat.

It should be apparent at this stage that while the doubling alluded to by the title of this novel is the eventual reduplication of Golyadkin himself, it might stand equally for a variety of reduplications at various levels which occur before the appearance of the double and which continue to manifest themselves after his arrival. From the first page where the fantasy of sleep and the reality of the waking world are confused, where everyday objects reflect back Golyadkin's gaze, and where a mirror offers him a specious moment of specular self-possession, doubling and duplicity become rampant. Doubling *and* duplicity, because every reduplication is seen to involve a treacherous loss. On his shopping expedition, Golyadkin takes his wad of high denomination notes to a money-changer. He comes away with a much thicker wallet-full of low-domination notes, having of course paid a commission on the exchange. Although he has lost by the transaction, it gives him the greatest satisfaction—the satisfaction, presumably, not only of appearing wealthier than he actually is, but also of a self-confirming exchange, the will to image the self and its true value being the same as the wish to image the true value of money in its bulk. It is a small moment, but one which neatly encapsulates the doubling process at work.[12]

Perhaps this structural description of *The Double* has begun to hint too at aspects of Eliot's work—particularly "The Love Song of J. Alfred Prufrock".[13] Prufrock in his balding and insignificant appearance certainly resembles Golyadkin far more than any other Dostoevskyian protagonist, least of all Raskolnikov, but it is parallels of structure rather than detail that most strongly suggest some kind of affinity.

The dramatic form of Prufrock, while it is drawn from a variety of traditions from the Elizabethan drama to Browning, serves, like the structure of *The Double*, to limit the perspective to that of the protagonist himself, a protagonist known therefore only by his language, his voice. What we learn about Prufrock's situation we know only from him, and his words seem often more symptomatic of his own malaise than indicative of any external reality—Prufrock imaging himself in his own discourse in that potentially endless exercise of attempted self-confirmation which constitutes the structural principle of Golyadkin's discourse. The opening words of "Prufrock", "Let us go then, you and I", while they speciously suggest a link with one English translation of Golyadkin's address to the double, "Let's go somewhere now, you and I",[14] are, more importantly, a key to the structural affinities and differences which link the two works.

If the words are read as Prufrock's own, which they need not be if it is not assumed that the poem is a dramatic monologue, then they might equally be addressed to his author, his reader, or to himself. If to himself, they suggest the gesture of self appropriation in the mirror which opens *The Double*. To whomever they might be addressed, they suggest that tone of attempted familiarity which characterizes one aspect of Golyadkin's relationship to others and especially to his double, an attempt to equate others with himself and to fix others, or the other, inside his own discourse. But no comfortable reading of these words is pos-

sible, as they are positioned with such wilful obscurity. They might be taken equally as the words of the author (or of a narrator) as of Prufrock himself, addressed possibly to the reader or to the protagonist. Suggesting all of these relationships without favouring any, the words come to stand generally for a language which seeks to appropriate the other to complete and satisfy the self, and in which the other, conversely, acquires a power to menace the self with what it has once taken to be its own image. Reader, author, Prufrock, and anyone else for that matter, are trapped in relationships of guilty complicity, drawn on and paralysed by specular images amongst the tawdry rubble of the godless city streets. Something like this is evidently how Eliot would have things, following quite a different brief from Dostoevsky in *The Double,* where author and reader alike are, despite superficial narrative complicity, placed at an aloof distance from Golyadkin's encroaching madness. Here, despite the humour at Prufrock's expense, there is a significant degree of endorsement of the Prufrockian position, not least by Eliot himself who, in a later interview, identified Prufrock as in part himself.[15]

Prufrock the frustrated prophet might not at first seem to have much in common with the socially unsituated Golyadkin, but on examination the similarities proliferate. In fact, Golyadkin fancies himself something of a prophet. Whenever he finds himself overtaken by some completely unpredictable circumstance, he offers himself the reassurance, manifestly untrue, that he has already foreseen it all. For instance, when the engagement with the double is already well developed, Golyadkin arrives home in a spirit of self-torment, and finds an unexpected letter, one which is possibly an illusion but which seems tangible enough. It is from a friend at the office, in connection with the scandal of the double, and comes in reply to an earlier letter of Golyadkin's which the latter had foreseen that his manservant had not delivered. Golyadkin contains his surprise on finding the latter: "However, I foresaw all this,' thought our hero, 'and now I foresee everything I shall find in the letter.'"[16] Having read the letter, Golyadkin is dazed and uncomprehending, but continues to reassure himself that he has foreseen it all while still puzzling the meaning of the words. Despite Golyadkin's puzzlement with the letter, in fact, there is no evidence that the letter is indeed real and not another projection. The language of the letter resembles closely Golyadkin's own self-dialogue and evasively accuses him of his most guilty action. Further, in the morning he looks again at the letter, and its meaning has changed in an unspecified way, somehow. Finally, looking in his pocket for the letter at a later stage, Golyadkin finds that it has disappeared, only to be replaced by a letter from the desired Carolina Ivanovna, rejecting her fiancé and inviting Golyadkin to elope; a letter which leads to his final destruction. The implication is that Golyadkin's self-proclaimed foresight is an attempt to contain a reality inimical to the self's desires, and perhaps a process of redefining that reality at first with subtlety and finally by outright alteration of the image of the world in the consciousness. On this analysis, the prime weapon of the self in its struggle with the other is its ability to substitute its own voice for the voice of others—a prophetic ability which Prufrock certainly shares, anticipating remarks about his hair and musculature, and anticipating also the scene of miscomprehension when his auditor remarks: "That is not it at all. That is not what I meant at all." At this point it is the voice of the other which rejects the appropriative strategy of the self and marks the self's inability to substitute its voice for the other.

Golyadkin too fears misprision, and is indeed always met by it in his attempted confidences, except for that single scene of the novel in which he finds himself contented, the night at home with the double, when the double, who comes to be known as Golyadkin Junior, unburdens himself to Golyadkin Senior, adopting the confidential and occasionally tearful manner of the latter. In the discourse of others, self-illusions have no purchase, and the romantic self is threatened with annihilation. It is the eyes of others which hold this power to annihilate the romantic self. For Prufrock there is the fore-knowledge of "The eyes that fix you in a formulated phrase" which pin him to the wall like an insect, and for Golyadkin, also compared to an insect in his moments of supreme abasement,[17] there is the "annihilating stare" of Andrey Phillipovich[18] for instance, and the recurrent fear of betrayal and loss of self possession in the conspiratorial words of others, words which he cannot hear. This fear is finally realized in the Judas-kiss of the double, and it is the person of the double who is finally construed as the enemy, a term which has to shift considerably in Golyadkin's discourse—he is at first sure that the double is the device of other unspecified enemies. But Golyadkin's social insecurity leads him to construe every social inferior as a betrayer, particularly as they never respond to his patronising manner, and Petrushka in particular will never show his master any respect. It is Petrushka who at the very opening of the novel is chatting and laughing with some other servants: Golyadkin fears that he has been "sold for nothing", a fear which compresses anxiety about annihilation in the discourse of others with anxiety about his own exchange value, and reveals perhaps a desire to be exchanged, like the desire to be made fully manifest, if only for the right price.

For Prufrock too there is betrayal, and humiliation before social inferiors. Here the footman is given a capital and made 'eternal', not only because in his manners he might seem that much more assured than Prufrock, but also because he is the archetypal other which fixes the self under its stare, and representative too of that absolute of revelation to which the prophet Prufrock aspires. Betrayal is writ large in "Prufrock." While Golyadkin is implicitly compared to Christ, Prufrock explicitly compares himself to John the Baptist, imagining his head "brought in upon a platter"—perhaps a tidier analogy than that of *The Double,* evoking the sexual factor, present in both works, as the motive of betrayal. Further, it serves to put Prufrock in his self-romanticization at one remove from Christ himself. John the Baptist merely foresees the coming of the one who shall be revealed as the Son of God, but the power of revelation is not his. In "Prufrock" as in *The Double,* rev-

elation is deferred or, as here, displaced, projected on to another. Revelation is the product in Eliot of a mystical timeless state, imagined as in many religions as a return to life from death, or a suspended state of death-in-life. Prufrock imagines himself saying "I am Lazarus, come from the dead, / Come back to tell you all. / I shall tell you all." Again, like Christ returning from the dead, but unlike Christ not possessed of any revelatory or prophetic power. Indeed, the Biblical Lazarus, anticlimactically, never says anything about having been dead. The possibility of Prufrock as prophet is all but obliterated by this deadening analogy, and in any case his wish to "have squeezed the universe into a ball" with its allusion to Marvell denotes a thorough confusion of the prophetic and the sexual urge to completion in a (Platonic and otherwise) ball. (For Golyadkin the wish to complete and summarize takes the form of a regret that he cannot cut off his finger as a means to settle the whole matter—a comically small sacrifice which nevertheless suggests castration and the mid-life impotence which the balding Golyadkin and Prufrock share—a diminutive version of Caligula's wish that the Roman Senate had only one throat which he could cut.)

Yet the possibility of the transcendent state is not dismissed in "Prufrock". It remains as an inaccessible possibility and recurs subsequently in much of Eliot's central work. *The Double* too deals with the death-in-life state, but does not offer it a refuge. Dostoevsky himself suffered from epilepsy, and Golyadkin is made to suffer bouts of epilepsy or perhaps madness in situations of acute stress. He is described as "more dead than alive"[19] and in reply to questions from his doctor about his current abode he miscomprehendingly replies: "I was living, Christian Ivanovich, I was living even formerly. I must have been, mustn't I?"[20] At the height of one of his attacks Golyadkin is "dumb and motionless, seeing nothing, hearing nothing, feeling nothing".[21] When less overwhelmed, he becomes tremendously distracted, his thoughts and conversation digress fantastically, and his mind becomes fixed on isolated images, much like the "sordid images" which brokenly fixate Eliotic protagonists. Golyadkin's death-in-life moments resemble nothing more than that moment in "The Burial of the Dead" in the presence of the "hyacinth girl".

> 'You gave me Hyacinths first a year ago;
> 'They called me the hyacinth girl.'
> —Yet when we came back, late, from the hyacinth
>   garden,
> Your arms full, and your hair wet, I could not
> Speak, and my eyes failed, I was neither
> Living nor dead, and I knew nothing,
> Looking into the heart of light, the silence.[22]

This is a complicated moment which begins from that basic Romantic premise which makes the woman that object which completes the man and offers him transcendence— just as the ultimate object of Golyadkin and Prufrock was sexual. Here, however, the scene is passed, the girl has no subjective recollection of it, and seems therefore an inadequate object of the man's rapture, while what the man recalls might equally be a fit of madness as of rapture, while the "heart of light" borrows the ineluctability of the "heart of darkness" to further veil the moment of transcendence.[23]

There is a crucial difference between Eliot and Dostoevsky on the point of romantic transcendence. For Eliot, while directing his full satirical tones against a weak romantic notion of transcendence in "Prufrock", there still seems to be always an escape clause. The possibility of transcendence is never disallowed—it is instead always deferred, delayed or otherwise displaced, remaining "a perpetual possibility / Only in a world of speculation."[24] We know that Eliot in his early period at least was very close to the philosophy of T. E. Hulme, and belief in the desirability at least of the concept of an Absolute, even if it were to be an entirely inaccessible one. Politically this idea manifested itself perhaps in Eliot's royalism, the concept of a state where the monarchy in mystical fashion secured social meaning, much like the framework satirized in *The Double* in which Golyadkin looks on the state and the highest officials of the state as a father who should secure his individuality by preventing what he calls "substitution"—meaning the substitution of the double for himself—in a chaos of social and semantic slippage. While Eliot harbours mysticism, Dostoevsky blows it away. While "Prufrock" defers the moment of transcendence, doubts it, but leaves it possible, *The Double* displays a rhetoric of self-revelation in a transcendent moment which is given the chance to play its last card. As *The Double* progresses, it becomes increasingly desireable for Golyadkin to make plain his case to some higher power, and in a late scene, having entered yet another social gathering uninvited, the chance at last arrives for him to explain to a supremo of the Civil Service known only as "His Excellency". "Well, what do you want?" asks His Excellency: "As I say, it's like this: I look on him as a father; I stand aloof in the whole affair—and protect me from my enemy! There you are!"[25] Golyadkin's reply ends with an exclamatory flourish which shows that he does indeed consider that he has made all plain. His Excellency of course is baffled, having heard nothing of Golyadkin's minor scandal, and in the face of incomprehension, Golyadkin breaks down and is taken away. When Golyadkin thinks he is revealing himself in a transcendent moment, all he reveals is that nexus of anxieties that has produced his discourse and actions throughout: his urge to completion and security, thought to be offered by the father: the repudiation of the self in the wish to stand outside it, elsewhere a wish to disappear or be annihilated: the fear for the safety of an incomplete self which, meeting only a hostile world which refuses it completion, projects enmity everywhere. It is a final testing of Golyadkin's rhetoric to which the subtler and more thoroughly scrutinized rhetoric of Prufrock is never subjected.

When Eliot selected a quotation from Conrad's "Heart of Darkness" as the original epigraph for *The Wasteland* he was challenged by Pound that it could not bear the weight which its position put on it. Contemporaries considered the work light, an evaluation which Pound seems to have shared, although Eliot, who took from it the epigraph to

"The Hollow Men", seemingly did not. It is an interesting disparity, because "Heart of Darkness" probably more than any modern work, relies on a rhetoric of ineffability which culminates in Kurtz's final words—"The horror! the horror!" For the early Romantic the transcendent moment might have been a union with God, but for Kurtz it produces a reduplicated vision of terror. At least this is what we are told by Marlow—for this is a displaced moment of vision. "Did he live his life again in every detail of desire, temptation, and surrender during that supreme moment of complete knowledge?" It is an unanswered question, even though it strongly suggests its own answer. For Marlow himself, although he seems to have lived through Kurtz's "last extremity", the summary is impossible—"I was within a hair's-breadth of the last opportunity for pronouncement, and I found with humiliation that probably I would have nothing to say."[26] Through a host of rhetorical devices, "Heart of Darkness" suggests complete revelation and summation in a transcendent moment which is however always on the other side of a ghostly line. For all its seriousness, the rhetoric of "Heart of Darkness", which places the word "horror" at its abysmal centre, has a buried affinity with the literature of Gothic horror, which must always employ a rhetoric of ineffability to maintain its power to horrify—it must in short refuse completion.

And in the manner of the horror fictionist—perhaps in that of his contemporary H. P. Lovecraft, whose language of ineffability owed much to Poe—Eliot deploys a rhetoric of displaced transcendence which has its roots in the first doubts of a Romanticism herded from the countryside and penned in the city, of which Coleridge is perhaps the earliest spokesman. Dostoevsky too deploys the Gothic—although never after *The Double* in the same unmitigated form—yet the notion of ineffability is demolished, the product of urban displacement and not its absolute though inaccessible meaning. It is a fundamental difference and one which makes the gap between *The Double* and "The Love Song of J. Alfred Prufrock" as wide as it could be. So finally, what is their subterranean connection?

> O keep the Dog far hence, that's friend to men,
> Or with his nails he'll dig it up again!

Notes

1. *To Criticize the Critic* (London: Faber and Faber, 1978), p. 27.

2. John C. Pope, "Prufrock and Raskolnikov", *American Literature* XVII (1945), 213–230.

3. "Prufrock and Raskolnikov Again: A Letter from Eliot", *American Literature* XXIII (1947), 319–321.

4. *Notes From Underground. The Double,* trans. Jessie Coulson (New York: Penguin Books Ltd., 1972), p. 127. I refer to the translation most readily available at the present moment. Subsequently referred to as *The Double.*

5. *The Double*, p. 127.

6. *The Double*, pp. 127–8.

7. *The Double*, p. 131.

8. *The Double*, p. 132.

9. *The Double*, pp. 132–3.

10. *The Double*, p. 133.

11. *The Double*, p. 158.

12. *The Double*, p. 144.

13. *The Complete Poems and Plays of T. S. Eliot* (London: Faber and Faber, 1969), pp. 13–17. As the poem is well known I have not given individual page references for each citation.

14. *The Double*, p. 250.

15. Interview in *Grantite Review* 24, No. 3 (1962), 16–20.

16. *The Double*, p. 223.

17. See e.g., *The Double*, p. 161.

18. *The Double*, p. 165.

19. *The Double*, p. 160.

20. *The Double*, p. 143.

21. *The Double*, p. 259.

22. *The Complete Poems and Plays of T. S. Eliot*, p. 62.

23. This interpretation is indebted to A. D. Moody, *Thomas Stearns Eliot: Poet*, (Cambridge: Cambridge University Press, 1979), p. 81.

24. *The Complete Poems and Plays of T. S. Eliot*, p. 171.

25. *The Double*, p. 269.

26. *Heart of Darkness* (London: Penguin, 1983), p. 112.

David Patterson (essay date 1988)

SOURCE: "Dostoevsky's *Dvoinik* per Lacan's Parole," in *The Affirming Flame: Religion, Language, Literature,* University of Oklahoma Press, 1988, pp. 58–73.

[*In the following essay, Patterson attempts to apply Lacan's concept of "parole" to* The Double.]

Having examined the implications of Lacan's *parole* for the literary critic, let us consider its implications for the critical approach to a specific literary text. As such an investigation, this [essay] provides an example of a response to a literary work in which personal presence achieved through the Word is an issue in the work itself. The [essay] demonstrates that Lacan's concept of the Word is applicable not only to the literary critic but to the literary character and the relationships that define him. For this purpose I have selected Dostoevsky's *Dvoinik,* or *The Double* (1846),[1] a novel in which the difficulty confronting the main character is fundamentally the same as the difficulty confronting the critic.

There have been numerous studies of *Dvoinik,* but all have failed to examine the structure of self represented by the protagonist, Golyadkin, as a structure of language. Dostoevsky's elder contemporary V. G. Belinsky, for example, describes Golyadkin by saying, "To live in the world would be quite unbearable for him; the black demon of his life, whom the hell of his insanity has transformed into a judge, is the pathological sensitivity and paranoia of his character."[2] Focusing on the "Mr. Hyde" who invades Golyadkin's "Dr. Jekyll," Belinsky defines Golyadkin's turmoil as the rise of a demonic judge who condemns from the start Golyadkin's every effort to find a place in the world. As the grim assessor becomes more and more powerful, he takes on a projected reality in the form of the double, who gradually eclipses every semblance of the "real" Golyadkin's personality. Finally, all that is left of Golyadkin is his psychosis.

More recently, Dyula Kirai has emphasized Golyadkin's social, psychological, and historical situation. In one article the Soviet critic states, "In *Dvoinik* Dostoevsky wanted to decipher a *social idea:* 'why people go out of their minds'";[3] and in another piece we read,

> The theme of the novel *Dvoinik* turns out to be rooted precisely in a shifting social-psychological situation; the development of an *idée fixe* within that situation lies in the disclosure of the social-psychological causes of insanity for a person living under the condition of the 1840s.[4]

Steeped in the methods of Marxist criticism, Kirai begins and ends by viewing the novel as a mirror of a historical, social environment. Insisting that the work is commenting only on a person living in 1840s Russia, Kirai's approach bears no ramifications and harbors no threat for the modern critic. Here the interest is not so much in the living individual as in the social situation that supposedly shapes the individual; the accent is on the social phenomenon, not on the personal crisis.

Other modern critics have underscored the inner life of Golyadkin but without pursuing a connection between the life within and its relation to the other without. Natalie Reber, for instance, explains that the double comes to the surface as the result of "a dread nourished by the powers of guilt consciousness," which in turn leads to paranoia.[5] She is more concerned with Golyadkin's behavioral symptoms than with his discourse or response capability, and like Belinsky, she wrongly identifies the double as Golyadkin's judge (as for who his judges really are, that will be established in the discussion below). Finally, in a rather lame Freudian analysis of Golyadkin, Charles C. Hoffmeister claims that the double is not a persecutor of conscience but a success figure for the hero, whose "id freely expresses itself in impulsive, irrational behavior that precludes thought-directed action."[6] Unlike Lacan, Hoffmeister fails to go beyond the literalism of Freud's system; he ignores the fragmentation signified by the double as well as the concurrent breakdown in Golyadkin's response capability.

Because we are here dealing with a Lacanian analysis of language in regard to Golyadkin, such an analysis must be distinguished from a purely linguistic approach. In the most prominent example of a linguistic approach, V. V. Vinogradov, in his book on Russian naturalism, closely examines both the language of *Dvoinik* in general and Golyadkin's manner of speech in particular. He concludes that Golyadkin's discourse has a twofold purpose: "first, it provides a means of stating his intentions and sensations, and, secondly, it serves as the accompaniment peculiar to his actions."[7] Vinogradov, however, does not mention the structure of self or intersubjective relationships. The critic in this case has made the mistake of concentrating on Golyadkin without looking at the character's relation to the *other* and the way language characterizes that relation. The one thinker who addresses this matter is Mikhail Bakhtin; he has correctly understood that "Golyadkin's speech strives above all to simulate total independence from the word of the other."[8] Although Bakhtin does not develop this insight as much as he might, it will be helpful to refer to him in the ensuing analysis.

Lacan has said that "the Word imparts meaning to the function of the individual,"[9] a remark that may guide our investigation of *Dvoinik,* for the loss of meaning and the onset of madness in Golyadkin's life are concurrent with his loss of the Word. To show that Golyadkin's madness is generated by a loss of the *parole,* I shall divide my remarks into three main sections: (1) the structure of the self; (2) the self and the other; and (3) judgment and the Word. These are the elements of Lacan's thinking that will take us the furthest in an analysis of Dostoevsky's *Dvoinik.*

THE STRUCTURE OF THE SELF

Lacan pictures the self as a dynamic of inter- and intrarelationships, as a structural *process,* which he represents in his simplified Schema L. It is easy to see how the Schema L may be used to describe Golyadkin. In *Dvoinik* a person (S) occupies a dwelling in Saint Petersburg. He (a') has a stake in establishing business and social relationships with certain people (a)—Andrey Filippovich and Anton Antonovich, for example. And there are those who serve as his judges (A), specifically Krest'yan Ivanovich and His Excellency. Bakhtin has, in fact, observed a similar structure of self in Golyadkin, claiming that his personality consists of three voices:

> His "I for myself" which is unable to do without the other and requires the other's recognition; his "I for the other" (his reflection in the other), that is, the voice which is Golyadkin's second substitute; and, finally, the voice of the Other who fails to acknowledge him and who at the same time has no real presence outside of him.
>
> [P. 372]

Applying the Schema L to Bakhtin's observations, we discover that Golyadkin's "I for myself" corresponds to Lacan's *moi* (a'), which seeks the recognition of the other through identification, through an effort to be like the other. His "I for the other" may be associated with Lacan's other (a), the alter ego or "second substitute" that com-

mands the attention of the *moi.* And "the voice of the Other" closely parallels Lacan's Other (A), which signifies both the "significant Other" whom the individual appeals to and the internalization of this Other. Bakhtin and Lacan, then, have very similar notions of the self.

It must be noted, again, that the term "self" here denotes a process of inter- and intrarelation. "The 'who' of Dasein," to use Wilden's paraphrase of Heidegger, "is the shifter 'I,' which is a locus and not a person."[10] Moreover, says Heidegger, "Dasein approaches itself from that which concerns it,"[11] so that whoever or whatever Golyadkin may be, he is structured by his relation to the other characters and by the way he perceives that relation. His longing for a place within the circle of the others is the longing of the self for itself. And the deeper the longing for acknowledgment, the greater the self's dependence on the other and the more severe the pending judgment. "The other is the indispensable mediator between me and myself," Sartre notes. "The very appearance of the other leads me to pronounce judgment on myself like an object, for it is as an object that I appear before the other."[12] Judgment, then, is an integral part of the process that constitutes the self.

The self as a process is a self as movement; insofar as Golyadkin is shaped by relation, he is shaped by action. To be sure, when he visits the doctor Krest'yan Ivanovich early in the novel, he stakes his claim to independence from others by explaining that even though he is "no master of eloquent speech," he compensates for it by being a man of action (p. 116). Thus, to use a phrase from Lacan's "Fonction," Golyadkin "makes an object of his action, but he does so in order to restore to it in due time its grounding function" (p. 285). Though he yearns for a relation, Golyadkin claims that he needs no support from others; instead, he cites his action as his support, so that his action becomes an object in itself. Yet in making this identification—that is, in making an object of his action—he is no longer engaged in action; he comes to a halt, and in doing so he loses the ability to speak. In his effort to justify himself, he is no master of speech, eloquent or otherwise, as is evidenced by his conversation with Krest'yan Ivanovich. Struggling to establish his selfhood, Golyadkin clings to the static ground-work of identity to avoid the ambiguity of process, in which he might create a self through the dialogical Word. Hence, in his effort to be himself he loses himself, since he is never able to engage in the action or to speak the Word that engenders the self. And so the seeds of madness are planted.

Michel Foucault has argued that "the function of the madman is to group all signs together in an endless proliferation of resemblance,"[13] and resemblance begins with the mirror. Because he is more concerned with identity than with process, Golyadkin remains before the mirror, where he stands at the end of the novel's opening paragraph: "Although the sleepy, nearsighted, and rather bald figure reflected in the mirror was so insignificant by itself that at first glance it did not really command any special attention, its owner evidently remained quite satisfied with everything he saw in the mirror" (pp. 109–10). The reassuring satisfaction that the nearsighted Golyadkin derives from the "insignificant" reflection in the mirror reveals an element of the imaginary in his relation to the mirror. To the extent that the figure in the mirror is the only one whom he can trust, the mirror is a kind of lure sustained by the imaginary. Indeed, this is a characteristic of Lacan's *stade du miroir.* Wilden explains: "In studying what he called 'paranoiac knowledge,' Lacan formed the view that the paranoiac alienation of the ego through the *stade du miroir* was one of the preconditions of human knowledge. Thus the *moi* is essentially paranoid; it is 'impregnated with the Imaginary'" (p. 173). Golyadkin's self-satisfaction is not only self-delusion; it is self-division. The thing about himself that he finds so satisfying is not something within but an image in the glass, something unreal, void of substance. Already, in Golyadkin's attraction to the mirror, we discover the elements of "paranoiac alienation." Already we encounter the division of self marked by the double: here is the man and there the mirror image that displaces him. Cut in half, Golyadkin is a wounded man who leaves the mirror to visit the doctor Krest'yan Ivanovich; he hopes for a source of healing but fears he will find only a seat of judgment.

Thus from the very beginning one can see the "alienation of the ego" in Golyadkin's painful awareness of how he looks and of what is proper. He "assumes the appropriate countenance" (p. 114), for example, before entering the doctor's office, and he places an order in a restaurant purely for the sake of propriety (p. 123). He is preoccupied with showing that he is "like everyone else" (p. 135), and he dreads giving himself a bad name (p. 160): nothing must violate the imaginary form he longs to assume. And, of course, the harder he tries to be like others and to look proper, the more miserably he fails. Like the man in the Hasidic story who knew where his clothes were but could not find himself, Golyadkin has the look, the gesture, and the dress of the crowd, but he has no sense of himself as an individual. In short, he has no self.

Lacan offers an insight that applies very nicely at this juncture: "For in this labor by which the subject endeavors to reconstruct a construct *for another,* he discovers again the fundamental alienation which made him construct it *like another,* and which has always destined it to be stripped from him *by another*" (p. 249). The "construct" in this instance is the self Golyadkin longs to be, the one of whom it may be said, "He is his own man, like everyone else." But to be one's "own man" is not to be like everyone else, and this is an important aspect of Golyadkin's failure to be or to find himself. We see him torn between these poles when he declares that he wears no masks and plays no sycophantic games (p. 124), an assertion that is itself a mask. His assuming such a mask *for* another and *like* another is symptomatic of the psychosis brewing within him. Further, the facade may be stripped from him *by* another because the game he plays is a *language* game; the construct he sets up is a language construct, and this makes it a public matter. Because it is a public matter, it is

alien to the Word, and this makes his language game self-alienating; instead of moving in the Word, he is stuck in the catchwords of *Das Man,* or "the They."

Here lies another touchstone in Lacan's "Fonction": "It is quite clear that the symptom is resolved entirely in an analysis of language, since it is itself structured like a language; for it is from language that the Word must be delivered" (p. 269). The difficulty for the self is to give voice to itself through the Word without losing itself to the objectifying constructs of language, without falling prey to the fixed formula that makes us like everyone else. If the self is a process, it is a process of speaking and responding; if the self is structured like language, it is structured according to its relation to the other. The idle talk and fixed phrases of the crowd are the opposite of the Word and preclude any response or relation to the other. For only the self who is at one with itself can be related to the other as an I related to a Thou; the self who is doubled or divided, fragmented by the discourse of the crowd, can generate no relation to the other.

THE SELF AND THE OTHER

The relation between the self and the other lies in the relation between the language of the self and the language of *Das Man,* or "the They." For *Das Man,* personal "reality" turns on identification within the coordinate system that comprises the world; here the person sees as the other sees and speaks as the other demands. In this way the language of *Das Man* provides the individual with a *Man-selbst,* or a They-self, contoured to fit into its proper slot in the crowd. The problem facing Golyadkin, then, is to accommodate himself to the categories of the other without getting lost in those categories; that is, he must speak the language of the other without slipping into a mimicry of the other. He must talk without being lured into idle talk; he must speak the language that relates him to the other while retaining the Word, which is the language of the self. And this is precisely what he cannot do. As soon as he sets out to speak the language of truth and openness, the language of the self, he gets trapped in the script that *Das Man* is forever following. And as the language of the self slips away, madness sets in.

"In the case of the madman," Lacan writes, "the absence of the Word manifests itself through the stereotypes of a discourse in which the subject, one might say, is spoken rather than speaking" (p. 280). One way in which this occurs in *Dvoinik* is through Golyadkin's repeated use of popular phrases. He often appends his remarks with the words "as they say" and "as the saying goes" (for example, pp. 119, 120, 121, 125). Indeed, Golyadkin is no master of eloquent speech and frequently has trouble getting his words out at all, even to the point of a virtual paralysis of the voice (for example, pp. 112, 124, 133–34). And, looking further, we never see Golyadkin so irrevocably in the grips of the other as when he shrinks into panicked flight upon encountering a colleague or a superior or, at times, even his servant, Petrushka (pp. 112, 113,

124). A slave to the language of the crowd, Golyadkin becomes a slave to the other since freedom lies in the capacity to freely respond with a word of one's own. Unable to respond to the other, he is unable to win the recognition of the other and is left to complete domination at the hands of the other.

If Golyadkin longs for a respectable position and a good name, like everyone else, it is not exactly because he wants to be like others or to fit into the crowd. Rather, as Lacan explains, the individual's desire "finds its meaning in the desire of the other, not so much because the other holds the key to the desired object, but because his primary object is to be recognized by the other" (p. 268). Perhaps the most revealing example of this is the fact that Golyadkin would sometimes dream of being in the company of distinguished and clever people, all of whom looked upon him with a favorable eye (p. 185). It is, however, just a dream; in reality Golyadkin's efforts to win the acclaim of others are at best fruitless, at worst destructive. And since he feels he is nothing without the recognition of the other, he ultimately reaches the point where he declares to himself, "There can be no doubt that I am ruined, that I have ceased to exist altogether" (p. 220).

In contrast to those critics who have wrongly identified the double as Golyadkin's judge, Bakhtin has accurately understood that "the basis of the plot lies in Golyadkin's attempt to find for himself a substitute for the other in the light of the utter lack of recognition of his self by others" (p. 368). This is where the double comes in; he is none other than the symbol or the personification of the conceptual other, what Foucault calls "the unthought" when he writes, "The unthought (whatever name we give it) is not lodged in man like a shrivelled-up nature or a stratified history; it is . . . the other that is not only a brother but a twin, born, not of man, nor in man, but beside him" (p. 326). The narrator of *Dvoinik,* in fact, refers to the double, in italics, as *drugoi,* or *the other* (p. 160). Golyadkin believes that the other, the double, is taking over his life, removing him from life, and this is just what it means to be both dominated and alienated by the other. Even in his dreams Golyadkin no sooner gains the recognition of the company surrounding him than the double appears and denounces him as the fraud he is (p. 186). From the moment he comes onto the scene, the double controls Golyadkin's every move to the point that Golyadkin cannot move at all. And because, as Lacan puts it, action "engenders the Word" (p. 271), the double's domination of Golyadkin's action amounts to a domination of the Word from Golyadkin's standpoint. It should also be noted that the discourse, or the *text,* that the double imposes on Golyadkin does not produce the imaginary relation—it controls it.

Thus we see that Golyadkin's lament that the double has imposed upon him the need to put everything into writing (pp. 175–76) is a lament over the loss of the Word. Writing, Derrida tells us, "menaces at once the breath, the spirit, and history as a revelation between self and spirit. It is their end, their finitude, their paralysis. Cutting short the breath, . . . it is the principle of death and difference."[14] Although Derrida intends this statement to be antilogocentric, we see that Golyadkin, frustrated by his failure to generate presence through the spoken Word, produces the written imprint that eclipses his voice. Unable to gain the spiritual presence embodied in the tone of the voice, he loses his voice to the atonal letter of the written word, the "letter written outside the man," as Saint Augustine calls it.[15] Just as when he stood before the mirror, Golyadkin now stands before the letter, gazing into the image that he continues to mistake for himself.

At this turn it should prove enlightening to consider the following observation concerning the *belle âme* from Wilden's essay on Lacan:

> The *belle âme* is a consciousness which judges others but which refuses action. In his vanity, the *belle âme* values his ineffective discourse above the facts of the world and expects it to be taken as the highest reality. . . . Thus the *belle âme* refuses the world and attains not being, but nonbeing, "an empty nothingness." . . . The *belle âme* fears the other because he wants so much to be the other, but being the other means losing himself. The whole paradox of identification is involved: seeking to be identical to the other, or seeking to possess the other's identity, is to lose one's own identity.
>
> [Pp. 289–90]

Golyadkin's longing both to be and not to be his double results in the loss of self because the all or nothing of identity or nonidentity precludes a relation to the other. Dominated, Golyadkin insists on dominating, and this produces a desire to be what he is not, a vain longing that adds to the fragmentation of self.

The self comes to itself by way of the other, and it creates a relation to the other by way of the Word. This is how we are to understand Lacan when he asserts:

> The form according to which language is expressed itself defines subjectivity. Language says, "You will go this way, and when you see that, you will turn there." To put it differently, language refers itself to the discourse of the other. It is enveloped as such in the highest function of the Word, insofar as the Word engages its author by investing the one to whom it is spoken with a new reality.
>
> [P. 298]

But Golyadkin seeks a new reality for himself without investing the other with a new reality; that is, he wants to be a greater human being without generating a relation with another human being. Like the *belle âme,* he is more concerned with identification than with relation, more interested in recognition than in response.

Golyadkin's one avenue to salvation lies in an appeal to an arbiter of truth, who occupies a third position between the other and himself, that is, between the double and himself. He must seek an audience, a *hearing,* in the presence of the Other, who, as Lacan explains, creates "the scene of the Word insofar as the scene of the Word is always in a third position between two subjects. This is simply to introduce the dimension of truth" (see Wilden, p. 269). Desperately hoping that his redeemer lives, Golyadkin seeks his redeemer in an attempt to regain his lost self, that is, in an effort to regain the Word. This brings us to our third item of concern.

JUDGMENT AND THE WORD

The doctor Krest'yan Ivanovich and the highest official Golyadkin works under, known as His Excellency, are the two main authorities of truth in the novel and as such represent the two figures of the Other. They are the two people from whom Golyadkin seeks a "diagnosis" or a response that will call him back to life. Let us consider, then, Golyadkin's relation to each of them.

It should first be noted that Golyadkin feels a need to communicate to Krest'yan Ivanovich something of the utmost importance, that he even thinks of the doctor as a kind of spiritual confessor (p. 113). The scene in the doctor's office, in fact, lays the groundwork for Golyadkin's loss of the Word and his degeneration into madness. It is here that Golyadkin's difficulty with words arises, along with his insistence that he is his own man. Yet apart from informing Golyadkin that he must change his life and his personality, the only significant reply Krest'yan Ivanovich gives Golyadkin is a series of long and "meaningful" intervals of silence (pp. 116–17). To be sure, Golyadkin continually meets with silence among his colleagues (p. 146) and even fears the silence of his servant (p. 144). So it is that in Golyadkin's attempt to speak, the first thing to make itself heard is the void, the trace of nothingness that outlines his tenuous presence.

In this regard Frederic Jameson has astutely called our attention to the fact that "the analyst's silence thus causes the structural dependency of the subject on the capital A of the Other's language to become visible as it never could in any concrete interpersonal situation."[16] Unable to speak the Word, Golyadkin is unable to elicit the Word from the doctor. Although he views the doctor as a confessor, he is entrenched in justification rather than confession. Instead of receiving a response that might absolve him, he meets with the silence that condemns him. For the silence of Krest'yan Ivanovich, again, points up the silent void, the absence of the Word, in Golyadkin himself.

Here the function of the Word in the psychoanalytic context begins to come into focus. Since "every Word calls for a reply," as Lacan says (p. 247), the Word makes a reply of the silence it encounters. The call of the Word and the silence of the void combine to establish the presence of the subject, a presence marked by what the subject is *not*. In his essay on Lacan, Wilden declares, "The subject *is* the binary opposition of presence and absence, and the discovery of One—the discovery of difference—is to be condemned to an eternal desire for the nonrelationship of zero, when identity is meaningless" (p. 191). Unable to

stand the weight of "being there" and the opposition it entails, Golyadkin slowly becomes his own executioner, crying, "I am my own murderer!" (p. 180). For the difference of presence and absence is just what Golyadkin cannot abide, and we see this in his desire to be his own man and to control the other, by whom he is controlled; he believes that if only he were in control, the difference that brings him into a collision with nothingness would be eliminated. Impotent to gain this upper hand, he proceeds to erect a monolith of narcissism. Hence the Word is reduced to an echo, and the self to an image in the mirror.

Golyadkin's struggle to regain himself culminates in a frustrated return to the Other, which comes in the form of an attempt to regain a relationship with His Excellency. Aloof yet dominating, His Excellency is the person whom Golyadkin views as a father and to whom he makes his final appeal in the name of the Father (p. 213). Though everyone else may fail to acknowledge him, if Golyadkin can win the recognition of His Excellency, then he can win redemption; then his existence will be legitimate. He believes that an audience with His Excellency, the figure of the Law, will set everything straight and restore him to his rightful self and to his proper place; the confusion created by the double's takeover will be dispelled. In this way he might win "the pardon of the Word," to borrow Lacan's phrase (p. 281). Hence, in his would-be return to a relation with the Word lie his longed-for redemption and salvation of self. And so he cries, "Your Excellency, I humbly request your permission to speak" (p. 217).

But this attempt also meets with silence. Once again, because Golyadkin seeks redemption through justification, he fails to respond and thus finds no response. In the final chapter he is turned over to Krest'yan Ivanovich, who in the end is much more than the Other as represented by the psychoanalyst; now he is the Other as god—or as devil. Now he is not "the Krest'yan Ivanovich of before; this is another Krest'yan Ivanovich! This is the terrible Krest'yan Ivanovich!" (p. 229). It is significant that immediately before the doctor's arrival, a silence falls over the gathering at the home of Berendeev, a silence that Golyadkin takes to be an occasion for prayer (p. 227). For prayer is the most extreme form of the appeal of the Word to the Other; in prayer the intense absence created by silence makes most intense the precarious presence of the self. Thus Golyadkin comes before his last judgment only to be condemned by the doctor, whose last words are "severe and terrible, like a judge's sentence" (p. 229).

CONCLUSION

The foregoing analysis has shown that Golyadkin begins in a state of narcissism in which the Word is absent. Throughout the remainder of the novel he is engaged in a struggle to regain the Word and, with it, his self. As his efforts prove increasingly impotent, he sinks deeper and deeper into madness. Continually erecting walls around himself and attempting to cover all his bases, he entrenches himself more and more in a compromising position, and this is another indication of his removal from the Word. "To the extent that language becomes more functional," says Lacan, "it is rendered improper for the Word" (pp. 298–99). Golyadkin is ultimately lost in the functional in that he is irrevocably turned over to negotiation and justification. In short, he loves no one, and that is what his torment consists of. What is hell? It is the inability to love, says Zosima in *The Brothers Karamazov.*[17]

Still another indication that Golyadkin has lost the Word lies in his inability to make any response that he can call his own. Because, as we have seen, every Word calls for a reply, a relation to the Word is constituted by the ability to reply. And because Golyadkin can only parrot the discourse of the other, he cannot respond either to the other or to himself; such is the result of being locked into a struggle to win the recognition of the other. Thus captured by the other—the double—the imaginary eclipses the real, and Golyadkin is condemned by the Other.

What, then, has been gained by examining Dostoevsky's *Dvoinik* per Lacan's *parole?* First of all, Golyadkin cannot be dismissed as a Jekyll-and-Hyde whose schizoid personality is aggravated by the appearance of the double. Secondly, his madness cannot be unraveled by deciphering a "social idea," if that means reducing such insanity to a strictly social phenomenon. Further, Golyadkin's is not simply a case of chronic angst, nor does he go mad over the appearance of the success figure he could never become. What has been learned, with the help of Lacan, is that this sort of investigation of the psyche must at some point deal with the language of the psyche; *Dvoinik* reveals a connection between *speaking* oneself and *being* oneself. That is to say, Lacan has enabled us to see the primacy of language and the Word in the way in which we see ourselves in relation to the world; we exist in a word-to-word structure and not in a word-to-reality network. However accurate or well argued other studies of *Dvoinik* have been, they have all failed to deal with this dimension of it. Thus Goethe's reversal of Saint John—in the beginning was the deed—is in turn reversed: Lacan writes, "It was the *verbe* that was in the beginning, and we live in its creation; but it is the action of our spirit that continues this creation by forever renewing it" (p. 271). Perhaps Buber says it best: "In the beginning was the relation."[18]

I cannot conclude, however, without addressing the question of my personal relation to *Dvoinik* and its main character. If I approach the novel as a critical curiosity or an *object* of analysis, then I have lost both the character and myself. It is only by responding to the living voice of the novel that I can generate a relation to it. Instead of isolating Golyadkin in 1840s Russia and maintaining the safety of objective distance, I must find my way to Golyadkin by assessing myself in the light of my assessment of him. Through the character, Dostoevsky summons me, and my relation to the character rests on the response I offer. Having completed the analysis of *Dvoinik* per Lacan's *parole,* I must shun the tempting illusion that I have made a response and have established a relation. To achieve a per-

sonal presence in relation to the novel, I must address my life in the way I have addressed the life of Golyadkin; I must determine my existential stake in my critical activity. This means raising for myself the questions I have raised for Golyadkin: What is the nature of my relation to the people around me? Is my discourse characterized by truthful and open response or by an effort to win recognition and domination? Am I preoccupied with looks, position, and self-justification, or is mine the language of response, embrace, and affirmation? And Dostoevsky himself reminds me that this last question is the one most needful. "You see," he writes, "I know that there is nothing higher than this thought of *embracing.*"[19]

Notes

1. Fyodor M. Dostoevsky, *Dvoinik,* vol. 1 of *Polnoe sobranie sochinenii* (Leningrad, 1972). Subsequent quotations are from this book.

2. V. G. Belinsky, *Polnoe sobranie sochinenii,* (Moscow, 1955), 9:563.

3. Dyula Kirai, "Kompozitsiya syuzheta romana 'Dvoinik. Priklyucheniya gospodina Golyadkina,'" *Acta Litteraria Academiae Scientiarum Hungaricae* 11 (1969): 364.

4. Dyula Kirai, "Syuzhetny parallizm v romane 'Dvoinik,'" *Studia Slavica* 15 (1969): 246.

5. Natalie Reber, *Studien zum Motiv des Doppelgängers bei Dostoevskij und E. T. A. Hoffman* (Giessen: Wilhelm Schmitz Verlag, 1964), p. 56.

6. Charles C. Hoffmeister, "'William Wilson' and *The Double:* A Freudian Insight," *Coranto* 9 (1974): 26.

7. V. V. Vinogradov, *Evolyutsiya russkogo naturalizma* (Leningrad, 1929), p. 277.

8. Mikhail Bakhtin, *Problemy poetiki Dostoevskogo,* 3d ed. (Moscow, 1972), p. 362. Subsequent quotations are from this book.

9. Jacques Lacan, "Fonction et champ de la parole et du language en psychoanalyse," in *Écrits* (Paris: Éditions du Seuil, 1966), p. 257. Subsequent quotations are from this book.

10. Anthony Wilden, "Lacan and the Discourse of the Other," in *The Language of the Self,* trans. with commentary by Anthony Wilden (Baltimore, Md.: Johns Hopkins University Press, 1968), p. 306. Subsequent quotations are from this book.

11. Martin Heidegger, *Sein und Zeit,* 2d ed. (Tübingen: Niemeyer, 1929), p. 337.

12. Jean-Paul Sartre, *L'Être et le néant* (Paris: Gallimard, 1943), p. 276.

13. Michel Foucault, *The Order of Things* (New York: Vintage Books, 1973), p. 49.

14. Jacques Derrida, *De la grammatologie* (Paris: Éditions de Minuit, 1967), pp. 40–41.

15. Quoted by Norman O. Brown, *Love's Body* (New York: Vintage Books, 1966), p. 224.

16. Frederic Jameson, "Imaginary and Symbolic in Lacan: Marxism, Psychoanalytic Criticism, and the Problem of the Subject," *Yale French Studies* 55–56 (1977): 369.

17. Fyodor M. Dostoevsky, *Brat'ya Karamazovy* (Petrozavodsk, 1970), p. 353.

18. Martin Buber, *Ich und Du,* in *Werke,* vol. 1 (Munich: Kösel-Verlag, 1962), p. 90.

19. Fyodor M. Dostoevsky, *Niezdanyi Dostoevsky—Zapiski knizhki i tetradi 1860–1881 gg.,* in *Literaturnoe nasledstvo,* vol. 30, ed. V. R. Shcherbina et al. (Moscow, 1971), p. 529.

John Herdman (essay date 1990)

SOURCE: "The Russian Double," in *The Double in Nineteenth-Century Fiction,* Macmillan, 1990, pp. 99–126.

[*In the following excerpt, Herdman examines* The Double *in the context of nineteenth-century European literature featuring doubles.*]

The age of Hoffmann and Hogg might be called the 'high noon' of the double in Western Europe; in the middle years of the century . . . the theme fell somewhat into abeyance as a serious literary preoccupation, to experience a new resurgence in the last years of the century, a fresh access of vitality which was related to a revival of the Gothic mode and to new scientific developments which cast a beguiling light on matters of duality and psychic division. In Russia, however, the hiatus was bridged, for the influence of Hoffmann and the 'Russian Hoffmannists' bore new fruit in the 1840s in the early work of Dostoevsky, who throughout his career continued pertinaciously to revert to the preoccupation with duality and self-division which had so fascinated him in his youth. In his last book, *The Brothers Karamazov,* the double proper was to surface again as a crucial dramatic motif.

By far the most influential Russian prose writer of the 1830s and early 1840s was Gogol. The inimitable mixture of social satire, fantastic humour and aberrant psychology which characterises his writing was a rich spawning-ground of dualistic obsession, and in some of his stories he verges on adopting the device of the double to carry these preoccupations. In his most famous story 'The Overcoat' (1842), the prized coat of the wretched clerk Akaky Akakievich becomes his 'companion', a kind of extension of his self, and hence a rudimentary double. In 'The Nose' (1836), Gogol had created a gruesome and evocative image of dissociation: Collegiate Assessor Kovalyov, an aspiring social climber, wakes up one morning to find that his nose has vanished, and when he later sees it in uniform and confronts it, it claims, 'I am a person in my own right!'

Charles E. Passage has seen this story as a 'bitter parody' of Hoffmann, a *'reductio ad absurdum'* of the habits of the writer whom Gogol had at first so unreservedly admired: the loss of Kovalyov's nose is absurdly analogous to Spikher's loss of his mirror-image in 'Die Abenteuer der Sylvesternacht', and its adventures are a burlesque of Hoffmann's *Doppelgänger* themes. The nose travels all over St Petersburg in the guise of a State Councillor, cutting a figure to which Kovalyov cannot attain; there are satirical references to the popularity of magnetism in the capital at that date. Eventually, the nose returns to the Collegiate Assessor's face as mysteriously as it had parted from it. Still earlier, in the farcical tale 'The Story of the Quarrel between Ivan Ivanovich and Ivan Nikiforovich' (1834), Gogol had used to great comic effect the motif of complementary opposites. The two absurd characters are 'friends the like of whom the world had never seen', of whom it was said that 'the devil himself tied Ivan Nikiforovich and Ivan Ivanovich together with a rope' (p. 51); but they become mortal enemies when, in the course of a crazy altercation, one of them calls the other a goose.

These essays on the theme of the double are fairly vestigial; the importance of Gogol in the present context lies in the immense influence which he exercised on Dostoevsky, who was to become one of the great masters of the double. Gogol's characters are typically viewed from without, sometimes, as in the case of Akaky Akakievich, with real compassion, but always with the detached, microscopic eye of a scientist examining a specimen. The reader is encouraged to deduce, as it were, the obscure movements of their souls from the very exact information which Gogol provides about their externals.

Dostoevsky, by nature a writer of passionate psychological inwardness, is also deeply interested in the clues provided by behaviour and appearance to the inner psychology of his characters. His early work inhabits the world of Gogol, the world of seedy, depressed, tyrannised government clerks and minor civil servants looked down upon as insects by the lofty superiors to whose altitude they hopelessly aspire. But from the start Dostoevsky was instinctively involved with the great passions of the human soul, though not, in his pre-Siberian days, from any consciously developed or deeply committed position. In his attempts to harness the style and tone of Gogol to the demands of a more emotional and inward-directed art he turned to the tale of terror, and drew on what he had imbedded from the example of writers such as Mrs Radcliffe, Eugene Sue and, above all, Hoffmann.

Yet if **The Double** (1846) was born of a marriage between Hoffmann and Gogol, Dostoevsky himself was very much more than just the midwife. His distinctive tone of voice and way of seeing things is already unmistakably present in this, his second novel. Greatly shaken in his high hopes for the book, and his confidence in its excellence, by the quite hostile response it provoked after the rapturous reception of **Poor Folk** by Belinsky and his circle, Dostoevsky continued to believe that the idea itself was first-rate and seminal, and that there were elements in it that were of great and permanent value. During the 1860s he planned to recast it in a radically new form to do the concept greater justice and to reflect his new ideological preoccupations; but this was never done. The revision which he undertook in 1866, resulting in the version with which we are familiar, was much less far-reaching: he cut out the original mock-heroic framework, simplified the plot, and strengthened the ending by making Golyadkin's ultimate fate more explicit. As Joseph Frank observes, 'Golyadkin is the ancestor of all Dostoevsky's great split personalities, who are always confronted with their doubles or quasi-doubles (whether in the form of other "real" characters, or as hallucinations) in the memorable scenes of the great novels.'

Dostoevsky's story introduces to the literature of the double the element of humour, which had earlier, if present at all, been merely marginal or incidental. The humorous tone derives from Gogol, though its particular *timbre* is already very much Dostoevsky's own: according to Passage, the idea for **The Double** had its origin in an attempt to amalgamate the spirit of Gogol's 'Diary of a Madman' with the framework of Hoffmann's 'Sylvesternacht', whence the important role of the mirror-image in **The Double.** It is a very funny book, combining the mock-heroic, the absurd, sometimes almost the grotesque, with an inspired inwardness which imparts to the comic vision an underlying realism. The horror of the tale is entirely internalised: its hero, Mr Golyadkin, does nothing outwardly wicked or outrageous, yet his humiliated soul is fertile in monstrous growths.

Dostoevsky's perception of his protagonist's weakness and vanity is relentless, and the narrative tone may seem cruel in its detachment, the mocking, parodic distance of its viewpoint, yet his power of entering imaginatively into the minute obscurities, hesitances and dubieties of the psyche involves a counterbalancing sympathy and understanding. The novel is also more 'psychological' in a modern scientific sense than anything we have yet encountered: we are now closer to the world of the neurosis, the complex and the case history. With Dostoevsky, though, psychology is never divorced from the moral consciousness. Mr Golyadkin does go mad, but his madness has its roots not only in the restrictions, frustrations and oppressions of his social situation, but in vanity, ambition, envy and wounded pride. Dostoevsky's *feuilleton* for the novel says that Golyadkin 'goes mad out of *ambition,* while at the same time despising ambition and even suffering from the fact that he happens to suffer from such nonsense as ambition'.

On the morning on which we first make the acquaintance of Mr Golyadkin, his first action on rising from his bed is to look in the mirror, and we are told that he is 'evidently quite satisfied with all that he saw there'. The world is smiling on him, and he responds with a 'complacent smile'. The first emotion he exhibits on contact with another human being, his servant, Petrushka, is 'righteous indignation'; riding in a carriage he assumes a 'sedate and decorous air' when he thinks he is being looked at. It is quickly apparent that Mr Golyadkin's dominant character-

istics are extreme self-consciousness, morbid suspiciousness and complacent vanity. When the head of the section of his Department passes in a droshky, he is utterly overcome with confusion, with 'indescribable anguish', for Mr Golyadkin does not usually ride in a carriage. Shall he acknowledge their acquaintance? he asks himself. 'Or shall I pretend it's not me but somebody else strikingly like me, and look as if nothing's the matter?' He raises his hat to Andrey Philippovich, but at the same time whispers to himself, 'It's quite all right; this is not me at all, Andrey Philippovich, it's not me at all, not me, and that's all about it' (p. 132). The psychic dissociation has already begun, and his flight from himself will become complete with the appearance of the double whom, by these words, he in a sense conjures up.

Mr Golyadkin's consciousness is riven by inner conflict and he swings constantly from arrogance and self-assertion to utter self-doubt, collapse of confidence and self-depreciation. He has two mechanisms of defence to which he recurrently resorts: 'a terrible challenging stare . . . a stare calculated to reduce all his enemies to dust' (p. 132), and an inner voice which, however sorry his plight, seeks to reassure him that in spite of everything he is really 'all right'. He believes that he has been invited to a very important dinner party, but on the way he feels suddenly impelled to visit his physician, Dr Rutenspitz, an impressive elderly gentleman 'with an expressive glittering eye' (p. 133). The description of Golyadkin's excruciating indecision and self-consciousness at the start of their interview—and even his paranoia—cannot fail to remind one of Dostoevsky's own sufferings in this respect during his tormented youth—for the novelist's crippling social gaucherie and sense of persecution apparently disappeared during his Siberian exile.

The hero protects himself with his 'annihilating' stare, however, a stare which 'fully conveyed Mr Golyadkin's independence, that is, it stated clearly that Mr Golyadkin didn't care, that he was his own master, like anybody else, and his life was his own' (p. 134). Dr Rutenspitz recommends 'something to take you out of yourself' and, getting to the heart of the matter, 'in a certain sense, a change in your character' (p. 135). Golyadkin responds with a confused, incoherent tirade which bears all the marks of envy, social resentment and incipient paranoia. He is, he tells the doctor, 'proud to be not a great man but a little man. I am not an intriguer—and I am proud of that too'. Ironically, in view of the fate that is soon to befall him, he claims not to like 'petty two-faced people . . . I only put on a mask at a masked ball, I don't wear one in public every day.' The source of Mr Golyadkin's troubles is securely outside himself: unexpectedly bursting into tears (a touch which arouses the reader's reluctant compassion), he confides to the doctor, 'I have enemies, Christian Ivanovich, I have enemies; I have bitter enemies who have sworn to ruin me' (p. 139).

Golyadkin's sense of a conspiracy against him centres on the promotion to the rank of Assessor of one Vladimir Semyonovich, an admirer of Clara Olsufyevna, who is the object of his own ambitious affections. Clara is the daughter of the distinguished Olsufi Ivanovich Berendeyev, a retired State Councillor and 'at one time Mr. Golyadkin's patron', to whom all in his office look up as to a god, and 'who had been deprived of the use of his legs by his long service' (p. 153). A dinner party followed by a ball is being held to celebrate Clara's birthday, but to his utter horror our hero is refused admission. After extraordinary fluctuations of mood and intention, however, Golyadkin determines to assert himself and gate-crash the party (or at least, somehow to insinuate himself into it), for, as he had told some young clerks earlier in the day, 'You all know me, gentlemen, but up to now you have only known one side of me' (p. 147).

Mr Golyadkin's enterprise issues in a nightmare of humiliation. After lurking for three hours in the passage from the back entrance to the flat amid trash and lumber, half-hidden behind a screen and awaiting the 'right moment' for his entry, he at last steps inside and mingles with the crowd. He makes a ludicrous speech of congratulation to Clara Olsufyevna, is rebuked by Andrey Philippovich, and after 'hopelessly striving at all costs to find a centre and a social status among the bewildered crowd' and finally attempting to dance with Clara, he is manhandled out of the building. Utterly crushed, he starts to run home in a driving blizzard, scarcely knowing what he is doing. 'Mr Golyadkin', we are told, 'looked as if he was trying to hide from himself, as if he wanted to run away from himself . . . to annihilate himself, to cease to be, to return to the dust' (p. 166). Occasionally he stops in bemusement, then runs madly on 'as though trying to escape from pursuit or an even more terrible disaster' (p. 167). Trying to escape from himself, he is about to encounter himself face to face.

At his very lowest moment of despair, 'beside himself' in fact, leaning on the parapet of the embankment above the Fontanka, it suddenly seems to him as if someone were standing beside him, someone who had even said something 'about a matter touching him nearly'. But there is no one there. Soon he hears the sound of a cannon and thinks to himself, 'Listen! isn't that a flood warning?—Evidently the water is rising very fast' (p. 168). He is about to be psychically overwhelmed. No sooner has he thought this than a figure approaches him, and the idea comes to him: 'perhaps this passer-by is—*he*, himself, perhaps he is here, and, what makes matters worse, he is not here for nothing'. The stranger passes him, disappears, passes him once more from the same direction. Mr Golyadkin knows him very well, but 'not for the greatest treasure in the world would he have been willing to name him' (p. 170).

Mr Golyadkin Junior, as he will come to be called, is the most completely identical double of all those we shall encounter in this study, with the exceptions of the second James Beatman and the second William Wilson. He has no basis in any character distinct from his original, as is the case with Medardus's double, Count Victor. He is not a

manifestation of the Devil, like Gil-Martin, and has no power to take on any form but that of Mr Golyadkin; he is not even, like Wilson's double, a personification of conscience. He is simply the second Mr Golyadkin, absolutely similar in every respect to the first, except that he does what the first wants to do but cannot do. He embodies the truth that the forces which destroy the hero come from within himself, yet have their own autonomy and are beyond his control.

There are perhaps stronger grounds than in the case of any other of our examples to suppose the double to be purely a figment of the protagonist's diseased imagination, since the novel is written in a mode of psychological realism rather than supernatural romance; but it is part of the craftiness of its design that while the reader may at times be tempted to this conclusion, it is never possible finally to accede to it—there are simply too many incidents in the book which depend upon the objective existence of Golyadkin Junior. Again, there can be no doubt that by the end of the story Golyadkin is mad; but is his double a symptom of his madness, or its cause—or, in some obscure way, both?

Golyadkin fears this encounter, this 'evil thing' that is about to befall him, but at the same time he desires it. As he runs along, a mongrel dog follows at his heels, shadowing him, and at the same time 'some far-off long-forgotten idea' hammers away in his head, refusing to leave him alone. He sees the stranger ahead of him, now going in the same direction as himself, and follows him to his own house, up the stairs and into his own flat; then, with horror in his heart he at last allows himself to recognise the figure sitting on his bed and nodding at him familiarly: 'Mr. Golyadkin's nocturnal acquaintance was none other than himself, Mr. Golyadkin himself, another Mr. Golyadkin, but exactly the same as himself—in short, in every respect what is called his double' (p. 173). The knowing tone indicates a fresh approach to the familiar theme. In Dostoevsky's **Double** there is an element of pastiche, and while the treatment is wholly convincing psychologically, he will also exploit in an innovatory way the humorous potential of the material.

On waking the next morning, Golyadkin explains this extraordinary development to himself in a paranoid manner: he 'had known for a very long time that something was being prepared, that there was *somebody else* in reserve' (p. 173). He decides, for the time being, to 'submit', an attitude which will become habitual. When, after much vacillation, he arrives at the office, he finds to his shame and horror that his double is there too, and has been put in the seat opposite him. To his fright, nobody shows any sign of surprise at this shameful and scandalous 'farce', so that Golyadkin begins to doubt his own identity. His double, on the other hand, sits 'staidly and peacefully'. It is only when it is explicitly pointed out to him that Anton Antonovich, Golyadkin's superior, sees the miraculousness of the likeness, and then, after encouragingly mentioning that his aunt had seen her double just before she died, suggests that the occurrence is God's will and that to murmur against it would be sinful. The hero's passivity is thus enjoined upon him by the authority he worships and fears.

The second Mr Golyadkin, like the shadow in Hans Christian Andersen's fable, is a usurping double. Though, as Chizhevsky acutely remarks, the 'place' from which his double squeezes him is almost completely illusory to begin with, as the successful embodiment of his original's hopeless aspirations he takes from the latter even the little that he has. 'For my part,' he tells the hero, 'I felt attracted to you at first sight'; and Golyadkin's first instinct is to appease him. Though feeling that 'It's putting my head into a noose of my own accord', he invites him in, listens to his double's long trivial history, and, when the latter asks for his friendship and protection, feels conciliated.

He discovers that they share the same name and patronymic—Iakov Petrovich—and come from the same province. They get drunk together and No. 1 asks No. 2 to stay the night; but in the morning the double has gone. Thereafter he treats his benefactor with increasing carelessness and insolence, exhibits the most odious officiousness, starts usurping his office functions and takes credit for Golyadkin Senior's work. The latter finds the situation impossible, but when he tries to confront his rival, the usurper, in full view of the clerks, pinches and tickles his cheek and prods him in the paunch. This is the other side of himself that Mr Golyadkin had earlier promised the clerks they would soon see.

Golyadkin vows revenge, but his resolution is always nullified by vacillation and indecision. His determination is rendered in biblical and mock-heroic terms: he will take a 'certain step' which will 'crush the serpent and bring low the horn of pride' (p. 206). Golyadkin Junior, however, is of course a projection of Golyadkin's Senior's own pride, and there are moments when he half admits it, and even attributes the whole mix-up to the Devil in the most traditional way: 'My God! What a hell-broth the Devil's concocted here! As for him, he's such a base and ignoble wretch, so mischievous and wanton, so frivolous and sycophantic and grovelling, such a Golyadkin! . . . And he'll supplant a man, supplant him—take his place as if he was nothing but an old rag, and never stop to think that a man's not an old rag' (p. 212). There are moments of high farce, as when Golyadkin goes into a restaurant and, having eaten one savoury patty, is charged for eleven; he starts to protest, but the veil is lifted from his eyes when he sees his double with the last piece of the tenth patty in his hand and about to enter his mouth. The original suffers a 'paroxysm of wounded pride'.

Under the influence of this emotion he writes to Mr Golyadkin Junior, linking his appearance to 'discourteous and unseemly treatment at the hands of enemies of mine' (p. 215). He has now found a new phrase with which to defend himself mentally from the violation which is occurring: 'I'm in the right.' In this way he continues to thrust responsibility from himself and project the origin of his woes upon external enemies and upon Fate. But his decisive and heroically conceived resolutions are perpetually nullified by the reality of his passivity and pusillanimity: his violent swings of mood toss him from assertion to abjection. Immediately regretting having written the letter, he castigates himself: 'Fool that I was, I let my pride run away with me! My pride drove me to it! That's what pride does for you, that's your proper pride, wretch that you are!' (p. 220). Even the servant, Petrushka, now experiences revulsion at his doubleness, and reproaches him in a speech which ironically echoes or parodies Golyadkin's complacent tirade to Dr Rutenspitz on people who wear 'masks': 'Good people live honestly,' says Petrushka, 'good people live without any faking, and they never come double' (p. 222).

All kinds of immoral and unseemly behaviour begin to be attributed to Mr Golyadkin. As was the case with Robert Wringhim and Gil-Martin, it never becomes altogether clear whether these actions have indeed been committed by the original, perhaps in a disordered state of mind, or whether, as he believes, they are the work of his double and represent a malicious campaign of character assassination on the part of the latter. The narrative voice, while utterly detached and ironical in its attitude towards Mr Golyadkin, limits itself progressively to describing events as they appear to the unfortunate Titular Councillor, whose consciousness is increasingly chaotic and distorted by projection. As his own mental condition deteriorates he protests that his double deserves the 'lunatic asylum'. He begins to have tortured dreams in which are mingled rebuffs, slights, his own mean tricks, and the arrogation of his life by his rival. The latter has Golyadkin's own character but succeeds where he fails and shows up his qualities as spurious. Thus he is the expression of both the fears and the conscience of the real and 'altogether rightful Mr Golyadkin'. In his dreams this mirror-image exhibiting himself to himself is hideously replicated, so that a long line of identical Golyadkins stretches back 'in a long file like a string of geese and scurrying after Mr Golyadkin, so that there was no escaping from perfect counterfeits of himself' (p. 232). 'Either you or I', Senior writes to Junior, 'but both of us together is impossible!' (p. 232).

Mr Golyadkin Junior has become immensely popular and important, and he behaves in reality just as he has in the dream. When Senior, who in some moods still seeks conciliation with his 'deadly enemy', attempts to shake his hand, that wretch snatches his hand away, shakes it in the air 'as though he had dirtied it in something extremely nasty', spits, and ostentatiously wipes his fingers with his handkerchief (p. 242). This is going a little too far, and the office clerks are momentarily disapproving, but the double once more turns the tables with an offensive jest. Further woes are at once heaped on Golyadkin's shoulders as Anton Antonovich accuses him of 'unbecoming conduct' towards Clara Olsufyevna and a German woman with whom he used to lodge (an element much more fully developed in the earlier version of the novel), and of 'slandering another person', that is, the second Mr Golyadkin. A confrontation with the double in a coffee house, during which Golyadkin's conversation consists mostly of high-flown but ludicrous inanities, ends when the usurper's behaviour becomes intolerably offensive. However Golyadkin manages to force his way into the latter's droshky, and when he is finally jolted off into the snow he finds himself in Olsufi Ivanovich's yard: his rival disappears into the house.

As Dostoevsky's tale moves towards its climax, his fable approaches more closely the model of the demonic double motif, with Mr Golyadkin Junior taking the part of the Mephistophilean tempter and Dr Rutenspitz that of Lucifer. As Golyadkin's psyche disintegrates, hallucination and reality become increasingly indistinguishable, and he descends into a delirium analogous to those of Medardus and Wringhim during the climactic days of their possession. After falling off the droshky, he finds in his pocket a letter delivered to him by the porter that morning; written by Clara, it is addressed to *one* of the Golyadkins, castigates the other as an intriguing scoundrel who has engineered her destruction, declares her love for the other, and invites him to elope with her. Whether this letter has any real existence is open to doubt, for later Mr Golyadkin cannot find it and wonders whether it has been purloined by his 'undeserving twin'.

The hero is thrown into utter confusion by the letter, and meanwhile his identity is crumbling and his life collapsing about his ears. In a tavern, he suddenly imagines that he is being poisoned; returning home, he is handed a letter from Andrey Philippovich instructing him to hand over all the business in his hands to Ivan Semyonovich. Even Petrushka is about to leave his service. He prepares for his parodic elopement, though terrified at the very thought of it: 'Here's a man on the way to destruction, a man is losing his identity, and he can hardly control himself—and you talk to him about a wedding!' (p. 265). Desperately determined to maintain his individuality and distinctness from his double, he goes to His Excellency's house to denounce the usurper; the latter is present, along with Dr Rutenspitz, whom, however, the crazed Golyadkin fails to recognise. After a fruitless and humiliating interview he is propelled towards the door and seen off the premises by his obnoxious rival.

Mr Golyadkin's hideous experience on the occasion of the first party at Olsufi Ivanovich's is now duplicated in an exaggerated form. He arrives with a carriage and awaits his lover for two hours in the courtyard in the bitter cold, beside a pile of logs. As he waits he talks out his torments, addressing himself mentally to Clara; he is more or less raving, but occasional flashes of distorted sense from time to time light up the confused darkness of his mind. He pays off the cabman and dashes off cheerfully: then immediately returns to the yard. All at once he realises that the entire company within is staring down at him from the windows. His double comes down the steps, and in spite of his protests the hero, 'feeling as though he was being roasted over a slow fire', is dragged up and into the drawing-room by this 'notorious detrimental' (pp. 280–1).

He is led up to the chair of Olsufi Ivanovich, and it now seems to him as if there were sympathetic tears in the eyes of all around him—'Or perhaps Mr Golyadkin only imagined all this because he himself had broken down and could distinctly feel the scalding tears running down his cold cheeks' (p. 282). In the structure of this episode, as Passage has noted, 'Dostoevsky is at pains to parallel a scene of heavenly justice pronounced upon a sinner.' Golyadkin tries to speak, but can only point to his heart. The crowd follow him about with curiosity and a certain enigmatic sympathy. Then he is led up to Mr Golyadkin Junior, who holds out his hand; Mr Golyadkin takes it, and they embrace, but even at the very moment of this 'Judas-kiss', he detects his double in a perfidious grimace and a conspiratorial wink to the crowd. In horror, he imagines 'that an endless string of Golyadkins all exactly alike were bursting in through the doors of the room; but it was too late. . . . The resounding treacherous kiss had been given, and . . .' (p. 284).

The scene that follows is one more variation on Faustus's carrying-off to hell by the avenging demons. Dr Rutenspitz appears, now grown terrible and unspeakably threatening, and is announced by Mr Golyadkin's twin, in whose face there shines 'an unseemly and sinister joy'. Dostoevsky could never have read Hogg, but there is a striking parallel with the gloating triumph of Gil-Martin as Wringhim goes to his doom. Golyadkin is led down to a closed carriage and the door opened by his double, and as he drives off with the doctor he is pursued in farewell by 'the piercing frantic yells of his enemies'. Mr Golyadkin Junior runs after the carriage, jumping up and blowing kisses. For a time the hero loses consciousness, then awakes to a new horror: 'two fiery eyes were watching him in the darkness, and they shone with malignant hellish joy. This was not Christian Ivanovich! Who was it?' For Mr Golyadkin, at least, Rutenspitz has become the Devil, and in truth the doctor is carrying him off to eternal torment. The latter's final words, which make it clear that their destination is an asylum, ring out in his ears 'like the stern and terrible sentence of a judge' (pp. 286–7).

Dostoevsky's masterly treatment of the theme of the double in this early novel thus combines a more clinically searching and carefully elaborated psychological realism than anything attempted by his predecessors (enhanced by a wonderful exploitation of the previously untapped comic potentiality of the motif), with the retention of essential traditional elements. The place of supernatural and fantastic causation in earlier double romances is here entirely supplied by the subjective and hallucinatory emanations of the protagonist's psyche (a development initiated by Hoffmann and Hogg, but in their work still ambiguously intertwined with the supernatural); but the independent existence of the double is safeguarded by a narrative structure which requires our acceptance of his objective presence, at least at some points in the story.

In later writers, as we shall see, this subjective-objective balance will be lost, largely due to changes in sensibility connected with scientific and psychological advance and altered attitudes to religious belief, changes which make it more difficult to render convincing such an interpenetration of the moral-spiritual and the physical worlds. Tales of the double then tend to divide off, on the one hand into pure moral allegory, which depends once more on the frankly fantastic, or on a scientism that is really glorified magic; and on the other into a merely clinical interpretation which lacks any spiritual dimension.

It is Dostoevsky's strength that his innovating development and extension of the psychological-realistic strand is securely based on traditional moral foundations. This is underlined by the pointed diablerie of the closing scenes, but the source of Golyadkin's troubles in his exclusive preoccupation with self is reverted to throughout the novel. He is not just an unfortunate victim of mental disorder, nor yet simply of social injustice, though that element is undoubtedly contributory. In spite of his being partly at the mercy of his social circumstances, of the autocratic, hierarchically repressive Russian society of his day, his character is relentlessly depicted by Dostoevsky as that of a man in whom vanity, pride, paltry ambition and envy have been allowed to develop monstrously and unchecked. The psychic disintegration which overtakes him is thus the fruit of what is traditionally called sin, and particularly of a variety of the sin of pride, which we have repeatedly observed to be the precondition for the appearance of a double.

Mr Golyadkin himself mutely acknowledges the connection between his mental collapse and his transgressions when, in the penultimate sentence of the book, he perceives the doctor as judge. Because *The Double* is a comic novel, this view may at first sight appear to be overstated, but the analogy of Dostoevsky's later work may persuade us otherwise. In his last novel he resorts once again to the device of the double to express one of the most important thematic ingredients of his narrative, and here, as in *The Double,* the appearance of the second self is associated with mental breakdown, this time quite explicitly arising from the dark, evil side of the subject's psyche, and specifically from the sin of pride.

Joseph Frank has expressed the view that Dostoevsky's final dissatisfaction with the form of his novel refers to its 'uncertain oscillation between the psychic and the supernatural', the fear that the objective aspect of Golyadkin's double was too troubling and mysterious for the reader. Feeling this as a weakness, Dostoevsky makes sure that this ambivalence in the status of the double does not recur in his later work: 'his doubles will either be clear-cut hallucinations, or what may be called "quasi-doubles"—characters who exist in their own right, but reflect some internal aspect of another character in a strengthened form'. This supposition is highly plausible, but it may well be that adverse criticism had caused Dostoevsky to question a procedure which his original artistic instinct had assured him could be both valid and effective. The ambivalence referred to is an inherent characteristic of the

supernatural double, and to realise that it can constitute its essential strength, indeed its *raison d'être,* we need look no further than Hoffmann's Coppelius or the *Justified Sinner.* In *The Double* it is partly this ambiguity which makes possible an analysis that is, as Chizhevsky puts it, both 'realistically' and 'transcendentally psychological', a successful interpenetration of naturalistic and fantastic modes. But Dostoevsky did move in the direction Frank indicates, and the results certainly cannot be any cause for regret.

Julian W. Connolly (essay date 1991)

SOURCE: "Madness and Doubling: From Dostoevsky's *The Double* to Nabokov's *The Eye,*" in *Russian Literature Triquarterly,* No. 24, 1991, pp. 129–39.

[*In the following essay, Connolly discusses* The Double *as a source of inspiration for Vladimir Nabokov's* The Eye.]

Vladimir Nabokov often expressed himself harshly when evaluating Fyodor Dostoevsky's abilities as a writer: "He was a prophet, a claptrap journalist and a slapdash comedian," he told an interviewer in 1963,[1] and in his *Lectures on Russian Literature* he stated that Dostoevsky was "not a great writer, but a rather mediocre one."[2] Not only did he criticize Dostoevsky in his lectures and interviews, he made fun of Dostoevsky in his fiction too, most notably in the novel *Despair (Otchainie)*, where his narrator Hermann Karlovich calls Dostoevsky's novel *Crime and Punishment* "Crime and Slime" and "Crime and Pun."[3] Yet Dostoevsky wrote one work that Nabokov professed to admire—*The Double (Dvoinik)*—which he termed in his *Lectures on Russian Literature* "the best thing he ever wrote" and "a perfect work of art."[4]

Significantly, Nabokov seems to have turned to *The Double* as an important source of inspiration for one of his own works, the novella *The Eye (Sogliadatai)*,[5] originally written in Russian and published in the journal *Sovremennye zapiski* in 1930.[6] A close reading of *The Eye* suggests that Nabokov was intrigued with the way Dostoevsky explores the transformation of reality in an insecure yet imaginative individual's mind. In *The Eye* Nabokov reworks Dostoevsky's vision of a character who first projects an image of an alter ego onto the surrounding world and then becomes obsessed with his created character's actions. Having extracted certain basic elements out of Dostoevsky's story, however, Nabokov reshaped them according to his own design, thereby creating a new work with an entirely different thrust. Whereas Dostoevsky's readers are plunged into a nightmarish world that probes human suffering with sober relentlessness,[7] Nabokov's readers encounter a buoyant narrative of shifting perspectives that Nabokov himself thought would be "excellent sport."[8] A reading of the two works together thus indicates the extent to which Nabokov was influenced by Dostoevsky's fiction and demonstrates the fundamental ways in which his artistic methods and world-view differ from Dostoevsky's.

The central point of similarity between the two works is the writers' investigation of a shared subject: a neurotic man's projection of an alter ego and his subsequent obsession with that alter ego. The central character of Dostoevsky's work is the government clerk Golyadkin who watches in consternation as his apparent double insinuates himself into Golyadkin's place at the office and in society. In Nabokov's tale, the central character is the narrator of the work. He describes how he watches the social interactions of a second character named Smurov. This Smurov, the reader gradually realizes, is in reality the narrator himself.

In both cases the protagonists' perception of an alter ego operating outside their core personalities indicates a profound dissatisfaction with their everyday selves. Each man imagines himself to be more worthy than his current position in the world would indicate, and each finds in his double his own perceived failings and strengths prominently displayed. The similarities between the two characters are so striking as to suggest that Nabokov has drawn upon Dostoevsky's portrait of Golyadkin for many of his own hero's personality traits. This can be demonstrated by a brief survey of the two characters' self-images and behavioral patterns.

To begin with, both characters see themselves as simple, decent, and modest individuals. Golyadkin tells his doctor: "I am a simple, unpretentious fellow,"[9] while the narrator of *The Eye* says of Smurov, "His manners were excellent," and he notes within Smurov a "noble and enigmatic modesty" (E 34; S 29). Beneath this simple facade, however, both men feel that they possess a dashing spirit. Dostoevsky mentions Golyadkin's "withering gaze," which had "the imaginary power of reducing all Mr. Golyadkin's enemies into dust and ashes" (*D* 155; *Dv* 115). The narrator of *The Eye* writes that Smurov was "obviously a person who, behind his unpretentiousness and quietness, concealed a fiery spirit. He was doubtless capable, in a moment of wrath, of slashing a chap into bits" (E 37; S 32). Moreover, each character believes himself capable of great wit and conversational charm. In a dream Golyadkin fancies that he "stands out because of his wit and gallantry, and everyone grows fond of him. . . . Everyone agrees that he is the most brilliant person in the company" (*D* 246; *Dv* 185). This corresponds to the narrator's observation about Smurov: "He spoke little, but everything he said was intelligent and appropriate, and his infrequent jokes, while too subtle to arouse roars of laughter, seemed to unlock a concealed door in the conversation, letting in an unexpected freshness" (E 34; S 29). In reality, however, neither character is as charming and attractive as he would like to believe, and in actual conversation both men seem hesitant or even incoherent. *The Double* is filled with examples of Golyadkin's difficulty in self-expression, and a dream sequence in *The Eye* reveals how confused the narrator becomes when trying to justify himself to Filip Khrushchov.[10]

More importantly, each character is extremely sensitive to the opinion of others about him, and each feels very vulnerable to outside criticism and potential embarrassment. Golyadkin frequently asks his colleagues if his superiors have said anything about him (e.g., *D* 250; *Dv* 189), and the narrator of *The Eye* not only asks people direct questions about Smurov (e.g., "'And how about you,' I asked Evgenia, 'what idea have *you* formed?'" [E 58; S 48]), but he even steals a letter in which information about Smurov might be found (see E 82–91; S 65–72).[11] In fact, it is the two men's sensitivity to social opinion and public embarrassment that leads to the initial projection of the double figure; this shall be discussed below.

In addition to basic similarities in self-image, the two protagonists evince common behaviors. Preoccupied with their self-images, for example, both men repeatedly look into mirrors (cf. D 148, 231, and 285 [*Dv* 109–10, 174, 216] and E 17 and 104 [S 16 and 82]). The first mirror scene in *The Double* is noteworthy, for it contains a transparent reference to Gogol's "The Nose." When Golyadkin fears that he will find "an unfamiliar pimple or some other unpleasant thing" one recalls that Major Kovalyov in "The Nose" discovers that his nose is missing when he looks in a mirror to check on a pimple. Nabokov perhaps echoes this incident in *The Eye* when his narrator notes that "a pimple glowed unpleasantly through the talc on Smurov's chin" (E 54; S 44).

Furthermore, both characters relate to women in similar ways. Both characters love a woman who is betrothed or attracted to another, and both men have liaisons with a German woman. Thus Golyadkin loves Klara Olsufievna, though she is drawn to Vladimir Semyonovich; Smurov loves a woman named Vanya, although she is engaged to Mukhin. Golyadkin had earlier been involved with a German woman named Karolina Ivanovna, while Smurov goes on to have an affair with a German maid named Gretchen or Hilda. Curiously, when each man is in the presence of the woman he loves, he finds himself moving toward her as if propelled by an involuntary force; at such moments each character seems to be denying true responsibility for his actions. The relevant scene in *The Double* occurs when Golyadkin sneaks into Klara Olsufievna's party. Single-mindedly concentrating on Klara's figure, he finds himself "simply propelled forward by that same spring which had pushed him uninvited into the ball . . . until he found himself in front of Klara Olsufievna herself" (*D* 178; *Dv* 133). In similar fashion, the narrator of *The Eye* describes how he came upon Vanya alone on her balcony: "I do not know how it started—there must have been some preparatory motions—but I remember finding myself perching on the wide wicker arm of Vanya's chair, and already clutching her wrist" (E 99; S 78).[12]

Though they are rebuffed in their actual attempts to win the affections of their beloved women, both characters imagine themselves capable of captivating a woman and covertly stealing off with her. Golyadkin becomes highly agitated by a letter which has supposedly been written by Klara and which asks him to wait under her window with a carriage to carry her off, while the narrator of *The Eye* fancies that Smurov was capable, in a moment of passion, "of carrying a frightened and perfumed girl beneath his cloak on a windy night to a waiting boat with muffled oar-locks" (E 37–38; S 32). In both cases, the men's fantasies are colored by literature they have read: Golyadkin recalls the signal a woman gave her lover in "some novel he had read long ago" (*D* 289; *Dv* 219), while the narrator's description of Smurov's hypothetical abduction concludes: "just as somebody did in Roman Bogdanovich's story" (E 38; S 32).[13]

As these fantasies suggest, the two characters seem more comfortable in the world of their dreams than in the real world. Indeed, at the beginning of *The Double* Golyadkin awakens from a dream to find that "he was not in some enchanted land of milk and honey, but in his apartment . . . in Petersburg." He then "shuddered and closed his eyes, apparently regretting his vanished dream and trying to recapture it for a moment at least" (*D* 147; *Dv* 109). In a crucial passage near the end of *The Eye,* the narrator expresses a similar sensation: "It is frightening when real life suddenly turns out to be a dream, but how much more frightening when that which one had thought a dream— fluid and irresponsible—suddenly starts to congeal into reality!" (E 104; S 82).

It is this predilection for dreaming that allows the two characters to slip so easily from the everyday world of the single personality into the fantastic world of multiple selves. And it is their extreme sensitivity, their inability to deal calmly with setbacks in the everyday world, that triggers their crucial flight into fantasy. Significantly, the sequence of events leading to the first sensation of doubling is roughly parallel in the two works. In both cases, the central character perceives a devastating blow to his self-esteem in front of others. This rebuff then precipitates a kind of extinction of the basic, integrated personality, and this is then followed by a strange new sensation of something like life after death, during which the core personality is reproduced or multiplied. The relevant episode in *The Double* begins at Klara Olsufievna's birthday party. After sneaking into the party, Golyadkin tries to dance with Klara, makes a fool of himself, and is bustled out of the house by the affronted guests; he then rushes away down the street. Dostoevsky's narrator remarks: "Golyadkin had been killed—actually killed in the full sense of the word, and if he still preserved the ability to run, it was through some sort of miracle" (*D* 184; *Dv* 138). It is directly after this impression of being killed that Golyadkin begins seeing his double.

In *The Eye* Nabokov takes a similar sequence of events and develops them further, giving certain elements of Dostoevsky's scheme a semblance of literalness. The moment of humiliation in Nabokov's work occurs when the narrator is thrashed in front of two boys by Kashmarin (whose name is derived from the Russian word for nightmare), who is angry at him for seducing his wife.[14] After his public humiliation the narrator rushes out of the apartment, runs home, points a revolver at himself, and pulls the trig-

ger, plunging into a deep swoon. This self-destructive act is a literal realization of a thought Golyadkin had had at Klara's party when he had "vaguely given himself his word of honor to shoot himself somehow that night" (*D* 179; *Dv* 133). Moreover, Dostoevsky's claim that Golyadkin had been killed after leaving the party becomes "reality" for the narrator of *The Eye,* for he states that he has in fact been killed, and when he awakens in a hospital setting, he cleverly invents the explanation that the surrounding world is only a creation of his thought process. He states: "it became clear that after death human thought lives on by momentum. . . . What a mighty thing was human thought, that it could hurtle on beyond death" (E 21; S 19).[15] It is in this post-suicide state that he first becomes aware of his alter ego Smurov.

Yet while Nabokov clearly models his hero's personality and actions after Dostoevsky's Golyadkin, he utilizes the concept of a bifurcated or dissociated self for significantly different purposes. This becomes particularly evident in the way in which each protagonist views his double. Golyadkin primarily sees in his double the representative of all that he loathes and fears in himself and in his society— dishonesty, egocentric cunning, a fawning attitude toward one's superiors, base flattery, etc. The element of unconscious self-recognition is marvelously evoked in Golyadkin's angry exclamation: "he's such a shifty, scheming fellow, such a boot-licker, such a toady, such a Golyadkin!" (*D* 229 [translation emended]; *Dv* 172). Confronted with the double's evident facility at manipulating these opportunistic qualities, Golyadkin experiences both envy and despair, for the double's apparent talent underscores his own feelings of inadequacy and impotence in society. For Golyadkin, then, the perception of a double represents a projection of his deepest insecurities, anxieties, and unresolved conflicts, and it develops into a source of extreme torment for him.

For the narrator of *The Eye,* however, the sensation of having an outside alter ego does not represent a threat to the core personality. Rather, he discovers in this sense of dissociation a possible means of protecting his personality. That is, no matter what happens to Smurov or what people may think of him, the narrator can comfort himself with the belief that he is insulated from such events and opinions, and that Smurov's encounters cannot have any harmful consequences for him. Of course, a major source of irony in the novel is the extent to which the narrator reveals that he *is* affected by Smurov's misfortunes.[16] Nevertheless, the doubles in the two works represent very different concepts for the two protagonists. While Golyadkin's double can be seen as an external manifestation of his own crumbling self-esteem, the narrator's double in *The Eye* represents the narrator's attempt to protect his self-esteem by uncoupling the core personality from its external shell.[17]

In fact, Nabokov seems to have taken for his central premise a concept that Golyadkin had pondered as a possible means of self-protection in *The Double.* The concept surfaces at two points in the tale. In chapter 1, as Golyadkin rides in a rented carriage he suddenly comes face to face with his superior riding in a different carriage. Embarrassed, he thinks: "Should I bow or shouldn't I? Should I acknowledge him? Admit that it is me? Or should I pretend I'm someone else, someone strikingly resembling me? . . . Yes, that's it; I'm not me and that's all there is to it" (*D* 151; *Dv* 113). Near the end of the narrative, when Golyadkin prepares to return to Klara Olsufievna's house, he arrives at a new variant of the same strategy: "I'll act as an outsider, as a spectator, nothing more, and whatever happens there—it won't be any fault of mine"; as an outsider, he will not be "in the least involved in the whole affair" (*D* 294; *Dv* 223). In both cases, Golyadkin perceives a potential source of immunity by imagining that the entity seen by the external world is not his true self. Yet even though he senses the potential benefit to be derived from this strategy, he does not manage to apply it with any consistency or success. In *The Eye*, however, it is precisely this strategy that the narrator adopts after his unsuccessful suicide attempt. Immediately after the suicide attempt, even before he has "met" Smurov, he states: "I saw myself from the outside" (E 23; S 21) and "in respect to myself I was now an onlooker" (E 28; S 24). His subsequent perception of the Smurov persona arises organically out of this.

The fundamental difference in the way the two protagonists view their doubles has further ramifications. Since Golyadkin's double surfaces as a visible reminder of the turmoil in his own soul, Golyadkin is terrified at the thought of having multiple doubles. When he dreams of running through the city and creating a new double with each step, he reacts with "horror," for "he realizes that there is no possible escape for him from the chain of exactly identical Golyadkins" (*D* 248; *Dv* 187). The narrator of *The Eye*, in contrast, welcomes the proliferation of new selves, for they represent both an extension and diversification of the basic self at no cost to that self. Throughout *The Eye*, he avidly collects the various images people have of Smurov and he concludes: "I do not exist; there exist but the thousands of mirrors that reflect me. With every acquaintance I make, the population of phantoms resembling me increases. Somewhere they live, somewhere they multiply" (E 109; S 86).

Clearly, then, there is a crucial difference between Dostoevsky's approach to the madness and doubling sequence and Nabokov's. For Dostoevsky, the idea that personal insecurity and mental instability can result in the creation of a double leads to an investigation of the dark recesses of a disturbed soul. For Nabokov, the very same concept provides an opportunity to explore how mental instability and inspired imagination can lead to a possible defense against the vicissitudes of "real" life. In both cases, the writers raise central issues that they develop in their subsequent fiction. Dostoevsky's exploration of a sensitive character's desperate longing for outside approval points the way toward such works as *Notes from the Underground* and *Crime and Punishment,* and his focus on a divided character "struggling for the integration" of his personality, as

Konstantin Mochulsky puts it, leads to the creation of such characters as Versilov, Stavrogin, and Ivan Karamazov.[18] Likewise, Nabokov's investigation of the way in which an imaginative transformation of the world can provide an illusion of security and control is further developed in such novels as *Despair* and *Pale Fire,* while his exploration of the possibilities inherent in creating multiple identities for oneself finds later reflection in *The Real Life of Sebastian Knight*[19] and *Pale Fire.*[20]

The basic difference in the approach Dostoevsky and Nabokov take toward a character's creation of an alter ego also surfaces in the endings of their two works. At the end of *The Double* Golyadkin returns to the scene of his initial humiliation at Klara's house and is led off in utter agony to an insane asylum. In *The Eye,* though, the narrator again meets his old persecutor Kashmarin, but this time the tables are turned. Kashmarin becomes deeply apologetic about having hit the narrator, confesses that his wife had been unfaithful before, and promises to obtain a new job for the narrator. The contrast between the psychological gloom of Dostoevsky's ending and the ironic reversal in Nabokov's last scene is striking, but Nabokov was too subtle an artist to leave the impression that his character had found complete peace. The final lines of his work sound a disquieting note. After asserting that he is content to have become an observer and that he has now attained a sense of invulnerability, the narrator cries out: "I am happy—yes, happy! What more can I do to prove it, how to proclaim that I am happy? Oh, to shout it so that all of you believe me at last, you cruel, smug people . . ." (E 111; S 87). This protestation reverberates with a hollow, shrill tone, and in the narrator's bravado one detects echoes of another voice from Dostoevsky's work—that of the insecure narrator of *Notes from the Underground.*[21] For all his professed confidence, the narrator still struggles with his basic insecurity in the face of implacable reality.

As this brief study of *The Eye* demonstrates, Nabokov's reservations about Dostoevsky's gift as a writer did not prevent him from absorbing valuable insights from Dostoevsky's work. Indeed, Nabokov's imagination was deeply stirred by Dostoevsky's portrait of an unbalanced man creating an alter ego in response to feelings of insecurity in the world. Having studied Dostoevsky's initial premise, however, Nabokov forged from it entirely different conclusions. In Nabokov's hands, Dostoevsky's grim exploration of obsessive human anxiety turns into a more playful and witty examination of the ways in which an imaginative individual attempts to transcend the travails of everyday life.[22] Nabokov's attitude toward Dostoevsky and his work is therefore not as simple as his critical pronouncements might suggest. Despite his doubts about Dostoevsky's general talent as a writer, Nabokov found in *The Double* a rich source of inspiration for his own artistic work. In *The Eye* he transforms Dostoevsky's vivid portrait of mental instability into the foundation for one of the most engaging and unusual creations in his entire *oeuvre.*

Notes

1. Vladimir Nabokov, *Strong Opinions* (New York: McGraw-Hill, 1973), p. 42.

2. Vladimir Nabokov, *Lectures on Russian Literature,* ed. Fredson Bowers (New York: Harcourt Brace Jovanovich, 1981), p. 98.

3. Vladimir Nabokov, *Despair* (New York: Capricorn Books, 1970), pp. 187 and 211. For a discussion of the role of such literary references in *Despair* see my article, "The Function of Literary Allusion in Nabokov's *Despair,*" *Slavic and East European Journal,* 26, No. 3 (Fall 1982), pp. 302–13.

4. Nabokov, *Lectures on Russian Literature,* pp. 100 and 104.

5. Although Andrew Field discusses the relationship of *The Eye* to other works by Dostoevsky, most notably *The Possessed,* he does not analyze the deep connections between *The Eye* and *The Double.* See Field, *Nabokov: His Life in Art* (Boston: Little, Brown and Co., 1967), p. 68. The most comprehensive introduction to the structure and themes of *The Eye* is D. Barton Johnson's article, "Eyeing Nabokov's *Eye,*" *Canadian-American Slavic Studies,* 19, No. 3 (Fall 1985), pp. 328–50. Johnson also discusses the literary allusions found in *The Eye* in his article, "The Books Reflected in Nabokov's *The Eye,*" *Slavic and East European Journal,* 29, No. 4 (Winter 1985), pp. 393–404.

6. Nabokov later translated the work into English with Dmitri Nabokov and published it in 1965.

7. D. S. Mirsky called the work an example of "cruel literature" in his *A History of Russian Literature* (New York: Vintage Books, 1958), p. 184.

8. Vladimir Nabokov, (New York: Pocket Books, 1966), p. x. All further quotations from this book will be noted in the text by a parenthetical reference using the abbreviation E and the page number. Corresponding passages in the Russian version will be keyed to the Ardis reprint of the 1938 edition of *Sogliadatai* (Ann Arbor: Ardis 1978) and will be noted by a parenthetical reference using the abbreviation S and the page number.

9. Fyodor Dostoevsky, *The Double,* in *Three Short Novels by Dostoevsky,* trans. Andrew R. MacAndrew (New York: Bantam Books, 1966), p. 157. All further quotations from this book will be noted by a parenthetical reference using the abbreviation D and the page number. Corresponding passages from the Russian will be keyed to the version of *Dvoinik* found in F. M. Dostoevskii, *Polnoe sobranie sochinenii v tridtsati tomakh,* I (Leningrad: Nauka, 1972), and will be noted in the text with the abbreviation Dv and the page number; this particular passage is found on page 116.

10. This explanatory scene, in which the narrator imagines himself refuting the assertion that he is a thief, recalls similar episodes in *The Double.* Both the narrator and Golyadkin protest that what others have said about them is false or slanderous (cf. E 95 [S 74], where the narrator swears that "every word of his is a lie" and D 225 [Dv 169], where Golyadkin sputters: "Who says that? My enemies must have said it."). In their attempts at self-justification both men make cryptic references to "certain people" without naming them, thus increasing the aura of intrigue they create around themselves (cf. *E* 93 [S 74] and D 243 [*Dv* 183]).

11. Likewise, both men claim to be the subject of rumors and intrigue (cf. *D* 162 [*Dv* 121] and *E* 54–56 [*S* 45–46]).

12. W. W. Rowe asserts in his book, *Nabokov's Spectral Dimension* (Ann Arbor: Ardis, 1981), pp. 94–95, that it is the spirit of the recently deceased Uncle Pasha who inspires the narrator's actions here. Rowe may be correct, but there are numerous other occasions on which the narrator acts in a similarly precipitous manner.

13. Despite the swashbuckling nature of their fantasies, the two characters display physical attributes that are somewhat less dashing: both men are described as walking with "mincing" steps (cf. *D* 254 and *E* 104). In the Russian original, Dostoevsky uses the word *presemenivaia* (Dv 192); Nabokov uses the word *semenil* (S 82).

14. Smurov's feeble protest to Kashmarin—"There must be a misunderstanding . . . Surely, a misunderstanding" (*E* 12; S 13)—recalls Golyadkin's statement to a servant trying to remove him from Klara's party: "You must be mistaken, I'm sure" (D 181; Dv 136). Both men once again try futilely to deny responsibility for their behavior.

15. The narrator's perception perhaps echoes an observation made in another Dostoevsky work, the sketch "Bobok," which appeared in his *Diary of a Writer* (*Dnevnik pisatelia*) in the journal *Grazhdanin* in 1873. The narrator of that work overhears voices emanating from the dead lying buried in a cemetery, and one such voice explains: "life continues as if by inertia. Everything is concentrated . . . somewhere in the consciousness and continues on for two or three months" (F. M. Dostoevskii, *Polnoe sobranie sochinenii v tridtsati tomakh,* vol. XXI). The similarity between Dostoevsky's and Nabokov's phrasing is more evident in Russian. In *Sogliadatai* one reads: "chelovecheskaia mysl' prodolzhaet zhit' po inertsii" (*S* 19). In "Bobok" Dostoevsky writes: "prodolzhaetsia zhizn' kak by po inertsii."

16. An example of such vulnerability occurs when the narrator searches Vanya's room for a photograph of her and Smurov. Finding it, he discovers that Smurov's image has been cropped out. He comments: "Shattering evidence! On Vanya's lace-covered pillow there suddenly appeared . . . the violent imprint

of my fist, and in the next moment I was already in the dining room . . . still trembling" (*E* 62; *S* 50).

17. Julia Bader perceives the essence of such a dynamic when she discusses the function of doubles in Nabokov's work; in her view, the double "can . . . represent a self which is deliberately detached from the material world, a self which can be contemplated from an aesthetic distance." *The Crystal Land: Artifice in Nabokov's English Novels* (Berkeley: University of California Press, 1972), p. 137.

18. Konstantin Mochulsky, *Dostoevsky: His Life and Work*, trans. Michael A. Minihan (Princeton: Princeton University Press, 1971), p. 50.

19. One recalls V.'s observation near the end of the novel that: "the soul is but a manner of being—not a constant state—that any soul may be yours, if you find and follow its undulations." And in an echo of what the narrator of *The Eye* achieves following his suicide attempt V. here continues: "The hereafter may be the full ability of consciously living in any chosen soul, in any number of souls." Vladimir Nabokov, *The Real Life of Sebastian Knight* (New York: New Directions, 1959), p. 204.

20. Charles Kinbote asserts near the end of *Pale Fire:* "I shall continue to exist. I may assume other disguises, other forms, but I shall try to exist." Vladimir Nabokov, *Pale Fire* (New York: G. P. Putnam's Sons, 1980), p. 300.

21. The narrator's exclamations in *Notes from the Underground* range from the coaxing "I suffered, gentlemen, I assure you" to the swaggering "Calm yourselves, gentlemen, I did not receive a slap, even though I really don't care what you might think about it" to the overheated "I will tell the whole world straight to its face! I have the right to speak in this way, because I myself will live to be sixty. I will live to be seventy! I will live to be eighty! . . . Wait! Let me catch my breath. . . ." F. M. Dostoevskii, *Polnoe sobranie sochinenii v tridtsati tomakh*, vol. V., pp. 108, 105, 101; the translations are mine.

22. It was Dostoevsky's predilection for grim moments of exposed human pain and degradation that Nabokov found particularly excessive. An example of such a moment in *The Double* occurs when Golyadkin lacerates himself for his shortcomings. The narrator comments: "To bait himself, and in this way to rub salt in his wounds was at this moment for Mr. Golyadkin a kind of deep satisfaction, almost a voluptuous delight" (Dv 170; the translation is mine, but is based on a translation by Constance Garnett). Nabokov found this kind of Dostoevskian glorification of self-humiliation distasteful. As he notes in his *Lectures on Russian Literature:* "the way he has of wallowing in the tragic misadventures of human dignity—all this is difficult to admire" (104).

Alba Amoia (essay date 1993)

SOURCE: "*The Double* (1846)," in *Feodor Dostoevsky*, Continuum, 1993, pp. 149–56.

[*In the following essay, Amoia discusses the importance of the characterization in* The Double *in the development of Dostoevsky's subsequent works.*]

Some of Dostoevsky's most significant characterizations and themes are developed in his six short novels. Among them are the paranoiac split personality whose double materializes before his incredulous eyes; the decrepit dotard with his impossible marital dream; the "perfectly good man" confronted with the despotic hypocrite in the microcosmic village of Stepanchikovo; the unloved, unloving "underground man" in his miserable mouse hole; the gambler whose ardor and vitality are focused on the treacherous revolutions of a roulette wheel; and, lastly, the respectable "eternal husband" who finds himself inexorably linked with his eternal rival.

The Double, which was written immediately after **Poor Folk,** is the earliest and probably the best known of Dostoevsky's short novels, not only because of its intrinsic fascination but also because its central figure has lent itself inexhaustibly to caricature by graphic artists. The pathologically ambivalent hero, Mr. Yakov Petrovich Golyadkin, offers a reflection of Dostoevsky's own agitated self as he existed in the mid-1840s. Just before completing the story, in February 1846, Feodor had written to his brother Mikhail: "My health is terribly unstrung; my nerves are sick and I'm afraid of a nervous fever. . . . I can't live in an orderly way, I'm so dissolute" (*Letters*, I, 123).

Accentuating Dostoevsky's internal turbulence was a feeling of dismay about the implications of the rigid bureaucratic order then prevailing in St. Petersburg government offices—a stultifying hierarchical system that smothered any aspirations to bureaucratic or social advancement such as those imputed to the "hero" of his story. In this novel, he chose to employ the Gothic device of the supernatural double as a means of exploring the attitudes, toward himself and others, of an abnormally shy, paranoiac petty employee who is subject to delusions.[1]

In an inept rebellion against the prevailing bureaucratic social order, the "ambitious" but pitifully weak Mr. Golyadkin becomes a victim of acute guilt feelings, mental distress, and a breakdown of his own psyche. In striving to assert himself in the real world, he is brought face-to-face with himself in the conviction that he has actually become two people.[2] In reality a purely psychic phenomenon, his inseparable doppelgänger paces alongside him, indistinguishable from the real Golyadkin, although inevitably one of them must be displaced by the other.

To twentieth-century readers, the progression from the splitting of Golyadkin's personality to the appearance of his actual double seems masterfully handled, even though

Dostoevsky's contemporaries apparently had difficulty in determining whether the double was a hallucination or really existed side by side with Golyadkin himself.

As one who insists upon his own genuineness and sincerity and "wears a mask only at masked balls," Golyadkin has been tormented by a suppressed desire to distinguish himself socially, at the same time straining to conceal those aspects of his character that he himself is unwilling to acknowledge. There is a part of his own nature that he disapproves of, fears, and cannot bear to contemplate. He is, in fact, the perfect example of the type that Luigi Pirandello so admirably portrayed in *Naked Masks:* the character divided between what he would like others to believe about him and what he really is.

The opening of Dostoevsky's haunting story finds Mr. Golyadkin engaged in ludicrous preparations to make an appearance at the birthday party of a young lady named Clara Olsufyevna, the daughter of a high official who has been Golyadkin's "benefactor and patron" but has no idea of receiving him socially. Thus far, Golyadkin has been frustrated in his desire to make a good social impression, obtain a promotion, and sue for Clara Olsufyevna's hand. Yet he truly believes himself deserving of esteem and recognition, attributing his lack of success thus far not to personal incapacity but to persecution by members of his entourage.

To convey him to the festive event, Golyadkin procures a hired blue hackney carriage decorated with a heraldic device. Petrushka, the servant, is outfitted in old, oversized livery adorned with tarnished gold lace. Golyadkin's own formal clothing is carefully pressed and perfumed. On the way to the party, however, he becomes conscious of an irresistible need to visit his doctor, for the heroic deed he is about to perform has filled the timid man with justified trepidation.

Having concluded the medical visit, where his abnormal behavior has been duly noted by the bemused physician, Golyadkin proceeds to the birthday party but is immediately turned away by the butler, who has had orders not to admit him. Returning humiliated to his blue carriage, he feels an irrational desire "to sink through the ground or hide himself, together with his carriage, in a mouse hole" (151) in defiance of all the laws of physics—an anticipation of the "mouse hole" to be met again in *Notes from Underground.*

After gathering courage for a second, bolder attempt to gain admission, Golyadkin barges straight into the refreshment room, proceeds thence to the drawing room, where he finds himself face-to-face with Clara, and astonishes himself and the entire gathering by his eccentric behavior. Crimson with the realization that he could never hope to achieve any kind of "social status" in this high-toned milieu, he tries to behave as though the situation had nothing to do with him, as though he were not the person who is about to be ejected.

It is here that the reader may discern the psychological origins of the "double" who will shortly begin tormenting this unhappy and uninvited guest. Crushed like an "utter insect," Golyadkin is summarily excluded from the sumptuous fête and breaks into flight to escape his "enemies." And now the wretched Mr. Golyadkin "senior"—the original Mr. Golyadkin—taking leave of himself, involuntarily stands to one side to make room for the "junior" who suddenly looms up beside him.

Once the double has materialized, the reader is privileged to observe the lengthy process whereby Golyadkin finally recognizes the stranger as "none other than himself." Over the ensuing days, his "infamous twin" and ignominious rival gradually supplants the original Mr. Golyadkin both at home and in the office—even obtaining Clara's consent to an elopement. His double having thus demonstrated that the original Mr. Golyadkin was nothing but a counterfeit, the weak and trembling senior is left out in the cold, both physically and morally. "[A] mere mosquito, if one could have existed in such weather in St. Petersburg, could very easily have knocked him down with one of its wings" (249).

Devastated by these fateful events, Golyadkin in due course is carried off to an insane asylum while his double pursues the carriage with cries of farewell. Finally, Mr. Golyadkin sinks into total madness and unconsciousness—at which his double vanishes.

Although the original subtitle of the novel was *The Adventures of Mr. Golyadkin,* in a revised version of 1866 it was changed to *A Poem of St. Petersburg.* Indeed, **The Double** may be read as a dramatic poem unfolding in the streets of the capital, not unlike the "story of St. Petersburg" narrated in Pushkin's famous poem about a "little hero" who is pursued through the city's streets by the statue of the "Bronze Horseman," Peter the Great.

Matching the main characters in Dostoevsky's "poem" are its two principal scenes of action, the one real and familiar, the other ideal and fanciful: the dirty green, smoke-begrimed, dusty domain of the downtrodden Golyadkin, and, in sharpest contrast, the fashionable drawing room of a Petersburg privy councillor, the ambiance to which he aspires but where he cannot realistically hope for acceptance.

The "real" place and time are established in Dostoevsky's opening sentence. In his bed at 8 A.M., the simple, uncomplicated Yakov Petrovich Golyadkin—who is, after all, a familiar Petersburg type—wakes from the slumber of the satisfied: a "sleepy, short-sighted, rather bald figure . . . of such insignificant character that nobody at all would have found it in the least remarkable." Scrutinizing himself in his mirror, the owner of the figure was "evidently quite satisfied with all he saw there" (127). The mirror will continue to play tricks on Mr. Golyadkin, projecting its reflection onto doorways that the hero will mistake for mirrors because his double is bewilderingly standing in them.

Mr. Golyadkin's awakening places the reader in the midst of one of Dostoevsky's typical evocations of the Petersburg scene, in which the city and its attributes are repeatedly personified. "[T]he dull, dirty, gray autumn day peered into the room at him through the cloudy windowpanes with a grimace so sour and bad-tempered that Mr. Golyadkin could no longer have the slightest doubt: he was not in some far-distant realm but in the capital" (127). Having duly peered into this gray soup, Mr. Golyadkin regales himself with an assortment of colors—actually a description of some ruble notes—in which lurks another personification. A shabby green wallet extracted from under some old yellowed papers reveals a "packet of green, gray, blue, red and rainbow-colored paper . . . [which] seemed to look back at Mr. Golyadkin in a friendly and approving fashion" (128).

A third personification is embodied in the samovar, which "was now raging and hissing fiercely, almost beside itself with anger and threatening to boil over any minute, gabbling away in its strange gibberish, lisping and babbling" (128–29). Complementary to the samovar is the comic figure of the servant, Petrushka, with his silly smile and ill-fitting livery, holding a gold-laced hat trimmed with green feathers and armed with a lackey's sword in a leather scabbard.

Mr. Golyadkin's good spirits quickly desert him as his hired carriage clatters, jingles, and creaks toward the home of Clara's father. Over his face comes a strangely anxious expression. He squeezes into the darkest corner of the hackney, for he has been espied by two young clerks who work in the same government department. They impudently point at him and loudly call him by name, to the chagrin of Golyadkin, who tries always to present himself with dignity and good breeding.

When Mr. Golyadkin's own department head catches sight of him from another carriage and stares incredulously, Golyadkin blushes to the roots of his hair, tormented all the while by nagging uncertainties about how he should conduct himself, whether he should pretend he is not himself but someone who looks strikingly like him, etc. The psychological roots of his "double" experience are already beginning to implant themselves in Mr. Golyadkin's mind. Before determining to speak to his doctor, he changes course several times or does just the opposite of what he intends—behavior that parallels the social ineptitude that is manifested in muttered words, vacuous smiles, blushes, and confusion ending in eloquent silence.

Like Dostoevsky himself, Golyadkin really prefers peace and quiet to the fashionable hubbub; he loathes gossip and scandalmongering. But even while reaffirming his social values in his conversation with the doctor, he is undergoing a strange transformation: "His gray eyes had a curious shine, his lips twitched, every muscle and every feature of his face seemed to be in fluid motion. He was shaking from head to foot. . . . His lips trembled, his chin quivered, and our hero unexpectedly burst into tears." "I have

bitter enemies who have sworn to ruin me," he tells the doctor in a frightened whisper (138–39).

His fears proliferate in opulent literary imagery as Mr. Golyadkin makes his successive approaches to the privy councillor's residence. On the first sally, he gains an impression that "everything whatever in Olsufi Ivanovich's house was staring at him through the windows" (personification), and he knows that "if he turned round he would die on the spot" (hyperbole) (151). At his second attempt to gain entrance, he oscillates between running like a rabbit (simile) and barging straight in.

Having once chosen the latter course, in a scene of pathetic humor he invites Clara to dance, sways, raises a leg, executes a kind of shuffle, then a kind of stamp, then stumbles (164). His next sensation is that of his overcoat being put on him and his hat pulled down over his eyes. Mr. Golyadkin is being reduced to a grotesque puppet costumed for the stage, passing down the dark stairs and into the cold courtyard, where he breaks into flight to escape the hail of social opprobrium, the shrieks of alarmed old women, the gasps and exclamations of the ladies, and his own chief's annihilating stare.

Nothing could be more dramatic than this humiliated man's attempts to run away from himself, hide from himself, free himself of the creature that is now gestating within him and seeking delivery at the cost of so much psychic pain.

> He stopped dead in the middle of the pavement and stood there motionless as though turned to stone; in those moments he died and disappeared off the face of the earth; then suddenly he would tear himself away from the spot like a madman and run, run without a backward glance, as though trying to escape from some pursuit or an even more horrible disaster. . . . Suddenly his whole body quivered, and involuntarily he leaped to one side. . . . It seemed to him that just now . . . somebody had been standing there, close to him, by his side . . . and—an extraordinary thing!—had even said something to him, something . . . not altogether understandable.
>
> (167)

Was it the wind's complaint? "The wind seemed to wail its long-drawn-out lament still more dolefully and drearily, like an importunate beggar whining for a copper coin" (168). The rainy, snowy November night churns around him in images that complement the personification of the grimacing, bad-tempered day in the opening chapter:

> It was a terrible night. . . . The wind howled in the empty streets, whipping the black water of the Fontanka higher than the mooring-rings . . . which in their turn echoed its wailing with the thin piercing squeak that makes up the endless whining, creaking concert so familiar to every inhabitant of St. Petersburg. . . . Jets of rainwater, broken off by the wind, prick[ed] and cut the wretched Mr. Golyadkin's face like thousands of pins and needles. In the nocturnal quiet, broken only

by the distant rumble of coaches, the howl of the wind and the squeaking of the swinging street lamps, the splash and murmur of the water running from every roof, porch, gutter, and cornice on to the granite flags of the pavement had a dismal sound.

(165–66)

As the wind, the rain, and the river continue their mockery, the wretched Mr. Golyadkin turns sharply to look at the stranger who has just passed him: "He turned about as though he had been twitched from behind, or as though the wind had whirled him round like a weathercock" (169).

The long, suspenseful drama of this meeting on a St. Petersburg street is temporarily resolved as Golyadkin falls into unconsciousness and awakens in his bed at eight the following morning, a mirror image of the novel's opening sentence. Henceforth, his portrait will be a double one, for there are now two persons in the dingy green room. "[T]he man now sitting opposite Mr. Golyadkin was Mr. Golyadkin's horror, he was Golyadkin's shame, he was Mr. Golyadkin's nightmare . . . ; in short, he was Mr. Golyadkin himself [and] nobody would have taken it on himself to say which was the old and which the new, which was the original and which the copy" (177).

Mr. Golyadkin's new guest at first exhibits familiar pangs of conscience and guilt feelings that actually elicit an upsurge of sympathy on the part of his involuntary host. Reluctant to try to evict the intruder by force, Mr. Golyadkin senior searches for "the politest way of showing the scoundrel the door"; but then, surprisingly, the meek, submissive double turns into a rude hypocrite, for he, too, has a split personality! To the confused Golyadkin, it appears that "people wearing masks have ceased to be a rarity . . . and . . . it is difficult nowadays to recognize the man under the mask" (199).

Shaken by his double's outlandish behavior, Golyadkin spends many a miserable night as the imagined victim of a universal conspiracy. Even his medicine is personified as an enemy: "The dark, reddish, disgusting-looking liquid shone with a evil gleam in Mr. Golyadkin's eyes." His nightmares feature "a certain person renowned for his ugliness and his satirical propensities," or "a certain person notorious for his disloyalty and swinish impulses." Armies of doubles haunt his dreams, "stretching out in a long file like a string of geese."

The double, meanwhile, has taken possession of Golyadkin's desk at the office and is doing excellent work, surpassing the highest expectations of his department head. His colleagues clearly prefer the new Golyadkin to the old one, and Mr. Golyadkin senior now realizes how foolish he has been in allowing himself to be used "as a doormat for people to wipe their dirty boots on." Yet in reproaching himself for his own baseness and cowardice, he feels "a kind of profound, indeed almost voluptuous satisfaction" (209)—a foretaste of the masochism described in such later works as *Notes from Underground* and *The Eternal Husband.*

The denouement of the story finds Mr. Golyadkin once again on a Petersburg street. "The weather was abominable: there had been a thaw, snow was falling thickly and it was raining as well—everything exactly as it was in the middle of that terrible, never-to-be-forgotten night when all Mr. Golyadkin's troubles had begun" (266). Once again, the mirror is held up to reflect two similar nights; and this, in turn, will be followed by still another mirror image.

Before being bundled off to the mental asylum, the sodden Mr. Golyadkin huddles for hours in Olsufi Ivanovich's courtyard awaiting the signal from Clara—who is now to elope with his double—while groups of people peer out of the windows at him. "Our hero would most gladly have crept then and there into some little mouse hole among the logs and crouched there in peace"—the same little mouse hole into which he would have liked to disappear with his hired carriage earlier in the story. Once again, the reader previews the melancholy domain of Dostoevsky's "underground man" in *Notes from Underground.*

The Double disappointed its readers when it appeared on the heels of *Poor Folk* in 1846, and Dostoevsky was dismayed by its poor reception after his assurances to Mikhail that it was "turning out superbly" and would be his "chef d'oeuvre" (*Letters,* I, 118). Playing with his character while the work was still in progress, he had cheerfully reported: "*Yakov Petrovich Golyadkin* is standing quite firm in character. A horrible scoundrel, he's unapproachable; refuses to move ahead at all, claiming that after all, he's not yet ready and that he's fine for the meanwhile just as things are. . . . He absolutely refuses to finish his career earlier than mid-November. . . . And he's putting me, his creator, in an extremely bad situation" (*Letters,* I, 113–14).

But by April 1846, after publication, the author writes: "Dear brother . . . everyone is displeased with me for Golyadkin" (*Letters,* I, 124). In fact, this experiment in the domain of the pathologically grotesque had been fully successful neither in style nor in characterization. It was, perhaps, too derivative and at the same time too original to be fully appreciated in its own era. Yet it has since been pointed out that, over and above its considerable literary merit, some of its episodes read almost like extracts from the classic studies of schizophrenia written half a century later.[3]

Notes

1. Ibid., 46–51.

2. There are many well-known archetypal figures of the double in world literature. Less familiar than the creations of E. T. A. Hoffmann, Gogol, and Poe, but closer to Dostoevsky's ambiance is the contribution of the Polish writer, Jan Potocki (1761–1815), who had held a diplomatic position in St. Petersburg. The theme of the double permeates the pages of his fantastic novel, *Manuscript Found at Saragossa* (written from ca. 1797–1815). Cf. *Manoscritto trovato a Saragozza* (Parma: Guanda, 1990).

3. Jessie Coulson, introduction to *Notes from Underground/The Double* (Harmondsworth: Penguin Books, 1972), 8.

Gary Rosenshield (essay date 1996)

SOURCE: "The Bronze Horseman and *The Double*: The Depoeticization of the Myth of Petersburg in the Young Dostoevskii," in *Slavic Review,* Vol. 55, Summer, 1996, pp. 399–428.

[*In the following essay, Rosenshield discusses Dostoevsky's role in the development of the nineteenth-century myth of Petersburg, as well as its representation in* The Double.]

In his discussion of *The Double,* Joseph Frank remarks that Dostoevskii's decision to change the original subtitle from *The Adventures of Mr. Goliadkin* (Prikliucheniia Gospodina Goliadkina) to *A Petersburg Poem* (Petersburgskaia poema) had, among other things, the "advantage of correctly assigning *The Double* its place in the Russian literary tradition initiated by *The Bronze Horseman.*"[1] If *The Double* is truly in the Petersburg tradition of *The Bronze Horseman,* it is curious that no one has studied the relationship between these works, each of which features a minor civil servant (*chinovnik*) who goes mad. The few comparative analyses of the Petersburg theme in Pushkin and Dostoevskii have invariably focused on the more obvious relationships between *The Queen of Spades* and *Crime and Punishment.*[2] Scholars have often compared *The Double* with other works—for example, the tales of E. T. A. Hoffmann[3] and Gogol's "Notes of a Madman," "The Nose," and *Dead Souls*[4] but not with those of Pushkin.

But, as I hope to show, *The Double* polemically engages *The Bronze Horseman* on the crucial question of Peter and his legacy in a way that distinguishes Dostoevskii's work, not only from other treatments of the Petersburg theme in Russian literature, but in some ways from Dostoevskii's later formulations as well. However ambivalently and ambiguously Pushkin presents Peter, Peter's legacy and the chinovnik hero, Evgenii, he poeticizes and mythologizes them throughout: he bathes them in his most moving poetry, incorporating them in a mythological universe in which empire and individual are inextricably bound. In his later works, Dostoevskii completely inverts the adulatory mythology that dominated the portrayal of Petersburg before Pushkin. But by demonizing his subject, he ultimately remythologizes—and repoeticizes—it. In *The Double,* however, Dostoevskii engages in a far more radical operation: he completely depoeticizes and demythologizes Peter, Peter's legacy, and Peter's victims, emptying his subject—in a sort of negative kenosis—of all mythological and sacred significance. Though no external evidence shows that *The Double* consciously engages *The Bronze Horseman* in a polemic over the significance of Peter the Great, I shall argue that we can best illuminate the rela-

tionship of these works by examining *The Double* as an implicit response to Pushkin's *The Bronze Horseman.*

In the first section of this [essay] I briefly discuss the nineteenth-century myth of Petersburg and Pushkin's and Dostoevskii's role in its formation. I then demonstrate *The Double*'s close thematic, narratological, and linguistic relationship—however parodic—to *The Bronze Horseman:* a relationship ultimately more profound than *The Double*'s ties to any of Gogol's works. The next section examines *The Double*'s relentless depreciation and depoeticization of Pushkin's Peter the Great—his figure, legacy, and vision—from the representation of the bureaucracy to the complete effacement of the tsar's image and mission from the Petersburg text. Finally, I show Dostoevskii's concomitant depoeticization of the Petersburg clerk through his parodic and sardonic treatment of the "hero's" love life, madness, and rebellion. *The Double* is not only unrelieved by the positive religious agenda of Dostoevskii's later work; it is as bereft as any twentieth-century text of the sacred and the heroic.

THE PETERSBURG MYTH

N. P. Antsiferov and Wacław Lednicki have shown that the image of Petersburg in Russian literature before Pushkin was essentially positive.[5] Peter was portrayed not as a spirit alien to Russian life, history, and culture but as the founder and creator of a holy city (*khram*), a northern Rome (Venice, Palmyra) that would replace its southern sister (Moscow). Petr Viazemskii described Peter as a god who created order (Petersburg) out of the primordial chaos (the Finnish bog). For eighteenth-century poets, Petersburg became a symbol of Russia's imperialistic mission, its new place among the nations, and its full entry into European civilization and history. Man, nature, and art existed in Petersburg in magnificent, though simple, peace and harmony.

Pushkin, as Antsiferov asserts, was the last bard to sing this bright side of Petersburg, the image of which became more somber with each passing year.[6] In the introductory ode (*Vstuplenie*) of *The Bronze Horseman,* the poet-persona brilliantly eulogizes the city, a symbol of Peter's far-seeing vision and idea (*Stoial on, dum velikikh poln/i vdal' gliadel,* 2-3). He loves its military might[7] and its mastery of the elements[8] no less than its beauty,[9] harmony,[10] space,[11] light,[12] sound,[13] and vitality.[14] He even loves its cruel winter (*zima tvoia zhestokaia,* 59). Further, he contrasts the city's present splendor, prowess, and fame with its dark, backward, ahistorical past, when it was surrounded by impenetrable forests and inhabited by poor Finnish fishermen.[15]

The second half of the poem is cast in an entirely different mode. The end of the Introduction announces a horrible time (*uzhasnaia pora*) and a sad story (*pechalen budet moi rasskaz*); in the first line of the narrative proper, Petersburg is darkened (*omrachennyi*) by an approaching storm. The *povest'* sympathetically portrays a hapless man

(Evgenii) who loses his beloved and goes mad as a result of the flood of 1824. He is presented as an innocent victim of the tsar's imperialistic ambitions and nature's terrible wrath. The words for horror, fury, gloom, darkness, and sadness dominate the entire narrative. Emphasizing the horrible sacrifices visited on the population by Peter's imperialistic visions, Pushkin introduces into the Petersburg text a new, foreboding element.

Although Pushkin opened the door (*prorubil okno,* as it were) for later authors to write more negatively about Petersburg, he did not determine the image. Gogol, Dostoevskii, Tolstoi, and Belyi had their own reasons for detesting the city. Nor did Pushkin repudiate Peter and his idea. *The Bronze Horseman* presents both Peter and Evgenii ambiguously and ambivalently. The rights of the state versus those of the individual are fundamentally irreconcilable, and however moved the narrator may be by the plight of his hero, he recognizes the necessity of Peter's mission and its attendant sacrifices. More important, he does not diminish the stature of his protagonists. Peter remains a larger, even more imposing figure, precisely because of his tyranny; Evgenii gains our sympathies as he begins to understand, through suffering and madness, the relationship between Peter's vision and his own unhappy fate; nature is tamed once more, but only temporarily. The protagonists all assume a larger role in Pushkin's mythic text; they are all elevated through the goddess of poetry. Any serious reduction of the protagonists would undercut the irresolvable and tragic tension that endows *The Bronze Horseman* with its tremendous power and suggestiveness.

Vladimir Toporov[16] maintains that the polar tensions between life and death, salvation and despair, light and darkness (like the dozens of antinomies discovered by generations of scholars)[17] define the Petersburg myth in Russian literature. But his synchronic definition of the Petersburg myth—which he implicitly bases on the Pushkinian text—reflects a clear pro-Petersburg agenda, a desire to see real hope for Russia—including contemporary Russia—in the slightest sign of light, harmony, or life in the anti-Petersburg text of writers like Dostoevskii, Tolstoi, and Belyi: "Petersburg mozhet okazat'sia nashim blizhaishim i nadezhneishim resursom, esli tol'ko my okazhemsia dostoinymi togo vechnogo i blagogo v nem, chto otkryto nam Petersburgskim tekstom" (223).[18] Rather, it is more often said that the essence of the Petersburg text reaches its apotheosis in Dostoevskii, specifically in *Crime and Punishment,* which Donald Fanger has called Dostoevskii's "greatest Petersburg work," the foundation for any poetics of the modern city.[19] But the myth of Petersburg in the mature Dostoevskii differs not only from Pushkin's mythic presentations but also from his own more radical treatment of the myth in *The Double.*

The dark vision of Petersburg in Dostoevskii's later work derives from Dostoevskii's Slavophile-Pochvennik agenda, with its rejection of much of Peter's legacy and its revulsion at the ills of the modern metropolis. For Dostoevskii, Petersburg is a city of dismal, dirty, cramped slums, rav-

aged by unemployment, alcoholism, and crime—a new Babylon, a window through which western evil continues to enter and poison the Russian land. According to the Underground Man, it is also the most rational and abstract place on earth. Even more, it is the most fantastic, insubstantial, alien (un-Russian), and unnatural of Russian cities: a city fated, one day, to dissipate with the fog.[20]

But in *Crime and Punishment* Dostoevskii does not so much demythologize as remythologize Peter. Peter and his city loom no less large in the mature Dostoevskii than they do in *The Bronze Horseman;* they are just negatively reproblematized—and demonized. The hero of *Crime and Punishment* is no Goliadkin, but a rational intellectual who dreams of becoming a world historical figure, a great man (*velikii chelovek*), a Napoleon who can in good conscience sacrifice thousands of human beings to achieve his mission—in other words, a nineteenth-century Peter the Great. For the late Dostoevskii, as for Pushkin in *The Bronze Horseman,* Peter the Great is still all too alive in his city; he is still inextricably tied up with Russia's destiny. In the epilogue of *Crime and Punishment,* Peter's legacy is represented in apocalyptic terms: men possessed of will and intelligence engage in internecine warfare that nearly results in the destruction of the human race.

Both the animus and apocalypticism associated with Peter and Petersburg are reflected in the few references that Dostoevskii later made to *The Bronze Horseman,* particularly in his nonfictional writings. Most of these references, alluding to line 16 of *The Bronze Horseman* (*V Evropu prorubit' okno*), are derogatory: some even paraphrase line 16 as *prorublennoe v Evropu okoshko* (*PSS,* 23:358). Dostoevskii presents the *okno/okoshko* not as Russia's window to Europe, but as a hole (*dyr'ia*) through which much that was bad (*durno*) and harmful (*vredno*) entered Russia, and he characterizes Petersburg as a Finnish bog (*chukhonskoe boloto*) separating the educated classes from the people. In an 1862 article, Dostoevskii writes that the reforms introduced German bureaucracy (officialdom—*chinovnichestvo*) into Russia and initiated the most horrible corruption of morals.[21] In the notes for a section of *A Diary of a Writer* for 1876, Dostoevskii, referring to Pushkin's lines, "Liubliu tebia, Petra tvoren'e," confesses: "Vinovat, ne liubliu ego" (*PSS,* 27:62).

Only two references in Dostoevskii's work mention the actual monument, the bronze horseman. In *A Raw Youth,* the narrator describes the city as a mirage that will disappear into thin air with the lifting fog. After the city disappears, only two things will remain: the Finnish swamp and, in the middle of it, "dlia krasy, bronzovyi vsadnik na zharko dyshashchem, zagnannom kone" (*PSS,* 13:113).[22] In the note to *A Diary of a Writer* mentioned above, Dostoevskii describes a Petersburg abandoned except for Germans, dilapidated buildings, and, in the middle of it all, Peter's monument (*pamiatnik Petra*).[23]

Though we have some confirmation that in 1862, four years before his revision of *The Double,* Dostoevskii still viewed bureaucracy as one of the most baleful results of Peter's reforms, the main note struck in almost all the above references is not bureaucracy, but the alienness, unreality, and *ephemerality* of Peter's reforms, city, and legacy. Further, prophesying the end of the Petersburg period of Russian history, Dostoevskii writes that among the few things left standing in the final days will be the monument to Peter. But now it will not be a Peter looking at the glory of his accomplishments and an even more glorious future, but a Peter surveying the ruins of his greatly mistaken venture, his sorry steed gasping and overdriven. But Peter remains great in his defeat, even as he overlooks the ruins of his mighty vision. Thus, in Dostoevskii's later work, the negative image of the Bronze Horseman continues to highlight Peter's tremendous role in Russian history—albeit a role that has played itself out. In contrast to Pushkin, Dostoevskii looks upon Petersburg's disappearance as the realization of Russia's highest destiny. But this apocalyptic optimism differs fundamentally from the pessimistic view of Petersburg that Dostoevskii creates in *The Double,* in which Peter's image and legacy are debunked and the common man—the chinovnik—is reduced to a reflection of his own nonbeing.

CORRESPONDENCES

Both *The Bronze Horseman* and *The Double* tell a story of aborted love resulting in the insanity of the chinovnik hero. At the end of *The Bronze Horseman,* Evgenii is found dead on one of the islands devastated in the flood of 1824; in *The Double,* the incurably insane Goliadkin is taken away to an asylum, where he will probably spend the rest of his life. The "love" plot in each work is divided into three parts, each developing the progressive derangement of the hero as he faces his unhappy fate. In the first episode of *The Bronze Horseman,* the flood forces Evgenii to take refuge on one of the marble lions. He is terrified not so much by his own precarious situation as by his fears for his fiancée Parasha, who lives in a flooded part of the city that was severely battered by the storm. As soon as the storm has considerably subsided, Evgenii braves the Neva to find Parasha; but his worst fears are confirmed: the storm has carried away his fiancée and her mother. He goes mad (*zakhokhotal,* 323).[24] But this episode does not denote a complete transformation from sanity to madness. Rather, it culminates a process begun when Evgenii first sat astride the marble lion amidst the flood. Evgenii enters the third and last stage of his derangement when he threatens the statue of Peter in word and gesture and then imagines the statue pursuing him all night through the streets of Petersburg. Not long after he is found dead on an island to which he very likely had fled in fear of the Bronze Horseman.

The story of Dostoevskii's Goliadkin bears several striking structural resemblances—though ironically refracted—to the story of Pushkin's Evgenii. From the very beginning of *The Double,* Goliadkin is suffering from severe psychological problems, both from a strained relationship with Karolina Ivanovna (she seems to have made some threat

against him), and from an unsuccessful attempt to court Klara Olsuf'evna, the daughter of his former superior, from whose house he has been barred. He has also just visited a doctor about his illness. Despite the apparent hopelessness of his situation, Goliadkin, in the second of his adventures, makes an abortive attempt to win Klara over by "crashing" her birthday party, from which he is forcibly and humiliatingly ejected. Returning home from the party, "he cracks"; he sees for the first time the double that will haunt him to the end of the novel.[25] As in *The Bronze Horseman,* the third episode shows the hero in the final stage of madness. He returns to the scene of his final humiliations (just as Evgenii finds himself for the third time by the marble lions and the Bronze Horseman) in an attempt to abduct Klara. When he is taken away this time, he is raving.

Each work, then, consists of three main episodes in which the hero becomes increasingly deranged—mutatis mutandis—as a result of his growing awareness of, and responsibility for, the loss of his beloved. Evgenii makes a valiant effort to visit Parasha as soon as the flood subsides; Goliadkin makes several attempts to "rescue" Klara, including a plan to elope with or abduct her. But there are even more striking parallels. Several aspects of the flood push Evgenii toward madness: his imagination of its ravages (episode one), its actual ravages (episode two), his thoughts about the one responsible for its ravages (episode three). In addition to the fury of the flood, in the second episode Pushkin emphasizes the gloomy, autumnal cold of November, the nocturnal darkness, and the plaintive wailing of the winds. Nouns and epithets of darkness, gloom, and horror (*mrak, t'ma, mgla, mrachnyi, unylyi,* and *uzhasnyi*) dominate the atmosphere of the poem proper; all perfectly accord with the madness that is soon to descend upon the hero as inexorably as the flood itself.[26]

It is precisely on such a night that Goliadkin, in the second main episode, loses Klara Olsuf'evna.

> It was a horrible [*uzhasnaia*] November night—damp, foggy, rainy, snowy, teeming with swollen faces, colds in the head, fevers, quinsies, ailments of all kinds and descriptions: that is to say, with all the gifts of a Petersburg November. The wind howled in the deserted streets, lifting up the black water of the Fontanka canal above the rings on the bank, and fitfully brushing against the lean lampposts which echoed its howling in a thin, shrill creak, constituting, as it were, an endless squeaky, jangling concert so familiar to every resident of Petersburg.[27]

> (509; 1:138)

After being ejected from Klara's birthday party, Goliadkin "suddenly set off again like mad and ran and ran without looking back, as though he were pursued, as though he were fleeing from some still more awful calamity. His situation was, indeed, horrible [*uzhasnoe*]" (510; 1:139).[28] Goliadkin, bemoaning the terrible weather, asks himself "whether there is going to be a flood" (*ne budet li navodneniia,* 512; 1:140); he thinks the water has risen so violently. At this moment Goliadkin meets not the Bronze Horseman but something far more frightening: himself, his double. Just like Evgenii (404), Goliadkin shudders (*On vzdrognul*, 1:141) after he hears "steps" behind him: "Suddenly through the howling of the wind and the uproar of the storm, the sound of steps very close at hand reached his ears again. He started and opened up his eyes" (512 1:141). We should not be surprised that he does not hear a *tiazhelo zvonkoe skakan'e* for, after all, it is Goliadkin's double, not Peter. But like Evgenii, he soon begins to run. Here Dostoevskii echoes almost exactly the text of *The Bronze Horseman* at perhaps the most critical point in Evgenii's story—immediately after he threatens the monument: Evgenii *vdrug stremglav / Bezhat' pustilsia* (438–39); Goliadkin *vdrug pustilsia bezhat' bez ogliadki* (1:142).

Although not quite so severe, the weather on the second crucial night (596; 1:213), just as in *The Bronze Horseman*, closely resembles that of the first night.[29] It is enough to remind Evgenii of the night of the flood, and to make Goliadkin imagine that he is now being pursued through the streets of Petersburg by innumerable copies of himself. After his confrontation with Peter, Evgenii spends his days wandering around the city. Likewise, Goliadkin spends his last day at large wandering around town, confused, disheveled, bedraggled, and deranged. When he is finally taken to the asylum, he is a completely broken man, hardly more alive than Evgenii's cold corpse at the end of *The Bronze Horseman*.[30]

PETER

Dostoevskii uses these structural similarities and verbal echoes—and they are quite significant—not to show his affinity with Pushkin, but rather to establish his source and then to dramatize the differences between his vision of Peter and Petersburg and Pushkin's. In *The Double*, Dostoevskii neither explores Pushkin's ambiguities nor emphasizes the tragic sacrifices made by the city's—and the country's—inhabitants in the service of Peter's mission; rather he consistently deflates Peter's image, legacy, and vision by emptying them of their grandeur and aura.

In *The Double*, Dostoevskii does not formulate the problem of Petersburg religiously, nor does he offer an apocalyptic solution based on Russia's path or potential for salvation.[31] The legacy of Peter has not been and will not be superseded because there is no longer anything monumental, substantial, or historically significant to be superseded. Aside from the inclement weather associated with the flood, Dostoevskii shows little, if any, of Pushkin's Petersburg. Pushkin's "Liubliu tebia, Petra tvoren'e," his magnificent paean of Peter and Petersburg in the Vstuplenie, is completely absent from *The Double*. Further, Dostoevskii reproduces almost none of Petersburg's grandeur, beauty, and dynamism: we see neither the white nights of summer nor the pinching frosts of winter, for his aim in his only "poem"[32] is to depoeticize his subject.[33] Whereas Evgenii ventures outside to the city's great squares and monuments—especially to the marble lions and the monument

of Peter—Goliadkin confines most of his activities to his dingy, dirty apartment in Shestilavochnaia Lane; we see only the insides of a few shops, restaurants, apartments, and offices. The Bronze Horseman is conspicuous in its absence from *The Double*, which includes not a single reference to the Falconet statue. The only praise of Petersburg in *The Double* comes from the lips of a mimicked Goliadkin. In one of his conversations with himself, Goliadkin Senior entertains his double, Goliadkin Junior, with anecdotes about the glories of the capital—an indiscriminate mélange, at best—concluding with readings from Baron Bambreus. Goliadkin cites the iron railing of the Summer Garden as Petersburg's greatest architectural attraction.

> When in good spirits, Mr. Goliadkin was sometimes fond of telling an interesting anecdote. Being now in such spirits, he told the visitor a great deal about the capital, about its entertainments and attractions, about the theater, the clubs, about Brülov's picture, and about the two Englishmen who came from England to Petersburg just to look at the iron railing of the Summer Garden, and then immediately returned home; about the office; about Olsufii Ivanovich and Andrei Filippovich; about the way that Russia was progressing, hour by hour, toward perfection; that "Arts and Letters flourish here today"; about an anecdote he had recently read in the *Northern Bee* concerning a boa-constrictor in India of extraordinary strength; about Baron Bambreus, and so on and so forth.
>
> (531; 1:156–57)

Both in the imagination of the poet in the panegyrical Introduction and in the imagination of the "insignificant" civil servant, Evgenii,[34] Peter the Great dominates *The Bronze Horseman*, whether he embodies Russian manifest destiny—that is, history itself[35]—or reveals himself to be a tyrant with little regard for human life.[36] Neither of these Peters appears in *The Double*.[37] Civil servants of the fifth and sixth rank, which seem infinitely above his own ninth rank, rule Goliadkin's world.[38] If Peter exists for Iakov *Petrovich* Goliadkin, for this "son of Peter," he takes the form of His Excellency, whom Goliadkin sees as the ultimate representative of the government, and therefore as his true father. The narrator, however, treats all these civil servants—especially their presence at Klara Olsuf'evna's birthday party—with mock-heroic irony.

> Oh, if I were a poet! of course, I mean, like Homer or Pushkin; with any lesser talent one would not venture; . . . I would describe for you . . . how the father Olsufii Ivanovich, a hale-looking old man and a state councilor, who had lost the use of his legs in his long years of service and been rewarded by fate for his zeal with investments, a modest house, some small estates, and a beautiful daughter, began to sob like a child and announced through his tears that His Excellency was a beneficent man.
>
> (499; 1:128–29)

The Double singles out these officials because it treats Peter primarily through his successors (the Russian officials described above) and his legacy (the bureaucratic order). Moreover, these officials hardly play the same role in Goliadkin's imagination as Peter does in Evgenii's. His Excellency does not emerge as a world historical personality, a "mighty figure," as Hegel described the type, who "must trample down many an innocent flower and crush to pieces many things in its path."[39] Peter's descendants, the department heads and His Excellencies do not ride horses over the abyss; they do not command armies and navies to realize Russia's manifest destiny: they walk from one office to another, commanding at best a detail of timorous civil servants.

Dostoevskii focuses most of all on Peter's true legacy, the bureaucracy, an institution that receives little attention in *The Bronze Horseman*. While Pushkin focuses on the cataclysmic events of the flood and the dramatic confrontation between his antagonists, Dostoevskii underscores the prosaic and undramatic: the bureaucratic "adventures" of a minor copy-clerk. *The Bronze Horseman* says little about Evgenii's work other than that he serves as a clerk in some unnamed ministry (*gde-to sluzhit*, 119). His position is not the most important thing in his life; it does not define him. Rather he dreams of family, independence, and a life out of Peter's—that is, out of harm's—way. On the other hand, Goliadkin's position in the bureaucracy constitutes his entire existence. A tragic dualism dominates Pushkin's world, in which the antagonists are separated by an unbridgeable gulf. A far more frightening monism rules the world of *The Double*; Goliadkin's main enemy turns out to be himself.

The tragic conflict in *The Bronze Horseman* is conveyed in binary oppositions;[40] it arises not from lack of definition, but from the sharp dividing lines that make impossible a reconciling Hegelian synthesis in which, in the end, the history of the world "represents the rationally necessary course of the World Spirit."[41] In the clairvoyance of madness, Evgenii understands the irreconcilability of the rights of the individual and the rights of the state. In *The Double*, however, the old lines have been effaced by the bureaucratic order. Goliadkin's position in the bureaucracy—and therefore, his very existence—is threatened, not by a great adversary, but by an alter ego who is even more petty, crass, and insignificant than he is.

The Double reduces Peter even in its representation of the clerk's fear. Evgenii is terrified of Peter the Great; he has the image of his monumental enemy indelibly stamped on his consciousness: he magnifies the figure of Peter in his crazed imagination. Goliadkin fears not only that others—his betters—can replace him, but that virtually anyone can replace him at any time, for he differs from others in no essential way. Most of all, he fears himself: he reduces his enemy to multiple, interchangeable debased images of himself, projections of his own self-hatred.

> Beside himself with shame and despair, the utterly ruined though perfectly just Mr. Goliadkin dashed headlong, at the whim of fate, but with every step, with every thud of his foot on the granite of the pavement,

there would leap up as though from beneath the earth an exactly identical Mr. Goliadkin, perfectly alike, and of a revolting depravity of heart. And all these perfectly similar Goliadkins immediately upon their appearance set to running after one another in a long chain, like a file of geese, hobbling after the real Mr. Goliadkin, so there was nowhere to escape from these perfect duplicates—so that Mr. Goliadkin, who was in every way deserving of compassion, was breathless with terror; so that at last a terrible multitude of perfect duplicates had sprung into being; so that the whole town was obstructed at last by duplicate Goliadkins, and a police officer, seeing such a breach of decorum, was obliged to seize all these perfect duplicates by the collar and to put them into the sentry box, which happened to be beside him.

(566; 1:186–87)

Dostoevskii presents the vision of the infinitely multiplying Goliadkins as horrible, but also as painfully prosaic. It takes but one police officer (a Peter seems unnecessary) to grab and place Goliadkin's doubles—more like a herd of geese than demons—in a space no larger than a policeman's watch-house. They seem to be a threat only to themselves.

For Pushkin, Peter still lives, "his will remains alive in the city";[42] for Evgenii, Peter is also alive. His greatness continues to live on as an integral part of the consciousness of all Russian subjects: the poet in *The Bronze Horseman* is no less a son of Peter's than Evgenii is. The tragic exists in Petersburg only because Peter, the spirit of Russian imperialistic history, is still destroying those who stand in his way. The dominating presence of the Bronze Horseman, the amplification of Peter in Evgenii's mind, and all Peter's antagonists—the rage of wind, rain, flood and sea engender a monumental Peter. In Dostoevskii's demythologized representation of the city, Peter lives—or rather survives—only through an aborted legacy, a soulless bureaucracy that parodies, if not mocks, his vain ambitions. *The Double*, thus, stands in a kenotic relationship to *The Bronze Horseman*: it enacts a desacralization—a humiliation—of Peter. Peter's necropolis is a city of dead souls.[43] This bureaucracy of "merit," with its attendant table of ranks, takes a higher toll than the ravages of nature (flood) and will (the Bronze Horseman). The institution has long stopped serving the interests of Peter's vision; it lives on despite, not for, Peter.

Gogol's "The Overcoat," a story that greatly influenced all Dostoevskii's early work, especially *Poor Folk,* also presents a disparaging view of the Petersburg bureaucracy; but Dostoevskii's derogation of Petersburg differs as significantly from Gogol's as from Pushkin's. Gogol depicts the bureaucracy neither as the central reality of an aborted Petrine legacy, nor as the root of all evil, but as the Russian incarnation of a universal desire to conceal falsehood and the death of the soul under an impressive facade. The devil figures no less prominently in the provincial world of *Dead Souls, The Inspector General,* or "Old World Landowners" than in Petersburg—the provincial bureaucracy is just smaller. Further, Gogol emphasizes the ridiculousness of bureaucracy—its "comic grotesque"[44]—not its horror. Since in Gogol's basically anti-Rousseauistic view, institutions do not corrupt man, but man corrupts institutions, one could hardly expect much of institutions run by dead souls.

In *The Double,* Dostoevskii presents a radically different view of institutions. In contrast to Gogol, he portrays the bureaucracy as an institution that has usurped the authority of human beings and now runs itself in its own interest. Elevating procedure over human feeling, treating human beings primarily in terms of function, the bureaucratic machine sees personality as expendable—at best. All Goliadkin's doubles are equally insignificant and interchangeable. All of Gogol's dead souls are dead in their own way; all Dostoevskii's souls in *The Double* are the same. They were not born that way; they are the products of Peter's bureaucratic legacy—a legacy as radically different from the one embodied by Gogol's Akakii Akakievich ("The Overcoat") and Kovalev ("The Nose") as the one embodied by Pushkin's Peter and Evgenii.

The process that Peter began continues at a dizzying speed; the doubles are multiplying faster and faster with no end in sight. In *The Double,* Peter's legacy may be reduced in stature, its monumentality continually undercut, its myth depoeticized, but its momentum remains undiminished. No great apocalypse will occur. Goliadkin's madness may even be wishful thinking. The novel implies an even worse horror: that these faceless, identical Goliadkins—all sons of Peter—will not go mad, but will function all too well within the system.

The novel's finale brilliantly conveys Dostoevskii's dark vision of Russia's fate. The figure of Peter may be absent in *The Double,* but the horse—or at least the horse-drawn carriage—is not. The first and last chapters begin with Goliadkin driving around Petersburg in a hired carriage (*kareta*).[45] In the first chapters, he makes some purchases, probably in preparation for an imagined marriage or elopement, visits his doctor who is treating him for a nervous condition, and then arrives at the place of his greatest humiliation, the house of the civil councilor Berendeev where Klara Olsuf'evna's birthday is being celebrated. In the last chapters, he once again hires a carriage, this time to elope with Klara; he is driven around town and then deposited before the house of Berendeev. This time he not only suffers a terrible humiliation but is whisked away in another carriage directly to the insane asylum.

In *The Bronze Horseman,* Peter pursues the hapless Evgenii on horseback; at the conclusion of *The Double,* the persecuting double runs after the horse-drawn carriage taking Goliadkin to the insane asylum. The narrator of *The Bronze Horseman* asks of the horse on which Peter sits: "Whither do you gallop, proud steed?" as does Gogol of the troika, Russia, at the end of *Dead Souls.* The question implies no knowledge of a destination but an assumption of a destination commensurate with Russia's immenseness

and potential. Even Poprishchin, the hero of Gogol's "Notes of a Madman," sees the carriage with horses not as a conveyance to but as the means of deliverance from the insane asylum, from insanity. Dostoevskii again presents Russia's fate more ominously than Gogol and Pushkin, but also less ambiguously. On route to his final destination, Goliadkin sees no immense perspectives, not even ruins—as in the later Dostoevskii—just nothingness.

> The carriage door slammed. One could hear a lash of the whip on the horses' backs . . . the horses jerked forward. . . . Everything dashed after Mr. Goliadkin. . . . He at last sank into unconsciousness. . . . When he came to himself, he saw the horses taking him along an unknown road. Dark forests appeared now on his left, now on his right; it was desolate and deserted [*bylo glukho i pusto*] he suddenly grew faint; two fiery eyes were staring at him in the darkness, and those two eyes were glittering with malignant, hellish, glee.
>
> (614–15; 1:229)

The horses allude to Peter's steed, as the unknown and uncharted road—Russia's path, if not her destiny—alludes to Peter's vision. But the road seems unfamiliar to Goliadkin only for a moment. Russia has entered a deep, dark forest. Everything around looms deserted, desolate, and empty: perhaps devoid of the unknown, but world-historical, Petrine meaning with which Pushkin had invested it. Goliadkin finally wakes up to the truth of his mysterious journey; the devil himself is conducting him—in the person of a German doctor with the ironic name of Krest'ian (Christian)—to the underworld. There is only one end, one destination for the sons of Peter: spiritual death. In this unrelievedly dark novel, perhaps the most modern of all Dostoevskii's work, the devil has the last laugh. It is understandable why some of Dostoevskii's contemporaries found *The Double* absolutely devastating.[46]

By conflating in his subtitle (*Petersburgskaia poema*) Pushkin's *Petersburgskaia povest'* and Gogol's *Poema,* Dostoevskii places his work in the tradition of both *The Bronze Horseman* and *Dead Souls* on the question of national origins and destiny. Dostoevskii's transformation of Pushkin's *povest'* to *poema* underlines, paradoxically, a comparison and not a contrast. Just like most members of his literary generation, Dostoevskii undoubtedly viewed *The Bronze Horseman*—as did Belinskii—as one of Pushkin's greatest *poemy,* and the subtitle *povest'* as alluding to the different or specific nature of *this* poema as opposed to Pushkin's other narrative poems (*poemy*).[47] *The Bronze Horseman* was not a traditional epic poema or Byronic poema (*povest' v stikhakh*) but a poema in which a prosaic tale and an unheroic hero play a prominent role.

On the other hand, by calling *Dead Souls* a poema, Gogol was asserting that his work had as much in common with the poema as with the novel.[48] Though *Dead Souls* deals with the prose of life, which the traditional poema eschews, it nevertheless treats the prosaic with the existential seriousness of the poema.[49] In *Dead Souls,* Gogol presents himself as transforming the prosaic into a "pearl of creation" (*perl sozdan'ia*) so that like the epic—and like Pushkin's poema, *The Bronze Horseman*—his novel can address seriously, through laughter, the most burning questions of national origins and destiny. Pushkin uses povest' to show how his poema differed from the traditional poema; Gogol uses poema to show how his povest' (or *roman*) differs from the traditional povest'.[50]

The numerous references in *The Double* to *Dead Souls,* the mock-epic chapter headings, and the subtitle of the 1846 version made, at that time, the subtitle poema superfluous. In 1866, however, when *The Double* could have been seen only as a povest' or novel, Dostoevskii saw the need to specify what kind of novel or povest' it was (just as Pushkin saw the need to indicate just what kind of poema *The Bronze Horseman* was), and more specifically, the need to relate his work to the Russian literary tradition embodied in the term *poema.* But Dostoevskii attempts a more radical departure from the traditional poema than Pushkin and Gogol; he creates a work of stunning existential, national, and universal significance from even more prosaic and insubstantial material than does Gogol, from material more reminiscent of "The Notes of a Madman" and "The Nose" than of *Dead Souls:* he grounds his poema in absence (Peter), shadow (Goliadkin), and fog (Petersburg)—in nothingness. As Donald Fanger writes: "Here is not even Gogolian *poshlost'*, but nothingness, raised by the quality of attention it receives to a higher power, where it becomes terror . . ."[51] Dostoevskii takes to its logical conclusion the way opened up by his literary fathers, transforming, even more than Gogol did, nothingness into "a pearl of creation," the depoeticization of the Petrine myth into a work of the most profound poetry.[52]

THE CLERK (CHINOVNIK): THE NARRATIVE STANCE

Dostoevskii's depreciation of Pushkin's common man, the Petersburg chinovnik, is just as important to his demythologizing agenda as is his reduction of Peter himself. Indeed, despite Peter's monumental presence in *The Bronze Horseman,* and his conspicuous absence in *The Double,* both works concentrate far more on their petty heroes, the progeny of Peter, than on Peter himself. *The Double* not only recounts in mock-epic fashion the adventures of Goliadkin; it engages Gogol and Pushkin just as in *Poor Folk,* through the representation of the clerk. Yet the implied comparison of Goliadkin with Evgenii plays as important a role in *The Double* as the more obvious comparisons of Goliadkin with Gogol's heroes. Although in *The Double,* Dostoevskii polemicizes with Gogol over the chinovnik much as he does in *Poor Folk,* he takes an entirely different approach to Pushkin not only by deconstructing the monument to Peter the Great (Peter's legacy) but also by consistently diminishing his son, Peter's progeny. In *Poor Folk,* Dostoevskii humanizes his clerk; in *The Double,* he dissolves his hero's personality and makes his very identity problematic.

Dostoevskii underlines his departure from Pushkin by radically transforming—if not deconstructing—three essential structural and thematic centers of *The Bronze Horseman:* narrative point of view (in particular the narrator's attitude toward his hero); the representation of madness; and the treatment of protest and rebellion—in *The Double* manifested primarily in the form of imposture (*samozvanstvo*).[53]

Even those critics who have taken "Peter's side" in *The Bronze Horseman*—or the side of historical necessity—interpret the narrator's attitude toward Evgenii as generally sympathetic.[54] The narrator certainly keeps an intellectual distance from Evgenii at all times, but he also becomes affectively involved with Evgenii as he tells his hero's sad tale. Evgenii, who bears the name of the hero of Pushkin's finest work, *Eugene Onegin,* is "our hero" (*nash geroi,* 109) and "my Evgenii" (*Evgenii moi,* 275). As misfortune strikes him, he is "the unfortunate" (*neschastnyi,* 296), "the poor man" (*bedniak,* 386), and as he goes mad, "the unfortunate madman" (*bednyi bezumets,* 425; *bezumets bednyi,* 452) and "my madman" (*bezumets moi,* 479). His name has a pleasant ring (*zvuchit priiatno,* 110) and hints at sound and healthy origins (Evgenii).[55] Unlike the more negatively characterized Germann of *The Queen of Spades*—Pushkin's other great work of 1833 in which the hero goes mad—Evgenii does not worry overmuch about fame and fortune, though his family name may be an ancient and respected one, and though he sometimes wonders why he was not fated to have an easier life.[56] He is, moreover—again in contrast to Germann—willing to secure his "independence" by means of hard work (*trudit'sia den' i noch' gotov,* 148). He dreams, not of a vast fortune of a thousand souls, or of a brilliant future, but of a humble and simple family life with his beloved, Parasha, "his dream" (*ego mechta,* 247) and of burial by his grandchildren. Seeing Evgenii's dream (*mechta*) in the context of Pushkin's life, we can more easily understand the sympathetic treatment of Evgenii, who desires honor, independence, simple pleasures, and freedom (*volia*) to be left in peace. Whereas in *The Queen of Spades* Pushkin places a considerable ironic distance between his narrative persona and the mad Germann, in *The Bronze Horseman* he bridges the emotional gap between narrator and character by depicting Evgenii's madness sympathetically, even as a precursor of truth.

Dostoevskii takes a much less sympathetic approach toward Goliadkin.[57] Goliadkin is not young, hale, and hearty but old, balding, and—from the very beginning of the novel—mentally ill. His name is not pleasing to the ear. He has neither family nor a real dream. Unlike Evgenii he does not think of marrying, having children, and being buried by his grandchildren. He has only himself, his servant, and later his double(s). His "romantic" attachment to Klara Olsuf'evna, similar to Poprishchin's in Gogol's "Notes of a Madman," constitutes a travesty of the sentimental romance. Further, the Klara Olsuf'evna that the reader sees is not the real person but a distorted image of Goliadkin's deranged imagination. Dostoevskii removes from *The Double* not only Pushkin's Peter with his "great thoughts" but also Evgenii with his more modest, but sympathetically presented, dream. Peter's monumental plans for empire destroy Evgenii's dream and drive him insane; in a scene as much comic as pathetic, the butler of Goliadkin's superior throws him down the stairs.[58]

Although several Soviet critics have argued that Goliadkin is basically a good man who is a victim of an oppressive social and political system,[59] most critics have found not only nothing of worth in Dostoevskii's hero but also no convincing social causes for his condition.[60] Victor Terras, describing everything about Goliadkin as petty, shabby, and trite, argues that he is Devushkin without any of Devushkin's positive attributes.

> The evil in Goliadkin Junior is as petty and wretched as the good in Goliadkin Senior is shabby and indifferent. Consequently, where the struggle between truly "romantic" *Doppelgängers* would reflect a struggle between heaven and hell, the struggle between the two Goliadkins is only a wretched intrigue, carried on by two underlings for nothing more than a snug little job. What difference does it make, which of the two—or if either—occupies a desk at the "department," a flat on Shestilavochnaia? . . . One wonders if Goliadkin is really entitled to a *Doppelgänger,* for in order to have a "dual personality," one must have a personality in the first place.[61]

Indeed, the narrator persistently reduces his hero by presenting his movements and speech as ridiculous. As Viktor Vinogradov and others have remarked, Goliadkin's abrupt movements make him appear more like a puppet on a string than a human being—not to speak of the hero of a novel.[62] Goliadkin is too timid to say anything briefly and directly; he makes endless, exasperating circumlocutions and even then does not say what he means. Although Mikhail Bakhtin and Vinogradov hold that in transcribing Goliadkin's consciousness and speech the narrator at times seems to fuse with his hero,[63] Terras and M. F. Lomagina demonstrate that the narrator distances himself from his hero even in those passages where the narrative voice seems to fuse most closely with that of Goliadkin or his double. In fact, Dostoevskii's use of *erlebte Rede,* which often gives the impression of false camaraderie, if not outright mimicry or mockery, only deepens the narrative irony.[64]

Whereas Pushkin suggests the possibility of the "little man" achieving an insight commensurate with the dream of his epic antagonist and arising even to challenge his enemy at the very center of his creation (Petersburg), Dostoevskii presents the prosaic adventures of Goliadkin in deflationary mock-epic style—a device that is far more obvious in the work's original journal form than in the revised version, from which Dostoevskii deleted the mock-epic headings for all the chapters.[65] We see Goliadkin on a shopping expedition, eating pies in a restaurant, riding in his carriage, "crashing" a party, being ejected from the party, and waiting in the rain to carry away an imagined fiancée—at best a series of nonadventures. The only Peter that Goliadkin ever meets is his servant Petrushka, a drunkard who, as in Gogol, occupies an even lower plane of social and moral being than his master.[66]

The poet of *The Bronze Horseman* sings of Evgenii as much as he sings of Peter; it behooves him to remember with compassion history's tragic casualties. Dostoevskii focuses on a diminished Goliadkin because he represents, both as Petrovich and as a Russian everyman, what has remained of Peter's legacy in nineteenth-century Russia. Dostoevskii seems to withdraw sympathy for Goliadkin even when his misfortunes increase. Even in suffering Goliadkin remains petty and unsympathetic.

Dostoevskii, however, must not reduce Goliadkin to the status of an Akakii Akakievich lest he erase his hero's national and universal significance. Goliadkin differs markedly not only from Devushkin in *Poor Folk* but also from innumerable chinovniki of the 1830s and 1840s, such as Gogol's Akakii Akakievich and Poprishchin. He occupies a responsible position as the assistant clerk in his office. He is literate, financially secure, ambitious, and for all we know, until his descent into madness, quite competent. Had his chief's nephew not worked in his office, he might even have received the promotion he desired. He has relationships with women. At times he cuts a ridiculous figure, but not nearly as ridiculous as Akakii Akakievich or Poprishchin. As Terras has shown, Goliadkin speaks more correctly than Devushkin; he is familiar with a good number of historical facts and anecdotes; and he has read quite a few journal articles and novels.[67] Konrad Onasch maintains that Goliadkin has even been affected by the ideas of the French Enlightenment and Jean-Jacques Rousseau.[68] The terrible significance of Goliadkin, like Evgenii, is that he is a Russian everyman.

THE CLERK: MADNESS AND REBELLION

Pushkin not only shows more sympathy for his mad hero than Dostoevskii, he also seems to valorize Evgenii's madness.[69] That the humble Evgenii could have threatened Peter only when he was mad points to a distinctly romantic conception of madness: only in madness can the truth break through the constraints of fear and reason and challenge the ultimate authority.[70] When Evgenii faces the Bronze Horseman for the first time after the flood, he is terrified precisely by the clarity of his thoughts—a clarity made possible by madness (*proiasnilis'/V nem strashno mysli,* 404–5).[71] His madness has undergone a romantic transformation, becoming a vehicle of a higher truth. Moreover, Evgenii's madness elevates him to Peter's level. He, too, now sees historically; he understands the goals for which the rights of individuals—his rights—have been sacrificed. He also becomes, for the reader, so much a part of Peter's story and the story of the Russian state that Peter seems almost inconceivable without him. If Evgenii's illumination, his insight into Peter and his creation, reflect nothing more than paranoia—as Richard Gregg argues[72]—both Peter's achievement and the terrible cost of that achievement would be severely diminished. Diminishing Evgenii seriously diminishes Peter.

Given his probable romantic interpretation of Evgenii's madness (Dostoevskii often interpreted Pushkin's works quite romantically), Dostoevskii needed to depoeticize, deromanticize, and devalue Goliadkin's madness in *The Double.* In nineteenth-century works featuring autoscopic doubles,[73] the double (even if it is exclusively a projection of the more negative or evil side of the self) often emerges as more interesting and venturesome—even more vital—than the original self. Goliadkin's double, however, is the very opposite of a higher self; it does not transform him into a poet, it does not give him any insight into Russian history, as Catharine Nepomnyashchy has argued for Pushkin's Evgenii and "all the downtrodden clerks and social nonentities in Russian literature."[74] On the contrary, Dostoevskii empties Goliadkin's madness, like madness in the Age of Reason, of all that is vital and elevating. It is a depoeticized madness as prosaic as Goliadkin himself. "Goliadkin's very madness," Terras concludes, "is ridiculous in its wretched pettiness, its lack of spirituality, its shallowness of feeling. Goliadkin's folly is a travesty of madness for really, there is nothing, but nothing at all, to go mad from."[75] According to Terras, Dostoevskii wisely did not invent for Goliadkin anything as imaginative as Poprishchin's King of Spain (in Gogol's "Notes of a Madman"), for "people who are dull and commonplace when sane remain just that when they become insane."[76] Petersburg has so reduced the spirit of man that "true" madness, the romantic last resort of protest and opposition, can no longer exist. Evgenii's crazed perception of the Bronze Horseman chasing him through the streets of Petersburg constitutes a magnificent flight of visionary madness worthy of Peter himself;[77] it is the very antithesis of seeing oneself chased through these same streets by exact replicas of one's shabby and repugnant self.

> "Bow or not? Answer or not? Recognize him or not?" our hero wondered in indescribable anguish. "Or pretend that it is not I, but somebody else, strikingly like me, and look as though nothing were the matter. It is simply not I, not I—and that's all there is to it," said Mr. Goliadkin, taking off his hat to Andrei Filippovich and keeping his eyes fixed upon him. "I'm . . . I'm entirely all right," he whispered with an effort; "I'm . . . quite all right. It's not I at all, Andrei Filippovich. It's not I at all, not I—and that's all there is to it."
>
> (481; 1:113)

Much like D. S. Merezhkovskii, Dostoevskii probably saw arising out of Evgenii's mad visions not only truth but the seeds of an effective rebellion, wherein an insignificant opponent breaks forever the seemingly imperturbable and majestic calm of the proud idol.[78] *The Bronze Horseman* suggests that the horseman, unmoved by the mighty flood, is so threatened by his lowly subject that he must descend from his pedestal to chase Evgenii through the streets of Petersburg. What is so potentially threatening to Peter—to the state—about Evgenii's madness (his higher sanity) is that it calls forth rebellion from one of Russia's most docile citizens, from a man whose ideal was to distance himself from affairs of state—to live a life, as it were, outside of historical time.[79] That Evgenii only imagines being chased by Peter does not significantly diminish his challenge; the act of imagination itself is crucial. Nor does it

matter that after uttering his threat, Evgenii experiences fear and trembling every time he encounters the statue in his wanderings around the city.[80] Once Evgenii questions Peter's mission and vision, Russian cultural and historical consciousness has taken a critical turn.

Thus, with the goal of demythologizing the Petersburg text, Dostoevskii not only deprives Goliadkin of Evgenii's visionary madness and sympathetic character, but also of his status as a serious rebel; he presents Goliadkin's rebellious thoughts—and his fear of those thoughts—as petty, conventional, and ridiculous, as virtually no different from his other ideas and concerns. In the revised version of *The Double,* the elimination of many passages relating to rebellion attenuated Dostoevskii's polemic with *The Bronze Horseman.*[81] But these cuts also obscured the reasons for Goliadkin's rebellious thoughts and his preoccupation with "freethinking" and imposture. As one of the deleted letters (a reflection of Goliadkin's guilty conscience) makes clear, complaints were soon going to be made—or already had been made—against Goliadkin; everyone, even his chief, would know about his disgraceful behavior toward Karolina Ivanovna. Goliadkin imagined that he would not only be publicly humiliated but would probably lose his position, his place of residence—and like Evgenii in *The Bronze Horseman*—be forced to wander the streets of Petersburg. All this is made explicit in a passage cut from the 1846 version, in which Vakhrameev, an intermediary through whom Goliadkin is conducting a correspondence concerning the plots of his enemies, excoriates Goliadkin for his scandalous behavior. (It is, of course, really Goliadkin writing to himself.)

> In conclusion, I must tell you that Karolina Ivanovna's petition regarding your affair [*delo*] has been submitted a long time ago, and that our mutual friend, Nikolai Sergeevich Skoroplekhin, has been busy working in Karolina Ivanovna's behalf. As a result of this affair being made public knowledge, you will no longer be able to find a place to live; you will be deprived of all credit and trust; and you will lose your position at work. For all your machinations have been anticipated and nullified by the petitions and supplications of Karolina Ivanovna before your chief. Finally, all your hopes and nonsensical ravings about Izmailovskii Bridge and thereabouts will come to nought all of themselves when your dissolute life is made fully public. Rejected by everyone, tormented by pangs of conscience, you will not know where to lay your head; you will be forced to wander the earth, nurturing in vain in your heart the viper of your own debauch and vengefulness.
>
> (1:414)

In the *Bronze Horseman,* the loss of his beloved unhinges Evgenii and eventually leads to his protest, his revolt. The narrator presents Evgenii's love in an understated manner, but he also expresses great sympathy for his hero, who is elevated by his suffering.[82] But in *The Double,* rather than ennobling his hero by a deeply moving relationship with a young girl—as he had done with Devushkin in *Poor Folk*—Dostoevskii involves Goliadkin in a rather shady relationship with a German woman.[83] Furthermore, Goliadkin's madness—in contrast to Evgenii's—is brought on not by the loss of his beloved but by fear of public exposure. By "depriving" Goliadkin of love and showing him to be the primary cause of his own misfortunes, Dostoevskii undercuts not only Goliadkin's intrinsic worth but also the justification for Goliakin's rebellion against his fate.

Dostoevskii also denigrates the anxiety Goliadkin experiences by his thoughts of rebellion. Having an inordinate, servile respect for authority, Goliadkin experiences great guilt whenever he thinks disrespectfully of his superiors—when, for example, he begins to feel envious, angry, and bitter after being passed over for promotion. But for Goliadkin to question the decisions of the authorities—thinking that one has the right to a position occupied by a rival—constitutes nothing less than a challenge to the entire system. Furthermore, Goliadkin's rebellion manifests itself not in outright defiance as in Evgenii's case, but in a debased form of imposture, samozvanstvo.[84] Samozvanstvo also constitutes a most serious threat to the state by challenging the religious, political, social, and cultural legitimacy of those who rule.[85] To forward his agenda in *The Double*—the debunking of the Petersburg text—Dostoevskii turns the theme of samozvanstvo into travesty.[86] In his little world, Goliadkin views any challenge to the existing order—albeit only the bureaucratic order—as the delegitimation of all authority and of "the place" of everyone who depends on that authority, including his own. Dostoevskii eliminated from the early version several passages in which Goliadkin remarks that Grishka Otrep'evs are no longer possible in our age (*nash vek*).[87] But Goliadkin protests too much; he knows his double is an imposter, a *samozvanets,* whom he cannot—must not—recognize as himself.

In the revised version of 1866, when Goliadkin brings up the topic of imposture, he applies it exclusively to his enemies who are "illegitimately" planning to displace him—the rightful, legitimate occupier of his position. But in the original journal text, Dostoevskii makes much clearer the reflexivity of Goliadkin's accusations of imposture against others, including his double. In the same letter of Vakhrameev-Goliadkin quoted above (1:414), Vakhrameev accuses Goliadkin of using the accusations of samozvanstvo as a means of slandering others but asserts that these accusations prove most of all that Goliadkin is more guilty of samozvanstvo than those whom he accuses: "Govoriu zhe ia sie, milostivyi moi gosudar', potomu chto sami deistvuete obmanom i samozvanstvom" (1:414).

By questioning the legitimacy of those in higher positions, Goliadkin lays himself open to the claims of those who occupy lower positions. In contrast to Evgenii, but in a typical Dostoevskian reduction—consistent with his deflation of the Petersburg clerk—Goliadkin begins to experience the challenge from *below* far more acutely than the one from *above.* He now comes to see himself—in the person of his double—as a pretender who has neither religious nor social legitimacy for the position that he presently occupies. It is thus not the mighty Peter who descends from *above* to crush Goliadkin, but petty demons—Goliadkin's legitimate place as titular councilor, a middling rank at best in the Russian civil service: "But with every step, with every thud of his foot on the granite of the pavement, there would leap up as though from beneath the earth an exactly identical Mr. Goliadkin, perfectly alike, and of a revolting depravity of heart" (566; 1:186–87). Peter is absent from the Petersburg text partly because he is no longer needed to crush such a paltry challenge to his authority; it is left to Goliadkin, or his imposter double-devil, to do it himself. As Uspenksii has argued, in the Russian cultural consciousness, the royal impostor owes his power to the devil, to the Antichrist; but so, by analogy, do all who engage in role playing and the donning of masks (samozvanstvo). Goliadkin's perception of being conducted to the underworld by the devil is, thus, condign punishment for his imagined imposture.[88]

Many nineteenth-century doubles are suicidal. To preserve its "legitimate" self, to crush the rebellion raging inside, the self must destroy its alter ego; but to do so necessarily entails the destruction of the "legitimate" self as well. Whereas for Evgenii rebellion is the greatest act of self-affirmation—for it is through his rebellion that Evgenii comes, willy-nilly, to play a role in Peter's story—for Goliadkin, the crisis of self not only stifles rebellion, samozvantsvo, but drives the self to madness bereft of truth.[89]

If the manifestation of the double emblemizes individual self-dissolution, Goliadkin's dream of all Petersburg inhabited by an endless stream of doubles perhaps universalizes the theme of imposture—of Grisha Otrep'ev—in the novel, where everyone—not only Goliadkin—is potentially in danger of being replaced by any one of his innumerable doubles. In a bureaucracy, nothing can stop the assembly line on which the double personality is created and infinitely reproduced. Dostoevskii's experiment leads to conclusions no less monumental than those dramatized in *The Bronze Horseman.* Goliadkin is living in a time of troubles beside which the threat of Peter or floods pales by comparison. The natural floods will pass; they may at some time even be completely tamed, but the hopes of containing the bureaucratic monster that Peter has created seem—especially in *The Double*—dim indeed.[90]

What is most unusual about Dostoevskii's disparaging diminution of Goliadkin as a freethinker and a rebel—and not only in terms of *The Bronze Horseman,* but in terms of Dostoevskii's later work as well—is that it undercuts the notion of even the possibility of rebellion from below. Evgenii could, at least in madness, threaten Peter. He sees the threat as something outside and alien to himself, and thus something that, *at some time,* can be confronted, even challenged—as his threatening gesture and words symbolize. In Goliadkin, both rebel and avenger are so completely internalized that they become two sides of the same self. What challenge can the Goliadkins of Russia, or of the world, offer when they internalize their own punishment and go mad by themselves? From the pessimistic point of view of *The Double,* both *The Bronze Horseman,* and *Notes from the Underground* present gross exaggerations of the human potential for rebellion in the modern world.

Few have resisted the temptation of seeing *The Double* as an interesting but unsuccessful experiment that paved the way for the achievements of the later novels. But the more romantically conceived heroes and novels of the 1860s and 1870s prophesy our own century much less than does *The Double* which ruthlessly undermines the myth of both the great and the common man. Indeed, *The Double* looks as fearlessly into the future as it does into the past; it challenges not only Pushkin but also the faith in man characteristic of some of Dostoevskii's later writings. It reminds twentieth-century readers of the terrifying, dream-like world of Kafka, in which the "individual," racked by guilt and angst, alienated, and trapped in a hopelessly unresponsive legal and administrative bureaucracy, ultimately turns on himself: Gregor Samsa metamorphoses into an insect, Goliadkin projects his self-repugnance onto innumerable nondistinctive copies of himself. If we look closely at Edvard Munch's surrealistic "Evening on Karl Johan Street"—one of our century's most horrific icons—can we fail to recognize likenesses, even doubles, of Mr. Goliadkin, as the people in the canvas come marching toward us, and again when, receding into the distance, they merge with the street and buildings?

Notes

1. Joseph Frank, *Dostoevsky: The Seeds of Revolt (1821–1849)* (Princeton: Princeton University Press, 1976), 310.

2. See, for example, A. L. Bem, "'Pikovaia dama' v tvorchestve Dostoevskogo," in A. L. Bem, ed., *U istokov tvorchestva Dostoevskogo* (Prague: Petropolis, 1936), 37–81; M. Al'tman, "Videnie Germanna (Pushkin i Dostoevskii)," *Slavia* 9 (1930–31): 792–800.

3. For Hoffmann's influence see Charles E. Passage, *Dostoevski the Adaptor: A Study in Dostoevski's Use of the "Tales of Hoffmann"* (Chapel Hill: University of North Carolina Press, 1954), 14–37; Ralph Tymms, *Doubles in Literary Psychology* (Cambridge: Bowes, 1947), 103–7; N. Reber, *Studien zum Motiv des Doppelgängers bei Dostoevskij und E. T. A. Hoffmann* (Giessen: Schmitz, 1964).

4. For Gogol's influence, see, for example, V. V. Vinogradov, "K morfologii natural'nogo stilia: Opyt lingvisticheskogo analiza poemy *Dvoinik*," *Izbrannye trudy* (Moscow: Nauka, 1976), 102–10; A. L. Bem, "'Nos' i 'Dvoinik,'" in Bem, ed., *U istokov tvorchestva Dostoevskogo*, 139–66; Konstantin Mochulsky, *Dostoevsky: His Life and Work*, trans. Michael A. Minihan (Princeton: Princeton University Press, 1967), 46–48; V. Shklovskii, "Dvoiniki i o 'Dvoinike,'" *Za i protiv: Zametki o Dostoevskom* (Moscow: Sovetskii pisatel', 1957), 62–63; G. M. Fridlender, "Primechaniia," in F. M. Dostoevskii, *Polnoe sobranie sochinenii* [hereafter *PSS*], ed. V. G. Bazanov et al., 30 vols. (Leningrad: Nauka, 1972–91), 1:486–87; Frank, *Dostoevsky: The Seeds of Revolt*, 298–300. Some critics received *The Double* with hostility (K. S. Aksakov, in particular) because they saw it as an uncreative, even slavish, imitation

of Gogol. For the contemporary reception of the work, see Fridlender, "Primechaniia," 489–93. Vladimir Nabokov, archly, found *The Double* to be "the best thing he [Dostoevskii] ever wrote" and "a perfect work of art." See his *Lectures on Russian Literature,* ed. Fredson Bowers (New York: Harcourt, 1981), 100, 104. For studies comparing Nabokov's treatment of the double—a favorite theme of Nabokov's—with Dostoevskii's in *The Double,* see Julian W. Connolly, "The Function of Literary Allusion in Nabokov's *Despair,*" *Slavic and East European Journal* 26, no. 3 (1982): 302–13; Julian W. Connolly, "Madness and Doubling: From Dostoevsky's *The Double* to Nabokov's *The Eye,*" *Russian Literature Triquarterly* 24 (1991): 129–39.

5. For the generally positive image of the city before Pushkin, see Antsiferov, *Dusha Petersburga* (Petersburg: Brokgauz-Efron, 1922), 45–62; Waclaw Lednicki, *Pushkin's "Bronze Horseman": The Story of a Masterpiece* (Berkeley: University of California Press, 1955), 43–51.

6. "Pushkin byl poslednim pevtsom svetloi Petersburga. S kazhdym godom vse mrachnee stanovitsia oblik severnoi stolitsy." See Antsiferov, *Dusha Petersburga,* 73.

7. Phrases will be given in the nominative case. *Otsel' grozit' my budem shvedu* (12); *derzhavnoe techen'e* (45); *Rossiia snova torzhestvuet . . . likuet* (80–83); *voennaia stolitsa* (75); *znamena pobednye* (72); *pobeda nad vragom* (79).

8. *Mosty povisli nad vodami* (36); *pobezhdennaia stikhiia* (87).

9. *Krasa* (22); *Krasuisia, grad Petrov* (84); *odnoobraznuiu krasivost'* (70).

10. *V ikh stroino zyblemom stroiu* (71); *stroinyi vid* (44).

11. *Prostor* (20).

12. *Blesk bezlunnyi* (49); *prozrachnyi sumrak* (49); *svetla / admiralteiskaia igla* (53–54); *zolotye nebesa* (56); *zaria* (57); *blesk* (63); *plamen' goluboi* (66).

13. *shum, i govor balov* (63); *grom* (76); *shipen'e penistykh bokalov* (65).

14. *Ozhivlennye berega* (30); *voinstvennaia zhivost'* (68).

15. The pathetic, lowly Finn (*ubogii chukhonets,* 8; *pechal'nyi pasynok prirody,* 26) lives in black huts (*cherneli izby,* 7) and plies his wretched boat (*bednyi cheln,* 4) with his worn-out net (*vetkhii nevod,* 29) along the low banks (*nizkie berega,* 27) of unknown waters (*nevedomye vody,* 28) and dark forests (*iz t'my lesov,* 23), impenetrable to the rays of the sun (*les, nevedomyi lucham v tumane spriatannogo solntsa,* 9–10).

16. V. N. Toporov, "Petersburg i petersburgskii tekst v russkoi literature," in Liubava Moreva, ed., *Metafizika Petersburga* (Petersburg: Eidos, 1993), 205–35.

17. For example, immortality/ephemerality, large/small, movement/stasis, will/fatalism, freedom/necessity,

rebellion/acquiescence, state/individual, social/ private, order/chaos, cosmos/chaos, order/nature, man/nature, natural/artificial, natural/unnatural, creation/destruction, birth/death, pagan/Christian, Petersburg/Moscow, nobility/people, tyrant/victim, center/periphery, land/water, future/past, reason/ madness, East/West, Russia/Europe, Russian/Finn, light/dark, dry/wet, empty/full, water/stone, land/ water, wind/stone, past/future.

18. The light that Toporov sees in Gogol's and Dostoevskii's Petersburg texts is, in fact, not associated with salvation. For Gogol, the brilliance of Petersburg represents a superficial cover over profound evil; for Dostoevskii it represents, at best, false hope. Devushkin is deceived by the Petersburg spring— which the narrator in "White Nights" describes as a consumptive young girl—and Raskol'nikov must get as far away from Petersburg as possible (Siberia) to be saved. In "Simvolika Petersburga i problemy semiotiki goroda," *Trudy po znakovym sistemam* 8 (1984): 30–45, Iu. M. Lotman, also basing his positive assessment of Petersburg on the city's inherent semiotic oppositions, contrasts Peter's ideal of a monolithic imperial capital to the historical reality of Petersburg's socially and ethnically heterogeneous population, a variety (*pestrota*) that gave birth to an exceptionally intense intellectual and spiritual life, "a phenomenon unique in the history of civilization" (45). Similarly, G. D. Gachev ("Kosmos Dostoevskogo," in *Natsional'nye obrazy mira* [Moscow: Sovetskii pisatel', 1988], 386) asserts that neither Petersburg nor Rus' constitutes the real Russia (*Rossiia*). Russia is a process, an unending dialogue between Petersburg and Rus'.

19. Donald Fanger, *Dostoevsky and Romantic Realism: A Study of Dostoevsky in Relation to Balzac, Dickens, and Gogol* (Chicago: University of Chicago Press, 1965), 184.

20. There is much myth about the myth of Petersburg. The idea of Petersburg as the most abstract city in the world has gained currency as almost the dominant topos of the Dostoevskian version of the myth. Although the Underground Man states that Petersburg is "the most abstract and intentional city in the whole world" (*samyi otvlechennyi i ymyshlennyi gorod na vsem zemnom share, PSS,* 5:101), few descriptions of Petersburg in Dostoevskii substantiate this claim. It is Belyi who picks up on the Underground Man's idea (with a little help from Tolstoi's Karenin) and integrates it into his novel about the city. Dostoevskii is far more apt to focus on the city's slums and phantasmagoric qualities. But even the phantasmagoric qualities of Petersburg, as Lotman shows ("Simvolika Petersburga i problemy semiotiki goroda," 35–40), were not the creations of Gogol or Dostoevskii (the canonizers of this idea), but the reworkings of longstanding popular stories and literary writings of the 1820s and 1830s—many by a group of writers (such as Odoevskii) close to Pushkin.

21. Dostoevskii unquestionably viewed Svidrigailov (the details of whose suicide recall *The Bronze Horseman,* see note 30) as an emblematic Petersburg creature who represented some of the worst aspects of Peter's legacy: *strashneishaia raspushchennost' nravov* (*PSS,* 20:14).

22. This, of course, is Dostoevskii's reduction of the last lines of the first part of *The Bronze Horseman.*

23. For other derogatory references to the *prorublennoe v Evropu okoshko* in the *Diary,* see especially the second chapter of the June 1876 issue, entitled "Moi paradoks" (*PSS,* 23:38–42).

24. The text and pagination of *The Bronze Horseman* is from the edition prepared by N. V. Izmailov, *A. S. Pushkin: Mednyi vsadnik* (Leningrad: Nauka, 1973). Izmailov was also responsible for the text of *The Bronze Horseman* in volume five (1948) of the Academy edition.

25. Evgenii's troubles also begin after returning home from visiting: *V to vremia iz gostei domoi / Prishel Evgenii molodoi* (106–7).

26. As Antsiferov shows, water has always symbolized the principle of primordial darkness and chaos, often in the form of a sea monster. Water, then, becomes an appropriate symbol in both Pushkin's and Dostoevskii's texts, not only for nature's revolt against Peter's order, but also for the mental dissolution of the heroes. N. P. Antsiferov, *Byl' i mif Petersburga* (Petrograd: Brokgauz-Efron, 1924), 57–60.

27. Fedor Dostoevsky, *The Short Novels of Dostoevsky,* trans. Constance Garnett (New York: Dial, 1945), 509. The passage continues for another eight lines to describe the weather: in particular, the howling of the wind and the rushing of the water. The English translations of *The Double* from the Garnett translation have been checked—and amended when necessary—with the Academy edition. The pagination from the English, followed by the Russian from the Academy edition, will appear in the text.

28. This is a clear literary echo. The narrator frequently uses *uzhasnyi* to describe Evgenii's experience. See lines 92 (*uzhasnaia pora*), 167 (*uzhasnyi den'*), 299 (*vidi uzhasnyi*), 350 (*uzhasnye potriaseniia*), 353 (*uzhasnye dumy*), 390 (*proshlyi uzhas*), 413 (*uzhasenon*).

29. "The weather was awful: there was a thaw; snow was coming down and it was raining—just as at that unforgettable time when at that terrible midnight hour all the misfortunes of Mr. Goliadkin had begun" (596; 1:213).

30. The most important indirect reference in the later works of Dostoevskii to *The Bronze Horseman* is probably Svidrigailov's suicide in *Crime and Punishment.* Dostoevskii revised *The Double* while still working on *Crime and Punishment.* Before his suicide, Svidrigailov wanders around town on a night very much like the one described in *The Double.* It is July, but nevertheless the night is pitch black, rainy,

cold, and damp with a chilling and howling wind. The following description alluding to a possible flood precedes Svidrigailov's second nightmare. "Through the nocturnal gloom and darkness there resounded a cannon shot, then another. 'Ah, the signal. The water is rising,' he thought; 'towards morning, it will pour out into the lower areas and streets, it will flood the basements and cellars, the sewer-rats will come up, and in the rain and the wind people will start, soaked and cursing, moving their rubbish to the upper floors'" (*PSS,* 6:392).

31. As he is carried off, in the end, to an insane asylum, Goliadkin, as we have seen, watches the doctor's fiery eyes flashing at him with malignant, hellish glee. One might—extravagantly—compare Goliadkin's vision here—seriously or parodically—with Evgenii's mad insight (*proiasnilis' mysli*) into the cause of his unhappy fate, but in *The Double,* God and the Devil are as absent as Peter the Great.

32. Fanger, *Dostoevsky and Romantic Realism,* 162.

33. On the other hand, Pushkin subtitled his *poema Petersburgskaia povest'*. Since the major parts of the poem are introduced as *povestvovan'e* (95) and *rasskaz* (96), the subtitle emphasizes the focus on Evgenii and the fact that Evgenii's story must be told in a different way than Peter's in the Introduction.

34. George Gutsche (*Moral Apostasy in Russian Literature* [DeKalb: Northern Illinois University Press, 1986], 31–35) has argued, from a moral perspective, for a less elevated Peter, who descends from his pedestal to the level of his insignificant subject, Evgenii.

35. Pushkin writes in a letter to Chaadaev (19 October 1836): "And Peter the Great, who in himself alone is universal history!" J. Thomas Shaw, ed., *The Letters of Alexander Pushkin* (Madison: University of Wisconsin Press, 1967), 780.

36. Hegel's famous "slaughter-bench at which the happiness of peoples, the wisdom of states, and the virtue of individuals have been victimized" (G. W. F. Hegel, *Reason in History: A General Introduction to the Philosophy of History,* trans. Robert S. Hartman [New York: Liberal Arts Press, 1953], 27).

37. The only "Peter" in *The Double* is Goliadkin's drunken, untrustworthy, and mocking servant Petrushka. He is usually not around when Goliadkin wants him: *Petrushki net.* Goliadkin is parodically cast as the true child (son) of Peter: Iakov Petrovich. It is, as Terras might say, another role in which Dostoevskii has cast Goliadkin, but a role which he is completely incapable of playing.

38. The Table of Ranks is, in fact, the only one of Peter's reforms that survived essentially intact to 1917.

39. Hegel, *Reason in History,* 43.

40. For a basically semiotic interpretation of *The Bronze Horseman* in terms of binary oppositions, see Svetlana Evdokimova, "'Mednyi vsadnik': Istoriia kak mif," *Russian, Croatian and Serbian, Czech and Slovak, Polish Literature* 28, no. 4 (1990): 441–60.

41. Hegel, *Reason in History,* 12.

42. Lednicki, *Pushkin's "Bronze Horseman,"* 50.

43. Freud argues that the double in primitive thought is a guarantee of immortality, but in the course of civilization it came increasingly to represent death. Sigmund Freud, "The 'Uncanny,'" in *Collected Papers,* 5 vols. (New York: Basic, 1959), 4:386–91.

44. Fanger contrasts Gogol's mastery of the "comic grotesque" with Dostoevskii's mastery of the "tragic grotesque" (*Dostoevsky and Romantic Realism,* 253).

45. For an analysis of the role of the horse or steed in Russian literature, see David Bethea, *The Shape of Apocalypse in Modern Russian Fiction* (Princeton: Princeton University Press, 1989), 44–61.

46. See Grigor'ev's remarks about the story in note 60.

47. For Belinskii's definitions of the poema and its distinction from other genres, see V. G. Belinskii, *Polnoe sobranie sochinenii,* 13 vols. (Moscow: AN SSSR, 1953–59), 6:414–15.

48. Gogol would probably have classified *Dead Souls* as an intermediary form between the epic and novel (*men'shii rod epopei*), in which the author employs a series of adventures to give an accurate and representative picture of the vices and foibles of an era. In citing Cervantes, Gogol points out that *Don Quixote* preserves its "lesser" epic form despite its lightness (*legkost'*), playful tone (*shutlivyi ton*), and prose narration. See N. V. Gogol, *Polnoe sobranie sochinenii,* 14 vols. (Moscow: AN SSSR, 1937–52) 8:478–79.

49. According to Belinskii (*Polnoe sobranie sochinenii*), the poema addresses only the most profound ideas and moral questions: "v noveishei poezii est' osobyi rod eposa, kotoryi ne dopuskaet prozy zhizni, kotoryi skhvatyvaet tol'ko poeticheskie, ideal'nye momenty zhizni i soderzhanie kotorogo sostavliaiut glubochaishie mirosozertsaniia i nravstvennye voprosy chelovechestva. Etot rod eposa odin uderzhal za soboiu imia 'poemy'" (415). "I epos novogo mira iavilsia preimushchestvenno v romane, kotorogo glavnoe otlichie ot drevneellinskogo eposa, krome khristianskikh i drugikh elementov noveishego mira, sostavliaet i *proza zhizni,* voshedshaia v ego soderzhanie i chuzhdaia drevneellinskomu eposu" (414).

50. The subtitles of Pushkin's and Gogol's works show an experimentation with genre typical of literary romanticism. In his discussion of *Evgenii Onegin,* Čiževsky cites Pushkin's novel in verse as a paradigm of the "free" romantic poem, in which the very subtitle (*roman*) constitutes "a deliberate challenge to classical poetics (xv)." Alexander Sergeevich Pushkin, *Evgenij Onegin: A Novel in Verse,* ed. Dmitry Čiževsky (Cambridge: Harvard University Press, 1967), xv–xx. For a discussion of *Dead Souls* as a mixed genre form, see Frederick T. Griffiths and Stanley J. Rabinowitz, *Novel Epics: Gogol, Dostoevsky and National Narrative* (Evanston: Northwestern University Press, 1990), 60–95.

51. Fanger, *Dostoevsky and Romantic Realism,* 162.

52. See Nabokov's positive assessment of *The Double* in his *Lectures on Russian Literature,* 100, 104.

53. Here I shall be relying on the last chapters of the 1846 journal version of *The Double,* since Dostoevskii considerably toned down the theme of rebellion in the revised version of 1866. For the most complete description and analysis of the differences between the 1846 and 1866 versions of *The Double,* see R. I. Avanesov, "Dostoevskii v rabote nad *Dvoinikom,*" in N. K. Piksanov, ed., *Tvorcheskaia istoriia: Issledovaniia po russkoi literature* (Moscow: Nikitinskie subbotniki, 1927), 154–91; Evelyn Harden, "Translator's Introduction," in Fyodor Dostoevsky, *"The Double": Two Versions* (Ann Arbor: Ardis, 1985), xxvi-xxxi. After the critical failure of *The Double* became apparent to him, Dostoevskii contemplated a radical revision of the novel. In the early 1860s he made some notes for revision (see *PSS,* 1:432–36), but they did not enter the 1866 version. In fact, what Dostoevskii did, for various reasons—financial as well as artistic—was to abandon his ambitious plans of transforming the old novel (which he always believed contained one of his most original ideas), and instead merely made cuts in the original: first by eliminating repetitions (Belinskii criticized the novel as exasperatingly repetitious) and then by deleting as much as possible those ideas of rebellion, "freethinking," and imposture (*samozvanstvo*) for which he already had envisioned other more appropriate novelistic forms. Most critics, like Avanesov, hold that the cuts that Dostoevskii made in the 1866 version harm the novel, and that the complete overhaul that Dostoevskii contemplated could never have been successfully achieved using the basic structure and characterization of the 1846 text. See, for example, Bem, "'Nos'" i 'Dvoinike,'" 159–61; W. J. Leatherbarrow, "The Rag with Ambition: The Problem of Self-Will in Dostoevsky's 'Bednyye lyudi' and 'Dvoinik,'" *Modern Language Review* 68 (1973): 616; Gyula Kiraly, "Kompozitsiia siuzheta romana *Dvoinik: Prikliucheniia Gospodina Goliadkina,*" Acta Litteraria Academiae Scientiarum Hungaricae 11 (Budapest: Magyar Tudomanyos Akademia, 1969), 239–56.

54. Perhaps the most notable exception is this regard is Richard Gregg's "The Nature of Nature and the Nature of Eugene in *The Bronze Horseman,*" *Slavic and East European Journal* 21, no. 2 (1977): 167–79.

55. For a different view of Evgenii's name, see Evdokimova, "'Mednyi vsadnik,'" 450. Evdokimova notes that Pushkin probably uses Evgenii's name ironically as "a semantic oxymoron." She further argues that eighteenth-century Russian writers often used *blagorodnyi* ironically, applying it to characters who did not live up to their names. On the other hand, Evdokimova (450) tends to see all similarities between Peter and Evgenii as fundamentally parodic.

56. Pushkin may have empathized with his hero's situation because he saw it as a metaphor of his own in

Russian society. On the other hand, though Evgenii may belong to the hereditary nobility, he seems far less concerned with the fate of his family line and class than was Pushkin. Pushkin, however, did not place family line or class over personal merit. For Pushkin's views on this matter, see Carl R. Proffer, ed., *The Critical Prose of Alexander Pushkin* (Bloomington: Indiana University Press, 1969), 118–20.

57. Dostoevskii's approach to Goliadkin has seemed to many even harsher in light of his sympathetic treatment of Devushkin, the hero of *Poor Folk,* his first novel. See, for example, Victor Terras, "Problems of Human Existence in the Works of the Young Dostoevsky," *Slavic Review* 23 (1964): 85; V. Ia. Kirpotin, *Molodoi Dostoevskii* (Moscow: Gikhl, 1947), 243–45. On the other hand, *The Double,* like *Poor Folk,* also parodies the works of Gogol—in this case, "The Nose," itself a parody of the theme of the double. Dostoevskii reintroduces the seriousness of the theme—the double—that Gogol had made ridiculous.

58. Critics have viewed Dostoevskii's consistent maintenance of both a sympathetic and deprecating stance toward Goliadkin as highly problematic. Frank (*Dostoevsky: The Seeds of Revolt,* 307) notes that "Dostoevsky's work of this period often contains a puzzling ambiguity of tone because a character is often shown simultaneously both as socially oppressed and yet as reprehensible and morally unsavory because he has surrendered too abjectly to the pressure of his environment." The grotesque effect of this point of view is also discussed by N. S. Trubetzkoy, *Dostoevskij als Künstler* (The Hague: Mouton, 1964), 49.

59. For Soviet critics who emphasize the disfiguring effects of the social environment on Goliadkin, see V. V. Ermilov, *F. M. Dostoevskii* (Moscow: Gikhl, 1956), 62–65; L. Grossman, *Dostoevskii* (Moscow: Molodaia gvardiia, 1962), 70–72; G. M. Fridlender, *Realizm Dostoevskogo* (Moscow: Molodaia gvardiia, 1962), 70–72; G. M. Fridlender, *Realizm Dostoevskogo* (Moscow: Nauka, 1964), 68–81; F. Evnin, "Ob odnoi istoriko-literatur-noi legende: Povest' Dostoevskogo 'Dvoinik,'" *Russkaia literatura* 7, no. 3 (1965): 3–26; V. E. Vetlovskaia, "Sotsial'naia tema v pervykh proizvedeniiakh Dostoevskogo," *Russkaia literatura* 3 (1984): 91–94. Many western critics also place a great deal of the blame for Goliadkin's situation on the social and political order in Russia under Nicholas I. See, for example, René Girard, *Dostoievski: Du double à l'unité* (Paris: Plon, 1963), 52–53; Rudolf Neuhäuser, *Das Frühwerk Dostojewkis, Literarische Tradition und gesellschaftliche Anspruch* (Heidelberg: Winter, 1979), 163–75; Dominique Arban, "Le statut de la folie dans les oeuvres de jeunesse de Dostoievski," *Zapiski russkoi akademicheskoi gruppy v SSHA* 14 (1981): 30; Frank, *Dostoevsky: The Seeds of Revolt,* 306–9.

60. Grigor'ev gave perhaps the most negative assessment of *The Double.* In an unpublished letter to Gogol of

17 November 1848, he describes the depressing effect that *The Double* had on his spirit. "As you read this monstrous work, you feel yourself devastated and thrilled as you merge with its absolutely insignificant hero. You come to feel sad that you are a human being and you become convinced that man could not be other than he is described here." Quoted in Kirpotin, *Molodoi Dostoevskii,* 248. Goliadkin has repelled many Soviet critics as well. See, for example, Kirpotin, *Molodoi Dostoevskii,* 242–46; Ermilov, *Dostoevskii,* 70–71.

61. Terras, "Problems of Human Existence," 84–85.

62. Vinogradov, "K morfologii," 111–13; N. S. Trubetzkoy, *Dostoevskij als Künstler,* 48–49; Terras, *The Young Dostoevsky (1846–1849)* (The Hague: Mouton, 1969), 128–33.

63. Vinogradov, "K morfologii," 113–40; Mikhail Bakhtin, *Problems of Dostoevsky's Poetics,* trans. Caryl Emerson (Minneapolis: University of Minnesota Press, 1989), 211–27.

64. Terras, *Young Dostoevsky,* 206–31; M. F. Lomagina, "K voprosu o pozitsii avtora v *Dvoinike* Dostoevskogo," *Filologicheskie nauki* 14, no. 5 (1971): 4–9. Space does not allow a detailed analysis of Dostoevskii's technique of transcribing consciousness. Basically, the narrative appears to be told by still another double of Goliadkin who has the feelings of Goliadkin Senior, but who, in contrast to Goliadkin Senior, can see through Goliadkin Junior's "treachery." In order to preserve his "innocence," Goliadkin Senior must pretend that he has no knowledge of Goliadkin Junior's designs until they are exposed. Alternatively, one might posit that the narration is a brilliant and unique example of *erlebte Rede* in which the narrator transcribes two different levels of Goliadkin's consciousness (and subconscious) simultaneously.

65. The subtitle for chapter 1 reads as follows: "How Titular Councilor Mr. Goliadkin woke up. How he fitted himself out and set off for where he was going. How Mr. Goliadkin justified himself in his own eyes and how later he came to the conclusion that it was better to act boldly, with an openness not devoid of nobility. How Goliadkin finally got to where he was going" (1:334).

66. Terras, *Young Dostoevsky,* 124.

67. Terras, *Young Dostoevsky,* 168–69.

68. Konrad Onasch, *Dostojewski als Verführer* (Zürich: EVZ, 1961), 28–29.

69. Just as evaluations of Evgenii have varied, depending on one's view of Peter and his mission, so have views of Evgenii's madness. Some have seen his madness as mere paranoia. According to Gregg in "The Nature of Nature," Evgenii is subject to "a fully paranoid obsession which in its final phase metamorphoses the illusion of persecution into the hallucination of actual physical pursuit. . . . For if the distinguishing trait of the insane mind is its inability to tell illusion from reality, and if a paranoiac is by definition someone who conjures up nonexistent persecutors, does not a realistic (as opposed to a romantic) reading of the scene suggest that Eugene's accusation is not a revelation of some 'higher reality' (pace Merežkovskij, Lednicki), but a paranoid attempt to escape from reality? . . . May we not, in short, surmise that in the depths of his disordered mind there is the uneasy perception that to have blamed Peter for his misfortunes and to have sworn personal vengeance on Russia's greatest sovereign was reckless, vain, and absurd" (174–75). For those who have seen Evgenii's madness as a higher, elevating poetic vision see, for example, D. S. Merezhkovskii, *Vechnye sputniki: Pushkin,* in *Polnoe sobranie sochinenii* (St. Petersburg: Wol'f, 1911): 13:342–45. Merezhkovskii (344) speaks of the *veshchii bred bezumtsa.* Valerii Briusov, *Moi Pushkin: Stat'i, issledovaniia, nabliudeniia,* ed. N. K. Piksanov (Moscow: Gikhl, 1929), 78–80; Lednicki, *Pushkin's "Bronze Horseman,"* 82–84; Catharine Theimer Nepomnyashchy, "The Poet, History and the Supernatural: A Note on Pushkin's 'The Poet' and *The Bronze Horseman,*" in A. Mandelker, ed., *The Supernatural in Slavic and Baltic Literatures: Essays in Honor of Victor Terras* (Columbus: Slavica, 1988), 34–46. The extent to which Pushkin romanticizes Evgenii's madness becomes apparent when one looks at the gradual diminishment of Evgenii through the drafts. By first reducing Evgenii to the diametric opposite of Peter, Pushkin makes Evgenii's later elevation all the more dramatic.

70. As is well known, because of problems with the censorship, including the personal notations on the manuscript made by Nicholas himself, Pushkin did not publish *The Bronze Horseman* in his lifetime. The version that Zhukovskii published in *Sovremennik* in 1837 had significant changes and deletions in lines 430–38. For Pushkin's lines 434–38—from his own revised version of 1836, which, of course, differs from the 1833 version of the poem—("I perst s ugrozoiu podniav / Shepnul, volnuem mysl'iu chernoi / 'Dobro, stroitel' chudotvornyi! / Uzhe tebe! . . .' No vdrug stremglav . . ."), Zhukovskii substituted: "I perst svoi na nego podniav / Zadumalsia. No vdrug stremglav." Pushkin's original lines (434–38) were restored in the 1857 Annenkov edition of Pushkin's works, with the exception of ellipses for "Uzhe tebe." For the journal version of *The Double,* Dostoevskii had at his disposal the 1841 edition of *The Bronze Horseman* (which was based on the version published by Zhukovskii in *Sovremennik* in 1837). For the revised version of *The Double* (1866), he had at his disposal the Annenkov and later editions of *The Bronze Horseman,* in which lines 434–38 were restored with the exception of "Uzhe tebe." Belinskii (*Polnoe sobranie sochinenii* [Moscow: AN SSSR, 1955], 7:542) in his 1846 review of *The Bronze Horseman* emphasized that Evgenii's words addressed to the monument had obviously been left out ("nedostaet slov, obrashchennykh Evgeniem k

monumentu") and that those words obviously contained the idea of the poem. Izmailov argues that Belinskii's words indicate that he knew the original lines, either through friends at *Sovremennik* or through those who prepared the first posthumous edition of Pushkin's works in 1841. Although Dostoevskii and other literary figures close to Belinskii may also have known the original lines, it is clear even in Zhukovskii's edition that Evgenii threatened the statue. Dostoevskii could hardly have been less perceptive than Belinskii about the omitted lines (*The Double* appeared in print before Belinskii's analysis of *The Bronze Horseman*), assuming that Belinskii did not know what had been omitted. For the most complete discussion of the publishing history of *The Bronze Horseman,* see Izmailov, *A. S. Pushkin,* 227–42.

71. For Briusov (*Moi Pushkin,* 79) this is not so much a return to sanity as *prozrenie.*

72. Gregg, "The Nature of Nature," 174–75.

73. Psychologists have often studied autoscopy, the hallucination that a mirror image of oneself exists outside the self. See Robert A. Rogers, *Psychoanalytical Study of the Double in Literature* (Detroit: Wayne State University Press, 1970), 14–15.

74. Nepomnyashchy, "Poet, History and the Supernatural," 43.

75. Terras, *Young Dostoevsky,* 256.

76. Ibid., 183.

77. Noting the solemnity of tone and the Slavonicisms used to describe Evgenii's most dramatic encounter with Peter, Briusov (*Moi Pushkin,* 80) sees that some type of equation has been temporarily achieved: "Eto uzhe ne 'nash geroi,' kotoryi 'zhivet v Kolomne, gde-to sluzhit'; eto sopernik 'groznogo tsaria,' o kotorom dolzhno govorit' 'tem zhe iazykom, kak o Petre.'"

78. Merezhkovskii, *Vechnye sputniki,* 344.

79. Critics have argued that the poem is at least in part a thinly disguised commentary on the Decembrist uprising. See, for example, D. D. Blagoi, *Sotsiologiia tvorchestva Pushkina: Etiudy* (Moscow: Federatsiia, 1929), 308–28; Gutsche, *Moral Apostasy,* 37–42, 158–60.

80. To Merezhkovskii, it was Evgenii's open threat to Peter that opened up the floodgates that would eventually bring an end to the Petersburg period of Russian history. Some critics have seen the threat as serious enough to force Peter to descend from his pedestal to quash it, even if Evgenii only imagines Peter descending from his pedestal—or even if Pushkin only imagines Evgenii imagining it. See, for example, David Bethea, "The Role of *Eques* in Pushkin's *The Bronze Horseman,*" in David M. Bethea, ed., *Puškin Today* (Bloomington: Indiana University Press, 1993), 117.

81. When Dostoevskii revised *The Double* in 1866, he had already become committed to the creation of more active, romantically conceived rebels. The foreboding notes and the figure of Germann in *The Queen of Spades* became the driving metaphors for his heroes and his depiction of Petersburg. In fact, Dostoevskii's notes for his revision of *The Double* reveal that he is no longer thinking of the meek Goliadkin, but rather of the proud Raskol'nikov. To transform, as Dostoevskii had planned, Goliadkin into an active revolutionary, a radical of the 1860s, involved more than revising the old story; it meant writing an entirely new novel.

82. For a negative evaluation of Evgenii's love for Parasha, see Evdokimova, "'Mednyi vsadnik,'" 452.

83. In his plans for revision (*PSS,* 1:435), Dostoevskii describes the German woman as a lame, exceedingly poor woman who had once helped Goliadkin. V. N. Zakharov notes that the novel never really shows Goliadkin in love. See his "Zagadka 'Dvoinika,'" *Problemy izucheniia Dostoevskogo* (Petrozavodsk: Petrozavodskii Gosudarstvennyi Universitet, 1978), 35.

84. In his notes for the revision of *The Double* (*PSS,* 1:432–36), Dostoevskii focuses on the relationship that should obtain between employees and their superiors (*nachal'stvo*). But as with many of these notes, they shed a great deal more light on Dostoevskii's projects of the 1860s than on the text of *The Double.* For an interpretation of these fragments, see Bem, "'Nos' i 'Dvoinik,'" 152–53. Imposture as rebellion is the subject of *Boris Godunov,* not *The Bronze Horseman.* For a discussion of samozvanstvo in Dostoevskii in terms of the demonic, see Harriet Murav, "Representations of the Demonic: Seventeenth-Century Pretenders and *The Devils,*" *Slavic and East European Journal* 35, no. 1 (1991): 56–70. For an especially insightful examination of the question of samozvanstvo in Pushkin, see Caryl Emerson, *Boris Godunov: Transpositions of a Russian Theme* (Bloomington: Indiana University Press, 1986), 88–141.

85. From an ancient biblical point of view, God alone is king in Israel. This view makes suspect the claims of even "legitimate" kings. In the eighth century B.C.E., killing one's predecessor was the most common path of succession to the throne. See Robert M. Seltzer, *Jewish People: Jewish Thought* (New York: Macmillan, 1980), 19–27.

86. Goliadkin's first name, Jacob (*Iakov*) further underscores the theme of imposture in *The Double.* In the Bible, Jacob, the younger brother, succeeds in usurping the position of his elder twin brother, Esau, by deceit, just as Goliadkin Junior usurps the position of Goliadkin Senior—at least in Goliadkin Senior's imagination. Esau calls attention to the importance of Jacob's name when he speaks to his father of Jacob's deception: "Was he, then, *named Jacob* that he might *supplant* me these two times? First he took away my birthright and now he has taken away my blessing" (Genesis 27:36). The Hebrew root *aqab* (supplant) is associated with the name Jacob. Whereas the Bible

treats the succession to the leadership of all Israel with requisite seriousness, *The Double* presents as travesty Goliadkin's being passed over for a petty position in the tsarist bureaucracy. Moreover, Goliadkin Senior and Junior, in contrast to Esau and Jacob, are not reconciled in the end.

87. See also the ridiculous occurrences of *Otrep'evy v nash vek nevozmozhny* in Klara Olsuf'evna's letter (1:416), clearly the most important deletions. See also 1:167, 1:191, 1:196, 1:212, 1:217.

88. See B. A. Uspenskii, "Tsar and Pretender: *Samozvanstvo* or Royal Imposture in Russia as a Cultural-Historical Phenomenon," trans. David Budgen, in Iu. Lotman and B. A. Uspenskii, *The Semiotics of Russian Culture,* ed. Ann Shukman (Ann Arbor: University of Michigan, 1984), 263, 272.

89. Caryl Emerson's (*Boris Godunov,* 123–26) characterization of Dimitrii as a risk-taker and adventurer, as a person who chooses to create himself—and thus a character rather dear in some ways to Pushkin's heart—highlights again the reductive and parodic nature of Dostoevskii's project with Goliadkin, whose greatest fear in life is imposture (samozvanstvo).

90. There is, of course, a critical approach to the poem that sees nature as the ultimate reality to which both Peter and Evgenii—and humankind in general—are subject. For the most detailed argument in favor of the primacy of nature in the poem, see A. D. Briggs, *A Comparative Study of Pushkin's The Bronze Horseman, Nekrasov's Red-Nosed Frost, and Blok's The Twelve* (Lewiston: Mellen, 1990). The visions of Petersburg presented at the end of Dostoevskii's "A Weak Heart" (1848), and later basically repeated in "Petersburg Dreams in Verse and Prose" (1861), represent some of the most brilliant examples of this position. The narrator of "A Weak Heart," describing Petersburg transformed in the winter twilight, concludes: "It seemed as if that entire world, with all its inhabitants, the strong and the weak, with all their habitations, the shelters of the poor, or the gilded palaces, the comfort of the strong of this world, resembled at that twilight hour a fantastic, bewitching vision, like a dream that in its turn would vanish and evaporate into the dark blue sky" (2:49). On the other hand, scholars have often identified Evgenii with the river, in terms of revolt. See, for example, Iurii Borev, *Iskusstvo interpretatsii i otsenki: Opyt prochteniia "Mednogo vsadnika"* (Moscow: Sovetskii pisatel', 1981), 382. Less common is the identification

of Peter with the river (in terms of birth). See Daniel Rancour-Laferriere, "The Couvade of Peter the Great: A Psychoanalytical Aspect of *The Bronze Horseman,*" in Bethea, ed., *Puškin Today,* 76–81.

FURTHER READING

Criticism

Anderson, Roger B. "*The Double*: Duality and Conflict." *Dostoevsky: Myths of Duality,* pp. 12–26. University of Florida Press, 1986.
Identifies contradictory elements in *The Double.*

Bakhtin, Mikhail M. "The Dismantled Consciousness: An Analysis of *The Double.*" *Dostoevsky: New Perspectives,* edited by Robert Louis Jackson, pp. 19–34. Englewood Cliffs, NJ: Prentice-Hall, 1984.
Examines speech and dialogue in *The Double.*

Gasperetti, David. "*The Double*: Dostoevski's Self-Effacing Narrative." *Slavic and East European Journal* 33 (1989): 217–34.
Discusses ways in which Dostoevski departed from the techniques of the Russian Natural School of fiction in *The Double* as well as his ambivalent opinion of the work throughout his life.

Jones, John. "*The Double.*" In *Dostoevsky,* pp. 47–106. Oxford and London: Oxford University Press, 1983.
Explores the poetic aspects of *The Double.*

Pachmuss, Temira. "The Technique of Dream-Logic." In *F. M. Dostoevsky: Dualism and Synthesis of the Human Soul,* pp. 18–190. Carbondale: Southern Illinois University Press, 1963.
Examines the blurring of objective and subjective reality in *The Double.*

Rosenthal, Richard J. "Dostoevsky's Experiment with Projective Mechanisms and the Theft of Identity in *The Double.*" In *Russian Literature and Psychoanalysis,* edited by Daniel Rancour-Laferriere, pp. 59–88. Amsterdam and Philadelphia: John Benjamins Publishing Company, 1989.
Discusses the psychoanalytic aspects of the dual personality in *The Double.*

Additional coverage of Dostoevsky's life and career is contained in the following sources published by the Gale Group: *DISCovering Authors; DISCovering Authors: British; DISCovering Authors: Canadian; DISCovering Authors Modules: Most-Studied Authors, Novelists; DISCovering Authors 3.0; Nineteenth-Century Literature Criticism,* Vols. 2, 7, 21, 33, 44; *Novels for Students,* Vols. 3, 8; *Short Stories for Students,* Vol. 8; and *World Literature Criticism.*

"A White Heron"

Sarah Orne Jewett

American short story writer, novelist, and poet. The following entry presents criticism on Jewett's short story "A White Heron" (1886). For additional coverage of Jewett's short fiction, see *SSC*, Vol. 6.

INTRODUCTION

"A White Heron" is one of Jewett's most well-known and often anthologized short story. In it, Jewett presents a nine-year-old girl's reaction to the intrusion of a young man into her feminine and natural world. The variety of narrative techniques, symbols, and imagery, as well as the ambiguous ending, have elicited much critical commentary by scholars. Several feminist scholars view this work as Jewett's rebellion against the realistic literature that male authors made the mainstream literature of the late nineteenth century. Although many of Jewett's short stories were first published in the *Atlantic Monthly,* the magazine's editor, William Dean Howells, declined this work for being too "romantic." Thus this favorite work, which Jewett referred to as "her" and professed "to love," was first published in 1886 in book form in *A White Heron, and Other Stories.*

PLOT AND MAJOR CHARACTERS

"A White Heron" opens in the evening as young Sylvia is searching for a milk cow astray in the woods of New England. She is startled by the sudden appearance of a young man with a gun, who proclaims that he is an ornithologist and has come to this rural land to hunt, kill, and stuff birds for his pleasure. When he entreats Sylvia's aid, she leads him to her grandmother's farm. Sylvia has come to live with Mrs. Tilley to both escape the industrial city where her mother struggles alone to support the family and to be a help and companion to her grandmother. The young stranger both charms the grandmother and interests the granddaughter and enlists their help, by offering much needed cash, in locating the nest of a rare white heron. Although the next day Sylvia docilely accompanies the young man on his quest, they fail to find their prey. At dawn on the following day, Sylvia awakes and scales a massive and ancient pine in search of the heron and its nest. From her vantage point atop the tree, Sylvia glimpses the heron, its nest, and its mate, and she experiences an epiphany. When she returns to the farm later that morning, Sylvia guards her secret.

MAJOR THEMES

Jewett was known as a local colorist whose stories often portrayed the ordinary aspects of life in works where mood or atmosphere preceed plot in importance. While the colorist elements are evident in "A White Heron," Sylvia's choice, or action of remaining silent, is the crucial element in the story. Commentators have interpreted Sylvia's choice between revealing or not revealing the location of the heron in various ways: expressing the conflict between urban/rural life, between child/adult perceptions of the world, or between male/female modes of artistic creation. Several critics see the work as a modern fairy tale in which the female declines to be rescued by a princely man, an ornithologist whose goal is symbolically to hunt and conquer women and display them in his home.

CRITICAL RECEPTION

Although contemporary commentators on "A White Heron" express qualified praise, it was not until the 1970s that critics seriously analyzed the story. Several scholars considered the possible influence of prior works, particularly Harriet Beecher Stowe's novel *The Pearl of Orr's Island* and Nathaniel Hawthorne's short story "Young Goodman Brown" on "A White Heron." The fact that Jewett expressed the personal importance "A White Heron" held for her has caused critics to treat it as a personal artistic credo and feminist document. They analyzed feminist subtexts, reversals of traditional fairy-tale formulas and coming-of-age stories, flight imagery, and narrative techniques. Several scholars explored the story's psycho-sexual and other symbols using Freudian or Jungian methods. Although critics debate various interpretations and the effectiveness of Jewett's efforts, they agree that "A White Heron" is worthy of study.

PRINCIPAL WORKS

Short Fiction

Play Days: A Book of Stories for Children 1878
Old Friends and New 1879
Country By-Ways 1881
The Mate of the Daylight, and Friends Ashore 1884
A White Heron, and Other Stories 1886
The King of Folly Island, and Other People 1888
Strangers and Wayfarers 1890
Tales of New England 1890
A Native of Winby, and Other Tales 1893
The Life of Nancy 1895
The Queen's Twin, and Other Stories 1899
Stories and Tales (novel and short stories) 1910
Lady Ferry 1950
The Country of the Pointed Firs, and Other Stories (omnibus volume) 1954
Deephaven, and Other Stories (omnibus volume) 1966
The Uncollected Short Stories of Sarah Orne Jewett 1971
Novels and Stories 1994
The Dunnet Landing Stories 1996
The Irish Stories of Sarah Orne Jewett 1996

Other Major Works

Deephaven (novel) 1877
A Country Doctor (novel) 1884
A Marsh Island (novel) 1885
Betty Leicester: A Story for Girls (juvenile fiction) 1890
Betty Leicester's English Xmas (juvenile fiction) 1894
The Country of the Pointed Firs (novel) 1896
The Tory Lover (novel) 1901
Verses (poetry) 1916
Sarah Orne Jewett Letters (letters) 1967

CRITICISM

Katharine T. Jobes (essay date 1974)

SOURCE: "From Stowe's *Eagle Island* to Jewett's 'White Heron,'" *Colby Library Quarterly,* Vol. 10, No. 8, December, 1974, pp. 515–521.

[*In the essay below, Jobes traces the influence of Harriet Beecher Stowe's novel* The Pearl of Orr's Island *on Jewett's art, particularly her self-definition as an artist.*]

Sarah Orne Jewett pointed out the influence of Harriet Beecher Stowe's Maine novel *The Pearl of Orr's Island* (1862) on her own writing and provided what has become the standard explanation of that influence. In her 1893 Preface to *Deephaven,* she acknowledges graciously that *The Pearl of Orr's Island* was the first work to show her how materials which she had known and loved from birth—Maine character, custom, landscape—could be used effectively in literature.

> It was, happily, in the writer's childhood that Mrs. Stowe had written of those who dwelt along the wooded seacoast and by the decaying, shipless harbors of Maine. The first chapter of *The Pearl of Orr's Island* gave the young author of *Deephaven* to see with new eyes, and to follow eagerly the old shore paths from one gray, weather-beaten house to another where Genius pointed her the way.[1]

Jewett's explanation has generally been echoed without substantial change by critics and biographers concerned with literary influences upon her writing.

I wish to point out another way in which *The Pearl of Orr's Island* seems to have influenced Jewett's developing art, which she and her critics have not noted: besides showing her the general material which would prove congenial to her, it provided—in the Eagle Island episode of Chapter 16—specific material which she would use in working out her self-definition as an artist. The Eagle Island episode expresses Stowe's conception of the nature of the artist. It does so through a brief narrative in which a sensitive girl demurs at a boy's plundering a birds' nest at the top of a tall tree and in an authorial explanation of the narrative. Evidently stirred by the episode to express her own conception of the nature of the artist, Jewett rewrote it twice—in **"The Eagle Trees"** (1882) and **"A White Heron"** (1886)—discovering in the process her own increasingly clearly defined artistic nature.

In her Eagle Island episode, Stowe conceives of the artist as one of a class of beings of unusual spiritual sensitivity who serve an essentially ministerial function as "priests and priestesses of the spiritual life, ordained of God to keep the balance between the rude but absolute necessities of physical life and the higher sphere to which that must at length give place."[2] Their spiritual giftedness is innate:

> But there are, both of men and women, beings born into this world in whom from childhood the spiritual and the reflective predominate over the physical. In re-

lation to other human beings, they seem to be organized much as birds are in relation to other animals. They are the artists, the poets, the unconscious seers, to whom the purer truths of spiritual instruction are open.

Stowe precedes her explanation with an exemplum, structured upon theological dialectic, in which she develops the spiritual artistic tendencies by contrast with the physical or "natural" tendency of those of more worldly calling. (In those editions of *The Pearl of Orr's Island* with chapter titles, Chapter 16 is entitled "The Natural and the Spiritual.") Stowe embodies the contrasting tendencies in Mara Lincoln and Moses Pennel. Mara is a gentle, idealistic, reflective creature of the spirit, the type of the artist/poet/seer; her playmate Moses is a vigorous, practical, active adventurer, the type of the natural man. They reveal their contrasting characters in a brief incident in which Moses climbs far up into a rugged old hemlock and plunders an eagles' nest, bringing its eggs down in his pocket. ("'I played their nest was a city and I spoiled it.'") Much as she loves and admires Moses, Mara is troubled by the eagles' distress and protests the spoiling. Though she is silenced by Moses' boyish bravado and belligerent rebuttal ("'I wish I had a gun now, I'd stop those old eagles' screeching'"; "'I am older than you, and when I tell you a thing's right, you ought to believe it'"), she will continue, Stowe predicts, to reflect upon the matter and will ultimately make Moses tremble before her sense of the right. Mara does indeed by the end of the novel exercise her spiritual suasion on Moses.

Stowe's own artistry in this Eagle Island episode is consistent with the conception she presents in it of the ministerial artist. She assumes the right to preach, taking her form—exemplum/explication—from the sermon and her dialectic structure from Christian theology. Her ministerial bent is not surprising, considering that she was daughter, sister, and wife to Congregational ministers and steeped in Calvinist theology.

In her two versions of Stowe's Eagle Island episode, Jewett retains the artist figure's sensitivity of spirit, but without theological formulation. The heart of the episode for Jewett is the instinctive sensitivity of the artist/poet/seer represented in the gentle Mara; Jewett stresses it in both her versions and uses the plot elements of the exemplum in order to do so. But Stowe's dialectic and didacticism were not natural to Jewett, who had not been bred, as Stowe had been, in Calvinism. Jewett's versions move away from the doctrinal and didactic toward the personal and lyric, seeking in the natural world familiar to Jewett the spiritual truths Stowe found in theology.

Jewett's first version, **"The Eagle Trees: To J[ohn] G[reenleaf] W[hittier],"** reveals Jewett reshaping Stowe's Eagle Island materials in several ways crucial to the success of the superior later version, **"A White Heron."** First, she casts an historical poet whom she greatly admired, Whittier, in Mara's role of artist/poet/seer. In so doing, she retains Mara's qualities of gentleness and sensitivity but

eliminates her theological connections. Whittier, as Jewett depicts him, does not take his poetic inspiration directly from God, like Stowe's artists ("ordained of God"), but rather from nature, which instructs him and has a metaphorical kinship with him:

> Was it the birds who early told
>   The dreaming boy that he would win
> A poet's crown instead of gold?
>   That he would fight a nation's sin,
>   On eagle wings of song would gain
>   A place that few might enter in,
>   And keep his life without a stain
>
> Through many years, yet not grow old?
> And he shall be what few men are,
>   Said all the pine trees, whispering low;
> His thought shall find an unseen star,
>   He shall our treasured legends know;
>   His words will give the way-worn rest
>   Like this cool shade our branches throw,
>   He, lifted like our loftiest crest,
> Shall watch his country near and far.[3]

Second, by personifying the great pines and the eagles and by making them the principal seers and the sources of poetic inspiration, Jewett has nature assume the leading role in this version of the narrative. Stowe's trees and eagles, in contrast, are merely props to illustrate her thesis about human nature. Jewett's animation of nature, like her image of the poet, modifies Stowe's contention that inspiration comes directly from God; moreover, it breaks down Stowe's physical/spiritual or natural/spiritual dialectic. The changes are important, because they help Jewett expand the province of regional materials from being merely local color to becoming an integral part of her aesthetic, as expressed in **"A White Heron"** and other New England stories.

Third, she re-characterizes another aspect of Stowe's dialectic—the equation of boy/girl in the narrative with active/passive, door/reflector—by making the poet a "dreaming *boy*" and by having her persona consider (but reject) Moses' active role of storming the eagles' nest (stanzas 3 and 4):

> High in the branches clings the nest
>   The great birds build from year to year
> And though they fly from east to west,
>   Some instinct keeps this eyrie dear
>   To their fierce hearts; and now their eyes
>   Glare down at me with rage and fear,
>   They stare at me with wild surprise
> Where high in air they strong-winged rest.
>
> I will not trespass in this place
>   Nor storm the eagles' castle-walls,
> Where winds have rocked the royal race
>   And taught the note the young bird calls
>   Rejoicing as he seeks the cloud,
>   And spreads his wings and never falls
>   Like weaker birds; but soaring proud
> A king at heart, he conquers space.

In stanza 4 lies the germ of the girl-poet who assumes some of Moses' active and decisive role in **"A White Heron."**

Finally, Jewett shifts the form of the Eagle Island material from exemplary prose narrative to lyric poetry. She is not a master of poetic form and diction, and she does not use Stowe's narrative elements coherently in **"The Eagle Trees."** In order to treat the Eagle Island material successfully, she returns to prose narrative in the form of the short story. But the poetic version serves the functions of shifting the tone from didactic to lyric and of reinforcing the emphatic role of nature in the narrative.

Having made these preparatory revisions, Jewett is then able to make Stowe's material fully her own in **"A White Heron."** The poet figure, Sylvia, is again a girl child, an "unconscious seer," much like Mara in her gentle spirituality and lonely reflectiveness, but Sylvia is able to assume, too, Moses' active role of making the heroic climb up the tall tree and of deciding the fate of the bird, in this version a rare white heron. (The hunter who seeks the heron, though he is on the whole sympathetically portrayed, retains Moses' possessive and destructive qualities; he seems to Sylvy at first acquaintance to be "the enemy.") Sylvy decides to save the heron instead of revealing him to her hunter friend and acknowledges in so doing her special kinship with nature. Her decision resolves a conflict which is not, as in Stowe's version, primarily dramatic and dialectic, but rather essentially private (in that Sylvy is seeking to define her own nature through her choice of allegiance) and lyric (in that Sylvy is reaching intuitively toward a highly personal and emotional union with nature).

Sylvy's nature points to a general conception of the artist quite different from Stowe's ministerial conception. Jewett's artist is not one of a class of passive spiritual mediums through whom God's truths flow to enlighten others; she is an active individual seeking to discover her own nature and its relationship to the world around her. Jewett images the discovery process in the difficult climb Sylvy makes up the tall tree "like a great main-mast to the voyaging earth"[4] whereby she becomes a seer of "this wonderful sight and pageant of the world" and finally of the spiritual essence of the natural world, as it is represented in the rare and beautiful white heron. The transcendent effort of seeing nature and of determining to preserve it inviolate rewards the seer, Jewett hopes, with spiritual sustenance: "Were the birds better friends than their hunter might have been,—who can tell? Whatever treasures were lost to her, woodlands and summer-time, remember! Bring your gifts and graces and tell your secrets to this lonely country child!"

Jewett's solicitude for the lonely country child is deeply felt. She is much closer personally to her image of the artist than Stowe is to hers. Sylvy is not, like Mara, an imagined type of the artistic spirit described with authorial detachment; she is a surrogate self for Jewett, a portrait of the artist as a young girl, whom the author describes and sometimes even addresses feelingly. Jewett depicts Sylvy as thriving in the country after her early years of wilting in a manufacturing town. Jewett herself had received similar sustenance from the New England countryside as a child; her doctor-father had taken her with him on his rounds so that her health might benefit from the fresh air. She continued to receive sustenance—now imaginative and spiritual—in her adulthood from the countryside she had loved as a child, and she notes wistfully changes brought about by time and by outsiders.[5] (The hunter in **"A White Heron"** is a city dweller who comes to the country with money and gun to try to possess and destroy its natural life.) And yet, like Sylvy, Jewett evidently found troubling the decision to commit herself fully—in her case in the form of her literary vocation—to preserving the New England countryside. In 1884, two years before **"A White Heron,"** she wrote the semi-autobiographical novel *A Country Doctor,* in which the heroine's conflict consists of whether to choose marriage or vocation. (She chooses vocation.) Still in the process of self-discovery, Jewett concludes her portrait of the artist not with an assertion, but with a question and a hope. The seer, the voyager on Jewett's great main-mast rooted firmly in New England, continuously looks out and questions and seeks.[6]

The successive versions of the Eagle Island episode record the growth of an independent artistic spirit away from her mentor. Retaining their common belief in the artist's sensitive spirit and their common use of New England materials, Jewett develops independently a quality of gentle questing in place of Stowe's earnest dogmatizing. She seeks in nature what Stowe finds in God. She speaks in lyric, poetic prose, while Stowe speaks in sermons. She envisions a wild, light, slender white heron instead of Stowe's protesting eagles.

Notes

1. Sarah Orne Jewett, Preface to *Deephaven* (Boston, 1894), 3-4. See also *Sarah Orne Jewett Letters,* ed. Richard Cary, enlarged and rev. ed. (Waterville, Maine, 1967), 40–41; 84–85.

2. *The Pearl of Orr's Island: A Story of the Coast of Maine,* 28th ed. (Boston, 1887), 179. Subsequent quotations are from pp. 178 and 177 of this edition.

3. The concluding stanzas (6 and 7) of the 1882 text of "The Eagle Trees: To J. G. W." quoted by Carl J. Weber in "Whittier and Sarah Orne Jewett." *New England Quarterly,* XVIII (September 1945), 404. Stanzas 3 and 4 below are from the same source, p. 403.

4. "A White Heron," in *The Best Stories of Sarah Orne Jewett,* ed. Willa Cather, Mayflower Ed. (Gloucester, Mass., 1965), II, 16. Subsequent quotations are from II, 18, and II, 21, in this edition.

   In Stowe's *Pearl,* Moses is an actual sea voyager.

5. See, for example, the 1893 Preface to *Deephaven,* p. 4: "it was easy to be much disturbed by the sad discovery that certain phases of provincial life were fast waning in New England. Small and old-fashioned

towns . . . were no longer almost self-subsistent, as in earlier times; and while it was impossible to estimate the value of that wider life that was flowing in from the great springs, many a mournful villager felt the anxiety that came with these years of change. . . . The new riches of the country were seldom very well spent in those days; the money that the tourist or summer citizen left behind him was apt to be used to sweep away the quaint houses, the roadside thicket, the shady woodland, that had lured him first." Jewett speaks here of her youthful anxieties; she professes to be more sanguine in 1893 about the survival of New England individuality. (Preface, p. 5.)

6. In "The Child in Sarah Orne Jewett," *Colby Library Quarterly,* VII (September 1967), reprinted in *Appreciation of Sarah Orne Jewett,* ed. Richard Cary (Waterville, Maine, 1973), Eugene Hillhouse Pool also reads "A White Heron" biographically, although somewhat differently. He argues that Jewett "chooses, psychologically, to remain a child with Sylvia," because she clings so intensely to her memory of her father and his love and thus "repudiates the offer of mature, passionate love that would be inherent in any acceptance of herself as a mature woman." (*Appreciation,* p. 225.)

Richard Brenzo (essay date 1978)

SOURCE: "Free Heron or Dead Sparrow: Sylvia's Choice in Sarah Orne Jewett's 'A White Heron,'" *Colby Library Quarterly,* Vol. 14, No. 1, March, 1978, pp. 36–41.

[*In this essay, Brenzo explains the symbolism of Sylvia's climb up the pine tree.*]

The use of a juvenile narrator or a child's point of view seems especially common in American literature (*What Maisie Knew, Huckleberry Finn,* "I Want to Know Why"). This technique provides a unique, often humorous view of the foibles of adult society, and, more profoundly, portrays the struggles of the child as he or she grows and tries to form a relationship with that society. In this tradition is one of Sarah Orne Jewett's finest stories, **"A White Heron,"** a thoughtful portrait of a nine-year-old girl who is suddenly forced to make a very difficult choice between a young man's approval and loyalty to herself and to nature. Because of the striking nature images—the forest, the pine tree, the heron, the hunted birds—and because of Sylvia's intense emotional response to the young hunter, a symbolic reading of the tale is inevitable, as most critical interpretations attest. Sylvia feels but cannot, of course, verbalize her awakening sexuality and growing self-awareness. However, Jewett's symbolic treatment universalizes and enriches the meaning of the girl's inner experiences.

Sylvia (her name derived from the Latin for "forest") is a recent transplant from "a crowded manufacturing town."[1]

Her grandmother, Mrs. Tilley, has asked the girl to come live with her at her small farm in the Maine woods. Sylvia finds it "a beautiful place to live in" (p. 141), and becomes so familiar with the woods that she can follow paths she cannot see, and finally becomes identified with the woods: "it made her feel as if she were a part of the gray shadows and the moving leaves" (pp. 141–42). Since Sylvia is "Afraid of folks" (p. 140) anyway, the solitude of the sylvan life is no burden. Several images underscore the fact that she is a shy, intensely private person. She is associated with her grandmother's cow, who loves to hide in the woods, with a hop-toad who tries to hide under the porch, and above all, with the white heron who dwells in a hidden nest in a remote swamp.

The story begins in the evening, as Sylvia walks the cow home. Just as she is thinking of "the great red-faced boy who used to chase and frighten her" (p. 142), she is "horror-stricken" (p. 142) to hear a boy's "determined, and somewhat aggressive" whistle (p. 142). Before she can hide, Sylvia is accosted by a young man carrying a rifle. This "enemy" (p. 142) asks her the way to the road in a "cheerful and persuasive tone" (p. 142). When she fails to answer, he explains "kindly" that he has been hunting birds, and needs "a friend very much" (p. 143). Sylvia is even more alarmed when he "gallantly" asks if he can spend the night at her home before going "gunning" (p. 143) in the morning. Jewett's language in this section establishes several of the themes and ironies developed later in her story. Sylvia's initial reaction to the young man is fear, partially sexual in nature, as the ambiguity of his requests indicates. His hunting of birds echoes Sylvia's memories of being chased by the frightening red-faced boy, which in turn is an obvious symbol for a fear of rape. At the same time, the girl's new acquaintance is actually "kind" and "gallant." Thus, Sylvia responds not only to what the youth is, but to what he (and his gun) represent; her fears have an internal as well as an external basis.

Interestingly, the author emphasizes Sylvia's sleepiness during this episode. Her awareness of external reality is blurred, so that her reactions are less objective and more emotional. Her waking consciousness is approaching a dream state. There is a dreamlike quality to much of the story's imagery.

Sylvia guides the young hunter to the homestead, where her grandmother's "long-slumbering hospitality" (p. 144) welcomes him to eat supper and remain overnight. It quickly becomes apparent that the youth is what he claims to be, a hunter of birds, an "ornithologist" (p. 147) who stuffs his specimens for display in his home. This also is a threatening idea for Sylvia, although the boy presents no overt physical danger. Her grandmother has already told the young man that "the wild creatur's counts her [Sylvia] one o' themselves" (p. 146), and that Sylvia is especially close to the birds of the forest. When the hunter asks if she has seen the white heron, her "heart gave a wild beat" (p. 147), for she has seen the bird in a bright, hot, swampy area, where her grandmother had warned her "she might sink in the soft black mud underneath and never be heard of more" (p. 148). Sylvia's identification with the things of the forest has moved from shadows and leaves to "creatur's," then birds, and finally the white heron. The fate of the heron is tied to Sylvia's own destiny.

A further association of girl and heron comes after the boy offers ten dollars to anyone who can show him the heron's nest. He speculates, "Perhaps it was only migrating, or had been chased out of its own region by some bird of prey" (p. 148). Of course this sentence can apply to Sylvia and her recollection of being chased by the red-faced boy in her first region, the city. At any rate, the ten dollars has its effect on Sylvia, arousing thoughts of the "many wished-for treasures" (p. 149) it could buy.

The next day Sylvia and the boy go on a hunting expedition. Now the girl loses "her first fear of the friendly lad" (p. 149), but she is still unable to understand "why he killed the very birds he seemed to like so much" (p. 149). Although she would like him better without his gun, she accepts his gift of a jackknife, thus associating herself with his own capacity for violence and bloodshed. Eventually her feeling for him becomes "loving admiration. She had never seen anybody so charming and delightful; the woman's heart, asleep in the child, was vaguely thrilled by a dream of love. Some premonition of that great power stirred and swayed these young foresters" (pp. 149–50). The sexuality and self-awareness beginning to stir within Sylvia are adult emotions; however, their subconscious aspect is underlined by "asleep" and "dream."

Sylvia is moving from an idea of sex as purely frightening and destructive, to a realization that generosity and kindness are also part of the male temperament. The author takes pains to show that the hunter has these virtues. Other traits are revealed by his words and actions. He is willing to devote considerable time and energy to his goal of shooting particular birds. He persuades with charm, and with gifts. He is described as a scientist, and although he enjoys the beauty of birds, he wants that beauty to be under his control and constantly accessible to him. The young man has become somewhat detached from his violent impulses, which he expresses through his love of shooting. Undoubtedly he is kind, gallant, and friendly, and these characteristics give him far more influence on Sylvia than a "great red-faced boy" could have. Yet he is a person determined to possess what he wants. This mixture of charm and forcefulness justifies Sylvia's continued ambivalent feelings towards him.

The tale's climax comes early the next morning, when Sylvia steals from her bed to find the nest of the white heron. For a lookout tower she plans to use "a great pinetree . . . the last of its generation" (pp. 150–51). Sylvia is sure she will see the whole world, and the nest as well, from the top of the tree. The girl believes this adventure will bring "triumph and delight and glory for the later morning when she could make known the secret! It was almost too real and too great for the childish heart to bear"

(p. 151). These last words suggest Sylvia feels herself on the verge of a transcendent experience, or perhaps a vision, more suited for an adult. And the author adds a cautionary note: "Alas, if the great wave of human interest which flooded for the first time this dull little life should sweep away the satisfaction of an existence heart to heart with nature and the dumb life of the forest!" (p. 152).

Sylvia is about to make a choice between two modes of living, thinking, and feeling. Clearly, what is at stake here is not only the heron, but Sylvia's own being. In the words of Richard Cary, "To divulge the secret of the heron would be to divulge the secret of self; to destroy one would be to destroy the other."[2] For Sylvia, betraying the heron would mean giving up her closeness to the forest, a closeness which is a profound, essential part of her identity. But to satisfy the boy's wishes, such a betrayal will be necessary.

Paul John Eakin sees Sylvia's scaling of the pine tree as a symbol of knowledge and experience.[3] Cary terms it a "rite of initiation leading to self-discovery" (p. 102). Fittingly, the climb takes place at dawn. The great tree is not only a road to knowledge and self-discovery, but also symbolizes the enduring strength of the past, not Sylvia's past in the stifling industrial town, but an ageless, archetypal past.

> The way was harder than she thought; she must reach far and hold fast, the sharp dry twigs caught and held her and scratched her like angry talons, the pitch made her thin little fingers clumsy and stiff as she went round and round the tree's great stem. . . .
>
> The tree seemed to lengthen itself out as she went up, and to reach farther and farther upward. . . . It must truly have been amazed that morning through all its ponderous frame as it felt this determined spark of human spirit wending its way from higher branch to branch. Who knows how steadily the least twigs held themselves to advantage this light, weak creature on her way! The old pine must have loved his new dependent.
>
> (pp. 153–54)

There is a sexual relationship indicated here between the hard, lengthening stem and the girl who grips and encircles it. The sex act is the most profound way of representing Sylvia's love of and identification with all of nature. At the beginning of her climb the twigs catch her— another reminder of the pursuit of the red-faced boy and the hunter's shooting of birds. But later, the tree becomes a friend who aids her ascent, as well as a father-lover with a new "dependent." Her subconscious fears of sex are lessened as a result of her climb.

At the end of her ordeal, Sylvia is, understandably, "trembling and tired but wholly triumphant, high in the treetop" (p. 154). Looking out towards the east, she sees not only the sea, but two hawks whose soaring makes her feel "as if she too could go flying away" (p. 155). To the west, she sees farms, villages, and churches, "a vast and awesome world" (p. 155). Atop the symbol of the past, she views, in the present, the world of nature and of men. For once in the story, these spheres are united in a total vision which is unmistakably spiritual and mystical.

But "was this wonderful sight and pageant of the world the only reward for having climbed to such a giddy height?" (p. 155). After this revelation of nature and mankind, Sylvia looks downward into the forest, her own habitat, to see the white heron, "like a single floating feather . . . with steady sweep of wing and outstretched slender neck" (p. 155). This glimpse sustains the grandeur and serenity of her earlier vision. The heron is an essential part of Sylvia—her animus, her soul, or her sexuality, or all three. Yet the serenity of mood is fragile: "an arrow of light and consciousness from your [Sylvia's] two eager eyes" (p. 156) might make him disappear. Here again, the dreamlike, subconscious quality of Sylvia's perceptions is stressed. The heron calling to his mate presents an image of a calm, harmonious marriage, far different from the relationships with the hunter and the red-faced boy.

Sylvia's vision is interrupted by the chattering of the catbirds, and soon she struggles down the tree. As she walks back to the house she wonders what the youth will think when she tells him "how to find his way straight to the heron's nest" (p. 156). Yet when she sees him she cannot give away the location. Sylvia thinks of the great pine's "murmur" and the harmony she felt with the heron, and "she cannot tell the heron's secret and give its life away" (p. 158). Why? The author's ironic question whether the girl will "thrust aside" the advances of the "great world . . . for a bird's sake" (pp. 157–58) cannot be taken at face value. Since the heron's secret is Sylvia's own, to sell that secret to the young man for ten dollars would be prostitution, in several respects. The holiness of her communion with the heron transcends monetary considerations.

And yet the story is not quite over. Sylvia has seen the "great world" as an "awesome" totality as she sat in the great pine, but she has also seen it in the form of the young hunter. She can never regain her childish contentment. Despite her loyalty to the woods and the heron, she would have "served and followed him [the hunter] and loved him as a dog loves!" (p. 158). And perhaps because of her symbolic ascent of the tree, "She even forgot her sorrow at the sharp report of his gun and the piteous sight of thrushes and sparrows dropping silent to the ground, their songs hushed and their pretty feathers stained and wet with blood" (p. 158). The images of defloration and death are no longer frightening, even if they are still strong. She continues to hear the boy's whistle, yet she remains a "lonely country child" (p. 158). And the author, at the end, urges "woodlands and summer-time" to bring their "gifts and graces" and "secrets" to compensate for the "treasures" Sylvia has lost (p. 158).

In light of the story's ending, it is difficult to evaluate Sylvia's experience. She has been true to herself and properly so; her vision is too intense and significant to be traded away. Her glimpse of the heron is also a glimpse of

a perfect, harmonious marriage. We cannot regret her decision to reject the young hunter's offer, since her yearning for him is depicted as servile and unhealthy. Yet there is also sadness and a sense of loss here. Perhaps the union of the two herons can only symbolize an inner harmony (which Sylvia lacks at the end of the story), not an actual marriage, which may mean a choice between a charming young hunter or a violent "red-faced boy." Her association with the woodlands cannot entirely replace heterosexual, human love, even when the relationship with the woodlands has sexual undertones. At the same time, Sylvia's vision from the top of the pine tree has literally broadened her horizons by showing the vastness of nature and its juxtaposition with human society. Perhaps she will not always have to lead an isolated life in a small area of the forest. The young man's haunting whistle is a constant reminder to Sylvia of the amorous mysteries of the adult world.

So the tale ends with Sylvia's conflicting emotions unreconciled. Several critics have seen this fictional conflict as a reflection of a similar struggle within Jewett herself. One such critic is Eugene Hillhouse Pool, who suggests the white heron represents the author's love for her father. The story thus shows how Jewett "chooses psychologically to remain a child with Sylvia." Pool believes the author, as well as Sylvia, "repudiates the offer of mature, passionate love that would be inherent in any acceptance of herself as a mature woman."[4] Paul John Eakin feels the tale's symbolism is inadequate for expressing Jewett's "unresolved feeling." "The image of violation and death provides an interesting contrast to the vision of life and beauty which the heron represents" (*Appreciation,* pp. 213, 214). Concurring with Pool, Ann Douglas Wood views Jewett's own rejection of marriage not as a sign of independence but as a shunning of adulthood,[5] although she does not cite **"The White Heron"** in support of her opinion.

Does Sylvia reject "adulthood," "mature, passionate love," or "an image of violation and death"? This reader's analysis of the story supports Eakin's view. There is a type of dominating, threatening lover, represented in this story by the young hunter, and Sylvia's ambivalent feelings towards him are understandable. She is both attracted by his charm and repelled by the ruthlessness beneath it. She feels a need to be someone's servant—and to be loyal to herself above all. No doubt Jewett presents a particularly unfavorable view of love and marriage in this tale. She gives Sylvia no glimpse of a male who might respect her privacy and wholeness. Her only choice is to allow herself to be caught, raped, killed, stuffed, and put on display in a man's house, a provocative satirical image of the condition of late nineteenth century wives. Who can blame Sylvia, if, like Jewett, she makes the painful decision to reject this role and preserve her integrity and independence?

Notes

1. *Tales of New England* (1894; rpt. Freeport. N.Y.: Books for Libraries Press, 1970), p. 140. All subsequent references to the story will be from this text.

2. *Sarah Orne Jewett* (New York: Twayne Publishers, Inc., 1962), p. 102.

3. "Sarah Orne Jewett and the Meaning of Country Life," *American Literature,* XXXVIII (Jan. 1967); rpt. in Richard Cary, ed., *Appreciation of Sarah Orne Jewett: Twenty-nine Interpretive Essays* (Waterville, Maine: Colby College Press, 1973), p. 214.

4. "The Child in Sarah Orne Jewett," *Colby Library Quarterly,* VII (Sept, 1967); rpt. in Richard Cary, ed., *Appreciation,* p. 225.

5. "The Literature of Impoverishment: The Women Local Colorists in America 1865–1914," *Women's Studies,* I, No. 1 (1972), 14.

Theodore R. Hovet (essay date 1978)

SOURCE: "America's 'Lonely Country Child': The Theme of Separation in Sarah Orne Jewett's 'A White Heron,'" *Colby Library Quarterly,* Vol. 14, No. 3, September, 1978, pp. 166–171.

[*In the following essay, Hovet analyzes "A White Heron" from a Freudian perspective, determining that the work portrays both the conflict between urban society and the natural world and also the separation of the adult world from that of the child.*]

When she was forty-eight years old, Sarah Orne Jewett thought back to 1857 and wrote, "This is my birthday and I am always nine years old." As F. O. Matthiessen shows, the "whole fading world" of pre-Civil War America as it was manifested in Maine continued to hold "the center of her affections."[1] But Jewett's love of her childhood and the past grew into much more than an astute observation of regional characteristics and the delicate rendering of a vanishing people and culture. As "A White Heron" reveals, Jewett discovered in the contrast between the distant world of the nine-year-old girl and the immediate industrial America of her adulthood the social enactment of the psychological drama of separation, the separation from bodily union with a nurturing environment which each individual must undergo in the process of maturation.

This drama of separation portrayed by Jewett is best explained by Norman O. Brown in *Life Against Death: The Psychoanalytical Meaning of History.* Brown's Freudian description of individual maturation rests on the premise that "the peculiar structure of the human ego results from its incapacity to accept reality, specifically the supreme reality of death and separation." He explains that "the primal act of the human ego is a negative one—not to accept reality, specifically the separation of the child's body from the mother's body." And, according to Brown, the "separation in the present is denied by reactivating fantasies of past union, and thus the ego interposes the shadow of the past between itself and the full reality of life and death in the present."[2] These fantasies of the past union motivate

the individual to search for substitutes with which to recapture that "loved reality," to engage in "an active attempt to alter reality" so as to regain the objects lost as a result of separation. The objects cannot, of course, be regained and thus the individual and the society as a whole are forced to sublimate, i.e., to substitute "nonbodily cultural objects" for the fantasy of bodily union. The quest for these objects by members of a society creates an essentially urban environment marked by "the new aggressive psychology of revolt against female principles of dependence and nurture."[3]

Jewett's **"A White Heron"** clearly portrays a similar view of the human ego and social development. Sylvia, living in the woodlands, remains at a stage of psychological development in which she is dependent upon bodily union with a nurturing environment whereas the young man and "the great world" from which he springs are engaged in an aggressive search for the objects of lost union. Thus the story portrays the fundamental rift in the modern human consciousness which has been so imaginatively explained in *Life Against Death.*

Sylvia spends her first eight years in "a crowded manufacturing town." There she is "afraid of folks" and feels that she is as dead as "the wretched dry geranium"[4] that belongs to a town neighbor. She willingly leaves her parents to live with her grandmother on a farm in a remote area. On this tiny farm in the woodlands, the "old place" as the grandmother calls it, Sylvia (sylvan) finds in nature the "Great Mother," a nurturing environment that she apparently never found in her biological mother.[5] The woodlands provide Sylvia her only food, mostly milk and berries, and a sense of physical union she had never found in the city. She lives "heart to heart with nature"; and "the wild creatur's," according to the grandmother, "counts her as one o' themselves" (pp. 168, 165). Sylvia concludes that it is "a beautiful place to live in and she should never wish to go home" (p. 162). The contrast of this life with that of the city is emphasized by her memory of the manufacturing town as a place where "the great red-faced boy" used "to chase and frighten her" (p. 163).

Into this primitive and feminine world blunders the young man, a redfaced boy grown mature and polished, carrying with him two dominant symbols of the modern world, money and a gun, with which to wrest his ornithological prizes from nature. The money, the economic surplus which creates cities, provides power over others. The young man will pay ten dollars to Sylvia for knowledge of the heron's whereabouts, a sum which she believes will make her and the grandmother "rich with money" (p. 170). The gun, one of the major technological achievements of the modern world, gives the young man power over nature as well. In short, the young man brings to the woodlands "the new masculine aggressive psychology" described by Brown.

The young man, who as an adult has by definition experienced the reality of separation, directs the aggression toward obtaining "nonbodily objects" which can be substituted, i.e., sublimated, for the lost union. But in the words of Freud, "after sublimation the erotic component no longer has the power to bind the whole of the destructive elements that were previously combined with it, and these are released in the form of inclinations to aggression and destruction."[6] Thus the young man's search for the lost objects of past union turns into a violent and destructive attempt "to alter reality" in the hope of regaining them. Sylvia witnessed "the sharp report of his gun and the piteous sight of thrushes and sparrows dropping silent to the ground, their songs hushed and their pretty feathers stained and wet with blood" (p. 171). Sylvia cannot understand why "he killed the very birds he seemed to like so much" (p. 166). This violent attempt to alter reality in order to regain what has been irrevocably lost also affects the male's approach to the woman. Jewett strongly hints that the fate of the birds—killed, stuffed, and displayed—is symbolic of the fate of a woman in the hands of the sublimating male. For example, the young man's aggressive confrontation of Sylvia in the woods causes her to hang "her head as if the stem were broken" (p. 163), a picture which clearly reflects the appearance of the dead birds in the young man's game bag. One cannot help but comment on Jewett's perception of the violence implied in the aggressor's tendency to mount women ("quails" or "birds" to use popular slang terms) on pedestals.

The hunt ("the fiery hunt" one might call it) for objects from the lost world of the self brings the modern world of masculine aggression into Sylvia's existence and threatens to alienate her from nature. The young man extends to Sylvia for the first time the hand "of the great world" and stirs in her "the woman's heart, asleep in the child" (pp. 170, 166). "Alas," the narrator interjects, 'if the great wave of human interest which flooded for the first time this dull little life should sweep away the satisfaction of an existence heart to heart with nature and the dumb life of the forest" (p. 168). The encounter in the woods between Sylvia and the young man becomes, therefore, an encounter of the adult with the lost world of childhood and, simultaneously, of modern society with the state of nature from which it has sprung. It is an encounter of the modern with its primitive past. As a result of this meeting, Sylvia is forced to affirm her relationship to nature and to face the realities of childhood. Viewed from Sylvia's perspective, the meeting is a confrontation of the old fashioned world of rural America with the forces of modern society.

To convey the significance of Sylvia's affirmation of her dependence on nature, Jewett turns to the mythic concept of what Joseph Campbell calls the "World Navel," the symbolic center of the universe.[7] This symbolic center is located in "a great pine-tree, the last of its generation" which is "like a great main-mast to the voyaging earth" (pp. 167, 169). Sylvia must climb this "tree of life" (one of the variant forms of the world navel) in order to locate the nest of the white heron, a climb which enacts the mythic trial by ordeal: "The way was harder than she thought. The sharp dry twigs caught and held her and

scratched her like angry talons, the pitch made her thin little fingers clumsy and stiff as she went round and round the tree's great stem, higher and higher upward" (p. 168). Perched at the top of the great pine like the great bird she is seeking, her identification with nature as complete as the human condition allows, Sylvia can see, in a sense, the whole world: "There was the sea with the dawning sun making a golden dazzle over it, and toward that glorious east flew two hawks with slow-moving pinions. . . . Westward, the woodlands and farms reached miles and miles into the distance; here and there were church steeples, and white villages; truly it was a vast and awesome world" (p. 169).

But the mere physical world is not what Sylvia seeks. As the narrator puts it, "was this wonderful sight and pageant of the world the only reward for having climbed such a giddy height?" (p. 169). The answer, of course, is no. Sylvia is initiated into the very secret of nature:

> Now look down again, Sylvia, where the green marsh is set among the shining birches and dark hemlocks; there where you saw the white heron once you will see him again; look, look! a white spot of him like a single floating feather comes up from the dead hemlock and grows larger, and rises, and comes close at last, and goes by the landmark pine with steady sweep of wing and outstretched slender neck and crested head. And wait! do not move a foot or a finger, little girl, do not send an arrow of light and consciousness from your two eager eyes, for the heron has perched on a pine bough not far beyond yours, and cries back to his mate on the nest, and plumes his feathers for the new day!

(p. 170)

Sylvia's vision encompasses the contrarieties of human existence—the golden light of the rising sun and the darkness of the swamp below, the natural world of sea and forest and the man-made world of towns and churches. These contrarieties are encompassed by the most fundamental one of all, the coexistence of birth and death. As the sun grows "bewilderingly bright," Sylvia sees the heron rise out of the nest by the dead hemlock. Thus having climbed the tree of life, Sylvia has been initiated into what Campbell calls "the miracle of vivification," "a culminating insight which goes beyond all pairs of opposites."[8] She has perceived that, to use Brown's words, "life and death are in some sort of unity at the organic level."[9]

With this vision of the unity of existence before her, Sylvia refuses to commit the act that would separate her from nature forever. She does not "send an arrow of light and consciousness" which would frighten the heron. Her refusal to separate herself from her union with the natural world is affirmed by her refusal to tell the young man of the "dead hemlock tree by the green marsh" which marks the location of the heron's nest. By declining the "triumph and delight and glory" as well as the ten dollars which the young man would bestow on her for this knowledge, Sylvia rejects the values of the great world beyond the woodlands in order to preserve her timeless, heart to heart existence with nature. And she also preserves a unified sensibility by not, as the young man has done, employing her consciousness to help to alter a living force into a nonbodily symbol. "She cannot tell the heron's secret and give its life away." In short, she, by aligning herself with the mother she has found in nature, refuses to cross the threshold into adulthood and the stream of modern history.

In this seemingly simple tale, then, the encounter between Sylvia and the young man becomes an encounter between two stages of psychological and, consequently, historical development in America. The young man, one of the rising generations of Americans building the new industrial order, is engaged in what Brown calls "the immortal project" of recovering his own childhood, a childhood which is irrevocably lost in the past "state of nature."[10] The young man's quest for the beautiful birds which modern social forces are making increasingly rare captures precisely the neurotic wellspring of the pursuit of progress. It is, to again quote Brown, a "forward-moving *recherche du temps perdu*."[11] In contrast, Sylvia reminds us of the passive, dependent timeless relationship to nature which exists before the crucial separation of child from mother, society from nature.

The outcome of the encounter is not encouraging. Sylvia possesses something of inestimable value, a recognition of our dependency on nature and the inextricable oneness of life and death. The young man also owns something of crucial importance, the scientific knowledge which potentially could increase human freedom by a purposeful action upon nature. But the value of what each possesses remains impotent without the other. Sylvia's knowledge of vivification is useless if it is not connected to purposeful action; the young man's technological and scientific knowledge is destructive without Sylvia's insight into the heart of nature. Sylvia "cannot speak" and the young man kills what he loves. And the story ends without an understanding by either character of what the other possesses. Sylvia suffers "a sharp pang" as the young man leaves "disappointed" (pp. 170–171). She remains the dependent child he can no longer be; he stays the aggressive adult she must become if she will live in the modern world.

Sarah Orne Jewett—the person who always felt nine years old even though she saw the great world and knew some of its great people—must have felt keenly the failure in **"A White Heron."** Perhaps her stories, like Sylvia's vision of the bird, became for her the means of preserving the lost world of childhood which could not be incorporated into the busy society beyond South Berwick, Maine. Or maybe the stories are, like the stuffed birds of the young man, the symbolic nonbodily objects which resulted from her own search for the lost life of childhood she had shared with her father and her aunts before the Civil War. In either case, in some profound depth of herself, Jewett understood the child and adult in her were writ large in the pockets of wilderness left in rural America and in the "unsatisfactory activity," as she once put it, of the cities.[12] She also felt that the history of modern America was being in-

creasingly determined by the failure to unite the meaning of the child and the adult. The story ends with the young man journeying off engaged in an endless and destructive quest for the lost world of childhood; Sylvia in the last words of the story, remains in the woodland, a "lonely country child," a haunting reminder of the forgotten world of union with nature which nestles in the heart of the American behemoth.

Notes

1. *Sarah Orne Jewett* (Boston: Houghton-Mifflin, 1929), pp. 30, 106. Richard Cary also describes Jewett's "unquenchable urge for things-as-they-were" and her "desire to remain a child" in *Sarah Orne Jewett* (New York: Twayne, 1962), p. 19.

2. *Life Against Death: The Psychoanalytical Meaning of History* (Middletown, Conn.: Wesleyan Univ. Press, 1959), pp. 159, 160, 162.

3. Brown, pp. 281–282.

4. "A White Heron" in *The Country of the Pointed Firs and Other Stories* (Garden City, N.Y.: Doubleday, 1956), p. 162. Subsequent references will appear in the text.

5. Brown briefly discusses the importance of the pre-Oedipal "Great Mother" to Freudian anthropology. See p. 126.

6. Quoted by Brown, p. 174.

7. *The Hero with a Thousand Faces* (Princeton, N.J.: Princeton Univ. Press, 1968), pp. 40–46.

8. Campbell, pp. 42, 44.

9. Brown, p. 100.

10. Brown, p. 84.

11. Brown, pp. 84, 83.

12. *The Country of the Pointed Firs*, p. 147.

Theodore R. Hovet (essay date 1978)

SOURCE: "'Once Upon a Time': Sarah Orne Jewett's 'A White Heron' as a Fairy Tale," *Studies in Short Fiction*, Vol. 15, No. 1, Winter, 1978, pp. 63–68.

[*In the essay below, Hovet demonstrates how "A White Heron" employs the fairy tale structure as defined by Vladimir Propp.*]

Sarah Orne Jewett's **"A White Heron"** is one of the most admired of nineteenth-century American short stories. It has frequently been praised for its delicate artistry and, more recently, for its treatment of the heroine.[1] In spite of its enduring critical reputation, however, the structure of the story has not been carefully analyzed. As a result, Jewett's use of the fairy tale form has been neither recognized nor appreciated. The application of "the morphology of the fairy tale," to use Vladimir Propp's phrase, not only describes the artistic structure of the story but also reveals how Jewett turned to the fairy tale in order to explore the mythic roots of the conflicts generated by the encounter of modern social forces with provincial America.

In his highly influential structural analysis of the fairy tale, Vladimir Propp has isolated "the chronological order of linear sequence of elements" in the fairy tale. This sequence arises out of the order of "the functions of the dramatis personae" in the tale. Function is defined by Propp "as an act of a character, defined from the point of view of its significance for the course of action."[2] Although the tale can move through as many as thirty-one such functions, many tales will end after twenty-two of them. Furthermore, many tales omit some of the functions, yet "the absence of certain functions does not change the order of the rest."[3] **"A White Heron"** follows the linear sequence of the first twenty functions described by Propp precisely. Jewett's story omits only the twenty-first and twenty-second functions and, as Propp predicts, these omissions in no way alter the sequence of the other nineteen functions. In the following analysis, the Roman numerals indicate the number of the function designated by Propp and the description of each function is quoted directly from his study. After each of these functions, a description is given of how the function appears in Jewett's story.

I. ONE OF THE MEMBERS OF THE FAMILY ABSENTS HIMSELF FROM HOME. (DEFINITION: ABSENTATION)

Sylvia, the protagonist in **"A White Heron,"** has left the home of her grandmother and entered a dark wood. This action conforms to the third category of absentation described by Propp in which a member of the younger generation absents herself from home.

II. AN INTERDICTION IS ADDRESSED TO THE HERO. (DEFINITION: INTERDICTION)

Sylvia has been ordered to bring home the grandmother's cow, Mistress Mooly.

III. THE INTERDICTION IS VIOLATED. (DEFINITION: VIOLATION)

At this point in the story, according to Propp, "a new personage, who can be termed the villain, enters the tale." In Jewett's story, Sylvia violates the interdiction by being tardy in bringing Mistress Mooly home. As a result, she encounters the new personage in the form of a "tall young man with a gun over his shoulder." Sylvia thinks of him as "the enemy."[4]

IV. THE VILLAIN MAKES AN ATTEMPT AT RECONNAISSANCE. (DEFINITION: RECONNAISSANCE)

One of the first types of such reconnaissance is the location of precious objects. The young man with the gun is hunting for birds, particularly the valuable and illusive white heron. He immediately begins to elicit information from Sylvia: "Speak up and tell me what your name is, and whether you think I can spend the night at your house, and go out gunning early in the morning (p. 163)?"

V. THE VILLAIN RECEIVES INFORMATION ABOUT HIS VICTIM. (DEFINITION: DELIVERY)

The first type of "delivery" is a direct answer to the villain's question. Sylvia answers his question by giving him her name and leading him to her grandmother's house.

VI. THE VILLAIN ATTEMPTS TO DECEIVE HIS VICTIM IN ORDER TO TAKE POSSESSION OF HIM OR HIS BELONGINGS. (DEFINITION: TRICKERY)

To do this, the villain assumes a disguise, often that of a handsome youth. In Jewett's story, the villain is disguised as a handsome youth. Sylvia's grandmother mistakes "the stranger for one of the farmer-lads of the region" (p. 163).

VII. THE VICTIM SUBMITS TO DECEPTION AND THEREBY UNWITTINGLY HELPS THE ENEMY. (DEFINITION: COMPLICITY)

The grandmother turns her house over to the villain and Sylvia agrees to accompany him on his hunting expedition.

VIII. THE VILLAIN CAUSES HARM OR INJURY TO A MEMBER OF A FAMILY. (DEFINITION: VILLAINY)

The fifth type of villainous function is that of plunder. The young man kills the birds of the forest who count Sylvia as "one o' themselves" (p. 165).

IX. MISFORTUNE OR LACK IS MADE KNOWN; THE HERO IS APPROACHED WITH A REQUEST OR A COMMAND; HE IS ALLOWED TO GO OR HE IS DISPATCHED. (DEFINITION: MEDIATION; THE CONNECTIVE INCIDENT)

According to Propp, this function brings the hero into the tale. The hero will be one of two types: the seeker or the victimized hero. Sylvia is transformed from a passive child to seeker-heroine when the young man (the villain, it is important to remember) expresses his lack: "I can't think of anything I should like so much as to find that heron's nest" (p. 166).

X. THE SEEKER AGREES TO OR DECIDES UPON COUNTERACTION. (DEFINITION: BEGINNING COUNTERACTION)

Sylvia decides to climb a great pine-tree in order "to discover whence the white heron flew, and mark the place, and find the hidden nest" (p. 167). She will then reveal its location to the young man.

XI. THE HERO LEAVES HOME. (DEFINITION: DEPARTURE)

Sylvia rises before dawn to climb the pine tree. At this point in the fairy tale, Propp's analysis shows, yet another personage (the donor) is introduced to the story. In **"A White Heron,"** the pine tree becomes such a donor: "The tree seemed to lengthen itself out as she went up, and to reach farther and farther upward. . . . The old pine must have loved his new dependent . . . and the tree stood still and held away the winds that June morning while the dawn grew bright in the east" (p. 169).

XII. THE HERO IS TESTED, INTERROGATED, ATTACKED, ETC., WHICH PREPARES THE WAY FOR HIS RECEIVING EITHER A MAGICAL AGENT OR HELPER. (DEFINITION: THE FIRST FUNCTION OF THE DONOR)

The first type of this function is the test of the hero by the donor. Sylvia must make a "dangerous pass" from an oak tree to the pine, and then struggle through the dry twigs ("angry talons") and pitch of the lower branches of the pine (p. 168).

XIII. THE HERO REACTS TO THE ACTIONS OF THE FUTURE DONOR. (DEFINITION: THE HERO'S REACTION)

The first type of this function consists of the hero withstanding the test. Sylvia makes the dangerous pass and climbs through the lower branches of the old pine.

XIV. THE HERO ACQUIRES THE USE OF A MAGICAL AGENT. (DEFINITION: PROVISION OR RECEIPT OF A MAGICAL AGENT)

The tree now helps Sylvia climb to the heights: "the least twigs held themselves to advantage . . . and the tree stood still and held away the winds of that June morning" (p. 169).

XV. THE HERO IS TRANSFERRED, DELIVERED, OR LED TO THE WHEREABOUTS OF AN OBJECT OF SEARCH. (DEFINITION: SPATIAL TRANSFERENCE BETWEEN TWO KINGDOMS, GUIDANCE)

As Propp explains it, "Generally the object of search is located in 'another' or 'different' kingdom. This kingdom may lie far away horizontally, or else very high up or deep down vertically." Sylvia from the supernatural height of the pine tree ("a great main-mast to the voyaging earth") can see "the vast and awesome world" (p. 169). Finally, she sees the white heron and watches it fly to its nest in the green marsh. The hero-seeker in Jewett's story has accomplished the quest.

XVI. THE HERO AND THE VILLAIN JOIN IN DIRECT COMBAT. (DEFINITION: STRUGGLE)

The struggle in **"A White Heron"** is, as one would expect in a story by a nineteenth-century realist, psychological rather than physical. The villain (the young man) tries to bribe Sylvia. He'll make her "rich with money" (p. 170). Sylvia, despite great internal agony, successfully withstands the young man and refuses to reveal the secret of the heron's nest to the young man.

XVII. THE HERO IS BRANDED. (DEFINITION: BRANDING, MARKING)

Since the combat has been psychological rather than physical, the wound received by Sylvia is internal. She suffers "a sharp pang" for withholding the information.

XVIII. THE VILLAIN IS DEFEATED. (DEFINITION: VICTORY)

The young man leaves "disappointed" without having killed the white heron.

XIX. THE INITIAL MISFORTUNE OR LACK IS LIQUIDATED. (PROPP GIVES NO DEFINING TERM FOR THIS FUNCTION)

Sylvia has the secret of the heron's nest and thus her lack of companionship is supplied by nature. She and the heron "watched the sea and the morning together" (p. 171) and the woodlands bring their "gifts," "Graces," and "secrets" to Sylvia (pp. 170–171).

XX. THE HERO RETURNS. (DEFINITION: RETURN)

Sylvia has completed her quest and returns to the woodlands from which the villain had attempted to alienate her.

Many fairy tales contain two more functions: the pursuit and rescue of the hero.[5] Jewett's story omits these two, although a shadow of their existence can be detected in the "haunting" of the pasture path by the memory of the young man and the possible rescue from that haunting by the "gifts and graces" of the woodlands. In any case, the sequence of the twenty functions in the story remains identical with those described by Propp and the tale logically concludes with the return of the hero.

Jewett's use of the structure of the fairy tale in **"A White Heron"** indicates far more than her love of childhood things or the employment of a convenient narrative device. The fairy tale, as Bruno Bettelheim has recently illustrated in *The Uses of Enchantment: The Meaning and Importance of Fairy Tales,* has served society for a long time as a means of initiating people into their more deep-seated conflicts, anxieties, and fears. Fairy tales provide the psychological distance necessary to deal with this region of human experience. Jewett's "fairy tale" permits her to explore sexual conflict in a way that a more explicit short story could not. The young birds the ornithologist kills and stuffs are thinly disguised symbols of what awaits the young girl who succumbs to masculine control. Sylvia initially sees the young man as "the enemy" who has "discovered her" as he has discovered the birds. When he speaks to her, Sylvia hangs "her head as if the stem of it were broken" (p. 163), an image which mirrors the dead birds in the young man's game sack. Finally, the picture of the birds "dropping silent to the ground, their songs hushed and their pretty feathers stained and wet with blood" (p. 171) presents a frightening symbol of the possible fate of the girl who succumbs to the sexual aggression of the male. There seems little doubt that a symbolic connection exists between the birds killed, stuffed, and mounted on the wall and the fate of the woman possessed by the modern American male and placed on the domestic pedestal. Sylvia's refusal to reveal the secret of the heron marks her refusal to place herself at the disposal of the masculine will. She withstands the attempt of the villain to destroy her feminine identity.

Moreover, fairy tales and myths can be, in the words of Michael Wood, "narrative vehicles for the display and displacement of what worries us."[6] Jewett, as Richard Cary has shown, was an unusually sensitive observer of "regional obsolesence" and "the invasion of rural standards" by an "urban industrial plutocracy."[7] She found much in this new order to distrust and fear. The gun and the money which the young man brings to the woodlands embody the imperialistic bent of industrial America. Sylvia's refusal to aid the young man not only protects her identity but also registers her rejection of a society which would convert nature into dead objects through technological force.

In the fairy tale, then, Jewett found the form which allowed her to explore parabolically the social and sexual tensions in nineteenth-century America. It also enabled her to convert regional materials into universal themes that illuminated the significance of modern cultural change. "A White Heron" is one of those rare tales which captures that almost imperceptible moment at which the human consciousness has to deal with the encroachment of the new upon traditional modes of thought and action. Once upon a time, the author tells us in her story, there yet existed a world in which a small girl could choose the nurturing power of nature rather than the materialistic exploitation of industrial America. Sarah Orne Jewett was one of the few nineteenth-century Americans who had the knowledge and sensitivity to cherish and depict that vanishing world.

Notes

1. For a good survey of these critical views, see Richard Cary, ed., *Appreciation of Sarah Orne Jewett: 29 Interpretive Essays* (Waterville, Maine: Colby College Press, 1973). For a discussion of the heroine see Annis Pratt, "Women and Nature in Modern Fiction," *Contemporary Literature,* 13 (Autumn 1972), 476–490.

2. *Morphology of the Folktale* (Austin: University of Texas Press, 1968), p. 21.

3. Propp, p. 22.

4. "A White Heron" in *The Country of the Pointed Firs and Other Stories* (Garden City, N. Y.: Doubleday and Co., 1956), p. 163. Subsequent page references will appear in the text.

5. That is if the tale ends after the twenty-second function. Some tales continue with the story through nine more functions.

6. "Hi ho Silver," *New York Review of Books,* July 15, 1976, p. 29.

7. *Sarah Orne Jewett* (New York: Twayne Publishers, Inc., 1962), pp. 16–17.

Michael Atkinson (essay date 1982)

SOURCE: "The Necessary Extravagance of Sarah Orne Jewett: Voices of Authority in 'A White Heron,'" *Studies in Short Fiction,* Vol. 19, No. 1, Winter, 1982, pp. 71–74.

[*In the following extract, Atkinson points out how Jewett portrayed the action in "A White Heron" from different viewpoints, including that of the main characters, the great pine tree anthropomorphized, and directly as the story's narrator.*]

"A White Heron" seems a simple story of simple people, in a simple time. Seems. But if we look more closely, we see that Jewett has used diverse and unusual devices to give this much anthologized[1] story the satisfying impact which puts us so at rest at its conclusion. In the next to last scene,[2] for example, she uses authorial voice and privilege in genuinely extravagant ways: a tree's thoughts are reported and given weight, and the author not only urgently whispers counsel to the main character but later exhorts the very landscape and seasons of the year in pantheistic prayer.[3] But these departures from "common sense" seem perfectly natural to us as we read the story, because they contribute so directly to the effect of the tale, the sense of which is a little uncommon. In fact, the work demands these extravagances.

"A White Heron" is a story of innocence, a theme calculated to move us deeply, loss of innocence being a mainstay of literature and myth from Genesis through Milton, Joyce, Salinger, and beyond—a theme of proven power. However, Jewett here writes not of innocence lost, but of innocence preserved, much rarer, yet in less obvious ways touching each of us in the corners of our lives where we remain uncalloused by experience, resignation, or cynicism. To make the story take, Jewett has to convince us emotionally that Sylvia's staying in the world of innocence is a positive step in her development as a person— not merely a cowering, a retreat, or a regression she must ultimately transcend.[4] And it is to this end that she employs her extravagant means.

The world of innocence in which Sylvia lives is a frail one, lacking strength. Both the girl and her grandmother, innocents of youth and age, their cottage a virtual "hermitage" (p. 8), seem vulnerable in a number of ways, living in a balance that could be upset by Sylvia's return to the city or by the intrusion of even the genuinely nice young hunter/ornithologist who loves birds but kills what he loves, to preserve them, offering money to find the path to his prize.[5] Our most immediate desire is that Sylvia remain in her innocent world, inviolate. But we also are made (by the impingement of threats from without) to want strength for her innocence that it might fend for itself—not a further retirement, but a compelling vision, an experience beside which anything promised by the thrill of infatuation for the hunter would pale.

And that vision is precisely what Jewett gives us in her management of the climactic scene, Sylvia's ascent of the great pine tree. As she climbs, our hopes and expectations are decidedly mixed: the climb is frightening, but the vision from the top tantalizing; the heron must be seen, but (contrary to Sylvia's conscious purpose in climbing) the hunter must not be told. In short, we want for her a transforming vision, but fear she will fail to attain it or will squander it. Something more than a glimpse of the heron's nest is needed here—some transcendent way of seeing, beyond the capacity of Sylvia, or her grandmother, or the hunter, each of whom in turn has been a center of consciousness through which this story has been reflected so far. And it is to fulfill this precise need that Jewett gives us the following passage:

> The tree seemed to lengthen itself out as she went up, and to reach farther and farther upward. It was like a great mainmast to the voyaging earth; it must have been truly amazed that morning through all its ponderous frame as it felt this determined spark of human spirit creeping and climbing from higher branch to branch. Who knows how steadily the least twigs held themselves to advantage this light, weak creature on her way! The old pine must have loved its new dependent. More than all the hawks, and bats, and moths, and even the sweet voiced thrushes, was the brave, beating heart of the solitary gray-eyed child. And the tree stood still and held away the winds that June morning while the dawn grew bright in the east
>
> (p. 17).

Sylvia's courage summons a response from the tree, a deep and intimate bond of trust in which nature rises to the needs of the girl without her asking, actively caring for the child and her birdlike soul, rare and wonderful, now hidden, like the heron, deeply and inaccessibly in nature itself.

Thus, it is not just that Sylvia has transcended her former viewpoint, symbolized (in the story's next paragraph) by her looking down upon the sea and the flying birds, but that the entire fiction has transcended its human limitations—and thus stepped outside the limits of human relationship which lured and threatened Sylvia. The validity of her remaining in nature and not forsaking its trust for human relationship is confirmed by the sentience of the tree, the towering and deeply rooted presence of nature embodied. Sylvia's final decision to keep her bond with nature inviolate is both anticipated and justified as we experience not just nature from her point of view, but her from nature's. She is its creature and child.

But another voice also makes itself heard in this scene, the voice of the tale's teller herself. Heretofore content to let the story tell itself by reflection through the consciousnesses of girl, grandmother, and hunter, and now tree, the narrator cannot keep silent at this crucial moment. She calls out to Sylvia silently, directly.

> There where you saw the white heron once you will see him again; look, look! a white spot of him like a single floating feather. . . . And wait! wait! do not

move a foot or finger, little girl, do not send an arrow of light and consciousness from your two eager eyes, for the heron has perched on a pine bough not far beyond yours

(p. 19).

The narrator's voice is given great power here, because as she directs, so Sylvia sees the long sought heron, the climactic moment of the climactic passage. The narrator's calling counsel is as unexpected as the articulated feelings of the tree. But it serves to confirm with human wisdom what the tree would show with natural intelligence. And like the consciousness of the tree, the voice of the narrator transcends other viewpoints in the story. She speaks from a wisdom greater than that possessed by the reader or any character in the tale. She is "older" and wiser than the grandmother, and sees what the old woman does not, representing a true maturity of innocence. She gives a voice to the reader's hopes, and in doing so extends and legitimates them—not by addressing *us* and telling *us* how it is, but by calling (as we in our wisest innocence might call out) to Sylvia.

This sudden cry of the narrator also prepares us for her speaking out in her own voice again at the end of the story.[6] She addresses our uncertainties by articulating them herself: "Were the birds better friends than their hunter might have been,—who can tell?" (p. 22). And then, closing the circle between the points of nature's intelligence and human wisdom, she addresses nature itself: "Whatever treasures were lost to her, woodlands and summertime, remember! Bring your gifts and graces and tell your secrets to this lonely country child!" (p. 22). The hushed and urgent whisper of this conspiracy of wisdom confirms for us the value of Sylvia's experience and her decision not to tell of the white heron, transferring maturity from the social back to the natural realm—profounder, deeper, never to be betrayed. Her innocence is preserved, extended; her soul is larger and steadier; and our experience, complete.

Notes

1. The story, always a favorite, now appears in two of the three most widely used anthologies of American literature and in one of the most popular general literary anthologies: *The American Tradition in Literature,* ed. Sculley Bradley et al, 4th ed. (New York: Grosset & Dunlap, 1974), II, 285–294; *Anthology of American Literature,* ed. George McMichael, 2nd ed. (New York: Macmillan, 1980), II, 197–203; *Anthology: An Introduction to Literature,* ed. Lynn Altenbernd (New York: Macmillan, 1977), pp. 55–63.

2. Sarah Orne Jewett, *A White Heron and Other Stories* (Boston: Houghton, Mifflin, 1886), pp. 17–20. Subsequent citations to this edition will be parenthetical.

3. The complexity of emotions and perceptions in Jewett's narrations is the subject of a study by Catherine Barnes Stevenson ("The Double Consciousness of the Narrator in Sarah Orne Jewett's Fiction," *Colby Library Quarterly,* 11, No. 1 [March 1975], 1–12).

But the double consciousness Barnes discusses in "A White Heron" is limited to the imagistic conflict of land values with values of the sea and air—the attractions of the land-locked hunter in the forest versus the free, airy, and seaward domain of the heron. The metaphysical and rhetorical shifts of consciousness from human to arboreal and from report to exhortation are not discussed. The remarkable projected account of the tree's emotions seems to have escaped critical notice or scrutiny by Jewett scholars. Even Robert D. Rhode ("Sarah Orne Jewett and the Palpable Present Intimate," in *Appreciation of Sarah Orne Jewett: 29 Interpretive Essays,* ed. Richard Cary [Watervill, Maine: Colby College Press, 1973], pp. 229–237), though he is concerned to show that the "special power [and] magic" of her art lie in the personification of "nature as a living force" (pp. 229–30), misses or omits this passage, the most radical personification in her work.

4. That the resolution of the conflict is crucial for the author as well as for the reader is made clear by Eugene Hillhouse Pool, ("The Child is Sarah Orne Jewett," in *Appreciation,* pp. 225–228). Taking a page from F. O. Matthiessen's biography of Jewett, Pool characterizes her life as "an uneasy middle road between childhood and adulthood": exceptional devotion to her father versus independent feminist political inclinations, children's stories versus adult fiction. In this view, Sylvia's choice is Sarah's choice, the choice of a woman who would, on turning forty-eight, announce "This is my birthday and I am always nine years old" (p. 224). Pool finds the story is a good one because it "is the expression of a situation closely paralleling her own personal problems, and thus contains her deepest feeling and surpassing attention" (p. 225).

5. "The woman's heart, asleep in the child, was vaguely thrilled by a dream of love . . . [though] Sylvia would have liked him better without his gun" (p. 12). But whatever sexual implications might be suggested by a young hunter with a ready gun who asks to spend the night, causing Sylvia pangs of unexplained guilt, are only latent, and remain so throughout the story—though this tale is a clear instance of the myth of the feminine bond between ancient woman and her young charge being threatened by male intrusion, a configuration that traces back to Demeter, Persephone, and Hades, and beyond.

6. For Paul John Eakin ("Sarah Orne Jewett and the Meaning of Country Life," in *Appreciation,* pp. 203–222), however, the story falters here. He sees the rhetorical interjection as a flaw, an anxious and desperate gesture of support for Sylvia's decision offered by an author too involved in the story's values to let the choice stand on its own. "The rhetoric of emotion suggests that the neat, symbolic pattern of the story was inadequate to resolve the complexity of the artist's feelings which it contains" (p. 214). But Eakin's reservation, like Pool's praise (see note 4),

interprets and judges the story primarily in terms of the writer's life, while the present study seeks to account for the strategies of the story in terms of their potential and actual rhetorical effects on readers.

Louis A. Renza (essay date 1984)

SOURCE: "'A White Heron' as a Nun-such," in *"A White Heron" and the Question of Minor Literature,* University of Wisconsin Press, 1984, pp. 73–117.

[*In the excerpt below, Renza discusses the pros and cons of a radical feminist reading of "A White Heron." Furthermore, he explores the father-daughter relationship and the psychosexual imagery evident in the story.*]

> They shut me up in Prose—
> As when a little Girl
> They put me in the Closet
> Because they liked me "still"—
>
> Still! Could themself have peeped—
> And seen my Brain—go round—
> They might as wise have lodged a Bird
> For Treason—in the Pound—
>
> Himself has but to will
> And easy as a Star
> Abolish his Captivity—
> And laugh—No more have I—
>
> —Emily Dickinson

This is my birthday and I am always nine years old.

> —Sarah Orne Jewett (circa 1897)

A child draws the outline of a body

She draws what she can, but it is white all through,

she cannot fill in what she knows is there.

> —Louise Glück

I

The ideological climate established by recent feminist critical theories regarding the "revision" of women's fiction, its writers as well as characters, encourages and even requires us to read **"A White Heron"** as a latent feminist document. To be sure, the story itself does not seem to request this kind of reading. From its publication in 1886 to the present, most critics have codified it in terms of the "local color" binary. . . . But this codification too, called for by the story's topos, theme, and the literary-historical setting in which it appears, can be apperceived as a screen partially concealing a nineteenth-century woman writer's protest against a patriarchal American society which controlled her means of literary production as well as her legal social status. Such a society undoubtedly would have made Jewett feel little older than her story's nine-year-old "minor" protagonist.[1]

To support this feminist rereading of Jewett's story, we can first point to her undoubtable awareness of the nineteenth-century woman's movement. John Neal, a fellow Maine writer who died in 1876, was one of this movements' most outspoken and prolific proponents.[2] Jewett herself was more than likely aware of Stanton's 1848 declaration at the Seneca Falls Convention; she was certainly aware of Mary Wollstonecraft's *Rights of Woman* and Margaret Fuller's *Woman in the Nineteenth Century,* both of which were reviewed in 1855 by George Eliot, an author whose "major" works she owned in her library.[3] Indeed, when she first began to write, Jewett had used the pseudonym "Alice Eliot," a name Cary thinks derives from the pseudonym of Mary Ann Evans.[4] Do we glimpse even here Jewett's early wish to reclaim feminine literary authority for her writing? "Alice Eliot" could easily constitute a refeminization of "George Eliot," itself representing the nineteenth-century woman writer's strategic use of a male signature to receive a fair reading of her works in a patriarchal society where women were precluded from being taken as "serious" writers.[5] In any case, we also find Jewett making a coded feminist allusion to the ideal of "universal suffrage" in a previously cited passage from **"River Driftwood"**; or in the 1881 **"From a Mournful Villager,"** arguing that "the sanctity of the front yard of . . . grandmothers" once connoted woman's secondary status, her "restricted and narrowly limited life," but now the "disappearance of many of the village front yards may come to be typical of the altered position of woman, and mark a stronghold on her way from the *much talked-of* slavery and subjection to a coveted equality."[6]

But the most telling sign of Jewett's ongoing concern with the nineteenth-century woman's grievance against, and attempt to rectify her position in, patriarchal society occurs in her 1884 work *A Country Doctor,* a novel which she later said she liked the "best" of all her "books."[7] As many critics have noted, in depicting the relationship between Nan Prince, the protagonist of this novel, and Dr. Leslie, the country doctor who becomes her mentor, Jewett here indirectly represents her own relationship with *her* country doctor father.[8] It is significant, then, that the story focuses on Nan's struggle to declare her female vocational independence, that is, to become a doctor in a male-dominated profession. As a child whose mother and grandmother have died, Nan becomes a member of Dr. Leslie's household. She eventually follows this childless widower on his rounds, just as Jewett did with her father, and gets smitten with the idea of becoming a doctor, an idea Dr. Leslie supports but, recognizing the difficulty she will encounter in trying to enter a male-dominated profession, encourages only cautiously. Nan ultimately realizes her desire, though not before she is made to doubt her vocational choice through the resistance of patriarchal males and females who think "a woman's proper place" is marriage. A woman, in fact, presents Nan with the greatest obstacle to realizing her vocational ambition. Nan's relatively wealthy paternal aunt Nancy, who lives in a city and whom Nan discovers after she has become an adult, not only tries to woo her away from the rural culture represented by Dr. Leslie, but staunchly maintains that Nan should get married.

The nineteenth-century feminist elements of *A Country Doctor* thus seem rather clear. On the one hand, we have a female protagonist who expresses her rights to enter a privileged profession from which women are systematically excluded and for which men are prepared from birth. Or as Nan herself remarks, given the same childhood backgrounds, still

> "everything helps a young man to follow his bent; he has an honored place in society, and just because he is a student of one of the learned professions, he ranks above the men who follow other pursuits. I don't see why it should be a shame and dishonor to a girl who is trying to do the same thing and to be of equal use in the world. God would not give us the same talents if what were right for men were wrong for women."[9]

On the other hand, Nan's reliance on a benign father figure (or on "God") to help her realize her social equality with men, however much it may have indicated one of "the larger effects of socialization, which . . . may govern the limits of expression or even of perception and experience itself" for women in other periods,[10] in this case reads like a gloss on Margaret Fuller. Unlike Nan's male suitor, for example, Dr. Leslie does not treat Nan as what Fuller termed an "article of property" or "an adopted child," i.e., in the way nineteenth-century men treated women.[11] Instead of treating the very young Nan with the deferential affection of a parent, "[he] did not like children *because they were children*" and thus comes to view her in the same light as one of his own "grown friends" (my italics).[12] In Dr. Leslie, Nan finds that "good father's early trust" that gives one of Fuller's enlightened woman friends "the first bias" for her "self-dependence, which was honored [in her by her father]," though "deprecated as a fault in most women" by other men.[13]

One could argue, then, that in fact and fiction Jewett perceived the woman's struggle for "self-dependence" along the same lines as her New England feminist precursor. Fuller had noted how feminine autonomy found its "preliminary [in] the increase of the class contemptuously designated as 'old maids.'"[14] Unmarried herself, her closest friends women, most especially Annie Fields, Jewett represents Nan's desire to become a doctor as requiring the rejection of marriage, an institution that Fuller and other nineteenth-century feminists deemed a patriarchal means for keeping women from realizing their own "spiritual" potential.[15] This desire is clearly that of a conscious feminist, although presented as that of a "New England nun." Nan thus does not make her vocational choice before entertaining serious doubts and being attracted to the possibility of marriage.[16] Moreover, in the sociohistorical context in which it appears, Nan's desire to become a physician also inescapably signifies a desire for a distinctively feminine as opposed to a general, i.e., less sexually conflictual, "self"-independence. Nan Prince's professional ambition clearly exists in precise opposition to established patriarchal norms of social behavior, an instance of which occurs when George Gerry, a prospective suitor, becomes threatened by her "unnatural" self-reliance: "It is in human nature to respect power; but all his manliness was at stake, and his natural rights would be degraded and lost, if he could not show his power to be greater than her own."[17]

But although Nan represents the ideal of female autonomy in *A Country Doctor,* the "virgin" who, in Fuller's words, would escape "the very fault of marriage . . . [namely] that the woman *does* belong to the man," her claim to social equality or the right to enter a male-dominated profession effectively buttresses rather than challenges the "power" of this patriarchically valued profession itself. Fuller had argued that the truly autonomous woman would remain radically "unrelated" to the established cultural roles valued by males. To become a doctor, after all, would hardly dispose of the elitist hierarchical comparisons Nan associates with patriarchal institutions: "Just because [one male] is a student of one of the learned professions, he ranks above the men who follow other pursuits." Nan's wish to become a *country* doctor like Dr. Leslie mitigates her complicity with such institutional elitism but remains no less related to the latter. Even the confrontational aspects of Nan's feminist ambition, and therefore of Jewett's novel, could frustrate the realization of a non-heterosexual or "virgin" female autonomy. Such confrontation would amount to engaging or even wanting to accept patriarchal values—a more moderate feminist idea which Fuller opposed but which also has radical feminist ramifications, as we shall see—and thus would retard women's attempts to develop a totally "unrelated" feminine culture or value system.[18]

What better way, then, to promulgate transcendentalist feminist values to other women than in an innocuous story with a nonadult and therefore nonfeminist "virgin" heroine whose silent refusal to be conscripted by a patriarchal ethos is bound to go unnoticed by male readers as a radical feminist declaration of independence? Precisely *because* it "isn't a very good magazine story" to Jewett, **"A White Heron,"** like the white heron in the story, eludes the determinate demands of the patriarchal "great world." In this sense, Jewett's story at once corroborates and exploits the fact that within a patriarchal society, women lead secret lives; that they have become used to concealing and suppressing their ideas; that instead of eliminating they should cultivate this secret apartness, that is, work to "leave off asking [men] and being influenced by them" and rather "retire within themselves" as women in "virgin loneliness."[19] Surely it is this "virgin loneliness," apt to be misread as a sentimental, even narcissistic denouement, that Sylvia represents with authorial encouragement at the story's end: "Bring your gifts and graces and tell your secrets to this lonely country child!" (xxiii).

At first, to be sure, the story does not seem to reverberate with coded feminist "secrets" so much as with modest feminist allusions. The exception to this surface modesty

may occur in the "canine servitude" that we have seen Annis Pratt argue Sylvia escapes, servitude to a hunter who here represents a rapacious patriarchal world that would make women as well as nature into objects of sexual and intellectual pleasure (see p. xxvii above). But with this possible exception, we do not need to rely heavily on feminist literary-critical tenets, such as Elaine Showalter's idea that women's fiction is a "double-voiced discourse, containing a 'dominant' and a 'muted' story" (the latter normally comprising the work's subcoded feminist connotations), to unearth the tale's images of female independence.[20] The cultural world Sylvia inhabits is a de facto matriarchy. Her father is dead or has left her mother; Mrs. Tilley's husband is dead, her son Dan gone off to seek his fortune in the West. Conversely, not only are the two adult women spared direct relations with patriarchal families—and relations to aggressive males within these families as exemplified by Dan and his father who "did n't hitch" (xvii)—they actively head these households as if men were unnecessary. Mrs. Tilley runs the farm at what appears to be a subsistent if not profit-making level: a "clean and comfortable" place suggesting "the best thrift of an old-fashioned farmstead, though on . . . a small scale" (xvi). Sylvia's mother supports a "houseful of children" back in that "crowded manufacturing town" (xiv), presumably by working in a factory. If only in a working-class way, both women demonstrate they can perform the economic functions traditionally assigned to *both* sexes.[21]

But the clearest indication of a feminist thematic in **"A White Heron"** lies in the little girl's encounter with the hunter. However benign he seems, in teaching Sylvia "about the birds," he also unconsciously comes to teach her "about the bees"—about a sublimated, aggressive male sexuality symbolized by his very project as well as the use of his gun. Where for the male critic, Sylvia's choice most often manifests her Thel-like turning away from the harsh realities of (a patriarchal American) society and/or sexuality, for the feminist critic this choice likely signifies a special brand of "heroinism."[22] By the end of the story, Sylvia, at the price of loneliness, has learned to recognize and avoid the ideologically coded willingness of even a "kind appealing" young male to violate a symbolically feminine and virginal nature for the sake of controlling "her," i.e., making her part of his "collection." As suggested by the etymology of her name (woods or forest) and her activities at the farm ("the wild creatur's counts her one o' themselves" [xvii]), this "nature" includes Sylvia herself.[23] Thus, both heron and heroine exist as mere objects within the hunter's field of perception; in terms of Fuller's definition of the woman's situation in patriarchal marriage, each is an interchangeable "article of property," items to be bought for ten dollars or seduced by the vague promise of romance. What Sylvia learns is that the hunter's quest for the heron "means murder" for herself as well as the bird; in turn, her identification with the heron comes to symbolize the desire of "the imprisoned girl-child to become a free adult."[24]

Ultimately, Jewett's narrative isolates Sylvia as the sole signifier of feminist ideology. Her mother and Mrs. Tilley, who will "rebuke" the girl for not telling the heron's secret to the hunter, show how women can duplicate male social roles but not act radically independent of American patriarchal values. Both women are not "free" but clearly if involuntarily remain inscribed within a patriarchal situation that thwarts their desires. Mrs. Tilley, for example, would "ha' seen the world . . . if it had been so I could" (xvi). It is against this stratum of feminine options as much as against the hunter's project that Sylvia appears as a "minor" because disguised symbol of radical feminist ideals. Precisely because she appears as no more than a child, she serves as a metaphorical "free *adult*" woman in whom female readers can see their only marginal relation to patriarchal determinations of their secondary social place. Thus, the "muted" story within Jewett's **"A White Heron"** concerns a white or pure feminine heroine who at the narrative's "dominant" level is described as "paler than ever," and thus subtly associated with the story's white heron. Or said another way, the little girl not only constitutes the story's secret and feminist anagrammatic title (white heron/white heroine), but also conveys its secret ideological life for those female readers who can revise what happens to her at the story's "dominant" or self-censored level. Like Annis Pratt, for example, such readers will immediately apprehend that Sylvia's feeling disappointment at not being able to "have served and . . . loved [the hunter] as a dog loves" (xxii-xxiii) signifies a deferred enslavement to a pejoratively construed patriarchal "great world."

More important, a strategic "mimetism," to use Mary Jacobus's term, pervades Jewett's representation of her feminist heroine's actions in the story. Mimetism entails the woman writer's "reproduction" of a "deliberately assumed" discursive practice pre-occupied by patriarchal values and myths about women; because she is unable to write "outside" a male literary tradition, there is no "alternative practice available to the woman writer apart from the process of undoing itself," even with regard to representing female heroines.[25] In this sense, we could argue that Jewett represents Sylvia with certain male-defined qualities in order to subtract them from or even reverse their assumed significance within the patriarchal ideological tradition which governs nineteenth-century literary representations. For example, by associating Sylvia with nature and especially the white heron, Jewett puts her in the role of the hunted object and thus seems to accede to the myth of the male as the active hunter, the traditional literary trope of males as the pursuers of women as well as natural creatures. Yet from the very beginning of the story, Jewett depicts *Sylvia* as a kind of hunter who becomes more successful in this activity than the hunter himself. She "had to hunt for" the cow, a *female* cow whose "pranks" she in turn assigns with "intelligent" or *active* meaning. Moreover, she knows the rural area around the farmstead as well as her uncle Dan whom Mrs. Tilley notes "she takes after": "There ain't a foot o' ground she don't know her way over" (xvii). And in attributing to her an ability to find the white heron, an ability that makes the hunter all but dependent on *her* prowess as a hunter, the story sub-

liminally defines Sylvia as an incomparable huntress and woodland explorer. In short, coupled with her "virgin" identity, these depictions allusively associate her with Artemis—a figure of radical feminine independence in the classical patriarchal tradition.[26]

This "muted" metamorphosis of a minor into a major female heroine, a metamorphosis that suggests both the ongoing feminist goal to live "outside" stereotypical patriarchal definitions of a woman's "proper place" and the story's own "secret" literary ambition, repeats itself in relation to two other patriarchal myths. One could argue that the hunter and Sylvia, for example, reenact the story of Apollo and Daphne from Ovid's *Metamorphoses*. In mythological tradition, Apollo is the archer, the overseer of birds (notably of the *white* swan), the inspirer of divine knowledge, and in Ovid's story, the love-obsessed god who pursues Daphne, a wood nymph, until she escapes from him by becoming a tree, thanks to the power of her river god father.[27] The mysterious "handsome stranger" of **"A White Heron"** is an expert marksman with his gun, as "when he brought down some unsuspecting singing creature from its bough" (xviii); an "ornithologist"; someone who knows all "about the birds and what they knew and where they lived and what they did with themselves" (xviii); and a godlike figure to Sylvia who, even though he inexplicably "killed the very birds he seemed to like so much" (and so holds the power of life and death in his hands), looks up to him "with loving admiration" (xviii) and treats him with awestruck deference, "the young man going first and Sylvia following, fascinated . . . her gray eyes dark with excitement" (xix). Most especially, of course, the hunter is obsessed with capturing the white heron which, as we have seen in this feminist reading of the story, becomes all but synonymous with the "white heroine."

But this last "muted" metamorphosis should alert us to how **"A White Heron"** itself becomes a marginal feminist version of a myth that effectively reduces the woman to a fixed or knowable natural object. The story quite clearly assigns Sylvia with Daphne-like attributes. Her name, her climbing the "great pine-tree," her final (treelike) silent stance before the hunter, even the "woodlands" the narrative suggests she will indefinitely inhabit as the story ends, all allude to this girl's virtual transformation into a tree. Yet Sylvia's transformation results from but is not the result of the Apollonian hunter's quest; it originates not out of anxiety, the sense of patriarchal pursuit, but out of her desire to "see all the world" from the tree, a desire, then, which like her name precedes and eventually supersedes the hunter's invasion of the farmstead. Thus, like the tree itself, the tree she regards "wistfully" not as a vehicle of escape but as a positive adventure, "the last of its generation," unaccountably left standing in the woods by (one assumes) past male settlers or shipbuilders, Sylvia remains beyond—or in Fuller's terms, "unrelated" to—the hunter's patriarchal code of understanding. But here she also replicates the status of the white heron that remains secret and literally beyond the hunter's vision. Sylvia *alone* climbs the tree, spots the heron and its secret nest, and ultimately refuses to divulge this experience to the hunter, i.e., to the patriarchal world both he and Sylvia's grandmother (as if she were a distraction from the confrontational sexual thematic of the story with its Apollo/Daphne allusion) represent.

In short, Sylvia's metamorphosis is variable, "free," elusive to any "proper" code of understanding. Indeed, the trope of "metamorphosis" may be considered a means for women writers to undo more traditional tropes like metaphor or simile which, for example, would make us perceive Sylvia *as* a displaced Daphne-like figure with a relatively stable significance.[28] No less than the story which allusively traces Ovid's, Sylvia becomes a site of purely possible signification, an interpretable "shy little" figure whose feminist significance remains secret but does not run away from male and female patriarchal readers.

But this "deliberately assumed" or traced revision of a classical patriarchal myth itself metamorphoses into a more major feminist revision of a less forgettable patriarchal myth. The tree that Sylvia climbs and which serves as the pivotal vehicle of her decision to save the heron obviously evokes comparison with the biblical Tree of Knowledge. In believing that "whoever climbed to the top of [the tree] could see the ocean . . . all the world" (xix), she assumes the trappings of an American Eve whose experience overturns the expectancies of the Puritan Judeo-Christian tradition that indicts the woman as the cause of Man's Fall, that is, because of her fatal curiosity about the Tree of Knowledge or Death.[29] The knowledge that the little girl gains from the tree results in life rather than death, in moral integrity rather than duplicity. Indeed, the heron Sylvia saves bears comparison with the peaceful "bird of paradise" found in many matriarchal creation myths. In this sense her action, far from being a sentimental Christian, i.e., patriarchal, homily on the value of life in general, symbolizes the return of a repressed feminine intentionality of nature.[30] Thus, both the story and Jewett's very writing of it could primarily concern this imaginary return to radical feminine origins or to a feminist perspective from which the "great pine-tree," say, symbolizes a gynocentric Tree of Knowledge precisely in opposition to its phallocentric usurpation and distortion in Western biblical tradition. Or just as the girl alone climbs the tree and sees the heron, so Jewett's "shy little" story entails a "secret" rhetorical transumption by which women can reclaim a gender-exclusive relation to the origins of life or the Edenic Garden in the face of patriarchal propaganda which would reduce such "knowledge" to a Fallen or ontological fetishism of nature—or to mere ontological naiveté.[31]

Of course, the relatively quiescent surface of **"A White Heron"** emits only faint signals of this sexual-biblical war; yet they appear in ways which bear the most extreme feminist interpretation. In Sylvia's tree-climbing episode, we hear echoes of Milton's rendition of Eve's experience in Book V of *Paradise Lost* where, thanks to the intervention of Satan disguised as a handsome "Guide" or "one of

those from Heav'n," she dreams of being transported to the top of the forbidden Tree of Knowledge:

> Forthwith up to the clouds
> With him I flew, and underneath behold
> The earth outstretched immense, a prospect wide
> And various: wond'ring at my flight and change
> To this high exaltation. . . .

(*Paradise Lost*, V, 86–90)

. . . when the last thorny bough was past . . . [Sylvia] stood trembling and tired but wholly triumphant, high in the tree-top. Yes, there was the sea with the dawning sun . . . and toward that glorious east flew two hawks. . . . [They] seemed only a little way from the tree, and Sylvia felt as if she too could go flying away among the clouds. Westward, the woodlands and farms reached miles and miles into the distance . . . truly it was a vast and awesome world.

(xxi)

The passage from Jewett's story glosses the Miltonic passage with strategic, ideologically motivated differences. Where Milton's Eve tells Adam of her dream (as she will later tell him of her disobedient deed), Sylvia will not tell the Adamic hunter what "knowledge" she has gained from this "flying away" experience despite her initial intention to do so. In fact, Jewett's "Eve" climbs the tree voluntarily and literally awake ("She forgot to think of sleep" [xix]), whereas it is "Adam" who has rehearsed within a dream the temptation of a sinful if pleasurable "knowledge": "The guest waked from a dream, and remembering his day's pleasure [i.e., to capture the heron] hurried to dress" (xxii). Jewett's Adam here represents the curiosity and desire for a kind of knowledge—of the heron he intends to kill and place in his ornithological collection—which almost, but not quite, seduces her feminist Eve into a Fall from her innocent relation to nature, and results in the latter's Fall as well, the reification of nature implicit in his stuffing birds. More, with his money and knowledge "about the birds" which, like Eve's knowledge after she eats the forbidden fruit, temporarily promotes an illusory or "vaguely thrilled" (xviii) intimacy with a sexual partner, *he* tempts the *woman* in this revised version of the biblical primal scene. Even Milton's masculine Satan, who produces Eve's dream by first disguising himself as a "Toad" (*Paradise Lost*, IV, 800), becomes neutralized and distanced as a tempter by the story's reduction of him to a mere "hop-toad in the narrow footpath" (xvii).

"A White Heron," then, (re)tells the story of how an exceptional woman—exceptional since even Mrs. Tilley accedes to the hunter's intention to "cage up" nature—resists such temptation and becomes representative of the woman radically "unrelated" to patriarchal stories of her inferior station in the order of creation. The male story of *Paradise Lost* here becomes a pretext for the female story of *Paradise Regained*. From the vantage of a subtly allusive Tree of Knowledge which the girl climbs by her "free will" or by her own "great design [which] kept her . . . awake and watching" (xix)—not, then, as in the Miltonic Eve's patriarchally produced dream—Jewett's Eve literally sees the "sea" for the first time; she sees "the *dawning* sun . . . and toward *that glorious east . . .* two hawks," images, like the child herself, resonating with prelapsarian echoes. In climbing this "great" tree, Sylvia encounters and triumphs over its phallic power and resistance to becoming occupied by a girl, "her thin little fingers clumsy and stiff as she" goes "round and round the tree's great stem, higher and higher upward" (xx). We could argue that the woman here symbolically overcomes the patriarchal tradition's phallocentrically privileged claim on all modes of knowledge and comes to know "a vast and awesome world" outside this tradition. And so, aside from the story's substituting a feminist heroic Eve for a dominant, privileged Adam, we find it also substituting the exclusive value of a feminine regenerative relation to a traditionally feminine nature for a woman-provoked Fallen relation to a traditionally patriarchal God. We could also argue that it performs these substitutions through the effective agency of a female authorial persona who appeals to this nature to assuage the necessary loneliness incurred by the vision of radical feminine independence, a vision that continually requires nature to "tell your secrets to this lonely country child!" (xxiii). Such an agency itself exists as a revision of Milton's surrogate male agency in *Paradise Lost,* the Raphaelite messenger of the Judeo-Christian patriarchal God who can promise Adam and Eve only a deferred surcease from their present spiritual loneliness, their alienation from a prelapsarian awareness of nature which in Jewett's story pertains *only* to the "disappointed" hunter.

As I have suggested, recent feminist critical theories not only license but request that we ascribe such unlikely, ideologically motivated revisions to texts written by women writers. These ascriptions pertain especially to fiction by and for women of the nineteenth century whose "feminism" would not likely lead them to be fully aware of the extent to which they indeed were revising patriarchal ideological norms of their social identity both within and outside their fiction. In this context, the implausibility of such revisions must itself be regarded as evidence for the "degraded" position of women in Western patriarchal society, a position Fuller registers when she paraphrases Plato's view "that Man, if he misuse the privileges of one life, shall be degraded into the form of Woman; and then, if he do not redeem himself, into that of a bird."[32] Through Sylvia's figurative and anagrammatic association with the white heron, Jewett clearly "mimics" this descent—but in order to create a space for the woman to declare her radical sociosexual independence. And further, she could be said to reinforce this strategic mimetism through her "elusive" (xix) representation of both heron and heroine. As we have seen, Sylvia becomes allusively associated with major feminine figures borrowed and revised from patriarchal tradition: Artemis, Daphne, and Eve. And were we to emphasize how Sylvia alone seeks and finds this white heron, she also would become a kind of Virgin Mary who here generates her own immaculate conception, namely through the agency of a Holy Ghost-like bird which both inspires her with a self-dependent vision of nature preclud-

ing intercourse with the values of "the great world," and itself eludes the discursive designs of patriarchal understanding as symbolized in "muted" fashion by the hunter's ornithological intentions.[33]

At the very least, as the tree-climbing episode almost literally proves, Sylvia as feminist heroine does not exhibit any fear of flying, that is, of determining her relation to life in terms which transcend her attraction to patriarchal terms, the "fancied triumph and delight and glory for the later morning when she could make known the secret!" (xix). Quite clearly a "child . . . brought up amid the teachings of the woods and fields, kept fancy-free by useful employment and a free flight into the heaven of thought,"[34] she exemplifies the ideal feminist "maiden" which Fuller had compared to a bird not unlike the "rare bird" that Sylvia becomes associated with in **"A White Heron."** Mothers, Fuller had gone on to say, should never "clip the wings of any bird that . . . finds in itself the strength of pinion for migratory flight unusual to its kind."[35] As mother to her story which she also refers to as a "her" (see p. 71 above), Jewett seems to have written a tale whose thematic referent interchangeably metamorphoses into a "heron," a "heroine," and a "her." Could there be a better way to demonstrate the "migratory flight" of a feminist literary text?

II

But at least three problems arise with this radical feminist revision of **"A White Heron."** The first has to do with the way even a feminist criticism can just as easily interpret the "secret," non-confrontational feminist propaedeutic and the story's allusive feminist revisions in terms of its as signs of an impotent capitulation to, co-option by, or perhaps de facto complicity with a patriarchal ethos. The second concerns the desire of such criticism to posit the feminist allegorical subtext of Jewett's production of her story as the "secret" site of its true textuality; this displacement occurs not only in defiance of the story's reduced and revised representational signs suggesting its own allusive feminist subtext, but also in spite of or in the face of this criticism's awareness of the difference between the "muted" and "dominant" elements of the text in question. The third problem relates to a contemporary critical aporia, namely the necessity of any critical theory to reproduce the text it criticizes in its own blind and insightful terms. Thus, one can question the radical or, in Adrienne Rich's terms, "lesbian" feminist critic's tendency to replace patriarchal standards of major literature, standards which have been invoked to reduce the value of women's writing, by gender-exclusive feminist standards which willy-nilly place a greater value on the act of feminist critical revision than on the literary text thus being used as a pretext for this critical narrative. In what if any sense could we maintain that **"A White Heron"** "deconstructs" its radical feminist meta-narrative—*after,* that is, one acknowledges its "deconstruction" of patriarchal appropriations?

As regards the first problem, radical feminist criticism should be only momentarily thwarted by a reactionary

feminist interpretation of **"A White Heron."** Such an in-
terprctation could doubtless stress the implausibility or
even egregious misreading which our exposition of the
story's feminist revisions clearly entails when compared
with its spare narrative surface; could perhaps cite the story's own implausible elements such as the child heroine's
temptation by a mere ten dollars, or the unrealistic possibility of romance with an older, at least adolescent, "young
man"; finally could point to the genteel literary context in
which Jewett wrote her stories, one of whose ideologemes
was a sentimentalized notion of childhood innocence.[36]
Thus, the girl's silent decision, a represented silence that
the narrative doubles by its own hesitant ("who can tell?")
paratactic silence regarding this decision, could be understood as a regressive *retreat* from any putative revisionary
feminist thematic. Instead of indicating "redemptive possibilities" or proffering an alternative feminine social model
to a profit-oriented patriarchal American society through,
say, an ideologically charged domestic topos, a viewpoint
Nina Baym adopts when reading American women novelists before 1868, the "muted" ideological silences of this
1886 story concerning a farm run by an elderly woman
may exemplify what Baym terms the "decline of women's
fiction into girl's fiction."[37] Or these silences may serve to
corroborate Ann Douglas's thesis about the "feminization"
of American patriarchal culture. Jewett's heroine, who effectively chooses to remain in her "hermitage" at the end
of the story, and even Jewett herself who relies on Margaret Fuller's *Woman in the Nineteenth Century,* a text virtually disregarded by late-nineteenth-century feminists concerned with more practical political matters, here seem to
deserve the pejorative rubric of "New England nun" insofar as they privilege a sentimentalized, idealistic moral
code and remain silent about the "real" social issues facing contemporary adult women.[38]

Yet with Nancy Miller, we could regard the story's silences as signs of its antipatriarchal inscriptions. We could
"italicize" both them and the story's *apparently* "unmoti-
vated and unconvincing" depiction of Sylvia and the hunter's romantic relationship and claim they are only "inau-
dible to the dominant [i.e., patriarchal] mode of
reception."[39] The little girl's silence throughout the story
and especially when she refuses to tell the heron's secret
would then touch on what Gilbert and Gubar identify as
the "aphasia and amnesia . . . which symbolically represent (*and parody*) the sort of intellectual incapacity patriarchal culture has traditionally required of women."[40] Similarly, even Sylvia's "vaguely" drawn erotic feelings toward
the hunter, feelings that generate the dilemma which
frames the girl's decision as decisive, also lead us to a
feminist register of meaning. Such erotic themes in wom-
en's fiction, according to Nancy Miller, actually conceal
and serve to repress the woman writer's own "impulse to
power . . . that would revise the social grammar in which
women are never defined as subjects."[41] Moreover, far
from constituting a descent "into girl's fiction" or representing Jewett's genteel acceptance of her proper, which is
to say minor, literary place, both the story's child heroine
and its diminutive genre invite us to revise them along the

lines of Adrienne Rich's interpretation of Emily Dickinson's abbreviated poems. Such poems constitute *acts* of
"self-diminutivization, almost to offset and deny—or even
disguise—[Dickinson's] actual dimensions as she must
have experienced them," that is, "under pressure of con-
cealment" from a patriarchal world.[42]

Feminist literary criticism, then, compels us to regard **"A
White Heron"** as a "muted" feminist story within an already "muted" feminist story. The heroine's dilemma concerns Jewett's own need to construct, in Myra Jehlen's
terms, "an enabling relationship with a language that of itself would deny [the woman writer] the ability to use it
creatively."[43] We saw evidence of this need in Jewett's *A
Country Doctor* where Nan Prince's obstacle-ridden attempt to become a physician—a vocation, like writing,
which was restrictively available to women in the nineteenth century—more than likely reflects the obstacles
Jewett encountered in choosing writing as a serious vocation.[44] Even the way Dr. Leslie encourages Nan to become
a doctor resembles the way Jewett's father encouraged her
to read books and especially "tell the things just as they
are" when writing them. Significantly for our present discussion, the novel ends at the point where Nan has not yet
begun a practice of her own—as if, that is, the choice of
vocation and not the vocational practice itself were its primary topic.

We could argue that **"A White Heron"** internalizes this
prevocational topic even more. In this context, Sylvia's refusal to tell the heron's secret locale to the hunter represents Jewett's own refusal to write a story she identifies as
feminine ("she isn't a very good magazine story, but I
love her") in terms of the prevailing esthetic mandates of
the patriarchal "great world" as represented by W. D. Howells and others. Howells's preference for social realism,
for example, presupposes access to major social issues
from which, as Virginia Woolf would later note, nineteenth-
century women were barred.[45] Jewett's story, then, here
becomes definable as an inverted feminist work which allegorizes its very mode of production. Her remarks in the
letter cited in the previous chapter (p. 71) suggest that as a
"romance" that deals with "every-day life after all," "she"
gets written precisely *not* to become "a very good magazine story," i.e., for the marketplace pre-occupied by male
editors, but rather to secure a "room of her own" for "her"
author. Moreover, even with regard to "her" diminutive literary genre, "she" reproduces or secretly parodies a mode
of fiction ironically intended to guarantee "her" minor literary fate before Jewett's canonically minded patriarchal
literary contemporaries and twentieth-century super-
sessors.[46] For the very reason that **"A White Heron"** could
so easily be reduced in terms of patriarchal literary standards, its secret feminist allegorization of its production
suggests that Jewett herself partakes of the girl's "spirit of
adventure [and] wild ambition" (xix). In other words, inscribed within the story is Jewett's wish to produce major
literature.[47]

In the end, however, such speculation about the story's
doubly subsumed feminist identity and its status as an al-

legorical prolegomenon to Sarah Orne Jewett's own "major" literary ambition belongs more to radical feminist criticism's discursive wish to transform **"A White Heron"** into an ironic minor literary text than to the "muted" sexual signals traced in the tale itself. A lesbian-feminist criticism like that espoused by Adrienne Rich must perform a supererogatory critical act that, even as it resituates Jewett's text within a recoverable "lesbian continuum," contradicts that same secret (and not merely "muted") feminist thematic which justifies the consideration of this text as a text of "major" feminist importance. Rich's perspective suggests that Jewett could not have written her stories except by converting the everyday moral and local color topics, topics with which she was most familiar as a restricted nineteenth-century woman, into the topic of the ways "women have always resisted male tyranny," or the "compulsory" (for the woman writer) patriarchal topic of heterosexual romance.[48] This perspective allows feminist critics alone to "ask how [a past woman writer] came to be for-herself and how she identified with and was able to use women's culture, a women's tradition"; and it allows women critics to "identify images, codes, metaphors, strategies, points of stress, unrevealed by conventional criticism which works from a male mainstream perspective."[49] Surely Sylvia's silent sacrifice of heterosexual romance with the hunter, not to mention her anxious memory of a "great red-faced boy who used to chase and frighten her," reveals such a point of stress, and thus justifies a radical feminist revision of Jewett's story.

But as Annette Kolodny argues, even a would-be revisionary feminist critic "must . . . be wary of reading literature as though it were a polemic and hence treating it as [she] would a manifesto or political tract."[50] To claim that Sylvia's silence has immanent gender-significant meaning in and through the narrative is not the same as claiming it has imminent referential meaning for women alone given their common experience of an underground secret life in patriarchal society. More important, to claim that this silence is gender determined as opposed to simply gender inflected within "a male mainstream perspective" is to violate its secret semiotic confrontation with male culture and/or its "lesbian" declaration of independence from this culture. The self-conscious metaphoricity that this self-conscious feminist critique would attribute to Sylvia's silence denies the very condition in terms of which it only *may* be appealing to a radical feminist mode of reception. For only if this secret *is* radical could it appear "unrelated" to any "male mainstream perspective." Or what amounts to the same thing, only if it can be read as if it were immediately accessible to such a perspective—after all, even patriarchal readers can apprehend the *relative* feminist significance of Sylvia's secret—can the story paradoxically signify its *doubly* secret or *radically* feminist scene of writing to women readers intent on constructing "her" coherent feminist subtext.

The danger for such criticism, then, lies in the way its self-conscious methodology risks opening up an irreconcilable breach between its own reflective act and the puta-

tive "lesbian" reading of the story which conditions this act on pain of its reduction to mere speculation. Such criticism must maintain the radical value of the story's esthetic surface, no matter how self-coherent and persuasive its ideological revision may seem to a feminist critical audience, lest it become exposed *to itself* as a *de facto* "polemic," a polemic that by definition would be no better than the variable critical avatars of "a male mainstream perspective." Can feminist criticism, for example, avoid transferring the meaning of Sylvia's silence from a patriarchal mode of reception to a feminist counterpatriarchal mode of reception whose "secret" significance ultimately depends on its contingent, literally and self-consciously maintained sexual inaccessibility to the male critic or reader?

Some recent feminist critics assert the impossibility of such a task. "In claiming value for the devalued term of an opposition," according to Elizabeth Berg, "one still allows the opposition to remain in place and to perpetuate the same order of relations."[51] In its "French" form, a feminist literary criticism would bracket women's writing as determined by literal gender differences, whether of authorship or characterizations. "Writing" alone expresses these differences, hence remains inaccessible both to traditional patriarchal modes of understanding and to their counterpatriarchal feminist revisions insofar as they polarize women's "essential" sexual identity. But even this notion of "writing," which views woman as a trope or a "reading effect . . . never stable, without identity," is comprehensible, as Alice Jardine argues, only to "the woman (feminist) reader."[52] Thus, although a feminist critic can recognize that her criticism "remains imbricated within the forms of [patriarchal] intelligibility . . . against which it pushes," she still insists on interpreting "a text that seems to do her arguing . . . for her," a text which—as Luce Irigaray claims, for example—"can only signify an excess or a deranging power" vis-à-vis patriarchal modes of writing.[53] It is the woman author's, critic's, and/or story's relation to what seems an always already prior patriarchal network of writing that prompts, and defines as such, the woman's perpetual deconstruction of such writing. In ideological terms, women's "writing" transumes rather than is consumed by naturalized images of women and women's writing purveyed by a repeated patriarchal discursive practice. Indeed, since the woman suppressed in society through patriarchal discourse constitutes a secret to herself as well as others, she has the unique if ironic ability to experience a dialectically privileged priority in relation to this discourse that would fix her identity to herself and other women.

"Mimetism," then, can apply to radical feminist critical practice as much as to the text it purports to explicate in feminist terms. And what looks like the conspicuous antithetical relation between a self-conscious feminist methodology and the "reading experience" of **"A White Heron"** here becomes feminist criticism's mimicking, at the level of critical discourse, of the story's esthetic expression of a secret feminism. The radical feminist codification of Jewett's story in terms of a counterpatriarchal critical discourse signifies less a self-conscious disagreement with what a patriarchal criticism would say or misrecognize about this story than a dialectically regained distance in "excess" of such criticism. In this sense, Jewett's heroine serves as an emblem for feminist criticism itself. On the one hand, she "*only followed* [the hunter], and there was no such thing as speaking first" (xix). On the other, she climbs the tree in secret and establishes a secret relation to the white heron. In the same way, the postgendered feminist critic mimics the teleological direction of patriarchal critical discourse to the extent of sometimes seeming complicit with it; but given her inconspicuous, relatively secret—even childlike—status within such discursive practice, she can climb above its openly propagated intentionalities of literary texts, intentionalities which minimize the value of literary texts written by and about women. More, she can establish a secret relation to **"A White Heron"** itself that remains beyond the epistemological ken of patriarchal understanding and critical discourse. Both feminist critic and woman writer thus concern themselves with uncovering discursive rooms of their own, secret spaces in excess of whatever critical paradigms exist at some given moment in literary as well as social patriarchal history. If only from this perspective, it becomes possible for the woman's literary text to communicate "without identity" to "the woman (feminist) reader" alone.[54]

But this postgendered feminist criticism must still signify to itself its act of tracing male-associated critical practices. To its women readers, it must emphasize its own unconventional citations of what Rich regards as already unconventional codes, metaphors, and strategies that permeate all women's literature. Otherwise, it would once more engage in the equivalent of a heterosexual romance with patriarchal criticism, albeit an unwitting, unwilling, if also subtly reactionary one. As it becomes more and more potentially misreadable by its own women readers, such criticism must acknowledge its "secret" relation to male-identifiable modes of criticism, that is, in ways that not only suggest its transcendence of them but also ensure that patriarchal criticisms can *never* know male *or* female literary texts as women readers and critics have ironically learned to do from their "compulsory" or coerced familiarity with masculine epistemologies. Thus, even a postgendered feminist criticism comes to depend on the gender-inflected signatures of its practitioners or tends to thematize its deconstructions of patriarchal projections of literary texts in gender-specific terms. And if only for the sake of economy, it concentrates its attention on women's literature traditionally overlooked in patriarchal canonical histories, a literature it would inversely elevate to "major" literary status according to standards immediately accessible to and apprehensible by women alone. Such self-identifying marks of an otherwise "without identity" or postgendered feminist criticism suggest that even the practice of mimetism, or, as Mary Jacobus recommends, ceaseless deconstruction, assumes a relatively secured or centered self-image of "woman" to perform such operations and to realize the sophisticated desideratum of a radically

secret or "lesbian" relation to a story, say, like Jewett's **"A White Heron."**

But perhaps such deconstruction could also lead to the extinction of the "woman," person *or* trope, as a pretext for subtly reprivileging or fetishizing the hierarchical binary of major and minor literature. After all, such a resurgent binary not only would bar male critics from custody rights over Jewett's story, but would ironically place these critics virtually in the same "minor" discursive position as feminist criticism would argue defines Jewett's in producing this story. In that case, who indeed could claim ideological custody of "her"? The question comes down to whether writers or critics, male *or* female, can ever arrive at a sexless and not merely nonsexist relation to a literary text and the issue of literary canonicity it seems perpetually to broach.

III

We could take the "muted" feminist elements of Jewett's story as one among other signs of its phenomenological retreat from radical feminist as well as patriarchal appropriations. A novitiate in her rural "hermitage," the little girl comes to exemplify the values of "virtuous womanhood," the reformist self-image of so-called nineteenth-century protestant nuns setting out to "tame" the perceived antisocial proclivities of males who would undermine the moral fabric of the family and, by extension, society at large.[55] These values, especially respect for the other, whether human or natural, are shown to endure in the face of male-caused crises, for example the conflict between Dan and his father; Dan's abandonment of the farm due to his wanderlust or fortune hunting; and the Civil War which perhaps accounts for the absence, i.e., death, of Sylvia's father, and her mother's need to support her family alone. Yet as seems quite obvious, Sylvia's choice has only a tangential sociological applicability to the situation of magazine readers in the city for whom male promiscuity and/or the disintegration of family values were more explicit concerns. In affirming Sylvia's life in the country ("Bring your gifts . . ."), the story's unidentified narrator also seems to affirm Jewett's stated preference for "persons [who] could make themselves quiet and solitary nests"—not unlike the white heron's "hidden nest"—"and never wish to go out into the busy world again."[56]

Jewett's writing thus seems to retreat from even the modest feminist elements suggested by her story. And this retreat becomes more noticeable in her representations of suggested adult heterosexual relationships. Writing to Willa Cather, she would later argue that the woman writer was unable to write from the first-person position of a "man's character," for to do so "must always, I believe, be something of a masquerade."[57] But this admission about her non-heterosexual imagination does not account for the way her third-person narrative representations of heterosexual relationships tend to be not only de-eroticized but blurred by certain verbal maneuvers which further mitigate the "otherness" of characters to each other and to the reader. George Gerry, the prospective suitor of Nan Prince in *A Country Doctor,* has a name as "two-dimensional" as Richard Cary argues Jewett's characterization of him is.[58] In *A Marsh Island,* a novel published one year before **"A White Heron,"** Jewett has two male characters—Dick Dale, a city-bred would-be artist, and Dan, a country boy— vie for the affections of Doris Owen, the daughter of a farmer who functions as a benign patriarchal figure for all three characters. Doris eventually chooses to marry Dan, but not before Dale's relationship to her is characterized as one of "brotherly" affection and her relationship to Dan Lester is based on his familiarity with the Owens' culture and family, particularly his having been the last person to see "his playmate," Doris's *brother,* "fall" during a Civil War battle.[59] Even these alliterative names, Doris, Dan, Dick Dale, George Gerry, strike one as unimaginative, blurring their gender distinctions or else underwriting their unimagined otherness as characters—as if they were children within the protective confines of a family rather than independent adults.

This process of regression to a childlike mode of representation, or said another way, this tendency of Jewett's writing to drift away from even the "virtuous" or modest feminist thematic, or the conventional heterosexual one, that *A Country Doctor* and *A Marsh Island* respectively invoke in the most explicit terms indicates Jewett's wish to produce a radical minor literature. Such literature *becomes* minor by the way she imagines its production, for example in the way she traces and tries to mitigate the feminist resonances of her representations. One way to write as if she were a child or literally a minor writer, that is, an ungendered persona whose imaginations are fictively in the process of avoiding impressment by adult sexual codes, is to reproduce a predominant child/parent relation either within her texts or in the very mode of her producing them. The expressions of this relation remain, of course, only latently autobiographical. Thus, the apparent irony of the feminist reference to the little girl's feeling in **"A White Heron"** that she could "have served and followed [the hunter] and loved him as a dog loves" becomes neutralized for Jewett, if not for the feminist critic, when apprehended first against the fictional precedent of the male Dan Lester's having "followed [Doris] about like a dog,"[60] and second against the precedent of her own childhood experience with her beloved father as he visited his patients: "I used to follow him about silently, like an undemanding dog."[61]

In her fiction written roughly around the time of **"A White Heron,"** this relation becomes thematically expressed in the way that Israel Owen, for example, the patriarch who defines the values in terms of which the other characters in *A Marsh Island* are judged, justifies his daughter's erratic behavior toward Dan by what could be apprehended as a stereotypical view of women: "Women's a kind of game: you've got to hunt 'em their own track, an' when you've caught 'em they've got to be tamed some."[62] Embedded in this stereotype of the male as hunter and the woman as huntable object lies the father's defending his daughter as an unconventional character—a subject who can only be

"tamed *some*" and for whom marriage, an option that she must concern herself with, "goes sort of against [her] natur'."[63] To Dr. Leslie in *A Country Doctor,* Nan Prince also exhibits "untamed wildnesses" as she is growing up.[64] As Nan's de facto father, he too appreciates his de facto daughter's difference from the other "village children," regardless of their gender; he thus tells Mrs. Graham, his longtime confidante in Oldfields who will later serve as Nan's reading companion, that given Nan's native "self-dependence and unnatural self-reliance," it "is a mistake for such a woman to marry. Nan's feeling toward her boy playmates is exactly the same as toward the girls she knows."[65] In both cases, then, though to different degrees, Jewett represents fathers whose "untamed" daughters they exempt from patriarchal institutions or conventions which these fathers thus only *appear* to represent by virtue of their social and/or sexual identities. And in the case of Dr. Leslie, as we have already seen, this exemption leads to the daughter's entering an elite profession by the end of the novel, but a profession which has not yet removed her from the "old fields" of his "country doctor" world.

Nan's daughterly relation to Dr. Leslie and his mode of professional practice quite obviously reflects Jewett's relation to her father and his homespun poetic advice to her to "tell the things just as they are," that is, in terms of her regionalist experiences or her familiarity as a woman with "every-day" topics. But *A Country Doctor* suggests that this relation itself can become the primary focus of Jewett's writing. In **"A White Heron,"** for example, Jewett-as-narrator, just like Dr. Leslie with Nan, allows Sylvia time to absorb the "gifts and graces" and "secrets" of nature by herself or before she will have to enter "the great world" of heterosexually defined relationships prefigured by her experience with the hunter. In this sense, the narrational modus operandi of the story thus internalizes the father/daughter relation.

But even supposing that a child/parent relation not only effectively displaces adult heterosexual and antiheterosexual representational occasions in Jewett's writing, but also generates the conditions which facilitate a phenomenological scene of "minor" writing at a step removed from being understood as a scene of minor or major feminist *righting,* why would a woman writer adopt a paternal as opposed to maternal authorial relation to a little girl character? Certainly Jewett's avowed "love" for her story—for "her"—suggests such a maternal relation.[66] Biographically speaking, though Jewett seldom refers to her in letters, her relation to her mother, an intelligent woman who encouraged her children to read,[67] hardly seems to have been troubled. And yet in the two novels and story under consideration, mothers and mother figures play secondary roles, and even appear as obstacles to their daughter's or daughter figure's "untamed wildnesses." The materialistically motivated Mrs. Owen, with her "undercurrent of dislike," encourages a match between Doris and the wealthy Dale, then accepts Dan as a mate for Doris when she learns he has inherited property.[68] Aunt Nancy, as I have suggested, functions as *A Country Doctor*'s melodramatic antagonist in attempting to make Nan abandon her vocational ambition for marriage. Mrs. Graham, who Cary thinks functions as Nan's mother and was in fact modeled after Jewett's mother,[69] exercises only an indirect influence on Nan and serves as a foil to Dr. Leslie who has a more central fatherly relation to her, as when she predicts the girl "will be a most lovely, daughterly, friendly girl, who will keep you from being lonely as you grow older."[70] And of course the otherwise benign Mrs. Tilley, the mother-substitute grandmother in **"A White Heron"** who in feminist terms could help the daughter gain her independence from her actual mother without devaluing the latter, "rebukes" Sylvia for her silence or failure to speak the language of "the great world."[71] Indeed, in this story and *A Country Doctor,* the mother per se literally vanishes from the text. Sylvia has left her mother and siblings to live with a grandmother from whom the girl becomes figuratively separate. Nan's mother dies in the first pages of the novel, her maternal grandmother a few pages later. Thus are emphasized Sylvia's exclusive relation to the narrator, and the widowed and childless Dr. Leslie's exclusive fatherly relation to Nan.

Doubtless we could account for Jewett's aversion in these works to representing the mother/daughter relation in neo-Freudian as well as ideological feminist terms. In a patriarchal society such as Jewett's, the father and not the mother holds privileged ("phallic") access to its forms. The girl thus wishes to identify with her father rather than with the socially castrated mother whom she can "resent" and come to "turn away from . . . altogether."[72] Or in more strict psychoanalytic terms, at the oedipal stage, a stage which establishes the paradigm that will govern her future adult relationships with men and women, the girl but not the boy "can transfer her sexual attentions from her mother to her father [and] can want first his phallus, and then by . . . analogy, his baby"[73]—or in the displaced sexual medium of a female literary artist, "his" text. But such a situation need mandate not so much the girl's resentment as her ambivalence toward the mother since, as Nancy Chodorow has argued, the daughter can more easily identify with her mother than the son with his father; only the son, that is, must give up or postpone the narcissistic project of wanting the mother.[74] In the normal course of ego development the girl must liberate herself from her infantile or egoless relation to the preoedipal mother so that at the oedipal stage she can desire the father's phallus, the symbol of power (rather than object of envy) which allows this liberation to occur.[75] The girl here splits her "internal image [of the preoedipal mother] into good and bad aspects" and goes on to free herself or gain self-identity from this "overwhelming" mother by "project[ing] all the good-object qualities . . . onto her father as an external object and onto her relationship to him."[76] But again, this transference of "libidinal" attachment from preoedipal mother to oedipal father does not require the devaluation of the female child's sense of her feminine identity; on the contrary, her love for her father literally depends on her prior relation to the mother, so that this love does not take place "at the expense of, or [as] a substitute for, her attachment to her mother."[77]

As her other works—especially *The Country of the Pointed Firs*—and her benign relation to her mother show in fact, so these explanations show in theory that the mother/daughter relation exists as a viable option for Jewett to have adopted in reproducing a "minor" relation to writing. If she privileges the father/daughter relation in these three works, it probably concerns more her wish to postpone her identification with adult or postoedipal mother figures than some outright aversion to such figures. For an adult woman, of course, such postponement would entail a fantasized regression, a replay of the little girl's energic transfer of love onto the father and also a return to a time when she could still postpone her "real" conscription into an adult womanhood which, as her women friends and close relationship to her two sisters show, she otherwise accepts and even embraces.[78] In imaginative terms, mother figures like Mrs. Owen, Mrs. Graham, Aunt Nancy, Sylvia's mother and grandmother signify the inevitability of the daughter's fate to become an adult woman. This fate, no doubt, seems all the more onerous because of its patriarchal restrictions and/or the possibility of the girl's becoming a mother herself with its attendant losses, as suggested by Mrs. Tilley's "family sorrows" and Sylvia's mother's economic plight in supporting her family by herself.[79] Conversely, a father figure like Dr. Leslie, though identifiable with this same fate, signifies a threshold situation for the daughter, that is, only the *possibility* of entering a world of adult heterosexual relationships. Indeed, Dr. Leslie's "country" practice entails a choice not to enter this world, for he rejects the advice of his medical colleagues to realize his scientific abilities in the city.[80]

Thus, we can argue that both Nan's prevocational status at the end of *A Country Doctor* and Sylvia's choice effectively to remain a preadolescent in **"A White Heron"** reflect their exclusive relations to "fathers"—the narrator in the case of this story. Such relations serve as screen images, in psychoanalytic terms, of these daughter figures's respective desires to return to and remain within that transitional psychosexual space between preoedipal and oedipal self-identity. Jewett's fictional fathers allow Nan, Sylvia, and to a lesser extent Doris (Mr. Owen accepts the possibility of her relationship to the cosmopolitan Dale even as she comes to choose the world of her father's Marsh Island through the brotherlike Dan) to glimpse and even choose "the great world" of adult heterosexual relationships, but in the end also to retain their preadult "untamed wildnesses" or identities.

Yet for Jewett, clearly, the presence of a father figure in either a representational *or* a concealed narrational sense must strike an incestuous semiotic note as well as connote, if only unconsciously, literal sex differentiations to an adult woman writer who so exclusively privileges the father/daughter relation. One could argue that the incest taboo functionally precludes, for example, her production of a text as "his" substitute "baby," in Mitchell's words.

But at the same time, such oedipal repression of a fantasized, fictionally mediated project of regression still leads the daughter to seek male substitutes, especially the adult "man . . . to give her [her father's] baby."[81] That this project appears *as* a project is clear from the way Jewett not only represents her heroines's choices of an exclusive father/daughter relationship over other adult hetero- and non-heterosexual options, but stresses these choices by banishing literal fathers just as much as mothers, without, nevertheless, erasing the crucial function of the father figure. In order *not* to write a "baby" text, in other words to distance her own awareness of the exclusive father/ daughter relation, she tries to make it a substitutive or only allusively inscribed relation, in this way pushing its immediate connotations of adult sexual differentiation out of representational sight.

Thus, like her mother, Nan's actual father is dead but substitutively present through her patronymic name, Prince. This patronymic further reminds us that her daughterly relation to Dr. Leslie is nonbiological, nonmandatory, hence a "distant" relation, also emphasized by the fact that he neither tries to adopt her legally nor assumes the conventional role of the authoritative patriarchal father in bringing her up. Moreover, Nan in effect rejects her patrimony by refusing to live permanently with her *paternal* Aunt Nancy, and in this way becomes distanced even further from her already dead father. A similar distancing relation obtains in **"A White Heron"** where a surnameless Sylvia, whose father may be dead but is in any case absent from the narrative, lives with her *maternal* grandmother, i.e., without a grandfather and apart from a mother whose husband the narrative would have had to account for as it does for Mrs. Tilley's husband. Even in *A Marsh Island* where a father plays a dominant role, we could argue that Doris's attraction to Dick Dale and Dan, both of whose fathers are dead, concerns, as we have seen, a "brotherly" duo that reminds us how in this patriarchal world the father/daughter relation has less value than what would have been a more primary father/son relation.

Still, as Mr. Owen and Dr. Leslie show, even the distanced substitute father figure can turn into a signifier of the daughter's inevitable transformation into an adult woman in fact (marriage) or in effect (vocation). Simply for a prose writer to "name the behavior of an individual," according to Sartre, involves "naming it to all others" who, at least in the case with Jewett's two novels, are synonymous with an adult understanding of these works.[82] Such naming, the sheer fact of representing father figures, inevitably must affect her very imagination of these works' putatively regressive projects. In an autobiographical sense, this "adult" recovery of the father as a median figure who helps introduce the daughter to nonpejorative heterosexual "behavior" but mitigates the necessity of her conforming to it equally applies to Jewett's representation of her substitute daughters. For example, on one level the already distanced daughter Nan's distanced relation to her patrimony works to repress—but in order, here, to *express*— the absent presence of a pure or preadult father/daughter

relation. But on another level, Dr. Leslie's support of her vocational desire—albeit a desire that must lead to a self-reliant kind of heterosexual adulthood—and her rejection of her patrimony would each risk reminding Jewett of her own situation as a writer, namely of *her* country doctor father's support of her vocation, and of the patrimony which, from the beginning of her career, allowed her to regard writing as "not a bread and butter affair with me."[83]

If the literal-minded "substitute" strategies of the two pre-**"A White Heron"** novels conspire to make fragile Jewett's desire to produce literature as a "minor" as opposed to an adult woman writer, that is, through a mantra-like projection of the father/daughter relation, such does not appear to be the case with **"A White Heron"** itself. Here, we have argued, a purely narrational or *anonymous* father/daughter relation helps constitute the story's "minor" mode of production. Or here Jewett relies on writing per se, writing in the (Lacanian) "name of the father" or of the linguistically dispersing Symbolic, to misrecognize the adult associations tied to any explicit representation of the father/daughter relation; to shred potential Imaginary identifications with maternal *or* paternal figures; in short, to elude "the biologistic reduction of the Law of the Dead Father to the rule of the actual, living male." or what amounts to the occasion of adult gender differentiations, even of a feminist or counterpatriarchal cast.[84] The Lacanian notion of "writing" can help us see how the story disperses rather than substitutes an explicit paternal position, if only to include this (non)position in a repressed or unconscious manner.

Doubtless we can attempt to rewrite **"A White Heron"** in terms of such "wild" psychoanalytic behavior. But if writing, in the words of Geoffrey Hartman, attenuates all "fixative spectral event[s]," and instead induces the writer to accept "the (absent) father . . . basically . . . the mediacy of words [and] a genuine recognition of difference," we will need to question even our identification of Jewett's anonymous, only surmisably paternal narrator as the fixed locus from which she inscribes a dyadic father/daughter relation in this story.[85] Writing endlessly retracts rather than compulsively repeats Imaginary projects like Jewett's; at the very least, writing in the name of the father should avert any unconscious desire to fetishize this "(absent)" paternal muse. In writing, then, Jewett cannot produce a guaranteed, unmitigated "minor" literature. Since writing precludes "some unique reduction to . . . one fixative spectral event,"[86] she cannot use it to reestablish even a discursively defined daughterly relation toward a metafatherly narrator who—just like the elliptically androgynous neo-Freudian father who represents, even as he displaces, the preoedipal mother for the little girl,—would regressively postpone her identity as a gender-differentiated, adult woman writer.

If Jewett cannot "write" from any secured position of the absent father, in this way becoming interchangeably "his" daughterly amanuensis, neither can she even indirectly represent this static but reversible dyadic relation through a writing-induced identification with Sylvia alone. This identification becomes apparent through her substitute narrator's "pathetic" interjections throughout the story (e.g., "look, look! . . . wait! wait! . . . little girl" [xxi]; through her avowed "love" for "her," the heroine-identified story itself; and through Jewett's middle-aged birthday confession of feeling "always nine years old," the age of Sylvia. Indeed, this identification verges on explicit self-reference, hence subject to Jewett's *adult* understanding and the demise of her "minor" project, that is, to write as if she *were* a minor shielded from adulthood by the protective father. Her own father died in 1878, a father whose poetic advice ("tell the things") we find her reiterating throughout her life—a father thus quite literally associated with her writing per se. If we date her own life from the date of her father's absence or death, she would have been virtually the same age as Sylvia when writing **"A White Heron"** in 1886.

In short, we could maintain that just as Sylvia can "look upon the cow's pranks as an intelligent attempt to play hide and seek" (xiii), so does Jewett need to deploy "writing" in relation to her feminized text. "Writing" serves to repress by dispersing and defetishizing the recognizable verbal sites of the father/daughter relation which would otherwise regenerate an apperceivable specular project, a compulsive narcissistic quest that in effect would promise to repeat her ensuing oedipalized growth into a sex-differentiated adult woman. Thus, the writing of **"A White Heron"** at best can realize her project to produce a "minor" literature only subliminally, whether because of the sexual-ideological allusions and possible readings of her text, or because of her own psychic temptations to specularize the dyad that would veto this "adult" semiosis.

In a sense, the precedent for examining **"A White Heron"** in such terms is afforded by *A Country Doctor.* There Jewett retreats from her father/daughter substitutions by "writing" and not only by mere representational distancing. There she inscribes her "minor" project by virtually tearing up her proper name, a "specular name" whose "repetition . . . gives rise to texts that seem to be anagrammatic or to conceal an unknown-unknowable key, a 'pure' signifier."[87] Nan Prince's very name suggests the father/daughter relation. "Prince" signifies both a patriarchal surname and superior masculine status in relation to other males, precisely the formulation used by Nan to defend the woman's right to enter a male-dominated profession (pp. 75–76 above). The feminine name "Nan" constitutes a diminutive form of "Nancy," the adult name by which the narrative refers to the already distanced mother figure, Aunt Nancy. "Nan Prince" thus virtually signifies daughter and father.

We could also maintain that since "Sarah" means "princess," Nan's last name reflects Jewett's unconscious paternalization of *her* first name, a paternalization rather than heterosexual masculinization since "*Prince*" points to a daughter's barely disguised sense of the father's privileged, capitalized—but not King-like—identity in relation to other adult males who are effectively excluded from this relation. Thus, "Nan Prince" figuratively tears up its already submerged "specular" allusion to a father/daughter relation and instead inscribes Jewett's own "unknown-unknowable" self-reference to a more intimate, more linguistically concealed father/daughter relation. Indeed, Jewett's actual but unused first name was Theodora, the feminization of her father's name Theodore. Quite literally, then, she would always be writing her name in the name of her absent father; or what here comes down to the same thing, she would always be reinvoking a relation whose unconscious "repetition" in a fictional character like Nan Prince remains as concealed from her as from friends and readers bound to identify her in terms of her sex-differentiating first name, the feminine "Sarah," and the patronymic "Jewett." Jewett's very signature thus helps her reproduce a childlike authorial anonymity, an absent father/daughter relation, which, far from indicating a "muted" feminist grievance, here momentarily eludes would-be feminist and patriarchal ideological conscriptions alike.

IV

Turning the dead father into the Dead Father, Jewett unconsciously deconstructs her story's potentially adult, which is to say potentially "major," sexual-ideological signs precisely in the act of writing "her." But Jewett's text must also deconstruct this deconstructive project lest *it* confess the adult perspective from which she desires to produce a pure minor literature. Otherwise, **"A White Heron"** would again become subject to the adult or major hierarchical codes of ideological significance that always have engendered this desire, codes which the story already seeks to displace by the more neutralized and neuterized binary thematic of a child's versus an adult's (Mrs. Tilley's as well as the hunter's) relation to nature. To be sure, **"A White Heron,"** as we have seen, invites the imposition of such adult codes. But it does so in a way that throws the burden on the reader, as if leaving the writer a space, albeit only momentarily since even this space can be ideologically reappropriated—for example, by feminist narratives of the woman writer's situation—in which she alone can sense the in-significance of her representations.

Thus, Jewett's text relies on a series of word-scattering tropes inviting, according to the conventions of her time, closures both simple and sophisticated. On one level, for example, Sylvia's decision not to tell either the hunter or Mrs. Tilley the heron's habitat strikes us as an adult decision in a possibly antipatriarchal as well as probably moral sense. Yet both the narrator's rhetorical question ("who can tell?") concerning the value of this decision and the girl's silence which "represents" it suggest its provisional status for the story's anonymously removed writer. More crucial is the narrative ellipsis between the time Sylvia climbs down from the tree intending to tell the stranger the heron's secret—she thinks about "what he would think when she told him" (xxii)—and the dramatic last scene where "she cannot tell the heron's secret and give its life away" (xxii). Again, the reader can attribute her change of mind to morality, sentiment, and/or American transcendentalism, in short the conventional ideological respect for nature indigenous to the historical and geographical situation of the story. But considering Jewett's avowed awareness of the conventions of "realism" surrounding this story's resistant "romance" identity, this ellipsis, marked as such by the text's spacing, signifies a narrative silence which not only duplicates Sylvia's in the next scene, but equally points to a withheld space in which the decision occurs not to represent her decision-making process, i.e., to let the reader do the decision making instead of the writer. Moreover, in the next scene the reader becomes further distracted from the elliptical or absent locus of "real" decision making when the narrative displaces Sylvia's decision by implying that it took place before her initial silence as she faces both her "fretfully" rebuking grandmother and "the young man's kind appealing eyes" (xxii). Only after this first silence, the putative result of her (unrepresented) thoughts when returning to the farm, does Sylvia remember "how the white heron came flying through the golden air" or the narrative suggest why she "cannot . . . give its life away" (xxii).

Such motivated rhetorical spacing occurs especially in relation to Jewett's inscription of the father/daughter relation. We could argue that Jewett first identifies and disidentifies with Sylvia by means of her name. The surnameless "Sylvia" stands as a torn up homonymic of "Sarah"—"S————a(h)"—a phonetic surrogate which the narrative deemphasizes by having Sylvia, no less than the two adults, refer to herself as "Sylvy." Such unnaming or even nonnaming reinvokes even as it invokes the father-as-author/daughter-as-character relation. It allows Jewett to unimagine herself *en passant* in the place of Sylvia, just as "writing" allows her to unimagine a paternalistic relation to the girl when as narrator she effectively adopts the position of Sylvia whom she helps discover the heron ("Now look down again, Sylvia . . . there where you saw the white heron once you will see him again" [xxi]) and both underwrites and identifies the moment the little girl makes her (contextually indeterminate) decision: "No, she must keep silence!" (xxii). Able to serve as a conduit through which the reader has the illusion of an unmediated apprehension of Sylvia in such scenes, Jewett's "pathetic" narrator also literally displaces the reader's proximity to the girl's thoughts or actions. This rhetorical stratagem interposes a space, a space occupied by a narrator bound to be overlooked as such and so still a space to the writer, that protects both the girl and the writer's relation to her from being regarded in adult, i.e., in explicit child/parent, terms. Moreover, in the scene where Sylvia climbs the tree, the narrative deploys an elusive spatiolinguistic imagery which refracts further the implicit child/parent relation between Sylvia and the narrator. Here the narrator adopts a childlike position and places Sylvia in the parental position by describing the girl at the top of the tree as if perceiving her "from the ground" (xxi).

Incipient metaphors and metamorphoses reducible to metonymies that displace the former's only possible and in any case prerepresentational objectifications of the father/daughter relation, such define the tropological strategies of **"A White Heron,"** its flight from adult determinations becoming as "elusive" as the bird it represents.[88] The story assiduously multiplies the various metaphorical adumbrations of this relation beyond the narrator's relation to Sylvia. For example, we have already seen how the narrative rhetorically tends to identify the "pale" heroine with the heron. Her birdlike associations are made explicit: when she climbs the tree, "her bare feet and fingers . . . pinched and held like bird's claws to the monstrous ladder reaching up" (xx). Atop the tree, "the solitary *gray*-eyed child" with a "brave, beating heart" like a bird's sees hawks with "*gray* feathers" and feels "as if she too could go flying away among the clouds" (xxi). But the possible metaphorical identification between Sylvia and the heron occurs most clearly when both of them perch on similar trees: "[the heron] comes close at last, and goes by the landmark pine with steady sweep of wing and outstretched slender neck and crested head. And wait! wait! . . . for the heron has perched on a pine bough not far beyond yours" (xxi).

This juxtaposition, this literal metonymy verging on metaphor or metamorphosis of Sylvia and the heron, could easily resolve itself into a metaphor of the father/daughter relation. Sylvia's "longed-for white heron" that here flies "beyond" her is not only male but assumes a royal or "crested" appearance to the girl and the narrator. He adumbrates a kind of princelike father figure previously discussed, in this story a figure to whom the daughter will—on the basis of a privileged, literally exclusive and privately witnessed relation to him—express more "loyalty" than to the adult hunter, the would-be heterosexual substitute of the father. At the same time, however, the vulnerability of the heron to the hunter, his obvious but also unconscious dependence on her for protection from adult designs and sheer survival, puts him in a childlike relation to her. Moreover, just as the reader begins to focus on this "close" spatiosymbolic identification of the heron and heroine in this scene, one also encounters the fact that he "goes by" and perches on another tree. In short, their potentially metaphorical relation literally *becomes* metonymical or contiguous. Even *this* relation gets displaced onto another when the heron "cries back to his mate on the nest" (xxi), a displacement which further subsumes yet one more possible father/daughter relation. After all, Sylvia must first "look down" to see "the white heron's nest in the sea of green branches" (xxi). Atop contiguous trees, then, both Sylvia and the male heron, like parents, are in the process of looking down to this necessarily smaller-appearing—and so childlike—"mate." Another white heron whose sex we can infer as female and whose nest will lead the reader quickly to suppose she is a mother or mother-to-be (since no young are mentioned), she nevertheless remains representationally sexless, thus a possible if improbable (hence "secret") adumbration of a daughter figure.

Jewett's story also traces this configuration with its other protagonistic "character," the "great pine-tree." As we have seen, Sylvia's name etymologically associates her with this tree; but more important, no less than the "longed-for white heron" the tree appears as an object of desire for her, especially at the moment she begins to climb it:

> She had always believed that whoever climbed to the top of it could see the ocean; and the little girl had often laid her hand on the great rough trunk and looked up wistfully at those dark boughs that the wind always stirred, no matter how hot and still the air might be below. Now she thought of the tree with a new excitement, for why, if one climbed it at break of day, could not one see all the world, and easily discover whence the white heron flew, and mark the place . . . ?
>
> (xix)

As I argued earlier, just as this tree becomes the means by which she sees the white heron, so in thematic terms does her implacable, tree-like silence become the means by which the reader apprehends the value of **"A White Heron"** itself.

But it is the narrative's deployment of the trope prosopopoeia, here, which "marks the place" or traces the Imaginary locus of **"A White Heron."** The male-personified tree resembles the trees Jewett in her earlier sketches often regards in parent/child and particularly fatherly terms: poplar trees that look like "a little procession of a father and mother and . . . children out for an afternoon walk";[89] a tree that, although apparently "stunted and dwarfed" when young, comes to "grow tall and strong, and in [its] wealth of usefulness [has become] like some of the world's great men who rose from poverty to kingliness. . . . The great tree is a protection to a thousand lesser interests."[90] In fact this "great tree" could easily be "an ancient pitch pine," the kind which Jewett likes "better than any trees in the world."[91] Clearly, the "stately head" of the "great" masculinized pitch pine in **"A White Heron"** that "towered above" all other trees in his vicinity (xix) could similarly connote attributes of fatherly "kingliness." Metaphorically speaking, like a father who "must have loved his *new dependent*," the "*old* pine" (xxi) also protects the little girl from "lesser interests" by exclusively taking her above the "hot and still" world synonymous with both the hunter's and Mrs. Tilley's human society.

But whether pertaining to the heron or the tree, this rhetorical figure of prosopopoeia humanizes and virtually makes present its non-human referent even as it invokes an "imaginary or absent person . . . represented as speaking or acting."[92] If it here invokes the absent father in relation to a little "solitary" daughterlike girl, Jewett's narrative also absents an already absent father by assigning the "*old* pine" with *grand*-fatherly connotations. Moreover, the narrative (dis)places this (absent) fatherly tree in relation to "the white oak tree that grew alongside" it (xx), in other words, in the same manner as the heron with his mate. Again the spatial arrangement of the two trees metonymically situates Sylvia and the paternal object above a smaller and non-sex-denominated object. The unpersoni-

fied oak tree's nestlike features (a bird nests there and Sylvia herself "was almost lost among the dark branches and the green leaves" [xx]), along with its much lesser physical size, also could suggest a maternal figuration. Indeed, we could maintain that in climbing this tree to get to the pine tree, Sylvia in effect outlines the daughter's process of eclipsing the mother (the mother whose presence in family romance interferes with the girl's exclusive claims on the father) here represented by the oak tree, one of whose "upper branches chafed against the pine trunk" (xx). Yet the tropological scattering of this relational situation also allows us to surmise that this genderless "*white oak*" represents an elusive signifier of the daughter, like Sylvia and like the white heron's mate in relation to their *en passant* (merely possible) father-personified signifiers.

In both cases, Sylvia as transcending the mother or as retracing her own daughterhood, the narrative focus here remains on the daughter's experience of the transition from a mother to father nature, an experience that will become doubled in her sighting of the white heron. This transition, this interchangeable occupation of the roles of father to daughter or daughter to father in the crucial scenes of the story and which we could thus cite as "her" displaced Imaginary scene of writing, ritualistically repeats an absent primal transfer of the daughter's affection from preoedipal mother to oedipal father. This transfer is fraught with the possibility that the tropologically subsumed father might disappear altogether, that is, might cancel the project before it has even begun to realize the daughter's regression to a presexual self-identity: "There, when [Sylvia] made the dangerous pass from one tree to the other, the great enterprise would really begin" (xx). Akin to a regression from a more immediate symbol of regression, the absent-fatherly pine tree itself constitutes only a transition to the absent-fatherly white heron whom Sylvia at this point in the story cannot be certain she will see.

In the second place, the very tropes which elicit this regression to a preadult-alias-preadolescent moment of self-identity could defeat this project by also serving as memos of co-possible configurations of adult sexuality. Who can miss not merely the general significance but the phenomenologically evocative details of Sylvia's climbing the phallic tree? She begins "with tingling, eager blood coursing the channels of her whole frame"; once begun, "the pitch made her thin little fingers clumsy and stiff as she went round and round the tree's great stem" until the "tree seemed to lengthen itself out as she went up" (xx). And once up the tree, quite clearly, she experiences a kind of climax, first with the two hawks, when she feels "as if she too could go flying away among the clouds," and then with the equally phallic white heron at the moment when to Sylvia he "grows larger, and rises, and comes close at last . . . with steady sweep of wing and outstretched slender neck and crested head." Such libidinal investments of the two central fatherly tropes of Jewett's story could be regarded as paradoxically lessening its psychosexual associations. For example, they also serve to displace the little girl's "vaguely thrilled" sexual relation to the adult hunter whose gun poses an explicit phallic threat to her and explicit sexual issue to "her," the narrative itself. Whereas the hunter's "determined, and somewhat aggressive" whistle (xv) and "the sharp report of his gun" overtly threaten Sylvia even by their very sounds, the tree's "sharp dry twigs" that "scratched her like angry talons" (xx) and the heron's sudden resurrection from the "dark hemlocks" (xxi) lead her to experience a sex-muted exclusive relation to nature in the guise of a radically sublimated absent father who, in the merely speculative terms of the narrative, "*must* have loved his new dependent."

Representationally, her closest physical contact with a phallus-associated figure occurs with the tree, that is, an inanimate object *least* associated with adult human sexuality. Similarly, as we have seen, the narrative displaces the phallic heron's epiphanic appearance before Sylvia by calling attention to his relation to his mate, his "cries" of love for another, an exclusive relation which, insofar as it also signifies a possible sexual relation, gets dispersed when "the solemn heron goes away" because "of shouting cat-birds" (xxi). More important, Sylvia's climactic apprehension of the heron's resurrected appearance occurs through metonymized or peripheral representations rather than as a focused metaphorical epiphany: "a white *spot of him like a single floating feather* comes up from the dead hemlock and grows larger" (xxi). Both Sylvia and the narrator do not properly focus on him until his sexual motion, as it were, has become quieted into the visually neutralized image of him "perched on a pine bough not far beyond." Indeed, the force of this scene as a climactic scene for the little girl's sublimated sexual desire, an unconscious desire to lose her virginity and thus enter the world of adolescence, has all along been deprivileged by prior narrative information that she "had once stolen softly near where [the heron] stood in some bright green swamp grass" (xvii) and that "where you saw the white heron once you will see him *again*" (xxi).

In short, the narrative's sex-lessening tropological movements, not to mention the girl herself, identify "her" as a "harmless housebreaker" (xx) into the sexual thematic associated with producing adult literature, a thematic the story simultaneously traces and withdraws from. No doubt we could add "emphasis," in Nancy Miller's words, to this withdrawal, just as we could revise Sylvia's climactic experience with the heron according to the aforementioned radical feminist positions. We could even displace it by an archetypal interpretation of this experience. Thus, Sylvia's climbing the "great main-mast to the voyaging earth" (xx), itself an archetypal figuration of primal intercourse between the sky and earth, leads to her divine, Leda-like rape by a swanlike heron from which she gains a transcendental or sacred vision of nature that she is incapable of communicating (hence, her silence) to the profane ears of the hunter and Mrs. Tilley.[93] But such an interpretation already constitutes a sublimation of the more phenomenologically contingent sexual connotations of the passage. And insofar as the story withdraws from this sexual thematic by reiterative tropological options, its absenting projections of the absent-father/absent-daughter relation, whether in terms of the trans-parental narrator, personified tree, or white heron, outline the narrative's project to tell its story from the Imaginary perspective of a time before such feminist and/or archetypal codifications would become necessary.

In this sense, the "lonely country girl" at the end of the story stands as the story's own desire for preoedipal or sex-less self-identity. If the girl's climbing the fatherly tree connotes anything, it is the "tingling, eager blood coursing the channels of" the *narrative's* "whole frame." In the same way, Sylvia's private climactic experience with the fatherly white heron allegorizes the narrative's own auto-erotic impulses, its exclusion from this representational scene not only of the hunter and Mrs. Tilley but also of the reader who putatively witnesses it with the narrator. As we have argued, the narrator's "look, look!" preempts the reader's position, his or her direct apprehension of the girl's here climactic moment. The narrator effectively keeps this scene private in the process of writing it. And insofar as the narrative attempts to situate itself in a time before sexual time began, this narrational masturbatory activity can also deny the supersession of masturbation within a woman's psychosexual history, its reduction to secondary status in adult women subliminally cognizant of its regressive, i.e., not vaginal, significance.[94] Indeed, this narrational figuration of a private masturbatory act "in the name of the father" can be considered yet another strategy for returning to the locus of the preoedipal daughter's effort "to differentiate her body from her mother's and to establish herself as an active, autonomous source of satisfaction."[95]

We can argue, then, that in **"A White Heron"** Jewett inscribes her wish to realize a sex-less site of literary production by substituting her heroine's experience with the heron, whom she chooses over the adult male hunter and Mrs. Tilley, and by means of tropes that objectify the father/daughter relation in veritably unconscious ways. But this objectification remains participial rather than "fixative." If Sylvia's tree climbing surrealistically outlines climbing the father from a child daughter's point of view, it also outlines a would-be daughterly writer's writing in terms of the metonymical proximity of an absent paternal figure "who" will allow her to grow up—just as Sylvia literally grows up when climbing the tree—in a way that quells any adult definitions of sexual self-identity. As long as she writes in terms of this adult-excluding dyad, Jewett can play at writing, can write as if she were indeed a "minor" writer in the same way that Sylvia plays with the cow as "amusement with a good deal of zest." She can even inscribe her name through the story's three protagonistic images: S-y-l-v-i-*a* as S-a-r-*a*-h; *heron* as anagram of *Orne;* the tree as a veritable *family* tree, a "great mainmast" metonym of the "Jewett" patrimony as first established by early patriarchal shipbuilders.[96] Significantly, this patrimony gives Jewett financial independence—a room of her own, as it were—to write without working and more important without getting married or entering "the great world" of heterosexuality and/or its feminist discontents.

On the one hand, the absent father allows such unconscious anagrammatic inscriptions to take place—here the scattered inscription of her name that signifies Jewett's desire to identify herself as a "minor" writer of this story once and for all. But on the other hand, as we have seen, this absent father requires constant invocation of his minimum still small voice, resurrected through submerged metonymies and prosopopoeias as well as narrational silences, lest "he" disappear and thus frustrate this project by leaving it open to adult sexual determinations—including Jewett's own—and leaving it also minus the (only past) father/daughter intentionality which once defined the production of **"A White Heron."** In short, here the issue of adult sexuality becomes coterminous with the issue of the story's possible textuality before others, a quite literal textuality that supersedes her "writing" and will lead Jewett defensively to remark, "But I love her," after she has written the story. As an allegory of its own production, **"A White Heron"** ultimately encounters the materiality of discourse interfering with its thus only contingent allegorization. Jewett's identification with Sylvia, for example, would reflect her desire to gain a "secret" relation to her story in the same way that the girl herself witnesses, but for some indefinite reason cannot tell, the white heron's secret: "What is it that suddenly forbids her and makes her dumb?" (xxii). Like Sylvia, Jewett cannot give away the secret father/daughter relation of the story without at the same time giving "*its* life away"; she cannot express without destroying her private relation to a paternal muse that "came flying through the golden air and how they watched the sea and the morning together" as she writes, that is, her unconscious memory of the pristine moment or "morning" of the girl's transition from preoedipal to oedipal daughter. The story, in fact, "forbids" these allegorical doublings. Jewett's identification with Sylvia remains possible, contingent, *en passant;* for otherwise it would betray the serious or explicit rather than secret "minor" intentionality of a story that in effect was being written *by* a minor, and not merely in the sense of one who, as a woman in patriarchal society, has a minority social self-identity.

In the same way, the relation between "writing" and its residual representational correlatives remains asymmetrically allegorical, allegorical in the sense of a discourse subsuming but not negating another discursive possibility. It is this possibility that makes Jewett's sex-lessening tropological maneuvers in **"A White Heron"** inadequate as ways to produce a totally pure minor literature. While it helps to neutralize all the imminent adult-alias-sexual ideological conscriptions of her text, writing in the name of the absent father in this particular intentional context cannot fully account for "her" coterminous exposure to other kinds of adult appropriations, especially those pertaining to the story's appearance as a literary text. Here the sheer exteriority of the *written* text makes it subject to such appropriations. And in turn, they make the "secret" intentionality of "her" production—an intentionality which constitutes this story's very "life," and which allows Jewett to "love her"—a continuing project that Jewett will have to reproduce in terms of these deferred possible readings.

In the end, to transpose the absent-father/absent-daughter relation to these other unaccounted-for discursive possibilities may lead us to regard Jewett as a kind of nun after all. **"A White Heron"** absolves her from identification as a genteel, reformist, or an ideologically protesting "New England nun." Instead it identifies her as a woman writer who would suspend the discourses of the great and busy world by constructing a verbal "hermitage" or scripting a private prayer. Or more precisely, "she," the story itself, would suspend discourses of any kind that strive to enlist "her" in a "great enterprise" greater than Jewett desires to propose here. Like the "shouting cat-birds" that chase away the white heron, these discourses would vex her project to produce a pure minor literature "in the name of the father."

Notes

1. Shulamith Firestone has emphasized this issue in her *The Dialectic of Sex,* a relevant version of which appears in her "On American Feminism" collected in Vivian Gornick and Barbara Moran, eds., *Woman in Sexist Society: Studies in Power and Powerlessness* (New York: Basic Books, 1971), esp. 486. Many feminist critics have discussed the woman writer's ambivalent situation in nineteenth-century patriarchal society wherein she could effectively produce *only* "minor literature," that is, literature conforming to male stereotypes about women's "proper place" or "nature." See, for example, Elizabeth Winston, "The Autobiographer and Her Readers," in Estelle C. Jelinek, ed., *Women's Autobiography: Essays in Criticism* (Bloomington: Indiana University Press, 1980), 95. I am also indebted to Mary Kelley for her work on "literary domestics," American woman novelists of the nineteenth century, which situates this issue in a specifically American cultural context. See her *Private Woman, Public Stage: Literary Domesticity in the Nineteenth Century* (New York: Oxford University Press, 1984).

2. Eleanor Flexner, *Century of Struggle: The Woman's Rights Movement in the United States,* rev. ed. (Cambridge: Belknap Press, 1975), 65. Flexner also argues that by "1848 [one year before Jewett was born], it was possible for women who rebelled against the circumstances of their lives to know that they were not alone" (77). Sheila M. Rothman also discusses the changing social milieu after the Civil War of women and the woman's movement in her *Woman's Proper Place: A History of Changing Ideals and Practices, 1870 to the Present* (New York: Basic Books, 1978).

3. Donovan, *Sarah Orne Jewett,* claims that "Eliot . . . was never a favorite, though Jewett's library included all Eliot's major works" (4). Jewett's objections to Eliot were likely on literary rather than ideological grounds (see Donovan, 24).

4. *Letters,* Cary, 17, fn. 3. Cary suggests that Jewett may have chosen this pseudonym "from George Eliot, whose life and works she wrote about."

5. Elaine Showalter, "Women Writers and the Double Standard," in *Woman in Sexist Society*, 325–27. Also see her *A Literature of Their Own: British Women Novelists from Brontë to Lessing* (Princeton: Princeton University Press, 1977), esp. 19 ff. and 36 et passim.

6. Quotation from "River Driftwood" occurs on p. 60, above. "From a Mournful Villager," 120–21; my italics. The issue of "suffrage" for women was complicated and even displaced—hence made more difficult for women—by the issue of abolition. Ellen Carol Du Bois, *Feminism and Suffrage: The Emergence of an Independent Women's Movement in America, 1848–1869* (Ithaca: Cornell University Press, 1978), discusses how the postbellum problem "for feminists was how to make progress for women suffrage in the face of abolitionists' reluctance to support them" (77).

7. Sarah Orne Jewett, *A Country Doctor* (Boston: Houghton Mifflin, 1884). Jewett's preference for this novel is noted in the Webers' *Bibliography*, 10.

8. Matthiessen quotes Jewett's own connection with this novel's father figure in *Sarah Orne Jewett*, 75–76.

9. Jewett, *A Country Doctor*, 282–83.

10. Annette Kolodny, "Some Notes on Defining a 'Feminist Literary Criticism,'" *Critical Inquiry* 2 (Autumn 1975):76. Flexner, *Century of Struggle*, discusses the somewhat tenuous political or practical influence of Fuller's *Woman in the Nineteenth Century* on the century's woman's movement (66). I am here more concerned with its literary-ideological influence on Jewett's production of "A White Heron."

11. Margaret Fuller, *Woman in the Nineteenth Century and Kindred Papers*, ed. Arthur Fuller (Boson: John P. Jewett, 1855), 63, 72, et passim.

12. Jewett, *A Country Doctor*, 52–54.

13. Fuller, *Woman in the Nineteenth Century*, 37 and 40; see pp. 120–21 for Fuller's example of a "bad" father who cares only to restrict his daughter's education. Fuller's enlightened friend Miranda and her relation to the "good" father are usually considered to represent Fuller's own early upbringing by *her* father. Paula Blanchard agrees with but also expresses some reservations about this connection in her *Margaret Fuller: From Transcendentalism to Revolution* (New York: Delacorte Press / Seymour Lawrence, 1978), 215–18.

14. Fuller, *Woman in the Nineteenth Century*, 96.

15. For a discussion of female friendships in the nineteenth century, see Carroll Smith-Rosenberg, "The Female World of Love and Ritual: Relations between Women in Nineteenth-Century America," *Signs* 1 (1975):9, 11, 14, et passim. Smith-Rosenberg notes that "homosocial" relations between women were encouraged by men; on the surface, that is, they posed no homosexual or gender-separatist threat to the patriarchy. Donovan, *Sarah Orne Jewett*, 13, briefly discusses Jewett's "life-long monogamous partnership" with Annie Fields. Showalter, "Women Writers and the Double Standard," 331 and 329, discusses how male critics and writers denigrated Victorian women writers by referring to them as "old maids" or "spinsters," women who did not confirm and conform to the patriarchal image of women as guardians of an idealized domestic life.

16. Jewett, *A Country Doctor*, 307.

17. Ibid., p. 295.

18. Fuller, *Woman in the Nineteenth Century*, 176, 129, 158.

19. Ibid., p. 121.

20. Elaine Showalter, "Feminist Criticism in the Wilderness," in Elizabeth Abel, ed., *Writing and Sexual Difference, Critical Inquiry* 8, no. 2 (Winter 1981):204.

21. Berthoff, *Fictions and Events*, makes an analogous if patriarchally coded point about the women represented in Jewett's later work, *Pointed Firs*. For the women left to face the "blight that has settled on the region" by themselves, "the only choice, the sacrifice required for survival, is to give up a *woman's proper life* and cover the default of the men to be guardians and preservers of a community" (250; my italics).

22. The term is Ellen Moers's from her *Literary Women* (Garden City: Doubleday, 1976), 122 ff. For a male critic like Berthoff, *Fictions and Events*, 250, Sylvia's choice entails her defensive desire to preserve the farmstead or region from the "grossness" of American society as represented by the hunter's "offering her money."

23. Martin, *Harvests of Change*, alludes to this etymology (144). For a discussion of Sylvia as a figure of nature within a patriarchal paradigm, see Chapter 3, pp. 121–22, below.

24. Moers, *Literary Women*, 250–51.

25. Mary Jacobus, "The Question of Language: Men of Maxims and *The Mill on the Floss*," in *Writing and Sexual Difference*, 210.

26. Fuller constantly alludes throughout *Woman in the Nineteenth Century* to ideal virgin and/or "self-sufficient" women in classical literature: for example to Sappho (47–48), the Sibyl (99), Cassandra (105–6), and especially the "Muse and Minerva" (115–16) as well as "Ceres" (121). As W.K.C. Guthrie notes in his *The Greeks and Their Gods*, rpt. ed. (Boston: Beacon Press, 1955), 101, the Greek goddess Demeter (in Roman mythology, Ceres) was assumed to be the mother of and sometimes Artemis herself, "an earth goddess, associated essentially and chiefly with the wild life and growth of the fields, and with human birth." In any case, Jewett's allusive association of Sylvia with a major feminine mythic figure, albeit inscribed within a patriarchal tradition, could easily

outline an exclusive feminine declaration in ways beyond my present argument. First, it appeals to the authority of this tradition, but only in the guise of its honorific, presently defunct or historically out-of-sight influence. Alluding to this inoperative literary-patriarchal tradition, the connection with Artemis effectively *dis*-associates Sylvia from a restrictive patriarchal conscription of this goddess and frees her to become an image for oppressed women of all times. Second, Jewett's use of this classical allusion, however subtle, amounts to her de facto declaration of woman's ability to know and make use of this learning, that is, her (here demonstrated) ability to conceive new and not simply reproduce "proper" meanings—in short, like Fuller's classical allusions, it is a demonstration of woman's intellectual capacities in the face of stereotypical male assumptions and restrictions concerning them (cf. Rothman, *Woman's Proper Place,* 29 et passim).

27. Oskar Seyffert, *A Dictionary of Classical Antiquities,* rev. and ed. by Henry Nettleship and J. E. Sandys (Cleveland: World, 1961), 43.

28. On the feminist use of "metamorphosis," see Nina Auerbach, "Magi and Maidens: The Romance of the Victorian Freud," in *Writing and Sexual Difference,* 294–97. Cf. Deleuze and Guattari's view of this trope's use by the "minor" writer, pp. 33–34, above. For a conservative view of how literature displaces myths by "credible" or "realistic" if still unconscious reconstructions, see Northrop Frye, "Myth, Fiction, and Displacement," *Fables of Identity,* esp. 34–37.

29. Judith Fryer, esp. 6, purports to use this "American Eve" framework in examining certain novels by male writers, *The Faces of Eve: Women in the Nineteenth Century American Novel* (New York: Oxford University Press, 1976).

30. Annis Pratt, "Women and Nature in Modern Fiction," argues that Sylvia's quest for the heron makes her emblematic of an ontological relation to nature decisively inaccessible to and different from the teleological paradigms of patriarchal quest literature and notions of self-identity (450; see p. xxvii, above). Annette Kolodny, "Turning the Lens on 'The Panther Captivity': A Feminist Exercise in Practical Criticism," in *Writing and Sexual Difference,* 343 et passim, also touches on this issue in discussing how this captivity narrative reveals "male figures of greed and violence . . . repeatedly breach[ing], or attempt[ing] to breach, the precincts of the lady's various Dream Gardens, her romantic trysting place, her person, and . . . her wilderness abode." In the same vein but with a particular focus on criticism, cf. Baym, "Melodramas of Beset Manhood."

31. Mary Daly, *Gyn/ecology: The Metaethics of Radical Feminism* (Boston: Beacon Press, 1978), 74–89, provides a context by which we could assert that the tree is a feminist archetype and the heron a possibly counter-patriarchal image inversely analogous to pa-

triarchal "rapes" of matriarchal orders. Fryer, *Faces of Eve,* quotes Otto Weininger to show patriarchal notions of woman's ontological naiveté: "Woman has no relation to the idea, she neither affirms nor denies it; she is neither moral nor anti-moral: mathematically speaking, she has no sign; she is purposeless, neither good nor bad . . . she is as non-moral as she is non-logical" (8). His depiction ironically turns out to be true for some feminist theorists discussed later.

32. Fuller, *Woman in the Nineteenth Century,* 102.

33. Fuller had argued that the pejorative representation of Eve in the Judeo-Christian tradition had been superseded by the transcendent representation of the Virgin Mary (47 and 56). Susan Gubar, "'The Blank Page' and the Issues of Female Creativity," in *Writing and Sexual Difference,* argues that the Virgin Mary allusion in women's literature might be viewed as a "revisionary metaphor" reclaiming the power of creativity for women (261).

34. Fuller, *Woman in the Nineteenth Century,* 135.

35. Ibid., p. 175.

36. One could argue that this ideological privileging of childhood permeates the writings of Howells and especially Twain, notably in the latter's "Old Times on the Mississippi." Childhood as a topos is also a "regionalist" ideologeme and could reflect the way Jewett's story reflects or even exploits the late-nineteenth-century American audience's interest in nostalgic representations of simpler if past modes of American life. In this sense, it seems no coincidence, perhaps, that as Matthiessen notes (*Sarah Orne Jewett,* 60–61), Jewett published a poem in an *Atlantic Monthly* of 1875, the edition in which Twain published the fifth section of "Old Times on the Mississippi."

37. Nina Baym, *Women's Fiction: A Guide to Novels by and about Women in America, 1820–1870* (Ithaca: Cornell University Press, 1978), 196.

38. Contrary to Baym and Mary Kelley, Ann Douglas discusses and criticizes the "feminization of American culture," the cooption of women writers, reduced to "sentimental" concerns in their fiction, by the patriarchal-clerical Christian tradition: *The Feminization of American Culture* (New York: Alfred A. Knopf, 1977), esp. 254 ff. Also cf. Cheri Register, "American Feminist Criticism: A Bibliographical Introduction, in Josephine Donovan, ed., *Feminist Literary Criticism* (Lexington: University Press of Kentucky, 1961), who argues that for "women like George Eliot and the Brontës, writing something other than sentimental novels was a rebellious act, and necessarily ideological and time-bound" (10).

39. Nancy C. Miller, "Emphasis Added: Plots and Plausibilities in Women's Fiction," *PMLA* 96, no. 1 (January 1981):36 and 39.

40. Sandra M. Gilbert and Susan Gubar, *The Madwoman in the Attic: The Woman Writer and the Nineteenth-*

Century Literary Imagination (New Haven: Yale University Press, 1979), 58; my italics.

41. Miller, "Emphasis Added," 41.

42. Adrienne Rich, "Vesuvius at Home: The Power of Emily Dickinson," *On Lies, Secrets, and Silence: Adrienne Rich, Selected Prose, 1966–1978* (New York: W. W. Norton, 1979), 166 and 162. Coppélia Kahn, "Excavating 'Those Dim Minoan Regions': Maternal Subtexts in Patriarchal Literature," *Diacritics* (Summer 1982), argues that contrary to male critics who assume genres to have universal significance, the "feminist reader consciously notes the gender perspective of this genre, and tries to learn from it about the working myths of patriarchal culture" (41). For a further discussion of the diminutive imagery used by women writers and its significance in their works, see Moers, *Literary Women,* 244 and 245. In this present context, it is ironic that Matthiessen, a male critic, maintains that Jewett and Emily Dickinson were for him at the time of his critical biography of Jewett "the two principal women writers America has had" (*Sarah Orne Jewett*), 152.

43. Myra Jehlen, "Archimedes and the Paradox of Feminist Criticism," *Signs* 6, no. 4 (Summer 1981):583.

44. Fuller, *Woman in the Nineteenth Century,* 221–22, associates these vocational options available to women. Also see Rothman, *Woman's Proper Place,* 30 ff.

45. Virginia Woolf, *A Room of One's Own* (New York: Harcourt, Brace & World, 1929; rpt. 1957), 74 et passim. Showalter also addresses this issue throughout her *A Literature of Their Own,* as does Annette Kolodny, "A Map of Rereading; or, Gender and the Interpretation of Literary Texts," *New Literary History* 11 (Spring 1980), esp. her discussion of Susan Glaspell's "A Jury of Her Peers," 460–63. Howells himself judged literature according to how it raised broad questions about life and society without giving self serving "romantic" answers: "What is our religion, what is our society, what is our country, what is our civilization? You cannot read [Tolstoy] without asking yourself these questions, and the result is left with you." W. D. Howells, "On Zola and Others," collected in Cleanth Brooks, R. W. B. Lewis, Robert Penn Warren, eds., *American Literature: The Makers and the Making,* Vol. 2 (New York: St. Martin's Press, 1973), 1370.

46. See n. 2, pp. 213–14, below.

47. Cf. Gilbert and Gubar's discussion of Anne Brontë's *The Tenant of Wildfell Hall* and of other women writers who inscribed their coerced but revolutionary status *as* writers within their works: "[the woman writer through her characters] produces a public art which she herself rejects as inadequate but which she secretly uses to discover a new aesthetic space for herself. In addition, she subverts her genteelly "feminine" works with personal representations which

endure only in tracings, since her guilt about the impropriety of self-expression has caused her to efface her private drawings just as it has led her to efface herself" (*Madwoman in the Attic,* 81). As I will try to argue, feminist critical narratives such as Gilbert and Gubar's themselves purport to be "secretly" gender-inflected discourses. For a further discussion of this issue, namely the virtual exclusion of male readers from a feminist if not feminine text, see Kolodny, "A Map of Rereading," esp. 463–65, and her "Reply to Commentaries," 588–89, in the same volume of *New Literary History.*

48. Adrienne Rich, "Compulsory Heterosexuality and Lesbian Existence," *Signs* 5, no. 4 (Summer 1980):652 et passim. For Rich, of course, the notion of "lesbian continuum," the subliminal resistance of all women in past and present patriarchal societies refers to "a range—through each woman's life and throughout history—of woman-identified experience; not simply the fact that a woman has had or consciously desired genital sexual experience with another woman" (648). Not only has "heterosexuality" been imposed on women as a norm to which they must conform, so has "heterosexual romance" for the woman writer; male critics, according to Rich in *On Lies, Secrets, and Silence,* privilege such representational romances as a "key to [the woman artist's] life and work" (158).

49. Rich, *On Lies, Secrets, and Silence,* 158.

50. Kolodny, "Some Notes on Defining a 'Feminist Literary Criticism,'" 90.

51. Elizabeth Berg, "The Third Woman," *Diacritics* (Summer 1982), 19.

52. Alice Jardine, "Gynesis," *Diacritics* (Summer 1982), 58. The difference between French and American feminisms becomes apparent when we see an American feminist critic like Josephine Donovan use the concept of an "authentic" feminine identity. See her "Afterword: Critical Re-vision," in *Feminist Literary Criticism,* 77 et passim. French feminist critics, on the other hand, seeming to adopt what to radical American feminist critics resembles a neoconservative position, would basically if reservedly agree with Julia Kristeva's warning in Elaine Marks and Isabelle de Courtivron, eds., *New French Feminisms: An Anthology* (Amherst: University of Massachusetts Press, 1980), "that certain feminist demands revive a kind of naive romanticism, a belief in identity (the reverse of phallocratism), if we compare them to the experience of both poles of sexual difference as is found in the economy of Joycian or Artaudian prose. . . . I pay close attention to the particular aspect of the [avant-garde] work . . . which dissolves . . . even sexual identities" (138).

53. Jacobus, "Question of Language," 211, 210.

54. Cf. Kolodny's discussion of the relation between feminist criticism and male critical paradigms like

Harold Bloom's, in "A Map of Rereading." Also cf. Gilbert and Gubar, *Madwoman in the Attic,* 73, and Mary Daly's feminist antimethod and/or self-conscious subversion of male-dominated discourses in *Gyn/ecology,* 22–29. In a different but no less revolutionary context, Deleuze and Guattari also argue for the sabotaging of the "major language" (see pp. 31–33, above).

55. See Rothman, *Woman's Proper Place,* 21–23.

56. *Letters,* Fields, 106.

57. Ibid., p. 246.

58. Cary, *Sarah Orne Jewett,* 141.

59. Sarah Orne Jewett, *A Marsh Island* (Boston: Houghton Mifflin, 1885), 181, 168. Dale explicitly notices the "patriarchal character to the [Owen] family" (109).

60. Ibid., p. 156.

61. *Letters,* Cary, 19, fn. 19. One should also note that Jewett's father practiced ornithology. Frost, *Sarah Orne Jewett* 22.

62. Jewett, *A Marsh Island,* 92.

63. Ibid.

64. Jewett, *A Country Doctor,* 270.

65. Ibid., pp. 133, 137.

66. Cf. Coppélia Kahn, "Excavating 'Those Dim Minoan Regions,'" who argues that feminist criticism should apply itself to discovering the maternal subtext of literary works, that is, should read "the text as the scene of interplay between infantile fantasy and manifest content" wherein the former "emanates from early childhood, when the child's most important relationship is with the mother" (36).

67. Frost, *Sarah Orne Jewett,* 22–23.

68. Jewett, *A Marsh Island,* 26, 64, 156, 154.

69. Cary, *Sarah Orne Jewett,* 138.

70. Jewett, *A Country Doctor,* 134.

71. For the significance of the grandmother in the girl's process of developing self-identity, see Elizabeth Abel, "(E)Merging Identities: The Dynamics of Female Friendship in Contemporary Fiction by Women," *Signs* 6, no. 3 (Spring 1981):427.

72. Juliet Mitchell, *Psychoanalysis and Feminism* (New York: Vintage Books, 1975), 96 and 57. In a way relevant to the position I will soon take, she also makes a "revised" Freudian perspective attentive to "the Minoan-Mycenean pre-Oedipal phase so crucial for femininity" (109 et passim).

73. Ibid., p. 97.

74. Nancy Chodorow, "Being and Doing: A Cross-Cultural Examination of the Socialization of Males and Females," in *Woman in Sexist Society,* 186.

75. Nancy Chodorow, *The Reproduction of Mothering: Psychoanalysis and the Sociology of Gender*

(Berkeley: University of California Press, 1978), 123. Chodorow goes on to stress that the girl's turning away from the mother to the father "is at most a concentration on her father of a girl's genital, or erotic, cathexis. But a girl never gives up her mother as an internal or external love object, even if she does become heterosexual" (127). Rich, of course, disagrees with Chodorow's heterosexual orientation ("Compulsory Heterosexuality and Lesbian Existence," 636). For another clinical corroboration of the Chodorow-like position, see Irene Fast, "Developments in Gender Identity: Gender Differentiation in Girls," *International Journal of Psycho-Analysis* 60 (1979): esp. 451 and 457.

76. Chodorow, *Reproduction of Mothering,* 123.

77. Chodorow, "Being and Doing," 191, 192; *Reproduction of Mothering,* 127.

78. Frost discusses Jewett's especially close relation to her older sister Mary (*Sarah Orne Jewett,* 75–76).

79. Larzer Ziff, *The American 1890s: Life and Times of a Lost Generation* (New York: Viking Press, 1966), 283, discusses the negative attitudes of women toward childbearing in general.

80. Jewett, *A Country Doctor,* 120, 122.

81. Mitchell, *Psychoanalysis and Feminism,* 97.

82. Jean-Paul Sartre, *What Is Literature?* 16. Cf. n. 39, p. 211, below, the passage cited from Barbara Herrnstein Smith's "Contingencies of Value."

83. *Letters,* Cary, 30.

84. Jane Gallop, "The Ghost of Lacan, the Trace of Language," *Diacritics* (Winter 1975): 24, a review of Mitchell's *Psychoanalysis and Feminism.* For further discussion of Lacanian psychoanalysis from a feminist viewpoint, see Gallop's *The Daughter's Seduction: Feminism and Psychoanalysis* (Ithaca: Cornell University Press, 1982), and Anika Lemaire's feminine if not feminist consideration, *Jacques Lacan,* trans. David Macey with preface by Jacques Lacan (London: Routledge & Kegan Paul, 1977), esp. 82 ff., where she discusses Lacan's notion of "the Name of the Father" as "paternal metaphor" or "representative of the law which founds humanity, [whose] speech must be recognized by [from the child's position, the preoedipal] mother."

85. Geoffrey H. Hartman, "Psychoanalysis: The French Connection," in Geoffrey H. Hartman, ed., *Psychoanalysis and the Question of the Text* (Baltimore: Johns Hopkins University Press, 1978), 92.

86. Ibid.

87. Ibid., p. 94.

88. I use Roman Jakobson's definition of these tropes from his "The Metaphoric and Metonymic Poles," in *Critical Theory since Plato,* 1113 and esp. 1114. My discussion of "A White Heron" from p. 102 to the end of this chapter follows in spirit, at least, the criti-

cal principles used by Roland Barthes in his examination of Balzac's "Sarrasine" in *S/Z*, trans. Richard Miller (New York: Hill and Wang, 1974), especially where he claims to initiate "a process of nomination which is the essence of the reader's activity: to read is to struggle to name, to subject the sentences of the text to a semantic transformation. This transformation is erratic; it consists in hesitating among several names. . . . The connotator refers not so much to a name as to a synonymic complex whose common nucleus we sense even while the discourse is leading us toward other possibilities, toward other related signifieds: thus, reading is absorbed in a kind of metonymic skid, each synonym adding to its neighbor some new trait, some new departure" (92).

89. Jewett, "River Driftwood," 19.

90. Jewett, "A Winter Drive," 169. One could add to this list of trees as parental tropes. In "An October Ride" she notes how "old pines" stand "a little way back watching their children march in upon their inheritance, *as if they were ready to interfere and protect and defend*" (98; my italics). Or again from "A Winter Drive," "It seems as if the tree [like an internalized cathected parent] remembered what we remember; it is something more than the fact of its having been associated with our past" (167).

91. Jewett, "A Winter Drive," 178.

92. Richard A. Lanham, *A Handlist of Rhetorical Terms* (Berkeley: University of California Press, 1968), 83.

93. Cf. Joseph Campbell who argues that in primitive societies, certain birds possess divine attributes which humans can attain by a kind of ritualistic imitation; thus, in climbing the tree, we could say, Sylvia metaphorically defines the place around it as holy ground, as a true "hermitage" or spiritual retreat consecrated as such by her vision of the heron. To quote from Campbell, *The Flight of the Wild Gander: Explorations in the Mythological Dimension* (New York: Viking Press, 1951; rpt. 1960), 167, "In many lands the soul has been pictured as a bird, and birds commonly appear as spiritual messengers: angels are modified birds. But the bird of the shaman is one of particular character and power, endowing him with an ability to fly in trance beyond all bounds of life, and yet return." Other "mythic" interpretations could be made of this after-all epiphanic moment with the white heron. Is it an allusion to the appearance of the New Testament angel—or even the Holy Ghost (Jewett was an Episcopalian), i.e., the Father's absent presence—announcing the Immaculate Conception to a Virgin Mary figure who will give birth to her own sacred innocence?

94. See Mitchell, *Psychoanalysis and Feminism*, 107: "The pre-Oedipal girl abandons her mother as love-object. . . . At the same time, she is likely to give up her clitoris too . . . her manual masturbation of it. She wants nothing to remind her of the wound to her narcissism—neither her all-responsible,

'castrated' mother, nor her own 'little penis.' The two go together. The girl realizes that she cannot possess her mother, hence the clitoris loses its active connotations, and when its sensitivity reemerges at puberty it is likely to be in a masturbatory role with passive aims . . . now either auto-erotic or as a preliminary to vaginal penetration."

95. Mary C. Rawlinson, "Psychiatric Discourse and the Feminine Voice," *Journal of Medicine and Philosophy* 8 (1982):172.

96. Jewett often alludes to South Berwick's shipbuilding past economy throughout her writings. See Jay Martin who discusses this topic in relation to an added section of *Pointed Firs,* "The Queen's Twin," (*Harvests of Change,* 143). Frost also mentions this shipbuilding patrimony in *Sarah Orne Jewett,* 1–3.

Elizabeth Ammons (essay date 1986)

SOURCE: "The Shape of Violence in Jewett's 'A White Heron,'" *Colby Library Quarterly,* Vol. 22, No. 1, March, 1986, pp. 6–16.

[*In the essay below, Ammons discusses the myths, narrative form, and themes of the story.*]

> Let us imagine that we live in a culture where time is a cycle, where the sand dollar lies beside its fossil (as it does). Where everything is seen to return, as the birds return to sight with the movement of the waves. As I return to the beach, again and again.
>
> Imagine that in that returning nothing stands outside; the bird is not separate from the wave but both are part of the same rhythm. Imagine that I know—not with my intellect but in my body, my heart—that I do not stand separate from the sand dollar or the fossil; that the slow forces that shaped the life of one and preserved the other under the deep pressure of settling mud for cycles upon cycles are the same forces that have formed my life; that when I hold the fossil in my hand I am looking into a mirror. . . . We are aware of the world as returning, the forms of our thoughts flow in circles, spirals, webs; they weave and dance, honoring the links, the connections, the patterns, the changes, so that nothing can be removed from its context.[1]

And now let us imagine that into this web—into this timeless cycle of birds and waves—walks a man with a gun.

I start with this quotation from the witch Starhawk because I want to suggest that **"A White Heron,"** on one level an interesting but "easy" story about the irreconcilable conflict between opposing sets of values: urban/rural, scientific/intuitional, civilized/natural, masculine/feminine, on a deeper level represents as radical—as sinister—a challenge to complacent heterosexual ideology as do the imaginings of a witch such as Starhawk. Indeed, it will be my contention that the arguments of **"A White Heron"** and of Starhawk, "birds" separated by a century (Jewett's story was published in 1886, Starhawk's book in 1982), have things in common. Specifically, after talking briefly about **"A White Heron"** as creation myth and as historical commentary, I will be arguing three things: that **"A White Heron"** is a story about resistance to heterosexuality; that the form Jewett adopts to express her idea is, quite appropriately, the fairy tale; and that despite her protests to the contrary Jewett shows in this fiction her ability to create conventional "plot"—that is, to use inherited masculine narrative shape—when she needs to.

Perhaps the most obvious meaning of **"A White Heron"** comes from the female creation, or re-creation, myth Jewett offers. The story presents a little girl whose world is entirely female. No brother, father, uncle, or grandfather lives in it; the men have feuded and left or died. Only she and her grandmother inhabit the rural paradise to which the child was removed after spending the first eight years of her life in a noisy manmade mill-town, the strongest memory (and perfect symbol) of which is a "great red-faced boy who used to chase and frighten her" as she walked home through the streets at night.[2] In the country with her grandmother she is safe. Named Sylvia (Latin for "woods") the girl feels that "she never had been alive at all before she came to live on the farm" (p. 228). Her grandmother says: there "never was such a child for straying out-of-doors since the world was made!" (p. 228). Clearly Sylvia is nature's child, a pristine or first female, repelled by the city but so at home in the woods that the birds and animals share their secrets and the earth itself, her true grand/mother, embraces her with gentle breezes and soft lullabies. Walking home through the woods one night (compare this with the experience she remembers from the city), she listens "to the thrushes with a heart that beat fast with pleasure" and senses "in the great boughs overhead . . . little birds and beasts . . . going about their world . . . [and] saying goodnight to each other in sleepy twitters. . . . It made her feel as if she were a part of the gray shadows and the moving leaves" (p. 229). As her grandmother boasts, "'the wild creatur's counts her one o' themselves'" (p. 230).

The whimsical and yet serious incarnation of this magical "natural" place to which the child has been restored, appropriately by her maternal grandmother, is a cow. Symbol of bountiful female nurture—a cow is a walking udder, a warm mobile milky mother (of a different species from us to be sure, but as this story shows, difference in species is not an important distinction to make in life)—the cow represents what the city is *not* and what the woods, healthy, wild, domestic, maternal, stands for in **"A White Heron."** In fact, Jewett opens the story by concentrating on the bond between this exaggeratedly female animal and her "little woods-girl" (p. 229). The two of them, the mature female (Mistress Moolly the cow) and nine-year-old Sylvia, amble together through the woods away from the western light (which means toward the rising moon, the heavenly body associated with women) in a wending nightly ritual of hide-and-seek that is almost a dance, the two partners know their steps so well. Played with the

wild but milky Mistress Moolly, this game of finding each other, situated as it is at the very opening of the story, serves as a metaphor for the whole realm of matrifocal happiness into which Jewett draws us. In this world females—human, bovine, it does not matter—*can* find each other. They can live together in fertile self-sufficiency and contentment, much as Jewett herself, of course, lived happily with her sisters and women friends within a complex and satisfying network of female support and intimacy into which men might wander, like the nameless intruder in this story, but always as strangers and never to stay.

Read historically, this Adamless Eden represents a response—mythic, spiritual—to the dramatic changes taking place in the lives of middle-class white American women toward the turn into the twentieth century. On the one hand, the middle-class nineteenth-century ideology of separate masculine and feminine spheres excluded women from competition and success in the public arena—medicine, commerce, high art, and the like. The ideology of separatism severely confined and limited women. At the same time, however, as Carroll Smith-Rosenberg points out in her classic study of middle-class, white, nineteenth-century female friendship in America, separatism strengthened women by honoring female bonding and intimacy. As Smith-Rosenberg explains, "women . . . did not form an isolated and oppressed subcategory in male society. Their letters and diaries indicate that women's sphere had an essential integrity and dignity that grew out of women's shared experiences and mutual affection and that, despite the profound changes which affected American social structure and institutions between the 1760s and 1870s, retained a constancy and predictability."[3]

Smith-Rosenberg's identification of the 1870s as the beginning of the end of this period of continuity for women highlights the fact that **"A White Heron,"** written in 1881, celebrates the ideology of separatism at the time historically that it was beginning to fall apart. As Josephine Donovan notes, the story speaks to "the profound ambivalence women of the late nineteenth century felt as they were beginning to move out of the female-centered world of the home into male-centered institutions."[4] Sylvia confronts and is tempted by the possibility of a new and traditionally masculine ethic for women. The hunter invites her to participate in his project. She can, like her sisters in the ranks of stenographers and typewriters smartly decking themselves out in shirtwaists and suit jackets to invade the nation's offices and boardrooms, bastions of male privilege and power previously off limits to women, identify with men. She can join the great masculine project of conquering and controlling ("harnessing") nature and agreeing on money as the best measure of worth and most effective medium of exchange between human beings. She can, in short, even though she is female, join in the great late nineteenth-century game of buying and selling the world.

She can—but she won't. Sylvia, and clearly Jewett as well, finds in the ideology of female separatism, despite its limitations, a better environment for women than that offered by the new ideology of integration, or identification with masculine values. The older ideology values compassion over profit and cooperation over competition. While the perfect bird for the ornithologist is a dead one, the perfect bird for the child is alive. Sylvia, choosing the past over the future, the bird over a ten dollar gold piece, says no to the temptation represented by the glamorous young scientist so eager to make a girl his partner. In the last paragraph the narrator concedes that the choice is not easy: "Were the birds better friends than their hunter might have been,—who can tell?" (p. 239). The young stranger with a gun is beautiful and powerful. "He can make them rich with money; he has promised it, and they are poor now. He is so well worth making happy" (p. 239). The stranger has great allure: the future is tempting. Indeed, Sylvia's grandmother is converted. But Sylvia is not. She may change when she is older; of that we cannot be certain. But the moment this story captures is the moment of her resistance. The moment of her saying no.

That resistance, I now want to argue, is not simply historical, not simply a matter of saying no to shirtwaists and coffee breaks. It is a matter of Sylvia's saying no to the erotic stirrings she feels for the handsome young man. Sylvia's resistance, in other words, is resistance to the institution of heterosexuality itself, which as Adrienne Rich explains with great care in "Compulsory Heterosexuality and Lesbian Existence" is the *sine qua non* of patriarchy. Rich argues: "If women are the earliest sources of emotional caring and physical nurture for both female and male children, it would seem logical, from a feminist perspective at least, to pose the following questions: whether the search for love and tenderness in both sexes does not originally lead toward women; *why in fact women would ever redirect that search;* . . . and why such violent strictures should be found necessary to enforce women's total emotional, erotic loyalty and subservience to men." Rich urges scholars to examine "the societal forces that wrench women's emotional and erotic energies away from themselves and other women and from woman-identified values" and states bluntly that "heterosexuality, like motherhood, needs to be recognized and studied as a *political institution*."[5] Prescribing and enforcing heterosexuality, she argues, is the essential task of patriarchy. Without that manipulation of women into transferring emotional and erotic allegiance from the mother to a man the system would crumble. Women would be free to remain woman-identified, emotionally and erotically, throughout life. For patriarchy to work society must realign woman's original, "natural" emotional/erotic attachment to her same-sex lover, mother—a complicated maneuver that Jewett, no less than Rich, understands.

Seen in this light **"A White Heron"** represents an anti-bildungsroman. It is a rite-of-passage story in which the heroine refuses to make the passage. Choosing the world of her grandmother over the world of the alluring young man, Sylvia chooses not to pass over into the world of adult female sexuality as it is defined by the culture. The nine-year-old child, a girl about to enter puberty, refuses to enter into the transaction that everyone—the hunter, her grandmother—expects her to make.

"A White Heron" says that heterosexuality requires the female to offer up body itself as prey. All Sylvia has to do is offer up the body of the bird—a free, beautiful creature like herself—to the hunter and she will receive in return money, social approval, and the affection of a man. Clearly the heron in this story symbolizes the heroine, and the exchange Sylvia is expected to make at the age of nine, with her heart set throbbing by the handsome young man, is the transition from childhood to the threshold of womanhood, the wrench from little girl identification with the mother (in this case the maternal earth itself) to big girl identification with a man. Sylvia is expected to offer her freedom, her true nature, indeed life itself to a predator, who will pierce, stuff, and then own and admire the beautiful corpse. (Ornithology as a metaphor for male heterosexual predation is one of the brilliant strokes of **"A White Heron."** The combination of violence, voyeurism, and commercialism contained in the gun-wielding science, the goal of which is to create living death, is chilling.)[6] Tempted—and Jewett *does* make the hunter with his money and charm and social privilege tempting—Sylvia says no.

In **"A White Heron"** Jewett creates a threshold story about choosing not to step across. Sylvia won't give the bird over to the hunter, won't give her self over to him, won't enter the body-for-money bargain the culture expects of her. She chooses the world of her grandmother, a place defined as free, healthy, and "natural" in this story, over the world of heterosexual favor and violence represented by the hunter.

Jewett's choice of a fairy tale to tell this story of resistance is perfect since one major purpose of the classic, white, western fairy tale is to teach heterosexuality.[7]

To illustrate, let me sketch the standard female coming-of-age story of fairy tale. A girl is stolen, taken, or in some other way separated from her mother and removed to live a lonely life (often deep in a secluded woods) where her only friends are birds and animals and her caretaker is an old woman. Until puberty the heroine stays in this magical and emphatically female world. (Rapunzel lives in the country with only the witch for company; Little Red Riding Hood journeys back and forth between her mother and grandmother; even Snow-White surrounded by men dwells in an ultra-domestic, "natural" place where the men are literally littler than the female.) Then near or at puberty the prince arrives: handsome, rich, heterosexual. His job is to rescue the heroine. He is to carry her away from this sylvan world, now carefully defined by the story-teller as wicked, aberrant—the realm of the dark, the evil, the overpossessive mother: in short, the witch. The tale ends—we've all read it: "Cinderella," "Rapunzel," "Little Snow-White," "Little Red Cap"—with the virile prince (often he is a hunter) delivering the heroine from this perverse same-sex realm into the luxury and "safety" of the heterosexual world.

These traditional fairy tales in which a sexy young man saves a sexually awakening heroine from an ugly witch assert the triumph of heterosexuality over matrisexuality. They show the transformation of the maternal realm, via the witch, into a sick (that is, a dangerous) place for a girl to stay past puberty. The normal, "healthy" thing to do is to follow a man out of it.

In obvious ways Jewett's story fits this paradigm. When **"A White Heron"** opens we meet a little girl who has been separated from her mother and taken to live in a lonely cottage deep in a woods. There her only friends are her grandmother and the birds, plants, and animals who have become her companions. Especially there is the cow, who plays hide and seek with Sylvia and is her "valued companion" (p. 227); but also there is the toad Sylvia plays with on the cottage path the night the young man comes (a jocular version of the young man himself on Jewett's part?), the heron and his mate, and the tree, personified as "his" (p. 236), which Sylvia climbs to see the bird. (I will return to the gender of both the tree and the bird.)

The woods, the lonely cottage, the grandmotherly caretaker, the isolated heroine, the humanized plants and animals: Jewett sets the stage perfectly for the rescuing prince to appear. And he does. As in conventional fairy tales ("Rapunzel," for example) Sylvia is at first afraid of him. Significantly, he shows up immediately following her memory of the ugly red-faced boy who "used to chase and frighten her" in town (p. 229). Still in the grip of this memory, the "little woods-girl is horror-stricken to hear a clear whistle not very far away. Not a bird's whistle, which would have a sort of friendliness, but a boy's whistle, determined, and somewhat aggressive." Sylvia feels that "the enemy had discovered her" (p. 229). But then, true to traditional fairy-tale transformations, the girl quickly overcomes her fear of the handsome stranger who, as if by magic, has dropped into her world. It takes only one day until Sylvia "watched the young man with loving admiration. She had never seen anybody so charming and delightful; the woman's heart, asleep in the child, was vaguely thrilled by a dream of love" (p. 233). Sylvia is ready to realign her passionate energies: she will offer up the bird to the stranger. She will cooperate in his project of making blood drip from its body so that he can stuff, own, and admire the carcass as "his."

Thus far Jewett's story follows fairy-tale logic,[8] but only thus far. Having evoked the classic female rite-of-passage drama of fairy tale, Jewett proceeds to deconstruct the very story she evokes. She writes her own fairy tale about female rite of passage and the theme she dramatizes, in contrast to inherited tradition, is resistance to the passage prescribed.

Supplied with all the appropriate totems and symbols (the deep woods, the symbolic animals, the pre-pubertal age of nine) Sylvia moves right to the brink of the passage into heterosexuality. She even enacts ritualistically that passage—journeying away from her grandmother's house to the outer edge of that maternal space, the place where it stops and some other territory begins. There, in unmistakably phallic imagery, Jewett shows her climbing a huge pine which seems "to lengthen itself out" as she mounts (p. 236) and causes her body pain as she embraces it and climbs. At the top of this ascent which sends "tingling, eager blood coursing the channels of her whole frame" (p. 235) she is able to see new worlds and societies (the sea, ships), and she has a glorious glimpse of heterosexual harmony (the herons). The journey into this new region is difficult but breathtaking. Sylvia is "well satisfied" (p. 238). Enacted symbolically and in nature the passage into heterosexuality looks marvelous.

But that journey, Jewett's story insists, is not the journey available to women in real life or in real time. The tree Sylvia climbs is very unusual.[9] It holds in its majestic branches fragile nests; along its mighty arms run all sorts of living creatures. Jewett tells us that the pine "was like a great main-mast to the voyaging earth," and clearly it is sentient and caring. "It must truly have been amazed that morning through all its ponderous frame as it felt this determined spark of human spirit [Sylvia] creeping and climbing from higher branch to branch. . . . The old pine must have loved his new dependent. More than all the hawks, and bats, and moths and even the sweet-voiced thrushes, was the brave, beating heart of the solitary gray-eyed child. And the tree stood still and held away the winds that June morning while the dawn grew bright in the east" (p. 236). In contrast to this lover, the male encountered by Sylvia in real life kills things. He is committed not to supporting life but to conquering and destroying it. The tree, Jewett is careful to tell us, is "the last of its generation" (p. 234). It is a relic from the past, an imagined possibility, an unrealistic (after all it is not even human) encounter.

The realistic encounter is the hunter, the ornithologist—the male who expects Sylvia to participate in his project of killing, stuffing, and appropriating the beautiful bird. Obviously the heterosexual experience existing for Jewett's heroine in real life derives not from nature but from invented human values of conquest, profit, and ownership. Stated simply, what Sylvia can choose, can literally buy into, is a system of carnal exchange in which the female represents game—the prized carcass—in the material power struggle between males.

This explains, I think, why the heron is male. In the first place, of course, it might simply be too obvious to make the bird female. The equation between Sylvia and the heron is clear enough without making them both female (its whiteness and her virginity, the wildness of them both, their closeness to nature and their shyness, etc.). The difference in gender makes Jewett's symbolism a little less blatant. Far more important, however, the maleness of the heron calls attention to the fact that the heterosexual contest as defined by the human male finally exists not between male and female, but between male and male—with the female as bait, weapon, spy. In heterosexual materialist society (which is what the alluring bird-stuffer represents) males aggress on each other—kill each other off (as the hunter wishes to kill the heron)—*through* the female, whose job it is to execute and display not her own but a man's authority and superiority.[10] Loyal to "her" man, the "good" woman helps carry out his assault on other males by finding out and carrying back the enemy's secrets, breaking up his home, and luring him into deadly space where "her" man can eliminate him—all of which is exactly what the ornithologist expects Sylvia to do for him.

Finally, of course, the heron is male in Jewett's story because ultimately the heterosexual contest is not simply through the female, but for her. The competition exists to establish which male will "win" the female. This game gets played in **"A White Heron."** Who will win Sylvia's allegiance, the heron or the hunter? Ironically, by showing the heron victorious, Jewett shows victory falling outside and antithetical to the human system the hunter, the introducer of the game, imports into the woods. In the end, when the male bird "wins" Sylvia's loyalty (even though he is oblivious to it—or so we assume), the victory translates into a victory—a "win"—for antimasculine values, for the values of Mother Earth.

As a fairy tale **"A White Heron"** argues against the maturation script assigned by the culture. To renounce matrisexual bonds for heterosexual love, this story says, is not to follow nature, as traditional fairy tales so artfully—and we should notice, nervously—insist. It is to ally oneself against nature, even against life. (Were Sylvia to follow the script the hunter and her grandmother promote, the heron would be dead.) Heterosexuality in **"A White Heron"** is no better or worse than matrisexuality. Nature contains both. What is bad—wrong—is the lie perpetuated in fairy tale after fairy tale that the *human institution* of heterosexuality is either natural or good, or for that matter inevitable. That fairy-tale fiction, Jewett's rewrite says, is a masculine plot. Literally. Which is why, I want to suggest in conclusion, Jewett could but usually chose not to write conventional "plot."

"A White Heron" has plot. Although Jewett lamented as a young writer, in a famous bit of posing, that she could not construct plot, **"A White Heron"** shows that she very well could and would. She wrote to Horace Scudder at the *Atlantic Monthly* when she was twenty-four: "But I don't believe I could write a long story as . . . you advise me in this last letter. In the first place, I have no dramatic talent. The story would have no plot. I should have to fill it out with descriptions of character and meditations. It seems to me I can furnish the theatre, and show you the actors, and the scenery, and the audience, but there never is any play!"[11] **"A White Heron"** not only shows Jewett's considerable dramatic talent; it conforms to classic inherited western plot structure. Sylvia lives happily with her grandmother (exposition). A stranger arrives who wants her to violate her own principles and show him where the heron nests (conflict). She falls in love with that stranger

(complication). She decides she *will* deliver the bird to him (climax). She reverses that decision and loses the man's flattering attention (resolution). The story, dramatically organized in terms of protagonist and antagonist, contains all the elements of conventional linear plot development: exposition, conflict, complication, climax, resolution. Indeed, structure could hardly be tighter. **"A White Heron"** is an almost perfect example of traditional "mainstream" western narrative structure.

That traditional inherited structure strikingly resembles the perceptual mode of men described by some modern psychologists. In *In a Different Voice: Psychological Theory and Women's Development* (1982), for example, Carol Gilligan explains that male and female developmental journeys and goals are not the same; we are taught to take different routes and to arrive at contrasting destinations. She finds that "while men represent powerful activity as assertion and aggression, women in contrast portray acts of nurturance as acts of strength" and says that men and women, translating these different definitions of successful development into pictorial images, tend to visualize their lives in very different terms. "The images of hierarchy and web," Gilligan says, "drawn from the texts of men's and women's fantasies and thoughts, convey different ways of structuring relationships and are associated with different views of morality and self." They "inform different modes of assertion and response: the wish [of men] to be alone at the top and the consequent fear that others will get too close; the wish [of women] to be at the center of connection and the consequent fear of being too far out on the edge."[12] As I have argued elsewhere, conventional western written narrative such as Jewett lamented not being able to reproduce corresponds in important ways to the hierarchical mode described here by Gilligan. Created by men, standard dramatic structure is linear (starts at one point and moves forward to another point); pinnacle-oriented (moves by stages or steps, often clearly identifiable, to a climactic top point); asymmetric (the high point usually occurs between the middle and the end); and relationally exclusive rather than accumulative (relationships compete with and replace each other to keep the action moving forward). The result is narrative structure that works on a ladder principle: action and tension mount as we progress through the fiction to its climax, its high point, situated close to the end.[13]

This traditional, masculine, narrative progression precisely describes the shape of **"A White Heron,"** a story about rejecting patriarchal prescriptions. In effect Jewett literally moves Sylvia through the very plot the girl must decide whether or not to be part of. To use Gilligan's images: onto Sylvia's world of web, a pattern grounded in affectional reciprocity rather than aggression, is superimposed a new pattern: one of hierarchy or ladder. Based not on relationality but on aggression,[14] this pattern is essentially masculine. Whereas Sylvia has been accustomed to meandering in loops and spirals with Mistress Moolly the cow, upon the stranger's arrival she is thrust into a new structure. It is one that *formally,* in the way it literally mounts toward its climax, reproduces the ethical and psychosexual journey that a girl heading into puberty is supposed to take. She is supposed to abandon her matrisexually structured life for a phallically dictated one. In **"A White Heron"** Sylvia tries the new pattern out. When she climbs the tree she actually scales the story's climax: content and form coalesce completely. Jewett makes Sylvia the protagonist of a plot classically masculine in its tight linear, climax-oriented structure.

After testing the pattern, after putting on the male-focused identity expected of her and traveling along the plotted line laid out for girls in heterosexual patriarchal culture, Sylvia resists. She returns to her circles of earthbound meanders with the cow—as does Jewett. Having perfectly reproduced traditional male-defined narrative structure she writes against it in her ultrafeminine last paragraph, full of flowery, personal invocations and hovering apostrophes. This flossy feminine paragraph rips the fiction formally very much as Sylvia's contrasting rhetoric—her complete silence—has already torn up the hunter's plot. Thematically and formally the conclusion of **"A White Heron"** rejects the shape of violence—the masculine plot—it has reproduced in order to challenge.[15]

"This is my birthday," Jewett wrote in 1897 at the age of 48, "and I am always nine years old."[16] To be nine years old in Jewett is not to be "arrested." It is to be poised on the edge of the most important decision a woman makes in life, whether or not to stay in the magical yet "natural" realm of the mother. In fairy tale terms, that is the realm of the witch and deciding to stay not only means deciding against the prince; it means deciding in favor of the witch. That figure in a nine-year-old, to come full circle and quote Starhawk as I end, is not a midwife or a hag. "She is the Maiden, the Virgin . . . belonging to herself alone, not bound to any man. She is the wild child, lady of the woods, the huntress, free and untamed—Artemis, Kore, Aradia, Nimue. White is her color."[17] Sylvia, Jewett's fairy tale says, is her name.

Notes

1. Starhawk, *Dreaming the Dark: Magic, Sex and Politics* (Boston: Beacon Press, 1982), pp. 15–16.

2. Sarah Orne Jewett, "A White Heron," in Sarah Orne Jewett, *The Country of the Pointed Firs and Other Stories,* ed. Mary Ellen Chase (New York: Norton, 1981), p. 229. All quotations from the story are from this edition.

3. Carroll Smith-Rosenberg, "The Female World of Love and Ritual: Relations between Women in Nineteenth-Century America," *Signs,* I (Autumn 1975), 9–10.

4. Josephine Donovan, *New England Local Color Literature: A Women's Tradition* (New York: Frederick Ungar, 1983), p. 109.

5. "Compulsory Heterosexuality and Lesbian Existence," *Powers of Desire: The Politics of Sexuality,* eds. Ann Snitow, Christine Stansell, and Sharon Thompson (New York: Monthly Review Press, 1983), pp. 182–83.

6. Richard Brenzo reads the profession similarly when he says that, symbolically, the ornithologist represents the choice for Sylvia of being "caught, raped, killed, stuffed, and put on display in a man's house." See "Free Heron or Dead Sparrow: Sylvia's Choice in Sarah Orne Jewett's 'A White Heron,'" *Colby Library Quarterly,* XIV (1978), 41.

7. For an excellent essay discussing this as well as other basic characteristics of traditional fairy tales from a feminist point of view, see Ellen Cronan Rose, "Through the Looking Glass: When Women Tell Fairy Tales," *The Voyage In: Fictions of Female Development,* eds. Elizabeth Abel, Marianna Hirsch, and Elizabeth Langland (Hanover, N.H.: Univ. Press of New England, 1983), pp. 209–27.

8. For interesting mention of the story's revision of "Cinderella" see Donovan, pp. 109–10. Also valuable as general discussions of the story are the essays on "A White Heron" in Gwen Nagel, *Critical Essays on Sarah Orne Jewett* (Boston: G. K. Hall, 1984); George Held, "Heart to Heart with Nature: Ways of Looking at 'A White Heron,'" pp. 58–68; and Gayle L. Smith, "The Language of Transcendence in Sarah Orne Jewett's 'A White Heron,'" pp. 69–76.

9. Possibly this stately, life-supporting tree was inspired by Jewett's reading of an odd book by P. A. Chadbourne called *Instinct: Its Office in the Animal Kingdom and Its Relation to the Higher Powers in Man* (1872, 1883), which she mentions with enthusiasm in a letter in 1872. (See Richard Cary, *Sarah Orne Jewett Letters* [Waterville, Maine, Colby College Press, 1967], p. 24.) Chadbourne talks in detail about the unbroken connection between human life and the life of the rest of the planet and argues that we are all—plant, animal, human—part of one vast complex system of interdependence. He seems to believe that if we allowed human nature to realize itself (instead of fighting against our "nature") we might create a human world that functioned as well as the natural one. He states, for example: "Every tree is a community of individuals" and says that trees depend on their environment to live but they also, his comparisons to coral and nests imply, give back to the community by supporting others. Whether or not Jewett had in mind this discussion in Chadbourne, her tree in "A White Heron" is just such a living organism, independent and yet fully integrated into and participating in the network of life around and in it. See P. A. Chadbourne (New York: G. P. Putnam's Sons, 1872, 1883), pp. 56–57.

10. The parallels here to Thorstein Veblen's theory of sexual economics are obvious. See Veblen, *The Theory of the Leisure Class: An Economic Study of Institutions* (1899).

11. Cary, *Letters,* p. 29.

12. Carol Gilligan, *In a Different Voice: Psychological Theory and Women's Development* (Cambridge, Mass.: Harvard Univ. Press, 1982), pp. 167–68, 62.

13. In this paragraph I borrow heavily from an earlier discussion of Jewett. See Ammons, "Going in Circles: The Female Geography of Jewett's *Country of the Pointed Firs*," *Studies in the Literary Imagination,* XVI (Fall 1983), 83–92. On Jewett's aesthetic also see Josephine Donovan, "Sarah Orne Jewett's Critical Theory: Notes toward a Feminine Literary Mode," *Critical Essays,* pp. 212–25.

14. See Gilligan, pp. 172, 46–47.

15. For a book-length deconstructionist reading of Jewett's story which offers as a feminist interpretation the psychoanalytic (and unquestioningly heterosexual) thesis that at the heart of this story is a "secret father/daughter relation" (p. 114), a thesis based on the "surmise" that the story's narrator is paternal (p. 102), see Louis A. Renza, *"A White Heron" and the Question of Minor Literature* (Madison: Univ. of Wisconsin Press, 1984).

16. Annie Fields, *Letters of Sarah Orne Jewett* (Boston: Houghton Mifflin, 1911), p. 125.

17. Starhawk, "Witchcraft and Women's Culture," *Womanspirit Rising,* eds. Carol P. Christ and Judith Plaskow (New York: Harper and Row, 1979), p. 263. I have written about witches in Jewett at length (though I say very little about "A White Heron") in "Jewett's Witches," *Critical Essays,* pp. 165–84.

Terry Heller (essay date 1990)

SOURCE: "The Rhetoric of Communion in Jewett's 'A White Heron,'" *Colby Library Quarterly,* Vol. 26, No. 3, September, 1990, pp. 182–194.

[*In the following essay, Heller explores Jewett's use of tense shifts, apostrophes to objects in the story, and direct address by the narrator, techniques that were found in sentimental fiction of Jewett's time but which she largely eschewed.*]

Readers have observed duplicity in the rhetoric of Sarah Orne Jewett's **"A White Heron"** (1886). On the one hand the story realizes a number of the conventions of realistic narrative, yet on the other hand there are several violations of these conventions, especially at the level of narrative voice. The violations consist of odd shifts between past and present tense, apostrophes to objects in the story, and direct addresses by the narrator to the reader and to Sylvia, the main character. Narrative activities such as these tend to be seen as violations of the rhetoric of realistic fiction for at least two interesting reasons. First, they are most commonly found during the nineteenth century in the sentimental fiction of "women's" magazines. For example, they occur frequently in Jewett's early magazine fiction

that appears in *The Uncollected Short Stories of Sarah Orne Jewett.* In such locations these rhetorical devices nearly always contribute to a moralizing tone, when "good" values or sentiments are enjoined upon the reader or a character. Second, as Wayne Booth illustrates in Part 1 of *The Rhetoric of Fiction,* such techniques were increasingly suspect among Jewett's realist contemporaries because they seemed to subvert what was becoming the central "rule" of realistic narrative, that the narrator who is not a character should seem invisible: "The novelist must not, by taking sides, exhibit his preferences. . . . He has . . . to render and not to tell. . . ." (Ford Madox Ford in Booth 25).

It is worth observing that Jewett gradually abandoned using tense shifts, direct addresses, and apostrophes, so that they appear rarely in the fiction she collected into books. **"A White Heron"** is virtually the lone exception among her better-known works, and it remains her single best-known and most popular piece of fiction. These two observations would tend to suggest that her choice to use techniques here that she had generally abandoned by the time she wrote this story was in some way a right choice. This story has held its own in a literary climate that has not, on the whole, been favorable to Jewett's works.

The apparent duplicity of Jewett's rhetoric in **"A White Heron"** has contributed to critical ambivalence about the story. We can see such a response in Jewett's difficulties finding a magazine publisher for what is now her most famous story. William Dean Howells, who published a number of Jewett's stories, rejected this one because it was too romantic (Griffith 22). In response to this rejection, Jewett wrote to her friend Annie Fields: "Mr. Howells thinks that this age frowns upon the romantic, that it is no use to write romance any more; but dear me, how much of it there is left in every-day life after all. It must be the fault of the writers that such writing is dull, but what shall I do with my **'White Heron'** now she is written? She isn't a very good magazine story, but I love her, and I mean to keep her for the beginning of my next book . . ." (Held in Nagel 58).

The early reviewers responded at least indirectly to this duplicity. They tended, even in praising the story, to belittle it with qualifications. For example, the reviewer for *Overland Monthly* said the story "is perfect in its way—a tiny classic. One little episode of a child life, among birds and woods, makes it up; and the secret soul of a child, the appeal of the bird to its instinctive honor and tenderness, never were interpreted with more beauty and insight" (in Nagel 34). While this is high praise, the author cannot resist using qualifiers—"in its way, tiny classic, little episode"—and referring to Sylvia as an "it." This language, especially neutering Sylvia, contrasts starkly with Jewett's personifying the story itself as female in her letter.

The doubleness of Jewett's rhetoric has earned negative criticism from recent critics, such as Richard Cary (101–02) and Josephine Donovan (70–71), and excuses about

Jewett's lack of control from readers such as George Held (in Nagel 58–60). Even the most interesting among the defenders of Jewett's rhetoric, Elizabeth Ammons, finds herself caught in its doubleness. However, turning to Ammons' reading of the story opens a rich perspective from which to consider what Jewett may have accomplished with her double rhetoric.

Ammons does not set out to defend Jewett's narrative technique, but she finds herself doing so when she explains the strange last paragraph in which the narrator says a number of puzzling things that seem not to connect very well with the rest of the story. Nine-year-old Sylvia has found and communed with the white heron that her visiting ornithologist so desires to add to his collection of stuffed specimens, but she has refused, despite strong temptation, to tell him where he can find the bird. Jewett's narrator ends the story with exclamations and apostrophes:

> Dear Loyalty, that suffered a sharp pang as the guest went away disappointed later in the day, that could have served and followed him and loved him as a dog loves! Many a night Sylvia heard the echo of his whistle haunting the pasture path as she came home with the loitering cow. She forgot even her sorrow at the sharp report of his gun and the piteous sight of thrushes and sparrows dropping silent to the ground, their songs hushed and their pretty feathers stained and wet with blood. Were the birds better friends than their hunter might have been,—who can tell? Whatever treasures were lost to her, woodlands and summertime, remember! Bring your gifts and graces and tell your secrets to this lonely country child!

(239)

The narrator pities Sylvia's sharp pang when the disappointed hunter leaves never to return. She explains that after this day Sylvia forgot his killing birds and, instead, missed him and dreamed of his return. The narrator asks a startling question when she wonders which is the better friend, after reminding the reader of Sylvia's now forgotten horror at the dead birds, for the story seems to have been saying all along. "Of course the birds were better friends!" But the narrator goes on to concede that Sylvia has lost "treasures" by being more loyal to the bird than to the man, and so admonishes woodlands and summer to compensate Sylvia for what she has given up. In this final passage Jewett seems to complicate matters that we might have thought simple and settled after we see Sylvia refuse to betray the heron to the hunter.

Ammons' position is that this paragraph illustrates Jewett's resistance to masculine impositions: "Having perfectly reproduced traditional male-defined narrative structure she writes against it in her ultrafeminine last paragraph, full of flowery, personal invocations and hovering apostrophes. This flossy feminine paragraph rips the fiction formally very much as Sylvia's contrasting rhetoric—her complete silence—has already torn up the hunter's plot" (Ammons, "White Heron" 16). Ammons' language seems curiously violent and ambivalent, and also

rather exaggerated here. It does not appear that she really approves of this "flossy feminine" paragraph that rips and tears. Furthermore, this paragraph "sticks out" in the story much less prominently than Ammons seems to imply, for Jewett has introduced unrealistic rhetoric earlier in the story. When Sylvia climbs the pine tree and communes with the heron, the narrative rhetoric completely does away with several major conventions of realistic narration. Before examining Jewett's narrative rhetoric in more detail, it will be helpful to place the story as a whole within the rich and enlightening context that Ammons provides.

Ammons characterizes a masculine plot as the traditional linear form including in this order: exposition, conflict, complication, crisis, climax, resolution. What does Ammons mean when she labels such a plot as masculine? This is the most common plot form in fiction because writing, publishing, and reviewing fiction have been dominated by a patriarchal ideology which favors plots that reflect conventional masculine gender roles. Traditionally, industrial man's function in life has been to go outside the family into another world and to struggle there until he succeeds or fails at some enterprise. Novel plots tend to imitate this significant masculine motion. In another essay Ammons contrasts this sort of plot with what she sees as the feminine plot of *The Country of the Pointed Firs*. That novel she sees as structured outward from a central location in space, time, and meaning, so that it forms a web of circular movements and social ties (Ammons, "*Pointed Firs*" 84–86).

In **"A White Heron,"** says Ammons, Jewett did a perfect imitation of a masculine plot in representing Sylvia's quest for the heron. Furthermore, this plot appears in the context of a fairy tale of feminine coming of age, but with a difference. In most such tales the young woman is rescued from the clutches of an evil older woman by a handsome young man. Ammons says the meaning of this plot is that when a girl reaches puberty, she is supposed to give up her attachments to her mother and girl-friends for heterosexual love (Ammons, "**White Heron**" 10–14). In Jewett's version the rescue fails because the young woman can have a better life by staying longer with older women, both her grandmother and Mother Nature. So, while following a traditional, masculine plot line, Jewett subverts the traditional events of one version of that plot. The final paragraph of the story is part of Jewett's subversion—with a feminine flourish—of the male plot. That plot should end when Sylvia rejects the hunter in favor of the heron, but Jewett extends it with her "flossy feminine" intrusions.

I think that Ammons is probably right to argue that in this story Jewett works against some patriarchal plots and ideas. We see a resistance of this kind in Jewett's comments on Howells' rejection of the story for his magazine. What he thinks is "real" in everyday life is not "really" all there is to see there. Jewett insists that "romance" is also "real." A detailed examination of Jewett's style would show that her rhetoric in this story works continuously against the masculine structure with which she organizes the events. Several critical essays that examine language and style in the story vividly demonstrate how much "fantasy" the story contains: rational cows, thinking pine trees, and a child who reads animals' minds (see especially Smith in Nagel). Furthermore, the quest plot is elaborately framed with a long introduction that sets up multileveled oppositions between the two paths open for Sylvia's immediate future. The strange final paragraph extends and closes the frame. About half the story's length is given to narrating Sylvia's quest, though rhetorical heightening may make this proportion seem greater.

Ammons, then, finds doubleness in **"A White Heron."** Jewett subverts a masculine plot by changing the way it ends and, also, with feminine rhetoric. I could not agree more except that I believe Ammons misunderstands or underestimates the extent and force of that rhetoric. Let us then turn to a close examination of the development of Jewett's unrealistic rhetoric in **"A White Heron."**

From the very beginning of the story, as Jewett's readers have pointed out, there are elements of the fanciful and of fantasy that form an undercurrent counter to realistic narrative. In the opening, for example, the narrator takes a childlike view of the milk cow's motives and behavior. This move unobtrusively but decisively identifies the reader with Sylvia's point of view, showing why she values the cow's companionship and what she gains from it. The narrative rhetoric gradually becomes more obtrusive, however, beginning with an arbitrary tense shift, proceeding through a direct address to the reader, and climaxing when Sylvia meets the heron in a complex set of tense shifts and direct addresses.

The first arbitrary tense shift breaks the narrative flow on several levels, including the grammatical level where it catches the reader's attention. It occurs as Sylvia drives the cow homeward. She thinks about her old life in town and remembers something unpleasant:

> [T]he thought of the great red-faced boy who used to chase and frighten her made her hurry along the path to escape from the shadow of the trees.

> Suddenly this little woods-girl is horror stricken to hear a clear whistle not very far away. Not a bird's whistle, but a boy's whistle, determined, and somewhat aggressive. Sylvia left the cow to whatever sad fate might await her, and stepped discreetly aside into the bushes, but she was just too late. The enemy had discovered her. . . .

> (229)

An unpleasant memory disturbs Sylvia's quiet and benign relations with the cow. The shift to present tense coincides with the reappearance of that threat in the present, forcing her actually to abandon her friend. This move to present tense signals disruptions in the narrative: in time, mood, and plot development. Except for time, these disruptions belong to a traditional plot in that they introduce conflict. If we assume that the shift is a deliberate rhetorical choice

rather than a lapse revealing Jewett's lack of expertise or control, how can we explain it? What positive effects may be gained from this shift?

Clearly the tense shift is not necessary to introduce conflict. And as a device for heightening tension at the moment of introducing conflict, it seems "cheap" and clumsy. Surely Jewett was well aware of this. The risk seems unnecessary, unless there is something really important to be gained. Were this the only such anomaly in the story, we could not make much of an argument in its defense. But since more such anomalies will follow this one, we can begin here to think about how they work on readers.

If we take the tense shift as thoughtfully chosen by the narrator, then we are forced to see the narrator as potentially a force in the story. Wayne Booth, for one, has pointed out that overt attempts to control a reader's reactions tend to expose a narration as an artificial construct (*The Rhetoric of Fiction* 205). By arbitrarily shifting tense, Jewett's narrator becomes visible, or comes into existence as an artificer. The narrator reveals to the reader one of her powers, to change the time relations between reader and story. Were we readers inclined simply to surrender to the rhetorical force of using the present tense, we would find ourselves more consciously participating in the enactment of narration.

The disruption of arbitrarily shifting the verb tense is likely to be felt as both right and wrong simultaneously. Past tense narration is, after all, only a convention of telling. It is exceedingly difficult to read any narration while maintaining a sense of its pastness, for the story is realized in the "present tense" of our acts of reading. Jewett's shift calls attention to the "real" condition of our reading. Insofar as we have allowed ourselves as readers to become intimately involved with Sylvia's contentment in her country refuge, we and she have entered the same experienced time. Insofar as the shift to present tense is felt as right, it draws us into deeper identification with Sylvia and, perhaps, with the narrator. We experience the violation of the dominant grammatical tense at the same instant that we share Sylvia's shock at the violation of her rural peace. Our sharing with the character is deepened and is pointedly placed in the same time as her shock, the present of our act of reading.

There is, of course, little reason to grant so much rhetorical power to the placement of the word "is" in a position where we expected "was" unless other more weighty parts of the story support these ways of handling this anomaly. While the major justification for this reading comes in the climactic scene with the heron, I must delay our discussion of the key scene a little longer in order to examine Jewett's second major disruption of the narrative flow. Doing so will show how she sets up the climactic scene and will allow an exploration of another kind of disruption, the address to the reader.

Jewett's narrator addresses the reader directly early in Part II of the story. The address occupies the position of a transition between Sylvia's going to the tree and beginning her climb:

> [S]he stole out of the house . . . listening with a sense of comfort and companionship to the drowsy twitter of a half-awakened bird, whose perch she had jarred in passing. Alas, if the great wave of human interest which flooded for the first time this dull little life should sweep away the satisfaction of an existence heart to heart with nature and the dumb life of the forest!
>
> (235)

Like the tense shift, this exclamation seems out of place and unnecessary. The previous sentence, in which Sylvia jars and disturbs the bird, effectively conveys the danger into which she is entering. She has found the young bird collector very attractive, and she is tempted to turn away from the comparatively isolated rural life in which she has blossomed for a year, back toward the more masculine, urban life that threatened to prevent her becoming a complete self. Though this turn would be a mistake, the story also conveys in several ways that such a turn is inevitable. Eventually, Sylvia must rejoin the larger human community, but only after she has successfully grown into a self in the way that seems best to suit her—on the quiet, slow farm with her grandmother. Because the story fairly obviously conveys these attitudes, it is superfluous for the narrator to make such a statement. Yet the narrator makes the statement and underlines its oddness by addressing it directly to the reader.

Surely Jewett was well aware of how this statement would jar the tone of the narrative, calling attention to itself and to a growing relationship between narrator and reader as observers in an eternal present of the narrated events. One further sign of Jewett's self-consciousness is that this second major departure from narrative distance echoes the first one. It disturbs the narrative as Sylvia disturbs the bird. It comes at a moment when Sylvia is in danger, though this time she is less aware of her danger. Indeed her lack of awareness seems to generate the address. We readers and the narrator think the same thought. This seems to me the main rhetorical effect of the address. It is as if the narrator and the reader looked each other in the eye and understood our agreement as we watch Sylvia ignorantly moving toward an undesirable fate. The address produces and explicitly acknowledges a moment of sympathy between two consciousnesses who are concerned for Sylvia. The narrative voice, then, claims to speak for the reader, voicing what should be the reader's thought. This amounts to an assertion of communion between narrator and reader as we contemplate Sylvia.

I have been describing how the two most disturbing, early diversions from a third-person, past-tense narration *might* work in **"A White Heron."** The shift to present tense and the direct address could be moves toward establishing the narrator and reader as self-conscious co-creators of the narration. Both intrusions could reduce the distance in time and mental location between narrator and reader; they could tend to move us into the same imaginative space and time. If we are willing to trust the author's skill, if we give in to these odd elements rather than resist them as signs of narrative weakness, we may at least find ourselves more disposed to let go of the conventional boundaries that tend to divide narrator, character, and reader from each other in realistic narrative. A close reading of Sylvia's adventure on the pine tree will show what we readers have to gain if we follow through with the disposition Jewett may have created.

Sylvia's climb, as we have seen, takes place in the context of a specific danger to her well-being. She goes to the pine to locate the heron: "[I]f one climbed it at break of day, could not one see all the world, and easily discover whence the white heron flew, and mark the place, and find the hidden nest" (234)? Sylvia has conceived the notion of taking all the world at once into her consciousness. If she succeeds, then she will be able to give a piece of that world to the attractive young hunter who wandered to her home two nights before. But, as the first address to the reader shows, the story has so controlled our reactions to the hunter and to Sylvia that we readers and the narrator want Sylvia to resist his desire to find the white heron. To give the heron away has become tantamount to sweeping away the progress she has made in discovering herself; it will amount to giving herself away, a great error, since she is as vast a world as the one she will see from atop the tree, and neither world really can be known in an instant. Her problem, as she climbs the tree, is that she has not yet discovered that she will lose herself if she flows now with the great wave of human interest that is flooding her little life for the first time. Jewett emphasizes this danger during the climb by repeatedly describing Sylvia as birdlike: her hands and feet like claws, her climbing upward as in first flight, her being at home in the trees, her desire to fly. And images emphasizing her paleness connect her specifically to the heron, as do images that connect both her and the heron with the rising sun.

Jewett prepares the reader for the strangeness of Sylvia's meeting the heron with more fantasy like that which opens the story. However, we do not see the tree from Sylvia's point of view as we did the cow. Here the narrator pointedly asks us readers to share with her imagining of the possible thoughts and actions of the pine:

> The tree . . . must truly have been amazed that morning through all its ponderous frame as it felt this determined spark of human spirit creeping and climbing from higher branch to branch. Who knows how steadily the least twigs held themselves to advantage this light, weak creature on her way! The old pine must have loved his new dependent. More than all the hawks, and bats, and moths, and even the sweet-voiced thrushes, was the brave, beating heart of the solitary gray-eyed child. And the tree stood still and held away the winds that June morning while the dawn grew bright in the east.
>
> (236)

Sylvia is to the tree as her blood is to her, "coursing the channels of her whole frame" (235). Sylvia and the tree seem one in consciousness and desire, though she may not herself be aware of this oneness. Contributing freely to her vitality, unconscious of danger, all living things abet Sylvia in what could turn out to be her greatest error. Implicit in such gifts from nature is an assurance that unity of spirit, the "existence heart to heart with nature," is the more powerful force in Sylvia's life and that it is even now asserting itself.

The reader is more directly exposed to that power after Sylvia attains her pinnacle and finally sees the "vast and awesome world" from the endless—seeming eastern sea to the also endless, settled westward land (238). The two paragraphs describing Sylvia's encounter with the heron subvert any pretense to a realistic rhetoric.

In the first paragraph, she sees the heron:

> At last the sun came up bewilderingly bright. Sylvia could see the white sails of ships out at sea, and the clouds that were purple and rose-colored and yellow at first began to fade away. Where was the white heron's nest in the sea of green branches, and was this wonderful sight and pageant of the world the only reward for having climbed to such a giddy height? Now look down again, Sylvia, where the green marsh is set among the shining birches and dark hemlocks; there where you saw the white heron once before you will see him again; look! look! a white spot of him like a single floating feather comes up from the dead hemlock and grows larger, and rises, and comes close at last, and goes by the landmark pine with steady sweep of wing and outstretched slender neck and crested head. And wait! wait! do not move a foot or a finger, little girl, do not send an arrow of light and consciousness from your two eager eyes, for the heron has perched on a pine bough not far beyond yours, and cries back to his mate on the nest, and plumes his feathers for the day!
>
> (238)

The first four sentences of this passage reenact the general pattern we observed in the first two disruptions of realistic narrative. We move from identifying with Sylvia's consciousness in the past tense, through a pair of questions that are at least ambiguous in their source, to a present tense address from the narrator to Sylvia. If Jewett's rhetoric has worked as a rhetoric of communion, then at this point in the story, we are well prepared to accept that the voice of our readerly sympathy coincides with the narrative voice. When that voice asks where the nest is, we see Sylvia's head scanning the marsh, but because the words are not Sylvia's spoken thoughts, we also feel the question as the narrator's and as our own. The second question moves us further in this direction, for how could Sylvia—overwhelmed as she is by the vision of all the world before her, exhilarated as she is by the sensation that she is flying out into that world—how could she feel or express disappointment? How could she ask whether this vision is her *only* reward? The reader and the narrator are the ones who want more for her, though we join the pine tree as

well in that what we want is to complete her communion with the world, for her to experience as fully as possible "the satisfaction of an existence heart to heart with nature and the dumb life of the forest." The second question *belongs* to us, a composite voice of narrator, reader, and nature. And it is this composite, communing voice that next speaks to Sylvia. We speak in the present tense, acknowledging that the moment of Sylvia's vision is eternally present and that we are in it together. In this moment we take over her body, directing her movements, our thoughts becoming her thoughts. We tell her where to look, and she looks there. We tell her not to move and to withhold her consciousness; she remains still and lets the impression of the moment flow in.

Only as the heron withdraws do we withdraw our restraining presence from her consciousness:

> The child gives a long sigh a minute later when a company of shouting cat-birds comes also to the tree, and vexed by their fluttering and lawlessness the solemn heron goes away. She knows his secret now, the wild, light, slender bird that floats and wavers and goes back like an arrow presently to his home in the green world beneath. Then Sylvia, well satisfied, makes her perilous way down again. . . .
>
> (238)

We leave her well satisfied, knowing fully the satisfaction of communion with nature, which has also been communion with us. Having helped her restrain the arrow of her consciousness, we have also helped the heron to *become* the arrow of her consciousness as it returns to its home in the green world, which is, on a metaphorical level, the current best home for her growing spirit. We have completed the identification that images and comparisons have been asserting between the brave, pale, light, slender girl and the wild, white, light, arrow-like bird.

Jewett then uses a fragmentary sentence to introduce a threat to Sylvia's achieved unity. "Wondering over and over again what the stranger would say to her, and what he would think when she told him how to find his way straight to the heron's nest" (238). This slight grammatical jar returns us to the past tense. We see the worried grandmother and the hunter who is anxious to compel Sylvia to tell the secret he believes she has discovered. However, as soon as we turn to Sylvia's consciousness, we return to the present tense:

> Here she comes now, paler than ever. . . . The grandmother and the sportsman stand in the door together and question her. . . .
>
> But Sylvia does not speak after all. . . .
>
> No, she must keep silence! What is it that suddenly forbids her and makes her dumb? Has she been nine years growing, and now, when the great world for the first time puts out a hand to her, must she thrust it aside for a bird's sake? The murmur of the pine's green branches is in her ears, she remembers how the white heron came flying through the golden air and how they

watched the sea and the morning together, and Sylvia cannot speak; she cannot tell the heron's secret and give its life away.

(239)

As the heron's cry back to its mate might suggest, there are, in fact, two great worlds. When Sylvia stands atop the pine, she can see them both: the world of settled humanity and the world of the dumb creatures of forest and sea. Given her tendency to quiet introspection, the latter world is the right one for her to grow up in, though she cannot avoid the former if she is finally to be happy. Most of Jewett's other works of fiction repeatedly emphasize the importance of human communion to human happiness. Sylvia needs first to discover herself apart from the kind of society represented by whistling boys, collecting hunters, and noisy catbirds. This is not the right time to take the proffered hand of the great world that is imaged as a "great wave of human interest."

The great world that Sylvia chooses by identification with its silence is the world that makes her dumb. In images, it consists of all that she has seen on her trip to find the heron. But rhetorically it consists of the narrator and the reader in concert with a sort of consciousness in nature. We have become nature's voice in the story. We have spoken inside Sylvia, controlling her body and her consciousness, and finally enforcing her silence. We have been the self that she is in the process of discovering and, in performing this function at the behest of Jewett's unusual rhetoric, we have communed with Sylvia, with the natural scenes she experiences, and with all who have ever or will ever read this story.

"A White Heron" is a great story, in part because Jewett found a rhetoric that could overcome the pretenses of separation between narrator, reader, and character that are characteristic of realistic fiction. Like the great American transcendentalists, Thoreau in *Walden* and Whitman in "Crossing Brooklyn Ferry," she sought and found means of using language to stimulate something like visionary experience in the reader.

I think we can now see that the last paragraph is consistent with the rhetoric of the whole story. It is probably wrong to say that this paragraph rips and tears at the rest of the story, though it may indeed do to the masculine plot what Sylvia's silence did to the hunter's plans for the white heron. Sylvia's silence, as we have seen, is not hers alone but is rather of a piece with the dumb life of the forest. That silence arises out of a communion we readers have experienced and is the means by which we acknowledge and treasure that communion. Our silence affirms the irreducible value and mystery of individual lives. Though one may try to take, possess, or collect such lives, one suffers under an illusion as long as one believes anything substantial is gained by the effort. This is the hunter's illusion, and it is the major sign of his incompletion. This incompletion is signaled both times he seems most threatening to Sylvia's growth, in the fragmentary sentence that

announces his whistle (229) and in the second fragmentary sentence when Sylvia anticipates telling him the heron's secret (238). When Sylvia gives him silence in response to his desire, she gives him the greatest gift she has for him, the same gift she has just received. This is the gift that can make him whole. The power of such a gift is hinted in Mrs. Tilley's account of how her son changed her husband's life by daring him and running away (232).

How is the ornithologist fragmented? Critics have tended to associate him with the greatest evils of Western civilization: Satan, sexism, commercial exploitation, cultural tyranny, materialism, matricide, and mad scientists. Yet most of these critics are forced to recognize that Sylvia, Mrs. Tilley, and *the narrator* find the hunter a personable and attractive person. The *only* serious problem Sylvia has with him is that he kills the birds he knows and loves so well (233). Taken out of the traditional context that establishes some personal or sacramental relationship with the hunted animal, the bird collector's actions do indeed seem reprehensible. Jewett reveals in him a dangerous aggressiveness by associating him with the pursuing red-faced boy, by making him an ornithologist who kills the birds he loves most for the purposes of knowing and possessing them, and by having him offer comfort and money in exchange for Sylvia's loyalty to her animal friends. He clearly threatens Sylvia by tempting her to leave her hermitage before she achieves a self. Still, he does not lack grace: "he told her many things about the birds and what they knew and where they lived and what they did with themselves" (233). The problem with the hunter is not that he is inherently evil; rather he is incomplete. Were everyone always to behave as the hunter does and never as Sylvia learns to in her vision, we would all always kill the things we love, or at least frighten them away with the arrows of our consciousness. If he shared fully the sacramental view of the heron that Sylvia gains, he would give up the gun and simply walk the woods to see the birds, valuing imaginative over literal possession. What the hunter needs is to be rescued from the excesses of his culture's ideology of masculinity, from the rigidity of his failed quest plot. He cannot complete that plot himself; therefore he sends Sylvia on his behalf after the bird. When she gives him silence instead of the bird, she still acts on his behalf though he does not yet understand this. For to be complete the hunter needs to learn another kind of possession, the kind of imaginative communion with a living spirit that Thoreau, in his chapter in *Walden* on "Higher Laws," says led him to give up his gun.

The story's final paragraph seems not to be about destruction but rather about redemption and healing. It completes an opposition that the story has sustained within its rhetoric and between its plot and rhetoric. Realistic rhetoric and plot have moved the story toward Sylvia's moment of decision when she may choose silence or speech. As Ammons shows, there are powerful traditional and conventional forces that would tend to affirm an ending in which Sylvia chooses human society over nature. One of these forces is the set of cultural values implicit in one kind of fairy tale of female coming of age in which the young woman leaves evil older women to place herself in the care of a questing man, e.g., "Snow White" and "Cinderella." However, we have seen that Jewett's rhetoric works consistently against such expectations and urgently engages us readers on the side of communion with nature. Of course there is another tradition, visible for example in Romantic transcendentalism, that would tend to make absolute the choice of communion with nature as preferable to communion with humanity. But Jewett's rhetoric also closes off any simplistic version of this response. Both conventional patriarchy and Romantic pantheism are incomplete. The former will prevent Sylvia from becoming a person capable of communion; the latter will cut her off from complex human relations so that she could eventually become like "poor" Joanna in *The Country of the Pointed Firs,* incapable of human relations. The story has sought to heal this division by means of visionary experience in which various "characters" experience communion while contemplating nature together.

Among the effects upon a reader of entering into the kind of communion Jewett offers in **"A White Heron"** is the experience of that communion. Such an experience can be redemptive. Readers tend to come to the story saturated with the rhetoric of realistic fiction, where the characters, however much we may sympathize with them, remain outside of and separate from ourselves. Jewett's rhetoric undoes such separations; it "rescues" us from loneliness and takes us into the human communion that writing essentially *is*. Our communion continues into the final paragraph, where we participate in further acts of healing.

In the last paragraph Jewett dramatizes human incompletion and acknowledges the value of human communion. That Sylvia wants to belong to both great worlds points to the incompleteness of each. Sylvia's legitimate desire to belong to the great world of human interest leads her to purify the hunter in her memory. The narrator rhetorically underlines what Sylvia forgets by detailing the violence of the dead and bloodied birds the hunter produced, yet grants and even admires the desire in Sylvia that forgets and so forgives. It really is not certain whether the birds were better friends to Sylvia than their hunter might have been. She *will* have lost treasures by rejecting the path he offered her. For one thing, she is a *lonely* country girl, and to love someone, even uncritically as a dog does, *may* be preferable to loneliness. Nevertheless, when the narrator prays to nature to bring gifts and graces to Sylvia, we readers are confident that nature will not cease to offer its gifts, just as we and Whitman are confident in the last movement of "Crossing Brooklyn Ferry" that the landscape of that poem will continue to give itself to the eye and to indicate what it "really" is to all who look with vision enhanced by Whitman's incantations.

Sylvia, in imagination, heals and redeems the hunter. Her silence toward him reenacts nature's silence toward her and so stands as an always-open offer to him of actual redemption if he will learn how to read her silence, how to look with her. Sylvia has become the focus of a visionary occasion of communion between narrator, reader, and nature; this occasion offers to heal the divisions valorized by the conventions of realistic narrative while offering redemption from the ideology of exploitation that corrupts the hunter. Jewett has created a moment of timeless unity between narrator, character, and reader by means of her rhetoric of communion. In doing so, she may reform and, thereby, alter the meaning of the masculine quest plot at the center of her story; she may create an imaginative space where masculine doing and feminine seeing may meet in temporary transcendence of their ancient opposition. That space is in the composite narrative voice of this story, where we readers may all be united for a moment—at least in our imaginations—with the wholeness of being that includes both nature and human will, both the feminine and the masculine, both seeing and doing.

Sources Cited and a Selection of Sources Consulted

Ammons, Elizabeth. "Going in Circles: The Female Geography of Jewett's *Country of the Pointed Firs.*" *Studies in Literary Imagination,* 16(2) (Fall 1983), 83–92.

———. "The Shape of Violence in Jewett's 'A White Heron.'" *Colby Library Quarterly,* 22(1) (March 1986), 6–16.

"Review of *A White Heron and Other Stories.*" *Harper's,* 74 (February 1887), 483.

Atkinson, Michael. "The Necessary Extravagance of Sarah Orne Jewett: Voices of Authority in 'A White Heron.'" *Studies in Short Fiction,* 19(1) (Winter 1982), 71–74.

Booth, Wayne C.*The Rhetoric of Fiction.* Chicago: Univ. of Chicago Press, 1961.

Brenzo, Richard. "Free Heron or Dead Sparrow: Sylvia's Choice in Sarah Orne Jewett's 'A White Heron.'"*Colby Library Quarterly,* 14 (1978), 36–41.

Cary, Richard.*Sarah Orne Jewett.* New York: Twayne, 1962.

Critical Essays on Sarah Orne Jewett. Ed. Gwen L. Nagel. Boston: Hall, 1984.

Donovan, Josephine.*Sarah Orne Jewett.* New York: Ungar, 1980.

Griffith, Kelley. "Sylvia as Hero in Sarah Orne Jewett's 'A White Heron.'"*Colby Library Quarterly,* 21(1) (March 1985), 22–27.

Hovet, Theodore. "America's 'Lonely Country Child': The Theme of Separation in Sarah Orne Jewett's 'A White Heron.'" *Colby Library Quarterly,* 14 (1978), 166–71.

———. "'Once Upon a Time': Sarah Orne Jewett's 'A White Heron' as a Fairy Tale."*Studies in Short Fiction,* 15 (Winter 1978), 63–68.

Jewett, Sarah Orne.*The Country of the Pointed Firs and Other Stories,* ed. Mary Ellen Chase. New York: Norton, 1982.

———. *The Uncollected Short Stories of Sarah Orne Jewett,* ed. Richard Cary. Waterville, Maine: Colby College Press, 1971.

Matthiessen, F. O.*Sarah Orne Jewett.* New York: Houghton Mifflin, 1929.

Pool, Eugene. "The Child in Sarah Orne Jewett." Rpt. in *Appreciation of Sarah Orne Jewett.* Ed. Richard Cary. Waterville, Maine: Colby College Press, 1973, 223–28.

Renza, Louis A. *"A White Heron" and the Question of Minor Literature.* Madison: Univ. of Wisconsin Press, 1984.

Singley, Carol. "Reaching Lonely Heights: Sarah Orne Jewett, Emily Dickinson, and Female Initiation." *Colby Library Quarterly,* 22(1) (March 1986), 75–82.

Stevenson, Catherine Barnes. "The Double Consciousness of the Narrator in Sarah Orne Jewett's Fiction." *Colby Library Quarterly,* 11 (1975), 1–12.

Jules Zanger (essay date 1990)

SOURCE: "'Young Goodman Brown' and 'A White Heron': Correspondences and Illuminations," *Papers on Language and Literature,* Vol. 26, No. 3, Summer, 1990, pp. 346–357.

[*In the following essay, Zanger compares and contrasts the themes, settings, narrative sequences, imagery, and dynamics of "A White Heron" with Nathaniel Hawthorne's short story "Young Goodman Brown" and suggests that these works illuminate each other.*]

It has become a commonplace of Sarah Orne Jewett criticism to observe, usually in passing, the parallels between her work and that of Nathaniel Hawthorne. Some critics find stylistic similarities, others thematic ones; there is general agreement about their shared concern with New England. Edward Garnett wrote that Jewett "ranked second only to Hawthorne in her interpretation of the spirit of New England Soil" (40–41). Van Wyck Brooks concluded his essay on Jewett in *New England: Indian Summer* by saying, "No one since Hawthorne had pictured this New England world with such exquisite freshness of feeling" (347–53). Other critics, notably Thompson (485–97), found traces of Hawthorne's influence in Jewett's **"The Gray Man"** and **"The Landscape Chamber."** More recently, Louis Renza makes a "bizarre" (his term) attempt to link Jewett's **"A White Heron"** to "The Minister's Black Veil" through the intermediary color coding of her **"The Gray Man"** and his "The Gray Champion" (142–52).

These adumbrations made, most critics have felt it unnecessary to identify, except in the most general and allusive ways, specific parallels, or influences, or variations linking one particular Hawthorne tale with one of Jewett's. I wish to demonstrate that such a detailed relationship does exist between what are probably two of the best known and most frequently anthologized stories of those writers: Jewett's **"A White Heron"** (1886) and Hawthorne's "Young Goodman Brown" (1835). A comparison of these stories reveals a series of shared elements: themes, settings, narrative sequences, images, and dynamics—whose extensiveness suggests the possibility that in **"A White Heron,"** at least, Jewett's indebtedness to Hawthorne, conscious or otherwise, extended well beyond the generalized relationships described above. The frequency and directness of these shared elements make it possible to read **"A White Heron"** as a personal variation upon the Hawthorne story: in the variations and transformations performed on "Young Goodman Brown" Jewett's particular vision is most fully revealed; at the same time, Jewett's story helps illuminate certain obscure elements in "Young Goodman Brown."

Both stories begin at sundown, Brown leaving Salem and Faith to walk upon a road "darkened by all the gloomiest trees of the forest." Sylvy, Jewett's protagonist, also first appears at sunset "going away from whatever light there was and striking deep into the woods." Almost immediately, both encounter the unnamed strangers with whom they will struggle. In both stories the strangers appear to be invoked by the fears of the characters. Brown, saying to himself, "What if the devil himself should be at my very elbow?" immediately afterward beholds the figure of the stranger with the staff. Sylvy, remembering the noisy town in which she lived before coming to her grandmother's farm, and recalling the great red-faced boy who used to chase and frighten her, is suddenly startled by the aggressive whistle of the young man with the gun. In both cases, the apprehension precedes the appearance.

Sylvy's stranger is linked to the "crowded manufacturing town" by the image of the red-faced boy who introduces him. Brown's stranger, he tells us in almost his first words, has just arrived from Boston. In the course of the stories, both these anonymous intruders are revealed to be hunters and tempters, offering knowledge, money, sexuality, a vision of the great world. Each potential victim accepts from his tempter his token, Satan giving Brown his staff, the hunter giving Sylvy his knife. Both protagonists, Brown and Sylvy, succumb to those temptations. Brown exclaims, "Come, devil, for to thee is this world given," and when the converts are called, "Goodman Brown stepped forth from the shadows of the trees and approached the congregation, with whom he felt a loathful brotherhood by the sympathy of all that was wicked in his heart" (86). Sylvy, after ascending to the pinnacle of the tree and "witnessing the wonderful sight and pageant of the world," descends fully committed to betraying the secret of the heron's nest to the hunter: "wondering over and over again what the stranger would say to her, and what he would think when she told him how to find his way straight to the heron's nest" (156).

Both, of course, change their minds, and they do this in ways which are remarkably similar. Brown, who until the moment of satanic baptism, has apparently acquiesced in the ritual, suddenly cries, "look up to heaven and resist the wicked one" (88). To this point we have been privy to

Brown's thoughts through the medium of the omniscient narrator; from the moment in which he and Faith stand before the altar, we are rigorously excluded from them, so that his decision to reject Satan comes as an inexplicable surprise. Between his joining the satanic congregation and his rejecting it, no single incident or insight is provided to motivate or explain Brown's change of heart. Indeed, the final element which had convinced him to join the Devil's party—his conviction of Faith's sin as ambiguously evidenced by the pink ribbon—now appears to be absolutely confirmed by her presence at the altar. Brown's reversion to virtue, if that is what it is, remains a mystery.

Sylvy's decision to deny to the hunter and the grandmother the location of the heron's nest is just as surprising and inexplicable as Brown's change of heart. Employing an omniscient narrator, Jewett permits the reader to share Sylvy's thoughts all through the long climb to the top of the pine, the subsequent discovery of the heron's nest, and the dangerous descent. At the end of that descent, "well-satisfied," she remains fully determined to reveal to the hunter the location of the nest. At that point, Jewett shifts her focus to the grandmother and the hunter waiting at the farm for Sylvy's news. "But Sylvy does not speak after all, though the old grandmother fretfully rebukes her, and the young man's kind, appealing eyes are looking straight into her own . . ." (157). That is, in the interval, marked appropriately by white space, between her descent from the tree and her arrival at the farm, something has happened to radically alter her intentions. We are told only after the fact that "the murmur of the pine's green branches is in her ears, she remembers how the white heron came flying through the golden air and how they watched the sea and the morning together, and Sylvy cannot speak. . . ." But this is no adequate explanation of her change of heart, since it was immediately after this remembered experience that she was most committed to revealing the secret. As with Brown's decision to reject Satan, we are faced again with a mystery. Without speculating as to whether these reversals may be read as illustrations of the interventions of a mysterious providence, I would suggest that as dramatic strategies intended to manipulate the reader's sensibility they are remarkably like each other, moving the reader first to apprehension, then to an unexpected though desired resolution.

In the actual conclusions of both these stories, however, we discover that the apparent resolutions are no resolutions at all. Brown's denial of Satan is at best an equivocal act and his subsequent life one of desperation and gloom. Hawthorne's ending is doubly inconclusive, leaving the reader with at least two questions: "Was it a dream?" and, more seriously, was Brown's single act of recantation worth the profound dislocation and isolation of his subsequent life? In the same way, Sylvy's refusal to tell the heron's secret, which appears to be both triumphant and conclusive, is immediately called into question by the intrusive narrator: "Were the birds better friends than their hunter might have been,—who can tell?" And this uncertainty is emphasized in the narrator's final adjuration: "Whatever

treasures were lost to her, woodlands and summertime, remember! Bring your gifts and graces and tell your secrets to this lonely country child" (158). This entreaty offers to the reader no positive resolution, formally balancing as it does "the treasures that were lost to her" against the gifts, graces, and secrets that Nature might bring. Both stories end in deliberate ambiguity, denying to the reader any easy moral or ideological closure or resolution.[1]

In the end, both characters return to communities with which they had enjoyed ties of affection and trust, ties now breached by their experiences in the forest. Brown's profound distrust of his wife and his townsfolk is echoed obliquely by Sylvy's unwillingness to trust the heron's secret to her grandmother and the hunter. As if to underline her isolation, the last words of the story are "this lonely country child."

All of these parallels—of settings, images, themes, strategies of rhetoric—link these otherwise quite different stories and suggest that Jewett wrote **"A White Heron"** out of profound familiarity with "Young Goodman Brown." Certainly the shared elements establish connections between the two which make it legitimate to regard Jewett's story, written a half century later, as a variation upon what was perhaps Hawthorne's best-known tale. In the transformations her distinctive vision imposed, we can discover illuminations of both stories.

On the most general level, it is as if Jewett had translated Hawthorne's symbolic allegory into the realistic mode of post-Civil War fiction. Certainly Hawthorne's tale, though localized by history and myth, shows little evidence of the local color writer's concern with the particulars of regional landscape, dialect speech, or economy, all of which we find in **"A White Heron."** Jewett's work displays many other characteristics usually associated with the local color movement and especially with the contemporary fiction of New England women writers like H. B. Stowe, Rose Terry Cooke, and Mary Wilkes Freeman, all of whom depict life in rural or village New England, focussing often on lower-class women, spinsters, and widows, and the unromantic and often painful particulars of their lives. Despite these affinities, **"A White Heron"** deviates in several significant ways from such realistic models. First, of course, is the presence of an intrusive narrator, not unlike the narrator in "Young Goodman Brown," whose role as a high-relief commentator, adjuror, and enthusiastic partisan violates the illusion of realistic fiction as a direct transcription from life. Secondly, the intensely circumscribed scene and cast of characters in **"A White Heron,"** the nameless hunter and the allegorically named sylvan child, the climactic uses of dusk and dawn, the opposition of wilderness and community, possess an immediately evident symbolic dimension, so that the story demands to be read on levels not normally appropriate to local color writing, thus linking it further to Hawthorne's model.

On the other hand, Jewett's wilderness is "real," as Hawthorne's never attempts to be, its reality continuously con-

firmed by particularizing details, including the unsenti-
mental presence of a purring cat, "fat with young robins."
Hawthorne's "wild beasts" never appear except as undifferentiated off-stage noises. Jewett's woods are vividly
populated with jaybirds and crows, squirrels and par-
tridges, sparrows and robins, whippoorwills and thrushes,
moths and toads.

Jewett's wilderness, as has often been pointed out, is an
essentially benevolent one, with no suggestion of that
lurking evil which haunts Hawthorne's postlapsarian forest. It is certainly possible to read these contrasting visions
of American nature as gender based, as has frequently
been done,[2] but surely another possible explanation can be
seen in the half century of historical change that separates
them. In 1835 the New England wilderness was much
closer to wildness than the settled, cutover, second growth
woodlands of 1885: railroads and post roads had pretty
well banished the last Indians and bears. Paradoxically,
Jewett's "real" forest is, in 1885, much more a metaphorical stage than was Hawthorne's symbolic wilderness half a
century before. Further, the moral nature of the wilderness
in these stories is at least partially defined against a particular human community. In "Young Goodman Brown"
that community which helps define the demonic wilderness is morning-lit Salem, offering at least the illusion of
peace and order, virtue and love. In **"A White Heron,"**
fifty years later, the alternative community is a "noisy,"
"crowded manufacturing town," against which the tamed
woodlands seem sanctuary-like. This was especially true
in the last decades of the century when "noisy" and
"crowded," applied to cities, had come to be code words
for the presence of undesirable ethnic types. That perception which opposed a beneficent, nurturing wilderness to
an aggressive, noisy, dangerous city was one of the commonplaces of the last decades of the nineteenth century,
being espoused by writers as various as Frederick Olm-
sted, Theodore Roosevelt, James Russell Lowell, and Mark
Twain. By reversing Hawthorne's equation of community
and nature, good and evil, Jewett was dramatizing that
widely held perception which was publicly expressing itself in the Garden Cemetery and National Park movements. In the half century separating the stories, Hawthorne's wilderness had become Jewett's Nature, and that
original sense of mission which had impelled the first settlers into the forest had turned on itself. Instead of that
older vision in which civilization transformed wilderness,
many Americans, taught by Thoreau and Emerson, and
later by George Perkins Marsh, John Muir, Louis Agassiz,
and others, had come to believe that civilization must
somehow be redeemed by learning from and about Nature.
In the opposition between these two perceptions dramatized by Jewett, the man with the gun is immediately recognizable as the dominant figure in the typology of wilderness central to the older vision. The child, on the other
hand, might well be construed as emblematic of the new
role in relation to Nature which the new vision required.[3]

Despite the differences between Jewett's presentation of
Nature and Hawthorne's, it should be recognized that for

both of them the forest and the attendant isolation it imposes serve as a setting for the encounters, testing, and
self-definition that each story involves. For both, the wilderness retains its traditional American nature as a locus
for individual striving: in 1835, Americans, most characteristically, strove against Nature; by 1885, it was becoming increasingly evident that Americans had to strive to
preserve the natural world, as Sylvy does.

More significant differences emerge as we move from the
settings to the characters. Brown and Sylvy, though both
the subjects of temptation, are in almost every other respect distinct from each other.

Unlike Sylvy, Young Goodman Brown is permitted by his
role and circumstance to act out of choice rather than necessity. We see him brush aside Faith's objections to his
trip into the woods, as he hastens to keep his appointment
with the Devil. Even in the debate with Satan, Brown determines the agenda, holding up each of his idols—grandfather and father, the good people of New England, his
own saintly minister—to be ritualistically knocked down
by Satan's predictable responses. These are clearly straw
men: at no point does Brown question, let alone reject, Satan's contentions that they are all of his party, beyond asking the Father of Lies, "Can this be so?" It is only the introduction of Faith into the debate that momentarily halts
Brown's systematic destruction of his idols, and that last
obstruction is overcome with his unquestioning acceptance
of the flimsy and ambiguous pink ribbon as evidence of
his wife's corruption. With each of these icons broken,
Brown has freed himself to pursue his evil purpose.

At the same time, Brown, a creature of Original Sin, is appropriately aware of the role of the past in shaping the
present. When he proposes to act virtuously, he bases his
virtue on that of his ancestors. When he permits himself to
be convinced that grandfather, father, minister, and Faith
are all of the Devil's party, he commits himself absolutely
to evil: "There is no good on earth; and sin is but a name.
Come, devil; for to thee is this world given" (83). At the
very last moment, he chooses once more, electing to deny
Satan, apparently as absolutely as he had affirmed him.

Sylvy, on the other hand, exists until the conclusion of
Jewett's story in a position of powerlessness. As a small,
dependent, timid, female child, she is dominated by both
her grandmother and the hunter. Her act of courage in discovering the heron's nest is performed as an act of propi-
tiation to another. Her domination is most clearly signified
by her silence; after reluctantly revealing her name at the
hunter's insistence when they first encounter each other,
Sylvy maintains an "awed silence" throughout the story:
"the sound of her own unquestioned voice would have terrified her" (150). Her silence, however, which traditionally
is a sign of subservience, becomes in the last scene of the
story an instrument of power.[4] After a year in the woods
and her adventure of the night before, the timid little town
girl has found the courage to defy her elders. Sylvy's submissive silence is transformed into the silence of defiance,

as she denies her grandmother and the hunter the knowledge she possesses. In a radical inversion of conventional order, Sylvy's denial turns the world upside down, silently declaring her independence.

Her act of denial is significantly different from Brown's and provides perspective on his rejection of Satan. About Brown's stranger there is no doubt in Brown's mind. He has announced his supernatural nature with his first words, and his snake-staff immediately establishes his identity. Though the careful reader may recognize ambiguities in his presentation, Brown believes he knows precisely with whom he is dealing. A sometime communicant of his saintly minister's church, Brown knows a whole body of appropriate, conditioned responses to the Evil One, to the Enemy, all of which support his ultimate denial. Rejecting Satan in the woods and then accepting his valuation of the world in the town, he in both instances acts consistently with the received knowledge and values of his community. Told by Satan in the woods that the nature of man is evil, Brown can well believe him because his venerable minister has preached exactly that tenet of faith in the town. Brown's brief involvement with Satanism is, as Gatsby might have said, only personal. In the absence of significant motivation, his denial of the Devil emerges as reflexive and communally conditioned by fear, not faith.

On the other hand, for Sylvy's young man there is no equivalent mechanism for rejection. Just the opposite: he is attractive, kindly, friendly; he has been welcomed as a guest by her grandmother. As a sportsman, as a scientist, he embodies some of the highest masculine values of his country and time. When Sylvy mysteriously changes her mind and decides not to reveal the heron's secret, she acts precisely against the received values of her community as they are represented by her grandmother and by the young man. She too acts personally, denying both the masculine "great world" apparently offered to her by the hunter and, at least as significantly, the matriarchal world of the grandmother who has cared for and protected her.

It is an act demanding much greater courage and sacrifice than Brown's last moment, trimmer's reversion to the safe and familiar. He, after all, saves only himself, leaving Faith behind at the altar, as he earlier left her behind in the village. "Sauve qui peut!" Sylvy, instead, sacrifices her grandmother's approval and the hunter's gratitude, reward, and friendship for the heron's sake and for the vision of Nature she has experienced at day-break from the top of the tree.

This response to experience is significantly different from Brown's, who throughout his story denies his own personal experience when confronted by authority. Accepting the Devil's contentions and illusions, he disregards his own living knowledge of his grandfather and father whom he had believed to be "honest men and Christians," of his minister, "a good old man," and of his wife Faith, "a blessed angel on earth." Nine-year-old Sylvy, however, awed as she is by the young man and indebted as she is to her grandmother, rejects both adults' authority to affirm her own private experience.

The double nature of this rejection is often neglected by critics who focus exclusively on Sylvy's denial of the hunter. Those interpretations of **"A White Heron"** which limit it to a conflict between an aggressive patriarchal system represented by the young man and a supportive matriarchal community represented by Sylvy (cf. Donovan) do so only by eliding any consideration of the third character in the story, the grandmother. It is she who is the actual center of the matriarchal community, and it is she who gives in to temptation and allies herself with the hunter against Sylvy. The ideological reductivism that ignores the grandmother's role does violence to the story and undervalues the artistic complexity of Jewett's achievement.

The scene Jewett has created for the climax of her story confronts Sylvy with two possible futures. The hunter represents a combination of masculine aggressiveness and scientific detachment linked to "a wave of human interest," an entry into "the great world," and a hazy promise of love. The grandmother offers very real love, but represents the alternative to the hunter's promise: a world of actual experience, of loss, penury, and pain. To the elderly widow, left behind by her children and living in poverty on her isolated hardscrabble farm, the ten dollar reward promised by the hunter represents, not the child's fantasy of wealth, but the harsh difference between buying new shoes for Sylvy or buying another cow, or none. It is the presence of the grandmother that prevents **"A White Heron"** from sliding into formulaic allegory and roots it in the actual world of 19th century, decaying New England. This old farm woman who has buried four children, whose daughter has moved away to the city, and whose last son has disappeared into the West, possesses a solidity and credibility that the nameless young man never achieves. If he vaguely implies some golden future, she, more realistically, suggests another not nearly so bright. If the young man suggests power and wonder, the old woman represents the restrictiveness of experience, Nature, and circumstance.

Confronted with grandmother and hunter, the Emersonian polarities of Fate and Will, Sylvy—perhaps childishly, perhaps because she is a child—refuses allegiance to either, committing herself instead to a transcendent unity with Nature, achieved by a denial of self. Her distance from Young Goodman Brown could hardly be greater.

On the strength of the correspondences between these stories, the differences that distinguish them acquire special significance. The contrasting perceptions of wilderness and town and the contrasting conceptions of allegiance and community suggest some of the intellectual and cultural developments that had changed American literature and American society in the fifty years that separated the stories.

Other differences provide insights, perhaps more personal, into the writers themselves. Hawthorne's "good" young man is presented to us in terms which, while characteristically ambivalent, finally ask us to judge him and to deny his solitary claim to godliness. Writing in a period much less certain of the verities, Jewett is more tentative: Sylvy's act of refusal appears to us to be unquestionably right, yet it too amounts to an act of withdrawal from the human community and the conditions that circumscribe it; its consequences remain uncertain to Sylvy and to the narrator. Hawthorne can follow Brown for us to the hour of his gloomy death. We must leave Sylvy at the age of nine, all of the problematical consequences of her choice still before her. Jewett, who at forty-eight wrote, "This is my birthday and I am always nine years old," apparently was to remain uncertain of the correctness of Sylvy's choice into her own maturity (*Letters* 125).

Taken together, these stories can rewardingly be read as foils for each other, each putting the other into sharper outline. If Brown seems a little darker and Sylvy a little brighter for this procedure, they both come together in realizing for us worlds in which moral choices have profound consequences and must be made, however uncertainly. Beyond that, the stories suggest that many of the conventional distinctions we make separating our romantic and realistic writers can be profitably reexamined.

Notes

1. Leo Marx points out in his description of the American pastoral that "the endings of these pastoral fables tend to be inconclusive if not deliberately equivocal" (301–02). Both "Young Goodman Brown" and "A White Heron" correspond to Marx's formulation to a very high degree.

2. The perception of nature as feminine and maternal and the corresponding perception of technology and destruction as masculine are discussed as dominating American metaphors by Kolodny.

3. For discussions of this shift in attitudes toward nature, see Huthe 87–104; Robertson 115–21.

4. Person discusses Hawthorne's use of silence as both a sign of submission and an instrument of revenge.

Works Cited

Brooks, Van Wyck. *New England: Indian Summer, 1865–1915*. New York: Dutton, 1940.

Fields, Annie, ed. *Letters of Sarah Orne Jewett*. Boston: n. P., 1911.

Garnett, Edward. "Books Too Little Known." *Academy and Literature* 11 July 1903: 40–41.

Hawthorne, Nathaniel. *Mosses from an Old Manse*. Columbus: Ohio State UP, 1974. 74–90

Huthe, Hans. *Nature and the American: Three Centuries of Changing Attitudes*. Los Angeles: U of California P, 1957.

Jewett, Sarah Orne. *Tales of New England*. Boston: Riverside, 1896. 138–58.

Kolodny, Annette. *The Lay of the Land*. Chapel Hill: U of North Carolina P, 1975.

Marx, Leo. *The Pilot and the Passenger*. New York: Oxford UP, 1988.

Person, Leland S., Jr. "Hester's Revenge: the Power of Silence in *The Scarlet Letter*." *Nineteenth-Century Literature* 43 (1989): 465–83.

Renza, Louis A. *"A White Heron" and the Question of Minor Literature*. Madison: U of Wisconsin P, 1984.

Robertson, James O. *American Myth, American Reality*. New York: Hill, 1980.

Thompson, Charles M. "The Art of Miss Jewett." *Atlantic Monthly* October 1904: 485–97.

Karen K. Moreno (essay date 1991)

SOURCE: "'A White Heron': Sylvia's Lonely Journey," *Connecticut Review,* Vol. 13, No. 1, Spring, 1991, pp. 81–85.

[*In the article below, Moreno explicates "A White Heron" as a feminist quest myth in which Sylvia's journey has a psychological, physical, and spiritual meaning that can be interpreted using Jungian terms.*]

In her short story **"A White Heron,"** Sarah Orne Jewett presents the quest myth in feminist terms. Since Sylvia, the protagonist, lives with her grandmother in the country, her bond with nature and the maternal is continually being formed and strengthened. Until the boy stranger, an ornithologist, enters the woods near her grandmother's farm, Sylvia's life is virtually devoid of male contact. (One previous encounter she had with a boy, "the great red-faced boy" of the city, was frightening to her.) But the young Sylvia is lured by the prospect of love and trusts the boy stranger. In an attempt to please him, she journeys alone into darkness in search of the elusive white heron, a symbol of spiritual transcendence. As Sylvia has no desire to dominate or destroy, she ultimately chooses to join nature instead of man. Through this journey, which may be seen as psychological, physical, and spiritual, Sylvia becomes one with the realm that the ornithologist endeavors to master through aggression but cannot.

In the opening scene, Sylvia dreamily drives a cow home through shadow-filled woods, which suggest the psychological process she must undergo. In Jungian psychology, the maturation process is called individuation. An aspect of this process involves the various parts of the self coming to terms with one another. Jung's colleague M.-L. von Franz states that in mythical terms the ego and the shadow, parts of the personality, are linked, the shadow being the darkness with which the ego is in conflict (Franz 168). Jung calls this conflict "the battle for deliverance" (Henderson 118). The shadow-filled woods through which Sylvia walks indicate she is engaged in this battle.

Sylvia's journey takes place in June: early adulthood on the calendar of human life. Jewett emphasizes Sylvia's age; she is a "little girl," nine years old, on the brink of puberty. Furthermore, Sylvia is juxtaposed with a cow in the opening scene, suggesting her close attachment to the maternal. The dichotomy of the maternal symbol and the child points to the adolescence which Sylvia is about to enter on her physical journey.

The number nine has spiritual as well as physical implications: Jung's colleague Jolande Jacobi states, "The nine has been a 'magic number' for centuries. According to the traditional symbolism of numbers, it represents the perfected form of the perfected Trinity in its threefold elevation" (Jacobi 297). Indicative of Sylvia's spiritual journey, her trial, is the direction she walks: eastward. But, as the sun is setting, she walks *away* from the light, not toward it. For she must first pass through the darkness of night in order to reach the light of dawn, as is typical in myth: the hero must go into darkness, which represents death (Henderson 118). Sylvia's symbolic death is her passing away from one physical stage/spiritual state, while her symbolic rebirth follows at the beginning of a new day: the day she finds the object of her quest, the white heron.

From the initial scene, Sylvia's journey involves her sensual/sexual encounter with nature. In the country, Sylvia experiences a physical awakening. She has come to the country from the city (perhaps symbolic of society and the lack of individual identity), and at the farm she feels alive for the first time, "as if she never had been alive at all" (Jewett 228). As she walks through the water in bare feet, her heart beats "fast with pleasure" (Jewett 229). Jewett sets the tone for Sylvia's physical journey with her sensual, strong imagery: "twilight moths struck softly against her . . . there was a stirring in the great boughs overhead . . . She was not often in the woods so late as this, and it made her feel as if she were a part of the gray shadows and the moving leaves" (Jewett 229). As Sylvia develops an affinity with nature, she also discovers her own identity.

Just as the reader becomes aware of Sylvia's bond with nature, the absence of men in Sylvia's life also becomes clear: Sylvia lives on the farm with her grandmother, who chose Sylvia out of her *daughter's* children to live with her in the country. No mention is ever made of Sylvia's father. She is completely surrounded by maternal figures and imagery, from her own mother, to her grandmother, to Mistress Moolly the cow, to the regenerative vegetation around her. She feels as much akin to the woodlands as she feels alienated from the masculine, mechanistic city.[1]

As Sylvia wanders home through the woods with the cow, "the thought of the great red-faced boy who used to chase and frighten her" causes her "to hurry along the path to escape from the shadow of the trees" (Jewett 229). Juxtaposed with this fear-evoking remembrance is the present threat of the boy stranger's whistle.[2] Jewett adds to the tension of this threat by switching from past to present tense: "suddenly this little woodsgirl is horror-stricken to hear a clear whistle not very far away. Not a bird's whistle, which would have a sort of friendliness, but a boy's whistle, determined, and somewhat aggressive" (Jewett 229). As the boy stranger intrudes on Sylvia's woods, Sylvia instinctively attempts to hide herself in the bushes as would a child in a mother's skirts when confronted by a stranger, or as would a white heron in the leaves of a tree when threatened by a hunter.

The boy stranger seems to represent male dominance and sexuality, and the human world as opposed to the natural world. He, perhaps, may be seen as a devil figure. The stranger is sexual: carrying a gun, an obvious phallic symbol; asking to spend the night at Sylvia's house; and demanding that Sylvia give him milk. The stranger also demands to know Sylvia's name, but he doesn't tell her his. The boy's aggressive whistle indicates the force of his desire to acquire Sylvia's knowledge of the whereabouts of the white heron, which he intends to kill. As the boy stranger speaks with Sylvia and her grandmother, he makes known his offer of money to anyone who can show him the heron's nest. He tempts Sylvia not only with money, but also with the promise of friendship. If, as Joseph L. Henderson suggests, ". . . the bird is the most fitting symbol of transcendence" (Henderson 151), then in effect the stranger is asking Sylvia to sell her soul.[3]

The second scene takes place the following day in the woods; Sylvia becomes more confident with the boy stranger and loses her initial fear of him. The stranger presents Sylvia with a jack-knife, another phallic symbol, a bribe for her to trust him. Jewett's language is implicitly sexual: "All day long he did not once make her troubled or afraid except when he brought down some unsuspecting singing creature from its bough" (Jewett 233). It is when he "brings down" a creature that Sylvia feels afraid, but she is nonetheless attracted to him. She "watched the young man with loving admiration. She had never seen anybody so charming and delightful; the woman's heart, asleep in the child, was vaguely thrilled by a dream of love" (Jewett 233). The sexual tone of the passage continues as "they pressed forward again eagerly, parting the branches,—speaking to each other rarely and in whispers; the young man going first and Sylvia following, fascinated . . . her gray eyes dark with excitement" (Jewett 233–34).

In the next scene, before sunrise the following morning, Sylvia sets off on her lonely journey into the woods to discover the white heron's nest. Her intention is to please the boy stranger with the knowledge he has been seeking. She is not aware as she begins her journey that it will lead to what Henderson terms a "release through transcendence," that her "lonely journey or pilgrimage" is indeed a spiritual pilgrimage, one of "release, renunciation, and atonement, presided over and fostered by some spirit of compassion" (Henderson 151).

When Sylvia mounts the tree from which she hopes to see the white heron, she abandons her passivity and experiences a physical and spiritual awakening. According to

Jung, the tree is a symbol of "evolution, physical growth or psychological maturation" (Jung 90). Jung suggests the tree may also symbolize the phallus. Essential to the sexual interpretation of this scene is Jewett's personification of the tree.[4] It is described as a "great tree . . . the last of its generation" (Jewett 234). When Sylvia approaches the tree, it sleeps, as if human. The tone of the passage is expressly sexual: Sylvia mounts the tree "with tingling, eager blood coursing the channels of her whole frame" (Jewett 235). The tree "seemed to lengthen itself out as she went up, and to reach farther and farther upward" (Jewett 236), as though it were a phallus becoming erect. At the top of the tree, Sylvia's heart is beating, her face is "like a pale star," and she stands "trembling and tired but wholly triumphant" (Jewett 236). When Sylvia sees the white heron, her ecstasy is spiritual as well as physical. She "gives a long sigh" and is "well satisfied" (Jewett 238).

Jewett switches verb tense in this scene from past to present imperative (the switch lends tension and immediacy to the scene just as the change of tense in the first scene does); the imperative voice seems to be that of a higher being, the divine, instructing her where to look in order to see the white heron. Or perhaps this imperative voice is the voice of the Self, about which Franz speaks: "How far [the psyche] develops depends on whether or not the ego is willing to listen to the messages of Self" (Franz 162). The voice tells Sylvia, "And wait! wait! do not move a foot or a finger, little girl, do not send an arrow of light and consciousness from your two eager eyes, for the heron has perched on a pine bough not far beyond yours, and cries back to his mate on the nest, and plumes his feathers for the new day!" (Jewett 238). While the words "light and consciousness" express Sylvia's transcendence to a higher level of spiritual consciousness, the heron's mate and nest reflect Sylvia's own maturing sexuality. The young girl has journeyed through the darkness of night to discover the white heron and emerges into the new day. She has taken a lonely journey from west to east and now faces the rising sun, which in many societies represents "man's indefinable religious experience" (Jung 22).

After coming down from the tree, Sylvia appears before the grandmother and the boy, her clothing torn and soiled by the semen-like pine pitch. Not until confronted by her grandmother and the ornithologist does Sylvia experience an epiphany. Since she intends to tell the boy the location of the white heron's nest, the time for her to speak is the "splendid moment" for which she has waited. But Sylvia finds she cannot speak, for she hears her lover whisper into her ear: "The murmur of the pine's green branches is in her ears, she remembers how the white heron came flying through the golden air and how they watched the sea and the morning together . . ." (Jewett 239). Although Sylvia has been tempted by the stranger and believes "he is so well worth making happy" (Jewett 239), she recalls her moment of ecstasy and finds she cannot betray nature, her spiritual lover. In so doing, she has allied herself with the natural world and rejected the human world.

Sylvia's lonely journey is an initiation into adulthood; she has experienced "that moment of initiation at which one must learn to take the decisive steps into life alone" (Henderson 152). On her quest for the white heron, she has defied the temptation of the boy stranger and has matured psychologically, physically, and spiritually. While the ornithologist attempts to dominate nature by destroying it, Sylvia joins nature and protects it in a loving embrace.

Notes

1. In his article "America's 'Lonely Country Child': The Theme of Separation in Sarah Orne Jewett's 'A White Heron,'" Theodore R. Hovet sees Sylvia's connection to the maternal in nature as her refusal to enter adulthood and the modern, pre-industrialized world. Hovet theorizes that Sylvia remains a dependent child, while the boy stranger has crossed into adulthood, lives in the modern world, but continues to search "in an endless and destructive quest for the lost world of childhood" (171).

2. Critic James Ellis states, "Clearly . . . this young man with his whistle is to be equated with the great red-faced boy of the town who used to chase and frighten her" (4). Ellis concurs that Sylvia ultimately takes nature as her lover instead of man.

3. It is interesting to note that William Butler Yeats saw the heron (or herne) as a symbol of the divine in his plays *The Herne's Egg* and *Calvary*.

4. Critic Gayle L. Smith in her essay "The Language of Transcendence in Sarah Orne Jewett's 'A White Heron'" maintains that the personification of the tree is part of the "transcendental vision" that Jewett uses throughout her story (73).

Works Cited

Ellis, James. "The World of Dreams: Sexual Symbolism in 'A White Heron.'" *Nassau Review: The Journal of Nassau Community College Devoted to Arts, Lettres & Sciences* 3 (1977): iii, 3–9.

Hovet, Theodore R. "America's 'Lonely Country Child': The Theme of Separation in Sarah Orne Jewett's 'A White Heron.'" *Colby Library Quarterly* 14 (1978): 166–71.

Jewett, Sarah Orne. "A White Heron." *The Country of the Pointed Firs and Other Stories*. Ed. Mary Ellen Chase. New York: Norton, 1981. 227–39.

Jung, Carl G., M.-L. von Franz, Joseph L. Henderson, Jolande Jacobi, and Aniela Jaffe. *Man and his Symbols*. Garden City: Doubleday, 1964.

Smith, Gayle L. "The Language of Transcendence in Sarah Orne Jewett's 'A White Heron.'" *Critical; Essays on Sarah Orne Jewett*. Ed. Gwen L. Nagel. Boston: G. K. Hall, 1984. 69–75.

FURTHER READING

Biographies

Cary, Richard. *Sarah Orne Jewett.* Twayne, 1962, 175 p.
  Critical biography by a notable Jewett scholar.

Frost, John Eldridge. *Sarah Orne Jewett.* Gundalow Club, 1960, 174 p.
  Extensive biographical study of Jewett.

Matthiessen, Francis Otto. *Sarah Orne Jewett.* Houghton Mifflin, 1929, 159 p.
  Early critical biography of Jewett.

Criticism

Eakin, Paul John. "Sarah Orne Jewett and the Meaning of Country Life." *American Literature* 38, No. 4 (January 1967): 508–531.
  Briefly discusses "A White Heron" as a part of Jewett's general espousal of country life over city life.

Stevenson, Catherine Barnes. "The Double Consciousness of the Narrator in Sarah Orne Jewett's Fiction." *Colby Library Quarterly* 10, No. 1 (March 1975): 1–12.
  Analyzes the perceptions of the narrators in Jewett's *Deephaven,* "A White Heron," and *The Country of the Pointed Firs.*

Additional coverage of Jewett's life and career is contained in the following sources published by the Gale Group: *Contemporary Authors,* **Vols. 108, 127;** *Contemporary Authors New Revision Series,* **Vol. 71;** *Dictionary of Literary Biography,* **Vols. 12, 74, 221;** *Something About the Author,* **Vol. 15;** *Short Stories for Students,* **Vol. 4;** *St. James Guide to Feminist Writers;* **and** *Twentieth-Century Literary Criticism,* **Vols. 1, 22.**

"Araby"

James Joyce

The following entry presents criticism on Joyce's short story "Araby" (1914). For additional coverage of Joyce's short fiction, see *SSC,* Vols. 3 and 26.

INTRODUCTION

Considered one of Joyce's best known short stories, "Araby" is the third story in his short fiction collection, *Dubliners,* which was published in 1914. It is perceived as a prime example of Joyce's use of epiphany—a sudden revelation of truth about life inspired by a seemingly trivial incident—as the young narrator realizes his disillusionment with his concept of ideal love when he attempts to buy a token of affection for a young girl. Critical interest in the story has remained intense in recent decades as each story in *Dubliners* has been closely examined within the context of the volume and as an individual narrative. As the third story, "Araby" is often viewed as an important step between the first two stories—"The Sisters" and "An Encounter"—and the rest of the collection.

PLOT AND MAJOR CHARACTERS

The narrator of "Araby" is a young boy living with his aunt and uncle in a dark, untidy home in Dublin that was once the residence of a priest, now deceased. The boy is infatuated with his friend's older sister, and often follows her to school, never having the courage to talk to her. Finally she speaks to him, asking him if he is going to attend a visiting bazaar, known as the "Araby." When she indicates that she cannot attend, he offers to bring her something from the bazaar, hoping to impress her. On the night he is to attend, his uncle is late coming home from work. By the time the young boy borrows money from his uncle and makes his way to the bazaar, most of the people have left and many of the stalls are closed. As he looks for something to buy his friend's sister, he overhears a banal young salesgirl flirt with two young men. When the disinterested salesgirl asks him if he needs help, he declines, and he walks through the dark, empty halls, disillusioned with himself and the world around him.

MAJOR THEMES

Each story in *Dubliners* contains an epiphanic moment toward which the controlled yet seemingly plotless narrative moves. Among the best-known epiphanies is the one that

occurs in "Araby," in which a young boy recognizes the vanity and falsity of ideal, romantic love. It has also been interpreted as a story about a boy's growing alienation with his family, religion, and the world around him. Moreover, it is viewed as autobiographical, reflecting Joyce's own disillusionment with religion and love. As such, *Dubliners* is considered a collection of stories that parallel the process of initiation: the early stories focus on the tribulations of childhood, then move on to the challenges and epiphanies of adulthood. A few critics have detected the theme of Irish nationalism, as Joyce employs Irish legends to indicate the vast discrepancy between the narrator's idealized view of the girl and the harsh reality of the bazaar. Moreover, the theme of the quest is a prevalent one in "Araby," as the young narrator embarks on a dangerous journey to win the hand of a young maiden.

CRITICAL RECEPTION

For many decades *Dubliners* was considered little more than a slight volume of naturalist fiction evoking the repressed social milieu of turn-of-the-century Dublin. When critics began to explore the individual stories in the collection, much attention was focused on the symbolism in "Araby," particularly the religious imagery and the surrounding of the bazaar. In fact, some commentators have invested the story with many layers of meaning and religious symbolism; others urge a more superficial reading. Literary allusions, influences, and autobiographical aspects of the story have also been a rich area for study; in fact, commentators have found traces of Geoffrey Chaucer's *The Canterbury Tales,* Dante's *Commedia,* and Homer's *The Odyssey* in Joyce's story. Much critical attention has focused on stylistic elements, especially the impact of the narrative voice in "Araby." As scholars continue to mine Joyce's *Dubliners* for critical study, "Araby" remains one of the most highly regarded and popular stories in the volume.

PRINCIPAL WORKS

Short Fiction

Dubliners 1914
The Portable James Joyce 1947
The Essential James Joyce 1948

Other Major Works

Chamber Music (poetry) 1907
A Portrait of the Artist As a Young Man (novel) 1916
Exiles (drama) 1918
Ulysses (novel) 1922
Poems Penyeach (poetry) 1927
Collected Poems (poetry) 1936
Finnegans Wake (novel) 1939
Stephen Hero (unfinished novel) 1944
Letters 3 Vols. (letters) 1955–1966
Critical Writings of James Joyce (criticism) 1959

CRITICISM

William Bysshe Stein (essay date 1962)

SOURCE: "Joyce's 'Araby': Paradise Lost," in *Perspective,* Vol. 12, No. 4, Spring, 1962, pp. 215–22.

[*In the following essay, Stein surveys the religious imagery in "Araby."*]

As L. A. G. Strong has observed in *The Sacred River,* "Christianity for Joyce is inescapable, and his critics cannot escape it either." And he is right. No matter the work, Joyce always views the order and disorder of the world in terms of the Catholic faith in which he was reared. Turn though he does at times to other sanctions for his beliefs, he never quite shakes off the power of "a symbol behind which are massed twenty centuries of authority and veneration." Only the life of Christ objectifies the absolute moral standards by which man can make sense out of life.

This is true, in particular, of **Dubliners.** In their egoistic preoccupation with temporal pleasures and aspirations, the protagonists in this collection of stories forget that the willing sacrifice of Christ promises them deliverance from all the agonizing frustrations and sufferings in the material universe of time and space. Prey to all the fears of their darkened spirit, they lack the will to deny the temptations of sin and therefore paralyze the vitality of their souls. But, paradoxically, even when enslaved by their perverse and perverting desires, they still yearn for true selfhood—for the state of Adam in Paradise before he forfeited the perfection with which God endowed him. Thus, in all of these stories, the pathos and tragedy of the human predicament are projected in the fruitless efforts of the protagonists to substitute material for spiritual values and to imbue the former with the enduring substance of the latter. The extremely popular **"Araby"** illustrates the manner in which Joyce integrates this pattern of action with the intricate symbolism of his Catholic background.

At the outset of the story the physical and seasonal setting establishes the necessity of the youthful hero's quest for a redemptive ideal. "An uninhabited house . . . at the blind end" of a street figures the spiritual inertia of the Irish Church. For when the boy prowls in the empty residence that formerly belonged to a now deceased priest, he is oppressed by its "musty" atmosphere. And when, in a littered room, he discovers Scott's "The Abbot" and "The Memoirs of Vidocq," here is evidence that the priest had shirked the full responsibilities of his ministry and sought escape from his pastoral trusts in chronicles of romance and adventure. The "yellow" cover of one of these volumes (Joyce's symbolic color of betrayal, decay, and corruption) sustains this interpretation. Moreover, outside the building this defection from divine guidance is crystallized in an image of a blighted Garden of Eden:

> The wild garden behind the house contained a central apple tree and a few straggling bushes under one of which I found the late tenant's rusty bicycle pump. He had been a very charitable priest; in his will he had left his money to institutions and the furniture of his house to his sister.

This passage, of course, reverberates with irony. In his preoccupation with worldly things the priest has ceased to heed the inspiration of the Holy Spirit. As the "rusty bicycle pump" (a parallel to the theosophical bicycle pump in the Circe episode of *Ulysses*) suggests, he had mechanized his responses to divine love. No wonder, then, that the familiar tree of temptation and death occupies a central position in the yard.

But even as this scene re-creates the moral paralysis of the boy's environment, it likewise offers a solution to his problem of disoriented faith. For in relating the dismal prospect to the seasonal setting in the next paragraph, "the short days of winter," Joyce unobstrusively calls attention to the turn of the liturgical year—the Advent. This cycle of the Christian Year marks the preparation for Christmas and takes note of the miracle of the Incarnation (man's assurance of deliverance from the curse of the Fall). It therefore operates to evoke the tense expectation that preceded the coming of the Messiah—His birth in Bethlehem. And here it is well to recall the liturgy of the Advent, the "re-collection" of the penance and loving prayer by which "the people that walked in darkness" expressed their longing for redemption from sin and death. For against this background of the annual re-living of the life of Christ, Joyce projects the next development of his story. His hero is in an equivalent state of darkness. But since a tragic velleity of soul grips the Irish world, his position is almost helpless. With his father dead (and by extension the priesthood and the Church), there is no guiding light of wisdom and love to reveal the path of faith. As a consequence, he allows his instincts to give direction to his yearning for selfhood. Like so many other protagonists in *Dubliners,* he attempts to substitute the ephemeral titillations of romantic passion for the ineffable ecstasy of mystical participation in the Holy Passion.

Appropriately, Joyce resorts to inversions of the guiding light to dramatize the boy's susceptibility to the temptations of lust. For whenever he espies the object of his carnal curiosity (Mangan's sister), she is bathed in an artificial radiance that exhibits her coquettish charms:

> She was waiting for us, her figure defined by the light from the half-opened door. Her brother always teased her before he obeyed and I stood by the railing looking at her. Her dress swung as she moved her body and the soft rope of her hair tossed from side to side.

In another such tableau Joyce divulges her evil influence upon the youth's mind as she ridicules the significance of Advent penance. Unlike the chore of "a retreat that week in her convent," he, she observes, will be able to go to a "splendid bazaar" (an analogue of the *pompa diaboli* so vehemently deplored by the Church Fathers, certainly a commonplace to Joyce). Of course, her feline sensuality again numbs his spiritual awareness:

> The light from the lamp opposite our door caught the white curve of her neck, lit up her hair that rested there, and, falling, lit up the hand upon the railing. It fell over one side of her dress and caught the white border of a petticoat, just visible as she stood at ease.

In a final mutation of this enticing pose, Joyce clearly associates the girl with the derelict morality of Ireland. The rubric in this case is the casual reference to "brown," a symbolic color in *Dubliners* that is always connected with inward and outward decay and stagnation. It likewise prefigures, I think, the bleak futility of the quest undertaken by the boy with her warm encouragement:

> I looked over at the dark house where she lived. I may have stood there for an hour, seeing nothing but the brown-clad figure cast by my imagination, touched discreetly by the lamplight at the curved neck, at the hand upon the railings and at the border below her dress.

The combination of lust and romantic illusion generated by these glimpses of Mangan's sister has an interesting parallel in **"The Dead."** Gabriel Conroy perceives his wife standing on the staircase in a similar position, and she too is rendered mysteriously enchanting by the play of light and shadow:

> He could not see her face but he could see the terra-cotta and salmon-pink panels of her skirt which the shadow made appear black and white.

And it is this vision that fires the sexual passion leading to an epiphany even more agonizing and disillusioning than the boy's.

In **"Araby"** the romantic and unconsciously wanton incarnation that woman assumes in the imagination of the hero enables Joyce to initiate a brilliant religious trope. Never discerned by any of his critics, it is signalled by the choric repetition of "name" and "word." Since the Advent is the liturgical setting of the story, the artist sets out to correlate the seasonal theme of the Incarnation with the boy's unvoiced passion. In this maneuver, even as in the execution of *Ulysses,* the action unfolds on several different levels of reality, at once paralleling and opposing one another, and it reflects the young protagonist's desperate effort to find an earthly replacement for the spiritual ideal denied him by his environment, as certainly this passage indicates: "I pressed the palms of my hands together until they trembled, murmuring: 'O love! O love!' many times." But in order to construe the moral implications of this transformation of desire, it must be approached "un-protestantly" through the doctrines of Catholic theology (certain assumptions of faith in regard to divine nature). Otherwise the critic cannot understand why Joyce is silent about the name of Mangan's sister. For whenever the hero conjures her vision, her name dies on his lips in mute rapture: "her name was like a summons to my foolish blood." This awe and reverence literally manifest an impulse towards deification—in the religious context of the story a blasphemous tendency. According to traditional Christian myth, only the One who from all eternity has existed ever commanded such love and veneration, the One whose secret and unutterable name was YHVH (Yahveh). So holy was this tetragrammaton that it was sacrilege for a layman to pronounce it. This pure being, in appearance the ineffable light of glory, was the Father who for always and always was generating and begetting the Son; and for always and always the Holy Spirit was proceeding from the Father and the Son. And it was the Holy Spirit that engendered not only the Creation but also Jesus the Son of Mary.

Here it must be remembered that the rites of the Incarnation, which occur on Christmas, are centered upon the mystery of the appearance of light in the depth of darkness, of God "who hast made this most sacred night to shine forth with the brilliance of true light," and of him who is begotten "from the womb before the day-star." Significantly, on this day, the third Mass celebrates the eternal generation of the Divine Word from the Father, since the Child born this day is He who in the beginning created all worlds:

> In the beginning was the Word,
> And the Word was with God;
> And the Word was God.
> He was made in the beginning with God.
> All things were made through Him,
> And without Him was made nothing that has been
>   made.
> In Him was life, and the life was the light of men.

> (John I, 1–4)

As the youth's preoccupation with the illuminated figure of Mangan's sister suggests, he has forgotten that only the true light can redeem him from his earthly frustrations. Indeed, he profanely equates her with the miracle of the Eucharist:

> These noises [the pandemonium of the Dublin streets] converged in a single sensation of life for me. I imagined that I bore my chalice safely through a throng of foes. Her name sprang to my lips in strange prayers and praises which I myself did not understand. My eyes were often full of tears (I could not tell why) and at times a flood from my heart seemed to pour itself out into my bosom. *I thought little of the future.*

> (Italics mine)

Moreover, to emphasize this shocking blasphemy, Joyce deliberately connects this "confused adoration" with the perversion of the hymns, "the songs of the Holy Spirit": "my body was like a harp and her words were like fingers running upon wires." The harp, of course, is the conventional symbol of the Book of Psalms and of all songs and music that honor God. Here it is converted into an analogue of sensuality, an explicit rejection of spiritual love.

This pattern of inverted piety is also directly related to the hero's dereliction in his Advent devotions and to his distorted conception of Paradise:

> I wished to annihilate the tedious intervening days. I chafed against the work of school. At night in my bedroom and by day in the classroom her image came between me and the page I strove to read. The syllables of the word *Araby* were called to me through the silence in which my soul luxuriated and cast an Eastern enchantment over me . . . I answered few questions in class. I watched my master's face pass from amiability to sternness; he hoped I was not beginning to idle.

Instead of suppressing his desire for earthly pleasures in accordance with the sacramental practices of the Church

during this cycle of the Christian year, the youth experiences only the mortifications of frustration and delinquency. No thought of self-denial crosses his mind. His unruly instincts, disguising themselves in romantic sentiments, paralyze his awareness of God's gift of grace. Yet, ironically, his delusive "Eastern enchantment" would become a reality if he actually surrendered to the genuine aspirations of his soul. In this allusion Joyce apparently improvises on the symbolism of the East so persistent in the writings of the Church Fathers, especially as influenced by its identification with Christ in Zacharias VI, 12 ("The Orient is His name.") and by the antiphon of the liturgy *O Oriens* (The great day of the everlasting life will no longer be illuminated by the visible sun, but by the true light, the sun of justice, which is called the Orient . . .). In any event, as the Advent season contemplates the nativity of Christ, it also looks forward to the Resurrection and the fulfillment of His promise of salvation, man's attainment of Heaven. As the Book of Revelation puts it, there will be a re-creation of the Garden of Paradise in Eden, "a new heaven." These associations stem inevitably from Joyce's earlier reference to the scene of the Fall of Man, for, as the action unfolds from this point, it centers on the hero's yearning for a temporal Paradise. Tempted by unconscious sexual cravings, he substitutes Araby and its brown madonna for Heaven and its vision of the Divine Mary.

The balance of the story deals with his futile quest to gain the favor of Mangan's sister with an offering from the mock paradise of Araby. His disappointment is foreshadowed, however, in what might appear to be a sequence of harmless allusions to time ("I sat staring at the clock"; "it was after eight o'clock"; "At nine o'clock I heard my uncle's latchkey in the halldoor.").

Actually Joyce here reveals his hero's infatuation with *nunc fluens*, the present which is always flying away, as distinct from *nunc stans*, the eternal present which is the boon of Heaven. And it is possible that the florin with which the uncle provides the boy is an ironical reflection of this insulated absorption; for, as Joyce with his philological curiosity doubtlessly knew, the "godless" or "graceless florin" was minted during the last half of the nineteenth century. It was so designated because during one stage of its coinage the motto, *Dei Gratia*, was dropped from its face. In any event, all of these delicate symbolic repercussions seem to integrate with the boy's experience at the bazaar, his exposure to the wiles of the devil as reflected in the *pompa diaboli*.

His first impression of Araby, for instance, is colored with satanic corruption: "In front of me was a large building which displayed the magical name." Magic, of course, implies a desire to circumvent divine omnipotence, and this idea is comprehended in the immorality of amusements designed to incite souls to their ruin, gaming "stalls" and musical entertainment at the "*Cafe* Chantant," the latter description probably disguising the cheap, indecent comedy of a burlesque show. And since the enterprise appears to be run by people with predominantly "English accents," the traditional enemies of the Irish are co-operating with the devil in promoting the moral degradation of the native population. Surely, in the youthful hero's glimpse of two men . . . "counting money on a salver," there is a teasing echo of the betrayal of the Savior by Judas. These details operate, then, to expose the boy's complete disregard for his own and his country's salvation. This radical dissociation of religious sensibility is finally crystallized in his blasphemous fancy that in the hall there reigns "a silence like that which pervades a church after service."

As the story terminates, Joyce continues to enlarge the dimensions of this gimcrack Eden. When the boy at last decides to buy a present for the object of his transcendent love, he is discouraged by the indifference of the female attendant who, ironically, is engaged in amorous play as futile as his own:

> Remembering with difficulty why I had come I went over to one of the stalls and examined porcelain vases and flowered tea-sets. At the door of the stall a young lady was talking and laughing with two young gentlemen.

Significantly, the objects attracting his attention are not devoid of symbolic meaning. In traditional Christian iconography a vase holding a lily often designates the Annunciation. Empty, however, it indicates a separation of the soul from the body. From another point of view, the vase and the imitation flowers reflect the pervasive secularization of the culture, its preoccupation with external vanities. After all, what is the bazaar but a huge symbol of Vanity Fair, and what is the boy but a hypocritical pilgrim.

In the final scene of the story Joyce accentuates the theme of paradise lost, not only of the hero's Araby but of Heaven itself. With his illusions about an exotic bazaar shattered, the boy surrenders to a paralysis of volition:

> Observing me the young lady came over and asked me did I wish to buy anything. The tone of her voice was not encouraging; she seemed to have spoken to me out of a sense of duty. I looked humbly at the great jars that stood like eastern guards at either side of the dark entrance to the stall . . .

The "eastern guards" in this context, it seems to me, are surrogates of the cherubim of Genesis, "placed at the east of the garden of Eden . . . to keep the way of the tree of life." For even as Adam and Eve heard the reprimanding "voice of the Lord God" just before their summary expulsion from Paradise, so the boy, in a mock parallel to this incident, is awakened to his fate:

> I heard a voice call from one end of the gallery that the light was out. The upper part of the hall was now completely dark.

> Gazing up into the darkness I saw myself as a creature driven and derided by vanity; and my eyes burned with anguish and anger.

But unlike the darkness which fell after the crucifixion of Christ, there is no promise of a return of redemptive light.

Instead of profiting by his folly, the hero relapses into self-pity and anger, a slave to his egoistic desires. Forgetting that hope, faith, and charity (love) are supernatural gifts of God that can fulfill man's infinite craving for happiness, he allows frustration to obscure his vision of the eternal light of salvation. And so paradise can be lost! And so the symbolic dialectic of **"Araby"** enunciates!

John O. Lyons (essay date 1964)

SOURCE: "James Joyce and Chaucer's Prioress," in *English Language Notes,* Vol. 2, No. 2, December, 1964, pp. 127–32.

[*In the following essay, Lyons considers the influence of Chaucer's* Prioress' Tale *on Joyce's "Araby."*]

When Joyce's commentators mention the influence of Chaucer, the detail they cite most frequently is the character of Molly Bloom, which reminds them in its licentiousness and common sense of the Wife of Bath.[1] I think it can be shown, however, that Joyce's use of Chaucer is more than casual. There is no doubt of his knowledge of and respect for the writings of Chaucer. In 1912 he wrote, as part of an examination for a degree from the University of Padua, an essay on "The Good Parson of Chaucer."[2] Six years earlier he had written to Grant Richards, who had requested that some allegedly obscene passages be deleted from **Dubliners** before he published it, ". . . I suspect that it [English literature] will follow the other countries of Europe as it did in Chaucer's time."[3] Joyce's reference to Chaucer in connection with **Dubliners** may have more significance than as a mere prop to his argument that the English are more prudish in literary matters than Continentals. Both *The Canterbury Tales* and **Dubliners** illustrate those alternating attitudes of irony and sympathy which have been seen by critics in the characterizations of Dame Alice and Molly Bloom. But beyond this, both of these works are collections of short stories in which real places and people are mixed with fiction, and in which the author (thinly disguised) is a participant.

The influence of Chaucer on Joyce appears to be more specific when a comparison is made of the *Prioress' Tale* with the often anthologized **"Araby."** Chaucer's Prioress tells a story presumably based on the martyrdom of Hugh of Lincoln, to whom she refers at the end. The tale concerns a little boy who bolsters his courage to walk to and from school through the ghetto by singing *Alma redemptoris.* One day his throat is slit by the Jews, but his widowed mother is able to find him in the pit where he is thrown because he continues to sing.[4] Joyce's **"Araby"** is virtually the prototype of the modern short story about a youth's initiation. It concerns a romantic little boy who secretly worships the sister of a playmate. He wishes to please her by bringing her a souvenir from *Araby,* a bazaar. His uncle has promised him money for this treat, but on the night he is to go his uncle gets home late. When the boy finally arrives at the bazaar the stands are closing and his romantic imaginings dissolve before the tawdry props and people of the closing carnival.

On the surface these stories seem to have little similarity except that both are about obsessed schoolboys. Yet the details of Joyce's story often parallel those of Chaucer's tale. Chaucer's youth is a fatherless orphan; Joyce's lives with his aunt and uncle. Chaucer's youth attends "A litel schole of cristen folk," which is "Doun at the ferther ende" (494–495).[5] Joyce's boy goes to "the Christian Brothers' School," and lives at the blind end of North Richmond Street (p. 33).[6] Chaucer's boy sings his Latin prayers out of uncomprehending but complete devotion: "Nought wiste he what this Latin was to seye, / For he so young and tendre was of age" (523–524). In the back drawing room the boy in **"Araby"** reads books left there by a priest, the former tenant. These include *The Abbot,* by Walter Scott, *The Devout Communicant* and *The Memoirs of Vidocq.* I liked the last best because its leaves were yellow" (p. 33). He too loves more than he understands.

Both of these nameless innocents express a romantic and uncomprehending love for an idea of sweet beauty which sustains them in a hostile world. And both of them express their praise in song. To and from school Chaucer's little boy sings his song to the Virgin.

> Twyes a day it passes thurgh his throte,
> To scoleward and homward whan he wente;
> On Cristes moder set was his entente.
>
> (548–550)

The idea of this song and of the boy's singing recurs as a knell throughout the *Prioress' Tale.* She begins by calling her story a song (487), and then during the tale itself the words *song* and *singing* occur twenty four times in the 202 verses. Chaucer also plays with the idea of the song issuing from the boy's heart and passing through his throat which, even when slit, is an opening for his song.

> The swetnes hath his herte perced so
> Of cristes moder, that to hir to preye,
> He can nat stinte of singing by the weye.
>
> (555–557)

In **"Araby"** the idea of *singing* and *heart* are also dominant in the early part of the story. Music is introduced obliquely when the coachman ". . . smoothed or combed the horse or shook music from the buckled harness" (p. 34). When the boy spies upon Mangan's sister he feels a song rise from his heart. "When she came out on the doorstep my heart leaped," and "her name was like a summons to all my foolish blood" (p. 35). As Chaucer's young martyr braves his way through the Jewish ghetto by singing the praises of the Virgin, Joyce's boy protects himself from a crude, adult, and urban world by harboring the image of his innocent love. "Her image accompanied me even in places the most hostile to romance" (p. 35). Only in this way can he stand

> . . . the curses of labourers, the shrill litanies of shopboys who stand on guard by the barrels of pigs' cheeks, the nasal chanting of street-singers, who sang a *come-you-all* about O'Donovan Rossa, or a ballad about the troubles in our native land.
>
> (p. 35)

Here the songs are attributed to the hard world, so it is coarse music—and the modern initiate keeps his own song of romantic praise to himself.

> These noises converged in a single sensation of life for me: I imagined that I bore my chalice safely through a throng of foes. Her name sprang to my lips at moments in strange prayers and praises which I myself did not understand. My eyes were often full of tears (I could not tell why) and at times a flood from my heart seemed to pour itself out into my bosom.
>
> (p. 35)

When he is alone his praise and prayer are open. "I pressed the palms of my hands together until they trembled, murmuring: 'O love! O love!' many times" (p. 36). When he waits for his uncle to come home so that he can go to the bazaar he goes "from room to room singing" (p. 38). And when he arrives at *Araby* there is the bitter irony that his disillusionment comes as he stands before a stall called the "Café Chantant" (p. 40).

The little boy in the *Prioress' Tale* is a Christian martyr, which Joyce's youth is not. Yet the religious images in **"Araby"** have often been noted. Cleanth Brooks emphasizes them in his analysis of the story.[7] The house at the blind end of North Richmond Street was occupied by a priest; the boy treats Mangan's sister as an object of his vocation and offers prayers to her; his priestly role is performed when he imagines himself bearing a chalice through the throng; the aunt is visited by a "pawnbroker's widow, who collected used stamps for some pious purpose" (p. 38); when he arrives at the closing bazaar it seems to him that he "recognized a silence like that which pervades a church after a service"; and the concessioners are "counting money on a salver" (p. 40). The boy's romanticism is partly doomed because he translates his normal pubescent longings into a religious context. This absurdity is extended in the boy's mind to the world about him, so that in the church-like atmosphere of the bazaar Joyce comments once again on the stultifying effect of Irish Catholicism.

At the end of the *Prioress' Tale* the images of *singing, heart,* and *blood* which signify the boy's mortality give way to images of precious stones which signify his immortality. When his weeping mother finds him singing in the pit he is called "This gemme of chastitee, this emeraude, / And eek of martirdom the ruby bright" (609–610). The boy confesses that the Virgin "leyde a greyn up-on my tonge" (662), and when it is removed by the priest he stops singing. They bury the youthful martyr "in a tombe of marbul-stones clere" (681).

Chaucer's story of martyrdom is about a little Christian boy in "Λsic" who is killed by vindictive Jews. Joyce's story is of a young and innocent romantic who is disillusioned at *Araby* by crass Englishmen. The imagery of **"Araby"** also moves from blood and song to hard precious objects. Here it is not the beauty and immortality of gems, but those coins which should be rendered unto Caesar. He goes to the bazaar with the florin his uncle gives him tightly gripped in his hand. When he arrives he cannot find a sixpenny entrance, and so squanders a shilling to a "weary-looking man" (p. 40). Then he sees the two men "counting money on a salver," and listens "to the fall of the coins" (p. 40). His imaginings of Eastern enchantment fade when he hears the young lady at the booth in a frivolous and flirtatious conversation and feels her coldness toward him. Instead of the "greyn" upon his tongue which allows him to sing in death, he has in his pocket two pennies and a sixpence which he allows to fall against each other as he lingers before the booth. The image of his virgin, Mangan's sister, deserts him in this last hour. In his own mind he had canonized the way in which "her dress swung as she moved her body and the soft rope of her hair tossed from side to side" (p. 34). She cannot go to the bazaar because there is a retreat that week in her convent; he does go to *Araby,* and is there deserted by her image. Marvin Magalaner wonders why Joyce does not give the Christian name of the girl.[8] Even her few words are given indirectly. If it were not so, and even if her name were given, the romantically deified image which the boy has of her would be diluted. In his disillusionment he is isolated from the doings of this world in a way which is analogous to the murder of Chaucer's little martyr.

The end of **"Araby"** might seem to be excessively hysterical for the small dimensions of the story.

> Gazing up into the darkness I saw myself as a creature driven and derided by vanity; and my eyes burned with anguish and anger.

(p. 41)

Yet when the story is seen as a complement to an earlier type of Christian martyrdom by its depiction of a martyrdom for romantic childhood idealism, this death of youth justifies such excess. When the abbot removes the "greyn" from the tongue of the Prioress' martyr his actions are much more extravagant.

> His salte teres trikled doun as reyn,
> And gruf he fil al plat up-on the grounde,
> And stille he lay as he had been y-bounde.

(674–676)

Compared to this, Joyce's youth is restrained when he sees the impious death in life which the adult world about him leads. And yet, as with Chaucer's overstatement of his innocent martyr's infant piety, there is an irony in the theological wording of the boy's self-condemnation. He is still as ignorant of his own motives as is the Prioress of some of the grotesqueness of her tale.

In *A Portrait of the Artist as a Young Man* Joyce shows Stephen Dedalus grow from precocious piety to worship for a young girl. **"Araby"** condenses this experience. In both, a youthful idealism is destroyed by a callous world. To enforce the sense that a romantic and pious youth is martyred by reality in **"Araby"** Joyce may well have gone to Chaucer's tale of a martyred youth. Where the stories differ those differences are complementary. The Christian world of the Prioress, like the ghetto in her tale, is "open at either ende" (494). The world of Joyce's little boy, like North Richmond Street at the end of which he lives, is blind.

Notes

1. Harry Levin, *James Joyce: A Critical Introduction* (Norfolk, Conn., (1941), p. 126. Richard M. Kain, *Fabulous Voyager: James Joyce's Ulysses* (Chicago, 1947), p. 100; William Y. Tindall, *James Joyce: His Way of Interpreting the Modern World* (New York and London, 1950), p. 38.

2. Richard Ellmann, *James Joyce* (New York, 1959), p. 332.

3. Quoted by Herbert Gorman, *James Joyce* (New York and Toronto, 1939), p. 150.

4. Bloom makes reference to the story during his meditations on death in Glasnavin Cemetery. "It's the blood sinking in the earth gives new life. Same idea those jews they said killed the christian boy." James Joyce, *Ulysses* (New York, 1961), p. 108.

5. *The Poetical Works of Chaucer,* ed. F. N. Robinson (Boston, 1933)—line numbers are indicated in the text.

6. James Joyce, *Dubliners* (New York, n.d.)—page numbers are indicated in the text.

7. Cleanth Brooks and Robert Penn Warren, *Understanding Fiction* (New York, 1948), pp. 420–423.

8. Marvin Magalaner and Richard M. Kain, *Joyce: The Man, the Work, the Reputation* (New York, 1956), p. 78.

Harry Stone (essay date 1965)

SOURCE: "'Araby' and the Writings of James Joyce," in *Antioch Review,* Vol. 25, No. 3, Fall, 1965, pp. 375–410.

[*In the following essay, Stone explores the literary allusions and symbolism found in "Araby," contending that Joyce "was careful to lacquer his images and actions with layer after layer of translucent, incremental meaning."*]

> Love came to us in time gone by
>   When one at twilight shyly played
> And one in fear was standing nigh—
>   For Love at first is all afraid.
> We were grave lovers. Love is past
>   That had his sweet hours many a one;

Welcome to us now at the last
    The ways that we shall go upon.

   —*Chamber Music*, XXX (written in 1904 or earlier).
And still you hold our longing gaze
With languorous look and lavish limb!
Are you not weary of ardent ways?
Tell no more of enchanted days.

   —*A Portrait of the Artist as a Young Man* (1904–14).
Lust, thou shalt not commix idolatry.

          —*Finnegans Wake* (1922–39).

"We walk through ourselves," says Stephen Dedalus in *Ulysses*. Stephen is trying to show how Shakespeare, or for that matter how any artist (creator of "Dane or Dubliner"), forever turns to the themes which agitate him, endlessly bodying forth the few crucial events of his life. "Every life is many days, day after day," says Stephen. "We walk through ourselves, meeting robbers, ghosts, giants, old men, young men, wives, widows, brothers-in-love. But always meeting ourselves." Stephen's theory may be an ingenious *jeu d'esprit*—though Joyce himself was heavily committed to such views. But whether or not Stephen's words are appropriate to Shakespeare, they are exactly appropriate to Joyce. In his writings, Joyce was always meeting himself—in ways which must at times have been beyond his conscious ordinance—and the pages of **"Araby"** are witness to that fact.

For **"Araby"** preserves a central episode in Joyce's life, an episode he will endlessly recapitulate. The boy in **"Araby,"** like the youthful Joyce himself, must begin to free himself from the nets and trammels of society. That beginning involves painful farewells and disturbing dislocations. The boy must dream "no more of enchanted days." He must forego the shimmering mirage of childhood, begin to see things as they really are. But to see things as they really are is only a prelude. Far in the distance lies his appointed (but as yet unimagined) task: to encounter the reality of experience and forge the uncreated conscience of his race. The whole of that struggle, of course, is set forth in *A Portrait of the Artist as a Young Man*. **"Araby"** is the identical struggle at an earlier stage; **"Araby"** is a portrait of the artist as a young boy.

II

The autobiographical nexus of **"Araby"** is not confined to the struggle raging in the boy's mind, though that conflict—an epitome of Joyce's first painful effort to see—is central and controls all else. Many of the details of the story are also rooted in Joyce's life. The narrator of **"Araby"**—the narrator is the boy of the story now grown up—lived, like Joyce, on North Richmond Street. North Richmond Street is blind, with a detached two-story house at the blind end, and down the street, as the opening paragraph informs us, the Christian Brothers' school. Like Joyce, the boy attended this school, and again like Joyce he found it dull and stultifying. Furthermore, the boy's surrogate parents, his aunt and uncle, are a version of Joyce's parents: the aunt, with her forbearance and her un-

examined piety, is like his mother; the uncle, with his irregular hours, his irresponsibility, his love of recitation, and his drunkenness, is like his father.

The title and the central action of the story are also autobiographical. From May fourteenth to nineteenth, 1894, while the Joyce family was living on North Richmond Street and Joyce was twelve, Araby came to Dublin. Araby was a bazaar, and the program of the bazaar, advertising the fair as a "Grand Oriental Fête," featured the name "Araby" in huge exotic letters, while the design as well as the detail of the program conveyed an ill-assorted blend of pseudo-Eastern romanticism and blatant commercialism. For one shilling, as the program put it, one could visit "Araby in Dublin" and at the same time aid the Jervis Street Hospital.

But the art of **"Araby"** goes beyond its autobiographical matrix. The autobiographical strands soon entwine themselves about more literary patterns and enter the fiction in dozens of unsuspected ways. For instance, embedded in **"Araby"** is a story, "Our Lady of the Hills," from a book that Joyce knew well, *The Celtic Twilight* (1893) by William Butler Yeats. "Our Lady of the Hills" tells how a pretty young Protestant girl walking through the mountains near Lough Gill was taken for the Virgin Mary by a group of Irish Catholic children. The children refused to accept her denials of divinity; to them she was "the great Queen of Heaven come to walk upon the mountain and be kind to them." After they had parted and she had walked on for half a mile, one of the children, a boy, jumped down into her path and said that he would believe she were mortal if she had a petticoat under her dress like other ladies. The girl showed the boy her two skirts, and the boy's dream of a saintly epiphany vanished into the mountain air. In his anguish, he cried out angrily, "Dad's a divil, mum's a divil, and I'm a divil, and you are only an ordinary lady." Then he "ran away sobbing."

Probably reverberating in **"Araby"** also are chords from one of Thomas De Quincey's most famous works, "Levana and Our Ladies of Sorrow." In "Levana," Our Lady of Tears (she bears the additional title, "Madonna") speaks about the child who is destined to suffer and to see, a type of the inchoate artist:

> "Lo! here is he whom in childhood I dedicated to my altars. This is he that once I made my darling. Him I led astray, him I beguiled, and from heaven I stole away his young heart to mine. Through me did he become idolatrous; and through me it was, by languishing desires, that he worshipped the worm, and prayed to the wormy grave. Holy was the grave to him; lovely was its darkness; saintly its corruption. Him, this young idolater, I have seasoned for thee, dear gentle Sister of Sighs!"

He who is chosen by the Ladies of Sorrow will suffer and be cursed; he will "see the things that ought *not* to be seen, sights that are abominable, and secrets that are unutterable," but he will also be able to read the great truths of the universe, and he will "rise again *before* he dies." In this manner, says Our Lady of Tears, we accomplish the commission we had from God: "to plague [the chosen one's] heart until we had unfolded the capacities of his spirit."

The ideas and images of "Levana" (witness the parody in *Ulysses*) had sunk deep into Joyce's imagination. His imagination had always sought out, always vibrated to, the Levanaesque constellation—a constellation that fuses religion, sexuality, idolatry, darkness, ascension, and art. "**Araby,**" both in its central idea and its characteristic imagery—in the image of Mangan's sister, in the boy's blind idolatry, and in the boy's ultimate insight and dawning ascension—is cognate with "Levana."

Other literary prototypes also contribute to "**Araby.**" In "**Araby**" as in Joyce's life, Mangan is an important name. In life Mangan was one of Joyce's favorite Romantic poets, a little-known Irish poet who pretended that many of his poems were translations from the Arabic although he was totally ignorant of that language. Joyce championed him in a paper delivered as a Pateresque twenty-year-old before the Literary and Historical Society of University College, Dublin, and championed him again five years later, in a lecture at the Università Popolare in Trieste, as "the most significant poet of the modern Celtic world, and one of the most inspired singers that ever used the lyric form in any country." In "**Araby**" Mangan is the boy's friend, but, what is more important, Mangan's sister is the adored girl. In each lecture Joyce discussed Mangan's poetry in words which could serve as an epigraph for the boy's mute, chivalric love for Mangan's sister and for his subsequent disillusionment and self-disdain. In the latter lecture, Joyce described the female persona that Mangan is constantly adoring:

> This figure which he adores recalls the spiritual yearnings and the imaginary loves of the Middle Ages, and Mangan has placed his lady in a world full of melody, of lights and perfumes, a world that grows fatally to frame every face that the eyes of a poet have gazed on with love. There is only one chivalrous idea, only one male devotion, that lights up the faces of Vittoria Colonna, Laura, and Beatrice, just as the bitter disillusion and the self-disdain that end the chapter are one and the same.

And one of Joyce's favorite poems by Mangan—a poem whose influence recurs in *A Portrait of the Artist as a Young Man, Ulysses,* and *Finnegans Wake*—is "Dark Rosaleen," a love paean to a girl who represents Ireland (Dark Rosaleen is a poetic name for Ireland), physical love, and romantic adoration. In "**Araby**" Joyce took Mangan's idealized girl as an embodiment of the artist's, especially the Irish artist's, relationship to his beloved, and then, combining the image of the girl with other resonating literary associations, wrote his own story of dawning, worshipful love.

III

It is easy to follow the external events of the story. A young boy becomes fascinated with his boyfriend's sister,

begins to dwell on her soft presence, and eventually adores her with an ecstasy of secret love. One day the girl speaks to him—it is one of the few times they have ever exchanged a word—and asks him if he is going to Araby. She herself cannot go, she tells him, for she must participate in a retreat. The boy says if he goes he will bring her a gift. When he finally visits the bazaar he is disillusioned by its tawdriness and by a banal conversation he overhears, and he buys no gift. Instead he feels "driven and derided by vanity" and his eyes burn with "anguish and anger."

"Driven and derided," "anguish and anger"—these reactions seem far too strong. Indeed they seem pretentious when compared to the trivial disillusionment which caused them. And they are pretentious, certainly they are inappropriate, if related only to their immediate external causes. But the boy is reacting to much more than a banal fair and a broken promise. He is reacting to sudden and deeply disturbing insights. These insights are shared by the attentive reader, for by the end of "**Araby**" the reader has been presented with all that he needs in order to resolve the story's intricate harmony into its component motifs.

Most of those motifs, both personal and public, are sounded at once. The former tenant of the boy's house, a house stale with the smell of mustiness and decay, had been a priest who had died in the back drawing room. In a litter of old papers in a waste room behind the kitchen the boy has found a few damp-stained volumes: "*The Abbot,* by Walter Scott, *The Devout Communicant,* and *The Memoirs of Vidocq.*" The only additional information Joyce gives us about these books is that the boy liked the last volume best because "its leaves were yellow." The musty books and the boy's response to them are doubly and trebly meaningful. Joyce chose works that would objectify the themes of "**Araby,**" works that would exemplify in the most blatant (yet unexpressed) manner the very confusions, veilings, and failures he was depicting in the priest and the boy. The books and their lurking incongruities help us arraign the priest and understand the boy. That the priest should leave a romance by Scott with a religious title that obscures the fact that it is the secular celebration of a worldly queen, Mary Queen of Scots, a queen enshrined in history as saint and harlot; a book of rules, meditations, anthems, and prayers for Holy Week by a Protestant clergyman named Abednego Seller, a clergyman who had written tracts against "Popish Priests," engaged in published controversy with a Jesuit divine, and was eventually relieved of his office; and a volume of lurid and often sexually suggestive memoirs by a notorious imposter, master of disguise, archcriminal, and police official—all this is a commentary on the priest and the religion he is supposed to represent. At the same time this literary debris objectifies the boy's confusions.

That Scott's unblemished romantic heroine, an idolized Catholic queen by the name of Mary, should also be (though not to Scott) a "harlot queen," a passionate thrice-married woman who was regarded by many of her contemporaries as the "Whore of Babylon," as a murderess who murdered to satisfy her lust—this strange dissonance, muted and obscured by Scott's presentation, is a version of the boy's strikingly similar and equally muted dissonances. That the dead priest's book of devotions is a Protestant manual by a man bearing the significant name, Abednego Seller—a name which combines in equal parts ancient religious associations (in particular associations of refusing to worship a golden image and of a faith strong enough to withstand a fiery furnace) with an ironically incongruous modern surname that has to do with selling and commercialism—this juxtaposition, also, is appropriate to the boy: it typifies one of his fundamental confusions.

That Vidocq should escape from a prison hospital disguised in the stolen habit of a nun, a veil over his face; that he should then assist a good-natured curé in celebrating mass, pretending to make the signs and genuflections prescribed for a nun—this is a version of what the boy will do. That *The Memoirs* should also contain the history of a beauty "who seemed to have been created as a model for the divine Madonnas which sprang from the imagination of Raphael," whose eyes "gave expression to all the gentleness of her soul," and who had a "heavenly forehead" and an "ethereal elegance"—but who, from the age of fourteen, had been a debauched prostitute who was ultimately caught by the police because, in the midst of committing a robbery, she and her accomplice became utterly engrossed in fornicating with one another—this, also, is a version, a grotesque extension, of the boy's confusions. The boy does not know, can not face, what he is. He gazes upon the things that attract or repel him, but they are blurred and veiled by clouds of romantic obfuscation: he likes *The Memoirs of Vidocq* best not because of what it is, a volume of exciting quasi-blasphemous criminal and sexual adventures, but because he finds its outward appearance, its yellowing leaves, romantically appealing. The boy, like the priest, or Vidocq's characters, or disguise-mad Vidocq himself, is, in effect, an imposter—only the boy is unaware of why he feels and acts as he does; the boy is an imposter through self-deception.

Joyce, in accordance with his practice throughout *Dubliners* (and for that matter, in accordance with his method throughout his writings) included these books so that we would make such generalizations about the priest and the boy. This is clear, not merely from his habitual usage in such matters or from the ironic significance of the books themselves, but from the highly directive import of the sentences which immediately follow these details. These sentences tell us that behind the boy's house was a "wild garden" containing a "central apple-tree"—images which strongly suggest a ruined Eden and Eden's forbidden central apple tree, a tree which has to do with man's downfall and his knowledge of good and evil: fundamental themes in **"Araby."** The last of the sentences is artfully inconclusive. "He had," concludes the narrator, "been a very charitable priest; in his will he had left all his money to institutions and the furniture of his house to his sister." Joyce's ambiguity suggests that the priest's charity may have been

as double-edged as other details in the opening paragraphs. Yet the possibility of an incongruity here never occurs to the boy. As usual he fails to examine beneath the veneer of outward appearances; he fails to allow for the possibility of a less public, more cynical interpretation of the priest's charity. If this worldly priest had been so "very charitable" why, at his death, was he able to donate "all his money" to institutions? His charity, so far as we know about it, began at his death.

These and other ambiguously worded ironies had already been sounded by the three opening sentences of **"Araby."** Joyce begins by telling us that North Richmond Street is blind. That North Richmond Street is a dead end is a simple statement of fact; but that the street is blind, especially since this feature is given significant emphasis in the opening phrases of the story, suggests that blindness plays a role thematically. It suggests, as we later come to understand, that the boy also is blind, that he has reached a dead end in his life. Finally, we are told that the houses of North Richmond Street "conscious of decent lives within them, gazed at one another with brown imperturbable faces." These words, too, are ironic. For the boy will shortly discover that his own consciousness of a decent life within has been a mirage; the imperturbable surface of North Richmond Street (and of the boy's life) will soon be perturbed.

In these opening paragraphs Joyce touches all the themes he will later develop: self-deluding blindness, self-inflating romanticism, decayed religion, mammonism, the coming into man's inheritance, and the gulf between appearance and reality. But these paragraphs do more: they link what could have been the idiosyncratic story of the boy, his problems and distortions, to the problems and distortions of Catholicism and of Ireland as a whole. In other words, the opening paragraphs (and one or two other sections) prevent us from believing that the fault is solely in the boy and not, to some extent at least, in the world that surrounds him, and still more fundamentally, in the nature of man himself.

IV

The boy, of course, contributes intricately to his own deception. His growing fascination for Mangan's sister is made to convey his blindness and his warring consciousness. Joyce suggests these confusions by the most artful images, symbolisms, and parallelisms. The picture of Mangan's sister which first sinks unforgettably into the boy's receptive mind is of the girl calling and waiting at her doorstep in the dusk, "her figure defined by the light from the half-opened door," while he plays in the twilight and then stands "by the railings looking at her." "Her dress," he remembered, "swung as she moved her body and the soft rope of her hair tossed from side to side."

This highly evocative, carefully staged, and carefully lit scene—it will recur throughout the story with slight but significant variations—gathers meaning as its many details take on definition and thematic importance. That importance was central to Joyce, and versions of the scene occur often in his writings. As his Mangan essay (1902) indicates, he had early chosen the adored female as an emblem of man's vanity, an emblem of false vision and self-delusion followed by insight and self-disdain. The female who appears in **"Araby"** (she appears again and again in his other writings) is such an emblem. The prototypical situation in all these appearances is of a male gazing at a female in a dim, veiled light. There are other features: the male usually looks up at the female; he often finds her standing half obscured near the top of some stairs and by a railing; he frequently notices her hair, her skirts, and her underclothes. But though the scene varies from appearance to appearance, the consequences are always the same. The male superimposes his own idealized vision upon this shadowy figure, only to have disillusioning reality (which has been there unregarded all the time) assert itself and devastate him. Joyce found this scene—with its shifting aureola of religious adoration, sexual beckoning, and blurred vision—infinitely suggestive, and he utilized it for major effects.

The prototypical scene occurs in Joyce's writings before **"Araby"** (1905). Around 1904, in *Chamber Music, XXX,* he depicted first-love as a "time gone by when one at twilight shyly played and one in fear was standing nigh," and then added punningly that "we were grave lovers" and "love is past." Later (around 1907), in **"The Dead,"** he drew another ambiguous lover. Gabriel Conroy stands in a dark hall at the foot of a dark staircase and gazes up through the gloom at a listening woman. His eyes linger on her shadowy skirt and shadowy form. The woman (who proves to be his wife, Gretta) is leaning on the stair railings. He is entranced by the grace and mystery of her attitude, "as if she were a symbol of something." But what, he asks, is a listening woman, standing on the stairs in the shadow, a symbol of? Then, with a blindness that will later be filled with terrible irony, he thinks how he would paint her if he were a painter: he would capture her in that attitude—leaning on the railings on the dark staircase—and he would feature her hair and her skirt. He would call the picture *Distant Music.* Gabriel's title is as deceptive as Gretta's pose. But insight and disillusionment are not far off. Gabriel will soon find out what distant music really means to his wife and to himself, and his life will never again be the same.

In *A Portrait of the Artist as a Young Man* (1904–14) the prototypical scene is conveyed through two girls. Stephen sees Emma, his beloved, standing under a grey "veiled sky" on the stairs of the library. He already doubts her constancy, and he takes "his place silently on the step below . . . turning his eyes towards her from time to time." While he gazes at her, she and her friends stand posing their umbrellas seductively and "holding their skirts demurely." Some days later Stephen is again standing on the steps of the library. The light has waned and he can hardly see. Suddenly his beloved is before him. He watches as she descends the steps of the library and bows to his sup-

planter, Cranly. "She had passed through the dusk. And therefore the air was silent save for one soft hiss that fell. . . . Darkness was falling." But though Stephen feels Emma betrays him, he uses her shadowy image to create the "Villanelle of the Temptress"—the only work of art he produces in *A Portrait,* and a poem which dwells on lures, fallen seraphim, chalices, longing gazes, lavish limbs, and the end of enchanted days.

These moments or vignettes from a fall, a fall which leads to insight and creation, are juxtaposed to an earlier episode in *A Portrait.* In the earlier scene, as Stephen strolls on the seashore, he hears the symbolic call to his destiny, the summons to become an artist. At this moment, in the "veiled grey sunlight," he sees a fair-haired birdlike girl wading in the sea, her slateblue skirts raised about her thighs, her softhued flesh girded by the "white fringes of her drawers." She feels the "worship of his eyes," and suffers his gaze, bending her eyes towards the stream. "Heavenly God!" cries Stephen to himself. In the "holy silence of his ecstasy," while "her image" passes "into his soul for ever," he commits himself "to live, to err, to fall, to triumph, to recreate life out of life!" But the ecstatic epiphany of the wading girl is soon deflated—not merely by the wasted sky and the grey sand which end the scene, but by the cold reality of its cognate, Emma's betrayal, to which the epiphany is juxtaposed. Paradoxically, the annunciatory visit of the birdgirl heralds only a hope; it is deflation, the beginning of betrayal, which stimulates creation.

Joyce's rejection of the romantic vision of the wading girl—and his continued interest in the voyeuristic scene of a male gazing at a shadowy female—is carried even further in the "Nausicaa" episode of *Ulysses* (1914–21) where he parodies this recurring scene with merciless brilliance. As the "Nausicaa" episode opens, dusk is falling. Bloom is sitting on Sandymount strand while a Benediction service (celebrated before a men's retreat) is going on in a nearby church. Bloom, too, is a celebrant; he is engaged in fervent devotions. He is gazing at Gerty MacDowell, "literally worshipping at her shrine." Gerty is eighteen and a virgin. From the nearby church, hymns of veneration ascend for the Host, for the Body, canticles of praise for Our Lady, for the Virgin Mary. Bloom concentrates on Gerty, who is enpedestaled on a rock by the water's edge. As he watches her settle her hair, swing her legs, and lift her skirts, his excitement grows. From the nearby Mirus bazaar (that is, "Wonderful" or "Perfumed" bazaar) which is raising funds for Mercer's hospital, a display of fireworks begins. Gerty uses the excuse of the fireworks to tempt Bloom, leaning back farther and farther, lifting her skirts higher and higher, and allowing him to see her thighs and her drawers. At almost the same moment, a hymn of adoration swells from the church; the priest kneels and looks up at the Blessed Sacrament, glorified now in the round ray-begirt opening of the monstrance, and displayed on high for all the venerating men to see. At this point Bloom's private service of veneration (like the one in the church) is coming to its conclusion. While Gerty lifts her skirts and displays herself, he masturbates to a climax. But having induced one deflation, he is about to undergo another. He realizes that Gerty is not what she seemed to be; she is a cripple, a lame, limping version of his self-inflated dream. And there are further abasements. Bloom's mind constantly circles back to the humiliating (yet strangely exciting) event of that afternoon: how Molly, his wife, displayed her lavish body before Blazes Boylan and brought that ardent lover to a more intimate climax. "Think you're escaping," muses Bloom, "and run into yourself." But now the distant music, the sacred incense, and the rapturous words "holy Mary holy virgin of virgins" have faded on the darkening air. The clock on the mantel of the priest's house concludes the deflation by uttering Shakespeare's absurd "word of fear."

> Cuckoo.
> Cuckoo.
> Cuckoo.

After the publication of *Ulysses,* Joyce explained that his method of writing in the "Nausicaa" episode was tumescence and detumescence; that the colors associated with the scene were blue (the color of the Virgin Mary—Gerty, a virgin who favors blue, is a parodic form of the Virgin Mary) and grey (the color of dusk); that the symbol of the chapter was the Virgin; that the organs involved in the episode were the nose (perfume and incense abound in the scene) and the eye (voyeurism); and that the art included in the section was painting.

V

"**Araby**" is a version—perhaps the most primordial version in Joyce—of this obsessively repeated scene. For in "**Araby**" the image of the worshipped girl is coterminous with, is a metaphor of, the entire story. The boy in "**Araby**," like Gabriel, will soon see that the portrait he has created—a romantic portrait that one might call *Young Adoration*—is a mockery, and his life will never again be the same. In "**Araby**" that portrait is of a girl in the dusk at her doorstep calling and waiting at her half-opened door, her figure defined by the light behind her. The picture is also of a boy standing by the railings looking up at her worshipfully. The suggestions evoked by the scene are of two utterly opposed sorts. On the one hand the image calls up associations of religious worship and spiritual adoration—the boy at the altar railing venerating a softly lit statue of the Virgin Mary—associations which will soon be powerfully underlined and elaborated. On the other hand, the image also suggests a seductive girl, even a harlot, calling and waiting at her half-opened door—the boy stares at her outlined figure, her swaying dress, her moving body, and her softly swinging hair—and these suggestions, too, will soon be underlined and elaborated. Lastly the image suggests Ireland, a country traditionally personified in Irish literature as a beautiful girl who is worshipped with mystical fervor. The two most famous literary embodiments of this personification are Cathleen ni Houlihan and Dark Rosaleen, the latter given its definitive popular form in "Dark Rosaleen," the poem by Mangan

that Joyce knew so well. In "**Araby**" Mangan's sister is adored and worshipped as Dark Rosaleen is in Mangan's poem, a parallel which many Irish readers would note at once, and a parallel which helps suggest that Mangan's sister is an embodiment of Ireland, is a new and more equivocal Dark Rosaleen. In "**Araby**" the girl is known only as Mangan's sister, an awkward and unaccountable substitute for a name (Mangan, the boy, is of no importance in the story) until one realizes that the circumlocution is designed to catch the reader's attention and direct his associations. Once the Mangan-"Dark Rosaleen" associations are called up, the parallels become charged with meaning. For Mangan's poem contains the same blend of physical love and religious adoration that Joyce makes the boy show for Mangan's sister. Dark Rosaleen has "holy, delicate white hands," is "my virgin flower, my flower of flowers," and can make the lover "kneel all night in prayer." Dark Rosaleen's name is like "lightning in my blood"; Mangan's sister's name is "like a summons to all my foolish blood." The poem exactly depicts the boy's unrest, his obsessive focus on the girl, his fusion of queen and saint, and his strange holy ardor:

> All day long, in unrest,
>   To and fro, do I move.
> The very soul within my breast
>   Is wasted for you, love!
> The heart in my bosom faints
>   To think of you, my Queen,
> My life of life, my saint of saints,
>   My Dark Rosaleen!
>   My own Rosaleen!
> To hear your sweet and sad complaints,
> My life, my love, my saint of saints,
>   My Dark Rosaleen!

Joyce begins, then, with a subtly evocative blend of spirituality, sexuality, and nationality; he immediately goes on to develop each motif in concert with the others. The boy remembers Mangan's sister as a "brown figure," and every morning, in an unvarying ritual, he actually prostrates himself before her image, lying on the floor in the front parlor and waiting for her to emerge so that he can follow her. This ritualistic abasement and prostration is appropriate to the boy's rapidly developing obsession. Like De Quincey's young boy, he has had his heart stolen away; he, too, has become idolatrous; through this girl, "by languishing desires," he has, all unknown to himself, "worshipped the worm, and prayed to the wormy grave."

For the boy has begun to worship Mangan's dark sister as all that is spiritual and holy and romantic; he has begun to utilize her idolatrously as an interceding saint, as a charm against the commercialism and materialism of the market place. When on Saturday evenings the boy accompanies his aunt in her marketing, the "image" of Mangan's sister is always with him. The language of the passage suggests that unconsciously, from the boy's point of view, two warring services are being conducted in the market place: the world's materialistic service in worship of mammon, and the boy's holy service in worship of his mild madonna.

The "flaring streets" are filled with their proper votaries: drunken men, bargaining women, and cursing laborers; they are also filled with an appropriate liturgical music: the "shrill litanies" of shopboys, the "nasal chanting" of street singers. In this materialistic world, so hostile to all that the boy imagines he believes in, he keeps himself inviolate by invoking his own secret service of worship. That service transmutes the stubborn commonplaces of everyday life into holy artifacts, holy strivings, and holy deeds of chivalry. The image of Mangan's sister becomes his sacred chalice; he guards it as he makes his way through the alien market place. "I imagined," he says, as he walks one Saturday evening through the market place, his mind fixed on the holy "image" of Mangan's sister, "that I bore my chalice safely through a throng of foes." This religious imagery continues to clothe and veil his impulses. He soon finds himself venerating his lady in "strange prayers and praises." His eyes often fill with tears, emotion floods from his heart; he wonders how he could ever tell her of his "confused adoration."

One evening, while in this excited state of sensual religiosity, the boy enters the back drawing room in which the priest had died. Thus begins the first of two vigils the boy will keep for Mangan's sister. The boy is about to lose himself in an ecstasy of devotion, and Joyce wants us to see that the boy is tenanting the same rooms and worshipping at the same shrines as the dead priest; that is, that the boy, like the priest, has begun to mix devotion with profanation, spirituality with materialism. The evening is dark and rainy. Through a broken pane the boy hears "the rain impinge upon the earth, the fine incessant needles of water playing in the sodden beds." The collocation of images is part of a cluster that Joyce used throughout his writings to suggest earthiness and bodily appetites (just before Mangan's sister's first appearance Joyce associated the boy with "dark dripping gardens where odours arose from the ashpits, [and] the dark odorous stables") and now, watching the rain and the earth and the sodden beds through his broken window, the boy again begins his confused adorations. Below him gleams "some distant lamp or lighted window"—Joyce continues to light his special scenes in ways equally suggestive of a sanctuary or a brothel—and then the blind boy, living on his blind street, looking through his broken window, says with deepest irony: "I was thankful that I could see so little."

In a moment the boy will be invoking love incarnate; senses veiled, swooning in self-delusion, palms pressed together in devotion, he will murmur his fervent prayers. Joyce conveys this tremulous sublimation—how the boy veils his sensual responses in the garment of religious ritual—by the most artfully directive language. "All my senses," says the boy, "seemed to desire to veil themselves and, feeling that I was about to slip from them, I pressed the palms of my hands together until they trembled, murmuring: '*O love! O love!*' many times." Every phrase is loaded with ironic meaning. The boy does not realize how truly his senses are veiling themselves (or for that matter, in what manner they are being veiled), nor does he understand, in the context, the religious connotations of the word "veil," or the physical connotations of the word "desire"; and slipping from his senses is what he emphatically is *not* doing as he tremblingly invokes Love.

The next sentence in the story, one which begins a new paragraph, is short and disconcerting: "At last she spoke to me." The abrupt transitionless juxtaposition of the boy's swooning invocation of Love, palms pressed prayerfully together, and the girl's sudden apparition is purposely ambiguous. Without saying so—without, that is, introducing the supernatural by having the girl materialize before him upon his prayerful invocation (for the remainder of the passage makes it clear that the girl did not speak to him that night), Joyce suggests, at least he gains the effect, that a visitation, an epiphany, has indeed occurred as a result of the boy's invocation. But whom has the boy invoked? Love? The Virgin? His Lady? Ireland? Levana? A harlot? He is too confused to know. The girl's first words to him—"Are you going to Araby?"—confound him. It will be a "splendid bazaar," she tells him; she would "love" to go, but she must attend a retreat in her convent. The boy is "so confused" he does "not know what to answer." His confusion is understandable. For here in epitome are correlatives of the very things that have confused and will continue to confuse him: materialism (the splendid bazaar), sensuality (love), and spirituality (the convent retreat).

As Mangan's sister speaks to him, she turns a "silver bracelet round and round her wrist." The boy stands "alone at the railings," gazing at this Madonna of the Silver Bracelet. "She held one of the spikes, bowing her head towards me. The light from the lamp opposite our door caught the white curve of her neck, lit up her hair that rested there and, falling, lit up the hand upon the railing. It fell over one side of her dress and caught the white border of a petticoat, just visible as she stood at ease."

This wonderfully evocative scene strikes the chords of commingled spirituality, sensuality, and materalism with increasing force. That commingling is central to **"Araby"**; it is also central to Joyce's life. As the story of his life makes clear, Joyce was a materialist, a man of almost paranoiac cupidity and selfishness. He was also a person strongly attracted to the spiritual and the sensual. He told his brother, Stanislaus, that his chief reason for not becoming a priest was that he could not remain chaste. In *A Portrait of the Artist as a Young Man* we learn of the dark ways and dark ladies that so early summoned his "foolish blood." When Stephen enters Nighttown for his first visit to a prostitute, he is seized by a trembling, his eyes grow dim, the yellow flares of gas burn "as if before an altar," and the people near the doors and in the lighted halls seem "arrayed as for some rite." That Joyce should render the loss of virginity as a religious rite is consonant with his outlook and his method. In his writings we are constantly privy to the perverse warfare of sacred and profane love, to the clamorous intermixings of doctrine and experience. In *Ulysses,* when Stephen sets off for Nighttown and the bawdyhouses, he thinks, "We . . . will seek the kips where shady Mary is." And in *Finnegans Wake* Joyce was fond of introducing such meldings as "Merryvirgin," "marrimount," "Hollymerry," "fingringmaries," and "hellmuirries."

One of the memorable scenes in *A Portrait*—it is a scene which dwells on the blasphemous conjoining of sacred and profane love—is that in which Stephen, fresh from the stews and with the savor of a harlot's kisses on his lips, kneels reverently at the altar to lead his sodality in their Saturday morning devotions to the Blessed Virgin Mary:

> Her eyes seemed to regard him with mild pity; her holiness, a strange light glowing faintly upon her frail flesh . . . The impulse that moved him was the wish to be her knight. If ever his soul, re-entering her dwelling shyly after the frenzy of his body's lust had spent itself, was turned towards her whose emblem is the morning star, "bright and musical, telling of heaven and infusing peace," it was when her names were murmured softly by lips whereon there still lingered foul and shameful words, the savour itself of a lewd kiss.

This deceptive fusion of knightly chivalry, spiritual devotion, and desecrating lust (all carefully lit)—it is Joyce's recurrent fusion, the fusion which reaches its culmination in the "Nausicaa" episode of *Ulysses*—had occurred even earlier in yet another evocation (in this case a striking premonition rather than a later extrapolation) of Mangan's shadowy sister. Between 1900 and 1903, that is, a few years before writing **"Araby,"** Joyce added to his slender collection of *Epiphanies* a scene in which the pose, the lighting, the physical features, the language, the connotations (the madonna allusion, and the conjoining of ape and martyrs' legends, for example)—all prefigure **"Araby."** Here is the epiphany in its entirety:

> She stands, her book held lightly at her breast, reading the lesson. Against the dark stuff of her dress her face, mild-featured with downcast eyes, rises softly outlined in light; and from a folded cap, set carelessly forward, a tassel falls along her brown ringletted hair . . .
>
> What is the lesson that she reads—of apes, of strange inventions, or the legends of martyrs? Who knows how deeply meditative, how reminiscent is this comeliness of Raffaello?

These recurrent comminglings help us establish the meaning of **"Araby"**; they show us that these fusions are intentional, that the aura of worship and desire, romanticism and corruption that Joyce casts over Mangan's sister is at the heart of **"Araby."**

VI

All women, for Joyce, are Eves: they tempt and they betray. He constantly fashions his women, fictional and real—Mangan's sister, Gretta, Mary Sheehy, Emma, Nora, Molly—into exemplars of this idea. By the same token, men, in their yearning to worship, contrive (perhaps even desire) their own betrayal and insure their own disillusionment. This paradox, which embodies Joyce's personal

needs and experiences, is at the center of *Exiles*. It also helps shape *A Portrait, Ulysses,* and *Finnegans Wake.* In the latter work the notion is universalized and multiplied. One of the primal forms of woman in *Finnegans Wake* is woman as temptress. She is portrayed most clearly as Isabel, the daughter of HCE and Anna Livia, and as the Maggies or Magdalenes (who appear in dozens of permutations: maudelenian, Margareena, Marie Maudlin, etc.), the two girls who tempted HCE to his fall in Phoenix Park, and who are often merged with Isabel. This archetypal temptress and goddess, blending and changing in a flux of protean metamorphoses (she is also Issy, Issis, Ishtar, Isolde—as Isolde of Ireland, an embodiment of Ireland) is frequently referred to as "Ysold," "I sold," "Issabil," "eyesoult," and "eyesalt." As her godlike role and legendary names imply, she combines worshipful love and sexual appeal (Isolde), with inevitable commercialism and betrayal (I sold), with bitter grief and disillusionment (eyesalt)—the combination and progression we also find in **"Araby."**

What Joyce is saying in **"Araby"** becomes more precise as the details accumulate and fall into patterns. This second evocation of the carefully lit figure of Mangan's sister, now in the guise of the Madonna of the Silver Bracelet, is worth examining once more, this time in the context of what we have just been tracing:

> While she spoke she turned a silver bracelet round and round her wrist. . . . I was alone at the railings. She held one of the spikes, bowing her head towards me. The light from the lamp opposite our door caught the white curve of her neck, lit up her hair that rested there and, falling, lit up the hand upon the railing. It fell over one side of her dress and caught the white border of a petticoat, just visible as she stood at ease.

This second evocation of Mangan's sister is again filled with strange harmonies. On the one hand the passage calls up Mary Magdalene and the Blessed Virgin Mary (both were present at the crucifixion) and soft overtones of a tender and dolorous *pietà;* one easily extracts and then extrapolates the appropriate images—the patient hand on the cruel spike, the gentle head bowed submissively, the mild neck arched in grief. But a coequal and co-ordinate pattern in the scene is the harlotry associations of Mary Magdalene, who, in Catholic liturgy, is specifically associated with exotic Near Eastern imagery, bracelets, and crossing the city in search of her love—all strong elements in **"Araby"**; while on the more personal level the name "Mary" is also the name of the girl Joyce regarded as his original "temptress" and "betrayer"—Mary Sheehy; and perhaps, at the same time, this "shady Mary" pattern is connected with the harlotry associations of still another Mary, the "harlot queen," Mary Queen of Scots, the heroine of the dead priest's book, *The Abbot,* who was executed in her petticoat. In any case, the negative pattern incorporated in the shadowy image of Mangan's sister combines hints of commercialism and sensuality with connotations of sexuality and betrayal—the turning and turning of the silver bracelet, the head bowing toward the boy, the white curve of the bare neck, the soft hair glowing in the light, the side of the dress accentuated by the dim glow, the white border of the petticoat just visible beneath the dress (one recalls the dream-shattering petticoat of the false Protestant madonna in "Our Lady of the Hills"), and the whole figure standing at ease in the dusk.

The boy now makes his pledge. "If I go," he says, "I will bring you something." The consequences of his pledge are immediately apparent. "What innumerable follies," writes the narrator in the very next sentence, "laid waste my waking and sleeping thoughts after that evening!" The shadowy "image" of Mangan's sister constantly comes between him and everything he undertakes; his schoolmaster, puzzled and then exasperated, hopes that he is "not beginning to idle"—a phrase which again, now punningly, underlines that the boy, like De Quincey's young boy, has indeed begun to worship false idols, that he is well on his way to Araby.

Araby—the very word connotes the nature of the boy's confusion. It is a word redolent of the lush East, of distant lands, Levantine riches, romantic entertainments, mysterious magic, "Grand Oriental Fêtes." The boy immerses himself in this incense-filled dream world. He tells us that "the syllables of the word *Araby* were called to me through the silence in which my soul luxuriated and cast an Eastern enchantment over me." That enchantment, or to put it another way, Near Eastern imagery (usually in conjunction with female opulence or romantic wish fulfillment), always excited Joyce. It reappears strongly in *Ulysses* in a highly intricate counterpoint, which is sometimes serious (Molly's Moorish attributes) and sometimes mocking (Bloom's dream of a Messianic Near Eastern oasis). But the boy in **"Araby"** always interprets these associations, no matter how disparate or how ambiguous they are, in one way: as correlatives of a baroquely beatific way of living. Yet the real, brick-and-mortar Araby in the boy's life is a bazaar, a market, a place where money and goods are exchanged. The boy is blind to this reality lurking beneath his enchanted dream. To the boy, his lady's silver bracelet is only part of her Eastern finery; his journey to a bazaar to buy her an offering is part of a romantic quest. But from this point on in the story the masquerading pretenses of the boy—and of his church, his land, his rulers, and his love—are rapidly underlined and brought into a conjunction which will pierce his perfervid dream world and put an end to "enchanted days."

The boy has arranged with his aunt and uncle that he will go to the bazaar on Saturday evening, that is, on the evening of the day specially set aside for veneration of the Virgin Mary. Saturday evening arrives but the boy's uncle is late from work and the boy wanders at loose ends through the empty upper reaches of his house. In the "high cold empty gloomy rooms" he begins his second vigil. Off by himself he feels liberated. He goes from room to room singing. Hidden, he watches his companions play and listens to their weakened, indistinct cries. Then he leans his forehead against a cool window pane and looks over at the "dark house" where Mangan's sister lives. "I may have

stood there for an hour, seeing nothing but the brown-clad figure cast by my imagination, touched discreetly by the lamplight at the curved neck, at the hand upon the railings and at the border below the dress."

When he goes downstairs again he is brought back from the isolated world of his imagination to the ordinary world of his everyday life. He finds Mrs. Mercer sitting at the fire. "She was an old garrulous woman, a pawnbroker's widow, who collected used stamps for some pious purpose." The sentence is packed with ironic meaning. The old lady's name—Mercer, that is, merchandise, wares, a small-ware dealer—links her to the commercial focus of the story. That her husband was a pawnbroker sharpens this focus, introducing as it does commercialism in its most abhorrent form from the church's point of view—commercialism as usury. But that the church accepts, even lives on, this same commercialism is also made clear: for garrulous old Mrs. Mercer (another embodiment of Ireland) is a pious woman with pious purposes; ironically, she expresses her piety in good works that depend upon empty mechanical acquisitiveness: she collects used stamps. (One recalls, in this connection, the "pious purpose" of the actual Araby bazaar—to collect money for a hospital; and one also recalls that the "Wonderful" or "Perfumed" bazaar in *Ulysses*—the bazaar that allowed Bloom to gaze worshipfully under Gerty's skirts while a choir celebrated the Host and hymned the Virgin Mary—was an attempt to collect money for another "pious purpose," for a hospital named "Mercer's.") Joyce is saying, in effect, that everyday religion and piety in Ireland are based upon self-deluding and mindless materialism. When Mrs. Mercer's unexamined commercial religion is remembered in conjunction with the boy's and then the dead priest's (one recalls that the priest's book of heretical devotions was by a man named "Seller")—we get some idea of how insidiously mammonistic is Ireland's religious bankruptcy.

The boy will soon have some insight into this and other bankruptcies, but at the moment he is taut with frustrated anticipation. "I am afraid," says his aunt, when his uncle still fails to appear, "you may put off your bazaar for this night of Our Lord"—counterpointing "bazaar" and "Our Lord," money and religion. Then, at nine O'clock, the uncle finally returns, tipsy and talking to himself. He has forgotten the bazaar, and he tries to put the boy off, but the aunt insists that he give the boy money for the bazaar, and he finally agrees, after the boy tells him twice that he is going to Araby. The word "Araby" sets the uncle's mind working. He asks the boy if he knows *The Arab's Farewell to His Steed,* and as the boy leaves the room, the uncle is about to recite the opening lines of the poem to his wife. Those lines never appear in the story, but they are fraught with thematic significance:

> My beautiful, my beautiful! that standeth meekly by,
>
> With thy proudly-arched and glossy neck, and dark and fiery eye!
>
> Fret not to roam the desert now with all thy wingèd speed;

I may not mount on thee again!—thou'rt sold, my Arab steed!

The notion of betrayal, of something loved and beautiful being sold for money, of something cherished and depended upon being lost forever, is central to what has already happened in **"Araby"** and what is about to take place. But the poem goes on with even greater cogency:

The stranger hath thy bridle-rein, thy master hath his gold;—

Fleet-limbed and beautiful, farewell!—thou'rt sold, my steed, thou'rt sold!

This cogency—turning the bridle reins over to a foreign master for money, saying farewell to a beautiful part of the past—has another and even more startling appropriateness. For the poem is by Caroline Norton, a great beauty and a member of a famous Irish family (her grandfather was Richard Brinsley Sheridan), who was sued for divorce by her husband, the Hon. George Chapple Norton, on the grounds that she had committed adultery with Lord Melbourne, then Home Secretary but at the time of the suit in 1836 prime minister of Great Britain. As Home Secretary, Lord Melbourne had been the minister responsible for Ireland, and in 1833, while still Home Secretary, he had supported the Coercion Bill, a bill of great severity aimed at Irish nationalists. The trial which ensued—one of the most notorious in the nineteenth century—was used by Dickens in the breach-of-promise suit in *Pickwick*, by Thackeray in the Lord Steyne-Becky Sharp relationship in *Vanity Fair*, and by Meredith in some of the climactic scenes of *Diana of the Crossways*. The jury found for the defendants, but chiefly on grounds other than Caroline Norton's constancy. The defendants won after conclusive testimony was introduced showing that Norton had been the chief advocate of his wife's liaison with Lord Melbourne, that he had initiated and perpetuated the liaison as a means of advancing himself, and that he had brought suit only after he had suffered reverses in that advancement.

That an Irish woman as beautiful as Caroline Norton should have been sold by her husband for English preferments; that she should have been sold to the man who, in effect, was the English ruler of Ireland; that she, in turn, should have been party to such a sale; that this very woman, writing desperately for money, should compose a sentimental poem celebrating the traitorous sale of a beautiful and supposedly loved creature; and that this poem should later be cherished by the Irish (the uncle's recitation is in character, the poem was a popular recitation piece, it appears in almost every anthology of Irish poetry)—all this is patently and ironically appropriate to what Joyce is saying.

So also is the next scene in **"Araby."** The boy leaves his house on the way to Araby with a florin, a piece of silver money, clutched tightly in his hand. That Joyce, out of all the coins and combinations of coins available to him, chose to have the boy clutch a florin is doubly meaningful. The

original florin, the prototype of all future coins bearing that name, was a gold coin, famed for its purity, minted in Florence in 1252. It received its name, "florin," that is, "flower," because, like many of its progeny, it bore a lily, the flower of Florence and of the Virgin Mary, on one side. On the other side it bore the figure of Saint John the Baptist in religious regalia, a man who gave his life rather than betray his religion. The florin the boy clutches, however, is a silver coin minted by the English with a head of Queen Victoria on one side and the Queen's coat of arms (including the conquered harp of Ireland) on the other. Owing to the fact that the customary "Dei Gratia, F. D." ("by the grace of God, defender of the faith") was omitted from the coin when originally issued in 1847, it became infamous as the "Godless and Graceless Florin" and aroused such a popular outcry that it had to be called in before the year was out. As a result, the Master of the Mint, a Roman Catholic, was dismissed, and a few years later a new but almost identical florin was issued with the usual motto. The malodorous genesis of the English coin, its association with a Catholic scapegoat, and the restitution of a motto which, from an Irish Catholic point of view, made the coin as idolatrous and offensive as the Godless version—all this is ideally suited to Joyce's purpose.

For the duped boy is now acting out his betrayal in the most emblematic way. We recall the intricate liturgy of his self-delusion. Despising the market place, he had summoned and protected the image of Mangan's sister as a holy chalice antithetical to all such worldly commerce; mistaking his impulses, he had transformed his sexual desires into prayers and praises for the Virgin, into worshipful Catholic devotions. That the boy who immersed himself in such ceremonious self-deception should be hastening to buy at a bazaar (where, incidentally, he will meet his English masters) and that he should be clutching an English florin, an alien and notorious silver coin sans Virgin's lily and sans Catholic saint but bearing instead symbols of his and Ireland's servitude and betrayal, is, of course, supremely ironic.

That irony continues and expands in what follows. It is Saturday night. The boy tells us that "the sight of streets thronged with buyers and glaring with gas recalled to me the purpose of my journey." The flaring streets "thronged with buyers" and the clutched silver coin call to the reader's mind a purpose far different from that which the boy thinks he is pursuing. The sights, the words, the Saturday evening, the silver florin, also recall that the last time the boy went into the flaring streets shopping through throngs of buyers on a Saturday night, he had said, speaking particularly of those buyers, "I imagined that I bore my chalice safely through a throng of foes." They recall also that Saturday is the day most particularly devoted to veneration of the Blessed Virgin Mary. We now see clearly what the boy bears through a throng of foes, what his chalice is: it is not the image of a mild spiritual madonna, it is money, the alien florin of betrayal—betrayal of his religion, his nation, his dream of supernal love; he, like his country, has betrayed himself for the symbolic piece of alien silver he clutches in his hand as he hurries on to Araby. We also begin to get a better notion of who the shadowy madonna is that he worships with such febrile spirituality. We recall that he is rushing headlong to a bazaar to buy his lady a token (he, too, is one of the throng of buyers), and then we recall how his madonna—could she be a false, sensual, materialistic madonna, a projection of his own complicated self-betrayal?—"turned a silver bracelet round and round her wrist."

The boy at last arrives at the large building which displays "the magical name" of *Araby*. In his haste to get into the closing bazaar, he passes through a shilling rather than a sixpenny entrance, handing the gatekeeper his silver coin as he goes through the turnstile. The interior of the building is like a church. The great central hall, circled at half its height by a gallery, contains dark stalls, dim lights, and curtained, jar-flanked sanctuaries. Joyce wants us to regard this temple of commerce as a place of worship. "I recognised a silence," says the boy as he stands in the middle of the hall, "like that which pervades a church after a service." The service is, of course, the worship of mammon, and Joyce, by his use of religious imagery here and throughout the story, lets us see both that the money-changers are in the temple (if one looks at the bazaar as a correlative of the church), and that the really devout worship which goes on in Ireland now, goes on in the market place: the streets thronged with buyers, the shrill litanies of shopboys, the silver-braceleted madonnas, the church-like bazaars. Even he who imagined that he bore his chalice safely through a throng of foes finds himself in the temple of the money-changers ready to buy. Shocked, and with growing awareness, the boy begins to realize where he is and what he is doing. In the half-dark hall, as the bazaar closes and the remaining lights begin to go out, he watches as two men work before a curtain lit overhead by a series of colored lamps upon which a commercial inscription is emblazoned. The two men "were counting money on a salver. I listened to the fall of the coins." The boy also has fallen. We recall the "wild garden" with its "central apple-tree," that the words "falling" and "fell" are crucial to the description of Mangan's sister during her epiphany before the boy, and that the word "fall" again recurs—again in connection with money—when the boy, in his penultimate action, an action reminiscent of how Judas let the silver of betrayal fall upon the ground after his contrition, allows "two pennies to fall against the sixpence" in his pocket as he finally turns to leave the bazaar. But right now the fallen boy is witnessing the counting of the collection before the sanctuary of this church of mammon (the curtain, the salver, the lamps, the inscription all suggest simultaneously the sanctuary of a Catholic church); he is listening to the music of this service of mammon, the clink of falling coins. The boy is so stupefied that he can remember only "with difficulty why [he] had come."

His shock and his disillusionment are not yet over. He sees a young saleslady standing at the door of one of the dark stalls. The reader, like the boy, instantly feels that he has viewed this scene before: the girl standing in the doorway, the dim lighting, the churchlike atmosphere. Then, suddenly, the reader realizes that the scene enforces a crucial juxtaposition; the waiting salesgirl is a parody of the boy's obsessive image of female felicity, she is a counterpart (an everyday, commercial counterpart) of Mangan's tenebrous sister. The boy looks steadily at this vulgar avatar of his longings; and then his other vision—his vision of a comely waiting presence, of a heavenly dolorous lady—dissolves and finally evaporates. The boy, at last, glimpses reality unadorned; he no longer deceives himself with his usual romanticizing. For the moment, at least, he truly sees. There before him stands a dull, drab, vacuous salesgirl; she is no mild Irish madonna, no pensive *pietà*, no mutely beckoning angel. He listens as she talks and laughs with two young gentlemen; the three of them have English accents:

"O, I never said such a thing!"

"O, but you did!"

"O, but I didn't!"

"Didn't she say that?"

"Yes, I heard her."

"O, there's a . . . fib!"

This snippet of banal conversation is Joyce's, the boy's, and now the reader's epiphany—the word "epiphany" used here in Joyce's special literary sense of "a sudden spiritual manifestation, whether in the vulgarity of speech or of gesture or in a memorable phase of the mind itself"—and the conversation the boy overhears bears an unmistakable resemblance to a well-defined type of epiphany which Joyce recorded (bald exchanges of fatuous, almost incoherent conversation), several examples of which have survived. But what we have here is the epiphany surrounded by all that is needed to give it significance; the private *quidditas* has been transformed into a public showing forth; the artist, the priest of the eternal imagination, has transmuted (to paraphrase another of Joyce's religious metaphors) the daily bread of experience into the radiant body of everliving art.

For what the boy now sees, and what we now know he sees, is that his worshipped madonna is only a girl, like the ordinary girl who stands before him, that his interest in his madonna is akin to the gentlemen's interest in the young lady before them, and that their pedestrian conversation about fibbing—the very word is a euphemism for "lying"—is only a banal version of his own intricate euphemisms, his own gorgeous lying to himself. Like the Catholic boy in Yeats' "Our Lady of the Hills," who sobs in anguish because his vision of a palpable madonna must give way to the reality of an ordinary Protestant girl, the boy in **"Araby"** can now also cry out angrily, "I'm a divil, and you are only an ordinary lady."

That this ordinary lady is an English lady is another shattering part of the boy's painful epiphany. The English accents are the accents of the ruling race, the foreign conquerors—Joyce makes much of this notion in *A Portrait* and more in *Ulysses*—and now the boy begins to understand that England, this nation which rules over him, is quintessentially vulgar, the servant par excellence of mammon. England is one with Ireland and Ireland's church, and the boy is one with all of these. He has felt the first stirrings of desire and converted them into masquerading religiosity; he has wanted to go shopping at a bazaar and has told himself that he is making an enchanted journey to fetch a chivalric token; he has been exposed to the debased vulgarities of *The Memoirs of Vidocq* and has admitted only that he liked its yellow pages. Yet he is no worse than the rest of Ireland—its dead priests (part of a dying church), its Mrs. Mercers, its faithless drunken surrogate fathers—and for that matter, no worse than Ireland's rulers. Ireland and Ireland's church, once appropriately imaged as a romantic lady or a sorrowful madonna, has now become cuckquean and harlot—she is sold and sells for silver.

Joyce returned to this theme again and again, often with startling repetitions of details and symbols. In *Ulysses,* for example, Ireland appears personified not as a young girl, but as an old milkwoman. She enters and leaves *Ulysses* in a page or two, yet within that cramped space, and despite the vast difference, on the realistic level, between the role she must play in *Ulysses* and the roles of those who appear in **"Araby,"** Joyce manages to associate her with many of the idiosyncratic features that characterize Ireland and Ireland's betrayal in **"Araby."** In *Ulysses* the old milkwoman is depicted as "an immortal serving her conqueror [Haines, the Englishman] and her gay betrayer [Mulligan, the Irishman], their common cuckquean." Mulligan sings a song about her "hising up her petticoats"; she tells him she is ashamed she must speak in foreign accents; she is depicted "slipping the ring of the milkcan on her forearm" (the silver bracelet again); and she is paid by Mulligan with a silver florin.

VII

Other elements in **"Araby"** are also connected to patterns that transcend the immediate action. The two most crucial events in the story, the two vigils, harmonize with specific occasions in the Roman Catholic liturgy. The first vigil—the one in which Mangan's sister appears after the boy's invocation, *"O love! O love!"*—suggests the Vigil of the Epiphany. The most striking passage in that Vigil tells how "in those childish days of ours we toiled away at the schoolroom tasks which the world gave us, till the appointed time came"—a passage which is exactly appropriate to how the boy, after his first visitation or epiphany (that is, after Mangan's sister has appeared to him and directed him to Araby—just as in the original Epiphany an angel appeared to Joseph directing him to go from Egypt to Israel) feels about the schoolroom tasks ("child's play, ugly monotonous child's play") while he waits for the time of his journey to Araby. But the "appointed time" spoken of in the Vigil is the time of the journey to Israel

and of the coming of the spirit of Jesus, not of a trip to Araby; it is the time when the spirit of Jesus cries out to a child, "Abba, Father," and he becomes no longer a child, a slave, but a son of God, entitled to "the son's right of inheritance." For the boy in **"Araby"** that cry and that inheritance turn out to be far different from what he believed them to be—he comes into a majority, but it is the disillusioning majority of the flesh, of all the sons of Adam, not of the spirit; he makes his journey, but it is a journey to Egypt, to Araby, to the market place, not back to the Holy Land.

These reverberating liturgical harmonies are continued in the boy's second vigil—the one he keeps during his long evening wait, and then during his journey to and sojourn in Araby. The connections here are with Holy Week (especially the Passion) and with Holy Saturday (the night before Easter Sunday). In **"Araby"** the trip to the bazaar takes place on a Saturday night; the boy's aunt refers to the Saturday night in question as "this night of Our Lord," an expression which can be applied to any Saturday (or Sabbath) night, but which calls up most particularly the pre-eminent Saturday "night of Our Lord," that is, Holy Saturday. The service appointed for this occasion is the Mass of Holy Saturday. This Mass, owing to its great beauty, and especially to the rich symbolism of the Tenebrae, haunted Joyce. (The whole of Book IV of *Finnegans Wake,* for example, takes place in the instant between Holy Saturday and Easter Sunday.) The Mass of Holy Saturday was the only Mass Joyce regularly tried to witness later in life, always leaving, however, before communion. Central to this Mass is the imagery of light and darkness, the extinguishing of the old lights and then the rekindling of new lights from new fire. On the other hand, prominent in the Passion is the notion of betrayal: Peter's lying threefold denial of Jesus, and Judas' selling of Jesus for thirty pieces of silver. The idea of profound betrayal, then the adumbration of awakening and rising, all combined with imagery of light and dark, and the whole counterpointed with liturgical overtones, informs the conclusion of **"Araby."**

The boy, for instance, comes to Araby with silver in his hand (with the idolatrous successor to the Godless Florin, it will be remembered); and he watches as the money of betrayal (his and his nation's) falls clinking on the salver. Like Peter's lying threefold denial of Jesus, the banal conversation about lying that the boy overhears also involves a threefold denial (the girl denies three times that she said what she is accused of saying). The foreign English accents continue the parallel, for Peter, like the English, is a foreigner, and his denials involve his accent. "Even thy speech betrays thee," he is told. When Peter recognized his betrayal (at the crowing of the cock) he "wept bitterly"; when the boy recognized his (at the call that the light was out) his "eyes burned with anguish and anger." In the service for Holy Saturday the lights are extinguished and then relit; in the service the boy witnesses there is no rekindling, the boy merely gazes "up into the darkness." And yet, of course, here too a new light is lit; for though an old faith is extinguished, we witness a dawning.

These liturgical and religious parallels and disparities (one could list other much more subterranean ones: the story of Abednego is told *in extenso* in the Holy Saturday Mass, and Abednego Seller's heretical *Devout Communicant* is a manual for Holy Week), these parallels lie unobtrusively in the background. They are not meant to be strictly or allegorically interpreted; they are meant to suggest, to hint, perhaps to condition. Unconsciously they tinge our associations and responses; they also harmonize with the more explicit motifs of the story.

The boy standing in front of the young lady's shadowy booth, listening to her bantering inanities, perceives all these significances only dimly. He is shocked, hurt, angered; but he intuitively feels, and will later understand, what the reader already comprehends. Yet even in his dim awareness he is ready to make one decision. While still at the "dark entrance" of the young lady's stall, he tells her he is no longer interested in "her wares." He lets the two pennies fall against the sixpence in his pocket; he has come to buy, but he has not bought. Someone calls that the light is out. The light is indeed out. Like De Quincey's young boy, the boy in **"Araby"** has been excluded from light, has worshipped the "lovely darkness" of the grave; he has (in the words of *Chamber Music*, XXX) been a "grave lover." But again like De Quincey's young boy, at last he has seen. He has risen again *before* he has died; he has begun to unfold "the capacities of his spirit." As *Chamber Music*, XXX, has it, he welcomes now "the ways that [he] shall go upon." For the boy has caught a glimpse of himself as he really is—a huddled, warring, confused paradox of romantic dreams, mistaken adorations, and mute fleshly cravings—and one portion of his life, his innocent, self-deluding childhood, is now behind him. In his pride and arrogance, and, yes, in his purity and innocence too, he had imagined that he bore his chalice safely through a throng of foes; instead, he had rushed headlong toward that which he thought he most despised. In a land of betrayers, he had betrayed himself. But now he understands some of this; and now, raising his eyes up into the blackness, but totally blind no more—the Christlike fusion here of ascent, of sight, and of agony is all-important—he can say, "Gazing up into the darkness I saw myself as a creature driven and derided by vanity; and my eyes burned with anguish and anger."

VIII

Joyce has succeeded, here, in taking the raw, rather humdrum, unpromising facts of his own life and transforming them into abiding patterns of beauty and illumination. He has taken a universal experience—a more or less ordinary experience of insight, disillusionment, and growth—and given it an extraordinary application and import. The experience becomes a criticism of a nation, a religion, a civilization, a way of existing; it becomes a grappling hook with which we can scale our own well-guarded citadels of self-delusion. Joyce does all this in six or seven pages. He manages this feat by endowing the simple phrases and actions of **"Araby"** with multiple meanings that deepen and enlarge what he is saying.

The image of Mangan's sister is a case in point. Joyce takes this shadowy image, this dark scene which fascinated and obsessed him and which he returned to again and again, and shapes it to his purposes. He projects this image so carefully, touches it so delicately and skillfully with directive associations and connotations, that it conveys simultaneously, in one simple seamless whole, all the warring meanings he wishes it to hold—all the warring meanings it held for him. The pose of the harlot is also the pose of the Virgin; the revered Lady of Romance (kin to Vittoria Colonna, Laura, Beatrice, Levana, Dark Rosaleen, and the beloved of any artist) is also Ireland and at the same time a vulgar English shopgirl. One need not belabor the point. These meanings are conveyed not merely by the juxtapositions and evocations of the chief images—of Mangan's dark sister and the English shopgirl, for example—but by the reiterated patterns, allusions, and actions which bind the whole work together: the dead priest's charitableness, Mrs. Mercer's used stamps, the fall of money on the salver; Araby, Eastern enchantment, the knightly quest for a chivalric token; the swaying dress, the veiled senses, the prayerful murmur, *"O love! O love!"* Scarcely a line, an evocation, an object—the central apple tree, the heretical book of devotions by Abednego Seller, "The Arab's Farewell to His Steed," the blind street—but adds its harmony to the whole and extends and clarifies the story's meaning.

The test of an explanation is its utility—how many facts can it order and make meaningful? The conception of **"Araby"** embodied in this essay accounts for thorny details as well as larger motifs. The conception also sheds light on recurrent scenes, ideas, and patterns in Joyce's writings; for example, it makes intelligible a heretofore impenetrable passage in *Finnegans Wake*. That passage, in turn, is part of a longer section which is amenable to similar exegesis, a section which contains lines such as "Never play lady's game for the Lord's stake"; "Lust, thou shalt not commix idolatry"; and "Collide with man, collude with money." But here is the passage itself:

> Remember the biter's bitters I shed the vigil I buried our Harlotte Quai from poor Mrs Mangain's of Britain Court on the feast of Marie Maudlin. Ah, who would wipe her weeper dry and lead her to the halter? Sold in her heyday, laid in the straw, bought for one puny petunia. Moral: if you can't point a lily get to henna out of here!

In the light of what we know about **"Araby,"** and paying attention only to those meanings which are pertinent to **"Araby,"** the passage might be freely construed as follows: Remember the bitter tears I shed, I the biter who was bitten, in that secret and buried vigil I kept—all was later shed and buried—for the Harlot Queen, for Mary Queen of Scots, for Mangan's sister, who lived, as all Ireland does, under the rule of Britain's Court. These and others, blended together, I venerated in my maudlin, sentimental way, as I also venerated Mary Magdalene, saint and prostitute (a weeper who wiped her weeping dry). To what end?—sacramental? (altar), noose or enslavement?

(halter), or merely a dead end? (halt her)? Ireland and Ireland's religion was sold in its heyday, laid low and prostituted in the straw, sold for one puny penny, for a petunia. Moral: if you can't accept Ireland's religion (lily), if you can't paint the lily (that is, gild the lily, romanticize Ireland, cover all with a veneer of gold—with a pun on "pointillism," and with sexual overtones), at least you can get the false dye (henna) out of her, and get the hell (Gehenna) out of here!

Obviously this is a bald transcription of something much richer and much more subtle. Obviously, too, the passage is wed to the patterns of *Finnegans Wake,* so that from the point of view of **"Araby,"** the passage is overlaid by considerations extraneous to the story. (For example, "Harlotte Quai"—that is, "Charlotte Quay"—and "Britain Court" are also actual places in Dublin.) But though **"Araby"** is not the *raison d'être* of the passage, it provides a key to the passage. For most of the meanings in the passage are so condensed and private, they can be satisfactorily read only in the light of their much plainer and more detailed conjunction in **"Araby."** How then does the passage come to be in *Finnegans Wake* at all? It is there because it is tied to a series of events which shaped some of Joyce's fundamental insights and concerns. Eventually that cluster of events and associations, given early literary coherence in **"Araby,"** became both matrix and correlative for such concerns. We see the cluster in *Finnegans Wake* as we see it in all his writings. Joyce, in truth, was always walking through and meeting himself.

We have already noticed that some portions of those original events and associations can be identified; other portions we can detect only as they filter again and again through Joyce's successive fictions. In *Finnegans Wake* these fragments of events and associations, truncated now and fantastically jumbled, have suffered a strange sea change, but they are still discernible, sometimes all the more so, and sometimes all the plainer in import, because of their laborious encrustations of meaning.

For one thing, as in **"Araby,"** the name "Mangan" (this is the only time it occurs in *Finnegans Wake*) again appears in female guise, now as "Mrs. Mangain." The changed spelling of the name is significant because it underlines the mercenary and sexual elements (Man-gain) which had played so large but so implicit a role in the boy's confused adoration of Mangan's dark sister. At the same time a whole group of associations sounded in **"Araby"** are also sounded here. "Harlotte Quai" and "Marie Maudlin" are a recrudescence of the virgin-harlot fusion embodied by Mangan's sister, the fusion of the "harlot queen" (Mary Queen of Scots) with Mary Queen of Heaven and Mary Magdalene. "Britain Court" again suggests courting Britain as well as submitting to British rule. "Vigil I buried" refers once more to the secret vigils the boy devoted to his false madonna, and to the ultimate deflation and burial of that self-deluding idolatry. While "biter's bitters" is another version of the boy's "anguish and anger"; as Joyce put it in his essay on Mangan, it is "the bitter disillusion

and self-disdain" which must end all such romantic projections; or, once again, as he put it in *Ulysses,* it is the "agenbite of inwit." (Note the striking repetition of words, meanings, and sounds, here—"anger," "anguish," "agenbite," "biter's," "bitters," "bitter," "inwit"—as though a constellation of sounds had become wedded to the archetypal event.) In a similar manner, the commingling of sex, selling one's self for money, and being brought low which is so central to **"Araby"** is epitomized in, "Sold in her heyday, laid in the straw, bought for one puny petunia." The sexual element is conveyed by "sold in her heyday" (punning on "hayday"), and "laid in the straw" (that is, made love to in the straw—"hayday" again), while engrafted upon the same words is the idea of selling one's self for money: "sold in her heyday," and "bought for one puny [that is, "one penny"] petunia" (with a pun on *pecunia*). And all this is conjoined with the ultimate deflation, the idea of being brought low: "laid in the straw"—a remark which, in the context, applies to Ireland and the Catholic religion as well as the narrator.

The last sentence in the passage is also packed with additional meanings analogous to those in **"Araby."** The lily is the predominent flower of Catholicism, but more particularly, in Catholic symbolism, it is the flower of the Virgin Mary. On the other hand, the plant, henna, in addition to producing a dye, that is, a masking substance, also produces a white flower connected with Mohammedan religious symbolism and used, like the dye, in Mohammedan religious and erotic rites—the word "henna" itself is of Arabic origin. Hence, in a manner analogous to the end of **"Araby,"** the line implies that Irish Catholicism, and in particular the worship of the Virgin Mary, is dyed or adulterated by money, sex, and "Arabian" exoticism; or to put it another way, if one can't have a religion devoid of henna, if one isn't allowed to paint the lily unless one gilds it, one must leave the religion and the country. But this statement, though its implications and even its images are redolent of **"Araby,"** goes beyond **"Araby."** For in *Finnegans Wake* Joyce is looking back; he can convey his moral from the distant pinnacle of exile and achievement. In **"Araby"** the boy has just discovered that he is confusing lilies and henna; in his moment of anguish he can not yet see that he must gild the lily or get out.

IX

Joyce's art in **"Araby,"** and in many of his other writings, may be likened to a palimpsest. Perhaps more than any artist of his era he was willing, for the sake of his over-all design, to obscure, even to wipe out rich nuances and powerful ironies. But at the same time, and again perhaps more than any contemporary artist, he was careful to lacquer his images and actions with layer after layer of translucent, incremental meaning. The finished palimpsest is rich with shimmering depths, strange blendings, and tantalizing hints: here something has been rubbed out, there a few faint lines coalesce meaningfully and then dwindle away, while in the center a figure, distinct, yet merging with myriads of dim underforms, swims slowly into focus and then turns and dissolves and re-forms before our gaze. Abednego Seller drops out of view, only the misleading, enigmatic *Devout Communicant* remains; England's silver florin gleams brightly in the boy's tight grasp, the ancient golden lily and golden saint glimmer darkly in the shaded depths; Saturday evening shopping trips and "this night of Our Lord" stand boldly in the foreground, the liturgical engrams of which they are a part loom faintly in the distance. Mangan's shadowy sister—a version of the darkling siren Joyce drew so often—is limned and limned again. Harlot and virgin, temptress and saint, queen and shopgirl, Ireland and England—she is a miracle of blendings, mergings, and montages. While a multitude of harmonizing designs, some clear, some dim, some just faintly discernible—Mary Queen of Scots, "Our Lady of the Hills," Dark Rosaleen, a criminal dressed as a nun, Levana, Eastern bazaars, Caroline Norton, and idolatrous vigils—complete the deceptive palimpsest.

In *Dubliners* we sometimes become fascinated by the more legible figures in the palimpsest. But the more obscure figures are there too, and Joyce, by his reticences, encourages us to seek them. We know at the end of **"Araby"** that something devastating has occurred, and we would like to know exactly what it is. Ultimately, the full radiance of sight, of meaning, is ours, not the boy's. He has caught a glimpse of reality, of himself as he really is; he can reject the old encumbering vision, he can decide to dream "no more of enchanted days," but he can not yet fashion a new life. As the story has it, the light is out; the boy must grapple in the dark. But like blind Oedipus, in the dark the boy finally sees: his moment of illumination is given to him as he gazes "up into the darkness." That moment of blinding sight is also the moment of artistic vision, of the unfolding of "the capacities of [the] spirit"; not merely because the moment is later seen and reseen with the clarity, the penetration, the rich ramification of the artist's eye, but because the moment itself is a *sine qua non* for the artist's eye. The boy's end is his beginning; he has walked through and met himself.

"Araby" is the rendering of a quintessential moment (and for Joyce, *the* quintessential moment) in a portrait of the artist as a young boy. It is as though the boy of the story has come to the end of a well-lighted dead-end road. He now confronts a tangle of dark paths. Perhaps one of those paths will eventually lead him to a brighter road and to a wider, steadier vision of the surrounding countryside. The boy has not yet chosen the path he will follow; he may very well choose the wrong path. But at least he has seen that his own comfortable well-worn road, well-lighted and thronged with travelers though it is, is a dead end. That insight makes further travel possible; he can "welcome . . . now at the last the ways that [he] shall go upon." North Richmond Street is blind, but Dublin perhaps has thoroughfares, and if not Dublin, then, as the conclusion of *A Portrait* tells us, the beckoning roads of all the world beyond Ireland: "white arms of roads" leading "beyond the sleeping fields to what journey's end?"

Robert P. ApRoberts (essay date 1967)

SOURCE: "'Araby' and the Palimpsest of Criticism or, Through a Glass Eye Darkly," in *Antioch Review,* Vol. 26, No. 4, Winter, 1967, pp. 469–89.

[*In the following essay, ApRoberts refutes Professor Stone's thesis in the essay reprinted above, asserting that "Araby" is a self-contained story and should be read at face value.*]

"You see how easy it is to deceive one who is an artist in phrases. Avoid them, Miss Dale; they dazzle the penetration of the composer. That is why people like Mrs. Mountstuart see so little; they are bent on describing so brilliantly."

—George Meredith, *The Egoist*

Vanity flee and verity fear.

—James Joyce, *Finnegans Wake*

Everywhere in modern criticism the tide of symbolic interpretation runs full. Exegetes search the literature of the Middle Ages for the four-fold levels of Dante's allegory and return from below the surface dives into the Miller's and the Reeve's tales bearing interpretations by which these stories undergo a sea-change into some thing which, if not rich, is at least strange. For several years now some critics have lived in the murky depths of symbolic interpretation of Shakespeare without ever emerging to breathe the fresh air or glimpse the light of common day. Many Dickensians scorn the judgment of the ordinary reader that Dickens is above all a comic writer (a judgment reflected in current musicals which transform villainous Fagins into Pickwickian grotesques) and find through the alchemy of symbolism, with the most solemn and unsmiling countenances, that his works are more Dostoyevskian and Kafkaesque than those of his two continental followers.

Of late there are signs that the tide may be ebbing. Protests are made that the *Troilus* which Professor D. W. Robertson, Jr., reads is not Chaucer's but the Parson's. Despite outraged cries of misunderstanding from G. Wilson Knight, Professor R. M. Frye's examination of the claims of the school of Knight is a telling *caveat* to the Christian symbolists of Shakespeare; and the symbolic interpreters of Dickens are being marked off, even by Dickensians, as a rather special breed. Professor Frank Kermode, examining one of Northrop Frye's archetypal flights, urges us to press our feet more firmly to the ground the farther Frye's balloons strain toward the stratosphere. The time is, then, certainly opportune for an examination of the claims of some of the symbolic critics, and fortunately there is at hand a rather pure and rather prettily limited instance of symbolic interpretation which we may use as a test case. This is an article by Professor Harry Stone entitled "'**Araby**' and the Writings of James Joyce" which makes an elaborate disclosure of the symbolism Mr. Stone finds in Joyce's short story.

Such an interpretation is not something new for Professor Stone, for he has written a number of studies offering symbolic interpretations of Dickens, though none of these has been on such a detailed scale as his interpretation of the Joyce story. Furthermore, his article bears the imprimatur of a distinguished review—an imprimatur made even more impressive through the fanfare accorded the article by the managing editor as breaking the twenty-five year tradition of the *Antioch Review* of not printing explications. The managing editor at once illustrated and justified the completeness of this momentous surrender by a lengthy quotation from the report of an Editor X who, without ever having read **"Araby,"** was convinced that the article not only told "the story in considerably more detail than Joyce gave" but was also "a demonstration of a method and a key to understanding not only Joyce as a whole, but the entire canon of twentieth-century allusive writers." Certainly a most alarming prospect is raised when this reaction is joined to the bemused wonder of the managing editor at the decision to publish Professor Stone's article: "Does it represent a major policy shift or a passing editorial aberration? Or is it, perhaps, capitulation in the face of the sheer number of explicatory articles submitted to us despite our protestations of non-interest?" Who can fail to feel alarm at the future that may face the editors if the decision is not rescinded? Will they be doomed to read such articles without necessarily reading the works they explicate? Will such a policy inaugurate a new dialogue at editorial meetings:

Q. (despairingly) "Have you read the 'Lake Isle of Innisfree'?"

A. (triumphantly) "No, but I've read the explication."

Is the "Editor's Shop Talk" a palimpsest beneath whose surface there is a cry for help from frightened people?

Whatever the real nature of the *Antioch* editors' reactions, they are at least a tribute to the effectiveness of Professor Stone's rhetoric. I myself would add to this tribute. Polished, finished, flowing, assured—rich and rolling on the tongue—almost it persuades. My conviction that there is not the slightest substance to the article only increases my admiration—no! my astonishment—at the audacity of the performance. Out of nothing Mr. Stone has created the illusion of something. But reason does have the power to resist the potent spell and to show that the fabric of the vision is baseless, that its cloud-capp'd towers and gorgeous palaces are an insubstantial pageant which, examined critically, dissolve and leave not an idea behind.

II

Let me declare at the outset that I do not understand what Mr. Stone's thesis is. Nowhere can I find an exact statement of it. But, clearly, whatever that thesis may be, one of its elements is the concept that in **"Araby"** are to be found, for the first time, ideas and themes which recur in Joyce's later work. Despite Professor Stone's curious claim that "in his writings Joyce was always meeting himself—in ways which must at times have been beyond his conscious

ordinance," surely the appearance of an idea in a later work of Joyce's is not proof of its existence in **"Araby."** The Joyce that wrote *Ulysses* and *Finnegans Wake* is the Joyce that had written **"Araby,"** but the Joyce that wrote **"Araby"** is not the Joyce who had written the later works. Just as clearly, before we can accept the claim that an idea in **"Araby"** recurs in a later work or is related somehow to its appearance in the work of another author, we must be convinced of its existence in **"Araby."**

We may, then, dismiss from consideration Mr. Stone's contention that Yeat's story "Our Lady of the Hills" is "embedded in 'Araby'" (whatever that means) or his suggestion that chords from "Levanna and Our Ladies of Sorrow" reverberate in it. In the absence of evidence external to **"Araby"**—evidence of the kind that would be provided by a statement of Joyce's that such linkages exist—both connections are dependent on the validity of Mr. Stone's reading of **"Araby."** We can also ignore Professor Stone's interpretation of "a heretofore impenetrable passage" from *Finnegans Wake* in the light of his reading of **"Araby"**—though we may admire the expertise that can distinguish the impenetrable passages of *Finnegans Wake* from the penetrable—for this interpretation also depends on the validity of that reading.

Just as the precise thesis of Mr. Stone's article is not clear, neither is his precise interpretation of **"Araby."** But it is clear that Mr. Stone believes that we are to see beneath the surface of the story certain themes, and that without such penetration we cannot understand the story. To an ordinary glance the final sentence of the story might seem the perfectly straightforward informing idea: "Gazing up into the darkness I saw myself as a creature driven and derided by vanity; and my eyes burned with anguish and anger." But Professor Stone counters any such idea at the very beginning of his discussion of the story:

> "Driven and derided," "anguish and anger"—these reactions seem far too strong. Indeed they seem pretentious when compared to the trivial disillusionment which caused them. And they are pretentious, certainly they are inappropriate, if related only to their immediate external causes. But the boy is reacting to much more than a banal fair and a broken promise. He is reacting to sudden and deeply disturbing insights. These insights are shared by the attentive reader, for by the end of **"Araby"** the reader has been presented with all that he needs in order to resolve the story's intricate harmony into its component motifs.

Professor Stone does not claim that the meanings he finds in the story are merely ancillary to, or concomitant with, the surface narrative. They are for him necessary to an understanding of the story. And, indeed, it must be so, for were these meanings merely underlying, then the attentive reader of Professor Stone's article might see no need to plunge into such murky depths when all seemed clear without arcane explanation. Professor Stone must and does claim that **"Araby"** can be fully understood only through the symbolic meanings he finds in it.

But though Professor Stone does not make his view of **"Araby"** clear, he does make clear his belief that a chief revelation of the story is that Irish Catholicism is decayed and corrupted, principally by mammonism. This indictment is first made by the details given about the dead priest, details which, according to Mr. Stone, were intended by Joyce to arraign the priest.

The case against the priest rests on two points. The first is the books he left behind. *The Abbot* has for its heroine that notoriously evil woman, Mary Queen of Scots. *The Memoirs of Vidocq* is "a volume of exciting quasi-blasphemous criminal and sexual adventures." *The Devout Communicant* is a devotional manual written, according to Mr. Stone, by a heretic and anti-Catholic, Abednego Seller, whose first name is that of one who would not worship the golden image and whose last suggests commercialism. The second point is the "highly directive import" Professor Stone finds in the "artfully inconclusive" final sentence about the priest.

> "He had," concludes the narrator, "been a very charitable priest; in his will he had left all his money to institutions and the furniture of his house to his sister." Joyce's ambiguity suggests that the priest's charity may have been . . . double edged. . . . If this worldly priest had been so "very charitable" why, at his death, was he able to donate "all his money" to institutions? His charity, so far as we know about it, began at his death.

From these two pieces of evidence Professor Stone deduces that the priest is an imposter, a finding of the greatest importance, for on it Professor Stone rears the superstructure of his article. He speaks of the first two paragraphs of the story in which the evidence appears as involving the themes of "decayed religion" and "mammonism" and as linking the story "to the problems and distortions of Catholicism and of Ireland as a whole," and he returns to these themes over and over, often referring to their relation to the priest and his defection from true religion. But their primary importance, of course, lies in their relation to the boy, for, as Mr. Stone tells us later, in worshipping the girl "the boy, like the priest, has begun to mix devotion with profanation, spirituality with materialism." And a principal revelation to the boy at the end of the story is that this worship is corrupt.

How well does the case against the priest stand examination? The attentive reader that Mr. Stone posits for **"Araby"** might naturally, in reading his article, wonder why, if it is so important for us to know that the author of *The Devout Communicant* was Abednego Seller, Joyce does not tell us. He does tell us that *The Abbott*—surely a somewhat more famous book—was by Walter Scott. Certainly Professor Stone attaches great importance not only to the paradox of the author's name but also to his having been a heretic and an anti-Catholic:

> When Mrs. Mercer's unexamined commercial religion is remembered in connection with the boy's and then the dead priest's (one recalls that the priest's book of

heretical devotions was by a man named "Seller")—we get some idea of how insidiously mammonistic is Ireland's religious bankruptcy.

> . . . the story of Abednego is told *in extenso* in the Holy Saturday Mass, and Abednego Seller's heretical *Devout Communicant* is a manual for Holy Week. . . .

> Scarcely a line, an evocation, an object—the central apple tree, the heretical book of devotions by Abednego Seller . . .—but adds its harmony to the whole and extends and clarifies the story's meaning.

Abednego Seller is the first piece of evidence Professor Stone adduces for the mammonism of the priest and hence of Ireland, and, if the arraignment of the priest is the foundation of Mr. Stone's article, Abednego Seller is its cornerstone.

Such emphasis might well lead the attentive reader to be curious about this author whose concealed name is of such paramount importance, a curiosity that would be further whetted by the discovery that no word-index or concordance to any work of Joyce's lists "Abednego Seller." If he were to satisfy this curiosity, he would find that Seller lived from about 1646 to 1705, that *The Devout Communicant* was first published in 1686, and that, after the sixth edition in 1695, there is no record of its having been reprinted under that title.

This information would raise for the attentive reader the question, "Could there be another religious manual with the same title of Roman Catholic provenance and published in Ireland?" Such an enquiry pursued would lead to the discovery that Pacificus Baker, a prominent English Franciscan, wrote such a manual in the eighteenth century. This *Devout Communicant* was first published in London and underwent a number of editions and reprintings—second edition (apparently the earliest extant) 1765, sixth edition 1798; reprintings in 1813, 1823 (Manchester), 1826, 1827, and 1828 (Liverpool). An edition without the author's name, revised and enlarged by William Gahan, an Augustinian, was printed in Cork in 1794 and a copy of this edition is the only copy of any work with the title *The Devout Communicant* in the National Library of Ireland. (There are also indications that the work was reprinted in Dublin at least twice during the nineteenth century.)

At this point the attentive reader would ask what proof Professor Stone can offer that Joyce knew of the existence of Abednego Seller's work? (The enquiries I have made have failed to locate a copy in Ireland, though these enquiries have been by no means exhaustive.) Even if Professor Stone can prove that Joyce knew of the seventeenth-century manual, how would he persuade the reader of the likelihood that the reference in **"Araby"** is to this work and not to the popular and often reprinted Roman Catholic work? In view of the realism of the Dublin setting with North Richmond Street and the Christian Brothers School, why should the attentive reader, supposing he knew of the two *Devout Communicants,* feel that Joyce refers to Abednego Seller's heretical manual rather than to Pacificus

Baker's orthodox one? If the title *The Abbot* were given alone without the name of the author, the reader might well assume that, because the book had belonged to a priest, it was a religious book. Any reader exerting the proper scholarly and critical attention that the attentive reader should exert would feel that he could not accept Mr. Stone's ascription of *The Devout Communicant* unless Mr. Stone could prove, first, that Joyce knew of Seller's work and, second, that Joyce was referring to this work and not to the Roman Catholic one. (We may note, in passing, that Professor Marvin Magalaner in his study *Time of Apprenticeship: The Fiction of Young James Joyce* (New York, 1959) ascribes the work to Pacificus Baker.)

The Devout Communicant is, then, not a piece of evidence which can be used to arraign the priest. What of the other books? The very most that can be said against a priest who reads works of the sort of *The Abbot* and *The Memoirs of Vidocq* is that he is guilty of venial sin, for they are vanities that stand in marked contrast to works entirely suitable for a priest to read, works such as *The Devout Communicant.*

Mr. Stone's other piece of evidence, which concerns the priest's charity, is easily disposed of. "If this worldly priest had been so 'very charitable' why, at his death, was he able to donate 'all his money' to institutions? His charity, so far as we know about it, began at his death." If Mr. Stone had only realized that his question is not a rhetorical one, he might have answered it himself. First, a secular priest is permitted to own property. Second, the priest may have given away vast sums during his life and still have left "all his money" to institutions. Finally, Mr. Stone's statement that the priest's charity, as far as we know, began at his death is an argument *ex silentio*. We might just as well say that the priest was unchaste on the grounds that we are told nothing at all about his chastity.

Once we think of this last point, we can see that Professor Stone missed a good opportunity to indict the priest for lust. Spiritually a priest might be regarded as both male and female, and for this the abandoned bicycle pump is a magnificent symbol. Its rustiness points to the waste of the priest's fertility. But underneath this obvious symbolism there is the more important idea of masturbation for which a pump is an unmistakable correlative, a symbolism reinforced when we recall Bloom's masturbation at the moment of the elevation of the Host—to which Mr. Stone refers in his article—a false priest elevating himself at the altar of lust. So too in **"Araby"** the priest is a false priest guilty of mammonism and fruitless lust just as we are to find the boy guilty of mammonism and fruitless lust. But there is still another layer of the palimpsest to be revealed. Such an article as a bicycle pump is clearly of British manufacture, for the Irish were not allowed to develop industry. It is then a symbol of the British commercial materialism which has corrupted Irish Catholicism—a symbol of Mammon, the strange god after whom the priest has gone a-whoring. This exegesis is not merely facetious; it illustrates a serious issue. A critic of Professor Stone's persuasion should find every detail in a story symbolic, for, if he admits that any detail is present for verisimilitude alone, he raises the question of how to distinguish such a detail from one which is symbolic.

But it is time to deliver a final verdict on the priest. And that verdict is not even "Not proven"; it is "Not guilty." And the other contentions dependent on the case topple with it like a file of upright dominoes falling with the first—the corruption of Irish religion, the other subliminal hints of this in the opening paragraphs, its parallel in the boy's worship of the girl, and the revelation to the boy at the end of the story that his worship is corrupt. The case has not provided a sound foundation for the interpretation of **"Araby"** let alone an Archimedean base from which to shift the understanding of the entire canon of twentieth-century allusive writers.

III

It would be simply tedious to expose the complete lack of substance of other and far less important readings by Professor Stone of the palimpsest of **"Araby."** Two of these baseless interpretations, however, are worth examining, for they illustrate beautifully the pitfalls that await the thesis-monger who grinds the axe of symbolic interpretation: false association and the creation of nonexistent facts.

Among those symbols of betrayal Mr. Stone finds everywhere in the story is the florin, the coin which the uncle gives the boy for the bazaar. "That Joyce, out of all the coins and combinations of coins available to him, chose to have the boy clutch a florin is doubly meaningful." The original florin of 1252, a gold coin noted for its purity, bore emblems of the Virgin and of John the Baptist. The boy's coin is silver and bears the emblems of Ireland's foreign masters. The first issue in England, coined in 1847, was known as the "Godless and Graceless Florin" because the title "Dei Gratia, F. D.," customary on coins, had been omitted by the Roman Catholic Master of the Mint, who was subsequently discharged for the offense. As Mr. Stone believes that the boy in his visit to the fair is "acting out his betrayal in the most emblematic way," he finds it "supremely ironic" that the boy "should be clutching an English florin, an alien and notorious silver coin sans Virgin's lily and sans Catholic saint but bearing instead symbols of his and Ireland's servitude and betrayal."

The reason why the seven stars are no more than seven is a pretty reason, and the reason why Joyce chose to have the boy clutch the florin is that he did not choose to have him clutch something else. What reader, no matter how attentive, would call to mind the history of the florin, even if he knew it, on the strength of its single mention in this sentence: "I held a florin tightly in my hand as I strode down Buckingham Street towards the station"? How many readers, well-read, cultivated, or attentive, know that history? Did Mr. Stone know it when he first read **"Araby"**? A florin is almost as common a coin for an Irishman or an Englishman as a fifty-cent piece is for an American (I say "almost" simply because the florin shares its equivalence to the fifty-cent piece with the half-crown), and no Irish or English reader would give a second thought to the single and simple mention of a florin any more than an American would to such a mention in a story of a fifty-cent piece, a coin which has associations as rich as those of the florin.

The colloquial designation "four-bits" arises from its relation to the Spanish "piece-of-eight"; its more formal designation of "half-dollar" relates it to the coins which first appeared in 1518 made of silver mined in Joachimsthal ("dollar" is a modified shortened form of *Joachimsthaler*) and bearing the effigy of the saint whose name appears in apocryphal writings as that of the father of the Virgin Mary. What an *embarras de richesses* for an explicator of Mr. Stone's kidney, if we add to these associations a fascinating history! When the Bank of England suspended payments in 1797, and the scarcity of coins was very great, a large number of Spanish pieces-of-eight, which were held by the Bank, were put into circulation after having been countermarked at the mint with a small oval bust of George III, such as used by the Goldsmith's company for marking. Others were simply over-stamped with the initials G. R. enclosed in a shield. In 1804 the Mandy penny head set in an octagonal compartment was employed. These coins were called "pieces-of-eight" because each was worth eight *reals* and were commonly referred to as "dollars." Several millions were distributed and were very largely used in the British North American colonies. By such a history our terms "four-bits" and "dollar" came into use. Let me disabuse the reader of any illusion that all this information is a display of erudition. It is readily at hand in the *Encyclopaedia Britannica*—from which I have taken the history practically verbatim—as is all the information Professor Stone provides about the florin.

Since Mr. Stone gives the history of the florin because he is searching the palimpsest of **"Araby"** for symbols of betrayal, we may remark here on his curious failure to note a word in the sentence containing "florin" much richer as such a symbol, a failure which illustrates how endless are the associations anyone can establish once he gives his fancy up unrestrainedly to symbol hunting. For the name of the street down which the boy hastens is Buckingham, a name rich in overtones of betrayal. I have no intention of exhausting these associations. Consider only those involved in the Buckingham who figures in *Richard III*—Richard's "second-self" in the practice of treachery and a traitor to Richard. How much more would this one association—an association within the knowledge of any cultivated reader—add to the irony Mr. Stone finds in the boy going to the bazaar bearing a coin symbolic of "his and Ireland's servitude and betrayal" by providing the further irony that to reach the bazaar the boy passes down a street with a name redolent of betrayal!

But our main point is that the significance Professor Stone sees in the word "florin" is an example of what I have called "false association." It is true that the florin has a history of association with the Virgin Mary and with the

idea of godlessness and gracelessness, but it is false to assume that these associations would be aroused in the reader by the bare mention of the name of an everyday coin.

The second misinterpretation involves the creation of a nonexistent fact to establish a false association. Mr. Stone says that when the boy "allows 'two pennies to fall against the sixpence' in his pocket," his action is "reminiscent of how Judas let the silver of betrayal fall upon the ground after his contrition." The context of this statement makes it quite clear that what establishes for Mr. Stone the association between Judas' act and the boy's is the action of "letting fall":

> The two men "were counting money on a salver. I listened to the fall of the coins." The boy also has fallen. We recall the "wild garden" with its "central apple-tree," that the words "falling" and "fell" are crucial to the description of Mangan's sister during her epiphany before the boy, and that the word "fall" again recurs—again in connection with money—when the boy, in his penultimate action, an action reminiscent of how Judas let the silver of betrayal fall upon the ground after his contrition, allows "two pennies to fall against the sixpence" in his pocket as he finally turns to leave the bazaar.

Judas did not let the silver of betrayal fall—he threw it down, he cast it down, he hurled it, he flung it, but he did not let it fall. In Matthew XXVII, 5, we are told that, after the betrayal of Jesus, Judas repented and attempted to return the thirty pieces of silver to the chief priests and elders in the temple. When they refused to take them back, Judas threw them away and went off and hanged himself. The words used to describe the action of throwing the money away are in the Greek original "rhipsas ta argyria en tō naō," in the Vulgate "projectis argenteis in templo," in the Challoner-Rheims revised "he flung the pieces of silver into the temple," in the King James "he cast down the pieces of silver in the temple," and in the Revised Standard "throwing down the pieces of silver in the temple." Nowhere in the original or in any standard translation is it said that Judas let the silver fall in the temple. Professor Stone finds an association which does not exist between the boy's act of letting his money fall and Judas' act of throwing away the money of betrayal.

IV

"Gazing up into the darkness I saw myself as a creature driven and derided by vanity; and my eyes burned with anguish and anger." Professor Stone, as we have seen, finds this final state of the narrator unconvincing in terms of what we might call the surface meaning of the story. It is with this judgment, from which Mr. Stone begins his examination of **"Araby,"** that the attentive reader of the article must take issue. For the final sentence records the reaction which the reader has been awaiting since the boy's entrance to the bazaar and which has been prepared for by all the details given after his entrance. Mr. Stone finds the reaction inappropriate to the triviality of the disillusionment, but what is important is not the triviality of the disillusionment but the strength of the illusion which led up to it. The occasion of the disillusionment is unimportant just as is the cause of the illusion. The important thing is the revelation to the boy of the triviality of what he had attached so much significance to. That revelation is universal and its truth is none the less keen for all its reputation over the centuries:

> Now I have seen the face of death and am sore afraid.
> One day too I shall be like Enkidu.

> Therefore I hated life; because the work that is wrought under the sun is grievous unto me: for all *is* vanity and vexation of spirit.

> her bifeoh læne,   her bifrēond læne,
> her bimon læne,   her bimaeg læne;
> eal pis eoran gesteal   idel weorpe!

> And thinketh al this world nis but a faire
> That passeth soone as floures faire.

> The boast of heraldry, the pomp of power,
> And all that beauty, all that wealth e'er gave,
> Awaits alike the inevitable hour.
> The paths of glory lead but to the grave.

> The Worldly Hope men set their Hearts upon
> Turns Ashes—or it prospers; and anon,
> Like Snow upon the Desert's dusty Face,
> Lighting a little hour or two—is gone.

> Man is in love and loves what vanishes
> What more is there to say?

The "anguish and anger" are the reactions of a young boy feeling this truth for the first time, and the self-centeredness and self dramatization are quite in keeping with his age and with the earlier creation by the boy of an inner world of love and hope at odds with reality. Our awareness that the story is told by a narrator who sees the boy's reaction in this way cuts against any tendency to find the reactions too strong, pretentious, or inappropriate—they are the reactions of a boy, and they are none the less important nor is the insight less true because in later life he will react differently.

Viewing the story in the light of its final revelation, we can see how beautifully every stroke prepares us for this revelation with the delicacy and simplicity of high art. The setting of a lower-middle-class district, though not of great importance, has a double appropriateness: it is a drab, respectable neighborhood whose inhabitants might well dream of a more beautiful environment; second, such a neighborhood does not crush the spirit out of its inhabitants as a working-class neighborhood might nor satisfy their longing for beauty as an upper-class neighborhood might. The more immediate and more important setting is not, however, the respectable bourgeois world of North Richmond Street but the world of boys which is described in much greater detail. The narrator has known a world occupied in school-time and play-time entirely by boys. In such a world women, old or young, have being only as

they relate to the members of this world—"John's mother wants him! Bill's aunt is calling him!" "Mangan's sister" is the girl's natural appellation here and not "an awkward and unaccountable substitute for a name . . . designed to catch the reader's attention and direct his associations" to James Mangan and Dark Rosaleen. (Granted the fame of James Clarence Mangan, why should the phrase direct an Irish reader to him when Mangan is such a common Irish name? Even if it did, why should "sister," which certainly has no connotations of romantic love, bring to mind Dark Rosaleen? The use of the last name rather than the first is the common practice in an English or Irish boy's school.)

The boy is at an age where his emotional fancies are strong and where he is experiencing a first awakening of a generalized impulse toward sexual love. Twelve years of age would fit very nicely and would accord with the biographical experience which the story no doubt reflects—Joyce was twelve in 1894 when his family lived in North Richmond Street. At this point in the boy's life a girl captures his attention. He has no idea of the mechanics of sex or that what he feels is the beginning of a period of strong sexual drive. What he notices are the precise details that such a boy would notice: the things that mark a girl as different externally from a boy—the dress with a petticoat showing at times below the hem, the long braid, the way she bends her head to one side, the way she holds the top of one of the iron uprights of the railing (no doubt swinging back and forth) and the common simple first piece of jewelry for a girl, a silver bracelet. Nothing could be more suggestive of girlhood and less suggestive of the "desecrating lust" and the "hints of commercialism and sensuality with connotations of sexuality and betrayal" which Mr. Stone finds in these details. And no one could be a less likely prototype of Gerty MacDowell or Molly Bloom or less suggestive of the harlot.

So too, nothing could be less suggestive of a response to sensuality and lust than the response the boy makes. His reaction is that of one who has been stirred by chivalric love in the tradition of the Arthurian romances. His love kept secret from the world becomes a treasure which he sees himself guarding safely from all harm, as a knight errant would guard the precious object of a quest (the most precious object in the Arthurian story is, of course, a chalice, the Holy Grail). His confused and generalized emotion is engendered as much by the exciting idea of being in love as it is by the object which calls forth such romantic intensity, a diffuseness which is shown when, in an ecstasy of feeling, he prays to the lord of terrible aspect with the intensity of a young Dante.

While he is in this feverish state, the girl speaks to him of Araby, and immediately her desire to go transfers to him with an intensity made greater because she cannot go and because he promises to bring her something from the fair—the knight now has a quest to undertake for his lady.

From this moment on suspense builds. The intervening days drag interminably until at last the appointed Saturday arrives. Knowing his uncle's habit of lingering late in a snug on a Saturday night, he reminds his uncle that he is going to the fair that night. The curt reply shows the irritation of a man acknowledging a request he does not want to carry out and it gives the boy a sense of foreboding. Arrived home, he waits feverishly for dinner and his uncle's return, cooling his forehead against the window which faces the house where the girl lives. When he comes downstairs he finds a Mrs. Mercer there for supper. To Professor Stone, Mrs. Mercer's name, her dead husband's occupation of pawnbroking, her collecting of stamps for a pious purpose all mean that "Joyce is saying, in effect, that everyday religion and piety in Ireland are based upon self-deluding and mindless materialism." But the function of every detail about Mrs. Mercer can be accounted for much more simply. What can be more infuriating when one is in a fever of doubt and expectation than to have to go through the formality of being polite to an outsider? How much more so when the outsider is a tedious person? How beautifully Joyce makes us feel this for the boy! The more trivial Mrs. Mercer, the greater our sense of the boy's anguish. She is the garrulous widow of a pawnbroker (pawnbroking is not the most glamorous of occupations) with nothing better to do than collect stamps for some "pious purpose" (the alliteration almost makes us hear the boy spitting out the words contemptuously). We feel the boy's relief when, after she takes her garrulous leave, he is able to walk up and down the room physically venting his anxiety.

Hope when the uncle at last appears is offset by the precautionary wait enforced by a drunkenness that may turn to nastiness before it is partially tempered by food. But at last, late though it is, the boy is off with money in his hand. At the same time that the complete emptiness of the train, the slowness of its journey, and the late hour of the arrival make us anticipate the disappointment to come, they heighten our sense of the boy's desperate anxiety not to miss the bazaar. Joyce could not have got him to Araby in a more feverishly anxious state.

And Joyce could not have got him there at a time when the contrast between his expectations of something wonderful and the reality of the bazaar would be greater—no bright lights but a half darkened fair, no gay noisy crowds but a nearly empty building about to close up, no busy booths with shouting hucksters but nearly all closed stalls and attendants counting their receipts before those still open. The one stall the boy stops before is hopelessly expensive for someone with eightpence in his pocket (four of which he would need for the train home). What price a present for his lady now? At this stall he overhears the most banal flirtatious talk, talk that bears as much relationship to a romantic love as his own exchange with the girl.

I do not see how Joyce could have achieved a greater build-up or a greater let-down. Not all boys would dream of romantic love in such bookish terms as the narrator, though surely the young Joyce would, but what boy has not experienced dreams of romantic love focussed on some

girl, dreams which grow and flourish in a secrecy guarded by shyness? What person has not felt the disillusionment that comes when an expected delight proves disappointing? What more than a fair or a circus promises a glamor it does not have—a fair is the very symbol of vanity; witness Bunyan's representation of the world as Vanity Fair. Then too, the boy's love for the girl is made to run parallel to his anticipation of the bazaar. Exciting enough in itself, the visit to the fair is made doubly exciting because it is a quest undertaken for his lady who longs to go and cannot, a quest from which he will bring back for her some wondrous object. Suspense mounts with the agonizing wait for the uncle and the intolerable slowness of the eleventh hour journey. The bazaar could never have lived up to the boy's expectations—no bazaar could have—but at no time could it have come less up to them than at the time of the boy's arrival.

At the end of the story we can see the true conflict and how details in the story reinforce our sense of its universality. The main conflict is between the desire of mankind for a perfection of beauty in life and the impossibility of realizing this desire. At first the boy feels a conflict between his "love" for the girl and his environment; he keeps his "love" to himself and protects it from the unworthy, hostile world—"I imagined that I bore my chalice safely through a throng of foes." This same conflict is involved in the case of the boy and the uncle—the uncle is indifferent to the intensity of the boy's desire to go to the bazaar. But at the end the boy realizes that the true conflict is not between himself and his environment, or at least not so much so, as it is between the enormous power of his fancy and the impossibility of reality ever corresponding to his fancy. "Vanity of Vanities, saith the preacher, all is vanity"—what the story is concerned with is the moment of first realization, the moment when its truth is most deeply felt.

V

Obviously, if we consider the symbol-making power of the mind, anything may become symbolic for a reader. The important questions for the critic are, "When is a particular symbolic perception acceptable? How does one check, restrain, discipline the symbol-making activity of the mind?" The whole of **"Araby"** is finally symbolic of the way in which men are driven and mocked by illusions. Some details in the story take on a symbolic cast and some do not, though this dichotomy is overly simple. It is more accurate to say that the details give verisimilitude and that, at the same time, some may take on symbolic significance in the light of the central idea of the story. Joyce suggests to us, at several points, that though men universally realize the truth the boy comes to experience, they never lose their vain desires. Of all men, a priest should be most keenly aware of the vanity of things, and yet the books the priest leaves behind are a mixture of a devout treatise and two highly romantic works. Even those whose lives are informed by an awareness of the contrast between the corruptible and the incorruptible are subject to the vanity of human wishes. The garden of the house is, as all gardens are, an attempt to achieve beauty, but its decayed condition shows a failure to achieve it or to maintain it even if it is momentarily achieved. This wild garden with its central apple tree may symbolize the vain aspiration of man to create beauty here where it cannot keep its lustrous eyes and may even, if some reader wishes, be taken as a symbolic allusion to the Garden of Eden, which man dreams of but can never achieve in his fallen condition. Again, the uncle, unresponsive though he is to the wild longing of the boy, is stirred by the name **"Araby"** to recite what, from the title alone, the reader recognizes would be a highly romantic poem. The ordered neighborhood with its "decent lives," the world of business and routine where adult men and women are preoccupied with making a living, checks and subdues the fancy but it never completely conquers it. Man still remains discontent with his condition—like the uncle, many men seek the public house "to see the world as the world's not" or they may become puritanical, as many Irish are, and seek to repress their vain desires, a reaction suggested when the boy feels anger at being driven and derided by vanity. Finally, there is the implication that one of the bases of religion, at least of Christianity, is the vanity of human wishes for which religion offers a consolation—the girl cannot go to the bazaar because her school is going to have a "retreat," a period devoted to a consideration of the difference between things eternal and things *sub species aeternitatis*.

Symbolic significances which supplement the central idea of a story, expand it, provide overtones for it, reinforce it, or in any way arise naturally from it are not to be objected to even if such significances might not occur to all readers. But symbolisms which run counter to the central idea, are discordant with it, are unrelated to it, or are claimed to be concurrent with it but to be perceived only by an understanding of an arcane network of unstated details obliquely connected with it are to be rejected unless evidence is adduced from outside the story to show that the author saw such symbolisms in the story. On this basis we must reject Mr. Stone's view that the girl with her silver bracelet holding one of the spikes of the area railing, head bowed and petticoat showing, is at once a symbol of the Virgin Mary as she appears in *pietàs* (in what *pietà* does she appear standing and holding one of the nails?) and of Mary Magdalene and hence, by the name "Mary" called up through this symbolism, to be associated with Mary Sheehy and Mary Queen of Scots. We reject the harlot symbolism, not merely because the associations reek of the lamp and would never occur to any reader however attentive, but rather because the idea of the girl as a harlot and of the boy's love for her as lust jars with the idea of a young boy's first romantic illusion of love. Our rejection of the Virgin symbolism would be based on Ockham's principle—the details beautifully bespeak young girlhood and need no further explanation. Or, again, we can reject the idea that the opening lines of "The Arab's Farewell to His Steed" "are fraught with thematic significance" and that the story of Caroline Norton, the author of the poem, "is patently and ironically appropriate to what Joyce is

saying." The story is self-contained and does not depend for its effect upon whether the reader knows these matters or not—the details that Joyce gives are the details the reader needs.

The flaw which stands at the very heart of Professor Stone's article is his basic assumption that **"Araby"** is not self-contained. He seeks to give substance to his belief by the idea that in this early story Joyce employs the allusive method of his later works. For Mr. Stone **"Araby"** cannot be understood by itself, and he proceeds to rewrite the story as Editor X unconsciously realized when he felt that, in reading Mr. Stone's article, he "was being told the story in considerably more detail than Joyce gave." Apparently neither Editor X or Mr. Stone conceived that, if Joyce had wanted to tell the story in more detail, he would have told it in more detail and that, if he had not done so, he would have written an imperfect story. If Joyce wanted the reader to arraign the priest, he would have made it clear that the priest was to be arraigned—if the arraignment were to depend upon the anomaly of Abednego Seller's name then Joyce would have made it clear that *The Devout Communicant* referred to was the one by Seller and not by any other.

The palimpsest Professor Stone sees in **"Araby"** is not in the story but in Professor Stone's mind, and what he takes for depths shimmering with rich, half-obscured images is a mirror wherein the figures of his own perfervid fancy glimmer and shift. Mr. Stone uses **"Araby"** as a sort of Rorschach test, a starting point for a long free association fantasy that might be of general human interest insofar as *humani nihil a me alienum*. However, it is quite alien to any academic discipline. For it is free association; there is no control whatsoever except the limit of what happens to be Mr. Stone's awareness.

Intellectually, Mr. Stone's approach to **"Araby"** is not different from Baconianism. It is only a jump—no, not even that—to move from the idea that the **"Araby"** Joyce wrote is not the **"Araby"** of the common reader but the **"Araby"** Mr. Stone reads beneath the surface, to the idea that it was written not by Joyce at all but by someone else as part of the Great Cryptogram. And the effect of such neo-Alexandrianism upon students, not to mention editors of reputable journals, may be a double disaster. It may either turn them into little apostles who see all works of art as double-acrostics and who are led to those displays of vanity against which Helen Gardner so sensibly warns us:

> The critic's task is to assist his readers to read for themselves, not to read for them. . . . He is not writing to display his own ingenuity, subtlety, learning or sensitiveness; but to display the work in a manner which will enable it to exert its own power.

Or it may drive them away from literature as something whose esoteric incomprehensibility repels the reason and destroys the humanistic illumination of art.

What some symbolic critics ask their readers to accept is that all fancies engendered by a work of art have validity.

They want complete exemption for such ideas from the requirements of evidence, common sense, and logic which ideas in other areas of human activity must meet before they are accepted. True, criticism is an art, though no one has ever claimed that it stands on the same footing as the original works it elucidates, but it is much more a science in that it must test its claims with the scrupulosity of science, and it must be as rigorous in the logic with which it advances them. Criticism is the product of reason enlightened by imagination and not of the free play of fancy released from the inhibitions imposed by logic and common sense. It is not the critic but the lunatic, the lover, and the poet who are allowed to give to airy nothing a local habitation and a name. Likewise, the true scholar checks out every fact to the end, never ignores any argument which stands against his thesis, even one which has never been advanced by another, and is tentative about every theory with a tentativeness that varies with its degree of probability. The true critic supports his interpretations by facts. Both are united in the pursuit of truth as something which they cannot alter to their own desires and which they pursue unwearyingly no matter how illusory the idea that they can ever say a final word.

> Quid est scholaris? Est homo discens virtutes cum solicitudine. . . . Qualis substantia est scholaris? Est substantia animata sensitiva scientiae et virtutem susceptibilis.

Bernard Benstock (essay date 1967)

SOURCE: "Arabesques: Third Position of Concord," in *James Joyce Quarterly,* Vol. 5, No. 1, Fall, 1967, pp. 30–9.

[*In the following essay, Benstock supports Professor Stone's thesis in the essay reprinted above, and agrees that "Araby" serves "as a vital introduction of many of the motifs of the later works of James Joyce."*]

> "You must say 'paragon': a paramour is,
> God bless us, a thing of naught."
>
> —A Midsummer-Night's Dream

> "I'm the Sheik of Araby,
> Your love belongs to me;
> At night when you're asleep,
> Into your tent I'll creep."
>
> —"The Sheik of Araby"

> ". . . (if you can spot fifty I spy
> four more) . . ."
>
> —Finnegans Wake

In the Fall '65 issue of the *Antioch Review* Harry Stone marched through James Joyce's **"Araby"** in hobnailed boots, kicking up many muddy chunks. In retaliation Robert P. ApRoberts in the Winter '66-'67 issue wafted over the same terrain, leaving hardly a trace. They collided but never met. If it is necessary to choose between their two approaches to the story (and I think it is), my preference is for the over-reacher rather than the under-achiever. In doing so I reject the Helen Gardner critical dictum quoted by Professor ApRoberts ("The critic's task is to assist his readers to read for themselves."); I see no reason for the critic to allow himself to be used as a crutch for those who cannot read for themselves in the first place. Instead I view the critic as an independent reader with a point of view of his own, with insights and outlooks shaped and sharpened by his overall view, who offers the reader the uniqueness of his reading. "Araby" will survive all of our critical comments, but the Joycean dialogue that is current today has been enriched by Professor Stone's speculations, rather than by Professor ApRoberts' insistence that we take the story at face value.

Self-contained as Joyce's story is, it is also a part of something else: both of a trio of tales of childhood, for which it serves as the culminating piece, and for the full *Dubliners* collection, for which it is germinal. Harry Stone is precise in citing those last phrases of the story ("'Driven and derided,' 'anguish and anger'—these reactions seem far too strong," he comments); his critic is flailing the wrong horse when he cites this passage against him. The final sentence of **"Araby"** serves as a recording of the boy's moment of self-awareness because of his experiences with Mangan's sister and the Araby bazaar that proves to be a vital link with her. But even larger is this revelatory instance for all the childhood experiences from **"The Sisters"** through **"An Encounter"** and **"Araby."** In each of the previous cases the boy is too young to comprehend fully the meaning to himself of the particular occurrence that disturbs him. The death of Father Flynn and the consequent gossip that floods in at its wake inundates the stunned child: his suspicions are aroused and he reserves judgment, having failed to make a pattern of the pieces. In the second story the boy is somewhat older but still prepubescent: he knows enough to be frightened by the encounter with the pederast, but not enough to understand the exact nature of the danger to him embodied in the "queer old josser." Instead he records a partial awareness of himself in relation to his friend Mahony: "He ran as if to bring me aid. And I was penitent; for in my heart I had always despised him a little." Compare this conclusion first to that of **"The Sisters"** (where the story is given over at the end completely to a literal reproduction of the words of the adults, without the boy venturing any real comment), and then to **"Araby"** (where the boy's reactions are squarely on target, although exaggerated). **"Araby"** is as self-contained an artistic entity as "The Mookse and The Gripes," but it is also as much a part of *Dubliners* as the latter is of *Finnegans Wake.*

To preserve that entity Joyce recapitulated in the third childhood vignette those important elements of the first two, hence the dead priest that Professor ApRoberts takes such pains to exonerate from sin. That nameless cleric is a remanifestation of the dead Father Flynn, with a sister to inherit after him—lest we miss the connection between the two stories. (Professor ApRoberts will probably demand *two* sisters for a perfect analogy, but James Joyce rarely honors such demands for slavish literalness; in fact, Joyce's subtleties may often go unnoticed for decades—and perhaps forever—but the primary levels are clear enough here, the secondary allusions perceptible to more careful readings, and tertiary ones dependent upon unusual insights or accidental discoveries.) It should be apparent from the "background material" that organized religion in the shape of the Roman Catholic Church of Ireland is already a dead end for the young tenant of North Richmond Street: all of **"The Sisters"** and the first two paragraphs of **"Araby"** independently serve to make that point. The same is equally true for the freedom of open adventure: the Pigeon House was never reached; on the road inexplicable danger presented itself. This romantic young heart may continue to dream of Persia or the Wild West, or of Araby, but his physical confines will remain the streets of Dublin, "places the most hostile to romance." Other important sources for his direct participation in active life are just as arid: like the boy in **"The Sisters"** he is the ward of an aunt and uncle (no parents of any kind are mentioned in the middle story). He comes to realize himself superior to and divorced from his casual playmates (as the boy in **"An Encounter"** felt toward Mahony), and with the awakening of puppy love, even his aptitude in school begins to dim as any actual achievement worth his attention: "I watched my master's face pass from amiability to sternness; he hoped I was not beginning to idle." The full composite of his hopes and interests now centers about Mangan's sister and the Araby bazaar that was to him her temple. When this house of cards collapses, it represents a kind of total destruction from which he may never spiritually recover. If he fails to go on to absorb a sophisticated education, he faces a future like that of Thomas Chandler (**"A Little Cloud"**); if he diligently returns to his schoolwork but remains unable to re-establish ties with other people, he runs the risk of a dead life similar to that of James Duffy (**"A Painful Case"**). At best he can hope to survive his disillusionment on the surface at least, remaining somewhat cautious when it comes to "real" commitments—in which case he may well share the painful awakening of Gabriel Conroy (**"The Dead"**). *Dubliners* in toto is a self-contained artistic entity.

With the final sentence of **"Araby,"** then, we are given the boy's assessment of the totality of his experiences: "Gazing up into the darkness I saw myself as a creature driven and derided by vanity; and my eyes burned with anguish and anger." Despite the succinct quality of his self-evaluation, there are important connectives still missing. We have seen the protagonist as the victim of delusion, having assumed that there was something in this world pure and perfect, and worthy of his adoration. All of the dammed-up streams of parental love, religious involvement, adventurous spirit, and individuality had made a madonna of Mangan's sister and a chalice-bearing Knight Templar of her worshipper. When the glorious temple proves to be a dreary commercial enterprise, and its priestess (a surrogate for the Adored One) a drably flirtatious salesgirl, painful disillusion sets in. The extreme reaction

that he has is concomitant with the total commitment that he had made to the ideal of a personal religion based on Mangan's sister as his goddess. Yet his self-accusation of vanity is something of an enigma, since obviously it is the world around him that has failed him, that has proven tawdry and cheap throughout, and that at most he is guilty of childish naivete rather than vanity. Unless there is actually something else that the boy learns (something about himself, which he feels at that moment but does not openly explain), other than that he is confined like all others within the limitations of his environment. Is there some personal guilt that he has become aware of? The technique of first-person narration precludes our receiving all the information directly, yet that careful reading provides all the necessary information.

The locus of the boy's sudden awareness is in the snatch of conversation overheard, a technique familiar to readers of Joyce aware of the epiphanies he recorded from just this sort of eavesdropping. That the accents of the two young men indicate that they are English is significant, the clue throughout *Dubliners* of the external domination of the Irish by their British masters: Mr. Alleyne's "piercing North of Ireland accent" (**"Counterparts"**), Gallaher returned from London sporting an orange tie (**"A Little Cloud"**), Routh's triumph at cards when the Irish Jimmy Doyle is the heavy loser (**"After the Race"**), and so forth. The local shopgirl is in the process of selling herself to the Englishmen, who obviously possess a good deal more money than the meager eight pence that the boy has with which to buy a present that will win the love of Mangan's sister (this situation is comparable to that of Farrington in **"Counterparts,"** who loses at Indian wrestling to the English Weathers and then watches the London actress walk out, aware that his "want of money" prevents him from approaching her). The contrast to the boy is apparent: his was an exalted love, while the flirtation in the bazaar is unspeakably vulgar. Yet how different actually were these two instances? To what extent had he kept hidden from himself the common denominator that underscores the two? He had assumed that his beloved was radically different from the run on the mill female—but was she? He had also assumed that he was vastly superior to the young men on the make—but is he? He had directly associated a gift that he would purchase with the successful wooing of the girl he loved. We have seen him during his moments of ecstasy, pressing his trembling hands together and "murmuring, '*O love! O love!*' many times"—and the combined religious fervor and sexual excitement should have been apparent throughout to the adult reader, however disguised it may have been to the early adolescent undergoing the experience. "Every morning I lay on the floor in the front parlour watching her door"; "her name was like a summons to all my foolish blood"; "Her name sprang to my lips at moments in strange prayers and praises which I myself did not understand"; "my body was like a harp and her words and gestures were like fingers running upon the wires"; "All my senses seemed to desire to veil themselves": these are the verbalized sensations and attitudes of the young protagonist (although the language in which they are couched is already somewhat removed from his own vocabulary at the time). It requires no Freudian come from Vienna to read these phrases to us with the obvious emphases. The boy himself makes the analogy with religious devotion, yet it is clear to the reader that he has transferred the familiar responses from the Virgin to Mangan's sister. Until the epiphanic moment engendered by the small talk of the shopgirl and her admirers, the boy has remained unaware of the degree to which it is his awakening sexuality that is responding to the girl he adores. Having shrouded his pubescent desires in mystic mantles, he has watched them suddenly pierced during the encounter in the bazaar: his love was sensual and secular, and now openly reflected in the harsh English accents and the insipid female coyness.

That **"Araby"** is a story of the grossness of common sexuality does not alter the fact that it is a delicate narrative of a sensitive boy's disillusionment (a crucial stage in the development of the kind of paralysis that Joyce sought to dissect in his native city), any more than the fragile lyrics of *Chamber Music* lose either their fragility or lyricism from Joyce's often-stated explanation that his title included the tinkle of the chamber pot. It requires a prurient sensibility quite different from Joyce's to insist that one aspect cancels out the other. I will even go so far as to add my acceptance of the contention that Maria in **"Clay"** is polarized as both the Blessed Virgin and the Halloween Witch, so that at the center of the polarity she is merely a pitifully human Maria. The young James Joyce who wrote **Dubliners** may not yet have had the equipment to artifice a *Finnegans Wake,* but he already saw himself as a candidate for literary greatness, a potential genius waiting in the wings to be called onto the stage, and a rival of the God of the Creation. **"Araby"** is already well-encrusted with complexities and calculated contradictions. It is surprising, therefore, that Professor Stone, who plays this delicate harpsichord as if it were a Catherdral organ, should avoid the Freudian interpretations that have already appeared on **"Araby"**: "her figure defined by the light from the half-opened door" (yonic); "The rain impinges upon the earth, the fine incessant needles of water playing in the sodden beds" (phallic); "she turned a silver bracelet round and round her wrist" (yonic); "She held one of the spikes" (phallic); "I passed in quickly through a turnstile. . . . I found myself in a big hall" (yonic). One can only imagine the howls of anguish from Professor ApRoberts at such transgressions against "logic and common sense"; yet to the Freudian these elements obviously exist in the story and accurately supplement the surface concepts. The same Marvin Magalaner that Professor ApRoberts credits with the accurate identification of *The Devout Communicant* as that of Pacificus Baker has been responsible for a reading of **"Araby"** that would certainly be considered "illogical" by Professor ApRoberts.

The contest featuring Pacificus Baker against Abednego Seller is a main event destined to delight the hearts of Joycean enthusiasts for many years. In one corner, wearing the orange trunks of a heretical Protestant is Seller, championed by Harry Stone; in the other corner, sporting the ecclesiastically purple trunks of a devout Catholic, stands Baker, brought out of retirement by Robert P. ApRoberts for a comeback. Two *Devout Communicants* in an embarrassment of riches, comparable only to having two Saint Patricks. How careless of James Joyce to have failed to provide us with the author's name in this instance! He left no doubt that *The Abbot* was written by Sir Walter Scott, and of course Vidocq's name is embedded in his title and cannot be avoided; but here is a mysterious volume titled *The Devout Communicant* and no author's name attached to avoid confusion. The "true scholar" that Professor ApRoberts postulates (who "checks out every fact to the end") would now have to find a yellow-paged candidate to solve the enigma—if the enigma were actually intended by Joyce to be solved. Joyce was a rummager through secondhand bookstalls and has left us quite a list of those existing in the Dublin of his day (in **"The Dead"** we hear about "Hickey's on Bachelor's Walk," "Webb's or Massey's on Ashton's Quay," and "O'Clohissey's in the by-street"; in *Ulysses* we find the "hawker's cart" under "Merchant's arch," "an old one in Liffey street," "Clohissey's," and the "slanted bookcart")— could Joyce have noticed the disparate volumes at any of these? Professor ApRoberts checked the current catalogue of the National Library of Ireland; did he also canvass Marsh's Library in Dublin, or the Bibliothèque Nationale and Bibliothèque Sainte-Geneviève in Paris? Joyce frequented those as well prior to 1904. Can we credit the bibliophilic Joyce with purposely keeping the identity of the boy's yellow-paged find a mystery to invite just the sort of speculation that the Stone-ApRoberts controversy has produced? It would certainly be in keeping with Joyce's bizarre sense of humor. Obviously the author of the particular volume is of no concern to the boy in the story, anymore than its subject matter. He is preoccupied with the charisma of the yellow pages, which serves as a clue to his romantic disposition.

This in itself should indicate to the reader something about James Joyce's artistic attitudes: he engenders mysteries with great delight and sits back to watch the scholars scurry about for elucidation. At times he ventures forward to lend a hand; at other times he keeps himself refined out of existence: at first he refused to disclose the schema to *Ulysses;* later he relented. That entire second paragraph of **"Araby"** is veiled with such enigmas, as Professor Stone indicates as he plunges beneath the veil. It is devoted to the dead clergyman and his legacy, and should we dismiss it as mere exposition (it would be a rare luxury in the tales styled in "scrupulous meanness"), Joyce brings the priest back later in the story: "One evening I went into the back drawing-room in which the priest had died." In exonerating the priest Professor ApRoberts runs the risk of eradicating him altogether, although he understandably objects to the heavy-handed treatment that had been afforded this paragraph. What do those three books actually signify about the priest? Nothing that would stand up in a court of law. We know nothing about how he came to have them, what use he put them to, what he thought of them, or who abandoned them—the priest himself or his sister? Assuming that these were deleted from the rest of his books by the legatee, would Pacificus Baker's properly Catholic *Devout Communicant* be junked along with Scott and Vidocq? We are treated to fragments of evidence that do not tell their entire tale, and we are told only what the finder, the central intelligence of **"Araby,"** knows or cares about. He passes no judgment on the priest, sees no mock-Eden in the "wild garden" or its "apple-tree," and comes to no conclusion about the "rusty bicycle-pump" (even Freudian analysts have avoided concrete conjecturing on that suspicious object). The boy merely transmits without comment of his own the hearsay of adults: "He was a very charitable priest; in his will he had left all his money to institutions and the furniture of his house to his sister." The protagonist shows no awareness of irony here, although Professor Stone is correct in his suspicion of intended irony. It seems inconceivable that James Joyce would have perpetrated such a sentence without ironic intention, but Joyce's irony is often a delicate sort of understructure. The heavy array of bricks that Professor Stone piles upon this one may cause it to buckle dangerously.

We might allow this particular priest, despite his strange reading habits and his suspect generosity, to get off lightly were he not one in a succession of priests who are suspicious personages in *Dubliners.* They range from the unfortunately demented Father Flynn (**"The Sisters"**) to the black sheep Father Keon (**"Ivy Day in the Committee Room"**) and that proponent of the celestial double-entry ledger, Father Purdon (**"Grace"**). In fact, there is not a single Catholic cleric in all of *Dubliners* whose role is not in some way actually sinister, even in their negative existences: the Father Butler who is not likely to be at the Pigeon House (**"An Encounter"**), the nameless priest—his photograph is already "yellowing"—who has long since left for Australia (**"Eveline"**), and the Father Conroy whose absence from his aunts' annual fête causes no comment at all (**"The Dead"**). Professor ApRoberts' naivete about Joyce's priest would be understandable if **"Araby"** were so self-contained that not a single other piece of Joycean writing existed.

The Stone case for the "Godless and Graceless Florin," however, does not quite ring true, and the ApRoberts rebuttal carries weight. When so arbitrary a choice for a worthless piece of abandoned junk as a rusty bicycle-pump proves to be only a naturalistic element in the story, the common two-shilling coin seems intended for service only within the realm of verisimilitude. Of the possible single coins (I assume that the single coin here parallels the tribute exacted in **"Two Gallants"** and the bribe offered in **"The Dead"**), only the half-crown might have been a logical alternative, since a shilling alone would be insufficient for fare and entrance fee, and anything more than half-a-crown exorbitant. Yet the coin and the change derived therefrom do function tangentially as symbolic of commercialism and betrayal within the framework of **"Araby,"** although Professor Stone gratuitously attributes a Judas role to the boy who is actually the betrayed. Since

Professor ApRoberts discovered the origin of the florin in the *Encyclopedia Britannica,* and suspects that his predecessor might have done the same, it is only by logical extension to presume that Joyce preceded both of them to that source—he was an avid user of the *Encyclopedia Britannica* (particularly the eleventh edition). Is it not a typically scholastic attitude to assume that creative writers are not equipped to do the kind of minute research that the scholar does? In the case of James Joyce, I would conjecture that he left his thumbprint on more books than even the best of his commentators, and might well have been smiling to himself as he handed the boy his florin. But if he was, he made very little effort to share the irony with his readers, leaving Professor Stone almost no tangible evidence to support his assertions. But the commercial coin is a weighty symbol in *Dubliners.* The remaining eight pence in the boy's pocket (pitifully insufficient even in the original two-shilling state to buy a fitting tribute to the madonna of his dreams) are mocked at the bazaar by the larger amounts of money being counted on the salver, in the same sense that the boy is dwarfed by the "great jars that stood like eastern guards." The florin not only has its counterpart in the coin exacted by Corley from the slavey and the gratuity foisted on Lily by the embarrassed Gabriel Conroy, but the hard facts of economic existence and some of its concomitant sordidness dominate all the adult stories in the book (Mrs. Mercer and her pawnbroker-husband heralding an entire parade of the mercantile and the mercenary): Eveline's poverty; Jimmy Doyle's losses at cards; Bob Doran's "bit of stuff put by"; Chandler's envy of Gallaher's success; Farrington's pawned watch; Maria pauperized in the laundry; Mr. Duffy's speculations about embezzlement; the unpaid election canvassers; Mrs. Kearney's insistence that her daughter be paid in advance; Father Purdon's sermon to the business community; Freddy Malins' Christmas card shop. No matter how Godly and Graceful the florin in **"Araby"** may be, it serves as a symbol of buying and selling.

It is because Professor Stone makes such conclusive pronouncements on such tenuous evidence that he provides his adversary with so accessible a target. Yet the case for Mangan's sister being larger than life remains a strong one (I am dubious, however, about the "Dark Rosaleen" as the necessary evocation). As a designation for the loved one, "Mangan's sister" has a significant sound despite Professor ApRoberts' scoffing. It is true that the boy would refer to his schoolmate by last name as is traditional in school, but the sister is not a classmate of his, nor one of the boys. She must have a first name and the boy must know it, yet the awe with which he regards her is detrimental to actual familiarity. "Mangan's sister" is a title rather than a name: its corollary may well be "Christ's mother" in an Irish Catholic milieu. That the boy never sees her as the Mary or Rosie or Flossie that she actually is serves to underscore the romantically warped view that he has imposed upon the ordinary girl. "Mangan is such a common Irish name," Professor ApRoberts insists, but were it as common as Murphy (which it is not), it would still signify James Clarence Mangan to Joyce and should to any careful reader of Joyce. The romantic despondency associated with that unfortunate poet is the common Irish malady that Joyce sees in the Dublin world of **"Araby."**

In contrast to the bold assertions of Harry Stone, Professor ApRoberts avoids committing himself to any significant reading of the story. He maintains that there is no thesis to the Stone case, yet there is a very precise and excellent one: that **"Araby"** serves as a vital introduction of many of the motifs of the later works of James Joyce. It is unfortunate that in being so right Professor Stone manages to sound so wrong. The *Finnegans Wake* quotation is awkwardly pushed forward for explication, and it turns out to be an explication on only the most literal level and divorced from the context which enriches it many times over. That the "whole of Book IV of *Finnegans Wake* . . . takes place in an instant between Holy Saturday and Easter Sunday" is inaccurate: even if one assumes that the dream is taking place on Saturday night (and many *Wake* analysts now contend that it is Friday), the instant that divides one day from another is necessarily at midnight, while Book IV takes place unmistakably at dawn. I also question Professor Stone's assumption that the girl working in the bazaar is English. It is hardly likely that English sales help would be coming to work in economically deprived Dublin—the actual emigration went in the other direction (and still does). It is Joyce's vague antecedent that is actually responsible for the critic's misreading: "At the door of the stall a young lady was talking and laughing with two young gentlemen. I remarked their English accents. . . ." The men are English ("their" refers back to them alone); the girl most likely is local. The Joycean motif is of the Irish selling themselves to the English—like the slavey in **"Two Gallants"** giving both body and coin to Corley, "the son of an inspector of police." The same sort of casualness with antecedents might have resulted in Professor Stone's contention that the Gerty MacDowell of *Ulysses* is eighteen years old: we know that "Gerty would never see seventeen again," but that is hardly proof that she is only eighteen. The troublesome sentence is the one that reads: "Then they could talk about her till they went blue in the face, Bertha Supple too, and Edy, the spitfire, because she would be twenty-two in November." The next sentence begins, "She would care for him with creature comforts . . ."—an indication that the "she" who will be 22 is the she who will "care for him," that is, the Gerty who is "womanly wise." That she is past the first bloom of youth is important to our awareness of the repressed sensuality of the beautiful but lame Gerty, making her desire to marry the much younger Reggy Wylie that much more pathetic.

In the final analysis there may not really be much to choose between the extreme approaches to **"Araby"** offered by the two contenders. On one hand we have Robert P. ApRoberts asserting that "nothing could be less suggestive of a response to sensuality than the response the boy makes," while on the other Harry Stone contends that "Joyce was a materialist, a man of almost paranoiac cupidity and selfishness." In Joycean terminology the Stone

case "has the true scholastic stink" (we might remember that in *Exiles* Robert Hand claims to be able to swim "like a stone"), while the ApRoberts correctives are full of sound and fury, signifying very little. Between the muddy torrents and the shallow pool a third stream approach seems necessary. In *Finnegans Wake* the Four Old Men present their individual commentaries on the events of Chapter 16: Matt's is the "First position of harmony"; Mark offers "a second position of discordance"; Luke follows with his "Third position of concord," still leaving room for John's "Fourth position of solution." In the Great **"Araby"** Controversy we may still look forward to a non-synoptic gospeller.

Frank Turaj (essay date 1970)

SOURCE: "'Araby' and *Portrait*: Stages of Pagan Conversion, in *English Language Notes*, Vol. 7, No. 3, March 3, 1970, pp. 209–13.

[*In the following essay, Turaj finds a parallel between "Araby" and* Portrait of the Artist as a Young Man, *maintaining that the two works represent two different stages in Joyce's personal development.*]

"Araby" is regarded as the story of a boy for whom young love becomes mystical and religious. It is partly a story of his initiation into love, and it is partly a story of his conversion *from* orthodox religion. Besides being a principal theme in Joyce's writing, this dialogue of the world and the spirit is, of course, a main fact in his life. A striking resemblance between the devices and themes of **"Araby"** and Chapter IV of *A Portrait of the Artist as a Young Man* suggests the process of the resolution of this dialogue, this conflict, both in Joyce's fiction and in his personal conversion to esthetic worldliness in his own life, as he recollects this artistically. That is, the resemblance really shows two stages in the conversion from Catholicism to "Paganism" of Dedalus-Joyce.

Chapter IV of the novel, the pivotal chapter, focuses on Stephen Dedalus' visit to the director priest, who attempts to recruit him for the Catholic priesthood. It then changes focus to reveal the opposite drive in Stephen's life as he watches the bathers. The scene with the director is famous:

> The director stood in the embrasure of the window, his back to the light, leaning an elbow on the brown crossblind, and as he spoke and smiled, slowly dangling and looping the cord of the other blind. . . . The priest's face was in total shadow, but the waning daylight from behind him touched the deeply grooved temples . . . of the skull.

The significance of the scene is revealed in the language and the imagery. The priest's back was to the light. He leans on a "crossblind." He dangles a cord (noose?). His "face was in total shadow." There was "waning daylight."

The reference to "deeply grooved temples" possibly involves a pun on the word "temples." The priest's head is referred to as a skull.

Directly after leaving the rectory, Stephen sees some boys swimming. Now the living sensuous world attracts him: "This was the call of life to his soul, not the dull gross voice of the world of duties and despair, not the inhuman voice that had called him to the pale service of the altar." He sees a girl standing in the water (italics have been added):

> She seemed like one whom magic had changed into the likeness of a strange and beautiful seabird. Her long slender bare legs were delicate as a crane's and pure save where an emerald trail of seaweed had fashioned itself as *a sign upon the flesh*. Her thighs, fuller and softhued as ivory, were bared almost to the hips where the white fringes of her drawers were like featherings of soft white down. Her slateblue skirts were kilted boldly about her waist and *dovetailed* behind her. Her bosom was as a bird's soft and slight, slight and soft as the breast of some *darkplumaged dove*. But her long fair hair was girlish: and girlish, and touched with the wonder *mortal beauty*, her face.

> She was alone and still, gazing out to sea; and when she felt his presence and the *worship* of his eyes her eyes turned to him. . . .—*Heavenly God! cried Stephen's soul*, in an outburst of *profane joy*.

The italicized words indicate the religious-like response to a thing of simple mortal existence. The phrasing suggests the conventions from which Stephen derives responses, generally religious words and images, and also (these not italicized) pagan overtones deriving from some general symbols, e.g., "strange and beautiful seabird," "emerald trail of seaweed," "ivory," "featherings of soft white down," "long fair hair." Stephen's fervor is transferring from things perceived by religious perception to things perceived by sense perception.

The boy in **"Araby"** is in the process of an analogous transformation. Like Stephen, he carries a way of thinking, an indoctrination, into a different—but psychologically related—plot context. The religious motif is woven into the story from the very first line (italics added): "North Richmond Street, *being blind*, was a quiet street except at the hour when the *Christian* Brothers' School *set the boys free*. An uninhabited house of two stories [Old and New Testaments?] stood at the *blind end*, detached from its neighbors in a square of ground. . . . The former tenant of our house, *a priest, had died* in the back drawing-room." All this is purposeful. The suggestions are of things musty, dull, dim, dead. Compare the passage to the one quoted from *Portrait* where the priest is described in a context of blindness and death, "back to the light," "crossblind," "skull," etc.

In the next few lines of **"Araby"** the author, or implied author, brings himself into the story. He mentions immediately the books he found in the room where the priest had died, "*The Abbot* by Walter Scott, *The Devout Communicant* and *The Memoirs of Vidocq*." He likes the last best, a worldly memoir. He favors this over a romantic novel of religion and a religious manual. Immediately the reader is told, "The wild garden behind the house contained a central apple-tree. . . ." In the light of developments, the seduction of his emotions, the meaning of the "garden" is worth contemplating.

The boy becomes interested in the girl. So far in his life he has really only known one set of emotional responses, those taught him by the Christian Brothers. Since he doesn't have even a father or mother—he has an aunt and an uncle instead—he is still further removed from the normal emotional process, and the significance of his Christian Brothers education looms larger. He transfers his religious responses, the kind he knows, to the girl.

A moment of illumination in this story comes when the boy returns to the "drawing room in which the priest had died." He sees "some distant lamp or lighted window . . ." like a votive light in a church. Then, like Stephen Dedalus, the boy experiences a conversion, a pagan conversion: "All my senses seemed to desire to veil themselves and feeling that I was about to slip from them, I pressed the palms of my hands together until they trembled, murmuring: '*O love! O love!*' many times." He is less mature and less intellectually aware than Stephen, so he does not yet realize that it is precisely a thing of the senses to which he is responding. He has retained the proper attitude for prayer, but his god has changed.

The girl speaks to him of **"Araby,"** or a place where material delights, gifts to the senses, abound. We get this image of her: "The light from the lamp opposite our door caught the white curve of her neck, lit up her hair that rested there and, falling, lit up the hand upon the railing. It fell over one side of her dress and caught the white border of a petticoat, just visible as she stood at ease." The light seems to trace something like a marble statue. One thinks of the convention with which the Virgin is represented. But the image informs us of the nature of this goddess. She is quite mortal: "the white border of a petticoat." Recall the passage quoted from *Portrait* of the girl standing in the water. There are trace resemblances again, "the white fringes of her drawers," and other soft and subtle similarities.

In both instances, *Portrait* and **"Araby,"** the subject is in a border world where worship and piety are confused with worship and passion. In each case feminine attraction carries religious suggestion.

The boy plans to go to the bazaar, **"Araby."** His aunt hopes it will not be "some Freemason affair," some nonorthodox activity. But his purpose for going is quite worldly, in fact a sort of pagan quest to obtain an object for tribute. His aunt, at one point, suggests, "I'm afraid you may put off your bazaar for this night of our lord." It is ironically a "night of our lord," considering the boy's new objective for his worshipful pilgrimage.

Joyce describes the bazaar in terms suggesting a church. The boy enters in awe. A reaction forms: "Gazing up into the darkness I saw myself a creature driven and derided by vanity; and my eyes burned with anguish and anger." He gazes up, as one gazes up in prayer, but now finds "darkness." He is gazing up into the "darkness" of "vanity." He has not escaped the training of the Christian Brothers. It dogs him.

The boy is not old enough to interpret his experience, or realize it, or articulate it as Stephen does, but this is essentially what has happened: Indoctrinated and imbued with the true spirit of Irish Catholicism, he reacts toward romanticism. He could have gone in three more-or-less romantic directions, monastic as exemplified by Walter Scott, devout pietism as illustrated in the handbook, or worldly romance. His favorite of the three books indicates his particular bent.

One may change ideas, but it is difficult to alter a way of thinking. He approaches love religiously. It replaces or palliates the character of the street, Christian, dead, and blind. Since the change is gradual—we read the story only when the boy is already familiar with the books and has already known the girl through the window for awhile—we witness it at a critical time.

If we take into consideration the different contexts and stages of maturity, this experience anticipates what happens to Stephen Dedalus. The change in the adolescent predicts the more conscious, deliberate, intellectual change in Dedalus-Joyce. In effect, **"Araby"** shows Joyce's recollection of the time when his vision began to change, and *Portrait* shows him when he finally grasped the change and accepted it. Shows it, that is, within the license of art.

Edward Brandabur (essay date 1971)

SOURCE: "The Green Stem of Fortune," in *A Scrupulous Meanness: A Study of Joyce's Early Work,* University of Illinois Press, 1971, pp. 49–56.

[*In the following essay, Brandabur provides a thematic overview of "Araby."*]

From the harsher portrayals of Dublin's youth encountering perversity in the first two stories, Joyce turns to romance. For **"Araby"** displays characteristics of "Romance" described by Northrop Frye in *Anatomy of Criticism* most clearly as it concerns the hero's power of action: "If superior in *degree* to other men and to his environment, the hero is the typical hero of romance, whose actions are marvelous but who is himself identified as a human being. The hero of romance moves in a world in which the ordinary laws of nature are slightly suspended."[1] Although like all the stories in *Dubliners,* **"Araby"** falls most obviously into the ironic mode, for the reader finds himself "looking down on a scene of bondage, frustration, or absurdity,"[2] the protagonist attempts to transcend his

limitations by "romantic" means. He earnestly imagines a "eucharistic" suspension of the laws of nature. Of course, Joyce works most effectively by mingling the ironic and romantic modes, as he will mix the tragic and ironic in **"A Painful Case,"** the comic and ironic in **"The Dead."** In all three stories the "heroism" cannot be purely romantic, tragic, or comic because of the sadomasochistic motivations at work. These motivations undermine the archetypal "purity" of romantic, tragic, comic quests. For example, the romantic quest of the boy in **"Araby"** proves a delusion because the boy realizes his contempt for the romantic gratification he appears to want. He prefers frustration, though he wears the trappings of desire. In **"A Painful Case,"** Mr. Duffy cannot evoke an unequivocal pity because compulsively he engineers his own tragic isolation. In **"The Dead,"** Gabriel cannot be a "pure" comic hero because his desire for the comic bride, Gretta, is undercut by an inhibiting hatred for her. The "irony" of *Dubliners* is not in showing up how foolish these characters are for thinking they can pretend heroism in Dublin. Rather, it is in showing the reader's archetypal expectations as delusions. They will not bear up under the sharp gaze of Joyce, whose eyes are ours for the duration of our reading. A close look at **"Araby"** will reveal this special Joycean irony.

In **"Araby"** an adolescent boy is romantically attracted to a neighbor girl, although he does not communicate with her until in a casual meeting she asks him if he is going to a bazaar called **"Araby"**; he attends the bazaar to buy a gift for the girl but, delayed by his uncle, he arrives as it is closing and buys nothing.

The protagonist's goal appears to be the indirect manifestation of his feelings to the girl; he goes to **"Araby"** like a troubadour-knight in the service of his lady.[3] He is inhibited from expressing himself directly to her; like Chaucer's courtly Troilus he watches her from afar: "Every morning I lay on the floor in the front parlour watching her door. The blind was pulled down to within an inch of the sash so that I could not be seen" (p. 30). But his quest is more elaborate than a juvenile attempt to give a shy valentine. One must look at the sacramental element in the story to delineate this intricate quest.

The protagonist actually seeks union not with the girl directly but with her image, a surrogate both for the religious belief which he has virtually given up as dead and hopeless and for an actual relationship with a girl which is also so hopeless for him that he cannot bring himself even to consider it openly. the defining circumstances of his quest suggest both what it replaces and what its character as surrogate must be. The story begins with the description of North Richmond Street which, by synecdoche for all the ways of Dublin, is a dead-end street at the "blind end" of which stands an uninhabited house where a priest had died leaving behind the "old useless papers" of his career. Among these are Scott's *The Abbot, The Devout Communicant,* and *The Memoirs of Vidocq,* which in their uselessness evoke both the ineffectuality of religion and the futility of romance in Dublin. The futility of religion has been explored especially in **"The Sisters,"** as in this story the death of romance, but it is romance in a "sacramental" sense, even though the chivalric trappings are present. The youthful crusader's first encounter with his "lady" suggests the ritual of a courtly *donnoi:*

> She asked me was I going to *Araby.* . . . While she spoke she turned a silver bracelet round and round her wrist. She could not go, she said, because there would be a retreat that week in her convent. Her brother and two other boys were fighting for their caps and I was alone at the railings. She held one of the spikes, bowing her head towards me. The light from the lamp opposite our door caught the white curve of her neck, lit up her hair that rested there and, falling, lit up the hand upon the railing. It fell over one side of her dress and caught the white border of her petticoat, just visible as she stood at ease.
>
> (pp. 31–32)

The erotic implication of the bracelet and the spike is unmistakable, as is the suggestion of her acquiescence in his desire for her. But his quest is not simply erotic, nor even simply at the level of romantic transcendence. His quest for her is combined with his quest for a priestly role. Here, as in the courtly love tradition, religion and romance combine with the difference of course that the medieval system employed religious elements as a convention largely because they were readily available. But in this story and throughout Joyce's writing, religious elements, particularly the liturgical and sacramental, unite with romance in an order not primarily romantic or religious, but a new combination: the transubstantiation of experience which **"Araby"** describes.

This "sacramental" process can be shown in **"Araby"** by assuming from the start the boy's identification with the dead priest, in terms of which he carries out his peculiar and isolated adventure. If the story chiefly depicted shy adolescent love, overwrought and disappointed, one could not account for the attention given to these squalid relics of a dead priest. But the first two paragraphs focus on his abandoned house which is a parody of the ruined monastery essential to gothic tales, haunted by sacred ghosts. Joyce's Dublin is one of the first cities to be haunted by modern ghosts—wasteland figures from a past which was neither vital or romantic, living in houses with pretentious histories, like "the house on Usher's Island" in **"The Dead"**; or Mr. Duffy's parody of a hermitage in **"A Painful Case."** In Dublin, imagination must have its reliquaries, even at the cost of parody. The shy and curious protagonist had poked about in this house enough to describe with affection the objects left behind. He reveres especially the old "useless" books: "I liked the last [*The Memoirs of Vidocq*] best because its leaves were yellow" (p. 29). After these introductory descriptions, the story recounts the boy's infatuation with Mangan's sister, who, like the priest, affects him entirely from a distance: "I did not know whether I would ever speak to her or not or, if I spoke to her, how I could tell her of my confused adora-

tion. But my body was like a harp and her words and gestures were like fingers running upon the wires" (p. 31).

The tension built up by his "confused adoration" comes to a head when the boy goes into the room where the priest had died: "It was a dark rainy evening and there was no sound in the house. Through one of the broken panes I heard the rain impinge upon the earth, the fine incessant needles of water playing in the sodden beds. Some distant lamp or lighted window gleamed below me. I was thankful that I could see so little. All my senses seemed to desire to veil themselves and, feeling that I was about to slip from them, I pressed the palms of my hands together until they trembled, murmuring: *O love! O love!* many times" (p. 31). Just before this episode, the boy had described himself in a priestly role, listening to "the shrill litanies of shop-boys . . . the nasal chanting of street-singers," sounds which "converged in a single sensation of life for me: I imagined that I bore my chalice safely through a throng of foes. Her name sprang to my lips at moments in strange prayers and praises which I myself did not understand" (p. 31).

Priest-like, the boy carries his eucharist, the image of Mangan's sister. The intense incident in the priest's room implies the verging on a suprasensory transcendence of the conditions of reality. The climax of tension in his rubbing of his hands together is also an invocation, his murmuring "*O love! O love!* many times." Probably also it is an auto-erotic displacement. The boy does carry out his erotic desire for Mangan's sister in fantasy which includes eros and eucharist, though the girl is not thought of primarily with affection but with veneration. The sexual element appears mainly through symbolic suggestion, as she turns a bracelet idly on her wrist and holds a fence spike while bowing in assent towards him, like Polly in **"The Boarding House,"** an obscene madonna.[4] The masochistic aspect of this posture Joyce recognized in his own affairs. In a letter to Nora he desired flagellation along with the visual realization of her in the typical Joycean image of woman as an obscene madonna: "Tonight I have an idea madder than usual. I feel I would like to be flogged by you. I would like to see your eyes blazing with anger. I wonder is there some madness in me. Or is love madness? One moment I see you like a virgin or madonna the next moment I see you shameless, insolent, half-naked and obscene."[5]

In **"Araby,"** the moment of invocation leads at once to a description of the first actual encounter between the protagonist and Mangan's sister, with his promise to bring her something from **"Araby."** After this, "the syllables of the word *Araby* were called to me through the silence in which my soul luxuriated and cast an Eastern enchantment over me" (p. 32). An "Eastern enchantment" urges the boy once again into a posture of transcendence. On the night he goes to **"Araby"** the ticking clock annoyingly reminds him of the conditions of reality, from which he wishes to flee into his interior state of sacramental transcendence:

> I mounted the staircase and gained the upper part of the house. The high cold empty gloomy rooms liberated me and I went from room to room singing. From

the front window I saw my companions playing below in the street. Their cries reached me weakened and indistinct and, leaning my forehead against the cool glass, I looked over at the dark house where she lived. I may have stood there for an hour, seeing nothing but the brown-clad figure cast by my imagination, touched discreetly by the lamplight at the curved neck, at the hand upon the railings and at the border below the dress.

(p. 33)

Adequately to achieve his quest, the boy must escape the vivacious sounds and warmth of life, where the clock speaks of human limitation into a state where passion freezes through the operation of the intellect and imagination: "leaning my forehead against the cool glass, I looked over at the dark house where she lived."[6] As with Stephen Dedalus, in his relation with Emma at the end of *A Portrait,* here at work is "the spiritual—heroic refrigerating apparatus, invented and patented in all countries by Dante Alighieri" (*Portrait,* p. 252).

The story ends with his coming to **"Araby,"** a rapidly darkening hall where it appears that he is not so much disillusioned about the sham nature of his quest as about his desire for what the surrogate replaced. Both encounters with women in the story occur across symbolic barriers and the last, with the salesgirl, conduces to the epiphany. She is the terminus of the protagonist's quest from whom he will presumably buy a trinket to manifest his romantic feelings. But when he arrives at **"Araby"** she is talking with two young Englishmen. The protagonist finds himself at once in a traditionally inferior position with respect to the salesgirl, who is surrounded by objects symbolically erotic: "Observing me the young lady came over and asked me did I wish to buy anything. The tone of her voice was not encouraging; she seemed to have spoken to me out of a sense of duty. I looked humbly at the great jars that stood like eastern guards at either side of the dark entrance to the stall and murmured:—No, thank you" (p. 35). His turning away implies the rejection of an erotic commitment felt to be futile at least partially because of that feeling of sexual inadequacy typical of the Joycean male. The dominating English command her attention, and the protagonist achieves an epiphany constituted partially of his feeling of ultimate rejection by the woman and partially of awareness of his own crushed masculinity. "I lingered before her stall, though I knew my stay was useless, to make my interest in her wares seem the more real. Then I turned away slowly and walked down the middle of the bazaar. I allowed the two pennies to fall against the sixpence in my pocket. I heard a voice call from one end of the gallery that the light was out. The upper part of the hall was now completely dark" (p. 35). Once again, the principle of defeat in his quest resides in a pleasant and vicious area of the soul. The itch of masochism urges him finally to look into the sad darkness of self-awareness: "Gazing up into the darkness I saw myself as a creature driven and derided by vanity; and my eyes burned with anguish and anger" (p. 35).

Like most of the Dubliners, the protagonist in **"Araby"** turns back on the threshold of what he has apparently sought. Like Eveline, who refuses erotic possibilities at the barrier of "the black mass of the ship"; like Mr. Duffy, who flees from the woman with whom he had been cultivating an intimate relationship at the instant when her touch prepared for a consummation of intimacy; like Gabriel, in **"The Dead,"** whose desire for Gretta subsides when he is alone with her, the urge for self-defeat brings the protagonist in **"Araby"** to a final repudiation of what he had seemed to want.

Notes

1. Northrop Frye, *Anatomy of Criticism* (Princeton, 1957), p. 33.

2. *Ibid.,* p. 34.

3. Cleanth Brooks observed the symbolic character of the boy's actions: "The present he hopes to bring her from Araby would somehow serve as a means of communicating his feelings to her, a symbol for their relationship in the midst of the inimical world." Brooks and Robert Penn Warren, *Understanding Fiction* (New York, 1959), p. 190.

4. Mr. Harry Stone presents a long list of archetypal and literary elements in this story, among them the liaison of harlot and "Lady of Romance," as a "pose" on the part of Mangan's sister. "'Araby' and the Writings of James Joyce," *The Antioch Review* 25 (Fall, 1965): 375–410.

5. Joyce to Nora, September 2, 1909, *Letters,* vol. 2, p. 243.

6. Dennis Donoghue perceives a similar pattern in everything Joyce wrote: "Joyce's career is an instance . . . of the gradual abandonment of the finite order, the virtual rejection of the human, the dissolution of time and history." "Joyce and the Finite Order," *Sewanee Review* 68 (Spring, 1960): 270. Though an unqualified generalization about Joyce's work, it suggests something which Joyce criticizes in his compatriots, who invariably prefer to rise above the conditions of existence, the world of "fact," into the ornate realm of Irish imagination.

Epifanio San Juan, Jr. (essay date 1972)

SOURCE: "Araby," in *James Joyce and the Craft of Fiction: An Interpretation of Dubliners,* Fairleigh Dickinson University Press, 1972, pp. 54–67.

[*In the following essay, San Juan offers a stylistic analysis of "Araby."*]

Among the various reasons why the existing interpretations of **"Araby"** have failed to grasp the principle of organization informing the narrative, I would point to the wrong emphasis placed upon stylistic details—the texture of description, the rhetorical appeals of imagery and ambiguous allusions, symbols, and so on—and the distortion of form created by this emphasis.[1] For if the formal whole of the story resides in the parts, the verbal devices which constitute the means of representation, then we may ask why the narrative has to present events in a sequence. And why should such an experience, consisting not only of images or of thoughts but also of decisions leading to acts that change the situation of the protagonist—why should the boy's experience be arranged in the precise order of revelation that we find in the story?

We can clearly account for the kind of formal wholeness realized by the story if, assuming that the whole is composed of a meaningful sequence of parts, we can formulate the principle enabling the story to exercise its power upon us through its own aesthetic integrity. My concern then would be with the formal structure of the story, the disposition of parts—plot, character, thought, and diction—in order to achieve certain effects.

The plot of "Araby" is a dynamic and complex one, consisting of a change in the fortune of the protagonist from a passionate "lover," sensitive and obsessed with heroic possibilities, to a disappointed visitor of a bazaar. Put this way, one perceives the absence of any contradiction between the initial condition and the final state of the character. A reversal occurs on the level of expectation and its nonfulfillment: the boy promised Mangan's sister to bring her a gift if he should succeed in going to the bazaar. The conditional mode of expressing his intention clearly discounts any exaggerated vision of future accomplishment; but this effect is part of the marked contrast in tone between the dialogue and the emotional response surrounding this isolated exchange between the idolized girl and the idealizing sensibility of the boy:

—It's well for you, she said.

—If I go, I said, I will bring you something.

What innumerable follies laid waste my waking and sleeping thoughts after that evening!

and so on. Note the similar discrepancy, the curve of deflation, in the preceding paragraphs, with the paragraph beginning "One evening I went into the back drawing-room. . . ." That isolation, the feeling of acute empathy, accelerates into sublime rapture, only to be undercut by the factual transcript of the first verbal exchange:

All my senses seemed to desire to veil themselves and, feeling that I was about to slip from them, I pressed the palms of my hands together until they trembled, murmuring: "O love! O love!" many times.

At last she spoke to me. When she addressed the first words to me I was so confused that I did not know what to answer. She asked me was I going to *Araby*. I forgot whether I answered yes or no. It would be a splendid bazaar, she said she would love to go.

The nature of the boy's response provides a key to our understanding of why the experience in the bazaar should be an inevitable conclusion and the last statement a surprising but probable generalization of the boy's ordeal for himself.

We derive quite a different perception of the boy's predicament, a grasp of the limitations and possibilities of the epiphany uttered at the end, in our acquaintance with the movement of the plot. The action proper begins with the middle of the story, with the paragraph beginning "At last she spoke to me. . . ." Prior to this, the exposition gives us all the relevant facts and information needed to make the boy's actions most probable and his response both unexpected and most likely. An inverted-pyramid pattern holds the details of setting (from panoramic scope to gradual localization into scenic background: North Richmond Street to garden and drawing-room, etc.), of space and time, until, the external circumstances established, the boy's inner world is systematically disclosed, from past routine—the collective sharing of childhood games in habitual times and places—to emotional concentration on his affection for Mangan's sister. Then, with the interiorization of this particular person in the boy's consciousness, the narrator describes what consequences arose from this focus on her image, how the world's appearance varied, how the boy's attitudes and feelings toward his habitual ways and associations subsequently changed, until his commitment to a promise moves him to action. The order of the exposition is controlled by a rhetorical purpose: to arouse our sympathetic identification with the boy by a vivid, concrete actualization of his world in sensuous details and their appeal to the boy's awareness of value at this stage. Thus the objective recording of surface phenomena—houses with "brown imperturbable faces," "musty" air of the drawing room, curled and damp pages of books, and the like—entails the corresponding effects on the boy's mind implied by the emphasis on sensory qualities: visual, auditory, tactile, and olfactory sensations predominate.

As the exposition develops, the stages of temporal specification harmonize with the concurrent heightening of the boy's presence in such an environment. Environment becomes a world. The first two paragraphs consist of the general and the particular geography of the story; the next two paragraphs convey the general (season) and specific temporal duration of the boy's experience prior to the momentous Saturday, the journey/pilgrimage to *Araby*. Further narrowing or close-up in time is accomplished by the change from the customary "Every morning I lay on the floor in the front parlour" to the climactic "One evening I went into the back drawing-room," this transition bridged by a paragraph embodying the charismatic force of the girl's image on the boy's consciousness, the cathexis of energy somehow converting the series of events in the boy's Saturday evenings into a static configuration. The total impact reduces his existence to a poetic instrument: ". . . my body was like a harp and her words and gestures were like fingers running upon the wires."

The orientation of place and time functions chiefly to form our idea of character in revealing the boy's thoughts, ideas, attitudes, and feelings about the objects and persons around him. Description of place contains within itself the manner of perceiving and responding. The narrator renders the boy's solidarity with his peers, their sense of community and sportiveness, his awareness of affective qualities, without discrimination:

> The space of sky above us was the colour of ever-changing violet and towards it the lamps of the street lifted their feeble lanterns. The cold air stung us and we played till our bodies glowed. Our shouts echoed in the silent street. The career of our play brought us through the dark muddy lanes behind the houses where we ran the gauntlet of the rough tribes from the cottages, to the back doors of the dark dripping gardens where odours arose from the ashpits, to the dark odorous stables where a coachman smoothed and combed the horse or shook music from the buckled harness.

Our inferences about the boy's character may be formulated in relation to what happens later, in terms of capacities to do certain things and to react in a certain way.

One major inference, quite apart from the boy's sensitive temperament and vigorous constitution, is his growing interest in the female sex as a class. Although the class is here represented by Mangan's sister, the designation itself seeks to preserve the generality to which the boy's image of the girl conforms. Her "brown figure," her "image," "her name," refuse to crystallize into any individualized person. In fact, the two occasions in which the boy apprehends her presence yield evidence for his tendency to introject, or internalize, what is observed. The first description—"Her dress swung as she moved her body and the soft rope of her hair tossed from side to side"—brings about a rapturous and intensely idealized response radically out of proportion to his slight acquaintance with the girl. Premised on this slight acquaintance, the boy naturally draws out of his inner resources (where religious, sexual, romantic imagery mix; the Tristan-Isolde romance and the cult of courtly love condense all these attributes) the force to endow her image with life. And the testimony of her life depends not on her actual existence, her reality as perceived, but on the quality of his response to her image, her reality as conceived. Obviously she, as intentional object of devotion, seems overdetermined: her image becomes a sacred "chalice" to the grail-hero.

Given this intense, passionate attraction to an idealized presence, we can understand his promise to bring a gift from *Araby* and his anxiety to perform the steps necessary to confirm his vow. But if the impetus to stylized worship gives strong, compelling direction to the boy's impulses and his irrational vitality in inventing fantasies, it also removes him farther and farther from ordinary life. Such indeed is the effect he records after the promise. But even before the promise is given, the boy has already exiled or cast himself out from the vulgar and business world: recall his chivalric withdrawal as he walked through the "flaring streets."

This withdrawal from the ordinary world and the removal from the level of material circumstance, a logical result of the boy's concentration on his self-generated object of worship, serves to motivate his estrangement from his aunt and uncle, his anger at their unconcern, and his agonized yearning to reach the temple-like bazaar where he will finally obtain the "chalice" and thus fulfill the sacramental object of his quest. The reality of the "chalice" depends on his promise to bring back something. Mangan's sister acquires all sorts of religious associations in the course of time; likewise, the bazaar attracts all the energy of idealization the boy can sustain, his spirit inflamed by opposing forces. The feeling of frustration, anger, and despairing revolt that we see in the boy at the end can be comprehended only on the basis of these expectations.

But the concluding statement is not wholly that of the boy as narrator-participant; it is also properly that of himself as the adult narrator who is reconstructing an experience from which he is now detached in space and time. Since then, the narrator obviously has gained some knowledge of the world and of the complexity of life to be able to clarify the predicament of the boy in this meaningful way. Because of this peculiarity, the narrative exists on two planes: the boy-participant (an imaginative projection) and the narrator. The narrator is the central intelligence whose judgment of the boy's experience as he undergoes it is subtly fused with the structure of the plot and is, at many points, exposed by telling overt comment. Joyce's problem in composing **"Araby"** lies, I suggest, in contriving a method to combine the authoritative first-person account and the balanced poise of the narrator who has organized the account in precisely the order we have it. It is the old problem of reconciling the confessional, witnessing virtues of the first-person viewpoint with the rational distance and sense of the totality usually ascribed to the omniscient storyteller. As I have noted above, the style and tone of description is the mature narrator's, especially in conceptual treatment: "The other houses of the street, conscious of decent lives within them, gazed at one another with brown imperturbable faces." The animistic charge invested in the "face" of the houses manifests its continuity in the hostile aspect of *Café Chantant*'s front: "I looked humbly at the great jars that stood like eastern guards at either side of the dark entrance to the stall."

Seen in the light of this ambiguous narrative voice, the conclusion may then be construed as a product of two lines of force, one dramatized in the progression of the plot and the other implicit in all the opposing elements that form the countermovement to the plot and thus constitute the agent of the reversal. The conclusion marks the triumphant harmony of the two narrative spheres of subjective (sensory) experience and objective (conceptual) understanding:

> Gazing up into the darkness I saw myself as a creature driven and derided by vanity; and my eyes burned with anguish and anger.

Ironically, this act of recognition is expressed as an act of "gazing into the darkness," that is, a perception of actuality: "the lights of the upper part of the hall had been extinguished." Cognizing the external world, the boy immediately becomes the mature narrator and recognizes his previous state. He executes this leap in the transitive mode of separating what he was and what he is now; and in producing a reflection of himself, one the seer and the other the image of himself seen, he defines his situation by that metaphor of "reflection." The emotional implication of the concepts frees him from his mistake of sentimental exaggeration; he objectifies the cause of the mistake in the word "vanity." "Vanity" is the active force that has led him to form undue expectations; "vanity" has driven and derided him to that extreme, to the "darkness" that is the end of his boyish indulgence. He is a "creature" whose eyes, both the cause of the delusion and the liberator from that delusion, "burned with anguish and anger"—anguish at the sense of being responsible for his plight and accepting it as such, anger at his "blindness" in not realizing the nature of his plight. If the principle for the shaping of the narrative is logically prior to the temporal unfolding of the plot, then it remains now to trace how the principle of organization implied in the concluding statement guides the sequence of incidents and the cause-effect relation among the different elements comprising such incidents.

"Vanity" is etymologically "empty," hence futile or blind. Negativity pervades the sense of place in the beginning: "blind" street, uninhabited house, hollow middle-class residences, empty drawing room, dead priest, decaying books, wild garden, straggling bushes, rusty bicycle pump, winter dusk, "dark muddy lanes," uncle, shadow, "back doors of the dark dripping gardens where odours arose from the ashpits," and "dark odorous stables." One can isolate the analogical matrix of "darkness," vanity, anger, and anguish of the last sentence in the imagery and the connotations of words that convey the relation of the boy to his world. With these realistic details, a few more reality-oriented judgments that one can ascribe to the mature narrator establish the counterforce to the idealizing tendency of the boy's passion and subsequently effect the reversal. (For even here one can see that the boy's connection with the world of squalor and vulgar indifference guarantees the firm, inescapable background for his existence in the world.) Consider these insinuated judgments:

> her name was like a summons to all my *foolish* blood.
>
> Her name sprang to my lips at moments in *strange* prayers and praises which *I myself did not understand.*
>
> My eyes were often full of tears (*I could not tell why*) and at times a flood from my heart *seemed* to pour itself out into my bosom. . . . *I did not know* whether I would ever speak to her or not or, if I spoke to her, how I could tell her of my *confused* adoration (*emphasis supplied.*)

Apart from the negative references to surroundings, the priest's dubious life, and the lack of visualized clarity in the girl's figure as apprehended by the boy, one detects the uncertainty undermining his irresistible passion for the girl's image in his mind. Indeed, his adoration is "confused," in both senses.

The boy's confusion, the chaotic and undefined response to the outside world at this stage of his experience, infects the first verbal contact between him and Mangan's sister. Note the failure of memory—the key to the reversal:

> At last she spoke to me. When she addressed the first words to me I was so confused that I did not know what to answer. She asked me was I going to *Araby*. I forgot whether I answered yes or no.

The boy's confusion and the failure of his memory foreshadow his fate at the bazaar. Becoming aware of her presence—severely qualified, selectively filtered to produce what many have considered a madonna image—and directly though mildly encouraged by her, he utters his crucial vow: "If I go, I will bring you something."

From this point, the movement gathers force in the direction of fulfilling the vow. But here the conflict between potent impulsive inwardness and the indifferent world grows sharp and almost dominates the foreground of the boy's consciousness. Owing to the strength of the distracting force exerted by the aunt, the master of the class, Mrs. Mercer, and the uncle, the boy's memory seriously suffers a fatal decline. At first he wanted to destroy outer reality: "What innumerable follies laid waste my waking and sleeping thoughts after that evening." But even as he wishes "to annihilate the tedious intervening days," he acknowledges his "follies." Immediately after confessing *Araby*'s "Eastern enchantment," he mentions his Aunt's reluctance, suspecting some "Freemason affair," his master's strictness and suspicion of idleness. How shall we take these next two utterances except as 1) the actual state of the boy-participant at the moment of experience, and 2) the depreciating comment of the mature narrator:

> I could not call my wandering thoughts together. I had hardly any patience with the serious work of life which, now that it stood between me and my desire, seemed to me child's play, ugly monotonous child's play.

Finally, the momentous day arrives—a transitional stage from the end of the week, Saturday, to Sunday, the beginning of a new week, plus all other associations in Christian liturgy. Every detail concerning the uncle's behavior—fussing with hat-brush, his return at nine o'clock registered by the rocking of the hallstand as it receives the weight of his overcoat—climaxed with his forgetting of the boy's intention, works toward blocking the primary action of the plot. Framed within the departure of the uncle and his arrival, the boy's experience—his bad humor, his heart's misgiving, his irritation—shows how time becomes humanized, a lived duration, measured in the stream-of-consciousness. Not entirely, however, since the boy's almost complete engulfing by, and immersion in, clock-time is avoided when he easily affirms his imaginative freedom by going up to the "high cold empty gloomy rooms." The epithets almost epitomize the whole course of the plot. He stresses his alienation from the world outside, and in the very process reveals to us (but unheeded by himself) the cause of his temporary imbalance: the dangerous prevalence of the imagination. It is his imagination that affords life and value to Mangan's sister, not her real existence. Consequently, everything depends on the imagination, whose muse is memory:

> The high cold empty gloomy rooms liberated me and I went from room to room singing. From the front window I saw my companions playing below in the street. Their cries reached me weakened and indistinct and, leaning my forehead against the cool glass, I looked over at the dark house where she lived. I may have stood there for an hour, seeing nothing but the brown-clad figure cast by my imagination, touched discreetly by the lamplight at the curved neck, at the hand upon the railings and at the border below the dress.

That passage compresses the two occasions in the story where Mangan's sister is described.

When he goes downstairs, however, we realize that his imagination and its efficacy depend on the limitations of time and place, the specific locale of his existence. And this condition of his imagined passion he has not at all accepted as an *a priori* ground of experience. While his idealism may be qualified by his sharp observation of the world, the world presents itself as colored and transformed by the pressure of his emotions. Thus we note a foreshortening in the gap between desire and the fulfillment of desire which he envisions, anxious and angry at his uncle's dereliction and the joke of the verses "The Arab's Farewell to his Steed." But finally the florin—a big sum for him—reinforces the movement to the glamorized goal, the *Araby* of his imagination.

So far, we anticipate the trip to *Araby* in a general way, knowing the driving force of his affection for the girl. But he finds later that it was not affection but vanity that drove him. Having overcome the obstacle of the indifferent adults—the boy's orphanhood justifies his courage to initiate himself into experience and to seek for symbols of authority—he now seems headed for the successful accomplishment of his quest. But the development of the narrative continues to interweave with the surface-movement, the journey to *Araby,* the resisting force. Unable to prevent his departure from the house, this resisting force—call it the corrupt Mammon-worshiping world of reality, the paralyzed philistine public, or what you will—now accompanies the boy's trip as an ominous part of the environment. At first, environment vivifies memory, whose failure threatens to ruin the project of the imagination: "The sight of the streets thronged with buyers and glaring with gas recalled to me the purpose of my journey." But from then on, the details of awareness convey to us a meaning counter to the literal motion of events: third-class carriage of a deserted train, ruinous houses, and improvised wooden platform. The positive note, though present, is subdued: twinkling river, special train, lighted dial of a clock, magical name.

Before the boy overhears the conversation at the *Café Chantant,* we observe that the florin is split up and lowers in denomination. This dwindling of monetary value parallels the gradual destruction of any hope of buying a present. The boy feared that the bazaar would be closed; he sacrifices a shilling to enter his "magical" Castle Perilous. But the weary-looking man simply heralds more disillusioning aspects: closed stalls, dark hall. As a result of the boy's inability to summon up the girl's image, to clearly remember the reason for his trip, the world slowly encroaches upon his consciousness from the moment he enters *Araby.* Distracted by the fall of the coins, he sees two men counting money on a salver: "Remembering with difficulty why I had come I went over to one of the stalls and examined porcelain vases and flowered tea-sets." The frivolous rhythm of talk between men and lady about truth and falsehood, and the woman's unencouraging and dutiful tone, do not greatly differ from the recorded exchange between him and Mangan's sister. His reply to the lady, "No, thank you," simply punctuates his feeling of emptiness—the sense of vanity—registered by the material sound of his "two pennies falling against the sixpence" in his pocket. Victim of his bad memory (the Muse is memory herself), he is defeated by what he thought the world of *Araby* would be. Remembering the past clearly, the artist becomes the priest of his own sacrifice.

The pattern of emotional response outlined here by pursuing the plot as it moves in one direction, either speeded up or impeded by the acts and responses of the protagonist, illumines finally the meaning of the epiphanic vision at the end. It is a conclusion for the primary plot involving the boy's quest and his journey to *Araby* on a metaphorical dimension; it is a conclusion, too, for the countermovement of the plot that involves the conditions which make the boy's quest probable at first, and improbable and thus "wonderful" (in Aristotle's sense) in the end. For the boy's character, right from the first paragraph, contains its own problem and solution. And the dialectical movement from problem to solution, rendered in the plot, obeys the principle of telling a story to achieve a difficult effect that is both paradoxical and ironic: the boy's experience—virtually an ordeal in the interpretation of signs—rendered at the moment of happening from a perspective of knowledge and just comprehension. The boy is aware of things but not the meaning of things; the narrator obliquely delivers the meaning of things to us. Interpreted in this way, one perceives **"Araby"** as Joyce's finest accomplishment in holding justice and reality in a single luminous imitation of an action.

Note

1. This essay assumes the relevance and qualified validity of all the existing interpretations of "Araby." Confining myself strictly to a description of the structure of the plot and its function in determining the whole narrative action, I thus inquire—if my description is correct—into the premise or condition whereby any other evaluation of details would be considered valid or consistent with the larger subsuming structure. I therefore assume here the Aristotelian position regarding the primacy of plot in mimetic art. For the

elaboration of motifs and themes in the story, and their relation with Joyce's achievement, I refer the reader to the following works: Bernard Benstock, "Arabesques: Third Position of Concord," *James Joyce Quarterly* 5 (Fall 1967): 30–39; Harry Stone, "'Araby' and the Writings of James Joyce," *Antioch Review* 25 (Fall 1965): 375–410; Robert P. Roberts, "'Araby' and the Palimpsest of Criticism, or Through a Glass Eye Darkly," *Antioch Review* 26 (Winter 1966–67): 469–89; William York Tindall, *A Reader's Guide to James Joyce* (New York: Noonday Press, 1959), pp. 19–21; Marvin Magalaner, *Time of Apprenticeship: The Fiction of Young James Joyce* (New York: Abelard-Schuman, 1959), pp. 79, 87, 101; James A. Fuller, "A Note on Joyce's 'Araby,'" *CEA Critic* 20 (February 1958): 8.

Susan J. Rosowski (essay date 1976)

SOURCE: "Joyce's 'Araby' and Imaginative Freedom," in *Research Studies*, Vol. 44, No. 3, September, 1976, pp. 183–88.

[*In the following essay, Rosowski views the primary conflict in "Araby" "not between the child's and the adult's visions, but between psychological and factual realities."*]

Readers have long recognized the importance of **"Araby"** in Joyce's canon. The third and final story of the childhood phase of the *Dubliners* (before adolescence, maturity, and public life), **"Araby"** portrays an early stage of the struggle that Joyce develops later in *A Portrait of the Artist as a Young Man* and in *Ulysses*. The story is viewed usually as portraying the initiation of a young boy: the boy moves from the child's world of romance to the adult world of reality and, in the final lines, to disillusionment as he realizes himself trapped in "the hell of the world of reality."[1] Yet basic problems remain unresolved with this interpretation: the narrative voice is unnecessarily complicated; the relevance of the opening paragraphs to the whole is unclear; and, finally, the boy's reaction in the last line of the story far exceeds his recognition of "reality." I believe that in the last paragraph of the story the boy does not move to an "adult" world but, instead, continues the human cycle of tension between imaginative flight and factual realities by assuming a new romantic role. More basically, I believe that the primary conflict of the story is not between the child's and the adult's visions, but between psychological and factual realities.

In **"Araby"** the concrete, factual world is filtered through the transforming mind of the narrator. The subject of the story is that transformation. The boy's games in Dublin, his infatuation with Mangan's sister, and his trip to the bazaar are all vehicles by which Joyce portrays the psychological truth of human struggle for imaginative freedom. The terms of this struggle are established early, for the opening setting reveals tension between appearance and reality: "North Richmond Street, being blind, was a quiet street except at the hour when the Christian Brothers' School set the boys free."[2] Potential freedom is pitted against social form. The social facade of blindness and imperturbability covers the actuality of children yearning for flight.

Joyce makes this tension specific in the second paragraph by focusing upon the perspective of the boy. Here the basic technique of the story is established, as the reader sees the world through the imaginative lens of the child and vicariously participates in his imaginative transformation. Yet Joyce insures that the reader also remain separate from the child through the use of a double perspective. First, there is the narrator himself, a commentator removed in time from the child he once was; second, there is the child, through whom the narrator is telling the story. By drawing back periodically, the narrator reminds the reader that he is separated in time from the boy of the story. For example, after recounting his childhood experience of first speaking to Mangan's sister, the narrator writes, "What innumerable follies laid waste my waking and sleeping thoughts after that evening!" The result is a dual perspective of childhood immediacy combined with adult distance.

Two effects are created by this technique. First, there is a delightful comic effect, maintained throughout the story. Finding some "paper-covered books, the pages of which were curled and damp," the boy decides he "liked the last best because its leaves were yellow," and, in describing the "wild garden" behind his house with its "central apple-tree," he conveys overtones of Edenic myth. In these descriptions, Joyce is careful that we move beyond the child's vision of his world, both by the adult narrator discussed previously and by a careful selection of images. If the "wild garden" with its "central apple-tree" is, indeed, suggestive of Eden, then it would follow that the "late tenant's rusty bicycle-pump" which is found under one of the bushes in the garden is suggestive of the snake.[3] The incongruity between the reality and the imaginative transformation is inescapably comic. The mythic images are there, certainly, "images which strongly suggest a ruined Eden and Eden's forbidden central apple tree, a tree which has to do with man's downfall and his knowledge of good and evil,"[4] but we must recognize that they are themes in the boy's mind which lead to the larger theme that emerges from the story as a whole. This larger concern is with the imaginative transformation of such seemingly mundane subjects.

There is a second, equally important effect conveyed through the double perspective, for at the same time that we recognize the comedy of the boy's imaginative flights, we also recognize their value:

> Our shouts echoed in the silent street. The career of our play brought us through the dark muddy lanes behind the houses where we ran the gauntlet of the rough tribes from the cottages, to the back doors of the dark dripping gardens where odours arose from the ashpits, to the dark odorous stables where a coachman smoothed and combed the horse or shook music from the buckled harness.

The experience is, quite simply, beautiful, and the incongruity of this beauty with the physical reality of stables and Dublin streets is suppressed. Thus early in the story Joyce establishes the paradoxically complementary sides of man's imaginative existence—its comedy and its beauty—and posits these against the threat of imprisonment to physical reality.

The tension underlying this threat is developed in the next paragraphs, when the boy becomes a knight-errant-lover for Mangan's sister, a role for which the preliminary scenes have prepared the reader. In developing this role, Joyce increasingly emphasizes the separation between physical reality and imaginative perception; correspondingly, the narrator is increasingly comic. We encounter him lying on the floor, peeping through a crack in the window shade so he can see Mangan's sister, and, later, stalking her in the Dublin streets. Yet Joyce continues to convey the beauty of imaginative experience, for through his role the boy becomes a part of a transformed, unified setting: "These noises converged in a single sensation of life for me. . . ." By the end of this initial description by the narrator of himself in his childhood role as knight-lover, the comedy and the beauty of the romantic pose are interwoven:

> My eyes were often full of tears (I could not tell why) and at times a flood from my heart seemed to pour itself out into my bosom. I thought little of the future. I did not know whether I would ever speak to her or not or, if I spoke to her, how I could tell her of my confused adoration. But my body was like a harp and her words and gestures were like fingers running upon the wires.

This use of the opening paragraphs to prepare the reader for the boy's romantic role is one of the great achievements of the story. Had Joyce opened with the boy's comically conventional pose, his eyes brimming with tears so that "at times a flood from my heart seemed to pour itself out into my bosom," certainly the reader would have laughed immediately, or at least chuckled, and possibly stopped reading. Yet the story opens with the deceptively simple description of North Richmond Street, building gradually to the romantic pose through the more easily accepted transformation of the garden and physical setting: "When we met in the street the houses had grown sombre. The space of sky above us was the colour of ever-changing violet and towards it the lamps of the street lifted their feeble lanterns. The cold air stung us and we played till our bodies glowed." By the time that the narrator specifies the boy in the role of lover, we are prepared for his transforming even "places the most hostile to romance." We accept and value the boy's melodramatic pose.

Like the initial paragraphs, the story as a whole is structured carefully to convey the tension between imaginative freedom and factual restraint. Two major empirical realities provide two psychological crises. First, the narrator's meeting with Mangan's sister provides the crisis to the first part of the story; it represents the physical reality that will forever threaten imaginative freedom. Mangan's sister

is clearly not the ideal the boy is imagining: "the white border of a petticoat, just visible as she stood at ease," represents the reality of the girl. Throughout the story, however, the boy never perceives her in terms of this reality. She exists for him only as an imaginative projection of himself, as he indicates when he calls her "my desire," the "brown-clad figure cast by my imagination." Similarly, their actual meeting is not the spiritually purified event that the boy imagines. It is, after all, set against a background of childish play, in which "her brother and two other boys were fighting for their caps. . . ." Yet this meeting also represents the potential strength of the imagination, for the boy totally transforms the physical details of the scene: "the light from the lamp opposite our door caught the white curve of her neck, lit up her hair that rested there and, falling, lit up the hand upon the railing." The boy emerges from this meeting on a new imaginative height, saying "the syllables of the word *Araby* were called to me through the silence in which my soul luxuriated and cast an Eastern enchantment over me."

Second, the bazaar provides a crisis to the story as a whole. Once the boy has talked with Mangan's sister and committed himself to the journey and the quest, the basic conflict of the story becomes specific. With this commitment, the reader knows the form of factual reality that the boy must, ultimately, confront. Again, however, we must distinguish the boy's definition of that struggle from one that emerges from the story as a whole. The boy has committed himself to go to the bazaar and to bring back something worthy to Mangan's sister. Yet by this time the incongruity between his imaginative ideal and the reality of the actual world is so great that there is no possibility in the reader's mind for the success of the specific task. Instead, the more important struggle is defined by the reader—the struggle of the boy to translate a specific task involving physical reality into the beauty of imaginative experience.

Actually confronted with the bazaar itself, the boy moves rapidly toward crisis. Striving to maintain the vision of the religious supplicant, he "recognized a silence like that which pervades a church after a service," which is broken by "the fall of the coins" as "two men were counting money on a salver." Critics have seen the fall of the coins as the point at which the boy descends from his vision; but here the boy has not yet fallen when viewed in terms of overall struggle described in the story—that to maintain imaginative freedom. He is still able to transform the concrete reality around him, as revealed in his use of the richly connotative word *salver* and in his suggestion of the money lenders in the temple with the description of the noise of the coins. After this scene, he continues to translate the wares of the bazaar into his imaginative vision: "I looked humbly at the great jars that stood like eastern guards at either side of the dark entrance to the stall. . . ."

It is only with the next paragraph that the boy's fall occurs: "I lingered before her stall, though I knew my stay was useless, to make my interest in her wares seem the more real." Finally, the boy is unable to sustain his imaginative role against the physical reality of the bazaar: "Then I turned away slowly and walked down the middle of the bazaar. I allowed the two pennies to fall against the sixpence in my pocket. I heard a voice call from one end of the gallery that the light was out. The upper part of the hall was now completely dark." For the only time in the story, the boy subjects himself to physical reality. There is no transforming quality in these lines, and no tension behind them. Their content is completely factual, and their style is completely flat. In this paragraph, the reader's expectations are fulfilled—expectations that the boy's romantic pose will be deflated and that he will be entrapped by physical reality. Were the story to end here, the boy would, indeed, be caught in the web of the actual world.

However, the story does not end here. The last line of **"Araby"** carries us beyond the boy's perception to the reader's epiphany, for here Joyce unifies the story by demonstrating truth to human reality and, by doing so, develops a contrast with the inhuman subjection to empirical reality of the preceding sentences. Far from representing the human spirit entrapped in a hellish world of reality, the final line represents man's inconquerable striving for imaginative freedom. In this line, the boy transcends the flat details of the two pennies and the sixpence and returns to imaginative existence as he assumes a new role. He is no longer the archetypal lover. He has become the archetypal sinner: "Gazing up into the darkness I saw myself as a creature driven and derided by vanity; and my eyes burned with anguish and anger."

Joyce has prepared the reader carefully to recognize that the last sentence is not reality, to see the comedy—and the beauty—behind the boy's Miltonic pose. The "creature" described is, after all, a young boy who has imagined love for the first time and who inevitably has been unable to sustain his imaginary ideal. Yet like the boy, the reader is not content with such a description of reality, for it is also real that we value the emotional possibilities of human experience and that, as a result, people are capable of liberation through great imaginative transformations. In the last sentence of **"Araby,"** we see the boy reentering imaginative flight.

In **"Araby,"** the epiphany of the reader is directed back, finally, upon himself and his own seriousness. For, despite all the obvious comedy of the story, the reader does concentrate upon the boy's role—as countless articles on the Edenic imagery of the garden and the quest motifs of the journey reveal. By identifying with the boy, the reader reveals his or her own romantic predisposition, a predisposition shared with all humanity. By recognizing the combination of comedy and beauty in the boy's role, the reader affirms the qualities necessary for imaginative freedom.

With this reading of **"Araby"** we see that the ending of the short story is similar to that of *A Portrait of the Artist as a Young Man,* in that the "final" stage of the protagonist is not necessarily final, but is rather a dramatic, imaginative pose heralding a new stage of development. Thus the significance of **"Araby"** in terms of Joyce's later development lies not in its portrayal of disillusionment over human entrapment in factual reality, but rather in its exploration of the liberating human truth of psychological processes. It is this exploration of imaginative processes that Joyce will develop more fully in *A Portrait of the Artist as a Young Man* and in *Ulysses.* As Stephen Dedalus will say in *Ulysses,* "We walk through ourselves, meeting robbers, ghosts, giants, old men, wives, widows, brothers-in-law. But always meeting ourselves."

Notes

1. Ben L. Collins, "Joyce's 'Araby' and the 'Extended Smile,'" *JJQ,* IV (1967), 90.

2. James Joyce, "Araby," in *Dubliners,* ed. Robert Scholes in consultation with Richard Ellman (New York: Viking Press, 1967). All subsequent references to "Araby" will be to this edition.

3. Collins, p. 85.

4. Harry Stone, "'Araby' and the Writings of James Joyce," *Antioch Review* (Fall, 1965), p. 381.

John J. Brugaletta and Mary H. Hayden (essay date 1978)

SOURCE: "The Motivation for Anguish in Joyce's 'Araby'," in *Studies in Short Fiction,* Vol. 15, No. 1, Winter, 1978, pp. 11–17.

[*In the following essay, Brugaletta and Hayden question important plot elements of "Araby."*]

In his discussion of James Joyce's **"Araby,"** Epifanio San Juan, Jr. contributes to Joyce studies a predominantly valid discussion of plot.[1] We agree with San Juan in his assumption of the "relevance and *qualified* validity of all the existing interpretations of 'Araby.'"[2] Our only disagreement with this critic's view of the story—our point of departure from that of other critics who have discussed the story—is in the evidently universal assumption that the one crucial conversation between the narrator and Mangan's sister actually took place.[3] "The boy promised Mangan's sister to bring her a gift," San Juan believes, later referring to the central passage as a "factual transcript of the first verbal exchange."[4]

In our examination of **"Araby"** and of a pattern which relates it to certain other stories in *Dubliners* and *A Portrait of the Artist as a Young Man,*[5] we find little reason to believe that Joyce meant to represent the physical presence of Mangan's sister in that back room where the priest had died. Indeed, there is much evidence that her absence from that event is a fact which is vital to the experience of the story. Put simply, Mangan's sister was not there; the boy imagined her, her words and her actions.

When Joyceans mention **"Araby"** at all, they often refer to it with a hint of an apology for the supposedly exaggerated anguish of the narrator.[6] Joyce places this anguish, evidently with some care, at the end of the story. (It would have been easy enough for the author to have kept us with his protagonist a little longer, leaving him on the train home, or even arriving there, so as to emphasize the anguish less.) This placement combines with the strong terms used in describing the boy's emotions at the story's end ("driven," "derided," "my eyes burned," "anguish and anger") to give us a clear sense of this event's great significance, even apart from its epiphanic qualities.

Nevertheless, apparently many readers are struck with the notion that there is inadequate motivation for such intense anguish. It is easy enough to refer to the narrator's promise to Mangan's sister and of the frustrations he experiences in the ensuing quest as Joyce's explanation. Such motivation, however, must appear weak in contrast with the reaction they supposedly cause, the boy's youth and romanticism notwithstanding. If readers are not to chastise Joyce for offending their sense of psychological consistency, they will find themselves thinking, perhaps secretly, of the narrator's naiveté and childish idealism in order to explain away the disparity. This reading, of course, comes uncomfortably near to begging the question. Rather than allowing us to reread the story with satisfaction, it merely tells us we do not know enough, or remember enough from our own childhood, about the subject of the story.

When read carefully, however, **"Araby"** tells us exactly why the boy is so anguish-stricken; there is no need then to feel nearly so inadequate in our preparation for reading the story. We may begin by noting that the narrator and Mangan are peers, and that these boys are appreciably younger than Mangan's sister. This last is evident in the boys' hiding from her when she calls her brother in to tea, finally walking up to Mangan's steps "resignedly"; were they nearer to her in age they would openly challenge her authority, never bothering to hide, finally acquiescing, if at all, most probably with audible protests. It is also significant that they behave toward her under such circumstances much as they do toward the narrator's uncle, clearly an authority figure; if the girl exercises authority over the boys, she must be significantly older than they.

To pursue the disparity in ages between the narrator and Mangan's sister, we may also note that he watches covertly from the front parlor for her to leave her house each morning. Snatching up his books, he follows her in silence, walking up alongside the girl—still mute—at the last possible moment. He tells us he had virtually never spoken to her. Obviously he is fascinated by this older girl, awed to the point of speechlessness. The experience is a common one; nearly every post-pubescent boy has borne the image of some older girl through an everyday world which, in its harsh clashing of real things, seems very much like a "throng of foes." And nearly every older girl, thus idolized, reacts (when she recognizes the situation) not as the boy's peer but as his elder. Usually she will either humor the boy, enjoying the situation as a game, or she will ignore him for one reason or another (lack of interest, often, or as part of an attempt to discourage the attention out of concern for the boy's feelings).

It must strike us, therefore, as odd that Mangan's sister acts as she does while talking with the narrator. The nervous turning of her bracelet as she speaks betrays a lack of self-confidence in the younger narrator's presence which a real sixteen-to-eighteen-year-old girl is unlikely to have. And what she says, in effect, is hardly more in keeping with the older-girl/younger-boy relationship: her coy (but nervous) hints that he will be doing something which fascinates her, an implication of her interest in the narrator himself, are the components of a peer male-female relationship, not the relationship which exists in this story.

This "conversation" in the room where the priest died is indeed a curious one. We take the foregoing as what may be called soft evidence of the physical absence of Mangan's sister on that important occasion, "soft" because based upon what we take to be no more than generally recognized psychological facts about young people in general. But harder evidence for her absence is plentiful.

A review of this harder evidence must begin with Joyce's clear rhetorical framing of the curious conversation in the form of an anecdote: he begins the passage with "One evening . . ." and ends it (about thirty lines later) with ". . . that evening!" Except for the opening paragraph of the passage (a paragraph with its own crucial function as we shall see), the two participants speak throughout the passage. Clearly we are meant to see anecdotal integrity in this carefully framed section of the story. And yet halfway through the passage the narrator seems to be no longer in the back room but is viewing Mangan's sister at "the railing," at her own front door. We submit that this is physically impossible. If the narrator must lie on the floor "in the front parlour" in order to watch her door, then he cannot be watching her at her front door from the "back drawing room." This portion of the passage, at least, must be seen as occurring psychologically, not physically.[7]

But what of the remainder of this supposed rendezvous? Did Joyce mean for us to believe that this meeting, with its extremely awkward social implications for the participants, actually took place? Given the fact that the boy says he had spoken only "a few casual words" to her, did Joyce expect the reader to accept as literal fact this curious event with no hint whatsoever of arrangements made beforehand for the meeting, coincidental circumstances placing them together in such an odd room, or even a brief description of the girl's entering (or leaving) the room? Mangan's sister might just as well have materialized out of thin air for all Joyce tells us.

In point of fact, we believe that to be very close to what Joyce does tell us. Joyceans have not, heretofore, read the story carefully enough. Had they done so, they would have noted the carefully described retreat from the objective world on the narrator's part. This is the beginning paragraph of the passage, preparing the narrator (and the reader) for the subjectivity of the experience to follow. There was "no sound" in the house. He hears the soft patter of rain falling on the garden beds—a sound and no sound, a white noise, mesmerizing, shutting out other, possibly distracting, noises. There is a faint light of uncertain origin, yet it is "dark." The narrator comments on this diminution of the sensory functions, "I was thankful that I could see so little. All my senses seemed to desire to veil themselves . . . feeling that I was about to slip from them. . . ." We must not be satisfied to think these the mere exaggerations of a hypersensitive boy. Taken literally, they help immensely in making better sense of the story. He has situated himself sensuously and prepared himself emotionally for an encounter within the imagination.

In the previous paragraph he had said, "Her name sprang to my lips at moments in strange prayers and phrases which I myself did not understand." This is just such an instance, though something new has been added, doubtless due in part to his being no longer amid the cacophony of the "flaring streets." He has retreated entirely from the world of "curses," "shrill litanies of shop-boys" and "nasal chanting." His senses no longer assailed by stimuli, he can focus his attention wholly upon the image and imagined voice of Mangan's sister which have been building within him. He presses the palms of his hands together in the attitude of prayer and murmurs "O love! O love!" repeatedly.

To ignore the visionary nature of this experience is to ignore what Joyce tells us on more than one occasion about the psychological tendencies of this boy. On the night of the bazaar, he stares long at the empty front of the girl's house, "seeing nothing but the brown-clad figure cast by my imagination." And in the days following the supposed conversation, "her image came between me and the page I strove to read." These are but after-shocks of that first psychological earthquake, differing only in their lesser degree of intensity and realism. The girl's physical presence is not required in order for the boy to see her.

The youthful narrator is not alone among Joyce's characters in his visualizing of absent persons. While his crucial vision, with its high degree of realism, is not reproduced with precision elsewhere in Joyce's early fiction, it does fall within a clear pattern of events in *Dubliners,* as well as in *Stephen Hero* and *Portrait.*[8] In **"The Sisters,"** the boy-narrator is in the dark of his bedroom, when he reports,

> I imagined that I saw again the heavy grey face of the paralytic. I drew the blankets over my head and tried to think of Christmas. But the grey face still followed me. I murmured; and I understood that it desired to confess something. I felt my soul receding into some pleasant and vicious region; and there again I found it waiting for me. It began to confess to me in a murmuring voice and I wondered why it smiled continually and why the lips were so moist with spittle
>
> (*Dubliners,* p. 11).

In this instance, the envisioned, the priest who was guilty of simony, is dead, a fact which renders his presence impossible. It may well have been this incident which caused Joyce to place the **"Araby"** conversation in the room where the priest had died. The two events are of a kind, and the brief allusion serves to point up the similarity.

This attempt to avoid the dead by thinking of Christmas brings us inevitably from the first to the last story of *Dubliners,* to Gabriel Conroy's vision of another dead man. Here again, in another setting of near-darkness and silence, the absent one becomes—at least temporarily—more unavoidably real than the physical surroundings as Gabriel "imagined he saw the form of a young man standing under a dripping tree. Other forms were near. His soul had approached that region where dwell the vast hosts of the dead. . . . The solid world itself, which these dead had one time reared and lived in, was dissolving and dwindling. A few light taps upon the pane made him turn to the window. It had begun to snow again" (*Dubliners,* p. 223).

Surely we are not meant to believe it is the snow which is tapping on the pane. Snow, even Irish snow, rarely, if ever, taps. This is Michael Furey, now dead, who had thrown gravel against Gretta's window to call her down to him. The imagined figure in this case neither speaks nor murmurs, but it does repeat, in a pallid way, one detail of Gretta's account of its former self, a detail which adds audibility to visibility.

In **"A Painful Case,"** the imagined presence is perceived tangibly and perhaps audibly: "As the light failed and his memory began to wander he thought her hand touched his" (*Dubliners,* p. 116). "She seemed to be near him in the darkness. At moments he seemed to feel her voice touch his ear, her hand touch his" (p. 117). But minutes later, "He could not feel her near him in the darkness nor her voice touch his ear. He waited for some minutes listening. He could hear nothing: the night was perfectly silent. He listened again: perfectly silent. He felt that he was alone." (Ibid.) Emily Sinico is dead. James Duffy, having just read a newspaper account of her death, has imagined her presence under much the same circumstances as other *Dubliners* protagonists envision absent people: the pattern of relative darkness and silence remains consistent when the vision is successful. Indeed, in the third instance of **"A Painful Case,"** when the vision leaves Duffy, the silence was mightily disturbed only seconds earlier by a train with a "laborious drone" and a "pounding." Furthermore, the first instance in **"A Painful Case"** follows similar visions in **"The Sisters,"** **"Araby"** and **"The Dead"** in occurring in a bedroom.[9]

The four visions of *Dubliners* clearly are of a kind. It may even be seen as evidence of their unity that each of the four contains a factor not present in the other three: while in every other instance the imaginer has known and, in one sense or another, loved the imagined, in **"The Dead"** we are forced to think of Gretta's identity as fused with Gabriel's if we wish the pattern to remain consistent. In

"A Painful Case," tangibility has taken the place of visibility in the pattern. In "The Sisters," the imaginer evidently is frightened by his "dream"; this obtains in none of the other visions. And in "Araby" the imagined is not dead, as are the priest, Emily Sinico and Michael Furey. What is more—and this fact possibly has misled readers of "Araby" more than any other—Joyce records dialogue from the narrator's vision. The boy in "The Sisters" had heard a "murmuring voice," James Duffy had "felt" a voice, and Gabriel Conroy had heard taps on the window pane; but only in "Araby" are we given the exact words (or, more correctly, some of the exact words) of an imagined dialogue.

Two possible reasons for this last curiosity are not far to seek. First, the plot demands that the boy be led into promising the envisioned girl a gift from the bazaar. This would be difficult without at least some dialogue. But secondly—and this is more important in that it tells us exactly what we wish to know about the story—it goes a long way toward explaining the narrator's intense anguish later. Linked closely in a causal relationship with the unique dialogue is the narrator's evident acceptance of the vision as reality. He goes to Araby in order to make good the promise he thinks—and almost entirely believes—he has made. Direct quotation so nearly reifies the memory of Mangan's sister in the crucial passage that readers have thought her really there. The technique necessary for the character (the boy) has worked all too well on the reader.

Joyce's interest in the vision as literary device, now further developed, is sustained in *Portrait*. Here the pattern is associated with Stephen's obsession with his painfully ambivalent feelings for E. C. E. C.'s "virgin" image shames him in his lustful fantasies as he composes the "Villanelle of the Temptress" in his bedroom. He lies in his bed in the "dull white light" of a silent dawn, his senses "veiled," and recalls that she approached him once and begged him to sing one of his "curious songs" (*Portrait*, p. 219). Her image dances teasingly before him until he distorts her "fair image," confounding her with the whorish girls who have beckoned to him in his Dublin walks. Anger, and jealousy of the priest, whom he sees as his rival, consume him, yet he knows that "however he might revile and mock her image, his anger was also a form of homage" (p. 220). Like the narrator of "Araby," Stephen lives on images of the girl, transforming them into events which can function as reality. The younger boy's character and psychological tendencies are consistent with those of Stephen, and in fact prefigure them, as critics have noted.[10]

But the "Araby" vision is much more concrete than any of the other four visions. He carries her image (though weakened) with him as far as Araby on his assumed quest. Once there, however, the immediate object of his quest within easy reach, the ultimate object—her image—fades away. Or, to be more precise, the vision of Mangan's sister fades into the physical presence of the young woman at the bazaar. The idealized image and its setting fade into the harsh reality of the concrete and necessary world: the

soothing darkness of the upper room to the cavernous darkness of the upper part of the hall; the soft "silence" of fine rain to the sharp chink of coins on a salver; the gentle, somewhat coy dialogue of the vision to the flat contradictions and open flirting of the salesgirl and her English acquaintances; the shy (bracelet-twisting) admiration of the envisioned girl to the unencouraging, dutiful tones of the girl of flesh. And then the words which haul him back by the scruff of the neck from what little remains of his reveries: "O, I never said such a thing!" She did, perhaps, but her counterpart did not. And that fact no doubt suddenly bursts into clarity (and *claritas*) for the boy at that point, most occasions having informed against him.[11]

He has been attracted by the "magical name" of the bazaar and has travelled there for the greater glory of that other magical name, the name which springs to his lips in prayers and praises. The vision had been his alternative to the real world, had indeed become at one point so realistic as to apparently fuse with reality for him. But that vision, concrete though it was, proved too fragile for a world of real older girls, money, drunken and indifferent uncles, and the necessary crassness of a day-to-day existence. He had conjured up the spirit of love with an incantation ("O love! O love!") only to have that spirit dispelled by the clumsiness of a physical world. The light is out now, as the voice has called, the light from within, and the upper part of the universe is in darkness. Nothing whatever remains for him to do; this is paralysis indeed. Anguish, however intense, is a perfectly appropriate reaction.

Notes

1. *James Joyce and the Craft of Fiction: An Interpretation of "Dubliners"* (Rutherford, N. J.: Fairleigh Dickinson University Press, 1972), pp. 54–67.

2. San Juan, p. 54, footnote. Our emphasis.

3. "He talks to her only once. . . ." Cleanth Brooks and Robert Penn Warren, *Understanding Fiction* (New York: F. S. Crofts and Company, 1943), p. 421. "One day the girl speaks to him. . . ." Harry Stone, "'Araby' and the Writings of James Joyce," *Dubliners: Text, Criticism, and Notes*, eds. Robert Scholes and A. Walton Litz (New York: Viking, 1969), p. 349. Edward Brandabur seems less consistent about the girl's presence: "The intense incident in the priest's room implies the verging on a suprasensory transcendence of the conditions of reality" (p. 53). "In 'Araby,' the moment of invocation leads at once to a description of the first actual encounter between the protagonist and Mangan's sister . . ." (p. 54). *A Scrupulous Meanness* (Urbana, Ill.: University of Illinois Press, 1971).

4. pp. 55, 56.

5. Hereafter referred to as *Portrait*.

6. "'Driven and derided,' 'anguish and anger'—these reactions seem far too strong. Indeed they seem pretentious when compared to the trivial disillusionment which caused them." Stone, p. 349.

7. Of course one may read a chronological break between the paragraph which begins "One evening" and the subsequent paragraph which opens with, "At last she spoke to me." To do so, however, violates the integrity of the passage.

8. The novels date from 1904–5, the same year as the writing of "The Sisters," "A Painful Case," and "Araby."

9. The situations of "The Sisters" and "A Painful Case" are obvious. In "Araby," the priest had died in bed, making it the priest's bedroom, though not the boy's. "The Dead" similarly uses a variation upon the bedroom pattern: the hotel room is a bedroom for a price; not Gabriel's but anyone's bedroom.

10. As examples, see Brandabur, p. 37, and Stone, p. 345.

11. The girl is the familiar Joycean woman, the virgin/temptress, to Stephen "a figure of the womanhood of his country, a batlike soul waking to the consciousness of itself in darkness and secrecy and loneliness . . ." (*Portrait,* p. 221). Joyce's male protagonists usually idealize the female, but almost invariably display an attraction/repulsion response to her.

Donald E. Morse (essay date 1978)

SOURCE: "'Sing Three Songs of Araby': Theme and Allusion in Joyce's 'Araby,'" in *College Literature,* Vol. 5, No. 2, Spring, 1978, pp. 125–32.

[*In the following essay, Morse explores the different literary allusions found in "Araby."*]

> I'll sing three songs of Araby
> And tales of fair Cashmere,
> Wild tales to cheat thee of a sigh,
> Or charm thee to a tear
> And dreams of delight shall on thee break,
> And rainbow visions rise,
> And all my soul shall strive to wake
> Sweet wonder in thine eyes.
> And all my soul shall strive to wake
> Sweet wonder in thine eyes.
>
> —W. G. Wills, "Araby"[1]

Adults enjoy being reminded, at a safe distance, of their own successful voyage through the rites of passage; for time first blunts, then obscures, the pain of being rejected by the first usually inappropriate and always unapproachable love. Many of the excesses committed in the name of Love appear later quite ridiculous yet with what great earnestness they were originally carried out! The dawn of adolescence found most of us supremely confident of our rightful place at the center of the universe and, therefore, all our acts held intrinsic importance not for ourselves alone but for the world at large. Later stepping back to "see ourselves as others see us," we discovered that our emotional as well as physical universe was no longer Ptole-

maic but Copernican, with ourselves located nowhere near its center. As a character in Vonnegut's *Cat's Cradle* succinctly says: "Maturity is a disease for which no remedy exists unless laughter can be said to remedy anything." Small wonder, then, that stories of a young person's initiation into the world of experience retain an almost universal appeal for adults.

The boy in **"Araby"** cannot laugh at his disillusionment, however, for the event is too overwhelming and too immediate.[2] During his brief visit to the bazaar he discovers that there is no place in the adult world for his dream of love, so he stands poised on the brink of maturity, but does not cross over—he is still too young. As he earlier reacted too intensely to the brief encounters with Mangan's sister, creating out of them an idealized portrait which he "adores," so now he overreacts to his loss and sees himself "as a creature driven and derided by vanity." His "eyes burn with anguish and anger," for having invested so much of himself in his vision the discovery that it may exist only in dreams leaves him desolate. "Falling in love with love," as Rodgers and Hart chorused in the 1930's, "is falling for make-believe"; and in large measure this describes the boy's painful realization. Commenting on the story's conclusion, Robert apRoberts tellingly writes:

> The "anguish and anger" are the reactions of a young boy feeling this truth for the first time [that "Man is in love and loves what vanishes / What more is there to say?"], and the self-centeredness and self-dramatization are quite in keeping with the earlier creation by the boy of an inner world of love and hope at odds with reality.[3]

Joyce comments on the boy's "self-centeredness and self-dramatization" by comparing his activities, thoughts and emotions with those of characters in the story itself and in other literature. Within **"Araby"** there are suggestive parallels drawn between the boy and his uncle, the boy and the priest who used to occupy the house, and the boy and his playmates. Each comparison contains an implied criticism, warning or qualification of the youngster's actions, thoughts or feelings. When the boy fashions his ideal of love out of a few casual words and chance meetings, he acts as inappropriately as his uncle does later, when he seizes upon the mere mention of the bazaar's title, Araby, as an occasion for declaiming "The Arab's Farewell to His Steed"—a poem which sentimentalizes and exaggerates a man's relationship to his horse in much the same way that the boy exaggerates his relationship with Mangan's sister. The refrain typifies the poem's romantic overstatement:

> The stranger hath thy bridle rein, thy master hath
>   his gold—
> Fleet limbed and beautiful, farewell; thou'rt sold,
>   my steed, thou'rt sold.
> 'Tis false! 'tis false!—my Arab Steed! I fling them
>   back my gold![4]

Another, although different, kind of overstatement is similarly treated. The boy pays the girl far more devotion than is warranted by their tentative relationship: "Every morning," he confesses, "I lay on the floor in the front parlor watching her door. The blind was pulled down to within an inch of the sash so that I could not be seen." This ludicrous abasement proves but the prelude to his morning ritual:

> When she came out on the doorstep my heart leaped. I ran to the hall, seized my books and followed her. I kept her brown figure always in my eye and, when we came near the point at which our ways diverged, I quickened my pace and passed her. This happened morning after morning . . . her name was like a summons to all my foolish blood.
>
> (p. 30)

His extravagance towards Mangan's sister is duplicated later by the uncle, who gives him far more money to spend at the bazaar than his age and purpose would warrant.[5] This paralleling of the uncle's and nephew's actions helps emphasize the hyperbolic and self-indulgent aspects of the boy's worship.

Joyce also qualifies the boy's adoration by setting his confession of love in the room where the priest died, thus clearly associating the two incidents:

> One evening I went into the back drawing-room in which the priest had died. It was a dark rainy evening and there was no sound in the house. Through one of the broken panes I heard the rain impinge upon the earth, the fine incessant needles of water playing in the sodden beds. Some distant lamp or lighted window gleamed below me. I was thankful that I could see so little. All my senses seemed to desire to veil themselves and, feeling that I was about to slip from them, I pressed the palms of my hands together until they trembled, murmuring: *O love! O love!* many times.
>
> (p. 31)

The boy's generalized, vague emotion and lack of action are opposed by nature's clear, specific, fructifying activity in the back garden. Through the broken windowpane he hears "the rain impinge upon the earth, the fine incessant needles of water playing in the sodden beds." This description, suggesting as it does sexuality and fertility, contrasts with the youngster's remote adoration and the room's associations with death. Joyce earlier underlined some negative connotations of the priest when he carefully described the cleric's legacy to the boy as three faded, paper-covered books (one of which he likes best because of the romantic appearance of its yellowed leaves), and a bicycle pump which like Rip Van Winkle's gun—an analogous male sexual symbol—lies rusted from neglect and long disuse. These details suggest that, while his worship of the girl from afar is quite in keeping with his age and temperament, it also represents a temptation to follow the path away from life towards sterility and death. The boy does not declare his love in the fertile garden, but in the sterile house.

In the past, fecundity was noticeably absent from the house on North Richmond Street with its "brown imperturbable face" and is unlikely to return in the present. The uncle who comes home most nights with "a drop or two taken" combines with the indistinct aunt to make another infertile pair—at least as far as may be determined from the tale.[6] The brown color of the house's facade, echoed in Mangan's sister's school uniform, is synonymous throughout *Dubliners* with the city's decay. Details of setting in **"Araby"** conspire to suggest that the health and vitality of the boy would improve if he stopped mooning about the house idealizing a remote and perhaps unworthy object, and instead joined his playmates in the street to play "till our bodies glowed." But having fallen in love with love, he continues pacing the rooms of the house indulging in his hopeless emotions while watching from a distance his "companions playing below in the street." Since he loves "what vanishes" his infatuation must inevitably lead to disillusionment, but as so much of the story suggests, this process is necessary if he is to replace his passive worship of an ethereal object with an active participation in life.

A similar point is made through the several literary allusions used by the boy and the narrator. The youngster compares his exploits to those of a knight of the Holy Grail, while the narrator suggests certain parallels between the youngster and Dante. Like the knights of old he agrees to perform a task for his "lady": "If I go [to the bazaar]," he says, "I will bring you something." He does not succeed, however, hence cannot return to his lady. His failure is compounded, for he pictures himself not as any knight of romance but as the most famous knight, the one who achieved the Holy Grail. A Saturday afternoon shopping expedition with his aunt becomes the occasion for testing his purpose: "I imagined that I bore my chalice safely through a throng of foes." He maintains his purity of vision against "the shrill litanies of shop-boys . . . the nasal chanting of streetsingers" (p. 31). His choice of metaphor is overstated but consistent with his penchant for self-dramatization.

In contrast to his conscious choice—comparing himself with knights—is his unconscious selection of a simile to describe his feelings: "my body was like a harp and her words and gestures were like fingers running upon the wires" (p. 31). Beneath his platonic vision lies the stirrings of pre-adolescent sexuality of which he is not yet aware. The result is an unselfconscious mixing of metaphors drawn from romances, grail quests, religious worship and music that becomes a precise delineation of a young boy's first confused awakening to love:

> I imagined that I bore my chalice safely through a throng of foes [the Grail knight]. Her name sprang to my lips . . . in strange prayers and praises [religious worship] . . . My eyes were often full of tears (I could not tell why) and at times a flood from my heart seemed to pour itself out into my bosom [physical change, emotional confusion]. . . . I did not know . . . how I could tell her of my confused adoration [worship]. But my body was like a harp and her words and gestures were fingers running upon the wires [sexual attraction].
>
> (p. 31)

If his jumbled impressions provoke smiles, it will not be so much at his expense as at our own recollection of a time when we, too, were unable to draw such nice distinctions between romance, religion, physical change and sexual attraction.

Joyce comments clearly on the boy's failure to discriminate between his youthful flights of fancy and reality by comparing many of his actions, thoughts and words with those of Dante when meeting Beatrice. In *La Vita Nuova* Dante details in prose and poetry how his life was transformed through encountering Beatrice, "she who confers blessing." Although no word is spoken during their first meeting, Dante departs overcome with love: "from that time on Love governed my soul, which became so readily devoted to him and over which he reigned with such assurance and lordship given him through the power of my imagination that it became necessary for me to cater to his every pleasure . . . her image . . . remained constantly with me, was Love's assurance of holding me . . ." The boy in **"Araby"** uses similar language to describe his state. Although Mangan's sister has yet to speak directly to him, he too is "overcome with love" and so carries her image through crowded streets, noisy shops and distracting schoolrooms. When at last she does speak to him, the parallel between him and Dante emerges more forcibly:

> At last she spoke to me. When she addressed the first words to me I was so confused that I did not know what to answer . . .
>
> What innumerable follies laid waste my waking and sleeping thoughts.
>
> (pp. 31–32)
>
> . . . she greeted me so miraculously that I felt I was experiencing the very summit of bliss . . . I was so overcome with ecstasy that I departed from everyone as if intoxicated. I returned to the loneliness of my room and began thinking of this most gracious lady.
>
> (*La Vita Nuova*, Section III, pp. 4–5)

Each reacts to his lady's words with confusion. Each retreats from the company of others to contemplate his vision in private, and each begins to dwell on his lady's "image" at the expense of his everyday tasks. Dante writes that

> after that vision my vitality began to slacken in its working for I had become wholly absorbed in the thought of this most gracious lady. . . . I became so weak and so frail that many of my friends were concerned about my appearance; while others, full of malicious curiosity, were striving to learn about me that which above all I wished to keep secret.
>
> (Section IV, p. 7)

The boy in **"Araby"** experiences similar difficulties as his schoolmaster's "face pass[es] from amiability to sternness." The teacher suspects him of idleness, but despite such "malicious curiosity" he never betrays his secret, nor does he buckle down to his tedious school work: "I had

hardly any patience with the serious work of life which, now that it stood between me and my desire, seemed to me child's play, ugly monotonous child's play" (p. 32). The games of his former companions also appear frivolous, for only her image is real. The boy now experiences what Dante describes so clearly:

> The power of Love borne in my lady's eyes
> Imparts its grace to all she looks upon;
> The heart of him she greets is made to quake,
> His face to whiten, forcing down his gaze;
> He sighs as all his defects flash in mind.
>
> (Section XXI, p. 38)

But there is a great difference between their experience of love. Dante's love will remain with him after youth fades and his beloved dies. Through Beatrice's intercession he will ascend into the very presence of God. Afterwards drawing on his literary gifts he will find the means to share his experience with others. The boy's adventure ends, as it must, in anguish at the bazaar, for he has no way of sustaining his vision and, therefore, must painfully relinquish it. Later, recording his feelings about the incident in **"Araby,"** he rightly focuses on discovery and loss and not, like Dante, on discovery, loss *and rediscovery* beyond the grave.

By introducing the allusions to *La Vita Nuova*, Joyce increases the distance between the boy's and reader's perceptions of events. Comparing events in **"Araby"** with those in Dante's work, the reader gains precisely what the boy cannot have, a sense of perspective.

Joyce also helps define the limits and nature of the youngster's experience by introducing allusions to the hero's, particularly Dante's, descent into the Underworld. In much of the world's mythology the hero travels from the known into the unknown world by crossing over water, exactly as the boy passes over the River Liffey in the special train going to the bazaar. In classical mythology the way to the Underworld lies over the River Styx, which must be crossed alone in Charon's boat after paying the requisite fee. The boy is ferried over the Liffey "alone in his bare carriage," although "a crowd of people pressed to the carriage doors" eager to gain admittance. (Their behavior is like that of the souls who arrive at the Styx without their penny for Charon, hence must remain forever on the shore opposite the Underworld proper.) In common with the hero, the boy must search for an entrance, find it, throw a sop to the guardian of the gate, then hurry inside to confront his own mortality and learn of his fate. In this last section of **"Araby"** there are strong suggestions of Dante's experience in the *Inferno:* on the road before the entrance the boy checks the time by glancing upwards at the clock, as Dante tells time by looking upward at the stars; he sees the sign on the building which "displayed the magical name" **"Araby,"** as Dante reads the inscription over the gate of hell, "Abandon all hope / ye who enter here"; inside he finds himself in a large hall girdled round by a gallery, as Dante notes the conical shape of hell with its many galleries or circles for the damned; he hears "a voice call . . . that the light was out," as Dante discovers that there can be no light in hell, for by definition it is the place which is without light or hope or grace. Once within the hall, his dream of love, which had accompanied him everywhere and which he had maintained in purity of heart, fails. Instead of the music of romance, he hears the commercial harmonies of silver coins clinking against a salver—the shopkeeper's litany of the daily receipts. Araby, which promised "dreams of delight," turns out not to resemble a Persian palace where a knight might select trophies worthy of sending to his lady, but a place of business where two foreigners, Englishmen, flirt with a sales-girl. When the boy finds himself before her stand, which is one of the few remaining open at this late hour, he discovers that the goods on display are far beyond his means. The lights go out, leaving him alone in his torment. For the youngster with no worldly experience this is indeed hell, for the loss of his "rainbow vision" deprives him of light, grace and hope.

Although his loss is painfully real, it is a necessary first step if he is to move beyond illusion into a deeper understanding of love. Mature love implies, as a character in Camus' *Caligula* observes, being willing to grow old with another person; that is, being willing to accept whatever changes must inevitably take place not only in that person but in yourself as well. Such a long-term commitment is rarely made by the young and, it could be argued, is hardly ever kept by anyone. No character in *Dubliners* is able to make, accept or keep such a promise. In **"The Dead,"** Gretta Conroy's one, true "romance in her life" lies unconsummated in a western grave. In **"Eveline,"** a girl rejects the very possibility of a love freely offered, in favor of emotional starvation. Maria in **"Clay"** clings to her dream of a "knight of bended knee" while moving inexorably towards death. Mr. Duffy in **"A Painful Case"** rejects any suggestion of companionship that might involve emotional commitment in order to return to his more familiar isolation and impending death. Bob Doran in **"The Boarding House"** accepts a marriage arrangement which promises not love but the blight of sterility. Adults in *Dubliners* appear incapable of sustaining love relationships. There are no happy marriages, only infantile compromises, such as Little Chandler's in **"A Little Cloud,"** or shallow accommodations, such as Gretta and Gabriel Conroy's. Other relationships also remain incomplete or closed: Julia Morkan is "arrayed for the bridal" with her chosen groom, Death; Freddy Malins in **"The Dead"** and Farrington in **"Counterparts"** rely on drink rather than love to sustain them through the good times and the bad.

Besides failed marriages and isolated individuals, Joyce includes other examples of unfruitful relationships, like the harmlessly insane Father Flynn who lives with his two elderly sisters in **"The Sisters."** Unable to fulfill his chosen role while living, he spends most of his days in a back room shut away from other people and from his vocation. Only in death does he succeed in winning praise for making such "a beautiful corpse."⁸ The former tenants of the

boy's house in **"Araby,"** another priest and his sister, although their garden contained "a central apple tree," were not fruitful, neither did they multiply.

Given the Dublin setting and the context of *Dubliners* as a whole, it is doubtful if the boy in **"Araby"** will be able to go beyond the shattering of his illusions into the discovery of mature love, but such speculation really lies outside the tale itself. As the story ends, he has some notion of where he stands and perceives dimly through his tears the way he has travelled. Thus **"Araby"** succeeds in eliciting our sympathy for the boy's plight while amusing us with his excesses—a double vision which appears remarkably similar to the one most adults adopt towards their own first encounter with romantic love.

Notes

1. This popular song with music by Frederic Clay became the bazaar's theme song. Don Gifford and Robert Seidman, *Notes for Joyce: Dubliners and A Portrait of the Artist as a Young Man* (New York, 1967), p. 38. Gifford's notes for "Araby" are the most complete and useful of those available.

2. All references to Joyce's "Araby" are to the corrected text in James Joyce, *Dubliners* (New York, 1967), pp. 29–35.

3. "The Palimpsest of Criticism," *Antioch Review,* XXVI, 481. The occasion for apRoberts' article is a previous one by Harry Stone, "'Araby' and Joyce," *Antioch Review,* XXV, 375–410, which attempts to read backwards from Joyce's later works to "Araby," with misleading results which apRoberts carefully and accurately notes. Other critics have also done violence to Joyce's brief tale of interpreting grace notes as full dominant chords. See particularly Edward Brandabur's comments on the autoerotic elements in "Araby" or the boy's "itch of masochism," in *A Scrupulous Meanness: A Study of Joyce's Early Work* (Urbana & London, 1971), pp. 53, 56.

4. Poem by Caroline Norton (1808–1877), whose opening lines and refrain are quoted in Gifford, p. 41.

5. The uncle gives the boy a florin or two shillings. Gifford comments in 1967 that the money is "the equivalent of $5.00 to $6.00 in modern currency, a sizeable and generous sum for a boy who probably would be used to handouts of three pence or at the most six pence [a half shilling]," p. 41. The uncle's generosity is more evidence of his drinking.

6. Given the story's turn-of-the-century Dublin setting, the aunt and uncle are more likely to be brother and sister than husband and wife. In any event, as far as may be known from the story, they have no children.

7. Richard Ellmann, *James Joyce* (New York, 1959), writes that "Dante was perhaps Joyce's favorite author" (p. 2), and Joyce himself remarks that "Italian literature begins with Dante and finishes with Dante" (Ellmann, p. 226). That Joyce knew much of Dante's writings by heart is well known. He would, of course,

have read and memorized the original Italian. The quotations in the text are from *La Vita Nuova of Dante Alighieri,* trans. Mark Musa (New Brunswick, N.J., 1957). References to this translation give both page and section number. Section II, p. 4.

8. "He had a beautiful death, God be praised" and "such a beautiful corpse" are traditional phrases heard at wakes and funerals all over Ireland. Joyce chooses to include them, however, because their sentiments contrast so clearly with earlier descriptions of the Reverend James Flynn while alive.

Joseph J. Egan (essay date 1979)

SOURCE: "Romantic Ireland, Dead and Gone: Joyce's 'Araby' as National Myth," in *Colby Library Quarterly,* Vol. 15, 1979, pp. 188–93.

[In the following essay, Egan examines Joyce's utilization of Irish culture and history in "Araby."]

Although A. Walton Litz points out that a "careful analysis of the last pages of '**Araby**' shows how the boy's personal despair is extended symbolically until it encompasses religious and political failure,"[1] perhaps insufficient attention has been given to the story's national imagery drawn from Irish culture and history and set in motion by the narrator's love for Mangan's sister, "the brown-clad figure cast by my imagination."[2] The allusion here is to James Clarence Mangan, the nineteenth-century Irish poet, and primarily to his best-known work, the love song "Dark Rosaleen" (*Roisin Dubh* in Irish, or "Dark Little Rose")—in part a translation from the Gaelic of a lyrical address to a personified Ireland written by a sixteenth-century Tyrconnell minstrel (probably one of the MacAwards, the bardic retainers of the O'Donnells), but chiefly, in its present form, the poetic creation of Mangan himself. Ben L. Collins sanctions such an interpretation of Mangan's sister in "**Araby**": "To the world, Mangan is known, if at all, for his 'The Dark Rosaleen.' . . . By allusion to this poem, the themes of love and religion are reinforced and the theme of nationality—about which Joyce has already concerned himself by mention of the come-all-you's of O'Donovan Rossa and the ballads about the troubles of the country—is introduced. Modern Ireland is in a like situation, beset by England and in need of a hero."[3] Collins, however, does not explore the nationalism theme in "**Araby**" beyond this point and thus fails to mention its further reverberations in the story.

After inviting a reading of his story on the national level by the reference to Mangan's poem, Joyce renews the invitation by alluding subtly to other ideas and events fixed in the Irish consciousness. Throughout the story the Dark Rosaleen character is paralleled and varied by the mythic figure Kathaleen Ny-Houlahan, the traditional Irish heroine familiar to Joyce through Mangan's poem of that name and popularized in 1902 by W. B. Yeats's one-act play

"Cathleen ni Houlihan." In this patriotic allegory, derived from an eighteenth-century Jacobite song, Ireland again is personified, now as Kathaleen Ny-Houlahan (Kathaleen, daughter of Houlahan), the Lady Erin, who, enslaved by the foreign foe, draws followers to her service and devotion as she awaits deliverance. Notice the boy-narrator's thoughts about Mangan's sister: "I had never spoken to her, except for a few casual words, and yet her name was like a summons to all my foolish blood. . . . Her name sprang to my lips at moments in strange prayers and praises which I myself did not understand. . . . But my body was like a harp and her words and gestures were like fingers running upon the wires" (pp. 30, 31).

Of course, as might be expected, there is in Joyce's story no trace of the sentimentality and Celticism found in Mangan's poems and in Yeats's play, for Joyce employs the Irish legends to indicate the vast discrepancy between the romantic vision of Ireland symbolized by the Mangan's sister of the boy's imagination and the reality of cheapened modern Ireland, with her "places the most hostile to romance" (p. 31). The notion of frustration and malaise in Irish life is suggested not only by the blind, mundane inhibition a shabby Dublin existence imposes (darkness and shadow are with us from the outset of the story), but also by the sardonic puns and inversions that punctuate the boy's quest for love and beauty. One can, for example, view the entire story as an extension of Thomas Moore's "Love's Young Dream," from *Irish Melodies:*

> Oh! the days are gone, when
>   Beauty bright
>   My heart's chain wove;
> When my dream of life, from morn till night,
>   Was love, still love.
> Oh! 't was light that ne'er can shine again
>   On life's dull stream.
>
>   (from stanzas 1 and 3)[4]

Thus even Mangan's sister, though "defined by the light" (p. 30), remains a "brown figure" (p. 30) amid the surrounding darkness, and her idealization is merely the product of the narrator's self-deluding infatuation. As the boy realizes at last, a distinction must be drawn between the vision of Mangan's sister projected by himself as her naive young worshiper, and the actual girl, who is perhaps too fond of her silver bracelet and, in a veiled sign of sexuality, carelessly shows the border of her petticoat.

When the boy fails to buy the promised gift for Mangan's sister at the bazaar and, implicitly, renounces his adolescent attachment to her, we have another suggestion of the defeat at the core of Irish life and quite possibly a wry inversion of another old song that Joyce, an accomplished singer, was familiar with, "Oh, Dear! What Can the Matter Be?":[5]

> He promised to buy me a trinket to please me,
> And then for a kiss, O he vowed he would tease me,
> He promised to bring me a bunch of blue ribbons
> To tie up my bonnie brown hair.

Oh, dear! What can the matter be?
Johnny's so long at the fair.

(stanza 1 and refrain)[6]

The trenchant irony here, as the story's narrative tension and epiphany make clear, is not that the boy stays too long at the gaudy bazaar, but that he arrives there too late to buy a present for a rather ordinary girl who has, after all, no feeling for him.[7]

Although the reasons for Joyce's quarrel with Ireland and Irish life are various and complex, one can discover some of them through a reading of **"Araby."** Central to Joyce's disenchantment with his country is his belief that Ireland's connection with Roman Catholicism has not been fortunate. The religious symbolism in **"Araby"** has been the subject of extensive investigation;[8] suffice it to say here that the sacred and ecclesiastical imagery associated with Mangan's sister, as well as the convent-school retreat she makes, emphasizes the idea of the union of Ireland and the Catholic Church. Mangan's sister, then, is not only, as we have seen, the symbol of an idealized Ireland, but also a representation, equally unreal, of the Roman Church as Virgin Madonna: "At night in my bedroom and by day in the classroom her image came between me and the page I strove to read. The syllables of the word *Araby* were called to me through the silence in which my soul luxuriated and cast an Eastern enchantment over me" (p. 32). Accordingly, the sales-girl at the bazaar, which is described in terms of an Eastern "church after a service" (p. 34), functions as a foil to Mangan's sister: in her silly, vulgar flirtation with the two gentlemen at her stall, she becomes the Catholic Church as scarlet woman, the Whore of Babylon, who shows the boy "her wares" (p. 35), and also presents the image of a sordid contemporary Ireland. Still another, if incidental, national figure—an ironic Shan Van Vocht, "the poor old woman" Ireland commemorated in the song of the 1798 insurgents—is Mrs. Mercer, "an old garrulous woman, a pawnbroker's widow, who collected used stamps for some pious purpose" (p. 33), the visitor to the narrator's home on the night of his fateful trip to Araby. Her dead husband's surname and trade and Mrs. Mercer's own hypocritical charity suggest that Ireland has become mercenary and petty, "poor" now in spirit.

In fact, the vagueness surrounding Mangan's sister herself (she has no first name and even her last is given indirectly), the hint of sexual blemish in her show of petticoat, and the idea that she is making "a retreat"—all call attention to the pervading vision of the story on the national level. Ireland, "the Western World," has lost her identity and integrity because of the exploitation of foreign, "eastern" influences—England, as well as Rome, as Joyce suggests by the "English accents" (p. 35) of the salesgirl and her gentlemen friends.[9] In the cogent historical link between the two exploitations is the origin of the abiding national tragedy of Ireland. In 1155 Henry II of England asked Pope Adrian IV—Nicholas Breakspear, the only English pontiff in the history of the Church—for permission to conquer Ireland. At this juncture, according to some authorities, the Pope, influenced by rather exaggerated accounts of the fallen state of religion in Ireland, issued a bull, *Laudabiliter,* authorizing Henry to take possession of Ireland in the name of the Church. The king did not act immediately; but in 1166, when Dermot MacMurrough, ruler of Leinster, having been driven from Ireland by his enemies, appealed to him for aid, Henry directed him to raise an army of invasion from among the Norman vassals of Richard de Clare, earl of Pembroke, known in Irish history as Strongbow. The authenticity of the bull *Laudabiliter* has been challenged by many writers, but the fact that England invaded Ireland with some sort of papal approval—later, in 1172, reinforced by letters from Pope Alexander III—seems beyond doubt. The Irish historian Edmund Curtis makes this pertinent observation:

> The grant of Ireland by the Papacy to Henry II constituted a "moral mission" under which Adrian and Alexander III constituted Henry king or lord of Ireland for certain purposes. Too much stress can hardly be laid on the moral and legal terms which accompanied the grant, especially the preservation of the rights of the Irish Church. When Alexander praises the lay princes for receiving Henry willingly, he assumes a bargain which had to be kept. Later generations of Irishmen right up to the seventeenth century fully accepted the papal donation as a fact—witness the Remonstrance of the Irish chiefs to the Pope in 1317—but both then and later they accused the Crown of England of having violated the rights of the Irish Church and the Irish people.[10]

Thus, in one of the many ironic twists of Irish history, the Church, as well as the Irish nation, came to rue what Rome itself had originally sanctioned—the English presence in Ireland. Ironically, too, Ireland remained loyal to Catholicism, whereas England, of course, disassociated herself from the authority of the Roman Church during the Reformation.

A recurring source of disillusionment in Joycean fiction is the grim truth that, in forwarding the destruction of Ireland's independence and integrity, the "foreigner" is aided by the Irish themselves; one can surmise that to Joyce's mind the treachery of MacMurrough—Dermot na Gall (of the Foreigners), as he is remembered in Irish history—was repeated by those later Irish "traitors" who, with the support of the Church once again, broke with Parnell, Ireland's "uncrowned king." The East ever encroaches upon the West; though not actually quoted in the story itself, the first stanza of "The Arab's Farewell to His Steed," the poem about to be recited by the narrator's drunken uncle on the night of the journey to Araby, the Oriental bazaar, obliquely indicates Ireland's betrayal at the hands of base self-interest:

My beautiful! my beautiful!
    That standest meekly by
With thy proudly arched and glossy neck,
    And dark and fiery eye;
Fret not to roam the desert now,
    With all thy winged speed—
I may not mount on thee again—

Thou'rt sold, my Arab steed!
The stranger hath thy bridle rein—
    Thy master hath *his* gold—
Fleet-limbed and beautiful! farewell!—
Thou'rt sold, my steed—thou'rt sold![11]

At the end of this poem, written by the celebrated Irish beauty Caroline Norton, the Arab, overcome with remorse, refuses to sell his beloved mount:

Who said that I had given thee up?—
    Who said that thou wert sold?
'Tis false,—'tis false, my Arab steed!
    I fling them back their gold!

(from final stanza)

Alas, no such renewal of selfless love and loyalty altered Ireland's fate.

These observations return us to the beginning of our discussion—to Mangan's "Dark Rosaleen" and, in the context of **"Araby,"** to the bitter irony of its opening stanza, wherein the supposed speaker, the late-sixteenth-century Tyrconnell chief, Red Hugh O'Donnell, comforts his mistress Ireland with the prospect of military aid from Rome and its ally, Catholic Spain, against the depredations of a now Protestant England:

Oh! my dark Rosaleen,
Do not sigh, do not weep!
The priests are on the ocean green,
They march along the deep.
There's wine from the royal Pope
Upon the ocean green,
And Spanish ale shall give you hope,
My dark Rosaleen!
My dark Rosaleen!
Shall glad your heart, shall give you hope,
Shall give you health, and help, and hope,
My dark Rosaleen![12]

Early in **"Araby"** mention is made of the priest who died in a back room of the narrator's house, leaving behind a rusty bicycle pump and a few paperback books—*The Abbot*, by Scott, *The Devout Communicant*, and *The Memoirs of Vidocq*—the first two of romantic and/or religious matter, the last, significantly, about a thief. These images, together with the closing reference to the extinguished light in the upper part of the bazaar hall—that is, the altar, with its darkened sanctuary lamp signifying the loss of the Real Presence—testify expressively, though mutely, to the "theft," through her relationship with the Church of Rome, of Ireland's vitality, aspiration, and hope. When the salesgirl, the figure of debased modern Irish life, coquettishly charges the two gentlemen at her stall with lying—"O, there's a . . . fib!" (p. 35)—her accusation has symbolic reference to the various lies and deceptions practiced against Ireland herself. From the pervasive gloom of Joyce's short story emerges the mythic vision of a country, the victim of "a throng of foes" (p. 31), stripped of her nationality by folly and self-delusion and sacrificed to exploitative foreign power.

Notes

1. *James Joyce* (New York: Twayne, 1966), p. 52.

2. James Joyce, "Araby," in *Dubliners: Text, Criticism, and Notes,* ed. Robert Scholes and A. Walton Litz (New York: Viking, 1969), p. 33. Subsequent citations to Joyce's story will be to this edition.

3. Ben L. Collins, "Joyce's 'Araby' and the 'Extended Simile,'" *James Joyce Quarterly,* IV (1967), 84–90; rpt. as "'Araby' and the 'Extended Simile'" in *Twentieth Century Interpretations of Dubliners,* ed. Peter K. Garrett (Englewood Cliffs, N.J.: Prentice-Hall, 1968), p. 96. Among critics of "Araby," Collins is somewhat exceptional in urging Mangan primarily as *nationalist* poet, though Harry Stone also mentions in passing Mangan's sister as "Dark Rosaleen." (See "'Araby' and the Writings of James Joyce," *Antioch Review,* XXV [1965], 375–410; rpt. in *Dubliners: Text, Criticism, and Notes,* p. 348.) Others have called attention to Mangan the Orientalist and thus to the relationship between Mangan's sister and the eastern imagery in Joyce's story. (See, e.g., Herbert Howarth, *The Irish Writers: 1880–1940* [New York: Hill and Wang, 1958], p. 262; and Homer Obed Brown, *James Joyce's Early Fiction: The Biography of a Form* [Cleveland: Case Western Reserve Univ. Press, 1972], pp. 54–55, n. 5.) Although the Oriental motif is certainly allied to the boy-narrator's dream of exotic romantic enchantment, there is also an element of ironic indirection here, similar to that in the title *Travels into Several Remote Nations of the World,* the major satire of another Irishman, Jonathan Swift; that is, in "Araby" eastern influences are not all "remote" from Irish affairs, as we shall discover.

4. *Poems of Thomas Moore,* 2 vols. (New York: Collier, 1902).

5. References to "Dark Rosaleen," "Love's Young Dream," and "Oh Dear, What Can the Matter Be?" in other of Joyce's works have been thoroughly documented in Matthew J. C. Hodgart and Mabel P. Worthington, *Song in the Works of James Joyce* (New York: Columbia Univ. Press, 1959). Joyce also devoted an essay and a lecture to Mangan and his poetry.

6. *Heritage Songster,* ed. Leon and Lynn Dallin (Dubuque, IA: Brown, 1966).

7. Incidentally, the reference to "porcelain vases" (p. 35) and "great jars that stood like eastern guards at either side of the dark entrance to the stall" (p. 35) prompts a recollection of "Ode on a Grecian Urn"; but, whereas the search for beauty and meaning is successful in Keats's poem, the boy-narrator of "Araby" encounters only blank despair at the end of his search, when the "light" of love and hope is extinguished.

8. For a summary of the relevant criticism, see Florence L. Walzl, "The Liturgy of the Epiphany Season and the Epiphanies of Joyce," *PMLA,* LXXX (1965), 445 and n. 50.

9. Cf. the ambivalent attitude of Gabriel Conroy, that anglicized Gael in "The Dead," towards the values of the "West."

10. *A History of Ireland,* 6th ed. (London: Methuen, 1950), p. 57.

11. As quoted in *Dubliners: Text, Criticism, and Notes,* pp. 468–69. An interesting discussion of the symbolic relationship between the poem and events in Caroline Norton's own life can be found in Stone, pp. 357–58.

12. *Poems,* ed. D. J. O'Donoghue (Dublin: O'Donoghue, 1903).

L. J. Morrissey (essay date 1982)

SOURCE: "Joyce's Narrative Strategies in 'Araby,'" in *Modern Fiction Studies,* Vol. 28, No. 1, Spring, 1982, pp. 45–52.

[*In the following essay, Morrissey analyzes Joyce's narrative techniques.*]

In his analysis of Roland Barthes's poetics of the novel, Jonathan Culler points to a "major flaw" in Barthes: "the absence of any code relating to narration (the reader's ability to collect items which help to characterize a narrator and to place the text in a kind of communicative circuit)."[1] Yet, "identifying narrators is one of the primary ways of naturalizing fiction."[2] Paradoxically, Culler decides that although "the identification of narrators is an important interpretive strategy, . . . it cannot itself take one very far."[3] By examining Joyce's narrative strategies in *Dubliners,* we can challenge Culler's notion that "the identification . . . cannot . . . take one very far" in the interpretation of a text. We may also be able to make some tentative suggestions about the poetics of narration.

Any careful reader of *Dubliners* is struck by the strength and oddity of **"Araby."** Though it is shorter than **"An Encounter,"** which precedes it, or **"A Little Cloud,"** eight stories into the collection, **"Araby"** is far more memorable. The reason can be found in the narration. The first two stories in *Dubliners* are straightforward first-person narratives. "I" is the seventeenth word in **"The Sisters,"** a story about a boy-narrator's isolated struggle to comprehend the mystery of religion, rumor, and insanity. **"An Encounter"** begins with the collective "us" (eleven words in) and shifts to the personal "I" as the boy moves from a diminishing group to his private, half-comprehended sexual encounter. **"Araby,"** the third story, is the puzzle. It begins with its narrative code telling the reader that it is a third-person story: "North Richmond Street, being blind, was a quiet street except at the hour when the Christian Brothers' School set the boys free. An uninhabited house. . . ."[4] The narrator, distant, uninvolved, clearly not one of "the boys," critically views a fragment of smug, lower-middle-class Dublin. From the first line, with its clear epic

preterite signal ("being" present preferent, "was" past tense) there should be no doubt that this will be a third-person tale. First-person narrators generally identify themselves immediately: "I was born in the year 1632, in the city of York . . ." (*Robinson Crusoe*); "My father's family name being Pirrip, and my Christian name Philip . . ." (*Great Expectations*); "Call me Ishmael . . ." (*Moby Dick*); "What's it going to be then, eh? There was me, that is Alex . . ." (*Clockwork Orange*). In the few instances where the first-person narrator does not immediately identify himself, the tale is usually about tale-telling itself, for instance, Conrad's *Heart of Darkness.* Even there, we are given a subtle signal that we have an involved narrator.[5] In **"Araby"** there is no such signal. The opening is perfect third-person. Then suddenly, sixty-seven words into the story, a possessive adjective shifts our expectations: "the former tenant of *our* house." Thirty-nine words later there can be no doubt of the shift into first-person narration: "Among these *I* found. . . ." Either Joyce has made a serious mistake in his narration, or he intends something by this shift.

As we read on in the story, we first notice a mixing of simple first-person "I" ("I found," "I liked," "I wished") and the collective pronoun ("Our house," "we met," "sky above us," "our shouts"). Gradually, the isolated "I" emerges, and the collective disappears. Very much the same progress occurs in **"An Encounter"** where, from paragraph thirteen through sixteen, the "I" gradually disengages himself from his companion Mahony for fear the man will think him as stupid as his friend. In **"An Encounter"** the disengagement is essential; the actual and the figurative encounter can only happen to the boy alone. This separation of the ego also suggests that growing up is a process of isolation, of separation from the group. Thus, Joyce is clearly not unsubtle in his use of narrative codes; so there must be some explanation for this mixture of first- and third-person and for the shift from collective to isolated first-person in **"Araby."**

If we go to the next tale in the collection, part of the answer emerges. **"Eveline,"** the story of a girl "over nineteen" (p. 38) who tries, and fails, to flee from a stifling father and from Ireland, is told by a sympathetic, omniscient third-person narrator: "She sat at the window. . . . She was tired . . . she heard footsteps. . . . One time there used to be a field there in which they used to play . . ." (p. 36). Then in the last lines of the story, the narrator coolly withdraws his sympathy and merely observes her from without, judging her failure: "She set her white face to him, like a helpless animal. Her eyes gave him no sign of love or farewell or recognition" (p. 41). She is now one of the damned, like Gabriel from **"The Dead,"** and Joyce's narrative code demonstrates this. The following story, **"After the Race,"** is about the son of a Dublin "merchant prince" (p. 43), actually a butcher, who tries to keep up with the international racing set. For this tale Joyce uses his characteristically detached narrator, who stays mostly outside his characters, occasionally making aloof, damning judgments ("Rapid motion through space elates one; so does notoriety; so does the possession of money. There were three good reasons for Jimmy's excitement" [p. 44]) or relating the characters' confusion and anguish with his fine mixture of naturalistic, disparaging detail and moral censoriousness ("He knew that he would regret in the morning but at present he was glad of the rest, glad of the dark stupor that would cover up his folly. He leaned his elbow on the table and rested his head between his hands, counting the beats of his temple" [p. 48]).

Clearly **"Araby"** is the mediation between first and third person stories in the collection. It also mediates between those characters who are free of restraints, or who try to free themselves, and those who give up, who succumb to Dublin and Ireland.[6] Until **"Araby,"** the children tell their own stories; after **"Araby,"** the narrator tells the tales of the lost souls. The half-man, half-child of **"Araby"** emerges slowly from the third person narration to tell his own tale.

In Joyce's fiction (perhaps in all fiction) the choice of first- or third-person narration is at least the expression of an author's moral relationship to his characters. Just as inevitably, the narrative stance implies reader responsibility. As the author becomes active as a judge, readers become passive. We need not judge lower-middle-class Dublin if the author judges it for us by describing a "blind" street with houses personified as having a "brown imperturbable face" or "conscious of decent lives within" (p. 29). But as the author becomes passive and apparently allows characters to tell their own tales, readers become morally active. We must decide how the boy really reacts to the bazaar, to the young lady at the door of the stall, to the money counting. Joyce has opened **"Araby"** by discouraging the reader's moral alertness, only to make extraordinary demands on it by the end of the tale. This shift in reader responsibility is the reason for some of the strong reader response to the tale. Even this is too simple a description of **"Araby."** It describes its place in the collection and its mixture of narrative codes, but it does not describe the full narrative complexity of the tale nor the reason for the mixture.

The first-person narrator in **"Araby"** is not one character, but three (or better, three moods of a developing adolescent). Appropriately, Joyce does not imagine that a character develops simply, moving from one stage to another and abandoning all of his old characteristics. Instead Joyce creates a tale of a boy at the edge of manhood, who has within him a simple naif, a poetic romantic, and a harsh adult censor. We can distinguish these three in their perceptions.

It is easy enough to distinguish between the naif and the romantic perceptions syntactically. The naif is actively engaged with particular events, and his direct sentences (with no internal modification) reflect this: "I found a few paper-covered books" (p. 29); "I like the last best because . . ." (p. 29); "the cold air stung us and we played in the streets" (p. 30); "If my uncle was seen turning the corner we hid

. . ." (p. 30). In his romantic mood, the boy lovingly interprets and describes events; thus the simple subject/verb sentence structure is interrupted with internal modifiers: "Air, *musty from having been long enclosed,* hung in all the rooms, and the waste room *behind the kitchen* was littered . . ." (p. 79); "The space *of sky above us* was of ever-changing violet and towards it the lamps *of the street* lifted their feeble lanterns" (p. 30); "the street light *from the kitchen windows* had filled the areas" (p. 30).

The two perceptions of these two moods of the boy are also clearly distinct. The naif is very matter-of-fact. He has found "the late tenant's rusty bicycle pump" (p. 29) under one of the bushes in the back yard. He prefers *The Memoirs of Vidocq* to Scott's *The Abbot,* not because *Memoirs* is more salacious and less romantic, but because its "curled and damp . . . leaves were yellow" (p. 29). He does not personify the books with the usual "whose pages"; instead, it is "the pages of which." He reports what must have been an ironic comment by adults as though it were simple fact: "He had been a very charitable priest; in his will he had left all his money to institutions and the furniture of his house to his sister" (p. 29). The innocent "very" changes the whole tone of this adult sneer. By contrast, in his romantic mood, it is all hearts leaping, "confused adoration" (p. 31), borne chalices, "litanies" (p. 31), and prayers to "O love! O love!" (p. 31).

These two moods are never absolutely separated; they merge in the early part of the story. At times the sentiment of the romantic is syntactically phrased like an innocent's: "When she came out on the doorstep my heart leaped" (p. 30). But the two tones are quite clearly there, overlapping though they be. The romantic loves personification ("the houses had grown sombre"; "all my senses seemed to veil themselves" [p. 31]; "the lamps . . . lifted their feeble lanterns" [p. 30]); excessive adjectives ("the high cold empty gloomy rooms" [p. 33]), and melodramatic situations, kneeling on a "dark rainy evening" (p. 31) in the room where the priest had died and praying to the girl. Perhaps the two tones can be best distinguished in the paragraph which describes the boy(s) waiting for the bazaar. First there is the overcharged rhetoric and the complex syntax of the romantic: "At night in my bedroom and by day in the classroom her image came between me and the page I strove to read. The syllables of the word. . . ." Then suddenly the simplicity of the child returns: "I asked for leave to go to the bazaar on Saturday night. My aunt was surprised and hoped it was not some Freemason affair" (p. 32). This is typical; he has two lives, one imaginative and the other literal and factual. In the latter, he reports the colloquial Irish phrasing of the aunt and uncle (pp. 33–34); even the girl's speech is reported in lilting Irish phrasing ("She asked me was I going to Araby" [p. 31]); and his actual encounter with her lacks all of the melodrama of the paragraph just before it in which he prays to her. It is first "murmuring: O love! O love! many times." And then: "At last she spoke to me. When she addressed the first words to me I was so confused that I did not know what to answer. She asked me was I going to Araby. I forget whether I answered yes or no" (p. 31).

Not surprisingly, the innocent active boy is part of a group of boys (thus the collective pronoun in the early part of the story) whose "shouts [echoed]" as they "ran the gauntlet," and who "played until our bodies glowed" (p. 30). The romantic prays by himself in the dark, watches the girl every morning from under the blind, and isolates himself from his "companions playing below in the streets" (p. 33) on the night of the bazaar. Thus the same maturing isolation that we saw in **"An Encounter"** goes on here. In isolation, or in his imagination, he is romantic, a knight bearing his "chalice safely through a throng of foes" (p. 31). In fact, he is a young boy only slightly better off than "the rough tribes from the cottages" (p. 30), living with an uncle given to drink. Notice that although the realist and the romantic form a clear contrast in the story, both are actively engaged with life, one with living and sensing it, the other with translating it.

On the night he visits the bazaar, he begins as a romantic: "The high cold empty rooms liberated me and I went from room to room singing. . . . I may have stood there for an hour, seeing nothing but the brown-clad figure cast by my imagination . . ." (p. 33). By nine o'clock when he has had to cajole his drunken uncle for the florin, the romantic has been replaced by the realist. The syntax shifts to that of the active boy: "I took my seat . . ."; "After an intolerable delay the train moved out . . ."; "It crept . . ."; "I remained . . ."; "I passed out . . ."; "I could not find . . ."; "I found . . ."; "I recognized"; "I walked" (p. 34); "I went . . ." (p. 35). In frustration, anxiety, and anger, the character pays a shilling to get in, leaving him only eight pence for a gift and the trip home. Even before he realizes this, the romance of Araby has turned into a nightmare of anxiety and failure, and he can only "[remember] with difficulty why I had come" (p. 35). The lights are going out; he is alone (he was "alone in the bare carriage" [p. 34], and at the bazaar he is excluded from the flirtatious group gathered around the young lady "at the door of the stall" [p. 35]); only fragments of his fantasy remain ("I looked humbly at the great jars that stood like eastern guards at either side of the dark entrance to the stall" [p. 35]). At that moment the character turns into harsh censor: "Gazing up into the darkness I saw myself as a creature driven and derided by vanity; and my eyes burned with anguish and anger" (p. 35). This final sentence has both the force and directness of the naive boy ("I saw myself"; "my eyes burned") and the poetic personifying capacity of the romantic ("a creature driven and derided by vanity").

We have heard this third voice throughout the tale, as a kind of warning undertone. At times it is the neutral voice of a more knowing boy. When he says, "My eyes were often full of tears (I could not tell why) . . ." (p. 31), the parenthesis suggests that a wiser human could. Much the same is true when he says, "Her name sprang to my lips at moments in strange prayers and praise which I myself did not understand" (p. 31). At other times, the censor is brutally frank in his judgments: "Yet her name was like a summons to all my *foolish* blood" (p. 30); "I thought little of the *future*" (p. 32); "What innumerable *follies laid waste*

my waking and sleeping thoughts" (p. 32). The voice of this censor begins to undercut the romantic musings of the character. The very word "imagined" takes on a new tone for the reader in the context of this censorious teller. This teller even censors the character's physical sensations: "My heart *seemed* to pour itself out into my bosom" (p. 31); "All my senses *seemed* to desire to veil themselves" (p. 31). Here is the priestly bourgeois voice of the harsh cynic with its concern for the "future" and its willingness to call love "vanity," folly, a "summons to . . . foolish blood." This voice has acted as a subtle narrative commentary on both the naive and the romantic moods of the boy. It has been particularly harsh with the romantic boy. The tragedy of the tale is that all three moods, or voices, coalesce in the final sentence, and it appears that the voice of the censor is dominant.[7] He has taken on the strong syntax of the naive boy, and he has turned the romantic's poetry back into social and religious rhetoric that judges and rejects the romantic impulse. The boy has escaped the group of wild, free boys only to fall under the repressive spell of adulthood in Ireland.

It is now clear why Joyce opens the tale in the third-person. It is to aid, perhaps to check, the reader. It is too easy for the reader to reject the romantic boy's excesses and follow the knowing, intimidating voice of the bourgeois cynic. If we are so foolish, we will feel no tragic sensations at the end of the story; we will simply agree with the "wiser" boy. But we should feel tragic sensations, and we should know what it is that has been lost. Here the opening narration helps us. Its rhetoric is exactly that of the romantic boy, under better control. The sentences are internally modified, subjects separated from verbs by verbal and prepositional phrases and adjective clauses: "street, *being blind,* was"; "house *of two storeys* stood"; "houses *of the street, conscious of decent lives within them,* gazed." Inanimate objects are personified: "houses gazed . . . with . . . imperturbable faces." This romantic voice judges bourgeois and priestly values, but not with the crudity of the boy's censor, who was essentially a name caller. In other tales this same narrator will be as harsh as the boy's censor, but here he uses poetic perception for criticism; he sees the smugness of the houses; he perceives in colloquial language a truth about this place. A street without an exit is "blind"; this is both metaphorically and symbolically appropriate for bourgeois Dublin. The poetic antithesis between the Christian Brothers and the freed boys is the opposition on which the story is built, and it is given to us immediately by the morally active third-person narrator. This antithesis is the Irish conflict, and it is internalized in the boy: on one side, the deadly caution of the censor and, on the other, the vibrant life of a boy of two moods, one realistically recording the odors of the ashpit and stable, the other romantically translating curses, sales litanies, or Mangan's sister into beauty.

With this one text, the identification of the narrative code has taken us very far indeed. It has explained both its oddity and its strength. By helping us judge the several moods of the boy, it has determined the tone of the story. It has also allowed us to speculate about the poetics of narration: about shifts in author-reader responsibility, about the moral responsiveness of the reader, and about the way narrative codes affect the reader.

Notes

1. Jonathan Culler, *Structuralist Poetics: Structuralism Linguistics and the Study of Literature* (London: Routledge & Kegan Paul, 1975), p. 203. Jean Ricardou has recently set out a brief structuralist code of narration ("Time of the Narration, Time of the Fiction," *James Joyce Quarterly,* 16, [1978–79], 7–15), but it is concerned with the backward and forward movements in time, the speed of narration, simultaneity, and repetition rather than with narrative stance. For a discussion (without resolution) of the complexities of narration in "Araby," see the article by the MURGE group in *James Joyce Quarterly,* 18 (1981), 237–254.

2. Culler, p. 200.

3. Culler, p. 202.

4. "Araby," in *Dubliners: Text, Criticism and Notes,* ed. Robert Scholes and A. Walton Litz (Harmondsworth: Penguin, 1976), p. 29. All other references in this article will be to this edition and will be cited in the text. I have occasionally added italics to the quoted text.

5. See L. J. Morrissey, "The Tellers in *Heart of Darkness:* Conrad's Chinese Boxes," *Conradiana,* 13 (1981), 142.

6. A number of studies have examined the theme of entrapment and freedom in this collection; see, for example, Arnold Goldman, *The Joyce Paradox: Form and Freedom in His Fiction* (London: Routledge & Kegan Paul, 1966), pp. 1–21.

7. Although he does not discuss narrative moods, David E. Jones in "Approaches to *Dubliners:* Joyce's," *James Joyce Quarterly,* 15 (1978), sees the boy caught between "quagmire" and "fantasy," with Joyce the final mediator (p. 114). He rather surprisingly concludes that the boy is "saved by a measure of self-realization" (p. 115). He ignores how clearly the tale fits the tragic mythos of autumn in which obstacles triumph over human will and endeavor.

David W. Robinson (essay date 1987)

SOURCE: "Narration of Reading in Joyce," in *Texas Studies in Literature and Language,* Vol. 29, No. 4, Winter, 1987, pp. 387–92.

[*In the following essay, Robinson considers the imagery in "Araby" and its relationship to the narrator of the story.*]

. . . Of the three opening stories in *Dubliners,* **"Araby"** presents by far the clearest framing of narrated events

within the controlling viewpoint of a definite narrator. Here, finally, is a narrator whose relation to his early self can be confidently gauged and whose interpretation of the past has some claim to authoritativeness—or so it seems. A fairly consistent level of ironic detachment helps us locate the narrator, who then serves as a model for what we might think about the young boy's adolescent passion. Like the other two stories, **"Araby"** is largely about interpretation—reading—whether of the written word or of signs encountered or acted out in society. As readers we are offered a chance to read these signs more skillfully than does the narrator himself.

As the last story of the opening triad, **"Araby"** unites the preceding focuses of desire (for the exotic, for the mysterious, for meaning, for truth) in the culminating symbol of sexual desire, Mangan's sister, who becomes the occasion or site, finally, of the boy's imaginative "writing"; that is, he responds to her unattainability as an object of desire by directing his energies toward a replica of her within his imagination. This is part of a logical movement from childhood to adolescence, with interest in the opposite sex displacing more childish games; but naturalism is superseded by the insistent gnomonic references in the opening pages and beyond. As the first paragraph of **"The Sisters"** described a "lighted square of window" (*Dubliners,* 9), so **"Araby"** begins with a series of physical objects delineating flawed rectangles and empty cubes which become associated with the earlier themes of physical and mental paralysis:

> North Richmond Street, being blind, was a quiet street except at the hour when the Christian Brothers' School set the boys free. An uninhabited house of two storeys stood at the blind end, detached from its neighbors in a square ground. The other houses of the street, conscious of decent lives within them, gazed at one another with brown imperturbable faces.
>
> (*Dubliners,* 29)

Words both as sounds and ideas tie this paragraph to passages in the preceding stories. The blindness mentioned in the first sentence is of course not the physiological variety, but the word is strikingly situated, and by the paragraph's end the inanimate houses on this inanimate street will be credited with human minds and human faces. "Blind" is a word straining against its context, furthering a series of references to physical debility (paralysis) and, in **"An Encounter,"** to blindness in particular. The layout of the street, so carefully described, consists of a row of houses on either side, forming a rectangle, so that the vacant house at the end, "detached from its neighbors in a square ground," serves as the removed portion of a gnomonic parallelogram whose flawed remainder will be the setting of the story. The house in which the boy lives contains a vacant back room on the first floor, and a number of "high cold empty rooms" (*Dubliners,* 33) on the second, which are not only abandoned, but were formerly inhabited by a now-dead priest (again) whose absence the boy seems eager to fill. The boy is already trapped in a network of associations that link blindness, paralysis, vacancy, silence, and death, all variations of an absence that he attempts to remedy, first by reading the dead priest's books (cf. **"The Sisters"**), next by joining his friends playing outside in a deathlike world of dark winter cold ("Our shouts echoed in the silent street," *Dubliners,* 30; cf. **"An Encounter"**), and finally by pursuing the girl.

The description of this girl identifies her with the gnomons just described (the empty house, the silent street, the missing priest). The passage, "She was waiting for us, her figure defined by the light of a half-opened door" (*Dubliners,* 30), bears a curiously geometric stamp, as though we are seeing "defined" a certain class of "figure." The rectangle of light from the door (part of a larger, partly dark rectangle) and the shadowed silhouette of the girl within that light are both geometrically gnomonic, while a different sense of the word explains the behavior of the others when they see her:

> If Mangan's sister came out on the doorstep to call her brother in to his tea we watched her from our shadow peer up and down the street. We waited to see whether she would remain or go in and, if she remained, we left our shadow and walked up to Mangan's steps resignedly.

> (*Dubliners,* 30)

Mangan's sister indicates whether or not the evening's play is finished. Not only is she gnomonic in this sense, but so too are the boys, in other senses: they interpret the sign she gives them, doing so from within shadows of their own, and they carry as part of their identity the resignation resulting from the action being forced on them.

The narrating boy's relationship to Mangan's sister consists wholly of distanced representation of her. As soon as he begins watching the girl from the window, he begins also to blind himself to any real perception of her, substituting an "image": "Her image accompanied me even in places the most hostile to romance" (*Dubliners,* 31), including any place more substantial than his imagination. That floating word "blind" recurs when he looks through a window with drawn blinds, separating himself as much as possible from the girl he is nominally observing: "One evening I went into the back drawing-room in which the priest had died. It was a dark rainy evening and there was no sound in the house [. . .] I was thankful that I could see so little. All my senses seemed to desire to veil themselves" (*Dubliners,* 31). The boy is, of course, reenacting the priest's "death" to the material world upon the taking of his vows, and in reading *Dubliners* it is hard to miss the point that such a death is more than metaphorical. Imaginative activity, whether on the part of the boy or the reader, never accomplishes what it ostensibly sets out to do. Since substitutions follow substitutions without any conclusion but death, the pursuit of final meanings and sublime images is also a desire to escape the contingency of life, that is, to die. The pursuit of such meanings is, however, the most urgently *alive* activity in these stories, although the methods used in searching out meanings are

the same ones that delude so many of the book's characters. In order to adore his own blessed virgin, the boy must withdraw from the world of the senses and contemplate an image that substitutes itself for fleshly desire without wholly obscuring its origin. The boy wills his own blindness, which in the context of these stories means that he has entered a metonymy beginning with desire for meaning and ending only with death. Somewhere along this chain the reader, too, can be found, trapped, like the boy, by its necessities. But not trapped in an overall paralysis like the boy, whose world is crowded with the dead and whose fellow citizens are hardly alive. Readers can live to read another day, writers to write; the boy, as a fictional character, is fixed, even when the story involves him in a struggle to read his own experience.

Balancing the symbolic afflatus of the story's first half, the second half chronicles the steady collapse of the boy's imaginative inflations (which have blinded him to some rather urgent interpretive necessities) as they are pricked on hard-edged reality. Each narrated event is in some way a disappointment, beginning with the rude awakening from reverie that greets the boy in Mrs. Mercer. The boy plummets from an evocation of the Virgin Mary, celebrated priestlike as he walks about in the upper rooms of the house singing, to a monstrous parody of youth, beauty, and holiness: "She was an old garrulous woman, a pawnbroker's widow, who collected used stamps for some pious purpose" (*Dubliners,* 33). The boy next waits impatiently until his uncle arrives—drunk. When he finally procures the money and prepares to leave, the uncle is on the verge of reciting *The Arab's Farewell to His Steed,* a debasement of everything the boy associates with the word "*Araby.*" The train that takes him to the bazaar is "deserted" (*Dubliners,* 34)—a fitting state of affairs for any *real* Araby. Once he arrives, his haste forces him to squander money on an expensive entrance. And once inside, he finds not a center of exotic life, but a tremendous gnomon: "Nearly all the stalls were closed and the greater part of the hall was in darkness. I recognised a silence like that which pervades a church after a service" (*Dubliners,* 34).

The irony of the story's conclusion is that the boy completely fails, until the very last, to interpret accurately the relation, and distance, between his desires and physical reality. He fails, in effect, to interpret himself, even though perfectly competent to interpret other signs, as when his uncle enters the house: "At nine o'clock I heard my uncle's latchkey in the halldoor. I heard him talking to himself and heard the hallstand rocking when it had received the weight of his overcoat. *I could interpret these signs*" (*Dubliners,* 33; my emphasis). The interpretation itself, that the uncle is drunk, remains unstated, suggesting that the boy's evident attention to his surroundings cloaks a continued reluctance to confront sordid reality head on, at least insofar as he is personally affected (for this effect is what he would like to deny). The one reality he cannot ignore, and the one he could most easily have "interpreted" had he wished to, is money, specifically the lack of it— four pence left at the story's end (deducting return train fair) with which to buy a gift. Money turns out to be the one potent signifier in the simoniacal society the boy has tried from the beginning to evade. As an arbitrarily fixed symbol, it stands for the power of society to determine meaning (hence value) with unchallengeable force, and thus reflects the boy's paralysis in a world of action which, once recognized, so completely negates individual meanings that the boy sees himself drained altogether of reality. Just as the money in his pocket will buy him nothing, the thirdhand romantic narratives that constitute his view of the world will do nothing to recoup the lack that he senses, and without those narratives, he is himself as much a blank spot as Mangan's sister (like her, he is nameless) or, for that matter, as Father Flynn. Hence: "Gazing up into the darkness *I saw myself* as a creature driven and derided by vanity; and my eyes burned with anguish and anger" (*Dubliners,* 35; my emphasis). Looking at the darkness that is himself, he is "driven" from within by desire, "derided" from without by alien signifier chains such as money. The empty vision comes to him in a dark, silent hall like the blind, dark, cold, silent street at the story's beginning and the silent, empty houses. The boy appears to have gone nowhere, to be trapped in the same web of deadness as before, having won at most an equivocal awareness of his condition. If the boy recognizes the banality of his predicament in the epiphanic conversation at the story's end, we recognize the boy's continued lack of self-knowledge (and by implication, our own similar lack as readers) in his final rethematizing of the events in the story.

The boy's ambiguous deflation occurs precisely where a close reading of the opening symbol structures leads one to think it would. Setting aside for a moment the dense gnomonic references I have already discussed, no reader can escape noticing the odd pattern that presents itself as the narrator describes the garden:

> The wild garden behind the house contained a central apple-tree and a few straggling bushes under one of which I found the late tenant's rusty bicycle-pump. He had been a very charitable priest; in his will he had left all his money to institutions and the furniture of his house to his sister.
>
> (*Dubliners,* 29)

Without a doubt we are handed the Garden of Eden in this passage; the problem is, what should we do with it? Thematically, the Eden allegory fits, since the story depicts the boy's fall into sexual awareness. There is even the brief moment when Mangan's sister acts like (though not much like) a temptress on pages 31–32. Yet Eden and the Fall seem *excessively* potent symbols, too rich in associations to be used in such an offhand way. One wishes that a stronger thread of allegory could be followed through the rest of the story.

But it cannot be, I believe, and the fact that it cannot sends me back to the passage just quoted, which contains the datum that the boy found, under one of those vaguely

Edenic bushes, "the late tenant's rusty bicycle pump." This surely is the last straw: the temptation to allegorize the pump into, at the very least, a snake, is irresistible, but also ridiculous. Rusty or not, this pump is too far-fetched a symbol to be taken seriously. Who would care to claim that this is no ordinary bicycle pump, but that it is really (on some allegorical plane) Satan himself, the great tempter, *disguised* as a bicycle pump? Yet the symbol is also obviously *there.* In an attempt to arbitrate between critics who would read **"Araby"** naturalistically and those who habitually pursue symbols, Bernard Benstock once said of the pump that "even Freudian analysts have avoided concrete conjecturing on that suspicious object" and dismisses it as nothing more than a naturalistic detail. Benstock is not far from right (indeed, no critic would want to be stuck with such a symbol), but it may be unwise to pigeonhole the detail into an ostensibly neutral category. The pump is not a very good symbol, but it *does* have a definite impact on the reader who notices it with alarm while trying to make sense of the other Edenic resonances. The pump, being of Joycean manufacture, *deflates* the allegorical afflatus which the combined hints about Eden have conjured in the mind of the reader. First we are invited to form an abstractable meaning; then we are mocked by the absurdity of what we have created. The dual meanings of *gnomon* have reached their fullest development by the end of **"Araby,"** where the explicit meaning introduced in **"The Sisters"** (a geometric figure defined by lack) has become a general, implicit background for the action, and the originally implicit meaning (an interpreter, a knower) has assumed a dominant role, defining the functions of boy, narrator, and reader with considerable power.

The stance of the narrating "voice" in the remaining twelve stories in **Dubliners,** a fluctuating omniscience which judges or withholds judgment irregularly, may be understood through the object lesson of the first three stories— that even the simplest kind of narration is grounded on an imposture, which exposes itself in the course of any sufficiently complex work. The first-person narrative mode is exhausted and destroyed by the end of **"Araby,"** turned inside out after beginning in **"The Sisters"** as a mere hint, the mannerisms of the speaking voice, and developing into a fully articulated stance of detached yet interested irony. The fictiveness of the narrator, once established, prepares the reader for the ensuing, even more disingenuous stories. In these, and in his later books, Joyce throws us at the mercy of the language by subverting every hint of authorial or narratorial intention. Yet the fertility of the language constantly implies deliberate arrangement, and the text, besides, is not a natural, found object—somebody wrote it. The special flavor of Joyce's work comes from the frustration that attends every effort to construe specific intentions, that is, meanings, which half appear wherever one looks. The texts are always booby-trapped. In view of this, the interpretive hypotheses we base on Joyce's language ought, ideally, to collapse rather quickly back into the protean possibilities of words, instead of assuming a permanence the text itself never claims.

Phillip F. Herring (essay date 1987)

SOURCE: "Trials of Adolescence," in *Joyce's Uncertainty Principle*, Princeton University Press, 1987, pp. 3–38.

[*In the following excerpt, Herring reveals the structural and thematic links between Joyce's "Araby" to "The Sisters" and "An Encounter."*]

"Araby" is the last in a set of three stories about how a youth is thwarted in his quest for transcendence. Each of the stories begins in the tedious surroundings of home or school, in reaction to which boys set for themselves idealized destinations involving eastward journeys: in one case it is a mystical state of mind associated with the priesthood, exotic dreams, and Persia; in the next story it is the Pigeon House at the most easterly point of Dublin's harbor (and anything that might symbolize). In the third story a bazaar named "Araby" casts an eastern enchantment over an adolescent mind. A further common characteristic is that the boys lack a kind of enlightenment necessary for their graduation to a more advanced stage of maturity; this they may eventually achieve, but the greatest benefit of their shocking *rites de passage* will be to illustrate the uncertainty principle of life itself.

"Araby" immediately reveals structural and thematic links to its two predecessors:

> North Richmond Street, being blind, was a quiet street except at the hour when the Christian Brothers' School set the boys free. An uninhabited house of two storeys stood at the blind end, detached from its neighbors in a square ground. The other houses of the street, conscious of decent lives within them, gazed at one another with brown imperturbable faces.
>
> (29)

Metaphorically speaking, the most serious problem for the young boys in *Dubliners* is their blindness, i.e., a youthful naiveté accompanied by introversion, sensitivity, and romanticism (as the protagonists understand the term) that makes them shun the tedious reality of their daily lives. Blindness was, of course, literally Joyce's most enduring affliction, and the biographical strain in the stories is salient enough to remind us that for him this condition had a special meaning. (In *A Portrait,* for instance, the breaking of Stephen's eyeglasses on the cinder path brings him unjust punishment and humiliation, primary determining factors in his evolution as an artist. In the temporary dimness of vision Stephen sees for the first time his powerlessness.)

To describe the boy's street in **"Araby"** Joyce could have written "cul-de-sac," the standard term on Irish street signs, or even "dead end" in the American sense, equally suggestive, but he used "blind" to foreshadow the boy's fruitless quest. (Later the boy spies on Mangan's sister from beneath a window blind.) This blind street may indeed be a "synecdoche for all the ways of Dublin" as Edward Brandabur suggests (51), but North Richmond was also a real "cul-de-sac," and Joyce lived on it in 1894 when he was

twelve, during which time the "Araby" bazaar was a featured attraction in Dublin.[1]

Joyce uses the street to illuminate oppositions in ironic ways. Geometrically it resembles a *gnomon*—a parallelogram disabled at one side for traffic to pass while the other end is closed off.[2] On the blind end of the street is an uninhabited house "in a square ground"; a neighboring house is occupied by surrogate parents apparently blind to the implications of a boy's restless spirit. On the weak, open-ended side of the *gnomon,* facing the vacant house is the exit through which he will travel to **"Araby"** on an errand that will force him to see that he has been a romantic fool and that the bazaar is a place that caters to such as he.

In addition to blindness and seeing, closed and open, there are other dichotomies. The street is quiet except after school. During school hours the boys are confined, so that when they are released they celebrate their freedom noisily. One house is empty, the others are inhabited. The inhabited houses are conscious of decent lives within, while by implication some Dublin houses must be conscious of indecent lives within, or perhaps some are just unconscious. The strategy of personification may imply that houses must be inhabited to be conscious, since the segregated house seems distinct from its neighbors as much in its lack of awareness as in its location at the blind end. Occupied houses see the reality of their inhabitants' lives; the vacant one has neither inner light nor tenants to be conscious about.

The boy is likewise set apart from his neighbors, oblivious of the inner lives of people he meets—dislocated too through a self-conscious and adolescent romanticism from more typically extroverted boys with whom he has ceased to play. Like the boys in **"The Sisters"** and **"An Encounter,"** he knows he is different, but unlike them his psychological isolation depends upon blindness to the epiphanies of his world that point vulgarly toward the antiromantic nature of reality. In geometric terms his vision creates gnomonic structures, illuminating one level of experience while blocking out others;[3] if *gnomon* can be a metaphor for inadequacy, as in the case of Father Flynn, then we are dealing with a figure who lacks the vision, experience, and maturity to play the role he has chosen for himself.

The second paragraph reinforces the imagery and opposition of the first by stressing vacancy and decay, and by introducing a protagonist-narrator who seems attracted to the musty smells of vacant rooms. The dead priest, so charitable to institutions, has left behind useless papers, three old books, and a rusty bicycle pump that would fit neatly into T. S. Eliot's "Rhapsody on a Windy Night." Stone (344–67) and Atherton (**"Araby"**) labor to show that each of the books is a thematic key, but the titles probably have just enough relevance to encourage readers to inflate them with meaning. (After all, Joyce supplied the pump.) There is no indication that the boy has read them, especially since he views them as physical objects, preferring the one with yellow leaves. Like his predecessors in *Dubliners,* what he seeks is not to be found in books but in the daily life around him.

Despite his affinity for darkness, enclosed spaces, and musty smells, the protagonist enjoys playing outdoors. Yet rough play with the neighborhood children, though exhilarating, loses its appeal as he succumbs to a more mature, more private kind of stimulation. Joyce's imagery of light and darkness, often remarked upon, serves not so much to emphasize the gloom of Dublin seasons as to highlight the confused tensions in the lives of his characters. When dusk falls, the houses grow somber; feeble lanterns stretch out to a violet sky. In this obscurity the children play till their "bodies [glow]." There are "dark muddy lanes," "dark dripping gardens"; "light from kitchen windows" shines through the darkness; when the uncle returns or Mangan's sister appears to call her brother to dinner, the children elude them by hiding in the shadow. From there the protagonist peers at another shadowy figure—Mangan's sister—"her figure defined by the light from the half-opened door." (Voycuristic scenes in *A Portrait* and *Ulysses* are, of course, foreshadowed.) In door and window Joyce chooses to reemphasize gnomonic shape along with the interplay of light and darkness, vision and blindness, though in the window he has reversed the dark-light aspect to form a shaded rectangle with light entering the lower section: "The blind was pulled down to within an inch of the sash so that I could not be seen" (30).

Unlike Stephen and Bloom who were only momentarily enchanted, respectively, by the "bird girl" and Gerty MacDowell, the hero of **"Araby"** feels a passionate commitment of many days duration; but like them he too will find that silent encounters with feminine beauty provide insight, though neither gratification nor commitment. In each case the silent language of adoration is more prayerful Mariology than Petrarchan laudation, with fantasy playing an important role. This somewhat obtrusive religious imagery of **"Araby"** conforms to the movements of expectation and disappointment, the central journey pattern in the stories of youth (just as it is in most of Joyce's narrative units describing maturation). Imitating a courtly love tradition of which he is presumably ignorant, the boy creates a false madonna and worships her fervently; upon arriving at the bazaar on "this night of Our Lord" (33), he immediately recognizes "a silence like that which pervades a church after a service" (34), and might well be reminded of the money-changers in the Temple, as several critics surmise.

Brooks and Warren note that during the latter part of **"Araby"** the boy's confusion is emphasized. It is a condition he actively magnifies, believing it necessary to romantic euphoria, a confusion of the senses prefigured both by the play upon blindness and by his misuse of the language of prayerful adoration. True, it is the only vocabulary the youth has for praising feminine virtue, but he uses it for self-intoxication rather than wooing: "her name was like a summons to all my foolish blood" (30); "her name sprang to my lips at moments in strange prayers and praises which I myself did not understand"; "how could I tell her of my confused adoration"; "I was thankful that I could see so little. All my senses seemed to desire to veil themselves"; "when she addressed the first words to me I was so confused that I did not know what to answer" (31). But like the bird girl and Gerty MacDowell, Mangan's sister hears no words of praise.

Confusion gives way to an intense determination to reach **"Araby."** Obstacles impede his way, but he completes the third journey of the *Dubliners* collection. His counterpart in **"The Sisters"** while paying his respects to the dead sought to clarify the nature of his friendship with the priest; in **"An Encounter"** the boy seeks through adventure to transcend the daily tedium of his life; for his part, the protagonist of **"Araby"** sets out to purchase a trophy that will make him seem desirable to Mangan's sister. Whether the vehicle for transcendence is religion, adventure, or romantic encounter, the result of each journey is displacement, shock, self-ridicule, and a new awareness of self and world (in **"The Sisters"** a process implied rather than described).

In **"Araby"** one sign that the destination is a mirage not of desert sands but of cityscape is the story's title, with its suggestion of a music-hall backdrop; another is the boy's use of an unexpected bazaar entrance. Clearly he has encountered in the external world a carefully devised confusion to balance the internal one he has nurtured. The purpose of the bazaar is to make money by providing an exotic atmosphere that appeals to the Dubliners' need for adventure or romance, hence the imagery of usury (Mrs. Mercer; the constant clink of coins; the buying and selling of wares). The boy's blindness to reality, his incessant confusion, his use of Mangan's sister to promote a sustained euphoria—the pressures of adolescence have steered him into a very antiromantic, commercial port of call.

In **"Araby"** Joyce's delicate balancing of the particular elements of the boy's romantic expectation with those present in the bazaar was a brilliant achievement. Quester and goal are each gnomonic shapes that complete each other. The enamored youth deludes himself, the bazaar deludes the populace; the false romance of the youth's delusion encounters the bogus romance of the Café Chantant and **"Araby"**; his earlier blindness to all that inhibited his romantic vision is finally dispelled by epiphany, the sudden clarity of insight being timed to match his waning view of this darkening vanity fair.

Since the first three *Dubliners* stories form a trilogy of youth, the key words on the first page were made to unlock meanings in all three stories, but they must be stretched slightly to fit the context, just as the boy in **"The Sisters"** does, until they reinforce a unity of design and help to unravel the three enigmatic endings. Although we are not always told precisely what the boys feel, they seem momentarily to share in the paralysis discovered before turning hurriedly away in a panic of self-awareness. (The ending of **"The Sisters"** does not show this, but any projection of geometric lines beyond the final ellipses would likely show parallels with the next two endings.) The boys of **"The Sisters"** and **"Araby"** obviously have simoniacal relationships, since some kind of commercial exchange is involved in their attachment to priest and madonna figures. As we have seen, gnomonic structures, accompanied by the interplay of light and dark images, become essential components in the boy's "seeing" both sweetheart and bazaar. An incomplete figure himself due to romantic blindness and immaturity, he travels in the rectangular shape of "a third-class carriage of a deserted train" and en route spies "the lighted dial of a clock" (34), the tardy hour of which forecasts the hopelessness of his journey. No series of ellipses is necessary to call our attention to what is missing in either the romantic impulse or in the structure he imagines to be the instrument of his fulfillment.

"Araby" turns out to be "a large building"; inside is "a big hall girdled at half its height by a gallery"; "the greater part of the hall was in darkness" (34). It is within this spacious *gnomon*—loosely definable here as an incomplete structure with one section in darkness—that illumination occurs, much as it must have come to Father Flynn in the darkened confessional. As the upper hall gradually darkens, ironically providing the ideal atmosphere for spying on girls and priming the imagination, the boy turns his back on **"Araby"** now more fully conscious of sight as a faculty that leads one from innocence to experience through disillusionment: "Gazing up into the darkness I saw myself as a creature driven and derided by vanity; and my eyes burned with anguish and anger" (35). Blindness is no more. This exit from Munsalvaesche should allow our young Parzival eventually to shed his fool's costume.

In the preceding *Dubliners* stories epiphany is accompanied by trite or deceptive language, meaning residing in silence or elliptical language rather than in the verbal camouflage that is the oil of social intercourse. Joycean epiphanies take one unawares, provoked by commonplace events and vacuous language that seem to belie the fact that for the initiate this is a primal scene of discovery. So it is in **"Araby"**:

> "I remarked their English accents and listened vaguely to their conversation:
>
> —O, I never said such a thing!
>
> —O, but you did!
>
> —O, but I didn't!
>
> —Didn't she say that?
>
> —Yes. I heard her.
>
> —O, there's a . . . fib!"
>
> (35)

The keenness of the boy's disappointment is commensurate with his sensitivity to language. Like his prototype in **"The Sisters,"** he orients himself by means of totem words that seem to reveal alternative worlds. It is as much the name of **"Araby"** as the girl's attraction to its wares that lures him to the bazaar.

Brewster Ghiselin is not quite on the mark when he says, "The response of the boy to the name *Araby* and his journey eastward across the city define his spiritual orientation, as his response to the disappointing reality of the bazaar indicates his rejection of a substitute for the true object of the soul's desire (328)."[4] Such a view diminishes the boy's personal responsibility for his disappointment, and suggests that he is clear about what he expects to find. Harry Stone is similarly wide of the mark in neglecting this aspect of the story. Stone writes convincingly of Yeats's story "Our Lady of the Hills" as a source for Joyce's portrayal of the girl in **"Araby"** as false madonna, yet it must also be emphasized that no falseness is discoverable in the girl herself as both Stone and Ben L. Collins (97) suggest.

As in the Yeats story, in his imagination the boy makes of the girl something she is not—an unrealistic figure of idolatry. The seven veils of mystery in which the boy cloaks her probably hide an ordinary Dublin girl of her age. Falseness resides, rather, in the voyeurism and mysticism that engender the reaction of an inexperienced lover who must learn about life the hard way, by looking for sustenance to a commercial establishment that matches his own temperament for falseness, a shabby bazaar that trades on the gullibility of wide-eyed locals by cloaking itself in the name (but not even the borrowed robes) of oriental exoticism. Neither boy nor reader mistakes the facade of Duessa's castle, realizing that falseness lies within both quester and goal, and deliverance is not from any "throng of foes" (31), but from illusions tenaciously held.

Notes

1. See Ellmann, *James Joyce,* 110, Plate III; and Atherton, "Araby" (40).
2. Cf. Friedrich, "The Perspective": 73.
3. A prerequisite for this selective blindness is isolation, a topic emphasized in Brooks and Warren. Meaningful interaction or communication with others is avoided since apparently the boy believes nobody can help him find his way.
4. Like most *Dubliners* stories, "Araby" teaches a lesson: not that lovers are fools, or that romantic feeling is only for experienced lovers, but that love is both spiritual and carnal. In a famous love letter to Nora, Joyce wrote, "One moment I see you like a virgin or madonna the next moment I see you shameless, insolent, half naked and obscene" (*Letters* 2: 243). The boy in "Araby" has been captivated by an illusion that human love is only spiritual.

Albert Wachtel (essay date 1992)

SOURCE: "The First Trinity," in *The Cracked Looking Glass: James Joyce and the Nightmare of History,* Susquehanna University Press, 1992, pp. 23–37.

[In the following excerpt, Wachtel views "Araby" as the third story in a trilogy—the other two being "The Sisters"

and "An Encounter"—and deems it an important transition to the other stories included in Dubliners.]

Although they depict the meanness, entrapment, and blindness of the citizenry, the first two stories of *Dubliners* are actually about the discovery of those same qualities in the protagonists. **"Araby,"** third in the series, is the final example of such self-scrutiny before the authorial voice presents the victims and the struggling might-have-beens of Dublin life.

Until the protagonists of the first stories discover and acknowledge their errors, it seems to them possible to direct their disapproval at others. In **"The Sisters,"** the boy resents Old Cotter and refuses the offering of the old woman. In **"An Encounter,"** the protagonist disdains Mahony and the Dillon boys. Similarly, in **"Araby"** the sources of failure appear at first to reside outside, in certain relatives or sales people, in streets or houses or the bazaar where the fragment of conversation we alluded to earlier (p. 21 above) actually occurs:

—O, I never said such a thing!

—O, but you did!

—O, but I didn't!

—Didn't she say that?

—Yes. I heard her.

—O, there's a . . . fib!

(p. 35)

What the exchange means to the speakers we cannot say, but a reconstruction of the protagonist's store of attitudes and memories when it occurs can reveal what it means to him.

Just as the narrative voices of the other stories often adopt the limitations and styles of their protagonists, the narrator of **"Araby"** adapts his story at critical points to the patterns of thought he had as a child. In the first paragraph, for example, streets and houses are given human attributes. North Richmond Street is a "quiet street" because it is "blind." Taken by itself, the sentence escapes pathetic fallacy: "blind" can be read as a synonym for dead-end; "quiet" as descriptive rather as an attribution. But what follows forces the issue. A school, we are told, sets the boys free, and the uninhabited house on the block is an outsider, exiled from its "neighbours." "The other houses of the street, *conscious* of decent lives within them, *gazed* at one another with brown *imperturbable faces*" (p. 29, my italics). The images are elegant and consistent, but self-consciously poetical. The anthropomorphic attributions constitute the first clue to the nature of the boy's problem, a romantic tendency to impose his vision on his environment.

As if to reassert that the father-priest figures who influenced the boys in the earlier stories are irrelevant here, the clergyman in **"Araby"** is dead. The books and the priest-like men who appear in **"The Sisters"** and **"An Encounter"** are alluded to in the early references to a dead priest and his unread volumes, both secular and religious. Too young to be moved by Scott's romance, free of the dangerous attractions of *The Devout Communicant,* too innocent sexually to respond to *The Memoirs of Vidocq,* the boy lets his fancy work upon the material properties of the books. He prefers Vidocq "because its leaves [are] yellow" (p. 29). His fantasies cannot be attributed to the influences of individual men or books; they arise from within himself.

He is attracted to the girl who lives across the street but does not know how to approach her. Lacking a firm model upon which to pattern his reactions, he gets his responses reversed. In the case of Vidocq's book, he ignores the words and reacts to the entity in which they appear; in the case of Mangan's sister, rather than responding to the girl herself, he idolizes her name—an ephemeral sound, so insignificant finally that it is not included in the story at all. He becomes her "devout communicant." "[H]er name was like a summons to all my foolish blood" (p. 30). He sublimates his personal feelings and his sexual appetite into a romantic, religious, and mawkish sentimentality: "I pressed the palms of my hands together until they trembled, murmuring, *O love! O love!* many times" (p. 31, Joyce's italics).

Joyce set himself the task of transforming the bread of everyday life into the host of art by exposing its essential nature. Carrying the frail image of the girl through the streets, the boy in **"Araby"** disdains common life. "The shrill litanies of shop-boys" and the "chanting of street singers" seem neither spiritually nor aesthetically significant to him. He explicitly rejects living itself: "These noises converged in a single sensation of life for me: I imagined that I bore my chalice safely through a throng of foes" (p. 31). His unexamined emotions alienate him from himself, turning his language into a babble of "prayers and praises which I myself did not understand." Like the deviate of **"An Encounter"** he is caught up and hypnotized by his own words, relinquishing his hold on the "real world" in which the story occurs.

Mangan's sister, on the other hand, deftly applies secular conventions to the situation. Not only does she know her own mind; she notices the boy's admiration for her as well, and well she should: he has been trailing her to school for months. Insufficient attention has been paid to what she tells him when they finally exchange words.

At last she spoke to me. When she addressed the first words to me I was so confused that I did not know what to answer. She asked me was I going to *Araby,* I forget whether I answered yes or no. It would be a splendid bazaar she said; she would love to go.

(p. 31)

Mangan's sister is generously offering to accompany the boy to the bazaar, but she lays herself open indirectly, in keeping with common social practice. Blind to her intent, however, the boy misses the hint and asks why she *can't* attend. He misunderstands what "I would love to go" can mean. Rebuffed, the girl toys with her bracelet, cooking up a response: "She could not go, she said, because there would be a retreat that week in her convent" (p. 32).

Though the symbolic import and the allusive suggestiveness of the scene, linking her to both virgin queen and archetypal temptress, are undeniable, they are less vital to the exchange than an understanding of the basic failure in communication that occurs. Whatever the girl's role may be in relation to the temptress of earlier fictions, her basic intent is to make herself available to the boy as a friend.

Armed with this awareness, we return to the flirtation between the salesgirl and the two English youths at the bazaar. Hearing them, the boy has only to link their situation to his exchange with Mangan's sister in order to reach an illuminating realization. Imagine it as he would: a girl has hinted at her willingness to be approached; her young man and his friend, immature, though more perceptive than the protagonist has been, tease her for offering a date; embarrassed, but shielded by her indirect approach, she responds, "O, I never said such a thing!" And the rest follows until, "Observing me the young lady came over and asked me did I wish to buy anything" (p. 35). This time the question is direct, but Mangan's sister too had asked if he wished to buy anything. Although his fidelity to an amalgam of romantic and religious rituals was matched by her obedience to the constricting social convention that girls must communicate indirectly, she at least was aware of his interest and tried to oblige him. He, blinded by unassimilated sensual desire and misplaced religious ecstasy, failed to read the meaning of her words. Like Stephen Dedalus in the *Portrait,* the boy failed to take a gift for "which he had only to stretch out his hand" (p. 69).

The bazaar itself, no matter how tawdry, is insufficient to have destroyed his illusions. It is true that when he arrives he finds money changers defiling a salver with their coins, but a bazaar is not a temple and he does not react adversely to the sight. It is also true that the exchange between the salesgirl and the young men is mundane and that the men have English accents. But since the flirtation at the booth can as easily be linked to the "throng of foes" as to Mangan's sister, the boy need not feel disappointed unless he has made some such connection as we have suggested between his conversation and theirs.

Critics have persisted in claiming that the bazaar disillusions him, but the boy's initial response to it, like his response to Mangan's sister, has religious overtones. The bazaar has "a silence like that which pervades a church after a service" (p. 34). And after the salesgirl approaches him he looks "humbly at the great jars that stood like eastern guards at either side of the dark entrance to the stall . . ." (p. 35). Even when deserted, the bazaar retains an element of mystery, but the boy has come to realize that he has lost an opportunity. The flirtation between the salesgirl and the

Englishmen is hardly epiphanic in its own right; rather, when the protagonist perceives the consonance between it and his earlier conversation with Mangan's sister, both the former and the latter are clarified for him. The boy realizes that by failing to understand and take advantage of Mangan's sister's subtle offer, he had missed an opportunity to be with her. Araby is, perhaps, disappointingly, just another bazaar, but the boy has been more importantly disillusioned about himself.

The nature of his failure becomes clearer if we depart from the text for a moment and contrast it with a related success. Joyce is said to have regretted that he had limited powers of invention, that he could not generate a fictional event without a strong basis in fact. But the faculty of invention is innate; we all create and live within sometimes fanciful fictions by which we try to understand and reconcile ourselves to the world. But some of us accurately chart the terrain of our experiences, while others obscure it. The advantage of the latter is that they temporarily insulate their believers against suffering; their liability is that they open them to the pain of having their fancies destroyed, exposing them to the subsequent anguish of working raw-nerved upon a harsh world.

There is no ultimate escape from fictions, then, but the possibility exists that destructive effects of the delusive kind can be minimized by an imaginative—that is, shaping—power, the same faculty Coleridge had in mind when he distinguished two varieties of imagination from fancy—in his scheme, the faculty by which degenerating memories are given new order, by placing the head of a woman on the body of a horse, for instance. The first of the imaginative powers, on the other hand, is the singular ability to create a sense of the whole of something real by means of partial perceptions. On a limited, visual scale this "primary" imagination is what we use every day in supplying full round heads to all the faces we see. This power, and the secondary ability to exercise it upon invented circumstances, Joyce had in abundance. The boy in **"Araby"** has not yet developed the primary power with regard to his life. Instead of working openly and imaginatively upon the real world to enlarge his understanding and fulfill his desires, he imposes what Coleridge would call fancy upon it: he conceives of houses as people, sees a girl as a saint, and love as a chalice. **"Araby"** tracks the destruction of his false notion about the "holy spirit" of secular love. It describes a necessary cutting away from vain romantic roles and blind assumptions.

In the end, the boy recognizes himself as "a creature driven and derided by vanity," but even here he overdramatizes his failure. Caught in an artificial world in which spiritual values are confounded with romantic aspirations, he is defeated by an egotistical belief in the singularity and sacredness of his feelings. The love he has cherished is a product of fancy, compounded of an urge to possess the girl and of the degenerating memory traces of religious feeling. Like the Virgin's head on the body of a Venus, the combination is interesting, perhaps, but disconcerting. For no such object of love exists outside the mind that concocts it.

A similar attitude was alive in Joyce: "My love for you allows me to pray to the spirit of eternal beauty and tenderness mirrored in your eyes or to fling you down under me, . . ." he confesses to his wife, and he goes on to describe a lustful and self-consciously animalistic coupling (p. 181). Thanks to the dimension of time, his conflicting feelings admit of satisfaction; he can worship Nora at one moment and abuse her as the eternal sow the next. Joyce may never have reconciled himself morally to such paradoxes of love, but in his art he understood them. In like manner, the narrator of **"Araby"** (if we indulge ourselves momentarily and imagine him real) may fail to develop a consistent vision of his lovers, but as artist he both perceives and embodies what he takes to be his youthful failure.

Neither Araby nor Mangan's sister is his primary obstacle. Instead, he learns, he himself has failed. The possibility of friendship was offered him and he myopically declined. Childishly, he attributes a finality to his failure which it need not have, but for the moment it crushes him. His story is less about disillusionment with the world than about the disabusing of the self, a lifting of the blinds through which a boy has peeped at life.

The protagonists of **"The Sisters," "An Encounter,"** and **"Araby"** understand their own roles in the situations they recollect and have to that extent freed themselves from complicity in their defeat. Each is an artist now, a storyteller, but was a boy when the action occurred. Their histories constitute a thematic unit and, though we shall not do so here, they can be read as phases in a single life. Each story seems to be about a failing in someone or something that the narrator once encountered in the world at large but each ends with the recognition that whatever the state of the external world there has been a more crucial failure within the boy himself. In the course of his microcosmic history he gains an important insight, and he atones for his sins by confessing them, not to the representative of some putative god, but within himself and to us. The boy's development is the crucial concern in each of the first three stories, and in each the addressable questions the story raises and the fictional base it develops direct us back to the boy and his experience of enlightenment, dispelling at the same time the perplexing and insoluble problems that might otherwise trouble the reader. As we shall see, the adult protagonists in *Dubliners* either cannot see, or refuse to acknowledge, their affinity for defeat. Those who cannot see are victimized; those who choose to remain ignorant become willing slaves.

Garry M. Leonard (essay date 1993)

SOURCE: "The Question and the Quest: the Story of Mangan's Sister," in *Reading* Dubliners *Again: A Lacanian Perspective*, Syracuse University Press, 1993, pp. 73–94.

[*In the following essay, Leonard utilizes the theories of Jacques Lacan to analyze the depiction of Mangan's sister in "Araby."*]

The displacement of the signifier determines the subjects in their acts, in their destiny, in their refusals, in their blindness, in their end and in their fate.

(Lacan 1988c, 43–44)

Gazing up into the darkness I saw myself as a creature driven and derided by vanity; and my eyes burned with anguish and anger.

(*Dubliners*; hereafter cited as *D* 35)

I had read **"Araby"** several times before I noticed and became curious about the fact that the Araby Bazaar is really the place where Mangan's sister wishes to go. The surprise and confusion of the boy's aunt when he asks if he may go makes it clear that he has not mentioned the event until after his conversation with Mangan's sister. She is the one who introduces "the magical name" that is also the title of the story, but what is her story? If she is not the protagonist of the story, can she be seen as the contagonist whose powerful absence makes the boy's presence in his own narrative possible?

Blanche Gelfant, in her introduction to a panel entitled "A Frame of Her Own: Joyce's Women in *Dubliners* Reviewed" at the Ninth Joyce Symposium, cites the boy's fantasy relationship to Mangan's sister as typical of what male critics have done with the women they have come upon in Joyce's fiction: "The reader can see Mangan's sister only as she has been appropriated by a male viewer—indeed, three male viewers: the deluded boy, the retrospective narrator, and the author. A fourth must be added, the male critic, whose objectivity as observer of Joyce's women has until recently gone unchallenged" (1988, 263). One has only to look over some of the male commentaries on **"Araby"** from the sixties and seventies to see that Gelfant's indictment of the male critic is justifiable.[1]

But is Joyce really the third male appropriator standing between the reader and Mangan's sister? I do not think so, and Marilyn French, in the panel that Gelfant introduces, also suggests otherwise: "Joyce's women are not mere mythic figures, types, such as appear in the work of so many other male authors. They have a reality of their own which is palpable even though the men who occupy the foreground of the stories largely ignore it" (1988, 267). Male critics have often appropriated the women in Joyce's fiction with at least as much ingenuity as any of the male characters in *Dubliners*. Mangan's sister, for example, has been featured as a virgin, a whore, Ireland, simony, and so on, in various essays. Like the boy of the story, male essayists have too often discovered that Mangan's sister represents the very thing they fear is lacking in their own arguments. And yet it is her frustrated desire that calls the boy into being. I suggest that her unspoken story speaks to who the narrator becomes in the course of what he presents as his story.[2]

The narrator says, "I kept her brown figure always in my eye." Once readers refuse to take his word for it, they see that this is not so. What he always keeps, as the symmetry of this phrase suggests, is his *I*, which is constructed in relation to the representation of Mangan's sister that he has appropriated by his "eye." It is this that allows him to believe in the fictional unity of his masculine identity, which in turn grants him the illusion of bearing his chalice (his presumed subjectivity) safely through a throng of foes (what Lacan terms the Real).[3] I go even further and suggest that the subject of **"Araby"** is the desire of Mangan's sister in the sense that her function in the boy's narration as absence and lack is what permits his subjective presence. He represses awareness of the question of her desire by incorporating it into what he presents as his quest. As a result, what he takes to be his identity has been constructed relative to another (Mangan's sister) and is destined to be taken apart in relation to someone else (the shop girl at the bazaar). The appropriating gaze he directs to Mangan's sister is reflected back to him—in an inverted and disorienting form—by the indifferent gaze of the shop girl who asks if he wants to buy something. As the delirious subjectivity when setting out on his quest founders, the question of woman returns, and the boy becomes the object of another's gaze: "Once or twice the young lady glanced at me over her shoulder. I lingered before her stall, though I knew my stay was useless, to make my interest in her wares seem the more real" (*D* 35). The masculine quester becomes the feminine question—masquerading to appear "more real."

By moving from the subject controlling the gaze to the object controlled by it, the narrator moves from the exhilaration of having the Phallus to the more debilitating posture of consciously pretending to be the Phallus for the benefit of another's desire ("I lingered . . . to make my interest in her wares seem the more real"). More real for whom? Certainly not the narrator; although he now knows he is pretending, earlier he knew he was the real thing, both of these moments equally represent reality inasmuch as both misrepresent the Real. The illusion of having the phallus (based on the lack of Mangan's sister—her inability to satisfy her desire to go to the Araby Bazaar) allows the boy to emerge as the only one worthy to go in search of the one, true (nonexistent) object of desire (the Holy Grail). He is a selected signifier destined to bring back the elected signified. Certainly the narrator feels found out by the end of this story (which was never his story), but his final epiphany is a new pose. Like so many of Joyce's characters, he is learning that in the masque of subjectivity—in disguising the face of the slave—sincerity is crucial; once you can fake that you have it made.

The boy sees Mangan's sister as a representation of what Lacan calls the woman; he imagines who he has become by positing his completeness on her lack.[4] He lives in a world of words, rather than the world itself—what Lacan calls the Real—which is whatever has not been represented, distorted, interpreted, or reconstructed in the Symbolic Order of language. In this kingdom of words he is able to imagine himself as king, and this allows him to believe in himself as a subject. But in the world of words, the subject is a signifier with no signified. The subject takes its place in a signifying chain and is, henceforth,

forced to model its very being on the moment of the signifying chain that traverses consciousness. A woman who appears to the masculine subject as feminine—as the Woman—appears as the locus of the question about the masculine subject's identity. She seems to represent the response given by the subject to the question of knowing what he is for the 'other.' Essentially, the Other is a concept designating the reference point from which one establishes identity—between consciousness and unconsciousness, between others and language, somewhere between one's sense of what is inside and outside. If the masculine subject could only possess the *original* signifier—which does not exist and which Lacan calls the Phallus—then he would no longer be merely a signifier that acts as a signifier for another signifier in a chain that goes on forever. But this can never be because there is nothing certain in the Symbolic Order—nothing that directly corresponds to the Real—that is capable of stopping the chain reaction.

For the narrator, Mangan's sister is a representation of femininity—the opposite of masculinity—which is to say she does not exist for him except as the representation of lack that confirms the fullness and authenticity of his masculine subjectivity. The Woman represents to the masculine subject the Other, which is the locus from which the subject's question of his existence is presented to him. This question can bathe and support the subject, but it can also invade him and tear him apart. When a woman is taken to be the Woman by a masculine subject, she is perceived as enigmatic and powerful because she appears to have the power to nurture or destroy—to confirm the authenticity of his identity or to undermine it. In fact, she has the power to do neither; the enigma of femininity merely reflects back to the masculine subject a division that already exists within him.

But does Mangan's sister exist outside the boy's "I/eye"—outside his representation of her as the Woman? Joyce shows us she does by allowing the possibility that, although the boy's narrative seeks to repress it, *she has noticed him looking and is looking back at him.* A commonplace criticism about this story is that the girl does not notice the narrator—perhaps because he is too young or, perhaps, because he has kept his confused adoration a secret. But I argue for the opposite assumption: she has seen him looking at her and that is why she begins their conversation (a fact as curiously easy to skip over as the fact that she brings up the subject of the Araby Bazaar). To begin with, he must have distinguished himself from her brother in her eyes because he consistently refuses to take part in his attitude of playful disobedience toward her: "Her brother always teased her before he obeyed and I stood by the railings looking at her" (*D* 30). Certainly, the narrator wishes to worship her in private, but he really has two impulses, and the second one has been insufficiently noted: one impulse is to remain unseen while seeing her (he pulls the window blind to within an inch of the sash), and the other is to have her see him while he appears to be looking elsewhere (every morning he contrives to cross her path as though by chance).

What can it mean, then, when he says *"at last* she spoke to me" (emphasis added) except that she has noticed him noticing her and has finally decided to act? And, when she does speak, her remarks (and the narrator heralds these remarks as "the first words," making it clear that he has been expecting something to begin), although narrated indirectly by the boy and, thus, apparently haphazard and indifferent are, in fact, rather cleverly designed to test the extent and nature of his attraction to her without risking embarrassment or rejection on her part. She is a girl curious about her recently discovered ability to attract the male gaze (a discovery selected by Molly Bloom as an extremely important one in a girl's life). The fact that the narrator is young and naïve is precisely the point; she would scarcely experiment with this new dimension of her being with someone like Blazes Boylan, because he would certainly lack the subtlety to interpret it in a manner flattering to herself. That her words to the boy come "at last" suggest that she has been fascinated by the game and even prolonged it. Finally, her choice of remark, asking him if he is going to an event that she cannot possibly attend, by rule of her parents, is not at all arbitrary but a clever way of drawing out his attention while at the same time protecting herself from it; she is still a little frightened of what his gaze might mean, but she longs to be nearer to it.

In an important essay, Devlin points out that a major component of Leopold Bloom's enjoyment of Gertie McDowell (his consumption of her image) depends on his belief that she is only stimulated by being looked at, not by looking at him: "Oddly enough, Bloom does not think of women being stimulated visually, through provocative sights, in an elision of the possibility of female scopophilia. . . . He fails to think of her as a voyeur or recognize the full extent of her own visual pleasure, refusing to see her as the pruriently viewing subject, himself as the exhibitionistic object. But after all, since when is a fairly overt masturbation not an exhibitionistic act?" (1988, 140).[5] The boy also exhibits himself to the girl morning after morning (although certainly less overtly than Bloom). My point is that the excitement of both Bloom and the narrator of **"Araby"** is contingent on the dynamic of their upholding their *I* by keeping the figure of a woman in their *eye*. But how is it possible to maintain this illusion about the unity of their subjectivity if the women they have appropriated for the purposes of stimulation have also or, in the case of Mangan's sister, have already appropriated their image in order to stimulate themselves?

Mangan's sister speaks to him first, and as she does so she turns a silver bracelet "round and round her wrist." Is this self-consciously sexual, a subtle variation of Gerty leaning farther back? Not necessarily, but I insist this shows that she is concentrating on what she is doing and saying and experimenting with her ability to direct the boy's gaze. The point is made that the narrator's two friends are fighting one another for each other's caps, and yet he is standing quietly before her staring at her hand and the movement of her bracelet. She would have to be conscious of his quiescent attitude against a backdrop of puerile high

jinks. She could not possibly confuse his attitude of reverence with their attitude of juvenile disregard. While she turns the bracelet, the narrator describes her as "bowing her head towards me" (*D* 32). This gesture is not the same thing, I would like to point out, as bowing her head down (as looking at the ground and away from him). I argue she is looking at him, even moving her face closer to him, and the proof is the curious absence in the narrator's extremely detailed description of any mention of her face or her eyes. Instead, he details the light of the lamp, her hand on the railing, the curve of her neck, and the border of her petticoat. Taken all in all, this is the observational standpoint of someone who is avoiding the gaze of the person he is looking at. She is watching him watch her and he, not wishing to understand this, looks elsewhere.[6]

After he is alone, the narrator gives the reader the impression that he has created an image of Mangan's sister in precise detail: "I may have stood there for an hour, seeing nothing but the brown-clad figure cast by my imagination, touched discreetly by the lamplight at the curved neck, at the hand upon the railings and at the border below the dress" (*D* 33). But this projection of her image is not a duplication at all; it has been edited significantly. There is no re creation, for example, of her hand turning her bracelet, nor is there any recollection of her head bowing toward him. That the narrator forgets these two movements is evidence that he has already repressed the question of her desire, which these gestures betray, in order to appropriate her image as the negative of his own. After dressing her in this image he needs to see, the boy strips her of language; although she brought up the subject of Araby, she is silent in his image of her while he burns with impatient desire to go to this same bazaar. Thus, the mediated image of Mangan's sister that Gelfant complains of is, in fact, the girl in the boy's imagination, but Mangan's sister exists alongside the boy's narration and can be glimpsed through those gaps in the text where the boy's story falters. Her desire is the subject of the story because it is the subject of the boy's unconscious where it directs right alongside but outside of his awareness—his conscious intentions that he misrecognizes as a call to destiny.

Having taken the unusual tack of discussing this story as though it were the story of Mangan's sister, I need to explain why she is absent from the narrator's story (although not from Joyce's). Pearce describes a narrative paradox that forces the reader, in the interest of wholeness, to present a narrative with holes. He gives several explanations for this, but one is most pertinent: "Some holes result from the failure to recognize or the need to suppress stories that are not valued or might be threatening; that is, the stories of woman." (1988, 79).

The boy in **"Araby"** must suppress the story of Mangan's sister (specifically of the awakening of her own confused desire) in order to tell his story—in order to have a story—so that he can believe in the myth of himself and, thus, bear his chalice safely through a throng of foes. This strategy will work until he comes upon another woman at the bazaar who is also enjoying and resisting the pleasure of looking and being looked at by two men. In essence, what was repressed returns because he has been displaced to a new position where he observes what he would not see when he was in the same position as the two men. He sees that the shop girl is looking back, that she is informing the structure of the conversation while appearing to be indifferent to it. In essence, he sees that she is looking, and in the only signifiers that are available to him (and too often to male critics) this makes her lewd, and himself as well, because it forces his earlier voyeurism into a strictly physical register unmitigated by the ennobling features of chivalry or courtly love. The shop girl's candid flirtation does not offend him—it indicts him. What the narrator retreats from in the closing moments of the story is the vague dread that something exists beyond the representations available to him—what Lacan calls the Real—that calls his being, (represented by his quest) into (quest)ion. The boy's concluding observation about himself is a reinterpretation of the Real and, thus, is no more true than his earlier perception of Mangan's sister, but it does restore reality to him because instead of the intolerable scenario of seeing himself being seen by Mangan's sister, and by the annoyed and distracted shop girl, he now reports *I saw myself* as a creature" (*D* 35). It is better to be his own creature than to be feminized by the objectifying gaze of a woman.

To reiterate, a woman is perceived by the masculine subject as what Lacan calls the Woman. A man comes upon this image and takes it to be the Other who has knowledge of the impossible signifier that gives meaning to the endless play of signifiers. For the masculine subject, the relief of discovering the Woman is something like the relief of a traveler, lost and bewildered in a snow storm that seems to represent first one thing and then another to him, who suddenly trips on something and, crouching down to examine it more closely, takes it to be his own doorstep. Marching resolutely through the storm of words that speak who he is, a man seeks the meaning of his own past in the future that the enigma of femininity seems to promise. The feminine mystery seems to contain for him something previous to, and outside of, the murderous signification of the Symbolic Order that, as Lacan puts it, speaks through him and directs him: "We make our destiny, because we talk. We believe that we say what we want, but it is what others wanted, most particularly our family, which speaks to us. . . . We are spoken, and because of that, we make of the accidents that push us, something 'plotted'" (Ragland-Sullivan 1988, 118).

Lacan designates this "something beyond" in the Woman as *jouissance*. This complex term refers to a sense of fusion and naturalness—before cultural myths, before speech—that is comparable to the infant's pleasure in the object constancy provided by his own mirror reflection. By making Mangan's sister fictional, the boy is able to plot the fact of his own destiny, which seems to harmonize his body in a manner outside the linguistic manipulations of the Symbolic Order: "My body was like a harp and her

words and gestures were like fingers running upon the wires" (*D* 31). Here, words and gestures—precisely what was elided from his fantasy image of her—return as confirmation of his identity rather than a challenge to it. A suggestion of a mirror response is in this description (every movement of the girl generates a reflective movement in the boy) except that he, not Mangan's sister, has become the mirror image constructed relative to another. Under the guise of worshipping her image, he is worshipping his image—the imaginary stage mirror reflection of fusion and wholeness outside and previous to the Symbolic Order (the mythical fusion, certainty and oneness of what Lacan calls the Imaginary Order). Significantly, he cannot account for her importance to him in language: "Her name sprang to my lips at moments in strange prayers and praises which I myself did not understand. My eyes were often full of tears (I could not tell why)" (*D* 31). We see from this passage that he knows her name, yet he withholds it from the story, for to name her would be to make her equivalent to a word, and this would once more close himself off from the prespeech fusion and sense of oneness that lies beyond representation. Gabriel Conroy's early love letters exhibit this same fear that using a woman's name will murder what is beyond the sign that seems to unify him: "Why is it that words like these seem to me so dull and cold? Is it because there is no word tender enough to be your name?" (*D* 214).

The overheard conversation of the shop girl—her display of desire beyond his representation of what the feminine is—subverts his fiction of Mangan's sister and would subvert his subjectivity as well if he did not reinterpret the real under the guise of self-enlightenment. At the conclusion of the story, he sees himself in order not to see that he is being seen and that his "self" is nothing but what he imagines the Other sees: "In the scopic field, everything is articulated between two terms that act in an antinomic way—on the side of things, there is the gaze that is to say, things look at me, and yet I see them. This is how one should understand those words, so strongly stressed, in the Gospel, *They have eyes that they might not see.* That they might not see what? Precisely, that things are looking at them" (Lacan 1981a, 109). For the boy to know that the shop girl has glanced at him once or twice, he must be, at least as far as he is aware, staring at her steadily. But this time the girl's sporadic glance overmasters his steady gaze because he knows that she knows that he is looking at her. "This is the phantasy to be found in the Platonic perspective of an absolute being to whom is transferred the quality of being all-seeing. At the very level of the phenomenal experience of contemplation this all-seeing aspect is to be found in the satisfaction of a woman who knows that she is being looked at, on condition that one does not show her that one knows that she knows" (Lacan 1981a, 75). Mangan's sister presents a more teasing and exciting image to the boy because it does not occur to him that she knows he is looking at her, yet, as I have already argued, every shift of posture is, on her part, a conscious reaction to the effect of being gazed upon. Likewise, in an antinomic way, there is nothing erotic, nothing supportive of the myth of the "self" in the exchange of looks because she sees that he knows that she knows that he is looking at her. Neither can pose as an object of desire for the other because it is the structure of desire that is based on a lack in being, not the illusion of an object that will satisfy and complete them, that has been made visible by their exchange of looks. "If I go I will bring you something" the narrator says to Mangan's sister (*D* 32), and it is the fact that the object is unnameable that gives it an alluring status as the thing that will complete him. Once he is standing before items for sale at the bazaar, however, he is faced with a simple and tawdry commercial transaction; it is not only the shop girl's dutiful surveillance that unnerves him but also her sudden demand that he say what he wants: "She asked me did I wish to buy anything" (*D* 35). Her realistic question, impossible to appropriate as a reflection of his own desire (he does not know what he wants), details his Real, and illusory, quest.

The advantage for the masculine subject of converting an individual woman into what Lacan calls the Woman—an image of femininity that does not exist—is that this image then operates (to extend the boy's analogy) as a chalice wherein the bread and wine of fragmented experience is converted into the body and blood of unified subjectivity. Accompanied by the sacred image of the Woman, the narrator is able to move through any scene, however variegated and threatening, without fear of dissolution. For the masculine subject, a woman becomes a symptom that helps ward off any discovery of how tenuous his subjectivity really is. Mangan's sister—somewhere beyond representation—plays the harp that is his body. If he did not imagine her, he could not believe in his masculine subjectivity as an instrument of certitude capable of endless harmony. The world is lost for the sake of the word. What is needed is possession of an object that will authenticate all other objects. The boy's quest for the Holy Grail is a search for what Lacan designates as the Phallus. It is not an anatomical object for several reasons—the primary one being that it does not exist. So rather than despair of finding it, the masculine subject embarks on a lifelong campaign of mistaking different objects for this primary signifier.

Indeed, when the subject looks for the Phallus, the search must result not in finding it or failing to find it (both alternatives lead toward psychosis) but in repeating the act of losing it. This repetition keeps alive the illusion that the Phallus exists and may yet be found again, and this illusion, in turn, creates a crucial effect on the masculine subject that is nothing less than the experience of consciousness. The mythical unity of this consciousness is always on the verge of being subverted by the unconscious, which exists not before it or underneath it but in tandem with it. Thus, the boy's spurious certitude is presented by Joyce as precariously balanced over an abyss of oblivion: "All my senses seemed to desire to veil themselves and, feeling that I was about to slip from them, I pressed the palms of my hands together until they trembled, murmuring: *O love! O love!* many times" (*D* 31). The word love, repeated like a chant, wards off the danger that the other for

whom the boy has constructed himself (Mangan's sister, who authenticates him) may be alien and dangerous. Because she confirms his unity, she is also uniquely capable of reminding him that he is permanently alienated into the otherness that exists in the gap between the word and the world. This impossible state of things that makes things possible is what Lacan calls desire.

Lacanian Desire, therefore, is essential and insatiable because it is the result of a fundamental lack-of-being that the subject consciously denies. The impossibility of satisfying desire actually permits the effect of subjectivity because it allows the subject to continue past each new object of desire as it inevitably proves fraudulent. The object of desire appears to frustrate the subject when, in fact, it contains within its structure the unbridgeable division that is always already present in the subject; the enigma of femininity, for example, merely reflects to the masculine subject the division that already exists within him. In patriarchal culture, an ideological world helps hide this fact and defines the feminine solely as that which is not masculine, as that negativity that authenticates masculine identity by embodying enigmatic anonymity. This same ideology relegates the female to an identity limbo where she is taught to mask her lack of identity to guarantee the spurious certitude of the masculine subject. The cultural praise she accrues for successfully doing this helps to mitigate the vertiginous effects of denying the problematics of her own sexual identity.

For Lacan, the Woman is a mythical species that, like Tinkerbell, does not exist beyond a masculine subject's belief in her. This imaginary being that confirms their fictional unity is then perceived by the masculine subject as either enchanting (Mangan's sister) or treacherous (the shop girl). Mangan's sister is enchanting in that she seems to promise wholeness only to the narrator, and the shop girl is treacherous in that she seems to offer wholeness to everyone but the narrator. From his displaced position as alienated observer at the Araby Bazaar, he witnesses the masquerade of femininity and sees how the masculine subjects participate in its construction (thus unconsciously directing the construction of themselves). He then loses faith in the Woman, which simultaneously deconstructs the myth of himself and forces him to begin telling his story anew, this time as a blinded and humbled Samson rather than Sir Lancelot. Femininity is absence, or lack, for the narrator—a placeholder like zero in the numerical system of the boy's narrative—it can neither betray nor bestow anything. But a masculine subject is compelled to view it as always doing one thing or the other in order to continue believing in the fictional unity of his subjective consciousness. In other words, it is the subject that is fraudulent not the object of desire. Put in the context of **"Araby,"** it is the narrator who is fictional, not Mangan's sister. Both Mangan's sister and the shop girl exist in his narrative and beyond it by remaining nameless, yet some part of them (jouissance) subverts the narrator's representation of them; it is their unrepresented story that writes his story.

In Lacan's analogy about how the subject constructs himself, he describes the subject as attaching himself at various points to the existing Symbolic Order the way upholstery is anchored to the existing wooden frame of a chair. This gives shape to an otherwise shapeless chair, just as attaching one's self to the existing Symbolic Order gives identity to an otherwise fragmented subject. The buttons that secure the upholstery to the frame (Lacan calls these buttons *points de capitons*) are key signifiers that anchor the subject to the existing linguistic code. The subject does not know what the key signifiers mean; he only knows they imbue him with a sense of meaning. And it is this buttoning down of the self to the linguistic code that generates a sense of being. The linguistic code to which the subject buttons himself, such as the representation of the Woman, takes on the role of the Other. It presents the question to which the subject imagines himself to be the answer. But if it imbues him with certitude, it can just as easily invade him with incertitude. It can hold him together or tear him apart. Neither state is based in the Real, although each may be said to represent the two poles of the subject's reality. What is real is that the strategies and avenues of fulfillment that are available to a given subject are given by this code and in many ways predetermine what the subject is often fond of calling his destiny.

The narrator tells Mangan's sister that if he goes to Araby he will bring back something for her. She has not asked him to go, and she does not tell him what she wants. He wants to get her what she does not even know to ask for, hoping that she will then give him what she does not possess; this is the powerful masquerade around a non-relation that Lacan calls love. Mangan's sister, as an object of desire, causes the narrator to desire, but she has no significance for him. Whatever he might bring her from the fair, it will not be what she wants, but only what he imagines she wants. The image of Mangan's sister as the Woman, in its metaphorical function as a symptom, has linked the narrator's conscious and unconscious desires in such a way that unconscious fantasy is able to force its way into the signifying chain in a fervent quest to obtain something he cannot name for someone who has not asked for it.

The result is a complete shift in the boy's interests, away from everything that has been of interest in the past toward a quest for what the Other knows about who he is. But there is no Other of the Other (even though the Woman would be this Other of the Other if she existed). Once a woman is transformed into the representation of the Woman, the search for the knowledge in the Other that verifies the masculine subject's existence is made possible. But, on the other hand, this same transformation, although it authorizes the quest, also makes absolute the impossibility of the subject ever completing it. So those moments where the narrator murmurs incoherent prayers to the image of Mangan's sister allow him to "bear his chalice safely through a throng of foes" because his belief in her, although she does not exist, is sufficient to cover the reality that he does not exist either (that the presumed unity of his masculine subjectivity is a fiction). By linking the narrator's conscious and unconscious desire, the image of the Woman connects subject and system as a point de capiton, and this determines both the necessity of his quest and the certainty of its failure. One does not find, or fail to find, the Phallus; one repeats the act of failing to have it, which is then understood as having lost it. Only through narration can the boy misrecognize this scenario of repetition as his destiny.

Unable to acknowledge the impossibility of satisfaction that the structure of desire has forced upon him, the narrator quickly introduces an obstacle to his goal by saying he will bring her something. In this way, the obstacle between him and what he takes to be the object of his desire will seem real and, therefore, surmountable rather than Real and, therefore, impossible to represent or overcome. He is caught in a structure in which the object of his desire becomes the signifier of his own impossibility. Every knight-in-armor, rather than face the debilitating nonrelation of the sexes, chooses to embark on a difficult and dangerous journey with an image of the Woman burning in his breast. The quest is a necessary obstacle, not an unfortunate one, on the interminable path to true love although it will be perceived as difficult and burdensome by the amorous knight. The male subject *must* go on a quest so that the inevitable failure to complete himself—to find the phallus—will seem to be the failure of the quest and not of the quest(ion) of his own subjectivity. In this way, the nonrelation of the sexes between the knight and his lady will be obscured by the erection of an impossible object (the Phallus). Put another way, by seeing femininity as an enigma, by seeing the desire of the Woman as inscrutably elsewhere, the knight is able to imagine a bridge over the unbridgeable division upon which he has founded the supposed unity of his subjective consciousness; the bridge will appear real as long as the Woman appears mythical. In short, the narrator of **"Araby"** has employed for himself the convention of courtly love that Lacan characterizes as "an altogether refined way of making up for the absence of sexual relation by pretending that it is we who put an obstacle to it. . . . For the man, whose lady was entirely, in the most servile sense of the term, his female subject, courtly love is the only way of coming off elegantly from the absence of sexual relation" (1982b, 141).

Femininity is not an essence; it is a representation. As such, it is a constructed identity—constructed by the male subject—and the representation does not contain or account for female desire. He desires it—the representation—rather than her because the masquerade of femininity appears to him as a lack-in-being that he gratefully defines as not masculine. The Woman masquerades as feminine—as the Phallus—to reassure a man that she does not have it, but at the same time her masquerade proves that it must—somewhere—exist or how could she know to imitate it? Of course, she has learned to perform what he needs to see, not anything that actually is, and so the masculine and the feminine waltz around the nonrelation of the sexes with a two-step of mutual misrecognition. Lacan says, "It is in order to be the phallus, that is to say, the signifier of the desire of the Other, that the woman will reject an essential part of her femininity, notably all its attributes through masquerade. It is for what she is not that she expects to be desired as well as loved. But she finds the signifier of her own desire in the body of the one to whom she addresses her demand for love" (1982, 84). A woman thus desires the Phallus, and so a man struggles to appear as if he has it. She desires the ability to bestow on him the gift he demands of her so that he can feel that he has had it all along. The Phallus can only play its role when it is veiled because there is nothing behind the veil. The erection of meaning that it enjoins on the masculine subject involves the subject in constant slippage because what is meaningful always contains its own vanishing point. In short, meaning does not reflect the sexual order; it compensates for a supposed unity that is fictional. Courtly love—the boy's quest on behalf of Mangan's sister—elevates her to a place where her inaccessibility disguises his lack. Thus, she becomes a symptom for him that wards off his unconscious and ensures the consistency of his relation to the phallic term.[7]

The Woman shows in her masquerade of femininity what she does not have by pretending that she has it and, thus, becomes what he desires but at the price of having no way to pronounce the quest(ion) of her own desire. She serves for the narrator as a metaphor for the phallus and, thus, becomes for him a symptom that disguises his lack. As a symptom standing in the place of the Other, Mangan's sister represents for him the initial signifier upon which his divided subjectivity is based. She appears to answer the question of who he is and this allows his self-ordained quest to subsume all previous concerns: "I could not call my wandering thoughts together. I had hardly any patience with the serious work of life which, now that it stood between me and my desire, seemed to me child's play, ugly monotonous child's play" (*D* 32). He has reinterpreted the Real to form a new reality, and the self-deprecating tone in this sentence will surface again at the close of the story when he does the same thing. The representation of femininity that the narrator worships is the only signifier that cannot signify anything. Because the image of Mangan's sister has been constructed to signify nothing, it can signify him.

In traveling to the Araby Bazaar, the boy boards a special train. People press against the doors in an attempt to enter, but they are pushed back and told that it is "a special train for the bazaar" (*D* 34). For the entire trip past "ruinous houses," the boy remains "alone in the bare carriage." At the end of the ride, the uniqueness of his journey persists as he steps out of the train on to "an improvised wooden platform" just recently constructed. Standing alone on the deserted platform, he sees in front of him "a large building which displayed the magical name." All these details suggest that the boy sees his journey as traveling to someplace other than Dublin. It is different from anywhere; it is magical. The boy's fantastic hope for the place gives it a fairy tale quality. The tawdry building seems enchanted to him only because of an enormous act of faith on his part.

Its status as magical is as tenuous as the fantastic unity of his subjective consciousness. The magical power of symbolization begins when a child realizes something is missing. The power of language to evoke what is not present depends on the feeling that something is lacking. His later realization that the bazaar is a commercial sham, perpetrated on the naïve for profit, will destroy the place as symbol but will have no effect on the powerful dynamic of symbolization. The narrator experiences his sexual awakening as the advent of unity, whereas Joyce's story of the presence of Mangan's sister outside the confines of the boy's narrative gives an opposite account of sexuality based solely on its divisions (division of the subject, division between subjects). It is her representation in the boy's narrative as the Woman and her absence from it as *a* woman that makes his story of himself possible. **"Araby"** is not about the loss or gain of this or that object, it is about the impossible structure of desire for both the masculine and feminine subjects.

The boy on the improvised platform sees displayed before him what is described as "the magical name" rather than the word "Araby." Like Mangan's sister, the bazaar implies something beyond what can be named or represented. What the narrator hopes he will see is the world before it has been crossed through by the word. The actual bazaar is irrelevant; in his own mind, he has traveled beyond time and space to the land of the Other, authorized to do so by a woman who, as The Woman, represents this land. This magical name does not exist anymore than she does. He hopes to discover the lost object that would end the primacy of the signifier over his subjectivity. He presumes she must desire this most precious of all signifiers because it was her appearance to him as lack—as feminine—that convinced him of the existence of a Holy Grail that could authenticate who he is. The magical bazaar could return him to the imaginary pristine duality of the mirror stage before he seized the false scepter of language and began to rule a world within the world where words are always ruling him (the boy, like Martha Clifford in *Ulysses*, does not like "that other world").

The Araby Bazaar is magical for the boy because he believes it will be a place beyond mere representation where the lost object he needs to complete himself will be found. This object is not hidden in a geometrical or an anatomical space; if that were so, he would have found it long ago. It is not hidden at all; it is always elsewhere "in" a symbolic structure that can only be perceived in its effect. In taking upon himself her pilgrimage, he is inevitably drawn into becoming the object of her desire, even as he tries to make her subject to his desire. Like the minister in Poe's story "The Purloined Letter," which Lacan analyzed, the narrator of **"Araby"** appears to be in control while he observes Mangan's sister; he understands everything she does relative to himself. But when he is displaced to her position at the close of the story, suddenly he demonstrates the traits of femininity (passivity and self-effacement) that he had previously attributed to her (likewise, after the minister steals the letter from the queen, he assumes her position, passively waiting for someone to steal it from him). The structural shift at the close of **"Araby"** makes the point that femininity and masculinity are effects of one's position in the Symbolic Order rather than inherently biological. Only the presence or absence of the phallus marks the distinction between the two positions. Whoever pretends to possess the Phallus is placed under the banner "feminine" and whoever struggles to represent it lines up under the banner "masculine" (which is why Lacan defines a man as someone who finds himself male without knowing what to do about it).

In front of the booth displaying the vases, the narrator witnesses another woman masquerading with two men as feminine in the sexual waltz of nonrelation; she has said something that the men want to possess. Curiously, they do not repeat what she has said (do not put it into words) but only insist that she has expressed it, each man calling on the other one to verify this, which, as one can see by now, is no verification at all. The boy is suddenly observing people who believe themselves to be unseen. In this new shift of position, he witnesses a scene of flirtation from which he is absent. In seeing the anonymous shop girl flirting with the two men—in seeing her looking at them—he is, in effect, seeing the earlier version of himself being watched when he had believed himself to be unseen. As Lacan makes clear, the Symbolic Order constitutes the subject, and if the subject's position within this order shifts, then the orientation of his subjectivity, which the subject receives from the itinerary of a signifier, will shift as well (1988c, 29). By watching and overhearing the girl and the two men, he views the earlier construct of his subjectivity, now revealed as imaginary, which, at the moment the quest began, he took to be himself. The look of Mangan's sister, repressed at that time for the sake of a seamless narrative, returns. The Real, which is the endless return of the moment of the subject's own impossibility, threatens to break through and show the fabric of his story to be no more complete than a complex weave that is made up of as many unconscious gaps as it is of conscious threads.

But this gap in subjectivity—what Lacan calls aphanisis—is equally present in his earlier conversation with Mangan's sister. When she asks him if he is going to the bazaar, he hears her saying, "Will you go and bring something back," thus transforming her question into his quest. Were he to tell her she has said this, she would have to respond, like the shop girl, "I never said such a thing!" What follows her question is, to my reading, the most significant sentence in the story: "I forget whether I answered yes or no." What a strange ellipsis in the narration of his story. He is not in doubt about anything else he has narrated up to this point. He forgets *what* he answers because he wishes to pose *as* the answer. At the moment the quest is inaugurated, the boy as subject (as question) disappears. He loses his authority at the precise moment she authorizes his quest. Later in his narration, as the meaningful dimension of the quest starts to fade, the boy's sense of his own subjectivity once more restricts him to the self-

conscious and the trivial rather than the unified and heroical: "Remembering with difficulty why I had come I went over to one of the stalls and examined porcelain vases and flower tea-sets. . . . I lingered before her stall, though I knew my stay was useless, to make my interest in her wares seem the more real" (*D* 35).

The narrator's consciousness flickers back and forth between these two moments of forgetfulness that mark the beginning and end of his quest. The two moments are threaded together by various acts of interpretation that are motivated by desire (indeed, Lacan says interpretation operates in the same manner as desire) and controlled by language. The quest, which he had hoped would untie the knot of the Symbolic Order, only succeeds in repeating the act of tying it. The boy's quest, which outlines the structure of desire, is impossible. He sets out to find the phallus/chalice because the desire of Mangan's sister, which he has appropriated as his desire, convinces him that it must exist and that it is the thing he requires to complete himself. What sets the quest in motion is the discovery that she lacks something. But in order for her to verify that he is something (masculine), she must be seen as nothing, (feminine). Put most simply, the divided structure that constitutes the narrator's subjectivity is inevitably reproduced in what becomes the unattainable object of his desire.

The conversation of the woman and the two men revolves around the issue of whether or not she has *said* something. "O, I never said such a thing!" the woman begins. "O, but you did!" one man counters. "O, but I didn't," she responds in perfect counterpoint. "Didn't she say that?" one man says to the other. "Yes. I heard her," he replies. "O, there's a . . . fib!" says the woman. Once more, one sees that it is the woman's desire that is unspoken. What has she said? The men keep her in a posture of negativity that allows them to affirm one another. ("Didn't she say that?" "Yes. I heard her.") There is another significant ellipsis when she says: "O, there's a . . . fib!" (*D* 35). What word does she veer away from? We cannot know, but certainly the word *lie* is a strong possibility. A fib is a lie, but it is a lie about something that is trivial in substance or significance. What has been made trivial (and she participates in this as part of the masquerade of femininity) is the substance of her desire. She is locked into a continual masquerade of absence that confirms their presence. In this conversation she is, in her essence, not all. The men repress the fact of her desire—her jouissance—by representing it themselves. Once more the unspeakable dictates what gets spoken in a Maypole dance around the nonexistent Phallus. "On the one hand," Lacan says, "the woman becomes, or is produced, precisely as what he is not . . . and on the other, as what he has to renounce, that is, *jouissance*" (1982b, 49). The men reserve for themselves the right to interpret, the woman supports that right by posing as enigmatic. The content of her statement—what she actually said—is not relevant, and this allows their narrative to become so.[8]

What the narrator wishes to find at the Araby Bazaar is something that will not set him forth on another repetition or shift him into a new register of signification that requires a fresh act of faith about his subjectivity. What he yearns for is an ending—the discovery of certitude beyond the forever shifting signifiers of language. Were he to find the Holy Grail/Phallus, his subjectivity would seem like a chalice that could neither be spilled nor declared empty. In beginning his search for what Mangan's sister lacks, for what she means, he has begun a search for what *he* means. But interpretation does not lead to knowledge (the two men are not interested in what the shop girl has actually said), it leads to the point where knowledge stumbles over the Woman. Her jouissance is an area of excess that is supplementary to male desire, not complementary to it, and knowledge, as it comes to the male subject, is merely the organized renunciation of jouissance. Most commentators on **"Araby"** agree that, by the end of the story, the narrator has learned something about himself. Yes, but this knowledge will become the new obstacle he will place between himself and the objects of his desire. It is not frustration of a particular desire of the narrator that occurs in this story—after all, he is never able to say what he wants—rather it is to use Lacan's phrase, "frustration by an object in which his desire is alienated and which the more it is elaborated, the more profound the alienation from its *jouissance* becomes for the subject" (1981h, 11).

Significantly, the boy's famous closing insight about himself is not presented in terms of looking inward but in terms of seeing himself: "Gazing up into the darkness I saw myself as a creature driven and derided by vanity; and my eyes burned with anguish and anger" (*D* 35). Far from putting an end to the myth of himself, he inaugurates a new fiction of what he imagines the gaze of the Other sees, which he has now learned must be who he is *really*. He reinterprets the Real, denigrates his earlier interpretation, and presents his new interpretation as the reality that was behind the appearances all along. But insight is just another guess at what it is the Other sees. The subject responds anew to the itinerary of the signifier in a manner that incorporates its directives while still preserving the subject's illusion of an autonomous identity and a satiable desire. "Epiphanic light," Ragland-Sullivan has stated in a recent overview of Joyce and Lacan, "is the return of the void into the Real of phallic meaning, where the void shows the place of division and the 'truth' of loss around which humans elaborate lives" (1988, 122). Elaborating on this, I would say the Joycean epiphany is the imaginary light that staves off Real darkness. The subject imagines himself to make the world real. In his new identity, the narrator is "derided by vanity." To be derided is to be laughed at contemptuously, to be subjected to ridicule. But how much better it is to be subjected to ridicule than not to be a subject at all. Who would not consent to wear a mask if the alternative was to have no face at all? Driven by vanity? The narrator will continue to be so driven. A vanity is a piece of furniture where a woman puts on her makeup, when she becomes a representation of femininity, when she is encouraged by the mirror to abandon the question of who she is and imagine herself instead as something that initiates a man's quest. At her vanity, a woman becomes the Woman; she masquerades as lack so the man can masquerade as completeness. Her vanity protects him from knowledge of his emptiness, that is, of *his* vanity. The two types of vanity are the two sides of the division over which he builds a bridge from one moment of forgetfulness to the next.

The necessity of the boy's humiliation, which he presents to himself as "knowledge," is certainly a painful realization, but it is one that protects him from realizing the greater pain of psychic and symbolic castration. Not perceiving his own castration, he feels free to act again, to set another scene where he will imagine himself as seeing a woman while remaining unseen. He does not hear the signifier that Lacan gives voice to as follows: "'You think you act when I stir you at the mercy of the bonds through which I knot your desires. Thus do they grow in force and multiply in objects, bringing you back to the fragmentation of your shattered childhood'" (Lacan 1988c, 52). In his final observation of himself, the boy's discovery of himself is, in fact, yet another discovery of who he is not. In telling readers who he is now, he is not lying, only telling a fib.

Notes

1. Harry Stone, to cite one example, is comfortable declaring that "all women, for Joyce, are Eves: they tempt and they betray" (1965, 392). Stone, like many male critics of the sixties and seventies, shows the same self-indulgent perspective on women as the narrator of "Araby," but I do not think this does justice to the complexity of Joyce's perspective.

2. Bernard Benstock writes: "Of all the fierce winds of controversy surrounding Joyce the most volatile remains that of the impact of the theories of Jacques Lacan" (1988b, 16). My approach here is informed by Lacanian theory, but my primary purpose is to problematize Joyce's representation of Mangan's sister and show it to be far more subtle than the perspective of the narrator.

3. As Ellie Ragland-Sullivan explains, "Lacan maintained that mind is not a unity; personal reality is built up by structures, effects, and the fragments of perceived fragmentations. Reality, therefore, is to be assessed in details, allusions and wisps of meaning" (1986, 187). The Real is what lies beyond representation; although it cannot be directly apprehended, it is always a threat to the subject's reality.

4. As Lacan explains, "When any speaking being whatever lines up under the banner of women it is by being constituted as not all that they are placed within the phallic function . . . except that The woman can only be written with The crossed through. . . . There is no such thing as The woman since of her essence . . . she is not all" (1982, 144).

5. Later in this same chapter, Devlin makes the general point, which I am also making in a more specific

way, that "the critical complaint that Joyce's women are male-defined seems to me one-sided" (1988, 143).

6. Devlin says of Bloom's attitude toward Gerty McDowell, "He does not envision the female eye as being possibly prurient, sexually intrusive, as being the organ of kinetic stimulation, as a compromising eye that secretly enjoys naughty sights" (1988, 137).

7. This is also how a woman comes to be seen as standing in the place of the Other and believed by the man to guarantee the reality of all his fantasies about himself and assure him of the authenticity of his masculine sexuality.

8. In a similar dynamic, one never sees the contents of the letter that changes hands in Poe's story. Because there is no certain signified, the signifier speaks through the subject.

Margot Norris (essay date 1995)

SOURCE: "Blind Streets and Seeing Horses: Araby's Dim Glass Revisited," in *Studies in Short Fiction,* Vol. 32, No. 3, Summer, 1995, pp. 309–18.

[*In the following essay, Norris explores stylistic elements of "Araby," particularly the narrative voice in the story.*]

Joyce's **"Araby"** not only draws attention to its conspicuous poetic language: it performatively offers the beauty of its art as compensation to the thematized frustrations of the story. The little boy whose heart is broken by a city "hostile to romance," transmutes his grief into a romance of language. Joyce, whose *Dubliners* stories tend to bear rhetorical titles, makes of **"Araby"** a rhetorical bazaar that outstrips in poetic exoticism the extravagant promise of the empty and sterile commercial confection that so disappoints the child. In an early essay on *Dubliners,* Frank O'Connor writes of **"Araby,"** "This is using words as they had not been used before in English, except by Pater—not to describe an experience, but so far as possible to duplicate it. Not even perhaps to duplicate it so much as to replace it by a combination of images—a rhetorician's dream, if you like, but Joyce was a student of rhetoric: (20). I construe this gesture of stylistic virtuosity less as an exercise in aestheticism than as a self-critical performance. The story's narrative performance of offering art as balm to heal the anguish of a modern city's paralysis enacts the quintessential Modernistic practice repeated in Eliot's "Waste Land" of turning to poetry for modern spiritual redemption. But by evoking literary traditions consonant with its chivalric preoccupations and temper, **"Araby"** intertextualizes itself with diverse nineteenth century medievalisms[1] whose archaic and mannered aestheticism Modernism generally abjures. To resolve this paradox of **"Araby"**'s incongruent Romantic appeal—a problem that *Portrait* criticism also confronts and resolves as stylistic imitation, parody, or ironic pastiche—I intend to treat the story's peculiar language as a multi-valenced textual performance: a self-incriminating narration whose rhetorical aims the text encapsulates and subjects to an immanent critique. This critique anticipates the later social criticism of aestheticism by Herbert Marcuse, and particularly his concept of "affirmative culture"—a notion recently used by Peter Buerger to criticize the self-contradiction in which Modernism implicates art—"art thus stabilizes the very social conditions against which it protests" (7). But I will argue that **"Araby"** critiques affirmative culture rather than abets it, and that the story destabilizes its own compensatory gesture by emptying its own rhetoric to restore it to the idiomatic, "marketplace" sense of "rhetoric" as a figure for elaborate but insubstantial speech. **"Araby"** the story, the ornate but empty narration, doubles "Araby," the ornate but empty bazaar. "If I go . . . I will bring you something" (32), the boy promises Mangan's sister, but he returns empty-handed—except for the story of their double, encapsulated, frustration. **"Araby,"** the story, offers readers a similar rhetorical empty-handedness.

I plan to track the story's compensatory strategy—its production of artful language to supplement unsatisfied desire—through a set of ontological operations by which the narrative consciousness attempts to constitute itself as a subject. "Gazing up into the darkness I saw myself as a creature driven and derided by vanity" (35). The story's closing moral turns on itself by concluding with a parabolic maneuver, by having the narrative consciousness turn itself into an allegorical figure, "a symbol of" something, as Gabriel Conroy might put it. The boy has been transformed by his own narrative voice into a figure of fable, of the mirrored emptiness that is Vanitas. **"Araby"** therefore doubles its thematic preoccupation with the chivalric quest implicit in its famous trope of the imperiled Grail ("I bore my chalice safely through a throng of foes" [31]) by further formally cloaking itself in the allegorical and parabolic rhetoric of chivalric literature. The question is whether the closing self-allegorization constitutes an epiphany[2]—a moment of illuminated enlightenment or transcendent anagnorisis—or whether the parabolic gesture enfolds other philosophical maneuvers within the story that offer knowledge and insight as reversible or retractable: the ocular voyeurism that turns upon itself as a "gaze;" the antonomasia of romance and desire that ricochets as a self-naming of its own failure; mythification oscillating with demythification. The reader confronts a variety of hermeneutical options at the end of the story—ranging from "straight" acceptance of the boy's self-estimation, to sympathy with the idealist's victimization by vulgar philistinism, to critique of the narrator's exploitations of the juvenile experience by turning it into an aestheticized social parable.

The curious figure of the reflective darkness ("Gazing up into the darkness I saw myself") of an extinguished dream ("the light was out"), suggests that this story will be illuminated by blindness, and that the boy who finds emptiness in **"Araby,"** the figure of romance, is in turn found empty, a personification rather than a person, by the story. This strange locution at the story's end, that has the darkened gallery of **"Araby"** appear to "see" the boy in a way that lets him see himself, as though it were a dark mirror catching him in its eye, recapitulates the strange topopoeia of the story's opening, where streets are personified as "blind" and houses as "seeing." This topographia frames the narration in a way that sets it up for a chiasmus: the story that opens with the 'real' estate of North Richmond Street closes with its antipode of the 'unreal' estate of **"Araby"**—but only after the two places have, as it were, traded places. What makes the crossing over possible is that **"Araby,"** the name of a longing for romance displaced onto a mythologized Oriental geography, suppresses the mediation of commerce and conceals the operations by which the fantasy of an exoticized and seductive East is a commercial fabrication produced by that realm the boy finds "most hostile to romance"—the marketplace. Commerce produces not only the trinkets and commodities the boy does not want, the vases and tea sets he spurns, and the parcels he bears like an irksome cross while shopping with his aunt every Saturday night. Commerce also produces fantasy and magic through language, "The syllables of the word *Araby* were called to me through the silence in which my soul luxuriated and cast an Eastern enchantment over me" (32). The narration of **"Araby"** is presumably neither a commodity, or a charity, like the ambiguously configured bazaar in the story.[3] But it resorts to the same power of language, the power to aestheticize and glamorize what is common and mean ("the magical name"), that the operation of advertising borrows from poetry. The narrative voice of **"Araby,"** with its gift for personification, could easily be that of Little Chandler, or rather "T. Malone Chandler," as he Celticizes himself—

> As he crossed Grattan Bridge he looked down the river towards the lower quays and pitied the poor stunted houses. They seemed to him a band of tramps, huddled together along the river-banks, their old coats covered with dust and soot, stupefied by the panorama of sunset and waiting for the first chill of night to bid them arise, shake themselves and begone. He wondered whether he could write a poem to express his idea
>
> (73)

The "Celtic note" of wistful sadness to which Chandler calculates to aspire ("The English critics, perhaps, would recognise him as one of the Celtic school by reason of the melancholy tone" [74]) can also be heard in the lapses into pathetic fallacy in **"Araby"** ("the lamps of the street lifted their feeble lanterns" [30]).

But the personifications of place in **"Araby"** transcend Little Chandler's affectations because of the complex temperamental and moral intersubjectivities the narration establishes between the boy and places of his habitation and imagination. North Richmond Street is introduced as blind, mute ("a quiet street"), with emptiness inside ("An uninhabited house . . . stood at the blind end" [29])—a proleptic figure of the boy at the end of the story. Much like the story with its confession of solipsistic interiority, the houses on North Richmond Street engage in both sober introspection ("conscious of decent lives within them") and

discreet censoriousness ("gazed at one another with brown imperturbable faces"). The story's solipsism and insularity is figured by the opening topography of North Richmond Street as "blind," as a cul de sac and dead end from which escape is baffled. The slippage of meaning that leads that figure of the "blind" from spatial to ocular closure, links the street, and its houses with their virtual hermetic seals, to the larger thematics of closed economies in which exchange, and communication, is doomed to recirculation. The boy's house—while not clearly identical with the uninhabited house at the end of the blind street—is figured as an enclosure of negativity, of death, waste rooms, waste papers, waste people and waste lives. The sealed rooms—"musty from having been long enclosed"—circulate as little air as the rusty bicycle pump abandoned in the garden. They in turn mirror that figure of closed economy: Mrs Mercer, the pawnbroker's widow, who extends her late husband's business of recycling used goods to her philanthropy ("collected used stamps for some pious purpose" [33]), and to her communication ("I had to endure the gossip"). Herself constructed like a closed system, Mrs Mercer, not surprisingly, feels herself endangered by fresh air ("the night air was bad for her"). The story's allusions to baffled pneumatic circulation itself circulates verbal bafflements, like an impaired pentecostal pneuma or wind, from other *Dubliners* stories ("one of them new-fangled carriages . . . them with the rheumatic wheels" [17]).

The slippage of "blind" continues to recirculate through the narration's tropological system. The narration describes the boy's voyeurism of Mangan's sister by slipping further meaning off the protective screen that is called a "blind," onto its meaning as an ocular shelter used by hunters to conceal or camouflage them from their prey ("The blind was pulled down . . . so that I could not be seen" [30]). This figurative transformation of the boy's house into a version of a duck or deer 'blind' is quite congruent with the boy's subsequent activity of essentially 'stalking' the girl, who is described as a "brown figure," a deer (or dear):

> Every morning I lay on the floor in the front parlour watching her door. The blind was pulled down to within an inch of the sash so that I could not be seen. When she came out on the doorstep my heart leaped. I ran to the hall, seized my books and followed her. I kept her brown figure always in my eye and, when we came near the point at which our ways diverged, I quickened my pace and passed her.
>
> (30)

Visually, the boy's voyeurism enacts a curious visual encapsulation that we might miss were it not for the introductory image of the 'seeing' houses. The nearly closed blind, with its slit for peeping, functions like an eyelid closed but for a slit—transforming the front parlor into an eye that harbors the peeping boy. The boy's own ocular gesture—"I kept her brown figure always in my eye"—is thus doubled, as the 'seeing' house keeps the boy in its eye. This strange figuration has complex ontological implications since an eye cannot see itself (except as mirrored or reflected, that is, as some other eye would see it). The boy in his hunter's "blind" thus looks out from a blind spot, what Jacques Lacan has termed a "scotoma." The implication of the boy doing his seeing from the site of his blind spot, is that he cannot see himself, cannot see himself as a voyeur or a stalker, for example, since he sees himself only as a worshiper or a lover. Unlike Stephen, whose peeping at girls or women may have earned him the threat of ocular extinction—"the eagles will come and pull out his eyes" (8)—this boy's eyes merely burn in anguish and anger at seeing his own solipsism.

My evocation of predatory images of the hunter emerging from a 'blind' to stalk his prey are intended to impugn the boy not for malignancy—since he clearly intends the girl no harm—but for the unwitting or blind psychological oppression that obsessives, including obsessive lovers, may inflict on their objects of desire. My intention is to complicate idealistic readings of the love story of **"Araby"**—"Palpably and poignantly a story of adolescent love, **'Araby'** rises to this still larger representation, of subjective division under the clash between the idealist's discriminating ardor and adverse insuperable circumstance" (Beck 106)—by exploring the maimed discourse produced by the boy's scotoma, his inability to see himself as the girl, for instance, might see him. Mangan's sister, whose name is both familiar and seductive to the narrator—"yet her name was like a summons to all my foolish blood" (30)—is nonetheless antonomastically displaced onto the rowdy boy who is her brother, and the rowdy poet ("between the drunkard and opium-eater"), who serves as her eponym.[4] Mangan's sister has difficulty in the story extricating herself as a person or a subject from the boy's image or imago of her because the narrative voice, like the boy, imagines itself as safe in its blind—able to peep and catch fleeting and fragmentary glimpses of her without having to imagine her as peeping back, and catching the voyeuristic boy, and the voyeuristic narration, in her own 'gaze.' Indeed, her world of peers organizes itself into such a peerage of boys peering at the girl from the shadows, as she peers for them in vain—"Or if Mangan's sister came out on the doorstep to call her brother in to his tea we watched her from our shadow peer up and down the street" (30).

As much as imagined "symbol of" something as Gretta Conroy on the stair, Mangan's sister is to the boy mute, blind, and empty, a cut-up fetish apprehended chiefly in metonymic parts as a rope of hair, a silver bracelet, a white curve of neck, an illuminated hand, a white border of petticoat. Her brown figure, like the somber brown houses on her street, is never interiorized or furnished with the thought and feeling that would make her come to life. The narration (like the boy) never stops to wonder whether the girl knows that she is followed every morning, or to contemplate how her knowledge—ensured by the boy's passing her to let her know he has been walking behind her—makes her feel. Does she suspect she is being watched through the slit in the blind? Does she recognize herself as an object of obsession—like Reggie Wylie, who may have stopped riding his bicycle in front of Gerty

MacDowell's garden to escape her infatuation? Or does the boy's strange behavior play music on her body, as hers does on his? These questions—which might have encompassed the function of her 'gaze,' her looking back and keeping the boy, and his narration, in her own eye—are never raised by a narration whose blind spots and solipsisms mirror the closed psychic system of the boy.

The subjectivity of the girl can be imagined at all, even if only extratextually, because she speaks. When Mangan's sister speaks, her speech is like a startling irruption in the boy's fantasy, and in the narration. He had dreamed of how it might be if he spoke to her—"I did not know whether I would ever speak to her or not or, if I spoke to her, how I could tell her of my confused adoration" (31)—but he did not dream that she would speak to him. Her subjectivity, her feelings, never enter into his fevered imaginings. Thus it is startling when she does speak directly to him, the more so because in her inaugural speech, she announces to him her desire. Indeed, she gives her desire a name—"*Araby . . .* It would be a splendid bazaar, she said; she would love to go" (31). In naming Araby as her desire, Mangan's sister appears to be speaking the extratextual fullness of her own name, as though she explicated and amplified her own magical name by endowing it with the interiority of her own desire. Joyce described James Clarence Mangan as a fabulist of Araby—"The lore of many lands goes with him always, eastern tales and memory of curiously printed medieval books which have rapt him out of his time" (*CW 77*)—with spiritual kinship to the fictional girl who bears his name. Mangan's sister, then, may be as much a romantic as the boy, although her desire is so thoroughly ingested and internalized by him that it becomes utterly expropriated from her. His gesture in embracing her desire and its name exoticizes her image—"The syllables of the word *Araby* were called to me through the silence in which my soul luxuriated and cast an Eastern enchantment over me" (32)—without leading him to her interiority, her feeling and intentions in calling to him the magical name.

Neither the boy, nor the narrative voice, wonders about her overture, which, unexplained, nonetheless issues a series of hermeneutical prods to the reader's speculation. Is the girl's convent retreat—like Stephen's in *Portrait*—scheduled to preempt and suppress sexual feeling in pubescent girls? Does the girl, whose silver bracelet betokens small vanities, resent ("It's well for you, she said" [32]) the Church displacing her dreams and scenes of romantic opulence and exotic splendor with impending puritanical strictures and punitive threats? Knowing that one of the neighborhood boys has been watching and following her, does she determine to initiate a conversation that she knows will serve as a romantic provocation? And what happens when the story ends? Does the boy return without a gift, without a romantic story to tell her, without a reciprocal speech of desire—or any speech? Will she neurotically attach herself to the memory of his unrenewed childish devotion as Gerty MacDowell does to Reggie Wylie ("He called her little one in a strangely husky voice and snatched a half kiss [the first!]" [13.203]), or as Gretta Conroy does to Michael Furey? This speculative retrieval of the girl's subjectivity and interiority rips the narration open, and would let fresh and stirring hermeneutical air circulate through our reading of the story's suffocating idealism if the text would let us escape its solipsistic enclosures. But as it is, the interiority of Mangan's sister is consigned to the fate of the brown houses on her street—destined to be furnished, perhaps during her convent retreats, with the leavings of dead priests ("He had been a very charitable priest; in his will he had left all his money to institutions and the furniture of his house to his sister" [29]). Judging from what we know of his house—that some of the "waste rooms . . . littered with old useless papers" were no more than giant wastepaper baskets—his gift seems a depressing and moribund legacy for any sister.

Yet the story does contain some apertures that would allow circulation along 'flaring' routes ("We walked through the flaring streets" [31]). Children's play and the marketplace are the two such open social systems that could allow bodies, activities, communication, and culture to circulate. The streets come alive with the noise in the street that is Stephen's Blakean god, when the Christian Brothers' School sets the boys free, or when the drunken men, bargaining women, cursing laborers, and nasal street singers teem over the shopping district on Saturday night. But the boy's temperament and ideology repeatedly repudiate these active social spaces, and his repulsion by the quotidian, by mass or crowd activities like children's play or the teeming marketplace figured as a "throng of foes" (31), as similates the boy's values to High Modernist ideology—the Arnoldian recoil from mass culture that surfaces in the aestheticist elitisms of Eliot and Pound. Critics too, consequently, tend to embrace these repudiations of the quotidien as the enemy of romance, without attending their possible interrogation or critique by the text. The boy, attracted to the Orientalism of **"Araby,"** fails to recognize in the Dublin street life the colorful gestures and music of an indigenous bazaar, more spontaneous in its diverse cultural productions ("the nasal chanting of street-singers, who sang a *come-all you* about O'Donovan Rossa,[5] or a ballad about the troubles in our native land" [31]) than the fran cophonic affectations of the staged commercial simulacrum, the *Café Chantant* (Gifford cites the Baedeker description of Paris coffeehouses as "a cut below the music halls" [48]) he finds in **"Araby,"** closed, its only music the fall of coins on the salver to announce its mercenary character. But the boy is clearly attuned to a different music, perhaps the lure of the uncited but silently glossed *Magic Flute* of Mozart which is, unquestionably, 'some Freemason affair' ("I asked for leave to go to the bazaar on Saturday night. My aunt was surprised and hoped it was not some Freemason affair" [32]). The opera, with its Eastern occultism, its romantic quest, and trial by gauntlet of spirits, could serve as an analogue for the boy's imagination, for the "dreams of delight" promised by the theme song ("I'll sing thee songs of Araby") of the historical "Grand Oriental Fête" held to benefit the Jervis Street

Hospital in May of 1894. We are left to imagine what songs were sounded, as the boy "went from room to room singing" (33) through the "cold empty gloomy rooms" of his house, on the afternoon of the bazaar.

The boy and narrator display far greater ambivalence toward the liberative potential of children's play, although the boy eventually repudiates that too, once he falls under the spell of eastern enchantment. The theme of romance is introduced circuitously, along the detour of old books and old gardens, as a slip along the verbal gloss of leaves, from yellow book leaves to green plant leaves, makes possible the transition from the musty, hermetically sealed house to the verdant garden and its mysteriously alive environs. Narratively, the yellow leaves of the dead priest's chivalric books leave their pages to drink in rain that lets them come to life again as "the dark dripping gardens redolent with living odours and resonant with the living music of live creatures—"the dark odorous stables where a coachman smoothed and combed the horse or shook music from the buckled harness" (30). The narrator replaces, in the suppler and more scrupulous prose of this lovely description, the florid and histrionic sentiment elided when the narration cuts short the uncle's impending recitation of Caroline Norton's *The Arab's Farewell to His Steed* ("The stranger hath thy bridle-rein, thy master hath his gold;—Fleet-limbed and beautiful, farewell!—thou'rt sold, my steed, thou'art sold!" [Gifford 47]). The children's play in the winter evenings is explicitly described as an exposure to fresh air, as a stimulus to circulation—"The cold air stung us and we played till our bodies glowed" (30). Conflict contributes to that stimulation—"we ran the gantlet of the rough tribes from the cottages" (30)—both in neighborhood play in the marketplace where the boy and his aunt run a gauntlet again, "I bore my chalice safely through a throng of foes" (31). This "mimic warfare," as it is called in **"An Encounter"** takes on the medievalistic colorations of the Crusades, with the gauntlet of "rough tribes" of (presumably) low-bred children from the working-class cottages representing some sort of infidels. But the boy's chivalric fascination with Mangan's sister strips the meaning of gauntlet, back to gantlet, to its archaic armorial form as a mail or metal glove, a rigid but protective barrier to touch or human contact. Thus the boy's adoration is figured in the solipsism implicit in the prayerful gesture—"I pressed the palms of my hands together until they trembled, murmuring: *O love! O love!* many times" (31)—that has him touch and speak to himself rather than to his beloved. Invoking the Grail legend a number of years before Eliot in "The Waste Land," the boy's romantic pilgrimage ends in a dark and silent hall likened to "a church after a service"—not unlike Eliot's ruined Chapel Perilous, "There is the empty chapel, only the wind's home" (l. 389).

Is the story or narration of **"Araby"** the very thing the boy was actually seeking: not a gift for the girl but a gift of idealism and spiritual healing for himself—a modernist poetry as Grail to redeem the paralytic philistinism of a moribund European capital? Does the narrator compensate the boy that is his disenchanted self, for having found the dream of romance empty, by rebuilding it in the form of a quest narrative in which he is re-aestheticized and re-idealized, the sensitive young man transformed into knight errant? Where does such a project leave Mangan's sister, except as a set of synecdochic (**"Araby"**) and metonymic images? What did the boy become, or what other identities implicitly cohabit his function as a poetic storyteller? Is he a romantical academic like Gabriel Conroy, or an intellectual celibate, like Mr Duffy, or a poet manqué like Little Chandler, or a priest? If **"Araby"** has become another version of the dead priest's chivalric books with their yellow leaves, an archaic and decadent aestheticism that will inspire other idealistic young boys—our own students, perhaps—to indulge their nostalgia for the solipsistic self-absorptions of first-love—then is it not itself a sort of dead priest's leavings? Each of these functions replicates the closed circuit of communication and exchange that thematizes the spiritual paralysis in this story less as a figure of motor cessation than as a pneuma of stale and trapped air. The boy's closing confession of vanity, which the narrative urges us to disbelieve, becomes the final rhetorical gesture of empty doubling: the creation of a moral fable with a specious moral.

Notes

1. See R. B. Kershner's extensive discussion of the dead priest's discarded books—especially Sir Walter Scott's *The Abbot*—and their curious gloss on the adventures of the boy in "Araby." "Scott's novel is peculiarly double-voiced; the ideology of nineteenth-century realism and Evangelical admonishment coexists uneasily with romantic ideology, so that Child Roland emerges as a figure both farcical and heroic, both chastened and victorious. The boy of 'Araby,' unfortunately, is trapped in a very different sort of narrative, where the idealism that is Roland's saving grace is exactly the quality responsible for the Irish boy's failure" (54).

2. Warren Beck, who delicately explores "Araby" as an adolescent love story, traces its movement "through self determining events to self-realization in a Joycean epiphany" (96) although he argues that the boy does not yet appreciate what he learns. "In 'Araby' the boy has been frustrated by externality, in the guises of the tardy drunken uncle and a slow train, but he is more lastingly grieved by discovery of a universal ineradicable flaw, the gap between idealization and its confined operation. This also is epiphany, but at first sight almost too appalling for him" (109).

3. The most detailed account of the 1894 Whitsuntide Araby bazaar to benefit the Catholic Jervis Street Hospital can be found in Donald Torchiana's *Backgrounds for Joyce's* Dubliners (56–60). But the charity function of the bazaar is elided in the story—suggesting that neither of the children, the boy or Mangan's sister, nor the boy's aunt (she "hoped it was not some Freemson affair" [32]) or uncle, are aware of this purpose. As a result, the thematic, symbolic, and ironic possibilities of "charity" as the boy's destination or purpose are difficult to determine, even in the context of a full extratextual history—which includes disreputable exploitations ("a number of people who ought to be respectable, with roulette tables, which they ran for the benefit, not of the hospital but of their own pockets" [quoted from the *Irish Times* by Torchiana 57]).

4. Gifford quotes two stanzas from one of James Clarence Mangan's most popular poems, "Dark Rosaleen." This poem's rhetoric of solipsistic address, that negates the interlocutory function of the woman who figurates the poet's inspiration, could serve as a model for the boy's adoration in "Araby."

5. The "come-all-you" about O'Donovan Rossa that the boy consigns to the throng of foes who threaten his chalice, might figure another 'breath of fresh air,' a topical and improvized art designed for spontaneous and mass circulation, to stand in contrast to archaic chivalric books of the sort that shape the boy's imagination and the narrator's rhetoric. The images and lore associated with Donovan—including dynamite (he was known as "Dynamite Rossa") and the circulation of exile (he was imprisoned, exiled to the United States, but returned to Ireland in 1891)—also make him a foil to the entrapped figures of the story.

Works Cited

Beck, Warren. *Joyce's* Dubliners: *Substance, Vision, and Art.* Durham, North Carolina: Duke UP, 1969.

Buerger, Peter. *Theory of the Avant-Garde.* Minneapolis: U of Minnesota P, 1984.

Gifford, Don. *Joyce Annotated: Notes for* Dubliners *and* A Portrait of the Artist as a Young Man. Berkeley: U of California P, 1982.

Joyce, James. *The Critical Writings.* Ed. Ellsworth Mason and Richard Ellmann. Ithaca, New York: Cornell UP, 1989.

———*Dubliners.* New York: Penguin, 1967.

Kershner, R. B. *Joyce, Bakhtin, and Popular Literature: Chronicles of Disorder.* Chapel Hill: U of North Carolina P, 1989.

Lacan, Jacques. "Of the Gaze as *Objet Petit a.*" *The Four Fundamental Concepts of Psycho-Analysis.* Ed. Jacques-Alain Miller. Trans. Alan Sheridan. New York: Norton, 1978.

O'Connor, Frank. "Work in Progress." In *Twentieth Century Interpretations of* Dubliners. Ed. Peter K. Garrett. Englewood Cliffs, New Jersey: Prentice, 1968.

Torchiana, Donald T. *Backgrounds for Joyce's* Dubliners. Boston: Allen, 1986.

Robert Fuhrel (essay date 1998)

SOURCE: "The Quest of Joyce and O'Connor in 'Araby' and 'The Man of the House,'" in *Frank O'Connor: New Perspectives,* edited by Robert C. Evans and Richard Harp, Locust Hill Press, 1998, 173–87.

[*In the following essay, Fuhrel discusses the motif of the quest in Frank O'Connor's "The Man of the House" and Joyce's "Araby" and contrasts the setting, tone, point of view, and themes of the two stories.*]

A young man narrates a tale about a time when, as a boy, old enough to leave the house and travel some distance by himself but innocent in matters of the heart, he had created an imaginary world in which he was a hero. Focusing on everyday matters is a continual problem for the boy. Desiring to please an older female, he recalls having traveled in quest of something for this lady. He reaches his destination and meets another woman, but he is sadly disappointed. Nothing turns out as he had imagined; as a result, his views of the world and himself significantly change. Though he fails to bring back anything for the woman, he has taken an important step toward maturity.

A reader familiar with the work of James Joyce immediately recognizes this summary of **"Araby,"** a story in *Dubliners.* Yet the motif of the quest, an important, recurring element in world literature, also underlies another important Irish short story, "The Man of the House" by Frank O'Connor, although the similarity ends with the plots. Like the unnamed narrator in **"Araby,"** Gus in "The Man of the House" is a young boy who goes on an errand for a loved one. On his travels he meets someone, and the experience, seen in retrospect, changes his ideas of himself and his world. However, given the authors' different ideas of their own roles as writers and of the sound and function of stories, the differences in setting, tone, point of view, and theme are both significant and understandable.

Joyce's story reflects his urban upbringing, his education, and the purposes he expressed in letters he wrote attempting to get *Dubliners* published. **"Araby"** is set in the Dublin of Joyce's youth, and the setting and plot are based on his experiences. The location of O'Connor's story is never specified, and, for all we know, the events could be entirely imaginary.

Joyce didn't consider himself imaginative, preferring to take notes on what he saw and heard around him, later arranging and transforming those notes into fiction, departing from fact when it suited him. Besides, his intention in *Dubliners* "was to write a chapter of the moral history of [his] country and [he] chose Dublin for the scene because that city seemed . . . the centre of paralysis. . . ."[1] Joyce believed that a person must be "a very bold man who dares to alter in the presentment, still more to deform, whatever he has seen and heard" (Scholes and Litz 267). A number of facts testify to Joyce's fidelity to his experience in writing **"Araby."**

First, the setting is entirely urban, essentially unrelieved by nature. The only exceptions are ruined remains, gardens described as either "wild" with "a few straggling bushes" and a "rusty bicycle pump" or "dark" and "dripping . . . where odours arose from the ashpits. . . ."[2] Ellmann's biography, *James Joyce,* reproduces the cover of the program for a real "Araby in Dublin," a "Grand Oriental Fete," which Joyce presumably attended in mid-May of 1894, when he was twelve, about the age of the protagonist.[3] Further, the Joyce family once lived on North Richmond Street, only a year later than the period when Joyce attended the Christian Brothers' School there, between two periods with the Jesuits. Given Joyce's praise of the Jesuits for instilling in him the rigorous habits of organization he demonstrated, and given his father's well-known preference for Jesuit education, it is entirely appropriate that this interim with the less worldly Christian Brothers, during his adolescence, is the setting for **"Araby."** For this is indeed, in the life of the protagonist, a dark, confused time, full of illusions and misunderstood emotions. Not surprisingly, all that is mentioned of the school is in terms of escape: the "blind street" was "quiet . . . except at the hour when the Christian Brothers School set the boys free" (29). "I chafed against the work of the school" (32). One notable departure from fact, though not from spirit, is that the boy in the story lives with an aunt and uncle rather than with his parents, but if we view the narrator as a portrayal of the youthful author, the behavior of Joyce's often drunken father helps to explain the boy's being an orphan in the story. For that matter, even the uncle in the story comes home late and at least slightly inebriated, causing a crucial delay in the boy's departure for the bazaar.

Frank O'Connor, very familiar with Joyce's work, approached the short story differently. According to William Tomory, "O'Connor often commented on Joyce's fiction—not just because Joyce was Irish and such a towering literary influence, but because he had come to be at odds with what Joyce's fiction represented."[4] While Joyce's story is narrated relatively straightforwardly in comparison to his later work, it is full of his typical allusions to obscure books such as *The Devout Communicant* and *The Memoirs of Vidocq* (29) and poems like "The Arab's Farewell to His Steed" (34). In contrast, Tomory points out that one "would search O'Connor's fiction in vain for stream of consciousness, interior monologue, or phantasmagorical dream sequences" because, as O'Connor says in *Towards an Appreciation of Literature:* "The nineteenth century novel still seems to me incomparably the greatest of the modern arts, the art in which the modern world has expressed itself most completely."[5]

Richard Ellmann greatly admired O'Connor as well as Joyce, and he, too, comments on O'Connor's lack of the experimentation that so characterizes Joyce, especially in the later work: "He saw that his own art must radiate out from a single nucleus, must not attempt detachment or alien centers of consciousness in the manner of James or Joyce."[6] In the same article, Ellmann discusses O'Connor's noted penchant for revision, one aspect of writing he shared with Joyce. However, Ellmann makes clear that even in this shared habit, O'Connor had a different purpose: "When he repeatedly revised his work . . . he did so not only to make it more wrought, but more free; for all that he had learned with desperate acquisitiveness stood in the way of primary apprehension."[7]

The reader's primary apprehension does not seem to have been a priority of Joyce, despite his efforts at self-promotion. Though he supplied charts and schemes to help a few selected critics understand his work and wrote detailed letters of explanation to his publishers and patrons, one suspects to help them more effectively publicize his writing, much of Joyce's technique is involved with puzzles and references obscure to the common reader, something O'Connor shunned. For example, in "The Man of the House," as opposed to Joyce's method in **"Araby,"** O'Connor tells in plain language a tale devoid of allusions to other works of literature. Also unlike the Dublin of **"Araby"** is the setting of O'Connor's story, which cannot be precisely determined. It seems to be far more rural, perhaps a small village or the outskirts of a city as it takes the boy no time to get out into the countryside. A similarity between the two stories involves the protagonists' attitudes toward school. Gus, in "The Man of the House," reflects that he "had always known a fellow could have his troubles, but if he faced them manfully, he could get advantages out of them as well. There was the school for instance. . . ." Gus doesn't go to school this day because of his mother's illness, but he walks by it while journeying to get medicine for her and notices "the chorus of poor sufferers through the open windows, and a glimpse of Danny Delaney's bald pate as he did sentry before the front door with his cane wriggling like a tail behind his back."[8] Neither boy seems particularly concerned with success in school, although the boy in **"Araby"** does comment on the concern of his teacher about the boy's daydreaming.

The urban setting of **"Araby"** is particularly grim, appropriate to Joyce's view of the city. One house is "uninhabited" and "detached from its neighbors." The other houses have "brown imperturbable faces." The boys play in "dark, muddy lanes" (29) and must run "the gauntlet of the rough tribes from the cottages," probably like the cottages where O'Connor's Gus lives.[9] Physically, in **"Araby"** the surroundings are bleak, but the boy's imagination transfigures all, however briefly, as it does in O'Connor's story as well. The insistent dreariness of the setting makes the reader wonder how any degree of imagination on the part of the boy can for long hold out against his surroundings, and in fact, the week is not out before the transfiguration, along with the boy's youthful naiveté, is shattered.

The boy in **"Araby"** thinks he is in love, and he goes on a quest in search of something for the lady he thinks he loves. Because of his attraction to his friend Mangan's[10] older sister, to whom he has never spoken "except for a few casual words," the boy is able to interject into "places the most hostile to romance" an element of magic. When he shops with his aunt, walking "through the flaring streets, jostled by drunken men and bargaining women, amid the curses of labourers" and "the shrill litanies of shop-boys" (30–31), he imagines, "I bore my chalice safely through a throng of foes" (31). The young boy in "The Man of the House," on the other hand, doesn't allow his imagination to rule him for long: for a brief moment only the world around him is transformed, and he feels "exalted, a voyager, a heroic figure" (187), but primarily he remains conscientious about sticking to his duty and finishing the errand for his mother. Nevertheless, he will also be distracted by a young lady, if only temporarily.

In **"Araby"** the boy is very confused, and he doesn't know whether he "would ever speak to [Mangan's sister] or not" or how he "could tell her of [his] confused adoration." His feelings are permeated with religious images, and in the chivalric image so similar to that in "The Man of the House," the boy blends his attraction for the girl with the thought of the divine. O'Connor's young protagonist has heard his mother describe him to her friend Mrs. Ryan as "'the best anyone ever reared.'" Mrs. Ryan responds by remarking, "'Why then, there aren't many like him. . . . The most of the children that's going now are more like savages than Christians'" (185). He wishes to please his mother and realizes that if he isn't careful, he will disappoint her. "One slip and I should be among those children that Minnie Ryan disapproved of, who were more like savages than Christians" (185). He, too, sees himself as the lone bearer of the sacred in a profane world.[11]

When the boy in **"Araby"** finally speaks to Mangan's sister, he promises rashly to bring her a gift from Araby, a "splendid bazaar," to which she off-handedly replies she would "love" to go, though she cannot because "there would be a retreat that week in her convent" (32). She has always been inaccessible, and he has watched her either from the street below, gazing up to where she has stood at the top of stairs in the doorway, or from across the street, peering voyeuristically at her through blinds. Always railings or walls have stood between them. But now Araby itself takes over his mind. "The syllables of the word 'Araby' were called to me through the silence in which my soul luxuriated and cast an Eastern enchantment over me" (32). Reaching Araby and winning this girl's love become his confused quest. In stark contrast, the young boy in "The Man of the House" has never before met the girl who momentarily leads him astray, and the quest he is on is for his mother. But this young lady is enticing. She urges him, after helping him to drink the bottle of cough medicine, to fill it up with water, and he cannot refuse her. "Mother was far away, and I was swept from anchorage into an unfamiliar world of spires, towers, trees, steps, and little girls who liked cough bottles. I worshiped that girl" (189). However, it takes but a moment and the empty bottle to bring him to his senses, and he "remembered my mother sick and the Blessed Virgin slighted, and my heart sank" (189).

Numerous critics have commented on the myth of the quest undertaken by "one who has been stirred by chivalric love in the tradition of the Arthurian romances."[12] Concepcion Dadaufalza points out that the quest itself was "meant to bring fertility to a blighted land."[13] This accurately describes Joyce's view of Dublin. The sterility of the Dublin setting, Dadaufalza explains, is reflected partly in the barrenness of the boy's relationships. Though he has playmates, they remain unnamed. His love is known only by her relationship to her brother. The boy himself lacks parents and lives in the home of an apparently childless aunt and uncle, surrounded by a "dead priest, an apparently unmarried sister, and a pawnbroker's widow." No wonder he seeks a Grail.

The boy in Joyce's tale does finally get to Araby after what seems to him an interminable delay caused by his uncle. He pays more than he had planned to get into the bazaar, which is about to close, and he "recognize[s] a silence like that which pervades a church after a service." He remembers only "with difficulty" why he had come and realizes he cannot buy anything. As he hears the English accents of a young woman and two men engaged in a most banal conversation, the boy's dream bursts. All his illusions about his maturity, about Mangan's sister and what he thought was her interest in him, about the exotic Araby, and, most significantly, about himself are destroyed, and the story concludes: "Gazing up into the darkness I saw myself as a creature driven and derided by vanity; and my eyes burned with anguish and anger" (35).

In order to understand Joyce's choice of setting, style, and theme, one must recall, again, that Joyce wrote this story as part of the whole of *Dubliners* "to betray the soul of that hemiplegia or paralysis which many consider a city," as he wrote in a letter to Constantine Curran reprinted in Scholes and Litz's volume (259). In other words, his purpose was moral in addition to artistic. Only by careful examination of conscience, such examination to be conducted by him, did Joyce believe the Irish could free themselves of the physical, intellectual, and spiritual paralysis he felt they were suffering. Had he remained in the home of his youth, as portrayed in **"Araby"** and the other *Dubliners* tales, he, too, would have fallen victim to Dublin's paralyzing influences; as self-exiled artist, it fell to him to aid in the cure of his countrymen.

None of this need to awaken his fellow Irishmen seems to have bothered Frank O'Connor. On the contrary, he is on record as having said about himself that "the thing this man likes best in the story is the story itself. . . . I like feeling that the story-teller has something to communicate, and if he doesn't communicate it he'll bust."[14]

Another aspect of **"Araby,"** its style, is a matter of debate. Joyce himself called it "for the most part a style of scrupulous meanness."[15] Joyce agreed only most begrudgingly to alter or omit certain phrases to which the printers had objected, but he was determined to change nothing else. Again, to his prospective publisher, Richards, Joyce wrote, "These details may now seem to you unimportant but if I took them away *Dubliners* would seem to me like an egg

without salt."[16] Further, he argued, "'You say that it is a small thing I am asked to do, to efface a word here and there. But do you not see clearly that in a short story above all such effacement may be fatal.'"[17]

While Joyce here certainly refers to particular words and phrases, his insistence by implication is that every word was deliberate and important, something O'Connor also demonstrated. In fact, O'Connor went further, revising his stories incessantly, both before and after publication. By "'scrupulous meanness,'" Joyce was not referring to a sparsity of detail, for the stories are thick with references to popular and classical culture, the history and rituals of Catholicism, and the history and culture of Ireland. A perhaps not entirely undeserved criticism of Joyce is directed at his display of erudition, an integral part of his method. If his writing relied on plot and character alone, his stories would be nowhere near as rich as they are, but then again, they wouldn't be his stories. As it is, the language is appropriate as the voice of an imaginative narrator, perhaps himself an artist, reflecting on his youth, but it is hardly ordinary life described in **"Araby."**

Frank O'Connor's "The Man of the House" is another story told in the first person by a narrator recalling his youth, but here we have the youth of an imaginative but plain-speaking person. He is younger at the time the story takes place than the twelve-year-old in **"Araby,"** for he tells us that when he reads the police court news to his mother, "I wasn't very quick about it because I was only at words of one syllable" (185). This boy, too, is fatherless, but in O'Connor's tale this detail is directly functional; it is the lack of an adult male in the family that motivates the boy to try to act maturely. On the other hand, the mother is more than present; she, not a peer, is the object of the boy's affection, for whom he ventures out into the potentially dangerous world. As in **"Araby,"** the boy's imagination transforms what he sees there. A "wooded gorge" becomes "the Rockies, Himalayas, or Highlands . . ." (185). The city below, seen from a hilltop, appears "more like the backcloth of a theatre than a real town," causing the boy to feel "exalted" (187). On his quest to bring back a bottle of medicine for his mother, he notices a "murmuring honeycomb of factory chimneys and houses" and a "gently rounded hilltop with a limestone spire and a purple sandstone tower rising out of it and piercing the clouds. It was so wide and bewildering a view that it was never all lit up at the same time" (187). The details described here are much more grounded in the boy's physical surroundings than are the descriptions in **"Araby,"** which much more often reflect the boy's emotional state.

At home, Gus sees himself as more manly, more useful, than he really is, but this self-perception is based on the desire to provide for and please his mother. He tells her he won't go to school but will care for her instead. He has a very practical imagination when focused on his duties. He notices her illness right away, orders her to bed, builds the fire properly, and makes her breakfast, though he is less than successful with the tea. He informs his mother's employer that he isn't sure if he will allow her to come to work, and he is elated when the boss agrees with his assessment of the situation. He successfully journeys to a nearby pub to get some whisky for his mother; in the pub he faces adults who threaten him, as the boy in **"Araby"** feels threatened by the crowds in the street. Gus sees a drunk in the pub, "grinning at me diabolically," who mistakes him for his "'old flower'" and calls him "'a thundering ruffian'" and "'the most notorious boozer in Capetown'" (186). As in **"Araby,"** here again youth is threatened by an inebriated adult.

When Gus gets home, with his mother is Minnie Ryan, "gossipy and pious" (185). She corresponds to Mrs. Mercer in **"Araby,"** who is described as "an old garrulous woman . . . who collected used stamps for some pious purpose. I had to endure the gossip of the tea table" (33). And when Gus goes out to play, he deliberately stays close to home, so as not to lose his concentration and be counted among the savages. Like the boy in **"Araby,"** Gus views himself as the saved one among the heathens.

Common to the two stories also is the theme of economic frustration. The boy in **"Araby"** cannot buy what he would like for his beloved, even if he could find something suitable, because he has spent too much on the special train to get to the bazaar and must still get home. In O'Connor's tale, the boy cannot both light a votive candle and buy candy. Before he can even go to the dispensary, he must visit the Poor Law guardian for the humiliating purpose of proving the family cannot pay for the doctor's visit. When the doctor arrives, apparently drunk, like the man in the pub, he does nothing but needlessly advise the boy to "'Look after your mother while you can,'" and then he writes a prescription. Presumably, more money would have provided a better physician, but Gus thinks little still of a doctor who "never washed his hands" (187).

So far, the details, including a poor, fatherless family with a sick mother and a boy who clearly dislikes school, another gossipy old lady, a man blindly drunk in a bar, and a doctor "like all the drunks of the medical profession" (186) seem to be as dismal as those in **"Araby."** But the sordidness of the description is undercut by the boy's acceptance of his world and his determination not to escape from it but to manage it maturely. Waiting for the bazaar, the boy in **"Araby"** is wont to wallow in self-pity and confusion, expressed in phrases like "I was thankful that I could see so little. All my senses seemed to desire to veil themselves. . . . I wished to annihilate the tedious intervening days. . . . I had hardly any patience with the serious work of life" (31–32). Gus, on the other hand, although aware of his shortcomings, still welcomes the challenges of the real world. He reads to his mother and successfully ventures to the pub, but both incidents are affected by his youth and inexperience. Even though, as he admits, he has begun "to feel the strain of my responsibilities," he knows that "Concentration . . . was what I had to practice" (185).

Later, he is sent to the dispensary for the cough-bottle. This trip is directly reminiscent of the quest of the boy in **"Araby."** Gus must go "through a thickly populated poor locality," down a "stoney pathway flanked on the one side by red-brick corporation houses and on the other by a wide common with an astounding view of the city" (187). The boy balances the poverty of state housing with the "astounding" view; he sees both the bad and good at once. Here, however, he starts to lose his concentration. The view is "bewildering." His thoughts turn to religion, as do the boy's in **"Araby,"** but this boy is far more practical if just as naive. Seeing a cathedral's spire and deciding to spend his penny on a candle to the Blessed Virgin, for his mother's recovery, he is "sure I'd get more value in a great church like that so close to heaven" than in an ordinary one down in the town (187).

Arriving at the dispensary, he meets the young lady who is destined to dispel his illusions. In **"Araby"** she was the banal shopkeeper flirting with two men, totally disregarding the boy, who brought him to his senses; in "The Man of the House," Gus is certainly paid attention to by the more experienced girl, but it becomes apparent to him that she only wants his cough-bottle. At first, he is attracted to her "pleasant, talkative" manner, her worldliness—"She obviously knew her way around"—and her green eyes (188). Gus is seduced from his mission and dismisses any need to light a candle. "In a queer way the little girl restored my confidence," he explains—a result quite different from the effect of the girl in **"Araby"** on that boy.

After they finish off the sweets he buys with the money he had intended to use to light "a candle to the Blessed Virgin in the cathedral on the hilltop for [his] mother's speedy recovery," the girl asks to try his mother's cough-bottle: "She took a long drink out of it, which alarmed me" (189). She then shares the rest with him and convinces him to "'Finish it and say the cork fell out.'" At this point, he realizes, "I had sacrificed both to a girl and she didn't even care for me" (189). But he can still hope for a miracle, and he goes into the nearest church, conveniently the cathedral with a shrine to the Blessed Virgin, and promises to buy a candle with his next penny. He returns home, broken in pocket and spirit (he, too, has wasted his substance on frivolities), thinking that his weakness, his failure to concentrate, has conquered him once more. But he phrases it quite differently than the boy in **"Araby"**; all Gus says is, "All the light had gone out of the day, and the echoing hillside had become a vast, alien, cruel world" (190).

When he arrives, he finds his mother still sick, and he breaks down in tears. She consoles him and says she was only concerned for his safety. This elicits from him the truth about the medicine; as a result, she mothers him even more. His lack of concentration, far from being the problem he has considered it, has forced her to resume her role as mother and protector. Although Gus is sure he is a failure, he has accomplished his mission in spite of himself. His return from his illusion of himself as a man to the realization that he is still a boy, in need of a mother, cures her, the very miracle he had sought.

We have what appears to be the same story told in two very different ways. The plot elements are remarkably alike though the characters differ, as do the writers' techniques. Joyce characteristically loads his tale with references to obscure books, popular ballads, and poems, but he undermines the references by having the narrator tell us the boy liked the books because they were old and yellow, putting the ballads in the mouths of nasal street singers, and having the boy leave while his uncle is just beginning to recite the poetry. "The Man of the House" is empty of such allusions, with the result that the boy comes across as a normal child instead of a budding artist. Joyce's tale is unrelievedly dark, from the blindness of the street at the beginning, through the short days of winter dusk, to the darkness of the empty hall at the conclusion; O'Connor's story begins on "a lovely summer morning" (184), and the boy has visions of himself as a knight on a hillside where "sunlight wandered across it as across a prairie" (187). These differences are significant, but more striking are the differences in the language of the two stories, differences that make **"Araby"** sound like the work of a writer and "The Man of the House" the work of a storyteller.

For example, consider this portion of the description of his surroundings given by the boy in **"Araby"**: "When we met in the street the houses had grown more somber. The space of sky above us was the colour of ever-changing violet and towards it the lamps of the street lifted their feeble lanterns" (30). O'Connor, in contrast, rejects almost all figurative language as he has his narrator say: "At the end of the lane was the limestone spire of Shandon; all along it young trees overhung the high, hot walls, and the sun, when it came out in hot, golden blasts behind us, threw our linked shadows onto the road" (189). Both boys are confused about their emotions, but the boy in **"Araby"** expresses himself in phrases such as: "Her name sprang to my lips at moments in strange prayers and praises which I myself did not understand. My eyes were often full of tears (I could not tell why) and at times a flood from my heart seemed to pour itself out into my bosom" (31). Gus is more likely to say things like "I worshiped that girl" (189). As opposed to Gus, who on more than one occasion "loses his concentration," the boy in **"Araby"** puts it differently: "What innumerable follies laid waste my waking and sleeping thoughts after that evening!" (32). When Gus realizes, very quickly, that he has been tricked by the young lady, he says, "I saw her guile and began to weep" (189). This is certainly more directly stated than the words of the boy in **"Araby"** at his awakening: "Gazing up into the darkness I saw myself as a creature driven and derided by vanity; and my eyes burned with anguish and anger" (35).

Here are two writers intensely interested in the word, but one seems more interested in the magical properties of it, the other in the functional. O'Connor relates one famous anecdote, often repeated, that illustrates the two authors' different attitudes. He says he had visited Joyce in Paris, and states, "I had admired an old print of Cork in the hall-way and wondered what the frame was made of. 'That's cork,' said Joyce. I said, 'I know it's Cork, but what's the frame made of?' 'That's cork,' Joyce repeated, and it was."[18] Hugh Kenner comments: "Being an old fashioned story teller for whom words have chiefly instrumental interest, O'Connor thought Joyce was going out of his mind."[19]

In any case, one of O'Connor's main interests was getting the voices right, as he made clear on many occasions. O'Connor, as he himself said, could not "pass a story as finished unless I know how everybody in it spoke. . . . If I use the right phrase and the reader hears the phrase in his head, he sees the individual."[20]

Different goals and attitudes about stories led Joyce and O'Connor to two very different treatments of essentially the same situation. While Joyce was primarily an experimenter interested in "Europeanizing" Irish literature, O'Connor seems more in the tradition of the Irish storyteller, the *shanachie,* though with the crucial difference that his art was certainly not one of improvisation. James D. Alexander discusses O'Connor's attitude about fiction and his differences with Joyce's methods. Regarding O'Connor's narrators, Alexander points out that they "may not be reliable—often . . . partly reliable—but his voice, even when ironic, confers the 'warmth' on the literary creation."[21] A perfect example is Gus in "The Man of the House." When he is giving and getting instructions from his mother at the start of the story, he suggests to her that eggs would be a good choice for dinner. Then, in one of his frequent asides to the reader, he informs us: "That was really only a bit of swank, because eggs were the one thing I could cook, but the mother told me to get sausages as well in case she was able to get up" (184). Also, according to Alexander, O'Connor used "the word 'cold' for Joyce's technique in *Dubliners* and *Ulysses,* to describe the quality of detachment he finds in Joyce. . . . Anything that gets in the way of the account, any reportage for its own sake, word play, allusion or symbol, struck O'Connor as sterile exhibitionism and was to be avoided."[22]

While no doubt an accurate assessment of O'Connor's feelings about Joyce's methods, this ignores the fact that Joyce was deliberately "cold" to many of his characters, whom he had not so much created as found in Dublin and in himself and whom he did not wish to portray sympathetically. Given such different ideas about the story and its purpose, it seems even more remarkable that the two writers would use the same quest motif in stories so similar in plot. One explanation of the similarity lies in O'Connor's undoubted respect for Joyce despite whatever criticism he might have leveled at him. In Eric Solomon's memoir of being O'Connor's student, he recalls that of O'Connor's many qualities, his lectures were exceptional, and Solomon states emphatically, "Frank O'Connor's classroom concert is what I recall best. He would read from Joyce's **'Araby.'**"[23]

Notes

1. This is from a letter Joyce wrote to Grant Richards on May 5, 1906, quoted in James Joyce, *Dubliners,* ed. Robert Scholes and A. Walton Litz (New York: The Viking Press, 1969), 269.

2. All references to "Araby" are to the Viking Critical Edition mentioned above. For these particular quotations, see 29–30. References hereafter will be cited in the text.

3. Richard Ellmann, *James Joyce* (New York: Oxford University Press, 1959), Plate III, following page 80.

4. William M. Tomory, *Frank O'Connor* (Boston: G. K. Hall and Co., 1980), 58.

5. Ibid., 57.

6. Quoted in "Michael-Frank" in *Michael/Frank,* ed. Maurice Sheehy (New York: Alfred A. Knopf, 1969), 26.

7. Ibid., 27.

8. All references to "The Man of the House" are to Frank O'Connor, *Collected Stories* (New York: Random House, 1981). This quote is from page 184.

9. That Joyce, like his protagonist in "Araby," was distinct from the "rough tribes" was emphasized by O'Connor in a projected broadcast scheduled for July 16, 1937, for Radio Eireann, a broadcast never made because of last-minute censorship. The transcript for the talk was published five days later in *The Irish Times.* In it, O'Connor says that the real tragedy of the Parnell split "was the desolation of the spirit it produced among the people, of whom Joyce is the very pattern. . . . This despair produced a violent overweening individualism" and "the desire to break forever with the tribe." This is discussed in Alan Cohn and Richard F. Peterson, "Frank O'Connor on Joyce and Lawrence: An Uncollected Text," *Journal of Modern Literature* 12 (1985): 211–20.

10. Most of *Dubliners* was written while Joyce was living in Trieste, when he was also writing overtly political newspaper articles for the Italian press. During this time, he also wrote in praise of James Clarence Mangan, author of "Dark Rosaleen," one of the better known personifications of Ireland. Perhaps naming the object of his young protagonist's infatuation "Mangan's sister" in some way identified her for Joyce with what many young men of the time desired, a more traditional Ireland, a desire the more mature Joyce did not share. Joyce at this time was also lecturing on Irish history and teaching conversational English; his teaching methods included much discussion of politics, as attested to by his former students in the documentary entitled *Is There One Who Understands Me?: The World of James Joyce* (Producer and Director Sean O'Mordha). Dublin: Radio Telcfis 1982. Dist. Princeton: Films for the Humanities and Sciences, FFH 897. Videocassette. 120 mm.

11. This image of bearing a chalice among enemies, more explicit in Joyce than in O'Connor, as one would expect, derives from stories of early Christian martyrs in Rome, particularly the story of Tarsicius, killed by a group of pagan boys as he tried to take the Blessed Sacrament to converts hiding in catacombs. See H. George Hahn, "Tarsicius: A Hagiographical Allusion in Joyce's 'Araby,'" *Papers on Language and Literature* 27 (1991): 381–85. According to Hahn, Joyce would have known about Tarsicius from a popular novel entitled *Fabiola: or, the Church of the Catacombs,* written by an Irish cardinal. Further, under the tutelage of the Jesuits, Joyce would have written narratives on the lives of the saints, and he certainly knew Butler's *Lives of the Saints,* where Tarsicius is linked with St. Stephen, the first martyr, about whom Joyce knew a great deal and to whom he alluded in a concurrent project, *A Portrait of the Artist as a Young Man,* going so far as to name the protagonist of that book Stephen. The story of Tarsicius also appeared in *Our Weekly Messenger,* a parochial elementary school publication, in the early 1950s, testimony to the staying power of the tale. My first reading of "Araby" made such an impression on me in part because I had read of Tarsicius in Philadelphia as a boy and identified with him. The legend would naturally have appealed to Joyce, who seems to have considered himself superior to his comrades in most respects.

12. Robert P. apRoberts, "'Araby' and the Palimpsest of Criticism or, Through a Glass Darkly," *Antioch Review* 26 (Winter 1966–67): 468–69.

13. Concepcion D. Dadaufalza, "The Quest of the Chalice-Bearer in James Joyce's 'Araby,'" *Dilman Review* 7 (1959): 317–25.

14. Frank O'Connor, "Writing a Story—One Man's Way," *The Listener* (23 July 1959): 139–40. Reprinted in *A Frank O'Connor Reader,* ed. Michael Steinman (Syracuse: Syracuse University Press, 1994), 312.

15. Quoted in Scholes and Litz, 269.

16. Ibid., 270.

17. Ibid., 273.

18. In Frank O'Connor, *A Short History of Irish Literature: A Backward Glance* (New York: Putnam, 1967), 211.

19. Hugh Kenner, *A Colder Eye: The Modern Irish Writers* (Baltimore: Johns Hopkins, 1983), 219.

20. "Frank O'Connor," *Writers at Work: The Paris Review Interviews,* ed. Malcolm Cowley (New York: The Viking Press, 1969), 169.

21. James D. Alexander, "Frank O'Connor's Joyce Criticism," *Journal of Irish Literature* 21 (1992): 40–53.

22. Ibid., 50.

23. Eric Solomon, "Frank O'Connor as Teacher," *Twentieth Century Literature* 36 (1990): 239–41.

FURTHER READING

Criticism

Atherton, J. S. "Araby." *James Joyce's Dubliners: Critical Essays,* edited by Clive Hart, pp. 39–47. New York: The Viking Press, 1969.

Discusses the ways in which "Araby" is typical of Joyce's oeuvre.

Brooks, Cleanth and Robert Penn Warren. "Araby." *Understanding Fiction,* pp. 414–24. East Norwalk, CT: Appleton-Century-Crofts, 1943.

Brooks and Warren explicate the major themes of Joyce's "Araby."

Collins, Ben L. "'Araby' and the 'Extended Simile.'" *Twentieth Century Interpretations of Dubliners: A Collection of Critical Essays,* edited by Peter K. Garrett, pp. 93–9. Englewood Cliffs, NJ: Prentice-Hall, 1968.

Originally published in 1967, finds parallels in "Araby" and Homer's *The Odyssey,* Dante's *Commedia,* and the biblical story of the Garden of Eden.

Dylan Thomas
1914–1953

(Full name Dylan Marlais Thomas) Welsh poet, dramatist, short story writer, and essayist. For additional criticism on Thomas's short fiction, see *SSC,* Volume 3.

INTRODUCTION

Remembered primarily as a poet who both created innovative poetry and lived a dissolute life, Thomas was also the author of such prose works as short stories, radio screenplays, novels, and a drama. Thomas's works, both prose and poetry, are intensely personal, a form of self-discovery. He often dealt with the same themes in varied genres, including the negative aspects of Welsh Christianity, Welsh folklore, fear of death, and sexuality. In his early prose, Thomas frequently relied on imagery rather than plot devices to advance the narrative. While Thomas's talent as a poet was recognized early in his career, his aptness as a writer of short fiction grew only when scholars attempted to assess his prose works in relationship to his entire oeuvre.

BIOGRAPHICAL INFORMATION

Born in Swansea, Wales, Thomas was the son of an English master at the Swansea Grammar School. English was his favorite academic subject, and he was the editor of the school literary magazine, in which his first short stories appeared. Otherwise, Thomas rebelled against the strictures of a formal education. When he failed his examinations in 1931, he left school at age sixteen. While working for the *South Wales Daily Post,* an evening newspaper, he acquired reporting skills that later proved useful in writing fiction. In 1934 he moved to London, where he lived a bohemian lifestyle and composed poems and short fiction, which were first published in magazines. In a pub in 1936 he met dancer Caitlin Macnamara, whom he married a year later, beginning a twelve-year relationship that eventually soured under the strain of poverty and Thomas's alcoholism. Alternating between London, where he indulged in excesses, and rural communities, where he wrote his works, Thomas turned to writing stories and radio screenplays to stave off indigency. During World War II, he wrote propaganda scripts for the British government. After the war, Thomas gave popular poetry readings, which turned into a more lucrative enterprise than prose writing. Nevertheless, he was continually on the verge of destitution and was often in an alcoholic stupor which interfered with his writing. While on an American poetry-reading tour in 1953, Thomas died from excessive alcohol consumption.

MAJOR WORKS OF SHORT FICTION

Known principally as a talented poet, Thomas devoted considerable time to writing short stories, the final versions of which he copied into his "Red Notebook," a personal journal from which he read aloud. In such stories as "Map of Love" and "A Prospect of the Sea" Thomas dealt with sexual initiation, while in "The Holy Six," "The Burning Baby," "The Enemies," and "The Tree," he portrayed Christianity run amok. These stories, from what commentators consider Thomas's early period, demonstrate a style that relies heavily on the fantastic, the poetic, and the shocking. They also have little use for plot in the traditional sense and rely instead on images and dreams to connect the action. Although Thomas attempted during the late 1930s to interest a publisher in a collection of short stories, he was unsuccessful because editors objected to what they considered vulgar language and offensive material. Consequently, while the collection *The Map of Love* appeared in 1939 and *Portrait of the Artist as a Young Dog* in 1940, it was not until after Thomas's death that a number of his more controversial stories appeared in book form. *Portrait of the Artist,* a collection of ten stories written while the couple lived in the Welsh coastal village of Laugharne in 1938 and 1939, marks the beginning of Thomas's more mature style. It reflects Thomas's experiences of marriage and family, as well as the outbreak of continental war. The stories focus on a single protagonist, Thomas, who recounts adventures in a more naturalistic style than his previously figurative prose style in which imagery dominated plot. In "The Peaches" the narrator learns of social class divisions, in "A Visit to Grandpa's" of old age and loneliness, in "Extraordinary Little Cough" of masculinity, and in "Old Garbo" of the tragic consequences of excessive drunkenness. During the 1940s Thomas wrote scripts for the BBC Wales Children's Hour, including "A Child's Memories of Christmas in Wales," which was later published in book form and became a children's classic. After writing the radio drama *Under Milk Wood* (1954), Thomas attempted to write an autobiographical novel, *Adventures in the Skin Trade,* but it was left unfinished at his death. Published posthumously in 1955 in a collection with several stories, *Adventures* is treated by some scholars as a series of short stories and by others as a novel.

CRITICAL RECEPTION

Thomas's short stories remain secondary to his poetry in critical acclaim. Derek Stanford judged Thomas's prose works valuable not on their own merits but because of the "clues they offer to Thomas's literary temperament, and the confirmation of his mode of thought in verse." Critics such as Jacob Korg have noted the progression of Thomas's style from the early stories to those published in *Portrait of the Artist* and later. Several critics, among them Stanford, John Ackerman, and Linden Peach, have focused on Thomas's use of imagery in his poetry and prose. According to Ackerman, in the stories written between 1934 and 1939, Thomas employed themes and techniques common to his early poetry: nostalgic childhood images and fantasies combined with biblical thought and imagery to make "a poet's prose—eloquent, sensuous, strongly rhythmic, and rich in metaphor." Both Rys Davies and Peter Levi, writing at opposite ends of a forty-year span, determined that Thomas never arrived at a mature prose style.

PRINCIPAL WORKS

Short Fiction

The Map of Love 1939
Portrait of the Artist as a Young Dog 1940
Quite Early One Morning 1954
Adventures in the Skin Trade, and Other Stories 1955
Selected Writings of Dylan Thomas 1970
Collected Stories 1980

Other Major Works

18 Poems (poetry) 1934
Twenty-Five Poems (poetry) 1936
New Poems (poetry) 1943
Collected Poems, 1934–1952 (poetry) 1952
Deaths and Entrances (poetry) 1952
In Country Sleep (poetry) 1952
Under Milk Wood (drama) 1954

CRITICISM

Derek Stanford (essay date 1954)

SOURCE: "Prose and Drama," in *Dylan Thomas,* Neville Spearman, 1954, pp. 155–88.

[*In the excerpt below, Stanford describes Thomas's provocative use of language in the stories of* Map of Love *and* Portrait of the Artist as a Young Dog.]

I

The seven stories in **The Map of Love** exhibit a typical young man's prose: not the prose of a young poet writing about poetry, but that of a poet using prose to convey what he has generally expressed in verse. (Remove the formal device of narrative and the tales in **The Map of Love** might all have been poems from that or previous volumes.) The value of these first stories, I should say, is that of Yeats' early stories. We read them, in retrospect, because they are the work of a fine poet, rather than because they succeed in themselves. But taken as a part of the poet's imaginary world, and read for the clues they offer to Thomas' literary temperament, and the confirmation of his mode of thought in verse, these tales are interesting enough. A second element in our just concern with them is that of their prophetic property—the way in which odd passages and phrases look forward to the objective consummation of the author's later prose.

The common quality in these seven stories is in the abnormal world they present. Some of them are fantasies; and others, while observing certain obligations to the claims of "reality", make good their escape from such ties by employing themes of dementia and madness. The setting, in each case, is in Wales, within range of "the Jarvis Hills" (a fictional topographical reference). Most of the stories have pastoral backgrounds; though in one of them an industrial town is featured. But, unlike the later tales in **Portrait of the Artist as a Young Dog,** the *genius loci* or spirit of the place is only evoked in the most general terms. Place in these early stories is not a matter of particular locality but of vague associative ideas.

A word as to their themes and plots. In **"The Visitor"** a dying poet is visited each night by his friend Callaghan. One evening, Callaghan comes to him, takes him naked from his bed, and—carrying him in his arms—flies through the darkened countryside with him. In their flight the poet sees the processes of nature working. The terms of his vision are grand and amplified:

> The moon, doubling and redoubling the strength of her beams, lit up the barks and the roots and the branches of the Jarvis trees, the busy lice in the wood, the shapes of the stones and the black ants travelling under them, the pebbles in the streams, the secret grass, the untiring death-worms under the blades.

Callaghan brings the poet back to his bed before the full breaking of the dawn. Rhianon the poet's wife "with a sweet, naked throat, stepped into the room.

> Rhianon, he said, hold my hand, Rhianon.
>
> She did not hear him, but stood over his bed and fixed him with an unbreakable sorrow.
>
> Hold my hand, he said. And then: Why are you putting the sheet over my face?

The figure of Callaghan (is he Death?) looks forward to "the Thief" in Thomas' poem "In country sleep."

"The Enemies" tells the story of an old clergyman who loses his way in the hills. He comes to the house of a young couple, where he stays for a meal and a rest. The wife spends much time staring in the crystal, and the husband is engaged in a lasting war with the endless weeds of his fecund garden. Between them, they symbolise the powers of darkness—of occult "pantheistic" forces. The man looks at the old clergyman and thinks, "He is afraid of the worm in the earth, of the copulation in the tree, of the living grease in the soil." The rector senses their pagan aura, and, feeling afraid, drops on his knees. "He stared and he prayed, like an old god beset by his enemies."

Anti-Christian, in another manner, is the parody of the Crucifixion in **"The Tree."**[1] A pious elderly gardener tells a little lonely boy about the tree on which Christ was crucified. In the boy's mind the story grows confused; and at night he creeps out of his bed to kneel and pray at the tree's foot. On Christmas Day, an idiot, who has been roaming the countryside, is found by the boy sitting under the tree. The boy gets him to stand up and raise his arms, then secures him to the tree with wire from the potting-shed. After which, he returns with a handful of "silver nails".

"The Map of Love" relates how a boy and girl are initiated into the mystery of sex by the ghost of "mad Jarvis" and his many sweethearts. His voice cries out to them from all the fields in which he has prosecuted his many amours.

"The Mouse and the Woman" recounts the dreams of an inmate of a lunatic asylum; while in **"The Dress"**[2] an escaped lunatic (who has cut off his wife's lips because she smiled at other men) goes to sleep with his head in the lap of a terrified woman, into whose cottage he has broken.

"The Orchards" describes the dreams of the poet Marlais, in which he falls in love with a female scarecrow and her beautiful sister. One day, walking in the country, he meets the girl out of his dream, and sees that the scarecrow is also there. I do not know whether this story owes anything to Walter de la Mare's tale of the scare-crow, in some meadows beyond a lonely house, that approaches a little nearer each day.

In the main, literary influence in these stories seems small. It is possible, but unlikely, that the adventures of Michael Robertes, in the tales of Yeats, may have impressed Thomas; and the tales from *The Mabinogion* may have contributed a touch here and there.

In his book *English Prose Style,* Sir Herbert Read has some remarks which help us to "place" these seven stories. "Fantasy," he observes, "is a product of thought, Imagination of sensibility. If the thinking discursive mind turns to speculation, the result is Fantasy; if, however, the sensible, intuitive mind turns to speculation, the result is Imagination. Fantasy may be visionary, but it is cold and logical; Imagination is sensuous and instinctive." This, I think, serves to distinguish the processes by which Thomas produced his verse and early prose. In both cases, his subject-matter is the same. The "pantheistic" "vegetable world", which "roared" under Mr. Owen's feet in **"The Enemies,"** is of the same universe as we encounter in Thomas' first two books of poems; but whereas the latter is the product of "the sensible, intuitive mind", the former has resulted from a lower-pressured "thinking". This may account for the "cold" unsubstantial quality of these tales which no show of rhetoric can hope to conceal.

But if the "Fantasy" of the seven tales does not succeed in creating the illusion of poetry, which it seems to wish to do, it fails also in achieving the element proper to its own genre—that "objectivity" which Sir Herbert Read posits as being its true distinguishing quality.

Disparate passages of "poetical" musing or of too self-conscious prose, drift like mists through the stories, depriving them of narrative economy and shape.

Lacking a grasp of particulars as being part of a general body, these tales do, however, occasionally evince that celebration of individual traits, that closeness to things, which the later prose reveals. "Upon town pavements," Thomas writes in **"The Orchards,"** "he saw the woman step loose, her breasts firm under a coat on which the single hairs from old men's heads lay white on black." His perception here is as shrewd as that of Maupassant or the de Goncourts.

Anticipative, too, is the vivid use of the "character" verb in the following sentence from **"The Enemies"**: "In her draughty kitchen Mrs. Owen grieved over the soup."

It is small points such as these that look forward to the pincer-like perception which we get in, say, **"A Story"** (1953): "The charabanc pulled up outside the Mountain Sheep, a small, unhappy public house with a thatched roof like a wig with ringworm."

II

Among other stories by Thomas which appeared about this time was one he contributed to *The New Apocalypse* (1939), a symposium of young writers. As this tale **"The Burning Baby"** was one which a number of people noticed, and as the group behind the anthology largely used the name and work of Thomas as sponsor and touchstone of their own movement, a few remarks may be devoted to it.

Revealing a greater flair for prose than any of the other tales in the volume, it has all the turgid morbidity—the pangs, and fits, and starts of a histrionic vision—which the work of the group as a whole displayed:

> They said that Rhys was burning his baby when a gorse bush broke into fire on the summit of the hill.

Spasmodically, though, the story manifests the inception of fresh prose qualities. There is the beginning of that humour which plays so large a part in Thomas' later stories. As yet, it shows itself concerned with obscene features or symptoms of decay—a kind of joyless Rabelaisianism:

> He took his daughter's hand as she lay in the garden hammock, and told her that he loved her. He told her that she was more beautiful than her dead mother. Her hair smelt of mice, her teeth came over her lip, and the lids of her eyes were red and wet.

or

> Rhys Rhys sat in his study, the stem of his pipe stuck between his fly-buttons, the bible unopened on his knees.

or consider the sadism of the tale's last paragraph:

> And the baby caught fire. The flames curled round its mouth and blew upon the shrinking gums. Flame round its red cord lapped its little belly till the raw flesh fell upon the heather. A flame touched its tongue. Eeeeeh, cried the burning baby, and the illuminated hill replied.

Judged as a Gothic extravaganza in the manner of Matthew Lewis' *The Monk,* **"The Burning Baby"** must be said to succeed; but success in so specious a category as this is no solid proof of literary distinction. . . .

The three chapters of Thomas' uncompleted novel *Adventures in the Skin Trade*[3] belongs to 1941, and later; and so represent more recent work than the stories in his book *Portrait of the Artist as a Young Dog* which was first published in 1940. I prefer, however, to take the former first,

since, genuinely entertaining as these chapters are, they do not display the 'vintage' qualities present in the earlier volume.

Adventures in the Skin Trade is an amusing fragment—a prologue to a sort of picaresque novel, in which the hero is a young provincial who entrains for London to seek for fame and women. Reading it, I was reminded of how Henry Miller said he went to Paris "to study vice". The twenty-year-old Samuel Bennet of the *Adventures* resorts to the metropolis for much the same purpose; but in the author's account of his quest there is none of that "dead-pan" earnestness of Miller, for whom the affairs of sex, one feels, are a Germanic substitute for philosophy. His adolescent aspirations of a somewhat disreputable nature are described with buoyancy, with a sympathetic spiritedness which does not exclude fun at the hero's expense. In fact, the wishes of the young poet (Samuel Bennet is clearly an alias for Thomas) to be thought a practised whoremonger, when he is as virgin as makes no difference, are mercilessly made the most of. Leering at a woman in the buffet at Paddington whom he assumes to be a prostitute (she smells, he decides, "of eau de cologne and powder and bed"), he succeeds only in being cold-shouldered, and in getting his little finger stuck in the neck of a Bass bottle. Befriended by an odd furniture-dealer, he is taken to a near by café, where a plain nymphomaniac with glasses escorts him upstairs to the bathroom to ease the bottle from his finger with soap. She finally gets him naked in the bath, makes him drink a glassful of Cologne, and then climbs in on top of him[4]. When he regains his mental composure, he sees the furniture-dealer and a friend standing by the bath considering him: the bottle is still on his little finger.

Shivering in the unwarmed water of the bath, as he waits in the darkened room for the girl to step in with him, the young man's thoughts are taken up, half with the natural fears of his situation and half with revenging himself on the far suburb that bore him:

> Come and have a look at impotent Samuel Bennet from Mortimer Street off Stanley's Grove trembling to death in a cold bath in the dark near Paddington Station.

The earlier part of this fragmentary novel describes the young man leaving home and his journey up in the train. During the night before his departure he creeps downstairs and does a lot of damage so that he can "never come back". He draws rude shapes on his father's papers, tears up the family photos, and breaks his mother's best china:

> A tureen cover dropped from his hand and smashed.

> He waited for the sound of his mother waking. No one stirred upstairs. 'Tinker did it', he said aloud [Tinker is the family pom], but the harsh noise of his voice drove him back into silence.

The gestures, the poses, the unconscious humour, and the grief of late adolescence are all here:

He burnt the edge of his mother's sunshade at the gas mantle, and felt the tears running down his cheeks and dropping on to his pyjama collar. Even in the moment of his guilt and shame, he remembered to put out his tongue and taste the track of his tears. Still crying, he said, "It's salt. It's very salt. Just like in my poems."

Sitting in the lavatory in the London train, he completes the process of burning his boats which he began earlier at home. From his note-book he tears out and destroys the names and addresses of people he can use as introductions to publishers and editors, leaving only the name and phone-number of a street-girl he has never met.

One sees that Samuel Bennet is quite set on "doing the Rimbaud" (as Thomas so well expresses it elsewhere); but unlike the French poet or his fictional counter-parts (Lafcadio, say, in André Gide's novel *Les Caves du Vatican*), there is no innocent belief behind this young man in a 'pure' cult of evil. Samuel Bennet would, no doubt, like to be wicked, and tries very hard to be so; but his youth and experience keep changing his audacities into bathos. It is this maturity of mind in Thomas, at back of his hatred of convention, which preserves a sense of proportion in its most corrective form: self-critical humour.

Since I have spoken in this high fashion of *Adventures in the Skin Trade,* and yet suggested that we shall not find the 'vintage' prose of Thomas here, it behoves me to give my reasons. The lack resides, I think, in his character-drawing. Samuel Bennet, his parents, and sister are well shown; but the off-setting group of bohemian figures, which the young man encounters in London, are rather too much to type. The character known as Mr. Allingham is something of an exception. A furniture-dealer who lives in a flat so fantastically crammed with his purchases that he has no room to turn round, and yet is furiously annoyed at the suggestion that the world is not sane, he has some of the Dickensian colour which Thomas gives to his later characters. On the other hand, the characters of George Ring (a poetry-loving pansy), Mrs. Dacey, and Polly have but small fetching likeness about them.

III

Portrait of the Artist as a Young Dog, a "touched-up" and thinly-veiled autobiography, consisting of ten stories, is a gem of humorous juvenile frankness. Allowing for its more disruptive plan, the book possesses a vivid truth similar to that of *Huckleberry Finn.* It has poetry, humour, psychological shrewdness, and an excellent swiftness in character-depiction.

In the description of farm-life and the country (see **"The Peaches"** and **"A Visit to Grandpa's"**) there are passages that prompt us to compare this aspect of Thomas with Alain-Fournier. Both have a like prose lyricism, and a kind of youthful nostalgia; but the Frenchman is more naively idealistic and sentimental than Thomas, and has not got his anodyne of humour.

Another comparison, or contrast perhaps, is to be found in the "William Brown" stories by Richmal Crompton. But the "I", the narrator in the *Portrait* (which commences with his adventures as a small child to the time when he becomes a junior reporter) begins where the popular figure leaves off. For the conventional "naughtiness" of William (smashing a pane of "old Jones'" green-house with his catapult or ball), Thomas substitutes a quite unbowdlerised catalogue of delinquencies:

> I let Edgar Reynolds be whipped because I had taken his homework; I stole from my mother's bag; I stole from Gwyneth's bag; I stole twelve books in three visits from the library, and threw them away in the park; I drank a cup of my water to see what it tasted like; I beat a dog with a stick so that it would roll over and lick my hand afterwards; I looked with Dan Jones through the keyhole while his maid had a bath; I cut my knee with a penknife, and put the blood on my handkerchief and said it had come out of my ears so that I could pretend I was ill and frighten my mother; I pulled my trousers down and showed Jack Williams; I saw Billy Jones beat a pigeon to death with a fire-shovel, and laughed and got sick; Cedric Williams and I broke into Mrs. Samuel's house and poured ink over the bedclothes.

In place of the young "doctored" protagonist—the prig disguised as a ragamuffin—which Richmal Crompton offers us, we have a real *enfant terrible,* a quite irrepressible junior Titan thirsting for the blood of all experience.

We see him, in **"Patricia, Edith and Arnold,"** playing-up the house-maid and listening to her talk; scrapping with a school-boy who becomes his best friend, and with whom he exchanges fantasies of future artistic greatness (in **"The Fight"**); pursuing, unsuccessfully, the caresses of school-girls (in **"Extraordinary Little Cough"**); getting drunk in the sailors' pubs as a "cub" reporter (in **"Old Garbo"**); and just missing a love-experience with a beautiful young street-walker (in **"One Warm Saturday"**).

But the various phases of growth through which the youthful hero passes are counter-parted, as it were, by the diversity of the book's other characters: foxy "Uncle Jim", in the course of trading his live-stock over the counter for liquor; cousin Gwilym, training for the ministry, who writes poems to actresses, practises his sermons from a cart in the barn, and masturbates himself in the farm privy while reading pornographic books; "Grandpa" who lights his pipe beneath the blankets, and sits up in bed driving imaginary horses; the drunk man who lost most of his posterior in a pit-accident (for which mischance he was awarded "Four and three! Two and three ha'pence a cheek"); the old begger who removes his cap and sets his hair on fire for a penny ("only a trick to amuse the boys", scornfully observes the young narrator)—these, and many others, vivify the *Portrait.*

And, in this book, we have proceeded from the half-mythical landscapes of *The Map of Love* to a real particularised Welsh world; not so compact and concentrated as that of Thomas' dramatic literature, yet still singularly present before the eyes. The optic nerve, on the watch for those individual splashes in the palette of local colour, vibrates finely in these stories:

> The rain had stopped and High Street shone. Walking on the tram-lines, a neat man held his banner high and prominently feared the Lord.

> **("Old Garbo")**

In all, this book evinces a closer direction of language over and above that of the first short stories. The elimination of marginal terms—of words that do not hit the bull's-eye of their object—is apparent if we take a passage from both books. Here is a specimen from *The Map of Love*:

> But there had been no woman in his dream. Not even a thread of a woman's hair had dangled from the sky. God had come down in a cloud and the cloud had changed to a snake's nest. Foul hissing of snakes had suggested the sound of water, and he had been drowned. Down and down he had fallen, under green shiftings and the bubbles that fishes blew from their mouths, down and down on to the bony floors of the sea.

> **("The Mouse and The Woman")**

and here a passage from the *Portrait*:

> Night was properly down on us now. The wind changed. Thin rain began. The sands themselves went out. We stood in the scooped, windy room of the arch, listening to the noises from the muffled town, a goods train shunting, a siren in the docks, the hoarse trams in the streets far behind, one bark of a dog, unplaceable sounds, iron being beaten, the distant creaking of wood, doors slamming from where there were no houses, an engine coughing like a sheep on a hill.

> **("Just like little dogs")**

How subtly, and truly, the words "unplaceable sounds" have been inserted in this exact catalogue of auditory impressions! Without them, the precision would have been unreal.

But the whittling accuracy of Thomas' thought behind his choice of terms is best demonstrated in the placing of one word:

> Uncle Jim [seated in his trap], in his black market suit with a stiff white shirt and no collar, loud new boots, and a plaid cap, creaked and climbed down.

Another author might well have written, ". . . climbed down, creaking", thus losing the exact connotation. The creaking preceded the climbing down, and was not simultaneous with it—the sound being caused by "Uncle Jim's" preliminary movements as he raised himself from a sitting position. With the one particular verb, in its particular place, Thomas conveys this straightaway.

Since the *Portrait* Thomas wrote a number of other stories and sketches in which the evocative use of language and the condensing of impressions were further developed. . . .

Notes

1. Because the poet felt both attraction and repulsion for the teaching of the Church, it is hard to say how far such a story as this is "anti-Christian" in intention. Indeed, the sympathy of the poet is clearly with the Christ-idiot figure, who is made to greet the boy as "Brother" as the wire cuts into his wrists. But the tale affects me as a travesty—a grim pathetic travesty, which replaces the story of the Crucifixion with a myth in which both parties are imbecilic.

2. Because of my low estimation of the tales in *The Map of Love,* I think it only fair to remark that the fine short-storyist Glyn Jones considers "The Dress" to be "one of the most beautiful of modern short stories."

3. Chapter one first appeared in *Folios of New Writing* no. 5 (Autumn, 1941); Chapters one and two (with the first section of Chapter one missing) in *Adam* no. 238 (1953); and Chapters one and two complete in *New World Writing* no. 2 (U.S.A.).

4. It is hard to say what, if anything, takes place. Indeed, from the story it is by no means certain that the girl *does* climb in. Perhaps this was part of Thomas' joke (on the basis of one type of *risqué* story which follows suspense with an anticlimax.)

John Ackerman (essay date 1964)

SOURCE: "A Prose Interlude: The Early Stories," in *Dylan Thomas: His Life and Work,* Oxford University Press, 1964, pp. 90-103.

[*In the following excerpt, Ackerman compares the themes and use of language in Thomas's early short stories, written between 1934 and 1939, to those of his early poetry.*]

Thomas's prose is essentially a poet's prose—eloquent, sensuous, strongly rhythmic, and rich in metaphor. It shares the usual Anglo-Welsh attitudes: it is nostalgic, impassioned, personal, and apocalyptic. The writing draws much upon Biblical thought and imagery, and childhood is a dominant theme. Its style owes much to Welsh pulpit oratory and, for its full subtlety, must be read aloud. Sometimes, it must be admitted, the magic of the word and the emotions of the author get the better of the sense.

This chapter considers the early stories written between 1934 and 1939, which differ significantly from the stories in *Portrait of the Artist as a Young Dog.* In both theme and technique these early stories are closely related to the early poetry. It seem that Thomas had, at this stage, yet to discover the dividing line between prose and poetry. The stories are introspective and subjective to an unusual degree, and only occasionally do they possess a dramatic form. **"After the Fair,"** probably the first story that Thomas wrote, has an unusually clear narrative outline. It begins:

The fair was over, the lights in the coco-nut stalls were put out, and the wooden horses stood still in the darkness, waiting for the music and the hum of the machines that would set them trotting forward. One by one, in every booth, the naphtha jets were turned down and the canvases pulled over the little gaming tables. The crowd went home, and there were lights in the windows of the caravans.

The story opens poignantly, with the closing of the fair, and the central character is a young girl who has left home:

Nobody had noticed the girl. In her black clothes she stood against the side of the roundabouts, hearing the last feet tread upon the sawdust and the last voices die in the distance. Then, all alone on the deserted ground, surrounded by the shapes of wooden horses and cheap fairy boats, she looked for a place to sleep. Now here and now there, she raised the canvas that shrouded the coco-nut stalls and peered into the warm darkness. . . . Once she stepped on the boards; the bells round a horse's throat jingled and were still; she did not dare breathe again until all was quiet and the darkness had forgotten the noise of the bells. . . . But there was nowhere, nowhere in all the fair for her to sleep.

The prose is lucid and musical. At the close of the story the girl, together with the Fat Man she has made friends with and a baby she tries to comfort, are described fantastically and irrationally riding, in the night, the speeding roundabout:

As the roundabout started, slowly at first and slowly gaining speed, the child at the girl's breast stopped crying and clapped its hands. The night wind tore through its hair, the music jangled in its ears. Round and round the wooden horses sped, drowning the cries of the wind with the beating of their hooves.

And so the men from the caravans found them, the Fat Man and the girl in black with a baby in her arms, racing round and round on their mechanical steeds to the ever-increasing music of the organ.

In his early stories Thomas often tends to move from realism to fantasy, from a disciplined handling of experience to a freer registering of emotions. **"A Prospect of the Sea"** is a further illustration of this. It opens in a style characteristic of Anglo-Welsh prose at its best:

It was high summer, and the boy was lying in the corn. He was happy because he had no work to do and the weather was hot. He heard the corn sway from side to side above him, and the noise of the birds who whistled from the branches of the trees that hid the house. Lying flat on his back, he stared up into the unbrokenly blue sky falling over the edge of the corn. The wind, after the warm rain before noon, smelt of rabbits and cattle. He stretched himself like a cat, and put his arms behind his head. Now he was riding on the sea, swimming through the golden corn waves, gliding along the heavens like a bird; in sevenleague boots he was springing over the fields; he was building a nest in the sixth of the seven trees that waved their hands from a bright, green hill.

The imagery is poetic ('the unbrokenly blue sky falling over the edge of the corn'), and the forms of natural life are blurred by a derangement of the senses ('swimming through the golden corn waves', 'trees that waved their hands').

Now he was a boy with tousled hair, rising lazily to his feet, wandering out of the corn to the strip of river by the hillside. He put his fingers in the water, making a mock sea-wave to roll the stones over and shake the weeds; his fingers stood up like ten tower pillars in the magnifying water, and a fish with a wise head and a lashing tail swam in and out of the tower gates. He made up a story as the fish swam through gates into the pebbles and the moving bed.

This is a communication of sensory experience, remarkable for its originality of perception. A little later in the story there is a typically Anglo-Welsh celebration of natural life:

The boy sent a stone skidding over the green water. He saw a rabbit scuttle, and threw a stone at its tail. A fish leaped at the gnats, and a lark darted out of the green earth. This was the best summer since the first seasons of the world. He did not believe in God, but God had made this summer full of blue winds and heat and pigeons in the house wood. There were no chimneys on the hills with no name in the distance, only the trees which stood like women and men enjoying the sun; there were no cranes or coal-tips, only the nameless distance and the hill with seven trees. He could think of no words to say how wonderful the summer was, or the noise of the wood-pigeons, or the lazy corn blowing in the half wind from the sea at the river's end. There were no words for the sky and the sun and the summer country.

Clearly Thomas has in mind the first splendour of creation. His description moves to an ecstatic idealization of the countryside of youth in which the chimneys, cranes, and coal-tips of industrial Swansea have no place. The landscape is witnessed in a vision: it is a summer country.

Towards the close of the story, as the poet describes the dying of the afternoon, again there is a tendency to blur the outlines of experience:

The afternoon was dying; lazily, namelessly drifting westward through the insects in the shade; over hill and tree and river and corn and grass to the evening shaping in the sea; blowing away; being blown from Wales in a wind, in the slow, blue grains, like a wind full of dreams and medicines; down the tide of the sun on to the grey and chanting shore where the birds from Noah's ark glide by with bushes in their mouths, and to-morrow and to-morrow tower over the cracked sandcastles.

The reference to Noah's ark is important, for the story ends on an apocalyptic, religious note, recalling Vernon Watkins's observation that Thomas's 'early stories explored the relation between immediate reality and archetypal symbols':

A raven flew by him, out of a window in the Flood to the blind, wind tower shaking in to-morrow's anger like a scarecrow made out of weathers.

'Once upon a time,' said the water voice.

'Do not adventure any more,' said the echo.

'She is ringing a bell for you in the sea.'

'I am the owl and the echo: you shall never go back.'

On a hill to the horizon stood an old man building a boat, and the light that slanted from the sea cast the holy mountain of a shadow over the three-storied decks and the Eastern timber. And through the sky, out of the beds and gardens, down the white precipice built of feathers, the loud combs and mounds, from the caves in the hill, the cloudy shapes of birds and beasts and insects drifted into the hewn door. A dove with a green petal followed in the raven's flight. Cool rain began to fall.

Such prose is very close to the style of Thomas's poems. There is little narrative outline and much of its meaning is implicit in the associations of the words, the strong rhythmic compulsion, and the sensory power of the language. The passage suggests the sacramental unity of all life, a unity that is outside time. This is the same creation, the same hope of regeneration as in the original story of the Flood. Contemporary life is interpreted in the light of traditional Christian mythology, and the dove and the raven are symbols, respectively, of redemption and regeneration ('with a green petal'), death and sin.

Another story which closely follows Old Testament mythology is **"The Tree,"** and here again the narrative outline is blurred at times. Its three characters—gardener, child, and idiot—possess a larger-than-life, primeval quality that recalls the work of Caradoc Evans. They inhabit a strange, impassioned world:

The gardener loved the Bible. When the sun sank and the garden was full of people, he would sit with a candle in his shed, reading of the first love and the legend of apples and serpents. But the death of Christ on the tree he loved most. . . . He would sit in his shed and read of the crucifixion, looking over the jars on his window-shelf into the winter nights. He would think that love fails on such nights, and that many of its children are cut down.

The gardener tells the child the Bible stories:

'Where is Bethlehem?'

'Far away,' said the gardener, 'in the East.'

To the east stood the Jarvis hills, hiding the sun, their trees drawing up the moon out of the grass.

The idiot is introduced in a manner reminiscent of Caradoc Evans's narrative style:

There was an idiot to the east of the country who walked the land like a beggar. Now at a farmhouse and now at a widow's cottage he begged for his bread.

Thomas suggests the idiot's innocence and holiness and the Welsh scene is identified with that of Christ's childhood:

'Bethlehem,' said the idiot to the valley, turning over the sounds of the word and giving it all the glory of the Welsh morning. He brothered the world around him, sipped at the air, as a child newly born sips and brothers the light. The life of the Jarvis valley, steaming up from the body of the grass and the trees and the long hand of the stream, lent him a new blood. Night had emptied the idiot's veins, and dawn in the valley filled them again.

'Bethlehem,' said the idiot to the valley.

There is a poet's delight in the sound of the word. It is significant that Thomas identifies the life of the idiot with the natural life around him ('He brothered the world around him'). On Christmas morning the idiot walked into the garden:

'Let me be,' said the idiot, and made a little gesture against the sky. There is rain on my face, there is wind on my cheeks. He brothered the rain.

So the child found him under the shelter of the tree, bearing the torture of the weather with a divine patience, letting his long hair blow where it would, with his mouth set in a sad smile. . . .

'Where do you come from?' asked the child.

'From the east,' answered the idiot.

The story moves to an apocalyptic, dramatic finish in which the biblical past superimposes its image on the present:

'Stand up against the tree.'

The idiot, still smiling, stood up with his back to the elder.

'Put out your arms like this.'

The idiot put out his arms.

The child ran as fast he could to the gardener's shed, and, returning over the sodden lawns, saw that the idiot had not moved but stood, straight and smiling, with his back to the tree and his arms stretched out.

'Let me tie your hands.'

The idiot felt the wire that had not mended the rake close round his wrists. It cut into the flesh, and the blood from the cuts fell shining on to the tree.

'Brother,' he said. He saw that the child held silver nails in the palm of his hands.

In this story biblical narrative has been interpreted in modern and personal terms, as in Thomas's early poetry. His idiot is in the romantic tradition of Wordsworth's idiot boy.

Some of the stories draw upon the magical, mystical, and primitive elements in Welsh folk-lore, and Thomas works out his violent themes of sin and death, revenge and redemption against a heavily coloured, almost Old Testament background. In his story **"The Enemies"** Mr. and Mrs. Owen emerge as vital, life-giving forces in a valley that is seen as primeval and barren:

> Up came the roots, and a crooked worm, disturbed by the probing fingers, wriggled blind in the sun. Of a sudden the valley filled all its hollows with the wind, with the voice of the roots, with the breathing of the nether sky. Not only a mandrake screams; torn roots have their cries; each weed Mr. Owen pulled out of the ground screamed like a baby. In the village behind the hill the wind would be raging, the clothes on the garden lines would be set to strange dances. And women with shapes in their wombs would feel a new knocking as they bent over the steamy tubs. Life would go on in the veins, in the bones, the binding flesh, that had their seasons and their weathers even as the valley binding the house about with the flesh of the green grass.

There is a similar perception of the germination of natural life, and of empathy with natural life, in the writing of Margiad Evans:

> Sifting the golden hazel and dark copper willow leaves, I saw and touched the earth. . . . It smelt of fermenting juices. Touching it I felt its clinging, living coldness mounting the veins of my arm, drawing me down into it. Under the dead bracken, the ivy, the celandine, and fox-glove it lay, lapping minute birth, minute decay. I saw the berry's kernel, the emptied broken nutshell, the flex of the shrivelled grass root like a nerve exposed.

The visitor to the valley in Thomas's story is old, afraid of death, and unable to accept the life-process in the way that Mr. and Mrs. Owen, more primitive characters, have accepted it:

> 'He is frightened of the dark,' thought Mrs. Owen, 'the lovely dark.' With a smile, Mr. Owen thought: 'He is frightened of the worm in the earth, of the copulation in the tree, of the living grease in the soil.' They looked at the old man, and saw that he was more ghostly than ever. . . . Suddenly Mr. Davies knelt down to pray. . . . He stared and he prayed, like an old god beset by his enemies.

Both Thomas's poetry and prose attempt to define similar modes of thought and feeling, and such sentences and phrases from these stories as 'felt desolation in his veins', 'desireless familiars', occur later in the poetry as 'Make desolation in the vein', 'A desireless familiar'.

These stories, to a greater extent than the poetry, owe something to surrealist techniques. Many of the unpublished stories are about lust, insanity, cruelty, and fear. They involve their author in a release of emotion, but whereas the surrealist creed encouraged merely the release of subconscious emotions, Thomas's interpretation of these emotions is essentially religious in character. T. S. Eliot has said that

Yeats's 'supernatural world' was the wrong supernatural world. It was not a world of spiritual significance, not a world of real Good and Evil, of holiness or sin, but a highly sophisticated lower mythology summoned, like a physician, to supply the fading pulse of poetry with some transient stimulant.

Unlike Yeats's supernatural world, the strange world of Thomas's stories is composed of Good and Evil—though, admittedly, the sense of evil tends to dominate.

Perhaps the most successful of these stories is **"The Burning Baby."** It is more dramatic in its emotions, more complex in its themes than the others, and it has a firmer narrative outline. I am indebted to Mr. Glyn Jones for information concerning the source of this story. On a visit to Aberystwyth to meet Caradoc Evans he told Dylan Thomas the story of Dr. Price of Llantrisant. The doctor, who died in 1893 at the age of ninety-three, defied in a most exhibitionist fashion the legal, religious, and moral conventions of his time. He called himself a druid and, on his public appearances, dressed in weird and highly-coloured costumes. He chanted pagan addresses to the moon and boasted of supernatural powers. His much-loved illegitimate son, whom he named Iesu Grist (Jesus Christ) and believed destined to recover the lost secrets of the druids, died at the age of five months. Price carried him to the top of a hill in Caerlan fields and, chanting wild laments over the body, burned it.

Thomas listened to this story lounging on his bed at their Aberystwyth hotel and by the end, Glyn Jones recalls, the bed-sheet was riddled with cigarette burns. Thomas's mind seized upon the incident of the child's cremation for **"The Burning Baby,"** which opens:

> They said that Rhys was burning his baby when a gorse bush broke into fire on the summit of the hill. The bush, burning merrily, assumed to them the sad white features and the rickety limbs of the vicar's burning baby. What the wind had not blown away of the baby's ashes, Rhys Rhys had sealed in a stone jar. With his own dust lay the baby's dust, and near him the dust of his daughter in a coffin of white wood.

In the second paragraph the vicar's elder son enters the story.

> They heard his son howl in the wind. They saw him walking over the hill, holding a dead animal up to the light of the stars. They saw him in the valley shadows as he moved, with the motion of a man cutting wheat, over the brows of the fields. In a sanatorium he coughed his lung into a basin, stirring his fingers delightedly in the blood. What moved with invisible scythe through the valley was a shadow and a handful of shadows cast by the grave sun.

One is reminded of Thomas's own tubercular symptoms. After these vigorous and dramatic paragraphs which set the scene, the narrative begins: 'It was, they said, on a fine sabbath morning in the middle of summer that Rhys Rhys fell in love with his daughter.' Thomas is morbidly obsessed with the corruption of the flesh:

> He moved his hand up and down her arm. Only the awkward and the ugly, only the barren bring forth fruit. The flesh of her arm was red with the smoothing of his hand. He touched her breast. From the touch of her breast he knew each inch of flesh upon her. Why do you touch me there? she said.

The vicar's son finds a dead rabbit and, as so often in these stories, a mutilated animal is used to release feelings of cruelty and horror.

> The rabbit's head was riddled with pellets, the dogs had torn open its belly, and the marks of a ferret's teeth were upon its throat. He lifted it gently up, tickling it behind the ears. The blood from its head dropped on his hand. Through the rip in the belly, its intestines had dropped out and coiled on the stone.

The boy is a changeling, an idiot, with long green hair. He, too, has been subject to strange sexual adventures, for his sister 'was to him as ugly as the sowfaced woman of Llareggub who had taught him the terrors of the flesh. He remembered the advances of that unlovely woman.' It is interesting to see the name Llareggub, that was to reappear as Llaregyb in *Under Milk Wood*, first coined in these stories of the mid-thirties. The earlier version is more suggestive of the word's etymology, a device employed also in Samuel Butler's title, *Erewhon*.

Rhys Rhys's daughter conceives a child by him, and it is this child which Rhys Rhys burns alive:

> Surrounded by shadows, he prayed before the flaming stack, and the sparks of the heather blew past his smile. Burn, child, poor flesh, mean flesh, flesh, flesh, sick sorry flesh, flesh of the foul womb, burn back to dust, he prayed.

Significantly, Thomas makes a minister of religion the central character in the story; as in such other tales of lechery, fear, and cruelty, as **"The Horse's Ha,"** **"The School for Witches,"** and **"The Holy Six."** Hypocrisy is the chief target of his ferocious satire:

> That night he preached of the sins of the flesh. O God in the image of our flesh, he prayed.

> His daughter sat in the front pew, and stroked her arm. She would have touched her breast where he had touched it, but the eyes of the congregation were upon her.

> Flesh, flesh, flesh, said the vicar.

The instinct to wound the Nonconformist clergy was as deeply rooted in Thomas as in Caradoc Evans. To attribute perverse desires to the religious and 'respectable' is a simple but effective method of attack, and Thomas is not slow to exploit its possibilities:

> Rhys Rhys sat in his study, the stem of his pipe stuck between his flybuttons, the bible unopened on his knees. The day of God was over, and the sun, like another sabbath, went down behind the hills. . . . Merry with desire, Rhys Rhys cast the bible on the floor. He reached for another book, and read, in the lamplit darkness, of the old woman who had deceived the devil. The devil is poor flesh, said Rhys Rhys.

The use of the Welsh background in the story **"The Holy Six"** is again imaginative rather than realistic. Thomas seeks to convey an atmosphere of primitive, sensual claustrophobia:

> The Holy Six of Wales sat in silence. The day was drawing to a close, and the heat of the first discussion grew cooler with the falling sun. All through the afternoon they had talked of nothing but the disappearance of the rector of Llareggub, and now, as the first lack of light moved in a visible shape and colour through the room, and their tongues were tired, and they heard the voices in their nerves, they waited only for the first darkness to set in. At the first signs of night they would step from the table, adjust their hats and smiles, and walk into the wicked streets. Where the women smiled under the lamps, and the promise of the old sickness stirred in the fingertips of the girls in the dark doorways, the Six would pass dreaming, to the scrape of their boots on the pavement, of the women throughout the town smiling and doctoring love. To Mr. Stul the women drifted in a maze of hair, and touched him in a raw place. The women drifted around Mr. Edger. He caught them close to him, holding their misty limbs to his with no love or fire. The women moved again, with the grace of cats, edging down the darker alleys where Mr. Vyne, envious of their slant-eyed beauty, would scrape and bow. To Mr. Rafe, their beauties, washed in blood, were enemies of the fluttering eyes, and moved, in what image they would, full-breasted, fur-footed, to a massacre of the flesh. He saw the red nails and trembled. There was no purpose in the shaping wombs but the death of the flesh they shaped, and he shrank from the contact of death, and the male nerve was pulled alone.

I have quoted at some length in order to indicate themes and technique that are typical of these stories. The Holy Six are at once clerical gentlemen and symbols of the same order as the mediaeval Seven Deadly Sins. The name Stul is an anagram of 'lust'; Edger of 'greed'; Vyne of 'envy'; and Rafe of 'fear'. In this paragraph Thomas suggests the various reactions of these characters towards sex: they are, respectively, reactions dominated by lust, greed, envy, and fear. Thus, to Mr. Rafe the women represent a 'massacre of the flesh': 'he saw the red nails and trembled'. For him 'the shaping wombs' meant 'the death of the flesh' and 'the male nerve was pulled alone'.

The link between these early stories and the early poetry is, very obviously, a fundamental one, both in theme and attitude. While **"The Holy Six"** deals with the subject of sexual man, **"The Horse's Ha"** is concerned with death in the form of a plague which enters a town. Again the language closely resembles that of the early poems, not least in its Biblical echoes:

> What is death's music? One note or many? The chord of contagion? Thus questioned the undertaker, the cup

three-quarters empty in his gloved hand. He who marks the sparrow's fall has no time for my birds, said ApLlewellyn. What music is death? . . .

So Mr. Montgomery was left alone, by the desolate church, under a disappearing moon. One by one the stars went out, leaving a hole in heaven. He looked upon the grave, and slowly removed his coat.

The emotional and moral attitudes behind such writing are conditioned by an essentially religious view of experience.

Thomas's early stories are essentially a by-product of his poetry. Their obsession with sexual themes, with cruelty, with death and decay has, in its total possession of the personality, something adolescent about it. The prose is distinguished more by its intense sensual power than by its subtlety. In the main tradition of Anglo-Welsh prose-writing Thomas aims at an imaginative—rather than a realistic—recreation of sensory experience, and packs his language with metaphor. He well understood what Rimbaud called 'the Alchemy of the word'. The stories, however, remain obsessively personal. They are solipsistic: each story brings the reader back to Thomas's own emotional conflicts, fears, and desires. They are imaginative projections of his own intuitions and feelings, bearing little relationship with the everyday, external world. He is hardly concerned with human relationships at all, for his interest in human life is essentially personal and isolated. He writes of the facts of love, death, happiness, and sorrow as they confront individual man. His concern with experience is not social but personal, not psychological but religious. The tales have the intensity and strangeness, in their wildest moments, of nightmare: and that nightmare, that phantasmagoria of images and perceptions, is offered as reality.

I have already suggested that Thomas was quick to draw upon the more arcane fantasies that the Welsh background and Welsh folk-lore presented to him. It is interesting to see, too, that in his stories, he usually put Welsh names in the final draft: thus, in **"The Visitor,"** the name Millicent was changed to Rhiannon; and in **"The Orchards"** the name Peter becomes—significantly—Marlais. **"The Orchards"** is a very personal piece, revealing something of Thomas's attitude to himself as a poet and his tendency to be overcome by the welter and conflict of his experience:

> The word is too much with us. He raised his pencil so that its shadow fell, a tower of wood and lead, on the clean paper. . . . The tower fell, down fell the city of words, the walls of a poem, the symmetrical letters. . . . 'Image, all image,' he cried to the fallen tower as the night came on. 'Whose harp is the sea? Whose burning candle is the sun?' An image of man, he rose to his feet and drew the curtains open. Peace, like a simile, lay over the roofs of the town. 'Image, all image,' cried Marlais, stepping through the window on to the level roofs. . . . He was a folk-man no longer but Marlais the poet walking, over the brink into ruin, up the side of doom, over hell in bed to the red left, till

he reached the first of fields where the unhatched apples were soon to cry fire in a wind from a half-mountain falling westward to the sea.

The impact on the poet of the town which he can see below him, of the nearby country and the sea, is through word and image. The conflict, in his mind, between the reality of the world before him and the reality of the word, is an ever-present one. These early stories present a poetic vision of adolescence and early manhood, with all the beauty and intensity, doubts and fears of that age of self-discovery.

Donald Tritschler (essay date 1971)

SOURCE: "The Stories in Dylan Thomas' *Red Notebook*," in *Journal of Modern Literature,* Vol. 2, No. 1, September, 1971, pp. 33–56.

[*In the excerpt below, Tritschler analyzes the changes made prior to the publication of the stories in* Red Notebook, *including the then unpublished "Gaspar, Melchior, Balthasar."*]

Dylan Thomas filled at least four copybooks with poetry and one, the **Red Notebook,**[1] with short stories by the time he was twenty. Though he had also written juvenilia that his mother carefully preserved,[2] these five notebooks contain early and late versions of most of his published poems and nine of his published short stories. Ralph Maud's publication of the four poetry copybooks,[3] which were nearly finished when Thomas began the **Red Notebook,** shows that he had already explored most of his major themes.

The ten **Notebook** stories likewise contain comparisons of divine, human and artistic creation and Thomas' obsessive paradox of creation as a destruction. They focus his sense of mankind's loss of innocence and love and the attendant ubiquity of evil and death in the world, and they present his criticism of the weak Christian religious practice that is unable to resolve the struggles of spirit and flesh. At least one of the stories was part of Thomas' first attempt to write a full-length novel. All of them seem to lie midway between the early poems and the later, more elaborate ones, perhaps because the time of composition was usually slightly later than most of the early poems, or because the short story form is roomier than the brief lyric and it obviously approaches the ideal of narrative that Thomas sought in his later poetry.

The **Notebook** itself is most interesting as a workbook. Several illuminating jottings, tables of contents and lists on the inside cover and on some of the final pages throw light on Thomas' publishing plans.[4] And because only one of the stories transcribed into it is unpublished, the differences between the **Notebook** and the published versions reveal much about Thomas' working methods and about the significance of the stories.

The first story, **"The Tree"** ("Finished December 28, 1933"), is included in each of the five tables of contents that are listed on the inside cover and the seven end pages of the *Red Notebook*. Its garden setting recalls the Creation—the gardener "knew every story from the beginning of the world"[5]—and the child's insistence on the specifics of the biblical stories leads him to recreate the Crucifixion. The boy's nature is imaginative and destructive, and his point of view, which can transform the lawn into a sea, the bushes into islands, birds into satanic omens, and the gardener into either a sinister figure or an "apostle," controls the structure of the story. The gardener himself views the biblical stories he tells the boy as examples of life and love in the earth. He is attuned to nature, a kind of minor deity of the microcosmic life in the garden, which is surrounded by the macrocosm of the Jarvis hills and the world they imply. He is aware of the fallen state of this world ("his god grew up like a tree from the apple-shaped earth"[6]), and he tells the boy, "God grows in strange trees" (p. 103). As a pantheist, he says, "Pray to a tree, *thinking of* Calvary and Eden" (p. 102—italics mine).

In this exchange, however, the boy insists the tree in their garden, that he sees as the one tree free of snow, is "the first tree," but the gardener politely overlooks his presumption by saying, "The elder is as good as another" (p. 103). The *Red Notebook* presented this as prudence: a star burned above the tree and the gardener would not confide in the stars of his god-infested world (p. 6a). In both versions the gardener attempts to repair the tines of the rake with a wire, and the boy suddenly sees him as sinister. Then he notices the gardener's pure white beard and sees him as an apostle telling of the stages of the cross. While the boy listens, he sees the noon shadows as blood staining the bark of the elder, in their garden. The tree stands as the Tree of Life at the beginning of the story and becomes the Cross of Calvary at the end.

The transformations of this tree trace the growth of metaphor in the boy's mind. When the gardener compares the tree to the Tree in the Garden, the boy extends the analogy to include Satan's entrance into Eden by interpreting a blackbird in the tree as "a monstrous hawk perched on a bough or an eagle swinging in the wind."[7] After hearing of Bethlehem and confusing it with the Jarvis hills to the east, the boy falls into a cavernous sleep, in which he dreams of descending among the "shadows" of the house (corrected from the more explicit "shades,"—p. 4a). After this descent into an underworld, he dreams of stepping into his own deceptive garden and of seeing his tree illuminated by a star burning brightly over it. The tree resembles a woman with frozen "arms" that bend "as to his touch," and now he kneels on its "blackened twigs" to pray (p. 100); "then, trembling with love *and* cold" (101—italics mine), he returns to the house. The other aspect of "the illuminated tree" is evident when it appears leafless and black— deathly.

Into this ambiguous setting the idiot enters on Christmas day, after the boy sees the star above the tree. When the idiot begs for water, his goodness is so evident that the people give him milk. When he simply says he is from the east, they trust him (p. 101). The next montage shot of the idiot shows him looking into the "immaculate" Jarvis valley. He hungers for light, which he tastes in the green life of the grass (p. 103). He is a brother to all things of the world, and he restores light to it; he believes he is entering Bethlehem as he answers the call of the world's voices in the Jarvis valley. The final episode of Christmas morning compares the idiot to Christ in His passion, which was included in the gardener's stories. He prays in the garden. Then its shapes seem hostile. The wind threatens, "raising a Jewish voice out of the elder boughs," and a voice within the idiot asks why he was brought here, somewhat as Christ momentarily seemed to question God. When the boy finds him, he shows "divine patience" (p. 106), even as the boy wires his arms to the limbs of the tree and prepares to nail him to it. The use of the wire shows what the naïve boy has learned from his own sinister vision of the gardener repairing the rake; the child's insistence on the specifics of the gardener's stories has finally led him to the crucifixion of innocence and love. Though the parallels to the life of Christ are sketchy—the "birth" and crucifixion both occur on Christmas day—they provide a context in which the latent evil of an "apple-shaped earth" can work through a naïve boy to murder innocence. The juxtaposition of the "birth" and crucifixion points one more ironic comment at the excesses of man's religious zeal.

The revisions of the *Red Notebook* version for publication are mainly routine retouches. There is almost no rearrangement, but many incidental changes reduce wordiness, and especially remove irrelevance and vagueness. Verbs are often strengthened by modifiers or by substitution of more vivid words ("he bent" for "he went"). Thomas is usually more specific in the final version—"apples and serpents" (p. 98) replaces "the first sin" (p. 2b)—and he is thereby more expressive, as in the replacement of "a darkness" by the more womby "spinning cavern" (p. 99). Another type of revision is the temperance of extravagant words ("rushing" of the sap instead of "roaring"—p. 98) and the removal of many examples of pathetic fallacy. Nevertheless, though the tower no longer "gave a benediction" (p. 8a), nature is animated in order to stress the force of life in the world that creates and cuts down its innocent children of love (p. 98).

While **"The Tree"** contains oblique references to Christ, the next story in the *Red Notebook,* **"The True Story"** (January 22, 1934), mentions various earthly visits to show its protagonist's naïveté: Martha is proud of her reading, and she vaguely recalls the stories of Zeus and Danaë, Satan's temptation of Eve, and Moses receiving God's commands from "a thing of fire" (p. 259). She thinks immediately of the dog she killed and buried under the manure at the end of the garden. That she wrote the epitaph and date backwards suggests "dog" is an inversion of *god*.[8] Surely her service to the old woman is mistaken. Like the biblical Martha, she selfishly makes it unthinking busywork, rather than service to her patient's being.[9] At the end of her reveries, in which she has plotted the old woman's death, she characteristically parodies the burial service with "in the midst of death. . . ." (p. 260).

During the exposition of the dull routine of service that Martha inherited from her mother, Martha associates the picking of currants with the money under the old woman's mattress. The next association is with the blood on her hands from chickens she has freshly killed. The first paragraph to focus on the present shows Martha's obsession with the fortune during this spring (which like Martha is "the undoer of winter,"—11a) of her twentieth year. In the manuscript Thomas emphasized "blood money," which stained in the same way the currants did (p. 10b). He may have removed this emphasis from the final version to avoid divulging the conclusion too quickly. Martha was surely more cold-blooded in the manuscript because her decision to murder was stated flatly and repeatedly. The published version startles the reader with her wish to fly in the window and suck the old woman's blood, her life's substance. The surprises that follow not only intensify the dreadful action, but the structure conveys the lack of values or feeling Martha's isolation fostered. The unfeeling combination of "One o'clock now, she said, and knocked the old woman's head against the wall"[10] renders her fatal naïveté exactly.

The plot of **"After the Fair"** (November 19, 1933) is simpler than those of the first two *Red Notebook* stories, and while their motivation is amoral, this plot develops from human kindness. The prospective tables of contents and Thomas' collections of his works he jotted in the *Notebook* show he did not think this one of his most important stories. Nor does he seem to have labored over it as much as he did some of the other stories because the manuscript version contains only a few, superficial, textual changes. The Fat Man's idea that the baby in the Astrologer's tent comes from looking at the stars is both humorous and significant; the girl's selection of the Fat Man to help her care for the baby, the policeman looking for her, and their soothing of the baby by riding a merry-go-round may suggest a flight into Egypt, but little is done with the parallel. **"The Enemies"** (Feb. 11. 1934), on the other hand, takes the reader to the strange heart of Thomas' mysterious Welsh valley.

The setting for Mr. and Mrs. Owen's cottage in the center of the Jarvis hills gives them a kind of proprietary interest—they came from their village to this isolated valley and fenced out the domestic cattle that grazed in it. Their valley has its special, hyperbolic identity: as Mr. Owen weeds, the descriptions of his garden and the surrounding hills suggest wars and oracles that are more human than vegetable. The grasses have heads and mouths (p. 90), and the green grass is flesh (p. 91). Mrs. Annis Pratt finds this valley in the heart of the fabulous Jarvis hills comparable to the immortal island of Welsh folklore, which she in turn relates to the personal mythology of initiation in **"The Map of Love"** and other stories.[11] In **"The Enemies,"** Reverend Davies is about to undergo an infernal initiation as he loses his way in this "wide world rocking from horizon to horizon" and comes upon a cottage that might have "been carried out of a village by a large bird and placed in the very middle of the tumultuous universe" (p. 92).

Such tumult fills the beginning of the story with images of separation—the bird from his mate and the valley by its stream (p. 89)—and it culminates in the dichotomy of flesh and spirit represented by Mr. and Mrs. Owen. Mr. Owen presides over the rise and fall of life in the garden (p. 90). He is a young, bearded Pan, lord of the concrete things of life, "of the worm in the earth, of the copulation in the tree, of the living grease in the soil" (p. 96). He cannot quite take Mrs. Owen's powers seriously, for they are intangible, dark powers from the other world. Her crystal ball gives up its dead like a grave; it is one of the abstractions, such as the sound of the wind and the shadow on the tablecloth, that indirectly reveal the nature of the world to her (p. 95). She resembles Mr. Owen only in that they both have superhuman powers and her strange, green eyes recall the green grass of his garden.

This dynamic, pagan world opposes Reverend Davies' pallid, Christian world. Mrs. Owen loves the dark that so frightens Mr. Davies. The old man loses his way in his own, dead world and enters their domain, where he senses both their conflicting forces as the hills seem to "storm" the sky and darkness gives him no comfort from the wind (p. 91). His black, clerical hat is replaced by a cloud as he moves out of Mrs. Owen's ball and into the fleshly valley of Mr. Owen, and while the rocks of the valley draw human blood from him, he becomes a shape among the stars in Mrs. Owen's crystal. In contrast to his powerful enemies, Mr. Davies is a white-haired phantom whose light is absorbed by Mrs. Owen's darkness—the world "had given under his feet" (p. 95).

Though the action is relatively static, the tense confrontation of enemies is a lyric poet's tableau of a world suffering the timeless clash of opposites. The clash of flesh and spirit in Mr. and Mrs. Owen, with all its related imagery mentioned briefly above, is complemented in another dimension: the clash of the Owens' pagan concentration on life and Mr. Davies' Christian preparation for death, as represented by dark and light imagery and other details. Mr. Davies reaches toward a blessed state in this clockless, roaring world, but his saintliness ambiguously emerges as a "ragged circle of light round his head" (p. 96). He is finally an insubstantial, ineffective "old god beset by his enemies" in the house of the proud flesh and the evil spirit.

Mrs. Owen's evil shows much more explicitly in **"The Holy Six,"** the sequel to **"The Enemies."** There she merges with *Miss* Myfanwy, as "Amabel Mary" (p. 203), and is pregnant with the fleshly child of Mr. Owen, though about to give virgin birth to the spiritual child of Mr. Davies. Apparently the child is the seventh and greatest sin, which is surrounded by the six sins that arrived at the Jarvis valley when Love's (Mr. Vole's) cart wrecked; their names are given as anagrams of lust, greed, envy, fear, cruelty and spite. In both stories the vitality of the world is too much for the ghostly Mr. Davies, and in the second one he takes his place among them. A weak god fails in this world, the house of sins.

Though **"The Holy Six"** unites the characters of **"The Enemies"** in a circle of sin, it is probably a different story from **"The Enemies United"** because both titles appear in two of the lists in the *Red Notebook.* (See note 4.) If **"The Enemies United"** was a third story about these characters, Thomas had written more of his short novel, *A Doom on the Sun,* than has been discovered. The phrase for this title first appeared in "Find meat on bones," for which the Lockwood library has a manuscript including corrections, dated July 15, 1933 and January, 1936. The earliest record of the projected novel was in a letter to Pamela Hansford Johnson on 2 May, 1934: "My novel—I've done the first chapter—will be, when and if I finish it, no more than the hotchpotch of a strayed poet, or the linking together of several short story sequences. I shall scrap it in a few days." He had just received a telegram from *New Stories* accepting **"The Enemies"** for publication, but the news was a mixed pleasure because they paid nothing for it. He had also transcribed into the *Red Notebook* two other stories, **"The Tree"** and **"The Visitors,"** which are explicitly set in the Jarvis hills.

Nine days later he wrote to Miss Johnson, "My novel of the Jarvis valley is slower than ever. I have already scrapped two chapters of it. It is as ambitious as the *Divine Comedy,* with a chorus of deadly sins, anagrammatized as old gentlemen, with the incarnated figures of Love & Death, an Ulyssean page of thought from the minds of two anagrammatical spinsters, Miss P. & Miss R. Sion-Rees, an Immaculate Conception, a baldheaded girl, a celestial tramp, a mock Christ, & the Holy Ghost." The two chapters would seem to be **"The Tree"** and **"The Visitors** [April, 1934]," for the old gentlemen appear in **"The Holy Six."** Two days later Thomas was still struggling: "My novel, tentatively, very tentatively, titled *A Doom on the Sun* is progressing, three chapters of it already completed [**"The Enemies," "The Holy Six"** and, perhaps, **"The Enemies United"**?]. So far, it is rather terrible, a kind of warped fable in which lust, greed, cruelty, spite etc., appear all the time as old gentlemen in the background of the story. I wrote a little bit of it early this morning—a charming incident in which Mr. Stripe, Mr. Edger, Mr. Stull, Mr. Thade and Mr. Strich watch a dog dying of poison. I'm a nice little soul, and my book is going to be as nice as me." Apparently the novel was approaching the "lived happily ever after" stage when he scrapped it.[12]

The few revisions of **"The Enemies"** give it a story-teller's polish, but the infrequent revisions of **"The Dress"** (March, 1934), the next story in the *Red Notebook,* are often to its key passages. The madman's pursuers sound like hounds baying after him, and he flees their bestial, adult world to recover an innocent relationship. The *Red Notebook* stressed a relationship with the mother: "As the moon rose, milkily it put a coat around his shoulders . . ." (p. 22b), and after the wish for shelter and food, "The mist was a mother, but he needed more than a mother's care. . . . He thought of the young woman being [*sic*] over the pot. He thought of her hair." The relationship the madman desires with the world is larger than a mother's comfort, and the ending shows it is also more general than lust.

The innocence of the madman's wish is not certain at first, and this uncertainty is artfully controlled to develop the reader's anticipation. Though several references to blood on the madman were deleted from the published version, the kinship he feels with the deadly owl is ominous. At the same time, he pities the hare killed by the weasel. Next his isolation is stressed in the encounter with the old man, who flees when the madman says it no night for the son of woman. His violence with the butcher's knife is mentioned, but he has flung it into a tree (a "male" object), discarded it with his anger over his wife, who smiled at other men.

The farm wife he comes upon knows he has cut off his wife's lips. In the *Red Notebook* he felt guilt, for he cut his own throat after he did it (p. 24b), but the omission of this detail in the final version leaves the frightful possibility that he may do violence without any apparent motivation or qualms. The affinity of the madman for the young wife emerges when he thinks of sleep as a girl who will give him her dress to lie on with her; the earth itself is the place of love, for the twigs rustle like her dress as he flees. Shortly after this fantasy, the first glimpse of the farm wife shows her trying on the new flowered dress she has sewn (p. 249). The descriptions of her and her dress, which has a lowcut bodice and which she leaves unbuttoned at the neck, heighten her sexuality. In the *Red Notebook* this was emphasized by her holding the dress up and saying, "Naughty frock" (p. 24a), but the omission of this comment makes her more innocent in the final version.

Instead of the guns the madman expects as he enters the farm house, he sees a fearful girl, but then he is dazzled by the flowers of her dress. The *Red Notebook* was unnecessarily explicit in this lovely ending: "With the moving of her arm, her dress, *like a summer field,* danced in the light" (italics mine). The need for sleep was also overstressed, and the *Notebook* stated "tired head," instead of the more significant "bewildered head." This story, which could be the banal account of a flight to innocence or simply the madman's search for sleep, becomes a delicate resolution of mad anger in gentle beauty.

"The Visitor" (April, 1934) is more complex than **"The Dress,"** for its opposing images of life and death interpenetrate. The description of awakening day at the beginning is pervaded by images of death, a condition that reverses at the end. The movement of time displaces life: the heart of Peter the poet is replaced by a clock and his hands move as mechanically as those of a clock. All the places and events of his life converge in this dry day, and he imagines his only release from this dwindled life could be in the ghost of the boy he was when he walked the Jarvis hills (p. 109). Later he makes from words an olive tree, a symbol of long life, that grows under the lake, somewhat as he wishes to lurk beneath the water, but it is only "a tree of words." Then Peter thinks of Christ, whose body was taken from a tree and prepared for burial and resurrection, somewhat as his being is cared for by Rhianon.[13]

Peter's companions help him reach his destination. He watches Rhianon tidying the room around him and thinks the dead are surprised by the bloom under the skin of the living. He supposes this while she sweeps dust from the picture of Mary, the "lying likeness" (cf. **"Our Eunuch Dreams"**) of his dead wife (p. 110), but the facts that his hands feel like stones on the sea of shrouds covering him and that he has had a vision of his own corpse in a coffin show that he, in his near-dead state, is the one surprised by life. His travelling companion, Callaghan, brings an enemy into his room that threatens to destroy his world. But while death can destroy the webs of life, the poet still retains the walls of memory around Mary (p. 111).

The death Peter anticipates is exotic—he is an "island of rich and miraculous plants" (p. 112). He thinks of submersion in the watery sounds of Rhianon's dress. When he says, "Water," he has Rhianon hold a glass of water before his eyes, for he wishes to become "a green place under [the water], staring around a dizzy cavern" (p. 113). Though his self is more passive than the wild self in "How shall my animal," a poem about creativity, the image shows him descending to the deepest level of his being. When Callaghan carries him into the valley, the frost is falling. He sees apocalyptic horrors before all life on the earth dissipates and fresh life springs up (p. 117). This dwindling and renewing of life in the valley anticipates the structure of the spiritual journey in **"A Winter's Tale."** Peter cries out in joy at this renewal of life before it again recedes and he and Callaghan must race away, as all spirits must, before the cocks crow.

As the story of a writer for whom words are as tangible as things, it shows the loss of poetic powers.[14] At the beginning, Peter tastes the blood of Rhianon's and Callaghan's battling words, but toward the end the words he makes are no longer flesh—they seem empty of life. In another sense, the story is about the microcosm within the macrocosm it implies. Peter's room itself is a world within a world, and within even that lies his inner microcosm (p. 110). Peter perceives this world when he hears the blinded birds singing songs of the world within their eyes. (p. 115; cf. "Because the pleasure-bird whistles.") Though Peter in death is losing his senses as a poet—he can't hear Rhianon's singing any longer (p. 112)—and though he is surprised when she finds him dead, he has experienced a blissful world he created on his journey over the naked hills within him, which are represented by the Jarvis hills.

The double movements of **"The Visitor"**—into and out of both life and death, and out of the world and into the universe of the self—are conveyed symmetrically. The predicament at the beginning, in which Peter is haunted by thoughts of his death, reverses at the end, in which he is filled with life and surprised by the sheet being drawn over his face. Again, an image of day at the beginning—"A man with a brush had drawn a rib of colour under the sun and painted many circles around the circle of the sun. Death was a man with a scythe, but that summer day no living stalk was to be cut down" (p. 110)—is balanced by one of night at the end—"A man with a brush had drawn a red rib down the east. The ghost of a circle around the circle of the moon spun through a cloud. . . . The cock cried again, and a bird whistled like a scythe through wheat" (pp. 118–119). By juxtaposing such organic and cosmic images as have been used elsewhere in the story, these passages emphasize the concentricity of the microcosm and the macrocosm. There are almost no significant revisions of the *Red Notebook* version for that in *Skin Trade,* but the *Criterion* deleted three passages, perhaps because an editor thought them too explicit, that were almost entirely restored when the story was collected by Thomas.[15]

Of those stories in the *Red Notebook* touching on derangement, **"The Vest"** (July 20. 1934) is most concerned with probing the sickness itself. The association of experiences that are logically unconnected, such as the boy in **"The Tree"** imposes and the madman in **"The Dress"** blissfully achieves, and amoral violence, such as Martha uses to escape her servitude, both occur in **"The Vest,"** but this story also investigates the immediate causes of sickness. The sight of a dog crushed by a car has bewildered the protagonist. The violence arouses pity in him, but also a glee upon touching the brain and blood, the inner being, of the animal. His mind then flickers between this violence and the violence he has done to his wife when he felt pain himself (p. 253). The confusion of the accident causes a fear in him that is represented by darkness, particularly by the large shadow in his house (p. 252). This shadow is a projection of the terrible self that he must release, and he does it blindly, insensitively, when he tears his wife's underclothes off. As he walks out of the house, he notices the shadow is broken into many pieces, in keeping with his character, which is represented by the many faces he sees in the mirror, each of which has "a section of his features" (p. 255).

He fears the mortality of the flesh. Women, particularly his wife, have betrayed him with their "blind, corrupted flesh" (p. 34a). When he learned of his mother-in-law's cancer, he felt it was his own face that was eaten by locusts. To avoid such corruption of the flesh, he imagined he lay by his wife's skeleton, but in the morning her flesh bloomed proudly with his love; he also made her skin blush when he beat her. The fantastic orgy of violence he imagines in the bar full of women confirms his perverted horror of the flesh. He seeks rational control of experience, as is suggested in the manuscript by his counting of steps and streetlamps and his measured ringing of the bell at the beginning of the story.

The published version deletes some of these opening details, which were presented in a more personal point of view than Thomas finally adopted. The final version is more consistent with the protagonist's cold formality: instead of "he smacked her face" (p. 34a), Thomas makes it "he struck her cheek." In the manuscript her name was Helen; in the final version, which is presented from his impersonal point of view, no name is mentioned. When he remembers her putting on her frock that morning, she is coldly described as an object, "thin in her nakedness, as a bag of skin and henna drifting out of the light" (p. 253). She has brought light into his life, and normally she would disperse the shadow in the house, she would comfort him, but any comforts he felt, such as heat from the dying fire, were removed from the manuscript.

The manuscript is more explicit about his feelings: thoughts of "poor dog" and his judgments of his own cruelty were removed, as were the graphic images of the slaughtered dog.[16] His reaction to the dog's accident there was "in the first darkness" (p. 34a). The manuscript also interpreted more explicitly the source of violence as his horror of human corruption. When the protagonist noticed the darkening room and tasted his sickness, he thought of man's fallen state, "all the pain of life, the pain of the damned, the pain of man . . ." (p. 34b).

In addition to removing many explicit statements, Thomas deleted unnecessary details. The removal of the names of bars, which began with the Duke of Wellington, went through the Rose, the Mason, the Men of Devon, and the Rising Sun, and ended significantly at the Waterloo, increases the anonymity of his lonely surroundings, as does the deletion of crowds seen near his destination. Large sections of the final orgy were transferred to that grotesquely humorous account of the fall of man as poet, "Prologue to an Adventure" (Summer, 1937). The man selling an almanac (a record of the temporal world), the girls dancing in sawdust (glass, in the *Red Notebook*) in that story's bar, the Seven Sins, and the Negress selling a pound of flesh (p. 212) are close to the passages in the *Red Notebook* (pp. 36b–37b).

The only unpublished story in the *Red Notebook*, "**Gaspar, Melchior, Balthasar**" (August 8. 1934), is another story of nightmarish violence, but on the grander scale of an island setting, such as England, in a class-conscious world. Since air raids and street fighting were dreadful possibilities in the economic struggles of the Thirties, "**Gaspar, Melchior, Balthasar**" is a *reductio ad absurdum* of the very real spiritual carnage in a sick society. The class war is a leveler of inequities—all die in the same gutters, all are hungry (p. 38b).

The conditions of this world seem the reverse of what they are supposed to be. The people starve (p. 38b; deletion by Thomas) because they lack love, the staff of life. The galvanic wheat, which death drove back into the bone, is bullets, "crow's food [that] sliced about them," and their sustenance, such as God gave to the chosen people, is the bombs they desire, "cupping their hands for the exploding manna. Two lovers, struck by the same shell, fell into bliss" in death, not in their love. The power elite, who slip gas masks onto faces that are used to wearing masks daily, who must even purchase sleep in this commercialized society, are surprised from their sybaritic preoccupations and their seedy occupations.[17] In their society life is denied (babies are starved), and money, leisure, and love are stolen. (These details were deleted.) In return, the workers to whom they give guns turn them greedily against their former "slave masters," and "the keys of hate [are found in the blood of] the opened pulses" (p. 39a; all deleted by Thomas). The new life born out of this strife is the ability to hate.

The story then shifts to the first person when two ghosts appear to search for something among the dead. All usual activity, such as commerce, travel, communication and ceremony, has halted in this barren world: "The ships were unloaded at the wharves, the engines cold in the stations, the printing presses silent, and the sentries before the island palace stiff, in their boxes" (p. 39a; deletion by Thomas). The speaker feels out of place in this land that has only the appearance of life; he is "a ghost" (pp. 39a-b; deletion by Thomas). Furthermore, this new world is only "the last of the first revolution" dying away as he enters "the first stages of the night" (p. 39b). The speaker draws nearer to the ghosts as they hunt the ruins and examine the corpses; he begins to take on the garb of a wise man—"I held my scarf to my face for the smell of the flowering dead" (p. 39b). Though these dead "flower," they are black plants, the ominous signs that "the hemlock & the upas sprouted for me from the gutter beds" (p. 39b).

Melodramatically, a minute before midnight, he sees a kind of "star of Bethlehem" at the end of the street. It is a lantern that first "was a red rose among the flowers that stank at my side"; this ironically Dantean image was changed to "It was bright & sweet among the flowers . . ." (p. 40a). The ghosts pass him and he follows them toward the lantern, "calling them by name," but revolutionists, "dark-eyed behind their lantern," stop him to ask, "Who are you, comrade?" When he says to let him pass because he is "of the wise men," they want to know where he is going. He knocks the lantern from their hands and runs past, pursued through a maze of alleys by shots from their revolvers.

When he reaches the ghosts in a moonlit square, "at their feet lay a dead woman, naked but for her shawl, with a bayonet wound in her breasts" (p. 40a). While he watches, "a miraculous life stirred in her belly, and the arms of the child in her womb broke, lifted, through the flesh" (p. 40b). The two ghosts bow down and offer gold and frankincense, and as the speaker kneels, his pursuers shoot him. Originally the ghosts were named Gaspar and Melchior and the speaker learned from them that his name was Balthasar when his ghost rose from him. But the names were deleted, "bitter as myrrh" was changed to "my blood streamed bitterly," and instead of anointing the mother's feet, his blood anoints "the emerging head." Such changes make the story less obvious but more maudlin. This quality and the over-intellectualized symbolism may have been among Thomas' reasons for abandoning the story, but still it is significant as one of many attempts to consider the Christian myth within a world such as ours, that reverses Christian values. Hate is born into this dark world. Though this bitter allegorical sketch of class warfare was clumsy, Thomas used some of the same imagery years later, in his brilliant elegies for man in World War II. The bitterness is still there, but it becomes more powerful when barely controlled by such understatement as is used in **"A Refusal to Mourn."**

The child born in **"The Burning Baby"** (September, 1934) is imagined by Rhys Rhys to be a Second Coming, but it is a child of the flesh, Vicar Rhy's supposed enemy. Like many Thomas characters in the **Red Notebook** and elsewhere, Rhys struggles with the flesh because of its mortal weaknesses, but he does not realize he has made it his god, somewhat as man has made God in his own fleshly image. Thomas treats this inverted relationship between God and man literally by suggesting sexuality is the "Word" of an anthropomorphic god when he has Rhys Rhys put the stem of his pipe in a "mouth" between his flybuttons (p. 130). He then casts down the Bible and reads in another book "of the old woman who had deceived the devil. [Since he thinks] the devil is poor flesh" (p. 131), he hopes to deceive it by producing a god from it, and he thereby deceives himself.

The woman who bore his daughter saw "the woman witch in his male eyes" and loved him passionately, but she died in childbirth. Then she stole the child of his second love and left a changeling in its place (p. 131), but this child is a shadow "cast by the grave sun," a pun that expresses an idea akin to what Thomas summarized in "Twenty-four years" as the "meat-eating sun." When the story opens, only the changeling survives to wander over the fields like a personification of death, "with the motion of a man cutting wheat" (p. 128). Rhys Rhys has been obsessed with this cutting of ripeness. He said in his sermons that the world was "ripe for the second coming of the son of man" (p. 129), but the ripeness was of the flesh, his daughter's flesh. On the morning that the gorse burst into flames, almost as miraculously as when God spoke from the burning bush, and Rhys desired his daughter, the **Red Notebook** had him thinking, "She was the failure of the flesh, & the skinny field. Poor flesh, he said, and touched her arm. She trembled at the heat in his fingers. Only the poor are beautiful. The poor soil shudders under the sun, he said" (p. 41b). The purpose of the incest, Rhys seems to rationalize, is to achieve the second coming and redeem the poor flesh that is burned daily by the "grave sun."

But the changeling, that resulted from a death, haunts Rhys with his symbols of death, the skins and skulls that he covets. On the day of the incestuous conception, Rhys takes a rabbit carcass from him and keeps it in his pocket while he seduces his daughter. The section ends with the changeling's words, "I want the little skull," and though it recalls the carcass, it may also refer to the child of the union. During her pregnancy the changeling watches his sister in her daily dying and imagines her skull nailed above his bed. In both cases Rhys attempts to trick death of its due: by burying the dust of his daughter near him, in a "virginal" white coffin, and by burning the body of the baby. The **Red Notebook** emphasized the paganized import of the ritual by stating, "He stacked the torn heathers in the midst of the druid Bard's Circle where the stones still howled on the witches' sabbaths" (p. 46b). Though Rhys Rhys has enacted a ritual of man's triumph over death, the self-deception is clear when the flesh of the baby screams from the flames.

The final story is more obviously autobiographical than any other in the **Red Notebook,** and it is also one of the more complicated ones. Originally called **"Mr Tritas on the Roofs"** (October. 1934), it became **"Anagram,"** a phantasy about the artist and thereby an anagram of what he does. The name Tritas is itself an anagram, but in the *Criterion* version he was renamed Peter—the name Thomas used for the poet in **"The Visitor"**—and for the *Map of Love* collection he became the more obviously autobiographical Marlais.[18] Another change was the setting of the story, which in the short **"Anagram"** version (five pages) was London, and in the expanded **"Orchards"** version was Swansea, Wales, and the world beyond. Thomas may have written **"Anagram"** in London, where as a freelance artist he began concentrating on fiction because of its greater commercial value; by publication time he had discovered how deep were his Welsh roots and turned to the notion of the artist as folk-hero adventuring through the land of his being. The additions to the beginning and end of the story (pp. 137–40 and 143–9) were the dream of the burning orchards and the artist's terrible journey through the dying world. Despite these changes, the story remains an anagram of the artist's struggle to unify his "three-cornered life" (pp. 49ab), the worlds of life, death and his own vision.

The burning apple orchards in his dream are his anagram of this life. The two scarecrows, "two fruit-trees out of a coal-hill" (p. 140), the sister trees in the vegetable garden, are the tree of knowledge, that is associated with light, and the tree of life (and death), that stands in a circular shadow with crows on her shoulders (p. 137). Marlais tries to write of his vision in which, "under the eyelids, where the inward night drove backwards, through the skull's base, into the wide, first world on the far-away eye, two love-trees smouldered like sisters" (p. 140). The artist looks inward at archetypal experience, from which comes "Marlais's death in life in the circular going down of the day" (p. 140; cf. "Author's Prologue."). When he steps onto the roofs (in a setting sometimes resembling Cwmdonkin Drive), he observes "below him, in a world of words, men on their errands moved to no purpose but the escape of time" (p. 141). As an artist standing halfway between the stars and the toy of the town below the roofs, on the one hand, and building images that touch both death and life,[19] on the other, he must involve himself by attempting to achieve a unity of awareness.

The unity is possible when, as a folk-hero or, in another part of this dream of man's fallen state, as an apple farmer, he adventures through eleven valleys. The first valley implies a unity of heaven and earth in its hills that are "unbroken walls, taller than the beanstalks that married a story on the roof of the world" (p. 146). Beyond these eleven valleys he realizes his own artistic vision when the orchards of time burst into flame at the edge of the sea. The three levels of the artist's awareness are represented, for example, in the three images of the moon: the shadow of the "mock moon" in the north, the real round moon shining on the earth, and "the half-moon of his thumb-nail rising and setting behind the leaden spire" (pp. 140–41). The struggle for unity of this awareness is stated directly in the final version—"It is all one, . . ." (p. 142)—and it was the revelation in the concluding lines of the manuscript:

> . . . he moved for the last answer (p. 142). And all was image and was image, but Mr Tritas on the roofs sought a cohesing image of the dead and the quick. So he came at last to a skylight by a chimney side, and leant over the leaded rim. There, in the attic, sitting upright in a dark coffin, a joyful gentleman smiled at the crowds of heaven and played on a violin.
>
> Death & life was one image & one anagram. Odd thief in the folds, cried Mr Tritas on the roofs.
>
> October. 1934[20]

Thomas removed this ending and added a much more elaborate anagram for **"The Orchards."**

The artist's predicament is that he makes life—he has "five-fingered life" before him (p. 142), but he also kills with words, which are lifeless abstractions. They are words, not flesh, and life intrudes on the death he would put into his story of a woman wailing beside Russian seas in a cold wind from Antarctica (p. 139). What Thomas would later call "the meat-eating sun" defeats his struggles with words (p. 140). The artist's imagination can make people and angels of the chimneys on the roofs, but somewhat like Lot's wife, they turn to stone as he attempts to fix their reality with words (p. 138). Though the artist may scramble over the lives in the rooms below, while he watches the images of life and death in the stars (p. 48b), "the word is too much with us." This half humorous parody of *Words*worth keynotes a story that summarizes the predicament of the artist, who lives with insubstantial words, on the rooftops of the world.

The anagram that concludes the story shows the artist, "our virgin Marlais," as his rooftop creations call him, entering life, experiencing first-hand the vision of the burning orchards that he dreamed before. Until now he has been a coward, hesitant to embrace the "unholy" women of Llanasia, romantically willing to settle for his dream of "a life too beautiful to break" (p. 143), but he steps from the rooftops into the falling world. He sees the barren coal-tables that embrace Llanasia like a grave. All life is dominated by the sun that has shown since man fell from innocence, as Marlais is now falling. When he begins his role as a folk-hero, he passes through myths that summarize man's nature: the revolt in Heaven, the Fall from Paradise, the Homeric vision of the "wine-coloured sea," the notion of a single source of the sea, the destruction of Sodom and Gomorrah, even Jack and the beanstalk. When he journeys to the last hour on the last hill down to the sea, he actually witnesses his dream image of burning life and finds the fair girl who possesses the being he has committed to life. At the end of the artist's life, which is all lives, Thomas says the story is more terrible than all those stories of the fictional Jarvis hills. The artist finally loves the world, but he is left with dead objects, in the embrace of a scare-crow, somewhat as the fisherman succumbs in "The furious ox-killing house of love" ("Ballad of the Long-legged Bait," 1. 200). Art and life must both be insufficient at last to survive the dry twig of death. Thomas' obsession with death is as prominent in the **Red Notebook** as in most of his poetry: processes of time dominate the worlds of **"Martha," "The Visitor," "The Vest," "The Burning Baby"** and **"The Orchards."** Because the artist attempts to stop time in art[21] he must struggle against life's inevitable self-consummation, and he therefore feels the effects of process acutely. Peter in **"The Visitor"** and Marlais in **"The Orchards"** both attempt to preserve their worlds in the artifice of words, but they, like (or as) the dead, are continually surprised by the encroachments of actual life, whether it gives the lie to the abstractions of their medium or it pushes them relentlessly toward death, the process is the odd thief in the fold. (Cf. The Thief of "In Country Sleep.") Others, such as the protagonist of **"The Vest,"** attempt to escape time and decay in violence or, obversely, flee violence in an attempt to recover past innocence, as does the madman of **"The Dress."**

Death is often shown in the other stories as one of the results of man's fallen state. Thomas rarely depicts innocence, as represented by the idiot in **"The Tree"**; rather, those such as the boy in that story or Martha in **"A True Story"** commit outrageous acts in their amorality. In other words, they share in the fallen state of man by acting as naïve agents of evil when the free-flowing evil in the world fortuitously infests them. Others commit evil acts more pointedly. More knowing than the boy in **"The Tree,"** the vicar Rhys in **"The Burning Baby"** has perverted Christian values with the narrow nonconformism so traditional in Wales. Another foolish cleric is the Reverend Davies, who wanders into the Jarvis valley, the heart of life forces that the Owens control. Their pagan power is too much for the weak Christian values of Davies. An early theme of Thomas, this weakness is represented in the poetry as the Christian God's indifference—especially in "Incarnate Devil"—or man's perversion of Christian values. He treats the distortion lightly in "Shall gods be said to thump the clouds," seriously in "The spire cranes," and bitterly in the manuscript of **"After the funeral,"**[22] where the insincere mourners stand in contrast to the natural goodness of dead Ann.

The treatment in fiction of themes that Thomas used in his poetry is not surprising, nor are the occasional verbal echoes in his works. He quite naturally used motifs in one work that he planned for another. Mr. Tritas stood on the roof with the dust of the streets filling his eyes, and (p. 48a) Thomas finally deleted this passage showing supersensitivity, that had been used in a much different context of the preceding story, **"The Burning Baby"**: "It was not her eyes that saw him proud before her, nor the eyes in her thumbs. Her blood was fluttering as he moved. The lashes of her fingers lifted. He saw the ball under the nail."[23] Another passage of the **"Orchards"** manuscript may have been used for phrases and images of "A grief ago":

> The sky is a strange land at night, where the seasons pass over in a drift of star & snow, and the dark, scythe-sided grasses in the lunar country drop at the dawn.
>
> (p. 48b)

The ***Red Notebook*** reveals much about Thomas' working habits and about his understanding of the artist's work. Though his first idea for a novel about the Jarvis hills and valley, *A Doom on the Sun,* was soon abandoned, it is not surprising that several of his stories, as well as his poems, use the Carmarthenshire setting around Fern Hill, the farm where he spent so much of his youth. **"The Dress," "The Burning Baby"** and **"Prospect of the Sea"** invoke a comparable setting. **"The Enemies," "The Tree," "The Visitor"** and **"The Holy Six"** name the Jarvis setting, and **"The Map of Love"** shows two children the love that remains of Jarvis himself and his baldheaded wife. His ambitious story **"The Orchards"** started from a sketch using an urban setting, but it was expanded to show the artist as folk-hero going out to a place even more dreadful than the magical Jarvis hills to encounter reality. Either of these strange places possesses life in its fullest sense and provides a counterpart to the conventionality of Llareggub, which is mentioned in some of these stories.

The heroism of the artist in **"The Orchards"** is his stepping out of a romanticized artistic world, one such as Thomas suspected in **"After the Funeral,"** into the tumult of life among the women of the street to seek the deepest resources of life and death in the last valley. The struggle to enter reality is a sustained theme in Thomas' works about the artist's creativity. The name of the artist in the *Criterion* version of **"The Orchards"** and in **"The Visitor"** evokes slang associations consistent with his advice to Charles Fisher (February, 1935): "Poetry . . . should be as orgiastic and organic as copulation, dividing and unifying . . . Men should be two tooled, and a poet's middle leg is his pencil. If his phallic pencil turns into an electric drill, breaking up the tar and the concrete of language worn thin by the tricycles tyres of nature poets and the heavy six wheels of the academic sirs, so much the better."[24] Thomas

almost identifies creation and procreation, and as the letter implies, violence, or at least violent wrenching of symbols, such as many of the dream-like ***Red Notebook*** stories use, is necessary to reach "the first beasts' island" in his map of Love.

Notes

1. "The Red Notebook" is so catalogued by its owner, the Poetry Collection of the Lockwood Memorial Library, State University of New York at Buffalo. The previously unpublished material quoted here is Copyright © by the Trustees for the Copyrights of Dylan Thomas, 1971. Both the Trustees and the library have kindly granted me permission to quote from it.

   The Notebook is a 7 ¾ × 6-inch copybook with a soft, deep-red cover that declares it "The ZENITH Exercise Book," and it advertises "Ruled Feint Lines" (twenty-two) and provides spaces for the student's name and school and the date (all unfilled). The back cover lists six [safety warnings] about playing near vehicles. If the schoolboy survived this first spelling lesson, he found on the inside back cover "Arithmetical Tables," tables of measures, and multiplication tables.

   The sheets of the Notebook, which are stapled at the center fold of the book, are numbered 2 through 53 (1 and 54 having been removed or lost) in the center of the headspace on the right-hand pages only. Most of the pages are numbered by Thomas in pencil, though almost all the writing in the book is in ink on both sides of the sheets. The first sheet apparently has been torn out by Thomas, for the second begins with "the clouds;" inked out, "in" overwritten with "In" as the beginning of the sentence, and "The Tree (Adelphi)." penciled beneath the page number.

2. The juvenilia and copious worksheets of some later works went to the University of Texas Humanities Research Center with the T. E. Hanley collection. The British Museum holds additional worksheets and typescripts of early poems; the Houghton Memorial Library at Harvard University holds the fourth major collection of manuscripts—copious worksheets of a few late poems. All four possess letters.

3. Ralph N. Maud, ed., *The Notebooks of Dylan Thomas* (New Directions, 1967).

4. The inside of the front cover provides a map of England. Its most striking entry is the words "The Birth," that Thomas penciled and framed with a rectangle between the Isle of Man and Northumberland. This may be a trial title, perhaps an alternative to "After the Fair," "The Visitor," or the unpublished "Gaspar, Melchior, Balthasar," where births of one sort or another occur. The stories in the Notebook and additional titles are listed in the North Sea. "The Witch," "Arecom [scratched] Genesis," "The Manor" and "The Knife" are inked in a column. These titles are probably the first jottings, because an additional title, "The Diarists," is penciled below that list. Tho-

mas mentioned this last story, in a Christmas (1932?) letter to Trevor Hughes, as one *The London Mercury* accepted but did not publish (*Selected Letters of Dylan Thomas,* ed. Constantine FitzGibbon [London: Dent, 1966], p. 8).

A table of contents directly west of this one is entirely in pencil and is almost the same as the order of stories in the Red Notebook:

The Tree

Martha

After The Fair

The Enemies

The Dress

The Visitors.

The Burning Baby

The Vest

Gaspar, Melchior, Balthazar

The two differences are that in the Notebook "The Burning Baby" follows "Gaspar, Melchior, Balthasar" and that the unlisted story, "Anagram," appears last in the "Notebook" and eventually constitutes the central section of "The Orchards."

The overleaf of sheet 53 also contains lists: three trials of a table of stories and a list headed by "Eighteen Poems." The next entry in this prospective list of "works" was originally "Ten Stories," the number in the Red Notebook, but the title of Thomas' next published book, "25 Poems" (Dent, 1936), has been inserted between these two. The insertion may date the lists in the Notebook. The rest of the list tries various titles: "Three Essays" (deleted), "Two Plays" (deleted), "Twenty Poems," "Six Stories" (deleted?), "Three Essays" (deleted), and "One Story" (deleted). The three versions of a table of contents for a collection of short stories on this overleaf not only show Thomas' uncertainty over what to include, but they indicate many other prose manuscripts were extant by this time.

The title of another elusive story, "An Uncommon Genesis," appears in most of these jotted tables. It was to be a short novel that Thomas began writing as early as 1932. He told Pamela Hansford Johnson it concerned "a man & a woman. And the woman, of course, is not human" (*Selected Letters,* p. 38; see also pp. 42 and 49). Mrs. Annis Vilas Pratt thinks the novelette probably became "The Mouse and the Woman," which does not appear in any of the lists of titles—"The Early Prose of Dylan Thomas," (Unpublished Ph.D. dissertation, Columbia University, 1964, p. 16.)

Other titles that appear somewhere in the Red Notebook but are not among its stories are:

The End of the River

The Horse's Ha

The Map of Love

Selmer

The Tramp

The Holy Six

The Enemies United.

5. Dylan Thomas, *Adventures in the Skin Trade* (New Directions, 1953), p. 98. Most future references to this volume will be noted parenthetically by page numbers in my text. References to the Red Notebook will likewise be noted, with the side of the leaf indicated by a or b.

6. *Skin Trade,* p. 98. His religious feeling was emphasized over the idea of the fall in the Red Notebook, where the phrase was "nave of the earth" (2b).

7. *Skin Trade,* p. 98. Cf. the "polar eagle" of "The Ballad of the Long-legged Bait."

8. Four months later (11 May, 1934) he despaired to Pamela Hasford Johnson, "All sentences fall when the weight of the mind is distributed unevenly along the holy consonants and vowels. In the beginning was a word I can't spell, not a reversed Dog, or a physical light, . . ." (*Selected Letters,* p. 127.)

9. The Red Notebook shows Thomas considered dropping the name Martha, which was also the original title of the story. For some reason he scratched most appearances of "Martha" in the Notebook and penciled "Helen." In a letter to John Davenport (31 August, 1938, according to *Selected Letters,* pp. 206–7), Thomas mentioned "'All Paul's Altar', the actual description of a murder committed by a naked woman (especially the phrase 'her head broke like an egg on the wall')," as one of the objectionable items for which puritanical standards had delayed publication of "The Burning Baby" volume. Eventually most of the selections proposed for that book were included in *The Map of Love.*

10. p. 261. The power of this understatement increased when Thomas removed "with a sudden movement" (p. 13a).

11. Annis Pratt, *Dylan Thomas' Early Prose: a Study in Creative Mythology* (University of Pittsburgh Press, 1970), Chapter II. She treats the Owens under her discussion of Thomas and the occult (Chapter IV).

12. *Selected Letters,* pp. 118, 126 and 130–81.

13. The name of the girl troubled Thomas. To Peter the poet it "meant nothing. It was a cool sound" (p. 113). In the fair copy of the Red Notebook it was to be "Millicent," but in two places he copied "Heather" and then changed it in pencil to "Hesther," apparently to support her characterization as like "a maiden out of the Old Testament." These were then corrected in ink to "Millicent," the name used in the version published by *Criterion,* XV (January, 1935), 251–9, and not entirely removed from *Skin Trade* (p. 111). The final name, "Rhianon," Mrs. Pratt relates to the

muse of poetry and learning by that name in *Y Bard-das,* ed. William Ab Ithel (London, 1862)—*Dylan Thomas' Early Prose,* p. 93.

14. Thomas also used "Peter" as the name of the poet in the *Criterion* version of "The Orchards," and it became "Marlais" for publication in *The Map of Love.* Thomas might have drawn "Peter" from his part in H. F. Rubinstein's "Peter and Paul," that Miss Ethel Ross says he acted with the Swansea Little Theater in Mumbles during March, 1933—"Dylan Thomas and the Amateur Theater," *The Swan,* II (March, 1958), 15–21. In the play Peter lost his poetic powers as he grew older and became involved in his happy family life. Such is the plight of the fisher-hero in "Ballad of the Long-legged Bait."

15. The passages deleted were:

> He was dead. Now he knew he was dead. (p. 116)

> He heard Callaghan's laughter like a rattle of thunder that the wind took up and doubled. [p. 118] Dead Peter, cried Callaghan, "I showed you death in the valley. And, Lord, you laughed (p. 32a—punctuation and corrections by Thomas.)

> There was the old rumour of Callaghan down his brain. From dawn to dark he had talked of death, had seen a moth caught in the candle, had heard the laughter that could not have been his ring in his ears (p. 199).

16. In the manuscript Thomas explicated the protagonist's sympathetic reaction to his mother-in-law's cancer: "He felt the locust of the cancer on his own face, in the mouth and the fluttering eyelid. He had knocked Helen over the mouth." (p. 34b—deletion by Thomas).

17. The "Red Notebook" reads, ". . . as they climbed out of a purchased sleep, puffed out of tenement offices, cupping their hands . . ." (p. 38b—deletion by Thomas.). It is difficult to ignore some of the many deletions in the manuscript. The description of the sky as a hangar was removed, apparently because it was confusing, and the explanatory "hangar of the shadow of death" may have been struck because it was stated too heavily. The trend of corrections on the first two pages removes much obvious sarcasm, but a guess about the corrections is risky because they are sometimes incomplete. The many inks and pencil used indicate Thomas tinkered with the story several times, even considered sending it to *Adelphi,* before he rejected it.

18. *Criterion,* XV (July, 1936), 614–22. The *Skin Trade* version did not excise "Peter" entirely. (*V.* p. 147.)

19. A passage in the Red Notebook stated, "The house-tops are a strange land where man might scramble over the easel and the typewriter.

> the mortal rooms, love and the winding-bed, contrasting their habitations with the heavens [original displays the latter six words as crossed through]. (P. 48b—corrections by Thomas.)

20. P. 50a. The last two lines and the change from "some" to "a," as well as the date, are in later pencil.

21. See my "The Metamorphic Stop of Time in 'A Winter's Tale,'" *PMLA,* LXXVIII (September, 1963), 422–30.

22. Held by the Lockwood Library and dated "Feb 10. '33." See *The Notebooks of Dylan Thomas,* pp. 168 and 302.

23. P. 45b) The second sentence, which was not consistent with the changeling's point of view, was removed from the published version.

24. *Selected Letters,* p. 151. This association of the phallus with the poet's pen is very likely a reason for his early selection of the name "Peter" for his fictional poets. See also note 14.

Peter Levi (review date 1983)

SOURCE: "Gruesome," in *Spectator,* London, July 9, 1983, pp. 22–3.

[*In the following review of Thomas's* Collected Stories, *Levi decides that Thomas never matured as a prose writer.*]

Dylan Thomas might have been alive today. He never lived to be 40; he died 30 years ago—of playing a role it is impossible to sustain through middle age, and perhaps hard to sustain at all in the modern world. Indeed the very idea of Dylan Thomas shows how our world has altered. The seedily respectable, prewar, provincial territory of Cwmdonkin Drive is more utterly lost now than the old moods of Soho or the purity of rural Wales.

You might flick through the leaves of his **Collected Stories** in search of a certain meaty Welsh realism, or the prose version of a rural poem. But Dylan Thomas spent many years refining and defining his subject matter, and if it were not for half a dozen, or at most a dozen poems, the climax of his life-work would really be *Under Milk Wood,* with humour and sentiment at last more or less under control, Freud and the Bible at last evaporating, and clarity beginning to be dominant over resonance. If it were not for the poems, Dylan Thomas would offer a quite common and simple graph of literary development, from sixth form genius, top heavy with adolescence, through journalism, precocious success and the school of life, to a capable, attractive writer becoming less mannered with age. He would be a healthy example of the good influence of the BBC. These stories would never have been reissued if he were not so famous, and so appealing to the bad taste most of us share.

We have already been given the complete **Early Prose Writings,** edited by Walford Davies in 1971. The edition that presents itself now has reprinted even the earliest stories rescued from juvenile note-books and school magazines, and over 100 pages more of stories written before the age of 24. They are gruesomely pretentious. With perhaps two early exceptions in which the water was already running clear, *Portrait of the Artist as a Young Dog,* a linked series of ten stories written on the eve of war and published in 1940, is the first and almost only success of this volume. *Adventures in the Skin Trade,* which followed, was three chapters of a curdled, unfinished book. They were written in the summer of 1941, and the joke of bohemian London had, no doubt, worn thin. *Horizon,* which had already begun in 1941 to print virtually the whole of his best poetry as soon as it was written, never chose to print a story by Dylan Thomas.

After *Adventures in the Skin Trade,* his stories gathered here were all written for broadcasting, the last one for television in 1953. They are terribly dated, only quite attractive. They are a clearing of the throat for *Under Milk Wood,* which took a long time getting written. I recollect that the begging letters (the one art form Dylan Thomas brought to near perfection) which were printed after his death by Principessa Caetani in *Botteghe Oscure,* referred to *Under Milk Wood* a long time before it was finished.

And yet one reads even these awful stories with a certain nostalgia. It is like coming upon old copies of *Argosy* in an attic, or like suddenly relishing again one of the horrible meals of boyhood, baked beans, for example, with H. P. sauce. Some of the stories contain clichés, once common, that I have not heard since 1948. Even Empson's review of the *Early Prose Writings* which was reprinted in the *Listener* anthology, looks pleasantly dated now. 'Most of the stories are about Welsh characters in an exalted state of religious mania, and they are full of fun in their own way, but the author does not seem to share in their exultation . . . He is uneasily trying to come to terms with life—not with being Welsh, as he simply thought better of Wales for producing such deep, extravagant types.'

Empson, with his merciless gentleness, detects a note of hysteria which is present on most pages of this book. In the early stories young Thomas is desperate about sex, and full of alarming fantasies. Later on he becomes panic-stricken about cities and his self-image is a terrified young man; the stories are sad and full of self-pity. Those private friends who knew Dylan Thomas best have always suggested there was far more to him than went into his stories. That sounds right. The stories are only giggling signs to ward off the evil of some nursery demon. As a writer in prose, Dylan Thomas never developed. In writers, as in civilisations, the true, admirable age of prose is often later to mature than the intoxicating age of poetry. Dylan Thomas did not live to be 40.

Brian Stonehill (review date 1985)

SOURCE: A review of *The Collected Stories,* in *Los Angeles Times Book Review,* January 6, 1985, p. 1, 5.

[*In the following review of* The Collected Stories, *Stonehill provides a brief appreciation.*]

What is the gift that some storytellers have of immediately enwrapping us? A walk through this collection by a story-teller better known as one of the great poets of our century offers a few clues to that question.

Dylan Thomas [in *The Collected Stories*] writes from the child in himself to the child in us, without disturbing the skeptical adult selves that stand sentry over precious childhood memories. He re-creates the intense colors, the distinctive odors, the absolutely human feel of everything we registered in our crustless youths. Yet the perspective is from here, today, looking back: We're not invited to escape so much as to measure our distance from how sensitive we once were, how much we once were able to perceive.

The evocation of youth is a kind of magic. What is gone, suddenly returns: presto! If Proust could pull vivid decades from a soggy cookie, Thomas suavely offers to perform a more robust, outdoor version of the trick. He'll pull his past out of a Welsh snowball:

> "I plunge my hands in the snow and bring out whatever I can find. In goes my hand into that wool-white bell-tongued ball of holidays resting as the rim of the carol-singing sea, and out come Mrs. Protero and the firemen."

The singing quality of Thomas' prose—that lilting rhythm and those fast-changing images—is one way he evades our defenses. "That's nice music," note our critical guards, perhaps recognizing Homer's stamp on the passport. "Artfully done. You may pass."

Then the child imprisoned in our imaginations grows restless and starts rattling its bars in time with Thomas' beat. "Hey, that's me! I recognize those sensations!" Then the meeting of our minds and the mind of the storyteller takes place, and "enchantment" best describes that feeling of being swept into—and away with—the story.

There's nothing naïve here, aesthetically or morally. Dylan Thomas observed the surrealists closely and walks part of the way with them, taking what he needs and then branching off. The world of the imagination embodies itself as commandingly as any other claim on our attention. No elves or dragons, but the fantastic flickering of our pasts across the screen of the present, with a narrative inventiveness that must please even the sternest of modernists.

On the moral level, Christian sentiment informs many of these stories, from **"The Tree,"** with its Crucifixion barely disguised by the writer at 19, to **"A Child's Christmas in Wales,"** written and recorded in Thomas' memorably rich voice, a few years before his death at 39, in 1953. What strikes one most, finally, about these stories, is their *generosity*. With a little distance from their alluring world, we're aware of Dylan Thomas mining this material from inside his *self*, excavating, polishing, and setting it asparkle before us.

There's nothing saccharine here, either. **"The Burning Baby"** is about incest and infanticide. Human failure casts its constant shadow. Deliberate destruction scars the soul, even of one who passed World War II telling stories for the BBC.

But Thomas feels the miraculous gifts of existence and consciousness with crucial intensity. His prose, his images, his stories all pulsate with life, with a beat and a variety that captivate, invigorate and clarify.

"He brothered the world around him, sipped at the air, as a child newly born sips and brothers the light." After the early stories, after *Portrait of the Artist as a Young Dog* and *Adventures in the Skin Trade,* this collection presents a story Dylan Thomas wrote for and read on TV. As Leslie Norris recalls in a fine foreword, "I saw Thomas tell this story on the old black and white screen. He filled it with action and colour with his unaided words."

Linden Peach (essay date 1988)

SOURCE: "Religion, Repression and Sexual Violence," in *The Prose Writing of Dylan Thomas,* Macmillan Press, 1988, pp. 15–45.

[*From a study of religion, repression, and sexual violence, Peach discusses in the essay below Thomas's use of imagery and symbolism to express the darker side of sexuality.*]

> Late in the Spring, Herzog had been overcome by the need to explain, to have it out, to justify, to put in perspective, to clarify, to make amends.
>
> (Saul Bellow, *Herzog*)

> Shall we never get rid of this Past. . . . In fact, the case is just as if a young giant were compelled to waste all his strength in carrying about the corpse of the old giant, his grandfather, who died a long while ago, and only needs to be decently buried.
>
> (Nathaniel Hawthorne, *The House of the Seven Gables*)

I

Dylan Thomas's early stories present a number of problems for the reader. They are unconventional even by the standards of Joyce and Chekhov. They contain few clearly defined characters, shift confusingly between symbolism and realism, and, in sometimes bizarre ways, tend to sexual violence.

There are parallels between the difficulties presented by the early prose and those presented by the early poems. In both Thomas fostered obscurity, as Moynihan says, 'as a structural device. . . . If newness or freshness could not be achieved by a statement of immediate force and compelling strength. . . . Then freshness might be achieved by a sense of verbal, thematic or imagistic struggle'. Hence, in the stories as in the early poems images jostle with each

other in what Thomas described himself in a letter to Vernon Watkins as 'a sequence of creations, recreations, destructions and contradictions'. But this is not the whole picture for there is an indigenous link between the seeming obscurity and compression. In the stories as Thomas once said of his poems 'everything it tightly packed away in a mad doctor's bag'. Indeed, to quote Moynihan, 'he reached a point where his language implied so much that it seemed to say nothing'.

The little critical attention that the early stories have received has regarded them as vehicles of expression for Thomas's innermost anxieties and obsessions. The lynchpin of this argument is that they do not delineate the exterior world in an empirical way but contain, as Walford Davies maintains, the 'fusion of objective realities like people, places and events' with 'the distorted vision made out of them by the poet's deeper fears'. The mawkish violence and often bizarre sexuality in the early stories constitute an interface between these two.

Walford Davies finds behind the farrago of the early stories 'the hysterical implosions of an imagination unable to accept order and control'. It is true that in Thomas's work there is a deep-rooted suspicion of order which borders on aversion and which even in the much later work, *Adventures in the Skin Trade,* belies Mr. Allingham's insistence 'that there's sense in everything'. But Walford Davies's explanation is not entirely satisfactory. The conflation of order and control with the negation of desire, of self-fulfilment and self-hood was not simply an 'hysterical implosion', but the result of Thomas's thinking about the repressive religious life of the narrow, rural communities. The recurring concern with sexual violence and perverse, secret desire which has been regarded only as an externalising of Thomas's personal obsessions is also an important part of Thomas's attempt, inspired at least partly by Caradoc Evans, to expose the hypocrisy and the sham of a dying Welsh chapel culture which he saw as a strait-jacket upon the Welsh people.

There is undoubtedly some truth in the thesis that the candid concern with sex in Thomas's work is part of an attempt on his part to confront, and come to terms with, his own subconscious anxieties about sex, as there is also in John Ackerman's assertion that surrealism and Freudian Psychology had an impact upon his young mind. However, it must be remembered that Caradoc Evans achieved considerable notoriety for his candid treatment of sex, too. Moreover, his work often deals with the conflict between sexual desire and a solipsistic, repressive, local culture that threatened either to stifle it or transform it into something shameful. In such a culture moral lapses received short shrift. Evans never forgot the way his own father, accused of adultery, suffered the public humiliation of 'Y Ceffyl Pren'—'The Wooden Horse'—in which he was tied astride a wooden pole and carried ignominiously through the village. The whole scene would have been accompanied by the kind of riotous procession Thomas Hardy describes accompanying the 'skimmington ride'—the West Country version in which effigies substituted for the real offenders—in *The Mayor of Casterbridge*.

Evans's women are often portrayed as sexually active and, in traditional terms, morally loose. Usually, he does not pass judgement upon them in the narrative as, for example, in his description of Maggy in "To Keep a Rainbow White":

> Maggy was thirty. Her cheeks were pink, her lips not thick or thin, her bosom full. Years before she was in the service of a Carmarthen auctioneer and begot a chance child, a male child.

He does, however, contrast their intense sexuality with the repressive, local culture in which they lived. And their intense sexuality is concomitant with feelings of guilt induced by that culture. So, eventually Maggy refrains from sex earning the nickname 'self-denial' in the hope of marrying a 'pure man'. Evans does not labour the irony, though it can hardly be missed, that while Maggy is looked down upon for her sexual freedom, she is also criticised by men for her abstinence. Evans is especially interested in the way men, ignoring their own complicity, shift the blame to the women as is clear from "An Offender in Siôn":

> He laid his hands on Rachel's shoulders, and he spoke flatteringly and made false promises. He said this also: 'Tidy, look you here, you are in your blood. Softening I am. Come you into the lower end and talk matters will we'.
>
> Rachel placed her trust carelessly in him; and it came to be that after Ianto had committed his sin he repented and rebuked Rachel: 'awful, serpent, in this you have done'.

In Evans's stories, as in some of Thomas's stories, to be seen to be respectable seems more important than respectability and integrity themselves. Also in Evans's work, as in Thomas's **"Old Garbo"**, the hypocritical are condemned not only for their hypocrisy but the brutality with which they turn upon others they see as wrong-doers. When Rachel, after Ianto has made her pregnant, threatens to expose him for his complicity, his response is sharp and violent: 'Jessabel', he said slowly, 'shut your chin, or kick your belly will I'. The Bible enables him to find convenient symbols of an evil which is really inside himself denouncing her as 'serpent' and 'Jessabel'.

It is not uncommon in literature which is the product of a repressive culture for sexual desires that are repressed to find expression in various degrees of sexually-tinged violence. We see it clearly in the work of Nathaniel Hawthorne and, to a lesser extent, Sir Walter Scott. Repressed sexuality is concomitant with violence in several of Thomas's early stories. In **"The Holy Six"** (1937) the religious life of the Six distorted their sexuality as Thomas unsubtly suggests when he says that 'the holy life was a constant erection to these gentlemen'. The repression colours their view of women, they are overconscious of, and

alarmed by, 'the wicked streets . . . where the women smiled under the lamps, and the promise of the old sickness stirred in the fingertips of the girls in the dark doorways'. Normal sexual energies are channelled into violence: 'Mr Lucytyre conducted an imaginary attack upon the maidenheads. Now here and now there he ripped the women, and kissing them, he bit into their lips.' None of the Holy Six is capable of enjoying a properly adjusted relationship with the opposite sex. Mr. Stul, an allegorical representation of lust as the anagram suggests, cannot read Mrs. Owen's letter without thinking that as she writes 'she feels the weight of her breasts on her ink-black arm'. It is he who 'thrusts his hand high up under Miss Myfanwy's skirt'. Lucytyre, again as the name suggests, can only relate to others through pain and violence, evident when he 'smiling at destruction, drove his fingers into her [Miss Myfanwy's] back until the knuckles tingled and the invisible flesh reddened with pain'. While walking from the overturned cart, Miss Myfanwy 'smelt the clover in the grass' while, characteristically, 'Mr. Lucytyre smelt only the dead birds.' A clue as to what Thomas believed had gone wrong in these lives is contained in a letter he wrote to Pamela Hansford-Johnson in 1933:

> During the period of adolescence, when the blood and seed of the growing flesh need, for the first time and more than ever again, communion and contact with the blood and seed of another flesh, sexual relationships are looked upon as being unnecessary and unclean. . . . So often the opportunity comes too late, the seed has soured, love has turned to lust, and lust to sadism.

This letter serves as a gloss on other stories, too, such as **"The True Story"** (1934) where, once again, sex denied a proper and natural outlet becomes as Thomas suggested in the letter, a sly and sinister force. Instead of eyes, the simple farm boy has 'two crafty cuts in his head' and is 'forever spying on the first shadows of Helen's [*sic*] breast'. The combination of 'crafty' meaning underhand and cunning with the sinister word 'cuts' projects a sense of menace accentuated by the use of 'spying' itself suggesting an intrusion upon not only what is secret but forbidden. The connotation is carried surreptitiously over into the first mention of Helen's sexuality.

Not only the simple farm boy, but Helen herself is the epitome of repressed sexuality. We are reminded that Helen is 'a woman under apron and pink frock', the apron being a symbol of the life of domesticity and drudgery she has been forced to assume in looking after the old woman. The fact that her frock is pink, like the pink ribbons in the hair of Faith in Hawthorne's "Young Goodman Brown", reminds us of her sexuality and pent-up passion. Helen's problem is again that which Thomas describes in the letter to Pamela Hansford-Johnson. Helen's transition from child to woman is described in virtually one sentence suggesting the speed with which time has passed and the way her sexuality has developed almost unnoticed even by herself.

II

The early stories are not simply delineations of sexual violence nor do they equate violence with sexual repression according to a simple formula. They betray a serious concern to try and understand the psychic origins of sexual violence. In **"The True Story"** the emphasis is as much upon the disturbed nature of Helen's mind as her repressed sexuality. In **"The Vest"** (1934), too, violence is a product of deep psychological problems. The killer, into whose mind the story takes us, tries to excuse his actions: 'when he hurt her, it was to hide his pain. When he struck her cheek until the skin blushed, it was to break the agony of his own head'. In **"The Dress"** (1934), Jack's murder of his wife might seem to stem, at first sight, from sexual jealousy: 'They said he had cut off her lips because she smiled at men.' But very subtly the story suggests that there are deeper problems: 'the mist was a mother to him, putting a coat around his shoulders where the shirt was torn and the blood dry on his blades'. At the very end of the story, the girl, rocking in her chair as an elderly mother in those days might, receives him as a mother would a frightened and hurt child: 'she sat before him, covered in flowers. "Sleep", said the madman. And, kneeling down, he put his bewildered head upon her lap'. The stories are strong on innuendo and short on theories, as they should be, for they deal with problems to which there are no easy solutions. The use of the word 'madman' is belied by the complexities to which the story as a whole points. In fact, there is a suggestion in the later *Adventures in the Skin Trade,* that Thomas remained throughout his life bewildered by sexual violence. The homosexual, George Ring,—Thomas's humour is often of this unsubtle kind—is told how one of the prostitutes was beaten by one of her clients who suddenly produced a clothes brush from a little bag. Allingham, the droll observer who has been ejected from a nightclub following a brawl, muses with a bewilderment that seems like the author's own: 'There's some people can't enjoy themselves unless they're knocking women down and licking them on the floor.'

The early stories make some interesting points about violence which might appear commonplace today, but were not so at the time at which Thomas wrote and for which Thomas's acuity deserves recognition. In several stories a connection is made between sexual violence and a desire to dominate. It is most candidly stated in **"The Vest"** in which the husband, in a lurid fantasy based on the relationship with the wife he has killed, orders her 'Take off your frock', slapping her and repeating the order when at first she does not obey. She is frightened and crying, but in the darkness he strips her of the rest of her clothes, and having humiliated her in this way, leaves. The incident is similar to one in **"The Burning Baby"** (1934) but, without the physical violence, where Rhys Rhys orders his daughter, 'step out of your shift'.

Thomas maintained in **"Replies to an Enquiry"** that his work 'must drag further into the clean nakedness of light more even of the hidden causes than Freud could realise'. In these early stories there is no gainsaying that the causes of sexual violence are complicated to unravel, itself a reflection of Thomas's concern to understand. In **"The Vest"**, especially, the urge to dominate is a symptom of a larger

misogynism. Hence, the husband who turns killer finds women repulsive because he cannot but see them as corrupt. In bed with his wife, 'he lay quietly by her skeleton. But she arose next morning in the corrupted flesh'. The language here has religious connotations. The use of the word 'skeleton' and the metaphor of rising from the dead reminds us of the resurrection and the way Christ was thought to have assumed a corrupt body. These connotations suggest that the origins of the man's distaste of women may be in his religious upbringing. This suggestion is not developed explicitly, but it is underlined by the way in which the man sees the inside of a bar, exaggeratedly, as "Sodom and Gomorrah":

> The bar was crowded. Women were laughing and shouting. They spilt their drinks over their dresses and lifted their dresses up. Girls were dancing on the sawdust. A woman caught him by the arm. . . . He could hear nothing but the voices of the laughing women and the shouting of the girls as they danced. Then the ungainly women from the seats and corners rocked towards him. He saw that the room was full of women. Slowly, still laughing, they gathered close to him.

This paranoid view is in sharp contrast to that at the end of the story when he offers his wife's blood-stained vest for sale and 'the meek and ordinary women in the bar' stand 'still, their glasses in their hands . . .'.

Rhys Rhys in **"The Burning Baby"** is similarly obsessed that flesh is corrupt, largely as a result of the guilt over his feelings for his daughter. Like the killer in **"The Vest"**, he is revolted by what always draws him magnetically. His daughter (at least in his eyes) is noticeably ugly: 'her hair smelt of mice, her teeth came over her lip, and the lids of her eyes were red and wet'. The madman in **"The Mouse and the Woman"** has killed the woman he loved because the female form repulsed him:

> They were . . . naked . . . Eve could not have been as beautiful. They ate with the devil, and saw that they were naked, and covered up their nakedness. In their good bodies they saw evil for the first time.

> Then you saw evil in me, she said, when I was naked. I would as soon be naked as clothed.

The phrase 'in their good bodies' is interesting because it is an intrusion championing the natural healthiness of the body, sensuality and sexuality and it is juxtaposed with a religious inspired view of sex, the body, and sensuality as evil. The woman is not the femme fatale of some of the other stories. She is innocently at ease with her nakedness. The reference to Eve, too, is deliberate for Thomas follows Blake in seeing the Fall as the beginning of sexual repression.

A similar thesis underpins some of the poems. In 'Unluckily For A Death' Dylan describes the chapel-going culture's stress on restricting sexuality as 'the choir and cloister / Of the wintry nunnery of the order of lust'. By contrast in physical love:

The ceremony of souls
Is celebrated there, and communion between suns.
Never shall my self chant
About the saint in shades while the endless breviary
Turns of your prayed flesh . . .

III

The sexual violence is part of a larger aspect of the early stories which can only be described by Herman Melville's term, 'the power of blackness' and which Melville observed 'derived its force from its appeal to the Calvinistic sense of Innate Depravity and Original Sin'. Nowhere is this more apparent than in **"The School for Witches"** (1936) which combines sexual desire, adolescent fraternising with the occult and the superstition of a remote rural community that owes more to the seventeenth century than the twentieth century.

In this story, as in others, it is not the author-narrator but a character who expresses the sense of an overwhelming evil most convincingly. Mrs. Price, the midwife, with a baby in her arms, screams: 'This is a wicked world.' The fact that she is a midwife and that she has a baby in her arms when she says this underscores the horror of the proclamation. She, like the witch, Mrs. Owen, in **"The Holy Six"**, is a type of character Thomas uses to express a thesis he is tempted towards himself but is not yet fully prepared to accept. Mrs. Owen described as 'wise to the impious systems', is able to see 'through the inner eye that the round but unbounded earth rotted as she ripened'. Thomas still hoped this was not the case.

Typically of the early stories, the doctor's daughter, Gladwys, in **"The School for Witches"** is a combination of overt passion and innocence: 'short and fat thighed; her cheeks were red; she had red lips and innocent eyes'. But this story is not concerned with the poignancy of innocence bent on it own destruction. Thomas is interested in the evil which she, having whipped herself up into a frenzy, brings down upon herself:

She saw, as clearly as the tinkers saw the spire, the towering coming of a beast in stag's skin, the antlered animal whose name read backwards, and the black, black, black wanderer climbing a hill for the seven wise girls of Cader.

Traditionally, the devil is the black bogey man of the forest—irrational prejudice against black people reaches deep into the communal psyche of Western societies—and in this story it is the black, itinerant blade sharpener who becomes the 'Evil One' with whom Gladwys enters into a relationship.

Gladwys' offering of herself is an episode deeply rooted in folklore. The black scissorman, an outsider because of his colour and his work, is the lusty, powerful blackman of white mythology. What is enacted here is a racial fear incredible to intelligent people today but unfortunately not uncommon in white gothic literature, the rape of a white virgin by a blackman:

And, like a god, the scissorman bent over Gladwys he healed her wound, she stood his ointment and his fire, she burned at the tower altar, and the black sacrifice was done.

Once again violence and dominance, are essential elements of the encounter, shrouded in religious imagery. Her sexual organs are a wound, she offers herself like a sacrifice and burns at the altar.

The sinister connotation of the scissors image is one which Thomas uses in his poetry. In "From Love's First Fever to her Plague" Thomas writes of 'the scissored caul'. In "When like a Running Grave", scissors are linked with time which 'comes, like a scissors stalking, tailor age'. Paul Ferris in his biography of Dylan Thomas claims the source of this image is *Struwwelpeter,* the illustrated book of children's stories which includes the tale, "Little Suck-a-Thumb", in which a child is punished by having his thumbs cut off by a grisly tailor with flying hair and an enormous scissors, 'the great, long, red-legged scissorman'. Certainly Thomas has *Struwwelpeter* in mind in **"The Mouse and the Woman"** (1936) where in one room of the asylum 'sat a child who had cut off his double thumb with a scissors'. In the passage from **"The School for Witches"** quoted above, the imagery is complicated, combining the idea of injury with the notion of healing, the concepts of healing and of baptism, and the concepts of baptism and of sacrifice. In **"A Prospect of the Sea"** (1937), where the scissors image is again used sexually, the context is not as ambivalent as in **"The School for Witches"**, the image is used with reference to the female and not the male and expresses the male's subconscious, sexual fears. In this story, a gypsy girl terrorises a young boy:

The stain on her lips was blood, not berries; and her nails were not broken but sharpened sideways, ten black scissor-blades ready to snip off his tongue.

The origin of the image for Thomas probably lay partly in the impact of *Struwwelpeter* upon his young imagination, partly in the innate appeal of the image as an expression of his own subconscious fear and partly in other sources. The image is afterall a universal one, associated as an attribute of the Fate, Atropos, with death—severing the thread of life—and whose adaptors include surrealist painters such as Robert Desnos in *Death of Max Morise.* The woman who dances alone in **"The Lemon"** is redolent of Atropos, she has a 'scissors dangling from the rope of her skirt' and the cutting of the lemon with the scissors signifies 'the coming of death of the interior world'. The closed scissors resembles a knife, traditionally associated with sacrifice, but the open scissors has quite potent sexual connotations. It admits into its depth what it then closes upon and severs. Moreover, as two blades acting as one, it has become an image of the union of two opposites. Part of its appeal as a sexual image may lie in its ability to arouse subconscious fears of castration, even impotence, fears which Paul Ferris believes may have indeed haunted Thomas.

The sense of innate depravity in Thomas's work stems from a fear that even though there is no gainsaying that suppressed desires find expression in dark and frequently violent ways, the emotions held in check may themselves be evil. As an older man writing *Under Milk Wood* (1954), Thomas, as we shall see, had become more confident about the unfettering of desire. However, at the time of writing his early short stories in the 1930s he was not convinced as Blake was, that the emotions released when the gates of repression were unlocked would prove inevitably healthy and unsinister. Consequently the early stories are peopled, like those of Poe, with dark and forbidding spectres of evil. However, the effect of the belief that possibly the evil arising from suppressed emotions was itself the manifestation of a much darker and innate evil is evident not only in character portrayal, but even the type of landscapes in which the stories are set. His obsession with what kind of reality lay beneath the 'perceived reality' gave him a jaundiced view not only of people, but nature, and, in stories such as **"The Holy Six"** and **"The School for Witches"**, almost of the universe itself. Dylan knew enough not to trust his eyes, but he was not able to refocus his vision. He wrote in July, 1935:

> My own eyes, I know, squint inwards when, and if, I looked at the exterior world, I see nothing or me . . . all I see is darkness, naked and not very nice.

This is especially close to the view of the world that pervades **"The Holy Six"**:

> There was a madman in each tree. This they did not know, seeing only the sanity of the trees on the broad back of the upper grasses.

As the Six clamber upward Thomas describes how 'the roots beneath their feet cried in the voices of the upspringing trees'. In **"The School for Witches"**, the doctor 'heard his daughter cry to the power swarming under the west roots'. Mr. Owen in Jarvis's valley in **"The Enemies"** (1934), hears how 'the vegetable world roared under his feet' and the word 'roaring' is both ambivalent and typical of Thomas. His pantheism is not the soothing kind of Wordsworth's "Tintern Abbey"; it almost assaults the senses. 'Roaring' suggests violence, anger, pain. Thomas observes later in **"The Enemies"**: 'Not only a mandrake screams; torn roots have their cries; each weed Mr. Owen pulled out of the ground screamed like a baby.' Nature always bleak in the early stories, is at best alien to man and usually hostile as in R. S. Thomas's poems. **"The School for Witches"** is focussed upon 'Cader Peak, half ruined in an enemy of weather' while in **"The Holy Six"** Thomas describes how 'shifting along the properties of the soil, man's chemic blood, pulled from him by the warring wind, mixed with the dust that the holy gentlemen, like six old horses, stamped into a cloud'.

Nothing summarises Thomas's sense of an innate evil more than the decision of the boy in **"The Tree"** to crucify the idiot. **"The Tree"** is indeed a dark and depressing story. The action takes place on the day before Christmas but before the end of the story, Christmas Day becomes Good Friday.

IV

The sinister world-view that threatens at times to overwhelm the early stories seems to be one aspect of Thomas's world-view which he was trying to keep at bay. There is little doubt that it was fuelled by a desire on his part to shock and by his reading in Gothic literature and the stories of Edgar Allan Poe. Although he read Poe avidly, the American writer's work seems far more tongue-in-cheek than Thomas's and once again, Thomas's work is closer to that of Caradoc Evans. Both share the satirical linking of violence with cynicism about a narrow-minded Welsh culture. Yet Thomas's work is different from Evans's in at least one important aspect. In Thomas's work there is an exploratory dimension the other lacks. While Evans delineates the deceit of which man is capable and portrays the violence which always seems to be beneath the surface and on the point of eruption, Thomas as we have said earlier, wanted to try and understand this violence.

Also, symbolism and innuendo are more fully developed as dramatic devices in Thomas's work than in Evans's work. What Evans demonstrates to us, sometimes in a rather heavy-handed fashion, Thomas dwells upon as only half-understood areas of experience. Thus, in the case of Coed's attempt to seduce Ianto, which we discussed earlier in this [essay . . .], no sooner are we aware of Coed's intentions than we are plunged into the violence of Ianto's reaction. Even though Thomas's early work lacks maturity and experience, it does display greater interest in characters who find themselves harbouring secret desires and in what this is doing to them than Evans achieves. Thus, however rough the edges of Helen's portraiture in **"The True Story"**, there is evidence of a more subtle involvement with character than in Evans's portrayal of Coed, even though at the end of the story it is the bizarre inexplicability of what she does that jolts the reader.

It must be admitted that the extent of Thomas's involvement with character, the complexities and perplexities of human motivation, is limited. It is held in check by the tendency to allegory. Of course, allegory although it leads to schematic portraits, is not entirely incompatible with conveying what it is that impels human behaviour. Hester in Hawthorne's *The Scarlet Letter*, for example, is both symbolic and a convincing portrayal of a mother deserted by her lover. But the failure to produce more convincing characters and to depart from allegory is evidence of the way in which Thomas's early prose was impelled by the ambition to explore through symbolism the relationship between individuality, on the one hand, and the influence of a repressive culture on the other.

The way in which Thomas achieved a subtler use of imagery and symbolism than Evans is evident from **"The Burning Baby"** where Thomas suggests how Rhys Rhys's desire for his daughter has consumed his entire being:

> In the church that morning he spoke of the beauty of the harvest, of the promise of standing corn and the

promise in the sharp edge of the scythe as it brings the corn low and whistles through the air before it cuts into the ripeness.

His concern with developing symbolism so that it could express the darker nuances of sexuality is evident from the way in which the images used here are adapted three years later to provide a backdrop for adolescent sexual yearnings in **"A Prospect of the Sea"** (1937):

> It was high summer, and the boy was lying in the corn. He was happy because he had no work to do and the weather was hot. He heard the corn sway from side to side above him, and the noise of the birds who whistled from the branches of the trees that hid the house. Lying flat on his back, he stared up into the unbrokenly blue sky falling over the edge of the corn.
>
> The wind, after the warm rain before noon, smelt of rabbits and cattle. He stretched himself like a cat, and put his arms behind his head. Now he was riding on the sea, swimming through the golden cornwaves, gliding along the heavens like a bird . . .

In this story the corn image is expanded within a fuller account of nature coming to fruition. There is almost mystical enjoyment of summer but there are also darker undertones in the picture which prepare us for the gypsy girl to whom we referred in the discussion of the scissors image. The sky may be unbrokenly blue but it falls—the word has sexual-biblical connotations and a comparison with Eden is explicitly developed later—over the edge of the corn. We have hints, albeit traditional ones, of the sexuality within nature through the reference to the birds whistling in the branches and the smell of rabbits. Slowly the passage evolves into a greater sexual awareness on the part of the boy. But the total image is still underpinned by an almost platonic innocence despite the physical verbs—riding, swimming—which surfaces in the last line where the boy glides 'along the heavens like a bird'. The reader is duped for soon the fears and pain of sexual knowledge which Thomas encapsulated in the earlier passage in the image of the sharp edge of the scythe 'which brings the corn low and whistles through the air before it cuts into the ripeness' undermine all this mystical innocence.

The process begins with the boy's next day dream. The fantasy is introduced by a transitional movement on the young lad's part: 'Now he was a boy with tousled hair, rising slowly to his feet, wandering out of the corn to the strip of river by the hillside'. 'Now he was a boy' refers to the return to reality—after the dream of gliding in the heavens—but also reminds us that he returns to the consciousness of an adolescent. It is a consciousness pervaded by half-understood sensations, and his sexual yearnings are expressed in images which are of violence as well as sexuality:

> He made up a story as the fish swam through the gates into the pebbles and the moving bed. There was a drowned princess from a Christmas book, with her shoulders broken and her two red pigtails stretched like strings of a fiddle over her broken throat; she was caught in a fisherman's net, and the fish plucked her hair.

The imagery is that of male adolescent fantasy. There is the echo of a girl, for example, helpless, vulnerable and dominated and the sexual dimension of the imagery really needs no elucidation. The boy is frustrated, confused, and Thomas, as elsewhere in the early stories, pursues the aspect of violence:

> The boy sent a stone skidding over the green water. He saw a rabbit scuttle, and threw a stone at its tail. A fish leaped at the gnats, and a lark darted out of the green earth.

Already what could have been a very traditional story is beginning to develop in original ways. The concept of innocence represented in a young boy meeting sexual knowledge in the form of an experienced and older girl is hardly new. But few stories have dwelt as Thomas does here on the violent, pent-up frustration. When the girl enters the story she does so with a candidness that undermines the traditional models and smacks of the young Thomas's desire to shock:

> The girl in the torn cotton frock sat down on the grass and crossed her legs; a real wind from nowhere lifted her frock, and up to her waist she was brown as an acorn.

This is tradition coloured by the kind of wish fulfilment of which adolescent tall stories are born. At the height of a boy's sexual frustration appears a girl who is not only experienced but seems to lack reservations. The key word here is 'real' and the candidness of the description is part of the contrast between the boy's fantasies and how he behaves in reality. Thus, the emphasis is not upon her brazen sexuality but his total lack of self-confidence:

> The boy, still standing timidly in the first shade, saw the broken, holiday princess die for the second time, and a country girl take her place on the live hill. Who had been frightened of a few birds flying out of the trees, and a sudden daze of the sun that made river and field and distance look so little under the hill? Who had told him the girl was as tall as a tree? She was no taller or stranger than the flowery girls on Sundays who picnicked in Whippet valley.

Critics who have written about Thomas's concern with sexuality and adolescence have tended not to notice the exploratory dimension of these early stories and that in passages such as this there is a third strong presence: the culture of the Welsh rural communities. Thus the interest is not so much in the sexuality as in what the culture has done to the sexuality. In the case of this boy, the primary influence is that of his uncle and here we must remember that Dylan's own uncle though never so influential was a minister. Thus when the girl eventually leans towards him her thick, red hair—which signifies her unfettered sexuality—pertinently blots out the golden cornfields (innocence and fruition) and his uncle's house.

Another dimension that distinguishes a story like this from those of Caradoc Evans is Thomas's ability, anticipating the stories of *Portrait of the Artist as a Young Dog,* to express the perceptions of an adolescent. Thus the way everything seems magnified by the senses captures the excitement of an adolescent in his/her first sexual experience heightened by fear. He also captures in wry comic terms the kind of new-found self-esteem that often accompanies attracting a girl for the first time:

> The boy awoke cautiously into a more curious dream, a summer vision broader than the one black cloud poised in the unbroken centre on a tower shaft of light; he came out of love through a wind full of turning knives and a cave full of flesh-white birds on to a new summit, standing like a stone that faces the stars blowing and stands no ceremony from the sea wind, a hard boy angry on a mound in the middle of a country evening; he put out his chest and said hard words to the world.

V

The general sense of evil pervading the early stories, and shrouding the repressive religiosity which enters directly or indirectly into them, is also conveyed in the way that Thomas ransacks the Bible for symbols.

Blind conviction and strict adherence to the fundamentals of the Bible protected the most zealous chapel-goers from self-doubt. They were like the young boy in the story **"In the Garden"** (1934) who tries to convince himself that the world in which he lives is the ultimate reality: 'that beyond the red curtains there lay nothing at all. . . . Only the bright room, his mother, and himself'. Thomas's stories challenge any such blind faith focussing upon what bothered most of those who admitted self-doubt: that maybe there was nothing beyond in a slightly different sense, i.e. nothingness, void. **"In the Garden"** is an allegorical portrayal of these fears. The boy is the believer who wants reassurance that there is something beyond death. Even when he opens the trunk and finds it empty he still refuses to believe that this is the ultimate reality:

> Once he had prised up the rusty padlock with his pocket knife and very fearfully opened the lid, to find only emptiness and the smell of rot. He felt sure that it must have a secret drawer somewhere that held precious stones as bright as the sun . . .

The image of the trunk here and the use made of it is not, of course, unique to Thomas, the box is a traditional life symbol. Its enclosure and darkness suggest the womb, while simultaneously, in its evocation of the coffin, it is an image of death.

"The Tree" (1933) is a similar allegory, but more fully expresses the horror and sense of desperation at the possibility of nothingness:

> Before it was dark, he and the child climbed the stairs to the tower, the key turned in the lock, and the door, like the lid of a secret box, opened and let them in. The room was empty. 'Where are the secrets?' Asked the child. . . . Over and over again he explored the empty

room, kicking up the dust to look for a colourless trap-door, tapping the unpanelled walls for the hollow voice of a room beyond the tower.

Both stories conclude with mock adaptations of images and incidents from the Bible. **"In the Garden"** employs not only the image of the sacred garden but the burning bush in which God revealed Himself to mortals: 'The door of the summer house swung back in the wind, and he saw that the trunk, lying upon its side, was full of fire'. At the end, the boy kneels like Paul on the road to Damascus before 'a blinding light', but this time of the moon instead of the sun. Thomas's own fears of death undoubtedly bear upon these stories but within the total context of the early writings they are also part of his all pervading quarrel with religion. The fact that a repressive religious code may after all be shielding not a divinely inspired universe but a void makes its repression sinister.

"The Tree" closes with a mock crucifixion, the epitome of evil, to which we referred earlier:

> The child ran as fast as he could to the gardener's shed, and, returning over the sodden lawns, saw that the idiot had not moved but stood, straight and smiling, with his back to the tree and his arms stretched out.
>
> 'Let me tie your hands'.
>
> The idiot felt the wire that had not mended the rake close round his wrists. It cut into the flesh, and the blood from the cuts fell shining on to the tree.
>
> 'Brother', he said. He saw that the child held silver nails in the palm of his hand.

While this passage anticipates Thomas's later concern with dominance and violence, it also betrays a fascination with the crucifixion that occurs in other stories. In **"The Visitor"** (1934) for example it is evoked to give breadth to Rhianon's capacity for sympathy and compassion: 'she had a strange name out of the Bible. Such a woman had washed the body after it had been taken off the tree, with cool and competent fingers that touched on the holes like ten blessings'.

Usually the fascination of the crucifixion for Thomas lay in its power as a symbol of death and evil. Thus the mock crucifixion with an idiot as the surrogate Christ belies traditional and sacred interpretations of the Messiah's death. In fact, it is typical of the way in which the surrealistic sequences of the early stories frequently overturn established associations and significances of Biblical myth and imagery. In **"The Holy Six"** (1937) Mr. Davies, the old, mad man, parodies Christ's washing of his disciples' feet:

> He knelt down in the wilderness of the tiny parlour, and off came the holy socks and boots. I, Davies, bathed their feet, muttered the grey minister. So that he might remember, the old, mad man said to himself, I, Davies, the poor ghost, washed the six sins in mustard and water.

This particular story becomes more blasphemous and outrageous as the sexually-perverse evil lurking behind the façade of religious respectability becomes more explicit. Thus we become aware of just how depraved a character is Stul when in fantasy 'he leapt out to marry Mary; all-sexed and nothing, intangible hermaphrodite riding the neuter dead, the minister of God in a grey image mounted dead Mary'. Outrage follows outrage until the final impact of a minister of God not only committing necrophilia but necrophilia with the Virgin Mary. But there is another level of blasphemy here, referred to throughout the story, in the way in which Stul represents natural instinct perverted by repression. He is a man whose 'manhood withered like the sap in a stick under a scarecrow's tatters' until he lost sexual identity and perspective as words like 'mounted' and descriptions of him as grey and as 'all-sexed and nothing' confirm.

Like Blake before him, Dylan Thomas tries to offer an alternative version of the Fall which in **"The Holy Six"** he refers to significantly as the 'first bewilderment'. This is especially obvious in **"The Mouse and the Woman"** (1936):

> A garden was planted eastward, and Adam lived in it. Eve was made for him, out of him, bone of his bones, flesh of his flesh. They were as naked as you upon the seashore, but Eve could not have been as beautiful. They ate with the devil, and saw that they were naked, and covered up their nakedness. In their good bodies they saw evil for the first time.

Thomas is beginning to develop here his conviction that the Welsh religious creed had prevented a healthy, sensuous enjoyment of life. The evil of this is underlined by the association of the young madman's fantasy with Good Friday and the crucifixion which we have already said attracted Thomas as a powerful symbol of darkness and death. The fantasy occurs 'one winter morning, after the last crowing of the cock, in the walks of his garden'. We are reminded of the cock that crowed after Peter's denial of Christ and of the Garden of Gethsemene. By turning Eden into Gethsemene, as it were, Thomas underlines the key thesis: the mismatch between nature and a repressive religious culture.

The argument is developed further in **"The Map of Love"** (1937). Here Beth Rib and Reuben enjoy swimming naked. The name Rib takes us back to Eden, to prelapsarian innocence. But, gradually, as Thomas describes Beth and Reuben's sensuous enjoyments and their new-found freedom, it is suggested that the pair cannot throw off the deeply ingrained sense of impropriety and guilt: 'Reuben, weed-bound, fought with the grey heads that fought his hands, and followed her back to the brink.' On one level, the grey heads are the weeds. On another level, they are old wisdom which has come down to him from the elders. The dichotomy between head and hand suggests the traditional battle between the mind and emotions while the boy's struggle with grey weeds—grey signifying age—suggests the conflict between youth and age. We are left in no doubt as to which will be the victor. Nor are we left in any doubt as to the lasting repressive influence Thomas at-

taches to religious teaching based on the myth of the Fall. As soon as the pair come out of the water they find it difficult to remain naked: 'First fear shot them back'. First here refers to time as 'first of all, fear shot them back' but also the so-called Original or first sin as in the 'First Fear'. There is a sense in which both Beth and Reuben are doomed. Like the Prodigal Son, the parable which Thomas evokes to describe their return, they will not simply return to, but conform with, the rest of the fold.

A number of the early stories suggest that youth has been misled by the old. The gardener's emphasis in **"The Tree"** upon the key which will unlock the tower is misleading because it is empty. The boy loves the tree in the garden and is encouraged in his worship of the tree by the gardener, yet the gardener has in mind not the actual tree loved by the boy but the tree of Calvary.

As Moynihan has aptly pointed out, Thomas's reaction against religion took several forms. He denies and mocks Christianity but at the same time builds with Biblical and religious symbols his personal mythology.

Margaret Moan Rowe (essay date 1990)

SOURCE: "Living 'under the shadow of the bowler': *Portrait of the Artist as a Young Dog,*" in *Dylan Thomas: Craft or Sullen Art,* edited by Alan Bold, Vision Press, 1990, pp. 125–36.

[*In the following excerpt, Rowe maintains that Thomas refashioned his own middle-class childhood in* Portrait of the Artist as a Young Dog *to make it more palatable.*]

Dylan Thomas is pre-eminently a rememberer; in both his poetry and prose, as John Wain has noted, 'his great theme is nostalgia'.[1] Indeed his best fiction, *Portrait of the Artist as a Young Dog,* is a celebration of his childhood, adolescence and young manhood in Swansea. The ten stories that make up the collection, published originally in 1940, have been described by Vernon Watkins as 'stories about human beings living and behaving exactly as they used to live and behave when he was a child'.[2] But the 'he' is Dylan Thomas of the flashing imagination, and the characters in his fiction are the creations of that imagination; the reader, therefore, must be wary of Watkins' 'exactly' when considering Thomas's most critically acclaimed fiction.

1

In *Portrait* Thomas does nothing less than shape and celebrate a past acceptable to him; he builds a world around the focusing of his sensibility. His raw material was his youth in Swansea spent in a middle-class family which Paul Ferris describes as 'the result of a common enough process, people growing away from a rural background into the life of cities'.[3] Thomas himself offers the most apt description of his status in one of the stories in *Portrait,*

"Where Tawe Flows". Therein Mr. Evans describes his fictional creation Mary Phillips who

> . . . wasn't a suburbanite from birth, she didn't live under the shadow of the bowler, like you or me. Or like me, anyway. I was born in 'The Poplars' and now I'm in 'Lavengro'. From bowler to bowler, though I must say, apropos of Mr. Humphries' diatribe, and I'm the first to admire his point of view, that the everyday man's just as interesting a character as the neurotic poets of Bloomsbury.[4]

Born and reared 'under the shadow of the bowler' Thomas may have been, but an everyday man he was not. In *Portrait* he creates a past worthy of the embryonic artist by selecting and heightening the eccentric even gothic elements in his background (perhaps best seen in his depiction of the child-grandparent relationship in **"A Visit to Grandpa's"**). More significantly, however, he celebrates his escape from those parts of his past not amenable to his artistic vocation, particularly the middle-class constrictions typified by the bowler.

2

Although a male image, the bowler's values are most effectively maintained in the domestic sphere dominated by women (with some help from evangelical clergy in **"The Fight"** and the judiciary in **"Just Like Little Dogs"**) in Thomas's stories. As a result, the domestic sphere is often presented as enemy terrain to be secured or avoided. Two stories, in particular, offer fascinating glimpses of male responses to the female sphere in *Portrait*.

"Just Like Little Dogs", a first-person narration, presents the narrator, presumably Dylan Thomas, as the romantic watcher:

> I was a lonely nightwalker and a steady stander-at-corners. I liked to walk through the wet town after midnight, when the streets were deserted and the window lights out, alone and alive on the glistening tramlines in dead and empty High Street under the moon, gigantically sad in the damp streets by ghostly Ebenezer Chapel.
>
> (p. 177)

As Jacob Korg has observed, 'Most of the stories [in *Portrait*] are about an observer or witness. . . .'[5] Such a rôle gives Thomas a way to underscore his artistic potential as the outsider in the ordinary life in Swansea. That rôle, too, allows Thomas to tweak, ever so gently, his own sense of difference, of specialness which he does in **"One Warm Saturday".**

During his watch in **"Just Like Little Dogs",** the narrator meets two other standers-at-corners and watchers, brothers Tom and Walter, and listens to their strange story. With Walter's help, Tom tells their 'love' story involving picking up two sisters, Doris and Norma, switching partners in the sand, facing paternity suits and marrying the wrong women (at least Tom does; Walter does not care for either

woman). Hence their nightly sojourns outdoors. As Walter describes it: 'We had to do the right thing by them, didn't we? That's why Tom won't go home. He never goes home till the early morning. I've got to keep him company. He's my brother' (p. 179). '. . . had to do the right thing' underscores the bowler's power, a power that turns the home into a place of confinement. Home here is no refuge for the brothers who prefer their own company to the company of wives or children.

The narrator, too, desires to escape the domestic sphere and keeps them company as he listens to the story; even more than that, he finds himself a voyeur in the story: 'I lay like a pimp in a bush by Tom's side and squinted through to see him round his hands on Norma's breast' (p. 179). All the sympathy in the story is extended to the men who have done 'the right thing' and to the male narrator who is constantly celebrating his curiosity: 'Fancy listening, I thought, to a long, unsatisfactory story in the frost-bite night in a polar arch' (p. 179). But listen he does as he gathers material for his own stories.

Inhospitable weather threatens neither listener nor speaker in **"Where Tawe Flows".** Indeed home and hearth seem to beckon Mr. Humphries, Mr. Roberts, and the much younger Mr. Thomas who journey to the suburban villa of Mr. Evans for their weekly Friday meeting. The four are involved in writing a novel about provincial life hence the need for an indoor setting. But significantly none of the real work can begin until Mrs. Evans retires:

> Mr. Humphries and Mr. Thomas arranged the chairs around the fire, and all four sat down, close and confidential and with full glasses in their hands. None of them spoke for a time. They gave one another sly looks, sipped and sighed, lit the cigarettes that Mr. Evans produced from a draughts box, and once Mr. Humphries glanced at the grandfather clock and winked and put his finger to his lips. Then, as the visitors grew warm and the wine worked and they forgot the bitter night outside, Mr. Evans said *with a little shudder of forbidden delight* [italics mine]: 'The wife will be going to bed in half an hour. Then we can start the good work. Have you all got yours with you?'
>
> (p. 182)

After Mrs. Evans' departure, 'the good work' can begin:

> Mr. Humphries and Mr. Thomas put notebooks on their knees, took a pencil each, and watched Mr. Evans open the door of the grandfather clock. Beneath the swinging weights was a heap of papers tied in a blue bow. These Mr. Evans placed on the desk.'
>
> (p. 185)

What follows is a wonderful piece of meta-fiction in which the four men elaborate their views on life and fiction. Indeed, Thomas is at such ease in this story that he is willing to joke about his own passion for the fantastic, a passion that led to many excesses and confusions in the stories in *The Map of Love* (1939). When the young Mr. Thomas in **"Where Tawe Flows"** wants to include a smattering of

the fantastic in the common effort, Mr. Humphries cries'
. . . let's get our realism straight. Mr. Thomas will be
making all the characters Blue Birds before we know
where we are' (p. 187).

But meta-fictional or no, **"Where Tawe Flows"** can also
be read as an example of what Thomas in **"Old Garbo"**
calls 'a great male moment' (p. 207), as male creators talk
about the problems of characterization involving mostly
female characters. (Throughout *Portrait* writing is a male
activity whether presented as Gwilym's religious/erotic
poetry in **"The Peaches"**, Arnold's prodigious letter writing in **"Patricia, Edith and Arnold"**, Dan's novels in
"The Fight", or Mr. Farr's editing in **"Old Garbo"**.) Even
the ordinary domestic setting is converted into a male
sanctuary with the departure of Mrs. Evans and the liberation of the manuscript from the grandfather clock. But the
transformation of setting is temporary as his memory that
'I promised Maud not after midnight' prompts Mr. Evans
to close the evening—with a little help from Mrs. Evans
above stairs calling 'Emlyn! Emlyn!' (pp. 194, 195).

Except in four stories—**"The Peaches"**, **"Patricia, Edith
and Arnold"**, **"Old Garbo"**, and **"One Warm Saturday"**—the domestic setting, associated with women and
the social order of the bowler, is a confining place in *Portrait*. The male sphere—whether the sanctuary secured
from Mrs. Evans in **"Where Tawe Flows"**, the polar night
in **"Just Like Little Dogs"**, the pub in **"Old Garbo"**, or
Rhossilli beach in **"Extraordinary Little Cough"** and
"Who Do You Wish Was With Us?"—is the preferred
setting in the collection. Male bonding—the 'great male
moment'—is also the central positive emotional experience in Thomas's stories. Women characters are often
marginalized by Thomas and generally associated with
'the choking houses' (p. 196) fled by the day hikers in
"Who Do You Wish Was With Us?" Women dust the
bowler just as they dust their sitting rooms.

3

Let me turn to the four stories which I cite as exceptions,
but let me make that turn by way of **"Where Tawe Flows"**.
Questioned by Mr. Humphries about his wife's whereabouts, Mr. Evans replies, 'In the kitchen'; to which
Humphries responds, 'A woman's only place . . . with
one exception' (p. 182)—a fair summation of the status of
women in **"The Peaches"**, **"Patricia, Edith and Arnold"**,
"Old Garbo", and **"One Warm Saturday"**. Thomas's
vocation may have made him different but his fantasies
about women were very ordinary. Locked in a conventional male fantasy, Thomas assigns central places to
women characters who serve his younger self.

The first story in *Portrait*, **"The Peaches"**, presents Dylan
Thomas as a young boy visiting his aunt and uncle—Jim
and Annie. Only his uncle's name is accompanied by a
family title; Annie is always Annie. She plays two rôles in
the story: goddess of the kitchen and keeper of the bowler.
But first to a rôle Thomas authorizes for women. After a

nightmarish, but imaginative foray with his 'Uncle Jim'
through town (with the frightened boy waiting outside a
pub) and over a sparsely inhabited landscape, Dylan is
greeted by Annie:

> . . . I ran into the kitchen and into Annie's arms. There
> was a welcome, then. The clock struck twelve as she
> kissed me, and I stood among the shining and striking
> like a prince taking off his disguise. One minute I was
> small and cold, skulking . . . ; the next I was a royal
> nephew in smart town clothes, embraced and wel-
> comed, standing in the snug centre of my stories and
> listening to the clock announcing me.
>
> (p. 125)

Annie—who 'fussed and clucked and nodded' (p. 125)—is
the instrument of transformation providing as she does the
emotional warmth and physical support that the boy needs.
His imaginative needs are fed by males in the story: Uncle
Jim, his cousin Gwilym, his friend Jack and Dylan, ever
given to crafting demon stories and shaping aristocratic
identities for himself.[6]

Annie's other rôle, as bowler-keeper, is less favorably presented in **"The Peaches"**; it is also a rôle that she plays
with considerable unease. Interestingly enough, she plays
that rôle for her nephew as she greets a more formidable
bowler-keeper, the rich and insensitive Mrs Williams,
mother of Dylan's friend Jack. Banished from the warmth
of the kitchen, Annie as bowler-keeper presides over 'the
best room', that sanctuary of family pieties:

> The best room smelt of moth balls and fur and damp
> and dead plants and stale, sour air. Two glass cases on
> wooden coffin-boxes lined the window-wall. . . . A
> case of china and pewter, trinkets, teeth, family
> brooches, stood beyond the brandy table; there was a
> large oil lamp on the patchwork table-cloth, a Bible
> with a clasp, a tall vase with a draped woman about to
> bathe on it, and a framed photograph of Annie, Uncle
> Jim, and Gwilym smiling in front of the fern-pot.
>
> (p. 129)

Saved for high days and holy days, 'the best room' transforms Annie, who 'dusted and brushed and polished there
once a week' (p. 130), into a hostess greeting the snobbish
Mrs. Williams. The transformation is a disaster as Mrs.
Williams, a former mayoress, refuses peaches, a long preserved delicacy in the straitened Jones's household.

Thomas handles the encounter skillfully to suggest at once
the deathlike hold of middle-class values caught in the description of 'the best room', the formidable bulk of the
awful Mrs. Williams, and the social pressure that momentarily transforms Annie into a liar who explains the absence of cake with 'we forgot to order it from the shop'
(p. 131). I want to stress the momentary change in Annie
because her central rôle in the story is as nurturer to 'a
royal nephew'—she is visibly ill at ease as she dusts the
bowler. Indeed, in the penultimate scene in the novel, Annie is back in the kitchen ministering to young Dylan:
'She forgave me when I drank tea from the saucer'
(p. 136).

"Patricia, Edith and Arnold" also presents a woman as ministering angel to a young boy, presumably Dylan. In this class-conscious third-person narration, Thomas presents a younger self as something of a spy in the life of Patricia, the family servant. '. . . listening carefully all the time' (p. 144), the boy observes the doings of Patricia and Edith, the servant next door, as they deal with the complexity of a shared beau. The young boy is both watcher and participant in the action; more than that, he is something of a competitor for Patricia's affection. He courts her with forbidden language; seeking her attention, he claims 'I'm dirty as Christ knows what' (p. 145). Responding to his taunt, Patricia 'made him change his suit in front of her', but the boy turns the apparent punishment into a sexual exhibition as 'He took off his trousers and danced around her, crying: Look at me, Patricia!' (p. 145).

The entire story is suffused with suggestions of a clammy closeness between the boy and the servant who frequently interchange rôles as comforter and comforted. Here any rules set by the servant (far from the bowler's power) are quickly ignored by the young boy, who invokes forbidden words like 'bottom' to secure Patricia's attention. Even more effectively, he invokes the truth—'. . . Arnold Matthews told lies. He said he loved you better than Edith, and he whispered behind your back to her' (p. 151)—and overthrows his rival. In the end, the boy Dylan triumphs as Patricia 'in the warm living-room' forgets her own sadness to minister to the princeling: 'There, that's better. The hurting's gone. You won't call the king your uncle in a minute' (p. 152).

Women in the domestic setting, then, are valued insofar as they conform to a male fantasy of woman as nurturer. Both Annie and Patricia serve so have a central rôle in Dylan Thomas's return to his past and his shaping of a personal myth.[7] But that myth takes Thomas from childhood to young manhood in Swansea, so women outside the domestic sphere also appear. Women outside the pale, outside 'the shadow of the bowler', find their places as nurturers of a different kind in *Portrait*'s final stories, **"Old Garbo"** and **"One Warm Saturday"**.

"Old Garbo" offers a particularly effective depiction of separate male and female spheres. The narrator is not the 'royal nephew' of **"The Peaches"** nor the curious boy of **"Patricia Edith, and Arnold"** but an older and world-hungry Dylan, junior reporter/reviewer for the *Tawe News*. The story is a celebration of 'a great male moment' when Dylan visits the town's underbelly, the *Fishguard* pub at the docks, with Mr. Farr 'the senior reporter' (206). (*Portrait* abounds with male mentors; the father's power is everywhere.) The world of respectability is typified by the Thomas household, his mother, and her bowler expectations: 'Going for a nice walk?' she asks as Dylan takes off for his pre-Christmas pub crawl with Mr. Farr.

The underside of that respectability is caught in the scene at the *Fishguard* where Dylan and Farr watch Mrs. Prothero—'We call her Old Garbo because she isn't like her,

see' (p. 214)—deal with news of her daughter's death in childbirth. No tip of the bowler to respectability in this scene, as mortician, Mrs. Prothero, and 'under a damp royal family, a row of black-dressed women on a hard bench sat laughing and crying, short glasses lined by their Guinnesses' (p. 214). Soon enough the party atmosphere which compels Dylan to leave his rôle as watcher and to participate in the drinking and singing gives way to re-criminations as the women discover that Mrs. Prothero's daughter is alive—unknown to the grieving mother who has left with their remaining shillings to share her grief at other pubs. Ever ladies—of sorts, 'In low voices the women reviled Mrs. Prothero, liar, adultress, mother of bastards, thief' (p. 216). Eventually Old Garbo kills herself.

What I want to underscore though is not Mrs. Prothero's sad end, but the comic and celebratory energy in the story. In **"Old Garbo"** Thomas praises freedom from respectability, what he records is at least a temporary getting out from 'under the shadow of the bowler'. In the *Fishguard*'s snuggery, surely a parodic 'best room', women of a lower class and suspect sexual mores have a place in Thomas's memories of his youth; indeed, they and liquor act as stimulants to his imagination:

> The rum burned and kicked in the hot room, but my head felt tough as a hill and I could write twelve books before morning and roll the 'Carlton' barmaid, like a barrel, the length of Tawe sands.
>
> (p. 214)

Even after the liquor wears off, Thomas the narrator is left with the memory of the free-wheeling people at the *Fishguard* and his certainty expressed to Mr. Farr, his mentor: 'I'll put them all in a story by and by, I said' (p. 218).

No male guide eases the way for the protagonist in **"One Warm Saturday"**; such an absence is fitting for the collection's final story, since Thomas clearly wants to depict a younger self on the verge, ready to break the fetters of the middle class. As the story opens the 'young man in a sailor's jersey' (p. 219) watches and waits. More of an outsider than ever, he draws a figure of a woman in the sand and foregoes participation in the holiday crowds around him. Having rejected his friends' invitations to join their pleasures—'rocking with the girls on the Giant Racer or tearing on the Ghost Train down the skeletons' tunnel' (p. 221)—he momentarily contents himself with his sense of difference.

> He thought: Poets live and walk with their poems; a man with vision needs no other company; Saturday is a crude day; I must go home and sit in my bedroom by the boiler.
>
> (p. 221)

But that sense of difference is quickly dispelled by the sense in which he is very like, especially sexually, all the other young men living 'under the shadow of the bowler': 'And what shall a prig do now?' he asks himself (p. 221).

Indeed, the 'bedroom by the boiler' which houses the beginning poet is also 'a bedroom that was full of his shames' (p. 226). Thomas brilliantly connects the young man's imaginative power with his masturbatory fantasies, and shows how both sensitivity and shame distance him from sexual experience.

That distance, however, is soon narrowed by Lou, the young prostitute who beckons him in the park and later, more successfully, in a saloon. As in **"Old Garbo"**, the chief setting in **"One Warm Saturday"** is the town's demi-monde—the saloon and Lou's room, a combination of the kitchen-bedroom settings authorized by male fantasy:

> She turned on the lights, and he walked with her proudly into her own room, into the room that he would come to know, and saw a wide bed, a gramophone on a chair, a wash-basin half-hidden in a corner, a gas fire and a cooking ring, a closed cupboard, and her photograph in a cardboard frame on the chest of drawers with no handles. Here she slept and ate.
>
> (p. 232)

What more perfect world for the young man seeking escape from the 'best room' and all it represents.

That escape, however, is not to be in **"One Warm Saturday"**—or in *Portrait of the Artist as a Young Dog* which, after all is Dylan Thomas's record of a younger self poised for, rather than accomplishing, escape. Lou's work in the person of Mr. O'Brien, 'her sugar daddy from old Ireland' (p. 230), and several other friends accompany Lou and the shy young man to the bower of bliss. As in **"Old Garbo"**, the drinking and singing lure the young man, but in **"One Warm Saturday"** those activities also keep him from Lou. In a marvellously comic turn, too much drink sends him on a grotesque search for a lavatory which he never finds; nor does he find the way back to the magic room.

The action moves toward failure with the young man's sexual quest never completed, as much because of the abstracting power of his imagination as anything else. Early in the story, Thomas captures the seductiveness of his own imaginative process:

> He saw her as a wise, soft girl whom no hard company could spoil, for her soft self, bare to the heart, broke through every defence of her sensual falsifiers. As he thought this, phrasing her gentleness, faithlessly running to words away from the real room and his love in the middle, he woke with a start and saw her lively body six steps from him, no calm heart dressed in a sentence, but a pretty girl, to be got and kept.
>
> (p. 229)

At the same time, the third-person point of view in the story privileges the power of imagination. Indeed, the incantatory power of Thomas's sentences in the internal views of the young man are nothing less than a celebration

of his difference, his poetic potential. In general, John Fuller is right when he observes that

> Thomas's prose is always sharp, observant and funny when he is writing about Wales and his childhood, and it is the richness and excitement of life which he communicates, rather than its holy rapture.[8]

Such is true of the details in **"One Warm Saturday"** when the narrative does not privilege the young man; I cite only two wildly comic scenes: the sexual banter in the Victoria saloon and the debate about whether or not Tenneyson had a hump. Alongside all the sharp observation, however, is precisely the 'holy rapture' which Fuller sees as missing. That rapture is there in the internal views of the young man as befits the portrait of a romantic poet's younger self.

That rapture is there, too, even at the end of **"One Warm Saturday"**, an ending that Richard Kelly reads as the young man's fall from 'his timeless, exotic dream of love to a decaying world'.[9] Lou is certainly lost, but women are expendable—even interchangeable—in Thomas's world; what is not expendable is the exercise of imagination, an exercise that the young man is involved in the story's final paragraph:

> For a long time he waited on the stairs, though there was no love now to wait for and no bed but his own too many miles away to lie in, and only the approaching day to remember his discovery. All around him the disturbed inhabitants of the house were falling back into sleep. Then he walked out of the house on to the waste space and under the leaning cranes and ladders. The light of the one weak lamp in a rusty circle fell across the brick heaps and the broken wood and the dust that had been houses once, where the small and hardly known and never-to-be-forgotten people of the dirty town had lived and loved and died and, always, lost.
>
> (p. 238)

Love may be lost, at least temporarily, but language is not as the solitary young man is once again the watcher, the rememberer 'faithlessly running to words'.

Notes

1. John Wain, "Druid of her Broken Body", *Dylan Thomas: New Critical Essays,* ed. Walford Davies (London: Dent, 1972), p. 17.

2. Vernon Watkins (ed.), *Dylan Thomas: Letters to Vernon Watkins,* (New York: New Directions, 1957), p. 20.

3. Paul Ferris, *Dylan Thomas* (London: Hodder & Stoughton, 1977), p. 24.

4. Dylan Thomas, "Where Tawe Flows", *The Collected Stories* (New York: New Directions, 1984), p. 188. Subsequent quotations from this edition will be cited by page number in the text.

5. Jacob Korg, *Dylan Thomas* (Boston: Twayne, 1965), p. 169.

6. For an interesting discussion of the workings of the imagination in "The Peaches" see Harold F. Mosher, "The Structure of Dylan Thomas's 'The Peaches'", *Studies in Short Fiction,* VI (Fall 1969), 536–47.

7. Walford Davies convincingly argues that Thomas is '. . . better at mythologizing the actual than at actualizing myth': "The Wanton Starer", *Dylan Thomas: New Critical Essays,* p. 139.

8. John Fuller, "The Cancered Aunt on Her Insanitary Farm", *Dylan Thomas: New Critical Essays,* p. 208.

9. Richard Kelly, "The Lost Vision in Dylan Thomas's 'One Warm Saturday'", *Studies in Short Fiction,* VI (Winter 1969), 209.

Jacob Korg (essay date 1992)

SOURCE: "Stories and Dramas," in *Dylan Thomas,* Twayne Publishers, 1992.

[*In the following essay, Korg analyzes the poetic and straightforward narrative styles that characterize Thomas's stories.*]

1

Thomas was as prolific a writer of prose as he was of verse. He published the first of his short stories, **"After the Fair,"** in March 1934, less than a year after his earliest poems had appeared, and he continued to write prose until his death. In addition to his numerous short stories, the uncompleted novel, ***Adventures in the Skin Trade,*** three prose dramas, the radio play, *Under Milk Wood,* and several film scripts, he wrote book reviews, radio talks, and descriptive essays, many of them collected in the posthumously published volume, ***Quite Early One Morning.***[1]

Thomas's fiction may be divided sharply into two classifications: vigorous fantasies in poetic style, a genre he discontinued after 1939, and straightforward, objective narratives. Until 1939 he seems to have thought of the short prose narrative as an alternate poetic form—as a vehicle for recording the action of the imagination in reshaping objective reality according to private desire. Almost every story of this period (the exceptions being **"After the Fair"** and **"The Tree"**) perceives actuality through the screen of an irrational mind. The main characters are madmen, simpletons, fanatics, lechers, and poets in love: people enslaved by the dictates of feeling. Their stories are narrated in a heavily poetic prose reflecting the confusion of actual and imaginary experiences that constitute their reality, so that the material and the psychological intersect without a joint, forming a strange new area of being. For example, as Mr. Davies, the deluded rector of **"The Holy Six,"** is washing the feet of his six colleagues, believing that he is performing a holy deed, we are told that "light brought the inner world to pass," that his misconception was transformed into actuality. Some of the stories seem transitional in style, enabling the reader to witness these transforma-

tions as an outsider. In **"The Dress,"** the fleeing madman who yearns for a chance to sleep thinks of sleep as personified by another object of desire—a girl. When he breaks into the cottage where the young housewife is sitting, he follows the logic of his delusion, mistakes her for sleep, and puts his head in her lap.

The setting of most of these stories is the seaside Welsh town wickedly called Llareggub (to be read backwards), which is also the scene of *Under Milk Wood,* with its neighboring countryside, including a valley named after Jarvis, a lecherous nineteenth-century landlord, some farms, and a mountain called Cader Peak. Among the inhabitants of this region are young men obsessed by unfulfilled love, as in **"The Mouse and the Woman"** and **"The Orchards"**; clergymen crazed by lust, as in **"The Holy Six"** and **"The Burning Baby"**; wise men or women who teach some cabalistic magic art, as in **"The Tree," "The Map of Love," "The School for Witches,"** and **"The Lemon"**; and enigmatic girls who rise from the sea or the soil as in **"The Mouse and the Woman"** and **"A Prospect of the Sea."** The fancies of these people, narrated in a manner rendering them indistinguishable from objective reality, fill the town and the countryside with visions, supernatural forces, and fantastic episodes recalling the world of fairy tale and of folklore. People and objects are whisked into new shapes, small and intimate experiences are magnified until they embody fundamental realities—"creation screaming in the steam of the kettle"—and the order of nature is constantly subjected to disruption. In this milieu the anomalous is the ordinary; at the end of **"Prologue to an Adventure,"** for example, the barroom where the two friends are standing runs down the drains of the town into the sea.

In one of his letters to Vernon Watkins, Thomas observes that the reader of verse needs an occasional rest but that the poet ought not to give it to him. In applying this principle to his stories, Thomas produced complex, involuted narratives with rich surfaces of language and imagery. At first impression they have no depths; but analysis reveals that the order of imagination operating in them is the one that produced Thomas's poetry. His stories, unlike his earliest poems, deal with recognizable people and places; but they are invested with the same mythic atmosphere found in the poems. As we have already observed, there are numerous and detailed affinities between the poems and these early, fantastic stories. Common themes—the burning of a child, the "falling" of time, the unity of life, and the verbal capacities of nature—provide subjects for both, and are also reflected in rhetorical details. But the most general resemblance is an awareness of the cosmic import of small events, a tendency to develop the significance of experiences by referring them to the absolute limits of the continuum of which they are a part. The lust of Rhys Rhys in **"The Burning Baby"** culminates in incest and in the murder of his child; the desire of the poet in **"The Mouse and the Woman"** raises a beautiful woman for him on the seashore; the vision of heaven the boy sees from the top of his ladder in **"A Prospect of the Sea"** is an endless Eden stretching to meet itself above and below.

2

In **"The Tree,"** which first appeared in *Adelphi* in December, 1934, within a week of the publication of *18 Poems*, the style typical of Thomas's fantastic stories is still at an early stage of its development, so it is possible to distinguish actual events from the delusions going on in the minds of the characters. The story also provides a convenient dramatization of the creative process at work in these stories. The gardener transmits his obsession to the boy; the boy, at the end of the story, tries to transform it into actuality. In writing his fantastic stories, Thomas, the narrator, acted the part of the boy. Borrowing delusions from his characters, Thomas produced in the narrative itself a version of reality corresponding to the delusions.

The gardener in the story is a naive religious man who, by one of those primitive metaphoric associations familiar to us from Thomas's poems, takes all trees as counterparts of the "tree" of the cross. As he tells the boy the story of Jesus, the child fixes on the elder tree in the garden as the scene of the crucifixion. When he is let into the locked tower as a Christmas gift, the boy is bitterly disappointed to find it empty; but he associates the Jarvis hills, which are visible through the window, with Bethlehem, for they, like Bethlehem, are toward the east. The idiot standing under the tree in the garden, exposed to the wind and rain, has already had Christlike intimations of his destiny when the boy finds him in the morning. And when the boy learns that he has come from the eastern hills that he has mistaken for Bethlehem, he fits the tree, the hills, and the idiot into the pattern described by the gardener, and sets about making the story of Jesus a reality. As the story closes, he has put the idiot against the tree and is crucifying him on it. The ultimate point of the story is the idiot's acceptance of his suffering; in the final scene the ignorant piety of the gardener is being transformed, through the imagination of the child and the love and humility of the idiot, into a reality.

The narrative style that blends actual and imagined worlds appears for the first time in **"The Visitor,"** whose main character, as he approaches death, perceives the continuity between the living and dead aspects of the cosmos. Because we know the actual world that is the background of his delusion, we can see that the first part of the narrative has a double structure, and we can easily separate Peter's delusions from external reality. His idea that the sheets are shrouds, that his heart is a clock ticking, and that he lacks feelings because he is dead are simply misinterpretations of sensory clues. Only occasionally does his mind drift into clear hallucination, as when he thinks he is looking down at his own dead face in the coffin. Otherwise his thoughts are perfectly intelligible; he recalls that his first wife died seven years earlier in childbirth, and the guilt he experiences is expressed in a remarkable metaphor: "He felt his body turn to vapour, and men who had been light as air walked, metal-hooved, through and beyond him."

In the second part of the story, however, we enter fully into Peter's dying delirium and the basis of fact offered by the external world fades away. In a region of pure fantasy, we are unable, like Peter himself, to distinguish the imaginary from the real or even to detect the moment of division between life and death. In his delirium, Callaghan, the visitor Peter has been expecting, comes and carries him away into a realm of essential being where the pulsations of alternate growth and destruction are perfectly visible in a stripped, transparent landscape. Here a new prose style, the one Thomas adopts as a means of objectifying mystical perception, presents itself. More descriptive than narrative, it is full of grotesque, clearly realized images. Sometimes rhapsodic, sometimes strangely matter of fact, it seeks to capture the disruption imposed upon nature by hallucinatory vision. As in the poems, metaphor becomes active, so that "the flowers shot out of the dead," and "the light of the moon . . . pulled the moles and badgers out of their winter."

The journey ends when Peter, suddenly returned to his sickbed again, feels restored to his body and speaks to his wife. But she does not hear him, and he does not realize he is dead until she pulls the sheet over his face. Just as he had the delusion, when he was living, that he was dead, he now has the delusion, when he is dead, that he is alive. The division between the two states is slight, and disembodied vitality persists so powerfully that moving from the aspect of being we call life to the one we call death hardly matters to it. As one of Thomas's poems concludes, "The heart is sensual, though five eyes break."

In **"The Visitor,"** Peter experiences actual and imaginary realms at different times; the two meet only at the boundary between them, where their edges are not clear. But in the further development of his narrative style, Thomas presented situations where imagined and actual events are super-imposed upon each other as single experiences. Two closely related short stories published in 1936, **"The Orchards"** and **"The Mouse and the Woman,"** illustrate this. Both have the same theme as "The Hunchback in the Park": the creation of an imaginary woman by a mind obsessed by the need for love. And both are tragedies of delusion, for they show that the dreamer is pitifully exposed to the demands of the actual world.

The woman loved by Marlais, the poet of **"The Orchards,"** comes to him in a dream in the form of a scarecrow who stands, with her sister in a landscape of burning orchards. When he wakes up, the memory of this dream persists and distracts him from his writing. Oppressed by the disparity between the passion of his dream thoughts and the dullness of the town outside his window, Marlais makes an effort of the imagination that leads him to mystic perception. What follows is perhaps Thomas's most complete description of mystic vision. The distinction between objective and subjective is canceled: "There was dust in his eyes; there were eyes in the grains of dust. . . ." Individual things seem parts of greater wholes, saturated with absolute significance: "His hand before him was five-fingered life." Opposites are reconciled: "It is all one, the loud voice and the still voice striking a common silence. . . ." Intoxicated with the feeling that he commands both spiritual and actual realms, so that he is "man among ghosts, and ghost in clover," Marlais now "moved for the last answer."

A second sleep shows him that the landscape of his dream and the woman he loves are still there; and when he wakes he goes out of the town to find it. The second half of the story, like that of **"The Visitor,"** is the journey of a mental traveler; but Marlais travels on the ground, not in the air, as Peter does. And his imagined world is spread over the real countryside, whose objective features emerge, like peaks rising out of the clouds of his thoughts. The Whippet valley, a part of the real countryside that has been destroyed by mining, is succeeded by a wood whose trees are said to spring from the legend of the Fall. As his walk continues, Marlais enters the realm of myth and becomes a myth himself; when he has penetrated into this imaginary world, he finds the orchards of his dream and the girl in it. An objective observer would probably say that Marlais had been invited to have a picnic tea with an ordinary girl; for the tablecloth, cups, and bread she produces are real enough. But as Marlais views the scene, the conditions of his dream impose themselves upon this objective reality, and the scene is transformed to correspond with it. The orchards break into fire; the girl is changed into a scarecrow and calls up her sister, as in the dream: and Marlais has his desire. But we have been warned at the beginning that Marlais's passion was "a story more terrible than the stories of the reverend madmen in the Black Book of Llareggub," and the conclusion tells us why. The fires of Marlais's dream are put out by "the real world's wind," and it becomes a fact, not a dream. The imaginative tide of his obsession recedes, leaving him stranded in actuality, kissing a scarecrow, and exposing his madness.

"The Mouse and the Woman" is a more elaborate treatment of the same theme: the betrayal of a poet by his obsession with love. In this story, as in **"The Orchards,"** the hero creates a dream woman, and he shuttles back and forth between a dream world and a waking world that seem equally real. But Thomas has added to the situation a moral aspect represented by the mouse. The story opens with a remarkable description of the madman in the lunatic asylum, and it then moves back in his memory to trace the steps of his alienation. As in **"The Orchards,"** the woman comes to him in a dream, and her memory persists when he is awake until he is caught between reality and delusion; he does not know whether to believe in her existence or not. He creates her by writing about her, "it was upon the block of paper that she was made absolute," thus surrendering to imagination; he then goes out on the beach to find her and bring her to his cottage. This begins the part of the story where hallucination is perfectly superimposed upon actuality. The girl is, of course, pure imagination, but the mouse, which is associated with evil, and the mousehole the hero nails up to keep it away seem representative of objective actuality. Oddly, within this waking dream the hero has nocturnal dreams containing frightening enigmatic symbols. When he strips the girl and becomes her lover, two related events follow: the mouse emerges from its hole, and the notion of original sin enters the consciousness of the lovers as the man tells the girl the story of the Fall. She realizes that he has felt evil in their relationship.

The mouse and what it represents are the seed of destruction in his euphoric delusion, for the woman leaves him. Though he pursues her, she will not have him back. Her rejection of him is marvelously conveyed in the fairy tale episode in which he lights upon her hand, like an insect, pleads with her, and is crushed as she closes her hand over him. Since he has created her by thought, he can kill her by thought. He writes "The woman died" on his writing pad, and we are told that "There was dignity in such a murder." He sees her dead body lying on the beach. But the knowledge that "he had failed . . . to hold his miracle" is too much for him, and he becomes the madman who appeared at the beginning of the story.

"The Mouse and the Woman" goes a step further than **"The Orchards,"** for it explains why the certainty offered by delusion should disappear. The poet's sense of guilt, emerging from within his mind as the mouse emerges from the walls of the house, poisons his dream. His derangements are no longer orderly and joyful, but confused: "The secret of that alchemy that had turned a little revolution of the unsteady senses into a golden moment was lost as a key is lost in the undergrowth." He has regained some contact with the objective world, but he wants to kill the woman. To do this, he must return to the world of imagination, where she exists. In killing her, he also kills the dream she dominates, on which his happiness depends. The mouse, now fully in possession of the kitchen, silently presides over the grief the poet feels at this self-destruction. Trapped between two systems and unable to commit himself to either, the poet can only howl at life from behind the bars of the asylum.

In four stories published in 1937 and 1938, the hallucinatory technique advances so far that it is no longer possible—or desirable—to disentangle imagined from actual episodes. External reality responds flexibly to the thoughts and feelings of the characters, so that the narrative amounts to a psychological allegory. This genre, it will be recalled, is the one to which "Ballad of the Long-Legged Bait" belongs, and two of the four stories now under discussion are so closely related to that poem that they seem to be prose sketches for it. The member of this group closest to the earlier stories is **"A Prospect of the Sea."** It has the same elements as **"The Orchards"** and **"The Mouse and the Woman"**: a girl who is encountered at the seashore and who disappears, and a delirious shuttling back and forth between different orders of reality.

In **"A Prospect of the Sea,"** the boy begins by enjoying the summer day and then makes up a story about a drowned princess, but this level of thought is intersected by another—the appearance of a country girl who confronts him in the actual landscape. This siren figure both tempts and terrifies him, for she has the power to make the world swell and shrink. His fantasies of death and disfigurement alternate with the actual events of her erotic advances. As evening comes, he yields himself to another daydream, a mystic's vision of power, piercing sight, and multiplied Edens. But the girl calls him into an actual world that is now strangely insubstantial: "she could make a long crystal of each tree, and turn the house wood into gauze." She leads him on a race through a mystically disrupted realm, and then, in the morning, in spite of his agonized protests, she walks into the sea and disappears. As he turns to walk inland, he confronts the elements of the Noah story: an old man building a boat, the beginning of rainfall, and a stream of animals entering the door. Apparently, then, the episodes of the story belong to the corrupt time God had determined to end by means of the Flood.

But **"A Prospect of the Sea"** is an innocent pastoral in comparison with **"Prologue to an Adventure,"** a chronicle of town sin, which is a subject that offers far richer opportunity for Thomas's grotesque metaphoric energies than the country scenes of the earlier stories. There is little action. The speaker wanders through the streets and, with an acquaintance named Daniel Dom—a variant of the name "Domdaniel" appearing in one of Thomas's unpublished poems "Fifty" (Notebook Poems, 176)—visits two bars; then, as in **"A Prospect of the Sea,"** destructive water comes in, as the scene is immersed by waves.

The interest of this story lies in the remarkable play of scenes and imagery conveying the feverish atmosphere of a night on the town. "Now in the shape of a bald girl smiling, a wailing wanton with handcuffs for earrings, or the lean girls that live on pickings, now in ragged women with a muckrake curtseying in the slime, the tempter of angels whispered over my shoulder."

As the speaker says, there is "more than man's meaning" in this torrent of fearsome Hieronymus Bosch-like visions, for holiness is caught up and debased in it. "I have the God of Israel in the image of a painted boy, and Lucifer, in a woman's shirt, pisses from a window in Damaroid Alley."

The two scenes in the bars are incoherent jumbles of fleeting images, glimpses of transcendental visions, and striking expressionistic effects. They look backward in technique and subject to the Circe scene of Joyce's *Ulysses* and forward to Thomas's *Doctor and the Devils* for their atmosphere of pinched debauchery. The speaker and his friend aspire for a moment to reach out of this welter of temptresses, oppressed children, and indifferent city streets to some heavenly goal, but they come instead to a new bar where, after joining the corrupt festivities, they turn to the window and witness the coming of the deluge. There are no alternate realms of reality in this story. It is all an inescapable mental reality, consisting entirely of representations of the desires, fears, suspicions, and other emotions of the narrator; for, as his visions tell him, "We are all metaphors of the sound of shape, of the shape of sound, break us we take another shape."

"In the Direction of the Beginning" and **"An Adventure from a Work in Progress"** are mythlike tales written in a hallucinatory style. The first, a short account of the creation, tells of the appearance of figures resembling Adam and Eve. Its enchanted, visionary prose presents a dizzying succession of images referring fleetingly to various seasons, ages, and episodes of history and legend. There is almost no physical action; the Fall is suggested as the man becomes entrapped by the woman's siren spell and as his obsession with her is projected through imagery showing that he feels her to be personified in every detail of the universe. The same obsession appears in **"An Adventure from a Work in Progress,"** an account of a man pursuing a shadowy woman through a strangely active archipelago where awesome cataclysms endanger him. At the climax of the story the woman merges with the mountain, just as the Eve in **"In the Direction of the Beginning"** merges with the soil. When the hero ultimately catches her, she undergoes a series of startling metamorphoses and shrinks to a tiny monster in the palm of his hand. After being thus betrayed by his obsession, like the lovers in **"The Orchards"** and **"The Mouse and the Woman,"** the hero returns from the imaginary world to the actual one, and sails away on "the common sea."

The "revolving islands and elastic hills" of this story show that it takes place in the realm that is more fully described in **"The Map of Love."** In the latter, the stages of sexual initiation are represented by a bewitched landscape; a curious animated map or model of this region exhibits its vital sexual properties, so that the children to whom it is being displayed blush at "the copulation in the second mud." The libido-charged landscape represented by the map is the world as it presents itself to the heroes of the last two stories, who find the women they love embodied in cliffs, seas, and mountains. The children in **"The Map of Love"** are guided by Sam Rib, who is named for the origin of love, and are encouraged by the spirit of their lecherous Great-Uncle Jarvis, who speaks to them from the fields where he has lain with ten different mistresses. But they never succeed in swimming up the river to the island of the first beasts of love. Apparently they are too shy, too lacking in lust; mere "synthetic prodigals" of Sam Rib's laboratory, they are unable to share the dangerous vitality of nature.

Four of the stories of this period form a separate subgroup: **"The Enemies," "The Holy Six," "The Burning Baby,"** and **"The School for Witches"** are all about the fictional town of Llareggub, and all are told in a narrative style that presents much objective material. Thomas has created a distinctive comic world in these stories, a world of lecherous, hypocritical clergymen and submissive girls, tumbling over an enchanted Welsh landscape into situations appropriate to myths and fairy tales. In **"The Enemies,"** Mr. Davies, the doddering rector of Llareggub, wanders onto the farm of Mr. and Mrs. Owen. The farmer and his wife are a strong pagan pair in tune with the fertility of the soil, and they feel pity for the poor rector who comes to them tired and bleeding, having been betrayed by the countryside where he has been lost. As they eat dinner in the pantheistic atmosphere of the Owen farm, Mr. Davies is suddenly struck by the inadequacy of his own faith, and he falls to his knees to pray in fear. The story ends: "He stared and he prayed, like an old god beset by his enemies." Thomas is distinguishing between the religion he saw represented in the churches of Wales and the one he saw embodied in "the copulation in the tree . . . the living grease in the soil."

In **"The Holy Six,"** a sequel to **"The Enemies,"** Mr. Davies's adventure is turned into channels that are both comic and more deeply religious. Six of his colleagues receive a letter from Mrs. Owen informing them of Mr. Davies's plight. These six are confirmed lechers. "The holy life was a constant erection to these six gentlemen." Much of the story consists of unproarious descriptions of the visions their evil minds project upon actuality. (An allusion to Peter, the poet of **"The Visitor,"** who lives in the Jarvis valley where the Owen farm is, suggests that Thomas thought of all the Llareggub stories as interrelated, though he makes little effort to establish links among them.) When the Six arrive at the Jarvis valley, they find the countryside alien to them, just as Mr. Davies did, and the opposition between their hypocritical faith and that of the Owen couple is developed as Mrs. Owen sees the truth of things in her crystal ball.

Mr. Davies is brought forward, strangely transformed. He has apparently learned the lesson of the fertile soil, but his newly discovered passions have merged with his religious habits of mind to form a grotesque compound of lust and devotion: "his ghost who laboured . . . leapt out to marry Mary; all-sexed and nothing, intangible hermaphrodite riding the neuter dead, the minister of God in a grey image mounted dead Mary." He performs the service of washing the feet of his colleagues, while the thoughts of each are described, forming a series of remarkable surrealist fantasies. When he has finished this task, Mr. Davies cryptically claims the paternity of the child in Mrs. Owen's womb. Though Mr. Owen smiles at this, it is clear that Mr. Davies is right, for their "ghosts" have consummated a spiritual love in a realm different from that of the love of husband and wife.

Religious hypocrisy and repression are condemned in **"The Holy Six"** and **"The Enemies"** mainly by comic means. But **"The Burning Baby"** treats this theme with a tragic force approaching grandeur. The spectacle of a child consumed by fire, as we know from his poems, impressed Thomas as the formulation of an ultimate question, for it involved the greatest imaginable suffering inflicted on the greatest imaginable innocence. Rhys Rhys, the vicar, who has been driven to seduce his daughter by an obsessive lust, burns the baby resulting from this union in an expurgatory ritual. The baby, like the devil, he considers "poor flesh," and he burns it to rid the earth of the fruit of the "foul womb" and of the evidence of his own sin. But Thomas, speaking in his own voice, corrects Rhys Rhys's view and insists on the spiritual symmetry of nature: "The

fruit of the flesh falls with the worm from the tree. Conceiving the worm, the bark crumbles. There lay the poor star of flesh that had dropped, like the bead of a woman's milk, through the nipples of a wormy tree." Though the child is dead, the flames awaken him to a shriek of protest that is significantly taken up by the landscape that witnesses his immolation.

"The Burning Baby" is probably the best-sustained and most carefully constructed of Thomas's early stories. Though it is about derangement, its style, with a few exceptions, is disciplined and objective. The moments when the emotions of the characters take over the story and shape the narration are clearly marked. For example, when Rhys Rhys is delivering his usual sermon, but thinking of his desire for his daughter, he thinks: "the good flesh, the mean flesh, flesh of his daughter, flesh, flesh, the flesh of the voice of thunder howling before the death of man." At the moment of the incestuous union, the disruption of the normal order of feelings is reflected by a disruption of the normal conditions of external reality: "The lashes of her fingers lifted. He saw the ball under the nail." Minor events predict what is to come. Rhys Rhys's son, whom he thinks is a changeling, brings in a dead rabbit, cradling it like a baby. The scene arouses Rhys Rhys's terrors, and he takes the dead rabbit away, thus appropriating death. But the changeling witnesses the seduction and the sacrifice of the baby, and he insanely reenacts them after the others are dead.

"The School for Witches" is another story having a baby as the victim of worship, but this worship is witchcraft, not Christianity. The cut accidentally inflicted on the black woman's baby at the moment of its birth is a warning that it is entering the "wicked world" of the school for witches where the black arts are taught. Most of the story is devoted to descriptions of the rituals, dances, and covens of the witches, the formalized evil that has risen from the cursed and bedeviled countryside. The doctor, the only lucid character, has bleak meditations as he and the midwife carry the baby back to his house: "What purpose there was in the shape of Cader Peak, in the bouldered breast of the hill and the craters poxing the green-black flesh, was no more than the wind's purpose that willy nilly blew from all corners the odd turfs and stones of an unmoulded world. The grassy rags and bones of the steep hill were . . . whirled together out of the bins of chaos by a winter wind." The baby's cry confirms this sadness, and rouses Mr. Griffiths, who thinks the sound is the scream of a mandrake being uprooted and goes out to investigate. When he finds the baby it is dead, lying neglected at the door of the house where all the other characters in the story are whirling in the mad dance of the witches' coven.

The regional folklore exploited in **"The School for Witches"** appears in subtler forms in the other fantastic tales. The fairy lady, the changeling, the devil rolling in a ball on the ground (as the lecherous clergymen do in **"The Holy Six"**), and the spontaneous metamorphoses of scenes and people all belong to the atmosphere of Welsh mythology. The plot of **"The Orchards"** and of **"The Mouse and the Woman,"** involving a man who meets and loses a fairy woman, is common in these myths. **"The Burning Baby"** begins in the manner of a folktale, for the story is offered as a heuristic explanation of the sudden bursting into flame of dry bushes. The presence of these borrowings in the stories suggests that there is a similar element in the poems Thomas was writing at this period. The poems contain a few references to folklore, such as the beliefs concerning the vampire and the mandrake. Thomas's interest in this subject raises the possibility that the mythic awareness we have observed in the poems has its ultimate roots in the legends of Wales.

The poems, it will be recalled, encompass two conceptions of time: the unmoving time of mysticism and the conventional notion of time as a power that changes and destroys. Time is also an important theme in at least four of the imaginative stories, for mystic insights or disruptions of the natural order, psychological or otherwise, are sometimes announced as disruptions of time. The derangement of the poet in **"The Mouse and the Woman"** takes the form of a decision that winter must be prevented from spoiling the beauty of the woman who has left him and maddened him with jealousy. He attacks "the old effigy" of time, flinging himself into a chaos of irrational images. There is a similar effect in **"The Horse's Ha."** When the undertaker drinks the magic brew intended to resurrect the dead, the movements of the sun and moon are disturbed, and the days pass with mysterious rapidity. One of the dreams of the boy in **"A Prospect of the Sea"** is a sweeping mystic vision in which he sees through time, relating remote things in a single historic unity. Finally, in **"An Adventure from a Work in Progress,"** the man's capture of the first woman he sees on the islands is accompanied by a phenomenon Thomas calls the falling of time. This event is echoed in "Ballad of the Long-Legged Bait." It involves a reversal of the development of living things, intense disturbances, including a windstorm, fires, and earthquakes, and, in fact, all the elements of chaos. Clearly, the timelessness of the poems is inappropriate to the world of the stories. The reason may be that the stories, unlike the early poems, are about human beings living their earthly lives and that the standard of conventional time is indispensable to them. When mortals seek to evade time in order to make love endure or to avoid death, as the boys do in "I see the boys of summer," chaos results.

3

Thomas was still working on the last of his fantastic narratives in 1938 when he began to write the realistic stories collected in *Portrait of the Artist as a Young Dog.* In March 1938 he wrote to Watkins that the first of "a series of short, straightforward stories about Swansea" had already been published. This statement must refer to **"A Visit to Grandpa's,"** which appeared in the *New English Weekly* on 10 March, 1938. The change in narrative style between these two groups of stories is, of course, a radical one; moreover, it paralleled the much more subtle change

in Thomas's poetic style that was going on at about the same time. Many of the casual details of these stories are drawn without change from Thomas's Swansea days, and some of the characters are based on actual people: the aunt in **"The Peaches"** is Ann Jones, and Dan Jenkyns in **"The Fight"** is Daniel Jones. In his "Poetic Manifesto," Thomas declared that the title he assigned to the collection was a variant, not of Joyce's title, but of one often given by painters to self-portraits. He admitted that the general influence of *Dubliners* might be felt in his stories, but he added that this was an influence no good writer of short stories could avoid ("Manifesto," 4–5).

The protagonist in all the stories is clearly Thomas himself, though the stories are narrated indifferently in first and third persons and though each presents him at a different age. They are about ordinary experiences: visits with relatives, excursions to the country, adventures with gangs of children, explorations of the town. In some of them the plot is so slight that the story approaches a reminiscence or cluster of impressions. Obviously written with only a loose unity in mind, they have no common theme, but taken as a group they seem to trace the child's emergence from his domain of imagination and secret pleasures into an adult world where he observes suffering, pathos, and dignity.

Most of the stories are about an observer or witness whose experience consists of awakening to the experiences of others. The events are presented in sharp, well-selected impressions. When he is observing a general scene, such as a boy's room or a crowded street, Thomas proceeds by piling up a lively list of the quintessential details or characteristic people. Sometimes the narrator's attitude toward people, places, and episodes is affectionate or amused; sometimes he finds grotesque nightmare evocations in them. But he encounters his strongest emotions in moments of solitude when he can hug his general impressions of the external world to himself as personal possessions—while walking down a street late at night, wandering in moody isolation on a noisy beach, or enjoying the atmosphere of an expensive bar.

The first three stories—**"The Peaches," "A Visit to Grandpa's"** and **"Patricia, Edith and Arnold"**—set the idyllic existence of a child side by side with the trials of adults. As the grownups suffer, the child remains indifferent or cruel; yet it appears at the end that he has understood and sympathized more than he knew, thus anticipating the ultimate union of the childish and adult points of view. **"The Peaches"** may be said to have "separateness" as an identifiable theme. Mrs. William, who brings her son for a holiday at the farm, is too superior to stay a moment longer than necessary, and refuses the precious canned peaches that have been saved for her visit. Jim curses her snobbery, but he cannot keep himself from drinking up the profits of the farm and distressing his wife. Gwilym, the son, who closely resembles the religious gardener in **"The Tree,"** is occupied with a vision of himself as a preacher and makes the barn into a church for his pretend sermons.

To these mutually uncommunicating attitudes toward life is added that of the boys who are busy with their games of wild Indian and indifferent to the concerns of the adults. But even here a division occurs when Jack Williams betrays his playmate by telling his mother an incriminating mixture of truth and falsehood about his treatment at the farm, and is taken away. At the end of **"The Peaches,"** the boy waves his handkerchief at his departing betrayer, innocent that any wrong has been done to him, or to his aunt and uncle.

In **"Patricia, Edith and Arnold,"** the child, at first cruelly indifferent to the pain felt by the two maidservants who have learned that the same young man has been walking out with both of them, gains some insight into adult sorrows. The story begins with a chaos of irreconcilable interests: the absorption of the girls in their love triangle and the rambunctious joy of the child who is all-conquering in his imaginary play world. But as the painful comedy of Arnold's entrapment is played out, the boy, uncomfortably cold and wet, feels his own distress and unconsciously comes to sympathize with Patricia. Returning to the shelter to retrieve his cap, he sees Arnold reading the letters he has written to the other girl, but he mercifully spares Patricia this knowledge. And his own experience of pain, a minor counterpart of the adult pain Patricia has suffered, comes when he thaws his cold hands at the fire. Patricia's final remark, "Now we've all had a good cry today," formulates both the similarity of their trials and their capacity to endure them.

Cruel jokes of the sort that life has played on Arnold occur in some of the other stories. In **"Just Like Little Dogs,"** the brothers exchange partners with each other in the middle of an evening of casual love. As a result, when the women become pregnant, it is not clear which brother is the father of their respective children. Two forced and loveless marriages take place, and now the two fathers spend their evenings in the street, standing hopelessly in the cold night air. In **"Old Garbo,"** the neighbors take up a collection for Mrs. Prothero, whose daughter is supposed to have died in childbirth; after Mrs. Prothero has drunk up the money, it is learned that the daughter has survived. The mother, ashamed at having taken the money under false pretenses, jumps into the river.

It is significant that in each of these stories the anecdotal nucleus is subordinated to the vehicle that conveys it. The impressive element of **"Just Like Little Dogs"** is the spectacle of the young men sheltering aimlessly from the night under the railway arch; they have no place more interesting to go and nothing more interesting to do. **"Old Garbo"** is, in reality, a story of initiation; the young reporter, eager to share the knowledge and maturity of the older one, follows him into the haunts where Mrs. Prothero's comic tragedy occurs. In this way he exchanges the boyish pastimes of the cinema and the novelty shop of the first part of the story for the more serious experience in the slum pub. He is not a qualified observer, for he becomes drunk, sick, and helpless, and the older reporter tells him, in an odd conclusion, that the story that has just been narrated has certain confused details. But he is still naively determined to put all the things the older reporter has shown him into a story.

Some of the stories have a note of personal futility and inadequacy that conspires with their prevailing comic tone to produce penetrating irony. The inferior boy who is the hero of **"Extraordinary Little Cough"** is bullied and mocked. But he turns his shy habit of running away when girls appear into a feat, for while the other boys are idling with the girls and yielding to romantic illusions, he runs the five miles of beach. As he falls to the ground exhausted at the end of the story, it is clear that he has risen nobly to a challenge, while the others have ended in frustration and petty animosity. The two boys who go for a country hike in **"Who Do You Wish Was With Us?"** feel they are escaping their town lives in the freedom of the country and the beach. But Ray, whose life has been full of terrible family misfortunes, is overtaken in the middle of his holiday by sorrow for his dead brother. The sea turns cold and threatening, and both boys feel that they cannot really escape the life they have fled.

The most powerful story about escape, and the most impressive one in the volume, is the last, **"One Warm Saturday."** Having rejected invitations to join his friends, the young man wanders despondently among the crowds on the beach, finding solace only in the face of a girl whom he flees shyly at first. Finally he again meets the girl, Lou, and as the two become involved in an oddly mixed group of drinkers, she promises him that his love for her will be fulfilled when they are alone. The party moves from the pub where it began to Lou's room in a huge ramshackle tenement. The young man's anxiety and Lou's demonstrations of affection are intensified, but the others show no signs of leaving. A grotesque frustration occurs when the young man goes out to the lavatory. He is unable to find his way back to Lou's room to claim the night of love she has promised him. Instead, he loses himself in the squalid maze of the tenement and stumbles into the rooms of other lodgers. Finally he gives up and wanders out into the street, having made the "discovery" during his search that all the obscure people of the town share his experience of loss.

Thomas's uncompleted novel, *Adventures in the Skin Trade,* may be considered a continuation of the quasi-autobiography loosely sketched in *Portrait of the Artist as a Young Dog,* though it is more broadly comic in style than any of the stories. It takes up the narrative of a life much like Thomas's at the point where the last of the stories ends, and its protagonist, Samuel Bennet, is not inconsistent with the wandering, imaginative youths found in the earlier book, though Bennet is much better defined. Thomas seems to have begun *Adventures* in 1940; although the first section was published in *Folios of New Writing* in 1941 under the title **"A Fine Beginning,"** and he was encouraged to continue with it, it remained a fragment at the time of his death in 1953.

The novel may be described as a farce based on the fact that Samuel Bennet and his world are excruciatingly uncomfortable with each other. On the night before he leaves his hometown for London, Samuel prepares a number of surprises for his family by breaking his mother's china, tearing up his sister's crochet work, and scribbling on the lessons that his father, a teacher, is correcting. But he does all this in tears, as if it were a painful necessity; and he says an affectionate farewell the next morning. On the other hand, he is not eager to see London; unwilling to make any decisions or to take any action, he lingers in the station cafe until a friend forces him to leave.

The London in which Samuel finds himself is a damp, angular, crowded, eccentric world, and it is both surprising and significant that he likes it as well as he does. The chaos he encounters is well represented by his first stop, a warehouse full of furniture piled up in unlikely heaps that nevertheless serves as living quarters for a number of people. The general technique of *Adventures* is suggested by the locked bathroom with its bird cages, where a strange girl makes an attempt on Samuel's virtue in a tub full of used bathwater, after drugging him with a drink of cologne. In the book, as in this scene, violent imaginative force explodes in a narrow enclosure filled with ordinary objects and people, toppling them into ludicrous attitudes and combinations. A mundane paraphernalia of Bass bottles, umbrellas, rubber ducks, boot polish, Worcestershire sauce, and Coca-Cola is juggled into patterns of uproarious private meaning, sometimes by Samuel's imagination, sometimes by the author's. Realism swims in a whirlpool of uninhibited fancy.

If the atmosphere of *Adventure* is found anywhere else, it is in Brinnin's accounts of the social events Thomas attended, where the poet, guided by some motivation of wit or self-dramatization, cunningly introduced chaos. In the novel, Mr. Allingham observes that the Bass bottle that has become wedged on Samuel's little finger is an enigma. Samuel, noticing that a barmaid looks like a duchess riding a horse, makes the irrelevant reply of "Tantivy" to some remark. But the curious thing is that Samuel, in spite of the hostility and defiance with which he confronts the world, is completely unready for the world's retaliation. As he is pushed and prodded from one place to another, drugged, undressed, bullied, and thrown out of a bar, he experiences terror and confusion. Samuel is too innocent to absorb what he sees. A stumbling, swooning, dreaming source of confusion, he is himself confused, and he seems destined to remain a timid and withdrawn picaro among the sharp and knowing characters who take possession of him. According to Robert Pocock, who discussed *Adventures* with Thomas, the novel was to end with Samuel stripped naked (except, no doubt, for the Bass bottle clinging enigmatically to his little finger) and arrested in Paddington Station.[2]

Notes

1. Thomas's book reviews and miscellaneous journalism are listed in J. Alexander Rolph, *Dylan Thomas: A Bibliography* (London: J. M. Dent, 1956), and much of this material has been reprinted in Walford Davies, ed., *Dylan Thomas: Early Prose Writings*

(New York: New Directions and London: J. M. Dent, 1971). For a list of unpublished prose, film scripts, and pieces written for radio broadcast, see Maud, *Entrances,* 121–48.

2. Robert Pocock, *Adam International Review* no. 238 (1953): 30–31.

FURTHER READING

Bibliographies

Gaston, Georg. *Dylan Thomas: A Reference Guide.* Boston: G. K. Hall, 1987, 213 p.
   A compilation of secondary sources.

Maud, Ralph. *Dylan Thomas in Print: A Bibliographical History.* Pittsburgh: University of Pittsburgh Press, 1970, 261 p.
   An extensive listing of primary and secondary sources.

Rolph, J. Alexander. *Dylan Thomas: A Bibliography.* London: J. M. Dent & Sons, 1956, 108 p.
   This early bibliography of works by and about Thomas includes illustrations.

Biographies

Ackerman, John. *Dylan Thomas: His Life and Work.* London: Oxford University Press, 1964, 201 p.
   In this critical biography, Ackerman stresses the importance of Thomas's Welsh heritage on his writings.

Davies, James A. *A Reference Companion to Dylan Thomas.* Westport, CT: Greenwood Press, 1998, 365 p.
   A biography and critical history covering Thomas's poetic and prose works.

Criticism

Cushman, Keith. "*Eight Stories* by Dylan Thomas." *Studies in Short Fiction* 31, No. 2 (Spring 1994): 265–67.
   Compares the stories in this collection favorably with those of *Dubliners* by James Joyce.

Davies, James A. *A Reference Companion to Dylan Thomas.* Westport, CT: Greenwood Press, 1998, 365 p.
   A combined biography and critical history covering Thomas's poetic and prose works. Includes critical histories focusing individually on Thomas's reputation in England, Wales, and North America.

Glick, Burton S. "A Brief Analysis of a Short Story by Dylan Thomas." *American Imago* 14, No. 2 (Summer 1957): 149–54.
   An analysis of "The Followers" from *Adventures in the Skin Trade, and Other Stories.*

Kelly, Richard. "The Lost Vision in Dylan Thomas' 'One Warm Saturday.'" *Studies in Short Fiction* 6, No. 2 (Winter 1969): 205–09.

> Compares and contrasts Thomas's "One Warm Saturday" from *Portrait of the Artist as a Young Dog* and James Joyce's "Araby" from *Dubliners*.

Morris, Frances. "The Man Who Loved and Haunted Himself." *Times Literary Supplement* (2 March 1984): 227.

> Maintains that Thomas's self-absorption is reflected in his short stories.

Mosher, Harold F., Jr. "The Structure of Dylan Thomas's 'The Peaches.'" *Studies in Short Fiction* 6, No. 5 (Fall 1969): 536–47.

> A structural analysis of "The Peaches" from *Portrait of the Artist as a Young Dog.*

Phillip, Neil. Review of *A Visit to Grandpa's and Other Stories. Times Educational Supplement,* No. 3564 (19 October 1984): 25.

> A short laudatory review of a new collection of stories, five of which originated in *Portrait of the Artist as a Young Dog.*

Additional coverage of Thomas's life and career is contained in the following sources published by the Gale Group: *Concise Dictionary of British Literary Biography, 1945–1960; Contemporary Authors,* Vols. 104, 120; *Contemporary Authors New Revision Series,* Vol. 65; *Dictionary of Literary Biography,* Vols. 13, 20, 139; *DISCovering Authors; DISCovering Authors: British; DISCovering Authors: Canadian; DISCovering Authors Modules: Dramatists, Most-studied Authors, Poets; DISCovering Authors 3.0; Major 20th-Century Writers,* Vols. 1, 2; *Poetry Criticism,* Vol. 2; *Poetry for Students,* Vol. 8; *Something about the Author,* Vol. 60; *Twentieth-Century Literary Criticism,* Vols. 1, 8, 45; and *World Literature Criticism.*

Israel Zangwill
1864–1926

(Also wrote under the pseudonym J. Freeman Bell) English novelist, short story writer, dramatist, essayist, critic, translator, lecturer, and poet.

INTRODUCTION

Known as the father of modern English-Jewish literature, Zangwill enjoyed international popularity in the late nineteenth and early twentieth centuries for his short stories and novels in which he realistically portrayed life in the Jewish ghetto of London. Zangwill's use of humor and his tendency for optimism distinguished his work from that of other realistic writers of the era. The short story collections *Ghetto Tragedies* (1893), *Ghetto Comedies* (1907), and the novella *The King of Schnorrers* (1894) number among his best-known works of short fiction.

BIOGRAPHICAL INFORMATION

The son of East European immigrant parents, Zangwill was born in the Whitechapel ghetto of London, although he later lived and was educated in Bristol. His talent and interest in writing came early, and by the time he was a teenager he had won first prize in a short story contest. After graduating from the Jews' Free School, Zangwill taught at that institution. In 1888 he quit teaching to pursue a full-time career as a writer, contributing a column to *The Jewish Standard* and writing novels and short stories. For two years he edited his own comic newspaper, *Ariel: The London Puck*. Worldwide recognition for Zangwill came upon the publication of *Children of the Ghetto* (1892), an episodic novel about the Jewish ghetto that had been commissioned by the Jewish Publication Society of America. After 1895, Zangwill became involved in a number or causes, including efforts to create a Jewish homeland and the women's suffrage movement. Also during this time he continued to write prolifically. Zangwill produced several dramas, which he used as vehicles to express his social and political ideas, as well as short stories and a volume of verse. Zangwill's last years were spent fraught with poor health and poorly received plays.

MAJOR WORKS OF SHORT FICTION

Over the course of his career, Zangwill published numerous works of short fiction. His stories, which included works on Jewish themes, non-Jewish themes, and mysteries, were often first published in periodicals and then

amassed in collections. *The Bachelors' Club* (1891) and its counterpart *The Old Maids' Club* (1892) deal with single people whose vows to avoid marriage fall humorously by the wayside. Although termed a novel, *Children of the Ghetto* is not a novel by the strictest definition; instead it is a series of scenes and sketches of Jewish life and characters. Thus some critics refer to this work as a collection of short stories. The short story collections *Ghetto Comedies* and *Ghetto Tragedies* similarly depict life in the Jewish section of London, blurring the distinction between the genres of the titles. *The King of Schnorrers* is also considered a long short story by some critics and a novella by others. In this work, Zangwill focused on a legendary Jewish character, the wily beggar who makes himself indispensable to the community. *Dreamers of the Ghetto* (1898) contains biographical sketches of prominent Jewish figures. Constants in Zangwill's works on Jewish themes are his affection for people and his use of humor. Zangwill's short fiction on non-Jewish themes, which includes mystery and other genre stories, is generally considered to be unremarkable.

CRITICAL RECEPTION

Zangwill's most successful works were his short stories and the novella *The King of Schnorrers*. While his novels often suffered from discursiveness, his short stories on Jewish topics well demonstrated the author's wit within the controlled length and form of the genre. Although early critics faulted Zangwill for what they termed a melodramatic style and ironic tone, others praised the exuberant, holistic treatment of Jews and Jewish life, and soulfulness of his short stories. While some scholars explored whether or not Zangwill was a realist, others focused on the themes of love, sacrifice, suffering, assimilation, and hope, as they manifest themselves in his stories. Several commentators expressed opinions on Zangwill's concern for Jewish survival and his ambivalence about Zionism. The novella *The King of Schnorrers* elicited much commentary, particularly about the history of the beggar figure in Jewish society and the debate over the quality of humor in Zangwill's work.

PRINCIPAL WORKS

Short Fiction

The Bachelors' Club 1891
The Old Maids' Club 1892
Ghetto Tragedies 1893
Merely Mary Ann 1893
The King of Schnorrers: Grotesques and Fantasies 1894
The Celibates' Club: Being the United Stories of the Bachelors' Club and the Old Maids' Club 1898
Dreamers of the Ghetto 1898
"They That Walk in Darkness": Ghetto Tragedies 1899
They Grey Wig: Stories and Novelettes 1903
Ghetto Comedies 1907

Other Major Works

The Ballad of Moses (poetry) 1882
The Premier and the Painter [with Louis Cowen, as J. Freeman Bell] (novel) 1888
Children of the Ghetto: Being Pictures of a Peculiar People. 3 vols. (novel) 1892
They Big Bow Mystery (novel) 1892
The Great Demonstration [with Louis Cowen] (drama) 1892
The Master (novel) 1895
The Mantle of Elijah (novel) 1900
The Melting Pot (drama) 1908
Italian Fantasies (travel essays) 1910
The War God (drama) 1911
The Next Religion (drama) 1912
The Principle of Nationalities (lecture) 1917
Jinny the Carrier (novel) 1919
The Voice of Jerusalem (essays) 1920
The Cockpit (drama) 1921
We Moderns (drama) 1921
The Forcing House; or, The Cockpit Continued (drama) 1922
The Collected Works of Israel Zangwill (novels, short stories, dramas, essays, and poetry) 1969

*This work was also published by the Jewish Publication Society of America in two volumes in 1892.

CRITICISM

The Nation (essay date 1898)

SOURCE: A review of *Dreamers of the Ghetto*, in *Nation*, Vol. 66, No. 1712, April 21, 1898, p. 310.

[*In the following review of* Dreamers of the Ghetto, *the anonymous critic faults Zangwill for his melodramatic style and ironic tone.*]

An application of the methods employed by Landor in his 'Imaginary Conversations,' and by Louisa Mühlbach in her historical novels, to some more or less famous Jewish worthies and unworthies of recent times, may redound to an author's credit for eccentricity but not sanity of genius. The result could not fail to be bizarre, particularly when, throughout, the jester's cap and bells seem to compete for mastery with the cynic's wail. The stories, too, it must be confessed, read better when they appeared "syndicated" in various magazines and weeklies than in the present collection; the tricks of phrase and style, the exaggerations in language and sentiment, the threadbare plush of rhetoric, and the flimsy ornamentation follow too rapidly and self-consciously as the chapters are successively analyzed. If the author, in addition to his undeniable gifts, had only possessed the gift of condensation, his work would have lost in bulk and exuberance, but it would have gained largely in merit.

Unlike novelists of the Ghetto such as Kompert, Bernstein, Mosenthal, Kohn, and Franzos, not to mention Berthold Auerbach, whose romance of 'Spinoza' anticipated Mr. Zangwill's **'The Master of Lenses,'** the author of **'Dreamers of the Ghetto'** essays a more ambitious rôle. They were, as a class, content to paint cameos or genre sketches of old-time Jewish life, and let the pictures, fantastic or realistic, speak for themselves. Mr. Zangwill aims at philosophy as well as fiction. We fear that he is too much inoculated with the very Aryanism which he deplores as ominous for the Jew, and is too much of a waverer himself to be a thoroughly trustworthy guide in any

philosophy of Judaism based upon the careers of the heroes in fact and fustian whom he exploits. How he can term Lassalle, Heine, and Disraeli "dreamers of the Ghetto," is a mystery indeed, especially in the case of Disraeli, who was a devout son of the Established Church, and never entered an English synagogue except when he acted as witness at a wedding of one of the Rothschilds. It was only after these worthies left the Ghetto—if they ever really belonged to it—that they became famous. Had they remained Ghetto youths, history might have been silent about them, and a Zangwill might never have employed them for text or pretext.

The volume, however, has its value in familiarizing the general public with a comparatively untrodden field—the inner history and workings of the Jews of recent centuries, and the currents and counter-currents among them due to opposing tendencies of the times. Under the guise of fiction, a goodly amount of modern Jewish history is thus unconsciously taught, which possibly can just now be imbibed in no other way. The author, too, is candid in exposing the faults of his brethren, and does not unduly idealize them. His own chief defect—which is becoming too painfully evident in the younger school of English fiction—is his quality of exaggeration. This makes his book glaringly melodramatic, and gives his "dreamers" often the tones and attitudes characteristic of burlesque. From this charge we must exclude his **"From a Mattress Grave,"** which is an exquisite vindication of Heine—a bit of Heine come to life again.

The Nation (essay date 1905)

SOURCE: "More Fiction," in *Nation*, Vol. 80, No. 2083, June 1, 1905, pp. 440–442.

[*In the following excerpt, the unnamed reviewer praises the exuberance of Zangwill's style in* The Celibates' Club.]

The **Celibates' Club** is a collection of extravagant tales and character sketches which probably first saw the light in a comic paper. Each separate chapter is good enough for such a medium of publication, but the book is no better than an exhibition of the journalistic talent for writing up exhaustively from the slightest foundation of facts or fancy. Mr. Zangwill's way of writing up a subject is very superior. He is extraordinarily fluent; he can do almost anything with words—make puns, paradoxes, epigrams, striking phrases, run on in an amusing fashion long after his subject or suggestion is buried out of sight and forgotten. Sometimes he runs off into unmitigated nonsense, and then, except for the purposes of the comic paper, he becomes an unmitigated bore—a fate that frequently threatens in his giddy flights provoked by the conception of a Bachelors' Club and an Old Maids' Club.

The nearest discoverable thing to a motive in his madness is an intention to satirize the general modern passion for

notoriety, finding most of his material in the world of actors, musicians, painters, and writers for the papers—a world that can hardly take offence at criticism which so obviously includes the author. All he says about this world expresses intimate acquaintance and personal identification with it, and a cheerfully cynical appreciation of life as he sees it, and lives it. Among his best sketches is that of Harry Slapup, a comic singer, who, quite against his will, was converted into Israfel Mondego, a warbler of sentimental ditties and darling of the drawing-room. The most amusing candidates for the Old Maids' Club is Frank Maddox, a celebrated critic of all the arts. "Few critics," says Mr. Zangwill, "possessed such charm of style and feature as Frank Maddox, who had a delicious retroussé nose, a dainty rosebud mouth, blue eyes, and a wealth of golden hair." The opening of the lady's discourse on her profession gives the tone of the best bits in the book:

> "You see, to be a critic it is not essential to know anything—you must simply be able to write. To be a great critic you must simply be able to write well. In my omniscience, or catholic ignorance, I naturally looked about for the subject on which I could most profitably employ my gift of style with the least chance of being found out. A moment's consideration will convince you that the most difficult branches of criticism are the easiest. Of musical and artistic matters not one person in a thousand understands aught but the rudiments; here, then, is the field in which the critical ignoramus may expatiate at large with the minimum danger of discovery. . . . Only say what you have got to say authoritatively and well, and the world shall fall down and worship you. The place of art in religion has undergone a peculiar historical development. First men worshipped the object of art; then they worshipped the artist; and nowadays they worship the art-critic."

Holbrook Jackson (essay date 1914)

SOURCE: "Israel Zangwill," in *Living Age*, Vol. 282, No. 3664, September 26, 1914, pp. 790–797.

[*In the excerpt below, Jackson approves of Zangwill's holistic portrayal of modern Jewish life, which reveals the soul of a people as well as that of the author.*]

[E]quipped with ability and a mind of his own, Israel Zangwill came to art. He did not come, however, as a business man marketing a gift. He had something to say and he desired to say it in the most effective manner; so he became a writer, recording at first the tragedy and achievement of the Jewish people and, later, interpreting the spirit of the age apropos of Hebrew and Christian morals and mysticism. Bare historic or philosophic statement could not have achieved his aim; indeed, that aim has been to give artistic form to the existing records of historian and philosopher plus the results of his own observation of ideas and happenings; where the former worked to impress the mind by intellectual processes, Zangwill sought to move the imagination by artistic processes. He goes so far as to distinguish, in a double sense, artistic from scientific truth. "Artistic truth is for me," he writes, "literally the highest truth: art may seize the essence of persons and movements no less truly, and certainly far more vitally, than a scientific generalization unifies a class of phenomena. Time and space are only the conditions through which spiritual facts struggle." The spiritual facts of Jewish history and of modern Jewish life have received their highest and most convincing expression in English, in such books as *Children of the Ghetto*, **Dreamers of the Ghetto, The King of Schnorrers,** and **They That Walk in Darkness.** From the point of view of art his great achievement is the restatement of the seemingly eternal tragedy of Israel in the light of modern experience and modern culture. And he has done this with fitting seriousness and a most gracious and refreshing sense of humor.

It is impossible to read this remarkable cycle of Jewish studies without being moved by the mastery of the Jews over life—yes, and death. Shakespeare, who had probably never seen a Jew, makes Shylock the mere symbol of an exacting business man who is permitted to claim relationship with the rest of humanity on the grounds of senses which are possessed in common. But there is nothing in Shylock's claims to human kinship which might not with equal logic have made him kin with cat or dog—nothing, save the claim that if a Jew is tickled he will laugh. It is clear that Shakespeare did not visualize the Jew as fully human. When he made Falstaff plead, "I am a Jew else, an Ebrew Jew," he associated himself with the popular conception of the Jew as rogue and outlaw. Dickens probably held a similar view when he created Fagin, but he sought to make amends in a later book by fashioning a Jew as impossibly good as Fagin was impossibly evil. Zangwill, on the other hand, having had the most intimate experience of Jews, and possessing both a sense of humor and a sense of fact, gives us a more convincing idea of his compatriots than we have yet had or are likely to have. But he does not give us only realistic portraiture, after the manner of the newer novelists of his early days; nor does he strive particularly to see the good and bad, and to apportion praise and blame, after the manner of pre-Meredithian novelists. He knows the Jew to be human, not only because he hath "hands, organs, dimensions, senses, affections, passions," but because he is capable of the same virtues and vices, the same splendors and the same littlenesses as other human beings; that he is in short compact of good and bad like the rest of us. But he does not commit the opposite folly of concluding therefore that the Jew is not different. That would have left us where Shakespeare and Dickens stood. He knows the Jew is different and that this difference is surmounted only by a genius for adaptability.

These differences are revealed in his Jewish studies, which have always astonished Gentiles by their fairness in recognizing the evil as well as the good among Jews. But that is no more an example of fairness than similar qualities in English or Scotch novelists. It is simply the faculties of observation and visualization crystallized in art. Israel Zangwill sees the Jew steadily and sees him whole. Any equally capable artist might have done the same; any equally capable artist in letters might have wrung our hearts with the pathos, or moved our souls with the tragedy of Jewry; just as any equally capable writer might have raised our eyebrows or our laughter by records of Jewish cunning or humor. Zangwill has done all of these things and more. He has realized the irony of the age-long drama of Israel in a world to which she has given inventors and scientists, philosophers and artists, poets and prophets and Gods, but without, as a race, providing herself with a place to lay her head. He draws the modern Jew in all his squalor, whether of poverty, in Whitechapel, or of luxury, in Park Lane (both squalors having sprung from like causes), on a background of race-splendor. He communicates to us his vivid consciousness of the tragedy of this dream-fed race which has poured into the world treasures of the spirit and the imagination, whilst forging the metal of its permanence in bondage, migration and oppression. [. . .]

Books live not because of any knowledge they contain, for knowledge soon becomes outmoded; neither do they live by reason of exquisite finish of workmanship, for art dies when the thing it meant is no longer a human need. Longevity is no test of art; a work of art should fill its time whether that time be a moment, an hour, a year, a century, or any number of centuries. But a book has a greater chance of life if it is a work of art revealing some unfathomable source of human ecstasy or power. Race has nothing to do with this, neither has nationality, nor religion. The thing that makes a work of art live is the same as that which determines the life of a race, or a nation, or a religion. It is spiritual power. Applying this test to the works of Israel Zangwill, and after making every allowance for what may be called the temporal delight one may glean from any or all of them, the laurels might be awarded to the following in the order named: **They That Walk in Darkness, Dreamers of the Ghetto, The King of Schnorrers,** *Children of the Ghetto,* and *Italian Fantasies.* Here are books drawn from the spiritual deeps; they reveal the soul of a people and the soul of a man. More, they add something tragic, something humorous, something carefully observed, and something honestly thought, to a literature already rich in these things, but not so rich as to be weary of receiving fresh treasures. There is equal art and fine intent in his other books, and they are as alive today as when they were first published, but the best things in them are better in the books named, and what remains remains for our day, and not for the far-away day when people will yet stay the tear over the **"Diary of a Meshumad," "Satan Mekatrig,"** and **"Incurable,"** and stop to marvel over **"Joseph the Dreamer," "The People's Saviour," "From a Mattress Grave,"** and **"The Joyous Comrade,"** and to laugh over Manasseh da Costa and his subject, Yankele.

Ira Eisenstein (essay date 1951–1952)

SOURCE: "Israel Zangwill," in *Jewish Book Annual*, Vol. 10, 1951–1952, pp. 37–42.

[In the excerpt below, Eisenstein briefly discusses two major themes evident in Children of the Ghetto *and several*

of Zangwill's stories: the tragic and noble character of the Jewish ghetto and the insurmountable schism between different generations of Jews.]

Two major themes seem to have occupied Zangwill: 1) the nobility and the tragedy of the ghetto; 2) the chasm that separates the generations from one another.

The first of these themes predominates in the *Children of the Ghetto*. With great tenderness, he described the seemingly bizarre conglomeration of pietists and radicals, charlatans and beggars, scholars and would-be scholars, philanthropists and the humble poor. I say "seemingly bizarre," because he always probed beneath the surface to uncover their essential humanity. His humor was always gentle, and oblique, never sharp and direct; for he regarded himself as an interpreter of the ghetto to the world, and he respected both.

One of my favorite passages is his description of the synagogue in "The Sons of the Covenant," who "sent no representatives to the club balls, wotting neither of waltzes nor of dress-coats, and preferring death to the embrace of a strange dancing woman." They occupied two large rooms, knocked into one, "the rear partitioned off for the use of the bewigged, heavy-jawed women who might not sit with the men lest they should fascinate their thoughts away from things spiritual."

"They prayed metaphysics, acrostics, angelology, Cabalah, history, exegetics, Talmudical controversies, menus, recipes, priestly prescriptions, the canonical books, psalms, love poems, and undigested hotch-potch of exalted and questionable sentiments, of communal and egoistic aspirations of the highest order. . . . If they did not always know what they were saying, they always meant it. If the service had been more intelligible it would have been less emotional and edifying. There was not a sentiment, however incomprehensible, for which they were not ready to die or to damn."

The "Grandchildren of the Ghetto" are more refined, more rational about their faith; but more materialistic, and soulless. The synagogues are now run "as a stock company for the sake of dividends," in a business-like way. And the "Children" are ridiculed for their uncouthness. Zangwill resented this rejection of the basic values of the ghetto. He conceded that there were even rogues among the ghetto characters; but they were lovable rogues, distinctive and colorful.

In the *King of the Schnorrers,* Zangwill reveals his love for a magnificent faker whose *hutzpah,* fortified by verses from the Torah, breaks down the stuffy and self-righteous tight-fistedness of the rich Jews. Among the beggars, whose "woebegone air was achieved almost entirely by not washing," the "King" stands out. His philosophy is that begging is noble because it gives Jews an opportunity to perform a *mitzvah.* So intent is he on raising their moral level that he virtually persecutes them into giving char-

ity—to him. When Grobstock, the rich man, looks through his old clothes to see whether anything was left in the pockets before handing them over to the "King," he is reviled in sermonic form. "What says Deuteronomy? 'When thou reapest thine harvest in thy field and hast forgot a sheaf in the field, thou shalt not go again to fetch it. It shall be for the fatherless and for the widows.' You will admit that Moses would have added a prohibition against searching minutely the pockets of cast-off garments, were it not that for forty years our ancestors had to wander in the wilderness in the same clothes . . .".

When a beau brummel gives him nothing, he shouts: "You will make a third at grace. Since the world was created only two men have taken their clothes with them to the world to come. One was Korah who was swallowed down, and the other was Elijah who was borne aloft. It is patent in which direction the third will go."

Zangwill clearly preferred the "King of the Schnorrers" to the self-hating grandchild of the ghetto, whom he describes in a story called **"The Jewish Trinity"**: "The Jew is a *patriot* everywhere, and a *Jew* everywhere, and an *anti-semite* everywhere. Passionate Hungarians, and true-born Italians, eagle-waving Americans and loyal Frenchmen. We are dispersed to preach the unity, and what we illustrate is the Jewish trinity."

The failure of the grandchildren to understand the ghetto leads to Zangwill's second major theme, the tragedy of the generations. In one of his most touching stories, **"Transitional,"** he deals with the problem of intermarriage. A father, torn between his devotion to Judaism and his daughter's happiness, sacrifices his principles for his child; she, recognizing his struggle, and his renunciation, catches a glimpse of the heights to which true piety can raise a man. In a letter to her fiancé, bidding him farewell, she writes:

> "If a religion that I thought all formalism is capable of producing such types of abnegation as my dear father, then it must, too, somewhere or other hold in solution all those ennobling ingredients, all those stimuli to self-sacrifice which the world calls Christian."

Zangwill clearly deplores the fact that it took a personal tragedy to enable a child to understand her father.

In other stories, such a final reconciliation fails to materialize. In the **"Diary of a Meshumed,"** a father is killed by his own converted son. In **"To Die in Jerusalem,"** a son, awakened at last to the fact that he has sinned against the faith of his fathers, travels to Palestine to receive his father's forgiveness and blessing. The father, sensing that his son needs him, rushes to England. The ships pass each other at sea. The son dies in Jerusalem, the father in London.

The failure of the fathers to transmit the heritage to the sons produces rootless and restless souls. In the characters, who suffer the pangs of this alienation, Zangwill puts his finger on the essential tragedy of contemporary Judaism.

In **"Hadgadyah,"** the son of a Venetian family ruminated during the Seder: "He wanted, he hungered after God, the God of his fathers. The three thousand years of belief could not be shaken off . . . but he could not have the God of his father—and his own God was distant and dubious, and nothing that modern science had taught him was yet registered in his organism." Nothing is left for the son but to throw himself into the canal.

Zangwill not only understood and felt the problem of the divided generations. He sensed the direction which Jewish religion would have to take if a reconciliation were to be effected. He anticipated some of the "reconstruction" which our generation has undertaken, by recognizing the need for an evolving religious faith, responsive to basic human needs and expressed in terms of contemporary experience. In **"A Modern Scribe in Jerusalem"** he says:

> "Absolute religious truth? How could there be such a thing? As well say German was truer than French, or that Greek was more final than Arabic. Its religion, like its speech, was the way that the deepest instincts of the race found expression, and like a language, a religion was dead when it ceased to change. Each religion gave the human soul something great to love, to live by and die for, and whoever lived in joyous surrender to some greatness outside himself had religion, even though the world called him atheist. The finest souls too easily abandoned the best words to the stupidest people. The time had come for a new religious expression, a new language for the old, everlasting emotions in terms of the modern cosmos. A religion that should contradict no fact and should check no inquiry, so that children should grow up again with no distracting divorce from their parents and their past, with no break in the sweet sanctities of childhood, which carry on to old age something of the freshness of early sensation, and are a fount of tears in the desert of life."

Milton Hindus (essay date 1954)

SOURCE: "Does Zangwill Still Live?" in *Commentary,* Vol. 17, 1954, p. 308.

[*In the following excerpt, Hindus points out the strengths and limitations in style of Zangwill's work as seen in* The King of Schnorrers.]

I began **The King of Schnorrers** with an anticipation based on a misty recollection of an old reading of Zangwill. The letdown I experienced was commensurate with my hopes. Perhaps to one who is more of an "outsider," **The King of Schnorrers** may seem, as Professor Bernard N. Schilling says in his introductory essay, "an extremely funny book." I find this hard to believe, however. Not that I think it a bad book, but it seems a good deal more humorous in intention than in fact.

And yet Zangwill has some solid literary virtues which are still discernible. He knew his Jewish subjects from within.

If his tone occasionally suggests that he is writing with an eye to the quaintness which appeals to tourists, it is the Jewish tourist whom he has in mind as well as the Gentile. Zangwill's Jewish knowledge is authentic, but I am afraid that it does not go too deep. It is a kind of journalistic smattering which seeks to impress the reader with a loose sprinkling of supposedly esoteric facts and colorful foreign words.

Zangwill possesses a sense of literary form which makes him scrupulous about connecting the beginning of his story with its end; he has an inventiveness of comic detail which, while not of the highest order, is distinctly above the mediocre; and best of all he cultivates a conciseness of expression which makes his style, if not classical, at least "studious of brevity." His style gives us the feeling of his being thoroughly at home in the English language; this, in spite of the greater example of Disraeli before him, was a flattering as it was surprising to the sensibilities of his fellow Jews in England in the last decade of the 19th century. What must have been doubly pleasing to them was the fact that he had used his sensitive ear for English not to make his way in the Gentile world, but had brought his gift "home" with him and used it for Jewish purposes.

His limitations as an artist appear most clearly when we compare him with Sholom Aleichem. Though the finer points of Sholom Aleichem's original Yiddish text defy the best-intentioned efforts to recapture them in any other idiom, yet even in the awkward gabardine of translation English he is distinctly funnier than Zangwill. It is perhaps a paradox that Sholom Aleichem, composing in a language which was accessible to Jews only, should have achieved a greater measure of universality than Zangwill did. I shan't attempt to say why this is so beyond remarking that Sholom Aleichem is never in doubt about his identity or his point of view, while Zangwill (in spite of an almost ostentatious feeling of ease in his English environment) betrays such doubts. Sometimes he is the Jew whom he is writing about, sometimes he is only one of the onlookers, and sometimes he falls between the two.

To those Jews whose native language is English, the name of Zangwill will always evoke a feeling of respect. This feeling [. . .] is probably based on an exaggeration of his actual merits. We tend to forget that while he brought his Jewish interests to the very border of English literary history, he never really took them across the line. The better part of his reputation lies in his attractive qualities as a person. He deserves his place in our pantheon, but it is not altogether without misgivings that we see his work being dusted off once more and offered to critical inspection.

Harold Fisch (essay date 1964)

SOURCE: "Israel Zangwill: Prophet of the Ghetto," in *Judaism,* Vol. 13, 1964, pp. 407–421.

[*In the essay below, Fisch contests the notion that Zangwill was a realist; instead he maintains that Zangwill used realist techniques to teach lessons about the Jews' epic struggle for survival, demonstrating at the same time his ambivalence about the Ghetto.*]

A hundred years is long enough to make and break an author's reputation. There is nothing surprising in this when we consider what has happened to Meredith, Swinburne, and even Kipling, all of whom enjoyed in their time a standing somewhat more eminent than that of Zangwill among English men of letters. But Zangwill's descent from near-classical eminence for the Jewish public of 1920 to the stage of being almost forgotten by 1964—the centenary of his birth—requires a little explanation. English-speaking Jewry is after all not quite so fertile in literary genius as to enable it to ignore so considerable a writer as Zangwill undoubtedly was. Moreover, Jews usually have a tendency to hoard the achievements of their past, even the deadest of Dead Sea scrolls: why then no more acclaim for such a master as Zangwill, who, unlike Mendelssohn, Heine, and Disraeli, devoted his genius to the portrayal of Jewish scenes and Jewish problems? An evaluation of his literary achievement may help us to answer this question.

I

Israel Zangwill is frequently classed as a realist; more particularly, a realist belonging to a recognizable group—the group of regional novelists who at the end of the nineteenth century were busy in different, well-established regions of the country. Zangwill was concerned with the detailed description of life in the East End of London, the Jewish Ghetto; Eden Phillpotts took in other areas of London; Arnold Bennett was concerned with the "Five Towns"; and then there were a number of Scottish novelists—Maclaren, Douglas, and others—helping to record the lives of the Lowland peasantry. But we would err in describing Zangwill as a realist, keen and accurate though his observation of East-End manners was. In an early lecture which he delivered in the United States at the end of the 90's, entitled "Fiction the Highest Form of Truth," he set himself explicitly against the current of realism stemming from Zola and Bennett, and pointed to an ideal beyond that of mere faithfulness to sordid fact. "If you examine your concept of Napoleon," he declares, "your attention concentrates itself not on the characteristics which Napoleon had in common with all other men, but on the points of difference—the indomitable will, *la gloire,* exile in St. Helena." He takes the steerage accommodation in a transatlantic liner as the typical subject matter for a realistic novel, and he points out "what a small fragment of total truth" would in fact be discovered by realistic treatment. All the hopes and fears, the idealism, the beauty would disappear. The naturalist, such as Zola, will portray a palace realistically by making it appear like a slum; Zangwill maintains, by contrast, that if the lens is properly focused a slum will be seen to be as glorious as a palace. That is the key to his portrayal of the life of the Ghetto. It is a realism which permits us to see grandeur, heroism, and beauty behind the tawdry and shabby exterior. The garret which the Ansell family inhabits in *Children of the Ghetto* becomes during the moments of spiritual illumination a corner of paradise. "There can be much love in a little room," Zangwill remarks in his description of this pauper residence.

Zangwill in this respect may be said to voice a Jewish protest against the doctrine of realism. It is a protest which is heard also in the writings of his friend Max Nordau, whose book *Degeneration (Entartung),* criticizing all the decadence of *fin-de-siècle* realism, burst on England "like a bombshell" in its translation of 1895. Zangwill indeed had helped to popularize Nordau's book, which greatly appealed to him when he first saw it. And it is obvious why it should have appealed to him, for Nordau in that book was fiercely attacking the concept of realism, maintaining that as practiced in Europe, it represented an inverted "perishing romanticism." The "healthy poet" indeed observes accurately, but he does not depress by concentrating on brothels and lunatic asylums; he does not destroy vision through an accumulation of sordid detail: he allows his vision to shine through and irradiate the detail. Such is the way of the "healthy poet," and such, according to Nordau, is the only worthwhile type of realism.

Now Zangwill, it may be maintained, is a "healthy poet" in the sense demanded by Max Nordau. He maintains a firm hold on historical fact, on manners, on social environment—indeed, we know that from an early age he recorded his observations of the East-End scene in special notebooks from which he later spun out his novels. But his vision is by no means circumscribed by such observation. There is always "the indomitable will, *la gloire,* exile in St. Helena" or in Jewish terms, there is always the sense of a sanctity brooding over the lives of his Ghetto-dwellers, a radiance which is part of their folk-tradition. More than that, Zangwill, like most Jewish writers, is not afraid of having a *message*. In this sense he is, like George Bernard Shaw, a firm opponent of art-for-art's-sake to which the realism of the late nineteenth century was a close relation. His hero Raphael Leon in *Grandchildren of the Ghetto*—speaking here for Zangwill himself without any doubt—declares, "Art is not a fetish . . . What degradation is there in art teaching a noble lesson." Again Nordau would have heartily agreed, as would Disraeli and Heine. Like them, Zangwill maintained, quite explicitly, that art is justified by its social and moral aims, and that in pursuance of them it in fact achieves its highest reaches. Here is a type of aesthetic which runs counter to most of the late nineteenth-century trends, though it echoes the earlier moral conception of art in Ruskin, Arnold, and Tolstoy.

Zangwill stands thus at a considerable distance from mere realism, and it seems to me that the type of novel he wrote requires in this respect considerable redefinition. Such redefinition would, for instance, involve the use of a non-realist term such as "epic." We may claim that Zangwill's writing is epic in the sense that though he describes individual lives, he is really concerned deeply with the destiny of a whole nation or community: there is always an undertone of universal reference. Thus Esther Ansell in *Children of the Ghetto* is more than a poor Jewish girl in London, more even than a *persona* of Zangwill himself (though she certainly is that).[1] She is ultimately a symbol for the Jew in an alien environment: she carries upon herself, consciously even, the burden of Jewish destiny, so that her movements to and from the Ghetto, her search for some principle of unity and integrity become a sort of diagram to represent the heroism, the triumph, and the shame which mark the life of the Jewish Ghetto in the West. This awareness of a broad historical and spiritual theme environing the lives of even his most humble characters lifts Zangwill's works from the level of mere regionalism and realism to that of the epic novel as practiced by George Eliot—and, in their different ways, Dickens and Scott.

There is another sense in which Zangwill's writings are epic, and that is in preserving a theological framework. The object of the epic, whether Christian or pre-Christian, had been "to justify the ways of God to man." Zangwill in his Jewish novels is trying to do just that. He visualizes human life as part of a providential pattern involving trial, suffering, and action. There is a certain parabolic quality in such a story as that of Levi (alias Leonard James) in *Children of the Ghetto* who leaves the Ghetto and his ancestral faith, passes some years in heathen gaiety amongst actors and actresses, and finally dies of typhoid in a hospital at Stockbridge whilst the aged Rabbi, his father, mutters the prayers for the dying over his bed. The theme is repeated in the short story **"To Die in Jerusalem."** The Jewish theme in *Dreamers of the Ghetto* is no mere matter of local color, or folklore: Zangwill is concerned there with the dialectic of alienation, apostasy, and repentance; idolatry and conflict. Zangwill has no assured theological position from which to utter a sermon, but he is everywhere grappling with the decisive problems of a people burdened with a divine task, a divine challenge, and whose history is consequently more difficult, more tormented than that of other peoples. This lends to his writing, in spite of its surface humor, a profound seriousness, and seriousness is surely the ultimate mark of the epic. The note of gravity in *Children of the Ghetto*, *Dreamers of the Ghetto*, and in his American play *The Melting Pot* is unmistakable. Behind his writing may be sensed the momentous outline of the Jewish world-sorrow, the Kishinev pogrom, the vast migrations from East to West, the eternal conflict in the history of Israel between the Law which makes one free, and the Freedom which enslaves. Behind all his writing is a dialogue in which his characters struggle with the meaning of their own history, a history indeed which transcends their individual fate and yet which is made manifest in the commonest and most trivial circumstances and choices of everyday.

What then are we to make of Zangwill's well-known talent for humor? He was surely the most brilliant *badchan*, or professional entertainer, of Anglo-Jewry. His *Ghetto Comedies* are genuine comedies, and his novel, *King of Schnorrers*, which is still reprinted from time to time, is surely an uproarious comedy from beginning to end. But here again, this gift of comedy is to be related to what we have just denominated his fundamental seriousness; for it is used most frequently to illuminate the paradox of Jewish existence in the Ghetto. Manasseh Bueno Barzillai Azavedo da Costa is a great comic character, and laughter is the medium through which he is viewed. But it is a laughter which helps us to hold together in one focus the two parts of his character. On the one hand, he is the quintessential *schnorrer*—a beggar with a home-made turban, a grotesque overcoat, his actions marked by deceit, sloth, and roguery; but on the other hand he is a King, for his dignity, his proud consciousness of his Sephardi descent, and his unfailing spiritual resource give him a true grandeur. There is the contrast between his Sabbath-day magnificence, when he grandly donates a hundred pounds sterling on the occasion of his daughter's marriage, and his Sunday-morning beggary when he goes around the community to collect the sum from his fellow-worshippers in order to save the synagogue from having a bad debt. At one level, this is an extravagant jest and no more; but from another angle, Manasseh is surely in this episode the symbol of the Jew in exile, raising himself through his spiritual power above the sordid world of old clo' and beggary, and showing even in his most degraded circumstances a certain moral independence. There is the same theme of double-lives in *Children of the Ghetto*, or **"Diary of a Meshumad,"** but here in *King of Schnorrers* it is given a comic rendering, whilst elsewhere it is portrayed as tragedy. But in both forms there is the same incongruity between the Jew as he conceives himself and the Jew as he outwardly is, between his historical role and his temporary circumstances. He is, on the one hand, the Chosen People, and on the other hand, he is the downtrodden, wretched, and frequently cringing shuffler through the world's slums, or the gaudy, conceited habitué of the world's night-clubs and music-halls. His outward bearing stands in sharp contrast to the inward message which he bears, the flame which he is destined to carry with him to the end of his history. Here is the double life of the Jew, and, in particular, the double life of the Ghetto Jew. Zangwill's blend of seriousness and levity is, at its best, the literary device for controlling this paradox.

That, of course, is to state his literary achievement at his best. But we must not ignore the serious faults which so frequently undermine it. They are faults connected both with his seriousness and with his gift of humor. The former has a tendency to degenerate into sentimentality, the latter into farce. It is not difficult to point to one of Zangwill's frequent lapses into sentimentality. In **"Joseph the Dreamer"** (*Dreamers of the Ghetto*), for instance, the two women who have loved Fra Giuseppe de Franchi meet over his grave. Miriam represents the Ghetto from which he had sprung, and Helena represents the Roman aristocratic Christian society to which he had aspired.

> Helena's tears flowed unrestrainedly. "Alas! Alas! the Dreamer. He should have been happy, happy with me, happy in the fullness of human love, in the light of the sun, in the beauty of this fair world, in the joy of art, in the sweetness of music."

"Nay, Signora, he was a Jew. He should have been happy with me, in the light of the Law, in the calm household life of prayer and study, of charity, and pity, and all good offices. I would have lit the Sabbath candles for him and set our children on his knee that he might bless them. Alas! Alas! the Dreamer!"

"Neither of these fates was to be his, Miriam. Kiss me, let us comfort each other."

Their lips met and their tears mingled.

"Henceforth, Miriam, we are sisters."

"Sisters," sobbed Miriam.

The quality of the emotion in that passage will not withstand much analysis. A gush of sentimentality covers over the lack of any real solution for the conflicts revealed. Instead of the honest acceptance of failure, of discord, we have the escape into the sentimental never-never-land where the two "sisters" embrace in tearful love. It is a false catharsis, and of course it is a break with realism of any kind. Such sentimental escapism is the origin also of the intermarriage theme so prominent in Zangwill, and even more in his successors, such as Louis Golding. The problem is that of Jewish separatism, alienation, the burden of peculiarity; but instead of seeking its solution along lines indicated by Jewish historical experience, the problem is sentimentally sidestepped through the "myth" of intermarriage. In Louis Golding's *Magnolia Street* (1932) this myth is employed with a kind of archetypal naiveté, the two sides of Magnolia Street representing the Jewish and gentile worlds tragically divided by their diverse histories and traditions, but sentimentally coming together through the occasional intermarriage between their respective offspring.

Then there is farce. This can be illustrated from many of Zangwill's slighter stories, such as **"Flutterduck,"** or **"Rose of the Ghetto"**; and there is much of it in another of Zangwill's comic characters, Melchizedek Pinchas, the Hebrew poet of the Ghetto (actually a somewhat unflattering pen-portrait of Naftali Herz Imber, the author of *Hatikvah*). Pinchas writes lyrics of Zion in the medieval style, but he supplements his income by composing the Hebrew propaganda for the missionary societies in the East End of London. The character of Melchizedek Pinchas, with his garbled pronunciation of English, his cunning, hypocrisy and avarice, is a joke in bad taste. It belongs to a recognizable literary genre which has its origin in a mocking gentile vision of the Jew. Pinchas suggests to Simon Wolf, the labor leader, that they should both try to get into Parliament for Whitechapel.

> "I'm afraid there's not much chance of that," sighed Simon Wolf.
>
> "Vy not? Dere are two seats. Vy should you not haf de oder?"
>
> "Ain't you forgetting about election expenses, Pinchas?"
>
> "Nein!" repeated the poet emphatically. "I forgets noding. Ve vill start a fund."

> "We can't start a fund for ourselves."
>
> "Be not a fool-man; of course not. You for me. I for you."

Farce and sentimentality are indeed the ultimate faults of Zangwill as a writer, and unfortunately they are not mere surface blemishes, but rather the result of a certain radical failure of vision, of a certain lack of integrity. Zangwill's humor at its best was, as we have said, a means of revealing the paradoxes of Jewish existence, but at its worst it is a way of making bad jokes about "Yids." It is a sign of a certain Jewish self-contempt from which Zangwill, strong as his roots were in Jewish history, was not wholly exempt.

II

It is therefore time to ask the direct question about Zangwill's ideological standpoint. Where does he stand in relation to the central problems of Jewish existence, the challenge of Emancipation, Jewish nationalism, Orthodoxy or Reform, and the other central issues of Jewish life at the close of the nineteenth and the beginning of the twentieth century? Perhaps such an inquiry may help to illuminate both the strengths and weaknesses of his writings.

The clearest statement of his position is to be found, I think, in one of his earliest (and best) essays, "English Judaism, a Criticism and a Classification," which he contributed to the first volume of the *Jewish Quarterly Review* in 1889. In attempting to answer the question, "What is Judaism?" and, more particularly, "What is there to justify our continued existence as Jews?", he arrives at the central factor without which neither Judaism nor Jewish existence can be understood, namely, Revelation. "For the keystone of Judaism, as it is now understood by the great majority, and as it has always been understood, is Revelation" (p. 380). The only factor which can ultimately preserve the community, he maintains, is its religious morale. It is not chicken soup (even with barley), or communal organizations, or researches in the Jewish past (such as those of Professor Graetz) which would provide a basis for a continued Jewish existence. "Judaism is not to be kept alive by researches in Pipe Rolls." He sees very clearly that if Judaism is worth keeping up, it is because, as our pious ancestors unhesitatingly believed, it is the revealed Word of God. It is not merely a good thing, an elevating moral system: it is a revelation, or more correctly, *the* Revelation of God to Man amid the thunders and lightnings of Mount Sinai. This faith and the conviction that it inspires as to the special mission and destiny of Israel were the basic reality governing Jewish life in the Ghetto. Zangwill is quite sure of this: the peculiar radiance which shone upon the life of the Jewish peasantry of Eastern Europe and the Jewish pauper of the London East End was explicable only in terms of the Jewish sense of a messianic destiny flowing from the possession of a revealed law.

> Some such spirit, as naïve and as burning, breathes through a myriad volumes of our post-exilian literature, and yet gladdens the simple heart of the Russian pau-

per as he sings the hymns of hope and trust after his humble Friday night's meal. Some such faith still solaces the foot-sore hawker amid the jeers and blows of the drunkard and the bully, and transfigures the squalid Ghetto with celestial light.

(pp. 406–7)

This passage, which forms part of the peroration with which the article on "English Judaism" closes, is characteristic of Zangwill's warm attachment to the simple and gregarious life of the Ghetto; but it is also marked by a certain tone of nostalgia. The fact is that Zangwill, whilst being sure that such was the faith of the Ghetto, the faith which made the life of the Ghetto meaningful, is equally sure that such a faith is no longer possible for the modern Jew emancipated from the conditions of the Ghetto! "Some such hope has been the inspiration of countless sacrifices and martyrdoms," he continues. The past tense is significant.

The Jew who would maintain such a faith in the world of Western European emancipation and in the light of modern scepticism and rationalism, is "like a mother who clasps her dead child to her breast, and will not let it go." The beliefs of the Ghetto are no longer valid, because

all over the world the old Judaism is breaking down . . . both Biblical and Rabbinical Judaism seem to have had their day.

(pp. 398–9)

The modern self-conscious Jew cannot recover that simple childlike devotion to the sacred text which enabled the Rabbis to perceive in it the repository of all Truth. His "spiritual imagination," he says, cannot weave itself around the Bible word; he would be too much aware that "the halo was round his own head."

There is a paradox here—the central paradox, I think, of Zangwill's life and work. On the one hand, he is fundamentally attached to the Ghetto, and attached to it precisely because of the special nourishment it afforded to his "spiritual imagination." The Ghetto was his true field, and only in relation to it could he express the richness of his sensibility. Yet he was sure that the life of the Ghetto would ultimately lead to moral and artistic claustrophobia. As early as 1893, he wrote to Clement Shorter, the famous editor of the *Illustrated London News,* saying, "I must resist the solicitations of editors to shut myself up in the Ghetto."[2] There is a certain tragic irony about this. It is not only that he senses an opposition between the Ghetto and the free world—that is a common experience—but he senses that the truths which make us genuinely free, to which we owe so to speak our human dignity, belong paradoxically to the Ghetto! On the one hand, the Ghetto where "the footsore Jewish hawker" shuffles along "amid the jeers and blows of the drunkard and the bully" is transfigured with celestial light; on the other hand, it is the antithesis of freedom, and hence the antithesis of art. The choice between the Ghetto and the free world is from one angle a

choice between slavery and freedom; from another angle it is a choice between holding a live baby to one's bosom and clasping a dead one.

From this central dilemma springs Zangwill's double vision of Jewish life. All his main characters are smitten with the disease of double-living. Esther Ansell makes herself understood to her grandmother in Yiddish, but doffs her Yiddish personality in the evening when she sits down to read the New Testament in the same garret where her father drones over the Talmud and its commentaries. Daniel Hyams is torn between the necessity of observing the Sabbath and the temptations of commercial advancement if he abandons it. Sidney Graham decides to bury his Jewish identity along with his family's name of Abrahams, but finds it again when he falls in love with his Orthodox cousin Adelie Leon. **"Diary of a Meshumad"** (*Ghetto Tragedies*) gives a peculiarly stark version of the theme. It portrays the contradictory attitudes of an apostate Jew who for years has concealed his Jewish past, and is now secretly reliving it. In one entry of his Diary he writes:

The thought of the men, of their gaberdines and their pious ringlets, of their studious dronings and their devout quiverings and wailings, of the women with their coarse figures and unsightly wigs; the remembrance of their vulgar dialect and their shuffling ways, and their accommodating morality, filled me with repulsion.

But in a later entry he writes:

Behind all the tangled network of ceremony and ritual, the larger mind of the man who has lived and loved sees the outlines of a creed grand in its simplicity, sublime in its persistence. The spirit has clothed itself with flesh as it must for human eyes to gaze on it and live with it. . . .

In such portraits, Zangwill projects his own inner contradictions into his writings.

The dualism of Zangwill's vision of Jewish life may be compared to the literary portraits of Jews that we find in non-Jewish writers. There, too, we may note what I have elsewhere termed a "Dual Image" of the Jew.[3] In Shakespeare, Marlowe, Scott, and George Eliot we find an interesting black-and-white phenomenon—a disreputable, or at least unattractive, old father juxtaposed with a white, charming, and morally inspiring daughter. To compensate for the avaricious or even murderous old Jew, we must have a symbol of purity and honor in the form of a young Jewess. Thus we have Jessica by the side of Shylock, Abigail by the side of Barabas, Rebecca by the side of Isaac of York, and Mirah to offset her disreputable father Lapidoth. I have suggested that in this way the imagination of the non-Jewish writer sought to project an unresolved conflict with regard to the status of the Jew in the world, and the moral claims he makes on the non-Jew's sense of charity and justice. Some similar necessity was evidently felt by Zangwill (as no doubt by many another Jewish writer of his time) with regard to the Jewish father-figure who is both hated and loved, reverenced and feared.

But in Zangwill's case, it is interesting to note that the paradigm is reversed. The old man is most often pious, simple, devout, and living the life of learning (for examples of this: Reb Shmuel and Moses Ansell in *Children of the Ghetto,* and the old Maggid in the short story, **"To Die in Jerusalem"**), whilst the younger generation are unsettled (Esther Ansell), or perfidious (Leonard James), or contemptible (Isaac Levinsky). It would seem that Zangwill locates the more positive elements of Judaism inevitably in the past whilst the non-Jewish poet sees the old Israel as wicked, avaricious and hateful, and looks forward to a regenerate scion of the New Israel which will one day blossom and bud and fill the face of the world with fruit. There is an illuminating contrast here in points of view; but the main fact to be insisted on is that Zangwill, like so many non-Jewish writers, is inevitably split in his basic spiritual affiliations. He is both situated in the Jewish world and outside it. His humor, as we have said, is the laughter of the Jew which marks his sense of freedom, his spiritual independence, but it is also a contemptuous laughter in the face of Jewish pusillanimity as viewed from the outside.

III

How does Zangwill overcome this dualistic tendency? For he was self-conscious enough to recognize it, and to acknowledge the need for an artistic resolution. If one looks at the Ghetto novels themselves, one sees what appear to be two contradictory solutions. In *Children of the Ghetto* (1892) the main characters, after various excursions and experiments, return to the Ghetto environment and discipline. This is the case with Esther Ansell, with Levi and Hannah, the son and daughter of Reb Shmuel, and with Daniel Hyams who finally succumbs to the law of the Sabbath and accepts the consequences. A few years later, however, in *Dreamers of the Ghetto,* we have the majority of the characters taking the opposite road, i.e. apostasy, whether it be that of a political credo (Lassalle), conversion (Joseph, Sabbatai Zevi, Heine), or philosophical revolt (Spinoza, Uriel Acosta). But we should be wrong in thinking that Zangwill in either instance is pointing to a genuine answer to the problem of double-living. The two "solutions," *viz.,* the return *to* the Ghetto, and the turning away *from* the Ghetto, are merely alternative postures adopted by the artist as a means of hiding from himself the fact of an unsolved, indeed insoluble dilemma. Hannah's mood in *Children of the Ghetto,* when she decides to remain with her family at their Seder-table and to spurn her lover who waits outside to offer her freedom and joy, is a characteristic decision. In fact it is no decision at all, but a kind of dull, trance-like surrender.

> Hannah sat lethargic, numb, unable to think, her strung-up nerves grown flaccid, her eyes full of bittersweet tears, her soul floating along as in a trance on the waves of familiar melody.

The psychological notation is very accurate and very revealing. In fact, we clearly have to do here with an *unsolved* problem. Similarly, the characters in *Dreamers of the Ghetto,* whilst seeming to make the opposite kind of

decision, have no joy from their apostasy. They are shown in the end disillusioned and forsaken (Sabbatai Zevi), dying (Heine), or in the act of suicide (the young Venetian in **"Chad Gadya"**).

Did Zangwill fare any better in tackling the issue at a non-artistic level, i.e. at the level of ideological reasoning and public policy? The early article on "English Judaism" already mentioned is here again very helpful. He there indicates one line of reasoning which was to be more and more emphasized in his later life and work. That is the idea there faintly hinted at in 1889 of a compromise between "the scientific morality of Moses and the emotional morality of Christ." In a later essay ("The Voice of Jerusalem," p. 142) he declares that "Judaism may now profitably widen itself" and that "the ancient intensity of that opposition of ideals, when each ideal had to develop itself, is no longer necessary." And towards the end of his life he preached the same ideal of religious amalgamation or assimilation involving the broadening of spiritual bases and the abandonment of Jewish particularity in his contribution to a symposium on the subject entitled *A Religion of Truth, Justice, and Peace* (ed., I. Singer, 1924). It is not difficult to see that this notion of a spiritual wedding between the "scientific morality of Moses and the emotional morality of Christ" is, translated into artistic terms, the source of the sentimental intermarriage theme between Jewish man and Christian maiden (and vice versa) as fully displayed in *The Melting Pot,* where we have David, survivor of the Kishinev pogrom, and Vera, daughter of the Russian officer who perpetrated it, meeting in America, land of liberty and the fusion of opposites, and falling passionately in love with one another! It seems to me that here we have the kernel of the sentimental, melodramatic side of Zangwill's writings (illustrated above in the passage quoted from *Joseph the Dreamer*) which, more than anything else, has caused Zangwill's writings to date so quickly in the forty years since his death.

Such sentimentality represents surely the attempt to pull away from the Ghetto (as in *Dreamers of the Ghetto*). It is as Zangwill would have said, "Judaism profitably widening itself"—though it may appear to us that it is being diluted away in a gush of watery sentiment. Realism is totally subverted.[4] But there is another solution equally unrealistic, though in a quite different way. And this other solution represents the opposite side of Zangwill's make-up—the deep atavistic pull of the Ghetto mode itself (as in *Children of the Ghetto*). In considering Zangwill's feeling for the Jewish future and the validity or invalidity of Jewish particularism founded on the belief in Revelation, we cannot overlook his highly problematical and ambiguous attitude to Zionism. Starting early on as a supporter (and perhaps, for England, *the* supporter) of Herzl, whom he in fact introduced to Anglo-Jewry on his first public appearance in England in 1895, Zangwill later on in 1905 broke away from the Zionist Organization, as is well known, and founded the ITO (or Jewish Territorial Organization) dedicated to the task of finding a territory, but *not* Palestine, where an autonomous Jewish society might be created.

Zangwill's aim in this was severely practical. He harshly insisted on the economic facts, refusing to countenance the "old religious Zionism" and claiming that sentiment and ideology must be kept out of the discussion of Jewish problems. Even after the issue of the Balfour Declaration Zangwill refused to be taken in by the promise of a Jewish National Home in Palestine, and he preferred to think of a Jewish future in Galveston, Texas, which would be "a much more practical and economic outlet for the swarming, impoverished, and tormented Jewries of Europe that can be provided by the tiny, half-ruined British-Arab territory in Palestine, where the mob that asks for bread cannot be put off with a stone however holy" (*The Voice of Jerusalem,* p. 293).[5] This quotation is drawn from an essay entitled "The Mirage of the Jewish State," a title which underlines very clearly another reason for the rapid fading of Zangwill's reputation. Setting himself up as a prophet in *The Voice of Jerusalem,* he has been given all too short a shrift by the muse of history. Prophets cannot afford to go wrong so badly as Zangwill did. ITO-land, whether in Uganda or Galveston or Biro-bidjan, has proved to be a mirage, whilst in Palestine indeed, in spite of Zangwill's forecast, a Jewish State has been born. The ignorant Jewish masses have proved more right than Zangwill. It is an odd situation, for when quite practical men like Weizmann and Ussishkin preferred to dream of a Jewish State in Palestine, Zangwill, poet and dreamer, preferred to be severely practical and to look away from the mirage of a Jewish State. How is that?

Here we return to Zangwill's central limitation both as artist and as a public man, *viz.,* his unqualified commitment to the Ghetto as both center and circumference of Jewish spirituality. What was ITO-land but a projection of the Ghetto mode on a vaster scale, a super-Ghetto in which the warm, gregarious, colorful Diaspora pattern might be perpetuated? Whilst on the one hand *the retreat from the Ghetto* proproduces extravagant unrealistic schemes for world-betterment and the magic assimilation of Judaism, Hellenism, and Christianity, on the other hand, *the return to the Ghetto,* which is Zangwill's major counter-theme, produces the idea of a permanent Ghetto to end all Ghettos. Zangwill had not seen the light of Sinai irradiating the sand of the desert, or shining upon the streets of Tel Aviv, nor did he particularly expect to see it there. He had seen it once and for all transfiguring the East-European and East-London Jewish quarter with a sombre beauty. It is interesting and significant that Zangwill also did not really believe in the revival of the Hebrew language. Long after Hebrew had established itself as the language of the new *Yishuv* in Eretz Yisrael, he was still saying (in *The Voice of Jerusalem,* 1920) that "it is to Yiddish that we must look for the truest repository of a specifically Jewish sociology" (p. 248). Here again is a sign of his unwillingness to risk that leap into the unknown future, that radical break with the Diaspora which the nationally-minded Jew has made.[6]

Zangwill's commitment to the Ghetto made it impossible for him to be a Zionist in this sense. This being so, it is doubly ironical that amongst the tributes paid to Zangwill during this centenary year, by far the warmest were heard during a commemorative gathering held at the official residence of the President of Israel on March 9th, when speaker after speaker went on to acclaim Zangwill as a Zionist dreamer and prophet! His post-1905 deviations were charitably ignored. Whilst he is now entirely forgotten in the East End of London, there is a street named after him in Tel Aviv! Zangwill himself would surely have enjoyed the irony of this, if by some reflexive act of the imagination he had succeeded in visualizing himself among his gallery of characters in the *Ghetto Comedies* or the *Ghetto Tragedies.*

IV

Zangwill belongs to a class of writers ultimately rather difficult to classify. He is a little like Matthew Arnold, a little like Carlyle, Disraeli, and George Eliot. I have already suggested that the term "epic" might be applicable to some of his writings. But I think there is a more accurate term which would be relevant here, and that is the term "prophetic." Zangwill was prophetic in a number of particular ways. His idea of art wedded to mission suggests the prophetic personality; and through his impatience with mere realism as practiced by Zola and Bennett, and his tendency to stress the universal historical frame environing the lives of his characters, he senses a background of great events. Moreover, he is consumed with a moral passion. This often strengthened his vision, but it also ruined his chances as a playwright. His plays were too strident, too hysterical; he was too much the preacher, burning with the desire to save mankind. Prophets do not in fact make good playwrights. But if Zangwill was a sort of prophet, it is also necessary to point out that he was, in the final analysis, a false prophet. He had disastrously committed himself to a partial ideal. His historical vision—and prophets are dependent on a true historical vision both of the past and future—was calamitously foreshortened.

In looking into himself, Zangwill felt that he belonged somehow to a bigger, wider world than that of his fellow-Jews. His vision was wider than theirs, and therefore he could not rest content with Jewish subjects, but had to make himself (in *The Masters* and other works) the novelist of the wide world. But he finds no ultimate satisfaction in such labors: what he finds is restlessness and conflict. He makes Heine say on his death bed: "Why was my soul wider than the Ghetto I was born in? Why did I not mate with my kind?" The autobiographical note is unmistakable. But Zangwill was much deceived if he thought his trouble was that he had a soul wider than the Ghetto he was born in. His case was quite the contrary of this, for his conflicts and difficulties flowed precisely from the fact that his vision of Judaism and the Jewish future was altogether too narrowly constrained by the Ghetto and its folkways, its heights and depths. It is this which led to his remarkable insistence on the continuing validity of the Ghetto-form of existence—and equally to his traumatic reactions against the confinements of Jewish particularism. They are two sides of the same coin. He could not get be-

yond the Ghetto in order to see the possibility of significantly rich Jewish meanings developing beyond it; he
could not see the flowering of Jewish particularity in a national messianic direction. George Eliot had in this matter
a sounder instinct.

If Zangwill was, as has been suggested, a prophet, then he
was perhaps a near-relation to the false prophet, Balaam.
He too, as we may remember, saw a vision of Israel—and
a true vision at that—but it was limited to Israel's temporary encampment in the wilderness. Seeing that, he declared, "How goodly are thy tents, O Jacob." He, too, was
entranced by the splendor of a "Ghetto." And if Zangwill,
like Balaam, could often see further and more clearly than
the leaders of the people who paid him for his fine words,
there were also times when, like Balaam, the ass he rode
on could see the plain facts more clearly than he could
himself.

Notes

1. The autobiographical aspect of this portrait is well
   brought out—with no little evidence—by Joseph
   Leftwich (*Israel Zangwill*, London, 1957, pp. 47–49;
   61).

2. From an unpublished letter in the Brotherton Collection, The University, Leeds.

3. H. Fisch, *The Dual Image: The Jew in English Literature* (London, 1959), *passim*. See also E. Rosenberg, *From Shylock to Svengali: Jewish Stereotypes
   in English Fiction* (London, 1961), p. 34.

4. Cf. M. Freund, *Israel Zangwills Stellung zum Juden-
   tum* (Berlin, 1927), pp. 56–57.

5. *The Voice of Jerusalem* was published in 1920, and it
   shows very clearly that by that date Zangwill had finally turned his back on Zionism after a short period
   of enthusiasm kindled by the issue of the Balfour
   Declaration. His final changes of viewpoint as he reacted to the changing political situation in the Holy
   Land are well reflected in the final section of
   Speeches, Articles, and Letters of Israel Zangwill, ed.
   M. Simon (London, 1937).

6. Oddly enough, Zangwill thought of the Zionists as
   the old-fashioned Jews, and felt strongly that he with
   his Territorialism had hitched his wagon to the future. "Zionism takes its vision and ideal from the
   past; Territorialism places them in the future" (*The
   Voice of Jerusalem*, p. 259).

Maurice Wohlgelernter (essay date 1964)

SOURCE: "Of Tragedy and Comedy," in *Israel Zangwill*,
Columbia University Press, 1964, pp. 71–91.

[*In the following essay from his book-length study of Zangwill, Wohlgelernter explores tragedy and comedy as
complementary aspects of Jewish ghetto life in such short
story collections as* Ghetto Tragedies, Ghetto Comedies,
The Celibates' Club, The Grey Wig, *and* The King of
Schnorrers.]

"Over all Zangwill's work, even the *King of Schnorrers,*"
writes the British poet, anthologist, and personal friend of
Zangwill, Thomas Moult, "broods tragedy—tragedy in the
Greek, the truer sense. It was instinctive in him to feel
tragedy pressing everywhere."[1] This brooding sense of
tragedy, added to the comic spirit, reveals itself most
clearly in the many short stories and novelettes included in
*Ghetto Tragedies, Ghetto Comedies, The Celibates' Club,
The Grey Wig,* as well as the play *Too Much Money* and
the comic tale *The King of Schnorrers.* To balance these
significant forces of tragedy and comedy and to show everywhere that they are closely related was Zangwill's ultimate aim in these stories. Before considering their interre-
lationship, however, we should examine the essence of
both tragedy and comedy.

Analyzing tragedy as a literary form, Aristotle says:

> A tragedy is the imitation of an action that is serious,
> complete, and also of a certain magnitude; in language
> embellished with each kind of artistic ornament, each
> kind brought in separately in the parts of the work; in
> the form of action, not of narrative; through pity and
> fear affecting the proper purgation of these emotions.[2]

What must be made unmistakably clear is that this definition of tragic, further elucidated in the *Poetics*, does not
apply in every detail to Zangwill's work. What does apply,
however, is the meaning of the Aristotelian term "serious"
as regards character, the necessity of tragic conflict, and
the reconciliation of the opposed and powerful influences
of pity and fear.

Consider, for example, the character of the protagonists in
the eleven stories that make up *Ghetto Tragedies*—Brum
in **"They That Walk in Darkness,"** Florence in **"Transitional,"** Peloni in **"Noah's Ark,"** Sruel in **"The Land of
Promise,"** Isaac Levinsky in **"To Die in Jerusalem,"** the
chaste girl in **"Bethulah,"** Sabrina Brill in **"The Keeper
of Conscience,"** Grinwitz in **"Satan *Mekatrig*,"** Demetrius in **"Diary of a *Meshumad* [Apostate],"** Sarah in
"The Incurable," the Polish woman in **"The Sabbath
Breaker"**—and you will find that all are simple people.
The same cobblers, dressmakers, capmakers, writers, and
poets who inhabit No. 1 Royal Street are presented in
these short stories. But if they do not conform to the accepted view that tragedy must concern itself with a character well above the common level, they are nevertheless
tragic. For, in harmony with his theory of art as an "imitation," Aristotle held that the gratification of art comes first
of all from "recognition." If so, then Zangwill would believe that there is a place in tragedy for the simple, ordinary man.

And Zangwill is anxious to impress us with the fact that,
given the stifling, suffocating nether world of the ghetto,
the struggles and sufferings of its inhabitants will provide
us with tragic exultation, not because they are eminent but
because they epitomize man's own lack of eminence. For
tragedy, Aristotle insists, involves "pity *and* fear," namely,
as Gassner writes, "our capacity to feel for others and fear

for ourselves, too, knowing that we share in their humanity and that they share in ours, which rules out the possibility of our ever dismissing humane considerations concerning other members of the species."[3] And that is precisely what Zangwill wanted to do: to arouse in all his readers that feeling of pity, of being able to experience the tragedy that rests at the heart of the ghetto. Throughout *Ghetto Tragedies,* then, we find ourselves experiencing a pity, or the profound going out of the spirit, in response to unmerited suffering in the futile attitude of bewildered grief. The struggles of these unfortunate victims of circumstance must be our struggles as well.

Moreover, it is not only from witnessing their struggles that we derive tragic exultation but more significantly from their triumph over these struggles that we are ennobled. For we must never forget that tragedy, essentially, is not an expression of despair but of triumph over despair and of confidence in the value of human life. As Edith Hamilton cogently says:

> The dignity and significance of human life—of these and these alone, tragedy will never let go. Without them there is not tragedy. . . . It is by our power to suffer, above all, that we are of more value than the sparrows. . . . Deep down, when we search out the reason for our conviction of the transcendent worth of each human being we know that it is because of the possibility that each can suffer so terribly.[4]

Though these inhabitants of the ghetto suffer, they do not despair; they transcend their suffering with dignity, showing themselves to be people, if not above the common in social status, then certainly of uncommon significance and value.

What, then, does Zangwill consider "the tragic flaw" in each of the characters in *Ghetto Tragedies?* What basic error leads to the catastrophic end? What mistake is committed that brings on the lurking enemy in the dark, ready and eager to spring and only waiting for a chance? A careful reading of these stories will reveal that each protagonist suffers from substituting trust in man for trust in God. This is not to say that Zangwill would deny that a belief in the greatness of man is not a prerequisite for the noble life; on the contrary, he readily admits it. But what he does deny is that such a faith is sufficient unto itself. Without an equal, if not greater, faith in God, the traditional God of the ghetto, faith in man will disintegrate.[5]

And nowhere is this faith better illustrated than in the story **"Transitional."** Florence, or "Schnapsie" as her father calls her, falls in love with Alfred, a handsome Christian, and anxious to flee the frustrating admonition of her God not to intermarry, decides to proclaim her nuptial vows with him in the pious hope that all differences between people will finally cease to exist. After a "long and passionate vigil," however, Florence, suffering terribly, writes a long letter to Alfred, telling him why, for the present, his love must remain unrequited:

> A new current of thought has been going in my mind. If a religion that I thought all formalism is capable of producing such types of abnegation as my dear father,

then it must, too, somewhere or other, hold in solution all those stimuli to self-sacrifice, which the world calls Christian. . . . Perhaps the prosaic epoch of Judaism into which I was born is only transitional, perhaps it only belongs to the middle classes, for I know I felt more of its poetry in my childhood; perhaps the future will develop (or recultivate) its diviner sides and lay more stress upon the beautiful, and thus all this blind instinct of isolation may prove only the conservation of the race for its nobler future, when it may still become, in very truth, a witness to the Highest, a chosen people in whom all the families of the earth may be blessed.[6]

When, Zangwill seems to be saying, "the events of the outward world do not correspond with the desires of the heart," faith in the love of man may ultimately be lost.

And when a faith in the greatness of God is replaced by a faith not in the greatness of man but in the greatness of the devil, the results are even more tragic. Such a fate overtakes Grinwitz in **"Satan *Mekatrig.*"** Like Faustus, Grinwitz makes a pact with the devil, not, to be sure, for power but for pleasure. When he accidentally drops the Holy Scroll because of nervous fright at the shattering thunder that pierces the house of worship, Grinwitz is admonished by the elders, because such calamities are the result not of fear but of impiety. Embarrassed, angry, and bitter, Grinwitz welcomes the devil's friendship and blasphemous utterance:

> Listen to Him no more; give not up the seventh day to idleness when your Lord worketh his lightnings thereon. Blind yourselves no longer over old-fashioned pages, dusty and dreary. Rise up against Him and His law, for He is moved with mirth at your mummeries. . . . What hath He done for His chosen people for their centuries of anguish and martyrdom? It is for His plaything that He hath chosen you. . . . Rouse yourselves, and be free men. Waste your lives neither for God nor man. Or, if you will, worship the Christ, whose ministers will pour gold upon you. Eat, drink, and be merry for tomorrow ye die.[7]

Grinwitz is comforted. But soon he finds himself torn, like Faustus, between an old faith represented in the person of his wailing wife, Rebecca, who, after a violent struggle, gains entry into the place where he is hiding, and the beckoning snares of the devil. In a paroxysm of fright, Grinwitz, clutching his new-born infant, utters the traditional affirmation of his faith: "Hear, O Israel, the Lord our God, the Lord is One." Having proclaimed this declaration of belief, Grinwitz falls dead as the "dark vapor lifted, and showed the three figures to the baleful, agonized eyes of the hunchback [devil] at the open door."

If in *Ghetto Tragedies* Zangwill appears rhapsodic by comparison with Aristotle's matter-of-fact notations, he is nevertheless "allied to the man-centered point of view in the *Poetics*." For, as Gassner has correctly stated, "tragic art predicates the *special* universality of man's capacity for greatness of soul and mind in spite of his *hamartia* or the flaw in his nature."[8] Central to all of these stories is a belief that tragedy is "a poetry of man":

The individual is exemplified by the highest reaches of his humanity in erring and bearing the consequences, willing and suffering, groping and arriving at decisions, collaborating in his destiny (becoming its dupe when necessary but never its puppet), and affirming his personality even in defeat and dissolution.[9]

And every one of these eleven children of the ghetto affirms his personality by recognizing that it is better to lose the world than one's soul; better to suffer torture than fail to collaborate with destiny; better to die than to live ignominiously. As Philo Buck sums up:

> The measure of the greatness of tragedy is the wealth of the personality displayed in the struggle. Personality is the recompense for suffering, and its varied manifestation is the secret of the exultation one experiences as one watches the agony of Lear or the bewilderment of Hamlet or Oedipus. What shall it profit a man if he gain the whole world and lose his soul? was a question once asked by a man who knew tragedy intimately. To lose the world but to gain one's soul, this is the profit of tragedy, as both history and art bear abundant witness. And the greater the victory, the greater the tragedy. For tragedy is life that plucks victory from the very jaws of defeat.[10]

Albeit of common birth, these ghetto dwellers have an uncommon, heroic destiny, because Zangwill the artist found himself "capable of considering and of making us consider that his people and their actions have that amplitude and importance which make them noble."[11] Fully aware of the calamities of life, these natives of the ghetto, like Zangwill, were supremely confident in the greatness of man. Hence over this, as over Zangwill's other works, there broods tragedy "in the Greek, the truer, sense."

But tragedy, we know, was not the only aspect of the ghetto that interested Zangwill; he was no less absorbed in its comic spirit and humor. He was convinced that both the comic spirit and humor, which always existed in the gloomy alleys of the ghetto, abetted the unconquerable faith that sustained his people in their struggle for survival. For, paradoxically, both the comic spirit and humor came out of a background of sorrow and evil and the need to accept them. Tragedy and comedy were, in fact, complementary aspects of ghetto life.

What, precisely, is the comic spirit? In his highly revealing "Essay on Comedy," Meredith tells us:

> Whenever they [men] wax out of proportion, overblown, affected, pretentious, bombastical, hypocritical, pedantic, fantastically delicate; whenever it sees them self-deceived or hood-winked into vanities, congregating in absurdities, planning short-sightedly, plotting dementedly whenever they are at variance with their professions, and violate the unwritten but perceptible laws binding them in consideration one to another; whenever they offend sound reason, fair justice; are false in humility or mined with conceit, individually or in the bulk; the Spirit overhead will look humanely malign, and cast an oblique light on them, followed by volleys of silvery laughter. That is the Comic Spirit.[12]

To be sure, Zangwill uses the term "humor" instead of "comedy" when he wishes to civilize the ghetto inhabitants by revealing the nature of their intellect. But, though "comedy" and "humor" are admittedly different in form, their ultimate interest, according to Zangwill, is the same. Both are interested in the influence of the social world upon the characters of men; both are less concerned with beginnings or endings or surrounding than with what men are now doing; both, in fact, laugh through the mind. Moreover, both contain a philosophic attitude that says, "whenever a man laughs humorously there is an element which, if his sensitivity were sufficiently exaggerated, would contain the possibility of tears. He is a man who has suffered or failed of something. And although in the humor of art he usually arrives at something else, in the humor of everyday life he frequently arrives at nothing at all."[13] Since the children of the ghetto arrived nowhere at all, humor became for them, Zangwill believed, an adroit and exquisite device by which their nerves outwitted the stings and paltry bitternesses of life.

That Zangwill considered humor absolutely essential for the novelist is certain. Anxious to impress us with the fact that, in his opinion, the naturalists were deficient as novelists precisely because they failed to include humor in their works, and, lacking it, failed to see life whole, Zangwill writes:

> Humor, whose definition has always eluded analysis, may, perhaps (to attempt a definition *currente calamo*), be that subtle flashing from one aspect to another, that turning the coin so rapidly that one seems to see simultaneously the face and the reverse, the pity and the humor of life, and knows not whether to laugh or weep. Humor is, then, the simultaneous revelation of the dual aspects of life; the synthetical fusion of opposites; the gift of writing with a double pen, of saying two things in one, of showing shine and shadow together.[14]

The tragic writer always produces a one-sided work because "he can only show one side of life at a time; the humorist alone can show both."

Desiring, therefore, to show both sides of life, Zangwill wrote comic stories and tales, notably such works as *The King of Schnorrers* and *Ghetto Comedies*. In the preface to the latter work, for example, Zangwill expressly informs us that he discarded the "usual distinction between tragedy and comedy" while writing these stories:

> In the old definition a comedy could be distinguished from a tragedy by its happy ending. Dante's Hell and Purgatory could thus appertain to a "comedy." This is a crude conception of the distinction between Tragedy and Comedy, which I have ventured to disregard, particularly in the last of these otherwise unassuming stories.[15]

By blurring the usual distinction between comedy and tragedy Zangwill was trying to say that comedy, like humor, should not necessarily be equated with raucous laughter, and that the "humorist" and the "funny man" are two distinct and separate people. The joy of Zangwill's comedy is thoughtful; its laugh is not noisy but "of the order of the smile, finely tempered, showing sunlight of the mind, mental richness rather than noisy enormity."[16]

Zangwill is not alone in his belief that humor, like comedy, is sufficiently strong to offset the extremities of life. In *The Sense of Humor,* Max Eastman also informs us of the positive value of humor in striking a healthy balance between pain and pleasure:

> Humor is the most philosophic of all emotions. It is a recognition in our instinctive nature of what our minds in their purest contemplation can inform us, that pleasure and pain are, except for the incidental purpose of preserving us, indifferent—that failure is just as interesting as success. Good and bad are but colored lights rayed out upon the things around us by our will to live, and since life contains both good and bad forever, that very will that discriminates them practically gives a deeper poetic indorsement to them both. Let us not take the discrimination, then, too seriously. So speaks the sense of humor with a gay wisdom among our emotions.[17]

Humor, then, has that philosophic attitude that, like comedy, will quickly discover the pretentiousness of men.

And where but in the ghetto were there so many men to whom failure was as interesting as success? Where, too, but in the ghetto, were "good and bad" so finely interwoven as to produce a fabric of life at once intricate and absorbing? Fortunately Zangwill, more than any other writer of his day, was better equipped to show both the tragic and comic sides of life in London's East End. First, because he knew intimately and at first hand the tragedy inherent in the lives of the children of the ghetto. And, second, we will remember, that Zangwill began his career as one of the "new humorists" who rallied around Jerome K. Jerome's *The Idler,* in which *The King of Schnorrers* was first published serially. These humorists, in the words of Zangwill, believed that "life was Janus-faced, and the humorist invests his characters with a double-mask; they stand for comedy as well as for tragedy."[18] In fact, *The Celibates' Club,* the series of humorous tales about bachelors and old maids, attracted considerable attention in London's literary circles in 1891, and its reception was one of the factors that led to his commission to write *Children of the Ghetto.* Because he was thus personally involved in the tragic and comic aspects of his life and times, Zangwill's *Ghetto Comedies,* like his other comic works, contains a mental richness rather than a noisy laughter, a finely tempered smile rather than a loud guffaw.

Read carefully, everyone of the fourteen stories in *Ghetto Comedies*—"The Model of Sorrows," "Anglicization," "The Jewish Trinity," "The Sabbath Question in Sudminster," "The Red Mark," "The Bearer of Burdens," "The *Luftmensch*," "The Tug of Love," "The Yiddish Hamlet," "The Converts," "Holy Wedlock," "Elijah's

Goblet," "The Hirelings," "*Samooborona*" (Self-Defense)—will show that its mirth is subdued; in fact, many of them lack any traces of humor at all. Why? Because Zangwill felt that comedy teaches us to look at life exactly as it *is.* It teaches us to be responsive, to be honest, to interrogate ourselves and correct our pretentiousness. Through the medium of comedy Zangwill chastened the children of the ghetto for their foolishness, stubbornness, self-deception, and failure to recognize the realities of life. This criticism, of course, was not the result of any rancor, for Zangwill, we know, had an abiding kinship with and affection for his people. He was able to ridicule those he loved without loving them less; he chastened without hating.[19] Zangwill, like Meredith, adored the comic spirit.

Surveying, therefore, the social impact of the ghetto on its inhabitants, Zangwill's "comic spirit" mocked the Jew for failing to understand the two basic needs for his survival: recapturing the true image of himself and heeding the call to action. Though most of the fourteen stories in *Ghetto Comedies* are variations on these themes, three of them—**"The Model of Sorrows," "The Hirelings,"** and **"Samooborona"**—exemplify the kind of offenses against reason committed by the Jew that the "comic spirit" set out to attack. The climax builds up with "volleys of silvery laughter."

"The Model of Sorrows" is the story of a painter "in love with the modern" who searches in reality for a model image of the Christ who sat in the synagogue of Jerusalem and walked about the shores of Galilee. He finally finds such an image in Israel Quarrier, "a frowsy gabardined Jew," on the streets of Brighton. In this odd figure the artist chanced on the very features, the haunting sadness and mystery that he had been so long seeking. On learning Quarrier's story—how he had fled Russia and arrived in England, how he was swindled of all his money by the rascally Elzas Kazelia, sustained his family on bread and water, was refused help by the Jewish Charity Board and was even shunned by the rabbi—the artist sees revealed in his model's tale of woe all the sordid details and tragedy of the Wandering Jew. The artist recognizes that he had erroneously removed "the lines of guile" from the face on his canvas and must perforce restore them. He had tried to idealize them out of existence, but now he sees the truth.

> For surely here at last was the true tragedy of the people of Christ—to have persisted sublimely, and to be as sordidly perverted; to be king and knave in one; to survive for two thousand years the loss of a fatherland and the pressure of persecution only to wear on its soul the yellow badge which had defaced its garments. . . . The true tragedy, the saddest sorrow, lay in the martyrdom of an Israel *unworthy of his sufferings.* And this was Israel the high tragedian in the comedy sock.[20]

To be a Jew, Zangwill believed, one must be "spotless as the dove." Only thus can the Jew be worthy of his suffering.

For the Jew to be worthy of suffering meant something more than just being kind, gracious, hospitable, and benevolent; he must be willing "to live and die with his own people."[21] Even when success in the arts, sciences, and professions brings the Jew into close contact with the world beyond the ghetto walls, he dare not ever forget his past and its associations. This Zangwill affirms in **"The Hirelings,"** in which Rozzenofski, the concert pianist, failing to impress his American audiences, returns home lonely and sad. Aboard ship he meets a leading patroness of the arts in America, Mrs. Andrew P. Wilhammer, and her maid, "a glorious young Jewess." Falling in love with the latter, he is inspired one afternoon to play a medley of ancient synagogue songs. Hearing him play so brilliantly, Mrs. Wilhammer invites him, despite his Semitic origins, to offer a recital at her home in Chicago and thus be assured of musical fortune. Torn between his love for "the hireling who first made him warmly conscious of his Semitic past and the wealthy patroness who would have him forget it," he chooses the latter:

> He had burst the coils of this narrow tribalism that had suddenly retwined itself around him; he had got back again from the dusty conventicles and the sunless ghettos—back to the spacious salons and radiant hostesses and the great free life of art. He drew deep breaths of sea air as he paced the deck, strewn so thickly with pleasant passengers to whom he felt drawn in a renewed sense of the human brotherhood.[22]

Rozzenofski himself became a hireling. To all of this, Zangwill's comic spirit has but one comment: *"Rishus* [evil], forsooth."[23]

Of far greater evil than this failure to seek identification with one's people was the failure to seek salvation. Zangwill was firmly convinced that the Jew, if he is to survive his hostile environment and its pogroms, must resort to the only course open to him: action. As Melchisedek Pinchas, the poet and playwright in these *Ghetto Comedies,* says on striking the actor Goldwater for tampering with his lines: "Action is greater than thought. Action is the greatest thing in the world."[24] Zangwill was deeply concerned about the failure of the Jew in the ghetto to comprehend the need for self defense. When, as so often happened, young men in the ghetto formed corps of armed volunteers to stand guard against the enemy, they met with derision, disdain, and worse still, disunity among their fellow Jews. Zangwill bemoaned this fact, and though he would have us believe that the failure to take up arms may have resulted from the stupor into which Jews fell after centuries of living in sunless ghettos, he reacted against it. He called the heroism of these brave volunteers *Samooborona.*

Like his Biblical namesake, David, the hero of this sad tale, is a man of action. Fearless, he seeks men for his corps who will not kiss the rod of "any moujik, any hooligan." Arriving in Milovka, "the next town on the pogrom route," he is unable to arouse the townspeople, who have grown accustomed after many years in the pale of settlement to mental and physical servitude. Only one among them, Ezekiel Leven, sees that in *Samooborona* lies their only salvation. But when David and Ezekiel approach the

leaders of the community, disclosing their Maccabean dreams and begging for moral, physical, financial support, and above all, unity, they find the people lost in a nebulous welter of separate parties and philosophies, each party groping toward its separate rays of light. Suddenly David has an illusion:

> [He has] a nightmare vision of bristling sects and pullulating factions, each with its Councils, Federations, Funds, Conferences, Party-Days, Agenda, Referats, Press-Organs, each differentiating itself with meticulous subtlety from all the other Parties, each defining with casuistic minuteness its relation to every contemporary problem, each equipped with inexhaustible polyglot orators speechifying through tumultuous nights.[25]

Powerless to unite these feuding factions, defenseless in the face of Russian artillery that bursts shells over the close-packed houses of the Milovka ghetto, David stands near the chimney pot of his temporary quarters, and with an "ironic *laugh*" turns his pistol on himself while the great guns boom on hour after hour.

> When the bombardment was over the peace of the devil lay over the ghetto of Milovka. Silent were all the fiery orators of all the letters of the alphabet; silent the Polish patriots and the lovers of Zion and the lovers of mankind; silent the bourgeois and the philosophers, the timber-merchants and the horse dealers, the Bankers and the Bundists, silent the Socialists and the Democrats; silent even the burly censor, and the careless Karaite and the cheerful *Chassid;* silent the landlord and his revolutionary infant in their fortified cellar; silent the Rabbi in his study, and the crowds in the market place.[26]

Zangwill was firmly convinced that if the Jew in the ghetto would "drift into vanities, congregate in absurdities, plan shortsightedly," and refuse to unite in self-defense, the comic spirit must look with "humane malignity" at him and in the end bring "the peace of the devil."

"The stroke of the great humorist," said Meredith, "is world wide, with lights of tragedy in his laughter."[27] In *Ghetto Comedies* the humorist Zangwill took a long look at the ghetto and found that it was filled with tragedy, which consisted either of an escape by some into the waiting arms of Christianity, or the refusal of others, like the Milovka settlers, to heed the call to action, allowing themselves to be slaughtered wantonly. In both instances the Jew was doomed to extinction. This, Zangwill, like all other believers in Jewish survival, wanted desperately to prevent. Hence, when he saw that the Jew in the ghetto refused to face reality, he invoked the comic spirit in order to cast an oblique eye upon him. Like Meredith, Zangwill considered comedy "the ultimate civilizer," hoping that by the use of this medium he would lead his people out of their misery. Zangwill hoped with these tales to clarify those issues that, he felt, were preventing the ghetto dwellers from achieving their freedom and felicity. Only the comic spirit could help Zangwill in his task, for, as the beautiful "hireling" said to the self-hating Rozzenofski, "with us Jews, tears and laughter are very close."[28]

The person who best typified the comic spirit was the ghetto *schnorrer,* immortalized by Zangwill in **The King of Schnorrers.** This short work is a vivid and humorous portrayal of a fictitious character—one Menasseh Bueno Barzilai Azevedo da Costa—who lords it in the London ghetto at the close of the eighteenth century. He is a Sephardic mendicant who has developed begging to a fine art and who combines with his audacious effrontery unfailing resourcefulness and ready repartee.

Zangwill tells the story of the *schnorrer* in a series of episodes that, taken together, are a minor classic of absurdity. These episodes pit the *schnorrer* Menasseh against three people: first, the philanthropist Grobstock; second, Yankele, a fellow *schnorrer* of Ashkenazic or northern European origin; and, finally, the Sephardic authorities, chiefly the *Mahamad,* a governing council of five elders of the synagogue. In each case what seems to be inferior actually wins out over something higher and greater than itself.

Menasseh is an odd combination of aristocrat, intellectual, and religionist. He is also a proud man who never lets anyone forget that he is a Sephardi, tracing his ancestry to the Spanish-Portuguese Jewish families who resettled in England in 1656 after having been expelled by Edward I in 1290. His very name, in fact, describes the properties that he possesses in abundance: scholarship, goodness, ancient family, wealth, and royal connections suited to Menasseh's concept of himself. It is no wonder, therefore, that on meeting with Joseph Grobstock, financier, East India Company director, treasurer of the Great Synagogue, and, as his German name would indicate, a solid, crude piece of common wood, Menasseh "towered over the unhappy capitalist, like an ancient prophet denouncing a swollen monarch."[29] And with an entertaining display of arrogance, vanity, and self-justification, he says to Grobstock:

> You are the immigrants of yesterday—refugees from the Ghettos of Russia and Poland and Germany. But, we, as you are aware, have been established here for generations; in the Peninsula our ancestors graced the courts of kings and controlled the purse-strings of princes; in Holland we held the empery of trade. Ours have been the poets and scholars of Israel. You cannot expect that we should recognize your rabble, which prejudices us in the eyes of England. We made the name of Jew honorable; you degrade it. You are as the mixed multitude which came with our forefathers out of Egypt.[30]

This natural feeling of superiority that seems "to ooze from every pore" of Menasseh is further developed in his attitude toward the problem of work. Since he identifies *schnorring* with "aristocracy," the *schnorrer* believes that he is forbidden to betray his calling by work in any form, just as he must avoid any of the other things by which people seem to become rich and successful. Work is an uncertain, insecure way of making a living. Hence, when Yankele ben Yitzchok, a "short Schnorrer even dingier

than da Costa," wishes to marry the latter's daughter, and tries to show that *schnorring* by synagogue-knocking brings in enough money to support her in style, Menasseh rebuffs him sharply:

> "What! To assist at the services for a fee! To worship one's Maker for hire! Under such conditions to pray is to work." His breast swelled with majesty and scorn. . . . "Surely you know that *schnorring* and work should never be mixed. . . . No, decidedly, I will not give my daughter to a worker, or to a *Schnorrer* who makes illegitimate profits."[31]

Schnorring, believed Menasseh, was the only occupation that is regular all year round. Only after Yankele submits to the supreme test of *schnorring* from "the king of guzzlers and topers, and the meanest of mankind," the miser Rabbi Remorse Red-herring, does Menasseh promise to become his father-in-law.

The intended union of Menasseh's daughter with a Polish Jew excites the liveliest horror in the breasts of the *Mahamad.* A Tedesco did not pronounce Hebrew as they did, hence he was inferior. Menasseh is therefore summoned before "these gentlemen who administered the affairs of the Spanish-Portuguese community, and [whose] oligarchy would undoubtedly be a byword for all that is arbitrary and inquisitorial but for the widespread ignorance of its existence," to show cause why he has consented to give his daughter's hand to an "inferior" Ashkenazic Jew. Using his sharp intellect, with its immense freight of apt quotation, allusion to ancient documents, and accumulated knowledge of the religious principles of the Jewish race, Menasseh demolishes the arguments of the elders. He proves, first, that no ancient *Ascama* (ordinance) ever forbade a Sephardi from marrying a Tedesco; and, second, that the takers and not the givers of charity "are the pillars of the synagogue." "Charity is the salt of riches," quotes Menasseh from the Talmud, "and, indeed, it is the salt that preserves your community." The *Mahamad* is "foiled by the quiet dignity of the beggar," who, proving the insecurity of their earthly power, emerges victorious at the intellectual level.[32]

With a final display of daring and bravado befitting only a king, Menasseh continues to lord it over the elders by promising to contribute to the synagogue an unbelievable sum of six hundred pounds, which he later extorts from a whole series of victims. This final episode in his career not only earns him his royal title but a permanent income as well. Illustrating his many-sided genius a few days after the royal wedding of Deborah and Yankele, Menasseh "strikes the Chancellor breathless" by handing him a bag containing all the money he promised.

> Stipulating only that it should be used to purchase a life-annuity (styled the DaCosta Fund) for a poor and deserving member of the congregation, in whose selection he, as donor, should have the ruling voice. . . . The donor's choice fell upon Menasseh Bueno Barzillai Azevedo Da Costa, thenceforward universally recognized, and hereby handed down to tradition, as the King of Schnorrers.[33]

Surely Zangwill meant to do more in this book than relate some simple episodes in the life of a beggar. As Bernard Schilling has already indicated, "the whole seems an ironic comment upon the absurdity of all human arrangements."[34] Beggary, the subject of this tale, implies a long history of poverty, injustice, and degradation, to which the Jew in the diaspora has been subjected. To offset the grim realities of the ghetto, there arose from the soil of Jewish life a determination to self-criticism that Freud called "tendency-wit." Humorous tales, subtle comments, witty anecdotes were directed, at times, against oneself or "against a person in whom one takes interest, that is, a composite personality such as one's own people."[35] These stories, invented by Jews themselves, mocked Jewish peculiarities and shortcomings and thus provided much psychic relief for the downtrodden of the ghetto. "From death and beggary themselves the Jews extracted the ludicrous."[36] Social stability, then, was achieved in the ghetto through "wise laughter."[37]

And wisdom is the key to the understanding of Menasseh's life and mind. Faced with the absurdities of the ghetto in which he, a learned man, is considered inferior, Menasseh exaggerates his value in order to build up his position among men who, for the moment, appear vastly superior. In this effort to achieve prominence he uses his intellect, which, because of his close study and vast knowledge of the Talmud, has been sharpened to deal ingeniously with all the vexing problems confronting him. Being more learned, Menasseh refuses to recognize any difference between master and servant, and insists, as Freud also recognized, "that the rich man gives him nothing, since he is obligated by [religious] mandate to give alms, and strictly speaking must be thankful that the schnorrer gives him an opportunity to be charitable."[38] Such arguments, at once audacious and humorous, offered psychic relief for all those anxious mendicants who, like Menasseh, roamed the streets of the ghetto in search of help.

The King of Schnorrers, therefore, underscores that special quality of Jewish humor that cures folly with folly, and, like the comic spirit, makes game of "serious" life. Menasseh's humor is "something intellectually quick whereby acuteness of mind may triumph over the actual facts and grim problems of life. Things are endurable only if the mind can find a twist, an element of relief or humor to obscure the hopeless wretchedness of life as it often is. So once more the Jews have been able better to accept life in the face of what it has done to them."[39] Heart *and* mind laugh with the King of Schnorrers.

Comedy heightened Zangwill's consciousness of the tragic in ghetto life. If, for example, Menasseh acts absurdly, it is only because he reflects the absurdity of his environment; if he has to use his mental skill to overpower his adversaries, it is only because these adversaries need to be overpowered; if, in short, his antics make us laugh, they also make us cry. Why? Because within the narrow radius of the ghetto reside a group of people who, as a result of the vicissitudes of migration and worship, and in spite of their tradition, worship the gruff, pompous, parsimonious financiers instead of the learned, the scholars, the intellectuals. Second, these very people who bear the cross of discrimination gain the dubious distinction of discriminating against their own brethren by forbidding, for example, a Sephardi to marry a Tedesco. And, finally, what seems far worse, we find Menasseh, who refuses himself to distinguish between master and servant, looking with disfavor on Yankele, a fellow mendicant, until the latter proves his worth as a *schnorrer.* It is this theme—disunity among Jews in the face of adversity, and their loss of a sense of values—that preoccupied so much of Zangwill's mind and that he often returned to in his writing, especially in **"Samooborona,"** the last of the *Ghetto Comedies.*

Acutely aware of the fact that the children of the ghetto were acting contrary to their welfare by "drifting into vanities" and "congregating in absurdities," Zangwill employed the comic spirit for the express purpose of controlling life.

> Comedy as well as tragedy can tell us that the vanity of the world is foolishness before the gods. Comedy dares seek the truth in the slums of Eastcheap or the crazy landscape Don Quixote wanders across or the enchanted Prospero isle. By mild inward laughter it tries to keep us sane in the drawing room, among decent men and women. It tells us that man is a giddy thing, yet does not despair of man.[40]

Because, as Thomas Moult reminds us, Zangwill was capable "of feeling tragedy everywhere while still maintaining faith in the nobility of man," he could, through comic perception, take a human view of the ghetto. It is this view, no doubt, that Zangwill expresses in a prologue to the dramatic version of *Children of the Ghetto,* "The Author to the Audience":

> But do not deem the Ghetto is all gloom
> The Comic Spirit mocks the age's doom
> And weaves athwart the woof of tragic drama
> The humors of the human panorama.[41]

This inward laughter at the absurdities of men that characterizes *Ghetto Comedies* and *The King of Schnorrers* finds personified reflection also in many of the heroes and heroines of his non-ghetto tales, novelettes, and stories. Hence in *The Grey Wig* and *The Celibates' Club* Zangwill applies the same comic art to the inhabitants of London's other rooms, other places, that he used so effectively in describing the blunders of his own children of the ghetto. Again, in these two latter works, Zangwill discovers that "truth is strong next to the Almighty and will not be put to worse when she grapples with falsehood in open encounter." To laugh at evil and error means we have surmounted them.

Consider, for example, any one of the "twelve apostles" of bachelorhood who, together with the teller of the tales, Paul Pry, make up the total membership of the Bachelors' Club. They are dedicated, we are told, to the principle that "marriage was a crime against woman for which no punishment not even exclusion from the Club could be suffi-ciently severe."[42] Of course, all of them—Osmund Bethel, Caleb Twinkletop, Eliot Dickray, Henry Robinson, Israfel Mondego, Joseph Fogson, M.D., O'Roherty, Oliver Green, Moses Fitz-Williams, Mandeville Brown, McGillicudy, and Pry—finally are forced, however hesitatingly, to marry. Delineating their checkered careers, Zangwill seems to be saying that what they at last learned, not without some mixed feelings of pain and pleasure, was that "love is not the only excuse that might induce a bachelor to marry . . . it is money, position, convenience, comfort, con-science, social pressure, and a thousand and one things that induce men to marry."[43] Not only does this apply to men, Zangwill tells us further, but also to women, who, despite possible membership in an Old Maids' Club, can-not truly profess ignorance of the "grammar of love." To resist marriage, therefore, is folly.

These truths, central to all these stories, are, Zangwill seems to be saying, occasionally forgotten, thus enabling him to declare: "No society is in good health without laughing at itself quietly and privately; no character is sound without self-scrutiny, without turning inward to see where it may have overreached itself."[44] This laughter, however, is also mixed with tears because the description of these forlorn characters, struggling to extricate them-selves from self-imposed celibacy, teaches us, like tragedy, "that the vanity of the world is foolishness before the gods."

Like *The Celibates' Club, The Grey Wig,* consisting of seven stories and one murder mystery, represents Zangwill at his comic best. The title story of the collection, for ex-ample, is brimful of "that sort of mirth which is above the mere coincidence of sound, which cannot and need not be put in the form of words because it springs from the inher-ent meaning of the situation."[45] It tells of two impecunious French women, Madame Dépine and Madame Valière, who, though living in the same boardinghouse, are not on speaking terms, and must therefore learn all about each other from Madame la Propriétaire. The two boarders wear brown wigs, the only things that time, writing "wrinkles enough on the brows of the two old ladies," does not touch. Because the owner comes down one day in a gray wig, both boarders, after burying their silence in order to wag about the new wig, decide to save their money together to buy a gray wig. Madame Dépine wins the tossup that de-cides who should wear the new wig first, but because Ma-dame Valière is going to a wedding, she is loaned the wig and a brooch by her friend. After Madame Valière leaves, the owner and Madame Dépine learn to their dismay that she is a "senescent kleptomaniac." Considered wealthy be-cause of the brooch, she is finally murdered by a thief.

In this, as in the other stories, Zangwill seems anxious to tinge the comic with sadness, for, as he concludes, "be-neath all these pretenses of content, lay [lies] a hollow sense of desolation." Lonely and aloof, these figures are deluded by visions of beauty and grandeur, seeking amid their ruins the love that is "the only reality" while recog-nizing that "everything else is a game played with counters." Hence, viewing the denuded body of her friend in the morgue, Madame Dépine is moved by "the great yearning for love and reconciliation and for the first time a grey wig seemed a petty and futile aspiration."[46]

Reviewing *The Grey Wig,* Abraham Cahan, the author of *The Rise of David Levinsky* and one of Zangwill's early and abiding admirers, correctly sums up the intention of these stories, namely, to evoke the inward laughter that takes the human, the double view of life that sees comedy and tragedy everywhere. "He cannot," says Cahan, "paint the ludicrous without tinging it with sadness—with the deep-rooted sadness of the Jewish race; nor can he give vent to his human sympathies without having the tragic note drowned in the uncontrollable rush of humor."[47] Hav-ing established a perspective, Zangwill, in these tales as well as in *Too Much Money*—a comedy written "during the tragic tension of World War I" and produced at the Ambassador's Theatre, London, on April 9, 1918—is able to tell us that man is a giddy person who seeks ephemeral things but of whom one does not despair. Hence Annabel Broadley, the major figure in this play, after gaining a for-tune in the stock market and not telling her wealthy hus-band, gains her soul by deciding to irrigate Mesopotamia. There is, Zangwill seems to be saying throughout these ghetto and non-ghetto works, a comic as well as a tragic road to wisdom and the future.

Notes

1. Moult, p. 290.

2. Aristotle, *Poetics,* ed. S. H. Butcher and with introd. by John Gassner (New York, 1951), p. 23.

3. Gassner, "Aristotelian Literary Criticism," introd. to *ibid.,* p. xiii.

4. Edith Hamilton, *The Great Age in Greek Literature* (New York, 1924), pp. 233–34.

5. A similar view is expressed by Joseph Wood Krutch in *The Modern Temper* (New York, 1929), p. 127.

6. *Ghetto Tragedies,* p. 74.

7. *Ibid.,* pp. 356–57.

8. Gassner, introd. to *Poetics,* p. lxvi.

9. *Ibid.,* p. lxvii.

10. Philo M. Buck, *Literary Criticism* (New York, 1930), p. 283.

11. Krutch, p. 122.

12. George Meredith, "An Essay on Comedy," *Comedy,* ed. Wylie Sypher (New York, 1956), p. 48.

13. Max Eastman, *The Sense of Humor* (New York, 1922), p. 21.

14. *Without Prejudice,* p. 84. See also Horace Kallen, *In-decency and the Seven Arts* (New York, 1930), p. 244.

15. *Ghetto Comedies,* p. i.

16. Meredith, "An Essay on Comedy," p. 48.

17. Eastman, *The Sense of Humor,* p. 22. The distinguished Canadian writer of humorous stories and tales, Stephen Leacock, once offered a definition of humor that, in essence, is not unlike Eastman's: "Such is the highest humor. It represents an outlook upon life, a retrospect as it were, in which the fever and fret of our earthly lot is contrasted with its shortcomings, its lost illusions and its inevitable end! The fiercest anger cools; the bitterest of hate sleeps in the churchyard; and over it all spread Time's ivy and Time's roses, preserving nothing but what is fair to look upon" (quoted in Max Eastman, *The Enjoyment of Laughter* [New York, 1937], p. 338).

18. *Without Prejudice,* p. 84. That the face of tragedy always lurked behind the mask of comedy, especially in his ghetto stories, is further confirmed in a letter Zangwill wrote from Florence, dated December 2, 1902, in which he stated: "I shall soon begin to write a new series of ghetto stories with an underlying comedy element, the comedy of course occasionally touching the deeps, for Jewish life is always tragicomedy."

19. Zangwill's humor, less filled with animus than with a deep sympathy for the oppressed and the weak, illustrates, interestingly, Thackeray's opinion: "The humorous writer professes to awaken and direct your love, your pity, your kindness—your scorn for untruth, pretension, imposture—your tenderness for the weak, the poor, the oppressed, the unhappy" (quoted in Buck, p. 294)

20. *Ghetto Comedies,* p. 55.

21. *Ibid.,* p. 410.

22. *Ibid.,* p. 425.

23. *Ibid.,* p. 425. The terms *Rishus,* meaning literally evil, was used colloquially by Zangwill in its Western Yiddish sense to mean anti-Semitism, evil, and viciousness. See Exodus ii. 14.

24. *Ibid.,* p. 332. Despite Zangwill's lament, the idea of Jewish self-defense as a fact of life was well known at the time that *Ghetto Comedies* was being written.

25. *Ibid.,* p. 481.

26. *Ibid.,* p. 487.

27. Meredith, "An Essay on Comedy," p. 45.

28. *Ghetto Comedies,* p. 407.

29. *The King of Schnorrers,* p. 10.

30. *Ibid.,* p. 13.

31. *Ibid.,* pp. 68–70.

32. *Ibid.,* pp. 105, 117, 121.

33. *Ibid.,* p. 156.

34. Schilling, introd. essay to *The King of Schnorrers,* p. xxiii.

35. Sigmund Freud, "Wit and the Unconscious," *Complete Psychological Works of Sigmund Freud,* ed. James Strachey, vol. VIII (London, 1960), p. 111. My translation of the original varies slightly from that of Mr. Strachey.

36. Schilling, p. viii.

37. That "wise laughter" serves as a catharsis and relieves the sense of guilt and anxiety is affirmed by Wylie Sypher in "The Meanings of Comedy," *Comedy,* p. 245.

38. Freud, *Complete Works,* VIII, 113.

39. Schilling, p. xxix.

40. Sypher, "The Meanings of Comedy," p. 254.

41. Zangwill, "The Author to the Audience" (sheet inserted in playbill distributed to audience), Theater Division, New York Public Library.

42. *The Celibates' Club,* p. 1.

43. *Ibid.,* p. 38.

44. Sypher, "The Meanings of Comedy," p. 252.

45. Cahan, "I. Zangwill's 'The Grey Wig,'" p. 256.

46. *The Grey Wig,* p. 43.

47. Cahan, "I. Zangwill's 'The Grey Wig,'" p. 256.

Bernard Winehouse (essay date 1973)

SOURCE: "Israel Zangwill's *The King of Schnorrers,*" in *Studies in Short Fiction,* Vol. 10, 1973, pp. 227–233.

[*In the essay below, Winehouse provides background and publication information as well as a critical overview of Zangwill's novella* The King of Schnorrers, *which he places among Zangwill's most competent comic works.*]

It is not difficult to understand the special interest of Zangwill, the ghetto upstart and social rebel, in the *schnorrer* and his picaresque adventures. In the traditional *schnorrer,* or Jewish beggar, was to be found a paradoxical, though peculiarly Jewish combination, of poverty and learning. His wit, erudition and incredible impudence were all used to cut across class barriers and to outwit his social superiors. The *nouveaux-riches* of Anglo-Jewry were the prime target of Zangwill's "King," whose funds of money were by no means always equalled by any fund of learning or religious piety. I like to see the King of Schnorrers as a literary extension of "Marshallik" (a Zangwill pseudonym), whose satire in columns of *The Jewish Standard* had plagued the Anglo-Jewish Philistines for some three years. "Marshallik," the traditional Jewish jester or fool, and the King of the Schnorrers are two of a kind, whose fictional masks Zangwill revelled in wearing.

The *schnorrer* had a long and proud history before he ever set foot on England's shores to become immortalized by Israel Zangwill. The word *schnorrer* comes, I believe, from the German word *schnurren,* which means to "buzz" or "whirr." The word was used to describe the musical instrument or *Schnurrpfeife* played by strolling beggars. By extension this came to mean to beg in an insolent way which was more humiliating to the almsgiver himself than to the beggar. The term *schnorrer* again might be connected with the German word *schnurre* meaning a comic tale or buffoonery. In the Middle Ages the *schnorrer* would eke out a living as an itinerant story-teller and retailer of anecdote and ghetto news. After the Khnielnicki pogroms in Poland (1648–1657), which rendered many thousands of Jews homeless, the *schnorrer* became an established and recognised institution in European Jewry.

Now the position of this species of Jewish beggar became in the course of time a very special and a very privileged one. Of the myriad of anecdotes and stories that exist about the *schnorrer,* most depend on the idea that the beggar was a vital necessity to the Jewish rich if they wished for a place in "the world to come." The performance of a religious duty, or *mitzva* as it is called in Hebrew, is considered a privilege for a Jew and the giving of charity is an absolutely fundamental *mitzva.* This explains the enormous pride the *schnorrer* exhibits in being the means by which the rich Jew can carry out his duty to God. This pride is further reinforced by the possession of an impeccable erudition which consists largely of a knowledge of all the references to charity in the scriptures. Learning has always been the status symbol *par excellence* amongst Jews. There is nothing "come-cap-in-hand" about the *schnorrer's* begging; such a beggar had never been seen in Christendom. Perhaps this is why the preposterous cheek of Zangwill's hero bewildered English readers. It is surprising that the author did not choose to give in a preface any of that fascinating background detail concerning the tradition of *schnorring,* which he had meticulously collected.

The King of Schnorrers was first published in Jerome K. Jerome's immensely popular magazine, *The Idler,* in 1893.[1] This magazine, incidentally, was the spiritual home of that prolific school of comic writing known in the eighteen-nineties as the "New Humor." It embraced such dissimilar writers as W. W. Jacobs, G. R. Sims, Eden Philpotts, Robert Barr and, of course, Zangwill. But the author's interest in the lore of the *schnorrer* went back at least five years before the serialization of the story in *The Idler.*

Writing in the *Jewish Standard* under the pseudonym of "Marshallik" in 1888, Zangwill expressed regret at the fact that charity, like everything else in the Jewish community, had become organized.[2] The handling of charitable works by communal bodies had, he noted with sadness, brought about the disappearance of the *schnorrer,* "that picturesque apparition, who used to turn up at all times and places, and display an ingenuity in extracting coins from reluctant pockets." The writer goes on to suggest that either Rabbi Gaster or Joseph Jacobs, both of whom were contemporary experts in Jewish folklore, should undertake such a work. "Marshallik," of course, could not resist the tempta-

tion of providing Messrs. Gaster and Jacobs with some grist for their mill in the form of two following *schnorrer* anecdotes, neither of which was to appear in **"King of Schnorrers."** A *schnorrer* once came to a wealthy Jew and complained of his very bad health. The *schnorrer* explained to the wealthy man that the doctors had advised a prolonged stay at some seaside resort. He completed his tale of woe by a request for an exorbitant sum of money in order to finance such a trip. The rich Jew gasps at the enormity of the sum involved: "I wish to go to Scarboro," the *schnorrer* replied.

"But Scarboro is the most expensive place you could select."

"Am I to consider expense where my health is concerned?"

The second anecdote which "Marshallik" had to offer tells the story of a Russian *schnorrer* who, when the rouble had fallen to its lowest level, bore a placard on which he had written; "Roubles received as if at par." Both these stories illustrate well the impudence with which the traditional *schnorrer* has always been associated.

The King of Schnorrers is, I think, as polished a piece of comic writing as Zangwill was ever to create. Professor B. N. Schilling refers to it in his book, which contains a very substantial section on *The King of Schnorrers,* as a "minor classic of absurdity."[3] Amongst Jewish readers of Zangwill it has always been a favourite and has been translated over the years into every European language. Jerome K. Jerome, who was ready to publish the work during the most critical period of *The Idler's* beginnings, saw the short novel as a gem. It is certainly worth the rest of Zangwill's prolific contribution to the school of "New Humour" put together.

Zangwill's own estimate of the story was quite different—but who would trust an author's evaluation of his own work? According to Mr. J. Leftwich, Zangwill had meant to "kill" the serialization of *The King of Schnorrers* halfway had not "J.K.J." insisted on its completion.[4] Writing, in 1893, to Philip Cowen, editor of the *American Hebrew,* who had asked for some writing from Zangwill, the author dismisses **"The King of Schnorrers"** as "entirely flippant." The work is then described with irony as being "perfectly harmless" for purposes of Jewish publication.[5] The reference here is to the huge rumpus caused a few months earlier in the American-Jewish press by the publication of *Children of the Ghetto.* Zangwill's apparent dismissal of *King of the Schnorrers* is very surprising. His diaries and letters of the period show that he had taken considerable pains to import verisimilitude of historical detail to the work. The adventures of his king-size *schnorrer* take place amongst the Jews of late eighteenth-century London. Zangwill's writing shows a scholarly intimacy with the social customs, rivalries and religious practices of Anglo-Jewry of this period.

Zangwill's story tells of the begging adventures of Manasseh Bueno Barsillai Azuedo da Costa, "King of the

Schnorrers." The very sonorous sound of his name informs us immediately that we have dealings with no ordinary beggar. Ragged yet dignified, poor but scholarly, Manasseh recalls in many ways that earlier picaresque hero, Fielding's Parson Adams; the resemblance is marked in the *schnorrer's* certainty of his righteousness. His colossal impudence, like Adams's piety, makes him totally oblivious to all class distinction. This *schnorrer* has every right to be proud, for is he not descended, so he tells us, from the cultured and rich "Sephardi" Jews of Spanish-Portuguese origin, who had for centuries been in England? *He* was no newly-arrived Eastern European "Ashkenazi." He is furthermore a scholar of Jewish law—especially, as I said, that part of it which relates to matters of almsgiving. Manasseh quotes lavishly from obscure parts of the Bible, *Midrash* and *Talmud* in order to justify his impertinent methods of begging. To aristocratic lineage and formidable learning Manasseh adds his religious devoutness. On all three counts he esteems himself vastly superior to those upstart, newly-rich "Ashkenazi" Jews from whom he begs. The status afforded by money means nothing to Manasseh; his delight and pride are in begging for, not receiving, the money. He had wheedled the rich Grobstock's entire wardrobe out of him and with no special desire to dress up, had unashamedly got his butler to deliver it to a dealer in second-hand clothes. Grobstock is much put out to discover that Manasseh has sold the clothes. For his part the *schnorrer* is amazed at Grobstock's lack of understanding: "You did not expect me to wear them? No, I know my station, thank God."

Earlier Grobstock had promised Manasseh a few items of his cast-off clothing. Both men now make their way to Grobstock's home where the *schnorrer* intends to gain richer prizes. The following episode illustrates Manasseh's method of proceeding with business: "Manasseh suddenly caught him [Joseph Grobstock] by a coat button.

'Stand still a second,' he cried imperatively.

'What is it?' murmured Grobstock, in alarm.

'You have spilt snuff all down your coat front,' Manasseh replied severely. 'Hold the bag a moment while I brush it off.' Joseph obeyed, and Manasseh scrupulously removed every particle with such patience that Grobstock's was exhausted.

'Thank you,' he said at last, as politely as he could. 'That will do.'

'No, it will not do,' replied Manasseh. 'I cannot have my coat spoiled. By the time it comes to me it will be a mass of stains if I don't look after it.'

'Oh, is that why you took so much trouble?' said Grobstock, with an uneasy laugh.

'Why else? Do you take me for a beadle, a brusher of gaiters?'"

A second *schnorrer,* Yankele, the *Ashkenazi,* is introduced as a foil to the master *schnorrer,* in the English comic tradition of comedian and stooge. As is usual in these rela-

tionships the stooge proves himself to be more skilful a trickster than his master. Yankele ends up by winning the coveted hand of Manasseh's daughter—but only after he has assured his father-in-law to be that he would not degrade the *schnorrer* tradition by accepting any manner of work.

The "King" had promised Yankele, as part of his daughter's dowry, "an estate in Jerusalem;" this turned out to be nothing more than a handful of earth from the Holy Land. Manasseh, pious Jew that he is, is quite genuine in his belief about the worthiness of such a marriage gift: "To a true Jew a casket of Jerusalem earth is worth all the diamonds in the world," he tells Yankele. He interprets Yankele's disgust at so small a wedding gift as being merely his doubt as to the *genuineness* of the holy soil. The second part of the dowry had consisted of a very definite promise of a "Province of England." Yankele, now very disappointed about the Jerusalem property, is eager to get some details about the location of this area of land: "Oh, you shall choose your own," replied Manasseh graciously. "We will get a large map of London, and I will mark off in red pencil the domain in which I *schnorr.* You will then choose any district in this—say, two main streets and a dozen byways and alleys—which shall be marked off in blue pencil, and whatever province of my kingdom you pick, I undertake not to *schnorr* in, from your wedding-day onwards."

The *schnorrer's* absurdities of impudence never degenerate into farce. Whether he is reviling his benefactor, Grobstock, or keeping the revered Circle of Elders of the *Sephardi* community waiting as they are about to sit in judgment of him, or over-indulging in appeals to the authority of the *Talmud,* Manasseh always remains convincing. His victims cringe before his learning, piety and his ancestry. He is secure in his belief that by accepting alms he fulfills a prime religious function—only this could explain his epic impudence. It is interesting to note that one hundred and sixty years later, a charitable organization's drive to get *schnorrers* off Israel streets met with fierce Rabbinic opposition. The Rabbis claimed that the beggars were necessary for the fulfilment of religious duties.[6]

All of Zangwill's novels from the *Premier & the Painter* (1888) to *Jinny The Carrier* (1919), are marked by their limited sense of structure. **The King of Schnorrers** is an episodic short novel; indeed it was probably written in monthly parts to meet the serial deadline of *The Idler.* The simplicities of an episodic structure were really the only ones Zangwill could handle competently at this stage. Manasseh, like Mr. Pickwick, remains the same character; no changed personality emerges from one episode to the next, his experiences have no effect on him at all. The four or five episodes that tell of the *schnorrer's* begging might be interchanged without any perceptible damage to the short novel. The close of the work merely relates yet another impudence in begging. One might charitably say that the progression from episode to episode is a cumulative one for the "King's" begging escapades grow in scope. For once, however, Zangwill knew when to stop. By the time we reach the account of the collection Manasseh makes from his clients in order to pay for his astoundingly generous wedding gift to the synagogue, we feel that we have had enough.

Both the serialization of *The King of Schnorrers* in *The Idler* and the book itself were well received. At one time *The King of Schnorrers* was listed among the twenty most popular books in the United States. But much of the richness of comedy in this work depends on an understanding of the niceties of Jewish tradition such as the *Ashkenazi-Sephardi* rivalries and the place of the charity and learning within the community. Zangwill does not do enough to explain these social *mores* in which the *schnorrer* thrived. Gentile readers were not certain as to whether Manasseh's escapades had any basis in reality, as in fact they did have. Here is part of the *Saturday Review's* critique of *King of Schnorrers.* The writer uses the royal plural so beloved by reviewers of the period: "We do know to what extent the whole art and etiquette of *schnorring,* as set forth in this amusing story, is to be accepted as a glorified transcript from the world of fact . . . Zangwill has created . . . a new figure in fiction, and a new type of humour. Dignity and impudence are commonly regarded as incompatible qualities."[7] "This book," wrote another contemporary critic, "is at times so technical as to be abstruse, so philological as to puzzle anyone but the mere man of science."[8] This, obviously, is an exaggeration, but many readers accustomed to the servility of the beggar were quite baffled.

The King of Schnorrers is, sadly, the only work in the Zangwill canon that has enjoyed separate publication in recent years. The short novel went into many editions and translations during the author's lifetime and was serialized once again in 1926 just a few months before he died. Zangwill's foreword to this publication of the work points to his life-long interest in the travels of his *schnorrer* and the varied work of illustration that accompanied the translations. Ever since that ubiquitous talent George Hutchinson, the first illustrator of the story, had created the "King" in the image of Zangwill himself, various European artists had followed his example. Zangwill's tall, ungainly figure, his strikingly Semitic features and proverbial untidiness, which so often made him a favourite of the caricaturist, served as a perfect model for the artist's *schnorrer.* I now quote from the foreword: "The King of Schnorrers has wandered far and wide since he first appeared in the *Idler* . . . There is hardly any European country in which he has not made his appearance, nor any language in the world in which he has not *Schnorred,* and I have been very amused to see how artists of different countries have created him pictorially. He has added the word *Schnorr* to the vocabulary of many languages as a verb, and *Schnorrer* is thus now conjugated even in French."[9]

Like some other of Zangwill's novels and short novels, *King of Schnorrers* was metamorphosed into a play—and not an especially good one if one must judge by the number of performances it enjoyed. Curiously enough the playscript had the distinction of being rejected by Harley Granville-Barker, who at the turn of the century was acting and producing at the Royal Court Theatre. His letter of refusal to Zangwill hints interestingly at the larger-than-life stature of Zangwill's creation: "Barzilai is a most fascinating character. He has stuck in mind ever since I read him in the *Idler* years ago. The difficulty of getting anyone to do him justice now that Irving is dead would be enormous. . . . I don't think *bravura* character and a necessarily *bravura* performance will sustain four acts of play."[10]

I have not been able to locate Zangwill's playscript of *King of Schnorrers.* It was never published as far as I know. One can well assume that the play would suffer from the episodic, and therefore repetitive, character of the novelette and its lack of climactic moment of any real force. Every play develops its myth and *The King of Schnorrers* is not without its own. During World War Two a group of French Jewish officers rotting in a German concentration camp composed a playscript from a French translation of "The King" which they had (unaccountably) with them. This script survives in a Jewish museum in Paris; one wonders whether those officers are still alive.

Zangwill, who came to love his *Schnorrer* so well, would be gratified to know that in the seventies his "King" yet bestrides two continents. In 1970 a musical comedy of the novelette was produced off Broadway. This year Israel will have its own Hebrew version of the comedy. Strangely enough, the work has much in it that may be allegorized by the Israeli public: "Ashkenazi"—"Sephardi" rivalries are a grim reality of Israeli social life; *schnorr* (begging) from the rich Jews of the world has allowed Israel to absorb its immigrants and settle its wastes.

Notes

1. 4 Aug., 1893—Jan., 1894.

2. "Morour and Charouseth," 1 (13 July 1888), p. 10.

3. *The Comic Spirit: Boccaccio to Thomas Mann*; (Detroit: Wayne State University Press, 1965), p. 151.

4. *Israel Zangwill* (London, 1957), p. 250.

5. Letter (14 July, 1893) in Philip Cowen, *Memories of an American Jew* (New York, 1932), p. 348.

6. v. Philip Gillon, "A Place for Beggars," *Jerusalem Post,* 6 Nov., 1964, p. 8.

7. *Saturday Review,* 3 March, 1894, p. 340.

8. *Black and White,* 17 March, 1894, p. 327.

9. "Author's Special Foreword," *Jewish Graphic,* 26 Feb., 1926, p. 12.

10. Letter dated 12 March, 1906, Central Zionist Archive, Jerusalem, Israel.

Joseph H. Udelson (essay date 1990)

SOURCE: "Literary Lion," in *Dreamer of the Ghetto: The Life and Works of Israel Zangwill,* University of Alabama Press, 1990, pp. 113–122.

[*In the following excerpt, Udelson demonstrates how Zangwill's preoccupation with Jewish survival, his doubts about*

Zionism, and his belief in the spiritual necessity of Judaism inform his short stories in Ghetto Comedics, Ghetto Tragedies, *and his novella* The King of Schnorrers.]

GHETTO TRAGEDIES

In 1893 **Ghetto Tragedies,** a collection of four short stories, appeared. An expanded version, containing an additional seven stories, was published under the title **They That Walk in Darkness** in 1899. Subsequently, in 1907, these eleven stories were reissued under the original title. Written in the Western "ghetto" literary tradition, the collection evokes the fading and poignant realities of the traditional Jewish world for a generation reaching maturity amid the glaring illumination of Western culture. Less didactic than most of his other fiction, this collection contains some of Zangwill's finest writing. Here his talent for description was allowed full expression and results in portraits that are animate and true. Yet the author's gnawing pessimism is also apparent; a common theme of many of these stories is the necessity for, despite the ironic futility of, self-sacrifice and noble ideals.

The original book contained two of Zangwill's most powerful early works, **"Satan Mekatrig"** and **"Diary of a Meshumad."** Added to these were two more recent stories. **"Incurables"** relates the story of an East End woman confined to a hospital and ignored by her unfaithful husband. Under pressure, he finally visits his wife and demands a divorce so as to be able to solemnize the affair with his paramour. The despairing woman agrees; her self-sacrifice is rewarded when the ex-husband's new bride begins visiting her invalid former rival.[1]

In **"The Sabbath-Breaker"** Zangwill tells the ironically maudlin story of a Jewish grandmother in Poland. One Sabbath eve forty years ago the woman had received a letter from her only son, who resided in a distant town; in the missive her son complained that he was feeling unwell. Distressed by this news, she decided to violate the Sabbath law to visit him, but she arrived too late, discovering that he had died that very Sabbath eve.[2] Ever since then, the woman had carried the fateful letter in her pocket, but now pulls it out and tells her departed son she is finally coming; so saying, she dies.[3]

Of the seven new stories in the later edition, three— **"Transition," "The Land of Promise,"** and **"The Keeper of Conscience"**—portray the decay of traditional Judaism when exposed to the freedoms of the West.[4] But in these stories Zangwill is still able to express the hope that this very disintegration is only the prelude to the truest yet flowering of the essence of Judaism:

> If a religion that I thought all formalism is capable of producing such types of abnegation as my dear old father, then it must, too, somewhere or other, hold in solution all those ennobling ingredients, all those stimuli to self-sacrifice, which the world calls Christian. Perhaps the prosaic epoch of Judaism into which I was born is only transitional . . . for I know I felt more of

its poetry in my childhood; perhaps the future will develop (or recultivate) its diviner sides and lay more stress upon a life beautiful and thus all this blind instinct of isolation may prove only the conservation of the race for its nobler future, when it may still become . . . a witness to the highest, a chosen people in whom all the families of the earth may be blessed.[5]

But this wistful, autobiographical passage equally expresses its author's subterranean sense of "isolation" from his "beautiful" childhood and his "prosaic" present and his pessimism regarding the future of his people, who twice- "perhaps" may yet recover.

Contrasting with the Jews' universalist mission is the theme of **"Noah's Ark,"** a fictionalized account of Mordecai Noah's attempt to found a Jewish homeland, Ararat, near Buffalo, New York.[6] In this story Zangwill clearly voices his rejection of Palestine as the likely site of a new Jewish national home; incredulously he remarks: "Re-erect Solomon's Temple in Palestine! A ruined country to regenerate a ruined people! A land belonging to the Turks, centre of the fanaticism of three religions and countless sects!"[7]

In despair the narrator, Peloni, cries in the throes of a fatal pessimism: "Israel had been too bent and broken by the dispersion and the long persecution; the spring snapped, he could not recover. . . . This pious patience—this rejection of the burden on to the shoulders of Messiah and Miracle—was it more than the veil of unconscious impotence? Ah, better sweep oneself away than endure the long ignominy."[8] Witnessing Noah's failure in America, believing Palestine an impossibility, Peloni commits suicide. And shortly after writing this story Zangwill joined the Zionist Movement!

This notion—that without a solution to the awful dilemma of the meaning of continued Jewish existence in the contemporary Western world only suicide, self-immolation, remained as an acceptable response—began to haunt Zangwill at this time. Implicit in this judgment is the estimation that unlike any other ethnic group, Jewish existence as a people for themselves would not provide sufficient justification for continued Jewish survival. Without possession of a recognizable significance, life for the Jew could no longer be sustained. But although the weight of doubt was proving too unbearable, the lack of firm identity too painful, Zangwill was not yet ready to surrender: he still believed in the efficacy of "hopes and dreams."

Although Zangwill in general rejected the nonrational in his fiction after **"Satan Mekatrig,"** two stories in this collection do explore this realm. **"They That Walk in Darkness"** relates the story of an East End family's only son, the prodigy Brum. On the eve of his bar mitzvah, the boy inexplicably becomes blind, and when physicians and rabbis despair of a cure, Brum's mother decides: "Science and Judaism had failed her: perhaps this unknown power, this heathen Pope, had indeed mastery over things diabolical."[9] So the distraught woman, taking her blind son, who is unaware of their destination, sets off for Rome. Along the way Brum insists on visiting the beautiful Christian sites and ponders how people could believe in pagan deities and the Pope, though neither were true. Upon arriving in Rome, the boy, still unaware, is led into the presence of the Pope: "His face was transfigured with ecstatic forevision," and he falls dead.[10] This theme—the beauty and hypnotic fatality of Christianity for the Jew—later emerges as the fundamental motif of Zangwill's *Dreamers of the Ghetto* and of his nationalist politics.

In **"Bethulah,"** Zangwill wrote one of his most impressive and profound short stories. It relates the story of an encounter between a modern American Jew and the beautiful daughter of an East European Chassidic *rebbe*. At first attracted by the picturesque Chassidim, the American decides to remain in the town for some time. But when he learns that a girl, the *rebbe*'s only child, is being held in seclusion because of her father's "Cabalistic mystifications," the Westernized narrator is horrified, for "Bethulah was not a being to be employed as a sort of supernatural advocate, but a sad, tender creature needing love and protection. . . . And for some fantastic shadow-myth a beautiful young life was to be immolated."[11]

The narrator has learned that this group of putative Chassidim believes that the messiah will be born "of her immaculacy," to a virgin (*betulah* in Hebrew) of the *rebbe*'s family. The American Jew is now determined to save her from such a fantastic fate and secretly arranges to meet her on the eve of Chanukah, which also happens to be Christmas eve. He offers to help her flee to America, but Bethulah adamantly refuses: her duty is to remain. The narrator, confessing the author's own uncomprehending absorption with the issue of Jewish survival, admits: "My passion [to rescue Bethulah from her "mission"] seemed suddenly prosaic and selfish. I was lifted up into the higher love that worships and abnegates."[12] Even many years later and after the dispersal of the "sect" members, the American finds Bethulah faithful to her duty.

Although the story has obvious Christian roots and the distorted portrait of these Chassidim is more accurately attributable to the Sabbatean heresy that so fascinated Zangwill (and is specifically mentioned in this story), there can be no doubt that **"Bethulah"** expresses its author's great attraction to the nonrational and mystical realm of religion. Whatever religious emotions he experienced emanated from these sources, offensive although they may have been to his own rationalism and his intellectualized view of Judaism.[13]

More so, **"Bethulah"** contrasts starkly with **"Noah's Ark."** In the latter, Jewish existence requires rational justification in terms of some universalist "Hebraic" mission, while in the former, Jewish survival is the manifest result of a mystical fidelity to a particularist "Judaic" sense of duty. How to find peace and unity through mediating between the opposing rigors of the "prosaic" rationalism of contemporary West and the "beautiful" devotionalism of traditional Juda-

ism was a dilemma that obsessed and, increasingly oppressed, Israel Zangwill.

Finally, in this collection of stories, of autobiographical interest is **"To Die in Jerusalem,"** which relates the story of a pious East European father and his alienated and contemptuous Anglicized son, so ashamed of his "grotesque parent." In lonely despair, the father departs "to die in Jerusalem." Eventually, however, remorse affects both father and son; the latter travels to Jerusalem seeking forgiveness while the former, unaware of the son's actions, returns to England to pardon his son in person. Never meeting, each dies exiled in the chosen land of the other; such is the bitter irony of travails of life.[14]

Ghetto Tragedies, the product of the antagonistic tensions within the author's psyche, displays Zangwill's artistic gifts at their finest. Skillful craftsmanship is coupled with evocative creativity to produce stories animated by the palpable realities of human experience. Here, too, is his preoccupation over continued Jewish survival, his doubts about Palestine as the site of a revived national homeland, and his belief in the universal spiritual mission of Judaism, as well as his "illicit" fascination with enigmatic mysticism. But no answers are suggested, no solutions proffered; only questions pleading for responses.

THE KING OF SCHNORRERS

The King of Schnorrers; Grotesques and Fantasies is probably Israel Zangwill's most enduring and popular book after *Children of the Ghetto*. It includes the novella of the title and fourteen short stories. Most originally appeared in the *Idler* and are in the New Humour genre; several, although not all, have Jewish characters.

Among the short stories the most interesting is **"Flutterduck, A Ghetto Grotesque."**[15] In the Western "ghetto," rather than "New Humour," tradition, it relates the sad biography of a flighty and impious ghetto housewife, ruined by the scruples of her observant husband, the rebelliousness of her assimilated daughter, and the general wickedness of the world. Closest to the author's experience and perceptions, it is the most truthful and effective piece in the book.

But it is the novella, ***The King of Schnorrers,*** that attracts the greatest attention.[16] Set in eighteenth-century London, it relates the story of Manasseh Bueno Barzillai Azevedo da Costa, "the King of Schnorrers" among the Jews of the capital. In episode after episode, Manasseh, a proud man of regal bearing, exacts his due as a *schnorrer* (beggar) by manipulating the foibles and weaknesses of the wealthy members of the Sephardi community. Manasseh wreaks havoc on the little community and its institutions as he deigns to accept its charity, and he triumphs in every test of wit he encounters. Through the adventures of this disdainful king, thumbing his nose at the bloated, pretentious grandees, Zangwill satirizes the wealthy and powerful who, behind their facades, are so insecure and feckless. Manasseh wins because he is imperious, determined, and clever—and never mean-spirited.[17]

The King of Schnorrers is Zangwill at his wittiest and is one of the best expressions of his skill as a New Humourist. It is not profound, but it is entertaining. And it could easily have been his own proud Manasseh who, when offered congratulations on his appointment as an editor, responded: "As regards the claims of the Jewish community on my gratitude, the only thing I have to be grateful to the Jewish community for, is that I have nothing for which to be grateful to it. This may seem a poor cause for gratitude, but the recollection of it has sweetened many hours otherwise bitter."[18]

GHETTO COMEDIES

Ghetto Comedies is a collection of fourteen short stories, the last Jewish fiction published by Israel Zangwill.[19] Coming at the end of his career as a story writer, after his entry upon his career as dramatist, essayist, nationalist leader, and social reformer, it well demonstrates Zangwill's exhausted creativity. The book is markedly uneven in quality, containing some stories that appear to be discarded, but charming, scraps of *Children of the Ghetto,* while others extend the "ghetto" portraits to the British provinces and America. Still others continue to proclaim their author's persistent pessimism over man's fate as he discovers himself unwitting victim of life's ironic perversions of his noblest wishes and intentions. Yet, many of these stories, although lacking the power of his previous Jewish stories, are still well worth reading.

What is most striking about this book, however, is Zangwill's increasingly overt identification of the Jews with the person and teachings of Jesus, his greatly altered views on the questions of intermarriage and of Jewish nationalism, and his conclusion that without drastic spiritual adaption to Western values the only proper response to continued Jewish existence is ethnic self-annihilation.

"The Model of Sorrows" is a tremendously bitter story of spiritual disillusionment. It relates how a painter seeking a model for his portrait of "the Man of Sorrows" discovers him in the person of a Russian Jewish immigrant to Britain, Israel Quarriar. The painter set out "to paint not the Christ that I started out to paint, but the Christ incarnated in a race, suffering."[20] But over the course of time the artist discovers that Israel is not quite the victim he claims to be but rather a petty swindler, and so in addition to the sorrow in the portrait he adds a touch of craft and guile:

> For surely here at least was the true tragedy of the people of Christ—to have persisted sublimely, and to be as sordidly perverted; to be king and knave in one; to survive two thousand years the loss of a fatherland and the pressure of persecution, only to wear on its soul the yellow badge which had defaced its garments. . . . The true tragedy, the saddest sorrow, lay in the martyrdom of an Israel *unworthy of his suffering.*[21]

Although no doubt in part reflecting Zangwill's own bitter struggle within, and his continuing early opposition to the Zionist Movement, the story even more reflects his Disraelian identification of the Jews with the mission and image of Jesus and his condemnation of Judaism's failure to remain faithful to these truths. Again, as in "Noah's Ark," Zangwill explicitly expresses his notion that, to survive, the Jewish people must prove "worthy"; extinction of separate identity is the only just alternative.

It is important to recognize that Israel Zangwill's insistence on the necessity of a justification for continued Jewish survival is not a mere idiosyncratic fixation. Instead it reflects the very real perception that while Western national identities represent a diversity within an encompassing cultural unity, his own Jewish and Western identities are intense and equal rivals, each wooing for his exclusive love and loyalty. What Zangwill is seeking is a reconciliation of his twinned identities by the creation of a new unity for Western Jews that will be congruent with that unitary identity found among ethnic Englishmen, Frenchmen, and Germans. To achieve this unity, he is seeking to placate both combatants by compressing somehow Jewish identity within the framework of the notion of "Western": Judaism is to represent the highest, the "spiritual," component of Western culture that was previously borne among the Gentile nations in the teachings of Jesus. Without such a niche defined within Western identity, a Jewish identity has no place: it must depart, either through total cultural assimilation or through physical separation.

In this exposition, Zangwill was choosing to analyze what others found uncongenial to notice, or indeed could not even see. But at the time he wrote "The Model of Sorrow," he was still groping toward this rationalist resolution of the conflict of identities. He comes to formulate it finally only to conclude that the combatants were irremediably intractable: no theoretical "middle path" between these rival identities could ever prove genuinely viable. Only the extreme solution—departure—might work.[22]

In "The Bearer of Burdens" Zangwill displays his new positive attitude toward Jewish-Christian intermarriage, adopting a theme reminiscent of Farjeon's *Solomon Isaacs.*[23] In this story, Henry Elkman, a child of the Spitalfields "ghetto," much to his mother's horror, marries a Christian girl; his elderly mother, the narrator pointedly observes, had failed to notice "the gradual process which had sapped Henry's instinct of racial isolation, or how he had passed from admiration of British ways into entire abandonment of Jewish."[24] His mother disowns Henry, and his non-Jewish wife dies in childbirth. Henry then marries a Jewish shrew to raise his young daughter, but, unable to endure his unpleasant spouse, he eventually deserts her and the child. Meanwhile, his mother discovers that her Jewish daughter-in-law is a drunken child-beater, the very opposite of the virtuous Christian woman she had replaced and the old lady had spurned. Horrified, Henry's elderly mother rescues her Christian granddaughter from the despicable Jewish stepmother and decides to raise the young girl herself: "this child was compensation for all [the old lady] had undergone, for all the years of trudging and grubbing and patching and turning. . . . The fusion of races had indeed made her [the granddaughter] sensitive and intelligent beyond the common."[25]

In **"Anglicization"** Zangwill explains how a Jewish boy like Henry could have lost his "instinct of racial isolation." Repeating almost exactly the description of Esther Ansell's youth, this narrator explains how it is that Solomon Cohn's son has come to join the British army in its fight against the Boers: "Anglicization had done its work: from his school days he had felt himself a descendant, not of Judas Maccabaeus, but of Nelson and Wellington."[26] Cohn's solution to the problems of white South Africa, interesting enough, is intermarriage of Britons and Boers.

Yet this same book that extols the universalism of a New Testament Judaism and the virtues of ethnic intermarriage simultaneously also powerfully advocates Jewish nationalism.[27] **"The Jewish Trinity,"** for instance, is the story of Leopold Barstein, a young Jewish sculptor who has joined the Zionist Movement and is courting the daughter of a wealthy Anglo-Jewish family; unfortunately for him, the girl's parents favor the "comforts" of a universalist interpretation of Judaism over the "threatening divisiveness" of Jewish nationalism. In the end Leopold's proposal of marriage is rejected by her "Podsnappian" father. Bitterly, Leopold reflects that this Anglo-Jew nabob is in reality a "Trinitarian": an Englishman, a Jew, and an anti-Semite.[28]

The story reflects Zangwill's impatience with the predominantly anti-Zionist attitude of Anglo-Jewry's leadership and sounds a new note of humorless stridency in his fictional writing hitherto absent from even his most scathing social criticisms, as, for instance, in his portrait of the Goldsmiths in **"Grandchildren of the Ghetto."** But Zangwill could be equally impatient with Jewish nationalists of all varieties, including his own Territorialist followers.

His urgent activist impulse pervades the final story in this collection, **"Samooborona,"** a late work reflecting Zangwill's matured position that abstract theorizing and "middle path" compromising were not practicable resolutions to the quandary of Western Jewry's sense of multiple identities.[29] In this piece, David Ben Amram learns of plans to provoke a pogrom in the little Polish town of Milouka. Rushing there, he hopes to arouse the local Jews to organize a self-defense force ("samooborona"). But his efforts prove fruitless. Religious and irreligious, Zionists and Territorialists, assimilationists and socialists, none trusts the others, and all are caught in webs of sophistical fantasies. Bemoans an uncomfortably perceptive and despairing David:

> [All these parties] each differentiating itself with meticulous subtlety from all the other Parties, each defining with casuistic minuteness its relation to every contemporary problem, each equipped with inexhaustible polyglot orators speechifying through tumultuous nights. . . .

> . . . The men of to-day had merely substituted for the world of the past the world of the future and so there had arisen logically perfect structures of Zionism without Zion, Jewish Socialism without a Jewish social order, Labour Parties without votes or a Parliament. The habit of actualities had been lost; what need of them when concepts provided as much intellectual stimulus?[30]

Zangwill's impatient condemnation extends from the quietism of traditional religious Judaism to the messianism of secular Jewish politics. For him what was most pressing was *action,* immediate action undertaken to rescue desperately imperiled Jewish people. It is this impulse that had driven him, before writing **"Samooborona,"** to champion Territorialism, that made him impatient with the Territorialists, and that later would make him such a strident opponent of the postwar Zionist leadership.

Zangwill explicitly traces the tragic immobility of all parties in the story to the Jews' confusion over their ethnic identity: "Poor bewildered Russian Jews, caught in the bewilderments both of the Russians and the Jews, and tangled up inextricably in the double confusion of interlacing coils."[31] This analysis of Westernized Jewry's malaise is incisive and ignored.

Defeated in his efforts to rescue the Jews of Milouka, David, like Alfred Hyams before him, retreats into bittersweet memories of childhood. Exhausted, he retreats into the local *beth hamedrash*:

> he would go back like a child to the familiar [religious] study-house of his youth, to the *Beth Hamedrash* where the grey beards poured over the great worm-eaten folios. . . . There lay the magic world of fantasy and legend that had been his people's true home, that had kept them sane and cheerful through eighteen centuries of tragedy—a water tight world into which no drop of outer reality could ever trickle. . . . Time and again he had raged against the artificiality of this quietist cosmos, accusing it of his people's paralysis, but tonight every fibre of him yearned for this respite from the harsh reality.[32]

But this retreat is only for a night: the present's reality will not be held at bay by the soothing fantasies of the past. The pogrom comes now inexorably to Milouka, victimizing indiscriminately members of all the squabbling parties. In despair, David commits suicide. Laments the narrator of this urgent, cautionary tale, "The same unconditional historic necessity had overtaken them all."[33]

Here, once again, is the Zangwillian twin response to the inescapable anguish of the Western Jew's conflict of identities: retreat for a time into the peaceful afterglow of dreamy childhood memories and, when implacable reality jars one awake, embrace the implacable immolation. This is the notion at the root of Zangwill's Jewish nationalism and, equally, of his intermarriage.

Notes

1. Israel Zangwill, "Incurable," in *Ghetto Tragedies* (London: McClure and Co., 1893), pp. 191–222.

2. The Sabbath law that is allegedly violated in this instance is that which prohibits one from traveling more than 2,000 cubits beyond a town boundary.

3. Zangwill, *Ghetto Tragedies,* pp. 225–36.

4. Israel Zangwill, *They That Walk in Darkness* (London: William Heinemann, 1899).

5. Ibid., p. 53.

6. Ibid., pp. 57–86.

7. Ibid., p. 81.

8. Ibid., p. 85.

9. Ibid., p. 15.

10. Ibid., p. 28.

11. Ibid., p. 143.

12. Ibid., p. 157.

13. Ibid., p. 131, where the narrator meets in Prague a group still devoted to the pseudomessiah Sabbatai Zevi; in *Dreamers of the Ghetto* Zangwill discusses him at length. If there is any Chassidic source at all for this story, it derives from a very distorted interpretation of the enigmatic figure, the Maid of Ludomir. However, the messianic doctrine expressed in the story has no normative Jewish source, and it is significant to note that Zangwill attributes such Christianized notions of the messiah to any group of Jews.

14. Zangwill, *Walk in Darkness,* pp. 111–26. In fact, Zangwill visited his father in Jerusalem on his trip to Palestine in 1897.

15. Israel Zangwill, "Flutter-duck, A Ghetto Grotesque," in *The King of Schnorrers* (London: William Heinemann, 1894), pp. 369–400. The story is illustrated by the author's brother, Mark.

16. Zangwill, "The King of Schnorrers," in ibid., pp. 3–156.

17. I would like to thank Abba Rubin for pointing out to me many of these observations.

18. Israel Zangwill, "Gratitude," *Jewish Chronicle,* 14 March 1890, p. 8. Zangwill was responding to the newspaper's 7 March congratulations to him on his appointment as editor of *Puck.*

19. Israel Zangwill, *Ghetto Comedies* (London: William Heinemann, 1907).

20. Ibid., p. 25. The identification of the Jews with Jesus and his teachings is treated extensively in the discussion of Zangwill's earlier work, *Dreamers of the Ghetto*; see Chapter 7.

21. Zangwill, *Ghetto Comedies,* p. 36. Emphasis in original.

22. See Chapter 7; and see Chapter 11 for a similar evolution by W. E. B. Du Bois.

23. Zangwill, *Ghetto Comedies,* pp. 193–221.

24. Ibid., p. 197.

25. Ibid., pp. 215–16.

26. Ibid., p. 62. In several places Zangwill identifies the Boers with the Jews.

27. For a discussion of Zangwill's marriage and an explanation for the paradoxical advocacy of Jewish assimilationism *and* Jewish nationalism see Chapters 7–9.

28. Zangwill, *Ghetto Comedies,* pp. 89–115.

29. Ibid., pp. 375–424.

30. Ibid., pp. 419–20.

31. Ibid., p. 420.

32. Ibid., p. 422.

33. Ibid.

FURTHER READING

Criticism

Adams, Elsie Bonita. "The Poetry of Mean Streets and Every-Day Figures'." *Israel Zangwill,* pp. 85–106. Twayne Publishers, 1971.
    Examines themes Zangwill treated in his short stories, including love, sacrifice, suffering, hope, assimilation, and failed dreams.

Benjamin, J. C. "Israel Zangwill: A Revaluation." *Jewish Quarterly* 24, No. 3 (1976): 3–5.
    Interprets Zangwill's writings as a defense of ethnic Judaism.

Bensusan, S. L. "Israel Zangwill." *Quarterly Review* (October 1926): 285–303.
    Reminiscing, the critic appreciatively highlights Zangwill's writings and social activism.

Gross, John. "Zangwill in Retrospect." *Commentary* 38, No. 12 (1964): 54–57.
    Deems *Dreamers of the Ghetto* a worthy introduction to Jewish history.

Leftwich, Joseph. "Israel Zangwill: On the Threshold of His Centenary." *Jewish Book Annual* 21 (1963–1964): 104–115.

An overview and reappraisal of Zangwill's critical reputation.

Review of *King of Schnorrers. Nation* 59, No. 1517 (July 26, 1894): 68.

    Although the anonymous critic praises Zangwill's wit and portrayal of Jewish character in the novella *The*

King of Schnorrers, he harshly criticizes his portrayal of English gentiles.

Payne, William Morton. Review of *Dreamers of the Ghetto. Dial* 25 (1898): 78–79.

    A brief, positive, contemporary review of *Dreamers of the Ghetto.*

Additional coverage of Zangwill's life and career is contained in the following sources published by the Gale Group: *Contemporary Authors,* **Vols. 109, 167;** *Dictionary of Literary Biography,* **Vols. 10, 135, 197;** *St. James Guide to Crime & Mystery Writers***; and** *Twentieth-Century Literary Criticism,* **Vol. 16.**

How to Use This Index

> **Calvino, Italo**
> 1923-1985 .... **CLC 5, 8, 11, 22, 33, 39,**
> **73; SSC 3**

list all author entries in the following Gale Literary Criticism series:

BLC = *Black Literature Criticism*
CLC = *Contemporary Literary Criticism*
CLR = *Children's Literature Review*
CMLC = *Classical and Medieval Literature Criticism*
DA = *DISCovering Authors*
DAB = *DISCovering Authors: British*
DAC = *DISCovering Authors: Canadian*
DAM = *DISCovering Authors: Modules*
     DRAM: Dramatists Module; MST: Most-Studied Authors Module;
     MULT: Multicultural Authors Module; NOV: Novelists Module;
     POET: Poets Module; POP: Popular Fiction and Genre Authors Module
DC = *Drama Criticism*
HLC = *Hispanic Literature Criticism*
LC = *Literature Criticism from 1400 to 1800*
NCLC = *Nineteenth-Century Literature Criticism*
NNAL = *Native North American Literature*
PC = *Poetry Criticism*
SSC = *Short Story Criticism*
TCLC = *Twentieth-Century Literary Criticism*
WLC = *World Literature Criticism, 1500 to the Present*

> See also CANR 23; CA 85-88;
> obituary CA116

list all author entries in the following Gale biographical and literary sources:

AAYA = *Authors & Artists for Young Adults*
AITN = *Authors in the News*
BEST = *Bestsellers*
BW = *Black Writers*
CA = *Contemporary Authors*
CAAS = *Contemporary Authors Autobiography Series*
CABS = *Contemporary Authors Bibliographical Series*
CANR = *Contemporary Authors New Revision Series*
CAP = *Contemporary Authors Permanent Series*
CDALB = *Concise Dictionary of American Literary Biography*
CDBLB = *Concise Dictionary of British Literary Biography*
DLB = *Dictionary of Literary Biography*
DLBD = *Dictionary of Literary Biography Documentary Series*
DLBY = *Dictionary of Literary Biography Yearbook*
HW = *Hispanic Writers*
JRDA = *Junior DISCovering Authors*
MAICYA = *Major Authors and Illustrators for Children and Young Adults*
MTCW = *Major 20th-Century Writers*
SAAS = *Something about the Author Autobiography Series*
SATA = *Something about the Author*
YABC = *Yesterday's Authors of Books for Children*

Literary Criticism Series
Cumulative Author Index

20/1631
See Upward, Allen

A/C Cross
See Lawrence, T(homas) E(dward)

Abasiyanik, Sait Faik 1906-1954
See Sait Faik
See also CA 123

Abbey, Edward 1927-1989 .... **CLC 36, 59**
See also CA 45-48; 128; CANR 2, 41; DA3;
MTCW 2; TCWW 2

Abbott, Lee K(ittredge) 1947- .... **CLC 48**
See also CA 124; CANR 51; DLB 130

Abe, Kōbō 1924-1993 ...... **CLC 8, 22, 53, 81;
DAM NOV**
See also CA 65-68; 140; CANR 24, 60;
DLB 182; MTCW 1, 2

Abelard, Peter c. 1079-c. 1142 ...... **CMLC 11**
See also DLB 115, 208

Abell, Kjeld 1901-1961 .... **CLC 15**
See also CA 111; DLB 214

Abish, Walter 1931- .... **CLC 22; SSC 44**
See also CA 101; CANR 37; DLB 130, 227

Abrahams, Peter (Henry) 1919 .... **CLC 4**
See also BW 1; CA 57-60; CANR 26; DLB
117, 225; MTCW 1, 2

Abrams, M(eyer) H(oward) 1912- ... **CLC 24**
See also CA 57-60; CANR 13, 33; DLB 67

Abse, Dannie 1923- .... **CLC 7, 29; DAB;
DAM POET**
See also CA 53-56; CAAS 1; CANR 4, 46,
74; DLB 27; MTCW 1

Achebe, (Albert) Chinua(lumogu)
1930- ...... **CLC 1, 3, 5, 7, 11, 26, 51, 75,
127; BLC 1; DA; DAB; DAC; DAM
MST, MULT, NOV**
See also AAYA 15; AW; BW 2, 3; CA 1-4R;
CANR 6, 26, 47; CLR 20; DA3; DLB
117; MAICYA; MTCW 1, 2; SATA 38,
40; SATA-Brief 38

Acker, Kathy 1948-1997 .... **CLC 45, 111**
See also CA 117; 122; 162; CANR 55

Ackroyd, Peter 1949- .... **CLC 34, 52, 140**
See also CA 123; 127; CANR 51, 74; DLB
155, 231; INT 127; MTCW 1

Acorn, Milton 1923-1986 .... **CLC 15; DAC**
See also CA 103; CCA 1; DLB 53; INT 103

Adamov, Arthur 1908-1970 .... **CLC 4, 25;
DAM DRAM**
See also CA 17-18; 25-28R; CAP 2; MTCW
1

Adams, Alice (Boyd) 1926-1999 .. **CLC 6, 13,
46; SSC 24**
See also CA 81-84; 179; CANR 26, 53, 75,
88; DLB 234; DLBY 86; INT CANR-26;
MTCW 1, 2

Adams, Andy 1859-1935 .... **TCLC 56**
See also AW 1; TCWW 2

Adams, Brooks 1848-1927 .... **TCLC 80**
See also CA 123; DLB 47

Adams, Douglas (Noel) 1952-2001 .. **CLC 27,
60; DAM POP**
See also AAYA 4, 33; BEST 89:3; CA 106;
CANR 34, 64; DA3; DLBY 83; JRDA;
MTCW 1; SATA 116

Adams, Francis 1862-1893 .... **NCLC 33**

Adams, Henry (Brooks)
1838-1918 .... **TCLC 4, 52; DA; DAB;
DAC; DAM MST**
See also CA 104; 133; CANR 77; DLB 12,
47, 189; MTCW 1

Adams, Richard (George) 1920- ... **CLC 4, 5,
18; DAM NOV**
See also AAYA 16; AITN 1, 2; AW; CA 49-
52; CANR 3, 35; CLR 20; JRDA; MAI-
CYA; MTCW 1, 2; SATA 7, 69

Adamson, Joy(-Friederike Victoria)
1910-1980 .... **CLC 17**
See also CA 69-72; 93-96; CANR 22;
MTCW 1; SATA 11; SATA-Obit 22

Adcock, Fleur 1934- .... **CLC 41**
See also CA 25-28R, 182; CAAE 182;
CAAS 23; CANR 11, 34, 69; DLB 40

Addams, Charles (Samuel)
1912-1988 .... **CLC 30**
See also CA 61-64; 126; CANR 12, 79

Addams, Jane 1860-1945 .... **TCLC 76**
See also AMWS 1

Addison, Joseph 1672-1719 .... **LC 18**
See also CDBLB 1660-1789; DLB 101

Adler, Alfred (F.) 1870-1937 .... **TCLC 61**
See also CA 119; 159

Adler, C(arole) S(chwerdtfeger)
1932- .... **CLC 35**
See also AAYA 4; AW; CA 89-92; CANR
19, 40; JRDA; MAICYA; SAAS 15;
SATA 26, 63, 102

Adler, Renata 1938- .... **CLC 8, 31**
See also CA 49-52; CANR 95; MTCW 1

Ady, Endre 1877-1919 .... **TCLC 11**
See also CA 107

A.E. TCLC 3, 10
See also Russell, George William

Aeschylus 525B.C.-456B.C. .. **CMLC 11; DA;
DAB; DAC; DAM DRAM, MST; DC 8**
See also AW; DLB 176

Aesop 620(?)B.C.-560(?)B.C. .... **CMLC 24**
See also CLR 14; MAICYA; SATA 64

Affable Hawk
See MacCarthy, Sir(Charles Otto) Desmond

Africa, Ben
See Bosman, Herman Charles

Afton, Effie
See Harper, Frances Ellen Watkins

Agapida, Fray Antonio
See Irving, Washington

Agee, James (Rufus) 1909-1955 ...... **TCLC 1,
19; DAM NOV**
See also AITN 1; CA 108; 148; CDALB
1941-1968; DLB 2, 26, 152; MTCW 1

Aghill, Gordon
See Silverberg, Robert

Agnon, S(hmuel) Y(osef Halevi)
1888-1970 .... **CLC 4, 8, 14; SSC 30**
See also CA 17-18; 25-28R; CANR 60;
CAP 2; MTCW 1, 2

Agrippa von Nettesheim, Henry Cornelius
1486-1535 .... **LC 27**

Aguilera Malta, Demetrio 1909-1981
See also CA 111; 124; CANR 87; DAM
MULT, NOV; DLB 145; HLCS 1; HW 1

Agustini, Delmira 1886-1914
See also CA 166; HLCS 1; HW 1, 2

Aherne, Owen
See Cassill, R(onald) V(erlin)

Ai 1947- .... **CLC 4, 14, 69**
See also CA 85-88; CAAS 13; CANR 70;
DLB 120

Aickman, Robert (Fordyce)
1914-1981 .... **CLC 57**
See also CA 5-8R; CANR 3, 72

Aiken, Conrad (Potter) 1889-1973 .... **CLC 1,
3, 5, 10, 52; DAM NOV, POET; PC 26;
SSC 9**
See also CA 5-8R; 45-48; CANR 4, 60;
CDALB 1929-1941; DLB 9, 45, 102;
MTCW 1, 2; SATA 3, 30

Aiken, Joan (Delano) 1924-1955 ...... **CLC 35**
See also AAYA 1, 25; CA 9-12R, 182;
CAAE 182; CANR 4, 23, 34, 64; CLR 1,
19; DLB 161; JRDA; MAICYA; MTCW
1; SAAS 1; SATA 2, 30, 73; SATA-Essay
109

Ainsworth, William Harrison
1805-1882 .... **NCLC 13**
See also DLB 21; SATA 24

Aitmatov, Chingiz (Torekulovich)
1928- .... **CLC 71**
See also CA 103; CANR 38; MTCW 1;
SATA 56

Akers, Floyd
See Baum, L(yman) Frank

Akhmadulina, Bella Akhatovna
1937- .... **CLC 53; DAM POET**
See also CA 65-68; CWW 2

Akhmatova, Anna 1888-1966 ..... **CLC 11, 25,
64, 126; DAM POET; PC 2**
See also CA 19-20; 25-28R; CANR 35;
CAP 1; DA3; MTCW 1, 2

Aksakov, Sergei Timofeyvich
1791-1859 .... **NCLC 2**
See also DLB 198

Aksenov, Vassily
See Aksyonov, Vassily (Pavlovich)

Akst, Daniel 1956- .... **CLC 109**
See also CA 161

Aksyonov, Vassily (Pavlovich)
1932- .... **CLC 22, 37, 101**
See also CA 53-56; CANR 12, 48, 77;
CWW 2

Akutagawa Ryunosuke
1892-1927 .... **TCLC 16; SSC 44**
See also CA 117; 154; DLB 180

Alain 1868-1951 .... **TCLC 41**
See also CA 163

Alain-Fournier TCLC 6
See also Fournier, Henri Alban
See also DLB 65

Alarcon, Pedro Antonio de
1833-1891 .... **NCLC 1**

Alas (y Urena), Leopoldo (Enrique Garcia)
1852-1901 .... **TCLC 29**
See also CA 113; 131; HW 1

Albee, Edward (Franklin III) 1928- . **CLC 1,
2, 3, 5, 9, 11, 13, 25, 53, 86, 113; DA;
DAB; DAC; DAM DRAM, MST; DC
11**
See also AITN 1; AW; CA 5-8R; CABS 3;
CANR 8, 54, 74; CDALB 1941-1968;
DA3; DLB 7; INT CANR-8; MTCW 1, 2

Alberti, Rafael 1902-1999 .... **CLC 7**
See also CA 85-88; 185; CANR 81; DLB
108; HW 2

Albert the Great 1193(?)-1280 ...... **CMLC 16**
See also DLB 115

Alcala-Galiano, Juan Valera y
See Valera y Alcala-Galiano, Juan

Alcayaga, Lucila Godoy
See Godoy Alcayaga, Lucila

Alcott, Amos Bronson 1799-1888 .... **NCLC 1**
See also DLB 1, 223

Alcott, Louisa May 1832-1888 . **NCLC 6, 58,
83; DA; DAB; DAC; DAM MST, NOV;
SSC 27**
See also AAYA 20; AMWS 1; AW; CDALB
1865-1917; CLR 1, 38; DA3; DLB 1, 42,
79, 223, 239, 242; DLBD 14; JRDA;
MAICYA; SATA 100

Aldanov, M. A.
See Aldanov, Mark (Alexandrovich)

Aldanov, Mark (Alexandrovich)
1886(?)-1957 .... **TCLC 23**
See also CA 118; 181

Aldington, Richard 1892-1962 .... **CLC 49**
See also CA 85-88; CANR 45; DLB 20, 36,
100, 149

Aldiss, Brian W(ilson) 1925- . **CLC 5, 14, 40;
DAM NOV; SSC 36**
See also CA 5-8R; CAAS 2; CANR 5, 28,
64; DLB 14; MTCW 1, 2; SATA 34

Alegria, Claribel 1924- .... **CLC 75; DAM
MULT; HLCS 1; PC 26**
See also CA 131; CAAS 15; CANR 66, 94;
CWW 2; DLB 145; HW 1; MTCW 1

Alegria, Fernando 1918- .... **CLC 57**
See also CA 9-12R; CANR 5, 32, 72; HW
1, 2

Aleichem, Sholom TCLC 1, 35; SSC 33
See also Rabinovitch, Sholem

Aleixandre, Vicente 1898-1984
See also CANR 81; HLCS 1; HW 2

Alepoudelis, Odysseus
See Elytis, Odysseus
See also CWW 2

Aleshkovsky, Joseph 1929-
See Aleshkovsky, Yuz
See also CA 121; 128

Aleshkovsky, Yuz CLC 44
See also Aleshkovsky, Joseph

Alexander, Lloyd (Chudley) 1924- ... **CLC 35**
See also AAYA 1, 27; CA 1-4R; CANR 1,
24, 38, 55; CLR 1, 5, 48; DLB 52; JRDA;
MAICYA; MTCW 1; SAAS 19; SATA 3,
49, 81

Alexander, Meena 1951- .... **CLC 121**
See also CA 115; CANR 38, 70

Alexander, Samuel 1859-1938 .... **TCLC 77**

Alexie, Sherman (Joseph, Jr.)
1966- .... **CLC 96; DAM MULT**
See also AAYA 28; CA 138; CANR 95;
DA3; DLB 175, 206; MTCW 1; NNAL

Alfau, Felipe 1902-1999 .... **CLC 66**
See also CA 137

Alfred, Jean Gaston
See Ponge, Francis

Alger, Horatio, Jr. 1832-1899 .... **NCLC 8, 83**
See also DLB 42; SATA 16

Algren, Nelson 1909-1981 ..... **CLC 4, 10, 33;
SSC 33**
See also CA 13-16R; 103; CANR 20, 61;
CDALB 1941-1968; DLB 9; DLBY 81,
82; MTCW 1, 2

Ali, Ahmed 1908-1998 .... **CLC 69**
See also CA 25-28R; CANR 15, 34

Alighieri, Dante
See Dante

Allan, John B.
See Westlake, Donald E(dwin)

Allan, Sidney
See Hartmann, Sadakichi

Allan, Sydney
See Hartmann, Sadakichi

Allen, Edward 1948- .... **CLC 59**

Allen, Fred 1894-1956 .... **TCLC 87**

Allen, Paula Gunn 1939- .... **CLC 84; DAM
MULT**
See also AMWS 4; CA 112; 143; CANR
63; DA3; DLB 175; MTCW 1; NNAL

Allen, Roland
See Ayckbourn, Alan

Allen, Sarah A.
See Hopkins, Pauline Elizabeth

Allen, Sidney H.
See Hartmann, Sadakichi

Allen, Woody 1935- .... **CLC 16, 52; DAM
POP**
See also AAYA 10; CA 33-36R; CANR 27,
38, 63; DLB 44; MTCW 1

Allende, Isabel 1942- . **CLC 39, 57, 97; DAM
MULT, NOV; HLC 1**
See also AAYA 18; AW; CA 125; 130;
CANR 51, 74; CWW 2; DA3; DLB 145;
HW 1, 2; INT 130; MTCW 1, 2

Alleyn, Ellen
See Rossetti, Christina (Georgina)

Allingham, Margery (Louise)
1904-1966 .... **CLC 19**
See also CA 5-8R; 25-28R; CANR 4, 58;
DLB 77; MTCW 1, 2

Allingham, William 1824-1889 ...... **NCLC 25**
See also DLB 35

Allison, Dorothy E. 1949- .... **CLC 78**
See also CA 140; CANR 66; DA3; MTCW
1

Allston, Washington 1779-1843 .... **NCLC 2**
See also DLB 1, 235

Almedingen, E. M. CLC 12
See also Almedingen, Martha Edith von
See also SATA 3

Almedingen, Martha Edith von 1898-1971
See Almedingen, E. M.
See also CA 1-4R; CANR 1

Almodovar, Pedro 1949(?)- .... **CLC 114;
HLCS 1**
See also CA 133; CANR 72; HW 2

Almqvist, Carl Jonas Love
1793-1866 .... **NCLC 42**

Alonso, Damaso 1898-1990 .... **CLC 14**
See also CA 110; 131; 130; CANR 72; DLB
108; HW 1, 2

Alov
See Gogol, Nikolai (Vasilyevich)

Alta 1942- .... **CLC 19**
See also CA 57-60

Alter, Robert B(ernard) 1935- .... **CLC 34**
See also CA 49-52; CANR 1, 47

Alther, Lisa 1944- .... **CLC 7, 41**
See also CA 65-68; CAAS 30; CANR 12,
30, 51; GLL 2; MTCW 1

Althusser, L.
See Althusser, Louis

Althusser, Louis 1918-1990 .... **CLC 106**
See also CA 131; 132; DLB 242

Altman, Robert 1925- .... **CLC 16, 116**
See also CA 73-76; CANR 43

Alurista
See Urista, Alberto H.
See also DLB 82; HLCS 1

Alvarez, A(lfred) 1929- .... **CLC 5, 13**
See also CA 1-4R; CANR 3, 33, 63; DLB
14, 40

Alvarez, Alejandro Rodriguez 1903-1965
See Casona, Alejandro
See also CA 131; 93-96; HW 1

Alvarez, Julia 1950- .... **CLC 93; HLCS 1**
See also AAYA 25; AMWS 7; CA 147;
CANR 69; DA3; MTCW 1

Alvaro, Corrado 1896-1956 .... **TCLC 60**
See also CA 163

Amado, Jorge 1912- .... **CLC 13, 40, 106;
DAM MULT, NOV; HLC 1**
See also CA 77-80; CANR 35, 74; DLB
113; HW 2; MTCW 1, 2

Ambler, Eric 1909-1998 .... **CLC 4, 6, 9**
See also BRWS 4; CA 9-12R; 171; CANR
7, 38, 74; DLB 77; MTCW 1, 2

Amichai, Yehuda 1924-2000 .. **CLC 9, 22, 57,
116**
See also CA 85-88; 189; CANR 46, 60;
CWW 2; MTCW 1

Amichai, Yehudah
See Amichai, Yehuda

Amiel, Henri Frederic 1821-1881 .... **NCLC 4**

Amis, Kingsley (William)
1922-1995 ...... **CLC 1, 2, 3, 5, 8, 13, 40,
44, 129; DA; DAB; DAC; DAM MST,
NOV**
See also AITN 2; BRWS 2; CA 9-12R; 150;
CANR 8, 28, 54; CDBLB 1945-1960;
DA3; DLB 15, 27, 100, 139; DLBY 96;
INT CANR-8; MTCW 1, 2

Amis, Martin (Louis) 1949- .... **CLC 4, 9, 38,
62, 101**
See also BEST 90:3; BRWS 4; CA 65-68;
CANR 8, 27, 54, 73, 95; DA3; DLB 14,
194; INT CANR-27; MTCW 1

Ammons, A(rchie) R(andolph)
1926-2001 ...... **CLC 2, 3, 5, 8, 9, 25, 57,
108; DAM POET; PC 16**
See also AITN 1; CA 9-12R; CANR 6, 36,
51, 73; DLB 5, 165; MTCW 1, 2

Amo, Tauraatua i
See Adams, Henry (Brooks)

Amory, Thomas 1691(?)-1788 .... **LC 48**

Anand, Mulk Raj 1905- .. **CLC 23, 93; DAM
NOV**
See also CA 65-68; CANR 32, 64; MTCW
1, 2

Anatol
See Schnitzler, Arthur

Anaximander c. 611B.C.-c.
546B.C. .... **CMLC 22**

Anaya, Rudolfo A(lfonso) 1937- ...... **CLC 23; DAM MULT, NOV; HLC 1**
See also AAYA 20; CA 45-48; CAAS 4; CANR 1, 32, 51; DLB 82, 206; HW 1; MTCW 1, 2

Andersen, Hans Christian
1805-1875 .... **NCLC 7, 79; DA; DAB; DAC; DAM MST, POP; SSC 6**
See also AW; CLR 6; DA3; MAICYA; SATA 100

Anderson, C. Farley
See Mencken, H(enry) L(ouis); Nathan, George Jean

Anderson, Jessica (Margaret) Queale
1916- .... **CLC 37**
See also CA 9-12R; CANR 4, 62

Anderson, Jon (Victor) 1940- . **CLC 9; DAM POET**
See also CA 25-28R; CANR 20

Anderson, Lindsay (Gordon)
1923-1994 .... **CLC 20**
See also CA 125; 128; 146; CANR 77

Anderson, Maxwell 1888-1959 .... **TCLC 2; DAM DRAM**
See also CA 105; 152; DLB 7, 228; MTCW 2

Anderson, Poul (William) 1926- .... **CLC 15**
See also AAYA 5, 34; CA 1-4R; 181; CAAE 181; CAAS 2; CANR 2, 15, 34, 64; CLR 58; DLB 8; INT CANR-15; MTCW 1, 2; SATA 90; SATA-Brief 39; SATA-Essay 106; SCFW 2

Anderson, Robert (Woodruff)
1917- .... **CLC 23; DAM DRAM**
See also AITN 1; CA 21-24R; CANR 32; DLB 7

Anderson, Sherwood 1876-1941 ..... **TCLC 1, 10, 24; DA; DAB; DAC; DAM MST, NOV; SSC 1**
See also AAYA 30; AW; CA 104; 121; CANR 61; CDALB 1917-1929; DA3; DLB 4, 9, 86; DLBD 1; GLL 2; MTCW 1, 2

Andier, Pierre
See Desnos, Robert

Andouard
See Giraudoux, (Hippolyte) Jean

Andrade, Carlos Drummond de CLC 18
See also Drummond de Andrade, Carlos

Andrade, Mario de 1893-1945 .... **TCLC 43**

Andreae, Johann V(alentin)
1586-1654 .... **LC 32**
See also DLB 164

Andreas-Salome, Lou 1861-1937 ... **TCLC 56**
See also CA 178; DLB 66

Andress, Lesley
See Sanders, Lawrence

Andrewes, Lancelot 1555-1626 .... **LC 5**
See also DLB 151, 172

Andrews, Cicily Fairfield
See West, Rebecca

Andrews, Elton V.
See Pohl, Frederik

Andreyev, Leonid (Nikolaevich)
1871-1919 .... **TCLC 3**
See also CA 104; 185

Andric, Ivo 1892-1975 .... **CLC 8; SSC 36**
See also CA 81-84; 57-60; CANR 43, 60; DLB 147; MTCW 1

Androvar
See Prado (Calvo), Pedro

Angelique, Pierre
See Bataille, Georges

Angell, Roger 1920- .... **CLC 26**
See also CA 57-60; CANR 13, 44, 70; DLB 171, 185

Angelou, Maya 1928- .... **CLC 12, 35, 64, 77; BLC 1; DA; DAB; DAC; DAM MST, MULT, POET, POP; PC 32**
See also AAYA 7, 20; AMWS 4; AW; BW 2, 3; CA 65-68; CANR 19, 42, 65; CDALBS; CLR 53; DA3; DLB 38; MTCW 1, 2; SATA 49

Anna Comnena 1083-1153 .... **CMLC 25**

Annensky, Innokenty (Fyodorovich)
1856-1909 .... **TCLC 14**
See also CA 110; 155

Annunzio, Gabriele d'
See D'Annunzio, Gabriele

Anodos
See Coleridge, Mary E(lizabeth)

Anon, Charles Robert
See Pessoa, Fernando (Antonio Nogueira)

Anouilh, Jean (Marie Lucien Pierre)
1910-1987 .... **CLC 1, 3, 8, 13, 40, 50; DAM DRAM; DC 8**
See also CA 17-20R; 123; CANR 32; MTCW 1, 2

Anthony, Florence
See Ai

Anthony, John
See Ciardi, John (Anthony)

Anthony, Peter
See Shaffer, Anthony (Joshua); Shaffer, Peter (Levin)

Anthony, Piers 1934- .... **CLC 35; DAM POP**
See also AAYA 11; AW; CA 21-24R; CANR 28, 56, 73; DLB 8; MTCW 1, 2; SAAS 22; SATA 84

Anthony, Susan B(rownell)
1916-1991 .... **TCLC 84**
See also CA 89-92; 134

Antoine, Marc
See Proust, (Valentin-Louis-George-Eugene-)Marcel

Antoninus, Brother
See Everson, William (Oliver)

Antonioni, Michelangelo 1912- .... **CLC 20**
See also CA 73-76; CANR 45, 77

Antschel, Paul 1920-1970
See Celan, Paul
See also CA 85-88; CANR 33, 61; MTCW 1

Anwar, Chairil 1922-1949 .... **TCLC 22**
See also CA 121

Anzaldua, Gloria (Evanjelina) 1942-
See also CA 175; DLB 122; HLCS 1

Apess, William 1798-1839(?) .... **NCLC 73; DAM MULT**
See also DLB 175; NNAL

Apollinaire, Guillaume 1880-1918 .. **TCLC 3, 8, 51; DAM POET; PC 7**
See also CA 152; MTCW 1

Appelfeld, Aharon 1932- ... **CLC 23, 47; SSC 42**
See also CA 112; 133; CANR 86; CWW 2

Apple, Max (Isaac) 1941- .... **CLC 9, 33**
See also CA 81-84; CANR 19, 54; DLB 130

Appleman, Philip (Dean) 1926- .... **CLC 51**
See also CA 13-16R; CAAS 18; CANR 6, 29, 56

Appleton, Lawrence
See Lovecraft, H(oward) P(hillips)

Apteryx
See Eliot, T(homas) S(tearns)

Apuleius, (Lucius Madaurensis)
125(?)-175(?) .... **CMLC 1**
See also DLB 211

Aquin, Hubert 1929-1977 .... **CLC 15**
See also CA 105; DLB 53

Aquinas, Thomas 1224(?)-1274 ..... **CMLC 33**
See also DLB 115

Aragon, Louis 1897-1982 .. **CLC 3, 22; DAM NOV, POET**
See also CA 69-72; 108; CANR 28, 71; DLB 72; GLL 2; MTCW 1, 2

Arany, Janos 1817-1882 .... **NCLC 34**

Aranyos, Kakay 1847-1910
See Mikszath, Kalman

Arbuthnot, John 1667-1735 .... **LC 1**
See also DLB 101

Archer, Herbert Winslow
See Mencken, H(enry) L(ouis)

Archer, Jeffrey (Howard) 1940- ...... **CLC 28; DAM POP**
See also AAYA 16; BEST 89:3; CA 77-80; CANR 22, 52, 95; DA3; INT CANR-22

Archer, Jules 1915- .... **CLC 12**
See also CA 9-12R; CANR 6, 69; SAAS 5; SATA 4, 85

Archer, Lee
See Ellison, Harlan (Jay)

Archilochus c. 7th cent. B.C.- .... **CMLC 44**
See also DLB 176

Arden, John 1930- .... **CLC 6, 13, 15; DAM DRAM**
See also BRWS 2; CA 13-16R; CAAS 4; CANR 31, 65, 67; DLB 13; MTCW 1

Arenas, Reinaldo 1943-1990 . **CLC 41; DAM MULT; HLC 1**
See also CA 124; 128; 133; CANR 73; DLB 145; GLL 2; HW 1; MTCW 1

Arendt, Hannah 1906-1975 .... **CLC 66, 98**
See also CA 17-20R; 61-64; CANR 26, 60; DLB 242; MTCW 1, 2

Aretino, Pietro 1492-1556 .... **LC 12**

Arghezi, Tudor CLC 80
See also Theodorescu, Ion N.
See also CA 167; DLB 220

Arguedas, Jose Maria 1911-1969 .... **CLC 10, 18; HLCS 1**
See also CA 89-92; CANR 73; DLB 113; HW 1

Argueta, Manlio 1936- .... **CLC 31**
See also CA 131; CANR 73; CWW 2; DLB 145; HW 1

Arias, Ron(ald Francis) 1941-
See also CA 131; CANR 81; DAM MULT; DLB 82; HLC 1; HW 1, 2; MTCW 2

Ariosto, Ludovico 1474-1533 .... **LC 6**

Aristides
See Epstein, Joseph

Aristophanes 450B.C.-385B.C. .... **CMLC 4; DA; DAB; DAC; DAM DRAM, MST; DC 2**
See also AW; DA3; DLB 176

Aristotle 384B.C.-322B.C. ..... **CMLC 31; DA; DAB; DAC; DAM MST**
See also AW; DA3; DLB 176

Arlt, Roberto (Godofredo Christophersen)
1900-1942 .... **TCLC 29; DAM MULT; HLC 1**
See also CA 123; 131; CANR 67; HW 1, 2

Armah, Ayi Kwei 1939- ...... **CLC 5, 33, 136; BLC 1; DAM MULT, POET**
See also BW 1; CA 61-64; CANR 21, 64; DLB 117; MTCW 1

Armatrading, Joan 1950- .... **CLC 17**
See also CA 114; 186

Arnette, Robert
See Silverberg, Robert

Arnim, Achim von (Ludwig Joachim von Arnim) 1781-1831 ..... **NCLC 5; SSC 29**
See also DLB 90

Arnim, Bettina von 1785-1859 .... **NCLC 38**
See also DLB 90

Arnold, Matthew 1822-1888 ..... **NCLC 6, 29, 89; DA; DAB; DAC; DAM MST, POET; PC 5**
See also AW; CDBLB 1832-1890; DLB 32, 57

Arnold, Thomas 1795-1842 .... **NCLC 18**
See also DLB 55

Arnow, Harriette (Louisa) Simpson
1908-1986 .... **CLC 2, 7, 18**
See also CA 9-12R; 118; CANR 14; DLB
6; MTCW 1, 2; SATA 42; SATA-Obit 47

Arouet, Francois-Marie
See Voltaire

Arp, Hans
See Arp, Jean

Arp, Jean 1887-1966 .... **CLC 5**
See also CA 81-84; 25-28R; CANR 42, 77

Arrabal
See Arrabal, Fernando

Arrabal, Fernando 1932- ... **CLC 2, 9, 18, 58**
See also CA 9-12R; CANR 15

Arreola, Juan Jose 1918- .... **SSC 38; DAM
MULT; HLC 1**
See also CA 113; 131; CANR 81; DLB 113;
HW 1, 2

Arrian c. 89(?)-c. 155(?) .... **CMLC 43**
See also DLB 176

Arrick, Fran CLC 30
See also Gaberman, Judie Angell

Artaud, Antonin (Marie Joseph)
1896-1948 . **TCLC 3, 36; DAM DRAM;
DC 14**
See also CA 104; 149; DA3; MTCW 1

Arthur, Ruth M(abel) 1905-1979 ..... **CLC 12**
See also CA 9-12R; 85-88; CANR 4; SATA
7, 26

Artsybashev, Mikhail (Petrovich)
1878-1927 .... **TCLC 31**
See also CA 170

Arundel, Honor (Morfydd)
1919-1973 .... **CLC 17**
See also CA 21-22; 41-44R; CAP 2; CLR
35; SATA 4; SATA-Obit 24

Arzner, Dorothy 1900-1979 .... **CLC 98**

Asch, Sholem 1880-1957 .... **TCLC 3**
See also CA 105; GLL 2

Ash, Shalom
See Asch, Sholem

Ashbery, John (Lawrence) 1927- .. **CLC 2, 3,
4, 6, 9, 13, 15, 25, 41, 77, 125; DAM
POET; PC 26**
See also Berry, Jonas
See also AMWS 3; CA 5-8R; CANR 9, 37,
66; DA3; DLB 5, 165; DLBY 81; INT
CANR-9; MTCW 1, 2

Ashdown, Clifford
See Freeman, R(ichard) Austin

Ashe, Gordon
See Creasey, John

Ashton-Warner, Sylvia (Constance)
1908-1984 .... **CLC 19**
See also CA 69-72; 112; CANR 29; MTCW
1, 2

Asimov, Isaac 1920-1992 ..... **CLC 1, 3, 9, 19,
26, 76, 92; DAM POP**
See also AAYA 13; AW; BEST 90:2; CA
1-4R; 137; CANR 2, 19, 36, 60; CLR 12;
DA3; DLB 8; DLBY 92; INT CANR-19;
JRDA; MAICYA; MTCW 1, 2; SATA 1,
26, 74; SCFW 2

Assis, Joaquim Maria Machado de
See Machado de Assis, Joaquim Maria

Astley, Thea (Beatrice May) 1925- .. **CLC 41**
See also CA 65-68; CANR 11, 43, 78

Aston, James
See White, T(erence) H(anbury)

Asturias, Miguel Ángel 1899-1974 .... **CLC 3,
8, 13; DAM MULT, NOV; HLC 1**
See also CA 25-28; 49-52; CANR 32; CAP
2; DA3; DLB 113; HW 1; MTCW 1, 2

Atares, Carlos Saura
See Saura (Atares), Carlos

Atheling, William
See Pound, Ezra (Weston Loomis)

Atheling, William, Jr.
See Blish, James (Benjamin)

Atherton, Gertrude (Franklin Horn)
1857-1948 .... **TCLC 2**
See also CA 104; 155; DLB 9, 78, 186;
TCWW 2

Atherton, Lucius
See Masters, Edgar Lee

Atkins, Jack
See Harris, Mark

Atkinson, Kate CLC 99
See also CA 166

Attaway, William (Alexander)
1911-1986 .... **CLC 92; BLC 1; DAM
MULT**
See also BW 2, 3; CA 143; CANR 82; DLB
76

Atticus
See Fleming, Ian (Lancaster); Wilson,
(Thomas) Woodrow

Atwood, Margaret (Eleanor) 1939- ... **CLC 2,
3, 4, 8, 13, 15, 25, 44, 84, 135; DA;
DAB; DAC; DAM MST, NOV, POET;
PC 8; SSC 2**
See also AAYA 12; AW; BEST 89:2; CA
49-52; CANR 3, 24, 33, 59, 95; DA3;
DLB 53; INT CANR-24; MTCW 1, 2;
SATA 50

Aubigny, Pierre d'
See Mencken, H(enry) L(ouis)

Aubin, Penelope 1685-1731(?) .... **LC 9**
See also DLB 39

Auchincloss, Louis (Stanton) 1917- .. **CLC 4,
6, 9, 18, 45; DAM NOV; SSC 22**
See also AMWS 4; CA 1-4R; CANR 6, 29,
55, 87; DLB 2; DLBY 80; INT CANR-
29; MTCW 1

Auden, W(ystan) H(ugh) 1907-1973 . **CLC 1,
2, 3, 4, 6, 9, 11, 14, 43, 123; DA; DAB;
DAC; DAM DRAM, MST, POET; PC
1**
See also AAYA 18; AMWS 2; AW; CA
9-12R; 45-48; CANR 5, 61; CDBLB
1914-1945; DA3; DLB 10, 20; MTCW 1,
2

Audiberti, Jacques 1900-1965 .... **CLC 38;
DAM DRAM**
See also CA 25-28R

Audubon, John James 1785-1851 . **NCLC 47**

Auel, Jean M(arie) 1936- .... **CLC 31, 107;
DAM POP**
See also AAYA 7; BEST 90:4; CA 103;
CANR 21, 64; DA3; INT CANR-21;
SATA 91

Auerbach, Erich 1892-1957 .... **TCLC 43**
See also CA 118; 155

Augier, Emile 1820-1889 .... **NCLC 31**
See also DLB 192

August, John
See De Voto, Bernard (Augustine)

Augustine 354-430 .... **CMLC 6; DA; DAB;
DAC; DAM MST**
See also AW; DA3; DLB 115

Aurelius
See Bourne, Randolph S(illiman)

Aurobindo, Sri
See Ghose, Aurabinda

Austen, Jane 1775-1817 ...... **NCLC 1, 13, 19,
33, 51, 81, 95; DA; DAB; DAC; DAM
MST, NOV**
See also AAYA 19; AW 1; CDBLB 1789-
1832; DA3; DLB 116

Auster, Paul 1947- .... **CLC 47, 131**
See also CA 69-72; CANR 23, 52, 75; DA3;
DLB 227; MTCW 1

Austin, Frank
See Faust, Frederick (Schiller)
See also TCWW 2

Austin, Mary (Hunter) 1868-1934 . **TCLC 25**
See also Stairs, Gordon
See also CA 109; 178; DLB 9, 78, 206, 221;
TCWW 2

Averroes 1126-1198 .... **CMLC 7**
See also DLB 115

Avicenna 980-1037 .... **CMLC 16**
See also DLB 115

Avison, Margaret 1918- .... **CLC 2, 4, 97;
DAC; DAM POET**
See also CA 17-20R; DLB 53; MTCW 1

Axton, David
See Koontz, Dean R(ay)

Ayckbourn, Alan 1939- ...... **CLC 5, 8, 18, 33,
74; DAB; DAM DRAM; DC 13**
See also BRWS 5; CA 21-24R; CANR 31,
59; DLB 13; MTCW 1, 2

Aydy, Catherine
See Tennant, Emma (Christina)

Ayme, Marcel (Andre) 1902-1967 ... **CLC 11;
SSC 41**
See also CA 89-92; CANR 67; CLR 25;
DLB 72; SATA 91

Ayrton, Michael 1921-1975 .... **CLC 7**
See also CA 5-8R; 61-64; CANR 9, 21

Azorin CLC 11
See also Martinez Ruiz, Jose

Azuela, Mariano 1873-1952 . **TCLC 3; DAM
MULT; HLC 1**
See also CA 104; 131; CANR 81; HW 1, 2;
MTCW 1, 2

Baastad, Babbis Friis
See Friis-Baastad, Babbis Ellinor

Bab
See Gilbert, W(illiam) S(chwenck)

Babbis, Eleanor
See Friis-Baastad, Babbis Ellinor

Babel, Isaac
See Babel, Isaak (Emmanuilovich)

Babel, Isaak (Emmanuilovich)
1894-1941(?) .... **TCLC 2, 13; SSC 16**
See also Babel, Isaac
See also CA 104; 155; MTCW 1

Babits, Mihaly 1883-1941 .... **TCLC 14**
See also CA 114

Babur 1483-1530 .... **LC 18**

Baca, Jimmy Santiago 1952-
See also CA 131; CANR 81, 90; DAM
MULT; DLB 122; HLC 1; HW 1, 2

Bacchelli, Riccardo 1891-1985 .... **CLC 19**
See also CA 29-32R; 117

Bach, Richard (David) 1936- .... **CLC 14;
DAM NOV, POP**
See also AITN 1; BEST 89:2; CA 9-12R;
CANR 18, 93; MTCW 1; SATA 13

Bachman, Richard
See King, Stephen (Edwin)

Bachmann, Ingeborg 1926-1973 .... **CLC 69**
See also CA 93-96; 45-48; CANR 69; DLB
85

Bacon, Francis 1561-1626 .... **LC 18, 32**
See also CDBLB Before 1660; DLB 151,
236

Bacon, Roger 1214(?)-1294 .... **CMLC 14**
See also DLB 115

Bacovia, George 1881-1957 .... **TCLC 24**
See also Bacovia, G.; Vasiliu, Gheorghe
See also DLB 220

Badanes, Jerome 1937- .... **CLC 59**

Bagehot, Walter 1826-1877 .... **NCLC 10**
See also DLB 55

Bagnold, Enid 1889-1981 ...... **CLC 25; DAM
DRAM**
See also CA 5-8R; 103; CANR 5, 40; DLB
13, 160, 191; MAICYA; SATA 1, 25

Bagritsky, Eduard 1895-1934 .... **TCLC 60**
Bagrjana, Elisaveta
　See Belcheva, Elisaveta
Bagryana, Elisaveta CLC 10
　See also Belcheva, Elisaveta
　See also CA 178; DLB 147
Bailey, Paul 1937- .... **CLC 45**
　See also CA 21-24R; CANR 16, 62; DLB
　14; GLL 2
Baillie, Joanna 1762-1851 .... **NCLC 71**
　See also DLB 93
Bainbridge, Beryl (Margaret) 1934- . **CLC 4,**
　5, 8, 10, 14, 18, 22, 62, 130; DAM NOV
　See also CA 21-24R; CANR 24, 55, 75, 88;
　DLB 14, 231; MTCW 1, 2
Baker, Elliott 1922- .... **CLC 8**
　See also CA 45-48; CANR 2, 63
Baker, Jean H. TCLC 3, 10
　See also Russell, George William
Baker, Nicholson 1957- .... **CLC 61; DAM**
　POP
　See also CA 135; CANR 63; DA3; DLB
　227
Baker, Ray Stannard 1870-1946 .... **TCLC 47**
　See also CA 118
Baker, Russell (Wayne) 1925- .... **CLC 31**
　See also BEST 89:4; CA 57-60; CANR 11,
　41, 59; MTCW 1, 2
Bakhtin, M.
　See Bakhtin, Mikhail Mikhailovich
Bakhtin, M. M.
　See Bakhtin, Mikhail Mikhailovich
Bakhtin, Mikhail
　See Bakhtin, Mikhail Mikhailovich
Bakhtin, Mikhail Mikhailovich
　1895-1975 .... **CLC 83**
　See also CA 128; 113; DLB 242
Bakshi, Ralph 1938(?)- .... **CLC 26**
　See also CA 112; 138; IDFW 3
Bakunin, Mikhail (Alexandrovich)
　1814-1876 .... **NCLC 25, 58**
Baldwin, James (Arthur) 1924-1987 . **CLC 1,**
　2, 3, 4, 5, 8, 13, 15, 17, 42, 50, 67, 90,
　127; BLC 1; DA; DAB; DAC; DAM
　MST, MULT, NOV, POP; DC 1; SSC
　10, 33
　See also AAYA 4, 34; AW; BW 1; CA 1-4R;
　124; CABS 1; CANR 3, 24; CDALB
　1941-1968; DA3; DLB 2, 7, 33; DLBY
　87; MTCW 1, 2; SATA 9; SATA-Obit 54
Bale, John 1495-1563 .... **LC 62**
　See also DLB 132
Ball, Hugo 1886-1927 .... **TCLC 104**
Ballard, J(ames) G(raham) 1930- . **CLC 3, 6,**
　14, 36, 137; DAM NOV, POP; SSC 1
　See also AAYA 3; CA 5-8R; CANR 15, 39,
　65; DA3; DLB 14, 207; MTCW 1, 2;
　SATA 93
Balmont, Konstantin (Dmitriyevich)
　1867-1943 .... **TCLC 11**
　See also CA 109; 155
Baltausis, Vincas 1847-1910
　See Mikszath, Kalman
Balzac, Honoré de 1799-1850 ... **NCLC 5, 35,**
　53; DA; DAB; DAC; DAM MST, NOV;
　SSC 5
　See also AW; DA3; DLB 119
Bambara, Toni Cade 1939-1995 ...... **CLC 19,**
　88; BLC 1; DA; DAC; DAM MST,
　MULT; SSC 35
　See also AAYA 5; AW; BW 2, 3; CA 29-
　32R; 150; CANR 24, 49, 81; CDALBS;
　DA3; DLB 38; MTCW 1, 2; SATA 112
Bamdad, A.
　See Shamlu, Ahmad
Banat, D. R.
　See Bradbury, Ray (Douglas)
Bancroft, Laura
　See Baum, L(yman) Frank

Banim, John 1798-1842 .... **NCLC 13**
　See also DLB 116, 158, 159
Banim, Michael 1796 1874 .... **NCLC 13**
　See also DLB 158, 159
Banjo, The
　See Paterson, A(ndrew) B(arton)
Banks, Iain
　See Banks, Iain M(enzies)
Banks, Iain M(enzies) 1954- .... **CLC 34**
　See also CA 123; 128; CANR 61; DLB 194;
　INT 128
Banks, Lynne Reid CLC 23
　See also Reid Banks, Lynne
　See also AAYA 6
Banks, Russell 1940- .... **CLC 37, 72; SSC 42**
　See also AMWS 5; CA 65-68; CAAS 15;
　CANR 19, 52, 73; DLB 130
Banville, John 1945- .... **CLC 46, 118**
　See also CA 117; 128; DLB 14; INT 128
Banville, Theodore (Faullain) de
　1832-1891 .... **NCLC 9**
Baraka, Amiri 1934- . **CLC 1, 2, 3, 5, 10, 14,**
　33, 115; BLC 1; DA; DAC; DAM MST,
　MULT, POET, POP; DC 6; PC 4
　See also Jones, LeRoi
　See also AMWS 2; AW; BW 2, 3; CA 21-
　24R; CABS 3; CANR 27, 38, 61; CDALB
　1941-1968; DA3; DLB 5, 7, 16, 38;
　DLBD 8; MTCW 1, 2
Barbauld, Anna Laetitia
　1743-1825 .... **NCLC 50**
　See also DLB 107, 109, 142, 158
Barbellion, W. N. P. TCLC 24
　See also Cummings, Bruce F(rederick)
Barber, Benjamin R. 1939- .... **CLC 141**
　See also CA 29-32R; CANR 12, 32, 64
Barbera, Jack (Vincent) 1945- .... **CLC 44**
　See also CA 110; CANR 45
Barbey d'Aurevilly, Jules Amedee
　1808-1889 .... **NCLC 1; SSC 17**
　See also DLB 119
Barbour, John c. 1316-1395 .... **CMLC 33**
　See also DLB 146
Barbusse, Henri 1873-1935 .... **TCLC 5**
　See also CA 105; 154; DLB 65
Barclay, Bill
　See Moorcock, Michael (John)
Barclay, William Ewert
　See Moorcock, Michael (John)
Barea, Arturo 1897-1957 .... **TCLC 14**
　See also CA 111
Barfoot, Joan 1946- .... **CLC 18**
　See also CA 105
Barham, Richard Harris
　1788-1845 .... **NCLC 77**
　See also DLB 159
Baring, Maurice 1874-1945 .... **TCLC 8**
　See also CA 105; 168; DLB 34
Baring-Gould, Sabine 1834-1924 ... **TCLC 88**
　See also DLB 156, 190
Barker, Clive 1952- ...... **CLC 52; DAM POP**
　See also AAYA 10; BEST 90:3; CA 121;
　129; CANR 71; DA3; INT 129; MTCW
　1, 2
Barker, George Granville
　1913-1991 .... **CLC 8, 48; DAM POET**
　See also CA 9-12R; 135; CANR 7, 38; DLB
　20; MTCW 1
Barker, Harley Granville
　See Granville-Barker, Harley
　See also DLB 10
Barker, Howard 1946- .... **CLC 37**
　See also CA 102; DLB 13, 233
Barker, Jane 1652-1732 .... **LC 42**
Barker, Pat(ricia) 1943- .... **CLC 32, 94**
　See also BRWS 4; CA 117; 122; CANR 50;
　INT 122

Barlach, Ernst (Heinrich)
　1870-1938 .... **TCLC 84**
　See also CA 178; DLB 56, 118
Barlow, Joel 1754-1812 .... **NCLC 23**
　See also AMWS 2; DLB 37
Barnard, Mary (Ethel) 1909- .... **CLC 48**
　See also CA 21-22; CAP 2
Barnes, Djuna 1892-1982 .... **CLC 3, 4, 8, 11,**
　29, 127; SSC 3
　See also Steptoe, Lydia
　See also AMWS 3; CA 9-12R; 107; CANR
　16, 55; DLB 4, 9, 45; GLL 1; MTCW 1,
　2
Barnes, Julian (Patrick) 1946- .... **CLC 42,**
　141; DAB
　See also BRWS 4; CA 102; CANR 19, 54;
　DLB 194; DLBY 93; MTCW 1
Barnes, Peter 1931- .... **CLC 5, 56**
　See also CA 65-68; CAAS 12; CANR 33,
　34, 64; DLB 13, 233; MTCW 1
Barnes, William 1801-1886 .... **NCLC 75**
　See also DLB 32
Baroja (y Nessi), Pio 1872-1956 ..... **TCLC 8;**
　HLC 1
　See also CA 104
Baron, David
　See Pinter, Harold
Baron Corvo
　See Rolfe, Frederick (William Serafino Aus-
　tin Lewis Mary)
Barondess, Sue K(aufman)
　1926-1977 .... **CLC 8**
　See also Kaufman, Sue
　See also CA 1-4R; 69-72; CANR 1
Baron de Teive
　See Pessoa, Fernando (Antonio Nogueira)
Baroness Von S.
　See Zangwill, Israel
Barres, (Auguste-) Maurice
　1862-1923 .... **TCLC 47**
　See also CA 164; DLB 123
Barreto, Afonso Henrique de Lima
　See Lima Barreto, Afonso Henrique de
Barrett, (Roger) Syd 1946- .... **CLC 35**
Barrett, William (Christopher)
　1913-1992 .... **CLC 27**
　See also CA 13-16R; 139; CANR 11, 67;
　INT CANR-11
Barrie, J(ames) M(atthew)
　1860-1937 .... **TCLC 2; DAB; DAM**
　DRAM
　See also AW 1; BRWS 3; CA 104; 136;
　CANR 77; CDBLB 1890-1914; CLR 16;
　DA3; DLB 10, 141, 156; MAICYA;
　MTCW 1; SATA 100
Barrington, Michael
　See Moorcock, Michael (John)
Barrol, Grady
　See Bograd, Larry
Barry, Mike
　See Malzberg, Barry N(athaniel)
Barry, Philip 1896-1949 .... **TCLC 11**
　See also CA 109; DLB 7, 228
Bart, Andre Schwarz
　See Schwarz-Bart, Andre
Barth, John (Simmons) 1930- ... **CLC 1, 2, 3,**
　5, 7, 9, 10, 14, 27, 51, 89; DAM NOV;
　SSC 10
　See also AITN 1, 2; CA 1-4R; CABS 1;
　CANR 5, 23, 49, 64; DLB 2, 227; MTCW
　1
Barthelme, Donald 1931-1989 ... **CLC 1, 2, 3,**
　5, 6, 8, 13, 23, 46, 59, 115; DAM NOV;
　SSC 2
　See also AMWS 4; CA 21-24R; 129; CANR
　20, 58; DA3; DLB 2, 234; DLBY 80, 89;
　MTCW 1, 2; SATA 7; SATA-Obit 62

Barthelme, Frederick 1943- ...... **CLC 36, 117**
See also CA 114; 122; CANR 77; DLBY 85; INT 122

Barthes, Roland (Gerard)
1915-1980 .... **CLC 24, 83**
See also CA 130; 97-100; CANR 66; MTCW 1, 2

Barzun, Jacques (Martin) 1907- ...... **CLC 51**
See also CA 61-64; CANR 22, 95

Bashevis, Isaac
See Singer, Isaac Bashevis

Bashkirtseff, Marie 1859-1884 .... **NCLC 27**

Basho
See Matsuo Basho

Basil of Caesaria c. 330-379 .... **CMLC 35**

Bass, Kingsley B., Jr.
See Bullins, Ed

Bass, Rick 1958- .... **CLC 79**
See also CA 126; CANR 53, 93; DLB 212

Bassani, Giorgio 1916-2000 .... **CLC 9**
See also CA 65-68; CANR 33; CWW 2; DLB 128, 177; MTCW 1

Bastos, Augusto (Antonio) Roa
See Roa Bastos, Augusto (Antonio)

Bataille, Georges 1897-1962 .... **CLC 29**
See also CA 101; 89-92

Bates, H(erbert) E(rnest)
1905-1974 . **CLC 46; DAB; DAM POP; SSC 10**
See also CA 93-96; 45-48; CANR 34; DA3; DLB 162, 191; MTCW 1, 2

Bauchart
See Camus, Albert

Baudelaire, Charles 1821-1867 . **NCLC 6, 29, 55; DA; DAB; DAC; DAM MST, POET; PC 1; SSC 18**
See also AW; DA3

Baudrillard, Jean 1929- .... **CLC 60**

Baum, L(yman) Frank 1856-1919 ... **TCLC 7**
See also CA 108; 133; CLR 15; DLB 22; JRDA; MAICYA; MTCW 1, 2; SATA 18, 100

Baum, Louis F.
See Baum, L(yman) Frank

Baumbach, Jonathan 1933- .... **CLC 6, 23**
See also CA 13-16R; CAAS 5; CANR 12, 66; DLBY 80; INT CANR-12; MTCW 1

Bausch, Richard (Carl) 1945- .... **CLC 51**
See also AMWS 7; CA 101; CAAS 14; CANR 43, 61, 87; DLB 130

Baxter, Charles (Morley) 1947- .... **CLC 45, 78; DAM POP**
See also CA 57-60; CANR 40, 64; DLB 130; MTCW 2

Baxter, George Owen
See Faust, Frederick (Schiller)

Baxter, James K(eir) 1926-1972 .... **CLC 14**
See also CA 77-80

Baxter, John
See Hunt, E(verette) Howard, (Jr.)

Bayer, Sylvia
See Glassco, John

Baynton, Barbara 1857-1929 .... **TCLC 57**
See also DLB 230

Beagle, Peter S(oyer) 1939- .... **CLC 7, 104**
See also AW; CA 9-12R; CANR 4, 51, 73; DA3; DLBY 80; INT CANR-4; MTCW 1; SATA 60

Bean, Normal
See Burroughs, Edgar Rice

Beard, Charles A(ustin)
1874-1948 .... **TCLC 15**
See also CA 115; 189; DLB 17; SATA 18

Beardsley, Aubrey 1872-1898 .... **NCLC 6**

Beattie, Ann 1947- ..... **CLC 8, 13, 18, 40, 63; DAM NOV, POP; SSC 11**
See also AMWS 5; BEST 90:2; CA 81-84; CANR 53, 73; DA3; DLBY 82; MTCW 1, 2

Beattie, James 1735-1803 .... **NCLC 25**
See also DLB 109

Beauchamp, Kathleen Mansfield 1888-1923
See Mansfield, Katherine
See also CA 104; 134; DA; DAC; DAM MST; DA3; MTCW 2

Beaumarchais, Pierre-Augustin Caron de
1732-1799 . **LC 61; DAM DRAM; DC 4**

Beaumont, Francis 1584(?)-1616 .... **LC 33; DC 6**
See also CDBLB Before 1660; DLB 58, 121

Beauvoir, Simone (Lucie Ernestine Marie Bertrand) de 1908-1986 .... **CLC 1, 2, 4, 8, 14, 31, 44, 50, 71, 124; DA; DAB; DAC; DAM MST, NOV; SSC 35**
See also AW; CA 9-12R; 118; CANR 28, 61; DA3; DLB 72; DLBY 86; MTCW 1, 2

Becker, Carl (Lotus) 1873-1945 ..... **TCLC 63**
See also CA 157; DLB 17

Becker, Jurek 1937-1997 .... **CLC 7, 19**
See also CA 85-88; 157; CANR 60; CWW 2; DLB 75

Becker, Walter 1950- .... **CLC 26**

Beckett, Samuel (Barclay)
1906-1989 .. **CLC 1, 2, 3, 4, 6, 9, 10, 11, 14, 18, 29, 57, 59, 83; DA; DAB; DAC; DAM DRAM, MST, NOV; SSC 16**
See also AW; BRWS 1; CA 5-8R; 130; CANR 33, 61; CDBLB 1945-1960; DA3; DLB 13, 15, 233; DLBY 90; MTCW 1, 2

Beckford, William 1760-1844 .... **NCLC 16**
See also DLB 39,213

Beckman, Gunnel 1910- .... **CLC 26**
See also CA 33-36R; CANR 15; CLR 25; MAICYA; SAAS 9; SATA 6

Becque, Henri 1837-1899 .... **NCLC 3**
See also DLB 192

Becquer, Gustavo Adolfo 1836-1870
See also DAM MULT; HLCS 1

Beddoes, Thomas Lovell
1803-1849 .... **NCLC 3**
See also DLB 96

Bede c. 673-735 .... **CMLC 20**
See also DLB 146

Bedford, Donald F.
See Fearing, Kenneth (Flexner)

Beecher, Catharine Esther
1800-1878 .... **NCLC 30**
See also DLB 1

Beecher, John 1904-1980 .... **CLC 6**
See also AITN 1; CA 5-8R; 105; CANR 8

Beer, Johann 1655-1700 .... **LC 5**
See also DLB 168

Beer, Patricia 1924- .... **CLC 58**
See also CA 61-64; 183; CANR 13, 46; DLB 40

Beerbohm, Max
See Beerbohm, (Henry) Max(imilian)
See also BRWS 2

Beerbohm, (Henry) Max(imilian)
1872-1956 .... **TCLC 1, 24**
See also CA 104; 154; CANR 79; DLB 34, 100

Beer-Hofmann, Richard
1866-1945 .... **TCLC 60**
See also CA 160; DLB 81

Begiebing, Robert J(ohn) 1946- .... **CLC 70**
See also CA 122; CANR 40, 88

Behan, Brendan 1923-1964 ...... **CLC 1, 8, 11, 15, 79; DAM DRAM**
See also BRWS 2; CA 73-76; CANR 33; CDBLB 1945-1960; DLB 13, 233; MTCW 1, 2

Behn, Aphra 1640(?)-1689 .... **LC 1, 30, 42; DA; DAB; DAC; DAM DRAM, MST, NOV, POET; DC 4; PC 13**
See also AW; BRWS 3; DA3; DLB 39, 80, 131

Behrman, S(amuel) N(athaniel)
1893-1973 .... **CLC 40**
See also CA 13-16; 45-48; CAP 1; DLB 7, 44

Belasco, David 1853-1931 .... **TCLC 3**
See also CA 104; 168; DLB 7

Belcheva, Elisaveta 1893-1991 .... **CLC 10**
See also Bagryana, Elisaveta

Beldone, Phil ''Cheech''
See Ellison, Harlan (Jay)

Beleno
See Azuela, Mariano

Belinski, Vissarion Grigoryevich
1811-1848 .... **NCLC 5**
See also DLB 198

Belitt, Ben 1911- .... **CLC 22**
See also CA 13-16R; CAAS 4; CANR 7, 77; DLB 5

Bell, Gertrude (Margaret Lowthian)
1868-1926 .... **TCLC 67**
See also CA 167; DLB 174

Bell, J. Freeman
See Zangwill, Israel

Bell, James Madison 1826-1902 ... **TCLC 43; BLC 1; DAM MULT**
See also BW 1; CA 122; 124; DLB 50

Bell, Madison Smartt 1957- ...... **CLC 41, 102**
See also CA 111, 183; CAAE 183; CANR 28, 54, 73; MTCW 1

Bell, Marvin (Hartley) 1937- ...... **CLC 8, 31; DAM POET**
See also CA 21-24R; CAAS 14; CANR 59; DLB 5; MTCW 1

Bell, W. L. D.
See Mencken, H(enry) L(ouis)

Bellamy, Atwood C.
See Mencken, H(enry) L(ouis)

Bellamy, Edward 1850-1898 ...... **NCLC 4, 86**
See also DLB 12

Belli, Gioconda 1949-
See also CA 152; CWW 2; HLCS 1

Bellin, Edward J.
See Kuttner, Henry

Belloc, (Joseph) Hilaire (Pierre Sebastien Rene Swanton) 1870-1953 ...... **TCLC 7, 18; DAM POET; PC 24**
See also AW 1; CA 106; 152; DLB 19, 100, 141, 174; MTCW 1; SATA 112

Belloc, Joseph Peter Rene Hilaire
See Belloc, (Joseph) Hilaire (Pierre Sebastien Rene Swanton)

Belloc, Joseph Pierre Hilaire
See Belloc, (Joseph) Hilaire (Pierre Sebastien Rene Swanton)

Belloc, M. A.
See Lowndes, Marie Adelaide (Belloc)

Bellow, Saul 1915- . **CLC 1, 2, 3, 6, 8, 10, 13, 15, 25, 33, 34, 63, 79; DA; DAB; DAC; DAM MST, NOV, POP; SSC 14**
See also AITN 2; AW; BEST 89:3; CA 5-8R; CABS 1; CANR 29, 53, 95; CDALB 1941-1968; DA3; DLB 2, 28; DLBD 3; DLBY 82; MTCW 1, 2

Belser, Reimond Karel Maria de 1929-
See Ruyslinck, Ward
See also CA 152

Bely, Andrey **TCLC 7; PC 11**
See also Bugayev, Boris Nikolayevich
See also MTCW 1

Belyi, Andrei
    See Bugayev, Boris Nikolayevich
Benary, Margot
    See Benary-Isbert, Margot
Benary-Isbert, Margot 1889-1979 .... **CLC 12**
    See also CA 5-8R; 89-92; CANR 4, 72;
    CLR 12; MAICYA; SATA 2; SATA-Obit
    21
Benavente (y Martinez), Jacinto
    1866-1954 .... **TCLC 3; DAM DRAM,
    MULT; HLCS 1**
    See also CA 106; 131; CANR 81; GLL 2;
    HW 1, 2; MTCW 1, 2
Benchley, Peter (Bradford) 1940- . **CLC 4, 8;
    DAM NOV, POP**
    See also AAYA 14; AITN 2; CA 17-20R;
    CANR 12, 35, 66; MTCW 1, 2; SATA 3,
    89
Benchley, Robert (Charles)
    1889-1945 .... **TCLC 1, 55**
    See also CA 105; 153; DLB 11
Benda, Julien 1867-1956 .... **TCLC 60**
    See also CA 120; 154
Benedict, Ruth (Fulton)
    1887-1948 .... **TCLC 60**
    See also CA 158
Benedict, Saint c. 480-c. 547 .... **CMLC 29**
Benedikt, Michael 1935- .... **CLC 4, 14**
    See also CA 13-16R; CANR 7; DLB 5
Benet, Juan 1927-1993 .... **CLC 28**
    See also CA 143
Benet, Stephen Vincent 1898-1943 . **TCLC 7;
    DAM POET; SSC 10**
    See also AW 1; CA 104; 152; DA3; DLB 4,
    48, 102; DLBY 97; MTCW 1
Benet, William Rose 1886-1950 .... **TCLC 28;
    DAM POET**
    See also CA 118; 152; DLB 45
Benford, Gregory (Albert) 1941- ..... **CLC 52**
    See also CA 69-72, 175; CAAE 175; CAAS
    27; CANR 12, 24, 49, 95; DLBY 82;
    SCFW 2
Bengtsson, Frans (Gunnar)
    1894-1954 .... **TCLC 48**
    See also CA 170
Benjamin, David
    See Slavitt, David R(ytman)
Benjamin, Lois
    See Gould, Lois
Benjamin, Walter 1892-1940 .... **TCLC 39**
    See also CA 164; DLB 242
Benn, Gottfried 1886-1956 .... **TCLC 3**
    See also CA 106; 153; DLB 56
Bennett, Alan 1934- .... **CLC 45, 77; DAB;
    DAM MST**
    See also CA 103; CANR 35, 55; MTCW 1,
    2
Bennett, (Enoch) Arnold
    1867-1931 .... **TCLC 5, 20**
    See also CA 106; 155; CDBLB 1890-1914;
    DLB 10, 34, 98, 135; MTCW 2
Bennett, Elizabeth
    See Mitchell, Margaret (Munnerlyn)
Bennett, George Harold 1930-
    See Bennett, Hal
    See also BW 1; CA 97-100; CANR 87
Bennett, Hal CLC 5
    See also Bennett, George Harold
    See also DLB 33
Bennett, Jay 1912- .... **CLC 35**
    See also AAYA 10; AW; CA 69-72; CANR
    11, 42, 79; JRDA; SAAS 4; SATA 41, 87;
    SATA-Brief 27
Bennett, Louise (Simone) 1919- ...... **CLC 28;
    BLC 1; DAM MULT**
    See also BW 2, 3; CA 151; DLB 117
Benson, E(dward) F(rederic)
    1867-1940 .... **TCLC 27**
    See also CA 114; 157; DLB 135, 153

Benson, Jackson J. 1930- .... **CLC 34**
    See also CA 25-28R; DLB 111
Benson, Sally 1900-1972 .... **CLC 17**
    See also CA 19-20; 37-40R; CAP 1; SATA
    1, 35; SATA-Obit 27
Benson, Stella 1892-1933 .... **TCLC 17**
    See also CA 117; 155; DLB 36, 162
Bentham, Jeremy 1748-1832 .... **NCLC 38**
    See also DLB 107, 158
Bentley, E(dmund) C(lerihew)
    1875-1956 .... **TCLC 12**
    See also CA 108; DLB 70
Bentley, Eric (Russell) 1916- .... **CLC 24**
    See also CA 5-8R; CANR 6, 67; INT
    CANR-6
Beranger, Pierre Jean de
    1780-1857 .... **NCLC 34**
Berdyaev, Nicolas
    See Berdyaev, Nikolai (Aleksandrovich)
Berdyaev, Nikolai (Aleksandrovich)
    1874-1948 .... **TCLC 67**
    See also CA 120; 157
Berdyayev, Nikolai (Aleksandrovich)
    See Berdyaev, Nikolai (Aleksandrovich)
Berendt, John (Lawrence) 1939- ...... **CLC 86**
    See also CA 146; CANR 75, 93; DA3;
    MTCW 1
Beresford, J(ohn) D(avys)
    1873-1947 .... **TCLC 81**
    See also CA 112; 155; DLB 162, 178, 197
Bergelson, David 1884-1952 .... **TCLC 81**
Berger, Colonel
    See Malraux, (Georges-)Andre
Berger, John (Peter) 1926- .... **CLC 2, 19**
    See also BRWS 4; CA 81-84; CANR 51,
    78; DLB 14, 207
Berger, Melvin H. 1927- .... **CLC 12**
    See also CA 5-8R; CANR 4; CLR 32;
    SAAS 2; SATA 5, 88
Berger, Thomas (Louis) 1924- .. **CLC 3, 5, 8,
    11, 18, 38; DAM NOV**
    See also CA 1-4R; CANR 5, 28, 51; DLB
    2; DLBY 80; INT CANR-28; MTCW 1,
    2; TCWW 2
Bergman, (Ernst) Ingmar
    1918-1997 .... **CLC 16, 72**
    See also CA 81-84; CANR 33, 70; MTCW
    2
Bergson, Henri(-Louis) 1859-1941 . **TCLC 32**
    See also CA 164
Bergstein, Eleanor 1938- .... **CLC 4**
    See also CA 53-56; CANR 5
Berkoff, Steven 1937- .... **CLC 56**
    See also CA 104; CANR 72
Berlin, Isaiah 1909-1997 .... **TCLC 105**
    See also CA 85-88; 162
Bermant, Chaim (Icyk) 1929-1998 ... **CLC 40**
    See also CA 57-60; CANR 6, 31, 57
Bern, Victoria
    See Fisher, M(ary) F(rances) K(ennedy)
Bernanos, (Paul Louis) Georges
    1888-1948 .... **TCLC 3**
    See also CA 104; 130; CANR 94; DLB 72
Bernard, April 1956- .... **CLC 59**
    See also CA 131
Berne, Victoria
    See Fisher, M(ary) F(rances) K(ennedy)
Bernhard, Thomas 1931-1989 ..... **CLC 3, 32,
    61; DC 14**
    See also CA 85-88; 127; CANR 32, 57;
    DLB 85, 124; MTCW 1
Bernhardt, Sarah (Henriette Rosine)
    1844-1923 .... **TCLC 75**
    See also CA 157
Berriault, Gina 1926-1999 .... **CLC 54, 109;
    SSC 30**
    See also CA 116; 129; 185; CANR 66;
    DLB 130

Berrigan, Daniel 1921- .... **CLC 4**
    See also CA 33-36R; CAAE 187; CAAS 1;
    CANR 11, 43, 78; DLB 5
Berrigan, Edmund Joseph Michael, Jr.
    1934-1983
    See Berrigan, Ted
    See also CA 61-64; 110; CANR 14
Berrigan, Ted CLC 37
    See also Berrigan, Edmund Joseph Michael,
    Jr.
    See also DLB 5, 169
Berry, Charles Edward Anderson 1931-
    See Berry, Chuck
    See also CA 115
Berry, Chuck CLC 17
    See also Berry, Charles Edward Anderson
Berry, Jonas
    See Ashbery, John (Lawrence)
    See also GLL 1
Berry, Wendell (Erdman) 1934- ... **CLC 4, 6,
    8, 27, 46; DAM POET; PC 28**
    See also AITN 1; CA 73-76; CANR 50, 73;
    DLB 5, 6, 234; MTCW 1
Berryman, John 1914-1972 ... **CLC 1, 2, 3, 4,
    6, 8, 10, 13, 25, 62; DAM POET**
    See also CA 13-16; 33-36R; CABS 2;
    CANR 35; CAP 1; CDALB 1941-1968;
    DLB 48; MTCW 1, 2
Bertolucci, Bernardo 1940- .... **CLC 16**
    See also CA 106
Berton, Pierre (Francis Demarigny)
    1920- .... **CLC 104**
    See also CA 1-4R; CANR 2, 56; DLB 68;
    SATA 99
Bertrand, Aloysius 1807-1841 .... **NCLC 31**
Bertran de Born c. 1140-1215 .... **CMLC 5**
Besant, Annie (Wood) 1847-1933 ..... **TCLC 9**
    See also CA 105; 185
Bessie, Alvah 1904-1985 .... **CLC 23**
    See also CA 5-8R; 116; CANR 2, 80; DLB
    26
Bethlen, T. D.
    See Silverberg, Robert
Beti, Mongo CLC 27; BLC 1; DAM MULT
    See also Biyidi, Alexandre
    See also CANR 79
Betjeman, John 1906-1984 ...... **CLC 2, 6, 10,
    34, 43; DAB; DAM MST, POET**
    See also CA 9-12R; 112; CANR 33, 56;
    CDBLB 1945-1960; DA3; DLB 20;
    DLBY 84; MTCW 1, 2
Bettelheim, Bruno 1903-1990 .... **CLC 79**
    See also CA 81-84; 131; CANR 23, 61;
    DA3; MTCW 1, 2
Betti, Ugo 1892-1953 .... **TCLC 5**
    See also CA 104; 155
Betts, Doris (Waugh) 1932- ...... **CLC 3, 6, 28**
    See also CA 13-16R; CANR 9, 66, 77;
    DLBY 82; INT CANR-9
Bevan, Alistair
    See Roberts, Keith (John Kingston)
Bey, Pilaff
    See Douglas, (George) Norman
Bialik, Chaim Nachman
    1873-1934 .... **TCLC 25**
    See also CA 170
Bickerstaff, Isaac
    See Swift, Jonathan
Bidart, Frank 1939- .... **CLC 33**
    See also CA 140
Bienek, Horst 1930- .... **CLC 7, 11**
    See also CA 73-76; DLB 75
Bierce, Ambrose (Gwinett)
    1842-1914(?) .... **TCLC 1, 7, 44; DA;
    DAC; DAM MST; SSC 9**
    See also AW; CA 104; 139; CANR 78;
    CDALB 1865-1917; DA3; DLB 11, 12,
    23, 71, 74, 186

Biggers, Earl Derr 1884-1933 .... **TCLC 65**
  See also CA 108; 153
Billings, Josh
  See Shaw, Henry Wheeler
Billington, (Lady) Rachel (Mary)
  1942- .... **CLC 43**
  See also AITN 2; CA 33-36R; CANR 44
Binyon, T(imothy) J(ohn) 1936- .... **CLC 34**
  See also CA 111; CANR 28
Bion 335B.C.-245B.C. .... **CMLC 39**
Bioy Casares, Adolfo 1914-1999 ... **CLC 4, 8,**
  13, 88; DAM MULT; HLC 1; SSC 17
  See also Miranda, Javier; Sacastru, Martin
  See also CA 29-32R; 177; CANR 19, 43,
  66; DLB 113; HW 1, 2; MTCW 1, 2
Bird, Cordwainer
  See Ellison, Harlan (Jay)
Bird, Robert Montgomery
  1806-1854 .... **NCLC 1**
  See also DLB 202
Birkerts, Sven 1951- .... **CLC 116**
  See also CA 128; 133; 176; CAAE 176;
  CAAS 29; INT 133
Birney, (Alfred) Earle 1904-1995 .. **CLC 1, 4,**
  6, 11; DAC; DAM MST, POET
  See also CA 1-4R; CANR 5, 20; DLB 88;
  MTCW 1
Biruni, al 973-1048(?) .... **CMLC 28**
Bishop, Elizabeth 1911-1979 ..... **CLC 1, 4, 9,**
  13, 15, 32; DA; DAC; DAM MST,
  POET; PC 3
  See also AMWS 1; CA 5-8R; 89-92; CABS
  2; CANR 26, 61; CDALB 1968-1988;
  DA3; DLB 5, 169; GLL 2; MTCW 1, 2;
  SATA-Obit 24
Bishop, John 1935- .... **CLC 10**
  See also CA 105
Bishop, John Peale 1892-1944 ..... **TCLC 103**
  See also CA 107; 155; DLB 4, 9, 45
Bissett, Bill 1939- .... **CLC 18; PC 14**
  See also CA 69-72; CAAS 19; CANR 15;
  CCA 1; DLB 53; MTCW 1
Bissoondath, Neil (Devindra)
  1955- .... **CLC 120; DAC**
  See also CA 136
Bitov, Andrei (Georgievich) 1937- ... **CLC 57**
  See also CA 142
Biyidi, Alexandre 1932-
  See Beti, Mongo
  See also BW 1, 3; CA 114; 124; CANR 81;
  DA3; MTCW 1, 2
Bjarme, Brynjolf
  See Ibsen, Henrik (Johan)
Bjoernson, Bjoernstjerne (Martinius)
  1832-1910 .... **TCLC 7, 37**
  See also CA 104
Black, Robert
  See Holdstock, Robert P.
Blackburn, Paul 1926-1971 .... **CLC 9, 43**
  See also CA 81-84; 33-36R; CANR 34;
  DLB 16; DLBY 81
Black Elk 1863-1950 .... **TCLC 33; DAM**
  MULT
  See also CA 144; MTCW 1; NNAL
Black Hobart
  See Sanders, (James) Ed(ward)
Blacklin, Malcolm
  See Chambers, Aidan
Blackmore, R(ichard) D(oddridge)
  1825-1900 .... **TCLC 27**
  See also CA 120; DLB 18
Blackmur, R(ichard) P(almer)
  1904-1965 .... **CLC 2, 24**
  See also AMWS 2; CA 11-12; 25-28R;
  CANR 71; CAP 1; DLB 63
Black Tarantula
  See Acker, Kathy

Blackwood, Algernon (Henry)
  1869-1951 .... **TCLC 5**
  See also CA 105; 150; DLB 153, 156, 178
Blackwood, Caroline 1931-1996 .... **CLC 6, 9,**
  100
  See also CA 85-88; 151; CANR 32, 61, 65;
  DLB 14, 207; MTCW 1
Blade, Alexander
  See Hamilton, Edmond; Silverberg, Robert
Blaga, Lucian 1895-1961 .... **CLC 75**
  See also CA 157; DLB 220
Blair, Eric (Arthur) 1903-1950
  See Orwell, George
  See also CA 104; 132; DA; DAB; DAC;
  DAM MST, NOV; DA3; MTCW 1, 2;
  SATA 29
Blair, Hugh 1718-1800 .... **NCLC 75**
Blais, Marie-Claire 1939- .... **CLC 2, 4, 6, 13,**
  22; DAC; DAM MST
  See also CA 21-24R; CAAS 4; CANR 38,
  75, 93; DLB 53; MTCW 1, 2
Blaise, Clark 1940- .... **CLC 29**
  See also AITN 2; CA 53-56; CAAS 3;
  CANR 5, 66; DLB 53
Blake, Fairley
  See De Voto, Bernard (Augustine)
Blake, Nicholas
  See Day Lewis, C(ecil)
  See also DLB 77
Blake, William 1757-1827 .... **NCLC 13, 37,**
  57; DA; DAB; DAC; DAM MST,
  POET; PC 12
  See also AW; CDBLB 1789-1832; CLR 52;
  DA3; DLB 93, 163; MAICYA; SATA 30
Blanchot, Maurice 1907- .... **CLC 135**
  See also CA 117; 144; DLB 72
Blasco Ibañez, Vicente
  1867-1928 .... **TCLC 12; DAM NOV**
  See also CA 110; 131; CANR 81; DA3; HW
  1, 2; MTCW 1
Blatty, William Peter 1928- .... **CLC 2; DAM**
  POP
  See also CA 5-8R; CANR 9
Bleeck, Oliver
  See Thomas, Ross (Elmore)
Blessing, Lee 1949- .... **CLC 54**
Blight, Rose
  See Greer, Germaine
Blish, James (Benjamin) 1921-1975 . **CLC 14**
  See also CA 1-4R; 57-60; CANR 3; DLB
  8; MTCW 1; SATA 66; SCFW 2
Bliss, Reginald
  See Wells, H(erbert) G(eorge)
Blixen, Karen (Christentze Dinesen)
  1885-1962
  See Dinesen, Isak
  See also CA 25-28; CANR 22, 50; CAP 2;
  DA3; MTCW 1, 2; SATA 44
Bloch, Robert (Albert) 1917-1994 .... **CLC 33**
  See also AAYA 29; CA 5-8R, 179; 146;
  CAAE 179; CAAS 20; CANR 5, 78;
  DA3; DLB 44; INT CANR-5; MTCW 1;
  SATA 12; SATA-Obit 82
Blok, Alexander (Alexandrovich)
  1880-1921 .... **TCLC 5; PC 21**
  See also CA 104; 183
Blom, Jan
  See Breytenbach, Breyten
Bloom, Harold 1930- .... **CLC 24, 103**
  See also CA 13-16R; CANR 39, 75, 92;
  DLB 67; MTCW 1
Bloomfield, Aurelius
  See Bourne, Randolph S(illiman)
Blount, Roy (Alton), Jr. 1941- .... **CLC 38**
  See also CA 53-56; CANR 10, 28, 61; INT
  CANR-28; MTCW 1, 2
Bloy, Leon 1846-1917 .... **TCLC 22**
  See also CA 121; 183; DLB 123

Blume, Judy (Sussman) 1938- .. **CLC 12, 30;**
  DAM NOV, POP
  See also AAYA 3, 26; CA 29-32R; CANR
  13, 37, 66; CLR 2, 15, 69; DA3; DLB 52;
  JRDA; MAICYA; MTCW 1, 2; SATA 2,
  31, 79
Blunden, Edmund (Charles)
  1896-1974 .... **CLC 2, 56**
  See also CA 17-18; 45-48; CANR 54; CAP
  2; DLB 20, 100, 155; MTCW 1
Bly, Robert (Elwood) 1926- .... **CLC 1, 2, 5,**
  10, 15, 38, 128; DAM POET
  See also AMWS 4; CA 5-8R; CANR 41,
  73; DA3; DLB 5; MTCW 1, 2
Boas, Franz 1858-1942 .... **TCLC 56**
  See also CA 115; 181
Bobette
  See Simenon, Georges (Jacques Christian)
Boccaccio, Giovanni 1313-1375 ... **CMLC 13;**
  SSC 10
Bochco, Steven 1943- .... **CLC 35**
  See also AAYA 11; CA 124; 138
Bodel, Jean 1167(?)-1210 .... **CMLC 28**
Bodenheim, Maxwell 1892-1954 .... **TCLC 44**
  See also CA 110; 187; DLB 9, 45
Bodker, Cecil 1927- .... **CLC 21**
  See also CA 73-76; CANR 13, 44; CLR 23;
  MAICYA; SATA 14
Boell, Heinrich (Theodor)
  1917-1985 ..... **CLC 2, 3, 6, 9, 11, 15, 27,**
  32, 72; DA; DAB; DAC; DAM MST,
  NOV; SSC 23
  See also AW; CA 21-24R; 116; CANR 24;
  DA3; DLB 69; DLBY 85; MTCW 1, 2
Boerne, Alfred
  See Doeblin, Alfred
Boethius 480(?)-524(?) .... **CMLC 15**
  See also DLB 115
Boff, Leonardo (Genezio Darci) 1938-
  See also CA 150; DAM MULT; HLC 1;
  HW 2
Bogan, Louise 1897-1970 .... **CLC 4, 39, 46,**
  93; DAM POET; PC 12
  See also AMWS 3; CA 73-76; 25-28R;
  CANR 33, 82; DLB 45, 169; MTCW 1, 2
Bogarde, Dirk
  See Van Den Bogarde, Derek Jules Gaspard
  Ulric Niven
Bogosian, Eric 1953- .... **CLC 45, 141**
  See also CA 138
Bograd, Larry 1953- .... **CLC 35**
  See also CA 93-96; CANR 57; SAAS 21;
  SATA 33, 89
Boiardo, Matteo Maria 1441-1494 .... **LC 6**
Boileau-Despreaux, Nicolas 1636-1711 . **LC 3**
Bojer, Johan 1872-1959 .... **TCLC 64**
  See also CA 189
Bok, Edward W. 1863-1930 .... **TCLC 101**
  See also DLB 91; DLBD 16
Boland, Eavan (Aisling) 1944- .. **CLC 40, 67,**
  113; DAM POET
  See also BRWS 5; CA 143; CANR 61; DLB
  40; MTCW 2
Böll, Heinrich
  See Boell, Heinrich (Theodor)
Bolt, Lee
  See Faust, Frederick (Schiller)
Bolt, Robert (Oxton) 1924-1995 ...... **CLC 14;**
  DAM DRAM
  See also CA 17-20R; 147; CANR 35, 67;
  DLB 13, 233; MTCW 1
Bombal, Maria Luisa 1910-1980 ...... **SSC 37;**
  HLCS 1
  See also CA 127; CANR 72; HW 1
Bombet, Louis-Alexandre-Cesar
  See Stendhal

Bomkauf
See Kaufman, Bob (Garnell)
Bonaventura NCLC 35
See also DLB 90
Bond, Edward 1934- .... **CLC 4, 6, 13, 23; DAM DRAM**
See also BRWS 1; CA 25-28R; CANR 38, 67; DLB 13; MTCW 1
Bonham, Frank 1914-1989 .... **CLC 12**
See also AAYA 1; AW; CA 9-12R; CANR 4, 36; JRDA; MAICYA; SAAS 3; SATA 1, 49; SATA-Obit 62; TCWW 2
Bonnefoy, Yves 1923- .. **CLC 9, 15, 58; DAM MST, POET**
See also CA 85-88; CANR 33, 75; CWW 2; MTCW 1, 2
Bontemps, Arna(ud Wendell)
1902-1973 ..... **CLC 1, 18; BLC 1; DAM MULT, NOV, POET**
See also BW 1; CA 1-4R; 41-44R; CANR 4, 35; CLR 6; DA3; DLB 48, 51; JRDA; MAICYA; MTCW 1, 2; SATA 2, 44; SATA-Obit 24
Booth, Martin 1944- .... **CLC 13**
See also CA 93-96; CAAE 188; CAAS 2; CANR 92
Booth, Philip 1925- .... **CLC 23**
See also CA 5-8R; CANR 5, 88; DLBY 82
Booth, Wayne C(layson) 1921- .... **CLC 24**
See also CA 1-4R; CAAS 5; CANR 3, 43; DLB 67
Borchert, Wolfgang 1921-1947 .... **TCLC 5**
See also CA 104; 188; DLB 69, 124
Borel, Petrus 1809-1859 .... **NCLC 41**
Borges, Jorge Luis 1899-1986 ... **CLC 1, 2, 3, 4, 6, 8, 9, 10, 13, 19, 44, 48, 83; DA; DAB; DAC; DAM MST, MULT; HLC 1; PC 22, 32; SSC 4, 41**
See also AAYA 26; AW; CA 21-24R; CANR 19, 33, 75; DA3; DLB 113; DLBY 86; HW 1, 2; MTCW 1, 2
Borowski, Tadeusz 1922-1951 .... **TCLC 9**
See also CA 106; 154
Borrow, George (Henry)
1803-1881 .... **NCLC 9**
See also DLB 21, 55, 166
Bosch (Gavino), Juan 1909-
See also CA 151; DAM MST, MULT; DLB 145; HLCS 1; HW 1, 2
Bosman, Herman Charles
1905-1951 .... **TCLC 49**
See also Malan, Herman
See also CA 160, DLB 225
Bosschere, Jean de 1878(?)-1953 ... **TCLC 19**
See also CA 115; 186
Boswell, James 1740-1795 ...... **LC 4, 50; DA; DAB; DAC; DAM MST**
See also AW; CDBLB 1660-1789; DLB 104, 142
Bottomley, Gordon 1874-1948 ..... **TCLC 107**
See also CA 120; DLB 10
Bottoms, David 1949- .... **CLC 53**
See also CA 105; CANR 22; DLB 120; DLBY 83
Boucicault, Dion 1820-1890 .... **NCLC 41**
Boucolon, Maryse
See Conde, Maryse
Bourget, Paul (Charles Joseph)
1852-1935 .... **TCLC 12**
See also CA 107; DLB 123
Bourjaily, Vance (Nye) 1922- .... **CLC 8, 62**
See also CA 1-4R; CAAS 1; CANR 2, 72; DLB 2, 143
Bourne, Randolph S(illiman)
1886-1918 .... **TCLC 16**
See also CA 117; 155; DLB 63

Bova, Ben(jamin William) 1932- ...... **CLC 45**
See also AAYA 16; CA 5-8R; CAAS 18; CANR 11, 56, 94; CLR 3; DLBY 81; INT CANR-11; MAICYA; MTCW 1; SATA 6, 68
Bowen, Elizabeth (Dorothea Cole)
1899-1973 . **CLC 1, 3, 6, 11, 15, 22, 118; DAM NOV; SSC 3, 28**
See also BRWS 2; CA 17-18; 41-44R; CANR 35; CAP 2; CDBLB 1945-1960; DA3; DLB 15, 162; MTCW 1, 2
Bowering, George 1935- .... **CLC 15, 47**
See also CA 21-24R; CAAS 16; CANR 10; DLB 53
Bowering, Marilyn R(uthe) 1949- .... **CLC 32**
See also CA 101; CANR 49
Bowers, Edgar 1924-2000 .... **CLC 9**
See also CA 5-8R; 188; CANR 24; DLB 5
Bowie, David CLC 17
See also Jones, David Robert
Bowles, Jane (Sydney) 1917-1973 ..... **CLC 3, 68**
See also CA 19-20; 41-44R; CAP 2
Bowles, Paul (Frederick) 1910-1999 . **CLC 1, 2, 19, 53; SSC 3**
See also AMWS 4; CA 1-4R; 186; CAAS 1; CANR 1, 19, 50, 75; DA3; DLB 5, 6; MTCW 1, 2
Box, Edgar
See Vidal, Gore
See also GLL 1
Boyd, Nancy
See Millay, Edna St. Vincent
See also GLL 1
Boyd, William 1952- .... **CLC 28, 53, 70**
See also CA 114; 120; CANR 51, 71; DLB 231
Boyle, Kay 1902-1992 .... **CLC 1, 5, 19, 58, 121; SSC 5**
See also CA 13-16R; 140; CAAS 1; CANR 29, 61; DLB 4, 9, 48, 86; DLBY 93; MTCW 1, 2
Boyle, Mark
See Kienzle, William X(avier)
Boyle, Patrick 1905-1982 .... **CLC 19**
See also CA 127
Boyle, T. C.
See Boyle, T(homas) Coraghessan
Boyle, T(homas) Coraghessan
1948- .... **CLC 36, 55, 90; DAM POP; SSC 16**
See also BEST 90:4; CA 120, CANR 44, 76, 89; DA3; DLBY 86; MTCW 2
Boz
See Dickens, Charles (John Huffam)
Brackenridge, Hugh Henry
1748-1816 .... **NCLC 7**
See also DLB 11, 37
Bradbury, Edward P.
See Moorcock, Michael (John)
See also MTCW 2
Bradbury, Malcolm (Stanley)
1932-2000 .... **CLC 32, 61; DAM NOV**
See also CA 1-4R; CANR 1, 33, 91; DA3; DLB 14, 207; MTCW 1, 2
Bradbury, Ray (Douglas) 1920- .... **CLC 1, 3, 10, 15, 42, 98; DA; DAB; DAC; DAM MST, NOV, POP; SSC 29**
See also AAYA 15; AITN 1, 2; AMWS 4; AW; CA 1-4R; CANR 2, 30, 75; CDALB 1968-1988; DA3; DLB 2, 8; MTCW 1, 2; SATA 11, 64; SCFW 2
Bradford, Gamaliel 1863-1932 .... **TCLC 36**
See also CA 160; DLB 17
Bradford, William 1590-1657 .... **LC 64**
See also DLB 24, 30

Bradley, David (Henry), Jr. 1950- ... **CLC 23, 118; BLC 1; DAM MULT**
See also BW 1, 3; CA 104; CANR 26, 81; DLB 33
Bradley, John Ed(mund, Jr.) 1958- . **CLC 55**
See also CA 139
Bradley, Marion Zimmer
1930-1999 .... **CLC 30; DAM POP**
See also Chapman, Lee; Dexter, John; Gardner, Miriam; Ives, Morgan; Rivers, Elfrida
See also AAYA 9; AW; CA 57-60; 185; CAAS 10; CANR 7, 31, 51, 75; DA3; DLB 8; MTCW 1, 2; SATA 90; SATA-Obit 116
Bradstreet, Anne 1612(?)-1672 ...... **LC 4, 30; DA; DAC; DAM MST, POET; PC 10**
See also AMWS 1; CDALB 1640-1865; DA3; DLB 24
Brady, Joan 1939- .... **CLC 86**
See also CA 141
Bragg, Melvyn 1939- .... **CLC 10**
See also BEST 89:3; CA 57-60; CANR 10, 48, 89; DLB 14
Brahe, Tycho 1546-1601 .... **LC 45**
Braine, John (Gerard) 1922-1986 . **CLC 1, 3, 41**
See also CA 1-4R; 120; CANR 1, 33; CDBLB 1945-1960; DLB 15; DLBY 86; MTCW 1
Bramah, Ernest 1868-1942 .... **TCLC 72**
See also CA 156; DLB 70
Brammer, William 1930(?)-1978 ...... **CLC 31**
See also CA 77-80
Brancati, Vitaliano 1907-1954 .... **TCLC 12**
See also CA 109
Brancato, Robin F(idler) 1936- .... **CLC 35**
See also AAYA 9; CA 69-72; CANR 11, 45; CLR 32; JRDA; SAAS 9; SATA 97
Brand, Max
See Faust, Frederick (Schiller)
See also TCWW 2
Brand, Millen 1906-1980 .... **CLC 7**
See also CA 21-24R; 97-100; CANR 72
Branden, Barbara CLC 44
See also CA 148
Brandes, Georg (Morris Cohen)
1842-1927 .... **TCLC 10**
See also CA 105; 189
Brandys, Kazimierz 1916-2000 .... **CLC 62**
Branley, Franklyn M(ansfield)
1915- .... **CLC 21**
See also CA 33-36R; CANR 14, 39; CLR 13; MAICYA; SAAS 16; SATA 4, 68
Brathwaite, Edward (Kamau)
1930- ...... **CLC 11; BLCS; DAM POET**
See also BW 2, 3; CA 25-28R; CANR 11, 26, 47; DLB 125
Brautigan, Richard (Gary)
1935-1984 .... **CLC 1, 3, 5, 9, 12, 34, 42; DAM NOV**
See also CA 53-56; 113; CANR 34; DA3; DLB 2, 5, 206; DLBY 80, 84; MTCW 1; SATA 56
Brave Bird, Mary
See Crow Dog, Mary (Ellen)
See also NNAL
Braverman, Kate 1950- .... **CLC 67**
See also CA 89-92
Brecht, (Eugen) Bertolt (Friedrich)
1898-1956 .... **TCLC 1, 6, 13, 35; DA; DAB; DAC; DAM DRAM, MST; DC 3**
See also AW; CA 104; 133; CANR 62; DA3; DLB 56, 124; MTCW 1, 2
Brecht, Eugen Berthold Friedrich
See Brecht, (Eugen) Bertolt (Friedrich)
Bremer, Fredrika 1801-1865 .... **NCLC 11**
Brennan, Christopher John
1870-1932 .... **TCLC 17**
See also CA 117; 188; DLB 230

Brennan, Maeve 1917-1993 .... CLC 5
See also CA 81-84; CANR 72
Brent, Linda
See Jacobs, Harriet A(nn)
Brentano, Clemens (Maria)
1778-1842 .... NCLC 1
See also DLB 90
Brent of Bin Bin
See Franklin, (Stella Maria Sarah) Miles
(Lampe)
Brenton, Howard 1942- .... CLC 31
See also CA 69-72; CANR 33, 67; DLB 13;
MTCW 1
Breslin, James 1935-1996
See Breslin, Jimmy
See also CA 73-76; CANR 31, 75; DAM
NOV; MTCW 1, 2
Breslin, Jimmy CLC 4, 43
See also Breslin, James
See also AITN 1; DLB 185; MTCW 2
Bresson, Robert 1901(?)-1999 .... CLC 16
See also CA 110; 187; CANR 49
Breton, Andre 1896-1966 .. CLC 2, 9, 15, 54;
PC 15
See also CA 19-20; 25-28R; CANR 40, 60;
CAP 2; DLB 65; MTCW 1, 2
Breytenbach, Breyten 1939(?)- .. CLC 23, 37,
126; DAM POET
See also CA 113; 129; CANR 61; CWW 2;
DLB 225
Bridgers, Sue Ellen 1942- .... CLC 26
See also AAYA 8; AW; CA 65-68; CANR
11, 36; CLR 18; DLB 52; JRDA; MAI-
CYA; SAAS 1; SATA 22, 90; SATA-Essay
109
Bridges, Robert (Seymour)
1844-1930 ... TCLC 1; DAM POET; PC
28
See also CA 104; 152; CDBLB 1890-1914;
DLB 19, 98
Bridie, James TCLC 3
See also Mavor, Osborne Henry
See also DLB 10
Brin, David 1950- .... CLC 34
See also AAYA 21; CA 102; CANR 24, 70;
INT CANR-24; SATA 65; SCFW 2
Brink, Andre (Philippus) 1935- . CLC 18, 36,
106
See also CA 104; CANR 39, 62; DLB 225;
INT 103; MTCW 1, 2
Brinsmead, H(esba) F(ay) 1922- ...... CLC 21
See also CA 21-24R; CANR 10; CLR 47;
MAICYA; SAAS 5; SATA 18, 78
Brittain, Vera (Mary) 1893(?)-1970 . CLC 23
See also CA 13-16; 25-28R; CANR 58;
CAP 1; DLB 191; MTCW 1, 2
Broch, Hermann 1886-1951 .... TCLC 20
See also CA 117; DLB 85, 124
Brock, Rose
See Hansen, Joseph
See also GLL 1
Brodkey, Harold (Roy) 1930-1996 ... CLC 56
See also CA 111; 151; CANR 71; DLB 130
Brodsky, Iosif Alexandrovich 1940-1996
See Brodsky, Joseph
See also AITN 1; CA 41-44R; 151; CANR
37; DAM POET; DA3; MTCW 1, 2
Brodsky, Joseph CLC 4, 6, 13, 36, 100; PC 9
See also Brodsky, Iosif Alexandrovich
See also CWW 2; MTCW 1
Brodsky, Michael (Mark) 1948- .... CLC 19
See also CA 102; CANR 18, 41, 58
Brome, Richard 1590(?)-1652 .... LC 61
See also DLB 58
Bromell, Henry 1947- .... CLC 5
See also CA 53-56; CANR 9
Bromfield, Louis (Brucker)
1896-1956 .... TCLC 11
See also CA 107; 155; DLB 4, 9, 86

Broner, E(sther) M(asserman)
1930- .... CLC 19
See also CA 17-20R; CANR 8, 25, 72; DLB
28
Bronk, William (M.) 1918-1999 .... CLC 10
See also CA 89-92; 177; CANR 23; DLB
165
Bronstein, Lev Davidovich
See Trotsky, Leon
Brontë, Anne 1820-1849 .... NCLC 4, 71
See also DA3; DLB 21, 199
Brontë, Charlotte 1816-1855 ...... NCLC 3, 8,
33, 58; DA; DAB; DAC; DAM MST,
NOV
See also AAYA 17; AW; CDBLB 1832-
1890; DA3; DLB 21, 159, 199
Brontë, Emily (Jane) 1818-1848 ... NCLC 16,
35; DA; DAB; DAC; DAM MST, NOV,
POET; PC 8
See also AAYA 17; AW; CDBLB 1832-
1890; DA3; DLB 21, 32, 199
Brontës
See Brontë
Brooke, Frances 1724-1789 .... LC 6, 48
See also DLB 39, 99
Brooke, Henry 1703(?)-1783 .... LC 1
See also DLB 39
Brooke, Rupert (Chawner)
1887-1915 .... TCLC 2, 7; DA; DAB;
DAC; DAM MST, POET; PC 24
See also AW; BRWS 3; CA 104; 132;
CANR 61; CDBLB 1914-1945; DLB 19;
GLL 2; MTCW 1, 2
Brooke-Haven, P.
See Wodehouse, P(elham) G(renville)
Brooke-Rose, Christine 1926(?)- ...... CLC 40
See also BRWS 4; CA 13-16R; CANR 58;
DLB 14, 231
Brookner, Anita 1928- . CLC 32, 34, 51, 136;
DAB; DAM POP
See also BRWS 4; CA 114; 120; CANR 37,
56, 87; DA3; DLB 194; DLBY 87;
MTCW 1, 2
Brooks, Cleanth 1906-1994 . CLC 24, 86, 110
See also CA 17-20R; 145; CANR 33, 35;
DLB 63; DLBY 94; INT CANR-35;
MTCW 1, 2
Brooks, George
See Baum, L(yman) Frank
Brooks, Gwendolyn 1917-2000 . CLC 1, 2, 4,
5, 15, 49, 125; BLC 1; DA; DAC;
DAM MST, MULT, POET; PC 7
See also AAYA 20; AITN 1; AMWS 3; AW;
BW 2, 3; CA 1-4R; CANR 1, 27, 52, 75;
CDALB 1941-1968; CLR 27; DA3; DLB
5, 76, 165; MTCW 1, 2; SATA 6
Brooks, Mel CLC 12
See also Kaminsky, Melvin
See also AAYA 13; DLB 26
Brooks, Peter 1938- .... CLC 34
See also CA 45-48; CANR 1
Brooks, Van Wyck 1886-1963 .... CLC 29
See also CA 1-4R; CANR 6; DLB 45, 63,
103
Brophy, Brigid (Antonia)
1929-1995 .... CLC 6, 11, 29, 105
See also CA 5-8R; 149; CAAS 4; CANR
25, 53; DA3; DLB 14; MTCW 1, 2
Brosman, Catharine Savage 1934- ..... CLC 9
See also CA 61-64; CANR 21, 46
Brossard, Nicole 1943- .... CLC 115
See also CA 122; CAAS 16; CCA 1; CWW
2; DLB 53; GLL 2
Brother Antoninus
See Everson, William (Oliver)
The Brothers Quay
See Quay, Stephen; Quay, Timothy
Broughton, T(homas) Alan 1936- ..... CLC 19
See also CA 45-48; CANR 2, 23, 48

Broumas, Olga 1949- .... CLC 10, 73
See also CA 85-88; CANR 20, 69; GLL 2
Broun, Heywood 1888-1939 .... TCLC 104
See also DLB 29, 171
Brown, Alan 1950- .... CLC 99
See also CA 156
Brown, Charles Brockden
1771-1810 .... NCLC 22, 74
See also AMWS 1; CDALB 1640-1865;
DLB 37, 59, 73
Brown, Christy 1932-1981 .... CLC 63
See also CA 105; 104; CANR 72; DLB 14
Brown, Claude 1937- .... CLC 30; BLC 1;
DAM MULT
See also AAYA 7; BW 1, 3; CA 73-76;
CANR 81
Brown, Dee (Alexander) 1908- . CLC 18, 47;
DAM POP
See also AAYA 30; CA 13-16R; CAAS 6;
CANR 11, 45, 60; DA3; DLBY 80;
MTCW 1, 2; SATA 5, 110; TCWW 2
Brown, George
See Wertmueller, Lina
Brown, George Douglas
1869-1902 .... TCLC 28
See also CA 162
Brown, George Mackay 1921-1996 ... CLC 5,
48, 100
See also CA 21-24R; 151; CAAS 6; CANR
12, 37, 67; DLB 14, 27, 139; MTCW 1;
SATA 35
Brown, (William) Larry 1951- .... CLC 73
See also CA 130; 134; INT 133
Brown, Moses
See Barrett, William (Christopher)
Brown, Rita Mae 1944- .... CLC 18, 43, 79;
DAM NOV, POP
See also CA 45-48; CANR 2, 11, 35, 62,
95; DA3; INT CANR-11; MTCW 1, 2
Brown, Roderick (Langmere) Haig-
See Haig-Brown, Roderick (Langmere)
Brown, Rosellen 1939- .... CLC 32
See also CA 77-80; CAAS 10; CANR 14,
44
Brown, Sterling Allen 1901-1989 ...... CLC 1,
23, 59; BLC 1; DAM MULT, POET
See also BW 1, 3; CA 85-88; 127; CANR
26; DA3; DLB 48, 51, 63; MTCW 1, 2
Brown, Will
See Ainsworth, William Harrison
Brown, William Wells 1815-1884 ... NCLC 2,
89; BLC 1; DAM MULT; DC 1
See also DLB 3, 50
Browne, (Clyde) Jackson 1948(?)- ... CLC 21
See also CA 120
Browning, Elizabeth Barrett
1806-1861 ...... NCLC 1, 16, 61, 66; DA;
DAB; DAC; DAM MST, POET; PC 6
See also AW; CDBLB 1832-1890; DA3;
DLB 32, 199
Browning, Robert 1812-1889 . NCLC 19, 79;
DA; DAB; DAC; DAM MST, POET;
PC 2
See also AW; CDBLB 1832-1890; DA3;
DLB 32, 163
Browning, Tod 1882-1962 .... CLC 16
See also CA 141; 117
Brownson, Orestes Augustus
1803-1876 .... NCLC 50
See also DLB 1, 59, 73
Bruccoli, Matthew J(oseph) 1931- ... CLC 34
See also CA 9-12R; CANR 7, 87; DLB 103
Bruce, Lenny CLC 21
See also Schneider, Leonard Alfred
Bruin, John
See Brutus, Dennis
Brulard, Henri
See Stendhal

Brulls, Christian
See Simenon, Georges (Jacques Christian)

Brunner, John (Kilian Houston)
1934-1995 .... **CLC 8, 10; DAM POP**
See also CA 1-4R; 149; CAAS 8; CANR 2,
37; MTCW 1, 2; SCFW 2

Bruno, Giordano 1548-1600 .... **LC 27**

Brutus, Dennis 1924- .... **CLC 43; BLC 1;
DAM MULT, POET; PC 24**
See also BW 2, 3; CA 49-52; CAAS 14;
CANR 2, 27, 42, 81; DLB 117, 225

Bryan, C(ourtlandt) D(ixon) B(arnes)
1936- .... **CLC 29**
See also CA 73-76; CANR 13, 68; DLB
185; INT CANR-13

Bryan, Michael
See Moore, Brian
See also CCA 1

Bryan, William Jennings
1860-1925 .... **TCLC 99**

Bryant, William Cullen 1794-1878 . **NCLC 6,
46; DA; DAB; DAC; DAM MST,
POET; PC 20**
See also AMWS 1; CDALB 1640-1865;
DLB 3, 43, 59, 189

Bryusov, Valery Yakovlevich
1873-1924 .... **TCLC 10**
See also CA 107; 155

Buchan, John 1875-1940 .... **TCLC 41; DAB;
DAM POP**
See also AW 2; CA 108; 145; DLB 34, 70,
156; MTCW 1

Buchanan, George 1506-1582 .... **LC 4**
See also DLB 152

Buchanan, Robert 1841-1901 .... **TCLC 107**
See also CA 179; DLB 18, 35

Buchheim, Lothar-Guenther 1918- .... **CLC 6**
See also CA 85-88

Büchner, (Karl) Georg 1813-1837 . **NCLC 26**

Buchwald, Art(hur) 1925- .... **CLC 33**
See also AITN 1; CA 5-8R; CANR 21, 67;
MTCW 1, 2; SATA 10

Buck, Pearl S(ydenstricker)
1892-1973 .... **CLC 7, 11, 18, 127; DA;
DAB; DAC; DAM MST, NOV**
See also AITN 1; AMWS 2; CA 1-4R; 41-
44R; CANR 1, 34; CDALBS; DA3; DLB
9, 102; MTCW 1, 2; SATA 1, 25

Buckler, Ernest 1908-1984 .... **CLC 13; DAC;
DAM MST**
See also CA 11-12; 114; CAP 1; CCA 1;
DLB 68; SATA 47

Buckley, Vincent (Thomas)
1925-1988 .... **CLC 57**
See also CA 101

Buckley, William F(rank), Jr. 1925- . **CLC 7,
18, 37; DAM POP**
See also AITN 1; CA 1-4R; CANR 1, 24,
53, 93; DA3; DLB 137; DLBY 80; INT
CANR-24; MTCW 1, 2

Buechner, (Carl) Frederick 1926- . **CLC 2, 4,
6, 9; DAM NOV**
See also CA 13-16R; CANR 11, 39, 64;
DLBY 80; INT CANR-11; MTCW 1, 2

Buell, John (Edward) 1927- .... **CLC 10**
See also CA 1-4R; CANR 71; DLB 53

Buero Vallejo, Antonio 1916-2000 ... **CLC 15,
46, 139**
See also CA 106; 189; CANR 24, 49, 75;
HW 1; MTCW 1, 2

Bufalino, Gesualdo 1920(?)-1990 ...... **CLC 74**
See also CWW 2; DLB 196

Bugayev, Boris Nikolayevich
1880-1934 .... **TCLC 7; PC 11**
See also Bely, Andrey
See also CA 104; 165; MTCW 1

Bukowski, Charles 1920-1994 ... **CLC 2, 5, 9,
41, 82, 108; DAM NOV, POET; PC 18**
See also CA 17-20R; 144; CANR 40, 62;
DA3; DLB 5, 130, 169; MTCW 1, 2

Bulgakov, Mikhail (Afanas'evich)
1891-1940 . **TCLC 2, 16; DAM DRAM,
NOV; SSC 18**
See also CA 105; 152

Bulgya, Alexander Alexandrovich
1901-1956 .... **TCLC 53**
See also Fadeyev, Alexander
See also CA 117; 181

Bullins, Ed 1935- .... **CLC 1, 5, 7; BLC 1;
DAM DRAM, MULT; DC 6**
See also BW 2, 3; CA 49-52; CAAS 16;
CANR 24, 46, 73; DLB 7, 38; MTCW 1,
2

**Bulwer-Lytton, Edward (George Earle
Lytton)** 1803-1873 .... **NCLC 1, 45**
See also DLB 21

Bunin, Ivan Alexeyevich
1870-1953 .... **TCLC 6; SSC 5**
See also CA 104

Bunting, Basil 1900-1985 ..... **CLC 10, 39, 47;
DAM POET**
See also CA 53-56; 115; CANR 7; DLB 20

Bunuel, Luis 1900-1983 .. **CLC 16, 80; DAM
MULT; HLC 1**
See also CA 101; 110; CANR 32, 77; HW
1

Bunyan, John 1628-1688 ... **LC 4; DA; DAB;
DAC; DAM MST**
See also AW; CDBLB 1660-1789; DLB 39

Burckhardt, Jacob (Christoph)
1818-1897 .... **NCLC 49**

Burford, Eleanor
See Hibbert, Eleanor Alice Burford

Burgess, Anthony **CLC 1, 2, 4, 5, 8, 10, 13,
15, 22, 40, 62, 81, 94; DAB**
See also Wilson, John (Anthony) Burgess
See also AAYA 25; AITN 1; AW; BRWS 1;
CDBLB 1960 to Present; DLB 14, 194,
DLBY 98; MTCW 1

Burke, Edmund 1729(?)-1797 .... **LC 7, 36;
DA; DAB; DAC; DAM MST**
See also AW; DA3; DLB 104

Burke, Kenneth (Duva) 1897-1993 ... **CLC 2,
24**
See also CA 5-8R; 143; CANR 39, 74; DLB
45, 63; MTCW 1, 2

Burke, Leda
See Garnett, David

Burke, Ralph
See Silverberg, Robert

Burke, Thomas 1886-1945 .... **TCLC 63**
See also CA 113; 155; DLB 197

Burney, Fanny 1752-1840 .... **NCLC 12, 54**
See also BRWS 3; DLB 39

Burney, Frances
See Burney, Fanny

Burns, Robert 1759-1796 . **LC 3, 29, 40; DA;
DAB; DAC; DAM MST, POET; PC 6**
See also AW; CDBLB 1789-1832; DA3;
DLB 109

Burns, Tex
See L'Amour, Louis (Dearborn)
See also TCWW 2

Burnshaw, Stanley 1906- .... **CLC 3, 13, 44**
See also CA 9-12R; DLB 48; DLBY 97

Burr, Anne 1937- .... **CLC 6**
See also CA 25-28R

Burroughs, Edgar Rice 1875-1950 . **TCLC 2,
32; DAM NOV**
See also AAYA 11; AW; CA 104; 132; DA3;
DLB 8; MTCW 1, 2; SATA 41

Burroughs, William S(eward)
1914-1997 .. **CLC 1, 2, 5, 15, 22, 42, 75,
109; DA; DAB; DAC; DAM MST,
NOV, POP**
See also Lee, William; Lee, Willy
See also AITN 2; AMWS 3; AW; CA
9-12R; 160; CANR 20, 52; DA3; DLB 2,
8, 16, 152; DLBY 81, 97; MTCW 1, 2

Burton, SirRichard F(rancis)
1821-1890 .... **NCLC 42**
See also DLB 55, 166, 184

Busch, Frederick 1941- .... **CLC 7, 10, 18, 47**
See also CA 33-36R; CAAS 1; CANR 45,
73, 92; DLB 6

Bush, Ronald 1946- .... **CLC 34**
See also CA 136

Bustos, F(rancisco)
See Borges, Jorge Luis

Bustos Domecq, H(onorio)
See Bioy Casares, Adolfo; Borges, Jorge
Luis

Butler, Octavia E(stelle) 1947- .... **CLC 38,
121; BLCS; DAM MULT, POP**
See also AAYA 18; AW; BW 2, 3; CA 73-
76; CANR 12, 24, 38, 73; CLR 65; DA3;
DLB 33; MTCW 1, 2; SATA 84

Butler, Robert Olen, (Jr.) 1945- ...... **CLC 81;
DAM POP**
See also CA 112; CANR 66; DLB 173; INT
112; MTCW 1

Butler, Samuel 1612-1680 .... **LC 16, 43**
See also DLB 101, 126

Butler, Samuel 1835-1902 . **TCLC 1, 33; DA;
DAB; DAC; DAM MST, NOV**
See also AW; BRWS 2; CA 143; CDBLB
1890-1914; DA3; DLB 18, 57, 174

Butler, Walter C.
See Faust, Frederick (Schiller)

Butor, Michel (Marie Francois)
1926- .... **CLC 1, 3, 8, 11, 15**
See also CA 9-12R; CANR 33, 66; DLB
83; MTCW 1, 2

Butts, Mary 1890(?)-1937 .... **TCLC 77**
See also CA 148

Buzo, Alexander (John) 1944- .... **CLC 61**
See also CA 97-100; CANR 17, 39, 69

Buzzati, Dino 1906-1972 .... **CLC 36**
See also CA 160; 33-36R; DLB 177

Byars, Betsy (Cromer) 1928- .... **CLC 35**
See also AAYA 19; CA 33-36R, 183; CAAE
183; CANR 18, 36, 57; CLR 1, 16; DLB
52; INT CANR-18; JRDA; MAICYA;
MTCW 1; SAAS 1; SATA 4, 46, 80;
SATA-Essay 108

Byatt, A(ntonia) S(usan Drabble)
1936- ...... **CLC 19, 65, 136; DAM NOV,
POP**
See also BRWS 4; CA 13-16R; CANR 13,
33, 50, 75, 96; DA3; DLB 14, 194;
MTCW 1, 2

Byrne, David 1952- .... **CLC 26**
See also CA 127

Byrne, John Keyes 1926-
See Leonard, Hugh
See also CA 102; CANR 78; INT 102

Byron, George Gordon (Noel)
1788-1824 .... **NCLC 2, 12; DA; DAB;
DAC; DAM MST, POET; PC 16**
See also AW; CDBLB 1789-1832; DA3;
DLB 96, 110

Byron, Robert 1905-1941 .... **TCLC 67**
See also CA 160; DLB 195

C. 3. 3.
See Wilde, Oscar (Fingal O'Flahertie Wills)

Caballero, Fernan 1796-1877 .... **NCLC 10**

Cabell, Branch
See Cabell, James Branch

Cabell, James Branch 1879-1958 .... **TCLC 6**
See also CA 105; 152; DLB 9, 78; MTCW
1

Cabeza de Vaca, Alvar Nunez
1490-1557(?) .... **LC 61**

Cable, George Washington
1844-1925 .... **TCLC 4; SSC 4**
See also CA 104; 155; DLB 12, 74; DLBD
13

Cabral de Melo Neto, João
1920-1999 .... **CLC 76; DAM MULT**
See also CA 151

Cabrera Infante, G(uillermo) 1929- . **CLC 5,**
25, 45, 120; DAM MULT; HLC 1; SSC
39
See also CA 85-88; CANR 29, 65; DA3;
DLB 113; HW 1, 2; MTCW 1, 2

Cade, Toni
See Bambara, Toni Cade

Cadmus and Harmonia
See Buchan, John

Caedmon fl. 658-680 .... **CMLC 7**
See also DLB 146

Caeiro, Alberto
See Pessoa, Fernando (Antonio Nogueira)

Cage, John (Milton, Jr.) 1912-1992 . **CLC 41**
See also CA 13-16R; 169; CANR 9, 78;
DLB 193; INT CANR-9

Cahan, Abraham 1860-1951 .... **TCLC 71**
See also CA 108; 154; DLB 9, 25, 28

Cain, G.
See Cabrera Infante, G(uillermo)

Cain, Guillermo
See Cabrera Infante, G(uillermo)

Cain, James M(allahan) 1892-1977 .. **CLC 3,**
11, 28
See also AITN 1; CA 17-20R; 73-76;
CANR 8, 34, 61; DLB 226; MTCW 1

Caine, Hall 1853-1931 .... **TCLC 97**

Caine, Mark
See Raphael, Frederic (Michael)

Calasso, Roberto 1941- .... **CLC 81**
See also CA 143; CANR 89

Calderon de la Barca, Pedro
1600-1681 .... **LC 23; DC 3; HLCS 1**

Caldwell, Erskine (Preston)
1903-1987 .. **CLC 1, 8, 14, 50, 60; DAM**
NOV; SSC 19
See also AITN 1; CA 1-4R; 121; CAAS 1;
CANR 2, 33; DA3; DLB 9, 86; MTCW
1, 2

Caldwell, (Janet Miriam) Taylor (Holland)
1900-1985 .. **CLC 2, 28, 39; DAM NOV,**
POP
See also CA 5-8R; 116; CANR 5; DA3;
DLBD 17

Calhoun, John Caldwell
1782-1850 .... **NCLC 15**
See also DLB 3

Calisher, Hortense 1911- ..... **CLC 2, 4, 8, 38,**
134; DAM NOV; SSC 15
See also CA 1-4R; CANR 1, 22, 67; DA3;
DLB 2; INT CANR-22; MTCW 1, 2

Callaghan, Morley Edward
1903-1990 ...... **CLC 3, 14, 41, 65; DAC;**
DAM MST
See also CA 9-12R; 132; CANR 33, 73;
DLB 68; MTCW 1, 2

Callimachus c. 305B.C.-c.
240B.C. .... **CMLC 18**
See also DLB 176

Calvin, John 1509-1564 .... **LC 37**

Calvino, Italo 1923-1985 .... **CLC 5, 8, 11, 22,**
33, 39, 73; DAM NOV; SSC 3
See also CA 85-88; 116; CANR 23, 61;
DLB 196; MTCW 1, 2

Cameron, Carey 1952- .... **CLC 59**
See also CA 135

Cameron, Peter 1959- .... **CLC 44**
See also CA 125; CANR 50; DLB 234;
GLL 2

Camoëns, Luis Vaz de 1524(?)-1580
See also HLCS 1

Camoes, Luis de 1524(?)-1580 .... **LC 62;**
HLCS 1; PC 31

Campana, Dino 1885-1932 .... **TCLC 20**
See also CA 117; DLB 114

Campanella, Tommaso 1568-1639 .... **LC 32**

Campbell, John W(ood, Jr.)
1910-1971 .... **CLC 32**
See also CA 21-22; 29-32R; CANR 34;
CAP 2; DLB 8; MTCW 1

Campbell, Joseph 1904-1987 .... **CLC 69**
See also AAYA 3; BEST 89:2; CA 1-4R;
124; CANR 3, 28, 61; DA3; MTCW 1, 2

Campbell, Maria 1940- .... **CLC 85; DAC**
See also CA 102; CANR 54; CCA 1; NNAL

Campbell, (John) Ramsey 1946- ..... **CLC 42;**
SSC 19
See also CA 57-60; CANR 7; INT CANR-7

Campbell, (Ignatius) Roy (Dunnachie)
1901-1957 .... **TCLC 5**
See also CA 104; 155; DLB 20, 225;
MTCW 2

Campbell, Thomas 1777-1844 .... **NCLC 19**
See also DLB 93; 144

Campbell, Wilfred TCLC 9
See also Campbell, William

Campbell, William 1858(?)-1918
See Campbell, Wilfred
See also CA 106; DLB 92

Campion, Jane CLC 95
See also AAYA 33; CA 138; CANR 87

Camus, Albert 1913-1960 ...... **CLC 1, 2, 4, 9,**
11, 14, 32, 63, 69, 124; DA; DAB;
DAC; DAM DRAM, MST, NOV; DC
2; SSC 9
See also AAYA 36; AW; CA 89-92; DA3;
DLB 72; MTCW 1, 2

Canby, Vincent 1924-2000 .... **CLC 13**
See also CA 81-84

Cancale
See Desnos, Robert

Canetti, Elias 1905-1994 .. **CLC 3, 14, 25, 75,**
86
See also CA 21-24R; 146; CANR 23, 61,
79; CWW 2; DA3; DLB 85, 124; MTCW
1, 2

Canfield, Dorothea F.
See Fisher, Dorothy (Frances) Canfield

Canfield, Dorothea Frances
See Fisher, Dorothy (Frances) Canfield

Canfield, Dorothy
See Fisher, Dorothy (Frances) Canfield

Canin, Ethan 1960- .... **CLC 55**
See also CA 131; 135

Cankar, Ivan 1876-1918 .... **TCLC 105**
See also DLB 147

Cannon, Curt
See Hunter, Evan

Cao, Lan 1961- .... **CLC 109**
See also CA 165

Cape, Judith
See Page, P(atricia) K(athleen)
See also CCA 1

Capek, Karel 1890-1938 ... **TCLC 6, 37; DA;**
DAB; DAC; DAM DRAM, MST, NOV;
DC 1; SSC 36
See also AW; CA 104; 140; DA3; MTCW
1; SCFW 2

Capote, Truman 1924-1984 . **CLC 1, 3, 8, 13,**
19, 34, 38, 58; DA; DAB; DAC; DAM
MST, NOV, POP; SSC 2
See also AMWS 3; AW; CA 5-8R; 113;
CANR 18, 62; CDALB 1941-1968; DA3;
DLB 2, 185, 227; DLBY 80, 84; GLL 1;
MTCW 1, 2; SATA 91

Capra, Frank 1897-1991 .... **CLC 16**
See also CA 61-64; 135

Caputo, Philip 1941- .... **CLC 32**
See also AW; CA 73-76; CANR 40

Caragiale, Ion Luca 1852-1912 ...... **TCLC 76**
See also CA 157

Card, Orson Scott 1951- ..... **CLC 44, 47, 50;**
DAM POP
See also AAYA 11; AW; CA 102; CANR
27, 47, 73; DA3; INT CANR-27; MTCW
1, 2; SATA 83

Cardenal, Ernesto 1925- .... **CLC 31; DAM**
MULT, POET; HLC 1; PC 22
See also CA 49-52; CANR 2, 32, 66; CWW
2; HW 1, 2; MTCW 1, 2

Cardozo, Benjamin N(athan)
1870-1938 .... **TCLC 65**
See also CA 117; 164

Carducci, Giosue (Alessandro Giuseppe)
1835-1907 .... **TCLC 32**
See also CA 163

Carew, Thomas 1595(?)-1640 . **LC 13; PC 29**
See also DLB 126

Carey, Ernestine Gilbreth 1908- ...... **CLC 17**
See also CA 5-8R; CANR 71; SATA 2

Carey, Peter 1943- .... **CLC 40, 55, 96**
See also CA 123; 127; CANR 53, 76; INT
127; MTCW 1, 2; SATA 94

Carleton, William 1794-1869 .... **NCLC 3**
See also DLB 159

Carlisle, Henry (Coffin) 1926- .... **CLC 33**
See also CA 13-16R; CANR 15, 85

Carlsen, Chris
See Holdstock, Robert P.

Carlson, Ron(ald F.) 1947- .... **CLC 54**
See also CA 105; CAAE 189; CANR 27

Carlyle, Thomas 1795-1881 .... **NCLC 22, 70;**
DA; DAB; DAC; DAM MST
See also CDBLB 1789-1832; DLB 55; 144

Carman, (William) Bliss
1861-1929 .... **TCLC 7; DAC**
See also CA 104; 152; DLB 92

Carnegie, Dale 1888-1955 .... **TCLC 53**

Carossa, Hans 1878-1956 .... **TCLC 48**
See also CA 170; DLB 66

Carpenter, Don(ald Richard)
1931-1995 .... **CLC 41**
See also CA 45-48; 149; CANR 1, 71

Carpenter, Edward 1844-1929 .... **TCLC 88**
See also CA 163; GLL 1

Carpentier (y Valmont), Alejo
1904-1980 ..... **CLC 8, 11, 38, 110; DAM**
MULT; HLC 1; SSC 35
See also CA 65-68; 97-100; CANR 11, 70;
DLB 113; HW 1, 2

Carr, Caleb 1955(?)- .... **CLC 86**
See also CA 147; CANR 73; DA3

Carr, Emily 1871-1945 .... **TCLC 32**
See also CA 159; DLB 68; GLL 2

Carr, John Dickson 1906-1977 .... **CLC 3**
See also Fairbairn, Roger
See also CA 49-52; 69-72; CANR 3, 33,
60; MTCW 1, 2

Carr, Philippa
See Hibbert, Eleanor Alice Burford

Carr, Virginia Spencer 1929- .... **CLC 34**
See also CA 61-64; DLB 111

Carrere, Emmanuel 1957- .... **CLC 89**

Carrier, Roch 1937- .... **CLC 13, 78; DAC;**
DAM MST
See also CA 130; CANR 61; CCA 1; DLB
53; SATA 105

Carroll, James P. 1943(?)- .... **CLC 38**
See also CA 81-84; CANR 73; MTCW 1

Carroll, Jim 1951- .... CLC **35**
See also AAYA 17; CA 45-48; CANR 42

Carroll, Lewis NCLC **2, 53**; PC **18**
See also Dodgson, Charles Lutwidge
See also AW; CDBLB 1832-1890; CLR 2,
18; DLB 18, 163, 178; DLBY 98; JRDA

Carroll, Paul Vincent 1900-1968 ...... CLC **10**
See also CA 9-12R; 25-28R; DLB 10

Carruth, Hayden 1921- ..... CLC **4, 7, 10, 18,
84**; PC **10**
See also CA 9-12R; CANR 4, 38, 59; DLB
5, 165; INT CANR-4; MTCW 1, 2; SATA
47

Carson, Rachel Louise 1907-1964 ... CLC **71**;
DAM POP
See also CA 77-80; CANR 35; DA3;
MTCW 1, 2; SATA 23

Carter, Angela (Olive) 1940-1992 ...... CLC **5,
41, 76**; SSC **13**
See also BRWS 3; CA 53-56; 136; CANR
12, 36, 61; DA3; DLB 14, 207; MTCW
1, 2; SATA 66; SATA-Obit 70

Carter, Nick
See Smith, Martin Cruz

Carver, Raymond 1938-1988 ..... CLC **22, 36,
53, 55, 126**; DAM NOV; SSC **8**
See also AMWS 3; CA 33-36R; 126; CANR
17, 34, 61; DA3; DLB 130; DLBY 84,
88; MTCW 1, 2; TCWW 2

Cary, Elizabeth, Lady Falkland
1585-1639 .... LC **30**

Cary, (Arthur) Joyce (Lunel)
1888-1957 .... TCLC **1, 29**
See also CA 104; 164; CDBLB 1914-1945;
DLB 15, 100; MTCW 2

Casanova de Seingalt, Giovanni Jacopo
1725-1798 .... LC **13**

Casares, Adolfo Bioy
See Bioy Casares, Adolfo

Casely-Hayford, J(oseph) E(phraim)
1866-1903 ...... TCLC **24**; BLC **1**; DAM
MULT
See also BW 2; CA 123; 152

Casey, John (Dudley) 1939- .... CLC **59**
See also BEST 90:2; CA 69-72; CANR 23

Casey, Michael 1947- .... CLC **2**
See also CA 65-68; DLB 5

Casey, Patrick
See Thurman, Wallace (Henry)

Casey, Warren (Peter) 1935-1988 .... CLC **12**
See also CA 101; 127; INT 101

Casona, Alejandro CLC **49**
See also Alvarez, Alejandro Rodriguez

Cassavetes, John 1929-1989 .... CLC **20**
See also CA 85-88; 127; CANR 82

Cassian, Nina 1924- .... PC **17**
See also CWW 2

Cassill, R(onald) V(erlin) 1919- ... CLC **4, 23**
See also CA 9-12R; CAAS 1; CANR 7, 45;
DLB 6

Cassiodorus, Flavius Magnus c. 490(?)-c.
583(?) .... CMLC **43**

Cassirer, Ernst 1874-1945 .... TCLC **61**
See also CA 157

Cassity, (Allen) Turner 1929- .... CLC **6, 42**
See also CA 17-20R; CAAS 8; CANR 11;
DLB 105

Castaneda, Carlos (Cesar Aranha)
1931(?)-1998 .... CLC **12, 119**
See also CA 25-28R; CANR 32, 66; HW 1;
MTCW 1

Castedo, Elena 1937- .... CLC **65**
See also CA 132

Castedo-Ellerman, Elena
See Castedo, Elena

Castellanos, Rosario 1925-1974 .... CLC **66**;
DAM MULT; HLC **1**; SSC **39**
See also CA 131; 53-56; CANR 58; DLB
113; HW 1; MTCW 1

Castelvetro, Lodovico 1505-1571 .... LC **12**

Castiglione, Baldassare 1478-1529 ...... LC **12**

Castiglione, Baldesar
See Castiglione, Baldassare

Castle, Robert
See Hamilton, Edmond

Castro (Ruz), Fidel 1926(?)-
See also CA 110; 129; CANR 81; DAM
MULT; HLC 1; HW 2

Castro, Guillen de 1569-1631 .... LC **19**

Castro, Rosalia de 1837-1885 ... NCLC **3, 78**;
DAM MULT

Cather, Willa
See Cather, Willa Sibert
See also TCWW 2

Cather, Willa Sibert 1873-1947 ...... TCLC **1,
11, 31, 99**; DA; DAB; DAC; DAM
MST, NOV; SSC **2**
See also Cather, Willa
See also AAYA 24; AW; CA 104; 128;
CDALB 1865-1917; DA3; DLB 9, 54, 78;
DLBD 1; MTCW 1, 2; SATA 30

Catherine, Saint 1347-1380 .... CMLC **27**

Cato, Marcus Porcius
234B.C.-149B.C. .... CMLC **21**
See also DLB 211

Catton, (Charles) Bruce 1899-1978 . CLC **35**
See also AITN 1; CA 5-8R; 81-84; CANR
7, 74; DLB 17; SATA 2; SATA-Obit 24

Catullus c. 84B.C.-c. 54B.C. .... CMLC **18**
See also DLB 211

Cauldwell, Frank
See King, Francis (Henry)

Caunitz, William J. 1933-1996 .... CLC **34**
See also BEST 89:3; CA 125; 130; 152;
CANR 73; INT 130

Causley, Charles (Stanley) 1917- .... CLC **7**
See also CA 9-12R; CANR 5, 35, 94; CLR
30; DLB 27; MTCW 1; SATA 3, 66

Caute, (John) David 1936- .... CLC **29**; DAM
NOV
See also CA 1-4R; CAAS 4; CANR 1, 33,
64; DLB 14, 231

Cavafy, C(onstantine) P(eter) TCLC **2, 7**;
DAM POET
See also Kavafis, Konstantinos Petrou
See also CA 148; DA3; MTCW 1

Cavallo, Evelyn
See Spark, Muriel (Sarah)

Cavanna, Betty CLC **12**
See also Harrison, Elizabeth Cavanna
See also JRDA; MAICYA; SAAS 4; SATA
1, 30

Cavendish, Margaret Lucas
1623-1673 .... LC **30**
See also DLB 131

Caxton, William 1421(?)-1491(?) .... LC **17**
See also DLB 170

Cayer, D. M.
See Duffy, Maureen

Cayrol, Jean 1911- .... CLC **11**
See also CA 89-92; DLB 83

Cela, Camilo Jose 1916- .... CLC **4, 13, 59,
122**; DAM MULT; HLC **1**
See also BEST 90:2; CA 21-24R; CAAS
10; CANR 21, 32, 76; DLBY 89; HW 1;
MTCW 1, 2

Celan, Paul CLC **10, 19, 53, 82**; PC **10**
See also Antschel, Paul
See also DLB 69

Celine, Louis-Ferdinand CLC **1, 3, 4, 7, 9,
15, 47, 124**
See also Destouches, Louis-Ferdinand
See also DLB 72

Cellini, Benvenuto 1500-1571 .... LC **7**

Cendrars, Blaise CLC **18, 106**
See also Sauser-Hall, Frederic

Cernuda (y Bidon), Luis
1902-1963 .... CLC **54**; DAM POET
See also CA 131; 89-92; DLB 134; GLL 1;
HW 1

Cervantes, Lorna Dee 1954-
See also CA 131; CANR 80; DLB 82;
HLCS 1; HW 1

Cervantes (Saavedra), Miguel de
1547-1616 .. LC **6, 23**; DA; DAB; DAC;
DAM MST, NOV; SSC **12**
See also AW

Cesaire, Aime (Fernand) 1913- . CLC **19, 32,
112**; BLC **1**; DAM MULT, POET; PC
25
See also BW 2, 3; CA 65-68; CANR 24,
43, 81; DA3; MTCW 1, 2

Chabon, Michael 1963- .... CLC **55**
See also CA 139; CANR 57, 96

Chabrol, Claude 1930- .... CLC **16**
See also CA 110

Challans, Mary 1905-1983
See Renault, Mary
See also CA 81-84; 111; CANR 74; DA3;
MTCW 2; SATA 23; SATA-Obit 36

Challis, George
See Faust, Frederick (Schiller)
See also TCWW 2

Chambers, Aidan 1934- .... CLC **35**
See also AAYA 27; AW; CA 25-28R; CANR
12, 31, 58; JRDA; MAICYA; SAAS 12;
SATA 1, 69, 108

Chambers, James 1948-
See Cliff, Jimmy
See also CA 124

Chambers, Jessie
See Lawrence, D(avid) H(erbert Richards)
See also GLL 1

Chambers, Robert W(illiam)
1865-1933 .... TCLC **41**
See also CA 165; DLB 202; SATA 107

Chamisso, Adelbert von
1781-1838 .... NCLC **82**
See also DLB 90

Chandler, Raymond (Thornton)
1888-1959 .... TCLC **1, 7**; SSC **23**
See also AAYA 25; AMWS 4; CA 104; 129;
CANR 60; CDALB 1929-1941; DA3;
DLB 226; DLBD 6; MTCW 1, 2

Chang, Eileen 1921-1995 .... SSC **28**
See also CA 166; CWW 2

Chang, Jung 1952- .... CLC **71**
See also CA 142

Chang Ai-Ling
See Chang, Eileen

Channing, William Ellery
1780-1842 .... NCLC **17**
See also DLB 1, 59, 235

Chao, Patricia 1955- .... CLC **119**
See also CA 163

Chaplin, Charles Spencer
1889-1977 .... CLC **16**
See also Chaplin, Charlie
See also CA 81-84; 73-76

Chaplin, Charlie
See Chaplin, Charles Spencer
See also DLB 44

Chapman, George 1559(?)-1634 .... LC **22**;
DAM DRAM
See also DLB 62, 121

Chapman, Graham 1941-1989 .... CLC **21**
See also Monty Python
See also CA 116; 129; CANR 35, 95

Chapman, John Jay 1862-1933 .... TCLC **7**
See also CA 104

Chapman, Lee
See Bradley, Marion Zimmer
See also GLL 1

Chapman, Walker
See Silverberg, Robert

Chappell, Fred (Davis) 1936- ..... **CLC 40, 78**
See also CA 5-8R; CAAS 4; CANR 8, 33, 67; DLB 6, 105

Char, Rene(-Emile) 1907-1988 .... **CLC 9, 11, 14, 55; DAM POET**
See also CA 13-16R; 124; CANR 32; MTCW 1, 2

Charby, Jay
See Ellison, Harlan (Jay)

Chardin, Pierre Teilhard de
See Teilhard de Chardin, (Marie Joseph) Pierre

Charlemagne 742-814 .... **CMLC 37**

Charles I 1600-1649 .... **LC 13**

Charriere, Isabelle de 1740-1805 .. **NCLC 66**

Charyn, Jerome 1937- .... **CLC 5, 8, 18**
See also CA 5-8R; CAAS 1; CANR 7, 61; DLBY 83; MTCW 1

Chase, Mary (Coyle) 1907-1981 .... **DC 1**
See also CA 77-80; 105; DLB 228; SATA 17; SATA-Obit 29

Chase, Mary Ellen 1887-1973 .... **CLC 2**
See also CA 13-16; 41-44R; CAP 1; SATA 10

Chase, Nicholas
See Hyde, Anthony
See also CCA 1

Chateaubriand, François Rene de 1768-1848 .... **NCLC 3**
See also DLB 119

Chatterje, Sarat Chandra 1876-1936(?)
See Chatterji, Saratchandra
See also CA 109

Chatterji, Bankim Chandra 1838-1894 .... **NCLC 19**

Chatterji, Saratchandra TCLC 13
See also Chatterje, Sarat Chandra
See also CA 186

Chatterton, Thomas 1752-1770 ..... **LC 3, 54; DAM POET**
See also DLB 109

Chatwin, (Charles) Bruce 1940-1989 . **CLC 28, 57, 59; DAM POP**
See also AAYA 4; BEST 90:1; BRWS 4; CA 85-88; 127; DLB 194, 204

Chaucer, Daniel
See Ford, Ford Madox

Chaucer, Geoffrey 1340(?)-1400 .. **LC 17, 56; DA; DAB; DAC; DAM MST, POET; PC 19**
See also AW; CDBLB Before 1660; DA3; DLB 146

Chavez, Denise (Elia) 1948-
See also CA 131; CANR 56, 81; DAM MULT; DLB 122; HLC 1; HW 1, 2; MTCW 2

Chaviaras, Strates 1935-
See Haviaras, Stratis
See also CA 105

Chayefsky, Paddy CLC 23
See also Chayefsky, Sidney
See also DLB 7, 44; DLBY 81

Chayefsky, Sidney 1923-1981
See Chayefsky, Paddy
See also CA 9-12R; 104; CANR 18; DAM DRAM

Chedid, Andree 1920- .... **CLC 47**
See also CA 145; CANR 95

Cheever, John 1912-1982 ..... **CLC 3, 7, 8, 11, 15, 25, 64; DA; DAB; DAC; DAM MST, NOV, POP; SSC 1, 38**
See also AMWS 1; AW; CA 5-8R; 106; CABS 1; CANR 5, 27, 76; CDALB 1941-1968; DA3; DLB 2, 102, 227; DLBY 80, 82; INT CANR-5; MTCW 1, 2

Cheever, Susan 1943- .... **CLC 18, 48**
See also CA 103; CANR 27, 51, 92; DLBY 82; INT CANR-27

Chekhonte, Antosha
See Chekhov, Anton (Pavlovich)

Chekhov, Anton (Pavlovich) 1860-1904 .... **TCLC 3, 10, 31, 55, 96; DA; DAB; DAC; DAM DRAM, MST; DC 9; SSC 2, 28, 41**
See also AW; CA 104; 124; DA3; SATA 90

Chernyshevsky, Nikolay Gavrilovich 1828-1889 .... **NCLC 1**
See also DLB 238

Cherry, Carolyn Janice 1942-
See Cherryh, C. J.
See also AW; CA 65-68; CANR 10

Cherryh, C. J. CLC 35
See also Cherry, Carolyn Janice
See also AAYA 24; DLBY 80; SATA 93

Chesnutt, Charles W(addell) 1858-1932 .. **TCLC 5, 39; BLC 1; DAM MULT; SSC 7**
See also BW 1, 3; CA 106; 125; CANR 76; DLB 12, 50, 78; MTCW 1, 2

Chester, Alfred 1929(?)-1971 .... **CLC 49**
See also CA 33-36R; DLB 130

Chesterton, G(ilbert) K(eith) 1874-1936 . **TCLC 1, 6, 64; DAM NOV, POET; PC 28; SSC 1**
See also CA 104; 132; CANR 73; CDBLB 1914-1945; DLB 10, 19, 34, 70, 98, 149, 178; MTCW 1, 2; SATA 27

Chiang, Pin-chin 1904-1986
See Ding Ling
See also CA 118

Ch'ien Chung-shu 1910- .... **CLC 22**
See also CA 130; CANR 73; MTCW 1, 2

Child, L. Maria
See Child, Lydia Maria

Child, Lydia Maria 1802-1880 .. **NCLC 6, 73**
See also DLB 1, 74; SATA 67

Child, Mrs.
See Child, Lydia Maria

Child, Philip 1898-1978 .... **CLC 19, 68**
See also CA 13-14; CAP 1; SATA 47

Childers, (Robert) Erskine 1870-1922 .... **TCLC 65**
See also CA 113; 153; DLB 70

Childress, Alice 1920-1994 .. **CLC 12, 15, 86, 96; BLC 1; DAM DRAM, MULT, NOV; DC 4**
See also AAYA 8; AW; BW 2, 3; CA 45-48; 146; CANR 3, 27, 50, 74; CLR 14; DA3; DLB 7, 38; JRDA; MAICYA; MTCW 1, 2; SATA 7, 48, 81

Chin, Frank (Chew, Jr.) 1940- ...... **CLC 135; DAM MULT; DC 7**
See also CA 33-36R; CANR 71; DLB 206

Chislett, (Margaret) Anne 1943- ...... **CLC 34**
See also CA 151

Chitty, Thomas Willes 1926- .... **CLC 11**
See also Hinde, Thomas
See also CA 5-8R

Chivers, Thomas Holley 1809-1858 .... **NCLC 49**
See also DLB 3

Choi, Susan CLC 119

Chomette, Rene Lucien 1898-1981
See Clair, Rene
See also CA 103

Chomsky, (Avram) Noam 1928- ..... **CLC 132**
See also CA 17-20R; CANR 28, 62; DA3; MTCW 1, 2

Chopin, Kate TCLC 5, 14; DA; DAB; SSC 8
See also Chopin, Katherine
See also AAYA 33; AMWS 1; AW; CDALB 1865-1917; DLB 12, 78

Chopin, Katherine 1851-1904
See Chopin, Kate
See also CA 104; 122; DAC; DAM MST, NOV; DA3

Chretien de Troyes c. 12th cent. - . **CMLC 10**
See also DLB 208

Christie
See Ichikawa, Kon

Christie, Agatha (Mary Clarissa) 1890-1976 .... **CLC 1, 6, 8, 12, 39, 48, 110; DAB; DAC; DAM NOV**
See also AAYA 9; AITN 1, 2; AW; BRWS 2; CA 17-20R; 61-64; CANR 10, 37; CDBLB 1914-1945; DA3; DLB 13, 77; MTCW 1, 2; SATA 36

Christie, (Ann) Philippa
See Pearce, Philippa
See also CA 5-8R; CANR 4

Christine de Pizan 1365(?)-1431(?) .... **LC 9**
See also DLB 208

Chubb, Elmer
See Masters, Edgar Lee

Chulkov, Mikhail Dmitrievich 1743-1792 .... **LC 2**
See also DLB 150

Churchill, Caryl 1938- .... **CLC 31, 55; DC 5**
See also BRWS 4; CA 102; CANR 22, 46; DLB 13; MTCW 1

Churchill, Charles 1731-1764 .... **LC 3**
See also DLB 109

Chute, Carolyn 1947- .... **CLC 39**
See also CA 123

Ciardi, John (Anthony) 1916-1986 . **CLC 10, 40, 44, 129; DAM POET**
See also CA 5-8R; 118; CAAS 2; CANR 5, 33; CLR 19; DLB 5; DLBY 86; INT CANR-5; MAICYA; MTCW 1, 2; SAAS 26; SATA 1, 65; SATA-Obit 46

Cicero, Marcus Tullius 106B.C.-43B.C. .... **CMLC 3**
See also DLB 211

Cimino, Michael 1943- .... **CLC 16**
See also CA 105

Cioran, E(mil) M. 1911-1995 .... **CLC 64**
See also CA 25-28R; 149; CANR 91; DLB 220

Cisneros, Sandra 1954- . **CLC 69, 118; DAM MULT; HLC 1; SSC 32**
See also AAYA 9; AMWS 7; AW; CA 131; CANR 64; DA3; DLB 122, 152; HW 1, 2; MTCW 2

Cixous, Helene 1937- .... **CLC 92**
See also CA 126; CANR 55; CWW 2; DLB 83, 242; MTCW 1, 2

Clair, Rene CLC 20
See also Chomette, Rene Lucien

Clampitt, Amy 1920-1994 .... **CLC 32; PC 19**
See also CA 110; 146; CANR 29, 79; DLB 105

Clancy, Thomas L., Jr. 1947-
See Clancy, Tom
See also CA 125; 131; CANR 62; DA3; DLB 227; INT 131; MTCW 1, 2

Clancy, Tom CLC 45, 112; DAM NOV, POP
See also Clancy, Thomas L., Jr.
See also AAYA 9; BEST 89:1, 90:1; MTCW 2

Clare, John 1793-1864 ... **NCLC 9, 86; DAB; DAM POET; PC 23**
See also DLB 55, 96

Clarin
See Alas (y Urena), Leopoldo (Enrique Garcia)

Clark, Al C.
See Goines, Donald

Clark, (Robert) Brian 1932- .... **CLC 29**
See also CA 41-44R; CANR 67

Clark, Curt
See Westlake, Donald E(dwin)

Clark, Eleanor 1913-1996 .... **CLC 5, 19**
See also CA 9-12R; 151; CANR 41; DLB 6

Clark, J. P.
See Clark Bekedermo, J(ohnson) P(epper)
See also DLB 117
Clark, John Pepper
See Clark Bekedermo, J(ohnson) P(epper)
Clark, M. R.
See Clark, Mavis Thorpe
Clark, Mavis Thorpe 1909- .... **CLC 12**
See also CA 57-60; CANR 8, 37; CLR 30;
MAICYA; SAAS 5; SATA 8, 74
Clark, Walter Van Tilburg
1909-1971 .... **CLC 28**
See also CA 9-12R; 33-36R; CANR 63;
DLB 9, 206; SATA 8
Clark Bekedermo, J(ohnson) P(epper)
1935- .. **CLC 38; BLC 1; DAM DRAM,
MULT; DC 5**
See also Clark, J. P.; Clark, John Pepper
See also BW 1; CA 65-68; CANR 16, 72;
MTCW 1
Clarke, Arthur C(harles) 1917- .... **CLC 1, 4,
13, 18, 35, 136; DAM POP; SSC 3**
See also AAYA 4, 33; AW; CA 1-4R; CANR
2, 28, 55, 74; DA3; JRDA; MAICYA;
MTCW 1, 2; SATA 13, 70, 115
Clarke, Austin 1896-1974 ... **CLC 6, 9; DAM
POET**
See also CA 29-32; 49-52; CAP 2; DLB 10,
20
Clarke, Austin C(hesterfield) 1934- .. **CLC 8,
53; BLC 1; DAC; DAM MULT**
See also BW 1; CA 25-28R; CAAS 16;
CANR 14, 32, 68; DLB 53, 125
Clarke, Gillian 1937- .... **CLC 61**
See also CA 106; DLB 40
Clarke, Marcus (Andrew Hislop)
1846-1881 .... **NCLC 19**
See also DLB 230
Clarke, Shirley 1925-1997 .... **CLC 16**
See also CA 189
Clash, The
See Headon, (Nicky) Topper; Jones, Mick;
Simonon, Paul; Strummer, Joe
Claudel, Paul (Louis Charles Marie)
1868-1955 .... **TCLC 2, 10**
See also CA 104; 165; DLB 192
Claudius, Matthias 1740-1815 .... **NCLC 75**
See also DLB 97
Clavell, James (duMaresq)
1925-1994 .. **CLC 6, 25, 87; DAM NOV,
POP**
See also CA 25-28R; 146; CANR 26, 48;
DA3; MTCW 1, 2
Cleaver, (Leroy) Eldridge
1935-1998 . **CLC 30, 119; BLC 1; DAM
MULT**
See also AW; BW 1, 3; CA 21-24R; 167;
CANR 16, 75; DA3; MTCW 2
Cleese, John (Marwood) 1939- .... **CLC 21**
See also Monty Python
See also CA 112; 116; CANR 35; MTCW 1
Cleishbotham, Jebediah
See Scott, Walter
Cleland, John 1710-1789 .... **LC 2, 48**
See also DLB 39
Clemens, Samuel Langhorne 1835-1910
See Twain, Mark
See also AW 2; CA 104; 135; CDALB
1865-1917; DA; DAB; DAC; DAM MST,
NOV; DA3; DLB 11, 12, 23, 64, 74, 186,
189; JRDA; MAICYA; SATA 100
Clement of Alexandria
150(?)-215(?) .... **CMLC 41**
Cleophil
See Congreve, William
Clerihew, E.
See Bentley, E(dmund) C(lerihew)

Clerk, N. W.
See Lewis, C(live) S(taples)
Cliff, Jimmy **CLC 21**
See also Chambers, James
Cliff, Michelle 1946- .... **CLC 120; BLCS**
See also BW 2; CA 116; CANR 39, 72;
DLB 157; GLL 2
Clifton, (Thelma) Lucille 1936- .... **CLC 19,
66; BLC 1; DAM MULT, POET; PC
17**
See also BW 2, 3; CA 49-52; CANR 2, 24,
42, 76; CLR 5; DA3; DLB 5, 41; MAI-
CYA; MTCW 1, 2; SATA 20, 69
Clinton, Dirk
See Silverberg, Robert
Clough, Arthur Hugh 1819-1861 ... **NCLC 27**
See also DLB 32
Clutha, Janet Paterson Frame 1924-
See Frame, Janet
See also CA 1-4R; CANR 2, 36, 76; MTCW
1, 2; SATA 119
Clyne, Terence
See Blatty, William Peter
Cobalt, Martin
See Mayne, William (James Carter)
Cobb, Irvin S(hrewsbury)
1876-1944 .... **TCLC 77**
See also CA 175; DLB 11, 25, 86
Cobbett, William 1763-1835 .... **NCLC 49**
See also DLB 43, 107, 158
Coburn, D(onald) L(ee) 1938- .... **CLC 10**
See also CA 89-92
Cocteau, Jean (Maurice Eugene Clement)
1889-1963 .... **CLC 1, 8, 15, 16, 43; DA;
DAB; DAC; DAM DRAM, MST, NOV**
See also AW; CA 25-28; CANR 40; CAP 2;
DA3; DLB 65; MTCW 1, 2
Codrescu, Andrei 1946- .... **CLC 46, 121;
DAM POET**
See also CA 33-36R; CAAS 19; CANR 13,
34, 53, 76; DA3; MTCW 2
Coe, Max
See Bourne, Randolph S(illiman)
Coe, Tucker
See Westlake, Donald E(dwin)
Coen, Ethan 1958 .... **CLC 108**
See also CA 126; CANR 85
Coen, Joel 1955- .... **CLC 108**
See also CA 126
The Coen Brothers
See Coen, Ethan; Coen, Joel
Coetzee, J(ohn) M(ichael) 1940- ...... **CLC 23,
33, 66, 117; DAM NOV**
See also AAYA 37; CA 77-80; CANR 41,
54, 74; DA3; DLB 225, MTCW 1, 2
Coffey, Brian
See Koontz, Dean R(ay)
Coffin, Robert P(eter) Tristram
1892-1955 .... **TCLC 95**
See also CA 123; 169; DLB 45
Cohan, George M(ichael)
1878-1942 .... **TCLC 60**
See also CA 157
Cohen, Arthur A(llen) 1928-1986 ...... **CLC 7,
31**
See also CA 1-4R; 120; CANR 1, 17, 42;
DLB 28
Cohen, Leonard (Norman) 1934- ...... **CLC 3,
38; DAC; DAM MST**
See also CA 21-24R; CANR 14, 69; DLB
53; MTCW 1
Cohen, Matt(hew) 1942-1999 .... **CLC 19;
DAC**
See also CA 61-64; 187; CAAS 18; CANR
40; DLB 53
Cohen-Solal, Annie 19(?)- .... **CLC 50**
Colegate, Isabel 1931- .... **CLC 36**
See also CA 17-20R; CANR 8, 22, 74; DLB
14, 231; INT CANR-22; MTCW 1

Coleman, Emmett
See Reed, Ishmael
Coleridge, Hartley 1796-1849 .... **NCLC 90**
See also DLB 96
Coleridge, M. E.
See Coleridge, Mary E(lizabeth)
Coleridge, Mary E(lizabeth)
1861-1907 .... **TCLC 73**
See also CA 116; 166; DLB 19, 98
Coleridge, Samuel Taylor
1772-1834 .... **NCLC 9, 54; DA; DAB;
DAC; DAM MST, POET; PC 11**
See also AW; CDBLB 1789-1832; DA3;
DLB 93, 107
Coleridge, Sara 1802-1852 .... **NCLC 31**
See also DLB 199
Coles, Don 1928- .... **CLC 46**
See also CA 115; CANR 38
Coles, Robert (Martin) 1929- .... **CLC 108**
See also CA 45-48; CANR 3, 32, 66, 70;
INT CANR-32; SATA 23
Colette, (Sidonie-Gabrielle)
1873-1954 . **TCLC 1, 5, 16; DAM NOV;
SSC 10**
See also Willy, Colette
See also CA 104; 131; DA3; DLB 65;
MTCW 1, 2
Collett, (Jacobine) Camilla (Wergeland)
1813-1895 .... **NCLC 22**
Collier, Christopher 1930- .... **CLC 30**
See also AAYA 13; CA 33-36R; CANR 13,
33; JRDA; MAICYA; SATA 16, 70
Collier, James L(incoln) 1928- .... **CLC 30;
DAM POP**
See also AAYA 13; CA 9-12R; CANR 4,
33, 60; CLR 3; JRDA; MAICYA; SAAS
21; SATA 8, 70
Collier, Jeremy 1650-1726 .... **LC 6**
Collier, John 1901-1980 .... **SSC 19**
See also CA 65-68; 97-100; CANR 10;
DLB 77
Collingwood, R(obin) G(eorge)
1889(?)-1943 .... **TCLC 67**
See also CA 117; 155
Collins, Hunt
See Hunter, Evan
Collins, Linda 1931- .... **CLC 44**
See also CA 125
Collins, (William) Wilkie
1824-1889 .... **NCLC 1, 18, 93**
See also CDBLB 1832-1890; DLB 18, 70,
159
Collins, William 1721-1759 . **LC 4, 40; DAM
POET**
See also DLB 109
Collodi, Carlo **NCLC 54**
See also Lorenzini, Carlo
See also CLR 5
Colman, George
See Glassco, John
Colt, Winchester Remington
See Hubbard, L(afayette) Ron(ald)
Colter, Cyrus 1910- .... **CLC 58**
See also BW 1; CA 65-68; CANR 10, 66;
DLB 33
Colton, James
See Hansen, Joseph
See also GLL 1
Colum, Padraic 1881-1972 .... **CLC 28**
See also CA 73-76; 33-36R; CANR 35;
CLR 36; MAICYA; MTCW 1; SATA 15
Colvin, James
See Moorcock, Michael (John)
Colwin, Laurie (E.) 1944-1992 .... **CLC 5, 13,
23, 84**
See also CA 89-92; 139; CANR 20, 46;
DLBY 80; MTCW 1

Comfort, Alex(ander) 1920-2000 .... **CLC 7;**
DAM POP
See also CA 1-4R; CANR 1, 45; MTCW 1

Comfort, Montgomery
See Campbell, (John) Ramsey

Compton-Burnett, I(vy)
1892(?)-1969 .... **CLC 1, 3, 10, 15, 34;**
DAM NOV
See also CA 1-4R; 25-28R; CANR 4; DLB
36; MTCW 1

Comstock, Anthony 1844-1915 ...... **TCLC 13**
See also CA 110; 169

Comte, Auguste 1798-1857 .... **NCLC 54**

Conan Doyle, Arthur
See Doyle, Arthur Conan

Conde (Abellan), Carmen 1901-
See also CA 177; DLB 108; HLCS 1; HW
2

Conde, Maryse 1937- .... **CLC 52, 92; BLCS;**
DAM MULT
See also BW 2, 3; CA 110; CANR 30, 53,
76; CWW 2; MTCW 1

Condillac, Etienne Bonnot de
1714-1780 .... **LC 26**

Condon, Richard (Thomas)
1915-1996 ...... **CLC 4, 6, 8, 10, 45, 100;**
DAM NOV
See also BEST 90:3; CA 1-4R; 151; CAAS
1; CANR 2, 23; INT CANR-23; MTCW
1, 2

Confucius 551B.C.-479B.C... **CMLC 19; DA;**
DAB; DAC; DAM MST
See also AW; DA3

Congreve, William 1670-1729 .... **LC 5, 21;**
DA; DAB; DAC; DAM DRAM, MST,
POET; DC 2
See also AW; CDBLB 1660-1789; DLB 39,
84

Connell, Evan S(helby), Jr. 1924- . **CLC 4, 6,**
45; DAM NOV
See also AAYA 7; CA 1-4R; CAAS 2;
CANR 2, 39, 76; DLB 2; DLBY 81;
MTCW 1, 2

Connelly, Marc(us Cook) 1890-1980 . **CLC 7**
See also CA 85-88; 102; CANR 30; DLB
7; DLBY 80; SATA-Obit 25

Connor, Ralph **TCLC 31**
See also Gordon, Charles William
See also DLB 92; TCWW 2

Conrad, Joseph 1857-1924 .... **TCLC 1, 6, 13,**
25, 43, 57; DA; DAB; DAC; DAM
MST, NOV; SSC 9
See also AAYA 26; AW; CA 104; 131;
CANR 60; CDBLB 1890-1914; DA3;
DLB 10, 34, 98, 156; MTCW 1, 2; SATA
27

Conrad, Robert Arnold
See Hart, Moss

Conroy, Pat
See Conroy, (Donald) Pat(rick)
See also MTCW 2

Conroy, (Donald) Pat(rick) 1945- ... **CLC 30,**
74; DAM NOV, POP
See also Conroy, Pat
See also AAYA 8; AITN 1; CA 85-88;
CANR 24, 53; DA3; DLB 6; MTCW 1

Constant (de Rebecque), (Henri) Benjamin
1767-1830 .... **NCLC 6**
See also DLB 119

Conybeare, Charles Augustus
See Eliot, T(homas) S(tearns)

Cook, Michael 1933-1994 .... **CLC 58**
See also CA 93-96; CANR 68; DLB 53

Cook, Robin 1940- .... **CLC 14; DAM POP**
See also AAYA 32; BEST 90:2; CA 108;
111; CANR 41, 90; DA3; INT 111

Cook, Roy
See Silverberg, Robert

Cooke, Elizabeth 1948- .... **CLC 55**
See also CA 129

Cooke, John Esten 1830-1886 .... **NCLC 5**
See also DLB 3

Cooke, John Estes
See Baum, L(yman) Frank

Cooke, M. E.
See Creasey, John

Cooke, Margaret
See Creasey, John

Cook-Lynn, Elizabeth 1930- . **CLC 93; DAM**
MULT
See also CA 133; DLB 175; NNAL

Cooney, Ray **CLC 62**

Cooper, Douglas 1960- .... **CLC 86**

Cooper, Henry St. John
See Creasey, John

Cooper, J(oan) California (?)- .... **CLC 56;**
DAM MULT
See also AAYA 12; BW 1; CA 125; CANR
55; DLB 212

Cooper, James Fenimore
1789-1851 .... **NCLC 1, 27, 54**
See also AAYA 22; CDALB 1640-1865;
DA3; DLB 3; SATA 19

Coover, Robert (Lowell) 1932- ...... **CLC 3, 7,**
15, 32, 46, 87; DAM NOV; SSC 15
See also AMWS 5; CA 45-48; CANR 3,
37, 58; DLB 2, 227; DLBY 81; MTCW
1, 2

Copeland, Stewart (Armstrong)
1952- .... **CLC 26**

Copernicus, Nicolaus 1473-1543 .... **LC 45**

Coppard, A(lfred) E(dgar)
1878-1957 .... **TCLC 5; SSC 21**
See also AW 1; CA 114; 167; DLB 162

Coppee, Francois 1842-1908 .... **TCLC 25**
See also CA 170

Coppola, Francis Ford 1939- ... **CLC 16, 126**
See also CA 77-80; CANR 40, 78; DLB 44

Corbiere, Tristan 1845-1875 .... **NCLC 43**

Corcoran, Barbara 1911- .... **CLC 17**
See also AAYA 14; CA 21-24R; CAAS 2;
CANR 11, 28, 48; CLR 50; DLB 52;
JRDA; SAAS 20; SATA 3, 77

Cordelier, Maurice
See Giraudoux, (Hippolyte) Jean

Corelli, Marie **TCLC 51**
See also Mackay, Mary
See also DLB 34, 156

Corman, Cid **CLC 9**
See also Corman, Sidney
See also CAAS 2; DLB 5, 193

Corman, Sidney 1924-
See Corman, Cid
See also CA 85-88; CANR 44; DAM POET

Cormier, Robert (Edmund)
1925-2000 .... **CLC 12, 30; DA; DAB;**
DAC; DAM MST, NOV
See also AAYA 3, 19; CA 1-4R; CANR 5,
23, 76, 93; CDALB 1968-1988; CLR 12,
55; DLB 52; INT CANR-23; JRDA; MAI-
CYA; MTCW 1, 2; SATA 10, 45, 83

Corn, Alfred (DeWitt III) 1943- .... **CLC 33**
See also CA 179; CAAE 179; CAAS 25;
CANR 44; DLB 120; DLBY 80

Corneille, Pierre 1606-1684 ..... **LC 28; DAB;**
DAM MST

Cornwell, David (John Moore)
1931- .... **CLC 9, 15; DAM POP**
See also le Carre, John
See also CA 5-8R; CANR 13, 33, 59; DA3;
MTCW 1, 2

Corso, (Nunzio) Gregory 1930-2001 . **CLC 1,**
11; PC 33
See also CA 5-8R; CANR 41, 76; DA3;
DLB 5, 16; MTCW 1, 2

Cortazar, Julio 1914-1984 ... **CLC 2, 3, 5, 10,**
13, 15, 33, 34, 92; DAM MULT, NOV;
HLC 1; SSC 7
See also CA 21-24R; CANR 12, 32, 81;
DA3; DLB 113; HW 1, 2; MTCW 1, 2

Cortes, Hernan 1485-1547 .... **LC 31**

Corvinus, Jakob
See Raabe, Wilhelm (Karl)

Corwin, Cecil
See Kornbluth, C(yril) M.

Cosic, Dobrica 1921- .... **CLC 14**
See also CA 122; 138; CWW 2; DLB 181

Costain, Thomas B(ertram)
1885-1965 .... **CLC 30**
See also CA 5-8R; 25-28R; DLB 9

Costantini, Humberto 1924(?)-1987 . **CLC 49**
See also CA 131; 122; HW 1

Costello, Elvis 1955- .... **CLC 21**

Costenoble, Philostene 1898-1962
See Ghelderode, Michel de

Cotes, Cecil V.
See Duncan, Sara Jeannette

Cotter, Joseph Seamon Sr.
1861-1949 ...... **TCLC 28; BLC 1; DAM**
MULT
See also BW 1; CA 124; DLB 50

Couch, Arthur Thomas Quiller
See Quiller-Couch, SirArthur (Thomas)

Coulton, James
See Hansen, Joseph

Couperus, Louis (Marie Anne)
1863-1923 .... **TCLC 15**
See also CA 115

Coupland, Douglas 1961- .... **CLC 85, 133;**
DAC; DAM POP
See also AAYA 34; CA 142; CANR 57, 90;
CCA 1

Court, Wesli
See Turco, Lewis (Putnam)

Courtenay, Bryce 1933- .... **CLC 59**
See also CA 138

Courtney, Robert
See Ellison, Harlan (Jay)

Cousteau, Jacques-Yves 1910-1997 .. **CLC 30**
See also CA 65-68; 159; CANR 15, 67;
MTCW 1; SATA 38, 98

Coventry, Francis 1725-1754 .... **LC 46**

Cowan, Peter (Walkinshaw) 1914- .... **SSC 28**
See also CA 21-24R; CANR 9, 25, 50, 83

Coward, Noël (Peirce) 1899-1973 . **CLC 1, 9,**
29, 51; DAM DRAM
See also AITN 1; BRWS 2; CA 17-18; 41-
44R; CANR 35; CAP 2; CDBLB 1914-
1945; DA3; DLB 10; IDFW 3; MTCW 1,
2

Cowley, Abraham 1618-1667 .... **LC 43**
See also DLB 131, 151

Cowley, Malcolm 1898-1989 .... **CLC 39**
See also AMWS 2; CA 5-8R; 128; CANR
3, 55; DLB 4, 48; DLBY 81, 89; MTCW
1, 2

Cowper, William 1731-1800 ..... **NCLC 8, 94;**
DAM POET
See also DA3; DLB 104, 109

Cox, William Trevor 1928- ... **CLC 9, 14, 71;**
DAM NOV
See also Trevor, William
See also CA 9-12R; CANR 4, 37, 55, 76;
DLB 14; INT CANR-37; MTCW 1, 2

Coyne, P. J.
See Masters, Hilary

Cozzens, James Gould 1903-1978 . **CLC 1, 4,**
11, 92
See also CA 9-12R; 81-84; CANR 19;
CDALB 1941-1968; DLB 9; DLBD 2;
DLBY 84, 97; MTCW 1, 2

Crabbe, George 1754-1832 .... **NCLC 26**
See also DLB 93

Craddock, Charles Egbert
See Murfree, Mary Noailles
Craig, A. A.
See Anderson, Poul (William)
Craik, Dinah Maria (Mulock)
1826-1887 .... NCLC **38**
See also DLB 35, 163; MAICYA; SATA 34
Cram, Ralph Adams 1863-1942 ..... TCLC **45**
See also CA 160
Crane, (Harold) Hart 1899-1932 .... TCLC **2, 5, 80; DA; DAB; DAC; DAM MST, POET; PC 3**
See also AW; CA 104; 127; CDALB 1917-1929; DA3; DLB 4, 48; MTCW 1, 2
Crane, R(onald) S(almon)
1886-1967 .... CLC **27**
See also CA 85-88; DLB 63
Crane, Stephen (Townley)
1871-1900 .... TCLC **11, 17, 32; DA; DAB; DAC; DAM MST, NOV, POET; SSC 7**
See also AAYA 21; CA 109; 140; CANR 84; CDALB 1865-1917; DA3; DLB 12, 54, 78
Cranshaw, Stanley
See Fisher, Dorothy (Frances) Canfield
Crase, Douglas 1944- .... CLC **58**
See also CA 106
Crashaw, Richard 1612(?)-1649 .... LC **24**
See also DLB 126
Craven, Margaret 1901-1980 .... CLC **17; DAC**
See also CA 103; CCA 1
Crawford, F(rancis) Marion
1854-1909 .... TCLC **10**
See also CA 107; 168; DLB 71
Crawford, Isabella Valancy
1850-1887 .... NCLC **12**
See also DLB 92
Crayon, Geoffrey
See Irving, Washington
Creasey, John 1908-1973 .... CLC **11**
See also CA 5-8R; 41-44R; CANR 8, 59; DLB 77; MTCW 1
Crebillon, Claude Prosper Jolyot de (fils)
1707-1777 .... LC **1, 28**
Credo
See Creasey, John
Credo, Alvaro J. de
See Prado (Calvo), Pedro
Creeley, Robert (White) 1926- .. CLC **1, 2, 4, 8, 11, 15, 36, 78; DAM POET**
See also AMWS 4; CA 1-4R; CAAS 10; CANR 23, 43, 89; DA3; DLB 5, 16, 169; DLBD 17; MTCW 1, 2
Crews, Harry (Eugene) 1935- ..... CLC **6, 23, 49**
See also AITN 1; CA 25-28R; CANR 20, 57; DA3; DLB 6, 143, 185; MTCW 1, 2
Crichton, (John) Michael 1942- .... CLC **2, 6, 54, 90; DAM NOV, POP**
See also AAYA 10; AITN 2; AW; CA 25-28R; CANR 13, 40, 54, 76; DA3; DLBY 81; INT CANR-13; JRDA; MTCW 1, 2; SATA 9, 88
Crispin, Edmund CLC **22**
See also Montgomery, (Robert) Bruce
See also DLB 87
Cristofer, Michael 1945(?)- ... CLC **28; DAM DRAM**
See also CA 110; 152; DLB 7
Croce, Benedetto 1866-1952 .... TCLC **37**
See also CA 120; 155
Crockett, David 1786-1836 .... NCLC **8**
See also DLB 3, 11
Crockett, Davy
See Crockett, David
Crofts, Freeman Wills 1879-1957 .. TCLC **55**
See also CA 115; DLB 77

Croker, John Wilson 1780-1857 .... NCLC **10**
See also DLB 110
Crommelynck, Fernand 1885 1970 .. CLC **75**
See also CA 189; 89-92
Cromwell, Oliver 1599-1658 .... LC **43**
Cronin, A(rchibald) J(oseph)
1896-1981 .... CLC **32**
See also CA 1-4R; 102; CANR 5; DLB 191; SATA 47; SATA-Obit 25
Cross, Amanda
See Heilbrun, Carolyn G(old)
Crothers, Rachel 1878(?)-1958 .... TCLC **19**
See also CA 113; DLB 7
Croves, Hal
See Traven, B.
Crow Dog, Mary (Ellen) (?)- .... CLC **93**
See also Brave Bird, Mary
See also CA 154
Crowfield, Christopher
See Stowe, Harriet (Elizabeth) Beecher
Crowley, Aleister TCLC **7**
See also Crowley, Edward Alexander
See also GLL 1
Crowley, Edward Alexander 1875-1947
See Crowley, Aleister
See also CA 104
Crowley, John 1942- .... CLC **57**
See also CA 61-64; CANR 43; DLBY 82; SATA 65
Crud
See Crumb, R(obert)
Crumarums
See Crumb, R(obert)
Crumb, R(obert) 1943- .... CLC **17**
See also CA 106
Crumbum
See Crumb, R(obert)
Crumski
See Crumb, R(obert)
Crum the Bum
See Crumb, R(obert)
Crunk
See Crumb, R(obert)
Crustt
See Crumb, R(obert)
Cruz, Victor Hernandez 1949-
See also BW 2; CA 65-68; CAAS 17; CANR 14, 32, 74; DAM MULT, POET; DLB 41; HLC 1; HW 1, 2; MTCW 1
Cryer, Gretchen (Kiger) 1935- .... CLC **21**
See also CA 114; 123
Csath, Geza 1887-1919 .... TCLC **13**
See also CA 111
Cudlip, David R(ockwell) 1933- .... CLC **34**
See also CA 177
Cullen, Countee 1903-1946 .... TCLC **4, 37; BLC 1; DA; DAC; DAM MST, MULT, POET; PC 20**
See also AMWS 4; AW; BW 1; CA 108; 124; CDALB 1917-1929; DA3; DLB 4, 48, 51; MTCW 1, 2; SATA 18
Cum, R.
See Crumb, R(obert)
Cummings, Bruce F(rederick) 1889-1919
See Barbellion, W. N. P.
See also CA 123
Cummings, E(dward) E(stlin)
1894-1962 .... CLC **1, 3, 8, 12, 15, 68; DA; DAB; DAC; DAM MST, POET; PC 5**
See also AW; CA 73-76; CANR 31; CDALB 1929-1941; DA3; DLB 4, 48; MTCW 1, 2
Cunha, Euclides (Rodrigues Pimenta) da
1866-1909 .... TCLC **24**
See also CA 123
Cunningham, E. V.
See Fast, Howard (Melvin)

Cunningham, J(ames) V(incent)
1911-1985 .... CLC **3, 31**
See also CA 1-4R; 115; CANR 1, 72; DLB 5
Cunningham, Julia (Woolfolk)
1916- .... CLC **12**
See also CA 9-12R; CANR 4, 19, 36; JRDA; MAICYA; SAAS 2; SATA 1, 26
Cunningham, Michael 1952- .... CLC **34**
See also CA 136; CANR 96; GLL 2
Cunninghame Graham, R. B.
See Cunninghame Graham, Robert (Gallnigad) Bontine
Cunninghame Graham, Robert (Gallnigad) Bontine 1852-1936 .... TCLC **19**
See also Graham, R(obert) B(ontine) Cunninghame
See also CA 119; 184; DLB 98
Currie, Ellen 19(?)- .... CLC **44**
Curtin, Philip
See Lowndes, Marie Adelaide (Belloc)
Curtis, Price
See Ellison, Harlan (Jay)
Cutrate, Joe
See Spiegelman, Art
Cynewulf c. 770-c. 840 .... CMLC **23**
Czaczkes, Shmuel Yosef
See Agnon, S(hmuel) Y(osef Halevi)
Dabrowska, Maria (Szumska)
1889-1965 .... CLC **15**
See also CA 106
Dabydeen, David 1955- .... CLC **34**
See also BW 1; CA 125; CANR 56, 92
Dacey, Philip 1939- .... CLC **51**
See also CA 37-40R; CAAS 17; CANR 14, 32, 64; DLB 105
Dagerman, Stig (Halvard)
1923-1954 .... TCLC **17**
See also CA 117; 155
Dahl, Roald 1916-1990 ...... CLC **1, 6, 18, 79; DAB; DAC; DAM MST, NOV, POP**
See also AAYA 15; AW; BRWS 4; CA 1-4R; 133; CANR 6, 32, 37, 62; CLR 1, 7, 41; DA3; DLB 139; JRDA; MAICYA; MTCW 1, 2; SATA 1, 26, 73; SATA-Obit 65
Dahlberg, Edward 1900-1977 .. CLC **1, 7, 14**
See also CA 9-12R; 69-72; CANR 31, 62; DLB 48; MTCW 1
Daitch, Susan 1954- .... CLC **103**
See also CA 161
Dale, Colin TCLC **18**
See also Lawrence, T(homas) E(dward)
Dale, George E.
See Asimov, Isaac
Dalton, Roque 1935-1975
See also HLCS 1; HW 2
Daly, Elizabeth 1878-1967 .... CLC **52**
See also CA 23-24; 25-28R; CANR 60; CAP 2
Daly, Maureen 1921-1983 .... CLC **17**
See also AAYA 5; AW; CANR 37, 83; JRDA; MAICYA; SAAS 1; SATA 2
Damas, Leon-Gontran 1912-1978 .... CLC **84**
See also BW 1; CA 125; 73-76
Dana, Richard Henry Sr.
1787-1879 .... NCLC **53**
Daniel, Samuel 1562(?)-1619 .... LC **24**
See also DLB 62
Daniels, Brett
See Adler, Renata
Dannay, Frederic 1905-1982 . CLC **11; DAM POP**
See also Queen, Ellery
See also CA 1-4R; 107; CANR 1, 39; DLB 137; MTCW 1
D'Annunzio, Gabriele 1863-1938 ... TCLC **6, 40**
See also CA 104; 155

Danois, N. le
See Gourmont, Remy (-Marie-Charles) de

Dante 1265-1321 .... **CMLC 3, 18, 39; DA; DAB; DAC; DAM MST, POET; PC 21**
See also AW; DA3

d'Antibes, Germain
See Simenon, Georges (Jacques Christian)

Danticat, Edwidge 1969- .... **CLC 94, 139**
See also AAYA 29; AW; CA 152; CANR 73; MTCW 1

Danvers, Dennis 1947- .... **CLC 70**

Danziger, Paula 1944- .... **CLC 21**
See also AAYA 4, 36; AW; CA 112; 115; CANR 37; CLR 20; JRDA; MAICYA; SATA 36, 63, 102; SATA-Brief 30

Da Ponte, Lorenzo 1749-1838 .... **NCLC 50**

Dario, Ruben 1867-1916 .... **TCLC 4; DAM MULT; HLC 1; PC 15**
See also CA 131; CANR 81; HW 1, 2; MTCW 1, 2

Darley, George 1795-1846 .... **NCLC 2**
See also DLB 96

Darrow, Clarence (Seward) 1857-1938 .... **TCLC 81**
See also CA 164

Darwin, Charles 1809-1882 .... **NCLC 57**
See also DLB 57, 166

Daryush, Elizabeth 1887-1977 ...... **CLC 6, 19**
See also CA 49-52; CANR 3, 81; DLB 20

Dasgupta, Surendranath 1887-1952 .... **TCLC 81**
See also CA 157

Dashwood, Edmee Elizabeth Monica de la Pasture 1890-1943
See Delafield, E. M.
See also CA 119; 154

Daudet, (Louis Marie) Alphonse 1840-1897 .... **NCLC 1**
See also DLB 123

Daumal, Rene 1908-1944 .... **TCLC 14**
See also CA 114

Davenant, William 1606-1668 .... **LC 13**
See also DLB 58, 126

Davenport, Guy (Mattison, Jr.) 1927- .... **CLC 6, 14, 38; SSC 16**
See also CA 33-36R; CANR 23, 73; DLB 130

Davidson, Avram (James) 1923-1993
See Queen, Ellery
See also CA 101; 171; CANR 26; DLB 8

Davidson, Donald (Grady) 1893-1968 .... **CLC 2, 13, 19**
See also CA 5-8R; 25-28R; CANR 4, 84; DLB 45

Davidson, Hugh
See Hamilton, Edmond

Davidson, John 1857-1909 .... **TCLC 24**
See also CA 118; DLB 19

Davidson, Sara 1943- .... **CLC 9**
See also CA 81-84; CANR 44, 68; DLB 185

Davie, Donald (Alfred) 1922-1995 .... **CLC 5, 8, 10, 31; PC 29**
See also CA 1-4R; 149; CAAS 3; CANR 1, 44; DLB 27; MTCW 1

Davies, Ray(mond Douglas) 1944- ... **CLC 21**
See also CA 116; 146; CANR 92

Davies, Rhys 1901-1978 .... **CLC 23**
See also CA 9-12R; 81-84; CANR 4; DLB 139, 191

Davies, (William) Robertson 1913-1995 .... **CLC 2, 7, 13, 25, 42, 75, 91; DA; DAB; DAC; DAM MST, NOV, POP**
See also Marchbanks, Samuel
See also AW; BEST 89:2; CA 33-36R; 150; CANR 17, 42; DA3; DLB 68; INT CANR-17; MTCW 1, 2

Davies, Walter C.
See Kornbluth, C(yril) M.

Davies, William Henry 1871-1940 ... **TCLC 5**
See also CA 104; 179; DLB 19, 174

Da Vinci, Leonardo 1452-1519 ..... **LC 12, 57, 60**

Davis, Angela (Yvonne) 1944- .... **CLC 77; DAM MULT**
See also BW 2, 3; CA 57-60; CANR 10, 81; DA3

Davis, B. Lynch
See Bioy Casares, Adolfo; Borges, Jorge Luis

Davis, B. Lynch
See Bioy Casares, Adolfo

Davis, Gordon
See Hunt, E(verette) Howard, (Jr.)

Davis, H(arold) L(enoir) 1896-1960 . **CLC 49**
See also CA 178; 89-92; DLB 9, 206; SATA 114

Davis, Rebecca (Blaine) Harding 1831-1910 .... **TCLC 6; SSC 38**
See also CA 104; 179; DLB 74, 239

Davis, Richard Harding 1864-1916 .... **TCLC 24**
See also CA 114; 179; DLB 12, 23, 78, 79, 189; DLBD 13

Davison, Frank Dalby 1893-1970 ..... **CLC 15**
See also CA 116

Davison, Lawrence H.
See Lawrence, D(avid) H(erbert Richards)

Davison, Peter (Hubert) 1928- .... **CLC 28**
See also CA 9-12R; CAAS 4; CANR 3, 43, 84; DLB 5

Davys, Mary 1674-1732 .... **LC 1, 46**
See also DLB 39

Dawson, Fielding 1930- .... **CLC 6**
See also CA 85-88; DLB 130

Dawson, Peter
See Faust, Frederick (Schiller)
See also TCWW 2, 2

Day, Clarence (Shepard, Jr.) 1874-1935 .... **TCLC 25**
See also CA 108; DLB 11

Day, Thomas 1748-1789 .... **LC 1**
See also AW 1; DLB 39

Day Lewis, C(ecil) 1904-1972 . **CLC 1, 6, 10; DAM POET; PC 11**
See also Blake, Nicholas
See also BRWS 3; CA 13-16; 33-36R; CANR 34; CAP 1; DLB 15, 20; MTCW 1, 2

Dazai Osamu **TCLC 11; SSC 41**
See also Tsushima, Shuji
See also CA 164; DLB 182

de Andrade, Carlos Drummond
See Drummond de Andrade, Carlos

Deane, Norman
See Creasey, John

Deane, Seamus (Francis) 1940- ...... **CLC 122**
See also CA 118; CANR 42

de Beauvoir, Simone (Lucie Ernestine Marie Bertrand)
See Beauvoir, Simone (Lucie Ernestine Marie Bertrand) de

de Beer, P.
See Bosman, Herman Charles

de Brissac, Malcolm
See Dickinson, Peter (Malcolm)

de Campos, Alvaro
See Pessoa, Fernando (Antonio Nogueira)

de Chardin, Pierre Teilhard
See Teilhard de Chardin, (Marie Joseph) Pierre

Dee, John 1527-1608 .... **LC 20**

Deer, Sandra 1940- .... **CLC 45**
See also CA 186

De Ferrari, Gabriella 1941- .... **CLC 65**
See also CA 146

Defoe, Daniel 1660(?)-1731 .... **LC 1, 42; DA; DAB; DAC; DAM MST, NOV**
See also AAYA 27; AW; CDBLB 1660-1789; CLR 61; DA3; DLB 39, 95, 101; JRDA; MAICYA; SATA 22

de Gourmont, Remy(-Marie-Charles)
See Gourmont, Remy (-Marie-Charles) de

de Hartog, Jan 1914- .... **CLC 19**
See also CA 1-4R; CANR 1

de Hostos, E. M.
See Hostos (y Bonilla), Eugenio Maria de

de Hostos, Eugenio M.
See Hostos (y Bonilla), Eugenio Maria de

Deighton, Len **CLC 4, 7, 22, 46**
See also Deighton, Leonard Cyril
See also AAYA 6; BEST 89:2; CDBLB 1960 to Present; DLB 87

Deighton, Leonard Cyril 1929-
See Deighton, Len
See also CA 9-12R; CANR 19, 33, 68; DAM NOV, POP; DA3; MTCW 1, 2

Dekker, Thomas 1572(?)-1632 . **LC 22; DAM DRAM; DC 12**
See also CDBLB Before 1660; DLB 62, 172

Delafield, E. M. **TCLC 61**
See also Dashwood, Edmee Elizabeth Monica de la Pasture
See also DLB 34

de la Mare, Walter (John) 1873-1956 ..... **TCLC 4, 53; DAB; DAC; DAM MST, POET; NOV**
See also AW; CA 163; CDBLB 1914-1945; CLR 23; DA3; DLB 162; MTCW 1; SATA 16

Delaney, Franey
See O'Hara, John (Henry)

Delaney, Shelagh 1939- .... **CLC 29; DAM DRAM**
See also CA 17-20R; CANR 30, 67; CD-BLB 1960 to Present; DLB 13; MTCW 1

Delany, Martin Robinson 1812-1885 .... **NCLC 93**
See also DLB 50

Delany, Mary (Granville Pendarves) 1700-1788 .... **LC 12**

Delany, Samuel R(ay), Jr. 1942- . **CLC 8, 14, 38, 141; BLC 1; DAM MULT**
See also AAYA 24; BW 2, 3; CA 81-84; CANR 27, 43; DLB 8, 33; MTCW 1, 2

De La Ramee, (Marie) Louise 1839-1908
See Ouida
See also SATA 20

de la Roche, Mazo 1879-1961 .... **CLC 14**
See also CA 85-88; CANR 30; DLB 68; SATA 64

De La Salle, Innocent
See Hartmann, Sadakichi

Delbanco, Nicholas (Franklin) 1942- .... **CLC 6, 13**
See also CA 17-20R; CAAE 189; CAAS 2; CANR 29, 55; DLB 6, 234

del Castillo, Michel 1933- .... **CLC 38**
See also CA 109; CANR 77

Deledda, Grazia (Cosima) 1875(?)-1936 .... **TCLC 23**
See also CA 123

Delgado, Abelardo (Lalo) B(arrientos) 1930-
See also CA 131; CAAS 15; CANR 90; DAM MST, MULT; DLB 82; HLC 1; HW 1, 2

Delibes, Miguel **CLC 8, 18**
See also Delibes Setien, Miguel

Delibes Setien, Miguel 1920-
See Delibes, Miguel
See also CA 45-48; CANR 1, 32; HW 1; MTCW 1

DeLillo, Don 1936- ..... **CLC 8, 10, 13, 27, 39, 54, 76; DAM NOV, POP**
See also AMWS 6; BEST 89:1; CA 81-84; CANR 21, 76, 92; DA3; DLB 6, 173; MTCW 1, 2

de Lisser, H. G.
See De Lisser, H(erbert) G(eorge)
See also DLB 117

De Lisser, H(erbert) G(eorge) 1878-1944 .... **TCLC 12**
See also de Lisser, H. G.
See also BW 2; CA 109; 152

Deloney, Thomas 1543(?)-1600 .... **LC 41**
See also DLB 167

Deloria, Vine (Victor), Jr. 1933- ...... **CLC 21, 122; DAM MULT**
See also CA 53-56; CANR 5, 20, 48; DLB 175; MTCW 1; NNAL; SATA 21

Del Vecchio, John M(ichael) 1947- .. **CLC 29**
See also CA 110; DLBD 9

de Man, Paul (Adolph Michel) 1919-1983 .... **CLC 55**
See also CA 128; 111; CANR 61; DLB 67; MTCW 1, 2

DeMarinis, Rick 1934- .... **CLC 54**
See also CA 57-60, 184; CAAE 184; CAAS 24; CANR 9, 25, 50

Dembry, R. Emmet
See Murfree, Mary Noailles

Demby, William 1922- .... **CLC 53; BLC 1; DAM MULT**
See also BW 1, 3; CA 81-84; CANR 81; DLB 33

de Menton, Francisco
See Chin, Frank (Chew, Jr.)

Demetrius of Phalerum c. 307B.C.- .... **CMLC 34**

Demijohn, Thom
See Disch, Thomas M(ichael)

Deming, Richard 1915-1983
See Queen, Ellery
See also CA 9-12R; CANR 3, 94; SATA 24

de Molina, Tirso 1580(?)-1648 .... **DC 13**
See also HLCS 2

de Montherlant, Henry (Milon)
See Montherlant, Henry (Milon) de

Demosthenes 384B.C.-322B.C. ...... **CMLC 13**
See also DLB 176

de Natale, Francine
See Malzberg, Barry N(athaniel)

de Navarre, Marguerite 1492-1549 ..... **LC 61**

Denby, Edwin (Orr) 1903-1983 .... **CLC 48**
See also CA 138; 110

Denis, Julio
See Cortazar, Julio

Denmark, Harrison
See Zelazny, Roger (Joseph)

Dennis, John 1658-1734 .... **LC 11**
See also DLB 101

Dennis, Nigel (Forbes) 1912-1989 ...... **CLC 8**
See also CA 25-28R; 129; DLB 13, 15, 233; MTCW 1

Dent, Lester 1904(?)-1959 .... **TCLC 72**
See also CA 112; 161

De Palma, Brian (Russell) 1940- ...... **CLC 20**
See also CA 109

De Quincey, Thomas 1785-1859 ..... **NCLC 4, 87**
See also CDBLB 1789-1832; DLB 110; 144

Deren, Eleanora 1917(?)-1961
See Deren, Maya
See also CA 111

Deren, Maya CLC 16, 102
See also Deren, Eleanora

Derleth, August (William) 1909-1971 .... **CLC 31**
See also CA 1-4R; 29-32R; CANR 4; DLB 9; DLBD 17; SATA 5

Der Nister 1884-1950 .... **TCLC 56**

de Routisie, Albert
See Aragon, Louis

Derrida, Jacques 1930- .... **CLC 24, 87**
See also CA 124; 127; CANR 76; DLB 242; MTCW 1

Derry Down Derry
See Lear, Edward

Dersonnes, Jacques
See Simenon, Georges (Jacques Christian)

Desai, Anita 1937- ..... **CLC 19, 37, 97; DAB; DAM NOV**
See also BRWS 5; CA 81-84; CANR 33, 53, 95; DA3; MTCW 1, 2; SATA 63

Desai, Kiran 1971- .... **CLC 119**
See also CA 171

de Saint-Luc, Jean
See Glassco, John

de Saint Roman, Arnaud
See Aragon, Louis

Desbordes-Valmore, Marceline 1786-1859 .... **NCLC 97**
See also DLB 217

Descartes, Rene 1596-1650 .... **LC 20, 35**

De Sica, Vittorio 1901(?)-1974 .... **CLC 20**
See also CA 117

Desnos, Robert 1900-1945 .... **TCLC 22**
See also CA 121; 151

Destouches, Louis-Ferdinand 1894-1961 .... **CLC 9, 15**
See also Celine, Louis-Ferdinand
See also CA 85-88; CANR 28; MTCW 1

de Tolignac, Gaston
See Griffith, D(avid Lewelyn) W(ark)

Deutsch, Babette 1895-1982 .... **CLC 18**
See also CA 1-4R; 108; CANR 4, 79; DLB 45; SATA 1; SATA-Obit 33

Devenant, William 1606-1649 .... **LC 13**

Devkota, Laxmiprasad 1909-1959 . **TCLC 23**
See also CA 123

De Voto, Bernard (Augustine) 1897-1955 .... **TCLC 29**
See also CA 113; 160; DLB 9

De Vries, Peter 1910-1993 ..... **CLC 1, 2, 3, 7, 10, 28, 46; DAM NOV**
See also CA 17-20R; 142; CANR 41; DLB 6; DLBY 82; MTCW 1, 2

Dewey, John 1859-1952 .... **TCLC 95**
See also CA 114; 170

Dexter, John
See Bradley, Marion Zimmer
See also GLL 1

Dexter, Martin
See Faust, Frederick (Schiller)
See also TCWW 2

Dexter, Pete 1943- .. **CLC 34, 55; DAM POP**
See also BEST 89:2; CA 127; 131; INT 131; MTCW 1

Diamano, Silmang
See Senghor, Leopold Sedar

Diamond, Neil 1941- .... **CLC 30**
See also CA 108

Diaz del Castillo, Bernal 1496-1584 .. **LC 31; HLCS 1**

di Bassetto, Corno
See Shaw, George Bernard

Dick, Philip K(indred) 1928-1982 ... **CLC 10, 30, 72; DAM NOV, POP**
See also AAYA 24; CA 49-52; 106; CANR 2, 16; DA3; DLB 8; MTCW 1, 2

Dickens, Charles (John Huffam) 1812-1870 .... **NCLC 3, 8, 18, 26, 37, 50, 86; DA; DAB; DAC; DAM MST, NOV; SSC 17**
See also AAYA 23; CDBLB 1832-1890; DA3; DLB 21, 55, 70, 159, 166; JRDA; MAICYA; SATA 15

Dickey, James (Lafayette) 1923-1997 .... **CLC 1, 2, 4, 7, 10, 15, 47, 109; DAM NOV, POET, POP**
See also AITN 1, 2; AMWS 4; CA 9-12R; 156; CABS 2; CANR 10, 48, 61; CDALB 1968-1988; DA3; DLB 5, 193; DLBD 7; DLBY 82, 93, 96, 97, 98; INT CANR-10; MTCW 1, 2

Dickey, William 1928-1994 .... **CLC 3, 28**
See also CA 9-12R; 145; CANR 24, 79; DLB 5

Dickinson, Charles 1951- .... **CLC 49**
See also CA 128

Dickinson, Emily (Elizabeth) 1830-1886 ..... **NCLC 21, 77; DA; DAB; DAC; DAM MST, POET; PC 1**
See also AAYA 22; CDALB 1865-1917; DA3; DLB 1; SATA 29

Dickinson, Peter (Malcolm) 1927- .. **CLC 12, 35**
See also AAYA 9; CA 41-44R; CANR 31, 58, 88; CLR 29; DLB 87, 161; JRDA; MAICYA; SATA 5, 62, 95

Dickson, Carr
See Carr, John Dickson

Dickson, Carter
See Carr, John Dickson

Diderot, Denis 1713-1784 .... **LC 26**

Didion, Joan 1934- .... **CLC 1, 3, 8, 14, 32, 129; DAM NOV**
See also AITN 1; AMWS 4; CA 5-8R; CANR 14, 52, 76; CDALB 1968-1988; DA3; DLB 2, 173, 185; DLBY 81, 86; MTCW 1, 2; TCWW 2

Dietrich, Robert
See Hunt, E(verette) Howard, (Jr.)

Difusa, Pati
See Almodovar, Pedro

Dillard, Annie 1945- .. **CLC 9, 60, 115; DAM NOV**
See also AAYA 6; AMWS 6; CA 49-52; CANR 3, 43, 62, 90; DA3; DLBY 80, MTCW 1, 2; SATA 10

Dillard, R(ichard) H(enry) W(ilde) 1937- .... **CLC 5**
See also CA 21-24R; CAAS 7; CANR 10; DLB 5

Dillon, Eilis 1920-1994 .... **CLC 17**
See also AW; CA 9-12R; 182; 147; CAAE 182; CAAS 3; CANR 4, 38, 78; CLR 26; MAICYA; SATA 2, 74; SATA-Essay 105; SATA-Obit 83

Dimont, Penelope
See Mortimer, Penelope (Ruth)

Dinesen, Isak CLC 10, 29, 95; SSC 7
See also Blixen, Karen (Christentze Dinesen)
See also MTCW 1

Ding Ling CLC 68
See also Chiang, Pin-chin

Diphusa, Patty
See Almodovar, Pedro

Disch, Thomas M(ichael) 1940- ... **CLC 7, 36**
See also AAYA 17; CA 21-24R; CAAS 4; CANR 17, 36, 54, 89; CLR 18; DA3; DLB 8; MAICYA; MTCW 1, 2; SAAS 15; SATA 92

Disch, Tom
See Disch, Thomas M(ichael)

d'Isly, Georges
See Simenon, Georges (Jacques Christian)

Disraeli, Benjamin 1804-1881 ... **NCLC 2, 39, 79**
See also DLB 21, 55

Ditcum, Steve
See Crumb, R(obert)

Dixon, Paige
See Corcoran, Barbara

Dixon, Stephen 1936- .... **CLC 52; SSC 16**
See also CA 89-92; CANR 17, 40, 54, 91;
DLB 130

Doak, Annie
See Dillard, Annie

Dobell, Sydney Thompson
1824-1874 .... **NCLC 43**
See also DLB 32

Doblin, Alfred TCLC 13
See also Doeblin, Alfred

Dobrolyubov, Nikolai Alexandrovich
1836-1861 .... **NCLC 5**

Dobson, Austin 1840-1921 .... **TCLC 79**
See also DLB 35; 144

Dobyns, Stephen 1941- .... **CLC 37**
See also CA 45-48; CANR 2, 18

Doctorow, E(dgar) L(aurence)
1931- .... **CLC 6, 11, 15, 18, 37, 44, 65,
113; DAM NOV, POP**
See also AAYA 22; AITN 2; AMWS 4;
BEST 89:3; CA 45-48; CANR 2, 33, 51,
76; CDALB 1968-1988; DA3; DLB 2, 28,
173; DLBY 80; MTCW 1, 2

Dodgson, Charles Lutwidge 1832-1898
See Carroll, Lewis
See also AW 2; CLR 2; DA; DAB; DAC;
DAM MST, NOV, POET; DA3; MAI-
CYA; SATA 100

Dodson, Owen (Vincent)
1914-1983 .... **CLC 79; BLC 1; DAM
MULT**
See also BW 1; CA 65-68; 110; CANR 24;
DLB 76

Doeblin, Alfred 1878-1957 .... **TCLC 13**
See also Doblin, Alfred
See also CA 110; 141; DLB 66

Doerr, Harriet 1910- .... **CLC 34**
See also CA 117; 122; CANR 47; INT 122

Domecq, H(onorio Bustos)
See Bioy Casares, Adolfo

Domecq, H(onorio) Bustos
See Bioy Casares, Adolfo; Borges, Jorge
Luis

Domini, Rey
See Lorde, Audre (Geraldine)
See also GLL 1

Dominique
See Proust, (Valentin-Louis-George-Eugene-
)Marcel

Don, A
See Stephen, SirLeslie

Donaldson, Stephen R. 1947- .. **CLC 46, 138;
DAM POP**
See also AAYA 36; CA 89-92; CANR 13,
55; INT CANR-13; SATA 121

Donleavy, J(ames) P(atrick) 1926- .... **CLC 1,
4, 6, 10, 45**
See also AITN 2; CA 9-12R; CANR 24, 49,
62, 80; DLB 6, 173; INT CANR-24;
MTCW 1, 2

Donne, John 1572-1631 .... **LC 10, 24; DA;
DAB; DAC; DAM MST, POET; PC 1**
See also AW; CDBLB Before 1660; DLB
121, 151

Donnell, David 1939(?)- .... **CLC 34**

Donoghue, P. S.
See Hunt, E(verette) Howard, (Jr.)

Donoso (Yanez), Jose 1924-1996 ... **CLC 4, 8,
11, 32, 99; DAM MULT; HLC 1; SSC
34**
See also CA 81-84; 155; CANR 32, 73;
DLB 113; HW 1, 2; MTCW 1, 2

Donovan, John 1928-1992 .... **CLC 35**
See also AAYA 20; AW; CA 97-100; 137;
CLR 3; MAICYA; SATA 72; SATA-Brief
29

Don Roberto
See Cunninghame Graham, Robert
(Gallnigad) Bontine

Doolittle, Hilda 1886-1961 . **CLC 3, 8, 14, 31,
34, 73; DA; DAC; DAM MST, POET;
PC 5**
See also H. D.
See also AMWS 1; AW; CA 97-100; CANR
35; DLB 4, 45; GLL 1; MTCW 1, 2

Dorfman, Ariel 1942- ...... **CLC 48, 77; DAM
MULT; HLC 1**
See also CA 124; 130; CANR 67, 70; CWW
2; HW 1, 2; INT 130

Dorn, Edward (Merton)
1929-1999 .... **CLC 10, 18**
See also CA 93-96; 187; CANR 42, 79;
DLB 5; INT 93-96

Dorris, Michael (Anthony)
1945-1997 .... **CLC 109; DAM MULT,
NOV**
See also AAYA 20; AW; BEST 90:1; CA
102; 157; CANR 19, 46, 75; CLR 58;
DA3; DLB 175; MTCW 2; NNAL; SATA
75; SATA-Obit 94; TCWW 2

Dorris, Michael A.
See Dorris, Michael (Anthony)

Dorsan, Luc
See Simenon, Georges (Jacques Christian)

Dorsange, Jean
See Simenon, Georges (Jacques Christian)

Dos Passos, John (Roderigo)
1896-1970 ... **CLC 1, 4, 8, 11, 15, 25, 34,
82; DA; DAB; DAC; DAM MST, NOV**
See also AW; CA 1-4R; 29-32R; CANR 3;
CDALB 1929-1941; DA3; DLB 4, 9;
DLBD 1, 15; DLBY 96; MTCW 1, 2

Dossage, Jean
See Simenon, Georges (Jacques Christian)

Dostoevsky, Fedor Mikhailovich
1821-1881 . **NCLC 2, 7, 21, 33, 43; DA;
DAB; DAC; DAM MST, NOV; SSC 2,
33, 44**
See also AW; DA3; DLB 238

Doughty, Charles M(ontagu)
1843-1926 .... **TCLC 27**
See also CA 115; 178; DLB 19, 57, 174

Douglas, Ellen CLC 73
See also Haxton, Josephine Ayres; Williamson, Ellen Douglas

Douglas, Gavin 1475(?)-1522 .... **LC 20**
See also DLB 132

Douglas, George
See Brown, George Douglas

Douglas, Keith (Castellain)
1920-1944 .... **TCLC 40**
See also CA 160; DLB 27

Douglas, Leonard
See Bradbury, Ray (Douglas)

Douglas, Michael
See Crichton, (John) Michael

Douglas, (George) Norman
1868-1952 .... **TCLC 68**
See also CA 119; 157; DLB 34, 195

Douglas, William
See Brown, George Douglas

Douglass, Frederick 1817(?)-1895 .. **NCLC 7,
55; BLC 1; DA; DAC; DAM MST,
MULT**
See also AMWS 3; AW; CDALB 1640-
1865; DA3; DLB 1, 43, 50, 79; SATA 29

Dourado, (Waldomiro Freitas) Autran
1926- .... **CLC 23, 60**
See also CA 25-28R; 179; CANR 34, 81;
DLB 145; HW 2

Dourado, Waldomiro Autran
See Dourado, (Waldomiro Freitas) Autran
See also CA 179

Dove, Rita (Frances) 1952- .... **CLC 50, 81;
BLCS; DAM MULT, POET; PC 6**
See also AMWS 4; BW 2; CA 109; CAAS
19; CANR 27, 42, 68, 76; CDALBS;
DA3; DLB 120; MTCW 1

Doveglion
See Villa, Jose Garcia

Dowell, Coleman 1925-1985 .... **CLC 60**
See also CA 25-28R; 117; CANR 10; DLB
130; GLL 2

Dowson, Ernest (Christopher)
1867-1900 .... **TCLC 4**
See also CA 105; 150; DLB 19, 135

Doyle, A. Conan
See Doyle, Arthur Conan

Doyle, Arthur Conan 1859-1930 .... **TCLC 7;
DA; DAB; DAC; DAM MST, NOV;
SSC 12**
See also Doyle, Sir Arthur Conan
See also AAYA 14; AW; CA 104; 122; CD-
BLB 1890-1914; DA3; DLB 18, 70, 156,
178; MTCW 1, 2; SATA 24

Doyle, Conan
See Doyle, Arthur Conan

Doyle, John
See Graves, Robert (von Ranke)

Doyle, Roddy 1958(?)- .... **CLC 81**
See also AAYA 14; BRWS 5; CA 143;
CANR 73; DA3; DLB 194

Doyle, Sir A. Conan
See Doyle, Arthur Conan

Doyle, Sir Arthur Conan
See Doyle, Arthur Conan
See also BRWS 2

Dr. A
See Asimov, Isaac; Silverstein, Alvin

Drabble, Margaret 1939- ...... **CLC 2, 3, 5, 8,
10, 22, 53, 129; DAB; DAC; DAM
MST, NOV, POP**
See also BRWS 4; CA 13-16R; CANR 18,
35, 63; CDBLB 1960 to Present; DA3;
DLB 14, 155, 231; MTCW 1, 2; SATA 48

Drapier, M. B.
See Swift, Jonathan

Drayham, James
See Mencken, H(enry) L(ouis)

Drayton, Michael 1563-1631 ..... **LC 8; DAM
POET**
See also DLB 121

Dreadstone, Carl
See Campbell, (John) Ramsey

Dreiser, Theodore (Herman Albert)
1871-1945 .... **TCLC 10, 18, 35, 83; DA;
DAC; DAM MST, NOV; SSC 30**
See also AW; CA 106; 132; CDALB 1865-
1917; DA3; DLB 9, 12, 102, 137; DLBD
1; MTCW 1, 2

Drexler, Rosalyn 1926- .... **CLC 2, 6**
See also CA 81-84; CANR 68

Dreyer, Carl Theodor 1889-1968 ...... **CLC 16**
See also CA 116

Drieu la Rochelle, Pierre(-Eugene)
1893-1945 .... **TCLC 21**
See also CA 117; DLB 72

Drinkwater, John 1882-1937 .... **TCLC 57**
See also CA 109; 149; DLB 10, 19, 149

Drop Shot
See Cable, George Washington

Droste-Hulshoff, Annette Freiin von
1797-1848 .... **NCLC 3**
See also DLB 133

Drummond, Walter
See Silverberg, Robert

Drummond, William Henry
1854-1907 .... **TCLC 25**
See also CA 160; DLB 92

Drummond de Andrade, Carlos
1902-1987 .... **CLC 18**
See also Andrade, Carlos Drummond de
See also CA 132; 123

Drury, Allen (Stuart) 1918-1998 .... **CLC 37**
See also CA 57-60; 170; CANR 18, 52; INT
CANR-18

Dryden, John 1631-1700 .... **LC 3, 21; DA; DAB; DAC; DAM DRAM, MST, POET; DC 3; PC 25**
See also AW; CDBLB 1660-1789; DLB 80, 101, 131

Duberman, Martin (Bauml) 1930- ..... **CLC 8**
See also CA 1-4R; CANR 2, 63

Dubie, Norman (Evans) 1945- .... **CLC 36**
See also CA 69-72; CANR 12; DLB 120

Du Bois, W(illiam) E(dward) B(urghardt) 1868-1963 ... **CLC 1, 2, 13, 64, 96; BLC 1; DA; DAC; DAM MST, MULT, NOV**
See also AMWS 2; AW; BW 1, 3; CA 85-88; CANR 34, 82; CDALB 1865-1917; DA3; DLB 47, 50, 91; MTCW 1, 2; SATA 42

Dubus, Andre 1936-1999 ..... **CLC 13, 36, 97; SSC 15**
See also AMWS 7; CA 21-24R; 177; CANR 17; DLB 130; INT CANR-17

Duca Minimo
See D'Annunzio, Gabriele

Ducharme, Rejean 1941- .... **CLC 74**
See also CA 165; DLB 60

Duclos, Charles Pinot 1704-1772 .... **LC 1**

Dudek, Louis 1918- .... **CLC 11, 19**
See also CA 45-48; CAAS 14; CANR 1; DLB 88

Duerrenmatt, Friedrich 1921-1990 ... **CLC 1, 4, 8, 11, 15, 43, 102; DAM DRAM**
See also CA 17-20R; CANR 33; DLB 69, 124; MTCW 1, 2

Duffy, Bruce 1953(?)- .... **CLC 50**
See also CA 172

Duffy, Maureen 1933- .... **CLC 37**
See also CA 25-28R; CANR 33, 68; DLB 14; MTCW 1

Dugan, Alan 1923- .... **CLC 2, 6**
See also CA 81-84; DLB 5

du Gard, Roger Martin
See Martin du Gard, Roger

Duhamel, Georges 1884-1966 .... **CLC 8**
See also CA 81-84; 25-28R; CANR 35; DLB 65; MTCW 1

Dujardin, Edouard (Emile Louis) 1861-1949 .... **TCLC 13**
See also CA 109; DLB 123

Dulles, John Foster 1888-1959 ...... **TCLC 72**
See also CA 115; 149

Dumas, Alexandre (pere)
See Dumas, Alexandre (Davy de la Pailleterie)

Dumas, Alexandre (Davy de la Pailleterie) 1802-1870 ...... **NCLC 11, 71; DA; DAB; DAC; DAM MST, NOV**
See also AW; DA3; DLB 119, 192; SATA 18

Dumas, Alexandre (fils) 1824-1895 .... **NCLC 9; DC 1**
See also AAYA 22; DLB 192; EW 1

Dumas, Claudine
See Malzberg, Barry N(athaniel)

Dumas, Henry L. 1934-1968 .... **CLC 6, 62**
See also BW 1; CA 85-88; DLB 41

du Maurier, Daphne 1907-1989 .. **CLC 6, 11, 59; DAB; DAC; DAM MST, POP; SSC 18**
See also AAYA 37; BRWS 3; CA 5-8R; 128; CANR 6, 55; DA3; DLB 191; MTCW 1, 2; SATA 27; SATA-Obit 60

Du Maurier, George 1834-1896 ..... **NCLC 86**
See also DLB 153, 178

Dunbar, Paul Laurence 1872-1906 . **TCLC 2, 12; BLC 1; DA; DAC; DAM MST, MULT, POET; PC 5; SSC 8**
See also AMWS 2; AW; BW 1, 3; CA 104; 124; CANR 79; CDALB 1865-1917; DA3; DLB 50, 54, 78; SATA 34

Dunbar, William 1460(?)-1520(?) .... **LC 20**
See also DLB 132, 146

Duncan, Dora Angela
See Duncan, Isadora

Duncan, Isadora 1877(?)-1927 .... **TCLC 68**
See also CA 118; 149

Duncan, Lois 1934- .... **CLC 26**
See also AAYA 4, 34; AW; CA 1-4R; CANR 2, 23, 36; CLR 29; JRDA; MAICYA; SAAS 2; SATA 1, 36, 75

Duncan, Robert (Edward) 1919-1988 .... **CLC 1, 2, 4, 7, 15, 41, 55; DAM POET; PC 2**
See also CA 9-12R; 124; CANR 28, 62; DLB 5, 16, 193; MTCW 1, 2

Duncan, Sara Jeannette 1861-1922 .... **TCLC 60**
See also CA 157; DLB 92

Dunlap, William 1766-1839 .... **NCLC 2**
See also DLB 30, 37, 59

Dunn, Douglas (Eaglesham) 1942- .... **CLC 6, 40**
See also CA 45-48; CANR 2, 33; DLB 40; MTCW 1

Dunn, Katherine (Karen) 1945- .... **CLC 71**
See also CA 33-36R; CANR 72; MTCW 1

Dunn, Stephen 1939- .... **CLC 36**
See also CA 33-36R; CANR 12, 48, 53; DLB 105

Dunne, Finley Peter 1867-1936 ...... **TCLC 28**
See also CA 108; 178; DLB 11, 23

Dunne, John Gregory 1932- .... **CLC 28**
See also CA 25-28R; CANR 14, 50; DLBY 80

Dunsany, Edward John Moreton Drax Plunkett 1878-1957
See Dunsany, Lord
See also CA 104; 148; DLB 10; MTCW 1

Dunsany, Lord TCLC 2, 59
See also Dunsany, Edward John Moreton Drax Plunkett
See also DLB 77, 153, 156

du Perry, Jean
See Simenon, Georges (Jacques Christian)

Durang, Christopher (Ferdinand) 1949- .... **CLC 27, 38**
See also CA 105; CANR 50, 76; MTCW 1

Duras, Marguerite 1914-1996 . **CLC 3, 6, 11, 20, 34, 40, 68, 100; SSC 40**
See also CA 25-28R; 151; CANR 50; CWW 2; DLB 83; MTCW 1, 2

Durban, (Rosa) Pam 1947- .... **CLC 39**
See also CA 123

Durcan, Paul 1944- .... **CLC 43, 70; DAM POET**
See also CA 134

Durkheim, Emile 1858-1917 .... **TCLC 55**

Durrell, Lawrence (George) 1912-1990 .... **CLC 1, 4, 6, 8, 13, 27, 41; DAM NOV**
See also BRWS 1; CA 9-12R; 132; CANR 40, 77; CDBLB 1945-1960; DLB 15, 27, 204; DLBY 90; MTCW 1, 2

Dürrenmatt, Friedrich
See Duerrenmatt, Friedrich

Dutt, Toru 1856-1877 .... **NCLC 29**
See also DLB 240

Dwight, Timothy 1752-1817 .... **NCLC 13**
See also DLB 37

Dworkin, Andrea 1946- .... **CLC 43, 123**
See also CA 77-80; CAAS 21; CANR 16, 39, 76, 96; GLL 1; INT CANR-16; MTCW 1, 2

Dwyer, Deanna
See Koontz, Dean R(ay)

Dwyer, K. R.
See Koontz, Dean R(ay)

Dwyer, Thomas A. 1923- .... **CLC 114**
See also CA 115

Dybek, Stuart 1942- .... **CLC 114**
See also CA 97-100; CANR 39; DLB 130

Dye, Richard
See De Voto, Bernard (Augustine)

Dylan, Bob 1941- .... **CLC 3, 4, 6, 12, 77**
See also CA 41-44R; DLB 16

E. V. L.
See Lucas, E(dward) V(errall)

Eagleton, Terence (Francis) 1943- .. **CLC 63, 132**
See also CA 57-60; CANR 7, 23, 68; DLB 242; MTCW 1, 2

Eagleton, Terry
See Eagleton, Terence (Francis)

Early, Jack
See Scoppettone, Sandra
See also GLL 1

East, Michael
See West, Morris L(anglo)

Eastaway, Edward
See Thomas, (Philip) Edward

Eastlake, William (Derry) 1917-1997 .... **CLC 8**
See also CA 5-8R; 158; CAAS 1; CANR 5, 63; DLB 6, 206; INT CANR-5; TCWW 2

Eastman, Charles A(lexander) 1858-1939 .... **TCLC 55; DAM MULT**
See also AW 1; CA 179; CANR 91; DLB 175; NNAL

Eberhart, Richard (Ghormley) 1904- .. **CLC 3, 11, 19, 56; DAM POET**
See also CA 1-4R; CANR 2; CDALB 1941-1968; DLB 48; MTCW 1

Eberstadt, Fernanda 1960- .... **CLC 39**
See also CA 136; CANR 69

Echegaray (y Eizaguirre), Jose (Maria Waldo) 1832-1916 .... **TCLC 4; HLCS 1**
See also CA 104; CANR 32; HW 1; MTCW 1

Echeverria, (Jose) Esteban (Antonino) 1805-1851 .... **NCLC 18**

Echo
See Proust, (Valentin-Louis-George-Eugene-)Marcel

Eckert, Allan W. 1931- .... **CLC 17**
See also AAYA 18; CA 13-16R; CANR 14, 45; INT CANR-14; SAAS 21; SATA 29, 91; SATA-Brief 27

Eckhart, Meister 1260(?)-1327(?) ... **CMLC 9**
See also DLB 115

Eckmar, F. R.
See de Hartog, Jan

Eco, Umberto 1932- .... **CLC 28, 60; DAM NOV, POP**
See also BEST 90:1; CA 77-80; CANR 12, 33, 55; CWW 2; DA3; DLB 196, 242; MTCW 1, 2

Eddison, E(ric) R(ucker) 1882-1945 .... **TCLC 15**
See also CA 109; 156

Eddy, Mary (Ann Morse) Baker 1821-1910 .... **TCLC 71**
See also CA 113; 174

Edel, (Joseph) Leon 1907-1997 .. **CLC 29, 34**
See also CA 1-4R; 161; CANR 1, 22; DLB 103; INT CANR-22

Eden, Emily 1797-1869 .... **NCLC 10**

Edgar, David 1948- .. **CLC 42; DAM DRAM**
See also CA 57-60; CANR 12, 61; DLB 13, 233; MTCW 1

Edgerton, Clyde (Carlyle) 1944- ...... **CLC 39**
See also AAYA 17; AW; CA 118; 134; CANR 64; INT 134

Edgeworth, Maria 1768-1849 .... **NCLC 1, 51**
See also BRWS 3; DLB 116, 159, 163; SATA 21

Edmonds, Paul
See Kuttner, Henry

Edmonds, Walter D(umaux)
1903-1998 .... **CLC 35**
See also CA 5-8R; CANR 2; DLB 9; MAI-
CYA; SAAS 4; SATA 1, 27; SATA-Obit
99

Edmondson, Wallace
See Ellison, Harlan (Jay)

Edson, Russell CLC 13
See also CA 33-36R

Edwards, Bronwen Elizabeth
See Rose, Wendy

Edwards, G(erald) B(asil)
1899-1976 .... **CLC 25**
See also CA 110

Edwards, Gus 1939- .... **CLC 43**
See also CA 108; INT 108

Edwards, Jonathan 1703-1758 .... **LC 7, 54;**
DA; DAC; DAM MST
See also DLB 24

Efron, Marina Ivanovna Tsvetaeva
See Tsvetaeva (Efron), Marina (Ivanovna)

Ehle, John (Marsden, Jr.) 1925- ...... **CLC 27**
See also CA 9-12R

Ehrenbourg, Ilya (Grigoryevich)
See Ehrenburg, Ilya (Grigoryevich)

Ehrenburg, Ilya (Grigoryevich)
1891-1967 .... **CLC 18, 34, 62**
See also CA 102; 25-28R

Ehrenburg, Ilyo (Grigoryevich)
See Ehrenburg, Ilya (Grigoryevich)

Ehrenreich, Barbara 1941- .... **CLC 110**
See also BEST 90:4; CA 73-76; CANR 16,
37, 62; MTCW 1, 2

Eich, Guenter 1907-1972 .... **CLC 15**
See also CA 111; 93-96; DLB 69, 124

Eichendorff, Joseph Freiherr von
1788-1857 .... **NCLC 8**
See also DLB 90

Eigner, Larry CLC 9
See also Eigner, Laurence (Joel)
See also CAAS 23; DLB 5

Eigner, Laurence (Joel) 1927-1996
See Eigner, Larry
See also CA 9-12R; 151; CANR 6, 84; DLB
193

Einstein, Albert 1879-1955 .... **TCLC 65**
See also CA 121; 133; MTCW 1, 2

Eiseley, Loren Corey 1907-1977 .... **CLC 7**
See also AAYA 5; CA 1-4R; 73-76; CANR
6; DLBD 17

Eisenstadt, Jill 1963- .... **CLC 50**
See also CA 140

Eisenstein, Sergei (Mikhailovich)
1898-1948 .... **TCLC 57**
See also CA 114; 149

Eisner, Simon
See Kornbluth, C(yril) M.

Ekeloef, (Bengt) Gunnar
1907-1968 ... **CLC 27; DAM POET; PC**
23
See also CA 123; 25-28R

Ekelöf, (Bengt) Gunnar
See Ekeloef, (Bengt) Gunnar

Ekelund, Vilhelm 1880-1949 .... **TCLC 75**
See also CA 189

Ekwensi, C. O. D.
See Ekwensi, Cyprian (Odiatu Duaka)

Ekwensi, Cyprian (Odiatu Duaka)
1921- ...... **CLC 4; BLC 1; DAM MULT**
See also BW 2, 3; CA 29-32R; CANR 18,
42, 74; DLB 117; MTCW 1, 2; SATA 66

Elaine TCLC 18
See also Leverson, Ada

El Crummo
See Crumb, R(obert)

Elder, Lonne III 1931-1996 .... **DC 8**
See also BLC 1; BW 1, 3; CA 81-84; 152;
CANR 25; DAM MULT; DLB 7, 38, 44

Eleanor of Aquitaine 1122-1204 ... **CMLC 39**

Elia
See Lamb, Charles

Eliade, Mircea 1907-1986 .... **CLC 19**
See also CA 65-68; 119; CANR 30, 62;
DLB 220; MTCW 1

Eliot, A. D.
See Jewett, (Theodora) Sarah Orne

Eliot, Alice
See Jewett, (Theodora) Sarah Orne

Eliot, Dan
See Silverberg, Robert

Eliot, George 1819-1880 ...... **NCLC 4, 13, 23,**
41, 49, 89; DA; DAB; DAC; DAM
MST, NOV; PC 20
See also AW; CDBLB 1832-1890; DA3;
DLB 21, 35, 55

Eliot, John 1604-1690 .... **LC 5**
See also DLB 24

Eliot, T(homas) S(tearns)
1888-1965 ...... **CLC 1, 2, 3, 6, 9, 10, 13,**
15, 24, 34, 41, 55, 57, 113; DA; DAB;
DAC; DAM DRAM, MST, POET; PC
5, 31
See also AAYA 28; AW; CA 5-8R; 25-28R;
CANR 41; CDALB 1929-1941; DA3;
DLB 7, 10, 45, 63; DLBY 88; MTCW 1,
2

Elizabeth 1866-1941 .... **TCLC 41**

Elkin, Stanley L(awrence)
1930-1995 .. **CLC 4, 6, 9, 14, 27, 51, 91;**
DAM NOV, POP; SSC 12
See also AMWS 6; CA 9-12R; 148; CANR
8, 46; DLB 2, 28; DLBY 80; INT
CANR-8; MTCW 1, 2

Elledge, Scott CLC 34

Elliot, Don
See Silverberg, Robert

Elliott, Don
See Silverberg, Robert

Elliott, George P(aul) 1918-1980 .... **CLC 2**
See also CA 1-4R; 97-100; CANR 2

Elliott, Janice 1931-1995 .... **CLC 47**
See also CA 13-16R; CANR 8, 29, 84; DLB
14; SATA 119

Elliott, Sumner Locke 1917-1991 ..... **CLC 38**
See also CA 5-8R; 134; CANR 2, 21

Elliott, William
See Bradbury, Ray (Douglas)

Ellis, A. E. CLC 7

Ellis, Alice Thomas CLC 40
See also Haycraft, Anna (Margaret)
See also DLB 194; MTCW 1

Ellis, Bret Easton 1964- ..... **CLC 39, 71, 117;**
DAM POP
See also AAYA 2; CA 118; 123; CANR 51,
74; DA3; INT 123; MTCW 1

Ellis, (Henry) Havelock
1859-1939 .... **TCLC 14**
See also CA 109; 169; DLB 190

Ellis, Landon
See Ellison, Harlan (Jay)

Ellis, Trey 1962- .... **CLC 55**
See also CA 146; CANR 92

Ellison, Harlan (Jay) 1934- ... **CLC 1, 13, 42,**
139; DAM POP; SSC 14
See also AAYA 29; CA 5-8R; CANR 5, 46;
DLB 8; INT CANR-5; MTCW 1, 2;
SCFW 2

Ellison, Ralph (Waldo) 1914-1994 .... **CLC 1,**
3, 11, 54, 86, 114; BLC 1; DA; DAB;
DAC; DAM MST, MULT, NOV; SSC
26
See also AAYA 19; AMWS 2; AW; BW 1,
3; CA 9-12R; 145; CANR 24, 53; CDALB
1941-1968; DA3; DLB 2, 76, 227; DLBY
94; MTCW 1, 2

Ellmann, Lucy (Elizabeth) 1956- ..... **CLC 61**
See also CA 128

Ellmann, Richard (David)
1918-1987 .... **CLC 50**
See also BEST 89:2; CA 1-4R; 122; CANR
2, 28, 61; DLB 103; DLBY 87; MTCW
1, 2

Elman, Richard (Martin)
1934-1997 .... **CLC 19**
See also CA 17-20R; 163; CAAS 3; CANR
47

Elron
See Hubbard, L(afayette) Ron(ald)

Eluard, Paul TCLC 7, 41
See also Grindel, Eugene

Elyot, Sir Thomas 1490(?)-1546 .... **LC 11**

Elytis, Odysseus 1911-1996 .... **CLC 15, 49,**
100; DAM POET; PC 21
See also Alepoudelis, Odysseus
See also CA 102; 151; CANR 94; CWW 2;
MTCW 1, 2

Emecheta, (Florence Onye) Buchi
1944- .. **CLC 14, 48, 128; BLC 2; DAM**
MULT
See also BW 2, 3; CA 81-84; CANR 27,
81; DA3; DLB 117; MTCW 1, 2; SATA
66

Emerson, Mary Moody
1774-1863 .... **NCLC 66**

Emerson, Ralph Waldo 1803-1882 . **NCLC 1,**
38; DA; DAB; DAC; DAM MST,
POET; PC 18
See also AW; CDALB 1640-1865; DA3;
DLB 1, 59, 73, 223

Eminescu, Mihail 1850-1889 .... **NCLC 33**

Empson, William 1906-1984 ... **CLC 3, 8, 19,**
33, 34
See also BRWS 2; CA 17-20R; 112; CANR
31, 61; DLB 20; MTCW 1, 2

Enchi, Fumiko (Ueda) 1905-1986 ..... **CLC 31**
See also CA 129; 121; DLB 182

Ende, Michael (Andreas Helmuth)
1929-1995 .... **CLC 31**
See also CA 118; 124; 149; CANR 36; CLR
14; DLB 75; MAICYA; SATA 61; SATA-
Brief 42; SATA-Obit 86

Endo, Shusaku 1923-1996 ..... **CLC 7, 14, 19,**
54, 99; DAM NOV
See also CA 29-32R; 153; CANR 21, 54;
DA3; DLB 182; MTCW 1, 2

Engel, Marian 1933-1985 .... **CLC 36**
See also CA 25-28R; CANR 12; DLB 53;
INT CANR-12

Engelhardt, Frederick
See Hubbard, L(afayette) Ron(ald)

Engels, Friedrich 1820-1895 .... **NCLC 85**
See also DLB 129

Enright, D(ennis) J(oseph) 1920- .. **CLC 4, 8,**
31
See also CA 1-4R; CANR 1, 42, 83; DLB
27; SATA 25

Enzensberger, Hans Magnus
1929- .... **CLC 43; PC 28**
See also CA 116; 119

Ephron, Nora 1941- .... **CLC 17, 31**
See also AAYA 35; AITN 2; CA 65-68;
CANR 12, 39, 83

Epicurus 341B.C.-270B.C. .... **CMLC 21**
See also DLB 176

Epsilon
See Betjeman, John

Epstein, Daniel Mark 1948- .... **CLC 7**
See also CA 49-52; CANR 2, 53, 90

Epstein, Jacob 1956- .... **CLC 19**
See also CA 114

Epstein, Jean 1897-1953 .... **TCLC 92**

Epstein, Joseph 1937- .... **CLC 39**
See also CA 112; 119; CANR 50, 65

Epstein, Leslie 1938- .... **CLC 27**
See also CA 73-76; CAAS 12; CANR
23, 69

Equiano, Olaudah 1745(?)-1797 .... **LC 16;**
BLC 2; DAM MULT
See also DLB 37, 50
Erasmus, Desiderius 1469(?)-1536 ...... **LC 16**
Erdman, Paul E(mil) 1932- .... **CLC 25**
See also AITN 1; CA 61-64; CANR 13, 43,
84
Erdrich, Louise 1954- .... **CLC 39, 54, 120;**
DAM MULT, NOV, POP
See also AAYA 10; AMWS 4; BEST 89:1;
CA 114; CANR 41, 62; CDALBS; DA3;
DLB 152, 175, 206; MTCW 1; NNAL;
SATA 94; TCWW 2
Erenburg, Ilya (Grigoryevich)
See Ehrenburg, Ilya (Grigoryevich)
Erickson, Stephen Michael 1950-
See Erickson, Steve
See also CA 129
Erickson, Steve CLC 64
See also Erickson, Stephen Michael
See also CANR 60, 68
Ericson, Walter
See Fast, Howard (Melvin)
Eriksson, Buntel
See Bergman, (Ernst) Ingmar
Ernaux, Annie 1940- .... **CLC 88**
See also CA 147; CANR 93
Erskine, John 1879-1951 .... **TCLC 84**
See also CA 112; 159; DLB 9, 102
Eschenbach, Wolfram von
See Wolfram von Eschenbach
Eseki, Bruno
See Mphahlele, Ezekiel
Esenin, Sergei (Alexandrovich)
1895-1925 .... **TCLC 4**
See also CA 104
Eshleman, Clayton 1935- .... **CLC 7**
See also CA 33-36R; CAAS 6; CANR 93;
DLB 5
Espriella, Don Manuel Alvarez
See Southey, Robert
Espriu, Salvador 1913-1985 .... **CLC 9**
See also CA 154; 115; DLB 134
Espronceda, Jose de 1808-1842 ..... **NCLC 39**
Esquivel, Laura 1951(?)- ... **CLC 141; HLCS**
1
See also AAYA 29; CA 143; CANR 68;
DA3; MTCW 1
Esse, James
See Stephens, James
Esterbrook, Tom
See Hubbard, L(afayette) Ron(ald)
Estleman, Loren D. 1952- ..... **CLC 48; DAM**
NOV, POP
See also AAYA 27; CA 85-88; CANR 27,
74; DA3; DLB 226; INT CANR-27;
MTCW 1, 2
Euclid 306B.C.-283B.C. .... **CMLC 25**
Eugenides, Jeffrey 1960(?)- .... **CLC 81**
See also CA 144
Euripides c. 485B.C.-406B.C. .... **CMLC 23;**
DA; DAB; DAC; DAM DRAM, MST;
DC 4
See also AW; DA3; DLB 176
Evan, Evin
See Faust, Frederick (Schiller)
Evans, Caradoc 1878-1945 ... **TCLC 85; SSC**
43
Evans, Evan
See Faust, Frederick (Schiller)
See also TCWW 2
Evans, Marian
See Eliot, George
Evans, Mary Ann
See Eliot, George
Evarts, Esther
See Benson, Sally

Everett, Percival
See Everett, Percival L.
Everett, Percival L. 1956- .... **CLC 57**
See also Everett, Percival
See also BW 2; CA 129; CANR 94
Everson, R(onald) G(ilmour)
1903-1992 .... **CLC 27**
See also CA 17-20R; DLB 88
Everson, William (Oliver)
1912-1994 .... **CLC 1, 5, 14**
See also CA 9-12R; 145; CANR 20; DLB
212; MTCW 1
Evtushenko, Evgenii Aleksandrovich
See Yevtushenko, Yevgeny (Alexandrovich)
Ewart, Gavin (Buchanan)
1916-1995 .... **CLC 13, 46**
See also CA 89-92; 150; CANR 17, 46;
DLB 40; MTCW 1
Ewers, Hanns Heinz 1871-1943 ..... **TCLC 12**
See also CA 109; 149
Ewing, Frederick R.
See Sturgeon, Theodore (Hamilton)
Exley, Frederick (Earl) 1929-1992 .... **CLC 6,**
11
See also AITN 2; CA 81-84; 138; DLB 143;
DLBY 81
Eynhardt, Guillermo
See Quiroga, Horacio (Sylvestre)
Ezekiel, Nissim 1924- .... **CLC 61**
See also CA 61-64
Ezekiel, Tish O'Dowd 1943- .... **CLC 34**
See also CA 129
Fadeyev, A.
See Bulgya, Alexander Alexandrovich
Fadeyev, Alexander TCLC 53
See also Bulgya, Alexander Alexandrovich
Fagen, Donald 1948- .... **CLC 26**
Fainzilberg, Ilya Arnoldovich 1897-1937
See Ilf, Ilya
See also CA 120; 165
Fair, Ronald L. 1932- .... **CLC 18**
See also BW 1; CA 69-72; CANR 25; DLB
33
Fairbairn, Roger
See Carr, John Dickson
Fairbairns, Zoe (Ann) 1948- .... **CLC 32**
See also CA 103; CANR 21, 85
Fairman, Paul W. 1916-1977
See Queen, Ellery
See also CA 114
Falco, Gian
See Papini, Giovanni
Falconer, James
See Kirkup, James
Falconer, Kenneth
See Kornbluth, C(yril) M.
Falkland, Samuel
See Heijermans, Herman
Fallaci, Oriana 1930- .... **CLC 11, 110**
See also CA 77-80; CANR 15, 58; MTCW
1
Faludi, Susan 1959- .... **CLC 140**
See also CA 138; MTCW 1
Faludy, George 1913- .... **CLC 42**
See also CA 21-24R
Faludy, Gyoergy
See Faludy, George
Fanon, Frantz 1925-1961 ... **CLC 74; BLC 2;**
DAM MULT
See also BW 1; CA 116; 89-92
Fanshawe, Ann 1625-1680 .... **LC 11**
Fante, John (Thomas) 1911-1983 ..... **CLC 60**
See also CA 69-72; 109; CANR 23; DLB
130; DLBY 83
Farah, Nuruddin 1945- .. **CLC 53, 137; BLC**
2; DAM MULT
See also BW 2, 3; CA 106; CANR 81;
DLB 125

Fargue, Leon-Paul 1876(?)-1947 .... **TCLC 11**
See also CA 109
Farigoule, Louis
See Romains, Jules
Farina, Richard 1936(?)-1966 .... **CLC 9**
See also CA 81-84; 25-28R
Farley, Walter (Lorimer)
1915-1989 .... **CLC 17**
See also AW; CA 17-20R; CANR 8, 29, 84;
DLB 22; JRDA; MAICYA; SATA 2, 43
Farmer, Philip Jose 1918- .... **CLC 1, 19**
See also AAYA 28; CA 1-4R; CANR 4, 35;
DLB 8; MTCW 1; SATA 93
Farquhar, George 1677-1707 ... **LC 21; DAM**
DRAM
See also DLB 84
Farrell, J(ames) G(ordon)
1935-1979 .... **CLC 6**
See also CA 73-76; 89-92; CANR 36; DLB
14; MTCW 1
Farrell, James T(homas) 1904-1979 . **CLC 1,**
4, 8, 11, 66; SSC 28
See also CA 5-8R; 89-92; CANR 9, 61;
DLB 4, 9, 86; DLBD 2; MTCW 1, 2
Farren, Richard J.
See Betjeman, John
Farren, Richard M.
See Betjeman, John
Fassbinder, Rainer Werner
1946-1982 .... **CLC 20**
See also CA 93-96; 106; CANR 31
Fast, Howard (Melvin) 1914- .. **CLC 23, 131;**
DAM NOV
See also AAYA 16; AW; CA 1-4R, 181;
CAAE 181; CAAS 18; CANR 1, 33, 54,
75; DLB 9; INT CANR-33; MTCW 1;
SATA 7; SATA-Essay 107; TCWW 2
Faulcon, Robert
See Holdstock, Robert P.
Faulkner, William (Cuthbert)
1897-1962 .... **CLC 1, 3, 6, 8, 9, 11, 14,**
18, 28, 52, 68; DA; DAB; DAC; DAM
MST, NOV; SSC 1, 35, 42
See also AAYA 7; AW; CA 81-84; CANR
33; CDALB 1929-1941; DA3; DLB 9, 11,
44, 102; DLBD 2; DLBY 86, 97; MTCW
1, 2
Fauset, Jessie Redmon
1882(?)-1961 .... **CLC 19, 54; BLC 2;**
DAM MULT
See also BW 1; CA 109; CANR 83; DLB
51
Faust, Frederick (Schiller)
1892-1944(?) .... **TCLC 49; DAM POP**
See also Austin, Frank; Brand, Max; Chal-
lis, George; Dawson, Peter; Dexter, Mar-
tin; Evans, Evan; Frederick, John; Frost,
Frederick; Manning, David; Silver, Nicho-
las
See also CA 108; 152
Faust, Irvin 1924- .... **CLC 8**
See also CA 33-36R; CANR 28, 67; DLB
2, 28; DLBY 80
Fawkes, Guy
See Benchley, Robert (Charles)
Fearing, Kenneth (Flexner)
1902-1961 .... **CLC 51**
See also CA 93-96; CANR 59; DLB 9
Fecamps, Elise
See Creasey, John
Federman, Raymond 1928- .... **CLC 6, 47**
See also CA 17-20R; CAAS 8; CANR 10,
43, 83; DLBY 80
Federspiel, J(uerg) F. 1931- .... **CLC 42**
See also CA 146

Feiffer, Jules (Ralph) 1929- ..... **CLC 2, 8, 64; DAM DRAM**
See also AAYA 3; CA 17-20R; CANR 30, 59; DLB 7, 44; INT CANR-30; MTCW 1; SATA 8, 61, 111

Feige, Hermann Albert Otto Maximilian
See Traven, B.

Feinberg, David B. 1956-1994 .... **CLC 59**
See also CA 135; 147

Feinstein, Elaine 1930- .... **CLC 36**
See also CA 69-72; CAAS 1; CANR 31, 68; DLB 14, 40; MTCW 1

Feldman, Irving (Mordecai) 1928- ..... **CLC 7**
See also CA 1-4R; CANR 1; DLB 169

Felix-Tchicaya, Gerald
See Tchicaya, Gerald Felix

Fellini, Federico 1920-1993 .... **CLC 16, 85**
See also CA 65-68; 143; CANR 33

Felsen, Henry Gregor 1916-1995 ..... **CLC 17**
See also CA 1-4R; 180; CANR 1; SAAS 2; SATA 1

Fenno, Jack
See Calisher, Hortense

Fenollosa, Ernest (Francisco)
1853-1908 .... **TCLC 91**

Fenton, James Martin 1949- .... **CLC 32**
See also CA 102; DLB 40

Ferber, Edna 1887-1968 .... **CLC 18, 93**
See also AITN 1; CA 5-8R; 25-28R; CANR 68; DLB 9, 28, 86; MTCW 1, 2; SATA 7; TCWW 2

Ferdowsi, Abu'l Qasem 940-1020 . **CMLC 43**

Ferguson, Helen
See Kavan, Anna

Ferguson, Niall 1967- .... **CLC 134**

Ferguson, Samuel 1810-1886 .... **NCLC 33**
See also DLB 32

Fergusson, Robert 1750-1774 .... **LC 29**
See also DLB 109

Ferling, Lawrence
See Ferlinghetti, Lawrence (Monsanto)

Ferlinghetti, Lawrence (Monsanto)
1919(?)- .... **CLC 2, 6, 10, 27, 111; DAM POET; PC 1**
See also CA 5-8R; CANR 3, 41, 73; CDALB 1941-1968; DA3; DLB 5, 16; MTCW 1, 2

Fern, Fanny
See Parton, Sara Payson Willis

Fernandez, Vicente Garcia Huidobro
See Huidobro Fernandez, Vicente Garcia

Fernandez de Lizardi, Jose Joaquin
See Lizardi, Jose Joaquin Fernandez de

Ferre, Rosario 1942- ...... **CLC 139; HLCS 1; SSC 36**
See also CA 131; CANR 55, 81; CWW 2; DLB 145; HW 1, 2; MTCW 1

Ferrer, Gabriel (Francisco Victor) Miro
See Miro (Ferrer), Gabriel (Francisco Victor)

Ferrier, Susan (Edmonstone)
1782-1854 .... **NCLC 8**
See also DLB 116

Ferrigno, Robert 1948(?)- .... **CLC 65**
See also CA 140

Ferron, Jacques 1921-1985 .... **CLC 94; DAC**
See also CA 117; 129; CCA 1; DLB 60

Feuchtwanger, Lion 1884-1958 .... **TCLC 3**
See also CA 104; 187; DLB 66

Feuillet, Octave 1821-1890 .... **NCLC 45**
See also DLB 192

Feydeau, Georges (Leon Jules Marie)
1862-1921 .... **TCLC 22; DAM DRAM**
See also CA 113; 152; CANR 84; DLB 192

Fichte, Johann Gottlieb
1762-1814 .... **NCLC 62**
See also DLB 90

Ficino, Marsilio 1433-1499 .... **LC 12**

Fiedeler, Hans
See Doeblin, Alfred

Fiedler, Leslie A(aron) 1917- .. **CLC 4, 13, 24**
See also CA 9-12R; CANR 7, 63; DLB 28, 67; MTCW 1, 2

Field, Andrew 1938- .... **CLC 44**
See also CA 97-100; CANR 25

Field, Eugene 1850-1895 .... **NCLC 3**
See also DLB 23, 42, 140; DLBD 13; MAI-CYA; SATA 16

Field, Gans T.
See Wellman, Manly Wade

Field, Michael 1915-1971 .... **TCLC 43**
See also CA 29-32R

Field, Peter
See Hobson, Laura Z(ametkin)
See also TCWW 2

Fielding, Henry 1707-1754 ..... **LC 1, 46; DA; DAB; DAC; DAM DRAM, MST, NOV**
See also AW; CDBLB 1660-1789; DA3; DLB 39, 84, 101

Fielding, Sarah 1710-1768 .... **LC 1, 44**
See also DLB 39

Fields, W. C. 1880-1946 .... **TCLC 80**
See also DLB 44

Fierstein, Harvey (Forbes) 1954- .... **CLC 33; DAM DRAM, POP**
See also CA 123; 129; DA3; GLL 1

Figes, Eva 1932- .... **CLC 31**
See also CA 53-56; CANR 4, 44, 83; DLB 14

Finch, Anne 1661-1720 .... **LC 3; PC 21**
See also DLB 95

Finch, Robert (Duer Claydon)
1900- .... **CLC 18**
See also CA 57-60; CANR 9, 24, 49; DLB 88

Findley, Timothy 1930- . **CLC 27, 102; DAC; DAM MST**
See also CA 25-28R; CANR 12, 42, 69; CCA 1; DLB 53

Fink, William
See Mencken, H(enry) L(ouis)

Firbank, Louis 1942-
See Reed, Lou
See also CA 117

Firbank, (Arthur Annesley) Ronald
1886-1926 .... **TCLC 1**
See also BRWS 2; CA 104; 177; DLB 36

Fisher, Dorothy (Frances) Canfield
1879-1958 .... **TCLC 87**
See also AW 1; CA 114; 136; CANR 80; DLB 9, 102; MAICYA

Fisher, M(ary) F(rances) K(ennedy)
1908-1992 .... **CLC 76, 87**
See also CA 77-80; 138; CANR 44; MTCW 1

Fisher, Roy 1930- .... **CLC 25**
See also CA 81-84; CAAS 10; CANR 16; DLB 40

Fisher, Rudolph 1897-1934 .. **TCLC 11; BLC 2; DAM MULT; SSC 25**
See also BW 1, 3; CA 107; 124; CANR 80; DLB 51, 102

Fisher, Vardis (Alvero) 1895-1968 ...... **CLC 7**
See also CA 5-8R; 25-28R; CANR 68; DLB 9, 206; TCWW 2

Fiske, Tarleton
See Bloch, Robert (Albert)

Fitch, Clarke
See Sinclair, Upton (Beall)

Fitch, John IV
See Cormier, Robert (Edmund)

Fitzgerald, Captain Hugh
See Baum, L(yman) Frank

FitzGerald, Edward 1809-1883 .... **NCLC 9**
See also DLB 32

Fitzgerald, F(rancis) Scott (Key)
1896-1940 .. **TCLC 1, 6, 14, 28, 55; DA; DAB; DAC; DAM MST, NOV; SSC 6, 31**
See also AAYA 24; AITN 1; AW; CA 110; 123; CDALB 1917-1929; DA3; DLB 4, 9, 86; DLBD 1, 15, 16; DLBY 81, 96; MTCW 1, 2

Fitzgerald, Penelope 1916-2000 . **CLC 19, 51, 61**
See also BRWS 5; CA 85-88; CAAS 10; CANR 56, 86; DLB 14, 194; MTCW 2

Fitzgerald, Robert (Stuart)
1910-1985 .... **CLC 39**
See also CA 1-4R; 114; CANR 1; DLBY 80

FitzGerald, Robert D(avid)
1902-1987 .... **CLC 19**
See also CA 17-20R

Fitzgerald, Zelda (Sayre)
1900-1948 .... **TCLC 52**
See also CA 117; 126; DLBY 84

Flanagan, Thomas (James Bonner)
1923- .... **CLC 25, 52**
See also CA 108; CANR 55; DLBY 80; INT 108; MTCW 1

Flaubert, Gustave 1821-1880 .... **NCLC 2, 10, 19, 62, 66; DA; DAB; DAC; DAM MST, NOV; SSC 11**
See also AW; DA3; DLB 119

Flecker, Herman Elroy
See Flecker, (Herman) James Elroy

Flecker, (Herman) James Elroy
1884-1915 .... **TCLC 43**
See also CA 109; 150; DLB 10, 19

Fleming, Ian (Lancaster) 1908-1964 . **CLC 3, 30; DAM POP**
See also AAYA 26; AW; CA 5-8R; CANR 59; CDBLB 1945-1960; DA3; DLB 87, 201; MTCW 1, 2; SATA 9

Fleming, Thomas (James) 1927- ...... **CLC 37**
See also CA 5-8R; CANR 10; INT CANR-10; SATA 8

Fletcher, John 1579-1625 .... **LC 33; DC 6**
See also CDBLB Before 1660; DLB 58

Fletcher, John Gould 1886-1950 .... **TCLC 35**
See also CA 107; 167; DLB 4, 45

Fleur, Paul
See Pohl, Frederik

Flooglebuckle, Al
See Spiegelman, Art

Flora, Fletcher 1914-1969
See Queen, Ellery
See also CA 1-4R; CANR 3, 85

Flying Officer X
See Bates, H(erbert) E(rnest)

Fo, Dario 1926- .... **CLC 32, 109; DAM DRAM; DC 10**
See also CA 116; 128; CANR 68; CWW 2; DA3; DLBY 97; MTCW 1, 2

Fogarty, Jonathan Titulescu Esq.
See Farrell, James T(homas)

Follett, Ken(neth Martin) 1949- ..... **CLC 18; DAM NOV, POP**
See also AAYA 6; BEST 89:4; CA 81-84; CANR 13, 33, 54; DA3; DLB 87; DLBY 81; INT CANR-33; MTCW 1

Fontane, Theodor 1819-1898 .... **NCLC 26**
See also DLB 129

Foote, Horton 1916- .... **CLC 51, 91; DAM DRAM**
See also CA 73-76; CANR 34, 51; DA3; DLB 26; INT CANR-34

Foote, Shelby 1916- ..... **CLC 75; DAM NOV, POP**
See also CA 5-8R; CANR 3, 45, 74; DA3; DLB 2, 17; MTCW 2

Forbes, Esther 1891-1967 .... **CLC 12**
See also AAYA 17; AW; CA 13-14; 25-28R;
CAP 1; CLR 27; DLB 22; JRDA; MAI-
CYA; SATA 2, 100
Forche, Carolyn (Louise) 1950- ...... **CLC 25,
83, 86; DAM POET; PC 10**
See also CA 109; 117; CANR 50, 74; DA3;
DLB 5, 193; INT 117; MTCW 1
Ford, Elbur
See Hibbert, Eleanor Alice Burford
Ford, Ford Madox 1873-1939 ... **TCLC 1, 15,
39, 57; DAM NOV**
See also Chaucer, Daniel
See also CA 104; 132; CANR 74; CDBLB
1914-1945; DA3; DLB 162; MTCW 1, 2
Ford, Henry 1863-1947 .... **TCLC 73**
See also CA 115; 148
Ford, John 1586-1639 .... **DC 8**
See also CDBLB Before 1660; DAM
DRAM; DA3; DLB 58
Ford, John 1895-1973 .... **CLC 16**
See also CA 187; 45-48
Ford, Richard 1944- .... **CLC 46, 99**
See also AMWS 5; CA 69-72; CANR 11,
47, 86; DLB 227; MTCW 1
Ford, Webster
See Masters, Edgar Lee
Foreman, Richard 1937- .... **CLC 50**
See also CA 65-68; CANR 32, 63
Forester, C(ecil) S(cott) 1899-1966 ... **CLC 35**
See also CA 73-76; 25-28R; CANR 83;
DLB 191; SATA 13
Forez
See Mauriac, Fran
Forman, James Douglas 1932- .... **CLC 21**
See also AAYA 17; AW; CA 9-12R; CANR
4, 19, 42; JRDA; MAICYA; SATA 8, 70
Fornés, María Irene 1930- . **CLC 39, 61; DC
10; HLCS 1**
See also CA 25-28R; CANR 28, 81; DLB
7; HW 1, 2; INT CANR-28; MTCW 1
Forrest, Leon (Richard) 1937-1997 ,, **CLC 4;
BLC3**
See also BW 2; CA 89-92; 162; CAAS 7;
CANR 25, 52, 87; DLB 33
Forster, E(dward) M(organ)
1879-1970 ..... **CLC 1, 2, 3, 4, 9, 10, 13,
15, 22, 45, 77; DA; DAB; DAC; DAM
MST, NOV; SSC 27**
See also AAYA 2, 37; AW; CA 13-14; 25-
28R; CANR 45; CAP 1; CDBLB 1914-
1945; DA3; DLB 34, 98, 162, 178, 195;
DLBD 10; MTCW 1, 2; SATA 57
Forster, John 1812-1876 .... **NCLC 11**
See also DLB 144, 184
Forsyth, Frederick 1938- .... **CLC 2, 5, 36;
DAM NOV, POP**
See also BEST 89:4; CA 85-88; CANR 38,
62; DLB 87; MTCW 1, 2
Forten, Charlotte L. TCLC 16; BLC 2
See also Grimke, Charlotte L(ottie) Forten
See also DLB 50
Foscolo, Ugo 1778-1827 .... **NCLC 8, 97**
Fosse, Bob CLC 20
See also Fosse, Robert Louis
Fosse, Robert Louis 1927-1987
See Fosse, Bob
See also CA 110; 123
Foster, Stephen Collins
1826-1864 .... **NCLC 26**
Foucault, Michel 1926-1984 . **CLC 31, 34, 69**
See also CA 105; 113; CANR 34; DLB 242;
GLL 1; MTCW 1, 2
**Fouque, Friedrich (Heinrich Karl) de la
Motte** 1777-1843 .... **NCLC 2**
See also DLB 90

Fourier, Charles 1772-1837 .... **NCLC 51**
Fournier, Pierre 1916- .... **CLC 11**
See also Gascar, Pierre
See also CA 89-92; CANR 16, 40
Fowles, John (Philip) 1926- .. **CLC 1, 2, 3, 4,
6, 9, 10, 15, 33, 87; DAB; DAC; DAM
MST; SSC 33**
See also BRWS 1; CA 5-8R; CANR 25, 71;
CDBLB 1960 to Present; DA3; DLB 14,
139, 207; MTCW 1, 2; SATA 22
Fox, Paula 1923- .... **CLC 2, 8, 121**
See also AAYA 3, 37; AW; CA 73-76;
CANR 20, 36, 62; CLR 1, 44; DLB 52;
JRDA; MAICYA; MTCW 1; SATA 17,
60, 120
Fox, William Price (Jr.) 1926- .... **CLC 22**
See also CA 17-20R; CAAS 19; CANR 11;
DLB 2; DLBY 81
Foxe, John 1517(?)-1587 .... **LC 14**
See also DLB 132
Frame, Janet CLC 2, 3, 6, 22, 66, 96; SSC 29
See also Clutha, Janet Paterson Frame
France, Anatole TCLC 9
See also Thibault, Jacques Anatole Francois
See also DLB 123; MTCW 1
Francis, Claude 19(?)- .... **CLC 50**
Francis, Dick 1920- .... **CLC 2, 22, 42, 102;
DAM POP**
See also AAYA 5, 21; BEST 89:3; CA 5-8R;
CANR 9, 42, 68; CDBLB 1960 to Present;
DA3; DLB 87; INT CANR-9; MTCW 1,
2
Francis, Robert (Churchill)
1901-1987 .... **CLC 15**
See also CA 1-4R; 123; CANR 1
Frank, Anne(lies Marie)
1929-1945 . **TCLC 17; DA; DAB; DAC;
DAM MST**
See also AAYA 12; CA 113; 133; CANR
68; DA3; MTCW 1, 2; SATA 87; SATA-
Brief 42
Frank, Bruno 1887-1945 .... **TCLC 81**
See also CA 189; DLB 118
Frank, Elizabeth 1945- .... **CLC 39**
See also CA 121; 126; CANR 78; INT 126
Frankl, Viktor E(mil) 1905-1997 ...... **CLC 93**
See also CA 65-68; 161
Franklin, Benjamin
See Hasek, Jaroslav (Matej Frantisek)
Franklin, Benjamin 1706-1790 .. **LC 25; DA;
DAB; DAC; DAM MST**
See also AW; CDALB 1640-1865; DA3;
DLB 24, 43, 73
**Franklin, (Stella Maria Sarah) Miles
(Lampe)** 1879-1954 .... **TCLC 7**
See also CA 104; 164; DLB 230; MTCW 2
Fraser, (Lady)Antonia (Pakenham)
1932- .... **CLC 32, 107**
See also CA 85-88; CANR 44, 65; MTCW
1, 2; SATA-Brief 32
Fraser, George MacDonald 1925- ...... **CLC 7**
See also CA 45-48, 180; CAAE 180; CANR
2, 48, 74; MTCW 1
Fraser, Sylvia 1935- .... **CLC 64**
See also CA 45-48; CANR 1, 16, 60; CCA
1
Frayn, Michael 1933- .... **CLC 3, 7, 31, 47;
DAM DRAM, NOV**
See also CA 5-8R; CANR 30, 69; DLB 13,
14, 194; MTCW 1, 2
Fraze, Candida (Merrill) 1945- .... **CLC 50**
See also CA 126
Frazer, J(ames) G(eorge)
1854-1941 .... **TCLC 32**
See also BRWS 3; CA 118
Frazer, Robert Caine
See Creasey, John
Frazer, Sir James George
See Frazer, J(ames) G(eorge)

Frazier, Charles 1950- .... **CLC 109**
See also AAYA 34; CA 161
Frazier, Ian 1951- .... **CLC 46**
See also CA 130; CANR 54, 93
Frederic, Harold 1856-1898 .... **NCLC 10**
See also DLB 12, 23; DLBD 13
Frederick, John
See Faust, Frederick (Schiller)
See also TCWW 2
Frederick the Great 1712-1786 .... **LC 14**
Fredro, Aleksander 1793-1876 .... **NCLC 8**
Freeling, Nicolas 1927- .... **CLC 38**
See also CA 49-52; CAAS 12; CANR 1,
17, 50, 84; DLB 87
Freeman, Douglas Southall
1886-1953 .... **TCLC 11**
See also CA 109; DLB 17; DLBD 17
Freeman, Judith 1946- .... **CLC 55**
See also CA 148
Freeman, Mary E(leanor) Wilkins
1852-1930 .... **TCLC 9; SSC 1**
See also CA 106; 177; DLB 12, 78, 221
Freeman, R(ichard) Austin
1862-1943 .... **TCLC 21**
See also CA 113; CANR 84; DLB 70
French, Albert 1943- .... **CLC 86**
See also BW 3; CA 167
French, Marilyn 1929- .... **CLC 10, 18, 60;
DAM DRAM, NOV, POP**
See also CA 69-72; CANR 3, 31; INT
CANR-31; MTCW 1, 2
French, Paul
See Asimov, Isaac
Freneau, Philip Morin 1752-1832 ... **NCLC 1**
See also AMWS 2; DLB 37, 43
Freud, Sigmund 1856-1939 .... **TCLC 52**
See also CA 115; 133; CANR 69; MTCW
1, 2
Friedan, Betty (Naomi) 1921- .... **CLC 74**
See also CA 65-68; CANR 18, 45, 74;
MTCW 1, 2
Friedlander, Saul 1932- .... **CLC 90**
See also CA 117; 130; CANR 72
Friedman, B(ernard) H(arper)
1926- .... **CLC 7**
See also CA 1-4R; CANR 3, 48
Friedman, Bruce Jay 1930- .... **CLC 3, 5, 56**
See also CA 9-12R; CANR 25, 52; DLB 2,
28; INT CANR-25
Friel, Brian 1929- .... **CLC 5, 42, 59, 115; DC
8**
See also BRWS 5; CA 21-24R; CANR 33,
69; DLB 13; MTCW 1
Friis-Baastad, Babbis Ellinor
1921-1970 .... **CLC 12**
See also CA 17-20R; 134; SATA 7
Frisch, Max (Rudolf) 1911-1991 ... **CLC 3, 9,
14, 18, 32, 44; DAM DRAM, NOV**
See also CA 85-88; CANR 32, 74;
DLB 69, 124; MTCW 1, 2
Fromentin, Eugene (Samuel Auguste)
1820-1876 .... **NCLC 10**
See also DLB 123
Frost, Frederick
See Faust, Frederick (Schiller)
See also TCWW 2
Frost, Robert (Lee) 1874-1963 .. **CLC 1, 3, 4,
9, 10, 13, 15, 26, 34, 44; DA; DAB;
DAC; DAM MST, POET; PC 1**
See also AAYA 21; CA 89-92; CANR 33;
CDALB 1917-1929; CLR 67; DA3; DLB
54; DLBD 7; MTCW 1, 2; SATA 14
Froude, James Anthony
1818-1894 .... **NCLC 43**
See also DLB 18, 57, 144
Froy, Herald
See Waterhouse, Keith (Spencer)

Fry, Christopher 1907- .... **CLC 2, 10, 14;**
DAM DRAM
See also BRWS 3; CA 17-20R; CAAS 23;
CANR 9, 30, 74; DLB 13; MTCW 1, 2;
SATA 66

Frye, (Herman) Northrop
1912-1991 .... **CLC 24, 70**
See also CA 5-8R; 133; CANR 8, 37; DLB
67, 68; MTCW 1, 2

Fuchs, Daniel 1909-1993 .... **CLC 8, 22**
See also CA 81-84; 142; CAAS 5; CANR
40; DLB 9, 26, 28; DLBY 93

Fuchs, Daniel 1934- .... **CLC 34**
See also CA 37-40R; CANR 14, 48

Fuentes, Carlos 1928- .. **CLC 3, 8, 10, 13, 22,**
41, 60, 113; DA; DAB; DAC; DAM
MST, MULT, NOV; HLC 1; SSC 24
See also AAYA 4; AITN 2; AW; CA 69-72;
CANR 10, 32, 68; CWW 2; DA3; DLB
113; HW 1, 2; MTCW 1, 2

Fuentes, Gregorio Lopez y
See Lopez y Fuentes, Gregorio

Fuertes, Gloria 1918-1998 .... **PC 27**
See also CA 178, 180; DLB 108; HW 2;
SATA 115

Fugard, (Harold) Athol 1932- . **CLC 5, 9, 14,**
25, 40, 80; DAM DRAM; DC 3
See also AAYA 17; CA 85-88; CANR 32,
54; DLB 225; MTCW 1

Fugard, Sheila 1932- .... **CLC 48**
See also CA 125

Fukuyama, Francis 1952- .... **CLC 131**
See also CA 140; CANR 72

Fuller, Charles (H., Jr.) 1939- .... **CLC 25;**
BLC 2; DAM DRAM, MULT; DC 1
See also BW 2; CA 108; 112; CANR 87;
DLB 38; INT 112; MTCW 1

Fuller, Henry Blake 1857-1929 .... **TCLC 103**
See also CA 108; 177; DLB 12

Fuller, John (Leopold) 1937- .... **CLC 62**
See also CA 21-24R; CANR 9, 44; DLB 40

Fuller, Margaret
See Ossoli, Sarah Margaret (Fuller marchesa
d')
See also AMWS 2

Fuller, Roy (Broadbent) 1912-1991 ... **CLC 4,**
28
See also CA 5-8R; 135; CAAS 10; CANR
53, 83; DLB 15, 20; SATA 87

Fuller, Sarah Margaret
See Ossoli, Sarah Margaret (Fuller marchesa
d')

Fulton, Alice 1952- .... **CLC 52**
See also CA 116; CANR 57, 88; DLB 193

Furphy, Joseph 1843-1912 .... **TCLC 25**
See also CA 163; DLB 230

Fussell, Paul 1924- .... **CLC 74**
See also BEST 90:1; CA 17-20R; CANR 8,
21, 35, 69; INT CANR-21; MTCW 1, 2

Futabatei, Shimei 1864-1909 .... **TCLC 44**
See also CA 162; DLB 180

Futrelle, Jacques 1875-1912 .... **TCLC 19**
See also CA 113; 155

Gaboriau, Emile 1835-1873 .... **NCLC 14**

Gadda, Carlo Emilio 1893-1973 .... **CLC 11**
See also CA 89-92; DLB 177

Gaddis, William 1922-1998 ... **CLC 1, 3, 6, 8,**
10, 19, 43, 86
See also AMWS 4; CA 17-20R; 172; CANR
21, 48; DLB 2; MTCW 1, 2

Gage, Walter
See Inge, William (Motter)

Gaines, Ernest J(ames) 1933- ...... **CLC 3, 11,**
18, 86; BLC 2; DAM MULT
See also AAYA 18; AITN 1; AW; BW 2, 3;
CA 9-12R; CANR 6, 24, 42, 75; CDALB
1968-1988; CLR 62; DA3; DLB 2, 33,
152; DLBY 80; MTCW 1, 2; SATA 86

Gaitskill, Mary 1954- .... **CLC 69**
See also CA 128; CANR 61

Galdos, Benito Perez
See Perez Galdos, Benito

Gale, Zona 1874-1938 .... **TCLC 7; DAM**
DRAM
See also CA 105; 153; CANR 84; DLB 9,
78, 228

Galeano, Eduardo (Hughes) 1940- . **CLC 72;**
HLCS 1
See also CA 29-32R; CANR 13, 32; HW 1

Galiano, Juan Valera y Alcala
See Valera y Alcala-Galiano, Juan

Galilei, Galileo 1564-1642 .... **LC 45**

Gallagher, Tess 1943- ...... **CLC 18, 63; DAM**
POET; PC 9
See also CA 106; DLB 212

Gallant, Mavis 1922- .. **CLC 7, 18, 38; DAC;**
DAM MST; SSC 5
See also CA 69-72; CANR 29, 69; CCA 1;
DLB 53; MTCW 1, 2

Gallant, Roy A(rthur) 1924- .... **CLC 17**
See also CA 5-8R; CANR 4, 29, 54; CLR
30; MAICYA; SATA 4, 68, 110

Gallico, Paul (William) 1897-1976 ..... **CLC 2**
See also AITN 1; CA 5-8R; 69-72; CANR
23; DLB 9, 171; MAICYA; SATA 13

Gallo, Max Louis 1932- .... **CLC 95**
See also CA 85-88

Gallois, Lucien
See Desnos, Robert

Gallup, Ralph
See Whitemore, Hugh (John)

Galsworthy, John 1867-1933 .... **TCLC 1, 45;**
DA; DAB; DAC; DAM DRAM, MST,
NOV; SSC 22
See also AW; CA 104; 141; CANR 75; CD-
BLB 1890-1914; DA3; DLB 10, 34, 98,
162; DLBD 16; MTCW 1

Galt, John 1779-1839 .... **NCLC 1**
See also DLB 99, 116, 159

Galvin, James 1951- .... **CLC 38**
See also CA 108; CANR 26

Gamboa, Federico 1864-1939 .... **TCLC 36**
See also CA 167; HW 2

Gandhi, M. K.
See Gandhi, Mohandas Karamchand

Gandhi, Mahatma
See Gandhi, Mohandas Karamchand

Gandhi, Mohandas Karamchand
1869-1948 .... **TCLC 59; DAM MULT**
See also CA 121; 132; DA3; MTCW 1, 2

Gann, Ernest Kellogg 1910-1991 ..... **CLC 23**
See also AITN 1; CA 1-4R; 136; CANR 1,
83

Garber, Eric 1943(?)-
See Holleran, Andrew
See also CANR 89

Garcia, Cristina 1958- .... **CLC 76**
See also CA 141; CANR 73; HW 2

Garcia Lorca, Federico 1898-1936 . **TCLC 1,**
7, 49; DA; DAB; DAC; DAM DRAM,
MST, MULT, POET; DC 2; HLC 2;
PC 3
See also Lorca, Federico Garcia
See also AW; CA 104; 131; CANR 81;
DA3; DLB 108; HW 1, 2; MTCW 1, 2

Garcia Marquez, Gabriel (Jose)
1928- .... **CLC 2, 3, 8, 10, 15, 27, 47, 55,**
68; DA; DAB; DAC; DAM MST,
MULT, NOV, POP; HLC 1; SSC 8
See also AAYA 3, 33; AW; BEST 89:1,
90:4; CA 33-36R; CANR 10, 28, 50, 75,
82; DA3; DLB 113; HW 1, 2; MTCW 1,
2

Garcilaso de la Vega, El Inca 1503-1536
See also HLCS 1

Gard, Janice
See Latham, Jean Lee

Gard, Roger Martin du
See Martin du Gard, Roger

Gardam, Jane 1928- .... **CLC 43**
See also AW; CA 49-52; CANR 2, 18, 33,
54; CLR 12; DLB 14, 161, 231; MAI-
CYA; MTCW 1; SAAS 9; SATA 39, 76;
SATA-Brief 28

Gardner, Herb(ert) 1934- .... **CLC 44**
See also CA 149

Gardner, John (Champlin), Jr.
1933-1982 ...... **CLC 2, 3, 5, 7, 8, 10, 18,**
28, 34; DAM NOV, POP; SSC 7
See also AITN 1; AMWS 5; CA 65-68; 107;
CANR 33, 73; CDALBS; DA3; DLB 2;
DLBY 82; MTCW 1; SATA 40; SATA-
Obit 31

Gardner, John (Edmund) 1926- ...... **CLC 30;**
DAM POP
See also CA 103; CANR 15, 69; MTCW 1

Gardner, Miriam
See Bradley, Marion Zimmer
See also GLL 1

Gardner, Noel
See Kuttner, Henry

Gardons, S. S.
See Snodgrass, W(illiam) D(e Witt)

Garfield, Leon 1921-1996 .... **CLC 12**
See also AAYA 8; AW; CA 17-20R; 152;
CANR 38, 41, 78; CLR 21; DLB 161;
JRDA; MAICYA; SATA 1, 32, 76; SATA-
Obit 90

Garland, (Hannibal) Hamlin
1860-1940 .... **TCLC 3; SSC 18**
See also CA 104; DLB 12, 71, 78, 186;
TCWW 2

Garneau, (Hector de) Saint-Denys
1912-1943 .... **TCLC 13**
See also CA 111; DLB 88

Garner, Alan 1934- ..... **CLC 17; DAB; DAM**
POP
See also AAYA 18; AW; CA 73-76, 178;
CAAE 178; CANR 15, 64; CLR 20; DLB
161; MAICYA; MTCW 1, 2; SATA 18,
69; SATA-Essay 108

Garner, Hugh 1913-1979 .... **CLC 13**
See also Warwick, Jarvis
See also CA 69-72; CANR 31; CCA 1; DLB
68

Garnett, David 1892-1981 .... **CLC 3**
See also CA 5-8R; 103; CANR 17, 79; DLB
34; MTCW 2

Garos, Stephanie
See Katz, Steve

Garrett, George (Palmer) 1929- .. **CLC 3, 11,**
51; SSC 30
See also AMWS 7; CA 1-4R; CAAS 5;
CANR 1, 42, 67; DLB 2, 5, 130, 152;
DLBY 83

Garrick, David 1717-1779 .... **LC 15; DAM**
DRAM
See also DLB 84

Garrigue, Jean 1914-1972 .... **CLC 2, 8**
See also CA 5-8R; 37-40R; CANR 20

Garrison, Frederick
See Sinclair, Upton (Beall)

Garro, Elena 1920(?)-1998
See also CA 131; 169; CWW 2; DLB 145;
HLCS 1; HW 1

Garth, Will
See Hamilton, Edmond; Kuttner, Henry

Garvey, Marcus (Moziah, Jr.)
1887-1940 ...... **TCLC 41; BLC 2; DAM**
MULT
See also BW 1; CA 120; 124; CANR 79

Gary, Romain CLC 25
See also Kacew, Romain
See also DLB 83

Gascar, Pierre CLC 11
See also Fournier, Pierre

Gascoyne, David (Emery) 1916- .... **CLC 45**
  See also CA 65-68; CANR 10, 28, 54; DLB
  20; MTCW 1
Gaskell, Elizabeth Cleghorn
  1810-1865 .... **NCLC 5, 70, 97; DAB;**
  DAM MST; SSC 25
  See also CDBLB 1832-1890; DLB 21, 144,
  159
Gass, William H(oward) 1924- . **CLC 1, 2, 8,**
  11, 15, 39, 132; SSC 12
  See also AMWS 6; CA 17-20R; CANR 30,
  71; DLB 2, 227; MTCW 1, 2
Gassendi, Pierre 1592-1655 .... **LC 54**
Gasset, Jose Ortega y
  See Ortega y Gasset, Jose
Gates, Henry Louis, Jr. 1950- .... **CLC 65;**
  BLCS; DAM MULT
  See also BW 2, 3; CA 109; CANR 25, 53,
  75; DA3; DLB 67; MTCW 1
Gautier, Theophile 1811-1872 .. **NCLC 1, 59;**
  DAM POET; PC 18; SSC 20
  See also DLB 119
Gawsworth, John
  See Bates, H(erbert) E(rnest)
Gay, John 1685-1732 .. **LC 49; DAM DRAM**
  See also DLB 84, 95
Gay, Oliver
  See Gogarty, Oliver St. John
Gaye, Marvin (Penze) 1939-1984 ..... **CLC 26**
  See also CA 112
Gebler, Carlo (Ernest) 1954- .... **CLC 39**
  See also CA 119; 133
Gee, Maggie (Mary) 1948- .... **CLC 57**
  See also CA 130; DLB 207
Gee, Maurice (Gough) 1931- .... **CLC 29**
  See also CA 97-100; CANR 67; CLR 56;
  SATA 46, 101
Gelbart, Larry (Simon) 1928- .... **CLC 21, 61**
  See also Gelbart, Larry
  See also CA 73-76; CANR 45, 94
Gelbart, Larry 1928-
  See Gelbart, Larry (Simon)
Gelber, Jack 1932- .... **CLC 1, 6, 14, 79**
  See also CA 1-4R; CANR 2; DLB 7, 228
Gellhorn, Martha (Ellis)
  1908-1998 .... **CLC 14, 60**
  See also CA 77-80; 164; CANR 44; DLBY
  82, 98
Genet, Jean 1910-1986 .. **CLC 1, 2, 5, 10, 14,**
  44, 46; DAM DRAM
  See also CA 13-16R; CANR 18; DA3; DLB
  72; DLBY 86; GLL 1; MTCW 1, 2
Gent, Peter 1942- .... **CLC 29**
  See also AITN 1; CA 89-92; DLBY 82
Gentile, Giovanni 1875-1944 .... **TCLC 96**
  See also CA 119
Gentlewoman in New England, A
  See Bradstreet, Anne
Gentlewoman in Those Parts, A
  See Bradstreet, Anne
Geoffrey of Monmouth c.
  1100-1155 .... **CMLC 44**
  See also DLB 146
George, Jean Craighead 1919- .... **CLC 35**
  See also AAYA 8; AW; CA 5-8R; CANR
  25; CLR 1; DLB 52; JRDA; MAICYA;
  SATA 2, 68
George, Stefan (Anton) 1868-1933 . **TCLC 2,**
  14
  See also CA 104
Georges, Georges Martin
  See Simenon, Georges (Jacques Christian)
Gerhardi, William Alexander
  See Gerhardie, William Alexander
Gerhardie, William Alexander
  1895-1977 .... **CLC 5**
  See also CA 25-28R; 73-76; CANR 18;
  DLB 36

Gerstler, Amy 1956- .... **CLC 70**
  See also CA 146
Gertler, T. **CLC 134**
  See also CA 116; 121
Ghalib **NCLC 39, 78**
  See also Ghalib, Hsadullah Khan
Ghalib, Hsadullah Khan 1797-1869
  See Ghalib
  See also DAM POET
Ghelderode, Michel de 1898-1962 ..... **CLC 6,**
  11; DAM DRAM
  See also CA 85-88; CANR 40, 77
Ghiselin, Brewster 1903- .... **CLC 23**
  See also CA 13-16R; CAAS 10; CANR 13
Ghose, Aurabinda 1872-1950 .... **TCLC 63**
  See also CA 163
Ghose, Zulfikar 1935- .... **CLC 42**
  See also CA 65-68; CANR 67
Ghosh, Amitav 1956- .... **CLC 44**
  See also CA 147; CANR 80
Giacosa, Giuseppe 1847-1906 .... **TCLC 7**
  See also CA 104
Gibb, Lee
  See Waterhouse, Keith (Spencer)
Gibbon, Lewis Grassic **TCLC 4**
  See also Mitchell, James Leslie
Gibbons, Kaye 1960- .... **CLC 50, 88; DAM**
  POP
  See also AAYA 34; CA 151; CANR 75;
  DA3; MTCW 1; SATA 117
Gibran, Kahlil 1883-1931 .... **TCLC 1, 9;**
  DAM POET, POP; PC 9
  See also CA 104; 150; DA3; MTCW 2
Gibran, Khalil
  See Gibran, Kahlil
Gibson, William 1914- .. **CLC 23; DA; DAB;**
  DAC; DAM DRAM, MST
  See also AW; CA 9-12R; CANR 9, 42, 75;
  DLB 7; MTCW 1; SATA 66; SCFW 2
Gibson, William (Ford) 1948- .. **CLC 39, 63;**
  DAM POP
  See also AAYA 12; CA 126; 133; CANR
  52, 90; DA3; MTCW 1
Gide, Andre (Paul Guillaume)
  1869-1951 . **TCLC 5, 12, 36; DA; DAB;**
  DAC; DAM MST, NOV; SSC 13
  See also AW; CA 104; 124; DA3; DLB 65;
  MTCW 1, 2
Gifford, Barry (Colby) 1946- .... **CLC 34**
  See also CA 65-68; CANR 9, 30, 40, 90
Gilbert, Frank
  See De Voto, Bernard (Augustine)
Gilbert, W(illiam) S(chwenck)
  1836-1911 .... **TCLC 3; DAM DRAM,**
  POET
  See also CA 104; 173; SATA 36
Gilbreth, Frank B., Jr. 1911-2001 .... **CLC 17**
  See also CA 9-12R; SATA 2
Gilchrist, Ellen 1935- ...... **CLC 34, 48; DAM**
  POP; SSC 14
  See also CA 113; 116; CANR 41, 61; DLB
  130; MTCW 1, 2
Giles, Molly 1942- .... **CLC 39**
  See also CA 126
Gill, Eric 1882-1940 .... **TCLC 85**
Gill, Patrick
  See Creasey, John
Gilliam, Terry (Vance) 1940- .... **CLC 21, 141**
  See also Monty Python
  See also AAYA 19; CA 108; 113; CANR
  35; INT 113
Gillian, Jerry
  See Gilliam, Terry (Vance)
Gilliatt, Penelope (Ann Douglass)
  1932-1993 .... **CLC 2, 10, 13, 53**
  See also AITN 2; CA 13-16R; 141; CANR
  49; DLB 14

Gilman, Charlotte (Anna) Perkins (Stetson)
  1860-1935 .... **TCLC 9, 37; SSC 13**
  See also CA 106; 150; DLB 221; MTCW 1
Gilmour, David 1949- .... **CLC 35**
  See also CA 138, 147
Gilpin, William 1724-1804 .... **NCLC 30**
Gilray, J. D.
  See Mencken, H(enry) L(ouis)
Gilroy, Frank D(aniel) 1925- .... **CLC 2**
  See also CA 81-84; CANR 32, 64, 86; DLB
  7
Gilstrap, John 1957(?)- .... **CLC 99**
  See also CA 160
Ginsberg, Allen 1926-1997 .... **CLC 1, 2, 3, 4,**
  6, 13, 36, 69, 109; DA; DAB; DAC;
  DAM MST, POET; PC 4
  See also AAYA 33; AITN 1; AMWS 2; AW;
  CA 1-4R; 157; CANR 2, 41, 63, 95;
  CDALB 1941-1968; DA3; DLB 5, 16,
  169; GLL 1; MTCW 1, 2
Ginzburg, Natalia 1916-1991 ...... **CLC 5, 11,**
  54, 70
  See also CA 85-88; 135; CANR 33; DLB
  177; MTCW 1, 2
Giono, Jean 1895-1970 .... **CLC 4, 11**
  See also CA 45-48; 29-32R; CANR 2, 35;
  DLB 72; MTCW 1
Giovanni, Nikki 1943- .... **CLC 2, 4, 19, 64,**
  117; BLC 2; DA; DAB; DAC; DAM
  MST, MULT, POET; PC 19
  See also AAYA 22; AITN 1; AW; BW 2, 3;
  CA 29-32R; CAAS 6; CANR 18, 41, 60,
  91; CDALBS; CLR 6; DA3; DLB 5, 41;
  INT CANR-18; MAICYA; MTCW 1, 2;
  SATA 24, 107
Giovene, Andrea 1904- .... **CLC 7**
  See also CA 85-88
Gippius, Zinaida (Nikolayevna) 1869-1945
  See Hippius, Zinaida
  See also CA 106
Giraudoux, (Hippolyte) Jean
  1882-1944 .... **TCLC 2, 7; DAM DRAM**
  See also CA 104; DLB 65
Gironella, Jose Maria 1917- .... **CLC 11**
  See also CA 101
Gissing, George (Robert)
  1857-1903 .... **TCLC 3, 24, 47; SSC 37**
  See also CA 105; 167; DLB 18, 135, 184
Giurlani, Aldo
  See Palazzeschi, Aldo
Gladkov, Fyodor (Vasilyevich)
  1883-1958 .... **TCLC 27**
  See also CA 170
Glanville, Brian (Lester) 1931- .... **CLC 6**
  See also CA 5-8R; CAAS 9; CANR 3, 70;
  DLB 15, 139; SATA 42
Glasgow, Ellen (Anderson Gholson)
  1873-1945 .... **TCLC 2, 7; SSC 34**
  See also CA 104; 164; DLB 9, 12; MTCW
  2
Glaspell, Susan 1882(?)-1948 . **TCLC 55; DC**
  10; SSC 41
  See also AMWS 3; AW 2; CA 110; 154;
  DLB 7, 9, 78, 228; TCWW 2
Glassco, John 1909-1981 .... **CLC 9**
  See also CA 13-16R; 102; CANR 15; DLB
  68
Glasscock, Amnesia
  See Steinbeck, John (Ernst)
Glasser, Ronald J. 1940(?)- .... **CLC 37**
Glassman, Joyce
  See Johnson, Joyce
Glendinning, Victoria 1937- .... **CLC 50**
  See also CA 120; 127; CANR 59, 89; DLB
  155
Glissant, Edouard 1928- . **CLC 10, 68; DAM**
  MULT
  See also CA 153; CWW 2

Gloag, Julian 1930- .... **CLC 40**
See also AITN 1; CA 65-68; CANR 10, 70
Glowacki, Aleksander
See Prus, Boleslaw
Gluck, Louise (Elisabeth) 1943- .. **CLC 7, 22, 44, 81; DAM POET; PC 16**
See also AMWS 5; CA 33-36R; CANR 40, 69; DA3; DLB 5; MTCW 2
Glyn, Elinor 1864-1943 .... **TCLC 72**
See also DLB 153
Gobineau, Joseph Arthur (Comte) de
1816-1882 .... **NCLC 17**
See also DLB 123
Godard, Jean-Luc 1930- .... **CLC 20**
See also CA 93-96
Godden, (Margaret) Rumer
1907-1998 .... **CLC 53**
See also AAYA 6; CA 5-8R; 172; CANR 4, 27, 36, 55, 80; CLR 20; DLB 161; MAI-CYA; SAAS 12; SATA 3, 36; SATA-Obit 109
Godoy Alcayaga, Lucila
1899-1957 .... **TCLC 2; DAM MULT; HLC 2; PC 32**
See also BW 2; CA 104; 131; CANR 81; HW 1, 2; MTCW 1, 2
Godwin, Gail (Kathleen) 1937- ..... **CLC 5, 8, 22, 31, 69, 125; DAM POP**
See also CA 29-32R; CANR 15, 43, 69; DA3; DLB 6, 234; INT CANR-15; MTCW 1, 2
Godwin, William 1756-1836 .... **NCLC 14**
See also CDBLB 1789-1832; DLB 39, 104, 142, 158, 163
Goebbels, Josef
See Goebbels, (Paul) Joseph
Goebbels, (Paul) Joseph
1897-1945 .... **TCLC 68**
See also CA 115; 148
Goebbels, Joseph Paul
See Goebbels, (Paul) Joseph
Goethe, Johann Wolfgang von
1749-1832 ...... **NCLC 4, 22, 34, 90; DA; DAB; DAC; DAM DRAM, MST, POET; PC 5; SSC 38**
See also AW; DA3; DLB 94
Gogarty, Oliver St. John
1878-1957 .... **TCLC 15**
See also CA 109; 150; DLB 15, 19
Gogol, Nikolai (Vasilyevich)
1809-1852 . **NCLC 5, 15, 31; DA; DAB; DAC; DAM DRAM, MST; DC 1; SSC 4, 29**
See also AW; DLB 198
Goines, Donald 1937(?)-1974 . **CLC 80; BLC 2; DAM MULT, POP**
See also AITN 1; BW 1, 3; CA 124; 114; CANR 82; DA3; DLB 33
Gold, Herbert 1924- .... **CLC 4, 7, 14, 42**
See also CA 9-12R; CANR 17, 45; DLB 2; DLBY 81
Goldbarth, Albert 1948- .... **CLC 5, 38**
See also CA 53-56; CANR 6, 40; DLB 120
Goldberg, Anatol 1910-1982 .... **CLC 34**
See also CA 131; 117
Goldemberg, Isaac 1945- .... **CLC 52**
See also CA 69-72; CAAS 12; CANR 11, 32; HW 1
Golding, William (Gerald)
1911-1993 ..... **CLC 1, 2, 3, 8, 10, 17, 27, 58, 81; DA; DAB; DAC; DAM MST, NOV**
See also AAYA 5; AW; BRWS 1; CA 5-8R; 141; CANR 13, 33, 54; CDBLB 1945-1960; DA3; DLB 15, 100; MTCW 1, 2
Goldman, Emma 1869-1940 .... **TCLC 13**
See also CA 110; 150; DLB 221
Goldman, Francisco 1954- .... **CLC 76**
See also CA 162

Goldman, William (W.) 1931- ...... **CLC 1, 48**
See also CA 9-12R; CANR 29, 69; DLB 44; IDFW 3
Goldmann, Lucien 1913-1970 .... **CLC 24**
See also CA 25-28; CAP 2
Goldoni, Carlo 1707-1793 .... **LC 4; DAM DRAM**
Goldsberry, Steven 1949- .... **CLC 34**
See also CA 131
Goldsmith, Oliver 1730-1774 . **LC 2, 48; DA; DAB; DAC; DAM DRAM, MST, NOV, POET; DC 8**
See also AW; CDBLB 1660-1789; DLB 39, 89, 104, 109, 142; SATA 26
Goldsmith, Peter
See Priestley, J(ohn) B(oynton)
Gombrowicz, Witold 1904-1969 .... **CLC 4, 7, 11, 49; DAM DRAM**
See also CA 19-20; 25-28R; CAP 2
Gomez de la Serna, Ramon
1888-1963 .... **CLC 9**
See also CA 153; 116; CANR 79; HW 1, 2
Goncharov, Ivan Alexandrovich
1812-1891 .... **NCLC 1, 63**
See also DLB 238
Goncourt, Edmond (Louis Antoine Huot) de
1822-1896 .... **NCLC 7**
See also DLB 123
Goncourt, Jules (Alfred Huot) de
1830-1870 .... **NCLC 7**
See also DLB 123
Gontier, Fernande 19(?)- .... **CLC 50**
Gonzalez Martinez, Enrique
1871-1952 .... **TCLC 72**
See also CA 166; CANR 81; HW 1, 2
Goodman, Paul 1911-1972 ..... **CLC 1, 2, 4, 7**
See also CA 19-20; 37-40R; CANR 34; CAP 2; DLB 130; MTCW 1
Gordimer, Nadine 1923- ...... **CLC 3, 5, 7, 10, 18, 33, 51, 70, 123; DA; DAB; DAC; DAM MST, NOV; SSC 17**
See also AW; BRWS 2; CA 5-8R; CANR 3, 28, 56, 88; DA3; DLB 225; INT CANR-28; MTCW 1, 2
Gordon, Adam Lindsay
1833-1870 .... **NCLC 21**
See also DLB 230
Gordon, Caroline 1895-1981 . **CLC 6, 13, 29, 83; SSC 15**
See also CA 11-12; 103; CANR 36; CAP 1; DLB 4, 9, 102; DLBD 17; DLBY 81; MTCW 1, 2
Gordon, Charles William 1860-1937
See Connor, Ralph
See also CA 109
Gordon, Mary (Catherine) 1949- .... **CLC 13, 22, 128**
See also AMWS 4; CA 102; CANR 44, 92; DLB 6; DLBY 81; INT 102; MTCW 1
Gordon, N. J.
See Bosman, Herman Charles
Gordon, Sol 1923- .... **CLC 26**
See also CA 53-56; CANR 4; SATA 11
Gordone, Charles 1925-1995 .... **CLC 1, 4; DAM DRAM; DC 8**
See also BW 1, 3; CA 93-96; 180; 150; CAAE 180; CANR 55; DLB 7; INT 93-96; MTCW 1
Gore, Catherine 1800-1861 .... **NCLC 65**
See also DLB 116
Gorenko, Anna Andreevna
See Akhmatova, Anna
Gorky, Maxim **TCLC 8; DAB; SSC 28**
See also Peshkov, Alexei Maximovich
See also AW; MTCW 2
Goryan, Sirak
See Saroyan, William

Gosse, Sir Edmund (William)
1849-1928 .... **TCLC 28**
See also CA 117; DLB 57, 144, 184
Gotlieb, Phyllis Fay (Bloom) 1926- .. **CLC 18**
See also CA 13-16R; CANR 7; DLB 88
Gottesman, S. D.
See Kornbluth, C(yril) M.; Pohl, Frederik
Gottfried von Strassburg fl. c.
1170-1215 .... **CMLC 10**
See also DLB 138
Gould, Lois .... **CLC 4, 10**
See also CA 77-80; CANR 29; MTCW 1
Gourmont, Remy (-Marie-Charles) de
1858-1915 .... **TCLC 17**
See also CA 109; 150; MTCW 2
Govier, Katherine 1948- .... **CLC 51**
See also CA 101; CANR 18, 40; CCA 1
Goyen, (Charles) William
1915-1983 .... **CLC 5, 8, 14, 40**
See also AITN 2; CA 5-8R; 110; CANR 6, 71; DLB 2; DLBY 83; INT CANR-6
Goytisolo, Juan 1931- .... **CLC 5, 10, 23, 133; DAM MULT; HLC 1**
See also CA 85-88; CANR 32, 61; CWW 2; GLL 2; HW 1, 2; MTCW 1, 2
Gozzano, Guido 1883-1916 .... **PC 10**
See also CA 154; DLB 114
Gozzi, (Conte) Carlo 1720-1806 .... **NCLC 23**
Grabbe, Christian Dietrich
1801-1836 .... **NCLC 2**
See also DLB 133
Grace, Patricia Frances 1937- .... **CLC 56**
See also CA 176
Gracian y Morales, Baltasar
1601-1658 .... **LC 15**
Gracq, Julien .... **CLC 11, 48**
See also Poirier, Louis
See also CWW 2; DLB 83
Grade, Chaim 1910-1982 .... **CLC 10**
See also CA 93-96; 107
Graduate of Oxford, A
See Ruskin, John
Grafton, Garth
See Duncan, Sara Jeannette
Graham, John
See Phillips, David Graham
Graham, Jorie 1951- .... **CLC 48, 118**
See also CA 111; CANR 63; DLB 120
Graham, R(obert) B(ontine) Cunninghame
See Cunninghame Graham, Robert (Gallnigad) Bontine
See also DLB 98, 135, 174
Graham, Robert
See Haldeman, Joe (William)
Graham, Tom
See Lewis, (Harry) Sinclair
Graham, W(illiam) S(idney)
1918-1986 .... **CLC 29**
See also CA 73-76; 118; DLB 20
Graham, Winston (Mawdsley)
1910- .... **CLC 23**
See also CA 49-52; CANR 2, 22, 45, 66; DLB 77
Grahame, Kenneth 1859-1932 ...... **TCLC 64; DAB**
See also AW 1; CA 108; 136; CANR 80; CLR 5; DA3; DLB 34, 141, 178; MAI-CYA; MTCW 2; SATA 100
Granovsky, Timofei Nikolaevich
1813-1855 .... **NCLC 75**
See also DLB 198
Grant, Skeeter
See Spiegelman, Art
Granville-Barker, Harley
1877-1946 .... **TCLC 2; DAM DRAM**
See also Barker, Harley Granville
See also CA 104

Grass, Guenter (Wilhelm) 1927- ... CLC 1, 2, 4, 6, 11, 15, 22, 32, 49, 88; DA; DAB; DAC; DAM MST, NOV
See also AW; CA 13-16R; CANR 20, 75, 93; DA3; DLB 75, 124; MTCW 1, 2

Gratton, Thomas
See Hulme, T(homas) E(rnest)

Grau, Shirley Ann 1929- . CLC 4, 9; SSC 15
See also CA 89-92; CANR 22, 69; DLB 2; INT CANR-22; MTCW 1

Gravel, Fern
See Hall, James Norman

Graver, Elizabeth 1964- .... CLC 70
See also CA 135; CANR 71

Graves, Richard Perceval
1895-1985 .... CLC 44
See also CA 65-68; CANR 9, 26, 51

Graves, Robert (von Ranke)
1895-1985 .. CLC 1, 2, 6, 11, 39, 44, 45; DAB; DAC; DAM MST, POET; PC 6
See also CA 5-8R; 117; CANR 5, 36; CD-BLB 1914-1945; DA3; DLB 20, 100, 191; DLBD 18; DLBY 85; MTCW 1, 2; SATA 45

Graves, Valerie
See Bradley, Marion Zimmer

Gray, Alasdair (James) 1934- .... CLC 41
See also CA 126; CANR 47, 69; DLB 194; INT 126; MTCW 1, 2

Gray, Amlin 1946- .... CLC 29
See also CA 138

Gray, Francine du Plessix 1930- ..... CLC 22; DAM NOV
See also BEST 90:3; CA 61-64; CAAS 2; CANR 11, 33, 75, 81; INT CANR-11; MTCW 1, 2

Gray, John (Henry) 1866-1934 ...... TCLC 19
See also CA 119; 162

Gray, Simon (James Holliday)
1936- .... CLC 9, 14, 36
See also AITN 1; CA 21-24R; CAAS 3; CANR 32, 69; DLB 13; MTCW 1

Gray, Spalding 1941- ..... CLC 49, 112; DAM POP; DC 7
See also CA 128; CANR 74; MTCW 2

Gray, Thomas 1716-1771 .... LC 4, 40; DA; DAB; DAC; DAM MST; PC 2
See also AW; CDBLB 1660-1789; DA3; DLB 109

Grayson, David
See Baker, Ray Stannard

Grayson, Richard (A.) 1951- .... CLC 38
See also CA 85-88; CANR 14, 31, 57; DLB 234

Greeley, Andrew M(oran) 1928- ..... CLC 28; DAM POP
See also CA 5-8R; CAAS 7; CANR 7, 43, 69; DA3; MTCW 1, 2

Green, Anna Katharine
1846-1935 .... TCLC 63
See also CA 112; 159; DLB 202, 221

Green, Brian
See Card, Orson Scott

Green, Hannah
See Greenberg, Joanne (Goldenberg)

Green, Hannah 1927(?)-1996 .... CLC 3
See also CA 73-76; CANR 59, 93

Green, Henry CLC 2, 13, 97
See also Yorke, Henry Vincent
See also BRWS 2; CA 175; DLB 15

Green, Julian (Hartridge) 1900-1998
See Green, Julien
See also CA 21-24R; 169; CANR 33, 87; DLB 4, 72; MTCW 1

Green, Julien CLC 3, 11, 77
See also Green, Julian (Hartridge)
See also MTCW 2

Green, Paul (Eliot) 1894-1981 .... CLC 25; DAM DRAM
See also AITN 1; CA 5-8R; 103; CANR 3; DLB 7, 9; DLBY 81

Greenberg, Ivan 1908-1973
See Rahv, Philip
See also CA 85-88

Greenberg, Joanne (Goldenberg)
1932- .... CLC 7, 30
See also AAYA 12; AW; CA 5-8R; CANR 14, 32, 69; SATA 25

Greenberg, Richard 1959(?)- .... CLC 57
See also CA 138

Greene, Bette 1934- .... CLC 30
See also AAYA 7; AW; CA 53-56; CANR 4; CLR 2; JRDA; MAICYA; SAAS 16; SATA 8, 102

Greene, Gael CLC 8
See also CA 13-16R; CANR 10

Greene, Graham (Henry)
1904-1991 .... CLC 1, 3, 6, 9, 14, 18, 27, 37, 70, 72, 125; DA; DAB; DAC; DAM MST, NOV; SSC 29
See also AITN 2; AW; BRWS 1; CA 13-16R; 133; CANR 35, 61; CDBLB 1945-1960; DA3; DLB 13, 15, 77, 100, 162, 201, 204; DLBY 91; MTCW 1, 2; SATA 20

Greene, Robert 1558-1592 .... LC 41
See also DLB 62, 167

Greer, Germaine 1939- .... CLC 131
See also AITN 1; CA 81-84; CANR 33, 70; MTCW 1, 2

Greer, Richard
See Silverberg, Robert

Gregor, Arthur 1923- .... CLC 9
See also CA 25-28R; CAAS 10; CANR 11; SATA 36

Gregor, Lee
See Pohl, Frederik

Gregory, Isabella Augusta (Persse)
1852-1932 .... TCLC 1
See also CA 104; 184; DLB 10

Gregory, J. Dennis
See Williams, John A(lfred)

Grendon, Stephen
See Derleth, August (William)

Grenville, Kate 1950- .... CLC 61
See also CA 118; CANR 53, 93

Grenville, Pelham
See Wodehouse, P(elham) G(renville)

Greve, Felix Paul (Berthold Friedrich)
1879-1948
See Grove, Frederick Philip
See also CA 104; 141, 175; CANR 79; DAC; DAM MST

Grey, Zane 1872-1939 . TCLC 6; DAM POP
See also CA 104; 132; DA3; DLB 212; MTCW 1, 2; TCWW 2

Grieg, (Johan) Nordahl (Brun)
1902-1943 .... TCLC 10
See also CA 107; 189

Grieve, C(hristopher) M(urray)
1892-1978 ..... CLC 11, 19; DAM POET
See also MacDiarmid, Hugh; Pteleon
See also CA 5-8R; 85-88; CANR 33; MTCW 1

Griffin, Gerald 1803-1840 .... NCLC 7
See also DLB 159

Griffin, John Howard 1920-1980 ..... CLC 68
See also AITN 1; CA 1-4R; 101; CANR 2

Griffin, Peter 1942- .... CLC 39
See also CA 136

Griffith, D(avid Lewelyn) W(ark)
1875(?)-1948 .... TCLC 68
See also CA 119; 150; CANR 80

Griffith, Lawrence
See Griffith, D(avid Lewelyn) W(ark)

Griffiths, Trevor 1935- .... CLC 13, 52
See also CA 97-100; CANR 45; DLB 13

Griggs, Sutton (Elbert)
1872-1930 .... TCLC 77
See also CA 123; 186; DLB 50

Grigson, Geoffrey (Edward Harvey)
1905-1985 .... CLC 7, 39
See also CA 25-28R; 118; CANR 20, 33; DLB 27; MTCW 1, 2

Grillparzer, Franz 1791-1872 .. NCLC 1; DC 14; SSC 37
See also DLB 133

Grimble, Reverend Charles James
See Eliot, T(homas) S(tearns)

Grimke, Charlotte L(ottie) Forten
1837(?)-1914
See Forten, Charlotte L.
See also BW 1; CA 117; 124; DAM MULT, POET; DLB 239

Grimm, Jacob Ludwig Karl
1785-1863 .... NCLC 3, 77; SSC 36
See also Grimm and Grimm
See also DLB 90; MAICYA; SATA 22

Grimm, Wilhelm Karl 1786-1859 .. NCLC 3, 77; SSC 36
See also Grimm and Grimm
See also DLB 90; MAICYA; SATA 22

Grimmelshausen, Johann Jakob Christoffel von 1621-1676 .... LC 6
See also DLB 168

Grindel, Eugene 1895-1952
See Eluard, Paul
See also CA 104

Grisham, John 1955- .... CLC 84; DAM POP
See also AAYA 14; CA 138; CANR 47, 69; DA3; MTCW 2

Grossman, David 1954- .... CLC 67
See also CA 138; CWW 2

Grossman, Vasily (Semenovich)
1905-1964 .... CLC 41
See also CA 124; 130; MTCW 1

Grove, Frederick Philip TCLC 4
See also Greve, Felix Paul (Berthold Friedrich)
See also DLB 92

Grubb
See Crumb, R(obert)

Grumbach, Doris (Isaac) 1918- . CLC 13, 22, 64
See also CA 5-8R; CAAS 2; CANR 9, 42, 70; INT CANR-9; MTCW 2

Grundtvig, Nicolai Frederik Severin
1783-1872 .... NCLC 1

Grunge
See Crumb, R(obert)

Grunwald, Lisa 1959- .... CLC 44
See also CA 120

Guare, John 1938- .... CLC 8, 14, 29, 67; DAM DRAM
See also CA 73-76; CANR 21, 69; DLB 7; MTCW 1, 2

Gudjonsson, Halldor Kiljan 1902-1998
See Laxness, Halldor
See also CA 103; 164; CWW 2

Guenter, Erich
See Eich, Guenter

Guest, Barbara 1920- .... CLC 34
See also CA 25-28R; CANR 11, 44, 84; DLB 5, 193

Guest, Edgar A(lbert) 1881-1959 ... TCLC 95
See also CA 112; 168

Guest, Judith (Ann) 1936- .... CLC 8, 30; DAM NOV, POP
See also AAYA 7; CA 77-80; CANR 15, 75; DA3; INT CANR-15; MTCW 1, 2

Guevara, Che CLC 87; HLC 1
See also Guevara (Serna), Ernesto

Guevara (Serna), Ernesto
1928-1967 .... **CLC 87; DAM MULT;**
HLC 1
See also Guevara, Che
See also CA 127; 111; CANR 56; HW 1
Guicciardini, Francesco 1483-1540 ..... **LC 49**
Guild, Nicholas M. 1944- .... **CLC 33**
See also CA 93-96
Guillemin, Jacques
See Sartre, Jean-Paul
Guillen, Jorge 1893-1984 .... **CLC 11; DAM**
MULT, POET; HLCS 1
See also CA 89-92; 112; DLB 108; HW 1
Guillen, Nicolas (Cristobal)
1902-1989 ... **CLC 48, 79; BLC 2; DAM**
MST, MULT, POET; HLC 1; PC 23
See also BW 2; CA 116; 125; 129; CANR
84; HW 1
Guillevic, (Eugene) 1907-1997 .... **CLC 33**
See also CA 93-96; CWW 2
Guillois
See Desnos, Robert
Guillois, Valentin
See Desnos, Robert
Guimarães Rosa, João 1908-1967
See also CA 175; HLCS 2
Guiney, Louise Imogen
1861-1920 .... **TCLC 41**
See also CA 160; DLB 54
Güiraldes, Ricardo (Guillermo)
1886-1927 .... **TCLC 39**
See also CA 131; HW 1; MTCW 1
Gumilev, Nikolai (Stepanovich)
1886-1921 .... **TCLC 60**
See also CA 165
Gunesekera, Romesh 1954- .... **CLC 91**
See also CA 159
Gunn, Bill CLC 5
See also Gunn, William Harrison
See also DLB 38
Gunn, Thom(son William) 1929- .. **CLC 3, 6,**
18, 32, 81; DAM POET; PC 26
See also BRWS 4; CA 17-20R; CANR 9,
33; CDBLB 1960 to Present; DLB 27;
INT CANR-33; MTCW 1
Gunn, William Harrison 1934(?)-1989
See Gunn, Bill
See also AITN 1; BW 1, 3; CA 13-16R;
128; CANR 12, 25, 76
Gunn Allen, Paula
See Allen, Paula Gunn
Gunnars, Kristjana 1948- .... **CLC 69**
See also CA 113; CCA 1; DLB 60
Gurdjieff, G(eorgei) I(vanovich)
1877(?)-1949 .... **TCLC 71**
See also CA 157
Gurganus, Allan 1947- . **CLC 70; DAM POP**
See also BEST 90:1; CA 135; GLL 1
Gurney, A(lbert) R(amsdell), Jr.
1930- ..... **CLC 32, 50, 54; DAM DRAM**
See also CA 77-80; CANR 32, 64
Gurney, Ivor (Bertie) 1890-1937 ... **TCLC 33**
See also CA 167
Gurney, Peter
See Gurney, A(lbert) R(amsdell), Jr.
Guro, Elena 1877-1913 .... **TCLC 56**
Gustafson, James M(oody) 1925- ... **CLC 100**
See also CA 25-28R; CANR 37
Gustafson, Ralph (Barker)
1909-1995 .... **CLC 36**
See also CA 21-24R; CANR 8, 45, 84; DLB
88
Gut, Gom
See Simenon, Georges (Jacques Christian)
Guterson, David 1956- .... **CLC 91**
See also CA 132; CANR 73; MTCW 2

Guthrie, A(lfred) B(ertram), Jr.
1901-1991 .... **CLC 23**
See also CA 57-60; 134; CANR 24; DLB
212; SATA 62; SATA-Obit 67
Guthrie, Isobel
See Grieve, C(hristopher) M(urray)
Guthrie, Woodrow Wilson 1912-1967
See Guthrie, Woody
See also CA 113; 93-96
Guthrie, Woody CLC 35
See also Guthrie, Woodrow Wilson
Gutierrez Najera, Manuel 1859-1895
See also HLCS 2
Guy, Rosa (Cuthbert) 1928- .... **CLC 26**
See also AAYA 4, 37; AW; BW 2; CA 17-
20R; CANR 14, 34, 83; CLR 13; DLB
33; JRDA; MAICYA; SATA 14, 62
Gwendolyn
See Bennett, (Enoch) Arnold
H. D. CLC 3, 8, 14, 31, 34, 73; PC 5
See also Doolittle, Hilda
H. de V.
See Buchan, John
Haavikko, Paavo Juhani 1931- .. **CLC 18, 34**
See also CA 106
Habbema, Koos
See Heijermans, Herman
Habermas, Juergen 1929- .... **CLC 104**
See also CA 109; CANR 85; DLB 242
Habermas, Jurgen
See Habermas, Juergen
Hacker, Marilyn 1942- ...... **CLC 5, 9, 23, 72,**
91; DAM POET
See also CA 77-80; CANR 68; DLB 120;
GLL 2
Haeckel, Ernst Heinrich (Philipp August)
1834-1919 .... **TCLC 83**
See also CA 157
Hafiz c. 1326-1389(?) .... **CMLC 34**
Hafiz c. 1326-1389 .... **CMLC 34**
Haggard, H(enry) Rider
1856-1925 .... **TCLC 11**
See also BRWS 3; CA 108; 148; DLB 70,
156, 174, 178; MTCW 2; SATA 16
Hagiosy, L.
See Larbaud, Valery (Nicolas)
Hagiwara Sakutaro 1886-1942 ..... **TCLC 60;**
PC 18
Haig, Fenil
See Ford, Ford Madox
Haig-Brown, Roderick (Langmere)
1908-1976 .... **CLC 21**
See also CA 5-8R; 69-72; CANR 4, 38, 83;
CLR 31; DLB 88; MAICYA; SATA 12
Hailey, Arthur 1920- ..... **CLC 5; DAM NOV,**
POP
See also AITN 2; BEST 90:3; CA 1-4R;
CANR 2, 36, 75; CCA 1; DLB 88; DLBY
82; MTCW 1, 2
Hailey, Elizabeth Forsythe 1938- ..... **CLC 40**
See also CA 93-96; CAAE 188; CAAS 1;
CANR 15, 48; INT CANR-15
Haines, John (Meade) 1924- .... **CLC 58**
See also CA 17-20R; CANR 13, 34; DLB
212
Hakluyt, Richard 1552-1616 .... **LC 31**
Haldeman, Joe (William) 1943- .... **CLC 61**
See also Graham, Robert
See also CA 53-56, 179; CAAE 179; CAAS
25; CANR 6, 70, 72; DLB 8; INT
CANR-6; SCFW 2
Hale, Sarah Josepha (Buell)
1788-1879 .... **NCLC 75**
See also DLB 1, 42, 73

Halévy, Elie 1870-1937 .... **TCLC 104**
Haley, Alex(ander Murray Palmer)
1921-1992 . **CLC 8, 12, 76; BLC 2; DA;**
DAB; DAC; DAM MST, MULT, POP
See also AAYA 26; BW 2, 3; CA 77-80;
136; CANR 61; CDALBS; DA3; DLB 38;
MTCW 1, 2
Haliburton, Thomas Chandler
1796-1865 .... **NCLC 15**
See also DLB 11, 99
Hall, Donald (Andrew, Jr.) 1928- ...... **CLC 1,**
13, 37, 59; DAM POET
See also CA 5-8R; CAAS 7; CANR 2, 44,
64; DLB 5; MTCW 1; SATA 23, 97
Hall, Frederic Sauser
See Sauser-Hall, Frederic
Hall, James
See Kuttner, Henry
Hall, James Norman 1887-1951 ..... **TCLC 23**
See also CA 123; 173; SATA 21
Hall, (Marguerite) Radclyffe
1880-1943 .... **TCLC 12**
See also CA 110; 150; CANR 83; DLB 191
Hall, Radclyffe 1880-1943
See Hall, (Marguerite) Radclyffe
See also MTCW 2
Hall, Rodney 1935- .... **CLC 51**
See also CA 109; CANR 69
Halleck, Fitz-Greene 1790-1867 .... **NCLC 47**
See also DLB 3
Halliday, Michael
See Creasey, John
Halpern, Daniel 1945- .... **CLC 14**
See also CA 33-36R; CANR 93
Hamburger, Michael (Peter Leopold)
1924- .... **CLC 5, 14**
See also CA 5-8R; CAAS 4; CANR 2, 47;
DLB 27
Hamill, Pete 1935- .... **CLC 10**
See also CA 25-28R; CANR 18, 71
Hamilton, Alexander
1755(?)-1804 .... **NCLC 49**
See also DLB 37
Hamilton, Clive
See Lewis, C(live) S(taples)
Hamilton, Edmond 1904-1977 .... **CLC 1**
See also CA 1-4R; CANR 3, 84; DLB 8;
SATA 118
Hamilton, Eugene (Jacob) Lee
See Lee-Hamilton, Eugene (Jacob)
Hamilton, Franklin
See Silverberg, Robert
Hamilton, Gail
See Corcoran, Barbara
Hamilton, Mollie
See Kaye, M(ary) M(argaret)
Hamilton, (Anthony Walter) Patrick
1904-1962 .... **CLC 51**
See also CA 176; 113; DLB 191
Hamilton, Virginia 1936- ...... **CLC 26; DAM**
MULT
See also AAYA 2, 21; AW; BW 2, 3; CA
25-28R; CANR 20, 37, 73; CLR 1, 11,
40; DLB 33, 52; INT CANR-20; JRDA;
MAICYA; MTCW 1, 2; SATA 4, 56, 79
Hammett, (Samuel) Dashiell
1894-1961 .... **CLC 3, 5, 10, 19, 47; SSC**
17
See also AITN 1; AMWS 4; CA 81-84;
CANR 42; CDALB 1929-1941; DA3;
DLB 226; DLBD 6; DLBY 96; MTCW 1,
2
Hammon, Jupiter 1720(?)-1800(?) . **NCLC 5;**
BLC 2; DAM MULT, POET; PC 16
See also DLB 31, 50
Hammond, Keith
See Kuttner, Henry
Hamner, Earl (Henry), Jr. 1923- ...... **CLC 12**
See also AITN 2; CA 73-76; DLB 6

Hampton, Christopher (James)
1946- .... CLC 4
See also CA 25-28R; DLB 13; MTCW 1

Hamsun, Knut TCLC 2, 14, 49
See also Pedersen, Knut

Handke, Peter 1942- .... CLC 5, 8, 10, 15, 38,
134; DAM DRAM, NOV
See also CA 77-80; CANR 33, 75; CWW
2; DLB 85, 124; MTCW 1, 2

Handy, W(illiam) C(hristopher)
1873-1958 .... TCLC 97
See also BW 3; CA 121; 167

Hanley, James 1901-1985 ..... CLC 3, 5, 8, 13
See also CA 73-76; 117; CANR 36; DLB
191; MTCW 1

Hannah, Barry 1942- .... CLC 23, 38, 90
See also CA 108; 110; CANR 43, 68; DLB
6, 234; INT 110; MTCW 1

Hannon, Ezra
See Hunter, Evan

Hansberry, Lorraine (Vivian)
1930-1965 ..... CLC 17, 62; BLC 2; DA;
DAB; DAC; DAM DRAM, MST,
MULT; DC 2
See also AAYA 25; AMWS 4; BW 1, 3; CA
109; 25-28R; CABS 3; CANR 58;
CDALB 1941-1968; DA3; DLB 7, 38;
MTCW 1, 2

Hansen, Joseph 1923- .... CLC 38
See also Brock, Rose; Colton, James
See also CA 29-32R; CAAS 17; CANR 16,
44, 66; DLB 226; GLL 1; INT CANR-16

Hansen, Martin A(lfred)
1909-1955 .... TCLC 32
See also CA 167; DLB 214

Hanson, Kenneth O(stlin) 1922- .... CLC 13
See also CA 53-56; CANR 7

Hardwick, Elizabeth (Bruce)
1916- .... CLC 13; DAM NOV
See also AMWS 3; CA 5-8R; CANR 3, 32,
70; DA3; DLB 6; MTCW 1, 2

Hardy, Thomas 1840-1928 .. TCLC 4, 10, 18,
32, 48, 53, 72; DA; DAB; DAC; DAM
MST, NOV, POET; PC 8; SSC 2
See also AW; CA 104; 123; CDBLB 1890-
1914; DA3; DLB 18, 19, 135; MTCW 1,
2

Hare, David 1947- .... CLC 29, 58, 136
See also BRWS 4; CA 97-100; CANR 39,
91; DLB 13; MTCW 1

Harewood, John
See Van Druten, John (William)

Harford, Henry
See Hudson, W(illiam) H(enry)

Hargrave, Leonie
See Disch, Thomas M(ichael)

Harjo, Joy 1951- ...... CLC 83; DAM MULT;
PC 27
See also CA 114; CANR 35, 67, 91; DLB
120, 175; MTCW 2; NNAL

Harlan, Louis R(udolph) 1922- .... CLC 34
See also CA 21-24R; CANR 25, 55, 80

Harling, Robert 1951(?)- .... CLC 53
See also CA 147

Harmon, William (Ruth) 1938- .... CLC 38
See also CA 33-36R; CANR 14, 32, 35;
SATA 65

Harper, F. E. W.
See Harper, Frances Ellen Watkins

Harper, Frances E. W.
See Harper, Frances Ellen Watkins

Harper, Frances E. Watkins
See Harper, Frances Ellen Watkins

Harper, Frances Ellen
See Harper, Frances Ellen Watkins

Harper, Frances Ellen Watkins
1825-1911 ...... TCLC 14; BLC 2; DAM
MULT, POET; PC 21
See also BW 1, 3; CA 111; 125; CANR 79;
DLB 50, 221

Harper, Michael S(teven) 1938- ... CLC 7, 22
See also BW 1; CA 33-36R; CANR 24;
DLB 41

Harper, Mrs. F. E. W.
See Harper, Frances Ellen Watkins

Harris, Christie (Lucy) Irwin
1907- .... CLC 12
See also CA 5-8R; CANR 6, 83; CLR 47;
DLB 88; JRDA; MAICYA; SAAS 10;
SATA 6, 74; SATA-Essay 116

Harris, Frank 1856-1931 .... TCLC 24
See also CA 109; 150; CANR 80; DLB 156,
197

Harris, George Washington
1814-1869 .... NCLC 23
See also DLB 3, 11

Harris, Joel Chandler 1848-1908 ... TCLC 2;
SSC 19
See also AW 1; CA 104; 137; CANR 80;
CLR 49; DLB 11, 23, 42, 78, 91; MAI-
CYA; SATA 100

**Harris, John (Wyndham Parkes Lucas)
Beynon** 1903-1969
See Wyndham, John
See also CA 102; 89-92; CANR 84; SATA
118

Harris, MacDonald CLC 9
See also Heiney, Donald (William)

Harris, Mark 1922- .... CLC 19
See also CA 5-8R; CAAS 3; CANR 2, 55,
83; DLB 2; DLBY 80

Harris, (Theodore) Wilson 1921- ..... CLC 25
See also BW 2, 3; CA 65-68; CAAS 16;
CANR 11, 27, 69; DLB 117; MTCW 1

Harrison, Elizabeth Cavanna 1909-
See Cavanna, Betty
See also AW; CA 9-12R; CANR 6, 27, 85

Harrison, Harry (Max) 1925- .... CLC 42
See also CA 1-4R; CANR 5, 21, 84; DLB
8; SATA 4; SCFW 2

Harrison, James (Thomas) 1937 ...... CLC 6,
14, 33, 66; SSC 19
See also Harrison, Jim
See also CA 13-16R; CANR 8, 51, 79;
DLBY 82; INT CANR-8

Harrison, Jim
See Harrison, James (Thomas)
See also TCWW 2

Harrison, Kathryn 1961- .... CLC 70
See also CA 144; CANR 68

Harrison, Tony 1937- .... CLC 43, 129
See also BRWS 5; CA 65-68; CANR 44;
DLB 40; MTCW 1

Harriss, Will(ard Irvin) 1922- .... CLC 34
See also CA 111

Harson, Sley
See Ellison, Harlan (Jay)

Hart, Ellis
See Ellison, Harlan (Jay)

Hart, Josephine 1942(?)- .... CLC 70; DAM
POP
See also CA 138; CANR 70

Hart, Moss 1904-1961 .... CLC 66; DAM
DRAM
See also CA 109; 89-92; CANR 84; DLB 7

Harte, (Francis) Bret(t)
1836(?)-1902 ... TCLC 1, 25; DA; DAC;
DAM MST; SSC 8
See also AMWS 2; AW; CA 104; 140;
CANR 80; CDALB 1865-1917; DA3;
DLB 12, 64, 74, 79, 186; SATA 26

Hartley, L(eslie) P(oles) 1895-1972 ... CLC 2,
22
See also CA 45-48; 37-40R; CANR 33;
DLB 15, 139; MTCW 1, 2

Hartman, Geoffrey H. 1929- .... CLC 27
See also CA 117; 125; CANR 79; DLB 67

Hartmann, Sadakichi 1869-1944 ... TCLC 73
See also CA 157; DLB 54

Hartmann von Aue c. 1170-c.
1210 .... CMLC 15
See also DLB 138

Hartmann von Aue 1170-1210 ...... CMLC 15

Haruf, Kent 1943- .... CLC 34
See also CA 149; CANR 91

Harwood, Ronald 1934- .... CLC 32; DAM
DRAM, MST
See also CA 1-4R; CANR 4, 55; DLB 13

Hasegawa Tatsunosuke
See Futabatei, Shimei

Hasek, Jaroslav (Matej Frantisek)
1883-1923 .... TCLC 4
See also CA 104; 129; MTCW 1, 2

Hass, Robert 1941- ... CLC 18, 39, 99; PC 16
See also AMWS 6; CA 111; CANR 30, 50,
71; DLB 105, 206; SATA 94

Hastings, Hudson
See Kuttner, Henry

Hastings, Selina CLC 44

Hathorne, John 1641-1717 .... LC 38

Hatteras, Amelia
See Mencken, H(enry) L(ouis)

Hatteras, Owen TCLC 18
See also Mencken, H(enry) L(ouis); Nathan,
George Jean

Hauptmann, Gerhart (Johann Robert)
1862-1946 .... TCLC 4; DAM DRAM;
SSC 37
See also CA 104; 153; DLB 66, 118

Havel, Václav 1936- ..... CLC 25, 58, 65, 123;
DAM DRAM; DC 6
See also CA 104; CANR 36, 63; CWW 2;
DA3; DLB 232; MTCW 1, 2

Haviaras, Stratis CLC 33
See also Chaviaras, Strates

Hawes, Stephen 1475(?)-1529(?) .... LC 17
See also DLB 132

Hawkes, John (Clendennin Burne, Jr.)
1925-1998 .. CLC 1, 2, 3, 4, 7, 9, 14, 15,
27, 49
See also CA 1-4R; 167; CANR 2, 47, 64;
DLB 2, 7, 227; DLBY 80, 98; MTCW 1,
2

Hawking, S. W.
See Hawking, Stephen W(illiam)

Hawking, Stephen W(illiam) 1942- . CLC 63,
105
See also AAYA 13; BEST 89:1; CA 126;
129; CANR 48; DA3; MTCW 2

Hawkins, Anthony Hope
See Hope, Anthony

Hawthorne, Julian 1846-1934 .... TCLC 25
See also CA 165

Hawthorne, Nathaniel 1804-1864 ... NCLC 2,
10, 17, 23, 39, 79, 95; DA; DAB; DAC;
DAM MST, NOV; SSC 3, 29, 39
See also AAYA 18; AW; CDALB 1640-
1865; DA3; DLB 1, 74, 223

Haxton, Josephine Ayres 1921-
See Douglas, Ellen
See also CA 115; CANR 41, 83

Hayaseca y Eizaguirre, Jorge
See Echegaray (y Eizaguirre), Jose (Maria
Waldo)

Hayashi, Fumiko 1904-1951 .... TCLC 27
See also CA 161; DLB 180

Haycraft, Anna (Margaret) 1932-
See Ellis, Alice Thomas
See also CA 122; CANR 85, 90; MTCW 2

Hayden, Robert E(arl) 1913-1980 . **CLC 5, 9, 14, 37; BLC 2; DA; DAC; DAM MST, MULT, POET; PC 6**
See also AMWS 2; BW 1, 3; CA 69-72; 97-100; CABS 2; CANR 24, 75, 82; CDALB 1941-1968; DLB 5, 76; MTCW 1, 2; SATA 19; SATA-Obit 26

Hayford, J(oseph) E(phraim) Casely
See Casely-Hayford, J(oseph) E(phraim)

Hayman, Ronald 1932- .... **CLC 44**
See also CA 25-28R; CANR 18, 50, 88; DLB 155

Hayne, Paul Hamilton 1830-1886 . **NCLC 94**
See also DLB 3, 64, 79

Haywood, Eliza (Fowler)
1693(?)-1756 .... **LC 1, 44**
See also DLB 39

Hazlitt, William 1778-1830 ...... **NCLC 29, 82**
See also DLB 110, 158

Hazzard, Shirley 1931- .... **CLC 18**
See also CA 9-12R; CANR 4, 70; DLBY 82; MTCW 1

Head, Bessie 1937-1986 .... **CLC 25, 67; BLC 2; DAM MULT**
See also BW 2, 3; CA 29-32R; 119; CANR 25, 82; DA3; DLB 117, 225; MTCW 1, 2

Headon, (Nicky) Topper 1956(?)- ..... **CLC 30**

Heaney, Seamus (Justin) 1939- ..... **CLC 5, 7, 14, 25, 37, 74, 91; DAB; DAM POET; PC 18**
See also AW; BRWS 2; CA 85-88; CANR 25, 48, 75, 91; CDBLB 1960 to Present; DA3; DLB 40; DLBY 95; MTCW 1, 2

Hearn, (Patricio) Lafcadio (Tessima Carlos)
1850-1904 .... **TCLC 9**
See also CA 105; 166; DLB 12, 78, 189

Hearne, Vicki 1946- .... **CLC 56**
See also CA 139

Hearon, Shelby 1931- .... **CLC 63**
See also AITN 2; CA 25-28R; CANR 18, 48

Heat-Moon, William Least CLC 29
See also Trogdon, William (Lewis)
See also AAYA 9

Hebbel, Friedrich 1813-1863 .... **NCLC 43; DAM DRAM**
See also DLB 129

Hebert, Anne 1916-2000 .... **CLC 4, 13, 29; DAC; DAM MST, POET**
See also CA 85-88; 187; CANR 69; CCA 1; CWW 2; DA3; DLB 68; MTCW 1, 2

Hecht, Anthony (Evan) 1923- ...... **CLC 8, 13, 19; DAM POET**
See also CA 9-12R; CANR 6; DLB 5, 169

Hecht, Ben 1894-1964 .... **CLC 8**
See also CA 85-88; DLB 7, 9, 25, 26, 28, 86; IDFW 3; TCLC 101

Hedayat, Sadeq 1903-1951 .... **TCLC 21**
See also CA 120

Hegel, Georg Wilhelm Friedrich
1770-1831 .... **NCLC 46**
See also DLB 90

Heidegger, Martin 1889-1976 .... **CLC 24**
See also CA 81-84; 65-68; CANR 34; MTCW 1, 2

Heidenstam, (Carl Gustaf) Verner von
1859-1940 .... **TCLC 5**
See also CA 104

Heifner, Jack 1946- .... **CLC 11**
See also CA 105; CANR 47

Heijermans, Herman 1864-1924 .... **TCLC 24**
See also CA 123

Heilbrun, Carolyn G(old) 1926- .... **CLC 25**
See also CA 45-48; CANR 1, 28, 58, 94

Heine, Heinrich 1797-1856 .... **NCLC 4, 54; PC 25**
See also DLB 90

Heinemann, Larry (Curtiss) 1944- .. **CLC 50**
See also CA 110; CAAS 21; CANR 31, 81; DLBD 9; INT CANR-31

Heiney, Donald (William) 1921-1993
See Harris, MacDonald
See also CA 1-4R; 142; CANR 3, 58

Heinlein, Robert A(nson) 1907-1988 . **CLC 1, 3, 8, 14, 26, 55; DAM POP**
See also AAYA 17; AW; CA 1-4R; 125; CANR 1, 20, 53; DA3; DLB 8; JRDA; MAICYA; MTCW 1, 2; SATA 9, 69; SATA-Obit 56

Helforth, John
See Doolittle, Hilda

Hellenhofferu, Vojtech Kapristian z
See Hasek, Jaroslav (Matej Frantisek)

Heller, Joseph 1923-1999 . **CLC 1, 3, 5, 8, 11, 36, 63; DA; DAB; DAC; DAM MST, NOV, POP**
See also AAYA 24; AITN 1; AMWS 4; AW; CA 5-8R; 187; CABS 1; CANR 8, 42, 66; DA3; DLB 2, 28, 227; DLBY 80; INT CANR-8; MTCW 1, 2

Hellman, Lillian (Florence)
1906-1984 .. **CLC 2, 4, 8, 14, 18, 34, 44, 52; DAM DRAM; DC 1**
See also AITN 1, 2; AMWS 1; CA 13-16R; 112; CANR 33; DA3; DLB 7, 228; DLBY 84; MTCW 1, 2

Helprin, Mark 1947- .... **CLC 7, 10, 22, 32; DAM NOV, POP**
See also CA 81-84; CANR 47, 64; CDALBS; DA3; DLBY 85; MTCW 1, 2

Helvetius, Claude-Adrien 1715-1771 .. **LC 26**

Helyar, Jane Penelope Josephine 1933-
See Poole, Josephine
See also CA 21-24R; CANR 10, 26; SATA 82

Hemans, Felicia 1793-1835 ...... **NCLC 29, 71**
See also DLB 96

Hemingway, Ernest (Miller)
1899-1961 .... **CLC 1, 3, 6, 8, 10, 13, 19, 30, 34, 39, 41, 44, 50, 61, 80; DA; DAB; DAC; DAM MST, NOV; SSC 1, 25, 36, 40**
See also AAYA 19; CA 77-80; CANR 34; CDALB 1917-1929; DA3; DLB 4, 9, 102, 210; DLBD 1, 15, 16; DLBY 81, 87, 96, 98; MTCW 1, 2

Hempel, Amy 1951- .... **CLC 39**
See also CA 118; 137; CANR 70; DA3; MTCW 2

Henderson, F. C.
See Mencken, H(enry) L(ouis)

Henderson, Sylvia
See Ashton-Warner, Sylvia (Constance)

Henderson, Zenna (Chlarson)
1917-1983 .... **SSC 29**
See also CA 1-4R; 133; CANR 1, 84; DLB 8; SATA 5

Henkin, Joshua CLC 119
See also CA 161

Henley, Beth CLC 23; DC 6, 14
See also Henley, Elizabeth Becker
See also CABS 3; DLBY 86

Henley, Elizabeth Becker 1952-
See Henley, Beth
See also CA 107; CANR 32, 73; DAM DRAM, MST; DA3; MTCW 1, 2

Henley, William Ernest 1849-1903 .. **TCLC 8**
See also CA 105; DLB 19

Hennissart, Martha
See Lathen, Emma
See also CA 85-88; CANR 64

Henry, O. TCLC 1, 19; SSC 5
See also Porter, William Sydney
See also AMWS 2; AW

Henry, Patrick 1736-1799 .... **LC 25**

Henryson, Robert 1430(?)-1506(?) ...... **LC 20**
See also DLB 146

Henry VIII 1491-1547 .... **LC 10**
See also DLB 132

Henschke, Alfred
See Klabund

Hentoff, Nat(han Irving) 1925- .... **CLC 26**
See also AAYA 4; CA 1-4R; CAAS 6; CANR 5, 25, 77; CLR 1, 52; INT CANR-25; JRDA; MAICYA; SATA 42, 69; SATA-Brief 27

Heppenstall, (John) Rayner
1911-1981 .... **CLC 10**
See also CA 1-4R; 103; CANR 29

Heraclitus c. 540B.C.-c. 450B.C. ... **CMLC 22**
See also DLB 176

Herbert, Frank (Patrick)
1920-1986 .... **CLC 12, 23, 35, 44, 85; DAM POP**
See also AAYA 21; AW; CA 53-56; 118; CANR 5, 43; CDALBS; DLB 8; INT CANR-5; MTCW 1, 2; SATA 9, 37; SATA-Obit 47; SCFW 2

Herbert, George 1593-1633 ..... **LC 24; DAB; DAM POET; PC 4**
See also CDBLB Before 1660; DLB 126

Herbert, Zbigniew 1924-1998 ..... **CLC 9, 43; DAM POET**
See also CA 89-92; 169; CANR 36, 74; CWW 2; DLB 232; MTCW 1

Herbst, Josephine (Frey)
1897-1969 .... **CLC 34**
See also CA 5-8R; 25-28R; DLB 9

Herder, Johann Gottfried von
1744-1803 .... **NCLC 8**
See also DLB 97

Heredia, Jose Maria 1803-1839
See also HLCS 2

Hergesheimer, Joseph 1880-1954 ... **TCLC 11**
See also CA 109; DLB 102, 9

Herlihy, James Leo 1927-1993 .... **CLC 6**
See also CA 1-4R; 143; CANR 2

Hermogenes fl. c. 175- .... **CMLC 6**

Hernandez, Jose 1834-1886 .... **NCLC 17**

Herodotus c. 484B.C.-429B.C. .... **CMLC 17**
See also DLB 176

Herrick, Robert 1591-1674 .... **LC 13; DA; DAB; DAC; DAM MST, POP; PC 9**
See also DLB 126

Herring, Guilles
See Somerville, Edith

Herriot, James CLC 12; DAM POP
See also Wight, James Alfred
See also AAYA 1; CA 148; CANR 40; MTCW 2; SATA 86

Herris, Violet
See Hunt, Violet

Herrmann, Dorothy 1941- .... **CLC 44**
See also CA 107

Herrmann, Taffy
See Herrmann, Dorothy

Hersey, John (Richard) 1914-1993 .... **CLC 1, 2, 7, 9, 40, 81, 97; DAM POP**
See also AAYA 29; CA 17-20R; 140; CANR 33; CDALBS; DLB 6, 185; MTCW 1, 2; SATA 25; SATA-Obit 76

Herzen, Aleksandr Ivanovich
1812-1870 .... **NCLC 10, 61**

Herzl, Theodor 1860-1904 .... **TCLC 36**
See also CA 168

Herzog, Werner 1942- .... **CLC 16**
See also CA 89-92

Hesiod c. 8th cent. B.C.- .... **CMLC 5**
See also DLB 176

Hesse, Hermann 1877-1962 ... **CLC 1, 2, 3, 6, 11, 17, 25, 69; DA; DAB; DAC; DAM MST, NOV; SSC 9**
See also AW; CA 17-18; CAP 2; DA3; DLB 66; MTCW 1, 2; SATA 50

Hewes, Cady
See De Voto, Bernard (Augustine)

Heyen, William 1940- .... **CLC 13, 18**
See also CA 33-36R; CAAS 9; DLB 5

Heyerdahl, Thor 1914- .... **CLC 26**
See also CA 5-8R; CANR 5, 22, 66, 73; MTCW 1, 2; SATA 2, 52

Heym, Georg (Theodor Franz Arthur)
1887-1912 .... **TCLC 9**
See also CA 106; 181

Heym, Stefan 1913- .... **CLC 41**
See also CA 9-12R; CANR 4; CWW 2; DLB 69

Heyse, Paul (Johann Ludwig von)
1830-1914 .... **TCLC 8**
See also CA 104; DLB 129

Heyward, (Edwin) DuBose
1885-1940 .... **TCLC 59**
See also CA 108; 157; DLB 7, 9, 45; SATA 21

Hibbert, Eleanor Alice Burford
1906-1993 .... **CLC 7; DAM POP**
See also BEST 90:4; CA 17-20R; 140; CANR 9, 28, 59; MTCW 2; SATA 2; SATA-Obit 74

Hichens, Robert (Smythe)
1864-1950 .... **TCLC 64**
See also CA 162; DLB 153

Higgins, George V(incent)
1939-1999 .... **CLC 4, 7, 10, 18**
See also CA 77-80; 186; CAAS 5; CANR 17, 51, 89, 96; DLB 2; DLBY 81, 98; INT CANR-17; MTCW 1

Higginson, Thomas Wentworth
1823-1911 .... **TCLC 36**
See also CA 162; DLB 1, 64

Highet, Helen
See MacInnes, Helen (Clark)

Highsmith, (Mary) Patricia
1921-1995 .... **CLC 2, 4, 14, 42, 102; DAM NOV, POP**
See also Morgan, Claire
See also BRWS 5; CA 1-4R; 147, CANR 1, 20, 48, 62; DA3; MTCW 1, 2

Highwater, Jamake (Mamake)
1942(?)- .... **CLC 12**
See also AAYA 7; CA 65-68; CAAS 7; CANR 10, 34, 84; CLR 17; DLB 52; DLBY 85; JRDA; MAICYA; SATA 32, 69; SATA-Brief 30

Highway, Tomson 1951- .... **CLC 92; DAC; DAM MULT**
See also CA 151; CANR 75; CCA 1; MTCW 2; NNAL

Hijuelos, Oscar 1951- .... **CLC 65; DAM MULT, POP; HLC 1**
See also AAYA 25; BEST 90:1; CA 123; CANR 50, 75; DA3; DLB 145; HW 1, 2; MTCW 2

Hikmet, Nazim 1902(?)-1963 .... **CLC 40**
See also CA 141; 93-96

Hildegard von Bingen 1098-1179 . **CMLC 20**
See also DLB 148

Hildesheimer, Wolfgang 1916-1991 .. **CLC 49**
See also CA 101; 135; DLB 69, 124

Hill, Geoffrey (William) 1932- ...... **CLC 5, 8, 18, 45; DAM POET**
See also BRWS 5; CA 81-84; CANR 21, 89; CDBLB 1960 to Present; DLB 40; MTCW 1

Hill, George Roy 1921- .... **CLC 26**
See also CA 110; 122

Hill, John
See Koontz, Dean R(ay)

Hill, Susan (Elizabeth) 1942- .... **CLC 4, 113; DAB; DAM MST, NOV**
See also CA 33-36R; CANR 29, 69; DLB 14, 139; MTCW 1

Hillerman, Tony 1925- . **CLC 62; DAM POP**
See also AAYA 6; AW; BEST 89:1; CA 29-32R; CANR 21, 42, 65; DA3; DLB 206; SATA 6; TCWW 2

Hillesum, Etty 1914-1943 .... **TCLC 49**
See also CA 137

Hilliard, Noel (Harvey) 1929-1996 ... **CLC 15**
See also CA 9-12R; CANR 7, 69

Hillis, Rick 1956- .... **CLC 66**
See also CA 134

Hilton, James 1900-1954 .... **TCLC 21**
See also CA 108; 169; DLB 34, 77; SATA 34

Himes, Chester (Bomar) 1909-1984 .. **CLC 2, 4, 7, 18, 58, 108; BLC 2; DAM MULT**
See also BW 2; CA 25-28R; 114; CANR 22, 89; DLB 2, 76, 143, 226; MTCW 1, 2

Hinde, Thomas **CLC 6, 11**
See also Chitty, Thomas Willes

Hine, (William) Daryl 1936- .... **CLC 15**
See also CA 1-4R; CAAS 15; CANR 1, 20; DLB 60

Hinkson, Katharine Tynan
See Tynan, Katharine

Hinojosa(-Smith), Rolando (R.) 1929-
See also CA 131; CAAS 16; CANR 62; DAM MULT; DLB 82; HLC 1; HW 1, 2; MTCW 2

Hinton, S(usan) E(loise) 1950- .... **CLC 30, 111; DA; DAB; DAC; DAM MST, NOV**
See also AAYA 2, 33; CA 81-84; CANR 32, 62, 92; CDALBS; CLR 3, 23; DA3; JRDA; MAICYA; MTCW 1, 2; SATA 19, 58, 115

Hippius, Zinaida **TCLC 9**
See also Gippius, Zinaida (Nikolayevna)

Hiraoka, Kimitake 1925-1970
See Mishima, Yukio
See also CA 97-100; 29-32R; DAM DRAM; DA3; MTCW 1, 2

Hirsch, E(ric) D(onald), Jr. 1928- .... **CLC 79**
See also CA 25-28R; CANR 27, 51; DLB 67; INT CANR-27; MTCW 1

Hirsch, Edward 1950- .... **CLC 31, 50**
See also CA 104; CANR 20, 42; DLB 120

Hitchcock, Alfred (Joseph)
1899-1980 .... **CLC 16**
See also AAYA 22; CA 159; 97-100; SATA 27; SATA-Obit 24

Hitler, Adolf 1889-1945 .... **TCLC 53**
See also CA 117; 147

Hoagland, Edward 1932- .... **CLC 28**
See also CA 1-4R; CANR 2, 31, 57; DLB 6; SATA 51; TCWW 2

Hoban, Russell (Conwell) 1925- . **CLC 7, 25; DAM NOV**
See also CA 5-8R; CANR 23, 37, 66; CLR 3, 69; DLB 52; MAICYA; MTCW 1, 2; SATA 1, 40, 78

Hobbes, Thomas 1588-1679 .... **LC 36**
See also DLB 151

Hobbs, Perry
See Blackmur, R(ichard) P(almer)

Hobson, Laura Z(ametkin)
1900-1986 .... **CLC 7, 25**
See also Field, Peter
See also CA 17-20R; 118; CANR 55; DLB 28; SATA 52

Hoch, Edward D(entinger) 1930-
See Queen, Ellery
See also CA 29-32R; CANR 11, 27, 51

Hochhuth, Rolf 1931- .. **CLC 4, 11, 18; DAM DRAM**
See also CA 5-8R; CANR 33, 75; CWW 2; DLB 124; MTCW 1, 2

Hochman, Sandra 1936- .... **CLC 3, 8**
See also CA 5-8R; DLB 5

Hochwaelder, Fritz 1911-1986 .... **CLC 36; DAM DRAM**
See also CA 29-32R; 120; CANR 42; MTCW 1

Hochwalder, Fritz
See Hochwaelder, Fritz

Hocking, Mary (Eunice) 1921- .... **CLC 13**
See also CA 101; CANR 18, 40

Hodgins, Jack 1938- .... **CLC 23**
See also CA 93-96; DLB 60

Hodgson, William Hope
1877(?)-1918 .... **TCLC 13**
See also CA 111; 164; DLB 70, 153, 156, 178; MTCW 2

Hoeg, Peter 1957- .... **CLC 95**
See also CA 151; CANR 75; DA3; MTCW 2

Hoffman, Alice 1952- ... **CLC 51; DAM NOV**
See also AAYA 37; CA 77-80; CANR 34, 66; MTCW 1, 2

Hoffman, Daniel (Gerard) 1923- . **CLC 6, 13, 23**
See also CA 1-4R; CANR 4; DLB 5

Hoffman, Stanley 1944- .... **CLC 5**
See also CA 77-80

Hoffman, William 1925- .... **CLC 141**
See also CA 21-24R; CANR 9; DLB 234

Hoffman, William M(oses) 1939- ...... **CLC 40**
See also CA 57-60; CANR 11, 71

Hoffmann, E(rnst) T(heodor) A(madeus)
1776-1822 .... **NCLC 2; SSC 13**
See also DLB 90; SATA 27

Hofmann, Gert 1931- .... **CLC 54**
See also CA 128

Hofmannsthal, Hugo von
1874-1929 ...... **TCLC 11; DAM DRAM; DC 4**
See also von Hofmannsthal, Hugo
See also CA 106; 153; DLB 81, 118

Hogan, Linda 1947- .. **CLC 73; DAM MULT**
See also AMWS 4; CA 120; CANR 45, 73; DLB 175; NNAL; TCWW 2

Hogarth, Charles
See Creasey, John

Hogarth, Emmett
See Polonsky, Abraham (Lincoln)

Hogg, James 1770-1835 .... **NCLC 4**
See also DLB 93, 116, 159

Holbach, Paul Henri Thiry Baron
1723-1789 .... **LC 14**

Holberg, Ludvig 1684-1754 .... **LC 6**

Holcroft, Thomas 1745-1809 .... **NCLC 85**
See also DLB 39, 89, 158

Holden, Ursula 1921- .... **CLC 18**
See also CA 101; CAAS 8; CANR 22

Hölderlin, (Johann Christian) Friedrich
1770-1843 .... **NCLC 16; PC 4**

Holdstock, Robert
See Holdstock, Robert P.

Holdstock, Robert P. 1948- .... **CLC 39**
See also CA 131; CANR 81

Holland, Isabelle 1920- .... **CLC 21**
See also AAYA 11; CA 21-24R, 181; CAAE 181; CANR 10, 25, 47; CLR 57; JRDA; MAICYA; SATA 8, 70; SATA-Essay 103

Holland, Marcus
See Caldwell, (Janet Miriam) Taylor (Holland)

Hollander, John 1929- .... **CLC 2, 5, 8, 14**
See also CA 1-4R; CANR 1, 52; DLB 5; SATA 13

Hollander, Paul
See Silverberg, Robert
Holleran, Andrew 1943(?)- .... CLC 38
See also Garber, Eric
See also CA 144; GLL 1
Holley, Marietta 1836(?)-1926 .... TCLC 99
See also CA 118; DLB 11
Hollinghurst, Alan 1954- .... CLC 55, 91
See also CA 114; DLB 207; GLL 1
Hollis, Jim
See Summers, Hollis (Spurgeon, Jr.)
Holly, Buddy 1936-1959 .... TCLC 65
Holmes, Gordon
See Shiel, M(atthew) P(hipps)
Holmes, John
See Souster, (Holmes) Raymond
Holmes, John Clellon 1926-1988 ...... CLC 56
See also CA 9-12R; 125; CANR 4; DLB 16
Holmes, Oliver Wendell, Jr.
1841-1935 .... TCLC 77
See also CA 114; 186
Holmes, Oliver Wendell
1809-1894 .... NCLC 14, 81
See also AMWS 1; CDALB 1640-1865;
DLB 1, 189, 235; SATA 34
Holmes, Raymond
See Souster, (Holmes) Raymond
Holt, Victoria
See Hibbert, Eleanor Alice Burford
Holub, Miroslav 1923-1998 .... CLC 4
See also CA 21-24R; 169; CANR 10; CWW
2; DLB 232
Homer c. 8th cent. B.C.- .. CMLC 1, 16; DA;
DAB; DAC; DAM MST, POET; PC 23
See also AW; DA3; DLB 176
Hongo, Garrett Kaoru 1951- .... PC 23
See also CA 133; CAAS 22; DLB 120
Honig, Edwin 1919- .... CLC 33
See also CA 5-8R; CAAS 8; CANR 4, 45;
DLB 5
Hood, Hugh (John Blagdon) 1928- . CLC 15,
28; SSC 42
See also CA 49-52; CAAS 17; CANR 1,
33, 87; DLB 53
Hood, Thomas 1799-1845 .... NCLC 16
See also DLB 96
Hooker, (Peter) Jeremy 1941- .... CLC 43
See also CA 77-80; CANR 22; DLB 40
hooks, bell CLC 94; BLCS
See also Watkins, Gloria Jean
See also MTCW 2
Hope, A(lec) D(erwent) 1907-2000 .... CLC 3,
51
See also CA 21-24R; 188; CANR 33, 74;
MTCW 1, 2
Hope, Anthony 1863-1933 .... TCLC 83
See also CA 157; DLB 153, 156
Hope, Brian
See Creasey, John
Hope, Christopher (David Tully)
1944- .... CLC 52
See also CA 106; CANR 47; DLB 225;
SATA 62
Hopkins, Gerard Manley
1844-1889 .... NCLC 17; DA; DAB;
DAC; DAM MST, POET; PC 15
See also AW; CDBLB 1890-1914; DA3;
DLB 35, 57
Hopkins, John (Richard) 1931-1998 .. CLC 4
See also CA 85-88; 169
Hopkins, Pauline Elizabeth
1859-1930 ...... TCLC 28; BLC 2; DAM
MULT
See also BW 2, 3; CA 141; CANR 82; DLB
50
Hopkinson, Francis 1737-1791 .... LC 25
See also DLB 31

Hopley-Woolrich, Cornell George 1903-1968
See Woolrich, Cornell
See also CA 13-14; CANR 58; CAP 1; DLB
226; MTCW 2
Horace 65B.C.- .... CMLC 39
See also DLB 211
Horatio
See Proust, (Valentin-Louis-George-Eugene-
)Marcel
Horgan, Paul (George Vincent
O'Shaughnessy) 1903-1995 . CLC 9, 53;
DAM NOV
See also CA 13-16R; 147; CANR 9, 35;
DLB 212; DLBY 85; INT CANR-9;
MTCW 1, 2; SATA 13; SATA-Obit 84;
TCWW 2
Horn, Peter
See Kuttner, Henry
Hornem, Horace Esq.
See Byron, George Gordon (Noel)
Horney, Karen (Clementine Theodore
Danielsen) 1885-1952 .... TCLC 71
See also CA 114; 165
Hornung, E(rnest) W(illiam)
1866-1921 .... TCLC 59
See also CA 108; 160; DLB 70
Horovitz, Israel (Arthur) 1939- ...... CLC 56;
DAM DRAM
See also CA 33-36R; CANR 46, 59; DLB 7
Horton, George Moses
1797(?)-1883(?) .... NCLC 87
See also DLB 50
Horvath, Odon von
See Horvath, Oedoen von
See also DLB 85, 124
Horvath, Oedoen von 1901-1938 ... TCLC 45
See also Horvath, Odon von; von Horvath,
Oedoen
See also CA 118
Horwitz, Julius 1920-1986 .... CLC 14
See also CA 9-12R; 119; CANR 12
Hospital, Janette Turner 1942- .... CLC 42
See also CA 108; CANR 48
Hostos, E. M. de
See Hostos (y Bonilla), Eugenio Maria de
Hostos, Eugenio M. de
See Hostos (y Bonilla), Eugenio Maria de
Hostos, Eugenio Maria
See Hostos (y Bonilla), Eugenio Maria de
Hostos (y Bonilla), Eugenio Maria de
1839-1903 .... TCLC 24
See also CA 123; 131; HW 1
Houdini
See Lovecraft, H(oward) P(hillips)
Hougan, Carolyn 1943- .... CLC 34
See also CA 139
Household, Geoffrey (Edward West)
1900-1988 .... CLC 11
See also CA 77-80; 126; CANR 58; DLB
87; SATA 14; SATA-Obit 59
Housman, A(lfred) E(dward)
1859-1936 .... TCLC 1, 10; DA; DAB;
DAC; DAM MST, POET; PC 2
See also AW; CA 104; 125; DA3; DLB 19;
MTCW 1, 2
Housman, Laurence 1865-1959 .... TCLC 7
See also CA 106; 155; DLB 10; SATA 25
Howard, Elizabeth Jane 1923- ..... CLC 7, 29
See also CA 5-8R; CANR 8, 62
Howard, Maureen 1930- .... CLC 5, 14, 46
See also CA 53-56; CANR 31, 75; DLBY
83; INT CANR-31; MTCW 1, 2
Howard, Richard 1929- .... CLC 7, 10, 47
See also AITN 1; CA 85-88; CANR 25, 80;
DLB 5; INT CANR-25
Howard, Robert E(rvin)
1906-1936 .... TCLC 8
See also CA 105; 157

Howard, Warren F.
See Pohl, Frederik
Howe, Fanny (Quincy) 1940- .... CLC 47
See also CA 117; CAAE 187; CAAS 27;
CANR 70; SATA-Brief 52
Howe, Irving 1920-1993 .... CLC 85
See also AMWS 6; CA 9-12R; 141; CANR
21, 50; DLB 67; MTCW 1, 2
Howe, Julia Ward 1819-1910 .... TCLC 21
See also CA 117; DLB 1, 189, 235
Howe, Susan 1937- .... CLC 72
See also AMWS 4; CA 160; DLB 120
Howe, Tina 1937- .... CLC 48
See also CA 109
Howell, James 1594(?)-1666 .... LC 13
See also DLB 151
Howells, W. D.
See Howells, William Dean
Howells, William D.
See Howells, William Dean
Howells, William Dean 1837-1920 .. TCLC 7,
17, 41; SSC 36
See also CA 104; 134; CDALB 1865-1917;
DLB 12, 64, 74, 79, 189; MTCW 2
Howes, Barbara 1914-1996 .... CLC 15
See also CA 9-12R; 151; CAAS 3; CANR
53; SATA 5
Hrabal, Bohumil 1914-1997 .... CLC 13, 67
See also CA 106; 156; CAAS 12; CANR
57; CWW 2; DLB 232
Hroswitha of Gandersheim c. 935-c.
1000 .... CMLC 29
See also DLB 148
Hsi, Chu 1130-1200 .... CMLC 42
Hsun, Lu
See Lu Hsun
Hubbard, L(afayette) Ron(ald)
1911-1986 .... CLC 43; DAM POP
See also CA 77-80; 118; CANR 52; DA3;
MTCW 2
Huch, Ricarda (Octavia)
1864-1947 .... TCLC 13
See also CA 111; 189; DLB 66
Huddle, David 1942- .... CLC 49
See also CA 57-60; CAAS 20; CANR 89;
DLB 130
Hudson, Jeffrey
See Crichton, (John) Michael
Hudson, W(illiam) H(enry)
1841-1922 .... TCLC 29
See also CA 115; DLB 98, 153, 174; SATA
35
Hueffer, Ford Madox
See Ford, Ford Madox
Hughart, Barry 1934- .... CLC 39
See also CA 137
Hughes, Colin
See Creasey, John
Hughes, David (John) 1930- .... CLC 48
See also CA 116; 129; DLB 14
Hughes, Edward James
See Hughes, Ted
See also DAM MST, POET; DA3
Hughes, (James) Langston
1902-1967 .... CLC 1, 5, 10, 15, 35, 44,
108; BLC 2; DA; DAB; DAC; DAM
DRAM, MST, MULT, POET; DC 3;
PC 1; SSC 6
See also AAYA 12; AMWS 1; AW; BW 1,
3; CA 1-4R; 25-28R; CANR 1, 34, 82;
CDALB 1929-1941; CLR 17; DA3; DLB
4, 7, 48, 51, 86, 228; JRDA; MAICYA;
MTCW 1, 2; SATA 4, 33
Hughes, Richard (Arthur Warren)
1900-1976 .... CLC 1, 11; DAM NOV
See also CA 5-8R; 65-68; CANR 4; DLB
15, 161; MTCW 1; SATA 8; SATA-Obit
25

Hughes, Ted 1930-1998 . **CLC 2, 4, 9, 14, 37, 119; DAB; DAC; PC 7**
See also Hughes, Edward James
See also AW; BRWS 1; CA 1-4R; 171; CANR 1, 33, 66; CLR 3; DLB 40, 161; MAICYA; MTCW 1, 2; SATA 49; SATA-Brief 27; SATA-Obit 107

Hugo, Richard F(ranklin)
1923-1982 .... **CLC 6, 18, 32; DAM POET**
See also CA 49-52; 108; CANR 3; DLB 5, 206

Hugo, Victor (Marie) 1802-1885 .... **NCLC 3, 10, 21; DA; DAB; DAC; DAM DRAM, MST, NOV, POET; PC 17**
See also AAYA 28; AW; DA3; DLB 119, 192; SATA 47

Huidobro, Vicente
See Huidobro Fernandez, Vicente Garcia

Huidobro Fernandez, Vicente Garcia
1893-1948 .... **TCLC 31**
See also CA 131; HW 1

Hulme, Keri 1947- .... **CLC 39, 130**
See also CA 125; CANR 69; INT 125

Hulme, T(homas) E(rnest)
1883-1917 .... **TCLC 21**
See also CA 117; DLB 19

Hume, David 1711-1776 .... **LC 7, 56**
See also BRWS 3; DLB 104

Humphrey, William 1924-1997 .... **CLC 45**
See also CA 77-80; 160; CANR 68; DLB 212; TCWW 2

Humphreys, Emyr Owen 1919- .... **CLC 47**
See also CA 5-8R; CANR 3, 24; DLB 15

Humphreys, Josephine 1945- ..... **CLC 34, 57**
See also CA 121; 127; INT 127

Huneker, James Gibbons
1860-1921 .... **TCLC 65**
See also DLB 71

Hungerford, Pixie
See Brinsmead, H(esba) F(ay)

Hunt, E(verette) Howard, (Jr.)
1918- .... **CLC 3**
See also AITN 1, CA 45-48; CANR 2, 47

Hunt, Francesca
See Holland, Isabelle

Hunt, Howard
See Hunt, E(verette) Howard, (Jr.)

Hunt, Kyle
See Creasey, John

Hunt, (James Henry) Leigh
1784-1859 .... **NCLC 1, 70; DAM POET**
See also DLB 96, 110, 144

Hunt, Marsha 1946- .... **CLC 70**
See also BW 2, 3; CA 143; CANR 79

Hunt, Violet 1866(?)-1942 .... **TCLC 53**
See also CA 184; DLB 162, 197

Hunter, E. Waldo
See Sturgeon, Theodore (Hamilton)

Hunter, Evan 1926- .... **CLC 11, 31; DAM POP**
See also CA 5-8R; CANR 5, 38, 62; DLBY 82; INT CANR-5; MTCW 1; SATA 25

Hunter, Kristin (Eggleston) 1931- .... **CLC 35**
See also AITN 1; AW; BW 1; CA 13-16R; CANR 13; CLR 3; DLB 33; INT CANR-13; MAICYA; SAAS 10; SATA 12

Hunter, Mary
See Austin, Mary (Hunter)

Hunter, Mollie 1922- .... **CLC 21**
See also McIlwraith, Maureen Mollie Hunter
See also AAYA 13; AW; CANR 37, 78; CLR 25; DLB 161; JRDA; MAICYA; SAAS 7; SATA 54, 106

Hunter, Robert (?)-1734 .... **LC 7**
Hurston, Zora Neale 1891-1960 .. **CLC 7, 30, 61; BLC 2; DA; DAC; DAM MST, MULT, NOV; DC 12; SSC 4**
See also AAYA 15; AW; BW 1, 3; CA 85-88; CANR 61; CDALBS; DA3; DLB 51, 86; MTCW 1, 2

Husserl, E. G.
See Husserl, Edmund (Gustav Albrecht)

Husserl, Edmund (Gustav Albrecht)
1859-1938 .... **TCLC 100**
See also CA 116; 133

Huston, John (Marcellus)
1906-1987 .... **CLC 20**
See also CA 73-76; 123; CANR 34; DLB 26

Hustvedt, Siri 1955- .... **CLC 76**
See also CA 137

Hutten, Ulrich von 1488-1523 .... **LC 16**
See also DLB 179

Huxley, Aldous (Leonard)
1894-1963 .... **CLC 1, 3, 4, 5, 8, 11, 18, 35, 79; DA; DAB; DAC; DAM MST, NOV; SSC 39**
See also AAYA 11; AW; CA 85-88; CANR 44; CDBLB 1914-1945; DA3; DLB 36, 100, 162, 195; MTCW 1, 2; SATA 63; SCFW 2

Huxley, T(homas) H(enry)
1825-1895 .... **NCLC 67**
See also DLB 57

Huysmans, Joris-Karl 1848-1907 ... **TCLC 7, 69**
See also CA 104; 165; DLB 123

Hwang, David Henry 1957- .. **CLC 55; DAM DRAM; DC 4**
See also CA 127; 132; CANR 76; DA3; DLB 212; INT 132; MTCW 2

Hyde, Anthony 1946- .... **CLC 42**
See also Chase, Nicholas
See also CA 136; CCA 1

Hyde, Margaret O(ldroyd) 1917- ..... **CLC 21**
See also CA 1-4R; CANR 1, 36; CLR 23; JRDA; MAICYA; SAAS 8; SATA 1, 42, 76

Hynes, James 1956(?)- .... **CLC 65**
See also CA 164

Hypatia c. 370-415 .... **CMLC 35**

Ian, Janis 1951- .... **CLC 21**
See also CA 105; 187

Ibanez, Vicente Blasco
See Blasco Iba

Ibarbourou, Juana de 1895-1979
See also HLCS 2; HW 1

Ibarguengoitia, Jorge 1928-1983 ...... **CLC 37**
See also CA 124; 113; HW 1

Ibsen, Henrik (Johan) 1828-1906 ... **TCLC 2, 8, 16, 37, 52; DA; DAB; DAC; DAM DRAM, MST; DC 2**
See also AW; CA 104; 141; DA3

Ibuse, Masuji 1898-1993 .... **CLC 22**
See also CA 127; 141; DLB 180

Ichikawa, Kon 1915- .... **CLC 20**
See also CA 121

Ichiyo, Higuchi 1872-1896 .... **NCLC 49**

Idle, Eric 1943-2000 .... **CLC 21**
See also Monty Python
See also CA 116; CANR 35, 91

Ignatow, David 1914-1997 .. **CLC 4, 7, 14, 40**
See also CA 9-12R; 162; CAAS 3; CANR 31, 57, 96; DLB 5

Ignotus
See Strachey, (Giles) Lytton

Ihimaera, Witi 1944- .... **CLC 46**
See also CA 77-80

Ilf, Ilya TCLC 21
See also Fainzilberg, Ilya Arnoldovich

Illyes, Gyula 1902-1983 .... **PC 16**
See also CA 114; 109; DLB 215

Immermann, Karl (Lebrecht)
1796-1840 .... **NCLC 4, 49**
See also DLB 133

Ince, Thomas H. 1882-1924 .... **TCLC 89**

Inchbald, Elizabeth 1753-1821 ...... **NCLC 62**
See also DLB 39, 89

Inclan, Ramon (Maria) del Valle
See Valle-Inclan, Ramon (Maria) del

Infante, G(uillermo) Cabrera
See Cabrera Infante, G(uillermo)

Ingalls, Rachel (Holmes) 1940- .... **CLC 42**
See also CA 123; 127

Ingamells, Reginald Charles
See Ingamells, Rex

Ingamells, Rex 1913-1955 .... **TCLC 35**
See also CA 167

Inge, William (Motter) 1913-1973 ..... **CLC 1, 8, 19; DAM DRAM**
See also CA 9-12R; CDALB 1941-1968; DA3; DLB 7; MTCW 1, 2

Ingelow, Jean 1820-1897 .... **NCLC 39**
See also DLB 35, 163; SATA 33

Ingram, Willis J.
See Harris, Mark

Innaurato, Albert (F.) 1948(?)- ... **CLC 21, 60**
See also CA 115; 122; CANR 78; INT 122

Innes, Michael
See Stewart, J(ohn) I(nnes) M(ackintosh)

Innis, Harold Adams 1894-1952 .... **TCLC 77**
See also CA 181; DLB 88

Ionesco, Eugene 1912-1994 ... **CLC 1, 4, 6, 9, 11, 15, 41, 86; DA; DAB; DAC; DAM DRAM, MST; DC 12**
See also AW; CA 9-12R; 144; CANR 55; CWW 2; DA3; MTCW 1, 2; SATA 7; SATA-Obit 79

Iqbal, Muhammad 1877-1938 .... **TCLC 28**

Ireland, Patrick
See O'Doherty, Brian

Irenaeus St. 130- .... **CMLC 42**

Iron, Ralph
See Schreiner, Olive (Emilie Albertina)

Irving, John (Winslow) 1942- ... **CLC 13, 23, 38, 112; DAM NOV, POP**
See also AAYA 8, AMWS 6; BEST 89:3; CA 25-28R; CANR 28, 73; DA3; DLB 6; DLBY 82; MTCW 1, 2

Irving, Washington 1783-1859 . **NCLC 2, 19, 95; DA; DAB; DAC; DAM MST; SSC 2, 37**
See also AW; CDALB 1640-1865; DA3; DLB 3, 11, 30, 59, 73, 74, 186

Irwin, P. K.
See Page, P(atricia) K(athleen)

Isaacs, Jorge Ricardo 1837-1895 ... **NCLC 70**

Isaacs, Susan 1943- .... **CLC 32; DAM POP**
See also BEST 89:1; CA 89-92; CANR 20, 41, 65; DA3; INT CANR-20; MTCW 1, 2

Isherwood, Christopher (William Bradshaw)
1904-1986 .. **CLC 1, 9, 11, 14, 44; DAM DRAM, NOV**
See also CA 13-16R; 117; CANR 35; DA3; DLB 15, 195; DLBY 86; MTCW 1, 2

Ishiguro, Kazuo 1954- . **CLC 27, 56, 59, 110; DAM NOV**
See also BEST 90:2; BRWS 4; CA 120; CANR 49, 95; DA3; DLB 194; MTCW 1, 2

Ishikawa, Hakuhin
See Ishikawa, Takuboku

Ishikawa, Takuboku
1886(?)-1912 ... **TCLC 15; DAM POET; PC 10**
See also CA 113; 153

Iskander, Fazil 1929- .... **CLC 47**
See also CA 102

Isler, Alan (David) 1934- .... **CLC 91**
See also CA 156

Ivan IV 1530-1584 .... **LC 17**

Ivanov, Vyacheslav Ivanovich
1866-1949 .... **TCLC 33**
See also CA 122

Ivask, Ivar Vidrik 1927-1992 .... **CLC 14**
See also CA 37-40R; 139; CANR 24

Ives, Morgan
See Bradley, Marion Zimmer
See also GLL 1

Izumi Shikibu c. 973-c. 1034 .... **CMLC 33**

J. R. S.
See Gogarty, Oliver St. John

Jabran, Kahlil
See Gibran, Kahlil

Jabran, Khalil
See Gibran, Kahlil

Jackson, Daniel
See Wingrove, David (John)

Jackson, Helen Hunt 1830-1885 .... **NCLC 90**
See also DLB 42, 47, 186, 189

Jackson, Jesse 1908-1983 .... **CLC 12**
See also BW 1; CA 25-28R; 109; CANR
27; CLR 28; MAICYA; SATA 2, 29;
SATA-Obit 48

Jackson, Laura (Riding) 1901-1991
See Riding, Laura
See also CA 65-68; 135; CANR 28, 89;
DLB 48

Jackson, Sam
See Trumbo, Dalton

Jackson, Sara
See Wingrove, David (John)

Jackson, Shirley 1919-1965 . **CLC 11, 60, 87;
DA; DAC; DAM MST; SSC 9, 39**
See also AAYA 9; AW; CA 1-4R; 25-28R;
CANR 4, 52; CDALB 1941-1968; DA3;
DLB 6, 234; MTCW 2; SATA 2

Jacob, (Cyprien-)Max 1876-1944 .... **TCLC 6**
See also CA 104

Jacobs, Harriet A(nn)
1813(?)-1897 .... **NCLC 67**
See also DLB 239

Jacobs, Jim 1942- .... **CLC 12**
See also CA 97-100; INT 97-100

Jacobs, W(illiam) W(ymark)
1863-1943 .... **TCLC 22**
See also CA 121; 167; DLB 135

Jacobsen, Jens Peter 1847-1885 .... **NCLC 34**

Jacobsen, Josephine 1908- .... **CLC 48, 102**
See also CA 33-36R; CAAS 18; CANR 23,
48; CCA 1

Jacobson, Dan 1929- .... **CLC 4, 14**
See also CA 1-4R; CANR 2, 25, 66; DLB
14, 207, 225; MTCW 1

Jacqueline
See Carpentier (y Valmont), Alejo

Jagger, Mick 1944- .... **CLC 17**

Jahiz, al- c. 780-c. 869 .... **CMLC 25**

Jakes, John (William) 1932- . **CLC 29; DAM
NOV, POP**
See also AAYA 32; BEST 89:4; CA 57-60;
CANR 10, 43, 66; DA3; DLBY 83; INT
CANR-10; MTCW 1, 2; SATA 62;
TCWW 2

James, Andrew
See Kirkup, James

James, C(yril) L(ionel) R(obert)
1901-1989 .... **CLC 33; BLCS**
See also BW 2; CA 117; 125; 128; CANR
62; DLB 125; MTCW 1

James, Daniel (Lewis) 1911-1988
See Santiago, Danny
See also CA 174; 125

James, Dynely
See Mayne, William (James Carter)

James, Henry Sr. 1811-1882 .... **NCLC 53**

James, Henry 1843-1916 ..... **TCLC 2, 11, 24,
40, 47, 64; DA; DAB; DAC; DAM
MST, NOV; SSC 8, 32**
See also AW; CA 104; 132; CDALB 1865-
1917; DA3; DLB 12, 71, 74, 189; DLBD
13; MTCW 1, 2

James, M. R.
See James, Montague (Rhodes)
See also DLB 156

James, Montague (Rhodes)
1862-1936 .... **TCLC 6; SSC 16**
See also CA 104; DLB 201

James, P. D. CLC 18, 46, 122
See also White, Phyllis Dorothy James
See also BEST 90:2; BRWS 4; CDBLB
1960 to Present; DLB 87; DLBD 17

James, Philip
See Moorcock, Michael (John)

James, William 1842-1910 .... **TCLC 15, 32**
See also CA 109

James I 1394-1437 .... **LC 20**

Jameson, Anna 1794-1860 .... **NCLC 43**
See also DLB 99, 166

Jami, Nur al-Din 'Abd al-Rahman
1414-1492 .... **LC 9**

Jammes, Francis 1868-1938 .... **TCLC 75**

Jandl, Ernst 1925-2000 .... **CLC 34**

Janowitz, Tama 1957- .. **CLC 43; DAM POP**
See also CA 106; CANR 52, 89

Japrisot, Sebastien 1931- .... **CLC 90**

Jarrell, Randall 1914-1965 .... **CLC 1, 2, 6, 9,
13, 49; DAM POET**
See also CA 5-8R; 25-28R; CABS 2; CANR
6, 34; CDALB 1941-1968; CLR 6; DLB
48, 52; MAICYA; MTCW 1, 2; SATA 7

Jarry, Alfred 1873-1907 . **TCLC 2, 14; DAM
DRAM; SSC 20**
See also CA 104; 153; DA3; DLB 192

Jawien, Andrzej
See John Paul II, Pope

Jaynes, Roderick
See Coen, Ethan

Jeake, Samuel, Jr.
See Aiken, Conrad (Potter)

Jean Paul 1763-1825 .... **NCLC 7**

Jefferies, (John) Richard
1848-1887 .... **NCLC 47**
See also DLB 98, 141; SATA 16

Jeffers, (John) Robinson 1887-1962 .. **CLC 2,
3, 11, 15, 54; DA; DAC; DAM MST,
POET; PC 17**
See also AMWS 2; AW; CA 85-88; CANR
35; CDALB 1917-1929; DLB 45, 212;
MTCW 1, 2

Jefferson, Janet
See Mencken, H(enry) L(ouis)

Jefferson, Thomas 1743-1826 .... **NCLC 11**
See also CDALB 1640-1865; DA3; DLB
31

Jeffrey, Francis 1773-1850 .... **NCLC 33**
See also DLB 107

Jelakowitch, Ivan
See Heijermans, Herman

Jellicoe, (Patricia) Ann 1927- .... **CLC 27**
See also CA 85-88; DLB 13, 233

Jemyma
See Holley, Marietta

Jen, Gish CLC 70
See also Jen, Lillian

Jen, Lillian 1956(?)-
See Jen, Gish
See also CA 135; CANR 89

Jenkins, (John) Robin 1912- .... **CLC 52**
See also CA 1-4R; CANR 1; DLB 14

Jennings, Elizabeth (Joan) 1926- ...... **CLC 5,
14, 131**
See also BRWS 5; CA 61-64; CAAS 5;
CANR 8, 39, 66; DLB 27; MTCW 1;
SATA 66

Jennings, Waylon 1937- .... **CLC 21**

Jensen, Johannes V. 1873-1950 ...... **TCLC 41**
See also CA 170; DLB 214

Jensen, Laura (Linnea) 1948- .... **CLC 37**
See also CA 103

Jerome, Jerome K(lapka)
1859-1927 .... **TCLC 23**
See also CA 119; 177; DLB 10, 34, 135

Jerrold, Douglas William
1803-1857 .... **NCLC 2**
See also DLB 158, 159

Jewett, (Theodora) Sarah Orne
1849-1909 .... **TCLC 1, 22; SSC 6, 44**
See also CA 108; 127; CANR 71; DLB 12,
74, 221; SATA 15

Jewsbury, Geraldine (Endsor)
1812-1880 .... **NCLC 22**
See also DLB 21

Jhabvala, Ruth Prawer 1927- . **CLC 4, 8, 29,
94, 138; DAB; DAM NOV**
See also CA 1-4R; CANR 2, 29, 51, 74, 91;
DLB 139, 194; INT CANR-29; MTCW 1,
2

Jibran, Kahlil
See Gibran, Kahlil

Jibran, Khalil
See Gibran, Kahlil

Jiles, Paulette 1943- .... **CLC 13, 58**
See also CA 101; CANR 70

Jimenez (Mantecon), Juan Ramon
1881-1958 .... **TCLC 4; DAM MULT,
POET; HLC 1; PC 7**
See also CA 104; 131; CANR 74; DLB 134;
HW 1; MTCW 1, 2

Jimenez, Ramon
See Jimenez (Mantecon), Juan Ramon

Jimenez Mantecon, Juan
See Jimenez (Mantecon), Juan Ramon

Jin, Ha
See Jin, Xuefei

Jin, Xuefei 1956- .... **CLC 109**
See also CA 152; CANR 91

Joel, Billy CLC 26
See also Joel, William Martin

Joel, William Martin 1949-
See Joel, Billy
See also CA 108

John, Saint 107th cent. -100 .... **CMLC 27**

John of the Cross, St. 1542-1591 .... **LC 18**

John Paul II, Pope 1920- .... **CLC 128**
See also CA 106; 133

Johnson, B(ryan) S(tanley William)
1933-1973 .... **CLC 6, 9**
See also CA 9-12R; 53-56; CANR 9; DLB
14, 40

Johnson, Benj. F. of Boo
See Riley, James Whitcomb

Johnson, Benjamin F. of Boo
See Riley, James Whitcomb

Johnson, Charles (Richard) 1948- .... **CLC 7,
51, 65; BLC 2; DAM MULT**
See also BW 2, 3; CA 116; CAAS 18;
CANR 42, 66, 82; DLB 33; MTCW 2

Johnson, Denis 1949- .... **CLC 52**
See also CA 117; 121; CANR 71; DLB 120

Johnson, Diane 1934- .... **CLC 5, 13, 48**
See also CA 41-44R; CANR 17, 40, 62, 95;
DLBY 80; INT CANR-17; MTCW 1

Johnson, Eyvind (Olof Verner)
1900-1976 .... **CLC 14**
See also CA 73-76; 69-72; CANR 34

Johnson, J. R.
See James, C(yril) L(ionel) R(obert)

Johnson, James Weldon
1871-1938 .. **TCLC 3, 19; BLC 2; DAM MULT, POET; PC 24**
See also BW 1, 3; CA 104; 125; CANR 82; CDALB 1917-1929; CLR 32; DA3; DLB 51; MTCW 1, 2; SATA 31

Johnson, Joyce 1935- .... **CLC 58**
See also CA 125; 129

Johnson, Judith (Emlyn) 1936- .... **CLC 7, 15**
See also Sherwin, Judith Johnson
See also CA 25-28R, 153; CANR 34

Johnson, Lionel (Pigot)
1867-1902 .... **TCLC 19**
See also CA 117; DLB 19

Johnson, Marguerite (Annie)
See Angelou, Maya

Johnson, Mel
See Malzberg, Barry N(athaniel)

Johnson, Pamela Hansford
1912-1981 .... **CLC 1, 7, 27**
See also CA 1-4R; 104; CANR 2, 28; DLB 15; MTCW 1, 2

Johnson, Robert 1911(?)-1938 .... **TCLC 69**
See also BW 3; CA 174

Johnson, Samuel 1709-1784 . **LC 15, 52; DA; DAB; DAC; DAM MST**
See also AW; CDBLB 1660-1789; DLB 39, 95, 104, 142

Johnson, Uwe 1934-1984 .. **CLC 5, 10, 15, 40**
See also CA 1-4R; 112; CANR 1, 39; DLB 75; MTCW 1

Johnston, George (Benson) 1913- .... **CLC 51**
See also CA 1-4R; CANR 5, 20; DLB 88

Johnston, Jennifer (Prudence) 1930- . **CLC 7**
See also CA 85-88; CANR 92; DLB 14

Joinville, Jean de 1224(?)-1317 ..... **CMLC 38**

Jolley, (Monica) Elizabeth 1923- ..... **CLC 46; SSC 19**
See also CA 127; CAAS 13; CANR 59

Jones, Arthur Llewellyn 1863-1947
See Machen, Arthur
See also CA 104; 179

Jones, D(ouglas) G(ordon) 1929- ..... **CLC 10**
See also CA 29-32R; CANR 13, 90; DLB 53

Jones, David (Michael) 1895-1974 ..... **CLC 2, 4, 7, 13, 42**
See also CA 9-12R; 53-56; CANR 28; CDBLB 1945-1960; DLB 20, 100; MTCW 1

Jones, David Robert 1947-
See Bowie, David
See also CA 103

Jones, Diana Wynne 1934- .... **CLC 26**
See also AAYA 12; AW; CA 49-52; CANR 4, 26, 56; CLR 23; DLB 161; JRDA; MAICYA; SAAS 7; SATA 9, 70, 108

Jones, Edward P. 1950- .... **CLC 76**
See also BW 2, 3; CA 142; CANR 79

Jones, Gayl 1949- ..... **CLC 6, 9, 131; BLC 2; DAM MULT**
See also BW 2, 3; CA 77-80; CANR 27, 66; DA3; DLB 33; MTCW 1, 2

Jones, James 1931-1978 ...... **CLC 1, 3, 10, 39**
See also AITN 1, 2; CA 1-4R; 69-72; CANR 6; DLB 2, 143; DLBD 17; DLBY 98; MTCW 1

Jones, John J.
See Lovecraft, H(oward) P(hillips)

Jones, LeRoi CLC 1, 2, 3, 5, 10, 14
See Baraka, Amiri
See also MTCW 2

Jones, Louis B. 1953- .... **CLC 65**
See also CA 141; CANR 73

Jones, Madison (Percy, Jr.) 1925- ...... **CLC 4**
See also CA 13-16R; CAAS 11; CANR 7, 54, 83; DLB 152

Jones, Mervyn 1922- .... **CLC 10, 52**
See also CA 45-48; CAAS 5; CANR 1, 91; MTCW 1

Jones, Mick 1956(?)- .... **CLC 30**

Jones, Nettie (Pearl) 1941- .... **CLC 34**
See also BW 2; CA 137; CAAS 20; CANR 88

Jones, Preston 1936-1979 .... **CLC 10**
See also CA 73-76; 89-92; DLB 7

Jones, Robert F(rancis) 1934- .... **CLC 7**
See also CA 49-52; CANR 2, 61

Jones, Rod 1953- .... **CLC 50**
See also CA 128

Jones, Terence Graham Parry
1942- .... **CLC 21**
See also Jones, Terry; Monty Python
See also CA 112; 116; CANR 35, 93; INT 116

Jones, Terry
See Jones, Terence Graham Parry
See also SATA 67; SATA-Brief 51

Jones, Thom (Douglas) 1945(?)- .... **CLC 81**
See also CA 157; CANR 88

Jong, Erica 1942- .... **CLC 4, 6, 8, 18, 83; DAM NOV, POP**
See also AITN 1; AMWS 5; BEST 90:2; CA 73-76; CANR 26, 52, 75; DA3; DLB 2, 5, 28, 152; INT CANR-26; MTCW 1, 2

Jonson, Ben(jamin) 1572(?)-1637 .. **LC 6, 33; DA; DAB; DAC; DAM DRAM, MST, POET; DC 4; PC 17**
See also AW; CDBLB Before 1660; DLB 62, 121

Jordan, June 1936- .... **CLC 5, 11, 23, 114; BLCS; DAM MULT, POET**
See also Meyer, June
See also AAYA 2; AW; BW 2, 3; CA 33-36R; CANR 25, 70; CLR 10; DLB 38; GLL 2; MAICYA; MTCW 1; SATA 4

Jordan, Neil (Patrick) 1950- .... **CLC 110**
See also CA 124; 130; CANR 54; GLL 2; INT 130

Jordan, Pat(rick M.) 1941- .... **CLC 37**
See also CA 33-36R

Jorgensen, Ivar
See Ellison, Harlan (Jay)

Jorgenson, Ivar
See Silverberg, Robert

Josephus, Flavius c. 37-100 .... **CMLC 13**

Josiah Allen's Wife
See Holley, Marietta

Josipovici, Gabriel (David) 1940- ...... **CLC 6, 43**
See also CA 37-40R; CAAS 8; CANR 47, 84; DLB 14

Joubert, Joseph 1754-1824 .... **NCLC 9**

Jouve, Pierre Jean 1887-1976 .... **CLC 47**
See also CA 65-68

Jovine, Francesco 1902-1950 .... **TCLC 79**

Joyce, James (Augustine Aloysius)
1882-1941 .. **TCLC 3, 8, 16, 35, 52; DA; DAB; DAC; DAM MST, NOV, POET; PC 22; SSC 3, 26, 44**
See also AW; CA 104; 126; CDBLB 1914-1945; DA3; DLB 10, 19, 36, 162; MTCW 1, 2

Jozsef, Attila 1905-1937 .... **TCLC 22**
See also CA 116

Juana Ines de la Cruz, Sor
1651(?)-1695 ...... **LC 5; HLCS 1; PC 24**

Juana Inez de La Cruz, Sor
See Juana Ines de la Cruz, Sor

Judd, Cyril
See Kornbluth, C(yril) M.; Pohl, Frederik

Juenger, Ernst 1895-1998 .... **CLC 125**
See also CA 101; 167; CANR 21, 47; DLB 56

Julian of Norwich 1342(?)-1416(?) . **LC 6, 52**
See also DLB 146

Junger, Ernst
See Juenger, Ernst

Junger, Sebastian 1962- .... **CLC 109**
See also AAYA 28; CA 165

Juniper, Alex
See Hospital, Janette Turner

Junius
See Luxemburg, Rosa

Just, Ward (Swift) 1935- .... **CLC 4, 27**
See also CA 25-28R; CANR 32, 87; INT CANR-32

Justice, Donald (Rodney) 1925- .. **CLC 6, 19, 102; DAM POET**
See also AMWS 7; CA 5-8R; CANR 26, 54, 74; DLBY 83; INT CANR-26; MTCW 2

Juvenal (?)-c. (?) .... **CMLC 8**
See also Juvenalis, Decimus Junius
See also DLB 211

Juvenalis, Decimus Junius 55(?)-c. 127(?)
See Juvenal

Juvenis
See Bourne, Randolph S(illiman)

Kabakov, Sasha CLC 59

Kacew, Romain 1914-1980
See Gary, Romain
See also CA 108; 102

Kadare, Ismail 1936- .... **CLC 52**
See also CA 161

Kadohata, Cynthia CLC 59, 122
See also CA 140

Kafka, Franz 1883-1924 . **TCLC 2, 6, 13, 29, 47, 53; DA; DAB; DAC; DAM MST, NOV; SSC 5, 29, 35**
See also AAYA 31; AW; CA 105; 126; DA3; DLB 81; MTCW 1, 2

Kahanovitsch, Pinkhes
See Der Nister

Kahn, Roger 1927- .... **CLC 30**
See also CA 25-28R; CANR 44, 69; DLB 171, SATA 37

Kain, Saul
See Sassoon, Siegfried (Lorraine)

Kaiser, Georg 1878-1945 .... **TCLC 9**
See also CA 106; DLB 124

Kaletski, Alexander 1946- .... **CLC 39**
See also CA 118; 143

Kalidasa fl. c. 400-455 .... **CMLC 9; PC 22**

Kallman, Chester (Simon)
1921-1975 .... **CLC 2**
See also CA 45-48; 53-56; CANR 3

Kaminsky, Melvin 1926-
See Brooks, Mel
See also CA 65-68; CANR 16

Kaminsky, Stuart M(elvin) 1934- ..... **CLC 59**
See also CA 73-76; CANR 29, 53, 89

Kandinsky, Wassily 1866-1944 .... **TCLC 92**
See also CA 118; 155

Kane, Francis
See Robbins, Harold

Kane, Henry 1918-
See Queen, Ellery
See also CA 156

Kane, Paul
See Simon, Paul (Frederick)

Kanin, Garson 1912-1999 .... **CLC 22**
See also AITN 1; CA 5-8R; 177; CANR 7, 78; DLB 7; IDFW 3

Kaniuk, Yoram 1930- .... **CLC 19**
See also CA 134

Kant, Immanuel 1724-1804 ..... **NCLC 27, 67**
See also DLB 94

Kantor, MacKinlay 1904-1977 .... **CLC 7**
See also CA 61-64; 73-76; CANR 60, 63; DLB 9, 102; MTCW 2; TCWW 2

Kaplan, David Michael 1946- .... **CLC 50**
See also CA 187

Kaplan, James 1951- .... **CLC 59**
See also CA 135**

Karageorge, Michael
See Anderson, Poul (William)
Karamzin, Nikolai Mikhailovich
1766-1826 .... **NCLC 3**
See also DLB 150
Karapanou, Margarita 1946- .... **CLC 13**
See also CA 101
Karinthy, Frigyes 1887-1938 .... **TCLC 47**
See also CA 170
Karl, Frederick R(obert) 1927- .... **CLC 34**
See also CA 5-8R; CANR 3, 44
Kastel, Warren
See Silverberg, Robert
Kataev, Evgeny Petrovich 1903-1942
See Petrov, Evgeny
See also CA 120
Kataphusin
See Ruskin, John
Katz, Steve 1935- .... **CLC 47**
See also CA 25-28R; CAAS 14, 64; CANR
12; DLBY 83
Kauffman, Janet 1945- .... **CLC 42**
See also CA 117; CANR 43, 84; DLBY 86
Kaufman, Bob (Garnell) 1925-1986 . **CLC 49**
See also BW 1; CA 41-44R; 118; CANR
22; DLB 16, 41
Kaufman, George S. 1889-1961 ...... **CLC 38;**
DAM DRAM
See also CA 108; 93-96; DLB 7; INT 108;
MTCW 2
Kaufman, Sue CLC 3, 8
See also Barondess, Sue K(aufman)
Kavafis, Konstantinos Petrou 1863-1933
See Cavafy, C(onstantine) P(eter)
See also CA 104
Kavan, Anna 1901-1968 .... **CLC 5, 13, 82**
See also CA 5-8R; CANR 6, 57; MTCW 1
Kavanagh, Dan
See Barnes, Julian (Patrick)
Kavanagh, Julie 1952- .... **CLC 119**
See also CA 163
Kavanagh, Patrick (Joseph)
1904-1967 .... **CLC 22; PC 33**
See also CA 123; 25-28R; DLB 15, 20;
MTCW 1
Kawabata, Yasunari 1899-1972 ..... **CLC 2, 5,**
9, 18, 107; DAM MULT; SSC 17
See also CA 93-96; 33-36R; CANR 88;
DLB 180; MTCW 2
Kaye, M(ary) M(argaret) 1909- .... **CLC 28**
See also CA 89-92; CANR 24, 60; MTCW
1, 2; SATA 62
Kaye, Mollie
See Kaye, M(ary) M(argaret)
Kaye-Smith, Sheila 1887-1956 .... **TCLC 20**
See also CA 118; DLB 36
Kaymor, Patrice Maguilene
See Senghor, Leopold Sedar
Kazakov, Yuri Pavlovich 1927-1982 . **SSC 43**
See also CA 5-8R; CANR 36; MTCW 1
Kazan, Elia 1909- .... **CLC 6, 16, 63**
See also CA 21-24R; CANR 32, 78
Kazantzakis, Nikos 1883(?)-1957 .... **TCLC 2,**
5, 33
See also CA 105; 132; DA3; MTCW 1, 2
Kazin, Alfred 1915-1998 ..... **CLC 34, 38, 119**
See also CA 1-4R; CAAS 7; CANR 1, 45,
79; DLB 67
Keane, Mary Nesta (Skrine) 1904-1996
See Keane, Molly
See also CA 108; 114; 151
Keane, Molly CLC 31
See also Keane, Mary Nesta (Skrine)
See also INT 114
Keates, Jonathan 1946(?)- .... **CLC 34**
See also CA 163

Keaton, Buster 1895-1966 .... **CLC 20**
Keats, John 1795-1821 ...... **NCLC 8, 73; DA;**
DAB; DAC; DAM MST, POET; PC 1
See also AW; CDBLB 1789-1832; DA3;
DLB 96, 110
Keble, John 1792-1866 .... **NCLC 87**
See also DLB 32, 55
Keene, Donald 1922- .... **CLC 34**
See also CA 1-4R; CANR 5
Keillor, Garrison CLC 40, 115
See also Keillor, Gary (Edward)
See also AAYA 2; BEST 89:3; DLBY 87;
SATA 58
Keillor, Gary (Edward) 1942-
See Keillor, Garrison
See also CA 111; 117; CANR 36, 59; DAM
POP; DA3; MTCW 1, 2
Keith, Michael
See Hubbard, L(afayette) Ron(ald)
Keller, Gottfried 1819-1890 .... **NCLC 2; SSC**
26
See also DLB 129
Keller, Nora Okja 1965- .... **CLC 109**
See also CA 187
Kellerman, Jonathan 1949- .. **CLC 44; DAM**
POP
See also AAYA 35; BEST 90:1; CA 106;
CANR 29, 51; DA3; INT CANR-29
Kelley, William Melvin 1937- .... **CLC 22**
See also BW 1; CA 77-80; CANR 27, 83;
DLB 33
Kellogg, Marjorie 1922- .... **CLC 2**
See also CA 81-84
Kellow, Kathleen
See Hibbert, Eleanor Alice Burford
Kelly, M(ilton) T(errence) 1947- ...... **CLC 55**
See also CA 97-100; CAAS 22; CANR 19,
43, 84
Kelman, James 1946- .... **CLC 58, 86**
See also BRWS 5; CA 148; CANR 85; DLB
194
Kemal, Yashar 1923- .... **CLC 14, 29**
See also CA 89-92; CANR 44; CWW 2
Kemble, Fanny 1809-1893 .... **NCLC 18**
See also DLB 32
Kemelman, Harry 1908-1996 .... **CLC 2**
See also AITN 1; CA 9-12R; 155; CANR 6,
71; DLB 28
Kempe, Margery 1373(?)-1440(?) ... **LC 6, 56**
See also DLB 146
Kempis, Thomas a 1380-1471 .... **LC 11**
Kendall, Henry 1839-1882 .... **NCLC 12**
See also DLB 230
Keneally, Thomas (Michael) 1935- ... **CLC 5,**
8, 10, 14, 19, 27, 43, 117; DAM NOV
See also BRWS 4; CA 85-88; CANR 10,
50, 74; DA3; MTCW 1, 2
Kennedy, Adrienne (Lita) 1931- ..... **CLC 66;**
BLC 2; DAM MULT; DC 5
See also BW 2, 3; CA 103; CAAS 20;
CABS 3; CANR 26, 53, 82; DLB 38
Kennedy, John Pendleton
1795-1870 .... **NCLC 2**
See also DLB 3
Kennedy, Joseph Charles 1929-
See Kennedy, X. J.
See also CA 1-4R; CANR 4, 30, 40; SATA
14, 86
Kennedy, William 1928- .. **CLC 6, 28, 34, 53;**
DAM NOV
See also AAYA 1; AMWS 7; CA 85-88;
CANR 14, 31, 76; DA3; DLB 143; DLBY
85; INT CANR-31; MTCW 1, 2; SATA
57
Kennedy, X. J. CLC 8, 42
See also Kennedy, Joseph Charles
See also CAAS 9; CLR 27; DLB 5;
SAAS 22

Kenny, Maurice (Francis) 1929- ..... **CLC 87;**
DAM MULT
See also CA 144; CAAS 22; DLB 175;
NNAL
Kent, Kelvin
See Kuttner, Henry
Kenton, Maxwell
See Southern, Terry
Kenyon, Robert O.
See Kuttner, Henry
Kepler, Johannes 1571-1630 .... **LC 45**
Kerouac, Jack CLC 1, 2, 3, 5, 14, 29, 61
See also Kerouac, Jean-Louis Lebris de
See also AAYA 25; AMWS 3; CDALB
1941-1968; DLB 2, 16; DLBD 3; DLBY
95; GLL 1; MTCW 2
Kerouac, Jean-Louis Lebris de 1922-1969
See Kerouac, Jack
See also AITN 1; AW; CA 5-8R; 25-28R;
CANR 26, 54, 95; DA; DAB; DAC; DAM
MST, NOV, POET, POP; DA3; MTCW 1,
2
Kerr, Jean 1923- .... **CLC 22**
See also CA 5-8R; CANR 7; INT CANR-7
Kerr, M. E. CLC 12, 35
See also Meaker, Marijane (Agnes)
See also AAYA 2, 23; CLR 29; SAAS 1
Kerr, Robert CLC 55
Kerrigan, (Thomas) Anthony 1918- .. **CLC 4,**
6
See also CA 49-52; CAAS 11; CANR 4
Kerry, Lois
See Duncan, Lois
Kesey, Ken (Elton) 1935- ..... **CLC 1, 3, 6, 11,**
46, 64; DA; DAB; DAC; DAM MST,
NOV, POP
See also AAYA 25; AW; CA 1-4R; CANR
22, 38, 66; CDALB 1968-1988; DA3;
DLB 2, 16, 206; MTCW 1, 2; SATA 66
Kesselring, Joseph (Otto)
1902-1967 .... **CLC 45; DAM DRAM,**
MST
See also CA 150
Kessler, Jascha (Frederick) 1929- ...... **CLC 4**
See also CA 17-20R; CANR 8, 48
Kettelkamp, Larry (Dale) 1933- .... **CLC 12**
See also CA 29-32R; CANR 16; SAAS 3;
SATA 2
Key, Ellen (Karolina Sofia)
1849-1926 .... **TCLC 65**
Keyber, Conny
See Fielding, Henry
Keyes, Daniel 1927- ..... **CLC 80; DA; DAC;**
DAM MST, NOV
See also AAYA 23; CA 17-20R, 181; CAAE
181; CANR 10, 26, 54, 74; DA3; MTCW
2; SATA 37
Keynes, John Maynard
1883-1946 .... **TCLC 64**
See also CA 114; 162, 163; DLBD 10;
MTCW 2
Khanshendel, Chiron
See Rose, Wendy
Khayyam, Omar 1048-1131 .... **CMLC 11;**
DAM POET; PC 8
See also DA3
Kherdian, David 1931- .... **CLC 6, 9**
See also CA 21-24R; CAAS 2; CANR 39,
78; CLR 24; JRDA; MAICYA; SATA 16,
74
Khlebnikov, Velimir TCLC 20
See also Khlebnikov, Viktor Vladimirovich
Khlebnikov, Viktor Vladimirovich 1885-1922
See Khlebnikov, Velimir
See also CA 117
Khodasevich, Vladislav (Felitsianovich)
1886-1939 .... **TCLC 15**
See also CA 115

Kielland, Alexander Lange
1849-1906 .... **TCLC 5**
See also CA 104

Kiely, Benedict 1919- .... **CLC 23, 43**
See also CA 1-4R; CANR 2, 84; DLB 15

Kienzle, William X(avier) 1928- ..... **CLC 25;
DAM POP**
See also CA 93-96; CAAS 1; CANR 9, 31,
59; DA3; INT CANR-31; MTCW 1, 2

Kierkegaard, Soren 1813-1855 ..... **NCLC 34,
78**

Kieslowski, Krzysztof 1941-1996 .... **CLC 120**
See also CA 147; 151

Killens, John Oliver 1916-1987 .... **CLC 10**
See also BW 2; CA 77-80; 123; CAAS 2;
CANR 26; DLB 33

Killigrew, Anne 1660-1685 .... **LC 4**
See also DLB 131

Killigrew, Thomas 1612-1683 .... **LC 57**
See also DLB 58

Kim
See Simenon, Georges (Jacques Christian)

Kincaid, Jamaica 1949- ..... **CLC 43, 68, 137;
BLC 2; DAM MULT, NOV**
See also AAYA 13; AMWS 7; AW; BW 2,
3; CA 125; CANR 47, 59, 95; CDALBS;
CLR 63; DA3; DLB 157, 227; MTCW 2

King, Francis (Henry) 1923- .... **CLC 8, 53;
DAM NOV**
See also CA 1-4R; CANR 1, 33, 86; DLB
15, 139; MTCW 1

King, Kennedy
See Brown, George Douglas

King, Martin Luther, Jr.
1929-1968 .... **CLC 83; BLC 2; DA;
DAB; DAC; DAM MST, MULT**
See also AW; BW 2, 3; CA 25-28; CANR
27, 44; CAP 2; DA3; MTCW 1, 2; SATA
14

King, Stephen (Edwin) 1947- .... **CLC 12, 26,
37, 61, 113; DAM NOV, POP; SSC 17**
See also AAYA 1, 17; AMWS 5; AW 1;
BEST 90:1; CA 61-64; CANR 1, 30, 52,
76; DA3; DLB 143; DLBY 80; JRDA;
MTCW 1, 2; SATA 9, 55

King, Steve
See King, Stephen (Edwin)

King, Thomas 1943- ... **CLC 89; DAC; DAM
MULT**
See also CA 144; CANR 95; CCA 1; DLB
175; NNAL; SATA 96

Kingman, Lee CLC 17
See also Natti, (Mary) Lee
See also SAAS 3; SATA 1, 67

Kingsley, Charles 1819-1875 .... **NCLC 35**
See also AW 2; DLB 21, 32, 163, 190

Kingsley, Sidney 1906-1995 .... **CLC 44**
See also CA 85-88; 147; DLB 7

Kingsolver, Barbara 1955- .... **CLC 55, 81,
130; DAM POP**
See also AAYA 15; AMWS 7; CA 129; 134;
CANR 60, 96; CDALBS; DA3; DLB 206;
INT 134; MTCW 2

Kingston, Maxine (Ting Ting) Hong
1940- .... **CLC 12, 19, 58, 121; DAM
MULT, NOV**
See also AAYA 8; AW; CA 69-72; CANR
13, 38, 74, 87; CDALBS; DA3; DLB 173,
212; DLBY 80; INT CANR-13; MTCW
1, 2; SATA 53

Kinnell, Galway 1927- ..... **CLC 1, 2, 3, 5, 13,
29, 129; PC 26**
See also AMWS 3; CA 9-12R; CANR 10,
34, 66; DLB 5; DLBY 87; INT CANR-
34; MTCW 1, 2

Kinsella, Thomas 1928- .... **CLC 4, 19, 138**
See also BRWS 5; CA 17-20R; CANR 15;
DLB 27; MTCW 1, 2

Kinsella, W(illiam) P(atrick) 1935- . **CLC 27,
43; DAC; DAM NOV, POP**
See also AAYA 7; CA 97-100; CAAS 7;
CANR 21, 35, 66, 75; INT CANR-21;
MTCW 1, 2

Kinsey, Alfred C(harles)
1894-1956 .... **TCLC 91**
See also CA 115; 170; MTCW 2

Kipling, (Joseph) Rudyard
1865-1936 .... **TCLC 8, 17; DA; DAB;
DAC; DAM MST, POET; PC 3; SSC 5**
See also AAYA 32; AW; CA 105; 120;
CANR 33; CDBLB 1890-1914; CLR 39,
65; DA3; DLB 19, 34, 141, 156; MAI-
CYA; MTCW 1, 2; SATA 100

Kirkland, Caroline M. 1801-1864 . **NCLC 85**
See also DLB 3, 73, 74; DLBD 13

Kirkup, James 1918- .... **CLC 1**
See also CA 1-4R; CAAS 4; CANR 2; DLB
27; SATA 12

Kirkwood, James 1930(?)-1989 .... **CLC 9**
See also AITN 2; CA 1-4R; 128; CANR 6,
40; GLL 2

Kirshner, Sidney
See Kingsley, Sidney

Kis, Danilo 1935-1989 .... **CLC 57**
See also CA 109; 118; 129; CANR 61; DLB
181; MTCW 1

Kissinger, Henry A(lfred) 1923- ..... **CLC 137**
See also CA 1-4R; CANR 2, 33, 66; MTCW
1

Kivi, Aleksis 1834-1872 .... **NCLC 30**

Kizer, Carolyn (Ashley) 1925- ... **CLC 15, 39,
80; DAM POET**
See also CA 65-68; CAAS 5; CANR 24,
70; DLB 5, 169; MTCW 2

Klabund 1890-1928 .... **TCLC 44**
See also CA 162; DLB 66

Klappert, Peter 1942- .... **CLC 57**
See also CA 33-36R; DLB 5

Klein, A(braham) M(oses)
1909-1972 . **CLC 19; DAB; DAC; DAM
MST**
See also CA 101; 37-40R; DLB 68

Klein, Norma 1938-1989 .... **CLC 30**
See also AAYA 2, 35; AW; CA 41-44R; 128;
CANR 15, 37; CLR 2, 19; INT CANR-
15; JRDA; MAICYA; SAAS 1; SATA 7,
57

Klein, T(heodore) E(ibon) D(onald)
1947- .... **CLC 34**
See also CA 119; CANR 44, 75

Kleist, Heinrich von 1777-1811 ...... **NCLC 2,
37; DAM DRAM; SSC 22**
See also DLB 90

Klima, Ivan 1931- .... **CLC 56; DAM NOV**
See also CA 25-28R; CANR 17, 50, 91;
CWW 2; DLB 232

Klimentov, Andrei Platonovich
1899-1951 .... **TCLC 14; SSC 42**
See also CA 108

Klinger, Friedrich Maximilian von
1752-1831 .... **NCLC 1**
See also DLB 94

Klingsor the Magician
See Hartmann, Sadakichi

Klopstock, Friedrich Gottlieb
1724-1803 .... **NCLC 11**
See also DLB 97

Knapp, Caroline 1959- .... **CLC 99**
See also CA 154

Knebel, Fletcher 1911-1993 .... **CLC 14**
See also AITN 1; CA 1-4R; 140; CAAS 3;
CANR 1, 36; SATA 36; SATA-Obit 75

Knickerbocker, Diedrich
See Irving, Washington

Knight, Etheridge 1931-1991 . **CLC 40; BLC
2; DAM POET; PC 14**
See also BW 1, 3; CA 21-24R; 133; CANR
23, 82; DLB 41; MTCW 2

Knight, Sarah Kemble 1666-1727 .... **LC 7**
See also DLB 24, 200

Knister, Raymond 1899-1932 .... **TCLC 56**
See also CA 186; DLB 68

Knowles, John 1926- . **CLC 1, 4, 10, 26; DA;
DAC; DAM MST, NOV**
See also AAYA 10; AW; CA 17-20R; CANR
40, 74, 76; CDALB 1968-1988; DLB 6;
MTCW 1, 2; SATA 8, 89

Knox, Calvin M.
See Silverberg, Robert

Knox, John c. 1505-1572 .... **LC 37**
See also DLB 132

Knye, Cassandra
See Disch, Thomas M(ichael)

Koch, C(hristopher) J(ohn) 1932- .... **CLC 42**
See also CA 127; CANR 84

Koch, Christopher
See Koch, C(hristopher) J(ohn)

Koch, Kenneth 1925- .... **CLC 5, 8, 44; DAM
POET**
See also CA 1-4R; CANR 6, 36, 57; DLB
5; INT CANR-36; MTCW 2; SATA 65

Kochanowski, Jan 1530-1584 .... **LC 10**

Kock, Charles Paul de 1794-1871 . **NCLC 16**

Koda Rohan
See Koda Shigeyuki

Koda Shigeyuki 1867-1947 .... **TCLC 22**
See also CA 121; 183; DLB 180

Koestler, Arthur 1905-1983 ... **CLC 1, 3, 6, 8,
15, 33**
See also BRWS 1; CA 1-4R; 109; CANR 1,
33; CDBLB 1945-1960; DLBY 83;
MTCW 1, 2

Kogawa, Joy Nozomi 1935- ..... **CLC 78, 129;
DAC; DAM MST, MULT**
See also CA 101; CANR 19, 62; MTCW 2;
SATA 99

Kohout, Pavel 1928- .... **CLC 13**
See also CA 45-48; CANR 3

Koizumi, Yakumo
See Hearn, (Patricio) Lafcadio (Tessima
Carlos)

Kolmar, Gertrud 1894-1943 .... **TCLC 40**
See also CA 167

Komunyakaa, Yusef 1947- .... **CLC 86, 94;
BLCS**
See also CA 147; CANR 83; DLB 120

Konrad, George
See Konrad, Gyorgy
See also CWW 2

Konrad, Gyorgy 1933- .... **CLC 4, 10, 73**
See also Konrad, George
See also CA 85-88; CWW 2; DLB 232

Konwicki, Tadeusz 1926- .... **CLC 8, 28, 54,
117**
See also CA 101; CAAS 9; CANR 39, 59;
CWW 2; DLB 232; IDFW 3; MTCW 1

Koontz, Dean R(ay) 1945- .... **CLC 78; DAM
NOV, POP**
See also AAYA 9, 31; AW; BEST 89:3,
90:2; CA 108; CANR 19, 36, 52, 95;
DA3; MTCW 1; SATA 92

Kopernik, Mikolaj
See Copernicus, Nicolaus

Kopit, Arthur (Lee) 1937- ..... **CLC 1, 18, 33;
DAM DRAM**
See also AITN 1; CA 81-84; CABS 3; DLB
7; MTCW 1

Kops, Bernard 1926- .... **CLC 4**
See also CA 5-8R; CANR 84; DLB 13

Kornbluth, C(yril) M. 1923-1958 .... **TCLC 8**
See also CA 105; 160; DLB 8

Korolenko, V. G.
See Korolenko, Vladimir Galaktionovich

Korolenko, Vladimir
   See Korolenko, Vladimir Galaktionovich
Korolenko, Vladimir G.
   See Korolenko, Vladimir Galaktionovich
Korolenko, Vladimir Galaktionovich
   1853-1921 .... TCLC 22
   See also CA 121
Korzybski, Alfred (Habdank Skarbek)
   1879-1950 .... TCLC 61
   See also CA 123; 160
Kosinski, Jerzy (Nikodem)
   1933-1991 .... CLC 1, 2, 3, 6, 10, 15, 53,
   70; DAM NOV
   See also AMWS 7; CA 17-20R; 134; CANR
   9, 46; DA3; DLB 2; DLBY 82; MTCW 1,
   2
Kostelanetz, Richard (Cory) 1940- .. CLC 28
   See also CA 13-16R; CAAS 8; CANR 38,
   77
Kotlowitz, Robert 1924- .... CLC 4
   See also CA 33-36R; CANR 36
Kotzebue, August (Friedrich Ferdinand) von
   1761-1819 .... NCLC 25
   See also DLB 94
Kotzwinkle, William 1938- ..... CLC 5, 14, 35
   See also AW; CA 45-48; CANR 3, 44, 84;
   CLR 6; DLB 173; MAICYA; SATA 24,
   70
Kowna, Stancy
   See Szymborska, Wislawa
Kozol, Jonathan 1936- .... CLC 17
   See also CA 61-64; CANR 16, 45, 96
Kozoll, Michael 1940(?)- .... CLC 35
Kramer, Kathryn 19(?)- .... CLC 34
Kramer, Larry 1935- .. CLC 42; DAM POP;
   DC 8
   See also CA 124; 126; CANR 60; GLL 1
Krasicki, Ignacy 1735-1801 .... NCLC 8
Krasinski, Zygmunt 1812-1859 .... NCLC 4
Kraus, Karl 1874-1936 .... TCLC 5
   See also CA 104; DLB 118
Kreve (Mickevicius), Vincas
   1882-1954 .... TCLC 27
   See also CA 170; DLB 220
Kristeva, Julia 1941- .... CLC 77, 140
   See also CA 154; DLB 242
Kristofferson, Kris 1936- .... CLC 26
   See also CA 104
Krizanc, John 1956- .... CLC 57
   See also CA 187
Krleza, Miroslav 1893-1981 .... CLC 8, 114
   See also CA 97-100; 105; CANR 50; DLB
   147
Kroetsch, Robert 1927- . CLC 5, 23, 57, 132;
   DAC; DAM POET
   See also CA 17-20R; CANR 8, 38; CCA 1;
   DLB 53; MTCW 1
Kroetz, Franz
   See Kroetz, Franz Xaver
Kroetz, Franz Xaver 1946- .... CLC 41
   See also CA 130
Kroker, Arthur (W.) 1945- .... CLC 77
   See also CA 161
Kropotkin, Peter (Aleksieevich)
   1842-1921 .... TCLC 36
   See also CA 119
Krotkov, Yuri 1917- .... CLC 19
   See also CA 102
Krumb
   See Crumb, R(obert)
Krumgold, Joseph (Quincy)
   1908-1980 .... CLC 12
   See also AW; CA 9-12R; 101; CANR 7;
   MAICYA; SATA 1, 48; SATA-Obit 23
Krumwitz
   See Crumb, R(obert)

Krutch, Joseph Wood 1893-1970 ..... CLC 24
   See also CA 1-4R; 25-28R; CANR 4; DLB
   63, 206
Krutzch, Gus
   See Eliot, T(homas) S(tearns)
Krylov, Ivan Andreevich
   1768(?)-1844 .... NCLC 1
   See also DLB 150
Kubin, Alfred (Leopold Isidor)
   1877-1959 .... TCLC 23
   See also CA 112; 149; DLB 81
Kubrick, Stanley 1928-1999 .... CLC 16
   See also AAYA 30; CA 81-84; 177; CANR
   33; DLB 26
Kueng, Hans 1928-
   See Kung, Hans
   See also CA 53-56; CANR 66; MTCW 1, 2
Kumin, Maxine (Winokur) 1925- ..... CLC 5,
   13, 28; DAM POET; PC 15
   See also AITN 2; AMWS 4; CA 1-4R;
   CAAS 8; CANR 1, 21, 69; DA3; DLB 5;
   MTCW 1, 2; SATA 12
Kundera, Milan 1929- . CLC 4, 9, 19, 32, 68,
   115, 135; DAM NOV; SSC 24
   See also AAYA 2; CA 85-88; CANR 19,
   52, 74; CWW 2; DA3; DLB 232; MTCW
   1, 2
Kunene, Mazisi (Raymond) 1930- ... CLC 85
   See also BW 1, 3; CA 125; CANR 81; DLB
   117
Kung, Hans CLC 130
   See also Kueng, Hans
Kunikida, Doppo 1869(?)-1908 ...... TCLC 99
   See also DLB 180
Kunitz, Stanley (Jasspon) 1905- .. CLC 6, 11,
   14; PC 19
   See also AMWS 3; CA 41-44R; CANR 26,
   57; DA3; DLB 48; INT CANR-26;
   MTCW 1, 2
Kunze, Reiner 1933- .... CLC 10
   See also CA 93-96; CWW 2; DLB 75
Kuprin, Aleksander Ivanovich
   1870-1938 .... TCLC 5
   See also CA 104; 182
Kureishi, Hanif 1954(?)- .... CLC 64, 135
   See also CA 139; DLB 194; GLL 2
Kurosawa, Akira 1910-1998 .... CLC 16, 119;
   DAM MULT
   See also AAYA 11; CA 101; 170; CANR 46
Kushner, Tony 1957(?)- .... CLC 81; DAM
   DRAM; DC 10
   See also CA 144; CANR 74; DA3; DLB
   228; GLL 1; MTCW 2
Kuttner, Henry 1915-1958 .... TCLC 10
   See also CA 107; 157; DLB 8
Kuzma, Greg 1944- .... CLC 7
   See also CA 33-36R; CANR 70
Kuzmin, Mikhail 1872(?)-1936 ...... TCLC 40
   See also CA 170
Kyd, Thomas 1558-1594 .... LC 22; DAM
   DRAM; DC 3
   See also DLB 62
Kyprianos, Iossif
   See Samarakis, Antonis
La Bruyere, Jean de 1645-1696 .... LC 17
Lacan, Jacques (Marie Emile)
   1901-1981 .... CLC 75
   See also CA 121; 104
Laclos, Pierre Ambroise Francois Choderlos
   de 1741-1803 .... NCLC 4, 87
La Colere, Francois
   See Aragon, Louis
Lacolere, Francois
   See Aragon, Louis
La Deshabilleuse
   See Simenon, Georges (Jacques Christian)
Lady Gregory
   See Gregory, Isabella Augusta (Persse)

Lady of Quality, A
   See Bagnold, Enid
La Fayette, Marie (Madelaine Pioche de la
   Vergne Comtes 1634-1693 .... LC 2
Lafayette, Rene
   See Hubbard, L(afayette) Ron(ald)
La Fontaine, Jean de 1621-1695 .... LC 50
   See also MAICYA; SATA 18
Laforgue, Jules 1860-1887 . NCLC 5, 53; PC
   14; SSC 20
Lagerkvist, Paer (Fabian)
   1891-1974 ...... CLC 7, 10, 13, 54; DAM
   DRAM, NOV
   See also Lagerkvist, Par
   See also CA 85-88; 49-52; DA3; MTCW 1,
   2
Lagerkvist, Par SSC 12
   See also Lagerkvist, Paer (Fabian)
   See also MTCW 2
Lagerkwist, Pär
   See Lagerkvist, Paer (Fabian)
Lagerloef, Selma (Ottiliana Lovisa)
   1858-1940 .... TCLC 4, 36
   See also Lagerlof, Selma (Ottiliana Lovisa)
   See also CA 108; MTCW 2; SATA 15
Lagerlof, Selma (Ottiliana Lovisa)
   See Lagerloef, Selma (Ottiliana Lovisa)
   See also CLR 7; SATA 15
La Guma, (Justin) Alex(ander)
   1925-1985 .... CLC 19; BLCS; DAM
   NOV
   See also BW 1, 3; CA 49-52; 118; CANR
   25, 81; DLB 117, 225; MTCW 1, 2
Laidlaw, A. K.
   See Grieve, C(hristopher) M(urray)
Lainez, Manuel Mujica
   See Mujica Lainez, Manuel
   See also HW 1
Laing, R(onald) D(avid) 1927-1989 . CLC 95
   See also CA 107; 129; CANR 34; MTCW 1
Lamartine, Alphonse (Marie Louis Prat) de
   1790-1869 . NCLC 11; DAM POET; PC
   16
Lamb, Charles 1775-1834 ..... NCLC 10; DA;
   DAB; DAC; DAM MST
   See also AW; CDBLB 1789-1832; DLB 93,
   107, 163; SATA 17
Lamb, Lady Caroline 1785-1828 ... NCLC 38
   See also DLB 116
Lamming, George (William) 1927- ... CLC 2,
   4, 66; BLC 2; DAM MULT
   See also BW 2, 3; CA 85-88; CANR 26,
   76; DLB 125; MTCW 1, 2
L'Amour, Louis (Dearborn)
   1908-1988 ...... CLC 25, 55; DAM NOV,
   POP
   See also Burns, Tex; Mayo, Jim
   See also AAYA 16; AITN 2; BEST 89:2;
   CA 1-4R; 125; CANR 3, 25, 40; DA3;
   DLB 206; DLBY 80; MTCW 1, 2
Lampedusa, Giuseppe (Tomasi) di TCLC 13
   See also Tomasi di Lampedusa, Giuseppe
   See also CA 164; DLB 177; MTCW 2
Lampman, Archibald 1861-1899 ... NCLC 25
   See also DLB 92
Lancaster, Bruce 1896-1963 .... CLC 36
   See also CA 9-10; CANR 70; CAP 1; SATA
   9
Lanchester, John CLC 99
Landau, Mark Alexandrovich
   See Aldanov, Mark (Alexandrovich)
Landau-Aldanov, Mark Alexandrovich
   See Aldanov, Mark (Alexandrovich)
Landis, Jerry
   See Simon, Paul (Frederick)
Landis, John 1950- .... CLC 26
   See also CA 112; 122
Landolfi, Tommaso 1908-1979 .... CLC 11, 49
   See also CA 127; 117; DLB 177

Landon, Letitia Elizabeth
1802-1838 .... NCLC 15
See also DLB 96
Landor, Walter Savage
1775-1864 .... NCLC 14
See also DLB 93, 107
Landwirth, Heinz 1927-
See Lind, Jakov
See also CA 9-12R; CANR 7
Lane, Patrick 1939- ... CLC 25; DAM POET
See also CA 97-100; CANR 54; DLB 53;
INT 97-100
Lang, Andrew 1844-1912 .... TCLC 16
See also CA 114; 137; CANR 85; DLB 98,
141, 184; MAICYA; SATA 16
Lang, Fritz 1890-1976 .... CLC 20, 103
See also CA 77-80; 69-72; CANR 30
Lange, John
See Crichton, (John) Michael
Langer, Elinor 1939- .... CLC 34
See also CA 121
Langland, William 1332(?)-1400(?) ... LC 19;
DA; DAB; DAC; DAM MST, POET
See also DLB 146
Langstaff, Launcelot
See Irving, Washington
Lanier, Sidney 1842-1881 ..... NCLC 6; DAM
POET
See also AMWS 1; DLB 64; DLBD 13;
MAICYA; SATA 18
Lanyer, Aemilia 1569-1645 .... LC 10, 30
See also DLB 121
Lao-Tzu
See Lao Tzu
Lao Tzu fl. 6046th cent. B.C.-490 ... CMLC 7
Lapine, James (Elliot) 1949- .... CLC 39
See also CA 123; 130; CANR 54; INT 130
Larbaud, Valery (Nicolas)
1881-1957 .... TCLC 9
See also CA 106; 152
Lardner, Ring
See Lardner, Ring(gold) W(ilmer)
Lardner, Ring W., Jr.
See Lardner, Ring(gold) W(ilmer)
Lardner, Ring(gold) W(ilmer)
1885-1933 .... TCLC 2, 14; SSC 32
See also CA 104; 131; CDALB 1917-1929;
DLB 11, 25, 86; DLBD 16; MTCW 1, 2
Laredo, Betty
See Codrescu, Andrei
Larkin, Maia
See Wojciechowska, Maia (Teresa)
Larkin, Philip (Arthur) 1922-1985 ... CLC 3,
5, 8, 9, 13, 18, 33, 39, 64; DAB; DAM
MST, POET; PC 21
See also BRWS 1; CA 5-8R; 117; CANR
24, 62; CDBLB 1960 to Present; DA3;
DLB 27; MTCW 1, 2
**Larra (y Sanchez de Castro), Mariano Jose
de** 1809-1837 .... NCLC 17
Larsen, Eric 1941- .... CLC 55
See also CA 132
Larsen, Nella 1893-1963 .... CLC 37; BLC 2;
DAM MULT
See also BW 1; CA 125; CANR 83; DLB
51
Larson, Charles R(aymond) 1938- ... CLC 31
See also CA 53-56; CANR 4
Larson, Jonathan 1961-1996 .... CLC 99
See also AAYA 28; CA 156
Las Casas, Bartolome de 1474-1566 ... LC 31
Lasch, Christopher 1932-1994 .... CLC 102
See also CA 73-76; 144; CANR 25; MTCW
1, 2
Lasker-Schueler, Else 1869-1945 ... TCLC 57
See also CA 183; DLB 66, 124
Laski, Harold J(oseph) 1893-1950 . TCLC 79
See also CA 188'

Latham, Jean Lee 1902-1995 .... CLC 12
See also AITN 1; AW; CA 5-8R; CANR 7,
84; CLR 50; MAICYA; SATA 2, 68
Latham, Mavis
See Clark, Mavis Thorpe
Lathen, Emma CLC 2
See also Hennissart, Martha; Latsis, Mary
J(ane)
Lathrop, Francis
See Leiber, Fritz (Reuter, Jr.)
Latsis, Mary J(ane) 1927(?)-1997
See Lathen, Emma
See also CA 85-88; 162
Lattimore, Richmond (Alexander)
1906-1984 .... CLC 3
See also CA 1-4R; 112; CANR 1
Laughlin, James 1914-1997 .... CLC 49
See also CA 21-24R; 162; CAAS 22; CANR
9, 47; DLB 48; DLBY 96, 97
Laurence, (Jean) Margaret (Wemyss)
1926-1987 . CLC 3, 6, 13, 50, 62; DAC;
DAM MST; SSC 7
See also CA 5-8R; 121; CANR 33; DLB
53; MTCW 1, 2; SATA-Obit 50
Laurent, Antoine 1952- .... CLC 50
Lauscher, Hermann
See Hesse, Hermann
Lautreamont, Comte de
1846-1870 .... NCLC 12; SSC 14
Laverty, Donald
See Blish, James (Benjamin)
Lavin, Mary 1912-1996 . CLC 4, 18, 99; SSC
4
See also CA 9-12R; 151; CANR 33; DLB
15; MTCW 1
Lavond, Paul Dennis
See Kornbluth, C(yril) M.; Pohl, Frederik
Lawler, Raymond Evenor 1922- .... CLC 58
See also CA 103
Lawrence, D(avid) H(erbert Richards)
1885-1930 .... TCLC 2, 9, 16, 33, 48, 61,
93; DA; DAB; DAC; DAM MST, NOV,
POET; SSC 4, 19
See also Chambers, Jessie
See also AW; CA 104; 121; CDBLB 1914-
1945; DA3; DLB 10, 19, 36, 98, 162, 195;
MTCW 1, 2
Lawrence, T(homas) E(dward)
1888-1935 .... TCLC 18
See also Dale, Colin
See also BRWS 2; CA 115; 167; DLB 195
Lawrence of Arabia
See Lawrence, T(homas) E(dward)
Lawson, Henry (Archibald Hertzberg)
1867-1922 .... TCLC 27; SSC 18
See also CA 120; 181; DLB 230
Lawton, Dennis
See Faust, Frederick (Schiller)
Laxness, Halldor CLC 25
See also Gudjonsson, Halldor Kiljan
Layamon fl. c. 1200- .... CMLC 10
See also DLB 146
Laye, Camara 1928-1980 ... CLC 4, 38; BLC
2; DAM MULT
See also BW 1; CA 85-88; 97-100; CANR
25; MTCW 1, 2
Layton, Irving (Peter) 1912- .... CLC 2, 15;
DAC; DAM MST, POET
See also CA 1-4R; CANR 2, 33, 43, 66;
DLB 88; MTCW 1, 2
Lazarus, Emma 1849-1887 .... NCLC 8
Lazarus, Felix
See Cable, George Washington
Lazarus, Henry
See Slavitt, David R(ytman)
Lea, Joan
See Neufeld, John (Arthur)

Leacock, Stephen (Butler)
1869-1944 .... TCLC 2; DAC; DAM
MST; SSC 39
See also CA 104; 141; CANR 80; DLB 92;
MTCW 2
Lear, Edward 1812-1888 .... NCLC 3
See also CLR 1; DLB 32, 163, 166; MAI-
CYA; SATA 18, 100
Lear, Norman (Milton) 1922- .... CLC 12
See also CA 73-76
Leautaud, Paul 1872-1956 .... TCLC 83
See also DLB 65
Leavis, F(rank) R(aymond)
1895-1978 .... CLC 24
See also CA 21-24R; 77-80; CANR 44;
DLB 242; MTCW 1, 2
Leavitt, David 1961- ..... CLC 34; DAM POP
See also CA 116; 122; CANR 50, 62; DA3;
DLB 130; GLL 1; INT 122; MTCW 2
Leblanc, Maurice (Marie Emile)
1864-1941 .... TCLC 49
See also CA 110
Lebowitz, Fran(ces Ann) 1951(?)- ... CLC 11,
36
See also CA 81-84; CANR 14, 60, 70; INT
CANR-14; MTCW 1
Lebrecht, Peter
See Tieck, (Johann) Ludwig
le Carre, John CLC 3, 5, 9, 15, 28
See also Cornwell, David (John Moore)
See also BEST 89:4; BRWS 2; CDBLB
1960 to Present; DLB 87; MTCW 2
Le Clezio, J(ean) M(arie) G(ustave)
1940- .... CLC 31
See also CA 116; 128; DLB 83
Leconte de Lisle, Charles-Marie-Rene
1818-1894 .... NCLC 29
Le Coq, Monsieur
See Simenon, Georges (Jacques Christian)
Leduc, Violette 1907-1972 .... CLC 22
See also CA 13-14; 33-36R; CANR 69;
CAP 1; GLL 1
Ledwidge, Francis 1887(?)-1917 .... TCLC 23
See also CA 123; DLB 20
Lee, Andrea 1953- ... CLC 36; BLC 2; DAM
MULT
See also BW 1, 3; CA 125; CANR 82
Lee, Andrew
See Auchincloss, Louis (Stanton)
Lee, Chang-rae 1965- .... CLC 91
See also CA 148; CANR 89
Lee, Don L. CLC 2
See also Madhubuti, Haki R.
Lee, George W(ashington)
1894-1976 .... CLC 52; BLC 2; DAM
MULT
See also BW 1; CA 125; CANR 83; DLB
51
Lee, (Nelle) Harper 1926- . CLC 12, 60; DA;
DAB; DAC; DAM MST, NOV
See also AAYA 13; CA 13-16R; CANR 51;
CDALB 1941-1968; DA3; DLB 6;
MTCW 1, 2; SATA 11
Lee, Helen Elaine 1959(?)- .... CLC 86
See also CA 148
Lee, Julian
See Latham, Jean Lee
Lee, Larry
See Lee, Lawrence
Lee, Laurie 1914-1997 .... CLC 90; DAB;
DAM POP
See also CA 77-80; 158; CANR 33, 73;
DLB 27; MTCW 1
Lee, Lawrence 1941-1990 .... CLC 34
See also CA 131; CANR 43
Lee, Li-Young 1957- .... PC 24
See also CA 153; DLB 165

Lee, Manfred B(ennington)
1905-1971 .... **CLC 11**
See also Queen, Ellery
See also CA 1-4R; 29-32R; CANR 2; DLB 137

Lee, Shelton Jackson 1957(?)- .... **CLC 105; BLCS; DAM MULT**
See also Lee, Spike
See also BW 2, 3; CA 125; CANR 42

Lee, Spike
See Lee, Shelton Jackson
See also AAYA 4, 29

Lee, Stan 1922- .... **CLC 17**
See also AAYA 5; CA 108; 111; INT 111

Lee, Tanith 1947- .... **CLC 46**
See also AAYA 15; AW; CA 37-40R; CANR 53; SATA 8, 88

Lee, Vernon TCLC 5; SSC 33
See also Paget, Violet
See also DLB 57, 153, 156, 174, 178; GLL 1

Lee, William
See Burroughs, William S(eward)
See also GLL 1

Lee, Willy
See Burroughs, William S(eward)
See also GLL 1

Lee-Hamilton, Eugene (Jacob)
1845-1907 .... **TCLC 22**
See also CA 117

Leet, Judith 1935- .... **CLC 11**
See also CA 187

Le Fanu, Joseph Sheridan
1814-1873 ..... **NCLC 9, 58; DAM POP; SSC 14**
See also DA3; DLB 21, 70, 159, 178

Leffland, Ella 1931- .... **CLC 19**
See also CA 29-32R; CANR 35, 78, 82; DLBY 84; INT CANR-35; SATA 65

Leger, Alexis
See Leger, (Marie-Rene Auguste) Alexis Saint-Leger

Leger, (Marie-Rene Auguste) Alexis Saint-Leger 1887-1975 .. **CLC 4, 11, 46; DAM POET; PC 23**
See also CA 13-16R; 61-64; CANR 43; MTCW 1

Leger, Saintleger
See Leger, (Marie-Rene Auguste) Alexis Saint-Leger

Le Guin, Ursula K(roeber) 1929- ..... **CLC 8, 13, 22, 45, 71, 136; DAB; DAC; DAM MST, POP; SSC 12**
See also AAYA 9, 27; AITN 1; CA 21-24R; CANR 9, 32, 52, 74; CDALB 1968-1988; CLR 3, 28; DA3; DLB 8, 52; INT CANR-32; JRDA; MAICYA; MTCW 1, 2; SATA 4, 52, 99

Lehmann, Rosamond (Nina)
1901-1990 .... **CLC 5**
See also CA 77-80; 131; CANR 8, 73; DLB 15; MTCW 2

Leiber, Fritz (Reuter, Jr.)
1910-1992 .... **CLC 25**
See also CA 45-48; 139; CANR 2, 40, 86; DLB 8; MTCW 1, 2; SATA 45; SATA-Obit 73; SCFW 2

Leibniz, Gottfried Wilhelm von
1646-1716 .... **LC 35**
See also DLB 168

Leimbach, Martha 1963-
See Leimbach, Marti
See also CA 130

Leimbach, Marti CLC 65
See also Leimbach, Martha

Leino, Eino TCLC 24
See also Loennbohm, Armas Eino Leopold

Leiris, Michel (Julien) 1901-1990 ..... **CLC 61**
See also CA 119; 128; 132

Leithauser, Brad 1953- .... **CLC 27**
See also CA 107; CANR 27, 81; DLB 120

Lelchuk, Alan 1938- .... **CLC 5**
See also CA 45-48; CAAS 20; CANR 1, 70

Lem, Stanislaw 1921- .... **CLC 8, 15, 40**
See also CA 105; CAAS 1; CANR 32; CWW 2; MTCW 1; SCFW 2

Lemann, Nancy 1956- .... **CLC 39**
See also CA 118; 136

Lemonnier, (Antoine Louis) Camille
1844-1913 .... **TCLC 22**
See also CA 121

Lenau, Nikolaus 1802-1850 .... **NCLC 16**

L'Engle, Madeleine (Camp Franklin)
1918- .... **CLC 12; DAM POP**
See also AAYA 28; AITN 2; CA 1-4R; CANR 3, 21, 39, 66; CLR 1, 14, 57; DA3; DLB 52; JRDA; MAICYA; MTCW 1, 2; SAAS 15; SATA 1, 27, 75

Lengyel, Jozsef 1896-1975 .... **CLC 7**
See also CA 85-88; 57-60; CANR 71

Lenin 1870-1924
See Lenin, V. I.
See also CA 121; 168

Lenin, V. I. TCLC 67
See also Lenin

Lennon, John (Ono) 1940-1980 .. **CLC 12, 35**
See also CA 102; SATA 114

Lennox, Charlotte Ramsay
1729(?)-1804 .... **NCLC 23**
See also DLB 39

Lentricchia, Frank (Jr.) 1940- .... **CLC 34**
See also CA 25-28R; CANR 19

Lenz, Siegfried 1926- .... **CLC 27; SSC 33**
See also CA 89-92; CANR 80; CWW 2; DLB 75

Leonard, Elmore (John, Jr.) 1925- . **CLC 28, 34, 71, 120; DAM POP**
See also AAYA 22; AITN 1; BEST 89:1, 90:4; CA 81-84; CANR 12, 28, 53, 76; DA3; DLB 173, 226; INT CANR-28; MTCW 1, 2; TCWW 2

Leonard, Hugh CLC 19
See also Byrne, John Keyes
See also DLB 13

Leonov, Leonid (Maximovich)
1899-1994 .... **CLC 92; DAM NOV**
See also CA 129; CANR 74, 76; MTCW 1, 2

Leopardi, Giacomo 1798-1837 .... **NCLC 22**

Le Reveler
See Artaud, Antonin (Marie Joseph)

Lerman, Eleanor 1952- .... **CLC 9**
See also CA 85-88; CANR 69

Lerman, Rhoda 1936- .... **CLC 56**
See also CA 49-52; CANR 70

Lermontov, Mikhail Yuryevich
1814-1841 .... **NCLC 5, 47; PC 18**
See also DLB 205

Leroux, Gaston 1868-1927 .... **TCLC 25**
See also CA 108; 136; CANR 69; SATA 65

Lesage, Alain-Rene 1668-1747 .... **LC 2, 28**

Leskov, Nikolai (Semyonovich)
1831-1895 .... **NCLC 25; SSC 34**

Lessing, Doris (May) 1919- ... **CLC 1, 2, 3, 6, 10, 15, 22, 40, 94; DA; DAB; DAC; DAM MST, NOV; SSC 6**
See also AW; BRWS 1; CA 9-12R; CAAS 14; CANR 33, 54, 76; CDBLB 1960 to Present; DA3; DLB 15, 139; DLBY 85; MTCW 1, 2

Lessing, Gotthold Ephraim 1729-1781 . **LC 8**
See also DLB 97

Lester, Richard 1932- .... **CLC 20**

Lever, Charles (James)
1806-1872 .... **NCLC 23**
See also DLB 21

Leverson, Ada 1865(?)-1936(?) .... **TCLC 18**
See also Elaine
See also CA 117; DLB 153

Levertov, Denise 1923-1997 .. **CLC 1, 2, 3, 5, 8, 15, 28, 66; DAM POET; PC 11**
See also AMWS 3; CA 1-4R; 178; 163; CAAE 178; CAAS 19; CANR 3, 29, 50; CDALBS; DLB 5, 165; INT CANR-29; MTCW 1, 2

Levi, Jonathan CLC 76

Levi, Peter (Chad Tigar)
1931-2000 .... **CLC 41**
See also CA 5-8R; 187; CANR 34, 80; DLB 40

Levi, Primo 1919-1987 . **CLC 37, 50; SSC 12**
See also CA 13-16R; 122; CANR 12, 33, 61, 70; DLB 177; MTCW 1, 2

Levin, Ira 1929- .... **CLC 3, 6; DAM POP**
See also CA 21-24R; CANR 17, 44, 74; DA3; MTCW 1, 2; SATA 66

Levin, Meyer 1905-1981 .... **CLC 7; DAM POP**
See also AITN 1; CA 9-12R; 104; CANR 15; DLB 9, 28; DLBY 81; SATA 21; SATA-Obit 27

Levine, Norman 1924- .... **CLC 54**
See also CA 73-76; CAAS 23; CANR 14, 70; DLB 88

Levine, Philip 1928- .. **CLC 2, 4, 5, 9, 14, 33, 118; DAM POET; PC 22**
See also AMWS 5; CA 9-12R; CANR 9, 37, 52; DLB 5

Levinson, Deirdre 1931- .... **CLC 49**
See also CA 73-76; CANR 70

Levi-Strauss, Claude 1908- .... **CLC 38**
See also CA 1-4R; CANR 6, 32, 57; DLB 242; MTCW 1, 2

Levitin, Sonia (Wolff) 1934- .... **CLC 17**
See also AAYA 13; AW; CA 29-32R; CANR 14, 32, 79; CLR 53; JRDA; MAICYA; SAAS 2; SATA 4, 68, 119

Levon, O. U.
See Kesey, Ken (Elton)

Levy, Amy 1861-1889 .... **NCLC 59**
See also DLB 156, 240

Lewes, George Henry 1817-1878 ... **NCLC 25**
See also DLB 55, 144

Lewis, Alun 1915-1944 .... **TCLC 3; SSC 40**
See also CA 104; 188; DLB 20, 162

Lewis, C. Day
See Day Lewis, C(ecil)

Lewis, C(live) S(taples) 1898-1963 .... **CLC 1, 3, 6, 14, 27, 124; DA; DAB; DAC; DAM MST, NOV, POP**
See also AAYA 3; BRWS 3; CA 81-84; CANR 33, 71; CDBLB 1945-1960; CLR 3, 27; DA3; DLB 15, 100, 160; JRDA; MAICYA; MTCW 1, 2; SATA 13, 100

Lewis, Janet 1899-1998 .... **CLC 41**
See also Winters, Janet Lewis
See also CA 9-12R; 172; CANR 29, 63; CAP 1; DLBY 87; TCWW 2

Lewis, Matthew Gregory
1775-1818 .... **NCLC 11, 62**
See also DLB 39, 158, 178

Lewis, (Harry) Sinclair 1885-1951 . **TCLC 4, 13, 23, 39; DA; DAB; DAC; DAM MST, NOV**
See also AW; CA 104; 133; CDALB 1917-1929; DA3; DLB 9, 102; DLBD 1; MTCW 1, 2

Lewis, (Percy) Wyndham
1884(?)-1957 .. **TCLC 2, 9, 104; SSC 34**
See also CA 104; 157; DLB 15; MTCW 2

Lewisohn, Ludwig 1883-1955 .... **TCLC 19**
See also CA 107; DLB 4, 9, 28, 102

Lewton, Val 1904-1951 .... **TCLC 76**
See also IDFW 3

Leyner, Mark 1956- .... **CLC 92**
    See also CA 110; CANR 28, 53; DA3;
    MTCW 2
Lezama Lima, Jose 1910-1976 .... **CLC 4, 10,**
    101; DAM MULT; HLCS 2
    See also CA 77-80; CANR 71; DLB 113;
    HW 1, 2
L'Heureux, John (Clarke) 1934- ...... **CLC 52**
    See also CA 13-16R; CANR 23, 45, 88
Liddell, C. H.
    See Kuttner, Henry
Lie, Jonas (Lauritz Idemil)
    1833-1908(?) .... **TCLC 5**
    See also CA 115
Lieber, Joel 1937-1971 .... **CLC 6**
    See also CA 73-76; 29-32R
Lieber, Stanley Martin
    See Lee, Stan
Lieberman, Laurence (James)
    1935- .... **CLC 4, 36**
    See also CA 17-20R; CANR 8, 36, 89
Lieh Tzu fl. 7th cent. B.C.-5th cent.
    B.C. .... **CMLC 27**
Lieksman, Anders
    See Haavikko, Paavo Juhani
Li Fei-kan 1904-
    See Pa Chin
    See also CA 105
Lifton, Robert Jay 1926- .... **CLC 67**
    See also CA 17-20R; CANR 27, 78; INT
    CANR-27; SATA 66
Lightfoot, Gordon 1938- .... **CLC 26**
    See also CA 109
Lightman, Alan P(aige) 1948- .... **CLC 81**
    See also CA 141; CANR 63
Ligotti, Thomas (Robert) 1953- ...... **CLC 44;**
    SSC 16
    See also CA 123; CANR 49
Li Ho 791-817 .... **PC 13**
Liliencron, (Friedrich Adolf Axel) Detlev
    von 1844-1909 .... **TCLC 18**
    See also CA 117
Lilly, William 1602-1681 .... **LC 27**
Lima, Jose Lezama
    See Lezama Lima, Jose
Lima Barreto, Afonso Henrique de
    1881-1922 .... **TCLC 23**
    See also CA 117; 181
Lima Barreto, Afonso Henriques de
    See Lima Barreto, Afonso Henrique de
Limonov, Edward 1944- .... **CLC 67**
    See also CA 137
Lin, Frank
    See Atherton, Gertrude (Franklin Horn)
Lincoln, Abraham 1809-1865 .... **NCLC 18**
Lind, Jakov **CLC 1, 2, 4, 27, 82**
    See also Landwirth, Heinz
    See also CAAS 4
Lindbergh, Anne (Spencer) Morrow
    1906-2001 .... **CLC 82; DAM NOV**
    See also CA 17-20R; CANR 16, 73; MTCW
    1, 2; SATA 33
Lindsay, David 1878(?)-1945 .... **TCLC 15**
    See also CA 113; 187
Lindsay, (Nicholas) Vachel
    1879-1931 . **TCLC 17; DA; DAC; DAM**
    MST, POET; PC 23
    See also AMWS 1; AW; CA 114; 135;
    CANR 79; CDALB 1865-1917; DA3;
    DLB 54; SATA 40
Linke-Poot
    See Doeblin, Alfred
Linney, Romulus 1930- .... **CLC 51**
    See also CA 1-4R; CANR 40, 44, 79
Linton, Eliza Lynn 1822-1898 .... **NCLC 41**
    See also DLB 18

Li Po 701-763 .... **CMLC 2; PC 29**
Lipsius, Justus 1547-1606 .... **LC 16**
Lipsyte, Robert (Michael) 1938- ..... **CLC 21;**
    DA; DAC; DAM MST, NOV
    See also AAYA 7; CA 17-20R; CANR 8,
    57; CLR 23; JRDA; MAICYA; SATA 5,
    68, 113
Lish, Gordon (Jay) 1934- ... **CLC 45; SSC 18**
    See also CA 113; 117; CANR 79; DLB 130;
    INT 117
Lispector, Clarice 1925(?)-1977 .... **CLC 43;**
    HLCS 2; SSC 34
    See also CA 139; 116; CANR 71; DLB 113;
    HW 2
Littell, Robert 1935(?)- .... **CLC 42**
    See also CA 109; 112; CANR 64
Little, Malcolm 1925-1965
    See Malcolm X
    See also BW 1, 3; CA 125; 111; CANR 82;
    DA; DAB; DAC; DAM MST, MULT;
    DA3; MTCW 1, 2
Littlewit, Humphrey Gent.
    See Lovecraft, H(oward) P(hillips)
Litwos
    See Sienkiewicz, Henryk (Adam Alexander
    Pius)
Liu, E 1857-1909 .... **TCLC 15**
    See also CA 115
Lively, Penelope (Margaret) 1933- .. **CLC 32,**
    50; DAM NOV
    See also CA 41-44R; CANR 29, 67, 79;
    CLR 7; DLB 14, 161, 207; JRDA; MAI-
    CYA; MTCW 1, 2; SATA 7, 60, 101
Livesay, Dorothy (Kathleen)
    1909-1996 . **CLC 4, 15, 79; DAC; DAM**
    MST, POET
    See also AITN 2; CA 25-28R; CAAS 8;
    CANR 36, 67; DLB 68; MTCW 1
Livy c. 59B.C.-c. 17 .... **CMLC 11**
    See also DLB 211
Lizardi, Jose Joaquin Fernandez de
    1776-1827 .... **NCLC 30**
Llewellyn, Richard
    See Llewellyn Lloyd, Richard Dafydd Viv-
    ian
    See also DLB 15
Llewellyn Lloyd, Richard Dafydd Vivian
    1906-1983 .... **CLC 7, 80**
    See also Llewellyn, Richard
    See also CA 53-56; 111; CANR 7, 71;
    SATA 11; SATA-Obit 37
Llosa, (Jorge) Mario (Pedro) Vargas
    See Vargas Llosa, (Jorge) Mario (Pedro)
Lloyd, Manda
    See Mander, (Mary) Jane
Lloyd Webber, Andrew 1948-
    See Webber, Andrew Lloyd
    See also AAYA 1; CA 116; 149; DAM
    DRAM; SATA 56
Llull, Ramon c. 1235-c. 1316 .... **CMLC 12**
Lobb, Ebenezer
    See Upward, Allen
Locke, Alain (Le Roy) 1886-1954 . **TCLC 43;**
    BLCS
    See also BW 1, 3; CA 106; 124; CANR 79;
    DLB 51
Locke, John 1632-1704 .... **LC 7, 35**
    See also DLB 101
Locke-Elliott, Sumner
    See Elliott, Sumner Locke
Lockhart, John Gibson 1794-1854 .. **NCLC 6**
    See also DLB 110, 116, 144
Lodge, David (John) 1935- ...... **CLC 36, 141;**
    DAM POP
    See also BEST 90:1; BRWS 4; CA 17-20R;
    CANR 19, 53, 92; DLB 14, 194; INT
    CANR-19; MTCW 1, 2
Lodge, Thomas 1558-1625 .... **LC 41**
    See also DLB 172

Lodge, Thomas 1558-1625 .... **LC 41**
Loennbohm, Armas Eino Leopold 1878-1926
    See Leino, Eino
    See also CA 123
Loewinsohn, Ron(ald William)
    1937- .... **CLC 52**
    See also CA 25-28R; CANR 71
Logan, Jake
    See Smith, Martin Cruz
Logan, John (Burton) 1923-1987 .... **CLC 5**
    See also CA 77-80; 124; CANR 45; DLB 5
Lo Kuan-chung 1330(?)-1400(?) .... **LC 12**
Lombard, Nap
    See Johnson, Pamela Hansford
London, Jack **TCLC 9, 15, 39; SSC 4**
    See also London, John Griffith
    See also AAYA 13; AITN 2; AW; CDALB
    1865-1917; DLB 8, 12, 78, 212; SATA
    18; TCWW 2
London, John Griffith 1876-1916
    See London, Jack
    See also CA 110; 119; CANR 73; DA;
    DAB; DAC; DAM MST, NOV; DA3;
    JRDA; MAICYA; MTCW 1, 2
Long, Emmett
    See Leonard, Elmore (John, Jr.)
Longbaugh, Harry
    See Goldman, William (W.)
Longfellow, Henry Wadsworth
    1807-1882 .... **NCLC 2, 45; DA; DAB;**
    DAC; DAM MST, POET; PC 30
    See also AW; CDALB 1640-1865; DA3;
    DLB 1, 59, 235; SATA 19
Longinus c. 1st cent. - .... **CMLC 27**
    See also DLB 176
Longley, Michael 1939- .... **CLC 29**
    See also CA 102; DLB 40
Longus fl. c. 2nd cent. - .... **CMLC 7**
Longway, A. Hugh
    See Lang, Andrew
Lonnrot, Elias 1802-1884 .... **NCLC 53**
Lopate, Phillip 1943- .... **CLC 29**
    See also CA 97-100; CANR 88; DLBY 80;
    INT 97-100
Lopez Portillo (y Pacheco), Jose
    1920- .... **CLC 46**
    See also CA 129; HW 1
Lopez y Fuentes, Gregorio
    1897(?)-1966 .... **CLC 32**
    See also CA 131; HW 1
Lorca, Federico Garcia
    See Garcia Lorca, Federico
Lord, Bette Bao 1938- .... **CLC 23**
    See also BEST 90:3; CA 107; CANR 41,
    79; INT 107; SATA 58
Lord Auch
    See Bataille, Georges
Lord Byron
    See Byron, George Gordon (Noel)
Lorde, Audre (Geraldine)
    1934-1992 ... **CLC 18, 71; BLC 2; DAM**
    MULT, POET; PC 12
    See also Domini, Rey
    See also BW 1, 3; CA 25-28R; 142; CANR
    16, 26, 46, 82; DA3; DLB 41; MTCW 1,
    2
Lord Houghton
    See Milnes, Richard Monckton
Lord Jeffrey
    See Jeffrey, Francis
Lorenzini, Carlo 1826-1890
    See Collodi, Carlo
    See also MAICYA; SATA 29, 100
Lorenzo, Heberto Padilla
    See Padilla (Lorenzo), Heberto

Loris
See Hofmannsthal, Hugo von
Loti, Pierre TCLC 11
See also Viaud, (Louis Marie) Julien
See also DLB 123
Lou, Henri
See Andreas-Salome, Lou
Louie, David Wong 1954- .... CLC 70
See also CA 139
Louis, Father M.
See Merton, Thomas
Lovecraft, H(oward) P(hillips)
1890-1937 ...... TCLC 4, 22; DAM POP;
SSC 3
See also AAYA 14; CA 104; 133; DA3;
MTCW 1, 2
Lovelace, Earl 1935- .... CLC 51
See also BW 2; CA 77-80; CANR 41, 72;
DLB 125; MTCW 1
Lovelace, Richard 1618-1657 .... LC 24
See also DLB 131
Lowell, Amy 1874-1925 .... TCLC 1, 8; DAM
POET; PC 13
See also CA 104; 151; DLB 54, 140;
MTCW 2
Lowell, James Russell 1819-1891 ... NCLC 2,
90
See also AMWS 1; CDALB 1640-1865;
DLB 1, 11, 64, 79, 189, 235
Lowell, Robert (Traill Spence, Jr.)
1917-1977 .... CLC 1, 2, 3, 4, 5, 8, 9, 11,
15, 37, 124; DA; DAB; DAC; DAM
MST, NOV; PC 3
See also AW; CA 9-12R; 73-76; CABS 2;
CANR 26, 60; CDALBS; DA3; DLB 5,
169; MTCW 1, 2
Lowenthal, Michael (Francis)
1969- .... CLC 119
See also CA 150
Lowndes, Marie Adelaide (Belloc)
1868-1947 .... TCLC 12
See also CA 107; DLB 70
Lowry, (Clarence) Malcolm
1909-1957 .... TCLC 6, 40; SSC 31
See also BRWS 3; CA 105; 131; CANR 62;
CDBLB 1945-1960; DLB 15; MTCW 1,
2
Lowry, Mina Gertrude 1882-1966
See Loy, Mina
See also CA 113
Loxsmith, John
See Brunner, John (Kilian Houston)
Loy, Mina CLC 28; DAM POET; PC 16
See also Lowry, Mina Gertrude
See also DLB 4, 54
Loyson-Bridet
See Schwob, Marcel (Mayer Andre)
Lucan 120-200 .... CMLC 33
See also AW 33; DLB 211
Lucas, Craig 1951- .... CLC 64
See also CA 137; CANR 71; GLL 2
Lucas, E(dward) V(errall)
1868-1938 .... TCLC 73
See also CA 176; DLB 98, 149, 153; SATA
20
Lucas, George 1944- .... CLC 16
See also AAYA 1, 23; CA 77-80; CANR
30; SATA 56
Lucas, Hans
See Godard, Jean-Luc
Lucas, Victoria
See Plath, Sylvia
Lucian c. 125-c. 200 .... CMLC 32
See also DLB 176
Ludlam, Charles 1943-1987 .... CLC 46, 50
See also CA 85-88; 122; CANR 72, 86

Ludlum, Robert 1927-2001 .... CLC 22, 43;
DAM NOV, POP
See also AAYA 10; BEST 89:1, 90:3; CA
33-36R; CANR 25, 41, 68; DA3; DLBY
82; MTCW 1, 2
Ludwig, Ken CLC 60
Ludwig, Otto 1813-1865 .... NCLC 4
See also DLB 129
Lugones, Leopoldo 1874-1938 ...... TCLC 15;
HLCS 2
See also CA 116; 131; HW 1
Lu Hsun TCLC 3; SSC 20
See also Shu-Jen, Chou
Lukacs, George CLC 24
See also Lukacs, György (Szegeny von)
Lukacs, György (Szegeny von) 1885-1971
See Lukacs, George
See also CA 101; 29-32R; CANR 62; DLB
242; MTCW 2
Luke, Peter (Ambrose Cyprian)
1919-1995 .... CLC 38
See also CA 81-84; 147; CANR 72; DLB
13
Lunar, Dennis
See Mungo, Raymond
Lurie, Alison 1926- .... CLC 4, 5, 18, 39
See also CA 1-4R; CANR 2, 17, 50, 88;
DLB 2; MTCW 1; SATA 46, 112
Lustig, Arnost 1926- .... CLC 56
See also AAYA 3; CA 69-72; CANR 47;
CWW 2; DLB 232; SATA 56
Luther, Martin 1483-1546 .... LC 9, 37
See also DLB 179
Luxemburg, Rosa 1870(?)-1919 ..... TCLC 63
See also CA 118
Luzi, Mario 1914- .... CLC 13
See also CA 61-64; CANR 9, 70; CWW 2;
DLB 128
Lyly, John 1554(?)-1606 .... LC 41; DAM
DRAM; DC 7
See also DLB 62, 167
L'Ymagier
See Gourmont, Remy (-Marie-Charles) de
Lynch, David (K.) 1946- .... CLC 66
See also CA 124; 129
Lynch, James
See Andreyev, Leonid (Nikolaevich)
Lyndsay, Sir David 1485-1555 .... LC 20
Lynn, Kenneth S(chuyler) 1923- ...... CLC 50
See also CA 1-4R; CANR 3, 27, 65
Lynx
See West, Rebecca
Lyons, Marcus
See Blish, James (Benjamin)
Lyotard, Jean-Francois
1924-1998 .... TCLC 103
See also DLB 242
Lyre, Pinchbeck
See Sassoon, Siegfried (Lorraine)
Lytle, Andrew (Nelson) 1902-1995 ... CLC 22
See also CA 9-12R; 150; CANR 70; DLB
6; DLBY 95
Lyttelton, George 1709-1773 .... LC 10
Maas, Peter 1929- .... CLC 29
See also CA 93-96; INT 93-96; MTCW 2
Macaulay, Catherine 1731-1791 .... LC 64
See also DLB 104
Macaulay, (Emilie) Rose
1881(?)-1958 .... TCLC 7, 44
See also CA 104; DLB 36
Macaulay, Thomas Babington
1800-1859 .... NCLC 42
See also CDBLB 1832-1890; DLB 32, 55
MacBeth, George (Mann)
1932-1992 .... CLC 2, 5, 9
See also CA 25-28R; 136; CANR 61, 66;
DLB 40; MTCW 1; SATA 4; SATA-Obit
70

MacCaig, Norman (Alexander)
1910-1996 .... CLC 36; DAB; DAM
POET
See also CA 9-12R; CANR 3, 34; DLB 27
MacCarthy, Sir(Charles Otto) Desmond
1877-1952 .... TCLC 36
See also CA 167
MacDiarmid, Hugh CLC 2, 4, 11, 19, 63; PC
9
See also Grieve, C(hristopher) M(urray)
See also CDBLB 1945-1960; DLB 20
MacDonald, Anson
See Heinlein, Robert A(nson)
Macdonald, Cynthia 1928- .... CLC 13, 19
See also CA 49-52; CANR 4, 44; DLB 105
MacDonald, George 1824-1905 .... TCLC 9
See also CA 106; 137; CANR 80; CLR 67;
DLB 18, 163, 178; MAICYA; SATA 33,
100
Macdonald, John
See Millar, Kenneth
MacDonald, John D(ann)
1916-1986 .. CLC 3, 27, 44; DAM NOV,
POP
See also CA 1-4R; 121; CANR 1, 19, 60;
DLB 8; DLBY 86; MTCW 1, 2
Macdonald, John Ross
See Millar, Kenneth
Macdonald, Ross CLC 1, 2, 3, 14, 34, 41
See also Millar, Kenneth
See also AMWS 4; DLBD 6
MacDougal, John
See Blish, James (Benjamin)
MacDougal, John
See Blish, James (Benjamin)
MacEwen, Gwendolyn (Margaret)
1941-1987 .... CLC 13, 55
See also CA 9-12R; 124; CANR 7, 22; DLB
53; SATA 50; SATA-Obit 55
Macha, Karel Hynek 1810-1846 .... NCLC 46
Machado (y Ruiz), Antonio
1875-1939 .... TCLC 3
See also CA 104; 174; DLB 108; HW 2
Machado de Assis, Joaquim Maria
1839-1908 ..... TCLC 10; BLC 2; HLCS
2; SSC 24
See also CA 107; 153; CANR 91
Machen, Arthur TCLC 4; SSC 20
See also Jones, Arthur Llewellyn
See also CA 179; DLB 36, 156, 178
Machiavelli, Niccolò 1469-1527 ..... LC 8, 36;
DA; DAB; DAC; DAM MST
See also AW
MacInnes, Colin 1914-1976 .... CLC 4, 23
See also CA 69-72; 65-68; CANR 21; DLB
14; MTCW 1, 2
MacInnes, Helen (Clark)
1907-1985 .... CLC 27, 39; DAM POP
See also CA 1-4R; 117; CANR 1, 28, 58;
DLB 87; MTCW 1, 2; SATA 22; SATA-
Obit 44
Mackenzie, Compton (Edward Montague)
1883-1972 .... CLC 18
See also CA 21-22; 37-40R; CAP 2; DLB
34, 100
Mackenzie, Henry 1745-1831 .... NCLC 41
See also DLB 39
Mackintosh, Elizabeth 1896(?)-1952
See Tey, Josephine
See also CA 110
MacLaren, James
See Grieve, C(hristopher) M(urray)
Mac Laverty, Bernard 1942- .... CLC 31
See also CA 116; 118; CANR 43, 88;
INT 118

MacLean, Alistair (Stuart)
   1922(?)-1987 .. **CLC 3, 13, 50, 63; DAM
   POP**
   See also CA 57-60; 121; CANR 28, 61;
   MTCW 1; SATA 23; SATA-Obit 50;
   TCWW 2
Maclean, Norman (Fitzroy)
   1902-1990 .... **CLC 78; DAM POP; SSC
   13**
   See also CA 102; 132; CANR 49; DLB 206;
   TCWW 2
MacLeish, Archibald 1892-1982 ... **CLC 3, 8,
   14, 68; DAM POET**
   See also CA 9-12R; 106; CANR 33, 63;
   CDALBS; DLB 4, 7, 45; DLBY 82;
   MTCW 1, 2
MacLennan, (John) Hugh
   1907-1990 . **CLC 2, 14, 92; DAC; DAM
   MST**
   See also CA 5-8R; 142; CANR 33; DLB
   68; MTCW 1, 2
MacLeod, Alistair 1936- .... **CLC 56; DAC;
   DAM MST**
   See also CA 123; CCA 1; DLB 60; MTCW
   2
Macleod, Fiona
   See Sharp, William
MacNeice, (Frederick) Louis
   1907-1963 .... **CLC 1, 4, 10, 53; DAB;
   DAM POET**
   See also CA 85-88; CANR 61; DLB 10, 20;
   MTCW 1, 2
MacNeill, Dand
   See Fraser, George MacDonald
Macpherson, James 1736-1796 .... **LC 29**
   See also Ossian
   See also DLB 109
Macpherson, (Jean) Jay 1931- .... **CLC 14**
   See also CA 5-8R; CANR 90; DLB 53
MacShane, Frank 1927-1999 .... **CLC 39**
   See also CA 9-12R; 186; CANR 3, 33; DLB
   111
Macumber, Mari
   See Sandoz, Mari(e Susette)
Madach, Imre 1823-1864 .... **NCLC 19**
Madden, (Jerry) David 1933- ...... **CLC 5, 15**
   See also CA 1-4R; CAAS 3; CANR 4, 45;
   DLB 6; MTCW 1
Maddern, Al(an)
   See Ellison, Harlan (Jay)
Madhubuti, Haki R. 1942- . **CLC 6, 73; BLC
   2; DAM MULT, POET; PC 5**
   See also Lee, Don L.
   See also BW 2, 3; CA 73-76; CANR 24,
   51, 73; DLB 5, 41; DLBD 8; MTCW 2
Maepenn, Hugh
   See Kuttner, Henry
Maepenn, K. H.
   See Kuttner, Henry
Maeterlinck, Maurice 1862-1949 ... **TCLC 3;
   DAM DRAM**
   See also CA 104; 136; CANR 80; DLB 192;
   SATA 66
Maginn, William 1794-1842 .... **NCLC 8**
   See also DLB 110, 159
Mahapatra, Jayanta 1928- .... **CLC 33; DAM
   MULT**
   See also CA 73-76; CAAS 9; CANR 15,
   33, 66, 87
Mahfouz, Naguib (Abdel Aziz Al-Sabilgi)
   1911(?)-
   See Mahfuz, Najib
   See also BEST 89:2; CA 128; CANR 55;
   CWW 2; DAM NOV; DA3; MTCW 1, 2
Mahfuz, Najib **CLC 52, 55**
   See also Mahfouz, Naguib (Abdel Aziz Al-
   Sabilgi)
   See also DLBY 88

Mahon, Derek 1941- .... **CLC 27**
   See also CA 113; 128; CANR 88; DLB 40
Mailer, Norman 1923- ... **CLC 1, 2, 3, 4, 5, 8,
   11, 14, 28, 39, 74, 111; DA; DAB;
   DAC; DAM MST, NOV, POP**
   See also AAYA 31; AITN 2; CA 9-12R;
   CABS 1; CANR 28, 74, 77; CDALB
   1968-1988; DA3; DLB 2, 16, 28, 185;
   DLBD 3; DLBY 80, 83; MTCW 1, 2
Maillet, Antonine 1929- .. **CLC 54, 118; DAC**
   See also CA 115; 120; CANR 46, 74, 77;
   CCA 1; CWW 2; DLB 60; INT 120;
   MTCW 2
Mais, Roger 1905-1955 .... **TCLC 8**
   See also BW 1, 3; CA 105; 124; CANR 82;
   DLB 125; MTCW 1
Maistre, Joseph de 1753-1821 .... **NCLC 37**
Maitland, Frederic William
   1850-1906 .... **TCLC 65**
Maitland, Sara (Louise) 1950- .... **CLC 49**
   See also CA 69-72; CANR 13, 59
Major, Clarence 1936- . **CLC 3, 19, 48; BLC
   2; DAM MULT**
   See also BW 2, 3; CA 21-24R; CAAS 6;
   CANR 13, 25, 53, 82; DLB 33
Major, Kevin (Gerald) 1949- . **CLC 26; DAC**
   See also AAYA 16; CA 97-100; CANR 21,
   38; CLR 11; DLB 60; INT CANR-21;
   JRDA; MAICYA; SATA 32, 82
Maki, James
   See Ozu, Yasujiro
Malabaila, Damiano
   See Levi, Primo
Malamud, Bernard 1914-1986 .. **CLC 1, 2, 3,
   5, 8, 9, 11, 18, 27, 44, 78, 85; DA;
   DAB; DAC; DAM MST, NOV, POP;
   SSC 15**
   See also AAYA 16; AMWS 1; AW; CA
   5-8R; 118; CABS 1; CANR 28, 62;
   CDALB 1941-1968; DA3; DLB 2, 28,
   152; DLBY 80, 86; MTCW 1, 2
Malan, Herman
   See Bosman, Herman Charles; Bosman,
   Herman Charles
Malaparte, Curzio 1898-1957 .... **TCLC 52**
Malcolm, Dan
   See Silverberg, Robert
Malcolm X **CLC 82, 117; BLC 2**
   See also Little, Malcolm
   See also AW
Malherbe, Francois de 1555-1628 .... **LC 5**
Mallarme, Stephane 1842-1898 ...... **NCLC 4,
   41; DAM POET; PC 4**
Mallet-Joris, Francoise 1930- .... **CLC 11**
   See also CA 65-68; CANR 17; DLB 83
Malley, Ern
   See McAuley, James Phillip
Mallowan, Agatha Christie
   See Christie, Agatha (Mary Clarissa)
Maloff, Saul 1922- .... **CLC 5**
   See also CA 33-36R
Malone, Louis
   See MacNeice, (Frederick) Louis
Malone, Michael (Christopher)
   1942- .... **CLC 43**
   See also CA 77-80; CANR 14, 32, 57
Malory, Thomas 1410(?)-1471(?) .... **LC 11;
   DA; DAB; DAC; DAM MST**
   See also AW; CDBLB Before 1660; DLB
   146; SATA 59; SATA-Brief 33
Malouf, (George Joseph) David
   1934- .... **CLC 28, 86**
   See also CA 124; CANR 50, 76; MTCW 2
Malraux, (Georges-)Andre
   1901-1976 .... **CLC 1, 4, 9, 13, 15, 57;
   DAM NOV**
   See also CA 21-22; 69-72; CANR 34, 58;
   CAP 2; DA3; DLB 72; MTCW 1, 2

Malzberg, Barry N(athaniel) 1939- ... **CLC 7**
   See also CA 61-64; CAAS 4; CANR 16;
   DLB 8
Mamet, David (Alan) 1947- .. **CLC 9, 15, 34,
   46, 91; DAM DRAM; DC 4**
   See also AAYA 3; CA 81-84; CABS 3;
   CANR 15, 41, 67, 72; DA3; DLB 7;
   MTCW 1, 2
Mamoulian, Rouben (Zachary)
   1897-1987 .... **CLC 16**
   See also CA 25-28R; 124; CANR 85
Mandelshtam, Osip
   See Mandelstam, Osip (Emilievich)
Mandelstam, Osip (Emilievich)
   1891(?)-1943(?) .... **TCLC 2, 6; PC 14**
   See also CA 104; 150; MTCW 2
Mander, (Mary) Jane 1877-1949 ... **TCLC 31**
   See also CA 162
Mandeville, John fl. 1350- .... **CMLC 19**
   See also DLB 146
Mandiargues, Andre Pieyre de **CLC 41**
   See also Pieyre de Mandiargues, Andre
   See also DLB 83
Mandrake, Ethel Belle
   See Thurman, Wallace (Henry)
Mangan, James Clarence
   1803-1849 .... **NCLC 27**
Maniere, J.-E.
   See Giraudoux, (Hippolyte) Jean
Mankiewicz, Herman (Jacob)
   1897-1953 .... **TCLC 85**
   See also CA 120; 169; DLB 26; IDFW 3
Manley, (Mary) Delariviere
   1672(?)-1724 .... **LC 1, 42**
   See also DLB 39, 80
Mann, Abel
   See Creasey, John
Mann, Emily 1952- .... **DC 7**
   See also CA 130; CANR 55
Mann, (Luiz) Heinrich 1871-1950 ... **TCLC 9**
   See also CA 106; 164, 181; DLB 66, 118
Mann, (Paul) Thomas 1875-1955 ... **TCLC 2,
   8, 14, 21, 35, 44, 60; DA; DAB; DAC;
   DAM MST, NOV; SSC 5**
   See also AW; CA 104; 128; DA3; DLB 66;
   GLL 1; MTCW 1, 2
Mannheim, Karl 1893-1947 .... **TCLC 65**
Manning, David
   See Faust, Frederick (Schiller)
   See also TCWW 2
Manning, Frederic 1887(?)-1935 ... **TCLC 25**
   See also CA 124
Manning, Olivia 1915-1980 .... **CLC 5, 19**
   See also CA 5-8R; 101; CANR 29; MTCW
   1
Mano, D. Keith 1942- .... **CLC 2, 10**
   See also CA 25-28R; CAAS 6; CANR 26,
   57; DLB 6
Mansfield, Katherine **TCLC 2, 8, 39; DAB;
   SSC 9, 23, 38**
   See also Beauchamp, Kathleen Mansfield
   See also AW; DLB 162; GLL 1
Manso, Peter 1940- .... **CLC 39**
   See also CA 29-32R; CANR 44
Mantecon, Juan Jimenez
   See Jimenez (Mantecon), Juan Ramon
Manton, Peter
   See Creasey, John
Man Without a Spleen, A
   See Chekhov, Anton (Pavlovich)
Manzoni, Alessandro 1785-1873 .... **NCLC 29**
Map, Walter 1140-1209 .... **CMLC 32**
Mapu, Abraham (ben Jekutiel)
   1808-1867 .... **NCLC 18**
Mara, Sally
   See Queneau, Raymond

Marat, Jean Paul 1743-1793 .... **LC 10**
Marcel, Gabriel Honore 1889-1973 . **CLC 15**
　See also CA 102; 45-48; MTCW 1, 2
March, William 1893-1954 .... **TCLC 96**
Marchbanks, Samuel
　See Davies, (William) Robertson
　See also CCA 1
Marchi, Giacomo
　See Bassani, Giorgio
Marguerite
　See de Navarre, Marguerite
Margulies, Donald **CLC 76**
　See also DLB 228
Marie de France c. 12th cent. - ..... **CMLC 8;
　PC 22**
　See also DLB 208
Marie de l'Incarnation 1599-1672 ...... **LC 10**
Marier, Captain Victor
　See Griffith, D(avid Lewelyn) W(ark)
Mariner, Scott
　See Pohl, Frederik
Marinetti, Filippo Tommaso
　1876-1944 .... **TCLC 10**
　See also CA 107; DLB 114
Marivaux, Pierre Carlet de Chamblain de
　1688-1763 .... **LC 4; DC 7**
Markandaya, Kamala **CLC 8, 38**
　See also Taylor, Kamala (Purnaiya)
Markfield, Wallace 1926- .... **CLC 8**
　See also CA 69-72; CAAS 3; DLB 2, 28
Markham, Edwin 1852-1940 .... **TCLC 47**
　See also CA 160; DLB 54, 186
Markham, Robert
　See Amis, Kingsley (William)
Marks, J
　See Highwater, Jamake (Mamake)
Marks-Highwater, J
　See Highwater, Jamake (Mamake)
Markson, David M(errill) 1927- .... **CLC 67**
　See also CA 49-52; CANR 1, 91
Marley, Bob **CLC 17**
　See also Marley, Robert Nesta
Marley, Robert Nesta 1945-1981
　See Marley, Bob
　See also CA 107; 103
Marlowe, Christopher 1564-1593 ...... **LC 22,
　47; DA; DAB; DAC; DAM DRAM,
　MST; DC 1**
　See also AW; CDBLB Before 1660; DA3;
　DLB 62
Marlowe, Stephen 1928-
　See Queen, Ellery
　See also CA 13-16R; CANR 6, 55
Marmontel, Jean-Francois 1723-1799 .. **LC 2**
Marquand, John P(hillips)
　1893-1960 .... **CLC 2, 10**
　See also CA 85-88; CANR 73; DLB 9, 102;
　MTCW 2
Marques, Rene 1919-1979 ..... **CLC 96; DAM
　MULT; HLC 2**
　See also CA 97-100; 85-88; CANR 78;
　DLB 113; HW 1, 2
Marquez, Gabriel (Jose) Garcia
　See Garcia Marquez, Gabriel (Jose)
Marquis, Don(ald Robert Perry)
　1878-1937 .... **TCLC 7**
　See also CA 104; 166; DLB 11, 25
Marric, J. J.
　See Creasey, John
Marryat, Frederick 1792-1848 .... **NCLC 3**
　See also DLB 21, 163
Marsden, James
　See Creasey, John
Marsh, Edward 1872-1953 .... **TCLC 99**
Marsh, (Edith) Ngaio 1899-1982 .... **CLC 7,
　53; DAM POP**
　See also CA 9-12R; CANR 6, 58; DLB 77;
　MTCW 1, 2

Marshall, Garry 1934- .... **CLC 17**
　See also AAYA 3; CA 111; SATA 60
Marshall, Paule 1929- .. **CLC 27, 72; BLC 3;
　DAM MULT; SSC 3**
　See also BW 2, 3; CA 77-80; CANR 25,
　73; DA3; DLB 33, 157, 227; MTCW 1, 2
Marshallik
　See Zangwill, Israel
Marsten, Richard
　See Hunter, Evan
Marston, John 1576-1634 .... **LC 33; DAM
　DRAM**
　See also DLB 58, 172
Martha, Henry
　See Harris, Mark
Martí (y Pérez), Jose (Julian)
　1853-1895 ...... **NCLC 63; DAM MULT;
　HLC 2**
　See also HW 2
Martial c. 40-c. 104 .... **CMLC 35; PC 10**
　See also DLB 211
Martin, Ken
　See Hubbard, L(afayette) Ron(ald)
Martin, Richard
　See Creasey, John
Martin, Steve 1945- .... **CLC 30**
　See also CA 97-100; CANR 30; MTCW 1
Martin, Valerie 1948- .... **CLC 89**
　See also BEST 90:2; CA 85-88; CANR 49,
　89
Martin, Violet Florence
　1862-1915 .... **TCLC 51**
Martin, Webber
　See Silverberg, Robert
Martindale, Patrick Victor
　See White, Patrick (Victor Martindale)
Martin du Gard, Roger
　1881-1958 .... **TCLC 24**
　See also CA 118; CANR 94; DLB 65
Martineau, Harriet 1802-1876 .... **NCLC 26**
　See also AW 2; DLB 21, 55, 159, 163, 166,
　190
Martines, Julia
　See O'Faolain, Julia
Martinez, Enrique Gonzalez
　See Gonzalez Martinez, Enrique
Martinez, Jacinto Benavente y
　See Benavente (y Martinez), Jacinto
Martinez Ruiz, Jose 1873-1967
　See Azorin; Ruiz, Jose Martinez
　See also CA 93-96; HW 1
Martinez Sierra, Gregorio
　1881-1947 .... **TCLC 6**
　See also CA 115
Martinez Sierra, Maria (de la O'LeJarraga)
　1874-1974 .... **TCLC 6**
　See also CA 115
Martinsen, Martin
　See Follett, Ken(neth Martin)
Martinson, Harry (Edmund)
　1904-1978 .... **CLC 14**
　See also CA 77-80; CANR 34
Marut, Ret
　See Traven, B.
Marut, Robert
　See Traven, B.
Marvell, Andrew 1621-1678 .. **LC 4, 43; DA;
　DAB; DAC; DAM MST, POET; PC 10**
　See also AW; CDBLB 1660-1789; DLB 131
Marx, Karl (Heinrich) 1818-1883 . **NCLC 17**
　See also DLB 129
Masaoka Shiki **TCLC 18**
　See also Masaoka Tsunenori
Masaoka Tsunenori 1867-1902
　See Masaoka Shiki
　See also CA 117

Masefield, John (Edward)
　1878-1967 ..... **CLC 11, 47; DAM POET**
　See also CA 19-20; 25-28R; CANR 33;
　CAP 2; CDBLB 1890-1914; DLB 10, 19,
　153, 160; MTCW 1, 2; SATA 19
Maso, Carole 19(?)- .... **CLC 44**
　See also CA 170; GLL 2
Mason, Bobbie Ann 1940- ... **CLC 28, 43, 82;
　SSC 4**
　See also AAYA 5; AW; CA 53-56; CANR
　11, 31, 58, 83; CDALBS; DA3; DLB 173;
　DLBY 87; INT CANR-31; MTCW 1, 2
Mason, Ernst
　See Pohl, Frederik
Mason, Lee W.
　See Malzberg, Barry N(athaniel)
Mason, Nick 1945- .... **CLC 35**
Mason, Tally
　See Derleth, August (William)
Mass, William
　See Gibson, William
Master Lao
　See Lao Tzu
Masters, Edgar Lee 1868-1950 .... **TCLC 2,
　25; DA; DAC; DAM MST, POET; PC
　1**
　See also AMWS 1; AW; CA 104; 133;
　CDALB 1865-1917; DLB 54; MTCW 1,
　2
Masters, Hilary 1928- .... **CLC 48**
　See also CA 25-28R; CANR 13, 47
Mastrosimone, William 19(?)- .... **CLC 36**
　See also CA 186
Mathe, Albert
　See Camus, Albert
Mather, Cotton 1663-1728 .... **LC 38**
　See also AMWS 2; CDALB 1640-1865;
　DLB 24, 30, 140
Mather, Increase 1639-1723 .... **LC 38**
　See also DLB 24
Matheson, Richard Burton 1926- .... **CLC 37**
　See also AAYA 31; CA 97-100; CANR 88;
　DLB 8, 44; INT 97-100; SCFW 2
Mathews, Harry 1930- .... **CLC 6, 52**
　See also CA 21-24R; CAAS 6; CANR 18,
　40
Mathews, John Joseph 1894-1979 .. **CLC 84;
　DAM MULT**
　See also CA 19-20; 142; CANR 45; CAP 2;
　DLB 175; NNAL
Mathias, Roland (Glyn) 1915- .... **CLC 45**
　See also CA 97-100; CANR 19, 41; DLB
　27
Matsuo Basho 1644-1694 .... **LC 62; DAM
　POET; PC 3**
Mattheson, Rodney
　See Creasey, John
Matthews, (James) Brander
　1852-1929 .... **TCLC 95**
　See also DLB 71, 78; DLBD 13
Matthews, Greg 1949- .... **CLC 45**
　See also CA 135
Matthews, William (Procter, III)
　1942-1997 .... **CLC 40**
　See also CA 29-32R; 162; CAAS 18; CANR
　12, 57; DLB 5
Matthias, John (Edward) 1941- .... **CLC 9**
　See also CA 33-36R; CANR 56
Matthiessen, F(rancis) O(tto)
　1902-1950 .... **TCLC 100**
　See also CA 185; DLB 63
Matthiessen, Peter 1927- ... **CLC 5, 7, 11, 32,
　64; DAM NOV**
　See also AAYA 6; AMWS 5; BEST 90:4;
　CA 9-12R; CANR 21, 50, 73; DA3; DLB
　6, 173; MTCW 1, 2; SATA 27
Maturin, Charles Robert
　1780(?)-1824 .... **NCLC 6**
　See also DLB 178

Matute (Ausejo), Ana Maria 1925- .. **CLC 11**
See also CA 89-92; MTCW 1

Maugham, W. S.
See Maugham, W(illiam) Somerset

Maugham, W(illiam) Somerset
1874-1965 ... **CLC 1, 11, 15, 67, 93; DA;
DAB; DAC; DAM DRAM, MST, NOV;
SSC 8**
See also AW; CA 5-8R; 25-28R; CANR 40;
CDBLB 1914-1945; DA3; DLB 10, 36,
77, 100, 162, 195; MTCW 1, 2; SATA 54

Maugham, William Somerset
See Maugham, W(illiam) Somerset

Maupassant, (Henri Rene Albert) Guy de
1850-1893 . **NCLC 1, 42, 83; DA; DAB;
DAC; DAM MST; SSC 1**
See also AW; DA3; DLB 123

Maupin, Armistead 1944- ..... **CLC 95; DAM
POP**
See also CA 125; 130; CANR 58, DA3;
GLL 1; INT 130; MTCW 2

Maurhut, Richard
See Traven, B.

Mauriac, Claude 1914-1996 .... **CLC 9**
See also CA 89-92; 152; CWW 2; DLB 83

Mauriac, François (Charles)
1885-1970 .... **CLC 4, 9, 56; SSC 24**
See also CA 25-28; CAP 2; DLB 65;
MTCW 1, 2

Mavor, Osborne Henry 1888-1951
See Bridie, James
See also CA 104

Maxwell, William (Keepers, Jr.)
1908-2000 .... **CLC 19**
See also CA 93-96; 189; CANR 54, 95;
DLBY 80; INT 93-96

May, Elaine 1932- .... **CLC 16**
See also CA 124; 142; DLB 44

Mayakovski, Vladimir (Vladimirovich)
1893-1930 .... **TCLC 4, 18**
See also CA 104; 158, MTCW 2

Mayakovsky, Vladimir
See Mayakovski, Vladimir (Vladimirovich)

Mayhew, Henry 1812-1887 .... **NCLC 31**
See also DLB 18, 55, 190

Mayle, Peter 1939(?)- .... **CLC 89**
See also CA 139; CANR 64

Maynard, Joyce 1953- .... **CLC 23**
See also CA 111; 129; CANR 64

Mayne, William (James Carter)
1928- .... **CLC 12**
See also AAYA 20; AW; CA 9-12R; CANR
37, 80; CLR 25; JRDA; MAICYA; SAAS
11; SATA 6, 68

Mayo, Jim
See L'Amour, Louis (Dearborn)
See also TCWW 2

Maysles, Albert 1926- .... **CLC 16**
See also CA 29-32R

Maysles, David 1932- .... **CLC 16**

Mazer, Norma Fox 1931- .... **CLC 26**
See also AAYA 5, 36; AW; CA 69-72;
CANR 12, 32, 66; CLR 23; JRDA; MAI-
CYA; SAAS 1; SATA 24, 67, 105

Mazzini, Guiseppe 1805-1872 .... **NCLC 34**

McAlmon, Robert (Menzies)
1895-1956 .... **TCLC 97**
See also CA 107; 168; DLB 4, 45; DLBD
15; GLL 1

McAuley, James Phillip 1917-1976 .. **CLC 45**
See also CA 97-100

McBain, Ed
See Hunter, Evan

McBrien, William (Augustine)
1930- .... **CLC 44**
See also CA 107; CANR 90

McCabe, Patrick 1955- .... **CLC 133**
See also CA 130; CANR 50, 90; DLB 194

McCaffrey, Anne (Inez) 1926- .... **CLC 17;
DAM NOV, POP**
See also AAYA 6, 34; AITN 2; BEST 89:2;
CA 25-28R; CANR 15, 35, 55, 96; CLR
49; DA3; DLB 8; JRDA; MAICYA;
MTCW 1, 2; SAAS 11; SATA 8, 70, 116

McCall, Nathan 1955(?)- .... **CLC 86**
See also BW 3; CA 146; CANR 88

McCann, Arthur
See Campbell, John W(ood, Jr.)

McCann, Edson
See Pohl, Frederik

McCarthy, Charles, Jr. 1933-
See McCarthy, Cormac
See also CANR 42, 69; DAM POP; DA3;
MTCW 2

McCarthy, Cormac CLC 4, 57, 59, 101
See also McCarthy, Charles, Jr.
See also DLB 6, 143; MTCW 2; TCWW 2

McCarthy, Mary (Therese)
1912-1989 .. **CLC 1, 3, 5, 14, 24, 39, 59;
SSC 24**
See also CA 5-8R; 129; CANR 16, 50, 64;
DA3; DLB 2; DLBY 81; INT CANR-16;
MTCW 1, 2

McCartney, (James) Paul 1942- . **CLC 12, 35**
See also CA 146

McCauley, Stephen (D.) 1955- .... **CLC 50**
See also CA 141

McClure, Michael (Thomas) 1932- ... **CLC 6,
10**
See also CA 21-24R; CANR 17, 46, 77;
DLB 16

McCorkle, Jill (Collins) 1958- .... **CLC 51**
See also CA 121; DLB 234; DLBY 87

McCourt, Frank 1930- .... **CLC 109**
See also CA 157

McCourt, James 1941- .... **CLC 5**
See also CA 57-60

McCourt, Malachy 1932- .... **CLC 119**

McCoy, Horace (Stanley)
1897-1955 .... **TCLC 28**
See also CA 108; 155; DLB 9

McCrae, John 1872-1918 .... **TCLC 12**
See also CA 109; DLB 92

McCreigh, James
See Pohl, Frederik

McCullers, (Lula) Carson (Smith)
1917-1967 .... **CLC 1, 4, 10, 12, 48, 100;
DA; DAB; DAC; DAM MST, NOV;
SSC 9, 24**
See also AAYA 21; AW; CA 5-8R; 25-28R;
CADS 1, 3; CANR 18; CDALB 1941-
1968; DA3; DLB 2, 7, 173, 228; GLL 1;
MTCW 1, 2; SATA 27

McCulloch, John Tyler
See Burroughs, Edgar Rice

McCullough, Colleen 1938(?)- .... **CLC 27,
107; DAM NOV, POP**
See also AAYA 36; CA 81-84; CANR 17,
46, 67; DA3; MTCW 1, 2

McDermott, Alice 1953- .... **CLC 90**
See also CA 109; CANR 40, 90

McElroy, Joseph 1930- .... **CLC 5, 47**
See also CA 17-20R

McEwan, Ian (Russell) 1948- .... **CLC 13, 66;
DAM NOV**
See also BEST 90:4; BRWS 4; CA 61-64;
CANR 14, 41, 69, 87; DLB 14, 194;
MTCW 1, 2

McFadden, David 1940- .... **CLC 48**
See also CA 104; DLB 60; INT 104

McFarland, Dennis 1950- .... **CLC 65**
See also CA 165

McGahern, John 1934- ... **CLC 5, 9, 48; SSC
17**
See also CA 17-20R; CANR 29, 68; DLB
14, 231; MTCW 1

McGinley, Patrick (Anthony) 1937- . **CLC 41**
See also CA 120; 127; CANR 56; INT 127

McGinley, Phyllis 1905-1978 .... **CLC 14**
See also CA 9-12R; 77-80; CANR 19; DLB
11, 48; SATA 2, 44; SATA-Obit 24

McGinniss, Joe 1942- .... **CLC 32**
See also AITN 2; BEST 89:2; CA 25-28R;
CANR 26, 70; DLB 185; INT CANR-26

McGivern, Maureen Daly
See Daly, Maureen

McGrath, Patrick 1950- .... **CLC 55**
See also CA 136; CANR 65; DLB 231

McGrath, Thomas (Matthew)
1916-1990 ..... **CLC 28, 59; DAM POET**
See also CA 9-12R; 132; CANR 6, 33, 95;
MTCW 1; SATA 41; SATA-Obit 66

McGuane, Thomas (Francis III)
1939- .... **CLC 3, 7, 18, 45, 127**
See also AITN 2; CA 49-52; CANR 5, 24,
49, 94; DLB 2, 212; DLBY 80; INT
CANR-24; MTCW 1; TCWW 2

McGuckian, Medbh 1950- .... **CLC 48; DAM
POET; PC 27**
See also BRWS 5; CA 143; DLB 40

McHale, Tom 1942(?)-1982 .... **CLC 3, 5**
See also AITN 1; CA 77-80; 106

McIlvanney, William 1936- .... **CLC 42**
See also CA 25-28R; CANR 61; DLB 14,
207

McIlwraith, Maureen Mollie Hunter
See Hunter, Mollie
See also SATA 2

McInerney, Jay 1955- .... **CLC 34, 112; DAM
POP**
See also AAYA 18; CA 116; 123; CANR
45, 68; DA3; INT 123; MTCW 2

McIntyre, Vonda N(eel) 1948- .... **CLC 18**
See also AW; CA 81-84; CANR 17, 34, 69;
MTCW 1

**McKay, Claude TCLC 7, 41; BLC 3; DAB;
PC 2**
See also McKay, Festus Claudius
See also DLB 4, 45, 51, 117; GLL 2

McKay, Festus Claudius 1889-1948
See McKay, Claude
See also AW; BW 1, 3; CA 104; 124;
CANR 73; DA; DAC; DAM MST, MULT,
NOV, POET; MTCW 1, 2

McKuen, Rod 1933- .... **CLC 1, 3**
See also AITN 1; CA 41-44R; CANR 40

McLoughlin, R. B.
See Mencken, H(enry) L(ouis)

McLuhan, (Herbert) Marshall
1911-1980 .... **CLC 37, 83**
See also CA 9-12R; 102; CANR 12, 34, 61;
DLB 88; INT CANR-12; MTCW 1, 2

McMillan, Terry (L.) 1951- .... **CLC 50, 61,
112; BLCS; DAM MULT, NOV, POP**
See also AAYA 21; AW; BW 2, 3; CA 140;
CANR 60; DA3; MTCW 2

McMurtry, Larry (Jeff) 1936- .. **CLC 2, 3, 7,
11, 27, 44, 127; DAM NOV, POP**
See also AAYA 15; AITN 2; AMWS 5;
BEST 89:2; CA 5-8R; CANR 19, 43, 64;
CDALB 1968-1988; DA3; DLB 2, 143;
DLBY 80, 87; MTCW 1, 2; TCWW 2

McNally, T. M. 1961- .... **CLC 82**

McNally, Terrence 1939- ... **CLC 4, 7, 41, 91;
DAM DRAM**
See also CA 45-48; CANR 2, 56; DA3;
DLB 7; GLL 1; MTCW 2

McNamer, Deirdre 1950- .... **CLC 70**

McNeal, Tom CLC 119

McNeile, Herman Cyril 1888-1937
See Sapper
See also CA 184; DLB 77

McNickle, (William) D'Arcy
1904-1977 .... CLC 89; DAM MULT
See also CA 9-12R; 85-88; CANR 5, 45;
DLB 175, 212; NNAL; SATA-Obit 22

McPhee, John (Angus) 1931- .... CLC 36
See also AMWS 3; BEST 90:1; CA 65-68;
CANR 20, 46, 64, 69; DLB 185; MTCW
1, 2

McPherson, James Alan 1943- .. CLC 19, 77;
BLCS
See also BW 1, 3; CA 25-28R; CAAS 17;
CANR 24, 74; DLB 38; MTCW 1, 2

McPherson, William (Alexander)
1933- .... CLC 34
See also CA 69-72; CANR 28; INT
CANR-28

McTaggart, J. McT. Ellis
See McTaggart, John McTaggart Ellis

McTaggart, John McTaggart Ellis
1866-1925 .... TCLC 105
See also CA 120

Mead, George Herbert 1873-1958 . TCLC 89

Mead, Margaret 1901-1978 .... CLC 37
See also AITN 1; CA 1-4R; 81-84; CANR
4; DA3; MTCW 1, 2; SATA-Obit 20

Meaker, Marijane (Agnes) 1927-
See Kerr, M. E.
See also AW; CA 107; CANR 37, 63; INT
107; JRDA; MAICYA; MTCW 1; SATA
20, 61, 99; SATA-Essay 111

Medoff, Mark (Howard) 1940- ... CLC 6, 23;
DAM DRAM
See also AITN 1; CA 53-56; CANR 5; DLB
7; INT CANR-5

Medvedev, P. N.
See Bakhtin, Mikhail Mikhailovich

Meged, Aharon
See Megged, Aharon

Meged, Aron
See Megged, Aharon

Megged, Aharon 1920- .... CLC 9
See also CA 49-52; CAAS 13; CANR 1

Mehta, Ved (Parkash) 1934- .... CLC 37
See also CA 1-4R; CANR 2, 23, 69; MTCW
1

Melanter
See Blackmore, R(ichard) D(oddridge)

Melies, Georges 1861-1938 .... TCLC 81

Melikow, Loris
See Hofmannsthal, Hugo von

Melmoth, Sebastian
See Wilde, Oscar (Fingal O'Flahertie Wills)

Meltzer, Milton 1915- .... CLC 26
See also AAYA 8; AW; CA 13-16R; CANR
38, 92; CLR 13; DLB 61; JRDA; MAI-
CYA; SAAS 1; SATA 1, 50, 80

Melville, Herman 1819-1891 ..... NCLC 3, 12,
29, 45, 49, 91, 93; DA; DAB; DAC;
DAM MST, NOV; SSC 1, 17
See also AAYA 25; AW; CDALB 1640-
1865; DA3; DLB 3, 74; SATA 59

Menander c. 342B.C.-c. 292B.C. ... CMLC 9;
DAM DRAM; DC 3
See also DLB 176

Menchú, Rigoberta 1959-
See also CA 175; HLCS 2

Mencken, H(enry) L(ouis)
1880-1956 .... TCLC 13
See also CA 105; 125; CDALB 1917-1929;
DLB 11, 29, 63, 137, 222; MTCW 1, 2

Mendelsohn, Jane 1965- .... CLC 99
See also CA 154; CANR 94

Mercer, David 1928-1980 .... CLC 5; DAM
DRAM
See also CA 9-12R; 102; CANR 23; DLB
13; MTCW 1

Merchant, Paul
See Ellison, Harlan (Jay)

Meredith, George 1828-1909 .. TCLC 17, 43;
DAM POET
See also CA 117; 153; CANR 80; CDBLB
1832-1890; DLB 18, 35, 57, 159

Meredith, William (Morris) 1919- .... CLC 4,
13, 22, 55; DAM POET; PC 28
See also CA 9-12R; CAAS 14; CANR 6,
40; DLB 5

Merezhkovsky, Dmitry Sergeyevich
1865-1941 .... TCLC 29
See also CA 169

Merimee, Prosper 1803-1870 ... NCLC 6, 65;
SSC 7
See also DLB 119, 192

Merkin, Daphne 1954- .... CLC 44
See also CA 123

Merlin, Arthur
See Blish, James (Benjamin)

Merrill, James (Ingram) 1926-1995 .. CLC 2,
3, 6, 8, 13, 18, 34, 91; DAM POET; PC
28
See also AMWS 3; CA 13-16R; 147; CANR
10, 49, 63; DA3; DLB 5, 165; DLBY 85;
INT CANR-10; MTCW 1, 2

Merriman, Alex
See Silverberg, Robert

Merriman, Brian 1747-1805 .... NCLC 70

Merritt, E. B.
See Waddington, Miriam

Merton, Thomas 1915-1968 ..... CLC 1, 3, 11,
34, 83; PC 10
See also CA 5-8R; 25-28R; CANR 22, 53;
DA3; DLB 48; DLBY 81; MTCW 1, 2

Merwin, W(illiam) S(tanley) 1927- ... CLC 1,
2, 3, 5, 8, 13, 18, 45, 88; DAM POET
See also AMWS 3; CA 13-16R; CANR 15,
51; DA3; DLB 5, 169; INT CANR-15;
MTCW 1, 2

Metcalf, John 1938- .... CLC 37; SSC 43
See also CA 113; DLB 60

Metcalf, Suzanne
See Baum, L(yman) Frank

Mew, Charlotte (Mary) 1870-1928 .. TCLC 8
See also CA 105; 189; DLB 19, 135

Mewshaw, Michael 1943- .... CLC 9
See also CA 53-56; CANR 7, 47; DLBY 80

Meyer, Conrad Ferdinand
1825-1905 .... NCLC 81
See also DLB 129

Meyer, June
See Jordan, June
See also GLL 2

Meyer, Lynn
See Slavitt, David R(ytman)

Meyer-Meyrink, Gustav 1868-1932
See Meyrink, Gustav
See also CA 117

Meyers, Jeffrey 1939- .... CLC 39
See also CA 73-76; CAAE 186; CANR 54;
DLB 111

Meynell, Alice (Christina Gertrude
Thompson) 1847-1922 .... TCLC 6
See also CA 104; 177; DLB 19, 98

Meyrink, Gustav TCLC 21
See also Meyer-Meyrink, Gustav
See also DLB 81

Michaels, Leonard 1933- .... CLC 6, 25; SSC
16
See also CA 61-64; CANR 21, 62; DLB
130; MTCW 1

Michaux, Henri 1899-1984 .... CLC 8, 19
See also CA 85-88; 114

Micheaux, Oscar (Devereaux)
1884-1951 .... TCLC 76
See also BW 3; CA 174; DLB 50; TCWW 2

Michelangelo 1475-1564 .... LC 12

Michelet, Jules 1798-1874 .... NCLC 31

Michels, Robert 1876-1936 .... TCLC 88

Michener, James A(lbert)
1907(?)-1997 .... CLC 1, 5, 11, 29, 60,
109; DAM NOV, POP
See also AAYA 27; AITN 1; BEST 90:1;
CA 5-8R; 161; CANR 21, 45, 68; DA3;
DLB 6; MTCW 1, 2

Mickiewicz, Adam 1798-1855 .... NCLC 3

Middleton, Christopher 1926- .... CLC 13
See also CA 13-16R; CANR 29, 54; DLB
40

Middleton, Richard (Barham)
1882-1911 .... TCLC 56
See also CA 187; DLB 156

Middleton, Stanley 1919- .... CLC 7, 38
See also CA 25-28R; CAAS 23; CANR 21,
46, 81; DLB 14

Middleton, Thomas 1580-1627 .... LC 33;
DAM DRAM, MST; DC 5
See also DLB 58

Migueis, Jose Rodrigues 1901- .... CLC 10

Mikszath, Kalman 1847-1910 .... TCLC 31
See also CA 170

Miles, Jack CLC 100

Miles, Josephine (Louise)
1911-1985 .. CLC 1, 2, 14, 34, 39; DAM
POET
See also CA 1-4R; 116; CANR 2, 55; DLB
48

Militant
See Sandburg, Carl (August)

Mill, John Stuart 1806-1873 .... NCLC 11, 58
See also CDBLB 1832-1890; DLB 55, 190

Millar, Kenneth 1915-1983 ... CLC 14; DAM
POP
See also Macdonald, Ross
See also CA 9-12R; 110; CANR 16, 63;
DA3; DLB 2, 226; DLBD 6; DLBY 83;
MTCW 1, 2

Millay, E. Vincent
See Millay, Edna St. Vincent

Millay, Edna St. Vincent
1892-1950 .... TCLC 4, 49; DA; DAB;
DAC; DAM MST, POET; PC 6
See also Boyd, Nancy
See also AW; CA 104; 130; CDALB 1917-
1929; DA3; DLB 45; MTCW 1, 2

Miller, Arthur 1915- ...... CLC 1, 2, 6, 10, 15,
26, 47, 78; DA; DAB; DAC; DAM
DRAM, MST; DC 1
See also AAYA 15; AITN 1; AW 1; CA
1-4R; CABS 3; CANR 2, 30, 54, 76;
CDALB 1941-1968; DA3; DLB 7;
MTCW 1, 2

Miller, Henry (Valentine)
1891-1980 .... CLC 1, 2, 4, 9, 14, 43, 84;
DA; DAB; DAC; DAM MST, NOV
See also AW; CA 9-12R; 97-100; CANR
33, 64; CDALB 1929-1941; DA3; DLB
4, 9; DLBY 80; MTCW 1, 2

Miller, Jason 1939(?)-2001 .... CLC 2
See also AITN 1; CA 73-76; DLB 7

Miller, Sue 1943- .... CLC 44; DAM POP
See also BEST 90:3; CA 139; CANR 59,
91; DA3; DLB 143

Miller, Walter M(ichael, Jr.)
1923-1996 .... CLC 4, 30
See also CA 85-88; DLB 8

Millett, Kate 1934- .... CLC 67
See also AITN 1; CA 73-76; CANR 32, 53,
76; DA3; GLL 1; MTCW 1, 2

Millhauser, Steven (Lewis) 1943- .... CLC 21,
54, 109
See also CA 110; 111; CANR 63; DA3;
DLB 2; INT 111; MTCW 2

Millin, Sarah Gertrude 1889-1968 ... CLC 49
See also CA 102; 93-96; DLB 225

Milne, A(lan) A(lexander)
1882-1956 ..... **TCLC 6, 88; DAB; DAC; DAM MST**
See also AW 1; CA 104; 133; CLR 1, 26; DA3; DLB 10, 77, 100, 160; MAICYA; MTCW 1, 2; SATA 100

Milner, Ron(ald) 1938- .... **CLC 56; BLC 3; DAM MULT**
See also AITN 1; BW 1; CA 73-76; CANR 24, 81; DLB 38; MTCW 1

Milnes, Richard Monckton
1809-1885 .... **NCLC 61**
See also DLB 32, 184

Milosz, Czeslaw 1911- ...... **CLC 5, 11, 22, 31, 56, 82; DAM MST, POET; PC 8**
See also AW; CA 81-84; CANR 23, 51, 91; CWW 2; DA3; MTCW 1, 2

Milton, John 1608-1674 .... **LC 9, 43; DA; DAB; DAC; DAM MST, POET; PC 19, 29**
See also AW; CDBLB 1660-1789; DA3; DLB 131, 151

Min, Anchee 1957- .... **CLC 86**
See also CA 146; CANR 94

Minehaha, Cornelius
See Wedekind, (Benjamin) Frank(lin)

Miner, Valerie 1947 .... **CLC 40**
See also CA 97-100; CANR 59; GLL 2

Minimo, Duca
See D'Annunzio, Gabriele

Minot, Susan 1956- .... **CLC 44**
See also AMWS 6; CA 134

Minus, Ed 1938- .... **CLC 39**
See also CA 185

Miranda, Javier
See Bioy Casares, Adolfo
See also CWW 2

Miranda, Javier
See Bioy Casares, Adolfo

Mirbeau, Octave 1848-1917 .... **TCLC 55**
See also DLB 123, 192

Miro (Ferrer), Gabriel (Francisco Victor)
1879-1930 .... **TCLC 5**
See also CA 104; 185

Mishima, Yukio CLC **2, 4, 6, 9, 27; DC 1; SSC 4**
See also Hiraoka, Kimitake
See also DLB 182; GLL 1; MTCW 2

Mistral, Frederic 1830-1914 .... **TCLC 51**
See also CA 122

Mistral, Gabriela
See Godoy Alcayaga, Lucila

Mistry, Rohinton 1952- .... **CLC 71; DAC**
See also CA 141; CANR 86; CCA 1

Mitchell, Clyde
See Ellison, Harlan (Jay); Silverberg, Robert

Mitchell, James Leslie 1901-1935
See Gibbon, Lewis Grassic
See also CA 104; 188; DLB 15

Mitchell, Joni 1943- .... **CLC 12**
See also CA 112; CCA 1

Mitchell, Joseph (Quincy)
1908-1996 .... **CLC 98**
See also CA 77-80; 152; CANR 69; DLB 185; DLBY 96

Mitchell, Margaret (Munnerlyn)
1900-1949 . **TCLC 11; DAM NOV, POP**
See also AAYA 23; AW 1; CA 109; 125; CANR 55, 94; CDALBS; DA3; DLB 9; MTCW 1, 2

Mitchell, Peggy
See Mitchell, Margaret (Munnerlyn)

Mitchell, S(ilas) Weir 1829-1914 .... **TCLC 36**
See also CA 165; DLB 202

Mitchell, W(illiam) O(rmond)
1914-1998 .. **CLC 25; DAC; DAM MST**
See also CA 77-80; 165; CANR 15, 43; DLB 88

Mitchell, William 1879-1936 .... **TCLC 81**

Mitford, Mary Russell 1787-1855 ... **NCLC 4**
See also DLB 110, 116

Mitford, Nancy 1904-1973 .... **CLC 44**
See also CA 9-12R; DLB 191

Miyamoto, (Chujo) Yuriko
1899-1951 .... **TCLC 37**
See also CA 170, 174; DLB 180

Miyazawa, Kenji 1896-1933 .... **TCLC 76**
See also CA 157

Mizoguchi, Kenji 1898-1956 .... **TCLC 72**
See also CA 167

Mo, Timothy (Peter) 1950(?)- ... **CLC 46, 134**
See also CA 117; DLB 194; MTCW 1

Modarressi, Taghi (M.) 1931- .... **CLC 44**
See also CA 121; 134; INT 134

Modiano, Patrick (Jean) 1945- .... **CLC 18**
See also CA 85-88; CANR 17, 40; CWW 2; DLB 83

Moerck, Paal
See Roelvaag, O(le) E(dvart)

Mofolo, Thomas (Mokopu)
1875(?)-1948 .. **TCLC 22; BLC 3; DAM MULT**
See also CA 121; 153; CANR 83; DLB 225; MTCW 2

Mohr, Nicholasa 1938- .... **CLC 12; DAM MULT; HLC 2**
See also AAYA 8; AW; CA 49-52; CANR 1, 32, 64; CLR 22; DLB 145; HW 1, 2; JRDA; SAAS 8; SATA 8, 97; SATA-Essay 113

Mojtabai, A(nn) G(race) 1938- ..... **CLC 5, 9, 15, 29**
See also CA 85-88; CANR 88

Moliere 1622-1673 .... **LC 10, 28, 64; DA; DAB; DAC; DAM DRAM, MST; DC 13**
See also AW; DA3

Molin, Charles
See Mayne, William (James Carter)

Molnár, Ferenc 1878-1952 .. **TCLC 20; DAM DRAM**
See also CA 109; 153; CANR 83; DLB 215

Momaday, N(avarre) Scott 1934- ...... **CLC 2, 19, 85, 95; DA; DAB; DAC; DAM MST, MULT, NOV, POP; PC 25**
See also AAYA 11; AMWS 4; AW; CA 25-28R; CANR 14, 34, 68; CDALBS; DA3; DLB 143, 175; INT CANR-14; MTCW 1, 2; NNAL; SATA 48; SATA-Brief 30

Monette, Paul 1945-1995 .... **CLC 82**
See also CA 139; 147; GLL 1

Monroe, Harriet 1860-1936 .... **TCLC 12**
See also CA 109; DLB 54, 91

Monroe, Lyle
See Heinlein, Robert A(nson)

Montagu, Elizabeth 1720-1800 .... **NCLC 7**

Montagu, Mary (Pierrepont) Wortley
1689-1762 .... **LC 9, 57; PC 16**
See also DLB 95, 101

Montagu, W. H.
See Coleridge, Samuel Taylor

Montague, John (Patrick) 1929- ..... **CLC 13, 46**
See also CA 9-12R; CANR 9, 69; DLB 40; MTCW 1

Montaigne, Michel (Eyquem) de
1533-1592 .... **LC 8; DA; DAB; DAC; DAM MST**
See also AW

Montale, Eugenio 1896-1981 ... **CLC 7, 9, 18; PC 13**
See also CA 17-20R; 104; CANR 30; DLB 114; MTCW 1

Montesquieu, Charles-Louis de Secondat
1689-1755 .... **LC 7**

Montessori, Maria 1870-1952 ...... **TCLC 103**
See also CA 115; 147

Montgomery, (Robert) Bruce 1921(?)-1978
See Crispin, Edmund
See also CA 179; 104

Montgomery, L(ucy) M(aud)
1874-1942 .... **TCLC 51; DAC; DAM MST**
See also AAYA 12; CA 108; 137; CLR 8; DA3; DLB 92; DLBD 14; JRDA; MAICYA; MTCW 2; SATA 100

Montgomery, Marion H., Jr. 1925- .... **CLC 7**
See also AITN 1; CA 1-4R; CANR 3, 48; DLB 6

Montgomery, Max
See Davenport, Guy (Mattison, Jr.)

Montherlant, Henry (Milon) de
1896-1972 ..... **CLC 8, 19; DAM DRAM**
See also CA 85-88; 37-40R; DLB 72; MTCW 1

Monty Python
See Chapman, Graham; Cleese, John (Marwood); Gilliam, Terry (Vance); Idle, Eric; Jones, Terence Graham Parry; Palin, Michael (Edward)
See also AAYA 7

Moodie, Susanna (Strickland)
1803-1885 .... **NCLC 14**
See also DLB 99

Moody, William Vaughan
1869-1910 .... **TCLC 105**
See also CA 110; 178; DLB 7, 54

Mooney, Edward 1951-
See Mooney, Ted
See also CA 130

Mooney, Ted CLC **25**
See also Mooney, Edward

Moorcock, Michael (John) 1939- ...... **CLC 5, 27, 58**
See also Bradbury, Edward P.
See also AAYA 26; CA 45-48; CAAS 5; CANR 2, 17, 38, 64; DLB 14, 231; MTCW 1, 2; SATA 93

Moore, Brian 1921-1999 ... **CLC 1, 3, 5, 7, 8, 19, 32, 90; DAB; DAC; DAM MST**
See also Bryan, Michael
See also CA 1-4R; 174; CANR 1, 25, 42, 63; CCA 1; MTCW 1, 2

Moore, Edward
See Muir, Edwin

Moore, G. E. 1873-1958 .... **TCLC 89**

Moore, George Augustus
1852-1933 .... **TCLC 7; SSC 19**
See also CA 104; 177; DLB 10, 18, 57, 135

Moore, Lorrie CLC **39, 45, 68**
See also Moore, Marie Lorena
See also DLB 234

Moore, Marianne (Craig)
1887-1972 ..... **CLC 1, 2, 4, 8, 10, 13, 19, 47; DA; DAB; DAC; DAM MST, POET; PC 4**
See also AW; CA 1-4R; 33-36R; CANR 3, 61; CDALB 1929-1941; DA3; DLB 45; DLBD 7; MTCW 1, 2; SATA 20

Moore, Marie Lorena 1957-
See Moore, Lorrie
See also CA 116; CANR 39, 83; DLB 234

Moore, Thomas 1779-1852 .... **NCLC 6**
See also DLB 96, 144

Moorhouse, Frank 1938- .... **SSC 40**
See also CA 118; CANR 92

Mora, Pat(ricia) 1942-
See also CA 129; CANR 57, 81; CLR 58; DAM MULT; DLB 209; HLC 2; HW 1, 2; SATA 92

Moraga, Cherrie 1952- .... **CLC 126; DAM MULT**
See also CA 131; CANR 66; DLB 82; GLL 1; HW 1, 2

Morand, Paul 1888-1976 .... **CLC 41; SSC 22**
See also CA 184; 69-72; DLB 65

Morante, Elsa 1918-1985 .... **CLC 8, 47**
See also CA 85-88; 117; CANR 35; DLB
177; MTCW 1, 2

**Moravia, Alberto CLC 2, 7, 11, 27, 46; SSC
26**
See also Pincherle, Alberto
See also DLB 177; MTCW 2

More, Hannah 1745-1833 .... **NCLC 27**
See also DLB 107, 109, 116, 158

More, Henry 1614-1687 .... **LC 9**
See also DLB 126

More, Sir Thomas 1478-1535 .... **LC 10, 32**

Moreas, Jean TCLC 18
See also Papadiamantopoulos, Johannes

Morgan, Berry 1919- .... **CLC 6**
See also CA 49-52; DLB 6

Morgan, Claire
See Highsmith, (Mary) Patricia
See also GLL 1

Morgan, Edwin (George) 1920- .... **CLC 31**
See also CA 5-8R; CANR 3, 43, 90; DLB
27

Morgan, (George) Frederick 1922- .. **CLC 23**
See also CA 17-20R; CANR 21

Morgan, Harriet
See Mencken, H(enry) L(ouis)

Morgan, Jane
See Cooper, James Fenimore

Morgan, Janet 1945- .... **CLC 39**
See also CA 65-68

Morgan, Lady 1776(?)-1859 .... **NCLC 29**
See also DLB 116, 158

Morgan, Robin (Evonne) 1941- .... **CLC 2**
See also CA 69-72; CANR 29, 68; MTCW
1; SATA 80

Morgan, Scott
See Kuttner, Henry

Morgan, Seth 1949(?)-1990 .... **CLC 65**
See also CA 185; 132

Morgenstern, Christian 1871-1914 .. **TCLC 8**
See also CA 105

Morgenstern, S.
See Goldman, William (W.)

Mori, Rintaro
See Mori Ogai
See also CA 110

Moricz, Zsigmond 1879-1942 .... **TCLC 33**
See also CA 165

Morike, Eduard (Friedrich)
1804-1875 .... **NCLC 10**
See also DLB 133

Mori Ogai 1862-1922 .... **TCLC 14**
See also CA 164; DLB 180

Moritz, Karl Philipp 1756-1793 .... **LC 2**
See also DLB 94

Morland, Peter Henry
See Faust, Frederick (Schiller)

Morley, Christopher (Darlington)
1890-1957 .... **TCLC 87**
See also CA 112; DLB 9

Morren, Theophil
See Hofmannsthal, Hugo von

Morris, Bill 1952- .... **CLC 76**

Morris, Julian
See West, Morris L(anglo)

Morris, Steveland Judkins 1950(?)-
See Wonder, Stevie
See also CA 111

Morris, William 1834-1896 .... **NCLC 4**
See also CDBLB 1832-1890; DLB 18, 35,
57, 156, 178, 184

Morris, Wright 1910-1998 .. **CLC 1, 3, 7, 18,
37**
See also CA 9-12R; 167; CANR 21, 81;
DLB 2, 206; DLBY 81; MTCW 1, 2;
TCLC 107; TCWW 2

Morrison, Arthur 1863-1945 .... **TCLC 72;
SSC 40**
See also CA 120; 157; DLB 70, 135, 197

Morrison, Chloe Anthony Wofford
See Morrison, Toni

Morrison, James Douglas 1943-1971
See Morrison, Jim
See also CA 73-76; CANR 40

Morrison, Jim CLC 17
See also Morrison, James Douglas

Morrison, Toni 1931- . **CLC 4, 10, 22, 55, 81,
87; BLC 3; DA; DAB; DAC; DAM
MST, MULT, NOV, POP**
See also AAYA 1, 22; AMWS 3; AW; BW
2, 3; CA 29-32R; CANR 27, 42, 67;
CDALB 1968-1988; DA3; DLB 6, 33,
143; DLBY 81; MTCW 1, 2; SATA 57

Morrison, Van 1945- .... **CLC 21**
See also CA 116; 168

Morrissy, Mary 1958- .... **CLC 99**

Mortimer, John (Clifford) 1923- ..... **CLC 28,
43; DAM DRAM, POP**
See also CA 13-16R; CANR 21, 69; CD-
BLB 1960 to Present; DA3; DLB 13; INT
CANR-21; MTCW 1, 2

Mortimer, Penelope (Ruth)
1918-1999 .... **CLC 5**
See also CA 57-60; 187; CANR 45, 88

Morton, Anthony
See Creasey, John

Mosca, Gaetano 1858-1941 .... **TCLC 75**

Mosher, Howard Frank 1943- .... **CLC 62**
See also CA 139; CANR 65

Mosley, Nicholas 1923- .... **CLC 43, 70**
See also CA 69-72; CANR 41, 60; DLB 14,
207

Mosley, Walter 1952- .... **CLC 97; BLCS;
DAM MULT, POP**
See also AAYA 17; BW 2; CA 142; CANR
57, 92; DA3; MTCW 2

Moss, Howard 1922-1987 ...... **CLC 7, 14, 45,
50; DAM POET**
See also CA 1-4R; 123; CANR 1, 44; DLB
5

Mossgiel, Rab
See Burns, Robert

Motion, Andrew (Peter) 1952- .... **CLC 47**
See also CA 146; CANR 90; DLB 40

Motley, Willard (Francis)
1912-1965 .... **CLC 18**
See also BW 1; CA 117; 106; CANR 88;
DLB 76, 143

Motoori, Norinaga 1730-1801 .... **NCLC 45**

Mott, Michael (Charles Alston)
1930- .... **CLC 15, 34**
See also CA 5-8R; CAAS 7; CANR 7, 29

Mountain Wolf Woman 1884-1960 .. **CLC 92**
See also CA 144; CANR 90; NNAL

Moure, Erin 1955- .... **CLC 88**
See also CA 113; DLB 60

Mowat, Farley (McGill) 1921- .... **CLC 26;
DAC; DAM MST**
See also AAYA 1; AW; CA 1-4R; CANR 4,
24, 42, 68; CLR 20; DLB 68; INT CANR-
24; JRDA; MAICYA; MTCW 1, 2; SATA
3, 55

Mowatt, Anna Cora 1819-1870 ..... **NCLC 74**

Moyers, Bill 1934- .... **CLC 74**
See also AITN 2; CA 61-64; CANR 31, 52

Mphahlele, Es'kia
See Mphahlele, Ezekiel
See also DLB 125, 225

Mphahlele, Ezekiel 1919- .... **CLC 25, 133;
BLC 3; DAM MULT**
See also Mphahlele, Es'kia
See also BW 2, 3; CA 81-84; CANR 26,
76; DA3; DLB 225; MTCW 2; SATA 119

Mqhayi, S(amuel) E(dward) K(rune Loliwe)
1875-1945 ...... **TCLC 25; BLC 3; DAM
MULT**
See also CA 153; CANR 87

Mrozek, Slawomir 1930- .... **CLC 3, 13**
See also CA 13-16R; CAAS 10; CANR 29;
CWW 2; DLB 232; MTCW 1

Mrs. Belloc-Lowndes
See Lowndes, Marie Adelaide (Belloc)

M'Taggart, John M'Taggart Ellis
See McTaggart, John McTaggart Ellis

Mtwa, Percy (?)- .... **CLC 47**

Mueller, Lisel 1924- .... **CLC 13, 51; PC 33**
See also CA 93-96; DLB 105

Muir, Edwin 1887-1959 .... **TCLC 2, 87**
See also CA 104; DLB 20, 100, 191

Muir, John 1838-1914 .... **TCLC 28**
See also CA 165; DLB 186

Mujica Lainez, Manuel 1910-1984 ... **CLC 31**
See also Lainez, Manuel Mujica
See also CA 81-84; 112; CANR 32; HW 1

Mukherjee, Bharati 1940- .... **CLC 53, 115;
DAM NOV; SSC 38**
See also BEST 89:2; CA 107; CANR 45,
72; DLB 60; MTCW 1, 2

Muldoon, Paul 1951- .... **CLC 32, 72; DAM
POET**
See also BRWS 4; CA 113; 129; CANR 52,
91; DLB 40; INT 129

Mulisch, Harry 1927- .... **CLC 42**
See also CA 9-12R; CANR 6, 26, 56

Mull, Martin 1943- .... **CLC 17**
See also CA 105

Muller, Wilhelm NCLC 73

Mulock, Dinah Maria
See Craik, Dinah Maria (Mulock)

Munford, Robert 1737(?)-1783 .... **LC 5**
See also DLB 31

Mungo, Raymond 1946- .... **CLC 72**
See also CA 49-52; CANR 2

Munro, Alice 1931- .... **CLC 6, 10, 19, 50, 95;
DAC; DAM MST, NOV; SSC 3**
See also AITN 2; AW; CA 33-36R; CANR
33, 53, 75; CCA 1; DA3; DLB 53; MTCW
1, 2; SATA 29

Munro, H(ector) H(ugh) 1870-1916
See Saki
See also AW; CA 104; 130; CDBLB 1890-
1914; DA; DAB; DAC; DAM MST, NOV;
DA3; DLB 34, 162; MTCW 1, 2

Murdoch, (Jean) Iris 1919-1999 ... **CLC 1, 2,
3, 4, 6, 8, 11, 15, 22, 31, 51; DAB;
DAC; DAM MST, NOV**
See also BRWS 1; CA 13-16R; 179; CANR
8, 43, 68; CDBLB 1960 to Present; DA3;
DLB 14, 194, 233; INT CANR-8; MTCW
1, 2

Murfree, Mary Noailles 1850-1922 ... **SSC 22**
See also CA 122; 176; DLB 12, 74

Murnau, Friedrich Wilhelm
See Plumpe, Friedrich Wilhelm

Murphy, Richard 1927- .... **CLC 41**
See also BRWS 5; CA 29-32R; DLB 40

Murphy, Sylvia 1937- .... **CLC 34**
See also CA 121

Murphy, Thomas (Bernard) 1935- ... **CLC 51**
See also CA 101

Murray, Albert L. 1916- .... **CLC 73**
See also BW 2; CA 49-52; CANR 26, 52,
78; DLB 38

Murray, Judith Sargent
1751-1820 .... **NCLC 63**
See also DLB 37, 200

Murray, Les(lie) A(llan) 1938- .... **CLC 40;
DAM POET**
See also CA 21-24R; CANR 11, 27, 56

Murry, J. Middleton
See Murry, John Middleton

Murry, John Middleton
1889-1957 .... **TCLC 16**
See also CA 118; DLB 149
Musgrave, Susan 1951- .... **CLC 13, 54**
See also CA 69-72; CANR 45, 84; CCA 1
Musil, Robert (Edler von)
1880-1942 .... **TCLC 12, 68; SSC 18**
See also CA 109; CANR 55, 84; DLB 81,
124; MTCW 2
Muske, Carol CLC 90
See also Muske-Dukes, Carol (Anne)
Muske-Dukes, Carol (Anne) 1945-
See Muske, Carol
See also CA 65-68; CANR 32, 70
Musset, (Louis Charles) Alfred de
1810-1857 .... **NCLC 7**
See also DLB 192
Mussolini, Benito (Amilcare Andrea)
1883-1945 .... **TCLC 96**
See also CA 116
My Brother's Brother
See Chekhov, Anton (Pavlovich)
Myers, L(eopold) H(amilton)
1881-1944 .... **TCLC 59**
See also CA 157; DLB 15
Myers, Walter Dean 1937- ..... **CLC 35; BLC
3; DAM MULT, NOV**
See also AAYA 4, 23; AW; BW 2; CA 33-
36R; CANR 20, 42, 67; CLR 4, 16, 35;
DLB 33; INT CANR-20; JRDA; MAI-
CYA; MTCW 2; SAAS 2; SATA 41, 71,
109; SATA-Brief 27
Myers, Walter M.
See Myers, Walter Dean
Myles, Symon
See Follett, Ken(neth Martin)
Nabokov, Vladimir (Vladimirovich)
1899-1977 .... **CLC 1, 2, 3, 6, 8, 11, 15,
23, 44, 46, 64; DA; DAB; DAC; DAM
MST, NOV; SSC 11**
See also AW; CA 5-8R; 69-72; CANR 20;
CDALB 1941 1968; DA3; DLB 2; DLBD
3; DLBY 80, 91; MTCW 1, 2
Naevius c. 265B.C.-201B.C. .... **CMLC 37**
See also DLB 211
Nagai, Kafu TCLC 51
See also Nagai, Sokichi
See also DLB 180
Nagai, Sokichi 1879-1959
See Nagai, Kafu
See also CA 117
Nagy, Laszlo 1925-1978 .... **CLC 7**
See also CA 129; 112
Naidu, Sarojini 1879-1949 .... **TCLC 80**
Naipaul, Shiva(dhar Srinivasa)
1945-1985 .... **CLC 32, 39; DAM NOV**
See also CA 110; 112; 116; CANR 33;
DA3; DLB 157; DLBY 85; MTCW 1, 2
Naipaul, V(idiadhar) S(urajprasad)
1932- .... **CLC 4, 7, 9, 13, 18, 37, 105;
DAB; DAC; DAM MST, NOV; SSC 38**
See also BRWS 1; CA 1-4R; CANR 1, 33,
51, 91; CDBLB 1960 to Present; DA3;
DLB 125, 204, 206; DLBY 85; MTCW 1,
2
Nakos, Lilika 1899(?)- .... **CLC 29**
Narayan, R(asipuram) K(rishnaswami)
1906-2001 .... **CLC 7, 28, 47, 121; DAM
NOV; SSC 25**
See also CA 81-84; CANR 33, 61; DA3;
MTCW 1, 2; SATA 62
Nash, (Frediric) Ogden 1902-1971 . **CLC 23;
DAM POET; PC 21**
See also CA 13-14; 29-32R; CANR 34, 61;
CAP 1; DLB 11; MAICYA; MTCW 1, 2;
SATA 2, 46
Nashe, Thomas 1567-1601(?) .... **LC 41**
See also DLB 167

Nashe, Thomas 1567-1601 .... **LC 41**
Nathan, Daniel
See Dannay, Frederic
Nathan, George Jean 1882-1958 .... **TCLC 18**
See also Hatteras, Owen
See also CA 114; 169; DLB 137
Natsume, Kinnosuke 1867-1916
See Natsume, Soseki
See also CA 104
Natsume, Soseki TCLC 2, 10
See also Natsume, Kinnosuke
See also DLB 180
Natti, (Mary) Lee 1919-
See Kingman, Lee
See also CA 5-8R; CANR 2
Naylor, Gloria 1950- .... **CLC 28, 52; BLC 3;
DA; DAC; DAM MST, MULT, NOV,
POP**
See also AAYA 6; AW; BW 2, 3; CA 107;
CANR 27, 51, 74; DA3; DLB 173;
MTCW 1, 2
Neihardt, John Gneisenau
1881-1973 .... **CLC 32**
See also CA 13-14; CANR 65; CAP 1; DLB
9, 54
Nekrasov, Nikolai Alekseevich
1821-1878 .... **NCLC 11**
Nelligan, Emile 1879-1941 .... **TCLC 14**
See also CA 114; DLB 92
Nelson, Willie 1933- .... **CLC 17**
See also CA 107
Nemerov, Howard (Stanley)
1920-1991 .... **CLC 2, 6, 9, 36; DAM
POET; PC 24**
See also CA 1-4R; 134; CABS 2; CANR 1,
27, 53; DLB 5, 6; DLBY 83; INT CANR-
27; MTCW 1, 2
Neruda, Pablo 1904-1973 .. **CLC 1, 2, 5, 7, 9,
28, 62; DA; DAB; DAC; DAM MST,
MULT, POET; HLC 2; PC 4**
See also AW; CA 19-20; 45-48; CAP 2;
DA3; HW 1; MTCW 1, 2
Nerval, Gerard de 1808-1855 ... **NCLC 1, 67;
PC 13; SSC 18**
Nervo, (Jose) Amado (Ruiz de)
1870-1919 .... **TCLC 11; HLCS 2**
See also CA 109; 131; HW 1
Nessi, Pio Baroja y
See Baroja (y Nessi), Pio
Nestroy, Johann 1801-1862 .... **NCLC 42**
See also DLB 133
Netterville, Luke
See O'Grady, Standish (James)
Neufeld, John (Arthur) 1938- .... **CLC 17**
See also AAYA 11; AW; CA 25-28R; CANR
11, 37, 56; CLR 52; MAICYA; SAAS 3;
SATA 6, 81
Neumann, Alfred 1895-1952 .... **TCLC 100**
See also CA 183; DLB 56
Neumann, Ferenc
See Moln
Neville, Emily Cheney 1919- .... **CLC 12**
See also AW; CA 5-8R; CANR 3, 37, 85;
JRDA; MAICYA; SAAS 2; SATA 1
Newbound, Bernard Slade 1930-
See Slade, Bernard
See also CA 81-84; CANR 49; DAM
DRAM
Newby, P(ercy) H(oward)
1918-1997 .... **CLC 2, 13; DAM NOV**
See also CA 5-8R; 161; CANR 32, 67; DLB
15; MTCW 1
Newlove, Donald 1928- .... **CLC 6**
See also CA 29-32R; CANR 25
Newlove, John (Herbert) 1938- .... **CLC 14**
See also CA 21-24R; CANR 9, 25
Newman, Charles 1938- .... **CLC 2, 8**
See also CA 21-24R; CANR 84

Newman, Edwin (Harold) 1919- ...... **CLC 14**
See also AITN 1; CA 69-72; CANR 5
Newman, John Henry 1801-1890 .. **NCLC 38**
See also DLB 18, 32, 55
Newton, (Sir)Isaac 1642-1727 .... **LC 35, 52**
Newton, Suzanne 1936- .... **CLC 35**
See also CA 41-44R; CANR 14; JRDA;
SATA 5, 77
Nexo, Martin Andersen
1869-1954 .... **TCLC 43**
See also DLB 214
Nezval, Vitezslav 1900-1958 .... **TCLC 44**
See also CA 123
Ng, Fae Myenne 1957(?)- .... **CLC 81**
See also CA 146
Ngema, Mbongeni 1955- .... **CLC 57**
See also BW 2; CA 143; CANR 84
Ngugi, James T(hiong'o) CLC 3, 7, 13
See also Ngugi wa Thiong'o
Ngugi wa Thiong'o 1938 .. **CLC 36; BLC 3;
DAM MULT, NOV**
See also Ngugi, James T(hiong'o)
See also BW 2; CA 81-84; CANR 27, 58;
DLB 125; MTCW 1, 2
Nichol, B(arrie) P(hillip) 1944-1988 . **CLC 18**
See also CA 53-56; DLB 53; SATA 66
Nichols, John (Treadwell) 1940- ...... **CLC 38**
See also CA 9-12R; CAAS 2; CANR 6, 70;
DLBY 82; TCWW 2
Nichols, Leigh
See Koontz, Dean R(ay)
Nichols, Peter (Richard) 1927- .... **CLC 5, 36,
65**
See also CA 104; CANR 33, 86; DLB 13;
MTCW 1
Nicolas, F. R. E.
See Freeling, Nicolas
Niedecker, Lorine 1903-1970 ..... **CLC 10, 42;
DAM POET**
See also CA 25-28; CAP 2; DLB 48
Nietzsche, Friedrich (Wilhelm)
1844-1900 .... **TCLC 10, 18, 55**
See also CA 107; 121; DLB 129
Nievo, Ippolito 1831-1861 .... **NCLC 22**
Nightingale, Anne Redmon 1943-
See Redmon, Anne
See also CA 103
Nightingale, Florence 1820-1910 ... **TCLC 85**
See also CA 188; DLB 166
Nik. T. O.
See Annensky, Innokenty (Fyodorovich)
Nin, Anaïs 1903-1977 ..... **CLC 1, 4, 8, 11, 14,
60, 127; DAM NOV, POP; SSC 10**
See also AITN 2; CA 13-16R; 69-72;
CANR 22, 53; DLB 2, 4, 152; GLL 2;
MTCW 1, 2
Nishida, Kitaro 1870-1945 .... **TCLC 83**
Nishiwaki, Junzaburo 1894-1982 .... **PC 15**
See also CA 107
Nissenson, Hugh 1933- .... **CLC 4, 9**
See also CA 17-20R; CANR 27; DLB 28
Niven, Larry CLC 8
See also Niven, Laurence Van Cott
See also AAYA 27; DLB 8; SCFW 2
Niven, Laurence Van Cott 1938-
See Niven, Larry
See also CA 21-24R; CAAS 12; CANR 14,
44, 66; DAM POP; MTCW 1, 2; SATA
95
Nixon, Agnes Eckhardt 1927- .... **CLC 21**
See also CA 110
Nizan, Paul 1905-1940 .... **TCLC 40**
See also CA 161; DLB 72
Nkosi, Lewis 1936- ... **CLC 45; BLC 3; DAM
MULT**
See also BW 1, 3; CA 65-68; CANR 27,
81; DLB 157, 225

Nodier, (Jean) Charles (Emmanuel)
1780-1844 .... **NCLC 19**
See also DLB 119

Noguchi, Yone 1875-1947 .... **TCLC 80**

Nolan, Christopher 1965- .... **CLC 58**
See also CA 111; CANR 88

Noon, Jeff 1957- .... **CLC 91**
See also CA 148; CANR 83

Norden, Charles
See Durrell, Lawrence (George)

Nordhoff, Charles (Bernard)
1887-1947 .... **TCLC 23**
See also CA 108; DLB 9; SATA 23

Norfolk, Lawrence 1963- .... **CLC 76**
See also CA 144; CANR 85

Norman, Marsha 1947- .... **CLC 28; DAM DRAM; DC 8**
See also CA 105; CABS 3; CANR 41; DLBY 84

Normyx
See Douglas, (George) Norman

Norris, Frank SSC 28
See also Norris, (Benjamin) Frank(lin, Jr.)
See also CDALB 1865-1917; DLB 12, 71, 186; TCWW 2

Norris, (Benjamin) Frank(lin, Jr.)
1870-1902 .... **TCLC 24**
See also Norris, Frank
See also CA 110; 160

Norris, Leslie 1921- .... **CLC 14**
See also CA 11-12; CANR 14; CAP 1; DLB 27

North, Andrew
See Norton, Andre

North, Anthony
See Koontz, Dean R(ay)

North, Captain George
See Stevenson, Robert Louis (Balfour)

North, Milou
See Erdrich, Louise

Northrup, B. A.
See Hubbard, L(afayette) Ron(ald)

North Staffs
See Hulme, T(homas) E(rnest)

Norton, Alice Mary
See Norton, Andre
See also MAICYA; SATA 1, 43

Norton, Andre 1912- .... **CLC 12**
See also Norton, Alice Mary
See also AAYA 14; AW; CA 1-4R; CANR 68; CLR 50; DLB 8, 52; JRDA; MTCW 1; SATA 91

Norton, Caroline 1808-1877 .... **NCLC 47**
See also DLB 21, 159, 199

Norway, Nevil Shute 1899-1960
See Shute, Nevil
See also CA 102; 93-96; CANR 85; MTCW 2

Norwid, Cyprian Kamil
1821-1883 .... **NCLC 17**

Nosille, Nabrah
See Ellison, Harlan (Jay)

Nossack, Hans Erich 1901-1978 .... **CLC 6**
See also CA 93-96; 85-88; DLB 69

Nostradamus 1503-1566 .... **LC 27**

Nosu, Chuji
See Ozu, Yasujiro

Notenburg, Eleanora (Genrikhovna) von
See Guro, Elena

Nova, Craig 1945- .... **CLC 7, 31**
See also CA 45-48; CANR 2, 53

Novak, Joseph
See Kosinski, Jerzy (Nikodem)

Novalis 1772-1801 .... **NCLC 13**
See also DLB 90

Novis, Emile
See Weil, Simone (Adolphine)

Nowlan, Alden (Albert) 1933-1983 . **CLC 15; DAC; DAM MST**
See also CA 9-12R; CANR 5; DLB 53

Noyes, Alfred 1880-1958 ...... **TCLC 7; PC 27**
See also CA 104; 188; DLB 20

Nunn, Kem CLC 34
See also CA 159

Nwapa, Flora 1931-1993 .... **CLC 133; BLCS**
See also BW 2; CA 143; CANR 83; DLB 125

Nye, Robert 1939- . **CLC 13, 42; DAM NOV**
See also CA 33-36R; CANR 29, 67; DLB 14; MTCW 1; SATA 6

Nyro, Laura 1947-1997 .... **CLC 17**

Oates, Joyce Carol 1938- .. **CLC 1, 2, 3, 6, 9, 11, 15, 19, 33, 52, 108, 134; DA; DAB; DAC; DAM MST, NOV, POP; SSC 6**
See also AAYA 15; AITN 1; AMWS 2; AW; BEST 89:2; CA 5-8R; CANR 25, 45, 74; CDALB 1968-1988; DA3; DLB 2, 5, 130; DLBY 81; INT CANR-25; MTCW 1, 2

O'Brien, Darcy 1939-1998 .... **CLC 11**
See also CA 21-24R; 167; CANR 8, 59

O'Brien, E. G.
See Clarke, Arthur C(harles)

O'Brien, Edna 1936- ..... **CLC 3, 5, 8, 13, 36, 65, 116; DAM NOV; SSC 10**
See also CA 1-4R; CANR 6, 41, 65; CD-BLB 1960 to Present; DA3; DLB 14, 231; MTCW 1, 2

O'Brien, Fitz-James 1828-1862 ..... **NCLC 21**
See also DLB 74

O'Brien, Flann CLC 1, 4, 5, 7, 10, 47
See also O Nuallain, Brian
See also BRWS 2; DLB 231

O'Brien, Richard 1942- .... **CLC 17**
See also CA 124

O'Brien, (William) Tim(othy) 1946- . **CLC 7, 19, 40, 103; DAM POP**
See also AAYA 16; CA 85-88; CANR 40, 58; CDALBS; DA3; DLB 152; DLBD 9; DLBY 80; MTCW 2

Obstfelder, Sigbjoern 1866-1900 .... **TCLC 23**
See also CA 123

O'Casey, Sean 1880-1964 .... **CLC 1, 5, 9, 11, 15, 88; DAB; DAC; DAM DRAM, MST; DC 12**
See also AW; CA 89-92; CANR 62; CD-BLB 1914-1945; DA3; DLB 10; MTCW 1, 2

O'Cathasaigh, Sean
See O'Casey, Sean

Occom, Samson 1723-1792 .... **LC 60**
See also DLB 175; NNAL

Ochs, Phil(ip David) 1940-1976 .... **CLC 17**
See also CA 185; 65-68

O'Connor, Edwin (Greene)
1918-1968 .... **CLC 14**
See also CA 93-96; 25-28R

O'Connor, (Mary) Flannery
1925-1964 .... **CLC 1, 2, 3, 6, 10, 13, 15, 21, 66, 104; DA; DAB; DAC; DAM MST, NOV; SSC 1, 23**
See also AAYA 7; AW; CA 1-4R; CANR 3, 41; CDALB 1941-1968; DA3; DLB 2, 152; DLBD 12; DLBY 80; MTCW 1, 2

O'Connor, Frank CLC 23; SSC 5
See also O'Donovan, Michael John
See also DLB 162

O'Dell, Scott 1898-1989 .... **CLC 30**
See also AAYA 3; AW; CA 61-64; 129; CANR 12, 30; CLR 1, 16; DLB 52; JRDA; MAICYA; SATA 12, 60

Odets, Clifford 1906-1963 ..... **CLC 2, 28, 98; DAM DRAM; DC 6**
See also AMWS 2; CA 85-88; CANR 62; DLB 7, 26; MTCW 1, 2

O'Doherty, Brian 1934- .... **CLC 76**
See also CA 105

O'Donnell, K. M.
See Malzberg, Barry N(athaniel)

O'Donnell, Lawrence
See Kuttner, Henry

O'Donovan, Michael John
1903-1966 .... **CLC 14**
See also O'Connor, Frank
See also CA 93-96; CANR 84

Ōe, Kenzaburō 1935- .... **CLC 10, 36, 86; DAM NOV; SSC 20**
See also CA 97-100; CANR 36, 50, 74; DA3; DLB 182; DLBY 94; MTCW 1, 2

O'Faolain, Julia 1932- .... **CLC 6, 19, 47, 108**
See also CA 81-84; CAAS 2; CANR 12, 61; DLB 14, 231; MTCW 1

O'Faolain, Sean 1900-1991 ...... **CLC 1, 7, 14, 32, 70; SSC 13**
See also CA 61-64; 134; CANR 12, 66; DLB 15, 162; MTCW 1, 2

O'Flaherty, Liam 1896-1984 .... **CLC 5, 34; SSC 6**
See also CA 101; 113; CANR 35; DLB 36, 162; DLBY 84; MTCW 1, 2

Ogilvy, Gavin
See Barrie, J(ames) M(atthew)

O'Grady, Standish (James)
1846-1928 .... **TCLC 5**
See also CA 104; 157

O'Grady, Timothy 1951- .... **CLC 59**
See also CA 138

O'Hara, Frank 1926-1966 .... **CLC 2, 5, 13, 78; DAM POET**
See also CA 9-12R; 25-28R; CANR 33; DA3; DLB 5, 16, 193; MTCW 1, 2

O'Hara, John (Henry) 1905-1970 . **CLC 1, 2, 3, 6, 11, 42; DAM NOV; SSC 15**
See also CA 5-8R; 25-28R; CANR 31, 60; CDALB 1929-1941; DLB 9, 86; DLBD 2; MTCW 1, 2

O Hehir, Diana 1922- .... **CLC 41**
See also CA 93-96

Ohiyesa 1858-1939
See Eastman, Charles A(lexander)

Okigbo, Christopher (Ifenayichukwu)
1932-1967 ... **CLC 25, 84; BLC 3; DAM MULT, POET; PC 7**
See also BW 1, 3; CA 77-80; CANR 74; DLB 125; MTCW 1, 2

Okri, Ben 1959- .... **CLC 87**
See also BRWS 5; BW 2, 3; CA 130; 138; CANR 65; DLB 157, 231; INT 138; MTCW 2

Olds, Sharon 1942- ... **CLC 32, 39, 85; DAM POET; PC 22**
See also CA 101; CANR 18, 41, 66; DLB 120; MTCW 2

Oldstyle, Jonathan
See Irving, Washington

Olesha, Yuri (Karlovich) 1899-1960 .. **CLC 8**
See also CA 85-88

Oliphant, Laurence 1829(?)-1888 .. **NCLC 47**
See also DLB 18, 166

Oliphant, Margaret (Oliphant Wilson)
1828-1897 .... **NCLC 11, 61; SSC 25**
See also Oliphant
See also DLB 18, 159, 190

Oliver, Mary 1935- .... **CLC 19, 34, 98**
See also AMWS 7; CA 21-24R; CANR 9, 43, 84, 92; DLB 5, 193

Olivier, Laurence (Kerr) 1907-1989 . **CLC 20**
See also CA 111; 150; 129

Olsen, Tillie 1912- .... **CLC 4, 13, 114; DA; DAB; DAC; DAM MST; SSC 11**
See also CA 1-4R; CANR 1, 43, 74; CDALBS; DA3; DLB 28, 206; DLBY 80; MTCW 1, 2

Olson, Charles (John) 1910-1970 .. **CLC 1, 2, 5, 6, 9, 11, 29; DAM POET; PC 19**
See also AMWS 2; CA 13-16; 25-28R; CABS 2; CANR 35, 61; CAP 1; DLB 5, 16, 193; MTCW 1, 2

Olson, Toby 1937- .... **CLC 28**
See also CA 65-68; CANR 9, 31, 84

Olyesha, Yuri
See Olesha, Yuri (Karlovich)

Ondaatje, (Philip) Michael 1943- .... **CLC 14, 29, 51, 76; DAB; DAC; DAM MST; PC 28**
See also CA 77-80; CANR 42, 74; DA3; DLB 60; MTCW 2

Oneal, Elizabeth 1934-
See Oneal, Zibby
See also AW; CA 106; CANR 28, 84; MAI-CYA; SATA 30, 82

Oneal, Zibby CLC 30
See also Oneal, Elizabeth
See also AAYA 5; CLR 13; JRDA

O'Neill, Eugene (Gladstone)
1888-1953 .... **TCLC 1, 6, 27, 49; DA; DAB; DAC; DAM DRAM, MST**
See also AITN 1; AW; CA 110; 132; CDALB 1929-1941; DA3; DLB 7; MTCW 1, 2

Onetti, Juan Carlos 1909-1994 ... **CLC 7, 10; DAM MULT, NOV; HLCS 2; SSC 23**
See also CA 85-88; 145; CANR 32, 63; DLB 113; HW 1, 2; MTCW 1, 2

O Nuallain, Brian 1911-1966
See O'Brien, Flann
See also CA 21-22; 25-28R; CAP 2; DLB 231

Ophuls, Max 1902-1957 .... **TCLC 79**
See also CA 113

Opie, Amelia 1769-1853 .... **NCLC 65**
See also DLB 116, 159

Oppen, George 1908-1984 ...... **CLC 7, 13, 34**
See also CA 13-16R; 113; CANR 8, 82; DLB 5, 165; TCLC 107

Oppenheim, E(dward) Phillips
1866-1946 .... **TCLC 45**
See also CA 111; DLB 70

Opuls, Max
See Ophuls, Max

Origen c. 185-c. 254 .... **CMLC 19**

Orlovitz, Gil 1918-1973 .... **CLC 22**
See also CA 77-80; 45-48; DLB 2, 5

Orris
See Ingelow, Jean

Ortega y Gasset, Jose 1883-1955 ... **TCLC 9; DAM MULT; HLC 2**
See also CA 106; 130; HW 1, 2; MTCW 1, 2

Ortese, Anna Maria 1914- .... **CLC 89**
See also DLB 177

Ortiz, Simon J(oseph) 1941- . **CLC 45; DAM MULT, POET; PC 17**
See also AMWS 4; CA 134; CANR 69; DLB 120, 175; NNAL

Orton, Joe CLC 4, 13, 43; DC 3
See also Orton, John Kingsley
See also BRWS 5; CDBLB 1960 to Present; DLB 13; GLL 1; MTCW 2

Orton, John Kingsley 1933-1967
See Orton, Joe
See also CA 85-88; CANR 35, 66; DAM DRAM; MTCW 1, 2

Orwell, George TCLC 2, 6, 15, 31, 51; DAB
See also Blair, Eric (Arthur)
See also AW; CDBLB 1945-1960; CLR 68; DLB 15, 98, 195; SCFW 2

Osborne, David
See Silverberg, Robert

Osborne, George
See Silverberg, Robert

Osborne, John (James) 1929-1994 .... **CLC 1, 2, 5, 11, 45; DA; DAB; DAC; DAM DRAM, MST**
See also AW; BRWS 1; CA 13-16R; 147; CANR 21, 56; CDBLB 1945-1960; DLB 13; MTCW 1, 2

Osborne, Lawrence 1958- .... **CLC 50**
See also CA 189

Osbourne, Lloyd 1868-1947 .... **TCLC 93**

Oshima, Nagisa 1932- .... **CLC 20**
See also CA 116; 121; CANR 78

Oskison, John Milton 1874-1947 .. **TCLC 35; DAM MULT**
See also CA 144; CANR 84; DLB 175; NNAL

Ossian c. 3rd cent. - .... **CMLC 28**
See also Macpherson, James

Ossoli, Sarah Margaret (Fuller marchesa d')
1810-1850 .... **NCLC 5, 50**
See also Fuller, Margaret; Fuller, Sarah Margaret
See also CDALB 1640-1865; DLB 1, 59, 73, 183, 223, 239; SATA 25

Ostriker, Alicia (Suskin) 1937- .... **CLC 132**
See also CA 25-28R; CAAS 24; CANR 10, 30, 62; DLB 120

Ostrovsky, Alexander 1823-1886 .. **NCLC 30, 57**

Otero, Blas de 1916-1979 .... **CLC 11**
See also CA 89-92; DLB 134

Otto, Rudolf 1869-1937 .... **TCLC 85**

Otto, Whitney 1955- .... **CLC 70**
See also CA 140

Ouida TCLC 43
See also De La Ramee, (Marie) Louise
See also DLB 18, 156

Ousmane, Sembene 1923- ... **CLC 66; BLC 3**
See also Sembene, Ousmane
See also BW 1, 3; CA 117; 125; CANR 81; CWW 2; MTCW 1

Ovid 43B.C.-17 . **CMLC 7; DAM POET; PC 2**
See also DA3; DLB 211

Owen, Hugh
See Faust, Frederick (Schiller)

Owen, Wilfred (Edward Salter)
1893-1918 .... **TCLC 5, 27; DA; DAB; DAC; DAM MST, POET; PC 19**
See also AW; CA 104; 141; CDBLB 1914-1945; DLB 20; MTCW 2

Owens, Rochelle 1936- .... **CLC 8**
See also CA 17-20R; CAAS 2; CANR 39

Oz, Amos 1939- ...... **CLC 5, 8, 11, 27, 33, 54; DAM NOV**
See also CA 53-56; CANR 27, 47, 65; CWW 2; MTCW 1, 2

Ozick, Cynthia 1928- .... **CLC 3, 7, 28, 62; DAM NOV, POP; SSC 15**
See also AMWS 5; BEST 90:1; CA 17-20R; CANR 23, 58; DA3; DLB 28, 152; DLBY 82; INT CANR-23; MTCW 1, 2

Ozu, Yasujiro 1903-1963 .... **CLC 16**
See also CA 112

Pacheco, C.
See Pessoa, Fernando (Antonio Nogueira)

Pacheco, Jose Emilio 1939-
See also CA 111; 131; CANR 65; DAM MULT; HLC 2; HW 1, 2

Pa Chin CLC 18
See also Li Fei-kan

Pack, Robert 1929- .... **CLC 13**
See also CA 1-4R; CANR 3, 44, 82; DLB 5; SATA 118

Padgett, Lewis
See Kuttner, Henry

Padilla (Lorenzo), Heberto
1932-2000 .... **CLC 38**
See also AITN 1; CA 123; 131; 189; HW 1

Page, Jimmy 1944- .... **CLC 12**

Page, Louise 1955- .... **CLC 40**
See also CA 140; CANR 76; DLB 233

Page, P(atricia) K(athleen) 1916- ...... **CLC 7, 18; DAC; DAM MST; PC 12**
See also Cape, Judith
See also CA 53-56; CANR 4, 22, 65; DLB 68; MTCW 1

Page, Stanton
See Fuller, Henry Blake

Page, Stanton
See Fuller, Henry Blake

Page, Thomas Nelson 1853-1922 .... **SSC 23**
See also CA 118; 177; DLB 12, 78; DLBD 13

Pagels, Elaine Hiesey 1943- .... **CLC 104**
See also CA 45-48; CANR 2, 24, 51

Paget, Violet 1856-1935
See Lee, Vernon
See also CA 104; 166; GLL 1

Paget-Lowe, Henry
See Lovecraft, H(oward) P(hillips)

Paglia, Camille (Anna) 1947- .... **CLC 68**
See also CA 140; CANR 72; GLL 2; MTCW 2

Paige, Richard
See Koontz, Dean R(ay)

Paine, Thomas 1737-1809 .... **NCLC 62**
See also AMWS 1; CDALB 1640-1865; DLB 31, 43, 73, 158

Pakenham, Antonia
See Fraser, (Lady)Antonia (Pakenham)

Palamas, Kostes 1859-1943 .... **TCLC 5**
See also CA 105

Palazzeschi, Aldo 1885-1974 .... **CLC 11**
See also CA 89-92; 53-56; DLB 114

Pales Matos, Luis 1898-1959
See also HLCS 2; HW 1

Paley, Grace 1922- .... **CLC 4, 6, 37, 140; DAM POP; SSC 8**
See also AMWS 6; CA 25-28R; CANR 13, 46, 74; DA3; DLB 28; INT CANR-13; MTCW 1, 2

Palin, Michael (Edward) 1943- .... **CLC 21**
See also Monty Python
See also CA 107; CANR 35; SATA 67

Palliser, Charles 1947- .... **CLC 65**
See also CA 136; CANR 76

Palma, Ricardo 1833-1919 .... **TCLC 29**
See also CA 168

Pancake, Breece Dexter 1952-1979
See Pancake, Breece D'J
See also CA 123; 109

Pancake, Breece D'J CLC 29
See also Pancake, Breece Dexter
See also DLB 130

Pankhurst, Emmeline (Goulden)
1858-1928 .... **TCLC 100**
See also CA 116

Panko, Rudy
See Gogol, Nikolai (Vasilyevich)

Papadiamantis, Alexandros
1851-1911 .... **TCLC 29**
See also CA 168

Papadiamantopoulos, Johannes 1856-1910
See Moreas, Jean
See also CA 117

Papini, Giovanni 1881-1956 .... **TCLC 22**
See also CA 121; 180

Paracelsus 1493-1541 .... **LC 14**
See also DLB 179

Parasol, Peter
See Stevens, Wallace

Pardo Bazan, Emilia 1851-1921 .... **SSC 30**

Pareto, Vilfredo 1848-1923 .... **TCLC 69**
See also CA 175

Paretsky, Sara 1947- .. **CLC 135; DAM POP**
See also AAYA 30; BEST 90:3; CA 125; 129; CANR 59, 95; DA3; INT 129

Parfenie, Maria
See Codrescu, Andrei

Parini, Jay (Lee) 1948- .... **CLC 54, 133**
See also CA 97-100; CAAS 16; CANR 32, 87

Park, Jordan
See Kornbluth, C(yril) M.; Pohl, Frederik

Park, Robert E(zra) 1864-1944 ..... **TCLC 73**
See also CA 122; 165

Parker, Bert
See Ellison, Harlan (Jay)

Parker, Dorothy (Rothschild)
1893-1967 .... **CLC 15, 68; DAM POET; PC 28; SSC 2**
See also CA 19-20; 25-28R; CAP 2; DA3; DLB 11, 45, 86; MTCW 1, 2

Parker, Robert B(rown) 1932- .... **CLC 27; DAM NOV, POP**
See also AAYA 28; BEST 89:4; CA 49-52; CANR 1, 26, 52, 89; INT CANR-26; MTCW 1

Parkin, Frank 1940- .... **CLC 43**
See also CA 147

Parkman, Francis, Jr. 1823-1893 .. **NCLC 12**
See also AMWS 2; DLB 1, 30, 186, 235

Parks, Gordon (Alexander Buchanan)
1912- .... **CLC 1, 16; BLC 3; DAM MULT**
See also AAYA 36; AITN 2; BW 2, 3; CA 41-44R; CANR 26, 66; DA3; DLB 33; MTCW 2; SATA 8, 108

Parmenides c. 515B.C.-c.
450B.C. .... **CMLC 22**
See also DLB 176

Parnell, Thomas 1679-1718 .... **LC 3**
See also DLB 94

Parra, Nicanor 1914- ...... **CLC 2, 102; DAM MULT; HLC 2**
See also CA 85-88; CANR 32; CWW 2; HW 1; MTCW 1

Parra Sanojo, Ana Teresa de la 1890-1936
See also HLCS 2

Parrish, Mary Frances
See Fisher, M(ary) F(rances) K(ennedy)

Parson
See Coleridge, Samuel Taylor

Parson Lot
See Kingsley, Charles

Parton, Sara Payson Willis
1811-1872 .... **NCLC 86**
See also DLB 43, 74, 239

Partridge, Anthony
See Oppenheim, E(dward) Phillips

Pascal, Blaise 1623-1662 .... **LC 35**

Pascoli, Giovanni 1855-1912 .... **TCLC 45**
See also CA 170

Pasolini, Pier Paolo 1922-1975 .. **CLC 20, 37, 106; PC 17**
See also CA 93-96; 61-64; CANR 63; DLB 128, 177; MTCW 1

Pasquini
See Silone, Ignazio

Pastan, Linda (Olenik) 1932- .... **CLC 27; DAM POET**
See also CA 61-64; CANR 18, 40, 61; DLB 5

Pasternak, Boris (Leonidovich)
1890-1960 .... **CLC 7, 10, 18, 63; DA; DAB; DAC; DAM MST, NOV, POET; PC 6; SSC 31**
See also AW; CA 127; 116; DA3; MTCW 1, 2

Patchen, Kenneth 1911-1972 .. **CLC 1, 2, 18; DAM POET**
See also CA 1-4R; 33-36R; CANR 3, 35; DLB 16, 48; MTCW 1

Pater, Walter (Horatio) 1839-1894 . **NCLC 7, 90**
See also CDBLB 1832-1890; DLB 57, 156

Paterson, A(ndrew) B(arton)
1864-1941 .... **TCLC 32**
See also CA 155; DLB 230; SATA 97

Paterson, Katherine (Womeldorf)
1932- .... **CLC 12, 30**
See also AAYA 1, 31; CA 21-24R; CANR 28, 59; CLR 7, 50; DLB 52; JRDA; MAICYA; MTCW 1; SATA 13, 53, 92

Patmore, Coventry Kersey Dighton
1823-1896 .... **NCLC 9**
See also DLB 35, 98

Paton, Alan (Stewart) 1903-1988 ...... **CLC 4, 10, 25, 55, 106; DA; DAB; DAC; DAM MST, NOV**
See also AAYA 26; AW; BRWS 2; CA 13-16; 125; CANR 22; CAP 1; DA3; DLB 225; DLBD 17; MTCW 1, 2; SATA 11; SATA-Obit 56

Paton Walsh, Gillian 1937- .... **CLC 35**
See also Walsh, Jill Paton
See also AAYA 11; AW; CANR 38, 83; CLR 2, 65; DLB 161; JRDA; MAICYA; SAAS 3; SATA 4, 72, 109

Paton Walsh, Jill
See Paton Walsh, Gillian

Patton, George S(mith), Jr.
1885-1945 .... **TCLC 79**
See also CA 189

Paulding, James Kirke 1778-1860 ... **NCLC 2**
See also DLB 3, 59, 74

Paulin, Thomas Neilson 1949-
See Paulin, Tom
See also CA 123; 128

Paulin, Tom CLC 37
See also Paulin, Thomas Neilson
See also DLB 40

Pausanias c. 1st cent. - .... **CMLC 36**

Paustovsky, Konstantin (Georgievich)
1892-1968 .... **CLC 40**
See also CA 93-96; 25-28R

Pavese, Cesare 1908-1950 .. **TCLC 3; PC 13; SSC 19**
See also CA 104; 169; DLB 128, 177

Pavic, Milorad 1929- .... **CLC 60**
See also CA 136; CWW 2; DLB 181

Pavlov, Ivan Petrovich 1849-1936 . **TCLC 91**
See also CA 118; 180

Payne, Alan
See Jakes, John (William)

Paz, Gil
See Lugones, Leopoldo

Paz, Octavio 1914-1998 . **CLC 3, 4, 6, 10, 19, 51, 65, 119; DA; DAB; DAC; DAM MST, MULT, POET; HLC 2; PC 1**
See also AW; CA 73-76; 165; CANR 32, 65; CWW 2; DA3; DLBY 90, 98; HW 1, 2; MTCW 1, 2

p'Bitek, Okot 1931-1982 .... **CLC 96; BLC 3; DAM MULT**
See also BW 2, 3; CA 124; 107; CANR 82; DLB 125; MTCW 1, 2

Peacock, Molly 1947- .... **CLC 60**
See also CA 103; CAAS 21; CANR 52, 84; DLB 120

Peacock, Thomas Love
1785-1866 .... **NCLC 22**
See also DLB 96, 116

Peake, Mervyn 1911-1968 .... **CLC 7, 54**
See also CA 5-8R; 25-28R; CANR 3; DLB 15, 160; MTCW 1; SATA 23

Pearce, Philippa CLC 21
See also Christie, (Ann) Philippa
See also CLR 9; DLB 161; MAICYA; SATA 1, 67

Pearl, Eric
See Elman, Richard (Martin)

Pearson, T(homas) R(eid) 1956- .... **CLC 39**
See also CA 120; 130; INT 130

Peck, Dale 1967- .... **CLC 81**
See also CA 146; CANR 72; GLL 2

Peck, John 1941- .... **CLC 3**
See also CA 49-52; CANR 3

Peck, Richard (Wayne) 1934- .... **CLC 21**
See also AAYA 1, 24; CA 85-88; CANR 19, 38; CLR 15; INT CANR-19; JRDA; MAICYA; SAAS 2; SATA 18, 55, 97; SATA-Essay 110

Peck, Robert Newton 1928- .... **CLC 17; DA; DAC; DAM MST**
See also AAYA 3; AW; CA 81-84, 182; CAAE 182; CANR 31, 63; CLR 45; JRDA; MAICYA; SAAS 1; SATA 21, 62, 111; SATA-Essay 108

Peckinpah, (David) Sam(uel)
1925-1984 .... **CLC 20**
See also CA 109; 114; CANR 82

Pedersen, Knut 1859-1952
See Hamsun, Knut
See also CA 104; 119; CANR 63; MTCW 1, 2

Peeslake, Gaffer
See Durrell, Lawrence (George)

Peguy, Charles Pierre 1873-1914 ... **TCLC 10**
See also CA 107

Peirce, Charles Sanders
1839-1914 .... **TCLC 81**

Pellicer, Carlos 1900(?)-1977
See also CA 153; 69-72; HLCS 2; HW 1

Pena, Ramon del Valle y
See Valle-Inclan, Ramon (Maria) del

Pendennis, Arthur Esquir
See Thackeray, William Makepeace

Penn, William 1644-1718 .... **LC 25**
See also DLB 24

PEPECE
See Prado (Calvo), Pedro

Pepys, Samuel 1633-1703 ..... **LC 11, 58; DA; DAB; DAC; DAM MST**
See also AW; CDBLB 1660-1789; DA3; DLB 101

Percy, Thomas 1729-1811 .... **NCLC 95**
See also DLB 104

Percy, Walker 1916-1990 .... **CLC 2, 3, 6, 8, 14, 18, 47, 65; DAM NOV, POP**
See also AMWS 3; CA 1-4R; 131; CANR 1, 23, 64; DA3; DLB 2; DLBY 80, 90; MTCW 1, 2

Percy, William Alexander
1885-1942 .... **TCLC 84**
See also CA 163; MTCW 2

Perec, Georges 1936-1982 .... **CLC 56, 116**
See also CA 141; DLB 83

Pereda (y Sanchez de Porrua), Jose Maria de 1833-1906 .... **TCLC 16**
See also CA 117

Pereda y Porrua, Jose Maria de
See Pereda (y Sanchez de Porrua), Jose Maria de

Peregoy, George Weems
See Mencken, H(enry) L(ouis)

Perelman, S(idney) J(oseph)
1904-1979 .. **CLC 3, 5, 9, 15, 23, 44, 49; DAM DRAM; SSC 32**
See also AITN 1, 2; CA 73-76; 89-92; CANR 18; DLB 11, 44; MTCW 1, 2

Peret, Benjamin 1899-1959 .... **TCLC 20; PC 33**
See also CA 117; 186

Peretz, Isaac Loeb 1851(?)-1915 ... **TCLC 16; SSC 26**
See also CA 109

Peretz, Yitzkhok Leibush
See Peretz, Isaac Loeb

Perez Galdos, Benito 1843-1920 ... **TCLC 27; HLCS 2**
See also CA 125; 153; HW 1

Peri Rossi, Cristina 1941-
See also CA 131; CANR 59, 81; DLB 145; HLCS 2; HW 1, 2

Perlata
See Peret, Benjamin

Perloff, Marjorie G(abrielle) 1931- .... **CLC 137**
See also CA 57-60; CANR 7, 22, 49

Perrault, Charles 1628-1703 ... **LC 3, 52; DC 12**
See also MAICYA; SATA 25

Perry, Anne 1938- .... **CLC 126**
See also CA 101; CANR 22, 50, 84

Perry, Brighton
See Sherwood, Robert E(mmet)

Perse, St.-John
See Leger, (Marie-Rene Auguste) Alexis Saint-Leger

Perutz, Leo(pold) 1882-1957 .... **TCLC 60**
See also CA 147; DLB 81

Peseenz, Tulio F.
See Lopez y Fuentes, Gregorio

Pesetsky, Bette 1932- .... **CLC 28**
See also CA 133; DLB 130

Peshkov, Alexei Maximovich 1868-1936
See Gorky, Maxim
See also CA 105; 141; CANR 83; DA; DAC; DAM DRAM, MST, NOV; MTCW 2

Pessoa, Fernando (Antonio Nogueira) 1898-1935 .... **TCLC 27; DAM MULT; HLC 2; PC 20**
See also CA 125; 183

Peterkin, Julia Mood 1880-1961 ...... **CLC 31**
See also CA 102; DLB 9

Peters, Joan K(aren) 1945- .... **CLC 39**
See also CA 158

Peters, Robert L(ouis) 1924- .... **CLC 7**
See also CA 13-16R; CAAS 8; DLB 105

Petofi, Sandor 1823-1849 .... **NCLC 21**

Petrakis, Harry Mark 1923- .... **CLC 3**
See also CA 9-12R; CANR 4, 30, 85

Petrarch 1304-1374 .... **CMLC 20; DAM POET; PC 8**
See also DA3

Petronius c. 20- .... **CMLC 34**
See also DLB 211

Petrov, Evgeny TCLC 21
See also Kataev, Evgeny Petrovich

Petry, Ann (Lane) 1908-1997 ... **CLC 1, 7, 18**
See also BW 1, 3; CA 5-8R; 157; CAAS 6; CANR 4, 46; CLR 12; DLB 76; JRDA; MAICYA; MTCW 1; SATA 5; SATA-Obit 94

Petursson, Halligrimur 1614-1674 .... **LC 8**

Peychinovich
See Vazov, Ivan (Minchov)

Phaedrus c. 15B.C.-c. 50 .... **CMLC 25**
See also DLB 211

Philips, Katherine 1632-1664 .... **LC 30**
See also DLB 131

Philipson, Morris H. 1926- .... **CLC 53**
See also CA 1-4R; CANR 4

Phillips, Caryl 1958- . **CLC 96; BLCS; DAM MULT**
See also BRWS 5; BW 2; CA 141; CANR 63; DA3; DLB 157; MTCW 2

Phillips, David Graham 1867-1911 .... **TCLC 44**
See also CA 108; 176; DLB 9, 12

Phillips, Jack
See Sandburg, Carl (August)

Phillips, Jayne Anne 1952- .... **CLC 15, 33, 139; SSC 16**
See also CA 101; CANR 24, 50, 96; DLBY 80; INT CANR-24; MTCW 1, 2

Phillips, Richard
See Dick, Philip K(indred)

Phillips, Robert (Schaeffer) 1938- .... **CLC 28**
See also CA 17-20R; CAAS 13; CANR 8; DLB 105

Phillips, Ward
See Lovecraft, H(oward) P(hillips)

Piccolo, Lucio 1901-1969 .... **CLC 13**
See also CA 97-100; DLB 114

Pickthall, Marjorie L(owry) C(hristie) 1883-1922 .... **TCLC 21**
See also CA 107; DLB 92

Pico della Mirandola, Giovanni 1463-1494 .... **LC 15**

Piercy, Marge 1936- .... **CLC 3, 6, 14, 18, 27, 62, 128; PC 29**
See also CA 21-24R; CAAE 187; CAAS 1; CANR 13, 43, 66; DLB 120, 227; MTCW 1, 2

Piers, Robert
See Anthony, Piers

Pieyre de Mandiargues, Andre 1909-1991
See Mandiargues, Andre Pieyre de
See also CA 103; 136; CANR 22, 82

Pilnyak, Boris TCLC 23
See also Vogau, Boris Andreyevich

Pincherle, Alberto 1907-1990 .... **CLC 11, 18; DAM NOV**
See also Moravia, Alberto
See also CA 25-28R; 132; CANR 33, 63; MTCW 1

Pinckney, Darryl 1953- .... **CLC 76**
See also BW 2, 3; CA 143; CANR 79

Pindar 518B.C.-442B.C. .... **CMLC 12; PC 19**
See also DLB 176

Pineda, Cecile 1942- .... **CLC 39**
See also CA 118; DLB 209

Pinero, Arthur Wing 1855-1934 ... **TCLC 32; DAM DRAM**
See also CA 110; 153; DLB 10

Piñero, Miguel (Antonio Gomez) 1946-1988 .... **CLC 4, 55**
See also CA 61-64; 125; CANR 29, 90; HW 1

Pinget, Robert 1919-1997 .... **CLC 7, 13, 37**
See also CA 85-88; 160; CWW 2; DLB 83

Pink Floyd
See Barrett, (Roger) Syd; Gilmour, David; Mason, Nick; Waters, Roger; Wright, Rick

Pinkney, Edward 1802-1828 .... **NCLC 31**

Pinkwater, Daniel Manus 1941- ...... **CLC 35**
See also Pinkwater, Manus
See also AAYA 1; AW; CA 29-32R; CANR 12, 38, 89; CLR 4; JRDA; MAICYA; SAAS 3; SATA 46, 76, 114

Pinkwater, Manus
See Pinkwater, Daniel Manus
See also SATA 8

Pinsky, Robert 1940- .... **CLC 9, 19, 38, 94, 121; DAM POET; PC 27**
See also AMWS 6; CA 29-32R; CAAS 4; CANR 58; DA3; DLBY 82, 98; MTCW 2

Pinta, Harold
See Pinter, Harold

Pinter, Harold 1930- .. **CLC 1, 3, 6, 9, 11, 15, 27, 58, 73; DA; DAB; DAC; DAM DRAM, MST**
See also AW; BRWS 1; CA 5-8R; CANR 33, 65; CDBLB 1960 to Present; DA3; DLB 13; IDFW 3; MTCW 1, 2

Piozzi, Hester Lynch (Thrale) 1741-1821 .... **NCLC 57**
See also DLB 104, 142

Pirandello, Luigi 1867-1936 ...... **TCLC 4, 29; DA; DAB; DAC; DAM DRAM, MST; DC 5; SSC 22**
See also AW; CA 104; 153; DA3; MTCW 2

Pirsig, Robert M(aynard) 1928- ... **CLC 4, 6, 73; DAM POP**
See also CA 53-56; CANR 42, 74; DA3; MTCW 1, 2; SATA 39

Pisarev, Dmitry Ivanovich 1840-1868 .... **NCLC 25**

Pix, Mary (Griffith) 1666-1709 .... **LC 8**
See also DLB 80

Pixerecourt, (Rene Charles) Guilbert de 1773-1844 .... **NCLC 39**
See also DLB 192

Plaatje, Sol(omon) T(shekisho) 1878-1932 .... **TCLC 73; BLCS**
See also BW 2, 3; CA 141; CANR 79; DLB 225

Plaidy, Jean
See Hibbert, Eleanor Alice Burford

Planche, James Robinson 1796-1880 .... **NCLC 42**

Plant, Robert 1948- .... **CLC 12**

Plante, David (Robert) 1940- ...... **CLC 7, 23, 38; DAM NOV**
See also CA 37-40R; CANR 12, 36, 58, 82; DLBY 83; INT CANR-12, MTCW 1

Plath, Sylvia 1932-1963 ...... **CLC 1, 2, 3, 5, 9, 11, 14, 17, 50, 51, 62, 111; DA; DAB; DAC; DAM MST, POET; PC 1**
See also AAYA 13; AMWS 1; AW; CA 19-20; CANR 34; CAP 2; CDALB 1941-1968; DA3; DLB 5, 6, 152; MTCW 1, 2; SATA 96

Plato 428(?)B.C.-348(?)B.C. ... **CMLC 8; DA; DAB; DAC; DAM MST**
See also AW; DA3; DLB 176

Platonov, Andrei
See Klimentov, Andrei Platonovich

Platt, Kin 1911- .... **CLC 26**
See also AAYA 11; CA 17-20R; CANR 11; JRDA; SAAS 17; SATA 21, 86

Plautus c. 254B.C.-184B.C. ... **CMLC 24; DC 6**
See also DLB 211

Plick et Plock
See Simenon, Georges (Jacques Christian)

Plieksans, Janis
See Rainis, Janis
See also CA 170; DLB 220

Plimpton, George (Ames) 1927- .... **CLC 36**
See also AITN 1; CA 21-24R; CANR 32, 70; DLB 185, 241; MTCW 1, 2; SATA 10

Pliny the Elder c. 23-79 .... **CMLC 23**
See also DLB 211

Plomer, William Charles Franklin 1903-1973 .... **CLC 4, 8**
See also CA 21-22; CANR 34; CAP 2; DLB 20, 162, 191, 225; MTCW 1; SATA 24

Plowman, Piers
See Kavanagh, Patrick (Joseph)

Plum, J.
See Wodehouse, P(elham) G(renville)

Plumly, Stanley (Ross) 1939- .... **CLC 33**
See also CA 108; 110; DLB 5, 193; INT 110

Plumpe, Friedrich Wilhelm 1888-1931 .... **TCLC 53**
See also CA 112

Po Chu-i 772-846 .... **CMLC 24**

Poe, Edgar Allan 1809-1849 ..... **NCLC 1, 16, 55, 78, 94, 97; DA; DAB; DAC; DAM MST, POET; PC 1; SSC 1, 22, 34, 35**
See also AAYA 14; AW; CDALB 1640-1865; DA3; DLB 3, 59, 73, 74; SATA 23

Poet of Titchfield Street, The
See Pound, Ezra (Weston Loomis)

Pohl, Frederik 1919- .... **CLC 18; SSC 25**
See also AAYA 24; CA 61-64; CAAE 188;
CAAS 1; CANR 11, 37, 81; DLB 8; INT
CANR-11; MTCW 1, 2; SATA 24; SCFW
2

Poirier, Louis 1910-
See Gracq, Julien
See also CA 122; 126; CWW 2

Poitier, Sidney 1927- .... **CLC 26**
See also BW 1; CA 117; CANR 94

Polanski, Roman 1933- .... **CLC 16**
See also CA 77-80

Poliakoff, Stephen 1952- .... **CLC 38**
See also CA 106; DLB 13

Police, The
See Copeland, Stewart (Armstrong); Sum-
mers, Andrew James; Sumner, Gordon
Matthew

Polidori, John William 1795-1821 . **NCLC 51**
See also DLB 116

Pollitt, Katha 1949- .... **CLC 28, 122**
See also CA 120; 122; CANR 66; MTCW
1, 2

Pollock, (Mary) Sharon 1936- .... **CLC 50;
DAC; DAM DRAM, MST**
See also CA 141; DLB 60

Polo, Marco 1254-1324 .... **CMLC 15**

Polonsky, Abraham (Lincoln)
1910-1999 .... **CLC 92**
See also CA 104; 187; DLB 26; INT 104

Polybius c. 200B.C.-c. 118B.C. ...... **CMLC 17**
See also DLB 176

Pomerance, Bernard 1940- ... **CLC 13; DAM
DRAM**
See also CA 101; CANR 49

Ponge, Francis 1899-1988 . **CLC 6, 18; DAM
POET**
See also CA 85-88; 126; CANR 40, 86

Poniatowska, Elena 1933- ... **CLC 140; DAM
MULT; HLC 2**
See also CA 101; CANR 32, 66; DLB 113;
HW 1, 2

Pontoppidan, Henrik 1857-1943 .... **TCLC 29**
See also CA 170

Poole, Josephine CLC 17
See also Helyar, Jane Penelope Josephine
See also SAAS 2; SATA 5

Popa, Vasko 1922-1991 .... **CLC 19**
See also CA 112; 148; DLB 181

Pope, Alexander 1688-1744 ...... **LC 3, 58, 60,
64; DA; DAB; DAC; DAM MST,
POET; PC 26**
See also AW; CDBLB 1660-1789; DA3;
DLB 95, 101

Porter, Connie (Rose) 1959(?)- .... **CLC 70**
See also BW 2, 3; CA 142; CANR 90;
SATA 81

Porter, Gene(va Grace) Stratton
(?)- .... **TCLC 21**
See also Stratton-Porter, Gene(va Grace)
See also CA 112

Porter, Katherine Anne 1890-1980 ... **CLC 1,
3, 7, 10, 13, 15, 27, 101; DA; DAB;
DAC; DAM MST, NOV; SSC 4, 31, 43**
See also AITN 2; CA 1-4R; 101; CANR 1,
65; CDALBS; DA3; DLB 4, 9, 102;
DLBD 12; DLBY 80; MTCW 1, 2; SATA
39; SATA-Obit 23

Porter, Peter (Neville Frederick)
1929- .... **CLC 5, 13, 33**
See also CA 85-88; DLB 40

Porter, William Sydney 1862-1910
See Henry, O.
See also AW 2; CA 104; 131; CDALB
1865-1917; DA; DAB; DAC; DAM MST;
DA3; DLB 12, 78, 79; MTCW 1, 2

Portillo (y Pacheco), Jose Lopez
See Lopez Portillo (y Pacheco), Jose

Portillo Trambley, Estela 1927-1998
See Trambley, Estela Portillo
See also CANR 32; DAM MULT; DLB
209; HLC 2; HW 1

Post, Melville Davisson
1869-1930 .... **TCLC 39**
See also CA 110

Potok, Chaim 1929- ... **CLC 2, 7, 14, 26, 112;
DAM NOV**
See also AAYA 15; AITN 1, 2; AW; CA 17-
20R; CANR 19, 35, 64; DA3; DLB 28,
152; INT CANR-19; MTCW 1, 2; SATA
33, 106

Potter, Dennis (Christopher George)
1935-1994 .... **CLC 58, 86, 123**
See also CA 107; 145; CANR 33, 61; DLB
233; MTCW 1

Pound, Ezra (Weston Loomis)
1885-1972 .. **CLC 1, 2, 3, 4, 5, 7, 10, 13,
18, 34, 48, 50, 112; DA; DAB; DAC;
DAM MST, POET; PC 4**
See also AW; CA 5-8R; 37-40R; CANR 40;
CDALB 1917-1929; DA3; DLB 4, 45, 63;
DLBD 15; MTCW 1, 2

Povod, Reinaldo 1959-1994 .... **CLC 44**
See also CA 136; 146; CANR 83

Powell, Adam Clayton, Jr.
1908-1972 .... **CLC 89; BLC 3; DAM
MULT**
See also BW 1, 3; CA 102; 33-36R; CANR
86

Powell, Anthony (Dymoke)
1905-2000 .... **CLC 1, 3, 7, 9, 10, 31**
See also CA 1-4R; 189; CANR 1, 32, 62;
CDBLB 1945-1960; DLB 15; MTCW 1,
2

Powell, Dawn 1897-1965 .... **CLC 66**
See also CA 5-8R; DLBY 97

Powell, Padgett 1952- .... **CLC 34**
See also CA 126; CANR 63; DLB 234

Powell, Talmage 1920-2000
See Queen, Ellery
See also CA 5-8R; CANR 2, 80

Power, Susan 1961- .... **CLC 91**
See also CA 160

Powers, J(ames) F(arl) 1917-1999 ..... **CLC 1,
4, 8, 57; SSC 4**
See also CA 1-4R; 181; CANR 2, 61; DLB
130; MTCW 1

Powers, John J(ames) 1945-
See Powers, John R.
See also CA 69-72

Powers, John R. CLC 66
See also Powers, John J(ames)

Powers, Richard (S.) 1957- .... **CLC 93**
See also CA 148; CANR 80

Pownall, David 1938- .... **CLC 10**
See also CA 89-92; 180; CAAS 18; CANR
49; DLB 14

Powys, John Cowper 1872-1963 ... **CLC 7, 9,
15, 46, 125**
See also CA 85-88; DLB 15; MTCW 1, 2

Powys, T(heodore) F(rancis)
1875-1953 .... **TCLC 9**
See also CA 106; 189; DLB 36, 162

Prado (Calvo), Pedro 1886-1952 ... **TCLC 75**
See also CA 131; HW 1

Prager, Emily 1952- .... **CLC 56**

Pratt, E(dwin) J(ohn)
1883(?)-1964 .... **CLC 19; DAC; DAM
POET**
See also CA 141; 93-96; CANR 77; DLB
92

Premchand TCLC 21
See also Srivastava, Dhanpat Rai

Preussler, Otfried 1923- .... **CLC 17**
See also CA 77-80; SATA 24

Prevert, Jacques (Henri Marie)
1900-1977 .... **CLC 15**
See also CA 77-80; 69-72; CANR 29, 61;
IDFW 3; MTCW 1; SATA-Obit 30

Prevost, Abbe (Antoine Francois)
1697-1763 .... **LC 1**

Price, (Edward) Reynolds 1933- ... **CLC 3, 6,
13, 43, 50, 63; DAM NOV; SSC 22**
See also CA 1-4R; CANR 1, 37, 57, 87;
DLB 2; INT CANR-37

Price, Richard 1949- .... **CLC 6, 12**
See also CA 49-52; CANR 3; DLBY 81

Prichard, Katharine Susannah
1883-1969 .... **CLC 46**
See also CA 11-12; CANR 33; CAP 1;
MTCW 1; SATA 66

Priestley, J(ohn) B(oynton)
1894-1984 ... **CLC 2, 5, 9, 34; DAM
DRAM, NOV**
See also CA 9-12R; 113; CANR 33; CD-
BLB 1914-1945; DA3; DLB 10, 34, 77,
100, 139; DLBY 84; MTCW 1, 2

Prince 1958(?)- .... **CLC 35**

Prince, F(rank) T(empleton) 1912- .. **CLC 22**
See also CA 101; CANR 43, 79; DLB 20

Prince Kropotkin
See Kropotkin, Peter (Aleksieevich)

Prior, Matthew 1664-1721 .... **LC 4**
See also DLB 95

Prishvin, Mikhail 1873-1954 .... **TCLC 75**

Pritchard, William H(arrison)
1932- .... **CLC 34**
See also CA 65-68; CANR 23, 95; DLB
111

Pritchett, V(ictor) S(awdon)
1900-1997 ...... **CLC 5, 13, 15, 41; DAM
NOV; SSC 14**
See also BRWS 3; CA 61-64; 157; CANR
31, 63; DA3; DLB 15, 139; MTCW 1, 2

Private 19022
See Manning, Frederic

Probst, Mark 1925- .... **CLC 59**
See also CA 130

Prokosch, Frederic 1908-1989 ...... **CLC 4, 48**
See also CA 73-76; 128; CANR 82; DLB
48; MTCW 2

Propertius, Sextus c. 50B.C.-c.
15B.C. .... **CMLC 32**
See also DLB 211

Prophet, The
See Dreiser, Theodore (Herman Albert)

Prose, Francine 1947- .... **CLC 45**
See also CA 109; 112; CANR 46, 95; DLB
234; SATA 101

Proudhon
See Cunha, Euclides (Rodrigues Pimenta)
da

Proulx, Annie
See Proulx, E(dna) Annie
See also AMWS 7

Proulx, E(dna) Annie 1935- .. **CLC 81; DAM
POP**
See also Proulx, Annie
See also CA 145; CANR 65; DA3; MTCW
2

Proust,
(Valentin-Louis-George-Eugene-)Marcel
1871-1922 . **TCLC 7, 13, 33; DA; DAB;
DAC; DAM MST, NOV**
See also AW; CA 104; 120; DA3; DLB 65;
MTCW 1, 2

Prowler, Harley
See Masters, Edgar Lee

Prus, Boleslaw 1845-1912 .... **TCLC 48**

Pryor, Richard (Franklin Lenox Thomas)
1940- .... **CLC 26**
See also CA 122; 152

Przybyszewski, Stanislaw
 1868-1927 .... **TCLC 36**
 See also CA 160; DLB 66
Pteleon
 See Grieve, C(hristopher) M(urray)
 See also DAM POET
Puckett, Lute
 See Masters, Edgar Lee
Puig, Manuel 1932-1990 .... **CLC 3, 5, 10, 28, 65, 133; DAM MULT; HLC 2**
 See also CA 45-48; CANR 2, 32, 63; DA3; DLB 113; GLL 1; HW 1, 2; MTCW 1, 2
Pulitzer, Joseph 1847-1911 .... **TCLC 76**
 See also CA 114; DLB 23
Purdy, A(lfred) W(ellington)
 1918-2000 .... **CLC 3, 6, 14, 50; DAC; DAM MST, POET**
 See also CA 81-84; 189; CAAS 17; CANR 42, 66; DLB 88
Purdy, James (Amos) 1923- .... **CLC 2, 4, 10, 28, 52**
 See also AMWS 7; CA 33-36R; CAAS 1; CANR 19, 51; DLB 2; INT CANR-19; MTCW 1
Pure, Simon
 See Swinnerton, Frank Arthur
Pushkin, Alexander (Sergeyevich)
 1799-1837 . **NCLC 3, 27, 83; DA; DAB; DAC; DAM DRAM, MST, POET; PC 10; SSC 27**
 See also AW; DA3; DLB 205; SATA 61
P'u Sung-ling 1640-1715 .... **LC 49; SSC 31**
Putnam, Arthur Lee
 See Alger, Horatio, Jr.
Puzo, Mario 1920-1999 .... **CLC 1, 2, 6, 36, 107; DAM NOV, POP**
 See also CA 65-68; 185; CANR 4, 42, 65; DA3; DLB 6; MTCW 1, 2
Pygge, Edward
 See Barnes, Julian (Patrick)
Pyle, Ernest Taylor 1900-1945
 See Pyle, Ernie
 See also CA 115; 160
Pyle, Ernie TCLC 75
 See also Pyle, Ernest Taylor
 See also DLB 29, MTCW 2
Pyle, Howard 1853-1911 .... **TCLC 81**
 See also AW; CA 109; 137; CLR 22; DLB 42, 188; DLBD 13; MAICYA; SATA 16, 100
Pym, Barbara (Mary Crampton)
 1913-1980 .... **CLC 13, 19, 37, 111**
 See also BRWS 2; CA 13-14; 97-100; CANR 13, 34; CAP 1; DLB 14, 207; DLBY 87; MTCW 1, 2
Pynchon, Thomas (Ruggles, Jr.)
 1937- ...... **CLC 2, 3, 6, 9, 11, 18, 33, 62, 72, 123; DA; DAB; DAC; DAM MST, NOV, POP; SSC 14**
 See also AMWS 2; AW; BEST 90:2; CA 17-20R; CANR 22, 46, 73; DA3; DLB 2, 173; MTCW 1, 2
Pythagoras c. 582B.C.-c. 507B.C. . **CMLC 22**
 See also DLB 176
Q
 See Quiller-Couch, SirArthur (Thomas)
Qian Zhongshu
 See Ch'ien Chung-shu
Qroll
 See Dagerman, Stig (Halvard)
Quarrington, Paul (Lewis) 1953- ..... **CLC 65**
 See also CA 129; CANR 62, 95
Quasimodo, Salvatore 1901-1968 ..... **CLC 10**
 See also CA 13-16; 25-28R; CAP 1; DLB 114; MTCW 1
Quay, Stephen 1947- .... **CLC 95**
 See also CA 189

Quay, Timothy 1947- .... **CLC 95**
 See also CA 189
Queen, Ellery CLC 3, 11
 See also Dannay, Frederic; Davidson, Avram (James); Deming, Richard; Fairman, Paul W.; Flora, Fletcher; Hoch, Edward D(entinger); Kane, Henry; Lee, Manfred B(ennington); Marlowe, Stephen; Powell, Talmage; Sheldon, Walter J.; Sturgeon, Theodore (Hamilton); Tracy, Don(ald Fiske); Vance, John Holbrook
Queen, Ellery, Jr.
 See Dannay, Frederic; Lee, Manfred B(ennington)
Queneau, Raymond 1903-1976 ..... **CLC 2, 5, 10, 42**
 See also CA 77-80; 69-72; CANR 32; DLB 72; MTCW 1, 2
Quevedo, Francisco de 1580-1645 .... **LC 23**
Quiller-Couch, SirArthur (Thomas)
 1863-1944 .... **TCLC 53**
 See also CA 118; 166; DLB 135, 153, 190
Quin, Ann (Marie) 1936-1973 .... **CLC 6**
 See also CA 9-12R; 45-48; DLB 14, 231
Quinn, Martin
 See Smith, Martin Cruz
Quinn, Peter 1947- .... **CLC 91**
Quinn, Simon
 See Smith, Martin Cruz
Quintana, Leroy V. 1944-
 See also CA 131; CANR 65; DAM MULT; DLB 82; HLC 2; HW 1, 2
Quiroga, Horacio (Sylvestre)
 1878-1937 .... **TCLC 20; DAM MULT; HLC 2**
 See also CA 117; 131; HW 1; MTCW 1
Quoirez, Francoise 1935- .... **CLC 9**
 See also Sagan, Francoise
 See also CA 49-52; CANR 6, 39, 73; CWW 2; MTCW 1, 2
Raabe, Wilhelm (Karl) 1831-1910 . **TCLC 45**
 See also CA 167; DLB 129
Rabe, David (William) 1940- ,. **CLC 4, 8, 33; DAM DRAM**
 See also CA 85-88; CABS 3; CANR 59; DLB 7, 228
Rabelais, François 1494-1553 .... **LC 5, 60; DA; DAB; DAC; DAM MST**
 See also AW
Rabinovitch, Sholem 1859-1916
 See Aleichem, Sholom
 See also CA 104
Rabinyan, Dorit 1972- .... **CLC 119**
 See also CA 170
Rachilde
 See Vallette, Marguerite Eymery
Racine, Jean 1639-1699 . **LC 28; DAB; DAM MST**
 See also DA3
Radcliffe, Ann (Ward) 1764-1823 ... **NCLC 6, 55**
 See also DLB 39, 178
Radiguet, Raymond 1903-1923 ...... **TCLC 29**
 See also CA 162; DLB 65
Radnoti, Miklos 1909-1944 .... **TCLC 16**
 See also CA 118
Rado, James 1939- .... **CLC 17**
 See also CA 105
Radvanyi, Netty 1900-1983
 See Seghers, Anna
 See also CA 85-88; 110; CANR 82
Rae, Ben
 See Griffiths, Trevor
Raeburn, John (Hay) 1941- .... **CLC 34**
 See also CA 57-60

Ragni, Gerome 1942-1991 .... **CLC 17**
 See also CA 105; 134
Rahv, Philip CLC 24
 See also Greenberg, Ivan
 See also DLB 137
Raimund, Ferdinand Jakob
 1790-1836 .... **NCLC 69**
 See also DLB 90
Raine, Craig 1944- .... **CLC 32, 103**
 See also CA 108; CANR 29, 51; DLB 40
Raine, Kathleen (Jessie) 1908- ..... **CLC 7, 45**
 See also CA 85-88; CANR 46; DLB 20; MTCW 1
Rainis, Janis 1865-1929 .... **TCLC 29**
 See also Plieksans, Janis
 See also CA 170; DLB 220
Rakosi, Carl CLC 47
 See also Rawley, Callman
 See also CAAS 5; DLB 193
Ralegh, SirWalter (?)-
 See Raleigh, SirWalter
Raleigh, Richard
 See Lovecraft, H(oward) P(hillips)
Raleigh, SirWalter 1554(?)-1618 .. **LC 31, 39; PC 31**
 See also CDBLB Before 1660; DLB 172
Rallentando, H. P.
 See Sayers, Dorothy L(eigh)
Ramal, Walter
 See de la Mare, Walter (John)
Ramana Maharshi 1879-1950 .... **TCLC 84**
Ramoacn y Cajal, Santiago
 1852-1934 .... **TCLC 93**
Ramon, Juan
 See Jimenez (Mantecon), Juan Ramon
Ramos, Graciliano 1892-1953 .... **TCLC 32**
 See also CA 167; HW 2
Rampersad, Arnold 1941- .... **CLC 44**
 See also BW 2, 3; CA 127; 133; CANR 81; DLB 111; INT 133
Rampling, Anne
 See Rice, Anne
 See also GLL 2
Ramsay, Allan 1686(?)-1758 .... **LC 29**
 See also DLB 95
Ramuz, Charles-Ferdinand
 1878-1947 .... **TCLC 33**
 See also CA 165
Rand, Ayn 1905-1982 ...... **CLC 3, 30, 44, 79; DA; DAC; DAM MST, NOV, POP**
 See also AAYA 10; AMWS 4; AW; CA 13-16R; 105; CANR 27, 73; CDALBS; DA3; DLB 227; MTCW 1, 2
Randall, Dudley (Felker) 1914-2000 . **CLC 1, 135; BLC 3; DAM MULT**
 See also BW 1, 3; CA 25-28R; 189; CANR 23, 82; DLB 41
Randall, Robert
 See Silverberg, Robert
Ranger, Ken
 See Creasey, John
Ransom, John Crowe 1888-1974 .. **CLC 2, 4, 5, 11, 24; DAM POET**
 See also CA 5-8R; 49-52; CANR 6, 34; CDALBS; DA3; DLB 45, 63; MTCW 1, 2
Rao, Raja 1909- ..... **CLC 25, 56; DAM NOV**
 See also CA 73-76; CANR 51; MTCW 1, 2
Raphael, Frederic (Michael) 1931- ... **CLC 2, 14**
 See also CA 1-4R; CANR 1, 86; DLB 14
Ratcliffe, James P.
 See Mencken, H(enry) L(ouis)
Rathbone, Julian 1935- .... **CLC 41**
 See also CA 101; CANR 34, 73

Rattigan, Terence (Mervyn)
  1911-1977 .... CLC 7; DAM DRAM
  See also CA 85-88; 73-76; CDBLB 1945-
  1960; DLB 13; IDFW 3; MTCW 1, 2
Ratushinskaya, Irina 1954- .... CLC 54
  See also CA 129; CANR 68; CWW 2
Raven, Simon (Arthur Noel) 1927- .. CLC 14
  See also CA 81-84; CANR 86
Ravenna, Michael
  See Welty, Eudora
Rawley, Callman 1903-
  See Rakosi, Carl
  See also CA 21-24R; CANR 12, 32, 91
Rawlings, Marjorie Kinnan
  1896-1953 .... TCLC 4
  See also AAYA 20; AW; CA 104; 137;
  CANR 74; CLR 63; DLB 9, 22, 102;
  DLBD 17; JRDA; MAICYA; MTCW 2;
  SATA 100
Ray, Satyajit 1921-1992 .. CLC 16, 76; DAM
  MULT
  See also CA 114; 137
Read, Herbert Edward 1893-1968 ..... CLC 4
  See also CA 85-88; 25-28R; DLB 20, 149
Read, Piers Paul 1941- .... CLC 4, 10, 25
  See also CA 21-24R; CANR 38, 86; DLB
  14; SATA 21
Reade, Charles 1814-1884 .... NCLC 2, 74
  See also DLB 21
Reade, Hamish
  See Gray, Simon (James Holliday)
Reading, Peter 1946- .... CLC 47
  See also CA 103; CANR 46, 96; DLB 40
Reaney, James 1926- .. CLC 13; DAC; DAM
  MST
  See also CA 41-44R; CAAS 15; CANR 42;
  DLB 68; SATA 43
Rebreanu, Liviu 1885-1944 .... TCLC 28
  See also CA 165; DLB 220
Rechy, John (Francisco) 1934- ...... CLC 1, 7,
  14, 18, 107; DAM MULT; HLC 2
  See also CA 5-8R; CAAS 4; CANR 6, 32,
  64; DLB 122; DLBY 82; HW 1, 2; INT
  CANR-6
Redcam, Tom 1870-1933 .... TCLC 25
Reddin, Keith CLC 67
Redgrove, Peter (William) 1932- . CLC 6, 41
  See also CA 1-4R; CANR 3, 39, 77; DLB
  40
Redmon, Anne CLC 22
  See also Nightingale, Anne Redmon
  See also DLBY 86
Reed, Eliot
  See Ambler, Eric
Reed, Ishmael 1938- .. CLC 2, 3, 5, 6, 13, 32,
  60; BLC 3; DAM MULT
  See also BW 2, 3; CA 21-24R; CANR 25,
  48, 74; DA3; DLB 2, 5, 33, 169, 227;
  DLBD 8; MTCW 1, 2; TCWW 2
Reed, John (Silas) 1887-1920 .... TCLC 9
  See also CA 106
Reed, Lou CLC 21
  See also Firbank, Louis
Reese, Lizette Woodworth 1856-1935 . PC 29
  See also CA 180; DLB 54
Reeve, Clara 1729-1807 .... NCLC 19
  See also DLB 39
Reich, Wilhelm 1897-1957 .... TCLC 57
Reid, Christopher (John) 1949- .... CLC 33
  See also CA 140; CANR 89; DLB 40
Reid, Desmond
  See Moorcock, Michael (John)
Reid Banks, Lynne 1929-
  See Banks, Lynne Reid
  See also AW; CA 1-4R; CANR 6, 22, 38,
  87; CLR 24; JRDA; MAICYA; SATA 22,
  75, 111

Reilly, William K.
  See Creasey, John
Reiner, Max
  See Caldwell, (Janet Miriam) Taylor
  (Holland)
Reis, Ricardo
  See Pessoa, Fernando (Antonio Nogueira)
Remarque, Erich Maria
  1898-1970 ... CLC 21; DA; DAB; DAC;
  DAM MST, NOV
  See also AAYA 27; CA 77-80; 29-32R;
  DA3; DLB 56; MTCW 1, 2
Remington, Frederic 1861-1909 ..... TCLC 89
  See also CA 108; 169; DLB 12, 186, 188;
  SATA 41
Remizov, A.
  See Remizov, Aleksei (Mikhailovich)
Remizov, A. M.
  See Remizov, Aleksei (Mikhailovich)
Remizov, Aleksei (Mikhailovich)
  1877-1957 .... TCLC 27
  See also CA 125; 133
Renan, Joseph Ernest 1823-1892 .. NCLC 26
Renard, Jules 1864-1910 .... TCLC 17
  See also CA 117
Renault, Mary CLC 3, 11, 17
  See also Challans, Mary
  See also DLBY 83; GLL 1; MTCW 2
Rendell, Ruth (Barbara) 1930- . CLC 28, 48;
  DAM POP
  See also Vine, Barbara
  See also CA 109; CANR 32, 52, 74; DLB
  87; INT CANR-32; MTCW 1, 2
Renoir, Jean 1894-1979 .... CLC 20
  See also CA 129; 85-88
Resnais, Alain 1922- .... CLC 16
Reverdy, Pierre 1889-1960 .... CLC 53
  See also CA 97-100; 89-92
Rexroth, Kenneth 1905-1982 .... CLC 1, 2, 6,
  11, 22, 49, 112; DAM POET; PC 20
  See also CA 5-8R; 107; CANR 14, 34, 63;
  CDALB 1941-1968; DLB 16, 48, 165,
  212; DLBY 82; INT CANR-14; MTCW
  1, 2
Reyes, Alfonso 1889-1959 .. TCLC 33; HLCS
  2
  See also CA 131; HW 1
Reyes y Basoalto, Ricardo Eliecer Neftali
  See Neruda, Pablo
Reymont, Wladyslaw (Stanislaw)
  1868(?)-1925 .... TCLC 5
  See also CA 104
Reynolds, Jonathan 1942- .... CLC 6, 38
  See also CA 65-68; CANR 28
Reynolds, Joshua 1723-1792 .... LC 15
  See also DLB 104
Reynolds, Michael S(hane)
  1937-2000 .... CLC 44
  See also CA 65-68; 189; CANR 9, 89
Reznikoff, Charles 1894-1976 .... CLC 9
  See also CA 33-36; 61-64; CAP 2; DLB 28,
  45
Rezzori (d'Arezzo), Gregor von
  1914-1998 .... CLC 25
  See also CA 122; 136; 167
Rhine, Richard
  See Silverstein, Alvin
Rhodes, Eugene Manlove
  1869-1934 .... TCLC 53
Rhodius, Apollonius c. 3rd cent.
  B.C.- .... CMLC 28
  See also DLB 176
R'hoone
  See Balzac, Honor
Rhys, Jean 1894(?)-1979 ...... CLC 2, 4, 6, 14,
  19, 51, 124; DAM NOV; SSC 21
  See also BRWS 2; CA 25-28R; 85-88;
  CANR 35, 62; CDBLB 1945-1960; DA3;
  DLB 36, 117, 162; MTCW 1, 2

Ribeiro, Darcy 1922-1997 .... CLC 34
  See also CA 33-36R; 156
Ribeiro, Joao Ubaldo (Osorio Pimentel)
  1941- .... CLC 10, 67
  See also CA 81-84
Ribman, Ronald (Burt) 1932- .... CLC 7
  See also CA 21-24R; CANR 46, 80
Ricci, Nino 1959- .... CLC 70
  See also CA 137; CCA 1
Rice, Anne 1941- .. CLC 41, 128; DAM POP
  See also Rampling, Anne
  See also AAYA 9; AMWS 7; AW; BEST
  89:2; CA 65-68; CANR 12, 36, 53, 74;
  DA3; GLL 2; MTCW 2
Rice, Elmer (Leopold) 1892-1967 ...... CLC 7,
  49; DAM DRAM
  See also CA 21-22; 25-28R; CAP 2; DLB
  4, 7; MTCW 1, 2
Rice, Tim(othy Miles Bindon)
  1944- .... CLC 21
  See also CA 103; CANR 46
Rich, Adrienne (Cecile) 1929- ... CLC 3, 6, 7,
  11, 18, 36, 73, 76, 125; DAM POET;
  PC 5
  See also AMWS 1; CA 9-12R; CANR 20,
  53, 74; CDALBS; DA3; DLB 5, 67;
  MTCW 1, 2
Rich, Barbara
  See Graves, Robert (von Ranke)
Rich, Robert
  See Trumbo, Dalton
  See also IDFW 3
Richard, Keith CLC 17
  See also Richards, Keith
Richards, David Adams 1950- .... CLC 59;
  DAC
  See also CA 93-96; CANR 60; DLB 53
Richards, I(vor) A(rmstrong)
  1893-1979 .... CLC 14, 24
  See also BRWS 2; CA 41-44R; 89-92;
  CANR 34, 74; DLB 27; MTCW 2
Richards, Keith 1943-
  See Richard, Keith
  See also CA 107; CANR 77
Richardson, Anne
  See Roiphe, Anne (Richardson)
Richardson, Dorothy Miller
  1873-1957 .... TCLC 3
  See also CA 104; DLB 36
Richardson (Robertson), Ethel Florence
  Lindesay 1870-1946
  See Richardson, Henry Handel
  See also CA 105; DLB 230
Richardson, Henry Handel TCLC 4
  See also Richardson (Robertson), Ethel Flo-
  rence Lindesay
  See also DLB 197
Richardson, John 1796-1852 .... NCLC 55;
  DAC
  See also CCA 1; DLB 99
Richardson, Samuel 1689-1761 ...... LC 1, 44;
  DA; DAB; DAC; DAM MST, NOV
  See also AW; CDBLB 1660-1789; DLB 39
Richler, Mordecai 1931- ...... CLC 3, 5, 9, 13,
  18, 46, 70; DAC; DAM MST, NOV
  See also AITN 1; CA 65-68; CANR 31, 62;
  CCA 1; CLR 17; DLB 53; MAICYA;
  MTCW 1, 2; SATA 44, 98; SATA-Brief
  27
Richter, Conrad (Michael)
  1890-1968 .... CLC 30
  See also AAYA 21; AW; CA 5-8R; 25-28R;
  CANR 23; DLB 9, 212; MTCW 1, 2;
  SATA 3; TCWW 2
Ricostranza, Tom
  See Ellis, Trey
Riddell, Charlotte 1832-1906 .... TCLC 40
  See also CA 165; DLB 156

Ridge, John Rollin 1827-1867 ...... **NCLC 82; DAM MULT**
See also CA 144; DLB 175; NNAL

Ridgway, Keith 1965- .... **CLC 119**
See also CA 172

Riding, Laura CLC 3, 7
See also Jackson, Laura (Riding)

Riefenstahl, Berta Helene Amalia 1902-
See Riefenstahl, Leni
See also CA 108

Riefenstahl, Leni CLC 16
See also Riefenstahl, Berta Helene Amalia

Riffe, Ernest
See Bergman, (Ernst) Ingmar

Riggs, (Rolla) Lynn 1899-1954 ..... **TCLC 56; DAM MULT**
See also CA 144; DLB 175; NNAL

Riis, Jacob A(ugust) 1849-1914 ..... **TCLC 80**
See also CA 113; 168; DLB 23

Riley, James Whitcomb 1849-1916 .... **TCLC 51; DAM POET**
See also CA 118; 137; MAICYA; SATA 17

Riley, Tex
See Creasey, John

Rilke, Rainer Maria 1875-1926 .. **TCLC 1, 6, 19; DAM POET; PC 2**
See also CA 104; 132; CANR 62; DA3; DLB 81; MTCW 1, 2

Rimbaud, (Jean Nicolas) Arthur 1854-1891 . **NCLC 4, 35, 82; DA; DAB; DAC; DAM MST, POET; PC 3**
See also AW; DA3

Rinehart, Mary Roberts 1876-1958 .... **TCLC 52**
See also CA 108; 166

Ringmaster, The
See Mencken, H(enry) L(ouis)

Ringwood, Gwen(dolyn Margaret) Pharis 1910-1984 .... **CLC 48**
See also CA 148; 112; DLB 88

Rio, Michel 19(?)- .... **CLC 43**

Ritsos, Giannes
See Ritsos, Yannis

Ritsos, Yannis 1909-1990 .... **CLC 6, 13, 31**
See also CA 77-80; 133; CANR 39, 61; MTCW 1

Ritter, Erika 1948(?)- .... **CLC 52**

Rivera, Jose Eustasio 1889-1928 ... **TCLC 35**
See also CA 162; HW 1, 2

Rivera, Tomas 1935-1984
See also CA 49-52; CANR 32; DLB 82; HLCS 2; HW 1; TCWW 2

Rivers, Conrad Kent 1933-1968 .... **CLC 1**
See also BW 1; CA 85-88; DLB 41

Rivers, Elfrida
See Bradley, Marion Zimmer
See also GLL 1

Riverside, John
See Heinlein, Robert A(nson)

Rizal, Jose 1861-1896 .... **NCLC 27**

Roa Bastos, Augusto (Antonio) 1917- .... **CLC 45; DAM MULT; HLC 2**
See also CA 131; DLB 113; HW 1

Robbe-Grillet, Alain 1922- .... **CLC 1, 2, 4, 6, 8, 10, 14, 43, 128**
See also CA 9-12R; CANR 33, 65; DLB 83; MTCW 1, 2

Robbins, Harold 1916-1997 .... **CLC 5; DAM NOV**
See also CA 73-76; 162; CANR 26, 54; DA3; MTCW 1, 2

Robbins, Thomas Eugene 1936-
See Robbins, Tom
See also CA 81-84; CANR 29, 59, 95; DAM NOV, POP; DA3; MTCW 1, 2

Robbins, Tom CLC 9, 32, 64
See also Robbins, Thomas Eugene
See also AAYA 32; BEST 90:3; DLBY 80; MTCW 2

Robbins, Trina 1938- .... **CLC 21**
See also CA 128

Roberts, Charles G(eorge) D(ouglas) 1860-1943 .... **TCLC 8**
See also CA 105; 188; CLR 33; DLB 92; SATA 88; SATA-Brief 29

Roberts, Elizabeth Madox 1886-1941 .... **TCLC 68**
See also CA 111; 166; DLB 9, 54, 102; SATA 33; SATA-Brief 27

Roberts, Kate 1891-1985 .... **CLC 15**
See also CA 107; 116

Roberts, Keith (John Kingston) 1935-2000 .... **CLC 14**
See also CA 25-28R; CANR 46

Roberts, Kenneth (Lewis) 1885-1957 .... **TCLC 23**
See also CA 109; DLB 9

Roberts, Michele (Brigitte) 1949- ..... **CLC 48**
See also CA 115; CANR 58; DLB 231

Robertson, Ellis
See Ellison, Harlan (Jay); Silverberg, Robert

Robertson, Thomas William 1829-1871 .... **NCLC 35; DAM DRAM**

Robeson, Kenneth
See Dent, Lester

Robinson, Edwin Arlington 1869-1935 ..... **TCLC 5, 101; DA; DAC; DAM MST, POET; PC 1**
See also CA 104; 133; CDALB 1865-1917; DLB 54; MTCW 1, 2

Robinson, Henry Crabb 1775-1867 .... **NCLC 15**
See also DLB 107

Robinson, Jill 1936- .... **CLC 10**
See also CA 102; INT 102

Robinson, Kim Stanley 1952- .... **CLC 34**
See also AAYA 26; CA 126; SATA 109

Robinson, Lloyd
See Silverberg, Robert

Robinson, Marilynne 1944- .... **CLC 25**
See also CA 116; CANR 80; DLB 206

Robinson, Smokey CLC 21
See also Robinson, William, Jr.

Robinson, William, Jr. 1940-
See Robinson, Smokey
See also CA 116

Robison, Mary 1949- .... **CLC 42, 98**
See also CA 113; 116; CANR 87; DLB 130; INT 116

Rod, Edouard 1857-1910 .... **TCLC 52**

Roddenberry, Eugene Wesley 1921-1991
See Roddenberry, Gene
See also CA 110; 135; CANR 37; SATA 45; SATA-Obit 69

Roddenberry, Gene CLC 17
See also Roddenberry, Eugene Wesley
See also AAYA 5; SATA-Obit 69

Rodgers, Mary 1931- .... **CLC 12**
See also CA 49-52; CANR 8, 55, 90; CLR 20; INT CANR-8; JRDA; MAICYA; SATA 8

Rodgers, W(illiam) R(obert) 1909-1969 .... **CLC 7**
See also CA 85-88; DLB 20

Rodman, Eric
See Silverberg, Robert

Rodman, Howard 1920(?)-1985 .... **CLC 65**
See also CA 118

Rodman, Maia
See Wojciechowska, Maia (Teresa)

Rodo, Jose Enrique 1871(?)-1917
See also CA 178; HLCS 2; HW 2

Rodriguez, Claudio 1934-1999 .... **CLC 10**
See also CA 188; DLB 134

Rodriguez, Richard 1944-
See also CA 110; CANR 66; DAM MULT; DLB 82; HLC 2; HW 1, 2

Roelvaag, O(le) E(dvart) 1876-1931 .... **TCLC 17**
See also Rolvaag, O(le) E(dvart)
See also CA 117; 171; DLB 9

Roethke, Theodore (Huebner) 1908-1963 .... **CLC 1, 3, 8, 11, 19, 46, 101; DAM POET; PC 15**
See also CA 81-84; CABS 2; CDALB 1941-1968; DA3; DLB 5, 206; MTCW 1, 2

Rogers, Samuel 1763-1855 .... **NCLC 69**
See also DLB 93

Rogers, Thomas Hunton 1927- .... **CLC 57**
See also CA 89-92; INT 89-92

Rogers, Will(iam Penn Adair) 1879-1935 ... **TCLC 8, 71; DAM MULT**
See also CA 105; 144; DA3; DLB 11; MTCW 2; NNAL

Rogin, Gilbert 1929- .... **CLC 18**
See also CA 65-68; CANR 15

Rohan, Koda
See Koda Shigeyuki

Rohlfs, Anna Katharine Green
See Green, Anna Katharine

Rohmer, Eric CLC 16
See also Scherer, Jean-Marie Maurice

Rohmer, Sax TCLC 28
See also Ward, Arthur Henry Sarsfield
See also DLB 70

Roiphe, Anne (Richardson) 1935- .. **CLC 3, 9**
See also CA 89-92; CANR 45, 73; DLBY 80; INT 89-92

Rojas, Fernando de 1475-1541 .... **LC 23; HLCS 1**

Rojas, Gonzalo 1917-
See also HLCS 2; HW 2

Rojas, Gonzalo 1917-
See also CA 178; HLCS 2

Rolfe, Frederick (William Serafino Austin Lewis Mary) 1860-1913 .... **TCLC 12**
See also CA 107; DLB 34, 156

Rolland, Romain 1866-1944 .... **TCLC 23**
See also CA 118; DLB 65

Rolle, Richard c. 1300-c. 1349 ...... **CMLC 21**
See also DLB 146

Rolvaag, O(le) E(dvart)
See Roelvaag, O(le) E(dvart)

Romain Arnaud, Saint
See Aragon, Louis

Romains, Jules 1885-1972 .... **CLC 7**
See also CA 85-88; CANR 34; DLB 65; MTCW 1

Romero, Jose Ruben 1890-1952 .... **TCLC 14**
See also CA 114; 131; HW 1

Ronsard, Pierre de 1524-1585 . **LC 6, 54; PC 11**

Rooke, Leon 1934- . **CLC 25, 34; DAM POP**
See also CA 25-28R; CANR 23, 53; CCA 1

Roosevelt, Franklin Delano 1882-1945 .... **TCLC 93**
See also CA 116; 173

Roosevelt, Theodore 1858-1919 ..... **TCLC 69**
See also CA 115; 170; DLB 47, 186

Roper, William 1498-1578 .... **LC 10**

Roquelaure, A. N.
See Rice, Anne

Rosa, Joao Guimaraes 1908-1967 ... **CLC 23; HLCS 1**
See also CA 89-92; DLB 113

Rose, Wendy 1948- .. **CLC 85; DAM MULT; PC 13**
See also CA 53-56; CANR 5, 51; DLB 175; NNAL; SATA 12

Rosen, R. D.
See Roscn, Richard (Dean)
Rosen, Richard (Dean) 1949- .... **CLC 39**
See also CA 77-80; CANR 62; INT
CANR-30
Rosenberg, Isaac 1890-1918 .... **TCLC 12**
See also CA 107; 188; DLB 20
Rosenblatt, Joe CLC 15
See also Rosenblatt, Joseph
Rosenblatt, Joseph 1933-
See Rosenblatt, Joe
See also CA 89-92; INT 89-92
Rosenfeld, Samuel
See Tzara, Tristan
Rosenstock, Sami
See Tzara, Tristan
Rosenstock, Samuel
See Tzara, Tristan
Rosenthal, M(acha) L(ouis)
1917-1996 .... **CLC 28**
See also CA 1-4R; 152; CAAS 6; CANR 4,
51; DLB 5; SATA 59
Ross, Barnaby
See Dannay, Frederic
Ross, Bernard L.
See Follett, Ken(neth Martin)
Ross, J. H.
See Lawrence, T(homas) E(dward)
Ross, John Hume
See Lawrence, T(homas) E(dward)
Ross, Martin -1915
See Martin, Violet Florence
See also DLB 135; GLL 2
Ross, (James) Sinclair 1908-1996 ... **CLC 13;**
DAC; DAM MST; SSC 24
See also CA 73-76; CANR 81; DLB 88
Rossetti, Christina (Georgina)
1830-1894 . **NCLC 2, 50, 66; DA; DAB;**
DAC; DAM MST, POET; PC 7
See also AW; DA3; DLB 35, 163, 240;
MAICYA; SATA 20
Rossetti, Dante Gabriel 1828-1882 . **NCLC 4,**
77; DA; DAB; DAC; DAM MST,
POET
See also AW; CDBLB 1832-1890; DLB 35
Rossner, Judith (Perelman) 1935- . **CLC 6, 9,**
29
See also AITN 2; BEST 90:3; CA 17-20R;
CANR 18, 51, 73; DLB 6; INT CANR-
18; MTCW 1, 2
Rostand, Edmond (Eugene Alexis)
1868-1918 .... **TCLC 6, 37; DA; DAB;**
DAC; DAM DRAM, MST; DC 10
See also CA 104; 126; DA3; DLB 192;
MTCW 1
Roth, Henry 1906-1995 ..... **CLC 2, 6, 11, 104**
See also CA 11-12; 149; CANR 38, 63;
CAP 1; DA3; DLB 28; MTCW 1, 2
Roth, (Moses) Joseph 1894-1939 ... **TCLC 33**
See also CA 160; DLB 85
Roth, Philip (Milton) 1933- ... **CLC 1, 2, 3, 4,**
6, 9, 15, 22, 31, 47, 66, 86, 119; DA;
DAB; DAC; DAM MST, NOV, POP;
SSC 26
See also AMWS 3; AW; BEST 90:3; CA
1-4R; CANR 1, 22, 36, 55, 89; CDALB
1968-1988; DA3; DLB 2, 28, 173; DLBY
82; MTCW 1, 2
Rothenberg, Jerome 1931- .... **CLC 6, 57**
See also CA 45-48; CANR 1; DLB 5, 193
Roumain, Jacques (Jean Baptiste)
1907-1944 ...... **TCLC 19; BLC 3; DAM**
MULT
See also BW 1; CA 117; 125
Rourke, Constance (Mayfield)
1885-1941 .... **TCLC 12**
See also AW 1; CA 107

Rousseau, Jean-Baptiste 1671-1741 ...... **LC 9**
Rousseau, Jean-Jacques 1712-1778 .... **LC 14,**
36; DA; DAB; DAC; DAM MST
See also AW; DA3
Roussel, Raymond 1877-1933 .... **TCLC 20**
See also CA 117
Rovit, Earl (Herbert) 1927- .... **CLC 7**
See also CA 5-8R; CANR 12
Rowe, Elizabeth Singer 1674-1737 ..... **LC 44**
See also DLB 39, 95
Rowe, Nicholas 1674-1718 .... **LC 8**
See also DLB 84
Rowley, Ames Dorrance
See Lovecraft, H(oward) P(hillips)
Rowling, J(oanne) K. 1966(?)- .... **CLC 137**
See also AAYA 34; CA 173; CLR 66; SATA
109
Rowson, Susanna Haswell
1762(?)-1824 .... **NCLC 5, 69**
See also DLB 37, 200
Roy, Arundhati 1960(?)- .... **CLC 109**
See also CA 163; CANR 90; DLBY 97
Roy, Gabrielle 1909-1983 .... **CLC 10, 14;**
DAB; DAC; DAM MST
See also CA 53-56; 110; CANR 5, 61; CCA
1; DLB 68; MTCW 1; SATA 104
Royko, Mike 1932-1997 .... **CLC 109**
See also CA 89-92; 157; CANR 26
Rozanov, Vassili 1856-1919 .... **TCLC 104**
Rozewicz, Tadeusz 1921- ..... **CLC 9, 23, 139;**
DAM POET
See also CA 108; CANR 36, 66; CWW 2;
DA3; DLB 232; MTCW 1, 2
Ruark, Gibbons 1941- .... **CLC 3**
See also CA 33-36R; CAAS 23; CANR 14,
31, 57; DLB 120
Rubens, Bernice (Ruth) 1923- .... **CLC 19, 31**
See also CA 25-28R; CANR 33, 65; DLB
14, 207; MTCW 1
Rubin, Harold
See Robbins, Harold
Rudkin, (James) David 1936- .... **CLC 14**
See also CA 89-92; DLB 13
Rudnik, Raphael 1933- .... **CLC 7**
See also CA 29-32R
Ruffian, M.
See Hasek, Jaroslav (Matej Frantisek)
Ruiz, Jose Martinez CLC 11
See also Martinez Ruiz, Jose
Rukeyser, Muriel 1913-1980 . **CLC 6, 10, 15,**
27; DAM POET; PC 12
See also AMWS 6; CA 5-8R; 93-96; CANR
26, 60; DA3; DLB 48; GLL 2; MTCW 1,
2; SATA-Obit 22
Rule, Jane (Vance) 1931- .... **CLC 27**
See also CA 25-28R; CAAS 18; CANR 12,
87; DLB 60
Rulfo, Juan 1918-1986 ...... **CLC 8, 80; DAM**
MULT; HLC 2; SSC 25
See also CA 85-88; 118; CANR 26; DLB
113; HW 1, 2; MTCW 1, 2
Rumi, Jalal al-Din 1207-1273 .... **CMLC 20**
Runeberg, Johan 1804-1877 .... **NCLC 41**
Runyon, (Alfred) Damon
1884(?)-1946 .... **TCLC 10**
See also CA 107; 165; DLB 11, 86, 171;
MTCW 2
Rush, Norman 1933- .... **CLC 44**
See also CA 121; 126; INT 126
Rushdie, (Ahmed) Salman 1947- .... **CLC 23,**
31, 55, 100; DAB; DAC; DAM MST,
NOV, POP
See also AW; BEST 89:3; BRWS 4; CA
108; 111; CANR 33, 56; DA3; DLB 194;
INT 111; MTCW 1, 2
Rushforth, Peter (Scott) 1945- .... **CLC 19**
See also CA 101

Ruskin, John 1819-1900 .... **TCLC 63**
See also CA 114; 129; CDBLB 1832-1890;
DLB 55, 163, 190; SATA 24
Russ, Joanna 1937- .... **CLC 15**
See also CA 5-28R; CANR 11, 31, 65; DLB
8; GLL 1; MTCW 1; SCFW 2
Russell, George William 1867-1935
See Baker, Jean H.
See also CA 104; 153; CDBLB 1890-1914;
DAM POET
Russell, (Henry) Ken(neth Alfred)
1927- .... **CLC 16**
See also CA 105
Russell, William Martin 1947- .... **CLC 60**
See also CA 164; DLB 233
Rutherford, Mark TCLC 25
See also White, William Hale
See also DLB 18
Ruyslinck, Ward CLC 14
See also Belser, Reimond Karel Maria de
Ryan, Cornelius (John) 1920-1974 ..... **CLC 7**
See also CA 69-72; 53-56; CANR 38
Ryan, Michael 1946- .... **CLC 65**
See also CA 49-52; DLBY 82
Ryan, Tim
See Dent, Lester
Rybakov, Anatoli (Naumovich)
1911-1998 .... **CLC 23, 53**
See also CA 126; 135; 172; SATA 79;
SATA-Obit 108
Ryder, Jonathan
See Ludlum, Robert
Ryga, George 1932-1987 .... **CLC 14; DAC;**
DAM MST
See also CA 101; 124; CANR 43, 90; CCA
1; DLB 60
Ryunosuke, Akutagawa
See Akutagawa Ryunosuke
S. H.
See Hartmann, Sadakichi
S. S.
See Sassoon, Siegfried (Lorraine)
Saba, Umberto 1883-1957 .... **TCLC 33**
See also CA 144; CANR 79; DLB 114
Sabatini, Rafael 1875-1950 .... **TCLC 47**
See also CA 162
Sabato, Ernesto (R.) 1911- .... **CLC 10, 23;**
DAM MULT; HLC 2
See also CA 97-100; CANR 32, 65; DLB
145; HW 1, 2; MTCW 1
Sa-Carniero, Mario de 1890-1916 . **TCLC 83**
Sacastru, Martin
See Bioy Casares, Adolfo
See also CWW 2
Sacastru, Martin
See Bioy Casares, Adolfo
Sacher-Masoch, Leopold von
1836(?)-1895 .... **NCLC 31**
Sachs, Marilyn (Stickle) 1927- .... **CLC 35**
See also AAYA 2; CA 17-20R; CANR 13,
47; CLR 2; JRDA; MAICYA; SAAS 2;
SATA 3, 68; SATA-Essay 110
Sachs, Nelly 1891-1970 .... **CLC 14, 98**
See also CA 17-18; 25-28R; CANR 87;
CAP 2; MTCW 2
Sackler, Howard (Oliver)
1929-1982 .... **CLC 14**
See also CA 61-64; 108; CANR 30; DLB 7
Sacks, Oliver (Wolf) 1933- .... **CLC 67**
See also CA 53-56; CANR 28, 50, 76; DA3;
INT CANR-28; MTCW 1, 2
Sadakichi
See Hartmann, Sadakichi
Sade, Donatien Alphonse Francois
1740-1814 .... **NCLC 3, 47**
Sadoff, Ira 1945- .... **CLC 9**
See also CA 53-56; CANR 5, 21; DLB 120

Saetone
 See Camus, Albert
Safire, William 1929- .... **CLC 10**
 See also CA 17-20R; CANR 31, 54, 91
Sagan, Carl (Edward) 1934-1996 .... **CLC 30, 112**
 See also AAYA 2; CA 25-28R; 155; CANR 11, 36, 74; DA3; MTCW 1, 2; SATA 58; SATA-Obit 94
Sagan, Francoise CLC 3, 6, 9, 17, 36
 See also Quoirez, Francoise
 See also CWW 2; DLB 83; MTCW 2
Sahgal, Nayantara (Pandit) 1927- .... **CLC 41**
 See also CA 9-12R; CANR 11, 88
Said, Edward W. 1935- .... **CLC 123**
 See also CA 21-24R; CANR 45, 74; DLB 67; MTCW 2
Saint, H(arry) F. 1941- .... **CLC 50**
 See also CA 127
St. Aubin de Teran, Lisa 1953-
 See Teran, Lisa St. Aubin de
 See also CA 118; 126; INT 126
Saint Birgitta of Sweden c. 1303-1373 .... **CMLC 24**
Sainte-Beuve, Charles Augustin 1804-1869 .... **NCLC 5**
Saint-Exupery, Antoine (Jean Baptiste Marie Roger) de 1900-1944 .... **TCLC 2, 56; DAM NOV**
 See also AW; CA 108; 132; CLR 10; DA3; DLB 72; MAICYA; MTCW 1, 2; SATA 20
St. John, David
 See Hunt, E(verette) Howard, (Jr.)
Saint-John Perse
 See Leger, (Marie-Rene Auguste) Alexis Saint-Leger
Saintsbury, George (Edward Bateman) 1845-1933 .... **TCLC 31**
 See also CA 160; DLB 57, 149
Sait Faik TCLC 23
 See also Abasiyanik, Sait Faik
Saki TCLC 3; SSC 12
 See also Munro, H(ector) H(ugh)
 See also MTCW 2
Sala, George Augustus 1828-1895 . **NCLC 46**
Saladin 1138-1193 .... **CMLC 38**
Salama, Hannu 1936- .... **CLC 18**
Salamanca, J(ack) R(ichard) 1922- .. **CLC 4, 15**
 See also CA 25-28R
Salas, Floyd Francis 1931-
 See also CA 119; CAAS 27; CANR 44, 75, 93; DAM MULT; DLB 82; HLC 2; HW 1, 2; MTCW 2
Sale, J. Kirkpatrick
 See Sale, Kirkpatrick
Sale, Kirkpatrick 1937- .... **CLC 68**
 See also CA 13-16R; CANR 10
Salinas, Luis Omar 1937- ..... **CLC 90; DAM MULT; HLC 2**
 See also CA 131; CANR 81; DLB 82; HW 1, 2
Salinas (y Serrano), Pedro 1891(?)-1951 .... **TCLC 17**
 See also CA 117; DLB 134
Salinger, J(erome) D(avid) 1919- .. **CLC 1, 3, 8, 12, 55, 56, 138; DA; DAB; DAC; DAM MST, NOV, POP; SSC 2, 28**
 See also AAYA 2, 36; CA 5-8R; CANR 39; CDALB 1941-1968; CLR 18; DA3; DLB 2, 102, 173; MAICYA; MTCW 1, 2; SATA 67
Salisbury, John
 See Caute, (John) David
Salter, James 1925- .... **CLC 7, 52, 59**
 See also CA 73-76; DLB 130
Saltus, Edgar (Everton) 1855-1921 . **TCLC 8**
 See also CA 105; DLB 202

Saltykov, Mikhail Evgrafovich 1826-1889 .... **NCLC 16**
 See also DLB 238:
Samarakis, Antonis 1919- .... **CLC 5**
 See also CA 25-28R; CAAS 16; CANR 36
Sanchez, Florencio 1875-1910 .... **TCLC 37**
 See also CA 153; HW 1
Sanchez, Luis Rafael 1936- .... **CLC 23**
 See also CA 128; DLB 145; HW 1
Sanchez, Sonia 1934- .... **CLC 5, 116; BLC 3; DAM MULT; PC 9**
 See also BW 2, 3; CA 33-36R; CANR 24, 49, 74; CLR 18; DA3; DLB 41; DLBD 8; MAICYA; MTCW 1, 2; SATA 22
Sand, George 1804-1876 ..... **NCLC 2, 42, 57; DA; DAB; DAC; DAM MST, NOV**
 See also AW; DA3; DLB 119, 192
Sandburg, Carl (August) 1878-1967 . **CLC 1, 4, 10, 15, 35; DA; DAB; DAC; DAM MST, POET; PC 2**
 See also AAYA 24; CA 5-8R; 25-28R; CANR 35; CDALB 1865-1917; CLR 67; DA3; DLB 17, 54; MAICYA; MTCW 1, 2; SATA 8
Sandburg, Charles
 See Sandburg, Carl (August)
Sandburg, Charles A.
 See Sandburg, Carl (August)
Sanders, (James) Ed(ward) 1939- ... **CLC 53; DAM POET**
 See also CA 13-16R; CAAS 21; CANR 13, 44, 78; DLB 16
Sanders, Lawrence 1920-1998 .... **CLC 41; DAM POP**
 See also BEST 89:4; CA 81-84; 165; CANR 33, 62; DA3; MTCW 1
Sanders, Noah
 See Blount, Roy (Alton), Jr.
Sanders, Winston P.
 See Anderson, Poul (William)
Sandoz, Mari(e Susette) 1900-1966 .. **CLC 28**
 See also CA 1-4R; 25-28R; CANR 17, 64; DLB 9, 212; MTCW 1, 2; SATA 5; TCWW 2
Saner, Reg(inald Anthony) 1931- .... **CLC 9**
 See also CA 65-68
Sankara 788-820 .... **CMLC 32**
Sannazaro, Jacopo 1456(?)-1530 .... **LC 8**
Sansom, William 1912-1976 .... **CLC 2, 6; DAM NOV; SSC 21**
 See also CA 5-8R; 65-68; CANR 42; DLB 139; MTCW 1
Santayana, George 1863-1952 .... **TCLC 40**
 See also CA 115; DLB 54, 71; DLBD 13
Santiago, Danny CLC 33
 See also James, Daniel (Lewis)
 See also DLB 122
Santmyer, Helen Hoover 1895-1986 . **CLC 33**
 See also CA 1-4R; 118; CANR 15, 33; DLBY 84; MTCW 1
Santoka, Taneda 1882-1940 .... **TCLC 72**
Santos, Bienvenido N(uqui) 1911-1996 .... **CLC 22; DAM MULT**
 See also CA 101; 151; CANR 19, 46
Sapper TCLC 44
 See also McNeile, Herman Cyril
Sapphire
 See Sapphire, Brenda
Sapphire, Brenda 1950- .... **CLC 99**
Sappho fl. 6256th cent. B.C.-570 .... **CMLC 3; DAM POET; PC 5**
 See also DA3; DLB 176
Saramago, Jose 1922- ..... **CLC 119; HLCS 1**
 See also CA 153
Sarduy, Severo 1937-1993 .... **CLC 6, 97; HLCS 1**
 See also CA 89-92; 142; CANR 58, 81; CWW 2; DLB 113; HW 1, 2

Sargeson, Frank 1903-1982 .... **CLC 31**
 See also CA 25-28R; 106; CANR 38, 79; GLL 2
Sarmiento, Domingo Faustino 1811-1888
 See also HLCS 2
Sarmiento, Felix Ruben Garcia
 See Dario, Ruben
Saro-Wiwa, Ken(ule Beeson) 1941-1995 .... **CLC 114**
 See also BW 2; CA 142; 150; CANR 60; DLB 157
Saroyan, William 1908-1981 ... **CLC 1, 8, 10, 29, 34, 56; DA; DAB; DAC; DAM DRAM, MST, NOV; SSC 21**
 See also AW; CA 5-8R; 103; CANR 30; CDALBS; DA3; DLB 7, 9, 86; DLBY 81; MTCW 1, 2; SATA 23; SATA-Obit 24
Sarraute, Nathalie 1900-1999 .... **CLC 1, 2, 4, 8, 10, 31, 80**
 See also CA 9-12R; 187; CANR 23, 66; CWW 2; DLB 83; MTCW 1, 2
Sarton, (Eleanor) May 1912-1995 ..... **CLC 4, 14, 49, 91; DAM POET**
 See also CA 1-4R; 149; CANR 1, 34, 55; DLB 48; DLBY 81; INT CANR-34; MTCW 1, 2; SATA 36; SATA-Obit 86
Sartre, Jean-Paul 1905-1980 . **CLC 1, 4, 7, 9, 13, 18, 24, 44, 50, 52; DA; DAB; DAC; DAM DRAM, MST, NOV; DC 3; SSC 32**
 See also AW; CA 9-12R; 97-100; CANR 21; DA3; DLB 72; MTCW 1, 2
Sassoon, Siegfried (Lorraine) 1886-1967 .... **CLC 36, 130; DAB; DAM MST, NOV, POET; PC 12**
 See also CA 104; 25-28R; CANR 36; DLB 20, 191; DLBD 18; MTCW 1, 2
Satterfield, Charles
 See Pohl, Frederik
Satyremont
 See Peret, Benjamin
Saul, John (W. III) 1942- ...... **CLC 46; DAM NOV, POP**
 See also AAYA 10; BEST 90:4; CA 81-84; CANR 16, 40, 81; SATA 98
Saunders, Caleb
 See Heinlein, Robert A(nson)
Saura (Atares), Carlos 1932-1998 .... **CLC 20**
 See also CA 114; 131; CANR 79; HW 1
Sauser-Hall, Frederic 1887-1961 ...... **CLC 18**
 See also Cendrars, Blaise
 See also CA 102; 93-96; CANR 36, 62; MTCW 1
Saussure, Ferdinand de 1857-1913 .... **TCLC 49**
Savage, Catharine
 See Brosman, Catharine Savage
Savage, Thomas 1915- .... **CLC 40**
 See also CA 126; 132; CAAS 15; INT 132; TCWW 2
Savan, Glenn 19(?)- .... **CLC 50**
Sayers, Dorothy L(eigh) 1893-1957 .... **TCLC 2, 15; DAM POP**
 See also BRWS 3; CA 104; 119; CANR 60; CDBLB 1914-1945; DLB 10, 36, 77, 100; MTCW 1, 2
Sayers, Valerie 1952- .... **CLC 50, 122**
 See also CA 134; CANR 61
Sayles, John (Thomas) 1950- . **CLC 7, 10, 14**
 See also CA 57-60; CANR 41, 84; DLB 44
Scammell, Michael 1935- .... **CLC 34**
 See also CA 156
Scannell, Vernon 1922- .... **CLC 49**
 See also CA 5-8R; CANR 8, 24, 57; DLB 27; SATA 59
Scarlett, Susan
 See Streatfeild, (Mary) Noel
Scarron 1847-1910
 See Mikszath, Kalman

Schaeffer, Susan Fromberg 1941- ..... **CLC 6, 11, 22**
  See also CA 49-52; CANR 18, 65; DLB 28; MTCW 1, 2; SATA 22

Schary, Jill
  See Robinson, Jill

Schell, Jonathan 1943- .... **CLC 35**
  See also CA 73-76; CANR 12

Schelling, Friedrich Wilhelm Joseph von
  1775-1854 .... **NCLC 30**
  See also DLB 90

Schendel, Arthur van 1874-1946 ... **TCLC 56**

Scherer, Jean-Marie Maurice 1920-
  See Rohmer, Eric
  See also CA 110

Schevill, James (Erwin) 1920- .... **CLC 7**
  See also CA 5-8R; CAAS 12

Schiller, Friedrich 1759-1805 . **NCLC 39, 69; DAM DRAM; DC 12**
  See also DLB 94

Schisgal, Murray (Joseph) 1926- .... **CLC 6**
  See also CA 21-24R; CANR 48, 86

Schlee, Ann 1934- .... **CLC 35**
  See also CA 101; CANR 29, 88; SATA 44; SATA-Brief 36

Schlegel, August Wilhelm von
  1767-1845 .... **NCLC 15**
  See also DLB 94

Schlegel, Friedrich 1772-1829 .... **NCLC 45**
  See also DLB 90

Schlegel, Johann Elias (von)
  1719(?)-1749 .... **LC 5**

Schlesinger, Arthur M(eier), Jr.
  1917- .... **CLC 84**
  See also AITN 1; CA 1-4R; CANR 1, 28, 58; DLB 17; INT CANR-28; MTCW 1, 2; SATA 61

Schmidt, Arno (Otto) 1914-1979 ...... **CLC 56**
  See also CA 128; 109; DLB 69

Schmitz, Aron Hector 1861-1928
  See Svevo, Italo
  See also CA 104; 122; MTCW 1

Schnackenberg, Gjertrud 1953- .... **CLC 40**
  See also CA 116; DLB 120

Schneider, Leonard Alfred 1925-1966
  See Bruce, Lenny
  See also CA 89-92

Schnitzler, Arthur 1862-1931 . **TCLC 4; SSC 15**
  See also CA 104; DLB 81, 118

Schoenberg, Arnold Franz Walter
  1874-1951 .... **TCLC 75**
  See also CA 109; 188

Schonberg, Arnold
  See Schoenberg, Arnold Franz Walter

Schopenhauer, Arthur 1788-1860 .. **NCLC 51**
  See also DLB 90

Schor, Sandra (M.) 1932(?)-1990 ..... **CLC 65**
  See also CA 132

Schorer, Mark 1908-1977 .... **CLC 9**
  See also CA 5-8R; 73-76; CANR 7; DLB 103

Schrader, Paul (Joseph) 1946- .... **CLC 26**
  See also CA 37-40R; CANR 41; DLB 44

Schreiner, Olive (Emilie Albertina)
  1855-1920 .... **TCLC 9**
  See also BRWS 2; CA 105; 154; DLB 18, 156, 190, 225

Schulberg, Budd (Wilson) 1914- .. **CLC 7, 48**
  See also CA 25-28R; CANR 19, 87; DLB 6, 26, 28; DLBY 81

Schulz, Bruno 1892-1942 .. **TCLC 5, 51; SSC 13**
  See also CA 115; 123; CANR 86; MTCW 2

Schulz, Charles M(onroe)
  1922-2000 .... **CLC 12**
  See also CA 9-12R; 187; CANR 6; INT CANR-6; SATA 10; SATA-Obit 118

Schumacher, E(rnst) F(riedrich)
  1911-1977 .... **CLC 80**
  See also CA 81-84; 73-76; CANR 34, 85

Schuyler, James Marcus 1923-1991 .. **CLC 5, 23; DAM POET**
  See also CA 101; 134; DLB 5, 169; INT 101

Schwartz, Delmore (David)
  1913-1966 ... **CLC 2, 4, 10, 45, 87; PC 8**
  See also AMWS 2; CA 17-18; 25-28R; CANR 35; CAP 2; DLB 28, 48; MTCW 1, 2

Schwartz, Ernst
  See Ozu, Yasujiro

Schwartz, John Burnham 1965- .... **CLC 59**
  See also CA 132

Schwartz, Lynne Sharon 1939- .... **CLC 31**
  See also CA 103; CANR 44, 89; MTCW 2

Schwartz, Muriel A.
  See Eliot, T(homas) S(tearns)

Schwarz-Bart, Andre 1928- .... **CLC 2, 4**
  See also CA 89-92

Schwarz-Bart, Simone 1938- . **CLC 7; BLCS**
  See also BW 2; CA 97-100

Schwitters, Kurt (Hermann Edward Karl Julius) 1887-1948 .... **TCLC 95**
  See also CA 158

Schwob, Marcel (Mayer Andre)
  1867-1905 .... **TCLC 20**
  See also CA 117; 168; DLB 123

Sciascia, Leonardo 1921-1989 .. **CLC 8, 9, 41**
  See also CA 85-88; 130; CANR 35; DLB 177; MTCW 1

Scoppettone, Sandra 1936- .... **CLC 26**
  See also Early, Jack
  See also AAYA 11; AW; CA 5-8R; CANR 41, 73; GLL 1; SATA 9, 92

Scorsese, Martin 1942- .... **CLC 20, 89**
  See also CA 110; 114; CANR 46, 85

Scotland, Jay
  See Jakes, John (William)

Scott, Duncan Campbell
  1862-1947 .... **TCLC 6; DAC**
  See also CA 104; 153; DLB 92

Scott, Evelyn 1893-1963 .... **CLC 43**
  See also CA 104; 112; CANR 64; DLB 9, 48

Scott, F(rancis) R(eginald)
  1899-1985 .... **CLC 22**
  See also CA 101; 114; CANR 87; DLB 88; INT 101

Scott, Frank
  See Scott, F(rancis) R(eginald)

Scott, Joanna 1960- .... **CLC 50**
  See also CA 126; CANR 53, 92

Scott, Paul (Mark) 1920-1978 ...... **CLC 9, 60**
  See also BRWS 1; CA 81-84; 77-80; CANR 33; DLB 14, 207; MTCW 1

Scott, Sarah 1723-1795 .... **LC 44**
  See also DLB 39

Scott, Walter 1771-1832 . **NCLC 15, 69; DA; DAB; DAC; DAM MST, NOV, POET; PC 13; SSC 32**
  See also AAYA 22; AW; CDBLB 1789-1832; DLB 93, 107, 116, 144, 159

Scribe, (Augustin) Eugene
  1791-1861 ..... **NCLC 16; DAM DRAM; DC 5**
  See also DLB 192

Scrum, R.
  See Crumb, R(obert)

Scudery, Madeleine de 1607-1701 .. **LC 2, 58**

Scum
  See Crumb, R(obert)

Scumbag, Little Bobby
  See Crumb, R(obert)

Seabrook, John
  See Hubbard, L(afayette) Ron(ald)

Sealy, I(rwin) Allan 1951- .... **CLC 55**
  See also CA 136

Search, Alexander
  See Pessoa, Fernando (Antonio Nogueira)

Sebastian, Lee
  See Silverberg, Robert

Sebastian Owl
  See Thompson, Hunter S(tockton)

Sebestyen, Ouida 1924- .... **CLC 30**
  See also AAYA 8; AW; CA 107; CANR 40; CLR 17; JRDA; MAICYA; SAAS 10; SATA 39

Secundus, H. Scriblerus
  See Fielding, Henry

Sedges, John
  See Buck, Pearl S(ydenstricker)

Sedgwick, Catharine Maria
  1789-1867 .... **NCLC 19**
  See also DLB 1, 74, 239

Seelye, John (Douglas) 1931- .... **CLC 7**
  See also CA 97-100; CANR 70; INT 97-100; TCWW 2

Seferiades, Giorgos Stylianou 1900-1971
  See Seferis, George
  See also CA 5-8R; 33-36R; CANR 5, 36; MTCW 1

Seferis, George CLC 5, 11
  See also Seferiades, Giorgos Stylianou

Segal, Erich (Wolf) 1937- . **CLC 3, 10; DAM POP**
  See also BEST 89:1; CA 25-28R; CANR 20, 36, 65; DLBY 86; INT CANR-20; MTCW 1

Seger, Bob 1945- .... **CLC 35**

Seghers, Anna CLC 7
  See also Radvanyi, Netty
  See also DLB 69

Seidel, Frederick (Lewis) 1936- .... **CLC 18**
  See also CA 13-16R; CANR 8; DLBY 84

Seifert, Jaroslav 1901-1986 .. **CLC 34, 44, 93**
  See also CA 127; DLB 215; MTCW 1, 2

Sei Shonagon c. 966-1017(?) .... **CMLC 6**

Sejour, Victor 1817-1874 .... **DC 10**
  See also DLB 50

Sejour Marcou et Ferrand, Juan Victor
  See Sejour, Victor

Selby, Hubert, Jr. 1928- .... **CLC 1, 2, 4, 8; SSC 20**
  See also CA 13-16R; CANR 33, 85; DLB 2, 227

Selzer, Richard 1928- .... **CLC 74**
  See also CA 65-68; CANR 14

Sembene, Ousmane
  See Ousmane, Sembene
  See also CWW 2

Senancour, Etienne Pivert de
  1770-1846 .... **NCLC 16**
  See also DLB 119

Sender, Ramon (Jose) 1902-1982 ...... **CLC 8; DAM MULT; HLC 2**
  See also CA 5-8R; 105; CANR 8; HW 1; MTCW 1

Seneca, Lucius Annaeus c. 4B.C.-c. 65 .... **CMLC 6; DAM DRAM; DC 5**
  See also DLB 211

Senghor, Leopold Sedar 1906- .... **CLC 54, 130; BLC 3; DAM MULT, POET; PC 25**
  See also BW 2; CA 116; 125; CANR 47, 74; MTCW 1, 2

Senna, Danzy 1970- .... **CLC 119**
  See also CA 169

Serling, (Edward) Rod(man)
  1924-1975 .... **CLC 30**
  See also AAYA 14; AITN 1; CA 162; 57-60; DLB 26

Serna, Ramon Gomez de la
  See Gomez de la Serna, Ramon

Serpieres
See Guillevic, (Eugene)

Service, Robert
See Service, Robert W(illiam)
See also DAB; DLB 92

Service, Robert W(illiam)
1874(?)-1958 .... **TCLC 15; DA; DAC; DAM MST, POET**
See also Service, Robert
See also AW; CA 115; 140; CANR 84; SATA 20

Seth, Vikram 1952- .... **CLC 43, 90; DAM MULT**
See also CA 121; 127; CANR 50, 74; DA3; DLB 120; INT 127; MTCW 2

Seton, Cynthia Propper 1926-1982 .. **CLC 27**
See also CA 5-8R; 108; CANR 7

Seton, Ernest (Evan) Thompson
1860-1946 .... **TCLC 31**
See also CA 109, CLR 59; DLB 92; DLBD 13; JRDA; SATA 18

Seton-Thompson, Ernest
See Seton, Ernest (Evan) Thompson

Settle, Mary Lee 1918- .... **CLC 19, 61**
See also CA 89-92; CAAS 1; CANR 44, 87; DLB 6; INT 89-92

Seuphor, Michel
See Arp, Jean

Sevigne, Marie (de Rabutin-Chantal)
Marquise de 1626-1696 .... **LC 11**

Sewall, Samuel 1652-1730 .... **LC 38**
See also DLB 24

Sexton, Anne (Harvey) 1928-1974 ..... **CLC 2, 4, 6, 8, 10, 15, 53, 123; DA; DAB; DAC; DAM MST, POET; PC 2**
See also AMWS 2; AW; CA 1-4R; 53-56; CABS 2; CANR 3, 36; CDALB 1941-1968; DA3; DLB 5, 169; MTCW 1, 2; SATA 10

Shaara, Jeff 1952- .... **CLC 119**
See also CA 163

Shaara, Michael (Joseph, Jr.)
1929-1988 .... **CLC 15; DAM POP**
See also AITN 1; CA 102; 125, CANR 52, 85; DLBY 83

Shackleton, C. C.
See Aldiss, Brian W(ilson)

Shacochis, Bob CLC 39
See also Shacochis, Robert G.

Shacochis, Robert G. 1951-
See Shacochis, Bob
See also CA 119; 124; INT 124

Shaffer, Anthony (Joshua) 1926- ..... **CLC 19; DAM DRAM**
See also CA 110; 116; DLB 13

Shaffer, Peter (Levin) 1926- .. **CLC 5, 14, 18, 37, 60; DAB; DAM DRAM, MST; DC 7**
See also BRWS 1; CA 25-28R; CANR 25, 47, 74; CDBLB 1960 to Present; DA3; DLB 13, 233; MTCW 1, 2

Shakey, Bernard
See Young, Neil

Shalamov, Varlam (Tikhonovich)
1907(?)-1982 .... **CLC 18**
See also CA 129; 105

Shamlu, Ahmad 1925-2000 .... **CLC 10**
See also CWW 2

Shammas, Anton 1951- .... **CLC 55**

Shandling, Arline
See Berriault, Gina

Shange, Ntozake 1948- .... **CLC 8, 25, 38, 74, 126; BLC 3; DAM DRAM, MULT; DC 3**
See also AAYA 9; AW; BW 2; CA 85-88; CABS 3; CANR 27, 48, 74; DA3; DLB 38; MTCW 1, 2

Shanley, John Patrick 1950- .... **CLC 75**
See also CA 128; 133; CANR 83

Shapcott, Thomas W(illiam) 1935- .. **CLC 38**
See also CA 69-72; CANR 49, 83

Shapiro, Jane CLC 76

Shapiro, Karl (Jay) 1913-2000 ...... **CLC 4, 8, 15, 53; PC 25**
See also AMWS 2; CA 1-4R; 188; CAAS 6; CANR 1, 36, 66; DLB 48; MTCW 1, 2

Sharp, William 1855-1905 .... **TCLC 39**
See also CA 160; DLB 156

Sharpe, Thomas Ridley 1928-
See Sharpe, Tom
See also CA 114; 122; CANR 85; DLB 231; INT 122

Sharpe, Tom CLC 36
See also Sharpe, Thomas Ridley
See also DLB 14

Shaw, Bernard
See Shaw, George Bernard
See also BW 1; MTCW 2

Shaw, G. Bernard
See Shaw, George Bernard

Shaw, George Bernard 1856-1950 .. **TCLC 3, 9, 21, 45; DA; DAB; DAC; DAM DRAM, MST**
See also Shaw, Bernard
See also AW; CA 104; 128; CDBLB 1914-1945; DA3; DLB 10, 57, 190; MTCW 1, 2

Shaw, Henry Wheeler 1818-1885 .. **NCLC 15**
See also DLB 11

Shaw, Irwin 1913-1984 .... **CLC 7, 23, 34; DAM DRAM, POP**
See also AITN 1; CA 13-16R; 112; CANR 21; CDALB 1941-1968; DLB 6, 102; DLBY 84; MTCW 1, 21

Shaw, Robert 1927-1978 .... **CLC 5**
See also AITN 1; CA 1-4R; 81-84; CANR 4; DLB 13, 14

Shaw, T. E.
See Lawrence, T(homas) E(dward)

Shawn, Wallace 1943- .... **CLC 41**
See also CA 112

Shea, Lisa 1953- .... **CLC 86**
See also CA 147

Sheed, Wilfrid (John Joseph) 1930- . **CLC 2, 4, 10, 53**
See also CA 65-68; CANR 30, 66; DLB 6; MTCW 1, 2

Sheldon, Alice Hastings Bradley
1915(?)-1987
See Tiptree, James, Jr.
See also CA 108; 122; CANR 34; INT 108; MTCW 1

Sheldon, John
See Bloch, Robert (Albert)

Sheldon, Walter J. 1917-1996
See Queen, Ellery
See also AITN 1; CA 25-28R; CANR 10

Shelley, Mary Wollstonecraft (Godwin)
1797-1851 ..... **NCLC 14, 59; DA; DAB; DAC; DAM MST, NOV**
See also AAYA 20; AW; BRWS 3; CDBLB 1789-1832; DA3; DLB 110, 116, 159, 178; SATA 29

Shelley, Percy Bysshe 1792-1822 .. **NCLC 18, 93; DA; DAB; DAC; DAM MST, POET; PC 14**
See also AW; CDBLB 1789-1832; DA3; DLB 96, 110, 158

Shepard, Jim 1956- .... **CLC 36**
See also CA 137; CANR 59; SATA 90

Shepard, Lucius 1947- .... **CLC 34**
See also CA 128; 141; CANR 81; SCFW 2

Shepard, Sam 1943- .... **CLC 4, 6, 17, 34, 41, 44; DAM DRAM; DC 5**
See also AAYA 1; AMWS 3; CA 69-72; CABS 3; CANR 22; DA3; DLB 7, 212; IDFW 3; MTCW 1, 2

Shepherd, Michael
See Ludlum, Robert

Sherburne, Zoa (Lillian Morin)
1912-1995 .... **CLC 30**
See also AAYA 13; AW; CA 1-4R; 176; CANR 3, 37; MAICYA; SAAS 18; SATA 3

Sheridan, Frances 1724-1766 .... **LC 7**
See also DLB 39, 84

Sheridan, Richard Brinsley
1751-1816 .... **NCLC 5, 91; DA; DAB; DAC; DAM DRAM, MST; DC 1**
See also AW; CDBLB 1660-1789; DLB 89

Sherman, Jonathan Marc CLC 55

Sherman, Martin 1941(?)- .... **CLC 19**
See also CA 116; 123; CANR 86

Sherwin, Judith Johnson
See Johnson, Judith (Emlyn)
See also CANR 85

Sherwood, Frances 1940- .... **CLC 81**
See also CA 146

Sherwood, Robert E(mmet)
1896-1955 .... **TCLC 3; DAM DRAM**
See also CA 104; 153; CANR 86; DLB 7, 26

Shestov, Lev 1866-1938 .... **TCLC 56**

Shevchenko, Taras 1814-1861 .... **NCLC 54**

Shiel, M(atthew) P(hipps)
1865-1947 .... **TCLC 8**
See also Holmes, Gordon
See also CA 106; 160; DLB 153; MTCW 2

Shields, Carol 1935- .... **CLC 91, 113; DAC**
See also AMWS 7; CA 81-84; CANR 51, 74; CCA 1; DA3; MTCW 2

Shields, David 1956- .... **CLC 97**
See also CA 124; CANR 48

Shiga, Naoya 1883-1971 ..... **CLC 33; SSC 23**
See also CA 101; 33-36R; DLB 180

Shikibu, Murasaki c. 978-c. 1014 ... **CMLC 1**

Shilts, Randy 1951-1994 .... **CLC 85**
See also AAYA 19; CA 115; 127; 144; CANR 45; DA3; GLL 1; INT 127; MTCW 2

Shimazaki, Haruki 1872-1943
See Shimazaki Toson
See also CA 105; 134; CANR 84

Shimazaki Toson TCLC 5
See also Shimazaki, Haruki
See also DLB 180

Sholokhov, Mikhail (Aleksandrovich)
1905-1984 .... **CLC 7, 15**
See also CA 101; 112; MTCW 1, 2; SATA-Obit 36

Shone, Patric
See Hanley, James

Shreve, Susan Richards 1939- .... **CLC 23**
See also CA 49-52; CAAS 5; CANR 5, 38, 69; MAICYA; SATA 46, 95; SATA-Brief 41

Shue, Larry 1946-1985 .... **CLC 52; DAM DRAM**
See also CA 145; 117

Shu-Jen, Chou 1881-1936
See Lu Hsun
See also CA 104

Shulman, Alix Kates 1932- .... **CLC 2, 10**
See also CA 29-32R; CANR 43; SATA 7

Shuster, Joe 1914-1992 .... **CLC 21**

Shute, Nevil CLC 30
See also Norway, Nevil Shute
See also MTCW 2

Shuttle, Penelope (Diane) 1947- .... **CLC 7**
See also CA 93-96; CANR 39, 84, 92; DLB 14, 40

Sidney, Mary 1561-1621 .... **LC 19, 39**

Sidney, SirPhilip 1554-1586 . **LC 19, 39; DA; DAB; DAC; DAM MST, POET; PC 32**
See also CDBLB Before 1660; DA3; DLB 167

Siegel, Jerome 1914-1996 .... **CLC 21**
See also CA 116; 169; 151

Siegel, Jerry
See Siegel, Jerome

Sienkiewicz, Henryk (Adam Alexander Pius) 1846-1916 .... **TCLC 3**
See also CA 104; 134; CANR 84

Sierra, Gregorio Martinez
See Martinez Sierra, Gregorio

Sierra, Maria (de la O'LeJarraga) Martinez
See Martinez Sierra, Maria (de la O'LeJarraga)

Sigal, Clancy 1926- .... **CLC 7**
See also CA 1-4R; CANR 85

Sigourney, Lydia Howard (Huntley) 1791-1865 .... **NCLC 21, 87**
See also DLB 1, 42, 73, 239

Sigüenza y Gongora, Carlos de 1645-1700 .... **LC 8; HLCS 2**

Sigurjonsson, Johann 1880-1919 ... **TCLC 27**
See also CA 170

Sikelianos, Angelos 1884-1951 ...... **TCLC 39; PC 29**

Silkin, Jon 1930-1997 .... **CLC 2, 6, 43**
See also CA 5-8R; CAAS 5; CANR 89; DLB 27

Silko, Leslie (Marmon) 1948- .... **CLC 23, 74, 114; DA; DAC; DAM MST, MULT, POP; SSC 37**
See also AAYA 14; AMWS 4; AW; CA 115; 122; CANR 45, 65; DA3; DLB 143, 175; MTCW 2; NNAL

Sillanpaa, Frans Eemil 1888-1964 ... **CLC 19**
See also CA 129; 93-96; MTCW 1

Sillitoe, Alan 1928- ... **CLC 1, 3, 6, 10, 19, 57**
See also AITN 1; BRWS 5; CA 9-12R; CAAS 2; CANR 8, 26, 55; CDBLB 1960 to Present; DLB 14, 139; MTCW 1, 2; SATA 61

Silone, Ignazio 1900-1978 .... **CLC 4**
See also CA 25-28; 81-84; CANR 34; CAP 2; MTCW 1

Silone, Ignazione
See Silone, Ignazio

Silver, Joan Micklin 1935- .... **CLC 20**
See also CA 114; 121; INT 121

Silver, Nicholas
See Faust, Frederick (Schiller)
See also TCWW 2

Silverberg, Robert 1935- .... **CLC 7, 140; DAM POP**
See also AAYA 24; CA 1-4R, 186; CAAE 186; CAAS 3; CANR 1, 20, 36, 85; CLR 59; DLB 8; INT CANR-20; MAICYA; MTCW 1, 2; SATA 13, 91; SATA-Essay 104; SCFW 2

Silverstein, Alvin 1933- .... **CLC 17**
See also CA 49-52; CANR 2; CLR 25; JRDA; MAICYA; SATA 8, 69

Silverstein, Virginia B(arbara Opshelor) 1937- .... **CLC 17**
See also CA 49-52; CANR 2; CLR 25; JRDA; MAICYA; SATA 8, 69

Sim, Georges
See Simenon, Georges (Jacques Christian)

Simak, Clifford D(onald) 1904-1988 . **CLC 1, 55**
See also CA 1-4R; 125; CANR 1, 35; DLB 8; MTCW 1; SATA-Obit 56

Simenon, Georges (Jacques Christian) 1903-1989 .... **CLC 1, 2, 3, 8, 18, 47; DAM POP**
See also CA 85-88; 129; CANR 35; DA3; DLB 72; DLBY 89; MTCW 1, 2

Simic, Charles 1938- .... **CLC 6, 9, 22, 49, 68, 130; DAM POET**
See also CA 29-32R; CAAS 4; CANR 12, 33, 52, 61, 96; DA3; DLB 105; MTCW 2

Simmel, Georg 1858-1918 .... **TCLC 64**
See also CA 157

Simmons, Charles (Paul) 1924- .... **CLC 57**
See also CA 89-92; INT 89-92

Simmons, Dan 1948- .... **CLC 44; DAM POP**
See also AAYA 16; CA 138; CANR 53, 81

Simmons, James (Stewart Alexander) 1933- .... **CLC 43**
See also CA 105; CAAS 21; DLB 40

Simms, William Gilmore 1806-1870 .... **NCLC 3**
See also DLB 3, 30, 59, 73

Simon, Carly 1945- .... **CLC 26**
See also CA 105

Simon, Claude 1913- .... **CLC 4, 9, 15, 39; DAM NOV**
See also CA 89-92; CANR 33; DLB 83; MTCW 1

Simon, (Marvin) Neil 1927- ... **CLC 6, 11, 31, 39, 70; DAM DRAM; DC 14**
See also AAYA 32; AITN 1; AMWS 4; CA 21-24R; CANR 26, 54, 87; DA3; DLB 7; MTCW 1, 2

Simon, Paul (Frederick) 1941(?)- ..... **CLC 17**
See also CA 116; 153

Simonon, Paul 1956(?)- .... **CLC 30**

Simpson, Harriette
See Arnow, Harriette (Louisa) Simpson

Simpson, Louis (Aston Marantz) 1923- ...... **CLC 4, 7, 9, 32; DAM POET**
See also CA 1-4R; CAAS 4; CANR 1, 61; DLB 5; MTCW 1, 2

Simpson, Mona (Elizabeth) 1957- .... **CLC 44**
See also CA 122; 135; CANR 68

Simpson, N(orman) F(rederick) 1919- .... **CLC 29**
See also CA 13-16R; DLB 13

Sinclair, Andrew (Annandale) 1935- . **CLC 2, 14**
See also CA 9-12R; CAAS 5; CANR 14, 38, 91; DLB 14; MTCW 1

Sinclair, Emil
See Hesse, Hermann

Sinclair, Iain 1943- .... **CLC 76**
See also CA 132; CANR 81

Sinclair, Iain MacGregor
See Sinclair, Iain

Sinclair, Irene
See Griffith, D(avid Lewelyn) W(ark)

Sinclair, Mary Amelia St. Clair 1865(?)-1946
See Sinclair, May
See also CA 104

Sinclair, May TCLC 3, 11
See also Sinclair, Mary Amelia St. Clair
See also CA 166; DLB 36, 135

Sinclair, Roy
See Griffith, D(avid Lewelyn) W(ark)

Sinclair, Upton (Beall) 1878-1968 ..... **CLC 1, 11, 15, 63; DA; DAB; DAC; DAM MST, NOV**
See also AMWS 5; AW; CA 5-8R; 25-28R; CANR 7; CDALB 1929-1941; DA3; DLB 9; INT CANR-7; MTCW 1, 2; SATA 9

Singer, Isaac
See Singer, Isaac Bashevis

Singer, Isaac Bashevis 1904-1991 .. **CLC 1, 3, 6, 9, 11, 15, 23, 38, 69, 111; DA; DAB; DAC; DAM MST, NOV; SSC 3**
See also AAYA 32; AITN 1, 2; AW; CA 1-4R; 134; CANR 1, 39; CDALB 1941-1968; CLR 1; DA3; DLB 6, 28, 52; DLBY 91; JRDA; MAICYA; MTCW 1, 2; SATA 3, 27; SATA-Obit 68

Singer, Israel Joshua 1893-1944 .... **TCLC 33**
See also CA 169

Singh, Khushwant 1915- .... **CLC 11**
See also CA 9-12R; CAAS 9; CANR 6, 84

Singleton, Ann
See Benedict, Ruth (Fulton)

Sinjohn, John
See Galsworthy, John

Sinyavsky, Andrei (Donatevich) 1925-1997 .... **CLC 8**
See also Tertz, Abram
See also CA 85-88; 159

Sirin, V.
See Nabokov, Vladimir (Vladimirovich)

Sissman, L(ouis) E(dward) 1928-1976 .... **CLC 9, 18**
See also CA 21-24R; 65-68; CANR 13; DLB 5

Sisson, C(harles) H(ubert) 1914- .... **CLC 8**
See also CA 1-4R; CAAS 3; CANR 3, 48, 84; DLB 27

Sitwell, DameEdith 1887-1964 ...... **CLC 2, 9, 67; DAM POET; PC 3**
See also CA 9-12R; CANR 35; CDBLB 1945-1960; DLB 20; MTCW 1, 2

Siwaarmill, H. P.
See Sharp, William

Sjoewall, Maj 1935- .... **CLC 7**
See also Sjowall, Maj
See also CA 65-68; CANR 73

Sjowall, Maj
See Sjoewall, Maj

Skelton, John 1460-1529 .... **PC 25**

Skelton, Robin 1925-1997 .... **CLC 13**
See also Zuk, Georges
See also AITN 2; CA 5-8R; 160; CAAS 5; CANR 28, 89; CCA 1; DLB 27, 53

Skolimowski, Jerzy 1938- .... **CLC 20**
See also CA 128

Skram, Amalie (Bertha) 1847-1905 .... **TCLC 25**
See also CA 165

Skvorecky, Josef (Vaclav) 1924- ...... **CLC 15, 39, 69; DAC; DAM NOV**
See also CA 61-64; CAAS 1; CANR 10, 34, 63; DA3; DLB 232; MTCW 1, 2

Slade, Bernard CLC 11, 46
See also Newbound, Bernard Slade
See also CAAS 9; CCA 1; DLB 53

Slaughter, Carolyn 1946- .... **CLC 56**
See also CA 85-88; CANR 85

Slaughter, Frank G(ill) 1908- .... **CLC 29**
See also AITN 2; CA 5-8R; CANR 5, 85; INT CANR-5

Slavitt, David R(ytman) 1935- ..... **CLC 5, 14**
See also CA 21-24R; CAAS 3; CANR 41, 83; DLB 5, 6

Slesinger, Tess 1905-1945 .... **TCLC 10**
See also CA 107; DLB 102

Slessor, Kenneth 1901-1971 .... **CLC 14**
See also CA 102; 89-92

Slowacki, Juliusz 1809-1849 .... **NCLC 15**

Smart, Christopher 1722-1771 .. **LC 3; DAM POET; PC 13**
See also DLB 109

Smart, Elizabeth 1913-1986 .... **CLC 54**
See also CA 81-84; 118; DLB 88

Smiley, Jane (Graves) 1949- ...... **CLC 53, 76; DAM POP**
See also AMWS 6; CA 104; CANR 30, 50, 74, 96; DA3; DLB 227, 234; INT CANR-30

Smith, A(rthur) J(ames) M(arshall) 1902-1980 .... **CLC 15; DAC**
See also CA 1-4R; 102; CANR 4; DLB 88

Smith, Adam 1723-1790 .... **LC 36**
See also DLB 104

Smith, Alexander 1829-1867 .... **NCLC 59**
See also DLB 32, 55

Smith, Anna Deavere 1950- .... **CLC 86**
 See also CA 133
Smith, Betty (Wehner) 1896-1972 .... **CLC 19**
 See also CA 5-8R; 33-36R; DLBY 82;
 SATA 6
Smith, Charlotte (Turner)
 1749-1806 .... **NCLC 23**
 See also DLB 39, 109
Smith, Clark Ashton 1893-1961 .... **CLC 43**
 See also CA 143; CANR 81; MTCW 2
Smith, Dave **CLC 22, 42**
 See also Smith, David (Jeddie)
 See also CAAS 7; DLB 5
Smith, David (Jeddie) 1942-
 See Smith, Dave
 See also CA 49-52; CANR 1, 59; DAM
 POET
Smith, Florence Margaret 1902-1971
 See Smith, Stevie
 See also CA 17-18; 29-32R; CANR 35;
 CAP 2; DAM POET; MTCW 1, 2
Smith, Iain Crichton 1928-1998 ...... **CLC 64**
 See also CA 21-24R; 171; DLB 40, 139
Smith, John 1580(?)-1631 .... **LC 9**
 See also DLB 24, 30
Smith, Johnston
 See Crane, Stephen (Townley)
Smith, Joseph, Jr. 1805-1844 .... **NCLC 53**
Smith, Lee 1944- .... **CLC 25, 73**
 See also CA 114; 119; CANR 46; DLB 143;
 DLBY 83; INT 119
Smith, Martin
 See Smith, Martin Cruz
Smith, Martin Cruz 1942- .... **CLC 25; DAM
 MULT, POP**
 See also BEST 89:4; CA 85-88; CANR 6,
 23, 43, 65; INT CANR-23; MTCW 2;
 NNAL
Smith, Mary-Ann Tirone 1944- .... **CLC 39**
 See also CA 118; 136
Smith, Patti 1946- .... **CLC 12**
 See also CA 93-96; CANR 63
Smith, Pauline (Urmson)
 1882-1959 .... **TCLC 25**
 See also DLB 225
Smith, Rosamond
 See Oates, Joyce Carol
Smith, Sheila Kaye
 See Kaye-Smith, Sheila
Smith, Stevie **CLC 3, 8, 25, 44; PC 12**
 See also Smith, Florence Margaret
 See also BRWS 2; DLB 20; MTCW 2
Smith, Wilbur (Addison) 1933- .... **CLC 33**
 See also CA 13-16R; CANR 7, 46, 66;
 MTCW 1, 2
Smith, William Jay 1918- .... **CLC 6**
 See also CA 5-8R; CANR 44; DLB 5; MAI-
 CYA; SAAS 22; SATA 2, 68
Smith, Woodrow Wilson
 See Kuttner, Henry
Smolenskin, Peretz 1842-1885 .... **NCLC 30**
Smollett, Tobias (George) 1721-1771 ... **LC 2,
 46**
 See also CDBLB 1660-1789; DLB 39, 104
Snodgrass, W(illiam) D(e Witt)
 1926- .... **CLC 2, 6, 10, 18, 68; DAM
 POET**
 See also CA 1-4R; CANR 6, 36, 65, 85;
 DLB 5; MTCW 1, 2
Snow, C(harles) P(ercy) 1905-1980 ... **CLC 1,
 4, 6, 9, 13, 19; DAM NOV**
 See also CA 5-8R; 101; CANR 28; CDBLB
 1945-1960; DLB 15, 77; DLBD 17;
 MTCW 1, 2
Snow, Frances Compton
 See Adams, Henry (Brooks)

Snyder, Gary (Sherman) 1930- . **CLC 1, 2, 5,
 9, 32, 120; DAM POET; PC 21**
 See also CA 17-20R; CANR 30, 60; DA3;
 DLB 5, 16, 165, 212; MTCW 2
Snyder, Zilpha Keatley 1927- .... **CLC 17**
 See also AAYA 15; AW; CA 9-12R; CANR
 38; CLR 31; JRDA; MAICYA; SAAS 2;
 SATA 1, 28, 75, 110; SATA-Essay 112
Soares, Bernardo
 See Pessoa, Fernando (Antonio Nogueira)
Sobh, A.
 See Shamlu, Ahmad
Sobol, Joshua **CLC 60**
 See also CWW 2
Socrates 470B.C.-399B.C. .... **CMLC 27**
Soderberg, Hjalmar 1869-1941 ...... **TCLC 39**
Södergran, Edith (Irene)
 See Soedergran, Edith (Irene)
Soedergran, Edith (Irene)
 1892-1923 .... **TCLC 31**
Softly, Edgar
 See Lovecraft, H(oward) P(hillips)
Softly, Edward
 See Lovecraft, H(oward) P(hillips)
Sokolov, Raymond 1941- .... **CLC 7**
 See also CA 85-88
Solo, Jay
 See Ellison, Harlan (Jay)
Sologub, Fyodor **TCLC 9**
 See also Teternikov, Fyodor Kuzmich
Solomons, Ikey Esquir
 See Thackeray, William Makepeace
Solomos, Dionysios 1798-1857 .... **NCLC 15**
Solwoska, Mara
 See French, Marilyn
Solzhenitsyn, Aleksandr I(sayevich)
 1918- .. **CLC 1, 2, 4, 7, 9, 10, 18, 26, 34,
 78, 134; DA; DAB; DAC; DAM MST,
 NOV; SSC 32**
 See also AITN 1; AW; CA 69-72; CANR
 40, 65; DA3; MTCW 1, 2
Somers, Jane
 See Lessing, Doris (May)
Somerville, Edith 1858-1949 .... **TCLC 51**
 See also DLB 135
Somerville & Ross
 See Martin, Violet Florence; Somerville,
 Edith
Sommer, Scott 1951- .... **CLC 25**
 See also CA 106
Sondheim, Stephen (Joshua) 1930- . **CLC 30,
 39; DAM DRAM**
 See also AAYA 11; CA 103; CANR 47, 67
Song, Cathy 1955- .... **PC 21**
 See also CA 154; DLB 169
Sontag, Susan 1933- .... **CLC 1, 2, 10, 13, 31,
 105; DAM POP**
 See also AMWS 3; CA 17-20R; CANR 25,
 51, 74; DA3; DLB 2, 67; MTCW 1, 2
Sophocles 496(?)B.C.-406(?)B.C. .... **CMLC 2;
 DA; DAB; DAC; DAM DRAM, MST;
 DC 1**
 See also AW; DA3; DLB 176
Sordello 1189-1269 .... **CMLC 15**
Sorel, Georges 1847-1922 .... **TCLC 91**
 See also CA 118; 188
Sorel, Julia
 See Drexler, Rosalyn
Sorrentino, Gilbert 1929- .. **CLC 3, 7, 14, 22,
 40**
 See also CA 77-80; CANR 14, 33; DLB 5,
 173; DLBY 80; INT CANR-14
Soto, Gary 1952- .... **CLC 32, 80; DAM
 MULT; HLC 2; PC 28**
 See also AAYA 10, 37; AW; CA 119; 125;
 CANR 50, 74; CLR 38; DLB 82; HW 1,
 2; INT 125; JRDA; MTCW 2; SATA 80,
 120

Soupault, Philippe 1897-1990 .... **CLC 68**
 See also CA 116; 147; 131
Souster, (Holmes) Raymond 1921- .... **CLC 5,
 14; DAC; DAM POET**
 See also CA 13-16R; CAAS 14; CANR 13,
 29, 53; DA3; DLB 88; SATA 63
Southern, Terry 1924(?)-1995 .... **CLC 7**
 See also CA 1-4R; 150; CANR 1, 55; DLB
 2; IDFW 3
Southey, Robert 1774-1843 .... **NCLC 8, 97**
 See also DLB 93, 107, 142; SATA 54
Southworth, Emma Dorothy Eliza Nevitte
 1819-1899 .... **NCLC 26**
 See also DLB 239
Souza, Ernest
 See Scott, Evelyn
Soyinka, Wole 1934- .... **CLC 3, 5, 14, 36, 44;
 BLC 3; DA; DAB; DAC; DAM
 DRAM, MST, MULT; DC 2**
 See also AW; BW 2, 3; CA 13-16R; CANR
 27, 39, 82; DA3; DLB 125; MTCW 1, 2
Spackman, W(illiam) M(ode)
 1905-1990 .... **CLC 46**
 See also CA 81-84; 132
Spacks, Barry (Bernard) 1931- .... **CLC 14**
 See also CA 154; CANR 33; DLB 105
Spanidou, Irini 1946- .... **CLC 44**
 See also CA 185
Spark, Muriel (Sarah) 1918- ..... **CLC 2, 3, 5,
 8, 13, 18, 40, 94; DAB; DAC; DAM
 MST, NOV; SSC 10**
 See also AW; BRWS 1; CA 5-8R; CANR
 12, 36, 76, 89; CDBLB 1945-1960; DA3;
 DLB 15, 139; INT CANR-12; MTCW 1,
 2
Spaulding, Douglas
 See Bradbury, Ray (Douglas)
Spaulding, Leonard
 See Bradbury, Ray (Douglas)
Spence, J. A. D.
 See Eliot, T(homas) S(tearns)
Spencer, Elizabeth 1921- .... **CLC 22**
 See also CA 13-16R; CANR 32, 65, 87;
 DLB 6; MTCW 1; SATA 14
Spencer, Leonard G.
 See Silverberg, Robert
Spencer, Scott 1945- .... **CLC 30**
 See also CA 113; CANR 51; DLBY 86
Spender, Stephen (Harold)
 1909-1995 ...... **CLC 1, 2, 5, 10, 41, 91;
 DAM POET**
 See also BRWS 2; CA 9-12R; 149; CANR
 31, 54; CDBLB 1945-1960; DA3; DLB
 20; MTCW 1, 2
Spengler, Oswald (Arnold Gottfried)
 1880-1936 .... **TCLC 25**
 See also CA 118; 189
Spenser, Edmund 1552(?)-1599 ..... **LC 5, 39;
 DA; DAB; DAC; DAM MST, POET;
 PC 8**
 See also AW; CDBLB Before 1660; DA3;
 DLB 167
Spicer, Jack 1925-1965 .... **CLC 8, 18, 72;
 DAM POET**
 See also CA 85-88; DLB 5, 16, 193; GLL 1
Spiegelman, Art 1948- .... **CLC 76**
 See also AAYA 10; AW; CA 125; CANR
 41, 55, 74; MTCW 2; SATA 109
Spielberg, Peter 1929- .... **CLC 6**
 See also CA 5-8R; CANR 4, 48; DLBY 81
Spielberg, Steven 1947- .... **CLC 20**
 See also AAYA 8, 24; CA 77-80; CANR
 32; SATA 32
Spillane, Frank Morrison 1918-
 See Spillane, Mickey
 See also CA 25-28R; CANR 28, 63; DA3;
 DLB 226; MTCW 1, 2; SATA 66

Spillane, Mickey CLC 3, 13
    See also Spillane, Frank Morrison
    See also DLB 226; MTCW 2
Spinoza, Benedictus de 1632-1677 .. LC 9, 58
Spinrad, Norman (Richard) 1940- ... **CLC 46**
    See also CA 37-40R; CAAS 19; CANR 20,
    91; DLB 8; INT CANR-20
Spitteler, Carl (Friedrich Georg)
    1845-1924 .... **TCLC 12**
    See also CA 109; DLB 129
Spivack, Kathleen (Romola Drucker)
    1938- .... **CLC 6**
    See also CA 49-52
Spoto, Donald 1941- .... **CLC 39**
    See also CA 65-68; CANR 11, 57, 93
Springsteen, Bruce (F.) 1949- .... **CLC 17**
    See also CA 111
Spurling, Hilary 1940- .... **CLC 34**
    See also CA 104; CANR 25, 52, 94
Spyker, John Howland
    See Elman, Richard (Martin)
Squires, (James) Radcliffe
    1917-1993 .... **CLC 51**
    See also CA 1-4R; 140; CANR 6, 21
Srivastava, Dhanpat Rai 1880(?)-1936
    See Premchand
    See also CA 118
Stacy, Donald
    See Pohl, Frederik
Staël, Germaine de NCLC 91
    See also Staël-Holstein, Anne Louise Ger-
    maine Necker
    See also DLB 192
Staël-Holstein, Anne Louise Germaine
    Necker 1766-1817 .... **NCLC 3**
    See also Staël, Germaine de
Stafford, Jean 1915-1979 .. CLC 4, 7, 19, 68;
    SSC 26
    See also CA 1-4R; 85-88; CANR 3, 65;
    DLB 2, 173; MTCW 1, 2; SATA-Obit 22;
    TCWW 2
Stafford, William (Edgar)
    1914-1993 .. CLC 4, 7, 29; DAM POET
    See also CA 5-8R; 142; CAAS 3; CANR 5,
    22; DLB 5, 206; INT CANR-22
Stagnelius, Eric Johan 1793-1823 . NCLC 61
Staines, Trevor
    See Brunner, John (Kilian Houston)
Stairs, Gordon
    See Austin, Mary (Hunter)
    See also TCWW 2
Stairs, Gordon 1868-1934
    See Austin, Mary (Hunter)
Stalin, Joseph 1879-1953 .... **TCLC 92**
Stannard, Martin 1947- .... **CLC 44**
    See also CA 142; DLB 155
Stanton, Elizabeth Cady
    1815-1902 .... **TCLC 73**
    See also CA 171; DLB 79
Stanton, Maura 1946- .... **CLC 9**
    See also CA 89-92; CANR 15; DLB 120
Stanton, Schuyler
    See Baum, L(yman) Frank
Stapledon, (William) Olaf
    1886-1950 .... **TCLC 22**
    See also CA 111; 162; DLB 15
Starbuck, George (Edwin)
    1931-1996 .... **CLC 53; DAM POET**
    See also CA 21-24R; 153; CANR 23
Stark, Richard
    See Westlake, Donald E(dwin)
Staunton, Schuyler
    See Baum, L(yman) Frank
Stead, Christina (Ellen) 1902-1983 ... CLC 2,
    5, 8, 32, 80
    See also BRWS 4; CA 13-16R; 109; CANR
    33, 40; MTCW 1, 2

Stead, William Thomas
    1849-1912 .... **TCLC 48**
    See also CA 167
Steele, SirRichard 1672-1729 .... LC 18
    See also CDBLB 1660-1789; DLB 84, 101
Steele, Timothy (Reid) 1948- .... **CLC 45**
    See also CA 93-96; CANR 16, 50, 92; DLB
    120
Steffens, (Joseph) Lincoln
    1866-1936 .... **TCLC 20**
    See also CA 117
Stegner, Wallace (Earle) 1909-1993 .. CLC 9,
    49, 81; DAM NOV; SSC 27
    See also AITN 1; AMWS 4; BEST 90:3;
    CA 1-4R; 141; CAAS 9; CANR 1, 21,
    46; DLB 9, 206; DLBY 93; MTCW 1, 2;
    TCWW 2
Stein, Gertrude 1874-1946 .... TCLC 1, 6, 28,
    48; DA; DAB; DAC; DAM MST, NOV,
    POET; PC 18; SSC 42
    See also AW; CA 104; 132; CDALB 1917-
    1929; DA3; DLB 4, 54, 86, 228; DLBD
    15; GLL 1; MTCW 1, 2
Steinbeck, John (Ernst) 1902-1968 ... CLC 1,
    5, 9, 13, 21, 34, 45, 75, 124; DA; DAB;
    DAC; DAM DRAM, MST, NOV; SSC
    11, 37
    See also AAYA 12; CA 1-4R; 25-28R;
    CANR 1, 35; CDALB 1929-1941; DA3;
    DLB 7, 9, 212; DLBD 2; MTCW 1, 2;
    SATA 9; TCWW 2
Steinem, Gloria 1934- .... **CLC 63**
    See also CA 53-56; CANR 28, 51; MTCW
    1, 2
Steiner, George 1929- .. CLC 24; DAM NOV
    See also CA 73-76; CANR 31, 67; DLB 67;
    MTCW 1, 2; SATA 62
Steiner, K. Leslie
    See Delany, Samuel R(ay), Jr.
Steiner, Rudolf 1861-1925 .... **TCLC 13**
    See also CA 107
Stendhal 1783-1842 .... NCLC 23, 46; DA;
    DAB; DAC; DAM MST, NOV; SSC 27
    See also AW; DA3; DLB 119
Stephen, Adeline Virginia
    See Woolf, (Adeline) Virginia
Stephen, SirLeslie 1832-1904 .... **TCLC 23**
    See also CA 123; DLB 57, 144, 190
Stephen, Sir Leslie
    See Stephen, SirLeslie
Stephen, Virginia
    See Woolf, (Adeline) Virginia
Stephens, James 1882(?)-1950 .... **TCLC 4**
    See also CA 104; DLB 19, 153, 162
Stephens, Reed
    See Donaldson, Stephen R.
Steptoe, Lydia
    See Barnes, Djuna
    See also GLL 1
Sterchi, Beat 1949- .... **CLC 65**
Sterling, Brett
    See Bradbury, Ray (Douglas); Hamilton,
    Edmond
Sterling, Bruce 1954- .... **CLC 72**
    See also CA 119; CANR 44; SCFW 2
Sterling, George 1869-1926 .... **TCLC 20**
    See also CA 117; 165; DLB 54
Stern, Gerald 1925- .... **CLC 40, 100**
    See also CA 81-84; CANR 28, 94; DLB
    105
Stern, Richard (Gustave) 1928- ... CLC 4, 39
    See also CA 1-4R; CANR 1, 25, 52; DLBY
    87; INT CANR-25
Sternberg, Josef von 1894-1969 .... **CLC 20**
    See also CA 81-84
Sterne, Laurence 1713-1768 .. LC 2, 48; DA;
    DAB; DAC; DAM MST, NOV
    See also AW; CDBLB 1660-1789; DLB 39

Sternheim, (William Adolf) Carl
    1878-1942 .... **TCLC 8**
    See also CA 105; DLB 56, 118
Stevens, Mark 1951- .... **CLC 34**
    See also CA 122
Stevens, Wallace 1879-1955 ...... TCLC 3, 12,
    45; DA; DAB; DAC; DAM MST,
    POET; PC 6
    See also AW; CA 104; 124; CDALB 1929-
    1941; DA3; DLB 54; MTCW 1, 2
Stevenson, Anne (Katharine) 1933- .. CLC 7,
    33
    See also CA 17-20R; CAAS 9; CANR 9,
    33; DLB 40; MTCW 1
Stevenson, Robert Louis (Balfour)
    1850-1894 . NCLC 5, 14, 63; DA; DAB;
    DAC; DAM MST, NOV; SSC 11
    See also AAYA 24; CDBLB 1890-1914;
    CLR 10, 11; DA3; DLB 18, 57, 141, 156,
    174; DLBD 13; JRDA; MAICYA; SATA
    100
Stewart, J(ohn) I(nnes) M(ackintosh)
    1906-1994 .... **CLC 7, 14, 32**
    See also CA 85-88; 147; CAAS 3; CANR
    47; MTCW 1, 2
Stewart, Mary (Florence Elinor)
    1916- .... **CLC 7, 35, 117; DAB**
    See also AAYA 29; AW; CA 1-4R; CANR
    1, 59; SATA 12
Stewart, Mary Rainbow
    See Stewart, Mary (Florence Elinor)
Stifle, June
    See Campbell, Maria
Stifter, Adalbert 1805-1868 .. NCLC 41; SSC
    28
    See also DLB 133
Still, James 1906-2001 .... **CLC 49**
    See also CA 65-68; CAAS 17; CANR 10,
    26; DLB 9; SATA 29
Sting 1951-
    See Sumner, Gordon Matthew
    See also CA 167
Stirling, Arthur
    See Sinclair, Upton (Beall)
Stitt, Milan 1941- .... **CLC 29**
    See also CA 69-72
Stockton, Francis Richard 1834-1902
    See Stockton, Frank R.
    See also CA 108; 137; MAICYA; SATA 44
Stockton, Frank R. TCLC 47
    See also Stockton, Francis Richard
    See also DLB 42, 74; DLBD 13; SATA-
    Brief 32
Stoddard, Charles
    See Kuttner, Henry
Stoker, Abraham 1847-1912
    See Stoker, Bram
    See also CA 105; 150; DA; DAC; DAM
    MST, NOV; DA3; SATA 29
Stoker, Bram TCLC 8; DAB
    See also Stoker, Abraham
    See also AAYA 23; AW; BRWS 3; CDBLB
    1890-1914; DLB 36, 70, 178
Stolz, Mary (Slattery) 1920- .... **CLC 12**
    See also AAYA 8; AITN 1; AW; CA 5-8R;
    CANR 13, 41; JRDA; MAICYA; SAAS
    3; SATA 10, 71
Stone, Irving 1903-1989 . CLC 7; DAM POP
    See also AITN 1; CA 1-4R; 129; CAAS 3;
    CANR 1, 23; DA3; INT CANR-23;
    MTCW 1, 2; SATA 3; SATA-Obit 64
Stone, Oliver (William) 1946- .... **CLC 73**
    See also AAYA 15; CA 110; CANR 55
Stone, Robert (Anthony) 1937- ... CLC 5, 23,
    42
    See also AMWS 5; CA 85-88; CANR 23,
    66, 95; DLB 152; INT CANR-23;
    MTCW 1

Stone, Zachary
    See Follett, Ken(neth Martin)
Stoppard, Tom 1937- ... **CLC 1, 3, 4, 5, 8, 15,
    29, 34, 63, 91; DA; DAB; DAC; DAM
    DRAM, MST; DC 6**
    See also AW; BRWS 1; CA 81-84; CANR
    39, 67; CDBLB 1960 to Present; DA3;
    DLB 13, 233; DLBY 85; MTCW 1, 2
Storey, David (Malcolm) 1933- . **CLC 2, 4, 5,
    8; DAM DRAM**
    See also BRWS 1; CA 81-84; CANR 36;
    DLB 13, 14, 207; MTCW 1
Storm, Hyemeyohsts 1935- ..... **CLC 3; DAM
    MULT**
    See also CA 81-84; CANR 45; NNAL
Storm, Theodor 1817-1888 .... **SSC 27**
Storm, (Hans) Theodor (Woldsen)
    1817-1888 .... **NCLC 1; SSC 27**
    See also DLB 129
Storni, Alfonsina 1892-1938 . **TCLC 5; DAM
    MULT; HLC 2; PC 33**
    See also CA 104; 131; HW 1
Stoughton, William 1631-1701 .... **LC 38**
    See also DLB 24
Stout, Rex (Todhunter) 1886-1975 ..... **CLC 3**
    See also AITN 2; CA 61-64; CANR 71
Stow, (Julian) Randolph 1935- ... **CLC 23, 48**
    See also CA 13-16R; CANR 33; MTCW 1
Stowe, Harriet (Elizabeth) Beecher
    1811-1896 .... **NCLC 3, 50; DA; DAB;
    DAC; DAM MST, NOV**
    See also AMWS 1; AW; CDALB 1865-
    1917; DA3; DLB 1, 12, 42, 74, 189, 239;
    JRDA; MAICYA
Strabo c. 64B.C.-c. 25 .... **CMLC 37**
    See also DLB 176
Strachey, (Giles) Lytton
    1880-1932 .... **TCLC 12**
    See also BRWS 2; CA 110; 178; DLB 149;
    DLBD 10; MTCW 2
Strand, Mark 1934- .... **CLC 6, 18, 41, 71;
    DAM POET**
    See also AMWS 4; CA 21-24R; CANR 40,
    65; DLB 5, SATA 41
Stratton-Porter, Gene(va Grace) 1863-1924
    See Porter, Gene(va Grace) Stratton
    See also CA 137; DLB 221; DLBD 14;
    MAICYA; SATA 15
Straub, Peter (Francis) 1943- . **CLC 28, 107;
    DAM POP**
    See also BEST 89:1; CA 85-88; CANR 28,
    65; DLBY 84; MTCW 1, 2
Strauss, Botho 1944- .... **CLC 22**
    See also CA 157; CWW 2; DLB 124
Streatfeild, (Mary) Noel
    1897(?)-1986 .... **CLC 21**
    See also CA 81-84; 120; CANR 31; CLR
    17; DLB 160; MAICYA; SATA 20; SATA-
    Obit 48
Stribling, T(homas) S(igismund)
    1881-1965 .... **CLC 23**
    See also CA 189; 107; DLB 9
Strindberg, (Johan) August
    1849-1912 .... **TCLC 1, 8, 21, 47; DA;
    DAB; DAC; DAM DRAM, MST**
    See also AW; CA 104; 135; DA3; MTCW 2
Stringer, Arthur 1874-1950 .... **TCLC 37**
    See also CA 161; DLB 92
Stringer, David
    See Roberts, Keith (John Kingston)
Stroheim, Erich von 1885-1957 ..... **TCLC 71**
Strugatskii, Arkadii (Natanovich)
    1925-1991 .... **CLC 27**
    See also CA 106; 135
Strugatskii, Boris (Natanovich)
    1933- .... **CLC 27**
    See also CA 106

Strummer, Joe 1953(?)- .... **CLC 30**
Strunk, William, Jr. 1869-1946 ...... **TCLC 92**
    See also CA 118; 164
Stryk, Lucien 1924- .... **PC 27**
    See also CA 13-16R; CANR 10, 28, 55
Stuart, Don A.
    See Campbell, John W(ood, Jr.)
Stuart, Ian
    See MacLean, Alistair (Stuart)
Stuart, Jesse (Hilton) 1906-1984 ... **CLC 1, 8,
    11, 14, 34; SSC 31**
    See also CA 5-8R; 112; CANR 31; DLB 9,
    48, 102; DLBY 84; SATA 2; SATA-Obit
    36
Sturgeon, Theodore (Hamilton)
    1918-1985 .... **CLC 22, 39**
    See also Queen, Ellery
    See also CA 81-84; 116; CANR 32; DLB 8;
    DLBY 85; MTCW 1, 2
Sturges, Preston 1898-1959 .... **TCLC 48**
    See also CA 114; 149; DLB 26
Styron, William 1925- .... **CLC 1, 3, 5, 11, 15,
    60; DAM NOV, POP; SSC 25**
    See also BEST 90:4; CA 5-8R; CANR 6,
    33, 74; CDALB 1968-1988; DA3; DLB
    2, 143; DLBY 80; INT CANR-6; MTCW
    1, 2
Su, Chien 1884-1918
    See Su Man-shu
    See also CA 123
Suarez Lynch, B.
    See Bioy Casares, Adolfo; Borges, Jorge
    Luis
Suassuna, Ariano Vilar 1927-
    See also CA 178; HLCS 1; HW 2
Suckling, Sir John 1609-1642 .... **PC 30**
    See also DAM POET; DLB 58, 126
Suckow, Ruth 1892-1960 .... **SSC 18**
    See also CA 113; DLB 9, 102; TCWW 2
Sudermann, Hermann 1857-1928 .. **TCLC 15**
    See also CA 107; DLB 118
Sue, Eugene 1804-1857 .... **NCLC 1**
    See also DLB 119
Sueskind, Patrick 1949- .... **CLC 44**
    See also Suskind, Patrick
Sukenick, Ronald 1932- ...... **CLC 3, 4, 6, 48**
    See also CA 25-28R; CAAS 8; CANR 32,
    89; DLB 173; DLBY 81
Suknaski, Andrew 1942- .... **CLC 19**
    See also CA 101; DLB 53
Sullivan, Vernon
    See Vian, Boris
Sully Prudhomme 1839-1907 .... **TCLC 31**
Su Man-shu **TCLC 24**
    See also Su, Chien
Summerforest, Ivy B.
    See Kirkup, James
Summers, Andrew James 1942- .... **CLC 26**
Summers, Andy
    See Summers, Andrew James
Summers, Hollis (Spurgeon, Jr.)
    1916- .... **CLC 10**
    See also CA 5-8R; CANR 3; DLB 6
**Summers, (Alphonsus Joseph-Mary
    Augustus) Montague**
    1880-1948 .... **TCLC 16**
    See also CA 118; 163
Sumner, Gordon Matthew **CLC 26**
    See also Sting
Surtees, Robert Smith 1805-1864 .. **NCLC 14**
    See also DLB 21
Susann, Jacqueline 1921-1974 .... **CLC 3**
    See also AITN 1; CA 65-68; 53-56; MTCW
    1, 2
Su Shih 1036-1101 .... **CMLC 15**
Suskind, Patrick
    See Sueskind, Patrick
    See also CA 145; CWW 2

Sutcliff, Rosemary 1920-1992 .... **CLC 26;
    DAB; DAC; DAM MST, POP**
    See also AAYA 10; AW; CA 5-8R; 139;
    CANR 37; CLR 1, 37; JRDA; MAICYA;
    SATA 6, 44, 78; SATA-Obit 73
Sutro, Alfred 1863-1933 .... **TCLC 6**
    See also CA 105; 185; DLB 10
Sutton, Henry
    See Slavitt, David R(ytman)
Svevo, Italo **TCLC 2, 35; SSC 25**
    See also Schmitz, Aron Hector
Swados, Elizabeth (A.) 1951- .... **CLC 12**
    See also CA 97-100; CANR 49; INT 97-
    100
Swados, Harvey 1920-1972 .... **CLC 5**
    See also CA 5-8R; 37-40R; CANR 6; DLB
    2
Swan, Gladys 1934- .... **CLC 69**
    See also CA 101; CANR 17, 39
Swanson, Logan
    See Matheson, Richard Burton
Swarthout, Glendon (Fred)
    1918-1992 .... **CLC 35**
    See also AW; CA 1-4R; 139; CANR 1, 47;
    SATA 26; TCWW 2
Sweet, Sarah C.
    See Jewett, (Theodora) Sarah Orne
Swenson, May 1919-1989 ...... **CLC 4, 14, 61,
    106; DA; DAB; DAC; DAM MST,
    POET; PC 14**
    See also AMWS 4; CA 5-8R; 130; CANR
    36, 61; DLB 5; GLL 2; MTCW 1, 2;
    SATA 15
Swift, Augustus
    See Lovecraft, H(oward) P(hillips)
Swift, Graham (Colin) 1949- ...... **CLC 41, 88**
    See also BRWS 5; CA 117; 122; CANR 46,
    71; DLB 194; MTCW 2
Swift, Jonathan 1667-1745 ..... **LC 1, 42; DA;
    DAB; DAC; DAM MST, NOV, POET;
    PC 9**
    See also AW; CDBLB 1660-1789; CLR 53;
    DA3; DLB 39, 95, 101; SATA 19
Swinburne, Algernon Charles
    1837-1909 .... **CLC 8, 36; DA; DAB;
    DAC; DAM MST, POET; PC 24**
    See also AW; CA 105; 140; CDBLB 1832-
    1890; DA3; DLB 35, 57
Swinfen, Ann **CLC 34**
Swinnerton, Frank Arthur
    1884-1982 .... **CLC 31**
    See also CA 108; DLB 34
Swithen, John
    See King, Stephen (Edwin)
Sylvia
    See Ashton-Warner, Sylvia (Constance)
Symmes, Robert Edward
    See Duncan, Robert (Edward)
Symonds, John Addington
    1840-1893 .... **NCLC 34**
    See also DLB 57, 144
Symons, Arthur 1865-1945 .... **TCLC 11**
    See also CA 107; 189; DLB 19, 57, 149
Symons, Julian (Gustave)
    1912-1994 .... **CLC 2, 14, 32**
    See also CA 49-52; 147; CAAS 3; CANR
    3, 33, 59; DLB 87, 155; DLBY 92;
    MTCW 1
Synge, (Edmund) J(ohn) M(illington)
    1871-1909 . **TCLC 6, 37; DAM DRAM;
    DC 2**
    See also CA 104; 141; CDBLB 1890-1914;
    DLB 10, 19
Syruc, J.
    See Milosz, Czeslaw
Szirtes, George 1948- .... **CLC 46**
    See also CA 109; CANR 27, 61

Szymborska, Wislawa 1923- .... **CLC 99**
See also CA 154; CANR 91; CWW 2; DA3;
DLB 232; DLBY 96; MTCW 2

T. O., Nik
See Annensky, Innokenty (Fyodorovich)

Tabori, George 1914- .... **CLC 19**
See also CA 49-52; CANR 4, 69

Tagore, Rabindranath 1861-1941 ... **TCLC 3,
53; DAM DRAM, POET; PC 8**
See also CA 104; 120; DA3; MTCW 1, 2

Taine, Hippolyte Adolphe
1828-1893 .... **NCLC 15**

Talese, Gay 1932- .... **CLC 37**
See also AITN 1; CA 1-4R; CANR 9, 58;
DLB 185; INT CANR-9; MTCW 1, 2

Tallent, Elizabeth (Ann) 1954- .... **CLC 45**
See also CA 117; CANR 72; DLB 130

Tally, Ted 1952- .... **CLC 42**
See also CA 120; 124; INT 124

Talvik, Heiti 1904-1947 .... **TCLC 87**

Tamayo y Baus, Manuel
1829-1898 .... **NCLC 1**

Tammsaare, A(nton) H(ansen)
1878-1940 .... **TCLC 27**
See also CA 164; DLB 220

Tam'si, Tchicaya U
See Tchicaya, Gerald Felix

Tan, Amy (Ruth) 1952- . **CLC 59, 120; DAM
MULT, NOV, POP**
See also AAYA 9; AW; BEST 89:3; CA 136;
CANR 54; CDALBS; DA3; DLB 173;
MTCW 2; SATA 75

Tandem, Felix
See Spitteler, Carl (Friedrich Georg)

Tanizaki, Jun'ichiro 1886-1965 ... **CLC 8, 14,
28; SSC 21**
See also CA 93-96; 25-28R; DLB 180;
MTCW 2

Tanner, William
See Amis, Kingsley (William)

Tao Lao
See Storni, Alfonsina

Tarantino, Quentin (Jerome)
1963- .... **CLC 125**
See also CA 171

Tarassoff, Lev
See Troyat, Henri

Tarbell, Ida M(inerva) 1857-1944 . **TCLC 40**
See also CA 122; 181; DLB 47

Tarkington, (Newton) Booth
1869-1946 .... **TCLC 9**
See also CA 110; 143; DLB 9, 102; MTCW
2; SATA 17

Tarkovsky, Andrei (Arsenyevich)
1932-1986 .... **CLC 75**
See also CA 127

Tartt, Donna 1964(?)- .... **CLC 76**
See also CA 142

Tasso, Torquato 1544-1595 .... **LC 5**

Tate, (John Orley) Allen 1899-1979 .. **CLC 2,
4, 6, 9, 11, 14, 24**
See also CA 5-8R; 85-88; CANR 32; DLB
4, 45, 63; DLBD 17; MTCW 1, 2

Tate, Ellalice
See Hibbert, Eleanor Alice Burford

Tate, James (Vincent) 1943- ..... **CLC 2, 6, 25**
See also CA 21-24R; CANR 29, 57; DLB
5, 169

Tauler, Johannes c. 1300-1361 ...... **CMLC 37**
See also DLB 179

Tavel, Ronald 1940- .... **CLC 6**
See also CA 21-24R; CANR 33

Taylor, Bayard 1825-1878 .... **NCLC 89**
See also DLB 3, 189

Taylor, C(ecil) P(hilip) 1929-1981 .... **CLC 27**
See also CA 25-28R; 105; CANR 47

Taylor, Edward 1642(?)-1729 ..... **LC 11; DA;
DAB; DAC; DAM MST, POET**
See also DLB 24

Taylor, Eleanor Ross 1920- .... **CLC 5**
See also CA 81-84; CANR 70

Taylor, Elizabeth 1932-1975 ..... **CLC 2, 4, 29**
See also CA 13-16R; CANR 9, 70; DLB
139; MTCW 1; SATA 13

Taylor, Frederick Winslow
1856-1915 .... **TCLC 76**
See also CA 188

Taylor, Henry (Splawn) 1942- .... **CLC 44**
See also CA 33-36R; CAAS 7; CANR 31;
DLB 5

Taylor, Kamala (Purnaiya) 1924-
See Markandaya, Kamala
See also CA 77-80

Taylor, Mildred D(elois) CLC 21
See also AAYA 10; BW 1; CA 85-88;
CANR 25; CLR 9, 59; DLB 52; JRDA;
MAICYA; SAAS 5; SATA 15, 70

Taylor, Peter (Hillsman) 1917-1994 .. **CLC 1,
4, 18, 37, 44, 50, 71; SSC 10**
See also AMWS 5; CA 13-16R; 147; CANR
9, 50; DLBY 81, 94; INT CANR-9;
MTCW 1, 2

Taylor, Robert Lewis 1912-1998 .... **CLC 14**
See also CA 1-4R; 170; CANR 3, 64; SATA
10

Tchekhov, Anton
See Chekhov, Anton (Pavlovich)

Tchicaya, Gerald Felix 1931-1988 .. **CLC 101**
See also CA 129; 125; CANR 81

Tchicaya U Tam'si
See Tchicaya, Gerald Felix

Teasdale, Sara 1884-1933 .... **TCLC 4; PC 31**
See also CA 104; 163; DLB 45; GLL 1;
SATA 32

Tegner, Esaias 1782-1846 .... **NCLC 2**

Teilhard de Chardin, (Marie Joseph) Pierre
1881-1955 .... **TCLC 9**
See also CA 105

Temple, Ann
See Mortimer, Penelope (Ruth)

Tennant, Emma (Christina) 1937- .. **CLC 13,
52**
See also CA 65-68; CAAS 9; CANR 10,
38, 59, 88; DLB 14

Tenneshaw, S. M.
See Silverberg, Robert

Tennyson, Alfred 1809-1892 ... **NCLC 30, 65;
DA; DAB; DAC; DAM MST, POET;
PC 6**
See also AW; CDBLB 1832-1890; DA3;
DLB 32

Teran, Lisa St. Aubin de CLC 36
See also St. Aubin de Teran, Lisa

Terence c. 195B.C.-c. 159B.C. ...... **CMLC 14;
DC 7**
See also DLB 211

Teresa de Jesus, St. 1515-1582 .... **LC 18**

Terkel, Louis 1912-
See Terkel, Studs
See also CA 57-60; CANR 18, 45, 67; DA3;
MTCW 1, 2

Terkel, Studs CLC 38
See also Terkel, Louis
See also AAYA 32; AITN 1; MTCW 2

Terry, C. V.
See Slaughter, Frank G(ill)

Terry, Megan 1932- .... **CLC 19; DC 13**
See also CA 77-80; CABS 3; CANR 43;
DLB 7; GLL 2

Tertullian c. 155-c. 245 .... **CMLC 29**

Tertz, Abram
See Sinyavsky, Andrei (Donatevich)
See also CWW 2

Tesich, Steve 1943(?)-1996 .... **CLC 40, 69**
See also CA 105; 152; DLBY 83

Tesla, Nikola 1856-1943 .... **TCLC 88**

Teternikov, Fyodor Kuzmich 1863-1927
See Sologub, Fyodor
See also CA 104

Tevis, Walter 1928-1984 .... **CLC 42**
See also CA 113

Tey, Josephine TCLC 14
See also Mackintosh, Elizabeth
See also DLB 77

Thackeray, William Makepeace
1811-1863 ...... **NCLC 5, 14, 22, 43; DA;
DAB; DAC; DAM MST, NOV**
See also AW; CDBLB 1832-1890; DA3;
DLB 21, 55, 159, 163; SATA 23

Thakura, Ravindranatha
See Tagore, Rabindranath

Tharoor, Shashi 1956- .... **CLC 70**
See also CA 141; CANR 91

Thelwell, Michael Miles 1939- .... **CLC 22**
See also BW 2; CA 101

Theobald, Lewis, Jr.
See Lovecraft, H(oward) P(hillips)

Theodorescu, Ion N. 1880-1967
See Arghezi, Tudor
See also CA 116; DLB 220

Theriault, Yves 1915-1983 .... **CLC 79; DAC;
DAM MST**
See also CA 102; CCA 1; DLB 88

Theroux, Alexander (Louis) 1939- .... **CLC 2,
25**
See also CA 85-88; CANR 20, 63

Theroux, Paul (Edward) 1941- ..... **CLC 5, 8,
11, 15, 28, 46; DAM POP**
See also AAYA 28; BEST 89:4; CA 33-36R;
CANR 20, 45, 74; CDALBS; DA3; DLB
2; MTCW 1, 2; SATA 44, 109

Thesen, Sharon 1946- .... **CLC 56**
See also CA 163

Thevenin, Denis
See Duhamel, Georges

Thibault, Jacques Anatole Francois
1844-1924
See France, Anatole
See also CA 106; 127; DAM NOV; DA3;
MTCW 1, 2

Thiele, Colin (Milton) 1920- .... **CLC 17**
See also AW; CA 29-32R; CANR 12, 28,
53; CLR 27; MAICYA; SAAS 2; SATA
14, 72

Thomas, Audrey (Callahan) 1935- .... **CLC 7,
13, 37, 107; SSC 20**
See also AITN 2; CA 21-24R; CAAS 19;
CANR 36, 58; DLB 60; MTCW 1

Thomas, Augustus 1857-1934 .... **TCLC 97**

Thomas, D(onald) M(ichael) 1935- . **CLC 13,
22, 31, 132**
See also BRWS 4; CA 61-64; CAAS 11;
CANR 17, 45, 75; CDBLB 1960 to
Present; DA3; DLB 40, 207; INT CANR-
17; MTCW 1, 2

Thomas, Dylan (Marlais)
1914-1953 ...... **TCLC 1, 8, 45, 105; DA;
DAB; DAC; DAM DRAM, MST,
POET; PC 2; SSC 3, 44**
See also AW; BRWS 1; CA 104; 120;
CANR 65; CDBLB 1945-1960; DA3;
DLB 13, 20, 139; MTCW 1, 2; SATA 60

Thomas, (Philip) Edward
1878-1917 .... **TCLC 10; DAM POET**
See also CA 106; 153; DLB 98

Thomas, Joyce Carol 1938- .... **CLC 35**
See also AAYA 12; AW; BW 2, 3; CA 113;
116; CANR 48; CLR 19; DLB 33; INT
116; JRDA; MAICYA; MTCW 1, 2;
SAAS 7; SATA 40, 78

Thomas, Lewis 1913-1993 .... **CLC 35**
See also CA 85-88; 143; CANR 38, 60;
MTCW 1, 2

Thomas, M. Carey 1857-1935 .... **TCLC 89**

Thomas, Paul
See Mann, (Paul) Thomas

Thomas, Piri 1928- .... **CLC 17; HLCS 2**
See also CA 73-76; HW 1

Thomas, R(onald) S(tuart)
1913-2000 . **CLC 6, 13, 48; DAB; DAM POET**
See also CA 89-92; 189; CAAS 4; CANR 30; CDBLB 1960 to Present; DLB 27; MTCW 1

Thomas, Ross (Elmore) 1926-1995 .. **CLC 39**
See also CA 33-36R; 150; CANR 22, 63

Thompson, Francis (Joseph)
1859-1907 .... **TCLC 4**
See also CA 104; 189; CDBLB 1890-1914; DLB 19

Thompson, Francis Clegg
See Mencken, H(enry) L(ouis)

Thompson, Hunter S(tockton)
1939- ... **CLC 9, 17, 40, 104; DAM POP**
See also BEST 89:1; CA 17-20R; CANR 23, 46, 74, 77; DA3; DLB 185; MTCW 1, 2

Thompson, James Myers
See Thompson, Jim (Myers)

Thompson, Jim (Myers)
1906-1977(?) .... **CLC 69**
See also CA 140; DLB 226

Thompson, Judith **CLC 39**

Thomson, James 1700-1748 ... **LC 16, 29, 40; DAM POET**
See also BRWS 3; DLB 95

Thomson, James 1834-1882 .... **NCLC 18; DAM POET**
See also DLB 35

Thoreau, Henry David 1817-1862 .. **NCLC 7, 21, 61; DA; DAB; DAC; DAM MST; PC 30**
See also AW; CDALB 1640-1865; DA3; DLB 1, 223

Thorndike, E. L.
See Thorndike, Edward L(ee)

Thorndike, Edward L(ee)
1874-1949 .... **TCLC 107**
See also CA 121

Thornton, Hall
See Silverberg, Robert

Thucydides c. 460B.C.-399B.C. ..... **CMLC 17**
See also DLB 176

Thumboo, Edwin 1933- .... **PC 30**

Thurber, James (Grover)
1894-1961 .... **CLC 5, 11, 25, 125; DA; DAB; DAC; DAM DRAM, MST, NOV; SSC 1**
See also AMWS 1; CA 73-76; CANR 17, 39; CDALB 1929-1941; DA3; DLB 4, 11, 22, 102; MAICYA; MTCW 1, 2; SATA 13

Thurman, Wallace (Henry)
1902-1934 .... **TCLC 6; BLC 3; DAM MULT**
See also BW 1, 3; CA 104; 124; CANR 81; DLB 51

Tibullus c. 54B.C.-c. 18B.C. .... **CMLC 36**
See also DLB 211

Ticheburn, Cheviot
See Ainsworth, William Harrison

Tieck, (Johann) Ludwig
1773-1853 .... **NCLC 5, 46; SSC 31**
See also DLB 90

Tiger, Derry
See Ellison, Harlan (Jay)

Tilghman, Christopher 1948(?)- .... **CLC 65**
See also CA 159

Tillich, Paul (Johannes)
1886-1965 .... **CLC 131**
See also CA 5-8R; 25-28R; CANR 33; MTCW 1, 2

Tillinghast, Richard (Williford)
1940- .... **CLC 29**
See also CA 29-32R; CAAS 23; CANR 26, 51, 96

Timrod, Henry 1828-1867 .... **NCLC 25**
See also DLB 3

Tindall, Gillian (Elizabeth) 1938- ...... **CLC 7**
See also CA 21-24R; CANR 11, 65

Tiptree, James, Jr. **CLC 48, 50**
See also Sheldon, Alice Hastings Bradley
See also DLB 8

Titmarsh, Michael Angelo
See Thackeray, William Makepeace

Tocqueville, Alexis (Charles Henri Maurice Clerel 1805-1859 .... **NCLC 7, 63**

Tolkien, J(ohn) R(onald) R(euel)
1892-1973 .. **CLC 1, 2, 3, 8, 12, 38; DA; DAB; DAC; DAM MST, NOV, POP**
See also AAYA 10; AITN 1; BRWS 2; CA 17-18; 45-48; CANR 36; CAP 2; CDBLB 1914-1945; CLR 56; DA3; DLB 15, 160; JRDA; MAICYA; MTCW 1, 2; SATA 2, 32, 100; SATA-Obit 24

Toller, Ernst 1893-1939 .... **TCLC 10**
See also CA 107; 186; DLB 124

Tolson, M. B.
See Tolson, Melvin B(eaunorus)

Tolson, Melvin B(eaunorus)
1898(?)-1966 .... **CLC 36, 105; BLC 3; DAM MULT, POET**
See also BW 1, 3; CA 124; 89-92; CANR 80; DLB 48, 76

Tolstoi, Aleksei Nikolaevich
See Tolstoy, Alexey Nikolaevich

Tolstoy, Alexey Nikolaevich
1882-1945 .... **TCLC 18**
See also CA 107; 158

Tolstoy, Count Leo
See Tolstoy, Leo (Nikolaevich)

Tolstoy, Leo (Nikolaevich)
1828-1910 .. **TCLC 4, 11, 17, 28, 44, 79; DA; DAB; DAC; DAM MST, NOV; SSC 9, 30**
See also AW; CA 104; 123; DA3; DLB 238; SATA 26

Tomasi di Lampedusa, Giuseppe 1896-1957
See Lampedusa, Giuseppe (Tomasi) di
See also CA 111

Tomlin, Lily **CLC 17**
See also Tomlin, Mary Jean

Tomlin, Mary Jean 1939(?)-
See Tomlin, Lily
See also CA 117

Tomlinson, (Alfred) Charles 1927- .... **CLC 2, 4, 6, 13, 45; DAM POET; PC 17**
See also CA 5-8R; CANR 33; DLB 40

Tomlinson, H(enry) M(ajor)
1873-1958 .... **TCLC 71**
See also CA 118; 161; DLB 36, 100, 195

Tonson, Jacob
See Bennett, (Enoch) Arnold

Toole, John Kennedy 1937-1969 ..... **CLC 19, 64**
See also CA 104; DLBY 81; MTCW 2

Toomer, Jean 1892-1967 .... **CLC 1, 4, 13, 22; BLC 3; DAM MULT; PC 7; SSC 1**
See also Pinchback, Eugene; Toomer, Eugene; Toomer, Eugene Pinchback; Toomer, Nathan Jean; Toomer, Nathan Pinchback
See also AMWS 3; AW; BW 1; CA 85-88; CDALB 1917-1929; DA3; DLB 45, 51; MTCW 1, 2

Torley, Luke
See Blish, James (Benjamin)

Tornimparte, Alessandra
See Ginzburg, Natalia

Torre, Raoul della
See Mencken, H(enry) L(ouis)

Torrence, Ridgely 1874-1950 .... **TCLC 97**
See also DLB 54

Torrey, E(dwin) Fuller 1937- .... **CLC 34**
See also CA 119; CANR 71

Torsvan, Ben Traven
See Traven, B.

Torsvan, Benno Traven
See Traven, B.

Torsvan, Berick Traven
See Traven, B.

Torsvan, Berwick Traven
See Traven, B.

Torsvan, Bruno Traven
See Traven, B.

Torsvan, Traven
See Traven, B.

Tournier, Michel (Edouard) 1924- .... **CLC 6, 23, 36, 95**
See also CA 49-52; CANR 3, 36, 74; DLB 83; MTCW 1, 2; SATA 23

Tournimparte, Alessandra
See Ginzburg, Natalia

Towers, Ivar
See Kornbluth, C(yril) M.

Towne, Robert (Burton) 1936(?)- ..... **CLC 87**
See also CA 108; DLB 44; IDFW 3

Townsend, Sue **CLC 61**
See also Townsend, Susan Elaine
See also AAYA 28; SATA 55, 93; SATA-Brief 48

Townsend, Susan Elaine 1946-
See Townsend, Sue
See also AW; CA 119; 127; CANR 65; DAB; DAC; DAM MST; INT 127

Townshend, Peter (Dennis Blandford)
1945- .... **CLC 17, 42**
See also CA 107

Tozzi, Federigo 1883-1920 .... **TCLC 31**
See also CA 160

Tracy, Don(ald Fiske) 1905-1970(?)
See Queen, Ellery
See also CA 1-4R; 176; CANR 2

Traill, Catharine Parr 1802-1899 .. **NCLC 31**
See also DLB 99

Trakl, Georg 1887-1914 .... **TCLC 5; PC 20**
See also CA 104; 165; MTCW 2

Transtroemer, Tomas (Goesta)
1931- .... **CLC 52, 65; DAM POET**
See also CA 117; 129; CAAS 17

Transtromer, Tomas Gosta
See Transtroemer, Tomas (Goesta)

Traven, B. 1882(?)-1969 .... **CLC 8, 11**
See also CA 19-20; 25-28R; CAP 2; DLB 9, 56; MTCW 1

Treitel, Jonathan 1959- .... **CLC 70**

Trelawny, Edward John
1792-1881 .... **NCLC 85**
See also DLB 110, 116, 144

Tremain, Rose 1943- .... **CLC 42**
See also CA 97-100; CANR 44, 95; DLB 14

Tremblay, Michel 1942- .... **CLC 29, 102; DAC; DAM MST**
See also CA 116; 128; CCA 1; CWW 2; DLB 60; GLL 1; MTCW 1, 2

Trevanian **CLC 29**
See also Whitaker, Rod(ney)

Trevor, Glen
See Hilton, James

Trevor, William **CLC 7, 9, 14, 25, 71, 116; SSC 21**
See also Cox, William Trevor
See also BRWS 4; DLB 14, 139; MTCW 2

Trifonov, Yuri (Valentinovich)
1925-1981 .... **CLC 45**
See also CA 126; 103; MTCW 1

Trilling, Diana (Rubin) 1905-1996 . **CLC 129**
  See also CA 5-8R; 154; CANR 10, 46; INT
  CANR-10; MTCW 1, 2
Trilling, Lionel 1905-1975 .... **CLC 9, 11, 24**
  See also AMWS 3; CA 9-12R; 61-64;
  CANR 10; DLB 28, 63; INT CANR-10;
  MTCW 1, 2
Trimball, W. H.
  See Mencken, H(enry) L(ouis)
Tristan
  See Gomez de la Serna, Ramon
Tristram
  See Housman, A(lfred) E(dward)
Trogdon, William (Lewis) 1939-
  See Heat-Moon, William Least
  See also CA 115; 119; CANR 47, 89; INT
  119
Trollope, Anthony 1815-1882 ... **NCLC 6, 33;**
  DA; DAB; DAC; DAM MST, NOV;
  SSC 28
    See also AW; CDBLB 1832-1890; DA3;
    DLB 21, 57, 159; SATA 22
Trollope, Frances 1779-1863 .... **NCLC 30**
  See also DLB 21, 166
Trotsky, Leon 1879-1940 .... **TCLC 22**
  See also CA 118; 167
Trotter (Cockburn), Catharine
  1679-1749 .... **LC 8**
  See also DLB 84
Trotter, Wilfred 1872-1939 .... **TCLC 97**
Trout, Kilgore
  See Farmer, Philip Jose
Trow, George W. S. 1943- .... **CLC 52**
  See also CA 126; CANR 91
Troyat, Henri 1911- .... **CLC 23**
  See also CA 45-48; CANR 2, 33, 67;
  MTCW 1
Trudeau, G(arretson) B(eekman) 1948-
  See Trudeau, Garry B.
  See also CA 81-84; CANR 31; SATA 35
Trudeau, Garry B. CLC 12
  See also Trudeau, G(arretson) B(eekman)
  See also AAYA 10; AITN 2
Truffaut, Francois 1932-1984 ... **CLC 20, 101**
  See also CA 81-84; 113; CANR 34
Trumbo, Dalton 1905-1976 .... **CLC 19**
  See also Rich, Robert
  See also AW; CA 21-24R; 69-72; CANR
  10; DLB 26; IDFW 3
Trumbull, John 1750-1831 .... **NCLC 30**
  See also DLB 31
Trundlett, Helen B.
  See Eliot, T(homas) S(tearns)
Truth, Sojourner 1797(?)-1883 ...... **NCLC 94**
  See also DLB 239
Tryon, Thomas 1926-1991 .... **CLC 3, 11;**
  DAM POP
    See also AITN 1; CA 29-32R; 135; CANR
    32, 77; DA3; MTCW 1
Tryon, Tom
  See Tryon, Thomas
Ts'ao Hsueh-ch'in 1715(?)-1763 .... **LC 1**
Tsushima, Shuji 1909-1948
  See Dazai Osamu
  See also CA 107
Tsvetaeva (Efron), Marina (Ivanovna)
  1892-1941 .... **TCLC 7, 35; PC 14**
    See also CA 104; 128; CANR 73; MTCW
    1, 2
Tuck, Lily 1938- .... **CLC 70**
  See also CA 139; CANR 90
Tu Fu 712-770 .... **PC 9**
  See also DAM MULT
Tunis, John R(oberts) 1889-1975 ..... **CLC 12**
  See also AW; CA 61-64; CANR 62; DLB
  22, 171; JRDA; MAICYA; SATA 37;
  SATA-Brief 30

Tuohy, Frank CLC 37
  See also Tuohy, John Francis
  See also DLB 14, 139
Tuohy, John Francis 1925-
  See Tuohy, Frank
  See also CA 5-8R; 178; CANR 3, 47
Turco, Lewis (Putnam) 1934- ..... **CLC 11, 63**
  See also CA 13-16R; CAAS 22; CANR 24,
  51; DLBY 84
Turgenev, Ivan 1818-1883 .... **NCLC 21, 37;**
  DA; DAB; DAC; DAM MST, NOV;
  DC 7; SSC 7
    See also AW; DLB 238
Turgot, Anne-Robert-Jacques
  1727-1781 .... **LC 26**
Turner, Frederick 1943- .... **CLC 48**
  See also CA 73-76; CAAS 10; CANR 12,
  30, 56; DLB 40
Tutu, Desmond M(pilo) 1931- .... **CLC 80;**
  BLC 3; DAM MULT
    See also BW 1, 3; CA 125; CANR 67, 81
Tutuola, Amos 1920-1997 ...... **CLC 5, 14, 29;**
  BLC 3; DAM MULT
    See also BW 2, 3; CA 9-12R; 159; CANR
    27, 66; DA3; DLB 125; MTCW 1, 2
Twain, Mark TCLC 6, 12, 19, 36, 48, 59; SSC
  34
    See also Clemens, Samuel Langhorne
    See also AAYA 20; AW; CLR 58, 60, 66;
    DLB 11, 12, 23, 64, 74
Tyler, Anne 1941- . **CLC 7, 11, 18, 28, 44, 59,**
  103; DAM NOV, POP
    See also AAYA 18; AMWS 4; AW; BEST
    89:1; CA 9-12R; CANR 11, 33, 53;
    CDALBS; DLB 6, 143; DLBY 82;
    MTCW 1, 2; SATA 7, 90
Tyler, Royall 1757-1826 .... **NCLC 3**
  See also DLB 37
Tynan, Katharine 1861-1931 .... **TCLC 3**
  See also CA 104; 167; DLB 153, 240
Tyutchev, Fyodor 1803-1873 .... **NCLC 34**
Tzara, Tristan 1896-1963 ...... **CLC 47; DAM**
  POET; PC 27
    See also CA 153; 89-92; MTCW 2
Uhry, Alfred 1936- .. **CLC 55; DAM DRAM,**
  POP
    See also CA 127; 133; DA3; INT 133
Ulf, Haerved
  See Strindberg, (Johan) August
Ulf, Harved
  See Strindberg, (Johan) August
Ulibarri, Sabine R(eyes) 1919- .... **CLC 83;**
  DAM MULT; HLCS 2
    See also CA 131; CANR 81; DLB 82; HW
    1, 2
Unamuno (y Jugo), Miguel de
  1864-1936 ..... **TCLC 2, 9; DAM MULT,**
  NOV; HLC 2; SSC 11
    See also CA 104; 131; CANR 81; DLB 108;
    HW 1, 2; MTCW 1, 2
Undercliffe, Errol
  See Campbell, (John) Ramsey
Underwood, Miles
  See Glassco, John
Undset, Sigrid 1882-1949 .... **TCLC 3; DA;**
  DAB; DAC; DAM MST, NOV
    See also AW; CA 104; 129; DA3; MTCW
    1, 2
Ungaretti, Giuseppe 1888-1970 ... **CLC 7, 11,**
  15
    See also CA 19-20; 25-28R; CAP 2; DLB
    114
Unger, Douglas 1952- .... **CLC 34**
  See also CA 130; CANR 94
Unsworth, Barry (Forster) 1930- .... **CLC 76,**
  127
    See also CA 25-28R; CANR 30, 54;
    DLB 194

Updike, John (Hoyer) 1932- . **CLC 1, 2, 3, 5,**
  7, 9, 13, 15, 23, 34, 43, 70, 139; DA;
  DAB; DAC; DAM MST, NOV, POET,
  POP; SSC 13, 27
    See also AAYA 36; AW; CA 1-4R; CABS
    1; CANR 4, 33, 51, 94; CDALB 1968-
    1988; DA3; DLB 2, 5, 143, 227; DLBD
    3; DLBY 80, 82, 97; MTCW 1, 2
Upshaw, Margaret Mitchell
  See Mitchell, Margaret (Munnerlyn)
Upton, Mark
  See Sanders, Lawrence
Upward, Allen 1863-1926 .... **TCLC 85**
  See also CA 117; 187; DLB 36
Urdang, Constance (Henriette)
  1922-1996 .... **CLC 47**
  See also CA 21-24R; CANR 9, 24
Uriel, Henry
  See Faust, Frederick (Schiller)
Uris, Leon (Marcus) 1924- .... **CLC 7, 32;**
  DAM NOV, POP
    See also AITN 1, 2; BEST 89:2; CA 1-4R;
    CANR 1, 40, 65; DA3; MTCW 1, 2;
    SATA 49
Urista, Alberto H. 1947-
  See Alurista
  See also CA 45-48, 182; CANR 2, 32;
  HLCS 1; HW 1
Urmuz
  See Codrescu, Andrei
Urquhart, Guy
  See McAlmon, Robert (Menzies)
Urquhart, Jane 1949- .... **CLC 90; DAC**
  See also CA 113; CANR 32, 68; CCA 1
Usigli, Rodolfo 1905-1979
  See also CA 131; HLCS 1; HW 1
Ustinov, Peter (Alexander) 1921- .... **CLC 1**
  See also AITN 1; CA 13-16R; CANR 25,
  51; DLB 13; MTCW 2
U Tam'si, Gerald Felix Tchicaya
  See Tchicaya, Gerald Felix
U Tam'si, Tchicaya
  See Tchicaya, Gerald Felix
Vachss, Andrew (Henry) 1942- .... **CLC 106**
  See also CA 118; CANR 44, 95
Vachss, Andrew H.
  See Vachss, Andrew (Henry)
Vaculik, Ludvik 1926- .... **CLC 7**
  See also CA 53-56; CANR 72; CWW 2;
  DLB 232
Vaihinger, Hans 1852-1933 .... **TCLC 71**
  See also CA 116; 166
Valdez, Luis (Miguel) 1940- .. **CLC 84; DAM**
  MULT; DC 10; HLC 2
    See also CA 101; CANR 32, 81; DLB 122;
    HW 1
Valenzuela, Luisa 1938- .... **CLC 31, 104;**
  DAM MULT; HLCS 2; SSC 14
    See also CA 101; CANR 32, 65; CWW 2;
    DLB 113; HW 1, 2
Valera y Alcala-Galiano, Juan
  1824-1905 .... **TCLC 10**
  See also CA 106
Valery, (Ambroise) Paul (Toussaint Jules)
  1871-1945 ... **TCLC 4, 15; DAM POET;**
  PC 9
    See also CA 104; 122; DA3; MTCW 1, 2
Valle-Inclan, Ramon (Maria) del
  1866-1936 .... **TCLC 5; DAM MULT;**
  HLC 2
    See also CA 106; 153; CANR 80; DLB 134;
    HW 2
Vallejo, Antonio Buero
  See Buero Vallejo, Antonio
Vallejo, Cesar (Abraham)
  1892-1938 .. **TCLC 3, 56; DAM MULT;**
  HLC 2
    See also CA 105; 153; HW 1

Valles, Jules 1832-1885 .... NCLC **71**
  See also DLB 123

Vallette, Marguerite Eymery
  1860-1953 .... TCLC **67**
  See also CA 182; DLB 123, 192

Valle Y Pena, Ramon del
  See Valle-Inclan, Ramon (Maria) del

Van Ash, Cay 1918- .... CLC **34**

Vanbrugh, Sir John 1664-1726 .... LC **21;**
  DAM DRAM
  See also DLB 80

Van Campen, Karl
  See Campbell, John W(ood, Jr.)

Vance, Gerald
  See Silverberg, Robert

Vance, Jack CLC **35**
  See also Vance, John Holbrook
  See also DLB 8; SCFW 2

Vance, John Holbrook 1916-
  See Queen, Ellery; Vance, Jack
  See also CA 29-32R; CANR 17, 65; MTCW
  1

Van Den Bogarde, Derek Jules Gaspard
  Ulric Niven 1921-1999 .... CLC **14**
  See also CA 77-80; 179; DLB 19

Vandenburgh, Jane CLC **59**
  See also CA 168

Vanderhaeghe, Guy 1951- .... CLC **41**
  See also CA 113; CANR 72

van der Post, Laurens (Jan)
  1906-1996 .... CLC **5**
  See also CA 5-8R; 155; CANR 35; DLB
  204

van de Wetering, Janwillem 1931- ... CLC **47**
  See also CA 49-52; CANR 4, 62, 90

Van Dine, S. S. TCLC **23**
  See also Wright, Willard Huntington

Van Doren, Carl (Clinton)
  1885-1950 .... TCLC **18**
  See also CA 111; 168

Van Doren, Mark 1894-1972 .... CLC **6, 10**
  See also CA 1-4R; 37-40R; CANR 3; DLB
  45; MTCW 1, 2

Van Druten, John (William)
  1901-1957 .... TCLC **2**
  See also CA 104; 161; DLB 10

Van Duyn, Mona (Jane) 1921- ...... CLC **3, 7,**
  63, 116; DAM POET
  See also CA 9-12R; CANR 7, 38, 60; DLB
  5

Van Dyne, Edith
  See Baum, L(yman) Frank

van Itallie, Jean-Claude 1936- .... CLC **3**
  See also CA 45-48; CAAS 2; CANR 1, 48;
  DLB 7

van Ostaijen, Paul 1896-1928 .... TCLC **33**
  See also CA 163

Van Peebles, Melvin 1932- .... CLC **2, 20;**
  DAM MULT
  See also BW 2, 3; CA 85-88; CANR 27,
  67, 82

Vansittart, Peter 1920- .... CLC **42**
  See also CA 1-4R; CANR 3, 49, 90

Van Vechten, Carl 1880-1964 .... CLC **33**
  See also AMWS 2; CA 183; 89-92; DLB 4,
  9, 51

Van Vogt, A(lfred) E(lton)
  1912-2000 .... CLC **1**
  See also CA 21-24R; CANR 28; DLB 8;
  SATA 14

Varda, Agnes 1928- .... CLC **16**
  See also CA 116; 122

Vargas Llosa, (Jorge) Mario (Pedro)
  1936- .... CLC **3, 6, 9, 10, 15, 31, 42, 85;**
  DA; DAB; DAC; DAM MST, MULT,
  NOV; HLC 2
  See also CA 73-76; CANR 18, 32, 42, 67;
  DA3; DLB 145; HW 1, 2; MTCW 1, 2

Vasiliu, Gheorghe
  See Bacovia, George
  See also CA 123; 189; DLB 220

Vassa, Gustavus
  See Equiano, Olaudah

Vassilikos, Vassilis 1933- .... CLC **4, 8**
  See also CA 81-84; CANR 75

Vaughan, Henry 1621-1695 .... LC **27**
  See also DLB 131

Vaughn, Stephanie CLC **62**

Vazov, Ivan (Minchov) 1850-1921 . TCLC **25**
  See also CA 121; 167; DLB 147

Veblen, Thorstein B(unde)
  1857-1929 .... TCLC **31**
  See also AMWS 1; CA 115; 165

Vega, Lope de 1562-1635 .... LC **23; HLCS 2**

Vendler, Helen (Hennessy) 1933- ... CLC **138**
  See also CA 41-44R; CANR 25, 72; MTCW
  1, 2

Venison, Alfred
  See Pound, Ezra (Weston Loomis)

Verdi, Marie de
  See Mencken, H(enry) L(ouis)

Verdu, Matilde
  See Cela, Camilo Jose

Verga, Giovanni (Carmelo)
  1840-1922 .... TCLC **3; SSC 21**
  See also CA 104; 123

Vergil 70B.C.-19B.C. .... CMLC **9, 40; DA;**
  DAB; DAC; DAM MST, POET; PC 12
  See also AW; DA3; DLB 211

Verhaeren, Emile (Adolphe Gustave)
  1855-1916 .... TCLC **12**
  See also CA 109

Verlaine, Paul (Marie) 1844-1896 .. NCLC **2,**
  51; DAM POET; PC 2, 32

Verne, Jules (Gabriel) 1828-1905 ... TCLC **6,**
  52
  See also AAYA 16; CA 110; 131; DA3;
  DLB 123; JRDA; MAICYA; SATA 21

Very, Jones 1813-1880 .... NCLC **9**
  See also DLB 1

Vesaas, Tarjei 1897-1970 .... CLC **48**
  See also CA 29-32R

Vialis, Gaston
  See Simenon, Georges (Jacques Christian)

Vian, Boris 1920-1959 .... TCLC **9**
  See also CA 106; 164; DLB 72; MTCW 2

Viaud, (Louis Marie) Julien 1850-1923
  See Loti, Pierre
  See also CA 107

Vicar, Henry
  See Felsen, Henry Gregor

Vicker, Angus
  See Felsen, Henry Gregor

Vidal, Gore 1925- ...... CLC **2, 4, 6, 8, 10, 22,**
  33, 72; DAM NOV, POP
  See also AITN 1; AMWS 4; BEST 90:2;
  CA 5-8R; CANR 13, 45, 65; CDALBS;
  DA3; DLB 6, 152; INT CANR-13;
  MTCW 1, 2

Viereck, Peter (Robert Edwin)
  1916- .... CLC **4; PC 27**
  See also CA 1-4R; CANR 1, 47; DLB 5

Vigny, Alfred (Victor) de
  1797-1863 .. NCLC **7; DAM POET; PC**
  26
  See also DLB 119, 192

Vilakazi, Benedict Wallet
  1906-1947 .... TCLC **37**
  See also CA 168

Villa, Jose Garcia 1914-1997 .... PC **22**
  See also CA 25-28R; CANR 12

Villarreal, Jose Antonio 1924-
  See also CA 133; CANR 93; DAM MULT;
  DLB 82; HLC 2; HW 1

Villaurrutia, Xavier 1903-1950 ...... TCLC **80**
  See also HW 1

Villehardouin 1150(?)-1218(?) .... CMLC **38**

Villiers de l'Isle Adam, Jean Marie Mathias
  Philippe Auguste, Comte de
  1838-1889 .... NCLC **3; SSC 14**
  See also DLB 123

Villon, François 1431-1463(?) . LC **62; PC 13**
  See also DLB 208

Vine, Barbara CLC **50**
  See also Rendell, Ruth (Barbara)
  See also BEST 90:4

Vinge, Joan (Carol) D(ennison)
  1948- .... CLC **30; SSC 24**
  See also AAYA 32; AW; CA 93-96; CANR
  72; SATA 36, 113

Violis, G.
  See Simenon, Georges (Jacques Christian)

Viramontes, Helena Maria 1954-
  See also CA 159; DLB 122; HLCS 2; HW
  2

Virgil
  See Vergil

Visconti, Luchino 1906-1976 .... CLC **16**
  See also CA 81-84; 65-68; CANR 39

Vittorini, Elio 1908-1966 .... CLC **6, 9, 14**
  See also CA 133; 25-28R

Vivekananda, Swami 1863-1902 .... TCLC **88**

Vizenor, Gerald Robert 1934- .... CLC **103;**
  DAM MULT
  See also CA 13-16R; CAAS 22; CANR 5,
  21, 44, 67; DLB 175, 227; MTCW 2;
  NNAL; TCWW 2

Vizinczey, Stephen 1933- .... CLC **40**
  See also CA 128; CCA 1; INT 128

Vliet, R(ussell) G(ordon)
  1929-1984 .... CLC **22**
  See also CA 37-40R; 112; CANR 18

Vogau, Boris Andreyevich 1894-1937(?)
  See Pilnyak, Boris
  See also CA 123

Vogel, Paula A(nne) 1951- .... CLC **76**
  See also CA 108

Voigt, Cynthia 1942- .... CLC **30**
  See also AAYA 3, 30; AW; CA 106, CANR
  18, 37, 40, 94; CLR 13, 48; INT CANR-
  18; JRDA; MAICYA; SATA 48, 79, 116,
  SATA-Brief 33

Voigt, Ellen Bryant 1943- .... CLC **54**
  See also CA 69-72; CANR 11, 29, 55; DLB
  120

Voinovich, Vladimir (Nikolaevich)
  1932- .... CLC **10, 49**
  See also CA 81-84; CAAS 12; CANR 33,
  67; MTCW 1

Vollmann, William T. 1959- .. CLC **89; DAM**
  NOV, POP
  See also CA 134; CANR 67; DA3; MTCW
  2

Voloshinov, V. N.
  See Bakhtin, Mikhail Mikhailovich

Voltaire 1694-1778 .... LC **14; DA; DAB;**
  DAC; DAM DRAM, MST; SSC 12
  See also AW; DA3

von Aschendrof, BaronIgnatz 1873-1939
  See Ford, Ford Madox

von Daeniken, Erich 1935- .... CLC **30**
  See also AITN 1; CA 37-40R; CANR 17,
  44

von Daniken, Erich
  See von Daeniken, Erich

von Hartmann, Eduard
  1842-1906 .... TCLC **96**

von Heidenstam, (Carl Gustaf) Verner
  See Heidenstam, (Carl Gustaf) Verner von

von Heyse, Paul (Johann Ludwig)
  See Heyse, Paul (Johann Ludwig von)

von Hofmannsthal, Hugo
See Hofmannsthal, Hugo von

von Horvath, Odon
See Horvath, Oedoen von

von Horvath, Oedoen
See Horvath, Oedoen von
See also CA 184

von Liliencron, (Friedrich Adolf Axel) Detlev
See Liliencron, (Friedrich Adolf Axel) Detlev von

Vonnegut, Kurt, Jr. 1922- . CLC 1, 2, 3, 4, 5, 8, 12, 22, 40, 60, 111; DA; DAB; DAC; DAM MST, NOV, POP; SSC 8
See also AAYA 6; AITN 1; AMWS 2; AW; BEST 90:4; CA 1-4R; CANR 1, 25, 49, 75, 92; CDALB 1968-1988; DA3; DLB 2, 8, 152; DLBD 3; DLBY 80; MTCW 1, 2

Von Rachen, Kurt
See Hubbard, L(afayette) Ron(ald)

von Rezzori (d'Arezzo), Gregor
See Rezzori (d'Arezzo), Gregor von

von Sternberg, Josef
See Sternberg, Josef von

Vorster, Gordon 1924- .... CLC 34
See also CA 133

Vosce, Trudie
See Ozick, Cynthia

Voznesensky, Andrei (Andreievich) 1933- .... CLC 1, 15, 57; DAM POET
See also CA 89-92; CANR 37; CWW 2; MTCW 1

Waddington, Miriam 1917- .... CLC 28
See also CA 21-24R; CANR 12, 30; CCA 1; DLB 68

Wagman, Fredrica 1937- .... CLC 7
See also CA 97-100; INT 97-100

Wagner, Linda W.
See Wagner-Martin, Linda (C.)

Wagner, Linda Welshimer
See Wagner-Martin, Linda (C.)

Wagner, Richard 1813-1883 .... NCLC 9
See also DLB 129

Wagner-Martin, Linda (C.) 1936- .... CLC 50
See also CA 159

Wagoner, David (Russell) 1926- .... CLC 3, 5, 15; PC 33
See also CA 1-4R; CAAS 3; CANR 2, 71; DLB 5; SATA 14; TCWW 2

Wah, Fred(erick James) 1939- .... CLC 44
See also CA 107; 141; DLB 60

Wahloo, Per 1926-1975 .... CLC 7
See also CA 61-64; CANR 73

Wahloo, Peter
See Wahloo, Per

Wain, John (Barrington) 1925-1994 . CLC 2, 11, 15, 46
See also CA 5-8R; 145; CAAS 4; CANR 23, 54; CDBLB 1960 to Present; DLB 15, 27, 139, 155; MTCW 1, 2

Wajda, Andrzej 1926- .... CLC 16
See also CA 102

Wakefield, Dan 1932- .... CLC 7
See also CA 21-24R; CAAS 7

Wakoski, Diane 1937- ...... CLC 2, 4, 7, 9, 11, 40; DAM POET; PC 15
See also CA 13-16R; CAAS 1; CANR 9, 60; DLB 5; INT CANR-9; MTCW 2

Wakoski-Sherbell, Diane
See Wakoski, Diane

Walcott, Derek (Alton) 1930- .... CLC 2, 4, 9, 14, 25, 42, 67, 76; BLC 3; DAB; DAC; DAM MST, MULT, POET; DC 7
See also BW 2; CA 89-92; CANR 26, 47, 75, 80; DA3; DLB 117; DLBY 81; MTCW 1, 2

Waldman, Anne (Lesley) 1945- .... CLC 7
See also CA 37-40R; CAAS 17; CANR 34, 69; DLB 16

Waldo, E. Hunter
See Sturgeon, Theodore (Hamilton)

Waldo, Edward Hamilton
See Sturgeon, Theodore (Hamilton)

Walker, Alice (Malsenior) 1944- ... CLC 5, 6, 9, 19, 27, 46, 58, 103; BLC 3; DA; DAB; DAC; DAM MST, MULT, NOV, POET, POP; PC 30; SSC 5
See also AAYA 3, 33; AMWS 3; AW; BEST 89:4; BW 2, 3; CA 37-40R; CANR 9, 27, 49, 66, 82; CDALB 1968-1988; DA3; DLB 6, 33, 143; INT CANR-27; MTCW 1, 2; SATA 31

Walker, David Harry 1911-1992 ...... CLC 14
See also CA 1-4R; 137; CANR 1; SATA 8; SATA-Obit 71

Walker, Edward Joseph 1934-
See Walker, Ted
See also CA 21-24R; CANR 12, 28, 53

Walker, George F. 1947- . CLC 44, 61; DAB; DAC; DAM MST
See also CA 103; CANR 21, 43, 59; DLB 60

Walker, Joseph A. 1935- .... CLC 19; DAM DRAM, MST
See also BW 1, 3; CA 89-92; CANR 26; DLB 38

Walker, Margaret (Abigail) 1915-1998 .... CLC 1, 6; BLC; DAM MULT; PC 20
See also BW 2, 3; CA 73-76; 172; CANR 26, 54, 76; DLB 76, 152; MTCW 1, 2

Walker, Ted CLC 13
See also Walker, Edward Joseph
See also DLB 40

Wallace, David Foster 1962- ..... CLC 50, 114
See also CA 132; CANR 59; DA3; MTCW 2

Wallace, Dexter
See Masters, Edgar Lee

Wallace, (Richard Horatio) Edgar 1875-1932 .... TCLC 57
See also CA 115; DLB 70

Wallace, Irving 1916-1990 .... CLC 7, 13; DAM NOV, POP
See also AITN 1; CA 1-4R; 132; CAAS 1; CANR 1, 27; INT CANR-27; MTCW 1, 2

Wallant, Edward Lewis 1926-1962 ... CLC 5, 10
See also CA 1-4R; CANR 22; DLB 2, 28, 143; MTCW 1, 2

Wallas, Graham 1858-1932 .... TCLC 91

Walley, Byron
See Card, Orson Scott

Walpole, Horace 1717-1797 .... LC 49
See also DLB 39, 104

Walpole, Hugh (Seymour) 1884-1941 .... TCLC 5
See also CA 104; 165; DLB 34; MTCW 2

Walser, Martin 1927- .... CLC 27
See also CA 57-60; CANR 8, 46; CWW 2; DLB 75, 124

Walser, Robert 1878-1956 .... TCLC 18; SSC 20
See also CA 118; 165; DLB 66

Walsh, Gillian Paton
See Paton Walsh, Gillian

Walsh, Jill Paton CLC 35
See also Paton Walsh, Gillian
See also CLR 2, 65

Walter, Villiam Christian
See Andersen, Hans Christian

Wambaugh, Joseph (Aloysius, Jr.) 1937- .... CLC 3, 18; DAM NOV, POP
See also AITN 1; BEST 89:3; CA 33-36R; CANR 42, 65; DA3; DLB 6; DLBY 83; MTCW 1, 2

Wang Wei 699(?)-761(?) .... PC 18

Ward, Arthur Henry Sarsfield 1883-1959
See Rohmer, Sax
See also CA 108; 173

Ward, Douglas Turner 1930- .... CLC 19
See also BW 1; CA 81-84; CANR 27; DLB 7, 38

Ward, E. D.
See Lucas, E(dward) V(errall)

Ward, Mary Augusta 1851-1920 ... TCLC 55
See also DLB 18

Ward, Peter
See Faust, Frederick (Schiller)

Warhol, Andy 1928(?)-1987 .... CLC 20
See also AAYA 12; BEST 89:4; CA 89-92; 121; CANR 34

Warner, Francis (Robert le Plastrier) 1937- .... CLC 14
See also CA 53-56; CANR 11

Warner, Marina 1946- .... CLC 59
See also CA 65-68; CANR 21, 55; DLB 194

Warner, Rex (Ernest) 1905-1986 ...... CLC 45
See also CA 89-92; 119; DLB 15

Warner, Susan (Bogert) 1819-1885 .... NCLC 31
See also DLB 3, 42, 239

Warner, Sylvia (Constance) Ashton
See Ashton-Warner, Sylvia (Constance)

Warner, Sylvia Townsend 1893-1978 .... CLC 7, 19; SSC 23
See also CA 61-64; 77-80; CANR 16, 60; DLB 34, 139; MTCW 1, 2

Warren, Mercy Otis 1728-1814 ..... NCLC 13
See also DLB 31, 200

Warren, Robert Penn 1905-1989 .. CLC 1, 4, 6, 8, 10, 13, 18, 39, 53, 59; DA; DAB; DAC; DAM MST, NOV, POET; SSC 4
See also AITN 1; AW; CA 13-16R; 129; CANR 10, 47; CDALB 1968-1988; DA3; DLB 2, 48, 152; DLBY 80, 89; INT CANR-10; MTCW 1, 2; SATA 46; SATA-Obit 63

Warshofsky, Isaac
See Singer, Isaac Bashevis

Warton, Thomas 1728-1790 ..... LC 15; DAM POET
See also DLB 104, 109

Waruk, Kona
See Harris, (Theodore) Wilson

Warung, Price TCLC 45
See also Astley, William

Warwick, Jarvis
See Garner, Hugh
See also CCA 1

Washington, Alex
See Harris, Mark

Washington, Booker T(aliaferro) 1856-1915 ...... TCLC 10; BLC 3; DAM MULT
See also BW 1; CA 114; 125; DA3; SATA 28

Washington, George 1732-1799 .... LC 25
See also DLB 31

Wassermann, (Karl) Jakob 1873-1934 .... TCLC 6
See also CA 104; 163; DLB 66

Wasserstein, Wendy 1950- .. CLC 32, 59, 90; DAM DRAM; DC 4
See also CA 121; 129; CABS 3; CANR 53, 75; DA3; DLB 228; INT 129; MTCW 2; SATA 94

Waterhouse, Keith (Spencer) 1929- . **CLC 47**
　　See also CA 5-8R; CANR 38, 67; DLB 13, 15; MTCW 1, 2

Waters, Frank (Joseph) 1902-1995 .. **CLC 88**
　　See also CA 5-8R; 149; CAAS 13; CANR 3, 18, 63; DLB 212; DLBY 86; TCWW 2

Waters, Roger 1944- .... **CLC 35**

Watkins, Frances Ellen
　　See Harper, Frances Ellen Watkins

Watkins, Gerrold
　　See Malzberg, Barry N(athaniel)

Watkins, Gloria Jean 1952(?)-
　　See hooks, bell
　　See also BW 2; CA 143; CANR 87; MTCW 2; SATA 115

Watkins, Paul 1964- .... **CLC 55**
　　See also CA 132; CANR 62

Watkins, Vernon Phillips
　　1906-1967 .... **CLC 43**
　　See also CA 9-10; 25-28R; CAP 1; DLB 20

Watson, Irving S.
　　See Mencken, H(enry) L(ouis)

Watson, John H.
　　See Farmer, Philip Jose

Watson, Richard F.
　　See Silverberg, Robert

Waugh, Auberon (Alexander)
　　1939-2001 .... **CLC 7**
　　See also CA 45-48; CANR 6, 22, 92; DLB 14, 194

Waugh, Evelyn (Arthur St. John)
　　1903-1966 .. **CLC 1, 3, 8, 13, 19, 27, 44, 107; DA; DAB; DAC; DAM MST, NOV, POP; SSC 41**
　　See also AW; CA 85-88; 25-28R; CANR 22; CDBLB 1914-1945; DA3; DLB 15, 162, 195; MTCW 1, 2

Waugh, Harriet 1944- .... **CLC 6**
　　See also CA 85-88; CANR 22

Ways, C. R.
　　See Blount, Roy (Alton), Jr.

Waystaff, Simon
　　See Swift, Jonathan

Webb, Beatrice (Martha Potter)
　　1858-1943 .... **TCLC 22**
　　See also CA 117; 162; DLB 190

Webb, Charles (Richard) 1939- .... **CLC 7**
　　See also CA 25-28R

Webb, James H(enry), Jr. 1946- ...... **CLC 22**
　　See also CA 81-84

Webb, Mary Gladys (Meredith)
　　1881-1927 .... **TCLC 24**
　　See also CA 182; 123; DLB 34

Webb, Mrs. Sidney
　　See Webb, Beatrice (Martha Potter)

Webb, Phyllis 1927- .... **CLC 18**
　　See also CA 104; CANR 23; CCA 1; DLB 53

Webb, Sidney (James) 1859-1947 .. **TCLC 22**
　　See also CA 117; 163; DLB 190

Webber, Andrew Lloyd CLC 21
　　See also Lloyd Webber, Andrew

Weber, Lenora Mattingly
　　1895-1971 .... **CLC 12**
　　See also CA 19-20; 29-32R; CAP 1; SATA 2; SATA-Obit 26

Weber, Max 1864-1920 .... **TCLC 69**
　　See also CA 109; 189

Webster, John 1580(?)-1634(?) ... **LC 33; DA; DAB; DAC; DAM DRAM, MST; DC 2**
　　See also AW; CDBLB Before 1660; DLB 58

Webster, Noah 1758-1843 .... **NCLC 30**
　　See also DLB 1, 37, 42, 43, 73

Wedekind, (Benjamin) Frank(lin)
　　1864-1918 .... **TCLC 7; DAM DRAM**
　　See also CA 104; 153; DLB 118

Weidman, Jerome 1913-1998 .... **CLC 7**
　　See also AITN 2; CA 1-4R; 171; CANR 1; DLB 28

Weil, Simone (Adolphine)
　　1909-1943 .... **TCLC 23**
　　See also CA 117; 159; MTCW 2

Weininger, Otto 1880-1903 .... **TCLC 84**

Weinstein, Nathan
　　See West, Nathanael

Weinstein, Nathan von Wallenstein
　　See West, Nathanael

Weir, Peter (Lindsay) 1944- .... **CLC 20**
　　See also CA 113; 123

Weiss, Peter (Ulrich) 1916-1982 .. **CLC 3, 15, 51; DAM DRAM**
　　See also CA 45-48; 106; CANR 3; DLB 69, 124

Weiss, Theodore (Russell) 1916- ... **CLC 3, 8, 14**
　　See also CA 9-12R; CAAE 189; CAAS 2; CANR 46, 94; DLB 5

Welch, (Maurice) Denton
　　1915-1948 .... **TCLC 22**
　　See also CA 121; 148

Welch, James 1940- ..... **CLC 6, 14, 52; DAM MULT, POP**
　　See also CA 85-88; CANR 42, 66; DLB 175; NNAL; TCWW 2

Weldon, Fay 1931- . **CLC 6, 9, 11, 19, 36, 59, 122; DAM POP**
　　See also BRWS 4; CA 21-24R; CANR 16, 46, 63; CDBLB 1960 to Present; DLB 14, 194; INT CANR-16; MTCW 1, 2

Wellek, Rene 1903-1995 .... **CLC 28**
　　See also CA 5-8R; 150; CAAS 7; CANR 8; DLB 63; INT CANR-8

Weller, Michael 1942- .... **CLC 10, 53**
　　See also CA 85-88

Weller, Paul 1958- .... **CLC 26**

Wellershoff, Dieter 1925- .... **CLC 46**
　　See also CA 89-92; CANR 16, 37

Welles, (George) Orson 1915-1985 .. **CLC 20, 80**
　　See also CA 93-96; 117

Wellman, John McDowell 1945-
　　See Wellman, Mac
　　See also CA 166

Wellman, Mac CLC 65
　　See also Wellman, John McDowell; Wellman, John McDowell

Wellman, Manly Wade 1903-1986 ... **CLC 49**
　　See also CA 1-4R; 118; CANR 6, 16, 44; SATA 6; SATA-Obit 47

Wells, Carolyn 1869(?)-1942 .... **TCLC 35**
　　See also CA 113; 185; DLB 11

Wells, H(erbert) G(eorge)
　　1866-1946 . **TCLC 6, 12, 19; DA; DAB; DAC; DAM MST, NOV; SSC 6**
　　See also AAYA 18; AW; CA 110; 121; CD-BLB 1914-1945; CLR 64; DA3; DLB 34, 70, 156, 178; MTCW 1, 2; SATA 20

Wells, Rosemary 1943- .... **CLC 12**
　　See also AAYA 13; AW; CA 85-88; CANR 48; CLR 16, 69; MAICYA; SAAS 1; SATA 18, 69, 114

Welty, Eudora 1909- ...... **CLC 1, 2, 5, 14, 22, 33, 105; DA; DAB; DAC; DAM MST, NOV; SSC 1, 27**
　　See also AW; CA 9-12R; CABS 1; CANR 32, 65; CDALB 1941-1968; DA3; DLB 2, 102, 143; DLBD 12; DLBY 87; MTCW 1, 2

Wen I-to 1899-1946 .... **TCLC 28**

Wentworth, Robert
　　See Hamilton, Edmond

Werfel, Franz (Viktor) 1890-1945 ... **TCLC 8**
　　See also CA 104; 161; DLB 81, 124

Wergeland, Henrik Arnold
　　1808-1845 .... **NCLC 5**

Wersba, Barbara 1932- .... **CLC 30**
　　See also AAYA 2, 30; AW; CA 29-32R; 182; CAAE 182; CANR 16, 38; CLR 3; DLB 52; JRDA; MAICYA; SAAS 2; SATA 1, 58; SATA-Essay 103

Wertmueller, Lina 1928- .... **CLC 16**
　　See also CA 97-100; CANR 39, 78

Wescott, Glenway 1901-1987 .. **CLC 13; SSC 35**
　　See also CA 13-16R; 121; CANR 23, 70; DLB 4, 9, 102

Wesker, Arnold 1932- ... **CLC 3, 5, 42; DAB; DAM DRAM**
　　See also CA 1-4R; CAAS 7; CANR 1, 33; CDBLB 1960 to Present; DLB 13; MTCW 1

Wesley, Richard (Errol) 1945- .... **CLC 7**
　　See also BW 1; CA 57-60; CANR 27; DLB 38

Wessel, Johan Herman 1742-1785 .... **LC 7**

West, Anthony (Panther)
　　1914-1987 .... **CLC 50**
　　See also CA 45-48; 124; CANR 3, 19; DLB 15

West, C. P.
　　See Wodehouse, P(elham) G(renville)

West, Cornel (Ronald) 1953- .... **CLC 134; BLCS**
　　See also CA 144; CANR 91

West, (Mary) Jessamyn 1902-1984 ... **CLC 7, 17**
　　See also AW; CA 9-12R; 112; CANR 27; DLB 6; DLBY 84; MTCW 1, 2; SATA-Obit 37

West, Morris L(anglo) 1916-1999 ..... **CLC 6, 33**
　　See also CA 5-8R; 187; CANR 24, 49, 64; MTCW 1, 2

West, Nathanael 1903-1940 .... **TCLC 1, 14, 44; SSC 16**
　　See also CA 104; 125; CDALB 1929-1941; DA3; DLB 4, 9, 28; MTCW 1, 2

West, Owen
　　See Koontz, Dean R(ay)

West, Paul 1930- .... **CLC 7, 14, 96**
　　See also CA 13-16R; CAAS 7; CANR 22, 53, 76, 89; DLB 14; INT CANR-22; MTCW 2

West, Rebecca 1892-1983 ... **CLC 7, 9, 31, 50**
　　See also BRWS 3; CA 5-8R; 109; CANR 19; DLB 36; DLBY 83; MTCW 1, 2

Westall, Robert (Atkinson)
　　1929-1993 .... **CLC 17**
　　See also AAYA 12; CA 69-72; 141; CANR 18, 68; CLR 13; JRDA; MAICYA; SAAS 2; SATA 23, 69; SATA-Obit 75

Westermarck, Edward 1862-1939 . **TCLC 87**

Westlake, Donald E(dwin) 1933- .... **CLC 7, 33; DAM POP**
　　See also CA 17-20R; CAAS 13; CANR 16, 44, 65, 94; INT CANR-16; MTCW 2

Westmacott, Mary
　　See Christie, Agatha (Mary Clarissa)

Weston, Allen
　　See Norton, Andre

Wetcheek, J. L.
　　See Feuchtwanger, Lion

Wetering, Janwillem van de
　　See van de Wetering, Janwillem

Wetherald, Agnes Ethelwyn
　　1857-1940 .... **TCLC 81**
　　See also DLB 99

Wetherell, Elizabeth
　　See Warner, Susan (Bogert)

Whale, James 1889-1957 .... **TCLC 63**

Whalen, Philip 1923- .... **CLC 6, 29**
　　See also CA 9-12R; CANR 5, 39; DLB 16

Wharton, Edith (Newbold Jones)
1862-1937 .... TCLC 3, 9, 27, 53; DA;
DAB; DAC; DAM MST, NOV; SSC 6
See also AAYA 25; AW; CA 104; 132;
CDALB 1865-1917; DA3; DLB 4, 9, 12,
78, 189; DLBD 13; MTCW 1, 2
Wharton, James
See Mencken, H(enry) L(ouis)
**Wharton, William (a pseudonym) CLC 18,
37**
See also CA 93-96; DLBY 80; INT 93-96
Wheatley (Peters), Phillis
1753(?)-1784 ...... LC 3, 50; BLC 3; DA;
DAC; DAM MST, MULT, POET; PC 3
See also AW; CDALB 1640-1865; DA3;
DLB 31, 50
Wheelock, John Hall 1886-1978 .... CLC 14
See also CA 13-16R; 77-80; CANR 14;
DLB 45
White, E(lwyn) B(rooks)
1899-1985 . CLC 10, 34, 39; DAM POP
See also AITN 2; AMWS 1; CA 13-16R;
116; CANR 16, 37; CDALBS; CLR 1, 21;
DA3; DLB 11, 22; MAICYA; MTCW 1,
2; SATA 2, 29, 100; SATA-Obit 44
White, Edmund (Valentine III)
1940- .... CLC 27, 110; DAM POP
See also AAYA 7; CA 45-48; CANR 3, 19,
36, 62; DA3; DLB 227; MTCW 1, 2
White, Patrick (Victor Martindale)
1912-1990 ...... CLC 3, 4, 5, 7, 9, 18, 65,
69; SSC 39
See also BRWS 1; CA 81-84; 132; CANR
43; MTCW 1
White, Phyllis Dorothy James 1920-
See James, P. D.
See also CA 21-24R; CANR 17, 43, 65;
DAM POP; DA3; MTCW 1, 2
White, T(erence) H(anbury)
1906-1964 .... CLC 30
See also AAYA 22; AW; CA 73-76; CANR
37; DLB 160; JRDA; MAICYA; SATA 12
White, Terence de Vere 1912-1994 ... CLC 49
See also CA 49-52; 145; CANR 3
White, Walter
See White, Walter F(rancis)
See also BLC; DAM MULT
White, Walter F(rancis)
1893-1955 .... TCLC 15
See also White, Walter
See also BW 1; CA 115; 124; DLB 51
White, William Hale 1831-1913
See Rutherford, Mark
See also CA 121; 189
Whitehead, Alfred North
1861-1947 .... TCLC 97
See also CA 117; 165; DLB 100
Whitehead, E(dward) A(nthony)
1933- .... CLC 5
See also CA 65-68; CANR 58
Whitemore, Hugh (John) 1936- .... CLC 37
See also CA 132; CANR 77; INT 132
Whitman, Sarah Helen (Power)
1803-1878 .... NCLC 19
See also DLB 1
Whitman, Walt(er) 1819-1892 .. NCLC 4, 31,
81; DA; DAB; DAC; DAM MST,
POET; PC 3
See also AW 1; CDALB 1640-1865; DA3;
DLB 3, 64, 224; SATA 20
Whitney, Phyllis A(yame) 1903- ...... CLC 42;
DAM POP
See also AAYA 36; AITN 2; AW; BEST
90:3; CA 1-4R; CANR 3, 25, 38, 60; CLR
59; DA3; JRDA; MAICYA; MTCW 2;
SATA 1, 30
Whittemore, (Edward) Reed (Jr.)
1919- .... CLC 4
See also CA 9-12R; CAAS 8; CANR 4;
DLB 5

Whittier, John Greenleaf
1807-1892 .... NCLC 8, 59
See also AMWS 1; DLB 1
Whittlebot, Hernia
See Coward, No
Wicker, Thomas Grey 1926-
See Wicker, Tom
See also CA 65-68; CANR 21, 46
Wicker, Tom CLC 7
See also Wicker, Thomas Grey
Wideman, John Edgar 1941- ...... CLC 5, 34,
36, 67, 122; BLC 3; DAM MULT
See also BW 2, 3; CA 85-88; CANR 14,
42, 67; DLB 33, 143; MTCW 2
Wiebe, Rudy (Henry) 1934- .. CLC 6, 11, 14,
138; DAC; DAM MST
See also CA 37-40R; CANR 42, 67; DLB
60
Wieland, Christoph Martin
1733-1813 .... NCLC 17
See also DLB 97
Wiene, Robert 1881-1938 .... TCLC 56
Wieners, John 1934- .... CLC 7
See also CA 13-16R; DLB 16
Wiesel, Elie(zer) 1928- .... CLC 3, 5, 11, 37;
DA; DAB; DAC; DAM MST, NOV
See also AAYA 7; AITN 1; AW; CA 5-8R;
CAAS 4; CANR 8, 40, 65; CDALBS;
DA3; DLB 83; DLBY 87; INT CANR-8;
MTCW 1, 2; SATA 56
Wiggins, Marianne 1947- .... CLC 57
See also BEST 89:3; CA 130; CANR 60
Wight, James Alfred 1916-1995
See Herriot, James
See also AW; CA 77-80; SATA 55; SATA-
Brief 44
Wilbur, Richard (Purdy) 1921- ..... CLC 3, 6,
9, 14, 53, 110; DA; DAB; DAC; DAM
MST, POET
See also AMWS 3; CA 1-4R; CABS 2;
CANR 2, 29, 76, 93; CDALBS; DLB 5,
169; INT CANR-29; MTCW 1, 2; SATA
9, 108
Wild, Peter 1940- .... CLC 14
See also CA 37-40R; DLB 5
Wilde, Oscar (Fingal O'Flahertie Wills)
1854(?)-1900 .... TCLC 1, 8, 23, 41; DA;
DAB; DAC; DAM DRAM, MST, NOV;
SSC 11
See also AW; CA 104; 119; CDBLB 1890-
1914; DA3; DLB 10, 19, 34, 57, 141, 156,
190; SATA 24
Wilder, Billy CLC 20
See also Wilder, Samuel
See also DLB 26
Wilder, Samuel 1906-
See Wilder, Billy
See also CA 89-92
Wilder, Thornton (Niven)
1897-1975 .. CLC 1, 5, 6, 10, 15, 35, 82;
DA; DAB; DAC; DAM DRAM, MST,
NOV; DC 1
See also AAYA 29; AITN 2; AW 1; CA 13-
16R; 61-64; CANR 40; CDALBS; DA3;
DLB 4, 7, 9, 228; DLBY 97; MTCW 1, 2
Wilding, Michael 1942- .... CLC 73
See also CA 104; CANR 24, 49
Wiley, Richard 1944- .... CLC 44
See also CA 121; 129; CANR 71
Wilhelm, Kate CLC 7
See also Wilhelm, Katie (Gertrude)
See also AAYA 20; CAAS 5; DLB 8; INT
CANR-17; SCFW 2
Wilhelm, Katie (Gertrude) 1928-
See Wilhelm, Kate
See also CA 37-40R; CANR 17, 36, 60, 94;
MTCW 1
Wilkins, Mary
See Freeman, Mary E(leanor) Wilkins

Willard, Nancy 1936- .... CLC 7, 37
See also CA 89-92; CANR 10, 39, 68; CLR
5; DLB 5, 52; MAICYA; MTCW 1; SATA
37, 71; SATA-Brief 30
William of Ockham 1290-1349 ..... CMLC 32
Williams, Ben Ames 1889-1953 ..... TCLC 89
See also CA 183; DLB 102
Williams, C(harles) K(enneth)
1936- .... CLC 33, 56; DAM POET
See also CA 37-40R; CAAS 26; CANR 57;
DLB 5
Williams, Charles
See Collier, James L(incoln)
Williams, Charles (Walter Stansby)
1886-1945 .... TCLC 1, 11
See also CA 104; 163; DLB 100, 153
Williams, (George) Emlyn
1905-1987 .... CLC 15; DAM DRAM
See also CA 104; 123; CANR 36; DLB 10,
77; MTCW 1
Williams, Hank 1923-1953 .... TCLC 81
Williams, Hugo 1942- .... CLC 42
See also CA 17-20R; CANR 45; DLB 40
Williams, J. Walker
See Wodehouse, P(elham) G(renville)
Williams, John A(lfred) 1925- ..... CLC 5, 13;
BLC 3; DAM MULT
See also BW 2, 3; CA 53-56; CAAS 3;
CANR 6, 26, 51; DLB 2, 33; INT
CANR-6
Williams, Jonathan (Chamberlain)
1929- .... CLC 13
See also CA 9-12R; CAAS 12; CANR 8;
DLB 5
Williams, Joy 1944- .... CLC 31
See also CA 41-44R; CANR 22, 48
Williams, Norman 1952- .... CLC 39
See also CA 118
Williams, Sherley Anne 1944-1999 . CLC 89;
BLC 3; DAM MULT, POET
See also BW 2, 3; CA 73-76; 185; CANR
25, 82; DLB 41; INT CANR-25; SATA
78; SATA-Obit 116
Williams, Shirley
See Williams, Sherley Anne
Williams, Tennessee 1914-1983 . CLC 1, 2, 5,
7, 8, 11, 15, 19, 30, 39, 45, 71, 111; DA;
DAB; DAC; DAM DRAM, MST; DC 4
See also AAYA 31; AITN 1, 2; AW; CA
5-8R; 108; CABS 3; CANR 31; CDALB
1941-1968; DA3; DLB 7; DLBD 4;
DLBY 83; GLL 1; MTCW 1, 2
Williams, Thomas (Alonzo)
1926-1990 .... CLC 14
See also CA 1-4R; 132; CANR 2
Williams, William C.
See Williams, William Carlos
Williams, William Carlos
1883-1963 ... CLC 1, 2, 5, 9, 13, 22, 42,
67; DA; DAB; DAC; DAM MST,
POET; PC 7; SSC 31
See also CA 89-92; CANR 34; CDALB
1917-1929; DA3; DLB 4, 16, 54, 86;
MTCW 1, 2
Williamson, David (Keith) 1942- ..... CLC 56
See also CA 103; CANR 41
Williamson, Ellen Douglas 1905-1984
See Douglas, Ellen
See also CA 17-20R; 114; CANR 39
Williamson, Jack CLC 29
See also Williamson, John Stewart
See also CAAS 8; DLB 8; SCFW 2
Williamson, John Stewart 1908-
See Williamson, Jack
See also CA 17-20R; CANR 23, 70
Willie, Frederick
See Lovecraft, H(oward) P(hillips)

Willingham, Calder (Baynard, Jr.)
  1922-1995 .... **CLC 5, 51**
  See also CA 5-8R; 147; CANR 3; DLB 2,
  44; IDFW 3; MTCW 1
Willis, Charles
  See Clarke, Arthur C(harles)
Willy
  See Colette, (Sidonie-Gabrielle)
Willy, Colette
  See Colette, (Sidonie-Gabrielle)
  See also GLL 1
Wilson, A(ndrew) N(orman) 1950- .. **CLC 33**
  See also CA 112; 122; DLB 14, 155, 194;
  MTCW 2
Wilson, Angus (Frank Johnstone)
  1913-1991 . **CLC 2, 3, 5, 25, 34; SSC 21**
  See also BRWS 1; CA 5-8R; 134; CANR
  21; DLB 15, 139, 155; MTCW 1, 2
Wilson, August 1945- ... **CLC 39, 50, 63, 118;
  BLC 3; DA; DAB; DAC; DAM
  DRAM, MST, MULT; DC 2**
  See also AAYA 16; AW; BW 2, 3; CA 115;
  122; CANR 42, 54, 76; DA3; DLB 228;
  MTCW 1, 2
Wilson, Brian 1942- .... **CLC 12**
Wilson, Colin 1931- .... **CLC 3, 14**
  See also CA 1-4R; CAAS 5; CANR 1, 22,
  33, 77; DLB 14, 194; MTCW 1
Wilson, Dirk
  See Pohl, Frederik
Wilson, Edmund 1895-1972 .. **CLC 1, 2, 3, 8,
  24**
  See also CA 1-4R; 37-40R; CANR 1, 46;
  DLB 63; MTCW 1, 2
Wilson, Ethel Davis (Bryant)
  1888(?)-1980 .... **CLC 13; DAC; DAM
  POET**
  See also CA 102; DLB 68; MTCW 1
Wilson, Harriet E. Adams
  1827(?)-1863(?) .... **NCLC 78; BLC 3;
  DAM MULT**
  See also DLB 50
Wilson, John 1785-1854 .... **NCLC 5**
Wilson, John (Anthony) Burgess 1917-1993
  See Burgess, Anthony
  See also CA 1-4R; 143; CANR 2, 46; DAC;
  DAM NOV; DA3; MTCW 1, 2
Wilson, Lanford 1937- .... **CLC 7, 14, 36;
  DAM DRAM**
  See also CA 17-20R; CABS 3; CANR 45,
  96; DLB 7
Wilson, Robert M. 1944- .... **CLC 7, 9**
  See also CA 49-52; CANR 2, 41; MTCW 1
Wilson, Robert McLiam 1964- .... **CLC 59**
  See also CA 132
Wilson, Sloan 1920- .... **CLC 32**
  See also CA 1-4R; CANR 1, 44
Wilson, Snoo 1948- .... **CLC 33**
  See also CA 69-72
Wilson, William S(mith) 1932- .... **CLC 49**
  See also CA 81-84
Wilson, (Thomas) Woodrow
  1856-1924 .... **TCLC 79**
  See also CA 166; DLB 47
Winchilsea, Anne (Kingsmill) Finch Counte
  1661-1720
  See Finch, Anne
Windham, Basil
  See Wodehouse, P(elham) G(renville)
Wingrove, David (John) 1954- .... **CLC 68**
  See also CA 133
Winnemucca, Sarah 1844-1891 ..... **NCLC 79**
Winstanley, Gerrard 1609-1676 .... **LC 52**
Wintergreen, Jane
  See Duncan, Sara Jeannette
Winters, Janet Lewis CLC 41
  See also Lewis, Janet
  See also DLBY 87

Winters, (Arthur) Yvor 1900-1968 .... **CLC 4,
  8, 32**
  See also AMWS 2; CA 11-12; 25-28R; CAP
  1; DLB 48; MTCW 1
Winterson, Jeanette 1959- .... **CLC 64; DAM
  POP**
  See also BRWS 4; CA 136; CANR 58;
  DA3; DLB 207; GLL 1; MTCW 2
Winthrop, John 1588-1649 .... **LC 31**
  See also DLB 24, 30
Wirth, Louis 1897-1952 .... **TCLC 92**
Wiseman, Frederick 1930- .... **CLC 20**
  See also CA 159
Wister, Owen 1860-1938 .... **TCLC 21**
  See also CA 108; 162; DLB 9, 78, 186;
  SATA 62; TCWW 2
Witkacy
  See Witkiewicz, Stanislaw Ignacy
Witkiewicz, Stanislaw Ignacy
  1885-1939 .... **TCLC 8**
  See also CA 105; 162; DLB 215
Wittgenstein, Ludwig (Josef Johann)
  1889-1951 .... **TCLC 59**
  See also CA 113; 164; MTCW 2
Wittig, Monique 1935(?)- .... **CLC 22**
  See also CA 116; 135; CWW 2; DLB 83;
  GLL 1
Wittlin, Jozef 1896-1976 .... **CLC 25**
  See also CA 49-52; 65-68; CANR 3
Wodehouse, P(elham) G(renville)
  1881-1975 .... **CLC 1, 2, 5, 10, 22; DAB;
  DAC; DAM NOV; SSC 2**
  See also AITN 2; BRWS 3; CA 45-48; 57-
  60; CANR 3, 33; CDBLB 1914-1945;
  DA3; DLB 34, 162; MTCW 1, 2; SATA
  22
Woiwode, L.
  See Woiwode, Larry (Alfred)
Woiwode, Larry (Alfred) 1941- ... **CLC 6, 10**
  See also CA 73-76; CANR 16, 94; DLB 6;
  INT CANR-16
Wojciechowska, Maia (Teresa)
  1927- .... **CLC 26**
  See also AAYA 8; AW; CA 9-12R; 183;
  CAAE 183; CANR 4, 41; CLR 1; JRDA;
  MAICYA; SAAS 1; SATA 1, 28, 83;
  SATA-Essay 104
Wojtyla, Karol
  See John Paul II, Pope
Wolf, Christa 1929- .... **CLC 14, 29, 58**
  See also CA 85-88; CANR 45; CWW 2;
  DLB 75; MTCW 1
Wolfe, Gene (Rodman) 1931- .... **CLC 25;
  DAM POP**
  See also AAYA 35; CA 57-60; CAAS 9;
  CANR 6, 32, 60; DLB 8; MTCW 2; SATA
  118; SCFW 2
Wolfe, George C. 1954- .... **CLC 49; BLCS**
  See also CA 149
Wolfe, Thomas (Clayton)
  1900-1938 ...... **TCLC 4, 13, 29, 61; DA;
  DAB; DAC; DAM MST, NOV; SSC 33**
  See also AW; CA 104; 132; CDALB 1929-
  1941; DA3; DLB 9, 102; DLBD 2, 16;
  DLBY 85, 97; MTCW 1, 2
Wolfe, Thomas Kennerly, Jr. 1930-
  See Wolfe, Tom
  See also CA 13-16R; CANR 9, 33, 70;
  DAM POP; DA3; DLB 185; INT
  CANR-9; MTCW 1, 2
Wolfe, Tom CLC 1, 2, 9, 15, 35, 51
  See also Wolfe, Thomas Kennerly, Jr.
  See also AAYA 8; AITN 2; AMWS 3; BEST
  89:1; DLB 152
Wolff, Geoffrey (Ansell) 1937- .... **CLC 41**
  See also CA 29-32R; CANR 29, 43, 78
Wolff, Sonia
  See Levitin, Sonia (Wolff)

Wolff, Tobias (Jonathan Ansell)
  1945- .... **CLC 39, 64**
  See also AAYA 16; AMWS 7; BEST 90:2;
  CA 114; 117; CAAS 22; CANR 54, 76,
  96; DA3; DLB 130; INT 117; MTCW 2
Wolfram von Eschenbach c. 1170-c.
  1220 .... **CMLC 5**
  See also DLB 138
Wolitzer, Hilma 1930- .... **CLC 17**
  See also AW; CA 65-68; CANR 18, 40; INT
  CANR-18; SATA 31
Wollstonecraft, Mary 1759-1797 ..... **LC 5, 50**
  See also BRWS 3; CDBLB 1789-1832;
  DLB 39, 104, 158
Wonder, Stevie CLC 12
  See also Morris, Steveland Judkins
Wong, Jade Snow 1922- .... **CLC 17**
  See also CA 109; CANR 91; SATA 112
Woodberry, George Edward
  1855-1930 .... **TCLC 73**
  See also CA 165; DLB 71, 103
Woodcott, Keith
  See Brunner, John (Kilian Houston)
Woodruff, Robert W.
  See Mencken, H(enry) L(ouis)
Woolf, (Adeline) Virginia
  1882-1941 .. **TCLC 1, 5, 20, 43, 56, 101;
  DA; DAB; DAC; DAM MST, NOV;
  SSC 7**
  See also Woolf, Virginia Adeline
  See also AW; CA 104; 130; CANR 64; CD-
  BLB 1914-1945; DA3; DLB 36, 100, 162;
  DLBD 10; MTCW 1
Woolf, Virginia Adeline
  See Woolf, (Adeline) Virginia
  See also MTCW 2
Woollcott, Alexander (Humphreys)
  1887-1943 .... **TCLC 5**
  See also CA 105; 161; DLB 29
Woolrich, Cornell CLC 77
  See also Hopley-Woolrich, Cornell George
Woolson, Constance Fenimore
  1840-1894 .... **NCLC 82**
  See also DLB 12, 74, 189, 221
Wordsworth, Dorothy 1771-1855 .. **NCLC 25**
  See also DLB 107
Wordsworth, William 1770-1850 .. **NCLC 12,
  38; DA; DAB; DAC; DAM MST,
  POET; PC 4**
  See also AW; CDBLB 1789-1832; DA3;
  DLB 93, 107
Wouk, Herman 1915- ... **CLC 1, 9, 38; DAM
  NOV, POP**
  See also CA 5-8R; CANR 6, 33, 67;
  CDALBS; DA3; DLBY 82; INT CANR-6;
  MTCW 1, 2
Wright, Charles (Penzel, Jr.) 1935- .. **CLC 6,
  13, 28, 119**
  See also AMWS 5; CA 29-32R; CAAS 7;
  CANR 23, 36, 62, 88; DLB 165; DLBY
  82; MTCW 1, 2
Wright, Charles Stevenson 1932- ... **CLC 49;
  BLC 3; DAM MULT, POET**
  See also BW 1; CA 9-12R; CANR 26; DLB
  33
Wright, Frances 1795-1852 .... **NCLC 74**
  See also DLB 73
Wright, Frank Lloyd 1867-1959 .... **TCLC 95**
  See also AAYA 33; CA 174
Wright, Jack R.
  See Harris, Mark
Wright, James (Arlington)
  1927-1980 .... **CLC 3, 5, 10, 28; DAM
  POET**
  See also AITN 2; AMWS 3; CA 49-52; 97-
  100; CANR 4, 34, 64; CDALBS; DLB 5,
  169; MTCW 1, 2

Wright, Judith (Arandell)
1915-2000 .... **CLC 11, 53; PC 14**
See also CA 13-16R; 188; CANR 31, 76,
93; MTCW 1, 2; SATA 14; SATA-Obit
121

Wright, L(aurali) R. 1939- .... **CLC 44**
See also CA 138

Wright, Richard (Nathaniel)
1908-1960 .... **CLC 1, 3, 4, 9, 14, 21, 48,
74; BLC 3; DA; DAB; DAC; DAM
MST, MULT, NOV; SSC 2**
See also AAYA 5; AW; BW 1; CA 108;
CANR 64; CDALB 1929-1941; DA3;
DLB 76, 102; DLBD 2; MTCW 1, 2

Wright, Richard B(ruce) 1937- .... **CLC 6**
See also CA 85-88; DLB 53

Wright, Rick 1945- .... **CLC 35**

Wright, Rowland
See Wells, Carolyn

Wright, Stephen 1946- .... **CLC 33**

Wright, Willard Huntington 1888-1939
See Van Dine, S. S.
See also CA 115; 189; DLBD 16

Wright, William 1930- .... **CLC 44**
See also CA 53-56; CANR 7, 23

Wroth, LadyMary 1587-1653(?) .... **LC 30**
See also DLB 121

Wu Ch'eng-en 1500(?)-1582(?) .... **LC 7**

Wu Ching-tzu 1701-1754 .... **LC 2**

Wurlitzer, Rudolph 1938(?)- .... **CLC 2, 4, 15**
See also CA 85-88; DLB 173

Wyatt, Thomas c. 1503-1542 .... **PC 27**
See also DLB 132

Wycherley, William 1640-1716 ...... **LC 8, 21;
DAM DRAM**
See also CDBLB 1660-1789; DLB 80

Wylie, Elinor (Morton Hoyt)
1885-1928 .... **TCLC 8; PC 23**
See also AMWS 1; CA 105; 162; DLB 9,
45

Wylie, Philip (Gordon) 1902-1971 ... **CLC 43**
See also CA 21-22; 33-36R; CAP 2; DLB 9

Wyndham, John **CLC 19**
See also Harris, John (Wyndham Parkes
Lucas) Beynon
See also SCFW 2

Wyss, Johann David Von
1743-1818 .... **NCLC 10**
See also JRDA; MAICYA; SATA 29; SATA-
Brief 27

Xenophon c. 430B.C.-c. 354B.C. ... **CMLC 17**
See also DLB 176

Yakumo Koizumi
See Hearn, (Patricio) Lafcadio (Tessima
Carlos)

Yamamoto, Hisaye 1921- .... **SSC 34; DAM
MULT**

Yanez, Jose Donoso
See Donoso (Yanez), Jose

Yanovsky, Basile S.
See Yanovsky, V(assily) S(emenovich)

Yanovsky, V(assily) S(emenovich)
1906-1989 .... **CLC 2, 18**
See also CA 97-100; 129

Yates, Richard 1926-1992 .... **CLC 7, 8, 23**
See also CA 5-8R; 139; CANR 10, 43; DLB
2, 234; DLBY 81, 92; INT CANR-10

Yeats, W. B.
See Yeats, William Butler

Yeats, William Butler 1865-1939 .... **TCLC 1,
11, 18, 31, 93; DA; DAB; DAC; DAM
DRAM, MST, POET; PC 20**
See also AW; CA 104; 127; CANR 45; CD-
BLB 1890-1914; DA3; DLB 10, 19, 98,
156; MTCW 1, 2

Yehoshua, A(braham) B. 1936- .. **CLC 13, 31**
See also CA 33-36R; CANR 43, 90

Yellow Bird
See Ridge, John Rollin

Yep, Laurence Michael 1948- .... **CLC 35**
See also AAYA 5, 31; CA 49-52; CANR 1,
46, 92; CLR 3, 17, 54; DLB 52; JRDA;
MAICYA; SATA 7, 69

Yerby, Frank G(arvin) 1916-1991 . **CLC 1, 7,
22; BLC 3; DAM MULT**
See also BW 1, 3; CA 9-12R; 136; CANR
16, 52; DLB 76; INT CANR-16; MTCW
1

Yesenin, Sergei Alexandrovich
See Esenin, Sergei (Alexandrovich)

Yevtushenko, Yevgeny (Alexandrovich)
1933- .. **CLC 1, 3, 13, 26, 51, 126; DAM
POET**
See also CA 81-84; CANR 33, 54; CWW
2; MTCW 1

Yezierska, Anzia 1885(?)-1970 .... **CLC 46**
See also CA 126; 89-92; DLB 28, 221;
MTCW 1

Yglesias, Helen 1915- .... **CLC 7, 22**
See also CA 37-40R; CAAS 20; CANR 15,
65, 95; INT CANR-15; MTCW 1

Yokomitsu, Riichi 1898-1947 .... **TCLC 47**
See also CA 170

Yonge, Charlotte (Mary)
1823-1901 .... **TCLC 48**
See also CA 109; 163; DLB 18, 163; SATA
17

York, Jeremy
See Creasey, John

York, Simon
See Heinlein, Robert A(nson)

Yorke, Henry Vincent 1905-1974 ..... **CLC 13**
See also Green, Henry
See also CA 85-88; 49-52

Yosano Akiko 1878-1942 .... **TCLC 59; PC 11**
See also CA 161

Yoshimoto, Banana **CLC 84**
See also Yoshimoto, Mahoko

Yoshimoto, Mahoko 1964-
See Yoshimoto, Banana
See also CA 144

Young, Al(bert James) 1939- . **CLC 19; BLC
3; DAM MULT**
See also BW 2, 3; CA 29-32R; CANR 26,
65; DLB 33

Young, Andrew (John) 1885-1971 ...... **CLC 5**
See also CA 5-8R; CANR 7, 29

Young, Collier
See Bloch, Robert (Albert)

Young, Edward 1683-1765 .... **LC 3, 40**
See also DLB 95

Young, Marguerite (Vivian)
1909-1995 .... **CLC 82**
See also CA 13-16; 150; CAP 1

Young, Neil 1945- .... **CLC 17**
See also CA 110; CCA 1

Young Bear, Ray A. 1950- ..... **CLC 94; DAM
MULT**
See also CA 146; DLB 175; NNAL

Yourcenar, Marguerite 1903-1987 ... **CLC 19,
38, 50, 87; DAM NOV**
See also CA 69-72; CANR 23, 60, 93; DLB
72; DLBY 88; GLL 1; MTCW 1, 2

Yuan, Chu 340(?)B.C.-278(?)B.C. . **CMLC 36**

Yurick, Sol 1925- .... **CLC 6**
See also CA 13-16R; CANR 25

Zabolotsky, Nikolai Alekseevich
1903-1958 .... **TCLC 52**
See also CA 116; 164

Zagajewski, Adam 1945- .... **PC 27**
See also CA 186; DLB 232

Zamiatin, Yevgenii
See Zamyatin, Evgeny Ivanovich

Zamora, Bernice (B. Ortiz) 1938- .. **CLC 89;
DAM MULT; HLC 2**
See also CA 151; CANR 80; DLB 82; HW
1, 2

Zamyatin, Evgeny Ivanovich
1884-1937 .... **TCLC 8, 37**
See also CA 105; 166

Zangwill, Israel 1864-1926 ... **TCLC 16; SSC
44**
See also CA 109; 167; DLB 10, 135, 197

Zappa, Francis Vincent, Jr. 1940-1993
See Zappa, Frank
See also CA 108; 143; CANR 57

Zappa, Frank **CLC 17**
See also Zappa, Francis Vincent, Jr.

Zaturenska, Marya 1902-1982 ..... **CLC 6, 11**
See also CA 13-16R; 105; CANR 22

Zeami 1363-1443 .... **DC 7**

Zelazny, Roger (Joseph) 1937-1995 . **CLC 21**
See also AAYA 7; CA 21-24R; 148; CANR
26, 60; DLB 8; MTCW 1, 2; SATA 57;
SATA-Brief 39

Zhdanov, Andrei Alexandrovich
1896-1948 .... **TCLC 18**
See also CA 117; 167

Zhukovsky, Vasily (Andreevich)
1783-1852 .... **NCLC 35**
See also DLB 205

Ziegenhagen, Eric **CLC 55**

Zimmer, Jill Schary
See Robinson, Jill

Zimmerman, Robert
See Dylan, Bob

Zindel, Paul 1936- ..... **CLC 6, 26; DA; DAB;
DAC; DAM DRAM, MST, NOV; DC 5**
See also AAYA 2, 37; AW; CA 73-76;
CANR 31, 65; CDALBS; CLR 3, 45;
DA3; DLB 7, 52; JRDA; MAICYA;
MTCW 1, 2; SATA 16, 58, 102

Zinov'Ev, A. A.
See Zinoviev, Alexander (Aleksandrovich)

Zinoviev, Alexander (Aleksandrovich)
1922- .... **CLC 19**
See also CA 116; 133; CAAS 10

Zoilus
See Lovecraft, H(oward) P(hillips)

Zola, Emile (Edouard Charles Antoine)
1840-1902 ...... **TCLC 1, 6, 21, 41; DA;
DAB; DAC; DAM MST, NOV**
See also AW; CA 104; 138; DA3; DLB 123

Zoline, Pamela 1941- .... **CLC 62**
See also CA 161

Zoroaster 628(?)B.C.-551(?)B.C. ... **CMLC 40**

Zorrilla y Moral, Jose 1817-1893 .... **NCLC 6**

Zoshchenko, Mikhail (Mikhailovich)
1895-1958 .... **TCLC 15; SSC 15**
See also CA 115; 160

Zuckmayer, Carl 1896-1977 .... **CLC 18**
See also CA 69-72; DLB 56, 124

Zuk, Georges
See Skelton, Robin
See also CCA 1

Zukofsky, Louis 1904-1978 ... **CLC 1, 2, 4, 7,
11, 18; DAM POET; PC 11**
See also AMWS 3; CA 9-12R; 77-80;
CANR 39; DLB 5, 165; MTCW 1

Zweig, Paul 1935-1984 .... **CLC 34, 42**
See also CA 85-88; 113

Zweig, Stefan 1881-1942 .... **TCLC 17**
See also CA 112; 170; DLB 81, 118

Zwingli, Huldreich 1484-1531 .... **LC 37**
See also DLB 179

SSC Cumulative Nationality Index

ALGERIAN

Camus, Albert 9

AMERICAN

Abish, Walter 44
Adams, Alice (Boyd) 24
Aiken, Conrad (Potter) 9
Alcott, Louisa May 27
Algren, Nelson 33
Anderson, Sherwood 1
Auchincloss, Louis (Stanton) 22
Baldwin, James (Arthur) 10, 33
Bambara, Toni Cade 35
Banks, Russell 42
Barnes, Djuna 3
Barth, John (Simmons) 10
Barthelme, Donald 2
Beattie, Ann 11
Bellow, Saul 14
Benet, Stephen Vincent 10
Berriault, Gina 30
Bierce, Ambrose (Gwinett) 9
Bowles, Paul (Frederick) 3
Boyle, Kay 5
Boyle, T(homas) Coraghessan 16
Bradbury, Ray (Douglas) 29
Cable, George Washington 4
Caldwell, Erskine (Preston) 19
Calisher, Hortense 15
Capote, Truman 2
Carver, Raymond 8
Cather, Willa Sibert 2
Chandler, Raymond (Thornton) 23
Cheever, John 1, 38
Chesnutt, Charles W(addell) 7
Chopin, Kate 8
Cisneros, Sandra 32
Coover, Robert (Lowell) 15
Cowan, Peter (Walkinshaw) 28
Crane, Stephen (Townley) 7
Davenport, Guy (Mattison Jr.) 16
Davis, Rebecca (Blaine) Harding 38
Dixon, Stephen 16
Dreiser, Theodore (Herman Albert) 30
Dubus, Andre 15
Dunbar, Paul Laurence 8
Elkin, Stanley L(awrence) 12
Ellison, Harlan (Jay) 14
Ellison, Ralph (Waldo) 26
Farrell, James T(homas) 28
Faulkner, William (Cuthbert) 1, 35, 42
Fisher, Rudolph 25
Fitzgerald, F(rancis) Scott (Key) 6, 31
Freeman, Mary E(leanor) Wilkins 1
Gardner, John (Champlin) Jr. 7
Garland, (Hannibal) Hamlin 18
Garrett, George (Palmer) 30
Gass, William H(oward) 12
Gilchrist, Ellen 14
Gilman, Charlotte (Anna) Perkins
  (Stetson) 13
Glasgow, Ellen (Anderson Gholson) 34

Glaspell, Susan 41
Gordon, Caroline 15
Grau, Shirley Ann 15
Hammett, (Samuel) Dashiell 17
Harris, Joel Chandler 19
Harrison, James (Thomas) 19
Harte, (Francis) Bret(t) 8
Hawthorne, Nathaniel 3, 29, 39
Hemingway, Ernest (Miller) 1, 25, 36, 40
Henderson, Zenna (Chlarson) 29
Henry, O. 5
Howells, William Dean 36
Hughes, (James) Langston 6
Hurston, Zora Neale 4
Huxley, Aldous (Leonard) 39
Irving, Washington 2, 37
Jackson, Shirley 9, 39
James, Henry 8, 32
Jewett, (Theodora) Sarah Orne 6, 44
King, Stephen (Edwin) 17
Lardner, Ring(gold) W(ilmer) 32
Le Guin, Ursula K(roeber) 12
Ligotti, Thomas (Robert) 16
Lish, Gordon (Jay) 18
London, Jack 4
Lovecraft, H(oward) P(hillips) 3
Maclean, Norman (Fitzroy) 13
Malamud, Bernard 15
Marshall, Paule 3
Mason, Bobbie Ann 4
McCarthy, Mary (Therese) 24
McCullers, (Lula) Carson (Smith) 9, 24
Melville, Herman 1, 17
Michaels, Leonard 16
Mukherjee, Bharati 38
Murfree, Mary Noailles 22
Nabokov, Vladimir (Vladimirovich) 11
Nin, Anaïs 10
Norris, Frank 28
Oates, Joyce Carol 6
O'Connor, (Mary) Flannery 1, 23
O'Hara, John (Henry) 15
Olsen, Tillie 11
Ozick, Cynthia 15
Page, Thomas Nelson 23
Paley, Grace 8
Parker, Dorothy (Rothschild) 2
Perelman, S(idney) J(oseph) 32
Phillips, Jayne Anne 16
Poe, Edgar Allan 1, 22, 34, 35
Pohl, Frederik 25
Porter, Katherine Anne 4, 31, 43
Powers, J(ames) F(arl) 4
Price, (Edward) Reynolds 22
Pynchon, Thomas (Ruggles Jr.) 14
Roth, Philip (Milton) 26
Salinger, J(erome) D(avid) 2, 28
Saroyan, William 21
Selby, Hubert Jr. 20
Silko, Leslie (Marmon) 37
Singer, Isaac Bashevis 3
Stafford, Jean 26
Stegner, Wallace (Earle) 27

Stein, Gertrude 42
Steinbeck, John (Ernst) 11, 37
Stuart, Jesse (Hilton) 31
Styron, William 25
Suckow, Ruth 18
Taylor, Peter (Hillsman) 10
Thomas, Audrey (Callahan) 20
Thurber, James (Grover) 1
Toomer, Jean 1
Twain, Mark 6, 26
Updike, John (Hoyer) 13, 27
Vinge, Joan (Carol) D(ennison) 24
Vonnegut, Kurt Jr. 8
Walker, Alice (Malsenior) 5
Warren, Robert Penn 4
Welty, Eudora 1, 27
Wescott, Glenway 35
West, Nathanael 16
Wharton, Edith (Newbold Jones) 6
Williams, William Carlos 31
Wodehouse, P(elham) G(renville) 2
Wolfe, Thomas (Clayton) 33
Wright, Richard (Nathaniel) 2

ARGENTINIAN

Bioy Casares, Adolfo 17
Borges, Jorge Luis 4, 41
Cortazar, Julio 7
Valenzuela, Luisa 14

AUSTRALIAN

Jolley, (Monica) Elizabeth 19
Lawson, Henry (Archibald Hertzberg) 18
Moorhouse, Frank 40
White, Patrick (Victor Martindale) 39

AUSTRIAN

Grillparzer, Franz 37
Kafka, Franz 5, 29, 35
Musil, Robert (Edler von) 18
Schnitzler, Arthur 15
Stifter, Adalbert 28

BRAZILIAN

Lispector, Clarice 34
Machado de Assis, Joaquim Maria 24

CANADIAN

Atwood, Margaret (Eleanor) 2
Bellow, Saul 14
Gallant, Mavis 5
Hood, Hugh (John Blagdon) 42
Laurence, (Jean) Margaret (Wemyss) 7
Leacock, Stephen (Butler) 39
Lewis, (Percy) Wyndham 34
Metcalf, John 43
Munro, Alice 3
Ross, (James) Sinclair 24
Thomas, Audrey (Callahan) 20

CHILEAN

Bombal, Maria Luisa 37
Donoso (Yanez), Jose 34

CHINESE

Chang, Eileen **28**
Lu Hsun **20**
P'u Sung-ling **31**

COLOMBIAN

Garcia Marquez, Gabriel (Jose) **8**

CUBAN

Cabrera Infante, G(uillermo) **39**
Calvino, Italo **3**
Carpentier (y Valmont), Alejo **35**

CZECH

Capek, Karel **36**
Kafka, Franz **5, 29, 35**
Kundera, Milan **24**

DANISH

Andersen, Hans Christian **6**
Dinesen, Isak **7**

ENGLISH

Aldiss, Brian W(ilson) **36**
Ballard, J(ames) G(raham) **1**
Bates, H(erbert) E(rnest) **10**
Bowen, Elizabeth (Dorothea Cole) **3, 28**
Campbell, (John) Ramsey **19**
Carter, Angela (Olive) **13**
Chesterton, G(ilbert) K(eith) **1**
Clarke, Arthur C(harles) **3**
Collier, John **19**
Conrad, Joseph **9**
Coppard, A(lfred) E(dgar) **21**
de la Mare, Walter (John) **14**
Dickens, Charles (John Huffam) **17**
Doyle, Arthur Conan **12**
du Maurier, Daphne **18**
Forster, E(dward) M(organ) **27**
Fowles, John (Philip) **33**
Galsworthy, John **22**
Gaskell, Elizabeth Cleghorn **25**
Gissing, George (Robert) **37**
Greene, Graham (Henry) **29**
Hardy, Thomas **2**
Huxley, Aldous (Leonard) **39**
James, Montague (Rhodes) **16**
Jolley, (Monica) Elizabeth **19**
Kipling, (Joseph) Rudyard **5**
Lawrence, D(avid) H(erbert Richards) **4, 19**
Lee, Vernon **33**
Lessing, Doris (May) **6**
Lowry, (Clarence) Malcolm **31**
Mansfield, Katherine **9, 23, 38**
Maugham, W(illiam) Somerset **8**
Morrison, Arthur **40**
Naipaul, V(idiadhar) S(urajprasad) **38**
Pritchett, V(ictor) S(awdon) **14**
Rhys, Jean **21**
Saki **12**
Sansom, William **21**
Trollope, Anthony **28**
Warner, Sylvia Townsend **23**
Waugh, Evelyn (Arthur St. John) **41**
Wells, H(erbert) G(eorge) **6**
White, Patrick (Victor Martindale) **39**
Wilson, Angus (Frank Johnstone) **21**
Wodehouse, P(elham) G(renville) **2**
Woolf, (Adeline) Virginia **7**
Zangwill, Israel **44**

FRENCH

Ayme, Marcel (Andre) **41**
Balzac, Honoré de **5**
Barbey d'Aurevilly, Jules Amedee **17**
Baudelaire, Charles **18**
Beauvoir, Simone (Lucie Ernestine Marie
    Bertrand) de **35**
Beckett, Samuel (Barclay) **16**

Camus, Albert **9**
Colette, (Sidonie-Gabrielle) **10**
Duras, Marguerite **40**
Flaubert, Gustave **11**
Gautier, Theophile **20**
Gide, Andre (Paul Guillaume) **13**
Jarry, Alfred **20**
Laforgue, Jules **20**
Lautreamont, Comte de **14**
Maupassant, (Henri Rene Albert) Guy de **1**
Mauriac, François (Charles) **24**
Merimee, Prosper **7**
Morand, Paul **22**
Nerval, Gerard de **18**
Nin, Anaïs **10**
Sartre, Jean-Paul **32**
Stendhal **27**
Villiers de l'Isle Adam, Jean Marie Mathias
    Philippe Auguste, Comte de **14**
Voltaire **12**

GERMAN

Arnim, Achim von (Ludwig Joachim von
    Arnim) **29**
Boell, Heinrich (Theodor) **23**
Goethe, Johann Wolfgang von **38**
Grimm, Jacob Ludwig Karl **36**
Grimm, Wilhelm Karl **36**
Hauptmann, Gerhart (Johann Robert) **37**
Hesse, Hermann **9**
Hoffmann, E(rnst) T(heodor) A(madeus) **13**
Kleist, Heinrich von **22**
Lenz, Siegfried **33**
Mann, (Paul) Thomas **5**
Storm, (Hans) Theodor (Woldsen) **27**
Tieck, (Johann) Ludwig **31**

INDIAN

Mukherjee, Bharati **38**
Narayan, R(asipuram) K(rishnaswami) **25**

IRISH

Beckett, Samuel (Barclay) **16**
Bowen, Elizabeth (Dorothea Cole) **3, 28**
Joyce, James (Augustine Aloysius) **3, 26,
    44**
Lavin, Mary **4**
Le Fanu, Joseph Sheridan **14**
McGahern, John **17**
Moore, George Augustus **19**
O'Brien, Edna **10**
O'Connor, Frank **5**
O'Faolain, Sean **13**
O'Flaherty, Liam **6**
Trevor, William **21**
Wilde, Oscar (Fingal O'Flahertie Wills) **11**

ISRAELI

Agnon, S(hmuel) Y(osef Halevi) **30**
Appelfeld, Aharon **42**

ITALIAN

Boccaccio, Giovanni **10**
Calvino, Italo **3**
Levi, Primo **12**
Moravia, Alberto **26**
Pavese, Cesare **19**
Pirandello, Luigi **22**
Svevo, Italo **25**
Verga, Giovanni (Carmelo) **21**

JAPANESE

Akutagawa, Ryunosuke **44**
Dazai Osamu **41**
Kawabata, Yasunari **17**
Mishima, Yukio **4**
Ōbe, Kenzaburō **20**
Shiga, Naoya **23**
Tanizaki, Jun'ichiro **21**

MEXICAN

Arreola, Juan Jose **38**
Castellanos, Rosario **39**
Fuentes, Carlos **24**
Rulfo, Juan **25**

NEW ZEALANDER

Frame, Janet **29**
Mansfield, Katherine **9, 23, 38**

POLISH

Agnon, S(hmuel) Y(osef Halevi) **30**
Conrad, Joseph **9**
Peretz, Isaac Loeb **26**
Schulz, Bruno **13**
Singer, Isaac Bashevis **3**

PUERTO RICAN

Ferre, Rosario **36**

RUSSIAN

Babel, Isaak (Emmanuilovich) **16**
Bulgakov, Mikhail (Afanas'evich) **18**
Bunin, Ivan Alexeyevich **5**
Chekhov, Anton (Pavlovich) **2, 28, 41**
Dostoevsky, Fedor Mikhailovich **2, 33, 44**
Gogol, Nikolai (Vasilyevich) **4, 29**
Gorky, Maxim **28**
Kazakov, Yuri Pavlovich **43**
Klimentov, Andrei Platonovich **42**
Leskov, Nikolai (Semyonovich) **34**
Nabokov, Vladimir (Vladimirovich) **11**
Pasternak, Boris (Leonidovich) **31**
Pushkin, Alexander (Sergeyevich) **27**
Solzhenitsyn, Aleksandr I(sayevich) **32**
Tolstoy, Leo (Nikolaevich) **9, 30**
Turgenev, Ivan **7**
Zoshchenko, Mikhail (Mikhailovich) **15**

SCOTTISH

Oliphant, Margaret (Oliphant Wilson) **25**
Scott, Walter **32**
Spark, Muriel (Sarah) **10**
Stevenson, Robert Louis (Balfour) **11**

SOUTH AFRICAN

Gordimer, Nadine **17**

SPANISH

Cervantes (Saavedra), Miguel de **12**
Pardo Bazan, Emilia **30**
Unamuno (y Jugo), Miguel de **11**

SWEDISH

Lagerkvist, Par **12**

SWISS

Hesse, Hermann **9**
Keller, Gottfried **26**
Walser, Robert **20**

TRINIDADIAN

Naipaul, V(idiadhar) S(urajprasad) **38**

UKRAINIAN

Aleichem, Sholom **33**

URUGUAYAN

Onetti, Juan Carlos **23**

WELSH

Evans, Caradoc **43**
Lewis, Alun **40**
Machen, Arthur **20**
Thomas, Dylan (Marlais) **3, 44**

YUGOSLAVIAN

Andric, Ivo **36**

SSC-44 Title Index

"Absorbed in Letters" (Akutagawa) **44**:44, 47, 54

"Access" (Abish) **44**:20, 26

Adolescent (Dostoevsky)
  See *Podrostok*

"An Adventure from a Work in Progress" (Thomas) **44**:357, 359

Adventures in the Skin Trade, and Other Stories (Thomas) **44**:323-24, 334, 341-42, 344, 354, 360-61

"After the Fair" (Thomas) **44**:325, 332, 354

"After the Funeral: In Memory of Anne Jones" (Thomas) **44**:338

"After the Race" (Joyce) **44**:263, 288

"The Aged Susano-ono-mikoto" (Akutagawa) **44**:62

"Anagram" (Thomas) **44**:336

"Anglicization" (Zangwill) **44**:378, 390

"Araby" (Joyce) **44**:235-319

"Ardor/Awe/Atrocity" (Abish) **44**:7-9, 12, 15, 19

"Aru ahō no isshō" (Akutagawa) **44**:44, 69, 83-4, 89

"The Autumn Mountain" (Akutagawa)
  See "Shūzan zu"

"The Ball" (Akutagawa)
  See "Butōkai"

"The Bandits" (Akutagawa)
  See "Chūtō"

"The Bearer of Burdens" (Zangwill) **44**:378, 389

Bednye lyudi (Dostoevsky) **44**:95, 111, 116, 122-24, 147, 157, 160, 162, 165, 167-69

"Bethulah" (Zangwill) **44**:375, 388

"Bisei no shin" (Akutagawa) **44**:90

"The Boarding House" (Joyce) **44**:269, 284

"The Burning Baby" (Thomas) **44**:323, 328, 336-38, 342, 344, 346, 354, 357-59

"Butōkai" (Akutagawa) **44**:64, 78

The Celibates' Club (Zangwill) **44**:365, 375, 378, 381-82

"Chad Gadya" (Zangwill) **44**:373

"A Child's Christmas in Wales" (Thomas) **44**:341

"Chūtō" (Akutagawa) **44**:74-5

"Clay" (Joyce) **44**:264, 284

"A Clod of Earth" (Akutagawa)
  See "Ikkai no Tsuchi"

"A Clod of Soil" (Akutagawa)
  See "Ikkai no Tsuchi"

"Cogwheel" (Akutagawa)
  See "Haguruma"

The Collected Stories (Thomas) **44**:340-41

"The Converts" (Zangwill) **44**:378

"Counterparts" (Joyce) **44**:263, 284

"Creative Frenzy" (Akutagawa) **44**:64

"Crossing Friends" (Abish) **44**:2

"Crossing the Great Void" (Abish) **44**:10, 16, 19-20

"Daidōji Shinsuke no Hansei" (Akutagawa) **44**:54, 82

"The Dead" (Joyce) **44**:236, 244, 263-65, 268-70, 279, 284, 288

"Death of a Martyr" (Akutagawa)
  See "Hōkyōnin no Shi"

"Death Register" (Akutagawa)
  See "Tenkibo"

The Devil and Tobacco (Akutagawa)
  See *Tabako to Akuma*

"The Diary of a Meshumad" (Zangwill) **44**:366-67, 370, 372, 375, 387

"The Dog Shiro" (Akutagawa) **44**:53

A Doom on the Sun (Thomas) **44**:333

The Double (Dostoevsky)
  See *Dvoynik*

"Doubts" (Akutagawa) **44**:45

Dowa (Akutagawa) **44**:69

"The Dragon" (Akutagawa) **44**:57-8

"The Dream of Lusheng" (Akutagawa) **44**:57-8

"Dreams" (Akutagawa) **44**:51

"Dreamers of the Ghetto" (Zangwill) **44**:364

Dreamers of the Ghetto (Zangwill) **44**:366, 370, 373, 388

"The Dress" (Thomas) **44**:322, 333-34, 337-38, 344, 354

Dubliners (Joyce) **44**:235-36, 238, 243, 254, 262-65, 268, 275, 277, 279, 282, 284, 288, 291-97, 299-303, 3-5-09, 313, 315, 317

Dvoinik (Dostoevsky)
  See *Dvoynik*

Dvoynik (Dostoevsky) **44**:93-177

"The Eagle Trees" (Jewett) **44**:179-81

"The Early Life of Daidōji Shinsuke" (Akutagawa)
  See "Daidōji Shinsuke no Hansei"

Early Prose Writings (Thomas) **44**:340-41

"Elijah's Goblet" (Zangwill) **44**:378

"An Encounter" (Joyce) **44**:262-63, 265, 288, 290-92, 294-95, 297, 299, 311

"The Enemies" (Thomas) **44**:322, 328, 332-33, 338, 346, 357-58

"The Enemies United" (Thomas) **44**:333

"The English Garden" (Abish) **44**:4-5, 8-9, 12-13, 15, 29

The Eternal Husband (Dostoevsky)
  See *Vechny muzh*

"Eveline" (Joyce) **44**:265, 284, 288

"Extraordinary Little Cough" (Thomas) **44**:324, 351, 360

"The Faith of Wei Cheng" (Akutagawa)
  See "Bisei no shin"

"The Fight" (Thomas) **44**:324, 350-51

"A Fine Beginning" (Thomas) **44**:360

"Flatcar" (Akutagawa) **44**:52

"Flutter-Duck" (Zangwill)
  See "Flutter-duck, A Ghetto Grotesque"

"Flutter-duck, A Ghetto Grotesque" (Zangwill) **44**:371, 388

"A Fool's Life" (Akutagawa)
  See "Aru ahō no isshō"

"From a Mattress Grave" (Zangwill) **44**:365-66

"From a Mournful Villager" (Jewett) **44**:193

"From Yasukichi's Notebooks" (Akutagawa)
  See "Yasukichi no Technō kara"

Future Perfect (Abish)
  See *In the Future Perfect*

"Gaspar, Melchior, Balthasar" (Thomas) **44**:335

"Geijutsu sono ta" (Akutagawa) **44**:89

"The General" (Akutagawa)
  See "Shōgun"

"Genkaku Sanbō" (Akutagawa) **44**:44, 46, 81-2

"Genkaku's Villa" (Akutagawa)
  See "Genkaku Sanbō"

"Gesaku Zammai" (Akutagawa) **44**:76-7

Ghetto Comedies (Zangwill) **44**:370, 374-75, 377-79, 381, 389

Ghetto Tragedies (Zangwill) **44**:372, 374-76, 387-88

"Grace" (Joyce) **44**:265

"Grandchildren of the Ghetto" (Zangwill) **44**:390

"The Gray Man" (Jewett) **44**:226

The Grey Wig: Stories and Novelettes (Zangwill) **44**:375, 381-82

Grotesques and Fantasies (Zangwill)
  See *The King of Schnorrers: Grotesques and Fantasies*

"Hadgadyah" (Zangwill) **44**:368

"Haguruma" (Akutagawa) **44**:44, 46, 49, 51, 54-5, 61, 79, 83-4, 89-90

"Hana" (Akutagawa) **44**:41, 45, 49-50, 56-8, 60-1, 73, 75-6, 88-9

"The Handkerchief" (Akutagawa)
  See "Hankechi"

"Hankechi" (Akutagawa) **44**:50, 78

"Heichu, the Amorous Genius" (Akutagawa) **44**:50

"The Hell Screen" (Akutagawa)
  See "Jigokuhen"

"Heresy" (Akutagawa) **44**:62

"The Hirelings" (Zangwill) **44**:378-79

"Hōkyōnin no Shi" (Akutagawa) **44**:53, 62, 76-7

"The Holy Six" (Thomas) **44**:329, 332-33, 338, 343, 345-46, 348-49, 354, 357-58

"Holy Wedlock" (Zangwill) **44**:378

"The Horse's Ha" (Thomas) **44**:329, 359

"How the comb gives meaning to the hair" (Abish) **44**:19

"Ikkai no Tsuchi" (Akutagawa) **44**:46, 53, 81

"Ill Omens" (Akutagawa)
  See "Kyō"

"Imogayu" (Akutagawa) **44**:50, 57, 76

"In Memory of Ann Jones" (Thomas)
  See "After the Funeral: In Memory of Anne Jones"

"In So Many Words" (Abish) **44**:5, 8-9, 12, 29

"In the Direction of the Beginning" (Thomas) **44**:357

"In the Future Perfect" (Abish) **44**:9, 13

In the Future Perfect (Abish) **44**:4-5, 10, 12-13, 19-21, 24, 26, 29, 38
"In the Garden" (Thomas) **44**:348
"The Incurable" (Zangwill) **44**:366, 375, 387
"Inside Out" (Abish) **44**:12, 37
"Interpretation" (Akutagawa) **44**:50
"The Istanbul Papers" (Abish) **44**3, 11:
"Ivy Day in the Committee Room" (Joyce) **44**:265
"The Jewish Trinity" (Zangwill) **44**:367, 378, 390
"Jigokuhen" (Akutagawa) **44**:44-5, 47, 51-4, 56, 65, 68, 72, 76-8, 81
"Joseph the Dreamer" (Zangwill) **44**:366, 370, 373
"The Joyous Comrade" (Zangwill) **44**:366
"Juliano Kichisuke" (Akutagawa) **44**:62
"Just like Little Dogs" (Thomas) **44**:325, 350-51, 360
"Kaika no Satsujin" (Akutagawa) **44**:78
"Karenoshō" (Akutagawa) **44**:44, 64, 75, 88-90
"The Keeper of Conscience" (Zangwill) **44**:375, 387
"Kesa and Moritō" (Akutagawa) **44**:51, 63
"Khozyaika" (Dostoevsky) **44**:98
"The King of Schnorrers" (Zangwill) **44**:384
The King of Schnorrers: Grotesques and Fantasies (Zangwill) **44**:366-68, 370, 375, 377-78, 380-81, 384-86, 388-89
"Kumonoito" (Akutagawa) **44**:52, 59-60, 75-6
"Kylin" (Akutagawa) **44**:54
"Kyō" (Akutagawa) **44**:80
"The Lady Roku-no-miya" (Akutagawa) **44**:50
"The Land of Promise" (Zangwill) **44**:375, 387
"The Landscape Chamber" (Jewett) **44**:226
"The Lemon" (Thomas) **44**:345, 354
Letters from the Underworld (Dostoevsky)
    See *Zapiski iz podpol'ya*
"Lice" (Akutagawa) **44**:42, 50, 57-8
"The Life of a Certain Idiot" (Akutagawa)
    See "Aru ahō no isshō"
"A Life Spent at Frivolous Writing" (Akutagawa)
    See "Gesaku Zammai"
"Life Uniforms" (Abish) **44**:20
"A Little Cloud" (Joyce) **44**:263, 284, 288
"Lord Susanoo" (Akutagawa) **44**:49
"Lucifer" (Akutagawa) **44**:62
"The *Luftmensch*" (Zangwill) **44**:378
"Mandarin Oranges" (Akutagawa) **44**:52
The Map of Love (Thomas) **44**:322, 332, 338, 349, 354, 357
The Map of Love (Thomas) **44**:321, 324-25, 336, 350
"The Marshland" (Akutagawa) **44**:64
"Martha" (Thomas) **44**:337
"The Master of Lenses" (Zangwill) **44**:364
Memoirs from Underground (Dostoevsky)
    See *Zapiski iz podpol'ya*
"Mensura Zoili" (Akutagawa) **44**:64
"Messages" (Abish) **44**:19
"Mikan" (Akutagawa) **44**:80, 87-90
"Minds Meet" (Abish) **44**:2, 18, 20-21
Minds Meet (Abish) **44**:2-4, 11, 17, 19-20, 24-26, 28, 30
"The Mirage" (Akutagawa)
    See "Shinkirō"
"The Model of Sorrows" (Zangwill) **44**:378, 389
"A Modern Scribe in Jerusalem" (Zangwill) **44**:368
"More by George" (Abish) **44**:2
"The Mouse and the Woman" (Thomas) **44**:322, 325, 344-45, 349, 354-57, 359
"Mr Tritas on the Roofs" (Thomas) **44**:336
"A Murder During the Age of Enlightenment" (Akutagawa)
    See "Kaika no Satsujin"
The 99: New Meaning (Abish) **44**:12, 37-38
"Noah's Ark" (Zangwill) **44**:375, 387-89
"Non-Site" (Abish) **44**:11

"Noroma Puppets" (Akutagawa) **44**:64
"The Nose" (Akutagawa)
    See "Hana"
Notebook (Thomas)
    See *Red Notebook*
Notes from the Underground (Dostoevsky)
    See *Zapiski iz podpol'ya*
Notes from Underground (Dostoevsky)
    See *Zapiski iz podpol'ya*
"Of Art and Other Things" (Akutagawa)
    See "Geijutsu sono ta"
"Ogata Ryōsai's Affidavit" (Akutagawa) **44**:53, 62
"Old Age" (Akutagawa)
    See "Rōnen"
"Old Garbo" (Thomas) **44**:324-25, 343, 351-53, 360
"The Old Man" (Akutagawa) **44**:56
"The Old Murder" (Akutagawa) **44**:53
"On Aspects of the Familiar World as Perceived in Everyday Life and Literature" (Abish) **44**:11
"On the Seashore" (Akutagawa) **44**:52-3, 64
"One Day of Oishiuchi Kuranosuke" (Akutagawa) **44**:63-4
"One Warm Saturday" (Thomas) **44**:324, 350-53, 360
"Oogawa no mizu" (Akutagawa) **44**:90
"The Orchards" (Thomas) **44**:322, 330, 336-38, 354-57, 359
"Our Eunuch Dreams" (Thomas) **44**:334
"A Painful Case" (Joyce) **44**:263, 268-69, 279-80, 284
"The Painting of an Autumn Mountain" (Akutagawa) **44**:51
"Parting Shot" (Abish) **44**:9, 16, 20, 29
"Patricia, Edith, and Arnold" (Thomas) **44**:324, 351-52, 359-60
"The Peaches" (Thomas) **44**:324, 351-52, 359
"The People's Saviour" (Zangwill) **44**:366
"The Pipe" (Akutagawa) **44**:42
Podrostok (Dostoevsky) **44**:93, 96, 98, 112
Poor Folk (Dostoevsky)
    See *Bednye lyudi*
Portrait of the Artist as a Young Dog (Thomas) **44**:321, 323-25, 341-42, 348-52, 359-60
"Prologue to an Adventure" (Thomas) **44**:335, 354, 357
"A Prospect of the Sea" (Thomas) **44**:326, 338, 345, 347, 354, 356-57
"The Puppeteer" (Akutagawa) **44**:57
Quite Early One Morning (Thomas) **44**:354
"Rashōmon" (Akutagawa) **44**:41-2, 45, 49-50, 56-8, 60-1, 63, 73-5
The Raw Youth (Dostoevsky)
    See *Podrostok*
A Raw Youth (Dostoevsky)
    See *Podrostok*
"Read Only Memory" (Abish) **44**:15
"The Red Mark" (Zangwill) **44**:378
Red Notebook (Thomas) **44**:330-38
"A Refusal to Mourn the Death, by Fire, of a Child in London" (Thomas) **44**:336
"Replies to an Enquiry" (Thomas) **44**:344
"River Driftwood" (Jewett) **44**:193
"The Robbers" (Akutagawa) **44**:49, 52, 62
"Rōnen" (Akutagawa) **44**:73
"Rose of the Ghetto" (Zangwill) **44**:371
Roshomon and Other Stories (Akutagawa) **44**:42, 57
"The Sabbath Breaker" (Zangwill) **44**:375, 387
"The Sabbath Question in Sudminster" (Zangwill) **44**:378
"Saigo Takamori" (Akutagawa) **44**:62
"Samooborona" (Zangwill) **44**:378, 381, 390
"Satan *Mekatrig*" (Zangwill) **44**:366, 375-76, 387
"The School for Witches" (Thomas) **44**:329, 345-46, 354, 357-58

"The Second Leg" (Abish) **44**:2-3, 11, 28
"Self Defense" (Zangwill)
    See "Samooborona"
"The Sennin" (Akutagawa) **44**:71
"Shinkirō" (Akutagawa) **44**:52-4, 83
"Shisô" (Akutagawa) **44**:90
"Shōgun" (Akutagawa) **44**:50, 78
"Shuju no kotoba" (Akutagawa) **44**:89
"Shūzan zu" (Akutagawa) **44**:64, 72
"The Sisters" (Joyce) **44**:262-63, 265, 279-80, 284, 288, 291-97, 299
Skin Trade (Thomas)
    See *Adventures in the Skin Trade, and Other Stories*
"The Solitary Snipe" (Akutagawa) **44**:64
"The Spider's Thread" (Akutagawa)
    See "Kumonoito"
"St. Christopher's Life" (Akutagawa) **44**:53, 62
"Strange Island" (Akutagawa) **44**:52, 64
"Susano-ono-mikoto" (Akutagawa) **44**:62
Tales for Children (Akutagawa)
    See *Dowa*
"Tangerines" (Akutagawa)
    See "Mikan"
"Tenkibo" (Akutagawa) **44**:73, 82-3
"They That Walk in Darkness" (Zangwill) **44**:375, 387
They That Walk in Darkness (Zangwill) **44**:366, 387
"This Is Not a Film, This Is a Precise Act of Disbelief" (Abish) **44**:4, 11, 18, 26-8, 30
"Those Days" (Akutagawa) **44**:64
"The Thread of the Spider's Web" (Akutagawa)
    See "Kumonoito"
"The Three Treasures" (Akutagawa) **44**:53
"To Die in Jerusalem" (Zangwill) **44**:367, 370, 373, 375, 388
"Tobacco and the Devil" (Akutagawa) **44**:62
Tobacco and the Devil (Akutagawa)
    See *Tobako to Akuma*
Tobako to Akuma (Akutagawa) **44**:42, 57-9
"Torokko" (Akutagawa) **44**:71, 79
"Toshishun" (Akutagawa) **44**:69-72
"Transitional" (Zangwill) **44**:367, 375-76, 387
"The Tree" (Thomas) **44**:322, 327, 331, 333-34, 337-38, 341, 346, 348-49, 354-55, 359
"The Truck" (Akutagawa)
    See "Torokko"
"A True Story" (Thomas)
    See "The True Story"
"The True Story" (Thomas) **44**:331, 343-44, 346
"Tu tzuch'un" (Akutagawa) **44**:52
"The Tug of Love" (Zangwill) **44**:378
"Two Gallants" (Joyce) **44**:265-66
The Uncollected Short Stories of Sarah Orne Jewett (Jewett) **44**:219
Vechny muzh (Dostoevsky) **44**:160
"The Vest" (Thomas) **44**:334, 337, 344
"A Visit to Grandpa's" (Thomas) **44**:324, 350, 359
"The Visitor" (Thomas) **44**:322, 330, 333-34, 336-38, 348, 355-58
"The Visitors [April '34]" (Thomas) **44**:333
"The Wandering Jew" (Akutagawa) **44**:62
"What Else" (Abish) **44**:12, 37
"Where Tawe Flows" (Thomas) **44**:350-51
"The White Heron" (Jewett)
    See "A White Heron"
"A White Heron" (Jewett) **44**:179-232
"Who Do You Wish Was with Us" (Thomas) **44**:351, 360
"Wine Worm" (Akutagawa) **44**:42, 57-8
"A Winter's Tale" (Thomas) **44**:334
"With Bill in the Desert" (Abish) **44**:11
"Withered Fields" (Akutagawa)
    See "Karenoshō"

"Within a Grove" (Akutagawa)
  See "Yabu no Naka"
"The Words of a Dwarf" (Akutagawa)
  See "Shuju no kotoba"
"Yabu no Naka" (Akutagawa) **44**:45, 51-2, 60,
  63, 78-9

"Yam Gruel" (Akutagawa)
  See "Imogayu"
"Yasukichi no Technō kara" (Akutagawa)
  44:79, 89
"A Yiddish 'Hamlet'" (Zangwill) **44**:378

"The Youth of Daidōji Shinsuke" (Akutagawa)
  See "Daidōji Shinsuke no Hansei"
"Youths and Death" (Akutagawa) **44**:56
Zapiski iz podpol'ya (Dostoevsky) **44**:112-13,
  155, 158, 160

Title Index